HAMILTON COUNTY, OHIO ROMAN CATHOLIC BAPTISM RECORDS

1850 – 1859
Part 1: A - L

Indexed by

Jeffrey G. Herbert and Julie M. Ross

Hamilton County Chapter of the
Ohio Genealogical Society

HAMILTON COUNTY, OHIO ROMAN CATHOLIC BAPTISM RECORDS

1850 – 1859
Part 1: A - L

Indexed by

Jeffrey G. Herbert and Julie M. Ross

for the

Hamilton County Chapter of the
Ohio Genealogical Society

Cincinnati, Ohio
2018

Published by the
Hamilton County Chapter, OGS
P.O. Box 15865
Cincinnati, OH 45215-0865
513-956-7078
http://hcgsohio.org

Printed in the United States of America.
ISBN-13: 978-1722654009
LCCN 2018951285

Table of Contents

Introduction

This index is intended to give the researcher another means of discovering information about early Hamilton County, Ohio ancestors who were born or baptized in the region between 1 January 1850 and 31 December 1859. Many families, while not settling here permanently, lived in the area for a time and had spouses and children who were baptized here while they were passing through this region. Traces of these early pioneer families are hard to find through cemetery, newspaper or court records during the first half of the nineteenth century. This index is intended to serve as another tool in the family history researcher's toolbox.

The title of this index is Hamilton County, Ohio, Roman Catholic Baptism Records because it is focused only on Roman Catholic parishes in the county. Previously published indexes cover the available non-Catholic baptismal records for Cincinnati and Hamilton County churches. Their titles are:

- Selected Hamilton County, Ohio Church Baptism Records - Early to 1859
- Selected Hamilton County, Ohio Church Baptism Records - 1860 – 1869
- Selected Hamilton County, Ohio Church Baptism Records - 1870 – 1879
- Selected Hamilton County, Ohio Church Baptism Records - 1880 – 1889
- Selected Hamilton County, Ohio Church Baptism Records - 1890 – 1899

And an earlier published index on Roman Catholic baptismal records,

- Hamilton County, Ohio Roman Catholic Baptism Records – Early to 1849

Please consult the Hamilton County Genealogical Society website, www.hcgsohio.org, for more information on individual prices and how to order these publications.

This index contains information for over **42,300** baptisms which occurred in Hamilton County between January 1850 and December 1859. The quality (both legibility and completeness) of the records varies greatly from church to church, from priest to priest, and from year to year. In most cases, birth and baptism dates were recorded along with the names of the godparents. While the date of baptism is recorded in the index because the baptismal register is usually chronological, the date of birth (usually a few days prior to the baptism) is typically also listed in the original register. If the mother's maiden name was mentioned, the information is recorded, otherwise it is denoted by "----". In many of the Irish parishes the names of the parents were recorded as John and Mary Smith, for example, and the maiden name of the mother was not recorded. If an entry cannot be read for certain, a best estimate of the name has been recorded with an "?" after it to denote that the name could not be accurately read. If a given parish numbered the pages in the baptismal register, these have been recorded under the "Page" column.

The source of information for this index is baptismal registers which were kept by the individual parish churches, and are stored on microfiche at the Archives of the

Archdiocese of Cincinnati. For more information on the process to request copies of the original register entries, consult the website, http://www.catholiccincinnati.org/ministries-offices/archives-office/genealogy/.

Requests for original copies should be made in writing either using the online form or directly submitting the request using the website. In the future, copies of these registers will be available on Findmypast.

The researcher should always check alternative spellings when using this or other alphabetical indices. During this time, the entries were recorded in Latin. The German churches kept their records in Latin also, but sometimes used the old German script, which complicates reading and interpretation of the information even further. Additional interpretation problems can arise due to bad handwriting, faded ink, ink blots on the page, yellowing and torn pages, and incomplete entries. In all cases, the best possible interpretation was used, and other sources were consulted, when available, to double-check a questionable interpretation or fill in missing information.

There may be a great deal of spelling variations in the way a first or last name was spelled. The priest recording the information might have had a hard time understanding and writing the name if the person speaking had a heavy foreign accent. Since many of the first or given names were also recorded in Latin, this can make translation into English difficult, and can result in several different possibilities for an equivalent name in English. For example, the name Jacob in Latin can be translated into English as either James or Jacob, while the name Joanna in Latin can be translated into English as Johanna, Joanne, Joan or Jane.

Common spelling variations include the frequent interchangeability of the letters C and K in names such as Carl and Karl, which can itself be a name in English, or can be translated into English as the equivalent name Charles. The same interchange can frequently be seen in spelling the Irish surname Cavanaugh or Kavanaugh.

German children typically had two or three given names, which could be recorded in any order in any entry. In a few cases, only one or two of the given names were recorded due to space considerations on the page.

The unique German letters and their usual English equivalents are listed below as an aid to the reader. Any unique German letter recorded, was used in this index to preserve the original name.
> ä usually translated into English as ae
> ö usually translated into English as oe
> ü usually translated into English as ue
> ß usually translated into English as ss

Some examples are Schäfer = Schaefer, Schröder = Schroeder, Müller = Mueller, and Bußmann = Bussmann.

List of Parishes and Codes

Code	Church	Dates
A	Holy Trinity	1850 - 1859
B	St. Peter in Chains Cathedral	1850 - 1859
C	Old St. Mary	1850 - 1859
D	St. John the Baptist	1850 - 1859
E	St. Francis Xavier	1850 - 1859
F	St. Joseph	1850 - 1859
G	Our Lady of Victory	1850 - 1859
H	St. James the Greater (White Oak)	1850 - 1859
J	St. Michael	1850 - 1859
K	St. Philomena	1850 - 1859
L	St. Paul	1850 - 1859
M	All Saints	1850 - 1859
N	St. Francis de Sales	1850 - 1859
P	St. Patrick	1850 - 1859
Q	St. Clement	1850 - 1859
R	Sts. Peter and Paul (Reading)	1851 - 1859
S	St. John the Baptist (Harrison)	1850 - 1859
T	St. Augustine	1853 - 1859
U	St. Boniface	1853 - 1859
V	St. Thomas	1853 - 1859
W	St. Peter (Lick Run)	1854 - 1859
X	St. Lawrence	1856 - 1859
Y	St. Francis Seraph	1859 - 1859
Z	Holy Angels	1859 - 1859
AA	St. Anthony (Madisonville)	1859 - 1859

Name of Child	Date of Baptism	Father	Mother	Church	Page
---- Sebastian	6, Apr. 1851		----, Elisabeth	D	260
----, (wife of James)	5, June 1852		adult	M	
----, Abraham	21, Nov. 1858	Edward	----, Bridget	M	
----, Ann	2, Aug. 1854	----	----, ----	M	
----, Ann	23, Aug. 1852		adult	M	
----, Ann Mary	11, Oct. 1856	?	?	B	35
----, Bernard Heinrich	10, Feb. 1853		adult - 42 years old	K	
----, Bridget	12, Apr. 1857	Daniel	----, Bridget	M	
----, Bridget	29, June 1856	Patrick	----, Mary	M	
----, Carl	20, Sept 1856	?	?	D	67
----, Carl Johan	13, Aug. 1859	?	?	D	144
----, Catharina	27, Sept 1855	Francis	----, Theresa	D	43
----, Catherine	22, Apr. 1851	----	----, ----	E	303
----, Catherine	18, July 1854	?	----, Ann	E	208
----, Catherine	1, Nov. 1852	?	?	B	274
----, Catherine	26, July 1852	?	?	B	266
----, Catherine	27, June 1858	Martin	----, Mary Ellen	M	
----, Catherine Elizabeth	5, Dec. 1856	Edward	----, Elizabeth	M	
----, Charles August	3, Apr. 1859	----	----, ----	E	615
----, Daniel	20, June 1856	----	----, ----	E	375
----, Daniel	16, May 1858	John	----, Bridget	M	
----, Edward	21, Dec. 1858	----	----, ----	E	588
----, Elisabeth Sophia	26, July 1858	Georg	Karre, Barbara	D	116
----, Ellen	13, July 1856	John	----, Mary	M	
----, Eva Margaretha	7, Oct. 1857	?	?	D	96
----, Francis	12, Nov. 1852	----	----, ----	E	34
----, Francis	30, Jan. 1859	----	----, ----	U	
----, Francis Joseph	28, Feb. 1859	----	----, ----	E	607
----, Friedrich?	29, May 1851	J. Christian	Holtmeyer, Anna Elisabeth	Q	1
----, George	5, Dec. 1853	?	?	B	304
----, Gerhard Heinrich	2, Jan. 1859	Herman	Renner, Sophia	T	
----, Hannah Ann	6, Nov. 1853		adult - 22 years old	P	58
----, James	31, July 1853	----	----, ----	R	
----, James	20, Apr. 1856	Christopher	----, Joanne	E	360
----, James	25, Sept 1859	Daniel	----, Bridget	M	
----, James	13, Oct. 1850	K.	Gilchrist, Margaret	M	
----, James	5, June 1852		adult	M	
----, Johan	13, Jan. 1856	?	?	K	
----, John	8, Sept 1850	----	----, ----	E	246
----, John	12, Nov. 1852	----	----, ----	E	34
----, John	31, July 1853	----	----, ----	R	
----, John	9, Aug. 1858	----	4 years old	U	
----, John	11, Aug. 1855	Daniel	----, Bridget	M	
----, John	30, Nov. 1851	James	----, Mary Ann	M	
----, John	20, Jan. 1859	James	----, Susan	M	
----, John	8, May 1859	John	----, Bridget	M	
----, John	10, Oct. 1859	John	----, Margaret	M	
----, John	22, Jan. 1854	Martin	----, Bridget	M	
----, John	25, Jan. 1857	Patrick	----, Mary	M	
----, John	14, June 1855	Philip	----, Mary	M	
----, John Edward	19, Jan. 1851	----	----, ----	E	277
----, John Joseph	16, Aug. 1854	----	----, ----	E	217
----, John William	15, July 1853	William	----, Catherine	E	107
----, Joseph	20, June 1856	----	----, ----	E	375
----, Joseph	27, Sept 1859	----	----, ----	E	658
----, Joseph	17, Jan. 1855	?	?	D	26
----, Joseph Aloysius	14, Dec. 1857	----	----, ----	E	501
----, Joseph Peter	3, May 1857		----, Sophia	N	
----, Julia	31, July 1853	----	----, ----	R	

Name of Child	Date of Baptism	Father	Mother	Church	Page
----, Margaret	16, June 1850	----	----, ----	E	224
----, Margaret	26, June 1853	?	?	B	294
----, Margaret	25, Feb. 1857	James	----, Catherine	M	
----, Margaret	15, Mar. 1854	Patrick	----, Margaret	M	
----, Margaret Theresa	17, Oct. 1858		adult - 13 years old	B	65
----, Maria	10, June 1854	----	----, ----	D	12
----, Maria	15, June 1855		adult - 20 years old	K	
----, Maria Bernardina	11, Dec. 1855	?	?	K	
----, Maria Margaretha	9, Oct. 1859	?	?	K	
----, Maria Philomena	16, Apr. 1850		14 years old	K	
----, Maria Theresa	20, Mar. 1857	?	?	K	
----, Martha	9, Aug. 1858	----	4 years old	U	
----, Martin	12, Dec. 1858	John	----, Mary	M	
----, Mary	26, Aug. 1851	----	----, ----	E	337
----, Mary	23, May 1853	----	----, ----	E	91
----, Mary	16, June 1851	?	?	B	234
----, Mary	28, Apr. 1854	?	?	B	314
----, Mary	3, Feb. 1857	John	----, Mary Ann	M	
----, Mary	19, Apr. 1856	Patrick	----, Bridget	E	360
----, Mary	29, Nov. 1850		adult - 58 years old	E	264
----, Mary	8, Mar. 1859	?	?	B	74
----, Mary Jane	8, June 1856		adult - 34 years old	P	182
----, Mary Josephine	2, Oct. 1852	?	?	B	271
----, Mary Josephine	7, Apr. 1851	?	?	B	229
----, Mary Magdalene	22, Jan. 1854	William	----, Magdalene	M	
----, Mary S.	1, July 1853	----	adult - 18 years old	E	103
----, Michael	11, July 1855	Francis	----, Bridget	M	
----, Michael	12, Sept 1858	Henry	----, Catherine	M	
----, Michael Ignatius	23, June 1850	----	----, ----	E	225
----, Patrick Joseph	24, Mar. 1858	?	?	B	57
----, Peter	26, Jan. 1853	?	?	B	281
----, Peter	3 Sept 1850	?	?	K	
----, Philomena Maria	17, June 1859		14 years old	K	
----, Philomena Susanna	17, June 1859		adult - 21 years old	K	
----, Richard	31, July 1853	----	----, ----	R	
----, Rose	22, Feb. 1855	Richard	----, Mary	M	
----, Samuel	13, May 1855	James	----, Mary Ann	M	
----, Sarah	29, May 1858	Patrick	----, Mary	M	
----, Sarah	21, Dec. 1856		adult	B	38
----, Sarah Ellen	12, June 1859	----	----, ----	M	
----, Sophia Carolina	21, Dec. 1858	Ludwig	----, Elisabeth	T	
----, Thomas	2, Dec. 1858	Thomas	----, Ann	M	
----, Thomas	30, Aug. 1857	Thomas	----, Bridget	M	
----, Wilhelm	9, Aug. 1858	----	3 years old	U	
----, William	17, Aug. 1850	----	----, ----	E	240
----, William	25, Dec. 1852	----	----, ----	P	32
----, William	8, Dec. 1858	----	1 year & 6 months old	U	
----, William Henry Joseph	22, Feb. 1857	?	?	B	41
----, William James	29, June 1856	?	?	B	30
----, William James	19, July 1857	William	----, Elizabeth	M	
----?, Apollonia Salomea	8, Feb. 1852	Nicolaus	Staub, Apollonia	K	
----?, Bridget	26, June 1856	Fe---	Needham, Mary	B	30
----?, Julia	14, Aug. 1853	William	----, Ellen	M	
----?, Sarah Jane	16, June 1856	William	O'Connor, Catherine	B	30
Aar, Jacob	9, Aug. 1856	Jacob	Pitlinger, Gertrud	D	64
Abel, Carl Wilhelm	7, Oct. 1859	Johan	Rettinger, Catharina	D	148
Abel, Carolina	28, Nov. 1852	Daniel	Sehir, Magdalena	K	
Abel, Carolina	8, July 1852	Heinrich	Wessel, Angela	J	16
Abel, Catherine	30, Mar. 1850	?	?	B	199

Name of Child	Date of Baptism	Father	Mother	Church	Page
Abel, Charles Henry	10, July 1853	James A.	Shockey, Mary Agnes	B	295
Abel, Daniel	28, Nov. 1852	Daniel	Sehir, Magdalena	K	
Abel, Elisabeth	18, May 1853	Francis H.	Elsen, Elisabeth	K	
Abel, Friedrich	28, Nov. 1852	Daniel	Sehir, Magdalena	K	
Abel, Gerhard Francis	14, Mar. 1855	Francis	Elsen, Elisabeth	K	
Abel, Heinrich	6, May 1854	Heinrich	Wessels, Angela	A	
Abel, Henry Robert	1, July 1855	James A.	Shockley, Mary Agnes	B	16
Abel, Herman August	25, May 1856	Heinrich	Lenfort, Anna Maria	J	36
Abel, Johan Theodor	7, Oct. 1859	Johan	Rettinger, Catharina	D	148
Abel, Joseph Gabriel	6, Apr. 1851	James	Shockley, Mary	B	229
Abel, Magdalena	28, Nov. 1852	Daniel	Sehir, Magdalena	K	
Abel, Marcellus	24, Apr. 1859	J. Georg	Kirsh, Maria	T	
Abel, Maria Gertrud	8, Aug. 1858	Heinrich	Lenfers, Maria	J	46
Abel, Maria Philomena	25, Dec. 1850	J. Joseph	Grobmeier, Maria Gertrud	A	
Abel, Melina	30, Sept 1857	Johan	Rettinger, Catharina	D	95
Abel, Severin	2, Mar. 1856	Johan	Rettinger, Catharina	D	53
Abel, Theresa	28, Nov. 1852	Daniel	Sehir, Magdalena	K	
Abeling, Anna Helena	12, Feb. 1856	J. Heinrich	Muckerheide, Anna	A	
Abeling, Bernard Heinrich	7, Feb. 1859	J. Heinrich	Borges, Helena	A	
Abeling, Francis Heinrich	27, June 1856	Heinrich	Lehmkuhle, Maria Anna	A	
Abeling, Joseph Gerhard	24, Feb. 1858	F. Heinrich	Muckerheide, Anna Helena	C	
Abeling, Peter Francis Heinrich	18, Jan. 1859	Francis	Muckerheide, Anna	A	
Abell, Mary Frances	10, June 1857	James	Shockley, Mary Ann	V	39
Abels, John	5, Feb. 1850		11 years old	B	195
Abert, Bernard	20, Mar. 1853	Bernard	----, Louise	B	286
Abigth, Johan Edward Adolph	9, Nov. 1857	Adolph	Deters, Agnes	K	
Abke, Johan Bernard	29, July 1857	Bernard	Pingsterauch, Elisabeth	C	
Abke, Maria Catharina	17, June 1850	B. Heinrich	Pingsterhaus, Maria Elisa	D	217
Abke, Wilhelmina Elisabeth Adelheid	26, Aug. 1853	Bernard H.	Pingsterhaus, Cahtarina Elis.	D	402
Achterkamp, Anna Maria Catharina	29, Dec. 1850	H. Dietrich	Werner, Maria Catharina	A	
Ackerman, Andreas	22, Nov. 1851	Mathias	----, Barbara	R	
Ackerman, Anna Elisabeth	16, May 1859	J. Bernard	Vedder, Elisabeth	R	
Ackerman, Barbara	2, Jan. 1857	Valentin	Müller, Christina	A	
Ackerman, Johan	16, Sept 1855	Valentin	Müller, Christina	A	
Ackerman, Susan	27, Aug. 1853	Mathias	Schütz, Barbara	R	
Ackermann, Anna Catharina	23, Feb. 1851	Simon	Eicher, Anna	F	
Ackermann, Anna Magdalena	5, Nov. 1854	Simon	Eicher, Anna	F	
Ackermann, Anna Maria Elisabeth	20, Mar. 1853	J. Theodor	Hoppe, Josephina	F	
Ackermann, Dominick Leo	10, July 1856	Theodor	Happe, Josephina	F	
Ackermann, Franz Herman	26, Dec. 1853	Bernard	Berling, Elisabeth	L	
Ackermann, Herman Heinrich	30, Sept 1854	Theodor	Hoppe, Josephina	F	
Ackermann, Johan Bernard Jacob	25, July 1850	J. Bernard	Determann, M. Catharina	L	
Ackermann, Mathias Wilhelm	7, Aug. 1858	J. Theodor	Hoppe, Josephina	F	
Ackermann, Rosa	28, Nov. 1852	Simon	Eicher, Anna	F	
Ackmann, Johan Christoph	15, May 1851	Heinrich	Hemann, Maria	L	
Acres, Mary Elizabeth	19, Nov. 1850	James	Fagan, Mary A.	B	219
Acton, Margaret	11, Aug. 1852	Patrick	Shields, Ellen	P	26
Adam, Anna Carolina	20, July 1850	Heinrich	Peter, Juliana	F	
Adam, Carl Michael	2, Mar. 1851	Francis	Remlinger, Theresa	C	
Adam, Carl Wilhelm	18, Apr. 1852	Michael	Schindler, Helena	J	16
Adam, Carolina Louisa	25, Sept 1853	Valentin	Schaller, Appolonia	F	
Adam, Francis Andreas	12, Mar. 1853	Francis	Remlinger, Theresa	C	
Adam, Francis Wendel	7, Dec. 1851	Thomas	Haver, Maria Magdalena	J	14
Adam, Georg Simon	15, Feb. 1857	Georg	Frick, Maria	F	
Adam, Heinrich Georg	9, Mar. 1851	Valentin	Schaller, Apollonia	F	
Adam, Laurenz Joseph	8, Apr. 1855	Michael	Schimler, Helena	F	
Adam, Robert	14, Aug. 1859	Lawrence	Lammers, Maria	F	
Adam, Rosa Martha	20, Mar. 1859	Valentin	Schaller, Appolonia	F	
Adam, Valentin Edward	25, Dec. 1856	Valentin	Schaller, Appolonia	F	

Name of Child	Date of Baptism	Father	Mother	Church	Page
Adam, Wilhelm Robert	31, May 1857	Lawrence	Lames, Maria	F	
Adams, Anna	5, Nov. 1854	Georg	Frick, Anna Maria	F	
Adams, Clemens Arnold	30, June 1853	Heinrich	Rechtin, Carolina	A	
Adams, Fanny Mary	28, May 1855	Alexander	White, Mary	E	289
Adams, Heinrich Eduard	15, June 1850	J. Peter	Höfer, Wilhelmina	D	217
Adams, James Monroe	8, Sept 1850	John Q.	Dorst, Mary Ann	B	213
Adams, Johan Vinant	28, Mar. 1854	Peter	Hoefer, Wilhelmina	L	
Adams, Johannetta	29, July 1855	Heinrich	Rechtine, Catharina	A	
Adams, John	1, Apr. 1851	John	Carr, Eliza	B	228
Adams, John William	16, Nov. 1858	John	Miller, Rody	P	267
Adams, Joseph	24, Sept 1859	John	Carr, Elizabeth	E	656
Adams, Joseph	16, Nov. 1858	John	Miller, Rody	P	267
Adams, Maria	28, Sept 1853	Lawrence	Lehmis, Maria	J	24
Adams, Mary	1, Sept 1857	John	Carr, Elizabeth	B	49
Adams, Mary	12, Dec. 1857	Silvester	Hass, Mary Ann	E	500
Ader, Anna Catharina Elisabeth	27, June 1858	Francis	Schmidt, Barbara	C	
Ader, Anton Johan	26, June 1856	Jacob	Metzler, Apollonia	C	
Ader, Carolina Anna Maria	23, Apr. 1854	Jacob	Meitzler, Apollonia	C	
Ader, Catharina	11, June 1858	Jacob	----, Apollonia	C	
Ader, Elisabeth	25, Apr. 1852	Jacob	Metzler, Apollonia	C	
Ader, Francis	7, Apr. 1850	Jacob	Meitzler, Appolonia	D	208
Ader, Georg Michael	18, Sept 1856	Francis	Sibert, Barbara	C	
Ader, Ludwig Jacob	26, Aug. 1859	Jacob	Meitzler, Apollonia	C	
Ader, Peter Anton	3, July 1858	Anton	Wagner, Eva	C	
Adler, Catharina	18, Apr. 1856	Leonard	Scheibel, Elisabeth	D	56
Adler, Simon	8, Nov. 1857	Leonard	Scheibel, Elisabeth	C	
Adlers, Maria Anna Elisabeth	6, Mar. 1852	Heinrich	Repling, Anna Maria	R	
Admire, John Baptist	25, May 1856	William	----, Mary	H	
Agen, Peter	11, Dec. 1859	Peter	Landen, Margaret	J	52
Agers, John	14, Mar. 1857	John	Kellegar, Ellen	E	439
Ahaus, Herman Heinrich	29, Aug. 1855	Bernard	Wulfhorst, Maria Clara	D	41
Ahaus, Johan Heinrich	16, Oct. 1857	J. Heinrich	Kuhlman, Maria Anna	A	
Ahaus, Johan Herman	11, Nov. 1854	J. Heinrich	Kuhlman, Maria Anna	A	
Ahaus, Maria Catharina	16, Oct. 1854	H. Joseph	Brinkman, Maria Elisabeth	A	
Ahaus, Maria Catharina Elisabeth	14, Aug. 1857	Herman	Wolke, Maria	D	92
Ahaus, Maria Elisabeth	22, Oct. 1852	Herman	Wulfhorst, Maria Clara	D	354
Ahaus, Maria Elisabeth	14, Apr. 1852	Joseph	Brinkman, Maria Elisabeth	A	
Ahaus, Mechtildis Wilhelmina	25, Feb. 1857	Joseph	Brinkman, Maria Elisabeth	A	
Ahaus, Wilhelm Heinrich	14, Oct. 1859	J. Heinrich	Kuhlman, Maria	A	
Ahearn, Catherine	2, Apr. 1854	Edward	O'Connor, Catherine	B	312
Ahearn, Edward James	28, Mar. 1855	Edward	O'Connor, Catherine	B	13
Ahearn, John	4, May 1852	John	Sheenan, Joanne	P	21
--aherbach, Anna Maria	28, Apr. 1858	Adam	Kapp, Margaretha	D	110
Ahern, Andrew	10, July 1853	Cornelius	----, Honora	U	
Ahern, Daniel	6, Nov. 1855	Cornelius	----, Honora	M	
Ahern, Edmund Patrick	16, Mar. 1851	Edward	O'Connor, Catherine	B	226
Ahern, Honora	7, Nov. 1858	Dennis	----, Catherine	M	
Ahern, John	3, Mar. 1858	Cornelius	----, Honora	M	
Ahern, John	29, Aug. 1852	Edward	O'Connor, Catherine	B	269
Ahern, Mau.	6, Mar. 1856	Dennis	----, Catherine	M	
Ahern, Maurice	4, Dec. 1859	John	Hennessey, Catherine	Z	
Ahern, Peter	2, Mar. 1851	John	Oldham, Mary Jane	B	228
Ahern, William	18, Sept 1857	Dennis	----, Catherine	M	
Ahleman, Johan	22, Oct. 1852	Johan	Stegg, Anna Maria	K	
Ahleman, Maria Anna Theresa	3, Sept 1853	Johan	Stich, Anna Maria	K	
Ahleman, Maria Paulina	8, June 1856	Johan	Stech, Anna Maria	K	
Ahlendick, Theodor Eduard	26, Aug. 1855	Herman	Rapke, Agnes	F	
Ahlendicke, Herman Franz	14, May 1851	Herman	Rapke, Agnes	F	
Ahler, Maria Gertrud	15, Jan. 1856	Herman	Tinker, Marianna	F	

Name of Child	Date of Baptism	Father	Mother	Church	Page
Ahlering, Carl Wilhelm	8, Feb. 1859	Friedrich	Ahrens, Elisabeth	K	
Ahlering, Friedrich Aloysius	6, Jan. 1851	Friedrich	Ahrnsen, Elisabeth	K	
Ahlering, Heinrich August Ludwig	1, Sept 1853	Friedrich	Ahrnzen, Maria Elisabeth	K	
Ahlering, Johan Bernard	13, Jan. 1856	Friedrich	Ahrens, Anna Maria	K	
Ahlers, Agnes Emma	21, Apr. 1857	J. Heinrich	Tiele, Bernardina	C	
Ahlers, Aloysius	15, May 1859	Carl	Bunnemeier, M. Cath.	L	
Ahlers, Amalia Adelheid Elisabeth	9, Oct. 1859	Heinrich	Willenbrink, Elisabeth	C	
Ahlers, Anna Maria Catharina	7, Apr. 1851	J. Heinrich	Heidelmann, Anna Maria	F	
Ahlers, Anna Maria Elisabeth	1, Aug. 1855	Carl Aug.	Bunnemeyer, Catharina	L	
Ahlers, Bernard	29, Feb. 1856	Bernard	Frass, Elisabeth	F	
Ahlers, Bernard	2, Aug. 1857	Herman	Junker, Adelheid	T	
Ahlers, Carl Arnold	10, May 1857	Carl Th.	Bunnemeier, M. Cath.	L	
Ahlers, Carl Francis	23, Nov. 1855	J. Heinrich	Thiele, Bernardina	C	
Ahlers, Clemens Edward	16, Nov. 1851	Heinrich	Thiele, Bernardina	C	
Ahlers, Herman Heinrich	1, June 1854	Herman H.	Tinkers, Marianna	F	
Ahlers, Johan Felix Ludwig	20, Nov. 1853	J. Heinrich	Thiele, Bernardina	C	
Ahlers, Louise	10, Apr. 1853	Herman	----, ----	U	
Ahlers, Philomena	22, Mar. 1854	Carl	Buenmeyer, Catharina	L	
Ahlers, Willibord Johan	16, Apr. 1853	J. Heinrich	Heilman, Maria	D	380
Ahlmark, Mary Adelheid	6, Feb. 1852	?	?	B	252
Ahls, Carolina Clementina	13, Feb. 1859	Johan	Bode, Augustina	F	
Ahman, Anna Maria Catharina	10, Oct. 1858	Wilhelm	Allers, Elisabeth	Q	29
Ahr, A. Maria	22, Nov. 1857	Jacob	Bittlinger, Gertrud	T	
Ahr, Bertha	14, Mar. 1858	Conrad	Mappes, Elisabeth	F	
Ahr, Josephina Theresa	27, Jan. 1856	Conrad	Mabbis, Elisabeth	F	
Ahr, Mathias	9, July 1854	Jacob	Batlinger, Gertrud	F	
Ahrens, Anna Maria Elisabeth	21, Aug. 1853	Heinrich	Bremermann, Maria	F	
Ahrens, Bernard Heinrich	8, Feb. 1857	Heinrich	Bremesmann, Maria	F	
Ahrens, Johan Gerhard	20, May 1852	Heinrich	Bremersmann, Maria	F	
Ahrens, Johan Gerhard	21, Nov. 1858	Johan H.	Bremersmann, Anna M.	T	
Ahrens, Maria Paulina Francisca	29, Nov. 1856	Gerhard	Krahmann, Margaretha	C	
Ahrens, Mathias Aloysius	19, Jan. 1854	J. Gerhard	Grammann, Elisabeth	C	
Ahrling, Anna Maria Elisabeth	13, July 1856	Francis H.	----, Maria Elisabeth	D	62
Ahrns, Maria Margaretha	27, Apr. 1851	Ludwig	Bremercamp, Maria	F	
Ahrsman, Joseph	13, Dec. 1855	Joseph	Bruneman, Elisabeth	D	48
Ahrsman, Maria Catharina	29, Dec. 1859	Joseph	Kest---, Anna Maria	D	153
Aigner, Johan Anton	29, Nov. 1854	John	Wagner, Francisca	N	26
Ainwright, Mary Helen	8, Dec. 1852	Cornelius	Bradish, Helen	B	277
Akenberg, Maria Anna	21, Feb. 1858	Francis	Jörling, M.B.	A	
Akenberg, Maria Catharina	10, Jan. 1855	Francis H.	Jörring, Maria Bernardina	A	
Akötter, Anna Maria Elisabeth	29, Mar. 1852	Anton	Koch, Gertrud	K	
Akötter, Herman Joseph	15, Aug. 1854	Anton	Koch, Anna Catharina	K	
Alban, Ludwig Peter	5, Oct. 1851	Ludwig	Dopler, Catharina	F	
Alber, Bernard Friedrich	11, Apr. 1850	J. Heinrich	Berns, Maria Catharina	D	208
Albers, Anna Maria Catharina	16, Mar. 1851	Gerhard H.	Linnemann, M. Catharina	L	
Albers, Bernard Clemens	9, Sept 1859	Clemens	Werman, Elisabeth	D	146
Albers, Bernard Friedrich Wilhelm	6, May 1859	Johan	Schnitteloh, Antonia C.	L	
Albers, Clemens	4, Sept 1854	Theodor	Hoppe, Elisabeth	K	
Albers, Heinrich Anton	3, May 1855	Heinrich	Runde, Maria	C	
Albers, Heinrich Francis	20, July 1854	Friedrich	Moller, Catharina	C	
Albers, Johan Clemens	26, Nov. 1857	Clemens	Werman, Elisabeth	D	99
Albers, Johan Heinrich	18, Nov. 1855	Clemens	Wehrman, Maria Elisabeth	A	
Albers, Johan Mathias	23, Aug. 1855	Gerhard H.	Lineman, Catharina Maria	D	41
Albers, Maria	7, June 1857	Theodor	Hoppe, Elisabeth	K	
Albers, Maria Agatha	4, Feb. 1856	Johan F.	----, Catharina	C	
Albers, Maria Anna	26, Mar. 1858	Friedrich	Miller, Catharina	C	
Albers, Maria Anna Francisca	25, Mar. 1853	Gerhard H.	Lindemann, Maria	L	
Albers, Maria Catharina	13, Oct. 1851	Friedrich	Moeller, Catharina	C	
Albers, Maria Catharina	8, July 1859	Johan G.H.	Lindeman, Anna Maria K.	D	141

Name of Child	Date of Baptism	Father	Mother	Church	Page
Albers, Maria Catharina Elisabeth	20, Sept 1852	Bernard H.	Gerdes, Maria Elisabeth	A	
Albers, Maria Clara	19, Sept 1853	Heinrich	Runde, Anna M.	C	
Albers, Maria Josephina	19, June 1851	Theodor	Hoppe, Elisabeth	K	
Albersman, Maria Elisabeth	9, Aug. 1854	Theodor	Schwartz, Margaretha	A	
Albersmann, Anna Maria	12, Nov. 1856	Theodor	Schwarte, Margaretha	C	
Albert, Adam	11, Oct. 1855	Martin	----, Victoria	H	
Albert, Dorothea	30, Oct. 1859	Martin	Schmidt, Victoria	T	
Albert, Eva Helena	19, Sept 1851	Hieronymus	Traut, Barbara	A	
Albert, Francis	20, Jan. 1858	Martin	Schwe---, Victoria	D	103
Albert, Francis Joseph	6, Aug. 1850	Hieronymus	Traut, Barbara	A	
Albert, Franz Joseph Albert	12, Apr. 1853	Hieronymus	Trauten, Barbara	F	
Albert, Maria Anna	1, Jan. 1852	Michael	Flick, Margaretha	D	300
Albert, Maria Carolina	16, Jan. 1859	Johan	Baldnof, Maria	T	
Albert, Maria Margaretha	31, Mar. 1850	Michael	Flick, Margaretha	D	207
Albertzahrt, Agnes Diedricka	15, July 1855	Herman	Krumpelbeck, Maria	L	
Albertzahrt, Johan Joseph Heinrich	30, Apr. 1854	Herman	Krumpelbeck, Magdalena	L	
Albertzart, Henrietta Johanna	31, July 1859	J. Herman	Krümmelbeck, M. Magdalena	A	
Albiger, Catharina	7, Feb. 1857	Jacob	Bodimer, Catharina	K	
Albiger, Elisabeth	6, Dec. 1852	Jacob	Bodimer, Catharina	K	
Albiger, Magdalena	21, Jan. 1855	Jacob	Bodemer, Catharina	K	
Alborn, Catharina Elisabeth	26, Feb. 1854	William	----, Elisabeth Catherine	F	
Albrecht, Josephina Catharina	13, Nov. 1859	Ignatius	Cammendzind, Catharina	K	
Albrecht, Magdalena Philomena	2, Mar. 1856	Ignatius	Konzing, Catharina	K	
Albrecht, Paulina Magdalena	4, Apr. 1858	Ignatius	Kaminzing, Magdalena	K	
Albrinck, Bernardina Anna	3, Mar. 1859	Friedrich	Schneider, Louisa	C	
Albrink, Herman Heinrich	17, June 1852	H. Heinrich	Kruse, Josephina	K	
---ald, Dennis	22, Nov. 1850	Thomas	Ahern, Honora	M	
Alden, Maria Margaretha	8, Sept 1850	Francis	Schloss, Theresa	K	
Alder, Johan	5, June 1856	Johan	Bayler, Carolina	C	
Alexand, William	10, Nov. 1852	William	adult - 25 years old	E	34
Alexander, Edward	13, June 1858	Joseph	Conlon, Honora	B	60
Alexander, Francis	19, Apr. 1854	Anthony	Flaherty, Mary	R	
Alexander, Francis	21, Sept 1856	George	----, Elisabeth	R	
Alexander, Helen	10, Apr. 1853	Robert	Murphy, Helen	B	288
Alexander, Hugh	18, Dec. 1855	Anthony	Flaherty, Mary	R	
Alexander, Joseph	22, Mar. 1857	Joseph	Connell, Honora	B	42
Alexander, William	10, Dec. 1854	Joseph	Conlon, Honora	P	109
Alexandre, Joseph David	19, Nov. 1852	Isaac	adult - 32 years old	E	36
Alf, Anna Maria	16, July 1851	Francis	Altenschulte, Anna Maria	F	
Alf, Anna Maria	12, Dec. 1853	J. Gerhard	Herzog, Elisabeth	D	420
Alf, Anna Maria	17, Feb. 1856	J. Theodor	Schipper, Anna M.	C	
Alf, Anna Maria	25, Jan. 1853	Wilhelm	Luehn, Adelheid	F	
Alf, Anna Maria Christina	25, Dec. 1854	Gerhard H.	Doll, Anna Maria	F	
Alf, Anna Maria Philomena	16, Mar. 1853	Theodor	Schipper, Maria	C	
Alf, Anna Maria Theresa	8, Sept 1853	Francis	Altenschulten, Maria	F	
Alf, Barbara Margaretha Veronica	13, June 1852	Johan	Latin, Maria Salome	L	
Alf, Bernard Dietrich	22, June 1852	G. Heinrich	Dall, Maria	K	
Alf, Bernard Herman	7, June 1851	G. Herman	Dull, Anna Maria	K	
Alf, Franz Theodor	18, Apr. 1856	Francis	Schulte, Anna Maria	F	
Alf, Johan Georg	10, Dec. 1858	Theodor	Schipper, Maria	C	
Alf, Johan Herman	15, Aug. 1857	Gerhard H.	Kleinhardt, Maria	F	
Alf, Johan Herman	16, Jan. 1859	Herman	Peters, Christina	C	
Alf, Johan Theodor	23, June 1851	Theodor	Schipper, Maria	C	
Alf, Johan Wilhelm	25, Dec. 1856		Alf, Regina	J	38
Alf, Maria Elisabeth	4, Nov. 1858	Francis	Altenschulte, A. Maria	F	
Alf, Maria Elisabeth	18, Oct. 1851	Gerhard	Herzog, Maria Elisabeth	D	287
Alf, Maria Elisabeth	19, July 1852	Herman	Debus, Anna Christina	D	340
Alf, Maria Elisabeth	28, Mar. 1858	Johan W.	Luehn, Maria Adelheid	F	
Alf, Maria Elisabeth Josephina	26, Aug. 1855	Wilhelm	Luehn, Adelheid	F	

Name of Child	Date of Baptism	Father	Mother	Church	Page
Alf?, Maria Theresa	3, Feb. 1852	J. Gerhard	Hammer, Catharina Theresa	K	
Alfers, Anna Maria	4, June 1856	J. Heinrich	Wolke, Anna	C	
Alfers, Anna Maria Elisabeth	20, July 1855	Herman	Daming, Johanna	N	
Alfers, Francis Heinrich	8, June 1858	J. Heinrich	Wolke, M. Catharina	C	
Alfers, Heinrich Gerhard	26, Oct. 1853	Herman	Daming, Johanna	N	17
Alfers, Johan Bernard Heinrich	11, Dec. 1857	B. Herman	Daming, Johanna	N	
Alfers, Joseph Heinrich	12, June 1853	Bernard	Wolke, Catharina	C	
Alfers, Maria Adelheid	27, June 1852	Herman	Daming, Johanna	N	7
Alfers, Maria Elisabeth	2, Nov. 1851	J. Heinrich	Wolke, Anna Maria	D	290
Alfred, Ida Catharina	8, Apr. 1855	Conrad	Schoepner, Ida	F	
Alfs, Anna Maria	3, Dec. 1855	Herman	Deters, Christina	C	
Algeier, Anna Catharina	25, Dec. 1855	Francis X.	Miggenburg, Gesina	D	49
Algeier, Anna Gertrud	13, Dec. 1857	Xavier	Mueggenburg, Gesina	T	
Algeier, Carolina	22, May 1856	Clemens	Vollmer, Maria Anna	D	59
Algemeier, Emma Maria Catharina	22, Aug. 1858	Andreas	Schmidt, Maria	D	117
Algemeier, Johan Julius	24, Dec. 1856	Andreas	Schmidt, Maria	D	75
Algenmeier, Heinrich Andreas	6, Aug. 1852	Heinrich A.	Schmid, Anna Maria	D	341
Alich, Catharina	17, Dec. 1854	J. Adam	Mueller, Margaretha	F	
Alich, Elisabeth	11, July 1852	Adam	Mueller, Margaretha	F	
Alich, Maria Barbara	11, Sept 1858	Johan A.	Mueller, Margaretha	F	
Alick, Adam	27, Feb. 1850	Adam	Müller, Margretha	D	203
Alig, Anna Maria	11, Sept 1853	Andreas	Gehrenbauer, Catharina	D	405
Alig, Johan Adam	17, Nov. 1850	Andreas	Gehrensbauer, Catharina	D	243
Aling, Francis Friedrich	22, Mar. 1854	Francis	Grote, Maria Elisabeth	D	7
Alkemeier, Eduard Francis	10, Oct. 1854	Andreas	Schmidt, Maria Elisabeth	D	19
Allart, Mary Catherine	4, May 1851	Louis	Lederey, Mary Catherine	E	305
Allen, John	28, Nov. 1855	William	Farley, Ann	T	
Allen, Julia	22, Oct. 1854	William	Hanlen, Catherine	E	234
Allen, Juliana	16, Feb. 1852	Alfred	Wel--, Margaret	B	253
Allen, Michael	17, Oct. 1852	Michael	McCabe, Bridget	E	28
Allen, Patrick	18, Oct. 1857	William	Farley, Ann	T	
Allendick, Herman Heinrich	23, Oct. 1853	Herman	Rupge, Agnes	F	
Allers, Johan Bernard	2, Sept 1851	Herman	Dunkers, Maria Anna	F	
Alley, Jean	31, May 1852	Andrew	----, Ann	E	421
Allgaier, William Sinclair	16, Apr. 1852	Sebastian	Snyder, Sarah	B	256
Allgan, Isabel Catherine	21, Mar. 1852	Richard	McFarland, Mary Ann	P	19
Allgeier, Aloisia	2, Nov. 1856	Paul	Reichert, Elisabeth	G	
Allgeier, Catharina Elisabeth	2, July 1854	Paul	Reichert, Elisabeth	F	
Allgeier, Christian	24, Apr. 1859	Paul	Reichard, Elisabeth	G	
Allgeier, Johan	30, Apr. 1854	Clemens	Vollmer, Maria Anna	D	9
Allgeier, Joseph	2, May 1858	Clemens	Vollmer, Maria Anna	D	110
Allgeyer, Theresa	20, Oct. 1850	Wendel	Beiler, Theresa	C	
Alligan, William	4, Oct. 1857	Richard	McFarlan, Mary Ann	P	**226**
Alliot, George	17, Mar. 1857	----	11 years old	U	
Alliot, William Andrew	17, Mar. 1857	----	6 years old	U	
Allman, Alice	19, Jan. 1859	Timothy	Doyle, Alice	B	70
Allman, John	7, Aug. 1855	John	Honer, Nancy	E	306
Allman, Margaret	7, Jan. 1855	Timothy	Doyle, Alice	B	9
Allman, Mary	21, Dec. 1856	Timothy	Doyle, Alice	B	38
Allo, (boy)	4, June 1854	Vincent	----, Catherine	E	196
Allow, John	5, Nov. 1854	William	David, Celia	P	102
Allwright, Mary Ann	11, Sept 1851	Francis	Maher, Bridget	B	240
Alsheimer, Carolina Barbara	10, Oct. 1858	J. Georg	Hartman, Margaretha	D	121
Alswaig, Bernard	3, Oct. 1856	Herman	Kraemer, Agnes	F	
Alswald, Johan Wilhelm	25, Apr. 1859	J. Herman	Kreiner, Agnes	F	
Alt, Adam	19, Feb. 1854	J. Gerhard	Welsch, Barbara	D	5
Alt, Johan	24, Feb. 1856	Gerhard	Welsch, Barbara	Q	13
Alt, Johan Peter	12, Apr. 1852	J. Gerhard	Welsch, Barbara	D	316
Alt, Johan Peter	9, May 1858	J. Gerhard	Welsch, Barbara	D	111

Name of Child	Date of Baptism	Father	Mother	Church	Page
Alt, Johan Peter	19, Dec. 1859	J. Gerhard	Welsch, Barbara	D	153
Alt, Johan Wilhelm	27, Apr. 1850	J. Gerhard	Welsch, Barbara	A	
Altbecker, Elisabeth Philomena	16, Jan. 1853	Joseph	Zahn, Catharina	D	365
Altbecker, Rosa Margaretha	25, Feb. 1855	Joseph	Sarn, Catharina	D	29
Altenau, Anna Bernardina Elisabeth	26, Dec. 1857	Wilhelm	Segnedi, Margaretha	F	
Altenau, Francis Anton	20, June 1858	Heinrich	Buddesmeyer, A. Catharina	A	
Altenau, Heinrich Herman	13, July 1856	J. Herman	Böckman, Agnes	A	
Altenau, Heinrich Jacob	11, Oct. 1855	Wilhelm	Schroeder, Margaretha	F	
Altenau, Heinrich Wilhelm	12, June 1859	Heinrich	Lahman, Anna Maria	A	
Altenau, Johan Gerhard Heinrich	28, Mar. 1851	Heinrich	Buddelmeier, M. Catharina	A	
Altenau, Josephina Carolina	19, July 1853	Heinrich	Buddemeier, Catharina	A	
Altenau, Marianna	16, Oct. 1859	Wilhelm	Sach, Margaretha	F	
Altenau, Wilhelm Heinrich	23, Feb. 1856	Heinrich	Buddelman, Maria Catharina	A	
Altenhoff, Elisabeth Sophia Henr.	5, Feb. 1854	Herman	Nuxol, Elisabeth	L	
Altenhoff, Herman Franz	8, Feb. 1852	Herman H.	Nuxel, M. Elisabeth	L	
Altenschulten, Catharina Francisca	20, Sept 1857	Bernard	Sendker, A. Angela	L	
Altenschulten, Herman Bernard	16, Nov. 1855	J. Bernard	Sendker, M. Engel	L	
Altenschulten, Johan Bernard	19, June 1859	J. Bernard	Sendker, M. Angela	L	
Altevers, Johan Heinrich	10, Oct. 1850	J. Herman	Krieger, Maria Anna	D	237
Altevers, Johan Herman	1, Oct. 1852	J. Heinrich	Krieger, Anna Maria	D	350
Altevers, Maria Catharina	26, Dec. 1856	J. Heinrich	Krieger, Maria Anna	D	75
Altevers, Nicolaus	7, Feb. 1855	J. Herman	Krieger, Maria Anna	D	28
Altevers, Theresa Josephina	25, Apr. 1859	Johan	Krieger, Johanna	F	
Altgilbers, Joseph Heinrich	18, Feb. 1852	Johan H.	Schulte, Susanna M.	F	
Althaus, Anton	4, Aug. 1851	Heinrich	Steinkamp, Elisabeth	F	
Altman, Jacob	20, Feb. 1859	Michael	Rapk, Salome	D	132
Altman, Magdalena	21, June 1857	Michael	Rapp, Salome	D	88
Altringer, Joseph Bernard	28, June 1857	Mathias	Plesser, Christina	A	
Altringer, Mathias Peter	4, Sept 1859	Mathias	Pleser, Christina	A	
Alwell, Ann	13, Mar. 1853	Michael	McKeown, Ann	B	286
Alwell, Margaret	2, Dec. 1855	Michael	McKeown, Ann	B	22
Alwell, Michael	25, June 1854	Michael	McKeown, Ann	B	1
Amand, Maria	18, Feb. 1855	Philipp A.	Luithart, Elisabeth	F	
Amandi, Francisca	24, Feb. 1852	Peter	Schrimme?, Barbara	D	309
Amann, Anna Maria	16, Feb. 1851		Amann, Anna Maria Gertrud	D	254
Amann, Bernard Aloyius Anton	6, Nov. 1855	Heinrich	Heet, Anna M.	C	
Amann, Emilia	19, May 1856	Philipp	Liefart, Elisabeth	A	
Amann, Johan Heinrich	26, Apr. 1853	Heinrich	Heet, Anna Maria	L	
Amann, Magdalena Dorothea	8, Feb. 1857	Conrad	Ankenbauer, Margaretha	A	
Amann, Maria	15, Apr. 1855	Conrad	Ankenbauer, Margaretha	A	
Ambrose, Daniel Joseph	15, May 1854	Patrick	Ftizgerald, Margaret	V	13
Ambrose, John	8, June 1856	Patrick	Fitzgerald, Margaret	E	372
Ambrose, Mary	2, Jan. 1853	Robert	Conners, Honora	E	50
Ambrose, Robert	13, Apr. 1851	Robert	Conners, Honora	P	7
Ambrose, Thomas	18, Apr. 1858	Patrick	Fitzgerald, Margaret	E	529
Amend, Margaret	15, May 1859	Valentin	Scanlin, Mary	R	
Amenskamp, Heinrich Joseph Aloysius	31, Sept 1855	Clemens	Tepe, Dina	K	
Amenskamp, Johan Francis	22, Aug. 1858	Clemens	Tepe, Bernardina	K	
Amer, Catharina	19, June 1859	Johan	Schr---, Catharina	S	
Amery, Henry	28, Feb. 1854	John	Phillips, Eliza	B	310
Ames, Felix	12, July 1851	William	Ronion, Mary	P	10
Ames, Maria Josephina	20, Feb. 1859	Joseph	Hagen, Mary	U	
Ames, Mary Medora	30, Jan. 1854	Fisher W.	DeShields, Mary T.	B	308
Ames, Matthew Charles	22, Feb. 1856	Joseph	Hagen, Mary	U	
Ames, William	15, May 1853	William	Rooney, Mary	E	90
Amiot, Philomina	14, Sept 1851	Francis	Leonard, Elizabeth	M	
Amman, Conrad	24, Oct. 1858	Conrad	Ankenbauer, Margaretha	A	
Amman, Dorothea	17, Apr. 1853	Conrad	Ankenbauer, Margaretha	J	22
Ammon, Dorothea	31, Jan. 1852	Conrad	Ankenbauer, Margaretha	D	304

Name of Child	Date of Baptism	Father	Mother	Church	Page
Ammon, Maria Catharina	10, Sept 1850	Hans	Auth, Maria Catharina	D	232
Amrein, Johan Adam	15, Aug. 1852	Bartholomew	----, Maria Anna	D	343
Amrein, Johan Michael	17, Sept 1854	Bartholomew	Fais, Maria	D	17
Amrein, Maria Anna	21, Nov. 1858	Bartholomew	Wem---, Maria	D	124
Amrein, Peter	2, Nov. 1856	Bartholomew	Wem---, Anna M.	D	71
Amschler, Johan	25, Mar. 1858	Joseph	Foster, Dorothea	U	
Amschler, Johan Georg	27, Apr. 1851	Joseph	Trestner, Dorothea	D	262
Amschler, Maria Dorothea	8, May 1853	Joseph	Köst, Dorothea	D	384
Amslacher, Pancratz	29, Apr. 1855	Johan	Stebelin, Barbara	U	
Amsler, A. Maria	21, Dec. 1857	John	Stablein, Barbara	T	
Anders---, Joseph Carl	2, Nov. 1858	Joseph C.	Schach---, Catharina	D	123
Anderson, Amanda	30, Mar. 1854	Robert	Arnold, Margaret	P	76
Anderson, Ann	22, Feb. 1855	William	Faron, Helen	B	11
Anderson, Catherine	24, Mar. 1850	John	Reagan, Ann	B	198
Anderson, Edward Francis	28, Nov. 1852	William	Feran, Helen	B	276
Anderson, Eliza	27, Mar. 1853	John	Reilly, Ann	B	287
Anderson, Ellen	26, Jan. 1851	Robert	----, Mary Ann	E	278
Anderson, James	18, Nov. 1855	William	McLane, Mary	E	327
Anderson, James Irwin	13, Mar. 1859	James	Irwin, Jane	B	72
Anderson, Josephine	25, Apr. 1851	John	Anderson, Sophia	M	
Anderson, Mary	22, Feb. 1855	William	Faron, Helen	B	11
Anderson, Mary Ann	4, June 1851	Samuel	----, Elizabeth	E	312
Anderson, Mary Anne	27, July 1851	John	----, Ann	E	328
Anderson, Mary Eliza	14, Aug. 1850	Robert	Arnold, Margaret	B	210
Anderson, Michael	2, Sept 1852	Michael	Martin, Mary	E	13
Anderson, Stephan John	3, Sept 1854	James	Irwin, Jane	B	5
Anderson, Susan Mary	13, Dec. 1855	James	Irwin, Jane	B	23
Anderson, Thomas	26, July 1857	James	Irwin, Jane	B	47
Andor, Albert	8, Aug. 1858	Adam	Albert, Dorothea	H	
Andre, Mary	21, Jan. 1855	Robert	Borland, Ann	P	117
Andre, William	21, Jan. 1855	Robert	Borland, Ann	P	116
Andreas, Catharina	9, Mar. 1856	Adam	Punt, Antonia	D	53
Andreas, Georg	31, Aug. 1858	Adam	Bunt, Antonia	T	
Andreas, Margaretha	3, Nov. 1850	Adam	Bund, Antonia	D	241
Andregan, James	2, May 1858	Michael	Shahan, Margaret	E	533
Andrer, Adam	29, Aug. 1852	Adam	Bund, Neta	Q	2
Andres, Fidel Andreas	22, Apr. 1855	Carl	Müller, Elisabeth	J	32
Andres, Maria Carolina	7, June 1852	Gabriel	Wilh---, Anna Maria	K	
Andress, Johan Baptist	22, Aug. 1858	Carl	Miller, Elisabeth	J	46
Andrews, Mary	26, Sept 1851	Marie	O'Brien, Bridget	E	346
Andrews, Mary A.	13, Aug. 1853	Edward	----, Sarah	E	117
Andrews, Samuel	29, Apr. 1850		adult - 35 years old	E	210
Angelbeck, Catharina Elisabeth	17, Dec. 1858	Joseph	Imsieke, Eliasbeth	K	
Angelbecke, Anna Maria Bernardina	13, Jan. 1856	Joseph	Imsike, Lisette	F	
Anger, Maria	23, Dec. 1855	Johan	Rudolf, Appolonia	D	48
Angert, Anna Margaretha	10, May 1854	Daniel	Ludwig, Anna Maria	D	10
Angert, Anna Maria	1, June 1858	Daniel	Ludwig, Anna Maria	D	112
Angert, Barbara	25, Aug. 1856	Daniel	Ludwig, Anna Maria	D	65
Angert, Barbara	7, Feb. 1858	Johan	Raedolf, Appolonia	D	104
Angert, Christina	25, Dec. 1851	Daniel	Ludwig, Anna Maria	D	298
Angert, Daniel	11, Dec. 1853	Peter	Baum, Maria Margaretha	D	419
Angert, Eva Maria	8, Apr. 1855	Michael	Patorf, Maria	D	33
Angert, Heinrich	25, Mar. 1858	Peter	----, Anna Maria	D	108
Angert, Johan	12, Aug. 1855	Peter	Baum, Maria	D	40
Angert, Margaretha	10, May 1850	Daniel	Ludwig, Anna Maria	D	212
Angst, Andreas	20, Nov. 1857	Andreas	Bach--, Juliana	D	99
Angst, Francis	25, Jan. 1857	Johan	Leupele, Martina	D	77
Angst, Jacob	25, Feb. 1855	Johan	Lepord, Martina	D	29
Angst, Simon Jacob	30, Nov. 1851	Jacob	Hoffmann, Regina	C	

Name of Child	Date of Baptism	Father	Mother	Church	Page
Angst, Wilhelm Joseph	31, Oct. 1852	Jacob	Hoffmann, Regina	C	
Angster, Johan	5, Sept 1858	Johan	Lepold, Maria	D	118
Ankenbauer, Aloysius	31, Mar. 1850	Georg	Runser, Magdalena	K	
Ankenbauer, Barbara	24, Oct. 1858	Georg	Kroeger, Bernardina	T	
Ankenbauer, Barbara	8, Aug. 1858	Georg	Runzinger, Magdalena	U	
Ankenbauer, Bernard Joseph Alex.	5, Sept 1852	Johan	Kamper, Maria	F	
Ankenbauer, Ferdinand	15, Nov. 1857	Joseph	----, Margaretha	R	
Ankenbauer, Francis Xavier	12, May 1851	Joseph	Bittner, Margaretha	F	
Ankenbauer, Georg	26, Sept 1852	Georg	Runzer, Magdalena	F	
Ankenbauer, Isabella	25, Mar. 1855	Georg	----, Margaretha	U	
Ankenbauer, Jacob	14, Jan. 1855	Joseph	adult - 26 years old	K	
Ankenbauer, Johan Martin	1, Sept 1850	Johan	Kemper, Maria	D	230
Ankenbauer, Margaretha	25, Sept 1853	Johan	Jacobs, Gesina	D	407
Ankenbauer, Margaretha	15, Feb. 1855	Joseph	Masket, Margaret	R	
Ankenbauer, Michael	28, Feb. 1858	Joseph	Friedel, Susanna	K	
Ankenberg, Johan Bernard	2, Oct. 1852	Herman	Joring, Anna	K	
Ankenbrock, Bernard Heinrich	27, June 1858	Heinrich	Kramer, Gertrud	L	
Ankenbrock, Johan Bernard	16, June 1851	Heinrich	Kramer, Gertrud	L	
Ankenbrock, M. Gertrud Elisabeth	1, Feb. 1857	J. Heinrich	Kramer, M. Gertrud	L	
Ankenbrock, Maria Anna Gertrud	5, Mar. 1854	Heinrich	Kramer, Gertrud	L	
Annafedder, Johan Friedrich	3, Feb. 1856	Conrad	Noetker, Antonia	C	
Annafedder, Josephina	29, Aug. 1857	Conrad	Noetker, Antoinette	C	
Annafedder, M Antoinette Henrietta	10, Apr. 1859	Conrad	Noetker, Antoinette	C	
Annafedders, Johan	22, July 1854	Conrad	Noetker, Antonia	C	
Ansbury, Edward	7, Sept 1856	Thomas	----, Joanne	M	
Ansbury, Mark John	5, Sept 1858	Thomas	Donagar, Joanne	E	560
Ansbury, Thomas	18, Dec. 1853	Thomas	----, Joanne	M	
Anselm, Jacob	13, July 1851	Joseph	Gottman, Catharina	D	272
Ansinger, Elisabeth	3, Dec. 1854	Francis J.	Ansinger, Maria	D	23
Anspaugh, John	12, Jan. 1858	James L.	----, Susan	E	509
Answer, Jacob	20, Dec. 1852	Thomas	Dundgen, Johanna	K	
Ante, Maria Catharina	25, May 1856	Philipp	Ewald, Louisa	L	
Ante, Philipp Ewald	26, Nov. 1857	Philipp	Ewald, Louisa	L	
Anthe, Joseph Heinrich	27, Nov. 1859	Heinrich	Pale---, Catharina	D	151
Anthe, Louisa Maria Susanna	25, Sept 1859	Joseph	Brandner, Susanna	F	
Anthony, Patrick Henry	15, Mar. 1859	Patrick	McCarthy, Emily	B	72
Anthony, Thomas	10, Nov. 1853	Patrick	Sparks, Emily	B	302
Anthony, Walter	10, Nov. 1853	Patrick	Sparks, Emily	B	302
Antke, Joseph Anton	22, Nov. 1857	Joseph	Brandner, Susan	N	
Anton, William	13, July 1856	Adam	Albert, Dorothea	H	
Antoni, Margaret	7, May 1857	Patrick	----, Emily	M	
Apel, Georg	26, Apr. 1857	Georg	Kechner, Anna Maria	D	83
Apel, Jacob	1, Aug. 1858	Jacob	Schneider, Anna Maria	D	116
Apke, Anna Maria	30, Apr. 1857	Wilhelm	Boekman, Anna Maria	A	
Apke, Heinrich Bernard	10, Feb. 1855	Wilhelm	Lahrman, Anna Maria	A	
Apke, Maria Elisabeth	21, June 1859	Wilhelm	Specker, Anna Maria	A	
Appel, Margaret	2, Apr. 1859	Conrad	Drösch, Catharina	R	
Appel, Maria Wilhelmina	28, Sept 1851	Francis	Baumann, Maria	F	
Aqua, Johan Bernard	14, Apr. 1854	Gerhard H.	Plake, Maria Elisabeth	F	
Araldi, Maria Carolina	8, July 1859	Vincent	Gelb, Agostina	K	
Arata, Catharina Philomena Rosa	19, Sept 1858	Johan	Lavasa, Rosa	K	
Arata, Isidore Michael	3, May 1858	Joseph	Arata, Roda	B	58
Arata, Philomena Maria Paulina	18, Sept 1856	Giovanni	Lavesa, Rosa	K	
Arch, Maria Theresa	16, Oct. 1859	Peter	Heckelsmüller, Theresa	Q	33
Arche, Heinrich	29, Mar. 1851	Bernard	Gönner, Lisetta	K	
Archer, Mary Josephine	8, Feb. 1850	Frederick	Cool, Sophia	E	196
Archinger, Anna Maria Clara	31, Jan. 1858	Georg Anna	Boh, Richardina	C	
Archinger, Georg Anton	2, Sept 1855	Georg A.	Boeh, Richardina	F	
Archinger, Joseph	13, Nov. 1853	Anton	Boehnat, Richardina	F	

Name of Child	Date of Baptism	Father	Mother	Church	Page
Archinger, Maria Anna	11, May 1851	Anton	Boeh, Elisabeth	F	
Aren, Adolph	27, Jan. 1850	Ludwig	Ruffin, Maria	K	
Arens, Maria Catharina	27, Aug. 1854	Francis	Graf, Maria	D	16
Arens, Maria Josephina	16, Jan. 1859	Francis	Weinman, Maria	D	129
Arkenau, Anna Gertrud	25, Nov. 1855	Heinrich	VonBoekern, Elisabeth	A	
Arkenau, Heinrich	23, Jan. 1859	Heinrich	VonBockern, Elisabeth	A	
Arkenberg, Johan Francis	6, Mar. 1857	J. Francis	Meyer, Maria Bernardina	A	
Arkenberg, Johan Heinrich	26, Feb. 1856	Clemens	Bamer, Angela	C	
Arkenberg, Maria Elisabeth	27, Nov. 1853	Clemens	Baumer, Maria Angela	D	417
Arkman, Bernard Wilhelm Augustine	17, Aug. 1859		----, Francisca	K	
--arlem, Nicolaus Edward	11, June 1852	Michael	Brome, Carolina	D	324
Arlinghaus, Joseph	11, Apr. 1858	Francis	Bickhoff, Maria	K	
Arlinghaus, Maria Elisabeth	2, Mar. 1856	F. Heinrich	Bröckhoff, Maria Christina	K	
Armand, Theresa	22, July 1855	Peter	----, Catherine	H	
Armand, Wilhelm	19, June 1859	Peter	Leibig, Catharina	T	
Armberger, Joseph	21, Jan. 1855	Joseph	Mittereder, Anna	Q	6
Armbrust, Catharina	11, Aug. 1850	Thomas	Welschhaan, Catharina	H	
Armbruster, Amalia	8, Nov. 1857	Johan	Meier, Elisabeth	D	98
Armbruster, Carolina	20, May 1855	Bernard	Abba, Anna Maria	F	
Armbruster, Carolina	15, May 1859	Cyrian	Kristner, Maria Anna	D	138
Armbruster, Clara	8, Oct. 1857	Bernard	Abba, Maria Anna	T	
Armbruster, Elisabeth	13, Feb. 1853	Bernard	Abba, Anna Maria	D	371
Armbruster, Georg	3, Feb. 1850	Bernard	Abba, Maria	D	202
Armbruster, Heinrich	1, Aug. 1850	Johan	Kramer, Maria Anna	D	226
Armbruster, Johan	16, Feb. 1851	Johan	Abba, Maria Anna	F	
Armbruster, Maria Magdalena	14, May 1854	Johan	Kramer, Maria	J	26
Armbruster, Maria Magdalena	31, Jan. 1856	Johan	Meier, Elisabeth	F	
Armbruster, Rosina Catharina	14, June 1852	Johan	Kramer, Maria	D	324
Armenser, Carl	16, Oct. 1859	Johan	Tor---, Anna	N	
Armleder, Johan	30, Nov. 1856	Johan	----, Maria	D	73
Armleder, Johan Victor	28, Feb. 1858	Johan	Gaiser, Maria	D	106
Armleder, Joseph Paul	11, July 1859	Johan	Gerser, Maria	D	142
Armsley, Ellen	29, Dec. 1850	Thomas	Agan, Catherine	E	272
Armstrong, Ann	20, Feb. 1854	Francis	----, Elizabeth	E	170
Armstrong, Ann	15, May 1853	John	Horan, Mary	P	41
Armstrong, Ann	11, Sept 1859	John	Larkin, Honora	Z	
Armstrong, Ann Elisa	6, Apr. 1850	R.G.	----, Mary Jane	E	207
Armstrong, Catherine	27, July 1851	John	Marchal, Matilda	E	327
Armstrong, Catherine	4, June 1854	Robert	Summons, Mary Jane	E	196
Armstrong, Catherine Alice	7, Nov. 1858	James	O'Donnell, Mary	B	66
Armstrong, Charles	2, July 1858	Francis	----, Elizabeth	E	545
Armstrong, Charles	13, Jan. 1855	John	Marshall, Matilda	E	256
Armstrong, Elenore Mary	28, May 1851	----	----, ----	E	311
Armstrong, Eliza	25, Mar. 1858	John	Larkin, Honora	B	57
Armstrong, Francis Joseph	8, Feb. 1857	John	Marshall, Matilda	E	432
Armstrong, Helen	27, Nov. 1856	John	Horan, Mary	P	200
Armstrong, Helen Virginia	3, Apr. 1852	Thomas	Gardener, Elizabeth	E	398
Armstrong, John Blair	29, Nov. 1851	Robert	Summons, Mary Jane	E	362
Armstrong, Joseph Patrick	28, Mar. 1856	Francis	----, Elizabeth	E	353
Armstrong, Mary Ann	5, Oct. 1857	James	Lamb, Ann	P	**226**
Armstrong, Mary Josephine	29, Sept 1850	Francis	----, Elizabeth	E	251
Armstrong, Robert	13, June 1855	Robert	Summers, Mary	E	293
Armstrong, Robert Alexander	27, Mar. 1853	William	----, Matilda	E	76
Armstrong, Susan	16, July 1852	Francis	----, Elizabeth	E	427
Armstrong, Thomas Michael	25, Jan. 1857	James	O'Donnell, Mary	B	39
Arnetz, Josephina Gertrud	21, Apr. 1853	Peter	Adam, Friedrica	D	381
Arnetz, Maria Magdalena	19, Feb. 1857	Peter	Adam, Friedrica	D	79
Arnetz, Peter	14, Dec. 1854	Peter	Adam, Friederica	D	24
Arnetz, Rosina Barbara	15, Jan. 1852	Peter	Adam, Friedrica	D	302

Name of Child	Date of Baptism	Father	Mother	Church	Page
Arnold, Adolph Anton	12, Jan. 1851	Johan	Schreck, Charlotte	F	
Arnold, Albert	24, Jan. 1858	Wendelin	Renz, Elisabeth	D	103
Arnold, Benedict Aloysius	23, Apr. 1855	Georg	Mayer, Elisabeth	D	33
Arnold, Carl	17, Apr. 1855	Carl	Ganz, Gertrud	C	
Arnold, Elisabeth	8, Aug. 1852	Andreas	Haun, Clara	F	
Arnold, Elisabeth	1, Oct. 1854	Johan	Schreck, Charlotte	F	
Arnold, Elisabeth Arnolda	22, Apr. 1852	Georg	Mayer, Elisabeth	D	317
Arnold, Ernst	7, Mar. 1858	Johan	Schreck, Carolina	T	
Arnold, Georg	18, Apr. 1853	Georg	Gschwind, Elisabeth	D	381
Arnold, Georg	19, Apr. 1857	Johan	Baldauf--, Anna Maria	D	83
Arnold, Georg Jacob	10, June 1858	Georg J.	----, Magdalena	D	112
Arnold, Gustav	11, Dec. 1859	Wendelin	Renz, Elisabeth	D	152
Arnold, Johan Baptist	19, May 1850	Simon	Baumer, Anna M.	C	
Arnold, Maria Elisabeth	23, Dec. 1858	Georg	Meier, Elisabeth	F	
Arnold, Maria Magdalena	19, Aug. 1852	Johan	Schrek, Charlotte	F	
Arnold, Nicolaus Arnold	10, Oct. 1852	Simon	Baumer, Anna M.	C	
Arnold, Peter	28, Mar. 1850	Philipp	Eberhard, Christina	D	207
Arnold, Philippina	3, Feb. 1856	Johan	Schreck, Charlotte	F	
Arns, Georg William	12, Sept 1859	Gerhard	Schuster, Margaretha	D	146
Arssmann, Maria Elisabeth	12, Nov. 1853	J. Caspar	Brunemann, Maria Elisabeth	F	
Art, Anna Margaretha	30, Apr. 1854	Andreas	Kramer, Anna Maria	K	
Art, Johan Gerhard	10, Apr. 1850	J. Heinrich	Grisen, Catharina	C	
Art, Johan Heinrich M.	8, Jan. 1852	----	----, ----	C	
Art, Maria Catharina Carolina	5, July 1857	J. Bernard	Hograve, M. Adelheid	T	
Arth, Maria Josephina Rosina	21, Apr. 1854	Johan H.	Griese, Maria Catharina	F	
Arting, Johan Bernard	17, May 1851	Francis H.	Grote, Elisabeth	D	265
Artman, Anna Maria Agnes	5, July 1855	Francis	Voss, Maria	A	
Artman, Bernard	22, Nov. 1857	Francis	Hochgröve, Anna Maria Ag.	A	
Artman, Bernard Georg	4, June 1851	Bernard	Meier, Maria Anna	A	
Artman, Bernardina Josephina	25, Dec. 1859	Francis	Hochgrawe, Maria	A	
Artman, Johan Bernard Francis	18, Aug. 1853	Francis	Hochgroeve, Maria Agnes	A	
Artman, Joseph	20, Jan. 1858	Bernard	Meier, Maria Anna	G	
Artman, Joseph	20, Jan. 1858	Bernard	Meier, Maria Anna	W	21
Artman, Joseph Bernard	2, Apr. 1854	Bernard	Meyer, Maria Anna	K	
Artmann, Bernard Carl	9, Sept 1855	Bernard	Meyer, Maria Anna	G	
Arzeno, James	18, Sept 1854	Joseph	Macchiavelli, Susanna	P	96
Arzeno, Mary Ann Magdalene	21, Oct. 1858	Joseph	Maccheacelli, Susan	B	66
Arzeno, Mary Caroline	9, Oct. 1855	Joseph	Macchiavelli, Susanna	P	155
Asbrock, Amalia Catharina	13, Apr. 1858	Francis	----, Ann	R	
Asbrock, Francis	28, Apr. 1855	Francis	Weber, Anna Maria	R	
Asbrock, Johan David	4, Aug. 1851	Francis H.	Weber, Anna Maria	L	
Asbrock, Joseph Heinrich	18, Jan. 1857	Francis	----, Anna Maria	R	
Asbrock, Maria Catharina	18, Apr. 1853	Francis H.	Weber, Anna Maria	R	
Asche, Bernardina Elisabeth	13, Apr. 1851	Heinrich	Imwalde, Julia	L	
Asche, Cath. Bernardina Philomena	18, Apr. 1859	Heinrich	Imwalde, Juliana	F	
Asche, Henrietta Elisabeth Mathilda	30, Jan. 1853	Heinrich	Imwalle, Julia	D	368
Asche, Johanna Mathilda Elisabeth	27, Nov. 1856	Bernard	----, Maria Elisabeth	D	73
Ascheberg, Christina Francisca	26, July 1857	Bernard	Hagel, Gertrud	C	
Aschen, Maria Elisabeth	18, Jan. 1857	Heinrich	Imwalle, Julianna	F	
Aschenbach, Theresa	17, Jan. 1858	Joseph	Funk, Maria	C	
Ascht, Maria Theresa Johanna	11, May 1856	Adam	Grass, Elisabeth	J	36
Asfert, Johan Herman	8, Oct. 1859	J. Herman	---, Maria Catharina	D	148
Ash, Catherine	17, Dec. 1854	Thomas	----, Bridget	E	247
Ash, John James	10, June 1853	Thomas	----, Bridget	E	96
Ashar, Maria	28, May 1856	William	Donohoe, Ellen	A	
Asher, Mary	10, Sept 1854	William	----, Ellen	M	
Ashford, Mary Elizabeth	27, Jan. 1856	Joseph	Boyle, Honora	U	
Ashorn, Anna Adelheid	18, June 1853	Joseph	Tieman, Anna Maria	K	
Aslage, Maria Carolina Francisca	14, July 1857	Heinrich	M---, Anna Helena	D	90

Name of Child	Date of Baptism	Father	Mother	Church	Page
Asman, Philomena	17, Feb. 1858	Johan	----, Maria Elisabeth	D	105
Asmann, Maria Theresa	23, May 1858	Bernard	----, ----	C	
Asmer, Johan Heinrich	25, Aug. 1859	Johan	Bruneman, Anna Maria	D	145
Aspenleiter, Magdalena	26, Sept 1852	Sebastian	Winterisch, Sophia	C	
Assman, Elisabeth	13, May 1855	Bernard	Gerke, Elisabeth	D	35
Assman, Johan Francis	15, Nov. 1853	J. Bernard	Gerke, Maria Elisabeth	D	415
Ast, Francis Martin	13, Nov. 1856	John Adam	Siegel, Helena	C	
Ast, Helena Francisca	27, Aug. 1854	Adam	Siegel, Helena	C	
Ast, Johan Adam	24, Oct. 1852	John Adam	Siegel, Helena	C	
Ast, Johan Heinrich	26, Oct. 1851	John Adam	Siegel, Helena	C	
Ast, Ribiana Barbara Maria	5, Dec. 1858	Johan	Siegel, Helena	C	
Asti, Mary	14, Oct. 1855	James	Rosasca, Rose	P	155
Astley, Mary Jane	19, July 1857	Eli	Mahoney, Catherine	V	40
Atchen, Catherine	17, July 1857	Henry	----, E.	E	466
Ath, Anna Maria Regina	7, Sept 1852	Johan H.	Krieven, Catharina	F	
Athens, Wilhelm Francis	14, Dec. 1856	Francis	Kleinman, Maria	D	74
Athner, William	4, Aug. 1852	Robert	adult - 34 years old	E	2
Atierle, Herman	20, Apr. 1856	Andreas	----, Sophia	F	
Atkinson, Catherine	5, Aug. 1858	Michael	Keegan, Mary	B	62
Atkinson, Sarah Ann	26, June 1854	Richard	Cobb, Almira	B	2
Attermeier, Maria Francisca	14, Oct. 1857	Heinrich	Früling, Maria Anna	D	97
Attermeier, Maria Sophia	3, Nov. 1854	Andreas	Hellebrand, Theresa	D	21
Attermeier, Theresa Josephina	7, Apr. 1853	Heinrich	Friling, Anna Maria	D	379
Auberg, Johan Ernst Paul	22, Aug. 1855	Johan	Lang, Adelheid	N	
Auberger, Johan Adam	17, Oct. 1853	Peter	Eisemann, Barbara	F	
Aubke, Catharina Elisabeth	23, Dec. 1851	G. Heinrich	Ossendorf, Maria Elisabeth	K	
Aubke, Catharina Elisabeth	9, Jan. 1854	Heinrich	Ossendarp, Anna M.	C	
Aubke, Georg Friedrich	4, Apr. 1852	Heinrich	Kolkmeyer, Catharina Elisabeth	C	
Aubke, Georg Heinrich	4, May 1855	Heinrich	Kolkmeyer, Catharina	C	
Aubke, Gerhard Heinrich	6, Oct. 1856	Friedrich	Schaefer, Regina	C	
Aubke, Johan Friedrich	8, Dec. 1850	Friedrich	Schaefer, Elisabeth	C	
Aubke, Johan Friedrich	20, Nov. 1859	Friedrich	Schaefer, Regina	C	
Aubke, Johan Friedrich	10, Jan. 1856	Heinrich	Ossendorf, M. Elisabeth	C	
Aubke, Johan Heinrich	7, June 1854	Francis	Kolkmeyer, Catharina E.	C	
Aubke, Maria Clara	14, Nov. 1852	Friedrich	Schaefers, Regina	C	
Aubke, Maria Louisa	12, Oct. 1857	Friedrich	Kolkmeyer, Catharina Elisabeth	C	
Aubke, Maria Sophia	29, Mar. 1859	Heinrich	Ossendorf, Maria Elisabeth	K	
Auburger, Adam	7, Apr. 1856	Peter	----, Barbara	D	56
Auch, Georg Adolph	11, Feb. 1855	Georg	Schweitz, Catharina	D	28
Auchter, Johan Georg	5, Aug. 1855	Nicolaus	Folz, Mechtildis	Q	9
Audisis, Clotilda	15, May 1859	Johan	Williams, Helen	K	
Auer, Anton	22, May 1859	Johan	Greh, Emilia	F	
Auer, Carl August	21, Dec. 1854	Anton	Rotker, Angela	C	
Auer, Jacob	16, Apr. 1854	Conrad	Doerfler, Anna	D	8
Auer, Johan	28, Mar. 1859	Conrad	Dörfler, Maria Anna	A	
Auer, Peter	8, May 1857	Conrad	Dörfler, Maria	A	
Aug, Jacob	9, Mar. 1853	Jacob	Isbach, Helena	D	375
Augustin, Ann	2, Aug. 1857	Lawrence	----, Bridget	M	
Augustin, Johan Heinrich	18, Sept 1850	Johan	Niehaus, Anna Catharina	D	233
Augustino, Giovanni Roberto	29, Mar. 1857	Giovanni	Bernazana, Maria	K	
Aul, August Lambert	16, Jan. 1853	Jacob	Wagner, Margaretha	F	
Aul, Carolina Elisabeth	15, Nov. 1857	Johan	Hall, Johanna	F	
Aul, Franz Alexander	24, Aug. 1851	Adam	Trikler, Friedricka	F	
Aul, Franz Jacob	17, Dec. 1854	Johan	Hall, Sarah	F	
Aul, Jacob Carl	15, May 1858	Jacob	Wagner, Margaretha	F	
Aul, Margaretha Juliana	7, June 1855	Jacob	Wagner, Margaretha	F	
Aul, Maria Margaretha	29, Oct. 1854	Adam	Gikler, Friedricka	C	
Aull, Albert John	5, Jan. 1853	Adam A.	Giglin, Frederica	B	280
Aull, Edward Conrad	6, Apr. 1851	James	Wagner, Margaret	B	229

Name of Child	Date of Baptism	Father	Mother	Church	Page
Aull, Wiliam Martin	4, July 1858	William	Graham, Mary	B	61
Aupke, Carl	20, May 1856		Aupke, Anna Maria	A	
Aupke, Johan Joseph	2, Jan. 1859	Friedrich	Schäfer, Regina	C	
Austerman, Maria Elisabeth	16, Dec. 1857	Theodor	Herzog, Anna Maria	K	
Austing, Bernard Heinrich	22, Apr. 1850	Bernard	Pardick, Angela	L	
Austing, Bernard Heinrich	11, Feb. 1851	Bernard	Wrocklage, Bernardina	L	
Austing, Clemens August	11, Apr. 1858	Bernard	Frocklage, Bernardina	L	
Austing, Johan Bernard Heinrich	4, Jan. 1858	Francis	Stuntebeck, Catharina	L	
Austing, Joseph Heinrich	29, Sept 1859	Francis	Stundtbeck, M. Cath.	L	
Austing, Maria Adelheid Bernardina	17, Mar. 1854	J. Bernard	Frocklage, Catharina	L	
Auth, Georg	9, May 1858	Michael	Kron--, Maria	D	111
Averbeck, Anna Maria	16, May 1858	Johan B.	Meyer, Anna Maria Jos.	A	
Averbeck, Anton A.	14, Dec. 1856	Herman	Dillman, Maria Agnes	A	
Averbeck, Francis	30, Oct. 1859	Friedrich	Lutkenhaus, Elisabeth	C	
Averbeck, Francis Heinrich	2, Oct. 1852	H. Heinrich	Dillman, Maria Agnes	A	
Averbeck, Henrietta Elisabeth	13, Feb. 1858	Friedrich	Lutkenhaus, Elisabeth	C	
Averbeck, Johan Gerhard	3, Aug. 1857	J. Gerhard	Berkemeier, Dina	K	
Averbeck, Maria Catharina	5, Sept 1858	H.H.	Dillman, Agnes	A	
Averbeck, Maria Elisabeth	12, Dec. 1853	Herman H.	Dillman, Agnes	A	
Averdeck, James Andrew	16, Jan. 1853	Henry	Egan, Jane	E	54
Avery, Charles Edward	20, July 1852	Charles	----, Mary	E	431
Axt, Carl	23, May 1858	Vincent	Pflleger, Barbara	D	111
Axt, Carlina	12, Oct. 1859	Vincent	Pfleger, Barbara	D	148
Axt, Elisabeth	12, Oct. 1856	Johan	Pfleger, Barbara	D	69
Axt, Friedrich Thaddeus	20, Nov. 1854	Vincent	Pfleger, Barbara	K	
Aylward, John	22, Sept 1856	John	----, Mary	R	
Aylward, William	15, Nov. 1854	John	Flinn, Mary	R	
Ayres, Albert Clarence	31, May 1859	Albert	Billerbeck, Mary	B	76
B----, Maria Catharina	13, Sept 1850	Johan	Diner, Theresa	D	232
B----, Mary Jane	18, Sept 1859	Robert	----, Mary	M	
Babb, Daniel	23, June 1851	Daniel	Back, Mary	E	318
Babbitt, Joseph William	9, Feb. 1856	David	Spelmeyer, Catherine	E	343
Babbitt, Mary Elizabeth	6, Mar. 1853	David	Spelmeyer, Catherine	E	68
Baber, Mary Ann	21, Apr. 1852		adult	B	257
Baber, Mary Eliza	19, Mar. 1850	John	Tanner, Mary	B	198
Babst, John George	12, Dec. 1858	Philip	Bizle, Rose	H	
Bacagalupo, Bartholomew	22, Nov. 1859	Charles	----, Catherine	E	672
Baccericco, Maria Carolina Theresa	21, Sept 1859	Joseph	Ginoccia, Carolina	K	
Bacciacchi, Mary Josephine	17, Jan. 1854	Vincent	Fannan, Catherine	B	307
Bacciacco, Maria Aloysia	14, Oct. 1855	Santino	Zanone, Catherine	B	20
Bacciocca, Antonio Joseph	3, Mar. 1856	Joseph	Ginocchio, Carolina	K	
Bacciocco, Anton Santin John	27, Apr. 1852	Santino	Zanoni, Mary Catherine	B	258
Bacciocco, Giovanni Guiseppe Carlo	18, Nov. 1857	Guiseppi	Ginocchia, Carolina	K	
Bacciocco, Mary Ann Augustine	21, Nov. 1858	Santino	Zanone, Catherine	B	67
Bacciocco, Peter Stephen Bartholomew	26, Aug. 1857	Santino	Zanone, Catherine	B	48
Baccioco, Dominick John Thomas	27, Aug. 1851	John	Longinotti, Maria	B	239
Baccioco, Mary Virginia	28, Oct. 1855	John	Longinotti, Mary Rose	B	21
Bacciogo, Angelo Anthony Matthew	3, Dec. 1853	John	Longenotti, Mary Rose	B	303
Bach, Catharina	20, Nov. 1853	Ignatius	Hipf, Cunigunda	D	416
Bach, Charles Robert	1, May 1854	Herman	----, Margaret	M	
Bach, Philomena	13, May 1850	Herman	Seufert, Margaretha	K	
Bachelder, George Clifford	28, Mar. 1855	George H.	Avis, Susan	B	13
Bächle, Wendel	18, Jan. 1857	Ferdinand	Lipps, Rosa	K	
Bachman, Amalia	19, June 1851	Robert	Kammerer, Theresa	D	269
Bachman, Anna Maria	24, Apr. 1853	Nicolaus	Kunkel, Gertrud	D	382
Bachman, Carl	18, Nov. 1855	Johan	Flach, Anna	D	47
Bachman, Catharina	18, Feb. 1855	Nicolaus	Kunkel, Gertrud	D	29
Bachman, Eva Catharina	25, Oct. 1857	Adam	Borger, Anna Maria	Q	24
Bachman, Francis Carl	25, Apr. 1852	Johan	Flach, Anna	D	317

Name of Child	Date of Baptism	Father	Mother	Church	Page
Bachman, Gertrud	31, May 1857	Johan	Kunkel, Catharina	D	86
Bachman, Jacob	7, Mar. 1859	Georg	Zinn, Felicia	J	48
Bachman, Nicolaus	29, May 1859	Nicolaus	Kunkel, Gertrud	D	139
Bachman, Peter	27, July 1856	Michael	Scheck, Maria	D	63
Bachman, Peter	12, Oct. 1851	Nicolaus	Kunkel, Gertrud	D	286
Bachman, Wilhelmina	4, Oct.1857	Nicolaus	Kunkel, Gertrud	D	96
Bachmann, Carolina Christina	13, Apr. 1858	Peter	Auberger, Catharina	F	
Bachmann, Genofeva	31, May 1853	Andreas	Ruhmann, Margaretha	L	
Bachmann, Georg	10, Oct. 1852	Peter	Schuler, Elisabeth	L	
Bachmann, Johan	7, Feb. 1855	Peter	Auberger, Catharina	F	
Bachmann, Margaretha	11, Feb. 1850	Peter	Schuler, Elisabeth	F	
Bachmann, Margaretha	25, Dec. 1859	Peter	Schuler, Elisabeth	L	
Bachmann, Maria Catharina	1, Apr. 1855	Peter	Schuler, Elisabeth	L	
Bachmann, Maria Magdalena	24, Aug. 1851	Gervasius	Widerli, Magdalena	G	
Bachmann, Peter	19, Jan. 1851	Peter	Auberger, Catharina	F	
Bachmann, Peter	30, Aug. 1857	Peter	Schuler, Elisabeth	L	
Back, Anton Wilhelm	18, Oct. 1857	Anton	Rouger, Maria	T	
Back, Carolina	9, Oct. 1859	Anton	Ruske, Anna Maria	F	
Back, Clemens	30, Jan. 1855	Heinrich	Brinkmann, Margaretha	C	
Back, Elizabeth Ottilia	1, Feb. 1852		adult - 19 years old	B	251
Bäcker, Gerhard Heinrich	4, Aug. 1859	Eugene	Lageman, Gertrud	A	
Backer, John B.	3, Apr. 1853	John	----, Elizabeth	H	
Backer, Maria Catharina	22, Apr. 1858	Jacob	Kunkel, Josephina	T	
Bäcker, Maria Sophia Florentina	26, May 1852	Heinrich	Sander, Johanna	D	321
Backes, Michael	29, Jan. 1854	Johan	Heck, Maria	F	
Backhaus, Johan Clemens	26, July 1857	Johan H.	Bernsen, Maria Magdalena	F	
Backhaus, M. Elisabeth Magdalena	13, Mar. 1859	J. Heinrich	Bernzen, Magdalena	L	
Backherm, Bernard August	25, Sept 1850	B. Heinrich	Kniefers, Maria L.	D	234
Backherms, Anna Helena	24, Mar. 1855	Bernard	Knuewers, Louisa	C	
Backherms, Herman Bernard	3, Oct. 1858	Bernard	Hauer, Maria	T	
Backherms, Johan Herman	10, Apr. 1853	Bernard	Knufe, M. Longina	L	
Backscheider, Anna Maria	6, Feb. 1859	Jacob	Megel, Anna Maria	G	
Backscheider, Anna Maria	10, Nov. 1856	Johan	Kaiser, Catharina	G	
Backscheider, Catharina	5, Feb. 1854	Nicolaus	Kaiser, Anna Maria	G	
Backscheider, Catharina Elisabeth	1, Feb. 1856	Nicolaus	Kaiser, Anna Maria	G	
Backscheider, Jacob	14, Mar. 1858	Nicolaus	Kaiser, Anna Maria	G	
Backscheider, Johan Balthasar	3, Oct. 1858	Johan	Kaiser, Catharina	G	
Bacon, Hugh Thomas	23, May 1855	James	O'Donnell, Bridget	B	15
Bad, Francis	18, Oct. 1853	Francis	Zaum, Margaretha	D	410
Badaraccio, Honora	7, May 1854	John	Peratto, Catherine	B	314
Badaraccio, Mary Louise	3, Aug. 1851	John	Peratsa, Catherine	B	238
Badaradeno, Angela Centina	5, Jan. 1857	John	Perazza, Catherine	B	38
Baddaracca, John Joseph	10, Mar. 1851	Santino	Devoto, Maria Julia	B	226
Baddarotti, Petra Givanna Antonia	20, July 1856	Santino	Devoto, Maria	B	31
Baddelnach, Mary Magdalene Catheine	15, Jan. 1854	Santino	Devoto, Mary	B	307
Badderick, Augustine Louigi	19, Dec. 1858	Santino	Devoto, Mary	B	68
Bader, John	18, Nov. 1855	John	Rogers, Ann	E	328
Baderacca, Johan Santino	18, Dec. 1854	Carl	Gatti, Antonia	K	
Bado, George	12, June 1853	Nicolaus	Green, Elizabeth	E	96
Badoet, John Baptist	28, Apr. 1851	Nicholas	Greene, Elizabeth	B	231
Badrast, Giovanni Bartolomeo Davide	20, Nov. 1859	John	Brazzi, Catherine	B	84
Baeck, Peter Benedict Johan	7, Mar. 1858	Johan	Schock, Maria Anna	D	106
Baecker, Francis Heinrich	19, Nov. 1857	Heinrich	Ross, Theresa	D	99
Baer, Laura Josephine	Aug. 1850	Ezra	Knott, Rosalia	B	212
Baerman, Andreas Johan	30, June 1850	Lawrence	Oehler, Catharina	D	219
Baermann, Adam	2, Oct. 1859	August	Greiner, Catharina	G	
Baermann, Clara	10, July 1858	Lawrence	Ehler, Catharina	G	
Baern, John	17, Oct. 1855	Michael	Greens, Sarah	N	
Baerndissel, Adam	13, Mar. 1857	Wendel	Egger, Magdalena	C	

Name of Child	Date of Baptism	Father	Mother	Church	Page
Baetscher, Johan Francis	25, Dec. 1854	Johan	Derflinger, Catharina	K	
Bager, Catharina Emma	3, Apr. 1859	Johan	Dobflinger, Catharina	T	
Bagge, Anna Josephina	1, Sept 1853	H. Joseph	Macke, Anna Maria	K	
Bagge, Anna Maria	19, Feb. 1851	Joseph	Mercke, Maria Anna	K	
Bagge, Anna Maria Bertha	13, June 1858	J. Heinrich	Macke, Maria Anna	L	
Bagge, Bernard Heinrich	24, Oct. 1855	Heinrich	Macke, Anna Maria	L	
Bagge, Heinrich Ludwig	16, June 1852	Heinrich	Busch, Angela	C	
Baggett, Thomas	27, Sept 1859	James	Collins, Catherine	E	658
Baggot, Martha Francisca	26, Aug. 1858	Francis	Rourck, Margaret	T	
Baggot, Walter	29, Oct. 1854	William	Phelan, Catharine	T	
Baggot, William	20, Feb. 1853	William F.	Phelan, Catherine	B	284
Baggott, Jane Margaret	13, Jan. 1850	William	Phelan, Catherine	B	194
Baggott, Thomas	2, June 1851	William	Phelan, Catherine	B	233
Bagot, Catharine	24, Aug. 1856	William	Whelan, Catharine	T	
Bahlman, Johan Bernard Christoph	14, Apr. 1858	J. Heinrich	Röttker, Maria Elisabeth	K	
Bahlman, Juliana	9, Sept 1854	Johan	Götzinger, Theresa	D	17
Bahlmann, Agnes	27, Oct. 1859	Joseph	Luening, Maria Agnes	L	
Bahlmann, Bernard	7, Sept 1856	Bernard	Wilke, Anna	F	
Bahlmann, Conrad Joseph Wilhelm	30, Apr. 1857	Conrad	Epping, Gertrud	F	
Bahlmann, Johan Anton Georg	9, Sept 1858	Anton	Kohlmann, Dorothea	F	
Bahlmann, Johan Heinrich	24, Feb. 1859	Bernard	Wilke, Marianna	F	
Bahlmann, Joseph	28, May 1855	Bernard	Wilke, Marianna	F	
Bahlmann, Joseph Ludwig Wilhelm	19, Sept 1859	Conrad	Eppig, Gertrud	F	
Bahlmann, Maria Elisabeth	23, July 1858	Gerhard J.	Luening, Maria Agnes	L	
Bahlmann, Maria Theresa	24, Apr. 1859	Heinrich	Schroeder, Maria	F	
Bahlmann, Marianna	22, Jan. 1858	Bernard	Wilke, Marianna	F	
Bahlmann, Marianna Catharina	22, Apr. 1856	Herman H.	Kohlmann, Dorothea	F	
Bahr, Carl Joseph	21, June 1857	Francis X.	Eschelbach, Catharina	C	
Bahr, Catharina Sophia	4, July 1858	F. Xavier	Esselbach, Catharina	C	
Baier, Anna Margaretha	20, July 1856	Gerhard H.	Hesskamp, Maria Gesina	F	
Baier, Herman Heinrich	21, Mar. 1858	Gerhard H.	Hesskamp, Gesina M.	F	
Baier, Johan Heinrich	15, Mar. 1855	Gerhard H.	Heskamp, Gesina Maria	F	
Baiersdorfer, Barbara	12, June 1853	Francis	----, Mary Catherine	H	
Baiersdorfer, Johan	1, Oct. 1856	Francis	Michel, Maria Catharina	H	
Baiersdorfer, Joseph	29, June 1850	Francis	Michel, Maria Catharina	H	
Baile, Agnes Joanne Cecilia	10, May 1857	Charles	Tappe, Theresa	H	
Baily, Catherine Ann	7, May 1853	John	----, Catherine	E	86
Baily, Elizabeth	15, Oct. 1859	Michael	Daly, Marcella	E	662
Baily, Louis	20, Oct. 1859	Francis	McCarthy, Margaret	E	664
Baily, Thomas	17, Mar. 1857	Francis	McCarthy, Margaret	E	441
Bain, Anna Maria	14, Nov. 1858	Nicolaus	Göbel, Anna Maria	D	124
Bain, James	8, Feb. 1852	John	Tuny, Bridget	E	380
Bain, Mary Ann	8, Dec. 1857	Michael	----, Eliza	E	499
Bain, Patrick	19, Feb. 1852	Patrick	Young, Joanne	E	384
Bainbridge, Hatty	23, Apr. 1858	Eusebius	Dixon, Sarah	B	58
Baines, Mary Frances	22, Sept 1850	Allen W.	O'Donnell, Ann	B	214
Bairer, Wilhelmina	24, May 1858	Johan N.	Sch---, Regina	D	112
Bairing, Herman Heinrich	22, Aug. 1850	Herman H.	Roewekamp, M. Catharina	F	
Baker, Andrwe	27, June 1856	Andrew	Merrit, Mary	V	31
Baker, Elisabeth	25, Sept 1856	Georg	Klingler, Anna	K	
Baker, Ellen	6, June 1858	William	Foot, Ann	E	540
Baker, Franz Wilhelm	11, Aug. 1856	Wilhelm	Neubauer, Dorothea	F	
Baker, Helena	23, Mar. 1854	Andrew	Baker, Mary	K	
Baker, Jacob	16, Aug. 1857	Ludwig	Geier, Maria	D	92
Bäker, Johan Heinrich	16, July 1857	Eugene	Lageman, Anna	K	
Ba---ker, Johan Wilhelm	22, June 1852	B. Theodor	Brink, Christina	D	326
Baker, John	8, Feb. 1852	Andrew	Morris, Mary	B	252
Baker, Maria Theresa	23, Feb. 1855	Georg	Klinger, Anna	K	
Baker, Mary Ann	22, Nov. 1854	William	Fuss, Ann	E	242

Name of Child	Date of Baptism	Father	Mother	Church	Page
Baker, Rose Ann	14, Apr. 1850	Andrew	----, Mary	E	207
Bakes, Barbara Josephina	20, Nov. 1859	Peter	Wurst, Catharina	F	
Bal, Edward	7, June 1858	Albert	----, Helena	C	
Baldwin, Clara	25, July 1852	Ludwig	Lied?, Clara	D	340
Baldwin, John	24, Feb. 1850	Joseph	Burke, Mary	E	198
Baldwin, Joseph	29, May 1851	William	----, Catherine	B	232
Balet, David Garret	1, June 1858	David	----, Catherine	E	539
Balgenort, Gerhard Heinrich	3, Oct. 1854	J. Heinrich	Peddenpohl, M. Elisabeth	L	
Balgenort, Johan Friedrich	22, Oct. 1856	J. Heinrich	Peddenpohl, M. Elisabeth	L	
Balgenort, Johan M. Franz Joseph	7, Nov. 1859	Herman	Peddenpohl, M. Elis.	L	
Ball, Charles	19, Oct. 1852	Dominick	Thompson, Mary	B	272
Ball, George William	6, Nov. 1853	Edward	----, Ann	E	142
Ball, Mary Ann	18, Mar. 1850	Bernard	Hagerty, Margaret	E	204
Ball?, Catharina	1, Mar. 1857	Joseph	Kle---, Catharina	D	80
Ballard, Alice	9, May 1853	Michael	Brogan, Ann	B	291
Ballard, Honora	3, Sept 1854	Michael	Reagin, Ann	B	5
Ballard, Thomas	23, Jan. 1859	Michael	----, Ann	E	598
Baller, Anna Maria	13, Nov. 1857	Herman	Palster, Maria	D	98
Baller, Elisabeth	22, Apr. 1855	Herman	Palster, Maria	D	33
Balles, Heinrich	20, Oct. 1850	Herman	Poltz, Maria	C	
Balles, Stephen	20, Mar. 1853	Herman	Polst, M. Anna	C	
Balley, Louise	23, Sept 1850	Peter	Mitchell, Pauline	B	214
Ballhaus, Philippina Ernestina	3, Oct. 1852	Heinrich	Meyer, Augusta	C	
Ballhausen, Christina	4, Sept 1851	Heinrich	Meyer, Augusta	C	
Ballhausen, Michael Emil	17, Sept 1854	Heinrich	Meyer, Augusta	C	
Balling, Maria Anna	8, June 1851	J. Georg	Gebauer, Catharina	A	
Balling, Maria Catharina	8, June 1851	J. Georg	Gebauer, Catharina	A	
Ballingall, Lawrence	3, June 1855		adult	B	15
Ballman, Anna Maria	14, Feb. 1852	Heinrich	Woestemeier, Maria	K	
Ballman, Anna Maria Theresa	20, Mar. 1856	Heinrich	Woestemeier, Maria Elisabeth	K	
Ballman, Johan Heinrich	3, Oct. 1853	J. Heinrich	Woestemeier, Maria Elisabeth	K	
Ballman, Maria Gertrud	16, Jan. 1853	J. Caspar	Hahnhorst, Maria Elisabeth	D	365
Ballmann, Johan Heinrich	20, Oct. 1859	J. Heinrich	Strotmann, Elisabeth	C	
Ballmann, M. Catharina Elisabeth	13, Dec. 1857	Christoph	Strodmann, Elisabeth	C	
Bals, Anna Margaretha	21, May 1854	Valentin	Fucht, Ottilia	D	11
Balster, Frnacis Heinrich	31, May 1853	H.	Hagener, Maria	L	
Balt, Francis	8, Jan. 1854	Johan	Hattil, Maria	D	1
Balt, Henry	19, June 1859	Johan	Hattel, Maria	D	140
Balt, Maria Anna	19, Oct. 1856	Johan	Hattel, Maria Anna	D	70
Balzer, Maria Engel	16, May 1852	Bernard	Annewehr, Anna Elisabeth	D	319
Bamann, Anna Maria	7, Feb. 1855	Richard	Bremann, Bridget	L	
Bambeck, Catharina Carolina	16, Jan. 1859	Sebastian	Reiter, Catharina	Q	30
Bambeck, Maria Elisabeth	28, Dec. 1856	Sebastian	Reider, Catharina	Q	18
Bamberger, Joseph	16, Sept 1855	Francis	Gibhard, Maria	F	
Bamberger, Louisa	7, June 1858	Johan	Kraemer, Regina	D	112
Bamberger, Maria Wilhelmina	12, Aug. 1853	Francis	Spraul, Genofeva	L	
Bambery, William	30, Oct. 1858	William	Shay, Bridget	E	573
Bambrey, Margaret	13, Apr. 1851	William	O'Donnell, Mary	B	229
Bamser, Francis	11, May 1856	Jacob	Lien, Theresa	D	58
Bamser, Nicolaus	11, May 1856	Jacob	Lien, Theresa	D	58
Banan, Thomas	28, Mar. 1858	Thomas	Nolan, Margaret	T	
Banes, Bridget	2, Mar. 1855	Patrick	Milel, Margaret	E	268
Banfiel, Margaret	6, Sept 1856	Patrick	Brogan, Mary	P	190
Banfield, Michael	1, Sept 1854	Patrick	Brogan, Mary	B	5
Bang, John Charles	10, May 1857	John	Luers, Maria	H	
Bange, Bernard Joseph	6, Jan. 1858	Joseph	Raterman, Catharina	A	
Bange, Maria Philomena	13, Mar. 1859	Joseph	Raterman, Maria Catharina	A	
Banks, Helen	17, Oct. 1858	James	Welsh, Mary	E	570
Banlein?, Helena	31, Oct. 1858	Michael	Schettle, Elisabeth	D	123

Name of Child	Date of Baptism	Father	Mother	Church	Page
Bann, James	6, June 1858	John	Kline, Ellen	E	540
Bann, Mary	24, Apr. 1853	John	Klein, Ellen	E	83
Bann, William	4, Nov. 1855	John	Klein, ----	E	325
Bannaghan, Catherine	27, Nov. 1859	John	Mally, Catherine	P	304
Bannaher, Mary	22, June 1858	John	Malley, Catherine	P	251
Bannan, Bridget	1, Feb. 1852	Redy	----, Catherine	M	
Bannan, Mary Jane	7, Jan. 1854	James	Murthagh, Margaret	P	64
Bannan, Thomas	3, Dec. 1852	Owen	Donahoe, Margaret	E	41
Banning, William	25, Mar. 1852	John	Banning Joanne	B	255
Bannister, George	26, Nov. 1858		adult - 25 years old	P	268
Bannon, Catherine	28, June 1853	Patrick	----, Mary	E	103
Bannon, Margaret	8, Dec. 1854	Eugene	Donahoe, Margaret	V	20
Bannon, Margaret	30, Oct. 1855	James	Murtow, Margaret	T	
Bannon, Margaret	6, Nov. 1851	Terence	Donohue, Ann	E	356
Bannon, Mary	8, Oct. 1859	Terence	Donahoe, Ann	V	60
Bannon, Terrence	30, May 1859	Andrew	Scally, Mary	E	629
Bannon, Thomas	30, July 1854	Benedict	Donahue, Ann	E	212
Bantsch, Maria Susanna	14, Dec. 1857	Francis H.	Quetner, Carolina	D	100
Baos, Henrica Bernardina	25, Nov. 1850	Bernard	Fels, Adelheid	L	
Bar, Andreas	30, Nov. 1856	Marc	Lipps, Sophia	K	
Barbaro, Anthony John Charles	13, Feb. 1859	Anthony	Valente, Rose	E	603
Barbau, Johan Caspar	4, June 1856	Heinrich	Gisken, Maria	D	60
Barber, John	21, Sept 1853	John	Quinn, Joanne	E	128
Barber, Joseph	8, Jan. 1856	Joseph	Nolier, Julia	E	336
Barbian, Margaretha	10, Apr. 1853	Peter	Zei, Walburga	F	
Barbian, Maria Catharina	11, Aug. 1850	Peter	Tschai, Walburga	F	
Barbier, Clementine Virginia	23, Jan. 1859	Claude D.	Baar, Barbe	V	52
Barcoli, Louis Hieronymus	18, July 1858	Dominick	Ralzy, Mary	E	551
Bardels, Lisetta Renarda Catharina	5, Feb. 1854	Carl	Timmerman, Catharina	D	4
Bardels, Maria Renata	2, Aug. 1857	Carl	Timmermann, Catharina	C	
Barden, James	23, June 1850	James	Jefferson, Letitia	E	226
Barden, Mary Josephine	4, Aug. 1856	Arthur	----, Mary Jane	U	
Barden, Thomas	21, May 1853	John	----, Bridget	B	292
Bardon, Alice Emily	13, June 1854	James	Barker, Ann	E	198
Bardon, Peter	30, June 1853	Michael	Fitzgerald, Ann	E	103
Bardsell, Anita	15, Feb. 1852	Henry	Morell, Anita	B	253
Bardsell, Joseph Mary	17, Mar. 1850	Henry	Morelles, Annita	B	198
Baren, Margaret	30, Jan. 1853	George	Rafferty, Margaret	B	282
Barenbrock, Sophia Catharina Adelheid	24, Nov. 1856	Anton	Engbering, Gesina Adelheid	N	
Bargazi, Maria Theresa	11, July 1859	Victor	Schaette, Maria	D	142
Bargoetzi, Maria	5, June 1855	Victor	Schaedle, Maria	F	
Bargoetzi, Victor	22, Nov. 1857	Victor	Schaedle, Maria	D	99
Bargötzi, Ludwig	27, July 1856	Victor	Schaettle, Maria	D	63
Barka, Johan Heinrich	15, Nov. 1853	J. Heinrich	Gisken, Maria Adelheid	D	415
Barkau, Maria Gertrud	4, Sept 1859	Heinrich	Giesle, M. Adelheid	T	
Barkeling, Anna Philomena	8, Nov. 1853	J. Heinrich	Tenge, Euphemia	L	
Barkeling, Herman Heinrich	12, Dec. 1850	J. Herman	Tenger, Euphemia	L	
Barkeling, Johan Heinrich	12, Sept 1856	J. Heinrich	Tenger, Euphemia	L	
Barker, William	12, June 1850	Nathaniel	adult - 53 years old	E	232
Barlage, Anna Adelheid	30, Nov. 1858	Francis	Ruberg, Maria Elisabeth	L	
Barlage, Anna Maria Catharina	25, Jan. 1856	Francis	Ruberg, Anna Maria	L	
Barlage, Clemens Francis Anna	6, Nov. 1850	Gerhard	Heidemann, Theresa	C	
Barlage, Elisabeth Henriette	21, Feb. 1858	Wilhelm	Ostendorf, Wilhelmina	A	
Barlage, Johan Gerhard Heinrich	15, June 1853	Francis	Ruberg, Anna Maria	L	
Barlage, Johan Heinrich	28, Oct. 1850	J. Gerhard	Reinke, Maria Margaretha	A	
Barlage, Johan Heinrich	18, Oct. 1858	Johan H.	Oelfken, Maria Angela	K	
Barlage, Johan Mathias Clemens	23, Nov. 1853	Gerhard	Heidemann, Theresa	C	
Barlage, Maria Catharina Elisabeth	13, Dec. 1858	Francis	Reutermann, Catharina	L	
Barlage, Maria Elisabeth	30, July 1855	Anton	Zecher, Josephina	A	

Name of Child	Date of Baptism	Father	Mother	Church	Page
Barlage, Maria Gertrud	3, Jan. 1851	Francis	Ruberg, Anna Maria	L	
Barleon, eduard	6, July 1856	Basil	Adam, Maria	W	15
Barleon, Elisabeth	17, Aug. 1851	Georg	Neithorst, Antonia	C	
Barleon, Francis Xavier	19, Dec. 1852	Basil	Adam, Anna Maria	J	20
Barleon, Georg	28, Aug. 1859	Basil	Adam, Anna Maria	W	26
Barleon, Wilhelm	31, Mar. 1850	Basil	Adam, Anna Maria	F	
Barlett, Margaret	15, June 1856	Daniel	Meagher, Ann	T	
Barlow, Mary Ann	17, Oct. 1852	Patrick	Milon, Helen	E	28
Bärman, Jacob Lawrence	7, Nov. 1852	Lawrence	Oehler, Catharina	J	18
Bärman, Thomas Martin	7, Nov. 1852	Lawrence	Oehler, Catharina	J	18
Barnbrock, Anton Heinrich	31, May 1859	Anton	Engebring, Adelheid	N	
Barnen, Michael	19, Apr. 1850	Roger	Costello, Catherine	B	201
Barnes, Elisabeth	22, July 1854	William	O'Donnell, Ann	T	
Barnes, James	1, Feb. 1852	John	C---man, Bridget	P	16
Barnes, Louise Agnes	10, Aug. 1851	Alfred	Rood, Florence	M	
Barnes, Margaret	31, Aug. 1852	Allen	O'Donnell, Ann	B	269
Barnes, Richard Thomas	24, July 1852	Thomas	Burns, Ann	B	265
Barnes, Richard Thomas	1, Aug. 1852	Thomas	Burnside, Ann	B	266
Barnes, Sikes	10, Apr. 1850		adult - 40 years old	E	209
Barnet, Mary	11, Aug. 1850	Henry	Milach, Isabell	B	209
Barnett, Helen	5, Sept 1850	Henry	Imlah, Isabel	E	245
Barnhorn, Agnes Elisabeth	15, Sept 1855	Clemens	Lammers, Agnes	L	
Barnhorn, Clara Josephina	14, May 1853	Clemens	Lammers, M. Agnes	L	
Barnhorn, Franz Anton	1, Aug. 1858	Clemens	Lammers, Agnes	L	
Barnhorn, Heinrich August	10, Jan. 1857	Clemens	Lammers, Agnes	L	
Barnhorn, Johan Clemens	10, Jan. 1857	Clemens	Lammers, Agnes	L	
Barnhorst, Gerhard Heinrich	13, June 1858	J. Heinrich	Stockhoff, Catharina Maria	K	
Barnhorst, Johan Bernard	24, Mar. 1856	Heinrich	Stockhoff, Maria	K	
Barnickel, Cunegunda	26, Oct. 1856	Johan	Parteimüller, Francisca	A	
Barreiter, Anna Maria	4, July 1853	Conrad	Bieler, Catharina	F	
Barreiter, Paulina	14, June 1857	Conrad	Biehler, Catharina	F	
Barret, Catherine	19, June 1853	John	Farrell, Margaret	R	
Barret, Catherine	15, Jan. 1853	Michael	Farrell, Mary	R	
Barret, Margaret	22, Apr. 1855	John	Farrell, Margaret	R	
Barret, Mary Bridget	16, Jan. 1855	John	Whelan, Ellen	B	10
Barret, Patrick	23, Nov. 1851	John	Farrell, Mary	R	
Barrett, Catherine	26, Mar. 1859	James	Earley, Catherine	B	73
Barrett, Francis Xavier	29, May 1850	Samuel	----, Mary	E	216
Barrett, John	24, Feb. 1850	Daniel	Keefe, Ellen	B	197
Barrett, John Richard	9, Feb. 1859	William	Lynch, Margret	E	602
Barrett, Margaret	27, Mar. 1859	Patrick	----, Mary	V	54
Barrett, Mary	18, Dec. 1856	John	----, Catherine	R	
Barrett, Mary	16, Apr. 1855	Michael	----, Margaret	E	280
Barrett, Mary	18, June 1857	Patrick	----, Mary	R	
Barrett, Mary	20, Mar. 1853	William	Murphy, Louise	V	2
Barrett, Michael	30, Mar. 1851	Richard	----, Catherine	E	296
Barrett, Patrick	27, Mar. 1853	John	Gleeson, Esther	B	287
Barrett, Sarah Jane	17, Aug. 1853	Cornelius	----, Margaret	E	119
Barrett, William	14, Oct. 1858	Michael	----, Margaret	E	570
Barrett, William	3, Nov. 1857	William	Lynch, Margaret	V	42
Barretta, Angel Andreas	24, Aug. 1856	J. Baptist	Gosta, Assunta	K	
Barrey, Catherine	6, May 1855	John	G---, Catherine	P	131
Barron, Catherine	28, May 1856	Daniel	Roy, Mary	E	370
Barron, Mary	7, Sept 1851	James	----, Ann	B	240
Barron, Mary Ann	22, June 1856	John	Crilly, Mary	B	30
Barron, Michael	6, Sept 1855	Michael	----, Ann	E	313
Barron, Patrick	27, July 1854	David	Moore, Sarah	V	15
Barron, Richard Aloysius	15, Aug. 1854	John	Crilly, Margaret	B	4
Barry, Ann	21, July 1850	Michael	Anderson, Mary	B	208

Hamilton County, Ohio Roman Catholic Baptism Records -- 1850 - 1859

Name of Child	Date of Baptism	Father	Mother	Church	Page
Barry, Ann Jane	10, Oct. 1852	John	Green, Catherine	B	271
Barry, Ann Mary	30, July 1859	Dennis	Sheehan, Catherine	B	78
Barry, Bridget	19, July 1854	John	Moran, Bridget	E	208
Barry, Bridget	25, Aug. 1856	William	Lynch, Margaret	V	36
Barry, Catherine	23, June 1850	John	Marshall, Sarah	B	205
Barry, Catherine	30, Aug. 1854	John	Moran, Mary	E	220
Barry, David	13, Feb. 1850	Humphrey	----, Dorothy	E	196
Barry, Edward	31, Dec. 1854	Thomas	----, Mary	E	251
Barry, Ellen Mary	5, Aug. 1855	Dennis	Sheehan, Catherine	B	17
Barry, Emily	15, Mar. 1858	August	----, Mary	E	522
Barry, George William	28, Mar. 1852	Garrett	Magget, Ann	B	255
Barry, Honora	9, Oct. 1859	Bartholomew	Beacher, Ellen	P	299
Barry, Honora	1, Feb. 1857	Dennis	Sheehan, Catherine	B	40
Barry, Honora	15, June 1856	Thomas	Brennan, Mary	V	31
Barry, Isabelle	6, Oct. 1850	Daniel	Field, Ann	E	252
Barry, James	2, Nov. 1851	James	Connaughly, Honora	B	244
Barry, James	26, Oct. 1856	Richard	Mahony, Honora	V	34
Barry, John	26, Sept 1853	Thomas	Brennan, Mary	V	6
Barry, Margaret	10, Nov. 1855	Bartholomew	Beecher, Helen	P	158
Barry, Margaret	19, Jan. 1851	Michael	Moroney, Mary	B	223
Barry, Margaret Ann	2, Oct. 1853	Dennis	Sheehan, Catherine	B	300
Barry, Mary	27, Sept 1857	John	Green, Catherine	B	50
Barry, Mary Angela	22, Sept 1850	Patrick	Hogan, Mary	B	214
Barry, Mary Helen	19, July 1858	William	Hocter, Mary	P	254
Barry, Michael	5, Mar. 1854	John	May, Bridget	E	172
Barry, Sarah	17, Oct. 1852	John	Marshall, Sarah	B	272
Barry, William	18, Feb. 1855	John	Marsh, Sarah	B	11
Barsken, Johan Herman	26, Oct. 1856	J. Heinrich	Wessel, M.A. Elisabeth	D	70
Bartels, Anna Margaretha	13, June 1858	Heinrich	Miller, Magdalena	K	
Bartels, Catharina Renata	10, Oct. 1852	Carl	Timmer, Catharina	D	352
Bartels, Joseph	21, Oct. 1850	Carl	Zimmerman, Catharina	D	239
Barth, Elisabeth	5, Dec. 1858	Johan B.	Bross, Anna Maria	G	
Barth, Johan Baptist	30, Nov. 1856	J. Baptist	Bross, Maria Anna	J	38
Barth, Louisa Friedrica	1, Sept 1856		adult - 22 years old	K	
Barth, Margaretha	21, Apr. 1850	Johan	----, ----	D	210
Barth, Maria	1, Jan. 1859	Johan	Knauer, Catharina	D	128
Barth, Maria Theresa	11, Mar. 1855	J. Baptist	Bross, Maria Anna	J	30
Barth, Maria Theresa	25, Mar. 1855	Marc	Lipps, Sophia	K	
Barth, Rosina	29, Sept 1853	Jacob	Bauman, Magdalena	A	
Bartholme, Johan	31, Aug. 1851	Johan	Girten, Catharina	D	280
Bartholomey, Elisabeth	9, Nov. 1852	Johan	Gierten, Catharina	L	
Bartholt, Mary Charlotte	16, Sept 1856		adult - 18 years old	B	34
Bartle, Thomas	8, Dec. 1853	Daniel	Connell, Bridget	B	304
Bartlett, William	8, Dec. 1857		adult - 50 years old	E	499
Bartley, Francis	21, Mar. 1851	Thomas	Quinn, Bridget	E	293
Bartley, John	25, July 1858	Daniel	Meagher, Ann	E	552
Bartley, John	7, Aug. 1850	John	----, Mary	E	238
Bartley, Thomas	31, Aug. 1853	Daniel	----, Ann	E	124
Bartley, Timothy	25, Dec. 1859	Daniel	Meahar, Ann	U	
Bartliff, Thomas	22, Apr. 1852		adult - 39 years old	E	405
Bartlon, Helen	23, May 1854	Thomas	Galbraith, Helen	V	14
Bartmann, Aloysius Heinrich	1, Oct. 1851	Francis	Eiserkamp, Elisabeth	C	
Bartram, Susanna	28, Sept 1851	Peter	Schendler, Christina	D	284
Basal, Maria Helena	31, Sept 1855	Ludwig	Basal, Margaretha	K	
Baschel, Joseph Heinrich	19, May 1850	Joseph	Hoping, M. Catharina	L	
Basel, Anna	8, Dec. 1853	Ludwig	Reising, Margaretha	D	418
Basel, Johan Jacob	17, May 1857	Aloysius	Reising, Margaretha	D	85
Baser, Maria Louisa	4, June 1854	Valentin	Väl, Carolina	D	11
Bashannan, Ann Elizabeth	6, Mar. 1853	Bartholomew	Maher, Margaret	P	37

Name of Child	Date of Baptism	Father	Mother	Church	Page
Bassman, Gertrud Catharina	5, Feb. 1854	Ferdinand	Fischer, Anna Catharina	A	
Bast, Georg Heinrich	27, July 1852	Johan	Hoffmann, Barbara	F	
Bast, Jacob	27, July 1852	Johan	Hoffmann, Barbara	F	
Bast, Joseph	7, Feb. 1858	Johan	Bar---, Margaretha	D	105
Bast, Margaretha	27, Aug. 1854	Johan	Hoffmann, Margaretha	F	
Bast, Maria Margaretha	13, Feb. 1859	Johan	Bar---, Margaretha	D	131
Bast, Maria Rosina	25, Jan. 1857	Johan	Hoffmann, Barbara	F	
Bast?, Carolina	19, July 1857	Albert	Sch---, Helena	D	91
Bateman, Mary Ann	9, Oct. 1852		adult	B	271
Bates, Charles Augustine	13, Mar. 1858	Charles	Kent, Lucy	P	242
Bates, William Albert	8, Jan. 1855	Charles	Dugan, Margaret	E	255
Bath, Johan	2, May 1858	Marc	Lipps, Sophia	K	
Bath, Josephina Elisabeth	22, Aug. 1850	David	Lapp, Victoria	C	
Bath, Margaretha	4, June 1859	J. Nicolaus	Schok, Henrietta	D	139
Bathalser, Maria Catharina	7, Aug. 1859	Sigismund	Ham--her, Theresa	D	143
Batt, Carl Philipp	14, May 1854	Philipp	Heid, Rosina	C	
Batter, Herman Dietrich	27, Aug. 1851	Bernard D.	Kettler, Antonette	L	
Batter, Maria Anna	23, June 1854	Dietrich	Strothmann, Maria A.	F	
Batter, Maria Catharina Paulina	7, Dec. 1850	Bernard	Herles, Anna Maria	L	
Battle, Bartholomew	8, July 1850	Daniel	----, Bridget	B	207
Battle, John	7, Jan. 1852	Daniel	Cummins, Bridget	B	249
Battle, Maritn	18, Nov. 1856	Daniel	Cummins, Bridget	P	199
Battle, Mary	28, Feb. 1859	Daniel	Cummins, Bridget	B	71
Battle, Thomas	12, May 1856	Patrick	Moyles, Helen	P	180
Battlinger, Anna Catharina	13, Apr. 1856	Mathias	Fey, Catharina	D	56
Bauer, Adam	20, Apr. 1852	Johan	Popp, Catharina	C	
Bauer, Aloysius	9, Sept 1859	Jacob	Jacobi, Maria	T	
Bauer, Andreas	17, Mar. 1850	Peter	Held, Anna	H	
Bauer, Anna	14, Jan. 1855	Caspar	----, Barbara	C	
Bauer, Anna Barbara	17, Jan. 1858	Philipp	Engelert, A. Maria	T	
Bauer, Anna Catharina	28, Jan. 1856	Johan	Winter, Anna	L	
Bauer, Anna Maria	6, Nov. 1854	Johan	Gahr, Maria	D	21
Bauer, Anton	20, Apr. 1851	Anton	Hörman, Maria Anna	D	261
Bauer, Anton Melchior	7, Dec. 1856	Georg	Kramer, Maria	N	
Bauer, August Wilhelm	25, Nov. 1855	Johan	Spitznagel, Felicitas	D	47
Bauer, Barbara	1, Jan. 1857	J. Peter	Schlegel, Margaret	H	
Bauer, Barbara Louisa	3, July 1859	Godfried	R---, Apollonia	D	141
Bauer, Carl	6, Mar. 1859	Joseph	Weis, Rosina	T	
Bauer, Carolina	13, Mar. 1853	Michael	Witter, Cunigunda	A	
Bauer, Carolina	6, May 1855	Michael	Witter, Cunigunda	A	
Bauer, Catharina	11, June 1857	Conrad	Schweiz, Louisa	D	87
Bauer, Catharina	7, Sept 1851	Ignatius	Breiwieser, Magdalena	F	
Bauer, Catharina	28, Aug. 1853	Michael	Callaghan, Mary	S	
Bauer, Catharina Christina	9, June 1856	Johan	Gahr, Maria	D	60
Bauer, Catherina	16, May 1852	Peter	----, Anna Maria	H	
Bauer, Emilia Angela	7, Mar. 1852	Anthony	Mera, Catherine	E	388
Bauer, Francis Anton	14, Aug. 1859	Aloysius	Mo---, Carolina	D	144
Bauer, Georg	28, Nov. 1858	Georg	Kramer, Maria Anna	N	
Bauer, Jacob	10, Apr. 1855	Anton	Knobel, Anna Maria	C	
Bauer, Jacob	3, Aug. 1855	Jacob	Jacobs, Anna Maria	D	39
Bauer, Jacob August	15, July 1855	Jacob	Lentobske, Theresa	D	38
Bauer, Johan	21, Oct. 1857	Johan	Garder, Maria	D	97
Bauer, Johan	12, Dec. 1858	Johan	Spitznagel, Felicitas	D	126
Bauer, Johan	13, June 1858	Michael	Hittler, Cunigunda	F	
Bauer, Johan	11, Sept 1859	Philipp	Englert, Anna Maria	T	
Bauer, Johan	26, Nov. 1851	Sebastian	----, Margaretha	J	12
Bauer, Johan Jacob	9, Nov. 1851	Adam	Zimmerman, Margaretha	D	291
Bauer, Johan Mathias	18, June 1854	Pancratz	Husman, Christina	J	28
Bauer, Johan Peter	3, Sept 1854	Johan	Winter, Anna	L	

Name of Child	Date of Baptism	Father	Mother	Church	Page
Bauer, Johan Robert	21, June 1857	Johan	Pfeifer, Catharina	C	
Bauer, Joseph	8, Apr. 1855	Ignatius	Breitwieser, Christina	F	
Bauer, Joseph	24, Sept 1854	Johan	Kammerle, Barbara	S	
Bauer, Joseph	10, Aug. 1859	Joseph	Vetter, Margaretha	T	
Bauer, Joseph	29, July 1855	Joseph	Weiss, Rosina	J	32
Bauer, Juliana	7, Apr. 1850	Michael	Witter, Cunigunda	A	
Bauer, Juliana Magdalena	5, June 1853	Ignatius	Breitweser, Christina	F	
Bauer, Leonard	2, July 1854	Peter	----, Anna Maria	H	
Bauer, Magdalena	16, Mar. 1856		Bauer, Magdalena	W	12
Bauer, Margaretha	18, Sept 1853	Caspar	Messingschlager, Barbara	D	406
Bauer, Margaretha	26, Dec. 1856	Johan	Spitznagel, Felicitas	D	75
Bauer, Margaretha Francisca	10, Mar. 1855	Leopold	Kobb, Maria Margaretha	D	30
Bauer, Maria Christina	27, Apr. 1851	Michael	Witter, Cunigunda	A	
Bauer, Maria Elisabeth Johanna	10, July 1859	Joseph	H---, Maria	D	141
Bauer, Maria Louisa	4, Apr. 1858	Ignatius	Breitweser, Christina	T	
Bauer, Martina	6, Aug. 1854	Joseph	----, Margaret	H	
Bauer, Paul	26, Sept 1858	Peter	Schlegel, Margaret	H	
Bauer, Rosalia	20, July 1856	Philipp	Englert, Anna Maria	D	63
Bauer, Susanna Maria	22, Mar. 1857	Joseph	Weis, Rosina	F	
Bauer, Theresa	23, Feb. 1859	Johan	Gahr, Maria	D	132
Bauer, Valentin	7, Nov. 1858	J. Conrad	Schweizer, Louisa	W	24
Bauer, William	2, Aug. 1857	Joseph	Veite, Margaret	H	
Bauerborn, Lawrence	25, July 1858	Johan	Hamerle, Barbara	S	
Bäuerlein, Carl Ludwig	6, Nov. 1859	Francis J.	----, Francisca	D	150
Bäuerlein, Joseph Francis	18, Oct. 1855	Michael	Strets, Anna Maria	D	44
Baul, Bernard Heinrich	18, Dec. 1855	Gerhard H.	Kussfeld, Sophia	F	
Baullie, Peter	16, Aug. 1857	John	----, Barbara	R	
Baum, Fran Herman	13, Feb. 1857	Herman	Renges, Sophia	F	
Bauman, Anna Maria	6, Aug. 1855	Michael	Volk, Anna Maria	D	40
Bauman, Barbara	4, Dec. 1856	Joseph	Scheiner, Barbara	D	73
Bauman, Carolina	22, Feb. 1858	Fidel	Schwanz, Maria	D	106
Bauman, Catharina Paulina	10, June 1855	Johan	Krusemeier, Francisca	K	
Bauman, Eliasbeth Antonia	20, Nov. 1859	Andreas	Condrath, Lisetta?	N	
Bauman, Elisabeth	23, Mar. 1856	Fidel	Schwanz, Maria	D	54
Bauman, Elisabeth	21, Sept 1851	Johan	Gressemeil, Francisca	K	
Bauman, Elisabeth	13, Jan. 1850	Johan	Krusemeier, Francisca	F	
Bauman, Francis	5, Sept 1853	Joseph	Scheiner, Barbara	D	404
Bauman, Friedrich	11, Dec. 1853	Michael	Volk, Maria	D	419
Bauman, Georg	6, Jan. 1850	Ignatius	Helmer, Magdalena	D	198
Bauman, Joseph	12, Jan. 1851	Ignatius	Volmer, Magdalena	D	248
Bauman, Louisa	27, Oct. 1856	Philipp	Schwarz, Maria	D	71
Bauman, Maria Elisabeth	12, Oct. 1851	Michael	Volk, Anna Maria	D	287
Bauman, Maria Francisca	27, Nov. 1855	Joseph	Scheiner, Barbara	D	47
Bauman, Maria Magdalena Josephina	25, Mar. 1851	Joseph	Scheiner, Barbara	D	258
Bauman, Nicolaus	8, Oct. 1855	G. Michael	Steger, Rosina	N	
Baumann, Carl Friedrich	12, Sept 1859	Friedrich	Franz Eva	L	
Baumann, Lucia Sophia F.	18, Oct. 1858	Friedrich	Franz, Eva	L	
Baumann, Magdalena	10, Feb. 1850	Daniel	Erhard, Barbara	F	
Baumeister, Anton	16, May 1852	Bernard	Kluesner, Elisabeth	F	
Baumeister, Rosalia Elisabeth	13, Mar. 1859	Caspar	----, Maria	T	
Baumer, Anna Maria Elisabeth	24, Dec. 1854	Bernard	Braune, Catharina	C	
Baumer, Bernard Ludwig	26, Aug. 1856	Bernard	Laue, Anna Maria	L	
Baumer, Bernard Wilhelm	28, Sept 1853	Theodor	Potter, Gertrud	A	
Baumer, Carolina Henrietta Elisabeth	27, Oct. 1853	Bernard	Dressmeyer, Elisabeth	C	
Bäumer, Catharina Maria Anna	8, Sept 1850	Joseph	Parlage, Maria	D	231
Baumer, Francis	1, Mar. 1859	Michael	Volk, Anna Maria	D	133
Bäumer, Johan Herman	9, Feb. 1859	Bernard	B---, Maria	D	131
Baumer, Maria Catharina	15, Oct. 1855	Theodor	Boetter, Gertrud	F	
Baumer, Maria Elisabeth	17, Aug. 1850	Joseph	Exler, Catharina	F	

Name of Child	Date of Baptism	Father	Mother	Church	Page
Bäumer, Mary Louisa	15, Aug. 1859	Henry	Dellman, Mary Anna	D	144
Baumer, Sara Catharina	19, Apr. 1850	J. Bernard	Deie, Catharina Elis.	F	
Baumer, Stephan Gerhard Heinrich	27, Dec. 1853	Bernard	Laue, A. Maria	L	
Baumgaertner, Eduard	27, Dec. 1857	Christian	Hauter, Margaretha	T	
Baumgärdner, Anna Sarah	15, Mar. 1857	Jacob	Hain, Catharina	D	80
Baumgardner, Sarah Louise	1, Dec. 1850	Joseph	----, Louise	B	219
Baumgarten, Anna Maria Catharina	7, Oct. 1858	Mathias	Kronlage, Catharina	L	
Baumgartner, Amalia	23, Dec. 1855	Georg	Ihl, Carolina	D	49
Baumgärtner, Anna Catharina	19, May 1859	Jacob	Heim, Catharina	D	138
Baumgärtner, Anna Maria	29, Sept 1858	Carl	Hammer, Anna Maria	J	48
Baumgärtner, Anna Theresa	9, Jan. 1853	Jacob	Hain, Catharina	D	364
Baumgartner, Catharina	1, Jan. 1850	Vincent	Albacker, Rosa	D	197
Baumgartner, Francis	2, May 1852	Joseph	Judy, Louise	B	264
Baumgartner, Johan	26, Jan. 1851	Benedict	Nolle, Friedricka	F	
Baumgärtner, Johan Wilhelm	15, June 1852	Carl	Hammer, Maria	J	16
Baumgärtner, Maria Caecilia	23, Apr. 1854	Carl	Hammer, Maria Anna	J	26
Baumgärtner, Maria Elisabeth	14, Sept 1856	Carl	Hammer, Maria	J	38
Baumgärtner, Maria Margaretha	13, May 1855	Jacob	Hein, Catharina	D	34
Baumgartner, Maria Theresa	17, Aug. 1858	Andreas	----, Theresa	C	
Baumgartner, Martha Anna	9, Feb. 1851	Jacob	Heim, Catharina	D	252
Baumgartner, Wilhelm Joseph	12, Feb. 1854	Joseph	Baumgartner, Louisa	K	
Baumhöhe, Catharina Gertrud	30, Oct. 1853	Adolph	Schmits, Gertrud	D	412
Baumkamp, Augustine	28, Aug. 1853	Heinrich	Egart, Catharina	N	19
Baumkamp, Johan Joseph	2, Sept 1857	Heinrich	Egard, Catharina	N	
Baumler, Anna Maria	12, Apr. 1857	Joseph	Schmidt, Eva	F	
Baumler, Barbara	26, Mar. 1854	Joseph	Rudolf, Barbara	F	
Baumler, Georg Carl	12, Oct. 1851	Joseph	Ehrensberger, Eva	D	286
Baumler, Maria Magdalena	25, Sept 1859	Joseph	Ehrensberger, Eva	T	
Baumschäfer, Maria Elis. Josephina	13, Feb. 1854	Bernard	Kulenberg, Maria Elisabeth	D	4
Baumschafer, Maria Elisabeth	12, Aug. 1852	Bernard	Kuhlenberg, Elisabeth	D	342
Baumstark, Maria Philomena	8, Feb. 1854	August	Bauer, Barbara	K	
Baunhorst, Anna Maria Elisabeth	3, May 1851		Baunhorst, Margaretha	K	
Baus, Anna Maria Magdalena	22, Mar. 1851	Johan	Olinger, Anna Maria	H	
Bausch, Anton Edward	6, Nov. 1859	Georg	Fraum, Johanna	S	
Bausher, Francis	20, May 1855	Johan	Rodemer, Maria Eva	N	
Baute, Bernardina	3, Oct. 1856	Francis	Schaefer, M. Elis.	L	
Baute, Franz Joseph	1, Apr. 1859	Eberhard	Holtmeyer, Anna Maria	L	
Baute, Heinrich	13, Oct. 1854	J. Heinrich	Faske, M. Elisabeth	L	
Baute, Johan Franz Heinrich	28, Apr. 1856	Heinrich	Faske, M Clara Elis.	L	
Baute, Johan Friedrich	7, July 1854	Friedrich	Schaefer, M. Elisabeth	C	
Baute, Johan Friedrich	7, Nov. 1852	Gerhard H.	Klefoth, Louisa	L	
Baute, Johan Friedrich	21, Aug. 1853	Johan H.	Vaske, M. Elisabeth	L	
Baute, Maria Angela	13, July 1857	Eberhard	Holtmeier, Anna M.	L	
Baxter, Henriette	13, July 1851	James	Nugent, Bridget	E	322
Baxter, John	13, Mar. 1853	James	----, Bridget	E	72
Baxter, Mary	23, Aug. 1858	James	Nugent, Bridget	E	559
Baxter, Wilhelm	16, Aug. 1856	James	Tensy?, Bridget	K	
Bay, Elisabeth	11, Jan. 1852	Peter	Molick, Elisabeth	D	301
Bayer, Christina	21, Oct. 1851	Martin	Kraus, Anna Maria	D	288
Bayer, Johan Mathias	3, Sept 1856	Martin	Kraus, Anna Maria	D	66
Bayer, Maria Veronica	22, Jan. 1859	Bernard	Lehmeyer, Theresa	C	
Bayer, Michael	27, Nov. 1858	Martin	Kraur, Anna Maria	D	124
Bayer, Valentin	14, Sept 1856	Valentin	Hecker, Anna M.	C	
Bayes, Margaretha	9, Mar. 1854	Martin	Kraus, Anna Maria	D	6
Bayler, Carl Martin	30, May 1858	Andreas	Lindener, Carolina	C	
Bayley, Joanne	10, Feb. 1854	Daniel	----, Margaret	E	166
Bayley, Michael Joseph	19, Sept 1856	Michael	----, Marcella	E	399
Beacon, Elizabeth	26, Sept 1850	William	Neal, Bridget	B	214
Beady, William	11, May 1851	King	Booth, Mary	E	306

Name of Child	Date of Baptism	Father	Mother	Church	Page
Bealer, George	4, Jan. 1858	Cornelius	Lowen, Mary	E	505
Bealer, Mary Alice	6, Feb. 1854	Peter	Scully, Mary	J	26
Bean, John	14, Jan. 1855	Michael	Kelly, Alice	E	256
Beans, James	26, Dec. 1852	Michael	----, Elizabeth	E	49
Beard, John	4, Dec. 1856	William	McAtey, Mary Liza	E	417
Beard, William	4, Dec. 1856	William	McAtey, Mary Liza	E	417
Bearn?, James	25, Feb. 1855	Owen	Lynch, Catherine	N	27
Bearns, Helen	20, Feb. 1853	John	Kyne, Bridget	V	1
Beasley, Mary	6, Sept 1850		adult - 18 years old	E	248
Beasley, Mary Martha	13, July 1854	Edmund	----, Sarah	E	206
Beathy, William	29, Dec. 1851	James	Bell, Mary	E	368
Beatson, Harriet Ann	30, Apr. 1856	William	McCarthy, Catherine	E	364
Beatson, Joseph	14, Mar. 1859	William	McCarthy, Catherine	E	611
Beatson, Margaret	29, Jan. 1857	William	McCarthy, Catherine	E	429
Beattie, (son)	16, Dec. 1851	Charles	Howell, Hannah	B	247
Beatty, Helen	14, June 1852	John	Gr---, Mary	B	260
Beber, Christian	2, Jan. 1859	Ludwig	Luneman, Catharina	D	128
Beberberg, Heinrich Herman	11, Oct. 1852	J. Bernard	Hohman, Maria Elisabeth	N	9
Bechel, Georg Theodor	16, Feb. 1852	Anton	Horth, Eva	A	
Bechert, Johan Wilhelm	25, June 1854	Johan	Staph, Maria Anna	K	
Bechlin, Christina Maria	4, Sept 1853		Bechlin, Maria	A	
Bechold, Elisabeth	15, May 1853	Ferdinand	Brokamp, Dina	F	
Becht, Andreas	22, Feb. 1856	Joseph	Mohr, Maria Eva	D	52
Becht, August Conrad	20, Mar. 1854	Conrad	Munsch, Magdalena	D	7
Becht, Georg Joseph	27, June 1852	Georg	Stubenrauch, Elisabeth	D	327
Becht, Johan Adam	19, Sept 1853	Joseph	Mohn, Maria Eva	D	406
Becht, Josephina	1, Oct. 1854	Joseph	Mohn, Maria Eva	D	19
Becht, Maria Louisa	28, Sept 1850	Georg	Stubenrauch, Elisabeth	D	235
Becht, Maria Magdalena	12, Mar. 1854		Becht, Margaretha	D	6
Becht, Maria Magdalena	9, July 1855		Becht, Margaretha	D	38
Bechter, Margaretha	28, Mar. 1858	Joachim	Bütz, Catharina	D	108
Bechthold, Christian Martin	6, Jan. 1850	Andreas	Pair, Barbara	D	198
Bechthold, Regina Margaretha	6, Feb. 1853	Joachim	Katz, Christina	D	369
Bechtold, Anna Maria	2, Nov. 1851	Andreas	Beier, Barbara	F	
Bechtold, Francisca	17, Feb. 1856	Joseph	Fürkers, Agnes	K	
Bechtold, Joseph	29, June 1851	Joachim	Katz, Christina	D	270
Bechtold, Maria	21, Nov. 1851	Ferdinand	Brokamp, Bernardina	F	
Bechtolt, Ludwig	22, Apr. 1855	Joachim	Katz, Christina	D	33
Beck, Andreas Jacob	27, Nov. 1853	Jacob	Winterholer, Theresa	D	417
Beck, Barbara	25, Apr. 1859	Georg	Schwei, Josephina	C	
Beck, Carl	4, Oct.1857	Andreas	Schulz, Christina	D	96
Beck, Carl Joseph Benedict	22, July 1858	Jacob	Winterholter, Tharsilla	D	115
Beck, Carl Mathias	25, Dec. 1855	Jacob	Winterholter, Tharsilla	D	49
Beck, Carolina	11, Apr. 1857	Georg	Schwey, Josephina	C	
Beck, Charles	29, Apr. 1855	Joseph	McGuire, Elizabeth	E	282
Beck, Charles	12, Oct. 1850	Richard	----, Ellen	E	253
Beck, Christina	19, July 1859	Lawrence	Vonberg, Louisa	D	142
Beck, Edwin Michael	9, Sept 1855	Joseph	Maguire, Elizabeth	B	19
Beck, Elisabeth	8, May 1859	Johan	Baier, Cunigunda	D	137
Beck, Emilia Elisabeth	16, Oct. 1853	Andreas	Schulz, Christina	D	410
Beck, Francis	16, Nov. 1855	Johan	Baier, Cunigunda	D	47
Beck, Georg	18, Apr. 1852	Johan	Beyer, Cunigunda	D	317
Beck, Gregor	27, Sept 1850	Jacob	Winterholer, Theresa	D	234
Beck, Heinrich	31, July 1853	Johan	Bayer, Cunigunda	D	398
Beck, Johan	30, Mar. 1853	Lawrence	Krebs, Anna Maria	F	
Beck, Johan Bernard Wilhelm	4, Dec. 1850	Lawrence	Krebs, Anna Maria	F	
Beck, John	18, July 1851	William	Arend, Elizabeth	E	325
Beck, Joseph Ferdinand	29, May 1859	Nicolaus	Niebling, Theresa	A	
Beck, Josephina	1, Apr. 1855	Georg	Schway, Josephina	K	

Name of Child	Date of Baptism	Father	Mother	Church	Page
Beck, Maria	4, Mar. 1855	Andreas	Schulz, Christina	D	30
Beck, Maria Magdalena	20, July 1851	Jacob	Winterholer, Theresa	D	274
Beck, Maria Martha	13, July 1851	Andreas	Schulz, Christina	D	273
Beck, Michael Joseph	3, Oct. 1858	Friedrich	Düri---, Maria	D	120
Beck, Peter	31, Oct. 1855	Daniel?	----, Ann	E	324
Beck, Peter Joseph	11, Dec. 1858	Nicolaus	Klein, Helen	D	125
Beck, Samuel	9, Dec. 1850	Samuel	Pryor, Ann	E	266
Beck, Thomas	22, July 1853	Samuel	----, Ann	E	111
Beckel, Anna Maria Adelheid	27, June 1850	Johan D.	Schulte, Anna Maria	C	
Beckener, Johan	29, Nov. 1856	Pancratz	Ott, Juliana	A	
Beckenhaupt, Adam	19, July 1859	Johan	Peter, Carolina	J	50
Beckenhaupt, August	21, Jan. 1855	Johan	Peter, Carolina	F	
Beckenhaupt, Fidel	2, Sept 1855	Felix	Rick, Maria	J	32
Beckenhaupt, Helena	10, May 1857	Johan	Peter, Carolina	A	
Beckenhaupt, Joseph Wendel	6, Oct. 1850	Johan	Peter, Carolina	F	
Beckenhaupt, Rosina Emerentia	21, Nov. 1852	Johan	Peter, Carolina	F	
Becker, Anna Maria	4, Oct. 1857	Aloysius	Mueller, Maria	F	
Becker, Anna Maria	4, Aug. 1859	Dietrich	Schulte, Anna Maria	F	
Becker, Anna Maria	16, Sept 1855	Joseph	Geier, Anna Maria	D	42
Becker, Anna Maria Agnes	23, Feb. 1858	Johan H.	Kruse, A.M. Bernardina	F	
Becker, Anton de Padua	4, July 1859	Joseph	Geier, Anna Maria	D	141
Becker, Anton Kash.	21, Mar. 1858	Ludwig	Bau---, Anna Maria	D	107
Becker, Barbara	28, May 1856	Jacob	Zahrt, Johanna	D	59
Becker, Bernard Heinrich	29, July 1856	Bernard	Lörfing, Philomena H.	A	
Becker, Catharina	22, June 1858	Anton	Wer---, Philippina	D	113
Becker, Catharina	22, May 1859	Johan	End, Elisabeth	H	
Becker, Catharina	30, Oct. 1853	Nicolaus	Becker, Barbara	F	
Becker, Catharine	18, Oct. 1857	Dennis	Heil, Maria Anna	T	
Becker, Christian Friedrich	5, Mar. 1854	Christian F.	Thesing, Elisabeth	A	
Becker, Dominica	16, Oct. 1859	Wilhelm	Watlen, Catharina	D	149
Becker, Elisabeth	20, Mar. 1859	Marcus	Linsenmeyer, Rosina	C	
Becker, Ferdinand	31, May 1857	Christoph	Ulmer, Anna Magdalena	A	
Becker, Francis	9, May 1852	Christoph	Ulmer, Magdalena	A	
Becker, Friedrich	15, July 1856	Francis	Sentelbach, Christina	U	
Becker, Friedrich	4, Feb. 1855	Friedrich	Weber, Margaretha	D	28
Becker, Friedrich	23, Mar. 1856	Justus	Biel, Catharina	D	54
Becker, Georg Friedrich	7, Apr. 1850	Dennis	Heil, Maria Anna	D	208
Becker, Isabel	27, Jan. 1850	Bernard	Witmer, Louise	B	196
Becker, Johan	3, Feb. 1850	Christoph	Ulmer, Magdalena	A	
Becker, Johan	25, Dec. 1852	Emil	Quickley, Sarah	C	
Becker, Johan	1, Feb. 1852	L. Jodocus	Geyer, Anna Maria	D	304
Becker, Johan Baptist	22, June 1859	Henry	Buss--, Theresa	D	140
Becker, Johan Bernard Gerhard	9, June 1853	J. Theodor	Schulte, Anna Maria	F	
Becker, Johan Bernard Heinrich	5, Sept 1854	Heinrich	Heilker, Catharina	C	
Becker, Johan Francis	14, Oct. 1850	Christoph	Macke, Maria Angela	D	238
Becker, Johan Gerhard Herman	2, Oct. 1853	Hildebran	Lange, Elisabeth	L	
Becker, Johan Heinrich	23, Feb. 1852	Christoph	Macke, Angela	D	308
Becker, Johan Heinrich Joseph	1, Feb. 1856	Johan H.	Kruse, Anna Dina	F	
Becker, Johan Herman	20, June 1858	Bernard T.	Schulte, Maria	F	
Becker, Johan Joseph	28, Feb. 1859	Heinrich	Heiker, Maria Anna	C	
Becker, Johan Peter	15, Dec. 1850	Adam	Hirt, Margaretha	D	247
Becker, Johanna Maria	24, Nov. 1851	J. Bernard	Lersing, Wilhelmina Friedr.	A	
Becker, Joseph	14, Mar. 1858	Francis	Sentelbach, Christina	U	
Becker, Joseph Heinrich	6, May 1854	J. Bernard	Lehring, Wilhelmina	A	
Becker, Josephina Francisca	21, Sept 1851	Christian	Thesing, Maria Elisabeth	A	
Becker, Josephina Friedricka	4, May 1859	Johan	Maag, Dina	C	
Becker, Juliana	25, Feb. 1855	Francis	----, Christine	U	
Becker, Juliana Elmira Catharina	28, Dec. 1851	Bernard	Witwer, Louisa	D	299
Becker, Magdalena	14, Feb. 1858	Joseph	Kahl, Catharina	D	105

Name of Child	Date of Baptism	Father	Mother	Church	Page
Becker, Magdalena	1, Apr. 1855	Wilhelm	Watlen, Catharina	D	32
Becker, Margaretha	21, June 1857	Wilhelm	Walle, Catharina	D	88
Becker, Maria Catharina	29, Oct. 1856	Heinrich	Hilger, Maria Anna	C	
Becker, Maria Elisabeth	25, May 1858	Christian	Thesing, Theresa	A	
Becker, Maria Josephina	6, Aug. 1854	Dennis	Heil, Maria Anna	F	
Becker, Maria Louisa	10, May 1857	Johan	Arnold, Elisabeth	H	
Becker, Maria Magdalena	12, June 1852	Dennis	Heil, Maria Anna	F	
Becker, Michael	3, Mar. 1850	Jodocus	Geyer, Anna Maria	D	204
Becker, Michael Philipp	2, Dec. 1850	Nicolaus	Kiefer, Philippina	C	
Becker, Nicolaus	18, Sept 1859	Hugh	Bühl, Catharina	U	
Becker, Nicolaus	15, June 1856	Joseph	Kahl, Catharina	D	61
Becker, Paulina Christina	21, Feb. 1858	F. Wilhelm	----, Margaretha	D	106
Becker, Peter	3, June 1855	Francis J.	Stern, Charlotte	F	
Becker, Peter	17, July 1853	Jodocus	Geiger, Anna Maria	D	395
Becker, Philipp	20, July 1856	F. Wilhelm	Weber, Margaretha	D	63
Becker, Susanna	16, Apr. 1857	Lawrence	-irels, Anna Maria	D	83
Becker, Theodor Heinrich	8, Apr. 1850	J. Theodor	Korpers, Maria Gesina	K	
Becker, Theresa	18, July 1858	Francis	Hern, Charlotte	T	
Becker, Valentin	7, Feb. 1855	Simon	Geerman, Elisabeth	K	
Becker, Wilhelmina Catharina	1, Mar. 1857	Nicolaus	Kepper, Wilhelmina	A	
Beckereis, Maria Anna	26, Dec. 1856	John	Beets, Ann	H	
Beckert, Carolina	3, July 1856	Francis J.	Sternjacob, Carolina	F	
Beckert, Catharina Philomena	4, Sept 1859	Adam	Fond, Catharina	K	
Becket, William Henry	23, Jan. 1859	James	Amick?, Laura	B	70
Beckhaus, Elisabeth Catharina	31, Mar. 1859	Bernard	Segbers, Catharina Elisabeth	N	
Beckhaus, Maria Anna	10, Oct. 1856	Bernard	Segbers, Catharina Elisabeth	N	
Beckhaus, Maria Catharina	29, Oct. 1857	Bernard	Segbers, Catharina	N	
Beckler, Herman Johan	30, Aug. 1852	Conrad	Bagster, Elisabeth	K	
Beckman, Anna Maria Elisabeth	8, Jan. 1851	Herman	Morwessels, Margaret Elis.	A	
Beckman, Anna Maria Lucia	17, Jan. 1858	Herman	Moorman, Elisabeth	A	
Beckman, Anna Maria Theresa	11, Oct. 1851	G. Herman	Striker, Anna Maria	K	
Beckman, Bernard Heinrich	18, Aug. 1856	G. Herman	Strieker, Anna Maria	K	
Beckman, Frances	6, Mar. 1855	Theodor	----, Gertrud	H	
Beckman, Francis Joseph	24, July 1853	Ludwig	Schuller, Barbara	D	396
Beckman, Georg Theodor	9, June 1850	Theodor	----, Gertrud	H	
Beckman, Heinrich Wilhelm	14, Dec. 1852	H. Wilhelm	Landig, Maria Gertrud	D	360
Beckman, Herman Heinrich	3, Nov. 1856	Herman	Nepper, Catharina	K	
Beckman, Johan Gerhard Heinrich	22, Oct. 1850	Heinrich	Dieker, Anna Christina	A	
Beckman, Johan Heinrich	25, Nov. 1852	G. Herman	Striker, J. Maria	K	
Beckman, Johan Herman	18, Jan. 1859	Herman	Neppe, Anna	K	
Beckman, Johan Herman Heinrich	3, Mar. 1851	Herman	Lambers, Theresa	A	
Beckman, Johan Joseph	22, Aug. 1852	Herman	Lammers, Theresa	A	
Beckman, Maria	23, Nov. 1856	Michael	Schaller, Maria	D	72
Beckman, Maria Elisabeth	6, Apr. 1854	Gerhard H.	Morwessel, Margaretha E.	A	
Beckman, Maria Francisca	9, June 1854	Theodor	Sprakl, Agnes	D	12
Beckman, Michael	17, Sept 1854	Michael	Schaller, Maria Anna	D	18
Beckman, Wilhelm Heinrich Johan	4, Sept 1855	Wilhelm	Langengeld, Maria Theresa	D	42
Beckmann, Anna Catharina Sophia	26, Apr. 1858	J. Heinrich	Hillebrand, Anna Theresa	C	
Beckmann, Anna Maria	8, July 1856	Theodor	Bramlage, Gertrud	C	
Beckmann, Apollonia Wilhelmina	23, Oct. 1852	Robert	Kammerer, Theresa	C	
Beckmann, Bernard Francis	21, May 1853	Heinrich	Hildebrant, Theresa	C	
Beckmann, Francisca Bertha	4, July 1858	Johan	Bur, Catharina	C	
Beckmann, Friedrich August	30, Aug. 1857	Francis	Bossenkamp, Anna M.	F	
Beckmann, Johan Bernard	22, Mar. 1851	Heinrich	Hildebrand, Theresa	C	
Beckmann, Maria Catharina	23, June 1858	Heinrich	Wiechers, Theresa	L	
Beckmann, Maria Josephina	19, Dec. 1855	Heinrich	Hillebrand, Theresa	C	
Beckmann, Maria Louisa	16, Dec. 1855	Ludwig	Schaller, Barbara	C	
Becknell, Catherine	3, Nov. 1855	John	Field, Ann	E	324
Becknell, Charles William	25, Feb. 1853	Leo	Smith, Mary Ann	E	66

Name of Child	Date of Baptism	Father	Mother	Church	Page
Beckner, Leo Francis	1, Aug. 1858	J. Heinrich	Beckman, Rebecca Margaret	D	116
Beckschmidt, Heinrich Julius	6, Nov. 1851	Heinrich	Kleemeyer, Maria Theresa	K	
Beckschmidt, Johan Francis	28, Nov. 1857	Heinrich	Kleemeyer, Theresa	K	
Beckschmidt, Maria Gertrud	9, Sept 1855	Heinrich	Kleimeier, Theresa	K	
Beckschmidt, Maria Theresa	17, Oct. 1850	Johan J.	Kleimeyer, Elisabeth	L	
Beckschmidt, Theresa Juliana	4, Nov. 1853	Heinrich	Klemeier, Theresa	K	
Beckschulte, Anna Maria	5, Sept 1859	Anton	Ossenbeck, Anna Maria	Q	32
Beckwerment, Johan Bernard	23, Nov. 1856	Wilhelm	Herzog, Bernardina	K	
Beckwerment, Johan Herman	3, Apr. 1857	Herman	Grabber, Maria Carolina	K	
Beckwermert, Anna Maria Carolina	11, Jan. 1853	G. Heinrich	Grabbel, Maria A. Carolina	K	
Beckwermert, Anna Maria Josephina	12, Dec. 1858	Herman	Grabbe, Carolina	K	
Beckwermert, Johan Bernard	17, July 1857	J. Gerhard	Heileman, Maria Anna	K	
Beckwermert, Johanna Philomena	25, May 1855	J. Bernard	Grabbe, Carolina	K	
Beckwermert, Maria Anna Philomena	2 Feb. 1852	Gerhard	Herzog, Agnes	K	
Beckwermert, Maria Anna Philomena	7, July 1856	H. Gerhard	Heileman, Maria Anna	K	
Beckwermert, Maria Louisa	24, Sept 1851	Herman	Grabber, Maria Carolina	K	
Beckwermeth, Gerhard Wilhelm	3, Sept 1854	Wilhelm	Herzog, Dina	K	
Beckweth, John	13, June 1855	Lamuel	----, Ann	E	292
Beckwith, John	14, Jan. 1852	John	Dosset, Mary	E	373
Bedacht, Dorothea	28, Nov. 1852	Georg	Götz, Barbara	J	18
Bedacht, Maria Genofeva	25, Sept 1854	Georg	Götz, Barbara	J	28
Bedel, Agnes	3, Aug. 1851	Andrew	Riester, Regina	H	
Bedel, Andrew	15, Oct. 1854	John	----, Mary	H	
Bedel, Anna Maria	30, Jan. 1853	Johan	Alich, Anna Maria	F	
Bedel, Catharina Regina	9, Oct. 1852	Joseph	Fischer, Elisabeth	D	351
Bedel, Catherine	16, Apr. 1854	Andrew	----, Regina	H	
Bedel, Engelbert Adolph	14, Nov. 1858	Johan	Alich, Anna Maria	F	
Bedel, Francis	9, Sept 1850	Jacob	Eneser, Rosina	C	
Bedel, Francis	11, Oct. 1857	Joseph	Fischer, Elisabeth	D	96
Bedel, Franz	10, Dec. 1854	Johan	Alich, Anna Maria	F	
Bedel, Jacob	10, Oct. 1852	Jacob	Ekelinger, Rosina	D	351
Bedel, Johan	5, Jan. 1851	Johan	Ahlig, Anna Maria	F	
Bedel, Johan	8, Dec. 1850	Joseph	Fischer, Elisabeth	D	246
Bedel, Joseph	19, Sept 1852	Andrew	----, Regina	H	
Bedel, Joseph	9, May 1858	Andrew	Ries---, Regina	D	110
Bedel, Margaretha	12, Oct. 1856	Johan	Alick, Maria	F	
Bedel, Margaretha	17, Dec. 1854	Joseph	Fischer, Elisabeth	D	24
Bedel, Michael	10, May 1857	Johan	Stenger, Maria	H	
Bedel, Paul	11, Mar. 1855	Jacob	Elsner, Rosina	D	30
Bedell, Margaret	11, July 1858	Joseph	Spitzfarber, Anna Maria	H	
Beder, Heinrich Sigismund	29, Mar. 1855	Amand	Schimmel, Barbara	F	
Bedger, Mary Ellen	15, Aug. 1859	Theodore	McDonald, Eliza	B	79
Bedini, Anna Frances	3, July 1858	Joseph	Lux, Catharina	H	
Beech, John	25, May 1854	B.H.	adult - 18 years old	E	194
Beecham, Mary Ann	21, June 1854	Garrett	Calaghan, Frances	P	85
Beel, Francis Wilhelm	10, June 1855	Francis	Meyer, Maria	D	36
Beel, Johan	20, Jan. 1856	Clemens	Schneider, Maria Anna	D	51
Beel, Johan	23, Nov. 1851	Francis	Meyer, Maria Anna	L	
Beer, Francis	2, Aug. 1855	Johan	Bad, Margaretha	D	39
Beerman, Catherine	13, May 1855	Michael	Krimm, Catherine	R	
Beerman, Margaretha Barbara	27, Apr. 1858	Friedrich	Mes--, Margaretha	D	110
Beetle, Charles Edward	31, Aug. 1851	Alfred	----, Elizabeth	E	338
Beetz, Crescentia	11, Oct. 1857	Ignatius	Zapf, Cunigunda	H	
Beetzel, George	3, June 1859	Ignatius	Zapf, Cunigunda	H	
Begley, Ann	16, Feb. 1854	Nicolaus	Vandergraft, Susan	P	69
Begley, Ann Catherine	16, Feb. 1854	Nicolaus	Vandergraft, Susan	P	69
Begley, Daniel	15, Apr. 1855	Patrick	Garent, Bridget	E	280
Begley, Hugh	17, Nov. 1857	Patrick	----, Bridget	E	494
Begley, John	7, July 1850	Patrick	----, Mary	E	229

Name of Child	Date of Baptism	Father	Mother	Church	Page
Begley, John	13, Nov. 1859	Patrick	Mulcaren, Bridget	E	670
Begley, John Henry	1, Apr. 1852	Thomas	----, Elizabeth	E	397
Begley, Joseph Henry	16, Feb. 1854	Nicolaus	Vandergraft, Susan	P	69
Begley, Margaret	26, June 1853	Patrick	----, Bridget	E	101
Begley, Mary Emma	9, Apr. 1854	Nicolaus	Vandergrift, Susan	P	78
Begley, Susan	25, Feb. 1854		adult - 28 years old	P	70
Begone, John	23, Apr. 1854	John	Welsh, Bridget	B	313
Behan, Margaret Ann	9, Oct. 1859	James	Judge, Bridget	B	82
Behle, Joseph	13, Apr. 1857	Urban	Bosch, Catharina	J	40
Behlemann, Anna Adelheid	24, Feb. 1859	Johan B.	Borg, Anna Maria	T	
Behlen, Carl August	21, May 1854	Carl	Erdt, Henrietta	C	
Behlen, Maria Emma Catharina	31, July 1855	Carl	Erd, Henrietta	C	
Behlen, Maria Magdalena	25, Aug. 1856	Carl	Erd, Henrietta	C	
Behlen, Maria Philomena	17, Feb. 1859	Carl	Erd, Henrietta	C	
Behlen, Maria Philomena	21, June 1859	Carl	Erdt, Maria	C	
Behler, Edwin	1, Nov. 1852	Peter	Scully, Mary	B	274
Behler, Francis Cleophas	25, Sept 1859	Johan	Klausing, Maria	K	
Behler, James Henry	27, Apr. 1852	Peter	Scully, Mary	B	258
Behler, Rosina	18, Mar. 1855	Urban	Bosch, Catharian	J	30
Behlman, Carl August	2, Mar. 1851		adult	K	
Behman, Elisabeth	16, June 1858	Balthasar	G---nman, Maria Elisabeth	D	113
Behman, John Henry	26, Sept 1852	Gregory	Hamet, Mary	H	
Behne, Francis Joseph	8, July 1853	Joseph	Harm, Maria Engel	A	
Behr, Adam Eduard	9, June 1850	Nicolaus	Kramer, Francisca	D	216
Behr, Francis Xavier	10, Oct. 1852	Nicolaus	Kramer, Francisca	D	352
Behr, Maria Amelia Theresa	7, Oct. 1855	Nicolaus	Kramer, Francisca	D	44
Behrens, Anna Maria	7, Sept 1858	Bernard J.	Niemeier, Catharina M	L	
Behrens, Elisabeth	12, Dec. 1858	Francis	Scholl, Regina	T	
Behrens, Friedrich August	22, Dec. 1854	F. August	Weiker, Catharina	K	
Behrens, Helena Juliana	20, June 1853	Dietrich	Kroeger, Helena	K	
Behrens, Johan Heinrich	11, Jan. 1857	Bernard	Niemeier, Catharina	L	
Behrens, Johan Heinrich	29, July 1852	F. August	Heiker, Catharina	L	
Behrens, Johan Joseph	8, Feb. 1851	Joseph	Barkhaus, Maria Gertrud	K	
Behrens, Johanna Elisabeth	26, Feb. 1854	Bernard	Niemeyer, Margaretha	L	
Behrens, Maria Anna	9, Aug. 1852	J. Joseph	Barkhaus, Maria Gertrud	K	
Behrens, Maria Francisca	17, June 1859	Dietrich	Kroeger, Helena	K	
Behrens, Maria Josephina Carolina	30, Apr. 1854	Joseph	Beckhaus, Gertrud	K	
Behrens, Maria Philomena	12, Jan. 1857	J. Dietrich	Kroeger, Helena	K	
Behring, Anna Louisa	26, Dec. 1852	Heinrich	Fischer, Helena Maria	F	
Behringer, Christina	28, Apr. 1855	Johan	Witting, Regina	D	34
Behrle, Joseph Albert	30, Oct. 1859	Lucas	Berger, Augusta Engel	F	
Behrman, Francis	30, Jan. 1853	Michael	Grim, Catharina	D	368
Behrman, Johan Peter	28, Mar. 1858	Michael	Grinn, Catharina	D	108
Behrman, Margaretha Juliana	28, Jan. 1855	Johan	Jung, Barbara	D	27
Behrman, Maria Elisabeth	8, Aug. 1854	Francis	Moss, Maria Angela	D	15
Behrman, Michael	25, Aug. 1850	Michael	Grinn, Catharina	D	230
Behrmann, Carolina	27, Feb. 1859	Philipp	Haberthuer, Theresa	G	
Behrmann, Clara Josephina	10, Mar. 1856	Francis	Moos, Maria Engel	F	
Bei, Carl Joseph	6, Mar. 1859	Joseph	Pinz, Stephania	D	133
Beierlein, Cunigunda	20, Nov. 1853	Johan	Will, Barbara	D	416
Beierlein, Elisabeth	29, Nov. 1857	Johan	Will, Barbara	D	99
Beierlein, Francis Joseph	10, May 1858	Francis J.	Metz, Francisca	D	111
Beierlein, Francisca	15, July 1855	Francis	Nerz, Francisca	D	38
Beierlein, Johan Valentin	22, Nov. 1853	Francis	Nörz, Francisca	D	416
Beierlein, Joseph August	28, Aug. 1853	Peter	Reser, Catharina	F	
Beil, Johan Joseph	24, Aug. 1857	Joseph	Fortmann, M. Anna	C	
Beil, Joseph Johan Heinrich	19, Mar. 1854	Joseph	Fortmann, M. Anna	C	
Beil, Maria Elisabeth	21, July 1851	Joseph	Fortmann, Anna M.	C	
Beile, Anna Maria Carolina	16, Oct. 1854	Gerhard	Bockhorst, Christina	L	

Name of Child	Date of Baptism	Father	Mother	Church	Page
Beile, Carolina Josephina	9, Mar. 1851	Carl	Tappe, Theresa	A	
Beile, Carolina Theresa	2, Dec. 1858	Johan G.	Fahrenhorst, Christina	L	
Beile, Gerhard Heinrich	6, Aug. 1850	Gerhard	Bockhorst, Christina	L	
Beile, Johan Wilhelm	5, Feb. 1856	J. Gerhard	Bokhorst, Christina	L	
Beile, Maria Catharina Agnes	25, Apr. 1852	Gerhard	Bockhorst, Christina	L	
Beiler, Anna Maria	4, Nov. 1852	Martin	Stelzer, Dominica	D	356
Beiler, Georg	15, June 1850	Martin	Stelzer, Dominica	D	217
Beiler, Maria Margaretha	11, June 1854	Martin	Stelser, Dominica	D	12
Beiman, Catharina	8, Dec. 1856	Francis J.	Metz, Francisca	D	74
Beimforde, Johan Heinrich Clemens	8, June 1859	Bernard	Meier, Elisabeth	L	
Beimforde, Maria Catharina Wilhelmina	17, Feb. 1853	Bernard	Meyer, Elisabeth	K	
Beimforde, Maria Wilhelmina	9, Feb. 1857	Bernard	Meier, Elisabeth	L	
Beiring, Maria Anna	11, June 1851	Johan H.	Fischer, A. Maria Helena	F	
Beiser, Elisabeth	20, Mar. 1853	Andreas	Tensing, Elisabeth	A	
Beiser, Joseph	16, Mar. 1851	Andreas	Theiering, Elisabeth	A	
Beiser, Ludwig	9, Mar. 1856	Andreas	Theiring, Elisabeth	F	
Beitmann, Anna Maria	7, Sept 1854	Carl	Giese, Francisca	C	
Beitmann, Franz Wilhelm Arnold	3, Apr. 1859	Carl	Giese, Francisca	L	
Beitmann, Gerhard Joseph Carl	13, Apr. 1851	Carl	Giese, Francisca	C	
Beitmann, Heinrich Joseph	24, Jan. 1850	Gerhard	Bockeling, Catharina	C	
Beitmann, Johan Bernard Carl	13, Feb. 1853	Carl	Giese, Francisca	C	
Beitmann, Maria Gertrud Louisa	20, Nov. 1856	Carl	Giese, Francisca	C	
Beitrag, Johan Bernard Heinrich	21, June 1852	Bernard	Brüggeman, Engel	D	326
Bekeler, Theresa Agnes	3, Aug. 1850	Bernard	Kohne, Catharina	C	
Bekieber, Rosa	18, Sept 1859	Johan	Their---, Magdalena	D	147
Belden, Julius Emil	18, Sept 1851	Francis J.	Reiser, Nymphorosa	K	
Beler, Francis	2, Feb. 1857	Peter	Scully, Mary	B	40
Belf---, John Edward	24, Aug. 1853	John	Burns, Eliza	B	297
Bell, Agnes	6, June 1851	John	Magennis, Ann	E	313
Bell, Elizabeth	16, July 1853	John	----, Ann	E	107
Bell, Julius Adolph	10, Apr. 1859	Conrad	Zeller, Anna	D	135
Bell, Mary Ann	9, Aug. 1859	John	McEnnis, Ann	E	646
Bell, Samuel Henry	30, Oct. 1851	John	Hughes, Bridget	B	244
Bell, Sarah	29, Mar. 1854	John	Delaney, Mary	P	76
Bellen, Gerhard Heinrich	19, Mar. 1851	Gerhard	Widdenkamp, Anna	C	
Beller, Gerhard Joseph	19, Mar. 1854	Gerhard	Wedenkamp, Anna	F	
Beller, Jacob	5, Apr. 1858	Georg	Ader, Elisabeth	C	
Bellew, Bridget	19, Dec. 1856	James	Sweeney, Catharine	T	
Bellew, Jacob	15, Aug. 1858	Jacob	Sheen, Catharine	T	
Bellew, Peter	13, Apr. 1856	Patrick	Murphy, Elizabeth	V	30
Bellew, Theresa	10, Dec. 1853	Patrick	Murphy, Elizabeth	V	8
Bellew, William	6, Mar. 1859	Patrick	Murphy, Elizabeth	E	609
Bellow, James	4, Nov. 1850	Patrick	----, Elizabeth	E	259
Bells, Alice	8, June 1856	John	Delany, Mary	P	182
Belscher, Charles	21, Aug. 1851	Charles	Bishop, Mary Elizabeth	E	334
Belt, Daniel	11, Oct. 1851	John	Miginis, Ann	E	349
Belton, Susan Louise	28, Nov. 1858	William	Moore, Elizabeth	J	48
Belton, Thomas	11, Mar. 1855	William	Moore, Elizabeth	G	
Belton, William	21, Sept 1856	William	Moore, Elizabeth	J	38
Belton, William Henry	26, May 1853	Christopher	McGuffy, Mary	B	292
Belzer, Anna Maria	12, Sept 1853	Bernard	Unnewehr, Elisabeth	C	
Bemis, Francis William	1, May 1859	John	Kerns, Matilda	B	74
Ben, Johan Peter	18, July 1858	Johan	Rihn, Catharina	D	115
Bencken, Johan Heinrich	7, Nov. 1854	Bernard T.	Kale, Theresa	C	
Benckhoff, Johan Gerhard	11, June 1854	Bernard J.	Bockweg, Maria Catharina	D	12
Bendel, Carl	21, Sept 1851	Mathias	Heitel, Genofeva	C	
Bender, Anna Maria Adelheid	2, Mar. 1855	Herman	Nabers, Gesina	A	
Bender, August Damien	9, Feb. 1851	Wilhelm	Stahl, Elisabeth	C	
Bender, Catharina	15, Feb. 1857	Johan	Schild, Catharina	L	

Name of Child	Date of Baptism	Father	Mother	Church	Page
Bender, Catharina	25, Aug. 1855	Johan	Schilt, Catharina	D	41
Bender, Friedrich Johan	16, Jan. 1852	Herman	Nabers, Gesina	A	
Bender, Henry	4, Sept 1859	Joseph	Geistner, Clara	D	145
Bender, Jacob	14, Aug. 1853	Johan	Schild, Catharina	D	400
Bender, Jacob Victor	8, Aug. 1858	Georg	Knohr, Margaretha	Q	28
Bender, Johan Baptist	30, Jan. 1859	Johan B.	Schild, Catharina	D	130
Bender, Johan Bartholomew	2, Jan. 1850	Bartholomew	Volk, Matilda	A	
Bender, Johan Gerhard Lambert	13, May 1853	Herman	Nabers, Gesina	D	385
Bender, Louisa	9, Nov. 1856	Joseph	Gerstner, Clara	D	72
Bender, Maria Catharina Elisabeth	1, Aug. 1853	Wilhelm	Bruel, Elisabeth	C	
Bender, Mary Elisabeth	27, Apr. 1851	Peter	Calkof, Elizabeth	H	
Bender, Mary Elizabeth	19, July 1857	George	Knorr, Margaret	U	
Bender, Robert	6, Aug. 1857	Robert	Wolf, Catherine	E	472
Bender, Wilhelm	25, May 1851	Johan	Stoecke, Catharina	K	
Benfield, Mary	17, Aug. 1853	Patrick	Brown, Mary	P	49
Bengeman, Maria Philomena	15, Jan. 1857	G. Bernard	Wilkemake, Anna Maria	Q	19
Bengeser, Catharina	22, Jan. 1854	Leonard	Schemmel, Carolina	D	2
Bengeser, Rosina	2, Mar. 1858	Leonard	Schemmel, Carolina	D	106
Bengesser, Leonard	25, May 1856	Leonard	Schemmel, Carolina	D	59
Bengholz, Maria Gertrud	30, July 1850	Bernard	Mairin, Elisabeth	D	226
Benken, Herman Bernard	1, Sept 1852	Bernard	Kahle, M. Theresa	C	
Benken, Maria Elisabeth	17, Oct. 1850	B. Theodor	Kahle, Theresa	C	
Benkert, Adalbert	25, Sept 1853	Adam	Arnold, Anna Mara	D	407
Benkert, Andreas	8, Oct. 1854	Adam	Arnold, Anna Maria	N	25
Benkert, Jacob	11, May 1856	Adam	Arnold, Anna Maria	N	
Benkert, Peter	25, Apr. 1858	Adam	Arnold, Anna	N	
Benkhof, Anna Maria Francisca	12, Feb. 1853	Heinrich	Roller, Gertrud	D	370
Benkhof, Bernard Wilhelm	23, May 1857	Bernard	Boekweg, Catharina	D	85
Benkhof, Herman Gerhard Heinrich	18, Nov. 1851	J. Bernard	Bockweg, Maria Catharina	D	293
Benkhof, Johan Francis	31, Jan. 1851	Heinrich	Rolles, Gertrud	D	251
Benn, Elizabeth	20, Apr. 1851	John	Cline, Helen	E	301
Benn, Johan Peter	19, Sept 1854	Johan	Kraemer, Wilhelmina	D	18
Benn, Rosa	27, Mar. 1859	John	----, Catharina	D	135
Benne, Catharina Maria	9, July 1858	Heinrich	Hegel, Margaretha	L	
Benne, Johan Conrad	29, Sept 1856	J. Heinrich	Hegel, Margaretha	L	
Benne, Margaretha Elisabeth	19, Jan. 1859	Francis	Tockmann, M. Elisabeth	C	
Benne, Maria Elisabeth	20, May 1855	Heinrich	Hegel, M. Adelheid	L	
Benne, Mathias	22, Dec. 1850	Ernst	Dickhaus, Anna M.	C	
Benneman, Anton Bernard	7, Apr. 1850	Anton	Kröthing, Christina	D	208
Benner, Catherine Alice	31, Jan. 1857	Herman	----, Gesina	R	
Benner, Herman Heinrich	18, Feb. 1859	Herman	Nabers, Gesina	R	
Bennet, Helen	13, July 1854	Patrick	McDonald, Catherine	P	88
Bennett, Catherine	30, Aug. 1852	Henry	----, Margaret	M	
Bennett, Mary	13, Feb. 1853	James	McCaul, Mary	P	35
Bennewitz, Josephine Rachel	21, Mar. 1859	Frederick	Womah, Philomena	E	612
Bennewitz, Mary Caroline	19, Jan. 1859	Frederick	Wimah, Philomena Wilhelmina	E	599
Benninghoff, Johan Gerhard	1, Aug. 1855	Gerhard	Niemeyer, Maria Adelheid	A	
Bensman, Anna Maria	22, Apr. 1852	Herman	Harmeyer, Anna Maria	J	16
Bensmann, Louisa	2, Oct. 1853	Herman	Harmeier, Anna Maria	F	
Bensmann, Margaretha Elisabeth	26, June 1853	Valentin	Boenings, Marg. Elis.	L	
Benson, Catherine	25, May 1854	Jeremiah	Kenny, Mary	E	192
Benssman, Eva	29, Dec. 1852	Francis	Speidel, Magdalena	D	362
Benten, Emilia Elisabeth	19, Nov. 1854	Herman	Rump, Elisabeth	C	
Benten, Wilhelmina Francisca	19, Nov. 1854	Herman	Rump, Elisabeth	C	
Bentz, Francis	13, Nov. 1853	Anton	Gutting, Margaretha	C	
Benz, Adam	1, Apr. 1855	Francis	Scholl, Regina	C	
Benz, August	3, Sept 1851	Francis	Scholl, Regina	D	280
Benz, Augustine	22, Sept 1850	Francis	Schoh, Regina	D	234
Benz, Catharina	2, May 1852	Ignatius	Jonas, Angelica	D	318

Name of Child	Date of Baptism	Father	Mother	Church	Page
Benz, Gustav	13, Nov. 1853	Francis	Scholl, Regina	D	414
Benz, Gustav	7, Dec. 1858	Georg	Linkenstein, Elisabeth	T	
Benz, Johan	27, Feb. 1859	Ignatius	Jonas, Angela	G	
Benz, Johan	3, Aug. 1856	Valentin	Becking, Elisabeth	J	36
Benz, Joseph	2, Dec. 1852	Francis	Scholl, Regina	D	359
Benz, Josephina	26, Jan. 1851	Ignatius	Jonas, Angelica	J	10
Benz, Maria Anna	8, Mar. 1857	Georg	Hiltebrand, Magdalena	C	
Benz, Maria Carolina	19, Apr. 1857	Ignatius	Jonas, Angela	G	
Benz, Maria Magdalena	22, Apr. 1855	Ignatius	Jonas, Angelica	J	32
Benz, Rosina	11, Sept 1853	Ignatius	Jonas, Angelica	J	24
Benzer, Michael	25, Sept 1851	John	Doyle, Catherine	B	241
Benzert, Catharina	29, June 1851	Johan	Stoekel, Maria	H	
Benzinger, Wilhelm	14, Dec. 1856	Bernard	Bauman, Carolina	D	74
Ber, Johan	20, Jan. 1850	Johan	Ether, Veronica	J	6
Beraths, Anna Christina	26, July 1859	Bernard	Al---, Maria Christina	D	143
Berauer, Barbara	27, Feb. 1859	Johan	Fröhlicher, Catharina	D	132
Berauer, Johan	21, Sept 1856	Johan	Froehlicher, Catharina	C	
Berauer, Theresa	6, Sept 1854	Johan	Fröhlicher, Catharina	D	17
Berber, Josephina	30, June 1850	Joseph	Gotier, Julia	K	
Berber, Maria	18, Jan. 1852	Joseph	Gothier, Juliana	K	
Berberich,	28, Aug. 1859	Ferdinand	Emmentraut, Sophia	W	26
Berberich, Carl Friedrich	11, Apr. 1859	Joseph	Meier, Margaretha	R	
Berberich, Emma Rosalia	29, Sept 1853	J. Joseph	Goetzinger, Theresa	F	
Berberich, Ferdinand Michael	25, Feb. 1855	Ferdinand	Ermantraut, Sophia	J	30
Berberich, Georg Sebastian	25, Dec. 1856	Ferdinand	Ermentraut, Sophia	W	17
Berberich, Johan Francis	10, July 1859	Francis	Roman, Kunigunda	K	
Berberich, John Stephan	10, Jan. 1856	Joseph	Meier, Margaretha	R	
Berberich, Joseph	28, Aug. 1859	Ferdinand	Emmentraut, Sophia	W	26
Berberich, Magadelan	3, June 1858	J. Joseph	Götzinger, Theresa	K	
Berberich, Maria Amelia	10, July 1859	Carl Joseph	Keller, Maria	D	142
Berberich, Maria Anna	5, Oct. 1851	Ferdinand	Ermantraud, Sophia	F	
Berberich, Rudolph	6, Jan. 1857	J. Joseph	Götzinger, Theresa	K	
Berberich, Sebastian	7, Dec. 1856	Joseph	----, Margaretha	R	
Berberick, Carl Joseph	6, Jan. 1857	Carl Jos.	Keller, Maria	C	
Berberinger, Johan	9, Oct. 1859	Ignatius	Krapf, Maria H.	A	
Berbermann, Gertrud Conradina L.	8, Sept 1858	Conrad	Koch, Gertrud	F	
Berbery, August	25, Aug. 1858	Ferdinand	----, Sophia	T	
Berchtold, Heinrich	26, Apr. 1857	Georg	Katz, Christina	D	83
Berding, Catharina Louisa	4, Nov. 1855	Johan H.	Bunnemeyer, Maria Elisabeth	R	
Berding, Heinrich	8, Nov. 1855	Wilhelm	Niehaus, Josephina	C	
Berding, Heinrich Nicolaus	26, Dec. 1857	Johan H.	----, Maria Elisabeth	R	
Berding, Johan Clemens	6, Feb. 1853	J. Heinrich	Bünnemeyer, Maria Elisabeth	R	
Berding, Johanna Elisabeth	6, Feb. 1851	J. Heinrich	Bennemeier, Maria Elisabeth	D	252
Berding, Maria Elisabeth	24, July 1853	Peter W.	Niehaus, Josephina	C	
Berding, Peter	11, Feb. 1858	Peter	Niehaus, Josephina	C	
Berdinghaus, Anna Elisabeth	15, Aug. 1854	Joseph	Teippel, Maria Anna	C	
Berdon, Margaretha	17, Jan. 1858	Michael	Vitzgeorl, Anna	D	103
Berens, Catharina	31, Aug. 1857	August	Heiker, Catharina	C	
Berensesn, Anna Catharina	20, Oct. 1853	J. Gerhard	Bölter, Anna Theresa	A	
Berg, Carolina	23, Oct. 1859	Cyprian	Schäfer, Maria	K	
Berg, Francisca Elisabeth	5, Apr. 1858	Clemens W.	VanHorst, Elisabeth	D	108
Berg, Gerhard Herman	7, Aug. 1855	Gerhard H.	Hessel, Gesina	L	
Berg, Maria Elisabeth	5, Apr. 1858	Philipp	Hessel, Maria Gesina	L	
Berg, Maria Francisca	11, Jan. 1857	Philipp	Hessel, Maria Gesina	L	
Bergan, John	28, Apr. 1857	James	Cavanney, Juliana	E	449
Bergan, Mary	29, May 1853	James	----, Bridget	M	
Bergan, Mary Ann	18, Sept 1854	John	----, Ellen	E	224
Bergan, Patrick	10, June 1859	Dennis	White, Mary	P	285
Bergen, George	27, June 1854		adult - 32 years old	E	202

Name of Child	Date of Baptism	Father	Mother	Church	Page
Bergen, Helen Mary	23, Mar. 1856	Frederick	adult - 17 years old	P	173
Bergen, Michael	27, Jan. 1856	William	Geoghegan, Catherine	V	29
Bergen, Sarah Louise	29 Aug. 1852	James	Bard, Sarah	E	12
Bergen, Thomas	6, Sept 1857	William	----, Catherine	E	478
Bergen, William	8, Apr. 1859	James	----, Bridget	M	
Berger, Albert	22, Jan. 1854	Francis J.	Godstein, Christina	C	
Berger, Anna Margaretha	14, Nov. 1850	Theodor	Taphorn, Anna Maria Dina	A	
Berger, Anna Maria	8, Jan. 1854	J. Herman	Buscher, Helena	A	
Berger, Anna Maria	8, May 1859	Peter	Koch, Elisabeth	K	
Berger, Catharina Elisabeth	29, Jan. 1857	Werner	Gallagher, Maria	F	
Berger, Elisabeth Augusta	4, Aug. 1850	Peter	Koch, Elisabeth	D	227
Berger, Francis Joseph	3, June 1858	Francis J.	Katz, Christina	D	112
Berger, Friedrich Ludwig	30, May 1856	Joseph	Gottsten, Christina	C	
Berger, Georg	10, Nov. 1850	Georg	Köhr, Magdalena	D	242
Berger, Georg Lawrence Peter	25, May 1855	Peter	Koch, Elisabeth	K	
Berger, Gerhard Heinrich	22, June 1856	J. Theodor	Taphorn, Anna M. Bernardina	A	
Berger, Herman Heinrich	9, Mar. 1856	Gerhard	Gausing, M Adelheid	L	
Berger, Johan Bernard	19, May 1858	Heinrich	Spikers, Margaretha	K	
Berger, Johan Joseph	3, Apr. 1859	J. Theodor	Taphorn, Anna Bernardina	A	
Berger, Johan Theodor	19, Nov. 1853	Theodor	Taphorn, Bernardina	A	
Berger, Juliana	12, Sept 1852	Peter	Koch, Elisabeth	K	
Berger, Maria Elisabeth	14, Oct. 1851	Johan	Buscher, Maria Helena	A	
Berger, Maria Theresa	10, Feb. 1854	Gerhard H.	Gausing, M. Adelheid	L	
Berger, Peter	27, July 1856	Peter	Koch, Elisabeth	K	
Berger, Philomena	15, June 1851	Florence	Galla, Catharina	D	268
Berger, Rosalia	14, Jan. 1855	Georg	Köhl, Magdalena	D	26
Berger, Wilhelm	29, Aug. 1858	Werner	Galliger, Mary	T	
Bergers, Georg Francis	22, Feb. 1857	J. Georg	Koehl, Magdalena	C	
Berges, Johan Joseph	23, May 1852	J. Georg	Koehl, Magdalena	D	320
Bergewisch, Anna Catharina	21, Aug. 1859	Arnold	Grote, Maria	C	
Bergfeld, Herman Bernard Heinrich	9, Apr. 1856	Heinrich	Rump, Margaretha	L	
Bergfeld, Johanna Catharina Elis.	10, Mar. 1854	Herman H.	Raters, M. Elisabeth	L	
Bergfeld, Maria Carolina Johanna	17, Mar. 1856	Johan	Elsen, Gertrud	L	
Bergfeld, Maria Magdalena	25, May 1858	Heinrich	Rump, Margaretha	L	
Berghaus, Anna Catharina	17, Jan. 1859	Bernard	Schnier, Elisabeth	F	
Berghaus, Johan Bernard	2, Feb. 1853	Bernard	Schmid, Elisabeth	A	
Berghaus, Maria Magdalena	14, June 1855	Bernard	Schnier, Elisabeth	A	
Berghaus, Marianna Elisabeth	30, Mar. 1857	Bernard	Schnier, Elisabeth	F	
Berghegge, Georg Friedrich	15, Aug. 1855	Friedrich	Mueller, Elisabeth	C	
Berghegge, Johan Francis	29, Nov. 1857	Friedrich	Mueller, Catharina Elisabeth	C	
Berghegge, Ludwig	12, Nov. 1850	Friedrich	Muellers, Catharina	C	
Berghegge, Maria Elisabeth	18, Dec. 1859	Friedrich	Mueller, Catharina Elisabeth	C	
Berghegger, Johan Peter	4, Jan. 1853	Friedrich	Mueller, Catharina Elisabeth	C	
Bergin, Catherine	21, Sept 1851	James	Dwyer, Bridget	M	
Bergin, Catherine	23, Dec. 1852	Michael	----, Ann	E	46
Bergin, Dennis	21, July 1859	Martin	O'Shaugnessy, Mary	E	641
Bergin, Elizabeth	13, Sept 1857	James	Birch, Sarah	B	49
Bergin, Honora	3, Apr. 1858	Patrick	Tracy, Bridget	E	526
Bergin, James	16, Aug. 1856	Patrick	Dunn, Margaret	E	390
Bergin, John	13, Apr. 1858	John	Ward, Joanne	E	529
Bergin, John	24, Aug. 1854	Michael	----, Ann	E	219
Bergin, John	31, Jan. 1858	Patrick	Dunn, Margaret	B	55
Bergin, Margaret	2, Nov. 1857	Patrick	Cashen, Joanne	E	490
Bergin, Mary	19, Feb. 1855	James	----, Bridget	M	
Bergin, Mary	25, Feb. 1857	James	----, Bridget	M	
Bergin, Mary	22, Oct. 1859	Patrick	Cashin, Joanne	E	665
Bergin, Mary	20, Sept 1856	Patrick	Tracy, Bridget	E	398
Bergin, Mary Agnes	17, Apr. 1859	Patrick	Dunn, Margaret	B	74
Bergin, Sarah	28, Aug. 1853	James	Bird, Sarah	B	298

Name of Child	Date of Baptism	Father	Mother	Church	Page
Bergin, Thomas	11, June 1859	Patrick	Tracy, Bridget	E	631
Bergin, William	17, Apr. 1856	John	----, Joanne	E	359
Bergin, William	5, Sept 1859	William	----, Catherine	E	651
Bergman, Anna Catharina	2, Aug. 1856	Conrad	Herr, Christina	D	63
Bergman, Anna Maria	11, Dec. 1859	Georg Adam	Fath---, Anna	D	152
Bergman, Catharina	7, July 1856	Heinrich	Sickman, Elisabeth	A	
Bergman, Francis Heinrich	4, Sept 1858	Heinrich	Sickman, Maria E.	A	
Bergman, Georg Adam	14, Aug. 1853	Conrad	Herr, Christina	D	400
Bergman, Georg Friedrich	10, Jan. 1858	Georg A.	----, ----	D	102
Bergman, Johan Friedrich	15, Apr. 1850	J. Heinrich	Sickman, Elisabeth	A	
Bergman, Maria Anna Elisabeth	24, Jan. 1854	J. Heinrich	Sickman, Maria Elisabeth	A	
Bergman, Maria Elisabeth	27, Apr. 1851	Heinrich	Sickman, Elisabeth	A	
Bergmann, Catharina	26, Sept 1858	Heinrich	Haucap, Anna Maria	G	
Bergmann, Francis Stephan	15, June 1856	Heinrich	Haucab, Anna Maria	G	
Bergmann, Johan Aloysius	6, Aug. 1853	Francis	Kemper, Elisabeth	C	
Bergmann, Johan Francis	24, Jan. 1855	Theodor	Bokos, Anna	C	
Bergmann, Johan Heinrich	6, July 1852	Theodor	Bokop, M. Anna	C	
Bergmann, Johan Heinrich Georg	9, Sept 1854	Francis	Kemper, Elisabeth	C	
Bergmann, M. Catharina Elisabeth	1, May 1854		Bergmann, Catharina	F	
Bergmann, Maria Elisabeth	16, Mar. 1854	J. David	Bloemer, M. Elisabeth	C	
Bergmeyer, Anna Maria	23, Sept 1852	Francis	Dillmann, Anna Maria	L	
Bergmeyer, Anna Maria Francisca	6, June 1854	Friedrich	Raps, Anna	A	
Bergmeyer, Anton	8, Dec. 1850	Francis	Dillmann, Gertrud	L	
Bergmeyer, Johan Theodor	29, Jan. 1857	Friedrich	Kautz, Anna Maria	A	
Bergtold, Catharina	29, Nov. 1857	Joseph	Vieger, Agatha	N	
Berheide, Maria Anna	30, Sept 1853	Wilhelm	Busse, Maria Bernardina	D	408
Berheide, Maria Francisca	12, July 1851	Wilhelm	Busse, Bernardina	D	272
Berheide, Wilhelm Joseph	17, July 1856	Wilhelm	Busse, Dina	D	63
Bering, Anna Rosina Helena	27, Oct. 1857	Johan	Fischer, Helena	F	
Bering, Jacob Joseph	7, Aug. 1853	Balthasar	Nauld, Maria	C	
Bering, Maria Philomena Dorothea	9, Aug. 1855	Francis	adult - 21 years old	K	
Bering, Mathias Frank	26, July 1850	Balthasar	Nauath, Anna Maria	C	
Beringer, Jacob	22, June 1851	Xavier	Klock, Catharina	K	
Beringer, Johan	22, May 1856	Xavier	----, Anna	K	
Berkemeier, Catharina Elisabeth	25, Nov. 1858	Georg	----, Elisabeth	F	
Berkemeier, Clara Maria Josephina	1, June 1852	Bernard H.	----, ----	A	
Berkemeier, Franz	10, May 1851	Georg	Dickhaus, Elisabeth	F	
Berkemeier, Heinrich Francis Xavier	20, Oct. 1853	Bernard H.	Funke, Elisabeth	A	
Berkemeier, Herman Joseph Heinrich	17, Aug. 1853	Joseph A.	Puttemeier, A.M. Cath.	L	
Berkemeier, Johan Anton	3, Aug. 1854	Anton G.	Dickhaus, Maria Elisabeth	F	
Berkemeier, Johan August	10, Mar. 1856	Georg A.	Dickhaus, Maria Elisabeth	F	
Berkemeier, Johan Bernard Joseph	20, Oct. 1853	Bernard H.	Funke, Elisabeth	A	
Berkemeier, Johan Heinrich Francis	9, Nov. 1850	Heinrich	Funke, Anna Elisabeth	A	
Berkemeyer, Carl Herman	14, May 1851	Herman	Nieberding, Catharina	C	
Berkemeyer, Clara Josephina	29, Apr. 1857	Alexander	Puttmeyer, Longina	L	
Berkemeyer, Dorothea Josephina	30, Nov. 1859	B.H.	Kronlage, Maria Elisabeth	A	
Berkemeyer, Herman Heinrich	23, July 1856	Heinrich	Kronlage, Elisabeth	A	
Berkemeyer, Johan B. Joseph	2, Mar. 1858	Johan H.	Kronlage, Elisabeth	A	
Berkemeyer, Maria Josephina	30, Mar. 1855	Joseph	Buschermühle, Elisabeth	A	
Berker, Joseph	4, Dec. 1850	Joseph	Renz, Catharina	D	245
Berkherms, Theodor Bernard	24, Oct. 1858	Johan H.	Latare, Margaretha	A	
Berkmer, Magdalena	17, May 1857	Johan	Meier, Magdalena	D	85
Berkwisch, Anna Maria Elisabeth	10, Feb. 1853	Arnold	Grote, Anna M.	C	
Berlage, Maria Catharina	22, July 1858	Heinrich	H---, Maria Helena	D	115
Berle, Regina Magalena	26, Mar. 1854	Michael	----, Anna Maria	H	
Berlier, Anna Amalia	13, Sept 1857	Michael	Braun, Maria Anna	J	42
Berlier, Jacob	29, Nov. 1857	Jacob	Tremer, Louisa	W	20
Berlier, Maria Anna	13, Sept 1857	Michael	Braun, Maria Anna	J	42
Berlier, Philipp	3, July 1859	Jacob	Thremes, Louisa	G	

Name of Child	Date of Baptism	Father	Mother	Church	Page
Berling, Anna Maria Elisabeth	28, Apr. 1858	Herman H.	Bene, A. Margaretha	T	
Berling, Georg Anton	25, July 1858	Anton	Sauer, Maria	D	115
Berling, Herman Gerhard	1, Feb. 1857	Gerhard	Westendorf, Gertrud	D	78
Berling, Johan Theodor	23, Mar. 1855	Gerhard	Westerhof, Gertrud	D	32
Berling, Maria Gertrud	27, Feb. 1852	Herman H.	Böhning, Maria	D	309
Berlinger, Gerhard Heinrich	18, Mar. 1855	J. Heinrich	Pund, Maria Margaretha	D	31
Berlinger, Maria	18, Sept 1855	Carl	Rodler, Theresa	D	43
Berman, Johan Peter	1, Mar. 1857	Johan	Jung, Barbara	D	80
Berman, Johan Wilhelm	3, Aug. 1856	Bernard	Greving, Anna Maria	A	
Berman, Louisa	22, Feb. 1859	J. Francis	Engel---, Maria	D	132
Berman, Michael Francis	21, Aug. 1859	Johan	Jung, Barbara	D	145
Bermann, Anna Maria	8, June 1856	Heinrich	Aul, Eva	C	
Bermann, Francis Heinrich	27, Mar. 1857	Friedrich	Junk, Anna Adelheid	C	
Bermann, M. Margaretha Francisca	4. Sept 1853	Bernard	Niemeyer, Francisca	L	
Bermann, Margaretha Elisabeth	8, June 1859	Friedrich	Jung, Anna	C	
Bernard, Ann Mary	15, Jan. 1854	Philipp	Gerette, Mary	E	160
Bernard, Anna Maria Theresa	19, June 1859	Anton	Braun, Elisabeth Margaretha	A	
Bernard, Catharina Mathilda	12, Jan. 1859	Christian	Honneberger, Barbara	D	128
Bernard, Emilia	14, Oct. 1857	Christian	Henneberger, Barbara	D	97
Bernard, John	12, May 1850	Philipp	Geris, Mary	E	213
Bernard, Margaretha	17, July 1851	Johan	Barnickel, Margaret	C	
Bernard, Maria Elisabeth	10, Feb. 1854	Hubert	Heiob, Anna Maria	D	4
Bernard, Mary	5, Jan. 1857	James	Corrett, Catherine	B	38
Bernard, Mary Ann	28, Apr. 1851	?	?	B	231
Bernard, Philipp	13, June 1852	Philipp	Jeres, Mary	B	260
Bernaro, John Anthony	19, May 1850	John	Raretta, Maria	B	203
Bernens, Heinrich Ludwig	2, Aug. 1857	Joseph	Backhaas, Catharina H.	A	
Berner, Anna Maria	26, July 1857	Hubert	Heiob, Mary Ann	U	
Berner, Georg	11, Feb. 1858	Sebastian	Hannam, Margaretha	J	44
Berner, Heinrich	5, Aug. 1855	Hubert	Heiob, Mary	U	
Berner, Johan	10, July 1859	Hubert	Heiob, Mary Hannah	U	
Bernhard, Carolina	10, Apr. 1853	Bernard	Huber, Genofeva	D	380
Bernhard, Elisabeth Josephina	22, June 1856	Paul	Miller, Josephina	D	61
Bernhard, Joseph Georg	10, Feb. 1850	Bernard	Huber, Genofeva	D	203
Bernhard, Maria Anna Elisabeth	26, Jan. 1851	Bernard	Huber, Genofeva	D	250
Bernhard, Michael	17, Jan. 1857	Bernard	Huber, Genofeva	D	76
Bernhard, Philipp Ludwig	7, Dec. 1851	Ludwig	Steiner, Barbara	D	296
Bernhard, Rosina	22, Feb. 1852	Bernard	Huber, Genofeva	D	308
Bernhard, Simon	7, Mar. 1858	Bernard	Huber, Genofeva	D	106
Bernhart, Anton	26, June 1859	Bernard	Huber, Genofeva	D	141
Bernhart, Carl Bernard	1, Aug. 1855	Bernard	Huber, Genofeva	D	39
Berning, Anna Maria Elisabeth	15, June 1856	J. Mathias	Fischer, Anna Helena	F	
Berning, Bernard Theodor	6, Sept 1857	Bernard	Hofhaus, Gertrud	N	
Berning, Caspar Heinrich	4, Feb. 1859	Caspar	Stüwe, Maria	A	
Berning, Clara Rosa	22, Nov. 1857	J. Bernard	Grote, Theresa	A	
Berning, Herman Heinrich	6, Sept 1854	Heinrich	Raas, Maria Adelheid	F	
Berning, Johan B.	28, July 1850	B.	Bulterman, Elisabeth	A	
Berning, Johan Bernard	11, Sept 1854	Anton	Roors, Antonette	A	
Berning, Johan Bernard Joseph	10, Aug. 1859	J. Bernard	Grote, Maria Theresa	A	
Berning, Johan Joseph	17, Dec. 1851	Anton	Roors, Antonette	A	
Berning, Joseph	30, Aug. 1852	Bernard	Bullermann, Elisabeth	F	
Berning, Maria	30, Aug. 1852	Bernard	Bullermann, Elisabeth	F	
Berning, Maria Anna	2, June 1853	Bernard	Schulte, Maria Anna	C	
Berning, Maria Carolina	6, May 1857	Caspar	Vael, Maria Engel	D	84
Berninger, Ann Rosina	25, Mar. 1856	Sebastian	Hartman, Ann	R	
Berninger, Maria Eva	7, May 1854	Sebastian	Hartman, Anna Maria	R	
Berra, Aemil	8, Jan. 1854	Johan	Wertner, Magdalena	K	
Berrell, Mary Ellen	20, Apr. 1851	George	Rafferty, Margaret	E	301
Berretti, Maria	2, Nov. 1854	Giovanni B.	Coster, Assunta	K	

Name of Child	Date of Baptism	Father	Mother	Church	Page
Berri, August	5, Mar. 1854	August	Schue, Maria Anna	K	
Berrigan, James	18, Jan. 1859	James	----, Julia	E	597
Berrigan, James	19, July 1857	James	Murray, Mary	B	47
Berringer, Carolina	22, May 1853	Johan	Pettinger, Regina	D	386
Berringer, Elizabeth	22, Sept 1859	Andrew	Coltrapp, Mary	E	655
Berron, Joseph Augustine	15, Apr. 1858	John	Reilly, Margaret	B	57
Berry, Ann	1, May 1859	John	Moran, Bridget	P	283
Berry, Catherine	8, Nov. 1856	John	Welsh, Ann	E	411
Berry, Clara	1, Dec. 1850	August	Schuh, Maria Anna	K	
Berry, Francis	13, Apr. 1856	August	Schuh, Maria Anna	K	
Berry, Johan	8, Aug. 1852	August	Schuh, Anna	K	
Berry, John Joseph	2, May 1858	James	Conaughton, Honora	B	58
Berry, Margaret	7, Aug. 1853	Luke	O'Neil, Ann	V	5
Berte, Catharina Josephina	5, Mar. 1851	Johan	VonLehm, Margaretha	K	
Bertel, Anna Maria Agnes	20, July 1854	Francis	Steinriede, Agnes	F	
Bertel, Josephina Elisabeth	29, July 1856	Francis	Steinriede, Agnes	F	
Bertel, Maria Elisabeth	13, July 1858	Francis	Steinriede, Agnes	F	
Berteling, Bernard Heinrich Joseph	25, Feb. 1858	Joseph	Bergman, Maria	A	
Berter, Maria Adelheid	9, Sept 1857	Theodor	Vening---, Christina	D	94
Berting, Bernard Joseph	25, Mar. 1851	Bernard	Garre, Elisabeth	L	
Berting, Francisca	22, Jan. 1859	Friedrich	Elsen, Catharina	T	
Bertk, Anna Catharina Francisca	28, July 1857	Anton	Schulte, Maria Gertrud	D	91
Bertke, Anna Maria Philomena	8, Sept 1856	J. Dietrich	Heitman, Maria	A	
Bertke, Johan Gerhard	24, Oct. 1851	Dietrich	Heidman, Anna Francisca	A	
Bertke, Maria Philomena	27, Aug. 1850	J. Dietrich	Heilman, Maria Francisca	K	
Bertlein, Barbara	3, Nov. 1850	Adam	Schmidt, Ursula	F	
Bertling, Adolph Heinrich	26, May 1850	Adolph	Renck, Eva Catharina	D	214
Bertling, Valentin	13, Aug. 1854	Adolph	Renk, Eva Catharina	S	
Bertram, Carl Heinrich	15, Aug. 1850	Leonard	Bach, Appollonia	D	228
Bertram, Elisabeth	8, Oct. 1854	Henry	----, Elisabeth	H	
Bertram, Eva Barbara	13, Apr. 1859	Heinrich	Breit---, Maria Elisabeth	D	136
Bertram, Francis	12, Feb. 1854	Leonard	Bach, Apollonia	W	1
Bertram, Georg	7, Sept 1851	Leonard	Bach, Appollonia	F	
Bertram, Henry	25, Dec. 1855	Henry	----, Elisabeth	H	
Bertram, Henry	1, Apr. 1855	Leonard	----, Apollonia	H	
Bertram, Henry	20, June 1858	Peter	Schied, Christine	H	
Bertram, Johan Heinrich Theodor	19, Mar. 1854	Heinrich	Speckman, Maria Anna	K	
Bertram, Maria	4, July 1858	Heinrich	Schuler, Elisabeth	T	
Bertram, Maria Anna	20, Apr. 1856	Leonard	Bach, Appollonia	W	12
Bertrand, Georg	13, Feb. 1853	Heinrich	Kuhlmann, Maria Gertrud	F	
Bertrum, Maria Francisca	24, Jan. 1853	Heinrich	Speckman, Gesina Maria	K	
Bertsy, Gerhard Herman	21, Mar. 1859	Herman	Loh, Elisabeth	F	
Berwanger, Barbara	20, June 1852	Michael	Schneider, Gertrud	D	325
Berwanger, Jacob	12, Feb. 1854	MIchael	----, Gertrud	U	
Berwanger, Michael Friedrich	28, Apr. 1850	Michael	Schneider, Gertrud	D	211
Berzen, Johan Bernard	17, Nov. 1851	Johan	Buddick, Anna Maria	A	
Bescher, Regina	25, Aug. 1850	Philipp	Schuler, Maria	D	229
Bescher, Regina	6, Oct. 1854	Philipp	Schuler, Maria	F	
Beske, Johan Heinrich	2, Mar. 1855	Johan H.	Wellbrock, Anna Maria	F	
Besken, August Friedrich	23, Apr. 1857	Johan	Wellbrock, Anna Maria	F	
Besken, Johan	28, Apr. 1859	Johan	Wellbrock, Maria	F	
Bessinger, Maria	22, Apr. 1855	Aloysius	Schuler, Crescentia	J	32
Bessler, Catharina	14, Sept 1850	Wolfgang	Schuh, Rosa	D	232
Bessler, Maria	12, Apr. 1852	Wolfgang	Schuh, Rosa	D	316
Bessler, Philipp	15, Jan. 1854	Wolfgang	Schuh, Rosa	D	2
Best, Ann Catherine	30, Apr. 1854	Francis	----, Ann Mary	U	
Best, Barbara	27, Mar. 1853	J. Joseph	Weber, Catharina	D	377
Best, Caroline	18, Oct. 1857	Francis	Sauer, Ann Mary	U	
Best, Francisca	25, May 1854	Joseph	Weber, Catharina	D	11

Name of Child	Date of Baptism	Father	Mother	Church	Page
Best, Johan	19, Oct. 1856	Joseph	Weber, Catharina	D	70
Best, Joseph	6, Apr. 1856	Francis	Sauer, Mary Ann	U	
Best, Magdalena	1, Mar. 1857	Carl	Weber, Rosina	D	80
Beste, Caspar	23, Jan. 1859	Joseph	Weber, Catherine	H	
Bester, Bernard Herman	12, July 1851	Herman	Buenning, Carolina	L	
Bester, Elisabeth	10, July 1859	Georg	Karkaran, Maria	A	
Besterman, Anna Rosalia	16, Nov. 1858	Bernard	Brugge, Louisa	K	
Besterman, Augusta Philomena	16, Nov. 1858	Bernard	Brugge, Louisa	K	
Besterman, Edward Martin	11, Dec. 1850	Heinrich	Borger, Veronica	K	
Besterman, Maria Louisa	12, Oct. 1851	Bernard	Brüggman, Maria Louisa	K	
Besterman, Maria Rosina	12, Mar. 1854	J. Bernard	Bruggeman, Maria L.	K	
Besterman, Maria Theresa Augusta	12, Oct. 1853	Heinrich	Börger, Veronica	K	
Besterman, Martha Catharina	13, Jan. 1856	Bernard	Brüggeman, Louisa	K	
Besthümer, Catharina	20, Sept 1857	Georg	Corcan, Mary	A	
Besuck, Johan	25, Dec. 1857	Francis	Jerusch, Maria	D	101
Betsch, Caecilia Louisa	13, Sept 1857	Conrad	Moran, Mary M.	D	94
Betsch, Georg	29, Aug. 1858	Valentin	Gross, Elisabeth	D	118
Betscheider, Heinrich	4, Oct. 1856	Heinrich	Forke, Margaretha	C	
Betscher, Adelheid Friedrica Alphonsa	25, Dec. 1859	Caspar	Meier, Adelheid	D	153
Betscher, Albert Gottlieb	22, Mar. 1857	Melchior	Koenzle, Christina	F	
Betscher, Carl Edward	21, June 1857	John	Dörflinger, Catharina	N	
Betscher, Francis Oscar	11, Apr. 1853	Caspar	Meyer, Adelheid	C	
Betscher, Francisca Amanda	6, May 1851	Caspar	Meier, Adelheid	A	
Betscher, Franz Joseph	8, Feb. 1857	Amand	Braun, Carolina	F	
Betscher, Friedrich Alphonse	18, Nov. 1855	Caspar	Meyer, Adelheid	W	10
Betscher, Ludiwg Sebastian	8, Apr. 1855	Melchior	Kensch, Christina	D	33
Betscher, Maria Anna Amalia	1, Feb. 1857	Joseph	Beising, Martha	H	
Betscher, Mary Magdalene	25, July 1858	Joseph	Beising, Martha	H	
Betscher, Xavier Oscar N.	24, May 1857	Caspar	Meier, Adelheid	D	85
Bettinger, Anna Margaretha	5, June 1852	Peter	Schmidt, Elisabeth	F	
Bettinger, Barbara Louisa	29, Nov. 1857	Peter	Schmidt, Elisabeth	A	
Bettinger, Carl	15, Dec. 1850	Michael	Angst, Elisabeth	L	
Bettinger, Catharina Carolina	24, Sept 1854	Peter	Schmidt, Elisabeth	A	
Bettinger, Joseph	21, Aug. 1856	Jacob	Dieringer, Elisabeth	D	65
Bettinger, Maria Elisabeth	11, Nov. 1850	Edward	Gerber, Elisabeth Catharina	A	
Bettinger, Maria Margaretha	20, Oct. 1850	Peter	Schmidt, Elisabeth	A	
Bettlinger, Catharina	23, Jan. 1859	Carl	Weitzel, Catharina	T	
Bettlinger, Elisabeth	18, Jan. 1857	Carl	Weizel, Catharina	D	76
Betton, Catharine	17, Apr. 1849	William	Moors, Elizabeth	S	
Betts, William	17, June 1859	William	Dwyer, Margaret	B	76
Bettscheider, Anna	28, Mar. 1853	Heinrich	Falger, Margaretha	D	378
Bettscheider, Bernard Heinrich	21, Feb. 1858	Heinrich	Farkel, Margaretha	C	
Bettscheider, Nicolaus	5, May 1854	Heinrich	Falk, Margaretha	D	9
Betz, Johan	27, Oct. 1850	Johan	Brand, Barbara	D	240
Betz, Margaretha	27, Dec. 1851	Ignatius	Zapf, Kunigunda	C	
Betz, Maria Anna	14, Jan. 1850	Ignatius	Zapf, Cunigunda	D	199
Betz, William	26, June 1856	William	Dwire, Margaret	E	377
Betzer, Johan Aloyis	29, June 1852	Aloysius	----, Johanna	C	
Betzi, Maria Elisabeth Philomena	4, Sept 1857	Gerhard H.	Lohe, M. Catharina Elisabeth	A	
Betzold, Anna Maria	25, Sept 1857	Joseph	Valerius, Wilhelmina	F	
Betzold, Catharina	2, Aug. 1857	Johan	Hess, Margaretha	W	19
Betzold, Elisabeth	25, Feb. 1855	Joseph	Valerius, Wilhelmina	C	
Betzold, Jacob	13, Feb. 1859	Johan	Heg---, Margaretha	D	131
Betzold, Johan	26, June 1853	Clemens B.	Reibl, Margaretha	D	391
Betzold, Michael	29, June 1851	Clemens	Reibel, Margaretha	D	270
Beumer, Anna Maria	28, Jan. 1852	Bernard	Blau, Anna Maria	L	
Beumer, Anna Maria	6, Sept 1852	Bernard	Day, Catharina Elisabeth	D	346
Beumer, Bernard Friedrich	15, May 1855	Bernard	Dressmeyer, Maria Elisabeth	U	
Beumer, Johan Heinrich	12, Mar. 1853	Joseph	Milles, Maria Anna	D	375

Name of Child	Date of Baptism	Father	Mother	Church	Page
Beumer, Maria Elisa	3, Mar. 1857	Bernard	Dressmayer, Maria Elisabeth	U	
Beumer, Wilhelm	25, May 1852	Wilhelm	Menge, Theresa	A	
Beuner, Heinrich Theodor	22, Sept 1857	Theodor	Better, Gertrud	F	
Beute, Eberhard Johan	11, Sept 1857	J. Heinrich	Vaske, Elisabeth	D	94
Bevermann, Theodor Ernst	14, Dec. 1856	Arnold	Koch, Gertrud	F	
Beyderhage, Johan Bernard	4, July 1855	J. Bernard	Brückman, Maria Engel	D	37
Beyrer, Heinrich Gustav	9, May 1856	Johan	Schmidt, Regina	D	58
Beyrer, Maria Louisa	9, May 1856	Johan	Schmidt, Regina	D	57
Bezol, Louise Caroline	10, Mar. 1857	Joseph	Derrick, Margaret	B	41
Bezold, Adam	13, Oct. 1855	Clemens	Reiser, Margaret	R	
Bezold, John	9, July 1859	Clemens	Renkel, Margaret	R	
B---g, Johan	31, Jan. 1858	Georg	---fer, Philippina	D	104
Bialazenitz, Joseph	18, Sept 1859	Thomas	Losos, Anna	C	
Bichelberger, Christina Carolina Elis.	24, Nov. 1853	Jacob	Kreiser, Carolina	D	416
Bichelberger, Johan Georg	14, Sept 1851	Jacob	Kreise, Carolina	D	282
Bick, Anna Maria Clara	21, June 1857	J. Heinrich	Bauten, Anna Maria Augusta	A	
Bick, Josephina	23, Sept 1850	Heinrich	Bunte, Angela	A	
Bick, Maria Margaretha	26, Apr. 1855	Philipp	Bordenni, Maria	D	34
Bicket, Joseph Purcell	17, Aug. 1851	John	Carnahan, Sabina	B	239
Bickler, Anna Maria	12, Aug. 1854	Joseph	Rentz, Catharina	L	
Bicksel, Maria Margaretha	10, Mar. 1850	Joseph	Meier, Elisabeth	D	205
Biddenharn, Johan	5, Aug. 1856	Heinrich	Feldman, Anna Maria	J	36
Bidenharn, Anna Maria Bernardina	30, May 1852	Heinrich	Feldman, Anna Maria	D	322
Bieber, Andreas Carl	15, Apr. 1855	Nicolaus	Daumeier, Maria Anna	D	33
Bieber, Gerhard Heinrich	7, Jan. 1859	Nicolaus	Ottmeier, Maria	D	128
Bieber, Rosa Maria	1, Feb. 1857	Nicolaus	Daumeier, Anna M.	D	78
Bieber, Rosalia Maria	30, July 1856	Nicolaus	Daumeier, Anna Maria	D	63
Biedenharn, Bernard Heinrich	18, Sept 1859	Bernard	Oevelgonne, Elisabeth	L	
Biedenharn, Johan Joseph	18, Oct. 1853	Friedrich	Nienaber, Maria Gertrud	F	
Biedenharn, M. Catharina Josephina	20, Oct. 1850	Heinrich	Feldmann, Maria	L	
Biedenoud, Gerhard Heinrich August	29, Aug. 1854	Heinrich	Feldmann, Anna Maria	F	
Biederhagen, Herman Heinrich	18, Feb. 1858	Gerhard	Hassy, Philomena	K	
Bieh, Michael	8, May 1859	Andreas	Huck, Aleid	K	
Biehle, Peter Martin	19, Dec. 1852	Martin	Lange, Barbara	A	
Biehler, Emma	7, Feb. 1858	Friedrich	Joseph, Francisca	F	
Biehn, Wilhelm	19, Apr. 1857	Andreas	Hugg, Apollonia	K	
Biele, Anna Theresa	29, Dec. 1850	Martin	Lange, Barbara	A	
Biele, Johan Francis	14, Jan. 1855	Martin	Lange, Barbara	A	
Biele, Johan Michael	27, July 1856	Martin	Lange, Barbara	A	
Biele, Margaretha Barbara	22, Aug. 1858	Martin	Keck, Barbara	A	
Bielefeld, Elisabeth Wilhelmina	6, Mar. 1859	Carl	Vögele, Rosa	A	
Bieler, Johan Jacob Heinrich	2, Mar. 1856	Johan	Rotering, Maria	A	
Bieler, Maria Barbara	18, June 1852	Benedict	Zimmerman, Josephina	K	
Bielle, Conrad Friedrich	21, Sept 1851	Friedrich	Joseph, Francisca	D	283
Biely, Constantin	16, Sept 1855	Friedrich	Joseph, Francisca	F	
Bierman, Anna Maria Catharina	17, Mar. 1852	Bernard	Gresing, Anna Maria	A	
Bierman, Johan Heinrich	12, Mar. 1854	Bernard	Henken, Maria Anna	A	
Bierman, Maria	10, Nov. 1851	Francis	Moss, Angela	A	
Bierman, Maria Francisca Wilhelmina	13, July 1851	Heinrich	Niemeier, Francisca	A	
Biermann, Antonia Elisabeth	3, Jan. 1859	Anton	Rattermann, M. Gertrud	F	
Biermann, Emilia Catharina	5, Sept 1858	Heinrich	Aul, Eva	F	
Bierwirth, Anna Maria Margaretha	7, Mar. 1857	Francis	Wilmers, Anna	L	
Bierwirth, Clara Carolina Josephin	18, Apr. 1855	J. Francis	Wilmes, Antonette	L	
Bierwirth, Maria Caecilia	25, Sept 1853	Francis	Wilms, Anna	C	
Bierz, Maria Anna	11, Apr. 1859	Gabriel	Hebig, Christina	Q	31
Biesenbach, Anna Maria Josephina	13, Jan. 1857	Adolph	Meyer, Maria Agnes	K	
Biesenbach, Maria Louisa	16, Dec. 1850	Adolph	Meyer, Maria Agnes	L	
Biesing, Thomas Stephen	3, June 1858	Caspar	Meis, Christina	C	
Biett, Carolina	25, Dec. 1855	Carl	Bantschuh, Elisabeth	C	

Name of Child	Date of Baptism	Father	Mother	Church	Page
Bigelow, John	12, May 1850		adult	B	202
Biggan, Catherine	2, Aug. 1858	Patrick	McMahon, Bridget	E	554
Biggers, Elisabeth	26, June 1859	Felix	Blaney, Mary	V	56
Bighe, Alexander	19, Dec. 1850	Fidel	Binniger, Carolina	K	
Bigolari, Charles John	3, Aug. 1856	John	Sutti, Catherine	B	32
Bihl, Catharina	17, July 1855	Nicolaus	Jacobs, Margaretha	D	38
Bihl, Peter	25, Mar. 1857	Nicolaus	Jacobs, Margaretha	D	81
Bihler, Theresa	17, Dec. 1854	Joseph	Mutner, Maria Anna	D	24
Bihn, Johan	16, Sept 1851	Andreas	Bart, Elisabeth	D	283
Bihn, Susanna Josephina	21, Aug. 1853	Andreas	Bart, Elisabeth	D	401
Bill, Barbara Susanna	19, Dec. 1858	Jacob	Stephan, Victoria	J	48
Bill, Carl Joseph	26, Mar. 1854	Johan	Jacobs, Elisabeth	A	
Bill, Catharina Adelheid	26, Nov. 1854	Jacob	Stephan, Victoria	J	30
Bill, Henrica Christina	5, Sept 1858	Heinrich	Verkamp, Bernardina	L	
Bill, Johan	29, Feb. 1852	Johan	Jacobs, Elisabeth	A	
Bill, Joseph	23, Feb. 1857	Johan	Jacobs, Elisabeth	A	
Bill, Louisa	22, Nov. 1857	Wilhelm	Gantner, Louisa	N	
Bill, Susanna	15, May 1853	Jacob	Stephan, Victoria	J	22
Bille, Johan Gerhard	20, Aug. 1851	J. Heinrich	Rinkess, Maria Elisabeth	C	
Billenbrink, Friedrich Joseph	28, Nov. 1853	Joseph	Wilberding, Bernardin	C	
Billes, Maria Francisca	7, Feb. 1857	Valentin	Miller, Maria	K	
Billet, Francis Arnold	3, Feb. 1856	Joseph	Brus, Maria Anna	D	51
Billhauz, Ann Maria	22, Dec. 1850	Augustine	Bä---, Magdalena	Q	1
Billiam, Anna Kunigunda	9, Mar. 1856	Georg	Roehle, Magdalena	C	
Billiam, Barbara	12, Sept 1858	J. Georg	Riele, Magdalena	N	
Billier, Johan	6, Oct. 1855	Mathias	Menge, Theresa	D	44
Billing, Joseph August	23, Jan. 1858	Adolph	Wese---, Anna	D	103
Billmeyer, Georg	19, June 1859	Georg	Blöss, Louise	S	
Bilo, Anna Catharina	29, Apr. 1859	Friedrich	Richter, Marianna	F	
Bilz, Margaretha	11, Sept 1859	Lawrence	Dick, Catharina	W	27
Binder, Anna Maria	11, Feb. 1855	Simon	Woertner, Josephina	G	
Binder, Anna Maria Carolina	2, June 1859	Simon	Woerter, Josephina	G	
Binder, Anna Sabina Wilhelmina	6, Apr. 1856	Johan	Dehner, Hedwig	W	12
Binder, Barbara	21, Sept 1856	Constantine	Kuebler, Eva	F	
Binder, Carl	20, Jan. 1854	Constantine	Klueber, Eva	F	
Binder, Constanz	29, May 1852	Constantine	Kluever, Eva	F	
Binder, Elisabeth	13, Apr. 1858	Johan	Geppert, Maria	G	
Binder, Francis Joseph	2, May 1852	Simon	Wärter, Josephina	J	16
Binder, Francis Xavier	2, Oct. 1853	Francis X.	Zintgraf, Wilhelmina	D	408
Binder, Freidrich Albert	4, Aug. 1850	Simon	Werder, Josephina	D	226
Binder, Hilarius Melchior	27, Apr. 1852	Johan	Dehner, Hedwig	F	
Binder, Joseph	16, Sept 1855	Xavier	Zinngraf, Wilhelmina	D	42
Binder, Joseph Edward	23, Sept 1855	Johan	Geppert, Magdalena	G	
Binder, Joseph Oswald	4, July 1852	Bernard	Geier, Elisabeth	L	
Binder, Margaretha	17, Mar. 1850	Johan	Satösker?, Barbara	D	206
Binder, Michael	16, Jan. 1854	Simon	Woerter, Josephina	G	
Binder, Peter	9, Nov. 1856	Simon	Woerter, Josephina	G	
Binder, Rosina Maria Agatha	17, Apr. 1854	Johan	Thener, Hedwig	W	3
Binder, Sarah Elisabeth	23, Aug. 1853	Johan	Geppert, Maria	G	
Binder, Theresa	27, Nov. 1859	Constantine	Klueber, Eva	T	
Bindler, Friedrich	16, Nov. 1856	Friedrich	Wolf, Crescentia	D	72
Bindler, Johan	2, Jan. 1859	Friedrich	Wolf, Crescentia	D	128
Bingstross, Anna Maria Gertrud	24, June 1850	J. Heinrich	Ultman, Maria Catharina	D	219
Binhaus, Bertha	21, Nov. 1858	Heinrich	Ehrhart, Salomea	N	
Binhaus, Heinrich	21, Nov. 1858	Heinrich	Ehrhart, Salomea	N	
Binsac, Francisca	3, Feb. 1853	Peter	Noll, Regina	F	
Binsack, Jacob	30, Oct. 1855	Peter	Nodel, Barbara	D	45
Binterim, Catharina Elisabeth	23, Nov. 1859	Georg	Gams, Adalheid	D	151
Binzer, Elisabeth Catharina Joesphina	19, Aug. 1853	Johan	Krümpelman, Catharina	J	24

Name of Child	Date of Baptism	Father	Mother	Church	Page
Binzer, Johan Carl Adam	7, Aug. 1855	Johan	Krümpelman, Catharina	J	32
Binzer, Maria Anna	5, June 1859	Johan	Krimpelmann, Catharina	G	
Bipon?, Mary Emma Julia Antonette	25, July 1858	John	Hammant, Julia	P	255
Birch, John	29, Jan. 1854	Richard	Hannefan, Mary	E	163
Birchler, Elisabeth Rosa	25, Dec. 1853	Meinrad	Schaedler, Elisabeth	L	
Birckel, Carl	24, July 1859	Joseph	----, Elisabeth	D	142
Birckenhauser, Franz	20, Dec. 1857	Philipp	Kraempfert, Margaretha	T	
Birckenhäuser, Herman Gustav	26, Mar. 1854	Philipp	Krampf, Barbara Walburga	D	7
Birckenhauser, Josephina	21, Dec. 1857	Philipp	Kraempfert, Margaretha	T	
Bird, Honora	26, Oct. 1853	John	Murphy, Margaret	E	138
Birdin, Mary	15, Aug. 1851	John	Coyne, Bridget	B	238
Birdsall, Charles Edward	19, Mar. 1851	Solomon	D----, Elizabeth	B	227
Birdsol, Emma Jane	21, Feb. 1853	Solomon	Denney, Elizabeth	B	284
Birer, Mary Josephine	30, May 1852	Joseph	Bicket, Mary A.	B	264
Birgi, Johan Wilhelm	17, Apr. 1859	Johan	---eng--, Theresa	D	136
Birk, Carl	7, May 1859	Carl	Munchenbach, Sibilla	L	
Birk, Catharina	3, Nov. 1850	Pius	----, Barbara	Q	1
Birk, Salome Theresa	27, Dec. 1857	Carl	Munchenber, Sibilla	K	
Birkhof, Anna Maria Christina	14, Nov. 1856	Gustav	Rudde, Christina	F	
Birkhofer, Joseph	18, July 1855	Joseph	Werry, Theresa	K	
Birkhofer, Josephina Eugenia	17, Aug. 1856	Joseph	Werny, Theresa	K	
Birkle, Augusta Carolina	27, Apr. 1856	Anton	Dieringer, Antonia	D	57
Birkle, Carolina	22, Aug. 1852	Andreas	Britsch, Theresa	D	345
Birkle, Elisabeth	5, Apr. 1858	Arbogast	Geisler, Victoria	D	109
Birkle, Friedrich Anton	27, Apr. 1856	Anton	Dieringer, Antonia	D	57
Birkle, Maria	23, Apr. 1854	Andreas	Britsch, Theresa	D	8
Birkle, Maria Agatha	22, Dec. 1850	Anton	Thieringer, Antonia	A	
Birkle, Maria Francisca	24, Dec. 1853	Anton	Dieringer, Antonia	D	421
Birmingham, Catherine	28, Apr. 1856	----	----, ----	P	177
Birmingham, James Lawrence	23, Oct. 1859	Martin	Quinlan, Ellen	B	82
Birmingham, Mary	12, June 1858	John	Hughes, Mary	E	541
Birmingham, Mary	17, Feb. 1855	Thomas	----, Catherine	E	265
Birmingham, William John	12, July 1857	Martin	Quinlen, Ellen	B	47
Bisch, Gertrud Rosina	11, Apr. 1858	Joseph	----, Rosina	R	
Bisch, Joseph	3, Nov. 1854	Joseph	Finn, Rosina	R	
Bisch, Maria Theresa	20, Apr. 1856	Joseph	----, Rosina	R	
Bisch, Mary Margaret	3, Oct. 1852	Joseph	Fenn, Rosina	R	
Bischer, Joseph	26, July 1857	Christoph	Glueck, Maria	C	
Bischof, Ann Elisabeth Margaret	21, May 1854	John	Steckenborn, Elisabeth	R	
Bischof, Francisca	9, Dec. 1852	Anton	Dickal, Maria	D	360
Bischof, Johan	20, June 1855	Christoph	Glueck, Anna M.	C	
Bischof, Johan Wilhelm	6, July 1850	J. Wilhelm	Schwers, Maria Elisabeth	K	
Bischof, Margaretha	26, Jan. 1851	Anton	Diehl, Maria Anna	D	250
Bischof, Maria Anna Henrietta	18, Feb. 1854	Wilhelm	Schweers, Maria Elisabeth	K	
Bischof, Maria Catharina	4, Aug. 1857	Johan	----, Elisabeth	R	
Bischof, Maria Elisabeth	10, Apr. 1852	Wilhelm	Schweerman, Maria Elisabeth	K	
Bischof, Maria Margaretha	6, Aug. 1857	Charles	Schulz, Rosina	L	
Bischof, Philipp Carl	15, June 1856	Anton	Decker, Maria Anna	D	60
Bischof, Sophia	17, Oct. 1858	Anton	Tickel, Anna Maria	D	122
Bischoff, Johan	18, Feb. 1855	Anton	Tickel, Maria Anna	D	29
Bisenth, Maria Margaretha	16, Jan. 1850	Johan	Spekmeni, Barbara	D	200
Bishof, Johan Wilhelm	6, Dec. 1855	Carl	Schulz, Rosina	L	
Bishof, Maria Josephina	16, Sept 1856	Wilhelm	Schweer, M. Elisabeth	L	
Bishop, Rosina	8, Nov. 1859	Charles	Shintz, Rosina	P	303
Bishop, Thomas	27, June 1850	John	Mahanan, Ann	E	232
Bising, Edward	26, Dec. 1859	Thomas	Hechinger, Clara	C	
Bising, Emma Magdalena Philippina	17, Aug. 1859	Coelestin	Gyr, Carolina	F	
Bitech, Angelica	9, June 1850	Marcus	Hicktenender, Maria Ottlia	F	
Bitt, Carolina	9, Nov. 1856	Carl	Bundschuh, Elisabeth	C	

Name of Child	Date of Baptism	Father	Mother	Church	Page
Bittel, Ann Theresa	25, May 1856	Joseph	----, Anna Maria	H	
Bittel, Elisabeth	24, Dec. 1851	Michael	Fleckenstein, Catharina	D	297
Bittel, Johan Baptist	1, Nov. 1853	Michael	Fleckenstein, Catharina	D	413
Bittenhond, Heinrich Joseph	19, June 1858	Bernard	Sieve, Elisabeth	F	
Bitter, Johan Augustine	13, Sept 1854	Anton	Nower, Catharina Maria	D	17
Bitterman, Maria Theresa	21, Dec. 1856	Johan	Geh---, Theresa	D	74
Bittinger, Georg Joseph	4, June 1854	Jacob	Duringer, Elisabeth	C	
Bittlinger, Amalia	23, May 1858	Mathias	Fey, Catharina	T	
Bittner, Adam	20, Jan. 1850	Andreas	----, Catharina	H	
Bittner, Elisabeth	8, Aug. 1852	Andreas	----, Catherina	H	
Bittner, Michael	2, Feb. 1854	Andreas	----, Catharina	H	
Black, Elisabeth	22, July 1855		adult	F	
Black, Jesse Mary	1, Feb. 1858	James	Byrnes, Mary	E	514
Black, Josephina	12, Apr. 1857	Ambrose	Hardin, Elisabeth	F	
Blackall, Ann Mary	13, Nov. 1859	Walter	Curley, Mary	B	83
Blackall, George	20, May 1856	Thomas	Bishop, Louise	E	367
Blackall, William Thomas	11, May 1857	Thomas	Bishop, Louise	E	452
Blaeser, Heinrich	28, Mar. 1858	Peter	Balkers, Rosalia	T	
Blaesi, Johan Blasius	26, June 1853		Blaesi, Catharina	F	
Blake, Catherine Theresa	7, Oct. 1855	James	Leonard, Ann	P	154
Blake, Elizabeth	20, Nov. 1859	James	Leonard, Ann	B	84
Blake, Helen Elizabeth	7, Sept 1851	James	Leonard, Ann	B	240
Blake, Mary Ann	11, Sept 1853	James	Leonard, Ann	P	51
Blake, Patrick	25, July 1851	Patrick	Heffeman, Bridget	B	236
Blake, Richard	14, Jan. 1850	James	Leonard, Ann	B	194
Blanck, Juliana	18, Apr. 1852	Johan	Hay, Margaretha	C	
Bland, Eliza	20, Jan. 1855	John	Gidding, Mary	E	258
Blank, Adalbert	20, Sept 1854	Georg	Blank, Anna	D	18
Blank, Francis Xavier	9, Dec. 1855	Mathias	Maurer, Rosa	J	34
Blank, Francisca	19, June 1851	J. Nepomuck	Rosemer, Maria Anna	J	12
Blank, Joseph Anton	6, Sept 1857	Mathias	Maurer, Rosa	J	42
Blank, Josephina Charlotte	1, Sept 1851	Georg	Blank, Anna	D	280
Blank, Maria Anna	30, June 1850	Johan	Heid, Margaretha	D	220
Blank, Maria Magdalena	19, Apr. 1854	Gregor	Maurer, Maria Anna	J	26
Blank, Maria Theresa	15, Aug. 1856	Gregor	Maurer, Maria Anna	J	38
Blank, Rosa Ottilia	16, Dec. 1855	Johan	Brosemer, Marianna	F	
Blank, Wilhelm Heinrich	15, Aug. 1853	Johan	Brosmer, Marianna	F	
Blankemeier, Herman Bernard Heinr.	1, July 1859	Heinrich	Gaus, Julia Anna	L	
Blankemeier, Maria Theresa	30, July 1857	Heinrich	Gauss, Julianna	L	
Blankemeyer, Longina H. Amalia	4, Mar. 1855	Alexander	Pullemeyer, Longina	L	
Blankman, Bernard Heinrich	10, Feb. 1853	Heinrich	Lucken, Maria Angela	A	
Bla---rbacher, Sophia	29, June 1858	Wenceslaus	Humla---, Anna	D	114
Blartl?, Margaretha Elisabeth	7, Nov. 1852	Roch?	Kachman, Maria	D	356
Blasehiere, Marie	13, May 1852	August	----, Mary	E	413
Blashiere, Alphonse Cornelius	13, May 1852	August	----, Mary	E	413
Blau, Maria Barbara	15, Jan. 1859	Stephan	Konz, Maria	F	
Blear, Margaret	12, May 1857	Robert	Borley, Helen	R	
Bleasby,	21, Oct. 1850		adult - 25 years old	E	256
Blech, August	5, Sept 1851	Ambrose	Harten, Elisabeth	J	12
Bleck, Catharina Maria	5, Apr. 1855	Ambrose	Hatten, Elisabeth	F	
Bleck, Joseph Rupert	21, Aug. 1853	Anton	Fiel, Elisabeth	F	
Bleck, Rosetta Clara	10, June 1855	Ambrose	Hadden, Elisabeth	F	
Bleckham?, Thomas	16, Dec. 1855	Thomas	Rensck, Mary	B	23
Bleckman, G. Herm. Heinrich Aloysius	9, July 1851	Friedrich	Botlerman, Anna Maria	K	
Bleckman, Maria Philomena Elisabeth	22, Dec. 1853	J. Friedrich	Butterman, Anna Maria	K	
Bleckmann, Anna Maria Elisabeth	13, Feb. 1853	Carl H.	Nienaber, Margaretha Elis.	F	
Bleckmann, Anna Philomena Elisabeth	19, Nov. 1851	Herman	Kallmeyer, Maria	C	
Bleckmann, Johan Friedrich H.	2, Dec. 1851	Heinrich	Nienhofen, Elisabeth	C	
Bleckmann, Johan Herman Heinrich	18, Nov. 1854	Herman H.	Kallmeier, Maria	F	

Name of Child	Date of Baptism	Father	Mother	Church	Page
Bleckmann, Josephina Angela	8, June 1853	J. Herman	Kallmeier, Maria Angela	F	
Bleckmann, Maria Catharina	29, Aug. 1856	Herman	Kohlmann, Marianna	F	
Bleckmann, Maria Catharina	29, July 1858	Herman H.	Niehaber, M. Elisabeth	F	
Bleckmann, Maria Elisabeth	28, Oct. 1855	Heinrich	Nienaber, Elisabeth	F	
Blegue, Peter James	6, Feb. 1853	Matthew	Creton, Bridget	E	61
Blehman, Franz Bernard	1, Jan. 1850	Andreas	Blehman, Margaretha	D	197
Blei, Antonia Elisabeth	24, Aug. 1856	Carl Wm.	Trikler, Theresa C.	F	
Blei, Johan Anton	15, May 1856	Anton	Warburg, Elisabeth	F	
Blei, Joseph Carl	11, Nov. 1858	Anton	Waerberg, Elisabeth	F	
Blei, Joseph Heinrich	2, Nov. 1857	Joseph	Darbeck, Clara	C	
Blei, Maria Catharina Augusta	29, Mar. 1859	Carl Wm.	Trickler, Carolina	F	
Blei, Maria Elisabeth	22, Dec. 1853	Anton	Warburg, Elisabeth	F	
Blei, Wilhelm Heinrich	5, Oct. 1857	Carl Wm.	Trikler, Carolina	F	
Bleibel, Carl August	9, Apr. 1854	Johan	Kramer, Walburga	A	
Bleibel, Fr. Joseph	24, Oct. 1858	Joseph	Krämer, Walburga	A	
Bleibel, Francis Joseph	23, Mar. 1856	Joseph	Krämer, Walburga	A	
Bleie, Johan August	12, Jan. 1853	Joseph	Darbeck, Clara	C	
Bleie, Maria Anna Clara	7, Sept 1855	Joseph	Darbeck, Clara	C	
Bleie, Maria Magdalena	13, Apr. 1851	Joseph	Darbeck, Clara	C	
Bleiman, Herman Heinrich	14, Jan. 1859	Bernard	Schwej---, Maria	D	129
Bleiman, Maria Adelheid Elisabeth	1, Oct. 1857	Bernard	Schwe--, Anna Maria	D	95
Bleistein, Johan Anton	10, Dec. 1854	Ignatius	Stub, Eva	D	23
Blese, Barbara	8, Dec. 1850	Christian	Anget, Anna Maria	D	246
Blese, Catharina	8, Nov. 1858	Gottlieb	Anget, Anna Maria	D	124
Blesi, Friedrich	30, Mar. 1856	Christian	Anger, Anna M.	D	55
Blesi, Maria	14, July 1853	Christian	Angeth, Maria	D	394
Blesser, Lawrence August	12, Mar. 1854	J. Peter	Baldus, Rosalia	D	6
Blesser, Maria Anna	8, July 1855	J. Peter	Paten, Rosalia	D	38
Blettner, Catharina	31, July 1859	Joseph	Zam, Elisabeth	C	
Blettner, Johan	13, Apr. 1856	Johan	Pfe---, Maria Anna	D	56
Blettner, Maria Elisabeth	13, Sept 1857	Joseph	Same, Elisabeth	C	
Blettner, Nicolaus Michael	12, Dec. 1858	Johan	Schend---, Maria Anna	D	126
Bley, Benrard Ferdinand	28, Nov. 1859	Joseph	Darbeck, Clara	A	
Blier?, Johan Gustav	15, June 1856	P---	Schul---, Catharina	D	61
Blisch, Maria Anna	2, Sept 1855	Reinhard	Radich, Theresa	R	
Block, Albina Elisabeth	6, Jan. 1850	Joseph	Jank, Elisabeth	A	
Block, Anna Catharina	8, Sept 1850	Johan	Stamm, Philomena	A	
Block, Carl	27, Mar. 1853	Johan	Stamm, Philippina	A	
Block, Johan	30, June 1854		Block, Elisabeth	A	
Block, Maria Elisabeth	16, Sept 1855	Stephan	Schäme, Elisabeth	A	
Block, Maria Elisabeth Henrica	16, Feb. 1852	Joseph	Johns, Maria Elisabeth	A	
Bloemer, Anna Maria	20, Sept 1853	Andreas	Vedders, Elisabeth	F	
Bloemer, Anna Maria	2, May 1858	Heinrich	Muggenburg, M. Anna	C	
Bloemer, Anna Maria Bernardina	18, May 1851	Bernard	Nodler, Bernardina	C	
Bloemer, Bernardina Catharina	9, Apr. 1856	Bernard	Nedner, Bernardina	C	
Bloemer, Johan Bernard	2, Jan. 1854	Bernard	Nedler, Anna Catharina	C	
Bloemer, Johan Heinrich	10, Feb. 1856	Johan	Muggenburg, Elisabeth	C	
Bloemer, Johanna Maria	6, Feb. 1853	Johan	Woppen, Johanna Maria	D	370
Blom, Maria Johana Philomena	13, Sept 1857	John W.	----, Engel	R	
Blome, Anna Maria Gertrud	29, July 1851	J. Heinrich	Hunighake, Maria Angela	A	
Blome, Bernard Herman	4, May 1851	J. Bernard	Jaske, M. Angela	C	
Blome, Francisca Louise	19, Oct. 1855	Wilhelm	Jaske, M. Angela	C	
Blome, Heinrich Wilhelm	12, Dec. 1852	J. Wilhelm	Jaske, Angela	C	
Blome, Herman Gerhard	13, July 1859	J. Wilhelm	Jaske, M. Angela	C	
Blome, Herman Heinrich	19, Oct. 1856	J. Heinrich	Huninghake, Maria Angela	A	
Blome, Johan Bernard	29, Oct. 1854	Bernard H.	Huninghake, Maria Engel	A	
Blöme, Joseph Heinrich	25, Dec. 1859	Heinrich	Hünighake, Maria Angela	A	
Blome, Maria Anna	13, June 1850	B.	Schroeder, Maria	A	
Blömer, Bernard	25, Dec. 1851	Bernard	Wehri, Catharina	D	298

Name of Child	Date of Baptism	Father	Mother	Church	Page
Blömer, Bernard	7, May 1851	J. Heinrich	Wegemer, Clara	K	
Blömer, Catharina Josephna	7, Feb. 1856	Bernard	Weri, Catharina	A	
Blömer, Francis Lawrence	15, Aug. 1853	F. Bernard	Wery, Catharina	D	400
Blömer, Herman Joseph	25, Dec. 1851	Bernard	Wehri, Catharina	D	298
Blömer, Johan Herman	9, Mar. 1859	Bernard	Nel---, Bernardina	D	133
Blomer, Margaretha Elisabeth	8, Mar. 1852	J. Heinrich	Heeman, A.	K	
Blondell, Caroline Sarah	1, Dec. 1856	Joseph	Reading, Mary	B	37
Blondell, Charles	5, Aug. 1850	Joseph	Redding, Mary Ann	B	209
Blondell, Charles William	29, July 1858	Joseph	Reading, Mary	B	62
Blondell, Mary	7, July 1853	Joseph	Redding, Mary Ann	B	294
Bloomer, Elisabeth	5, June 1853	John	----, Ann	H	
Bloomer, Mary Ann	7, Jan. 1855	John	----, Ann	U	
Bluet, James	2, June 1859	Matthew	Keegan, Bridget	E	630
Bluett, Charles John	27, Feb. 1859	Charles	Henny, Mary	E	607
Bluette, Charles	17, July 1857	Matthew	Keegan, Bridget	E	466
Blum, Agatha	15, July 1855	Peter	Fischer, Gertrud	J	32
Blum, Andrew	27, June 1858	Amand	Amans, Elizabeth	U	
Blum, Anna Maria	25, Feb. 1851		adult - 23 years old	K	
Blum, Elisabeth	27, Jan. 1850	Peter	Fischer, Gertrud	J	6
Blum, Johan Justin	4, May 1851	Daniel	Kloeber, Gertrud	F	
Blum, Joseph	3, Oct. 1852	Xavier	Wehrle, Catharina	F	
Blum, Maria	27, Sept 1851	Amand	Amann, Elisabeth	F	
Blum, Maria	19, July 1857	Peter	Fischer, Gertrud	G	
Blum, Maria	18, Dec. 1853	Peter	Fischer, Gertrud	J	24
Blum, Mary Theresa	9, Apr. 1856	Xavier	Wehrle, Catherine	U	
Blum, Peter	26, Mar. 1852	Peter	Fischer, Gertrud	J	16
Blum, William	27, June 1858	Amand	Amans, Elizabeth	U	
Blume, Christian Ludwig	17, July 1853	Georg L.	Deiser, Wilhelmina	F	
Blume, Clemens Franz Georg	2, Oct. 1856	Theodor	Tilly, Julia	L	
Blumer, Johan Gerhard Heinrich	28, Apr. 1851	Ludwig	Dreise, Wilhelmina	F	
Blumer, Peter	16, July 1850	Carl	Rottenkirch, Catharina	D	223
Boacke, Heinrich	18, Mar. 1856		adult - 22 years old	A	
Boberg, Anna Maria	18, Nov. 1854	Gerhard H.	Schluetters, Margaret	L	
Boberg, Heinrich Wilhelm	5, Aug. 1850	Wilhelm	Cofermann, Clara Elis.	L	
Boberg, Maria Wilhelmina	9, July 1858	Gerhard	Schulting, Maria	C	
Boberg, Susanna Margaretha	25, Aug. 1856	Heinrich	Schulte, Susanna M.	F	
Bobinacott, Ann	2, July 1854	Frederick	Farrell, Mary Ann	P	86
Bocciocco, John Baptist Charles Louis	3, Jan. 1858	John B.	----, ----	B	54
Boch, Maria Amalia	30, Mar. 1858	Friedrich	Tobbe, Maria	K	
Bochhorst, Maria Margaretha	8, Dec. 1850	Heinrich	Blomer, Catharina	C	
Bochman, Anna Maria	6, Dec. 1857	Heinrich	Dallner, Maria Anna	D	100
Bockding, Anna Philomena	21, May 1852	Bernard	Eifers, Elisabeth	D	320
Bockding, Marina Carolina	27, Oct. 1850	Gerhard	Schwing, Adelheid	D	240
Böckert, Carl	24, Aug. 1858	J. Georg	Klinger, Anna	K	
Bockert, Carolina	21, Dec. 1856	Johan	Fridl, Barbara	D	74
Bockgraf, Balthasar	17, Aug. 1856	Ludwig	Schel, Louisa	C	
Bockhorst, Anton Gerhard Heinrich	8, Feb. 1855	G. Heinrich	Blomer, Anna Margaretha	K	
Bockhorst, Catharina Elisabeth	19, Oct. 1852	J. Heinrich	Messman, Maria Catharina	K	
Bockhorst, Gerhard Heinrich	14, June 1857	J. Gerhard	Blömer, Anna Maria	K	
Bockhorst, Lisette Henrietta	17, Feb. 1853	Gerhard	Bloemer, Maria	L	
Bocklage, Anna Elisabeth	12, June 1859	Henry	Mas---, Anna Maria	D	140
Bocklage, Anna Margaretha	19, June 1858	H.H.	Closterman, Catharina	A	
Bocklage, Anna Maria Catharina	7, May 1854	Gerhard	Becker, Anna M.	C	
Bocklage, Clemens	22, Apr. 1854	H. Heinrich	Biedebecke, Maria Anna	K	
Bocklage, Elisabeth Josephina	14, Jan. 1857	J. Heinrich	Bünker, Catharina	A	
Bocklage, Francis Heinrich	17, Dec. 1850	H. Heinrich	Biderbecke, Gertrud	K	
Bocklage, Herman Heinrich	6, Nov. 1852	J. Heinrich	Bönker, Maria Catharina	A	
Bocklage, Johan Herman	27, Jan. 1852	Gerhard	Becker, Maria	C	
Bocklage, Johan Wilhelm Herman	12, Dec. 1859	J. Heinrich	Bönker, Catharina	A	

Name of Child	Date of Baptism	Father	Mother	Church	Page
Bocklage, Maria Anna	22, Feb. 1852	H. Heinrich	Biederbeck, Maria Gertrud	K	
Bocklage, Maria Anna Carolina	5, May 1856	Gerhard	Becker, Anna M.	C	
Bocklage, Maria Catharina	1, June 1854	J.H.	Bünker, Catharina	A	
Bocklage, Maria Elisabeth	3, Mar. 1850	Gerhard	Becker, Maria	C	
Bocklage, Maria Josephina	2, Jan. 1858	Heinrich	Bünker, Catharina	A	
Bocklage, Wilhelm Carl	22, Mar. 1859	Gerhard	Becker, Anna Maria	C	
Bocklegh, Anna Elisabeth Rosa	27, Oct. 1857	Heinrich	Moorman, Maria	D	97
Bocklet, Carl	16, Jan. 1859	Johan	Fidel, Barbara	T	
Bocklet, Johan	14, May 1854	Johan	Fridl, Barbara	D	10
Bockling, Otto Heinrich Albert	13, Mar. 1851	Anton	Borgess, Elisabeth	A	
Bocklo, Catharina Maria	24, Nov. 1859	Nicolaus	Steincke, Elisabeth	T	
Bockman, Anna Elisabeth	6, Mar. 1859	G.H.	Schwarz, Carolina	A	
Böckman, Anna Maria Christina	28, July 1854	Friedrich	Buschen, Maria Elisabeth	A	
Böckman, Anna Maria Elisabeth	21, Dec. 1852	Heinrich	Sicker, Anna Gesina	A	
Böckman, Catharina Philomena	29, Sept 1850	Gerhard	Bünger, Theresa	K	
Böckman, Herman	20, Nov. 1859	Heinrich	Sicker, Gesina	A	
Böckman, Johan Heinrich	28, Jan. 1855	Heinrich	Sicker, Gesina	A	
Bockman, Maria Anna	26, Dec. 1852	Gerhard	Bunger, Theresa	N	10
Böckman, Maria Elisabeth	16, Apr. 1854	J. Bernard	Wohnker, Maria Elisabeth	A	
Bockmann, Anna Maria Elisabeth	23, Aug. 1857	Bernard	Wenker, Elisabeth	L	
Bockmann, Carl	30, Sept 1857	Gerhard	Buenger, Theresa	L	
Bockting, Gerhard Heinrich	12, May 1851	Bernard	Elvers, Elisabeth	D	264
Bockwald, Joseph	27, June 1858	Andreas	Ermel, Anna	A	
Bockweg, Caroline	15, Nov. 1854	Henry	Wilhelm, Barbara	R	
Bockweg, Johan Gerhard	1, Jan. 1855	J. Bernard	Massman, Maria Anna	D	26
Bockweg, Maria Anna	3, July 1856	J. Heinrich	Massman, Gertrud	D	62
Bocle, Maria Irena	28, Feb. 1854	Francis	Schultz, Louisa	C	
Bode, Amelia Margaretha	31, Oct. 1858	G. Wilhelm	Fideley, Maria Catharina	Q	29
Bode, Anna Maria Theresa	9, Oct. 1859	Bernard	Tietmeier, Theresa	F	
Bode, Catharina Maria	29, Oct. 1854	Francis	Haverkamp, Margaretha	L	
Bode, Heinrich	10, Sept 1851	G. Wilhelm	Fidelday, Catharina Maria	D	282
Bode, Herman	19, Feb. 1857	G. Wilhelm	Fideldey, Maria Catharina	Q	20
Bode, Joseph	12, Jan. 1855	Gerhard W.	Fideldei, Catharina Maria	D	26
Bode, Maria Catharina	2, Apr. 1853	Francis	Haverkamp, Margaretha	L	
Bode, Philomena	12, June 1853	Gerhard W.	Fideldey, Catharina Maria	D	389
Bode, Wilhelm Johan	16, Mar. 1856	Francis	Haverkamp, Margaretha	L	
Bödecker, Anna Maria Elisabeth	23, Feb. 1850	J. Heinrich	Pille, Anna Maria	A	
Bödecker, Carolina Friederica	29, Apr. 1852	J. Heinrich	Pille, Maria Elisabeth	A	
Bödecker, Catharina Maria	13, May 1851	Herman	Lutmerding, Maria Agnes	A	
Bödecker, Gerhard Heinrich	17, Mar. 1857	J. Heinrich	Pille, Catharina	A	
Bödecker, Johan Herman Heinrich	9, June 1853	J. Herman	Lütmerding, Maria Agnes	A	
Bödeker, Anna Maria	29, Nov. 1858	Wilhelm	Qualbrink, Catharina	A	
Bödeker, Anna Maria Clara	4, Mar. 1858	J. Herman	Lutmerding, Maria Agnes	A	
Bödeker, Catharina Francisca	10, Feb. 1855	J. Heinrich	Pille, Elisabeth	A	
Bödel, Maria Anna	10, Feb. 1850	Stephan	Wiest, Elisabeth	D	203
Boden, Ann	7, Mar. 1858	John	Roger, Ann	E	520
Boden, Julia	30, Mar. 1851	John	----, Ann	E	296
Boden, Mary	7, Aug. 1853	John	----, Ann	E	115
Bodenstein, Anna Angela	29, Dec. 1856	Carl	Klenke, Anna	A	
Bodkin, Mary	21, June 1859	Samuel	----, Bridget	E	634
Bodry, Martin	4, June 1854	Stephan	----, Magdalene	M	
Boebinger, Elisabeth	22, May 1859	Wilhelm	Geiger, Catharina	D	138
Boecker, Anna Margaretha	2, Nov. 1856	Clemens	Bishof, Margaretha	L	
Boecker, Anna Maria Catharina	25, Nov. 1858	Clemens	Zurline, Theresa	L	
Boecker, Herman Heinrich	23, July 1856	Christian	Unnewehr, Maria Angela	F	
Boecker, Herman Heinrich	30, Nov. 1851	Herman	Gerwe, Marianna	F	
Boecker, Maria Catharina	24, May 1859	Johan	Bischof, Margaretha	L	
Boecker, Maria Theresa Carolina	6, Nov. 1853	Clemens	Zurline, Theresa	L	
Boeckling, Maria Christina	30, May 1855	Anton	Borgess, Elisabeth	C	

Name of Child	Date of Baptism	Father	Mother	Church	Page
Boeckman, Gerhard Heinrich	23, May 1855	Gerhard	Bünger, Theresa	K	
Boeckman, Johan Bernard	20, Apr. 1859	J. Bernard	Wönker, Elisabeth	K	
Boeckmann, Anton	6, Oct. 1854	Joseph	Redelmann, Elisabeth	L	
Boeckmann, Catharina Gertrud	4, Jan. 1857	Joseph	Redelmann, Cath. Elisabeth	L	
Boeckmann, Josephina	9, Feb. 1859	Joseph	Redelmann, M. Elisabeth	L	
Boeckmann, M Catharina Josephina	20, Jan. 1856	J. Bernard	Woehnker, M. Elisabeth	L	
Boedken, Marianna Catharina Elis.	18, Sept 1853	Wilhelm	Gerve, Marianna	F	
Boedker, Heinrich Wilhelm	9, Mar. 1859	Wilhelm	Gerwe, Theresa Elisabeth	T	
Boedker, Johan Heinrich Wilhelm	7, June 1855	Wilhelm	Gerwe, Maria	F	
Boedker, Joseph Gerhard	12, July 1857	Herman W.	Gerwe, Marianna	F	
Boedker, Marianna Francisca	22, Apr. 1857	Johan H.	Kruse, Margaretha	F	
Boedker, Wilhelm Herman	31, Aug. 1858	J. Heinrich	Kruse, Margaretha	T	
Boeger, Georg Joseph	11, July 1853	G. Valentin	Klingler, Anna	K	
Boeger, Mathias Otto	4, Oct. 1857	Johan	Stapf, Maria Anna	K	
Boeh, Johan Carl	31, Oct. 1858	Melchior	Jaeger, Francisca	C	
Boeh, Maria Louisa	18, May 1851	Melchior	Jaeger, Francisca	C	
Boehle, Maria Amalia	21, Feb. 1858	Georg	Volz, Emilia	D	105
Boehler, Georg Joseph	18, Feb. 1857	Joseph	Scherer, Clara	C	
Boehler, Heinrich Francis	24, June 1855	Francis	Schulz, Laura	C	
Boehler, Maria Christina	26, Jan. 1857	Francis	Stopp---, Anna Catharina	D	77
Boehles, Johan Francis	20, Oct. 1859	Joseph	Scherer, Clara	K	
Boehmel, Anna Maria	8, Jan. 1857	Michael	Knoblauch, Dorothea	F	
Boehmer, Anna Maria	20, Apr. 1857	Gerhard	Buenger, Theresa	L	
Boehmer, Bernard Francis Wilhelm	2, Mar. 1856	J. Wilhelm	Grave, M. Elisabeth	C	
Boehmer, Bernard Heinrich	23, Oct. 1852	Bernard H.	Brune, Catharine	C	
Boehmer, Bernard Joseph	2, May 1857	Bernard	Brune, Maria	L	
Boehmer, Catharina M. Elisabeth	30, Sept 1859	Bernard H.	Brune, Cath. M. Elis.	L	
Boehmer, Johan Bernard	13, Feb. 1859	Gerhard H.	Buecker, Thecla	C	
Boehmer, Johan Matthias	8, Dec. 1850	Herman	Brohne, Elisabeth	C	
Boehmer, Maria Anna Elisabeth	9, Aug. 1853	Engelbert	Heiart, Elisabeth	L	
Boehmer, Maria Elisabeth	29, Nov. 1854	Gerhard	Bueker, Thecla	C	
Boehne, Anna Maria Josephina	30, July 1853	Gerhard H.	Hedebeg, Catharina Gertrud	D	397
Boehne, Carl Heinrich	23, Nov. 1856	Bernard	Böh----, Agnes	D	72
Boehne, Heinrich Herman	12, July 1850	Theodor	Witte, Elisabeth	L	
Boehne, Johan Theodor Joseph	22, Dec. 1852	J. Theodor	Witte, Elisabeth	L	
Boehner, Adam Christian	25, Dec. 1855	Albert	Heiking, Gertrud	L	
Boehner, Bernard Heinrich D.	21, May 1858	Heinrich	Beu---, Catharina	D	111
Boehner, Johan Albert	25, Dec. 1855	Albert	Heiking, Gertrud	L	
Boehring, Anna Catharina	14, July 1854	J. Mathias	Fischer, A.M. Helena	F	
Boehringer, Carl	14, Jan. 1854	Carl	Schmalz, Leonora	D	1
Boehringer, Maria Elisabeth	30, Aug. 1857	Carl	Schmalz, Eleonora	Q	24
Boeker, A. Maria Catharina Elis.	10, Sept 1856	Clemens	Zurline, Theresa	L	
Boeker, Herman Friedrich	9, Dec. 1858	Christian	Unnevehr, Anna Maria A.	F	
Boelling, Catharina Elisabeth	23, Oct. 1859	F. Adolph	Wernsing, Anna	C	
Boellinger, Jacob	5, June 1859	Martin	Reis, Eva	T	
Boellner, Anna Maria	18, July 1852	J. Heinrich	Beckmann, Rebecca	C	
Boellner, Georg Heinrich	27, Dec. 1853	Heinrich	Beckmann, Maria	C	
Boellner, Johan Edmund	23, Dec. 1855	J. Heinrich	Beckmann, Rebecca	C	
Boemer, Susanna F. Elisabeth	5, Apr. 1857	Engelbert	Heuer, Elisabeth	L	
Boemersen, Maria	11, Sept 1853	Wilhelm	Praunfiel, Margaretha	K	
Boennemann, Anna Maria	20, July 1850	J. Heinrich	Fiege, M. Elisabeth	L	
Boerger, Anna Barbara	12, Oct. 1855	Johan	Selm, Anna Maria	L	
Boerger, Anna Maria	4, Oct. 1853	Johan	Sehm, Anna Maria	L	
Boerger, Friedrich Wilhelm	19, Nov. 1852	J. Bernard	Pellenwessel, Agnes	L	
Boerger, Johan Friedrich	27, Feb. 1856	Friedrich	Michael, Maria Agnes	L	
Boerger, Joseph Augustine	23, Nov. 1854	August	Helmkamp, Maria Anna	K	
Boerger, Maria	31, Jan. 1850	Friedrich	Michael, Maria Agnes	L	
Boerger, Maria Angelica	22, Nov. 1854	J. Bernard	Berling, M. Catharina	L	
Boerger, Maria Catharina	5, Mar. 1854	Friedrich	Michael, Agnes	L	

Name of Child	Date of Baptism	Father	Mother	Church	Page
Boerger, Maria Elisabeth	12, Nov. 1858	Friedrich	Michael, Agnes	L	
Boerger, Maria Engel Agnes	21, Dec. 1851	Friedrich	Michael, M. Agnes	L	
Boerger, Maria Philomena	10, Feb. 1856	H. Heinrich	Spieker, Anna Maria	K	
Boergman, Maria Agnes	18, July 1851	Friedrich	Stricker, Agnes	D	273
Böering, Bernard Herman	5, Dec. 1852	Herman	Brogman, Anna Catharina	D	359
Boerman, Wilhelm Heinrich	31, Jan. 1853	Wilhelm	Lux, Margaretha	D	368
Boes, Helena	8, Feb. 1857	Johan	Homan, Elisabeth	J	40
Boes, Louisa Catharina	20, Nov. 1854	J. Balthasar	Hohman, Elisabeth	K	
Boesch, Maria Rosa	28, Mar. 1858	Francis	Sig, Louisa	A	
Boescher, Francis Theodor	4, Nov. 1855	Clemens	Kneppe, Anna	C	
Boesten, Bernard Heinrich	26, Sept 1853	Herman	Büning, Carolina	D	407
Boet, Georg Edward	26, Feb. 1854	Melchior	Jaeger, Francisca	K	
Boethe, Franz Joseph	12, Apr. 1858	Bernard	Diepmeier, Theresa	F	
Boetting, Amalia Theresa	18, Oct. 1859	Gustav	Weiss, Jacobina	F	
Boettinger, Rosa	27, Jan. 1850	Mathias	Boettinger, Wilhelmina	C	
Boetzow, Wilhelmina Friedricka	21, Apr. 1850	Julius	Beil, Friedricka	C	
Boey, Clara Francisca	17, Aug. 1856	Melchior	Jaeger, Francisca	K	
Bogemann, Johan Herman Heinrich	14, Apr. 1854	Heinrich	Broxtermann, Elis.	L	
Bogenschuetz, Anna Maria	11, Sept 1849	Dennis	Schetter, Wilhelmina	S	
Bogenschuetz, Maria Margaretha	24, July 1853	Michael	Dorst, Catharina	S	
Bogenschuetz, Wilhelm	20, June 1852	Michael	Dorst, Catharina	S	
Bögershausen, Wilhelm Jacob Julius	13, Feb. 1859	Julius	Hölscher, Catharina Maria	K	
Boggiani, John Joseph	23, Apr. 1853	James	Massa, Maria Augustina	B	289
Boggiano, Dominick Charles	12, June 1851	Giacomo	Augustina, Maria	E	315
Boggiano, John Augustine	12, Jan. 1858	James P.	Massa, Augustina	B	54
Boggiano, Maria Paula	15, July 1855	Giacomo	Massa, Maria Augustina	B	16
Boggy, Mary	17, July 1856	John	Gatley, Margaret	E	381
Bogman, Johan Heinrich Ludwig	24, Aug. 1858	Luke	Thomas, Maria Anna	D	118
Bogner, Barbara	12, Feb. 1854	Johan	Heim, Anna	F	
Bogweg, Anna Maria Magdalena	8, Nov. 1851	J. Heinrich	Blummel, Anna Maria	D	291
Bohan, Catherine	11, Dec. 1853	John	Sweeney, Bridget	P	62
Bohan, Honora	30, July 1859	Dennis	Dwyer, Ann	B	78
Bohan, James	13, Nov. 1853	Cornelius	Kenny, Sarah	P	59
Bohan, James	4, May 1851	Thomas	Sweeney, Mary	B	231
Bohan, John	11, Dec. 1853	John	Sweeney, Bridget	P	62
Bohan, Mary Ann	20, Aug. 1857	William	Flemming, Ann	B	48
Bohan, William	10, Feb. 1858	Michael	Casny, Joanne	E	516
Bohberg, Johan Wilhelm	3, Sept 1859	Anton	Nordhaus, Maria Theresa	J	52
Bohde, Wilhelm Heinrich	8, May 1859	Wilhelm	Donahue, Sarah	J	50
Bohen, William	2, Aug. 1858	Charles	----, Nancy	E	554
Bohl, Elisabeth Philomena	24, Apr. 1851		12 years old	K	
Bohl, Johan	14, Mar. 1852	Peter	Conrad, Barbara	K	
Bohl, Johan Edward	10, Oct. 1858	Valentin	Madler, Maria	K	
Bohl, Margaret	24, Oct. 1852	Michael	----, Ann	H	
Bohl, Philomena	24, Aug. 1856	Cornelius	Boes, Helena	J	38
Bohl, Philomena	8, June 1850	Peter	Conrad, Barbara	K	
Bohl, Wilhelm Bernard Joseph	21, July 1859	Bernard H.	Heidelding, Maria C.	F	
Bohle, Nicolaus	14, May 1854	Michael	Wagner, Anna	H	
Bohlender, Carolina	21, July 1850	Valentin	Gort, Susanna	C	
Bohlender, Maria Louisa	15, Aug. 1852	Valentin	Gort, Susanna	C	
Bohlinger, Elisabeth	1, Feb. 1852	Martin	Reis, Eva	C	
Bohlinger, Francisca Eva	15, Dec. 1850	Martin	Reis, Eva	C	
Bohlinger, Georg Martin	7, May 1854	Martin	Reis, Eva	D	9
Bohlinger, Martin	17, Feb. 1856	Martin	Reis, Eva	C	
Bohlman, Johan Joseph	6, Sept 1856	Bernard	Swetker, Angela	J	38
Bohlman, Johan Theodor	9 Feb. 1851	J. Caspar	Haunhorst, Maria Elisabeth	D	252
Bohlman, Maria Margaretha	18, June 1858	Bernard	Swipker, Angela	J	46
Bohlmayer, Johan Heinrich	13, June 1855	Johan	Filiber, Louisa	D	36
Böhm, Francis	18, Oct. 1857	Francis	Sch---, Anna Maria	D	97

Name of Child	Date of Baptism	Father	Mother	Church	Page
Böhman, Johan Heinrich	27, Apr. 1851	Joseph	Albers, Maria Elisabeth	A	
Böhmer, Albert Heinrich	11, Dec. 1853	Albert	Baumer, Carolina	D	419
Bohmer, Anna Maria	13, Mar. 1859	Theodor	Potter, Gertrud	T	
Böhmer, Anna Maria	16, Mar. 1856	Heinrich	Böcher, Catharina	A	
Böhmer, Bernard Anton	12, June 1856	Albert	Krienpell---, Anna	D	60
Böhmer, Carl Albert	12, May 1851	Albert	Bäumer, Carolina	D	264
Böhmer, Engelbert Theodor	14, June 1851	Engelbert	Heiad, Elisabeth	D	268
Böhmer, Johan Bernard	15, June 1856	Joseph	Müller, Anna	D	61
Böhmer, Johan Bernard	24, Jan. 1853	Nicolaus	Taumeier, Maria	D	367
Böhmer, Johan Theodor	23, Nov. 1858	Wilhelm	Grawe, Elisabeth	K	
Böhmer, Maria Theresa	25, Apr. 1854	Bernard	Dey, Catharina Elisabeth	D	9
Bohn, Angela	31, Oct. 1858	Johan	Walter, Anna Maria	T	
Bohn, Ernst	9, Dec. 1855	Johan	----, Maria	C	
Bohn, Johan Anton	25, Aug. 1856	Johan	Knaber, Anna Maria	F	
Bohne, Anna Maria Theresa	13, July 1851	J. Heinrich	Strieker, Theresa	C	
Bohne, Franz	18, July 1853	Heinrich	Stricker, Theresa	L	
Böhne, Gerhard Heinrich	12, Dec. 1851	G. Heinrich	Hedebecke, Maria Gertrud	D	296
Bohne, Herman	4, Sept 1856	Heinrich	Stricker, Theresa	L	
Bohne, Maria Agnes Elisabeth	13, July 1856	Ferdinand	Wopkenberg, Elisabeth	A	
Bohne, Wilhelm	2, Aug. 1857	Bernard	Wuebken, Agnes	C	
Bohner, Carl	12, July 1852	Anton	Stahl, Margaretha	D	329
Bohner, Johan	13, Jan. 1855	Johan	Bohrer, Maria Anna	D	26
Bohnert, Carl Emil	27, Aug. 1854	Bernard	Ramloh, Maria Elisabeth	D	16
Bohnert, Carolina	22, Mar. 1857	Bernard	Straumber, Elisabeth	D	81
Bohnert, Johan Adam	21, Jan. 1855	Joseph	Degg, Anna Maria	D	27
Böhning, Francis	11, Sept 1851	Heinrich	Eppeke, Josephina	D	282
Bohrer, Francis Bernard	30, Jan. 1859	Joseph	Reinsen, Bertha	K	
Bohrer, Johan	16, Feb. 1851	Georg	Freund, Maria	Q	1
Böhrer, Johan Arnold Dennis	12, Dec. 1852	J. Caspar	Liennes, Anna Maria	D	360
Bohrer, Johan Baptist	20, Feb. 1853	Georg	Freund, Anna M.	D	373
Bohrer, Joseph Rainer	28, June 1856	Joseph	Rainser, Berta	D	61
Bohrer, Marcella	10, Oct. 1852	Johan	Bohrer, Anna Maria	D	352
Bohrer, Nicolaus	14, Sept 1856	Georg	Freund, Maria	D	67
Bohrer, Rosa	7, Mar. 1858	Georg	Freund, Maria	D	106
Bohrer, Sara Anna	14, Sept 1856	Georg	Freund, Maria	D	67
Böhringer, Carolina	5, Sept 1852	Carl	Schmalz, Leonora	D	346
Böhringer, Catharina Elisabeth	21, Sept 1856	A. Wolfgang	----, Wilhelmina	D	68
Böhringer, Rosina	19, Mar. 1855	Carl	Schmalz, Elenora	D	31
Boilean, Laura	15, Aug. 1859	Nutte	Gorman, Catherine	P	293
Boitman, Herman Gerhard	31, Mar. 1858	Gerhard	Borgeding, Catharina	K	
Bokers, Josephina Bernardina Julia	31, Dec. 1855	Bernard	Wilke, Bernardina	L	
Bolan, Ann	1, Aug. 1852	Patrick	McMahon, Sarah	P	25
Bolan, Bridget	3, Mar. 1850	John	Shea, Catherine	E	201
Bolan, James	29, Jan. 1854	Michael	Croshan, Ann	E	163
Bolan, James	18, Feb. 1859	Michael	Flinn, Bridget	P	276
Bolan, John	31, Mar. 1857	John	Rohan, Mary	P	209
Bolan, Mary	15, Aug. 1854	John	Rouen, Mary	B	4
Bolan, Rosanne	4, Jan. 1852	Charles	Murray, Elizabeth	P	15
Boland, Charles Mary	15, Aug. 1857	Michael	Flynn, Bridget	B	48
Boland, Conrad Georg	14, Dec. 1850	Heinrich	Schuhmacher, Maria	A	
Boland, John	11, Mar. 1858	Dennis	O'Brien, Bridget	P	242
Boland, Julia	4, Jan. 1852	Michael	Crossen, Ann	E	370
Boland, Mary	24, Nov. 1859	Dennis	O'Brien, Bridget	P	304
Boland, Mary	23, Oct. 1853	James	----, Mary	E	137
Boland, Maurice	23, Nov. 1851	James	----, Mary	M	
Boland, Patrick	3, June 1850	John	----, Margaret	E	219
Bolans, Eugene Justinian	12, Feb. 1854	James	----, Mary	E	167
Bolbert, Johan August	13, Oct. 1850	F. Martin	Miller, Maria Crescentia	D	237
Bold, Helena	11, Oct. 1857	Jacob	Scherer, Elisabeth	K	

Name of Child	Date of Baptism	Father	Mother	Church	Page
Bolger, Margaret	26, Oct. 1856	James	----, Julia	M	
Bolger, Mary Ann	27, Mar. 1853	James	----, Julia	M	
Bolin, Elisabeth	22, Mar. 1857	Aloysius	Schmidt, Elisabeth	F	
Bolinger, Ludwig Christian	28, Jan. 1851	Christian	Müller, Anna Maria	A	
Boljard, Johan Heinrich	1, Feb. 1857	Carl	Bachmann, Augusta	L	
Bolk, Gerhard Heinrich	9, Sept 1854	Lambert	Bunte, Maria Adelheid	A	
Bolke, Anna Maria Josephina Alwina	6, Sept 1857	Herman	Pellenwessel, Maria	A	
Bolke, Joseph Bernard	10, Sept 1853	Herman	Pellenwessel, Anna Maria	A	
Bolle, Philomena Carolina	27, Oct. 1853	Wilhelm	Kraemer, Agnes	C	
Boller, Georg	4, Mar. 1855	Johan	Humbel, Anna Ursula	D	30
Boller, Joseph August	15, Feb. 1852	Johan	Humbell, Anna Ursula	D	306
Boller, Josephina Barbara	15, May 1853	Johan	Humble, Anna Ursula	D	385
Bollinger, Adalbert	24, Apr. 1853	Bernard	Maier, Maria	D	382
Bollman, Bernard Theodor	30, Apr. 1852	Dietrich	Stoerig, Maria Elisabeth	K	
Bollman, Cecilia	13, Feb. 1851	Henry	Greves, Mary	E	283
Bollman, Johan Bernard	26, Dec. 1858	Dietrich	Stoerig, Maria	K	
Bollman, Johan Friedrich	26, Aug. 1856	Dietrich	Stoerig, Elisabeth	K	
Bollman, Oscar	2, July 1854	Henry	----, Mary	E	204
Bollman, Otto Henry Joseph	30, Aug. 1852	Henry	----, Mary	E	13
Bollmann, Anna Maria Gesina	2, Nov. 1853	J. Bernard	Rackel, A. Helena Adel.	L	
Bollmann, Bernard Friedrich M.	17, June 1852	Friedrich	Dame, Lina	L	
Bollmann, Joseph Bernard Anton	8, Dec. 1854	Fritz	Dahne, Lisette	L	
Bollmer, Johan Bernard	16, May 1856	J. Bernard	Rakel, Helena A.	L	
Bolmer, Catharina Maria	15, Dec. 1857	Bernard	Lahrman, Catharina Maria	A	
Bolmer, Johan Bernard Heinrich	12, May 1859	J. Bernard	Larman, Maria Elisabeth	A	
Bolster, Gerhard Heinrich	9, Dec. 1851	Gerhard H.	Lageman, Anna Maria	A	
Bolster, Johan Bernard	24, Nov. 1852	Heinrich	Brüning, Catharina	D	358
Bolster, Maria Anna	13, Jan. 1851	J. Heinrich	Bruning, Maria Catharina	A	
Bolt, Mary Dora	10, Apr. 1852	Jeffery	----, Mary	P	20
Bolte, Anna Margaretha Philomena	23, Dec. 1850		adult - 26 years old	K	
Bolte, Johan Bernard	5, Oct. 1851	Heinrich	Hebling, Maria Anna	L	
Bolte, Maria Adelheid	12, Jan. 1859	Heinrich	Kemper, Gesina	J	48
Boltin, John	28, July 1855	William	----, Elizabeth	M	
Boltin, Margaret	15, Mar. 1854	William	----, Elizabeth	M	
Boltin, William	31, Jan. 1858	William	----, Elizabeth	M	
Bolton, Lucy Jane	1, Nov. 1852	William	Moore, Elizabeth	B	274
Bomery, Ellen	3, May 1850	William	O'Donnell, Mary	E	210
Bömmel, Johan Michael	20, Aug. 1854	Michael	Knoblauer, Dorothea	D	16
Bonacum, Edward Joseph	22, July 1851	Edward	Small, Mary	B	236
Bonacum, James	18, Apr. 1853	Edward	Small, Mary	B	289
Bond, Ann Catherine	25, Nov. 1855	Thomas	----, Susan	M	
Bond, Mary Theresa Augusta	21, Sept 1856	John	Ginocchio, Catherina	P	192
Böne, Friedrich Heinrich	22, July 1855	Heinrich G.	Hodeker, Gertrud M.	D	39
Boner, Emilia	28, May 1850	Anton	Schans, Magdalena	L	
Bonin, Carl Adam	2, Oct. 1859	Theodor	Schneller, Magdalena	F	
Bonker, Anna Catharina	28, Aug. 1859	Johan	Köbbe, Theresa	A	
Bonker, Clemens Heinrich	3, Apr. 1856	Johan	Kobbe, Anna Maria Theresa	A	
Bönker, Johan Heinrich Theodo	5, Feb. 1854	J. Herman	Kobbe, Anna Theresa	A	
Bonlanger, Magloire Felix	2, Nov. 1854	Louis	Gouvignor, Maria	C	
Bonn, Andreas Hugo	4, Aug. 1850	A.	Goettings, Jenna	D	227
Bonn, Bertha Theresa	8, July 1852	J. Heinrich	Koetting, Maria Anna	D	328
Bonn, Elisabeth	30, June 1854	Johan	Walter, M. Anna	C	
Bonn, Elisabeth Theresa	4, Jan. 1858	Heinrich	Bauer, Elisabeth	C	
Bonn, Ida	17, Nov. 1859	Joseph	Weber, Catharina	D	151
Bonner, James	14, Mar. 1852	Stephan	Hanley, Lucy	B	254
Bonner, Joseph Maria	16, May 1858	Stephan	Hanley, Lucy	B	59
Bonner, Lucy Clara	2, Sept 1855	Stephan	Hanley, Lucy	B	18
Bonner, Michael	14, May 1854	Stephan	Hanley, Lucy	B	314
Bonnert, Friedrich	19, Jan. 1851	Valentin	----, Catharina	K	

Name of Child	Date of Baptism	Father	Mother	Church	Page
Bonnert, Mathilda Elisabeth	7, Mar. 1852	Joseph B.	Ramloch, Elisabeth	D	311
Bonnet, Catharina Maria	18, Oct. 1857	Joseph	Dürk--, Maria	D	97
Bonny, Catherine	23, Dec. 1855	Andrew	Carey, Catherine	P	163
Bonny, Elizabeth	13, Sept 1857	Andrew	Carey, Catherine	P	223
Bonny, Esther	6, Nov. 1859	Andrew	Carey, Catherine	P	302
Bonny, John	23, Apr. 1854	Andrew	Carey, Catherine	P	80
Boos, Heinrich	21, June 1857	Heinrich	Baute, Dina	D	88
Boran, Dennis	8, July 1858	John	Connors, Catherine	E	547
Boran, Mary	15, May 1858	John	Hogan, Margaret	E	535
Boran, Mary Ann	22, Sept 1854	John A.	Scully, Bridget	V	18
Borbender, Catharina	13, Jan. 1854	Martin	Krieger, Sophia	C	
Borchard, Mary Louise	15, June 1851	Wendel	Lehmbert, Margaret	H	
Borchett, Anna Maria Justina	29, Sept 1853	Friedrich	Grimme, A.M. Elisabeth	F	
Borden, John	8, Oct. 1854	John	Coine, Bridget	E	230
Bores, Catherine	24, Jan. 1853	James	Kelly, Ann	E	57
Börgeding, Bernardina Carolina P.	21, Nov. 1852	Francis	Rabe, Maria Carolina	K	
Borgeding, Heinrich Joseph	4, Aug. 1859	Heinrich	Plagge, Maria Elis.	T	
Borgeding, Johan Heinrich Francis	2, Mar. 1851	Francis H.	Bove, Cun.	K	
Borgeding, Lawrence Heinrich	12, Aug. 1854	Francis	Rabe, Maria Carolina	K	
Borgeding, Maria Catharina Amelia	25, Mar. 1856	Francis	Rabe, Carolina	K	
Borgelt, Maria Gertrud	25, Mar. 1852	Herman	Frie, Maria Anna	C	
Borgelt, Philipp Friedrich	7, June 1855	Philipp	Poggenborg, Anna	A	
Borgemenke, Bernard Heinrich	8, Mar. 1859	Christoph	Lueken, Maria	F	
Borgemenke, Johan Christoph	28, July 1853	Johan H.	Blumberg, Sophia	A	
Borgemenke, Johan Franz Christoph	7, May 1854	Christoph	Luecken, Anna Maria	F	
Borgemenke, Johan Franz Heinrich	25, Sept 1856	Christoph	Lueken, Anna Maria	F	
Borgen, Mary	22, Oct. 1854	Patrick	----, Margaret	U	
Borger, Albert	16, Mar. 1851	Cletus	Geier, Gertrud	A	
Börger, Anna Margaretha Josephina	5, Nov. 1851	H. Heinrich	Spieker, Anna Margaretha	K	
Borger, Anna Maria Elisabeth	7, Aug. 1859	Caspar	Schmidt, Elisabeth	L	
Borger, Anna Maria Theresa	9, Apr. 1854	Heinrich	Spicke, Margaretha	K	
Börger, Anna Maria Veronica	17, Mar. 1853	August	Helmkamp, Anna Maria	K	
Borger, Catharina	1, Jan. 1858	Friedrich	Dick, Wilhelmina	T	
Börger, Elisabeth Catharina	15, Mar. 1859	Joseph	Uhlen, Francisca	A	
Borger, Francis Joseph	13, June 1858	Joseph	Kaiser, Carolina	D	113
Börger, Johan Heinrich	12, Nov. 1857	Joseph	Egbers, Maria	K	
Borger, Joseph	14, Sept 1851	Johan	Selm, Anna Maria	D	282
Börger, Joseph Heinrich	8, Dec. 1852	Joseph	Egbert, Louisa	K	
Börger, Lucia Louisa	4, May 1855	Joseph	Egbers, Louisa	K	
Borger, Maria	15, Mar. 1850	Peter	Ruh, Anna Maria	D	205
Börger, Maria Anna Josephina Phil.	18, Sept 1850	Joseph	Egbers, Louisa	K	
Börger, Maria Philomena Josephina	12, Mar. 1857	August	Helmkamp, Maria	K	
Borger, Wilhelm	25, Dec. 1856	Valentin	Erdel, Marianna	F	
Borgers, Anna Maria Helena	3, July 1852	Johan	Gudmann, Elisabeth	C	
Borgert, Maria Apollonia	10, May 1857	Michael	Drenel, Margaretha	D	84
Borges, Bernardina	24, Sept 1854	Johan	Gutmann, Elisabeth	C	
Borges, Johan Bernard Anton	7, Apr. 1857	Johan	Gutmann, Elisabeth	C	
Borges, Johan Heinrich	27, Apr. 1851	Francis	Kramer, Bernardina	C	
Borget, Anna Maria	15, June 1856	Albert	Lindauer, Sophia	A	
Borget, Anton Luke	21, Feb. 1858	Luke	Wo---, Maria	D	105
Borget, Catharina Louisa	11, Mar. 1854	Herman	Fries, Marianna	D	6
Borget, Herman Joseph	20, June 1857	Herman	Frie, Maria Anna	D	88
Borget, Johan Joseph Heinrich	15, Sept 1855	Herman	Fey, Maria Anna	D	42
Borglet, Elizabeth	19, Apr. 1859	Elisha	----, Celestine	E	618
Borgman, Bernard Heinrich	26, June 1851	J. Heinrich	Niehaus, Maria Angela	D	270
Borgman, Johan	11, Sept 1853	G. Adam	Feth, Anna	D	405
Borgman, Johan	6, Oct. 1851	G. Adam	Miller, Anna	D	286
Borgman, Maria Katharina	11, Dec. 1850	Johan	Frühlink, Maria Anna	A	
Borgmann, Angela Philomena	12, Jan. 1851	Johan	Klinghammer, Anna Maria	L	

Name of Child	Date of Baptism	Father	Mother	Church	Page
Borgmann, Bernard J. Heinrich	28, Feb. 1853	Joseph	Klekamp, M. Catharina	L	
Borgmann, Franz Heinrich	17, Jan. 1858	Johan	Klinkhammer, Catharina	L	
Borgmann, Friedrica Bernardina S.	11, Jan. 1853	Herman	Stodeur, Johanna	F	
Borgmann, Johan	26, Jan. 1851	Herman	Stodeur, Johanna	F	
Borgmann, Johan	27, Jan. 1850	Johan	Klinghammer, Anna M.	L	
Borgmann, Johan Christoph	19, July 1854	Johan	Frilling, Anna Maria	F	
Borgmann, Johan Herman	18, Sept 1855	Joseph	Deters, Catharina	L	
Borgmann, Johanna Catharina Jos.	3, Mar. 1850	Joseph	Deters, M. Catharina	L	
Borgmann, Maria Catharina	9, Jan. 1853	Joseph	Deters, M. Catharina	L	
Borgmann, Maria Elisabeth	12, Oct. 1858	Joseph	Deters, M. Catharina	L	
Borgmann, Marianna Johanna	12, Sept 1852	Johan	Fulling, Anna Maria	F	
Borgo, Aloysius Angel	16, Dec. 1855	Gitone	Surrena, Lucy Ann	E	333
Borgo, Nicholas Charles	25, Jan. 1852	J. William	Commeny, Serina	E	376
Bork, Isabella Cornelia	1, May 1859	Jacob	Saterland, Sophia	L	
Bork, John	15, Feb. 1850	Henry	----, Ellen	E	196
Borkel, Caspar Heinrich	13, Dec. 1857	Gerhard H.	Behrens, Bernardina	A	
Borkhart, Johan Paul	18, Aug. 1850	Ferdinand	---chter, Rosa	A	
Borman, Adam	26, June 1859	Valentin	Eveling, Anna	A	
Borman, Anna Maria	8, Dec. 1850	Wilhelm	Lux, Margaretha	D	246
Borman, Heinrich	5, Feb. 1858	Wilhelm	Lux, Margaretha	D	104
Borman, Wilhelm	23, Apr. 1855	Wilhelm	Lux, Margaretha	A	
Born, Alphons	6, Jan. 1856	Johan	Ratzel, Magdalena	F	
Born, Maria Elisabeth	26, July 1857	Johan	Ratzel, Magdalena	C	
Borndick, Maria Anna Catharina	12, July 1851	Johan	Hatke, Maria Anna	D	272
Bornens, Johan Friedrich Aloysius	8, Nov. 1854	Johan	Pardick, Anna Maria	A	
Bornhorn, Maria Anna	12, Sept 1858	Heinrich	Krummer, Margaretha	K	
Bornhorst, Bernard Aloysius	22, Feb. 1851	Bernard	Storig, Margaretha	K	
Bornhorst, Maria Elisabeth	23, Feb. 1853	Bernard	Störig, Margaretha	K	
Bornhorst, Maria Philomena	3, June 1855	Bernard	Storig, Margaretha	K	
Bornkamp, Herman Engelbert	30, May 1852	Heinrich	Ehgott, Catharina	N	7
Bornmann, Elisabeth	12, July 1857	Carl	Matsch, Maria	F	
Bornmann, Maria Henrica	11, Sept 1858	Carl	Mutsch, Maria	F	
Borntraeger, Anna Elisabeth	30, May 1852	Valentin	Albert, Anna Maria	D	322
Borntraeger, Barbara Francisca	27, Apr. 1856	Valentin	Albert, Anna Maria	D	57
Borntraeger, Francis	19, Sept 1858	Ludwig	Dieckmann, M. Anna	C	
Borntraeger, Johan Heinrich	30, May 1850	Ludwig	Dieckmann, M. Anna	C	
Borntraeger, Maria Anna	5, Mar. 1858	Valentin	Albert, Anna Maria	D	106
Borntraeger, Valentin	23, Jan. 1853	Ludwig	Dieckman, Maria Anna	D	366
Borntrager, Maria Elisabeth	20, Jan. 1856	Louis	Dieckmann, M. Anna	C	
Bornträger, Maria Magdalena Louisa	19, Mar. 1854	Valentin	Albert, Maria Magdalena	D	7
Borr, Johan Bernard	22, Nov. 1857	Johan	Borr, Maria	D	99
Borrglet, Louisa Anna	12, Oct. 1856	Elisha	Caellon, Celestina	G	
Borrglet, Margaretha Coelestina	19, Nov. 1854	Elisha	Caillon, Celestina	G	
Borsch, Adam Albert	28, May 1854	Johan	Tilzer, Elisabeth	K	
Borsch, Johan Francis	26, Sept 1858	Johan	Dilser, Elisabeth	K	
Bortlein, Philip	19, Dec. 1852	John	----, ----	H	
Bosche, Elisabeth	6, Apr. 1858	Theodor	Helmsing, Gertrud	F	
Bosche, Henry	5, Oct. 1857	Henry	----, Barbara	R	
Bosche, Johan Baptist	14, Apr. 1850	Heinrich	Foos, Barbara	H	
Bosche, Lludwig	28, Mar. 1858	Heinrich	Foos, Barbara	C	
Bosche, Martin	28, Mar. 1858	Heinrich	Foos, Barbara	C	
Bosche, Philip	11, Nov. 1855	Henry	----, Barbara	H	
Bosche, Valentin Heinrich	10, Aug. 1851	Heinrich	Foos, Barbara	D	277
Boschert, Helena	6, June 1852	Bernard	Madlinger, Genofeva	C	
Boschet, Andreas	15, June 1851	Wendelin	Berg, Catharina	D	268
Boschet, Johan	23, Dec. 1855	Wendelin	Bragel, Catharina	D	49
Boschi, Fabian Sebastian	26, Mar. 1854	Henry	----, Barbara	H	
Boschi, Maria Magdalena	5, Mar. 1851	Johan	Mangold, Agnes	H	
Böse, Maria Agnes	11, Jan. 1852	Theodor	Wiegelman, Maria Anna	A	

Name of Child	Date of Baptism	Father	Mother	Church	Page
Bosehart, Anna Maria	6, Dec. 1850	Bernard	Mathlinger, Genofeva	C	
Boseke, Francis	3, Apr. 1858	Heinrich	Reinecke, Margaretha	C	
Bosel, Wilhelm Heinrich	12, July 1857	J. Friedrich	Fiereck, Sophia	N	
Bosfeld, Carolina	20, July 1850	Christian	Borgmann, Anna	F	
Bosfeld, Maria Francisca	18, Feb. 1853	Christian	Borgman, Lucia Anna	D	372
Bosfeld, Maria Philomena Gesina	12, May 1859	Christian	Bergman, Lucia	D	137
Bosh, Thomas Henry	17, June 1855	Frederick	Viersch, Sibilla	N	
Boske, Anna Maria Elisabeth	3, Mar. 1858	Clemens	Knobbe, Anna	A	
Boske, Johan Theodor	11, Nov. 1855	Theodor	Helmsing, Gertrud	F	
Bosse, Anna Maria Elisabeth	3, Sept 1851	Heinrich	Schmiesing, Agnes	A	
Bosse, Franz Heinrich	27, Aug. 1857	Francis	Wiesmann, Catharina	L	
Bosse, Gerhard Heinrich	29, Mar. 1855	Francis	Wiesmann, Catharina	L	
Bosse, Johan Heinrich	24, May 1853	J. Heinrich	Schmising, Maria Agnes	N	13
Bosse, Joseph	16, Nov. 1852	Francis	Wissmann, Catharina	L	
Bosse, Maria Catharina	13, July 1856	J. Heinrich	Schmiesing, Agnes	N	
Bossen, Maria Anna	11, Dec. 1859	Francis	Wissmann, M. Catharina	L	
Bost, Jacob	11, Aug. 1850	Johan	Kieser, Catharina	D	227
Botscher, Appolonia Henrietta	19, Aug. 1852	Hirlander	----, ----	D	344
Bottelt, Johan Francis	4, July 1852	Francis	Stinewiede, Agnes	A	
Botter, Bernard Heinrich	31, May 1857	Theodor F.	Kettler, Antoinette	L	
Botter, Johan Wilhelm	21, Mar. 1852	Wilhelm G.	Ahrens, Henrica	A	
Botter, Maria Longina	26, Sept 1859	Gerhard H.	Thiers, M. Theresa	L	
Botter, Maria Theresa Rosalia	18, July 1858	Gerhard H.	Thier, M. Theresa	L	
Botter, Theodor Lucas Bernard	20, Mar. 1851	Theodor	Hackman, Maria Anna	A	
Böttker, Heinrich Wilhelm	19, Aug. 1855	J. Heinrich	Kuhlman, Maria Catharina	D	41
Böttker, Maria Anna	15, Apr. 1855	Bernard	Schrichten, Catharina	D	33
Botto, Charles	9, Feb. 1853	James	Devoto, Thomasena	B	283
Bötz, Johan	4, Mar. 1855	Ignatius	Zapf, Cunigunda	D	30
Boudet, John Benjamin	9, July 1854	Francis	----, Mary	M	
Boudinot, Anna Maria Josephina	23, Nov. 1856	John	----, Margaret	R	
Boudinot, Julia Paulina	15, Apr. 1858	John B.	----, Margaret	R	
Boughen, William	27, July 1851	John	Sweeney, Bridget	B	237
Boughman, Daniel	27, May 1853	David	adult - 32 years old	E	94
Boulger, Bridget	14, Feb. 1858	James	Brady, Catherine	U	
Boulger, Mary	20, July 1856	James	Brady, Catherine	U	
Boulich, Maria Eva	7, Nov. 1851	Johan	Zapp, Barbara	D	291
Boullie, Georg Jacob	17, Feb. 1850	Johan	Zapp, Barbara	D	202
Boullie, Margaretha	17, May 1855	Georg	Zellner, Anna Maria	D	35
Boullie, Nicolaus	28, Oct. 1855	Johan	Zapp, Barbara	D	45
Boullie, Peter	22, Feb. 1854	Johan	Zapp, Barbara	D	5
Bourgignon, Ludwig	4, Feb. 1855	Joseph	Jux, Gertrud	F	
Bourke, Mary	11, Aug. 1850	John	----, Ann	E	238
Boutet, Charles	19, Jan. 1850	Francis	Lennox, Olive	E	193
Boutet, Henry	7, Dec. 1851	Francis	----, Mary Olive	M	
Boutte, Wilhelm	9, Nov. 1856	Francis	----, Maria Olive	K	
Bovere, Helena	11, May 1851	Valentin	Riedinger, Ursula	C	
Boveri, Johan Heinrich	4, Sept 1853	Valentin	Ridinger, Ursula	D	404
Bovery, Benedict	22, May 1856	Valentin	----, Ursula	H	
Bovery, James	26, July 1857	Valentin	Riedinger, Ursula	H	
Böving, Anna Maria Catharina	23, Mar. 1850	H. Heinrich	Bröker, Anna Maria Catharina	D	206
Böving, Herman August	27, July 1855	Herman	Bröker, Catharina	D	39
Bovinkel, Johan Heinrich	29, Apr. 1851	Johan	Evermann, Elisabeth	C	
Bowen, Mary	21, Mar. 1852	Thomas	Milark, Sarah	B	254
Bower, Mary	15, Oct. 1854	James	Hehenhem, Mary	E	233
Bower, Mary Ellen	24, Apr. 1858	John	----, Mary	E	531
Bowers, Danreeth	22, Sept 1859		adult - 36 years old	E	656
Bowers, Edward Wallace	15, June 1856	Joseph	Phillips, Rachael	B	30
Bowers, Nicolaus	29, Jan. 1854	Patrick	Harrigan, Catharine	S	
Bowers, Sarah Helen	24, Oct. 1858	Robert	Noonan, Mary Ann	P	265

Name of Child	Date of Baptism	Father	Mother	Church	Page
Bowling, Patrick	21, Mar. 1853	Patrick	----, Catherine	B	287
Box, Ernestina Agusuta	19, Apr. 1852	Philipp	Ballahuser, Ernestina	K	
Box, Henrietta Augusta	16, Oct. 1853	Philipp	Ballhausen, Ernestina	C	
Boyce, John	22, Feb. 1854	Edmund	Murphy, Helen	T	
Boyce, Julia	14, Mar. 1852	George	Murray, Catherine	B	254
Boyce, Mary	9, June 1850	Michael	----, Margaret	E	220
Boyce, William Joseph	30, Aug. 1857	George	----, Catherine	E	476
Boyd, Robert	8, July 1850		adult - 29 years old	E	230
Boyd, Sarah	3, Mar. 1858		adult	B	56
Boylan, Catherine	7, Mar. 1852	James	Hall, Margaret	E	389
Boyle, Ann	5, July 1857	Patrick	White, Catherine	E	463
Boyle, Ann Catherin	18, Nov. 1855	Edward	McKenzie, Margaret	P	160
Boyle, Bridget	18, July 1852	Michael	----, Margaret	E	429
Boyle, Catherine	5, Sept 1850	Michael	----, Ann	E	246
Boyle, Catherine	23, May 1858	Patrick	----, Joanne	R	
Boyle, Daniel	12, Apr. 1856	James	----, Mary	R	
Boyle, David	22, Mar. 1857	David	Dugan, Margaret	E	442
Boyle, Edward	29, Apr. 1852	Bernard	----, Mary	E	407
Boyle, Edward	23, May 1858	Stephan S.	Peterson, Elizabeth	X	
Boyle, Edward Purcell	26, June 1859	John	McCloskey, Elizabeth	B	76
Boyle, Elizabeth	18, Nov. 1853	Stephan	Peterson, Elizabeth W.	B	302
Boyle, Emma Frances	18, Jan. 1857	John	Doherty, Elizabeth	B	39
Boyle, Francis Henry	30, Mar 1856	Charles	----, Theresa	H	
Boyle, Helen	12, Apr. 1854	John	----, Mary	B	313
Boyle, Helen	14, Oct. 1853	John	Geyby, Helen	E	134
Boyle, James	2, Jan. 1859	John	Gillman, Ann	B	69
Boyle, James	12, Oct. 1854	Patrick	Fleming, Bridget	P	100
Boyle, John	25, Aug. 1850	George	----, Catherine	E	242
Boyle, John	9, Nov. 1854	John	----, Elizabeth	M	
Boyle, John	1, July 1855	Michael B.	Hart, Margaret	V	25
Boyle, Joseph Daniel	29, Aug. 1858	Edward	McKenzie, Margaret	B	63
Boyle, Margaret	27, Mar. 1853	G.?	Matthews, Sarah Ann	P	37
Boyle, Margaret	17, Feb. 1856	John	----, Mary	E	346
Boyle, Mary	13, Feb. 1859	David	Duger, Margaret	E	603
Boyle, Mary	18, Sept 1853	James	Harris, Mary	R	
Boyle, Mary	2, June 1850	Michael	Ryan, Bridget	B	204
Boyle, Mary Frances	19, June 1851	Stephan S.	Peterson, Elizabeth W.	B	234
Boyle, Mary Louise	26, Nov. 1852	Charles	----, Theresa	H	
Boyle, Niall	25, Nov. 1854	Patrick	Moran, Mary	V	20
Boyle, Peter	23, Mar. 1856	John	Reilly, Catherine	U	
Boyle, Samuel	11, Apr. 1852	Robert	Miles, Joanne	B	256
Boyle, Sarah	23, Nov. 1856	Patrick	----, Joanne	R	
Boyle, Sophia Elisabeth	28, May 1854	Charles	----, Theresa	H	
Boyle, Thomas	8, June 1851	Thomas	Fanning, Bridget	B	233
Boyle, William	1, May 1855	David	Dwyer, Margaret	E	283
Boyle, William	25, Dec. 1853	George	Murray, Catherine	E	155
Boyle, William James	24, May 1857	William	Walsh, Mary Ann	Q	22
Boyleston, Edward	1, July 1851	Conrad	----, Ellen	E	320
Boylson, Joseph	29, June 1856	Edward	Murphy, Helen	T	
Br---, William	19, Mar. 1854	Bradford	Morris, Mary	P	74
Brabender, Friedrich Wilhelm	5, June 1859	Martin	Kroeger, Sophia	T	
Brabender, Gerhard	29, Mar. 1857	Martin	Kragel, Josephina	D	82
Brabender, Hubert	29, Mar. 1857	Martin	Kragel, Josephina	D	82
Bräcken, Elisabeth Catharina	14, Oct. 1852	Wilhelm	Englisch, Louise Philomena	K	
Bracken, Maria Francisca	24, Oct. 1850	Wilhelm	Engels, Louisa	K	
Bracken, Maria Theresa	21, Oct. 1859	Wilhelm	Angler, Lucia Philomena	K	
Bracken, Mary	10, Jan. 1850	Dennis	Flynn, Mary	E	191
Bracken, Theodor Xavier	24, Oct. 1850	Wilhelm	Englos, Louisa	K	
Bracken, Thomas Friedrich	24, Oct. 1850	Wilhelm	Englor, Louisa	K	

Name of Child	Date of Baptism	Father	Mother	Church	Page
Bräcker, Martina Friederica	14, Nov. 1852	Friedrich	Lacher, Martina	K	
Brackmann, Caspar Ludwig August	5, June 1853	Caspar H.	Fibbe, Maria Elisabeth	F	
Bradbury, Frederick Winands	25, Mar. 1857	William E.	Hoban, Sarah	B	42
Bradbury, Vincent	17, July 1856		adult - 26 years old	V	32
Bradbury, Vincent Charles	27, Aug. 1859	Vincent	Cunningham, Jane	E	649
Bradbury, William Edward	4, Sept 1853	William E.	Hoban, Sarah	B	298
Braddock, Bernard	28, Aug. 1853		Braddock, Sarah	P	50
Bradford, Ann	4, Mar. 1852	John	----, ----	P	19
Bradford, Mary Jane	24, Feb. 1852		adult - 22 years old	B	253
Bradhuber, Peter	10, Sept 1856	Sebastian	Lindenfels, Cath.	L	
Bradley, Ann	27, Jan. 1851	John	Gillaspie, Margaret	B	224
Bradley, Catherine	26, Oct. 1858	Gil	Husey, Bridget	E	572
Bradley, Catherine	24, Aug. 1855	Timothy	Bradley, Mary	E	309
Bradley, Edward	31, Jan. 1854	John	Gillasky, Margaret	E	164
Bradley, Edward	23, Jan. 1855	Patrick	----, Mary	M	
Bradley, Ellen	22, May 1856	Patrick	----, Mary	M	
Bradley, George Frank	25, Sept 1850	Hiram	----, Dina	E	250
Bradley, James	1, Apr. 1854	Bernard	Doyle, Elizabeth	V	12
Bradley, James	13, Oct. 1858	Thomas	McLaughlin, Ann	E	569
Bradley, James Albert	23, Feb. 1852	Silvester	Shellows, Margaret	E	385
Bradley, John	10, Sept 1850	John	Conolan, Ellen	B	213
Bradley, John	29, Sept 1850	Thomas	Gilaspy, Margaret	B	215
Bradley, John Neil	28, July 1855	John	----, Margaret	E	303
Bradley, Louis	11, June 1850	John	Langley, Mary	E	221
Bradley, Margaret	3, Jan. 1854	Timothy	Bradley, Mary	V	9
Bradley, Mary	30, Dec. 1851	John	Larkin, Mary	E	368
Bradley, Mary	21, Mar. 1852	Timothy	----, Mary	E	394
Bradley, Mary	13, May 1851	Wurler?	Cunningham, Bridget	E	307
Bradley, Mary Ann	13, May 1858	Patrick	----, Mary	M	
Bradley, Mary Elizabeth	12, Dec. 1857	Thomas	Doherty, Mary	B	53
Bradley, Patrick Francis	26, Mar. 1851	Bernard	Lyons, Elizabeth	E	295
Bradley, Rosanne Catherine	17, Sept 1852	Bernard	Doyle, Eliza	E	18
Bradley, Rose Ann	27, Mar. 1859	Andrew	Roony, Alice	E	614
Bradley, Stephen	27, Dec. 1850	Timothy	----, Mary	E	271
Bradley, Thomas	23, Apr. 1854	Michael	Bradley, Elizabeth	P	79
Bradley, Thomas	14, Oct. 1854	Thomas	----, Ann	E	232
Bradley, Thomas Peter	25, July 1856	Thomas	Dougherty, Mary	B	31
Brady, Alice	26, Mar. 1854	Peter	Carroll, Sarah	P	76
Brady, Ann	25, Jan. 1852	James	Heffernan, Johanna	B	251
Brady, Ann	2, Sept 1851	Patrick	McGinn, Mary	B	240
Brady, Ann	4, Dec. 1859	Peter	Dwire, Ann	S	
Brady, Bernard	15, Dec. 1853	Daniel	Dowd, Bridget	V	8
Brady, Bernard	13, Jan. 1856	Edward	Edwards, Helen	P	166
Brady, Bridget	8, Aug. 1852	James	----, Mary	M	
Brady, Bridget Martha	24, Sept 1854	James	Lyons, Penelope	S	
Brady, Catharine	9, July 1850	Patrick	Gwires, Mary	D	222
Brady, Catherine	6, Nov. 1859	John	Leddy, Bridget	B	83
Brady, Catherine	30, Nov. 1856	Patrick	Haden, Ellen	E	416
Brady, Catherine	20, Mar. 1859	Patrick	Sullivan, Catherine	E	612
Brady, Catherine	26, Sept 1852	Philip	Glenn, Catherine	B	270
Brady, Catherine	28, Dec. 1852	Thomas	----, Fanny	E	49
Brady, Christopher	1, Jan. 1854	Philipp	Higgins, Elisabeth	T	
Brady, Dennis	13, July 1859	Patrick	Hayden, Ellen	E	639
Brady, Euphemia	26, Sept 1858	Simon	Mulligan, Ann	S	
Brady, James	8, June 1856	James	Heffernen, Joanne	B	29
Brady, James	4, Apr. 1858	Simon	Callaghan, Margaret	S	
Brady, John	2, June 1850	James	Heffernen, Joanne	B	203
Brady, John	11, Jan. 1857	John	Leddy, Bridget	B	39
Brady, John	2, Oct. 1852	Joseph	----, Margaret	E	23

Name of Child	Date of Baptism	Father	Mother	Church	Page
Brady, John	26, Sept 1858	Simon	Mulligan, Ann	S	
Brady, Margaret	22, May 1857	Edward	Edwards, Ellen	P	213
Brady, Margaret	18, Jan. 1857	James	Costillo, Catherine	E	428
Brady, Margaret	6, Nov. 1859	Peter	Tierney, Catherine	B	83
Brady, Margaret	16, Jan. 1855	Philip	Glenn, Catherine	B	10
Brady, Mary	7, July 1850	James	----, Mary	B	206
Brady, Mary	12, Sept 1857	Patrick	Sheridan, Catherine	S	
Brady, Mary	2, Aug. 1857	Philip	Glenn, Catherine	E	472
Brady, Mary Ann	24, July 1859	Francis	Nolan, Catherine	B	77
Brady, Mary Ann	4, July 1852	James	Brady, Penelope	B	265
Brady, Mary Ann	12, Dec. 1852	Patrick	Hayden, Helen	B	277
Brady, Mary Elizabeth	21, Nov. 1858	James	Heffenan, Joanne	B	67
Brady, Matthew Frederick	25, Oct. 1857	Francis	Nolan, Catherine	B	51
Brady, Michael	26, Feb. 1851	Philipp	----, Catharine	D	255
Brady, Michael Apolinarus	10, Aug. 1851	Philip	----, Elisabeth	H	
Brady, Moses Edward	8, June 1856	Cormick	----, Elizabeth	M	
Brady, Patrick	17, Mar. 1854	James	Heffernan, Joanne	P	74
Brady, Peter	5, Aug. 1855	John	Lilly, Bridget	B	17
Brady, Robert	2, Sept 1850	William	Cahill, Mary	B	213
Brady, Susan	29, Jan. 1855	Patrick	Haden, Helen	E	261
Brady, Thomas	24, Jan. 1858	Patrick	Furlong, Mary	E	512
Brady, Thomas	19, Jan. 1851	Patrick	Hayden, Helen	B	223
Brady, Thomas	6, Nov. 1859	Simon	Callaghan, Margaret	S	
Brady, William	31, Oct. 1854	William	----, Catherine	E	237
Braendel, Martin Peter	17, Jan. 1858	Peter	Huck, Rosina	D	103
Bragany, William	24, Mar. 1859	James	Hopkins, Ellen	E	613
Bräger, Joseph Fridolin	20, Sept 1857	Fridolin	Lecher, Martina	K	
Brainen, Mary	15, Oct. 1856	Patrick	Curran, Helen	E	404
Brakel, Wilhelm Joseph	21, Nov. 1855	Wilhelm	----, ----	K	
Braker, Maria Friedrica	29, Oct. 1854	Friedrich	Lacher, Martina	K	
Braker, Veronica Angela	6, July 1855	August	Holliday, Mary	B	16
Braller, Johan Martin	16, May 1859	Johan	Kohl, Agnes	K	
Bram, Maria Helena Josephina	2, Dec. 1857	J. Herman	Kebbe, Maria Carolina	K	
Bramer, Francis Heinrich	1, Oct. 1859	Francis	Mueller, M. Anna	C	
Bramlage, Ann Mary Frances	15, Feb. 1855	William	----, Elisabeth	H	
Bramlage, Anna Maria Elisabeth	13, May 1857	Wilhelm	Tangman, Elisabeth	H	
Bramlage, Dorothea Elisabeth	1, Nov. 1859	Wilhelm	Teickman, Elisabeth	H	
Bramlage, Johan Bernard William	29, July 1852	William	----, Elizabeth	H	
Bramlage, Wilhelm Joseph	14, Apr. 1850	Ludwig	Fangman, Catharina	A	
Brammers, Johan Heinrich	8, Dec. 1850	Ferdinand	Boinman, Anna Maria	D	246
Branan, Anne	3, Sept 1850	James	----, Margaret	E	245
Brand, Andreas	10, Oct. 1852	Johan	Kohler, Maria	D	352
Brand, Anna Elisabeth	19, Sept 1858	Joseph	Klein, Margaretha	D	119
Brand, Anna Maria Theresa	28, Apr. 1858	J. Heinrich	Schmieman, Maria Catharina	K	
Brand, Barbara	9, Nov. 1856	Johan	Faeth, Elisabeth	D	71
Brand, Catharina	10, July 1853	Joseph	Klein, Margaretha	D	394
Brand, Catharina Elisabeth	5, May 1857	Bernard	Pöttkötter, Elisabeth	A	
Brand, Elisabeth	9, Dec. 1855	Johan	Kohler, Margaretha	D	48
Brand, Georg	4, June 1859	Johan	Köhler, Margaretha	D	139
Brand, Johan	18, May 1851	Johan	Fee, Elisabeth	D	265
Brand, Johan	30, May 1858	Johan	H---, Margaretha	D	112
Brand, Johan Bernard	26, July 1854	Bernard	Pottkötter, Elisabeth	A	
Brand, Johan Heinrich	28, Nov. 1858	Bernard	Postkotter, Elisabeth	A	
Brand, Joseph	5, July 1852	Heinrich	Herzog, Maria	K	
Brand, Joseph	1, Aug. 1852	Johan	Faeth, Elisabeth	D	341
Brand, Joseph	5, Aug. 1855	Joseph	Klein, Margaretha	D	39
Brand, Leo	28, Feb. 1858	Johan	Kohler, Maria	D	106
Brand, Maria Catharina	3, Sept 1855	Bernard	Pottkotter, Elisabeth	A	
Brand, Martin	28, Feb. 1858	Johan	Faeth, Elisabeth	D	106

Name of Child	Date of Baptism	Father	Mother	Church	Page
Brand, Philipp	22, Jan. 1854	Johan	Faeth, Elisabeth	D	2
Brand, Theresa	29, June 1856	Michael	Leitner, Maria	K	
Brand, Wilhelm	18, Jan. 1857	Joseph	Klein, Margaretha	D	77
Brandel, Andrew	13, July 1851	Andrew	Zanner, Theresa	H	
Brändel, Joseph Wilhelm	22, Jan. 1854	Jacob	Geis, Catharina	D	2
Brandel, Peter	30, Mar. 1856	Peter	Hucker, Rosa	D	55
Brandenburg, Francis Joseph	15, Nov. 1858		Brandenburg, Margaretha	A	
Brandes, Joseph Heinrich	20, Jan. 1859	Heinrich	Brock, Catharina	L	
Brandewide, Johan Heinrich	13, Jan. 1853	Bernard	Beckheinrich, Maria Elis.	A	
Brandewiede, Anna Maria	2, Oct. 1855	Bernard H.	Beckhinrichs, Elisabeth	A	
Brandewiede, Anton Bernard	6, Oct. 1852	Bernard	Bornhorst, Elisabeth	L	
Brandewiede, Christian Heinrich	27, Aug. 1851	Christian	Behrens, Maria Johanna	A	
Brandhof, Anna Maria Philomena	11, Mar. 1853	Gerhard	Pe----, Theresa	K	
Brandhoff, Gerhard Herman	1, June 1851	Johan	Limke, Elisabeth	L	
Brandhol, Maria Johanna	26, July 1854	Georg	Pötter, Theresa	K	
Brandhuber, Francis Anton	5, Nov. 1854	Sebastian	Lindenfels, Catharina	C	
Brandner, Joseph	29, Mar. 1858	Anton	Spindler, Anna Maria	A	
Brandner, Maria Anna Catharina	8, June 1856	Anton	Spindler, Maria	A	
Brandstetter, Juliana	13, Jan. 1856	Isidor	Spinner, Juliana	F	
Brandstetter, Maria Theresa	14, Nov. 1857	Isidor	-uin---, Maria Anna	D	98
Brandt, August Herman	27, Sept 1854	John H.	Lee, Joanne	B	6
Brandt, Catharina Elisabeth	16, Nov. 1856	Erwin	Schmidt, Catharina	D	72
Brandt, Erwin	21, Mar. 1858	Erwin	Schmidt, Catharina	D	107
Brandt, Francisca	21, Aug. 1852	Christian	Unlander, M. Anna Lisette	C	
Brandt, George Frederick	6, Nov. 1859	Frederick	Langton, Mary	V	62
Brandt, Josephina Bernardina	31, Oct. 1858	Michael	Lohmann, Catharina	C	
Brandt, Sophia Jane	25, Feb. 1856	John H.	Lee, Jane	B	25
Brandt, Valentin	16, Oct. 1859	Erwin	Schmidt, Catharina	D	149
Braney, John	5, July 1855	Malachai	Tracy, Ann	E	297
Branigan, Mary Jane	19, Oct. 1851	Edward	Wilson, Mary	P	13a
Brannagan, Catherine	24, Mar. 1853	James	----, Alice	E	76
Brannagan, Catherine	20, Mar. 1858	Patrick	Gorman, Eliza	P	243
Brannagan, Patrick	19, Dec. 1854	Patrick	Gorman, Eliza	P	111
Brannan, Cornelius	20, May 1859	Patrick	Carney, Mary	P	283
Brannan, Elizabeth	20, Jan. 1858	Patrick	----, Ann	E	511
Brannan, Henriette	5, Mar. 1854	Richard	Berry, Ellen	E	174
Brannan?, Michael	7, Feb. 1854	Thomas	Dunn, Mary	P	68
Branneck, Rose Ann	9, Sept 1852	Edward	Deuber, Rose	E	16
Brannigan, Rosanne	25, Aug. 1850	Edward	Mitchell, Frances A.	B	212
Brannigan, Rosanne	29, Apr. 1852	Patrick	Gorman, Eliza	B	264
Branning, Johan	19, June 1853	Daniel	Corner, Margaret	J	22
Branolf, John	9, Nov. 1857	William	Pireau, Angela	E	492
Brant, Anna Philomina Catharina	30, May 1856	J. Peter	Schmieman, Catharina	K	
Brant, John Henry	1, June 1857	Henry	Lee, Jane	B	45
Branwende, Margaretha Sophia	9, July 1850	Martin	Dreyer, Sophia	D	222
Brasken, Charlotte	7, Dec. 1851	Daniel	S----, Susan	B	247
Brauch, Johan Georg Heinrich	17, May 1857	Wilhelm	Schmidt, Elisabeth	A	
Brauer, Christian	13, Oct. 1857	Michael	Horter, Magdalena	D	97
Brauer, Clemens	10, Apr. 1854	Carl Ant.	Vogelheimer, Marg. E.	L	
Brauer, Heinrich Anton	15, Dec. 1859	Friedrich	Knipper, Magdalena	C	
Brauer, Maria	28, Apr. 1859	Michael	Hoerter, Magdalena	D	137
Braun, Adam	13, Aug. 1855	Anton	Winterhold, Maria	D	40
Braun, Andreas	3, Feb. 1856	Anton	Liebel, Margaretha	D	51
Braun, Anna	15, Oct. 1854	Johan	Roeder, Susanna	C	
Braun, Anna Margaretha	1, Nov. 1855	Johan	Lutz, Anna Maria	D	46
Braun, Anton	28, Mar. 1858	Anton	Liebel, Margaretha	D	108
Braun, Bernard	25, Mar. 1858	Gregor	Werner, Agnes	C	
Braun, Carl	3, Aug. 1858	Ludwig	Teicker, Barbara	D	116
Braun, Carl Valentin	10, Oct. 1858	Valentin	Bengert, Henrietta	J	48

Name of Child	Date of Baptism	Father	Mother	Church	Page
Braun, Carolina	8, Dec. 1857	Friedrich	Müller, Margaretha	J	44
Braun, Carolina	21, Mar. 1853	Nicolaus	Koch, Catharina	K	
Braun, Carolina Gertrud	3, Sept 1854	J. Peter	Veith, Josephina Crescentia	D	17
Braun, Catharina	19, June 1859	Anton	Jacob, Maria	S	
Braun, Catharina	24, Nov. 1854		Braun, Maria Theresa	D	22
Braun, Elisabeth	31, July 1859	Anton	Liebel, Margaretha	D	143
Braun, Elisabeth	3, June 1855	Nicolaus	Kuh, Catharina	A	
Braun, Elisabeth Catherine	24, Dec. 1854	Michael	----, Anna Maria	H	
Braun, Ferdinand	19, Sept 1858	Anton	Winterhalter, Maria	K	
Braun, Francis	24, July 1854	Georg	Ridmaier, Anna	D	14
Braun, Francisca	21, June 1857	Francis	Buerkle, Francisca	F	
Braun, Francisca	18, Feb. 1855	J. Anton	Nicolau, Catharina	D	29
Braun, Francisca Carolina	17, Dec. 1854	Leopold	Vogt, Maria Magdalena	D	24
Braun, Friedrich	24, Sept 1852	Wendelin	Rongert, Henrietta	J	18
Braun, Georg	3, June 1856		Braun, Margaretha	C	
Braun, Henrietta	29, Apr. 1855	Friedrich	Müller, Margaretha	J	32
Braun, Jacob	10, Oct. 1850		Braun, Elisabeth	D	237
Braun, Johan	3, July 1850	Johan	Lutz, Anna Maria	D	220
Braun, Johan	29, Nov. 1857	Johan	Lutz, Anna Maria	D	99
Braun, Joseph	25, Nov. 1852	Friedrich	Miller, Margaretha	J	18
Braun, Joseph	30, Mar. 1851	Joseph	Denzbach, Catharina	D	259
Braun, Joseph Peter	29, Mar. 1857	Carl A.	Walz, Josephina	D	81
Braun, Josephina	30, May 1858	Nicolaus	Kern, Catharina	A	
Braun, Louisa	24, Aug. 1856	Leopold	Vogt, Magdalena	D	65
Braun, Louisa	24, Oct. 1852	Johan	Lutz, Anna Maria	D	355
Braun, Magdalena	2, Mar. 1858	Leopold	Vogt, Magdalena	D	106
Braun, Margaretha	12, May 1850	Nicolaus	Kuhn, Catharina	A	
Braun, Margaretha Henrietta	6, July 1856	Valentin	Bongert, Henrietta	J	36
Braun, Maria	20, June 1852	Joseph	Danzbach, Catharina	D	325
Braun, Maria Anna	30, Jan. 1853	Johan	Kraus, Eva	S	
Braun, Maria Anna	14, July 1850	Valentin	Bonert, Henrietta	A	
Braun, Maria Elisabeth	11, Dec. 1859	Mathias	Braun, Elisabeth	A	
Braun, Maria Elisabeth	17, Nov. 1850	Peter	Veit, Crescentia	D	243
Braun, Maria Eva	28, June 1857	Michael	Buettner, Anan Maria	H	
Braun, Maria Johanna	25, Aug. 1850	Peter	Young,	J	6
Braun, Maria Magdalena	2, June 1850	Friedrich	Müller, Margaretha	J	6
Braun, Maria Theresa	4, Oct. 1857	Urban	Huber, Helena	C	
Braun, Maria Veronica	25, July 1858	John	Wildes, Mary	H	
Braun, Mathias Joseph	11, Feb. 1855	Andreas	----, Carol	H	
Braun, Michael	22, Aug. 1850	Michael	Boettner, Maria	H	
Braun, Norbert	1, Jan. 1855	Bernard	Orkert, Catharina	K	
Braun, Peter	8, Sept 1852	Michael	----, Mary	H	
Braun, Philipp Ludwig	28, June 1857	Peter	Veit, Crescentia	D	88
Braun, Rosa	21, July 1857	Georg	Goetz, Carolina	C	
Braun, Rosalia	21, July 1857	Georg	Goetz, Carolina	C	
Braun, Theresa	25, Sept 1859	Jacob	R---, Francisca	D	147
Braun, Valentin	11, Oct. 1856	Anton	Windehard, Maria	D	69
Braunstein, Bernard Joseph	5, Sept 1857	F. Xavier	Schierberg, Maria Catharina	K	
Braunstein, Carl Borromeo	5, Feb. 1852	Francis X.	Schierberg, Maria Catharina	K	
Braunstein, Clara Elisabeth	6, Dec. 1853	Francis X.	Schierberg, Catharina	K	
Braunstein, Francis Xavier	2, Nov. 1855	Francis X.	Schierberg, Catharina	K	
Braunstein, Maria Catharina Theresa	25, Nov. 1859	F. Xavier	Schierberg, Catharina	K	
Braunstetter, Martin Ignatius	17, Apr. 1859	Isidor	Dumbacher, Maria Anna	N	
Braunwart, Adam Joseph	17, May 1858	Michael	Piek, Margaretha	C	
Brawley, John	13, Aug. 1850	Daniel	Foley, Mary	B	210
Bray, Albert M.	2, Aug. 1850	Aaron	Reeve, Mary Ann	E	236
Bray, John	2, Aug. 1850	Aaron	Reeve, Mary Ann	E	236
Brayne, John	28, July 1852	Peter	Riley, Joanne	B	266
Brecht, Francis Carl	30, June 1851	Carl	Eckel, Wilhelmina	C	

Hamilton County, Ohio Roman Catholic Baptism Records -- 1850 - 1859

Name of Child	Date of Baptism	Father	Mother	Church	Page
Brecht, Louise Barbara	5, Oct. 1851	Peter	Heidemann, Louise	C	
Brecht, Maria Hermina Carolina	8, Jan. 1850	Carl	Jeckel, Hermina	C	
Brechtel, Maria Francisca	14, Feb. 1853	Bernard	Bruder, Lutgardis	D	371
Breckey, Elizabeth	7, May 1851	John	McGrath, Ann	E	305
Brecks, Catharina	25, Oct. 1855	Wilhelm	Behrman, Maria Anna	A	
Bredestege, Herman Joseph	8, Apr. 1856	Joseph	Hinkelamet, Catharina	D	56
Bredestege, Johan Herman	8, Apr. 1856	Joseph	Hinkelamet, Catharina	D	56
Bredestege, Philomena Catharina	23, Feb. 1855	Joseph	Hinkelsman, M. Catharina	D	29
Bredestegge, Johan Herman Joseph	7, Feb. 1858	Joseph	Hinkelamet, Anna Maria	F	
Bree, Johan Joseph	2, Aug. 1853	Johan	Meier, Marianna	F	
Bree, Maria Catharina	26, May 1859	Johan A.	Meier, Maria	F	
Bree, Maria Gertrud	9, Feb. 1851	Johan	Meyer, M. Anna	C	
Breen, Bridget	26, Oct. 1858	John (+)	Fogarty, Bridget	E	572
Breen, Catherine	17, Sept 1859	James	----, Mary	E	654
Breen, Catherine	5, Oct. 1856	James	Tumilty, Mary	V	34
Breen, Catherine Cecilia	25, May 1856	Peter	Ward, Joanne	P	181
Breen, Charles	29, Jan. 1854	Peter	Reilly, Joanne	P	67
Breen, Cornelius	20, Aug. 1853	Patrick	Gill, Mary	E	120
Breen, Edmund	22, Jan. 1854	Edmund	Mulcahill, Peggy	E	161
Breen, Edward	24 May 1857	Edward	----, Ann	M	
Breen, Edward	19, Apr. 1857	Edward	Tracy, Margaret	V	38
Breen, Ellen	29, Dec. 1858	Patrick	Fitzgerald, Bridget	E	591
Breen, Ellen	20, Feb. 1859	Peter	Reilly, Jane	P	276
Breen, Honora	12, June 1859	Edward	Tracy, Margaret	B	76
Breen, Honora	20, July 1856	John	Fogerty, Bridget	E	382
Breen, John	27, Feb. 1859	Edward	----, Ann	M	
Breen, John	18, Apr. 1855	J.	----, Mary	E	280
Breen, Margaret	24, Apr. 1859	James	Tumulty, Mary	B	74
Breen, Margaret	10, Oct. 1854	John	Fogerty, Bridget	E	230
Breen, Mary	9, Dec. 1857	James	Tumilty, Mary	V	42
Breen, Mary	14, Jan. 1855	Patrick	Gill, Mary	E	256
Breen, William	17, Feb. 1850	Peter	O'Brien, Ann	B	196
Bregelmann, Anton Joseph	4, June 1852	Anton	Krogmann, M. Elisabeth	C	
Bregenzer, Elisabeth	1, Oct. 1857	Joseph	Sta---, Anna Maria	D	95
Brehe, Herman Heinrich Rudolph	12, June 1858	Rudolph	Strothmeier, Dorothea	L	
Brehm, Genofeva	19, Jan. 1855	Mathias	----, ----	F	
Brehm, Georg	31, Dec. 1857	Friedrich	Dein, Eva	D	101
Brehm, Maria Catharina	2, Aug. 1857	Andreas	Butscher, M. Anna	C	
Brehm, MariaKunigunda	20, Nov. 1859	Friedrich	Dein, Eva	D	151
Brehm, Nicolaus	21, Sept 1856	Friedrich	Deim, Eva	D	68
Brehmann, Johan Francis	17, Dec. 1854	Heinrich	Rebbers, Anna M.	C	
Brehn, Heinrich	13, Nov. 1853	Andreas	Butscher, Anna Maria	D	414
Breier, Carl	24, May 1857	Gregor	Buechele, Magdalena	F	
Breier, Francisca Magdalena	13, Mar. 1859	Gregor	Spiegele, Magdalena	F	
Breier, Franz	17, Apr. 1859	Francis	Adams, Margaretha	F	
Breigenherter, Francis Heinrich	23, Apr. 1857	Heinrich	Vernendiff?, Maria Anna	D	83
Breiling, Catharina Maria	10, Apr. 1856	Arnold	Seiler, Margaretha	F	
Breiling, Ludwig	12, Oct. 1854	Arnold	Seiler, Margaretha	F	
Breiling, Maria Margaretha	19, Aug. 1858	Arnold	Seiler, Margaretha	D	117
Brein---?, Catharina Philomena	18, Jan. 1852	J. Herman	Heitmeier, Catharina	D	303
Breinert, Catherine	25, Oct. 1857	Heinrich	----, Margaretha	U	
Breit, Josephina	15, Aug. 1858	Carl	Beer, Carolina	D	117
Breitelheim?, Francis Peter	5, Apr. 1857	Francis P.	Ell, Josephina	D	82
Breitenbach, Elis. Carolina Margaretha	22, June 1852	Ludwig	Nortman, Carolina	D	326
Breitenbach, Johan	1, May 1853	Adam	Jasker, Catharina	A	
Breitenbach, Johan Carl	5, Oct. 1856	August	Weber, Maria	F	
Breitenbach, Maria Magdalena	13, Dec. 1857	Ludwig	Nordman, Carolina	H	
Breitenbach, Walter Ludwig	7, Jan. 1855	Ludwig	Nordman, Charlotte	D	26
Breitenstein, Anna Maria	25, Sept 1856	Johan	Koch, Barbara	C	

Name of Child	Date of Baptism	Father	Mother	Church	Page
Breitenstein, Bertha	29, June 1858	Johan	Koch, Barbara	C	
Breitenstein, Heinrich Joseph	23, Feb. 1855	Luke	Lastenbier, Sophia	D	29
Breitenstein, Johan Ludwig	28, June 1857	Luke	Lorenbier, Sophia	D	88
Breitenstein, Ludwig	20, Apr. 1851	Lawrence	Enrich, Elisabeth	D	261
Breitenstein, Wilhelm	21, July 1854	Johan	Koch, Barbara	D	14
Breiter, Catharina	1, Oct. 1854	Conrad	Buehler, Catharina	F	
Brekers, Bernard Heinrich	24, Nov. 1858	Heinrich	Hünker, Maria	A	
Brels, Francisca Catharina	20, Apr. 1851	Peter	Steger, Catharina	D	261
Brelss, Peter	28, Feb. 1858	Peter	Steger, Catharina	D	106
Brelz, Maria Josephina	10, Oct. 1852	Peter	Steger, Catharina	D	352
Bremer, Maria Catharina Magalene	19, Dec. 1852	Emil	Wisker, Elisabeth	Q	2
Bremke, Armandte	22, Jan. 1855	Joseph	Unluecke, Antonette	L	
Bremke, Catharina Elisabeth	22, July 1857	Caspar	Eppenbrock, Elisabeth	C	
Bremke, Maria Mathilda	1, July 1857	Heinrich	Unluecke, Anna M.	L	
Bremm, Martin	1, Jan. 1857	Gregor	Beckel, Margaretha	D	76
Brenan, Michael	1, Oct. 1851	Simon	Donnelly, Margaret	B	242
Brenan, Michael	19, Sept 1850	Thomas	Haley, Mary	B	214
Brendel, Adam	11, Nov. 1855	Jacob	Geis, Catharina	D	46
Brendel, Andrew	2, Dec. 1855	Andrew	----, Theresa	H	
Brendel, Catharina Margaretha	16, Mar. 1855	Georg	Dombach, Christina	L	
Brendel, Johan	31, Dec. 1854	Georg	Dombach, Christina	L	
Brendel, Johan Wilhelm	27, Dec. 1857	Jacob	Geis, Catharina	D	101
Brendel, Maria Christina	1, Mar. 1857	J. Georg	Dumbach, Christina	C	
Brendl, Anna Catharina	29, May 1859	Valentin	----, Maria	D	139
Brendl, Clara	21, July 1857	Valentin	Hartman, Margaretha	D	91
Brendl, Wilhelm Valentin	20, Jan. 1856	Valentin	Hartman, Margaretha	D	50
Brenly, John	30, Oct. 1854	John	----, ----	E	236
Brennan, Ann	9, Feb. 1857	Patrick	----, Ann	E	432
Brennan, Ann	12, Dec. 1852	Patrick	Kalaher, Mary	B	277
Brennan, Bridget	21, Nov. 1852	James	King, Bridget	B	275
Brennan, Bridget	30, Nov. 1851	Martin	White, Joanne	B	246
Brennan, Catherine	28, July 1850	James	King, Bridget	B	208
Brennan, Catherine	15, Dec. 1850	John	Harris, Bridget	B	220
Brennan, Edward	28, Feb. 1858	Thomas	Quinn, Bridget	B	56
Brennan, Elizabeth	5, Feb. 1854	Edward	----, Margaret	M	
Brennan, Elizabeth	5, May 1859		Brennan, Catherine	E	622
Brennan, Francis Joseph	26, June 1855	John	Dunn, Joanne	P	137
Brennan, Henry William	24, June 1855	Timothy	Byrne, Sarah	B	16
Brennan, James	12, Mar. 1852	Edward	----, Margaret	M	
Brennan, James	15, Dec. 1854	Jeremiah	----, Mary	M	
Brennan, James	11, Apr. 1855	John	----, Margaret	M	
Brennan, John	14, Sept 1857	Christopher	Burns, Ann	P	224
Brennan, John	15, Feb. 1857	Patrick	Kearny, Mary	P	206
Brennan, John	3, Apr. 1859	Patrick	Murphy, Ellen	P	281
Brennan, John	20, Jan. 1856	Thomas	Quinn, Bridget	B	24
Brennan, Julia	11, Mar. 1855	Thomas	Carroll, Julia	P	124
Brennan, Luke	1, Dec. 1850	Patrick	----, Mary	B	219
Brennan, Margaret	13, Sept 1857	Timothy	Byrne, Sarah	P	224
Brennan, Mary	26, Oct. 1851	Patrick	Rooney, Eliza	B	244
Brennan, Mary	12, Mar. 1854	Edward	Coke, Bridget	B	311
Brennan, Mary	12, Nov. 1854	Patrick	Kehoe, Mary	B	7
Brennan, Mary	25, Dec. 1853	Thomas	Quinn, Bridget	B	305
Brennan, Mary Ann	18, Apr. 1852	Thomas	----, Julia	B	257
Brennan, Mary Ann	9, Mar. 1851	William	Collam, Ann	B	228
Brennan, Michael	22, Oct. 1855	John	Brennen, Ellen	E	322
Brennan, Michael Terrence	15, Apr. 1852	Patrick	Linch--, Ann	B	256
Brennan, Patrick	25, Jan. 1852	Thomas	Quinn, Bridget	B	251
Brennan, Patrick Joseph	23, May 1859	Patrick	Monroe, Ann	E	627
Brennan, Richard	10, Nov. 1850	Thomas	Carroll, Julia	B	218

Name of Child	Date of Baptism	Father	Mother	Church	Page
Brennan, Thomas	21, Dec. 1851	Daniel	Conn, Catherine	B	248
Brennan, Thomas	12, Apr. 1858	Edward	----, Margaret	R	
Brennan, Thomas	9, Feb. 1859	Patrick	O'Farrel, Ann	P	275
Brennan, Thomas James	1, Sept 1850	Timothy	----, Sarah	E	244
Brennan, Thomas William	3, Oct. 1858	James P.	Flynn, Catherine	B	65
Brennan, Timothy	11, Sept 1853	Timothy	Byrne, Sarah	P	52
Brennan, William	9, Mar. 1859	John	Livingston, Mary	E	610
Brennan, William	15, Mar. 1850	Martin	Brennan, Jane	B	198
Brennan, William	14, Aug. 1859	Thomas	Carroll, Julia	P	292
Brenneis, Maria Gertrud Philomena	29, Jan. 1856	Johan	Sohn, Maria Anna	K	
Brenneis, Maria Susanna	29, Nov. 1850	Johan	Sohn, Susanna	A	
Brennen, Emanuel	13, Nov. 1859	J. Georg	Bold, Josephina	C	
Brennen, Johan Carl	13, Nov. 1859	J. Georg	Bold, Josephina	C	
Brenner, Anton	14, June 1857	Conrad	Steuerwald, Gertrud	D	87
Brenner, Benedict Seraphin	16, Sept 1855	Johan	Schröder, Henrietta	D	42
Brenner, Elisabeth	24, Nov. 1856	Michael	----, Magdalena	H	
Brenner, Felicitas	27, Nov. 1853	Johan	Schroeder, Henrietta	D	417
Brenner, Franz Alexander	25, Oct. 1857	Georg J.	Bold, Josephina	F	
Brenner, Georg Friedrich	25, Mar. 1859	Conrad	Steigerwald, Gertrud	D	134
Brenner, Gertrud	11, Oct. 1857	Johan	Schroeder, Henrietta	D	96
Brenner, Heinrich	19, Oct. 1851	Johan	Schröder, Henrietta	D	288
Brenner, Heinrich	13, Dec. 1859	Johan	Schröder, Henrietta	D	152
Brenner, Helena	3, July 1859	Joseph	----, Rosalia	F	
Brenner, Johan	20, Jan. 1856	Conrad	Steigerwald, Gertrud	D	50
Brenner, Johan	14, Apr. 1850	Johan	Schröder, Henrietta	D	209
Brenner, Johan	10, Oct. 1852	Michael	Seibert, Magdalena	D	352
Brenner, Johan Carl	7, Sept 1856	Francis	Bolth, Johanna	C	
Brenner, Maria Magdalena	31, May 1857	Rudolph	Reisenm---, Theresa	D	86
Brenner, Rosalia	20, June 1858	Joseph	Sche---, Rosina	D	113
Bres, Johan Joseph	6, July 1856	Johan	Meyer, Marianna	F	
Breslahan, Cornelius	21, Feb. 1858	Daniel	Karney, Bridget	E	518
Breslan, Joanne	26, Sept 1852	John	Brown, Ellen	E	22
Breslan, Mary Jane	3, Oct. 1852	Jeremiah	Kenny, Mary	P	28
Breslehan, Joanne	12, Dec. 1853	Patrick	----, Margaret	E	152
Breslehan, Thomas	1, Feb. 1856	Patrick	----, Margaret	E	341
Bresler, Georg	19, Nov. 1854	Georg	Auer, Barbara	A	
Bresler, Mary	17, Jan. 1850	A.	Brophy, Mary	B	194
Breslin, Margaret	19, Oct. 1851	Patrick	Connell, Margaret	E	352
Bresnahan, Matthew	12, Sept 1859	Michael	McCarthy, Margaret	E	653
Bresser, Catharina Elisabeth	10, Aug. 1856	Theodor	Plaspohler, Elisabeth	C	
Bresser, Heinrich Lucas Johan	18, July 1858	Theodor	Flaspohl, Elisabeth	C	
Bresser, Heinrich Wilhelm	18, Oct. 1857	Heinrich	Flaspohler, M. Cath.	L	
Bresser, Johan Theodor	20, Apr. 1854	Bernard	Flaspohler, Catharina	C	
Bresser, Johan Theodor Bernard	5, Sept 1859	Gerhard H.	Flaspohler, M. Cath.	L	
Bresser, Maria Catharina Elisabeth	4, Jan. 1856	Gerhard	Flaspohler, Catharina	C	
Brette, Clement	16, Feb. 1851	Peter	Norten, Elisabeth	Q	1
Brettle, Joseph	6, Oct. 1859	Joseph	Stutters, Helen	E	661
Bretty, Philipp	4, Aug. 1852	Patrick	Mequaire, Maria	F	
Breuner, Christina	1, Jan. 1850	Joseph	Burkhard, Christina	D	197
Brewer, Catherine	1, May 1859	Philip	Caughlin, Ann	E	622
Brewer, Peter	28, May 1854		adult	B	315
Brewster, John	5, July 1850	John	Hilton, Julia	B	206
Brewster, John Randolph	Aug. 1850	John R.	Hilton, Julia	B	212
Brian, Catherine	3, Apr. 1859	Luke	Clifford, Hannah	B	73
Bricchetto, Maria Louisa Catharina	28, July 1858	Joseph	Arata, Johanna	B	62
Bricchetto, Maria Rosa Philomena	28, July 1858	Joseph	Arata, Johanna	B	62
Bricheti, Rosa Justina	19, Apr. 1857	Antonio	Nazana, Antonia	K	
Brichler, Gertrud	15, Oct. 1852	Georg	Wörz, Gertrud	D	353
Brichler, Margaretha	29, July 1855	Joseph	Müller, Mechtildis	A	

Name of Child	Date of Baptism	Father	Mother	Church	Page
Brichler, Nicolaus	20, Dec. 1857	Joseph	Miller, Julia	A	
Brick, Barbara	21, Mar. 1858	Nicolaus	Liebling, Theresa	A	
Brickerhoff, Francis Anton Ignatz	29, Oct. 1854	Johan	Trilling, Helena	C	
Brickler, Barbara	5, May 1850	Georg	Wirtz, Gertrud	C	
Brickley, Mary	12, Apr. 1850	John	McCarthy, Mary	B	200
Brickman, Georg	20, Nov. 1859	Johan	Resch, Elisabeth	U	
Bricknell, Mary Barter	14, Feb. 1857	William	Brough, Mary	T	
Brickwedde, Carl Wilhelm	20, Aug. 1858	Heinrich	Buschermuhle, Agnes	L	
Brickwedde, Carolina Dorothea	7, Feb. 1855	Heinrich	----, Bernardina	K	
Brickwede, Johan Heinrich	19, Nov. 1850	Nicolaus	Grozeschafer, Maria Elisabeth	D	243
Briede, Johan Gerhard Heinrich	15, Sept 1857	J. Theodor	Weller, Anna Maria	D	94
Brieden, Anna Maria Rosa	19, Oct. 1859	Theodor	Wellen, Anna Maria	D	149
Brielmeyer, Anna Maria	24, Dec. 1858	Anthony	Schmidt, Barbara	H	
Brien, Dennis	31, Dec. 1856	Michael	Brogan, Margaret	B	38
Brien, James	9, Dec. 1855	Patrick	Cohfield, Margaret	U	
Brien, Margaret	9, Oct. 1855	Michael	Stableton, Mary	U	
Brien, William	5, Mar. 1858		adult - 36 years old	E	519
Brieshof, Mary Elisabeth	19, Aug. 1859	Gerhard H.	Helmkamp, Anna Maria	D	144
Brige, Anna Agnes	3, Jan. 1858	Joseph	McGuire, Mary Ann	A	
Brigel, Johan Baptist	8, May 1851	Conrad	Memel, Cunigunda	H	
Brigel, Maria Veronica	20, Dec. 1855	Conrad	----, Cunigunda	H	
Briggeman, Maria Anna Wilhelmina	25, July 1858	Adolph	Stoer, Walburga	D	115
Briggman, Johan	15, Feb. 1857	Johan	R-fel, Elisabeth	D	79
Brighetti, Marianna	7, Aug. 1854	Antonio	Nadana, Antonia	P	91
Brigler, Anna Maria	17, Aug. 1851	Joseph	Jung, Barbara	A	
Brigman, Mary Angela	21, Nov. 1855	John A.	Baker, Angela	P	160
Brignola, Pietro Angelo Luigi	26, Mar. 1859	Michael	Querola, Annantiata	K	
Brill, Carl Heinrich	2, Mar. 1856	Georg	Seifert, Elisabeth	K	
Brill, Catharina Elisabeth	9, May 1858	Johan	Gehrich, Theresa	F	
Brill, Emanuel	21, Feb. 1858	Georg	Seifert, Elisabeth	D	105
Brill, Georg Joseph	2, May 1852	J.	Seifert, Elisabeth	K	
Brill, Johan Edward	22, Oct. 1854	Georg	Seifert, Elisabeth	K	
Brill, Johan Georg	25, May 1856	Johan	Gerig, Theresa	F	
Brill, Johan Wilhelm	24, Apr. 1853	Georg	Seiffert, Elisabeth	K	
Brill, Kunigunda	27, Nov. 1853	Johan	Gerig, Theresa	F	
Brill?, Philipp Wilhelm	24, June 1850	Johan	Oberding, Carolina	D	219
Brille, Carolina	6, Sept 1857	Johan	Kohl, Agnes	K	
Brille, Maria Louisa	1, Apr. 1856	Johan	Kohl, Agnes	K	
Brillmeyer, Barbara Amanda	31, Aug. 1856	Martin	Huppman, Catharina	H	
Brillmeyer, Eli Martin	18, Mar. 1855	Martin	----, Catherine	H	
Brillmeyer, Erhard Francis	28, Mar. 1858	Martin	Hoffman, Catherine	H	
Brimmelhaus, Herman Heinrich	27, Apr. 1851	Bernard H.	Bromerkamp, Maria Adelheid	A	
Brinckman, Maria Anna	15, Sept 1850	B.	Wiggerman, Agnes	A	
Brinckschneider, Anna Maria Elisabeth	4, Feb. 1852	Johan	Daming, Angela	K	
Bringelman, Maria Elisabeth	10, Feb. 1856	J. Bernard	Dreyer, Maria Catharina	A	
Bringelmann, Anna Maria Catharina	14, July 1854	Friedrich	Schottmer, Christina	L	
Bringelmann, Herman Heinrich	14, Oct. 1856	Friedrich	Schoetmer, A. Christina	L	
Bringelmann, Johan Bernard	12, Apr. 1852	Johan F.	Schoetmann, Christina	L	
Bringschneider, Gertrud	15, July 1858	Herman	Hildenhold, Gertrud	N	
Brink, Anna Maria Theresa	23, Oct. 1852	J. Heinrich	Niehaus, M. Anna	C	
Brink, Gerhard Franz	1, Jan. 1858	Gerhard	Picker, Catharina	F	
Brink, Johan Gerhard	22, Nov. 1852	Heinrich	Pundsak, Josephina	F	
Brink, Maria	26, Feb. 1855	Heinrich	Niehaus, M. Anna	C	
Brink, Maria Josephina	24, Feb. 1851	Johan H.	Sundsack, Josephina	F	
Brink, Marianna	12, July 1855	Gerhard	Becker, Catharina	F	
Brinke, Maria Anna	28, Jan. 1851	Heinrich	Niehaus, Maria Anna	D	251
Brinkelman, Anna Christina	4, Feb. 1850	Bernard	Dreyer, Catharina	A	
Brinkelman, Anna Maria Elisabeth	20, July 1852	Bernard	Dreiers, Maria Catharina	A	
Brinker, Bernard Theodor	9, Oct. 1859	Theodor	Wessendarp, Elisabeth	L	

Name of Child	Date of Baptism	Father	Mother	Church	Page
Brinker, Catharina Philomena	28, June 1858	Bernard	Wellen, Catharina	D	114
Brinker, Francis Joseph	28, Apr. 1853	Gerhard	VonderHeide, Bernardina	K	
Brinker, Friedrich Mathias	10, Mar. 1855	Gerhard	VonderHeide, Dina	K	
Brinker, Gerhard Heinrich	6, Sept 1859	Georg H.	VonderHeide, Bern.	C	
Brinker, Heinrich Franz	15, Apr. 1855	Heinrich	Pundsak, Josephina	F	
Brinker, Johan Heinrich	26, Jan. 1858	J. Heinrich	Fehrmann, Anna Maria	L	
Brinker, Margaretha Bernardina	6, Aug. 1857	Joseph	Geise, Bernardina	A	
Brinker, Maria Catharina Josephnia	5, Oct. 1850	Herman	Heitman, Catharina	D	236
Brinker, Maria Clara	12, Aug. 1856	Bernard	Wellen, Catharina	D	64
Brinker, Maria Elisabeth	31, May 1857	Georg	VonderHeide, Catharina	C	
Brinkers, Anna Maria Catharina	4, Aug. 1850	J. Heinrich	Fermanns, Anna M.	C	
Brinkers, Anna Maria Elisabeth	29, Dec. 1854	Johan H.	Birmann, A. Maria	L	
Brinkers, Anna Maria Margaretha	4, Dec. 1853	J. Bernard	Tebben, Euphemia	L	
Brinkers, Anna Philomena	20, Jan. 1857	J. Bernard	Teben, Euphemia	L	
Brinkers, Bernard Anton	3, Sept 1855	Bernard H.	Fricks, Euphemia	L	
Brinkers, Bernard Heinrich	6, Mar. 1853	J. Heinrich	Fermann, Anna Maria	L	
Brinkers, Euphemia Adelheid	17, Oct. 1858	J.H.	Graman, M. Agnes	A	
Brinkers, Herman Heinrich	5, July 1852	J. Bernard	Tebben, A. Margaretha	L	
Brinkers, Johan Bernard	1, Jan. 1850	J. Bernard	Tebben, Anna Margaretha	K	
Brinkers, Maria Catharina	23, Sept 1856	Bernard H.	Grahman, Anna Agnes	A	
Brinkers, Maria Josephina	27, Aug. 1858	J. Bernard	Tebben, A. Euphemia	L	
Brinkhaus, Anna Maria	22, June 1859	Francis	Linfert, Adelheid	D	140
Brinkhaus, Francis	19, Nov. 1857	Francis J.	Linfeld, Adelheid	D	99
Brinkhaus, Maria Gertrud	19, Mar. 1855	Francis	Linfert, Adelheid	D	31
Brinkley, Frances	24, Feb. 1850	John	Harnsen, Ellen	B	197
Brinkley, William	13, June 1852	James	----, ----	B	260
Brinkman, Anna Catharina	21, Sept 1858	Heinrich	Gausephol, Elisabeth	A	
Brinkman, Anna Maria	14, Dec. 1854	J. Heinrich	Kühlman, Anna Agnes	A	
Brinkman, Bernard	10, Sept 1854	Mathias	Schilmeier, Elisabeth	R	
Brinkman, Bernard Gerhard	8, Sept 1851	J. Gerhard	Remler, Margaretha	A	
Brinkman, Bernard Joseph	30, Jan. 1852	J. Joseph	Knagge, Catharina Elisabeth	A	
Brinkman, Elisabeth	18, May 1853	Mathias	Schildmeyer, Elisabeth	R	
Brinkman, Heinrich David	30, Nov. 1853	J. Heinrich	Kuhlman, Maria	A	
Brinkman, Johan Bernard Clemens	10, Jan. 1858	Clemens	Dickman, Catharina	A	
Brinkman, Johan Heinrich	30, July 1854	J. Heinrich	Gausepohl, Maria Elisabeth	A	
Brinkman, Johan Herman	4, Sept 1856	J. Heinrich	Gausepohl, Anna Maria E.	A	
Brinkman, Maria Elisabeth	5, Oct. 1852	J. Heinrich	Gausepohl, Maria Elisabeth	A	
Brinkman, Maria Gertrud	29, May 1852	Bernard	Wiegelman, Agnes	A	
Brinkmann, Anna Maria Agnes	18, Oct. 1857	Joseph	Knagge, Elisabeth	L	
Brinkmann, Anna Maria Elisabeth	12, May 1854	Francis	Winkelmann, Elisabeth	C	
Brinkmann, Bernard Christoph	5, Sept 1852	Bernard	Doecker, M. Elisabeth	F	
Brinkmann, Catharina Maria	18, Apr. 1857	J. Herman	Ukotter, M. Elisabeth	L	
Brinkmann, Elisabeth Henrietta Catharina	14, Nov. 1858	J. Heinrich	Timmermann, Elisabeth	C	
Brinkmann, Georg	10, Jan. 1858	Francis	Papenbrock, Clara	L	
Brinkmann, Herman Heinrich	4, May 1855	Herman	Timmermann, Elisabeth	C	
Brinkmann, Johan Alois	10, June 1856	Gerhard	----, Bernardina	C	
Brinkmann, Johan Bernard	11, Aug. 1855	J. Bernard	Habrock, Ida Cathrina	F	
Brinkmann, Johan Bernard Heinrich	8, Dec. 1859	J. Bernard	Vorjohann, M. Catharina	L	
Brinkmann, Johan Heinrich	5, Apr. 1852	Mathias	Schippmeyer, Elisabeth	L	
Brinkmann, Johan Mathias	16, Oct. 1858	Ferdinand	Niehaus, M. Gertrud	L	
Brinkmann, Joseph Heinrich	21, Oct. 1858	J. Heinrich	Steinkamp, Bernardina	L	
Brinkmann, M. Elisabeth Veronica	5, Feb. 1857	Herman H.	Timmermann, Elisabeth	C	
Brinkmann, Maria Anna Gertrud	22, Oct. 1850	Matthias	Schippmeyer, M. Elisabeth	L	
Brinkmann, Maria Aura	16, Feb. 1852	Heinrich	Hatke, Bernardina	C	
Brinkmann, Maria Cecilia	2, Aug. 1859	Jacob	Hatke, Bernardina	C	
Brinkmann, Maria Josephina	6, Oct. 1859	Heinrich	Fortmann, Maria	L	
Brinkmann, Maria Rosina	19, July 1858	Eberhard	Krafeld, C. Maria	C	
Brinkmann, Mathias	20, Mar. 1852	Francis H.	Winkelmann, Elisabeth	L	
Brinkmeier, Johan Francis Heinrich	17, Mar. 1854	Joseph	Engelberns, Maria	K	

Name of Child	Date of Baptism	Father	Mother	Church	Page
Brinkmeier, Johan Heinrich	10, July 1850	Gerhard H.	Schroers, Margaretha	C	
Brinkmeier, Maria Catharina Josephina	8, Apr. 1851	Joseph	Engelbert, Maria	K	
Brinkmeyer, A Catharina Margaretha	21, Feb. 1856	G. Heinrich	Schroer, Margaretha	C	
Brinkmeyer, Anna Maria Francisca	7, Jan. 1857	Francis J.	Engelbert, M. Cath.	L	
Brinkmeyer, Catharina Philomena	28, Dec. 1859	J. Heinrich	Adermeyer, Theresa	C	
Brinkmeyer, Gerhard Francis	8, Oct. 1858	Gerhard	Schroer, Margaretha	C	
Brinkmeyer, Gerhard Heinrich	4, Oct. 1852	Gerhard	Schroer, Margaretha	C	
Brinkmeyer, Gerhard Heinrich	28, July 1854	J. Heinrich	Adermeyer, Theresa	C	
Brinkmeyer, Johan Bernard	1, Aug. 1852	J. Heinrich	Attermeyer, Theresa	C	
Brinkmeyer, Johan Heinrich	7, Jan. 1857	J. Heinrich	Attermeyer, Theresa	C	
Brinkmeyer, Maria Louisa	4, Nov. 1855	Heinrich	Hemeyer, Theresa	C	
Brinkmeyer, Maria Theresa	10, Nov. 1850	J. Heinrich	Ademeyer, Theresa	L	
Brinsbach, Joseph	17, Oct. 1858	J. Georg	Flaig, Maria	D	122
Brinzbach, Maria Cunigunda	15, Apr. 1855	J. Georg	Flaig, Maria Anna	D	33
Brinzbach, Marianna	6, July 1856	J. Georg	Flaig, Marianna	F	
Briscoe, Eliza	19, Dec. 1852	Michael	Cunningham, Margaret	B	278
Briscoe, Michael	15, Oct. 1854	Michael	Cunningham, Margaret	T	
Brislan, John	27, July 1851	Jeremiah	Henny, Mary	B	237
Bristle, Michael	4, July 1858	Andreas	Lueders, Leonora	G	
Britt, Edward	22, Oct. 1850	Thomas	----, Mary	E	255
Britt, Margaret Ann	10, Oct. 1852	Thomas	----, Mary	E	26
Britt, Richard	15, May 1853	Michael	Cronin, Ann	B	291
Britt, Thomas	15, Oct. 1854	Thomas	Henry, Mary	E	232
Britt, Thomas	2, Dec. 1855	Thomas	Henry, Mary	E	331
Britten, Alfred	11, May 1854	Arthur	Moore, Mary	E	189
Britten, Barbara	4, Jan. 1851	Mathias	Bernd, Louise	Q	1
Britten, Margaretha	4, Apr. 1858	Mathias	Schütz, Catharina	N	
Britten, Maria	31, July 1859	Mathias	Schatz, Catharina	N	
Britten, Peter	1, Nov. 1853	Mathias	Bernd, Louisa	N	17
Brix, Carl	21, Nov. 1858	Wilhelm	Behrman, Maria	D	124
Brizzolara, Andreas Carlo Luigi	15, Jan. 1858	Luigi	Bogiana, Angela	K	
Brizzolari, Giovanni Stefano	26, June 1859	Giovanni	Sciutti, Catharina	K	
Brock, Aloysius Heinrich Anton	19, Apr. 1858	Joseph	Feldtrup, Anna	C	
Brock, Caspar Johan	12, Sept 1852	Jacob	Martin, Sarah	K	
Brock, Ferdinand	2, Jan. 1855	Joseph	Feldtrup, Anna	C	
Brock, Francisca Catharina	12, Sept 1852	Jacob	Martin, Sarah	K	
Brock, Heinrich Joseph Anton	7, Oct. 1859	Joseph	Feltrup, Maria Anna	L	
Brock, John James	4, Apr. 1854	James	Martin, Sarah	E	181
Brock, M. Gertrud Bernardina	19, June 1853	Joseph	Feltrup, Anna	C	
Brock, Robert	15, Dec. 1850	James	Martin, Sarah	E	267
Brockamp, Catharina Maria	29, Oct. 1850	Joseph	Felelmann, Elisabeth	L	
Brockamp, Francis Heinric	21, Apr. 1853	Francis	Timmer, Anna	C	
Brockamp, Francis Heinrich	19, Jan. 1855	Francis	Timmer, M. Anna	C	
Brockamp, Heinrich	13, Mar. 1850	Bernard	Wemhoff, Maria Anna	L	
Brockamp, Heinrich	28, Sept 1858	Heinrich	Rusche, Elisabeth	L	
Brockamp, Johan Francis Heinrich	18, May 1853	Johan H.	Lange, Elisabeth	A	
Brockamp, Johan Joseph	19, Feb. 1855	Heinrich	Lange, Elisabeth	A	
Brockamp, Maria Agnes	23, Sept 1851	Bernard	Wemhoff, Anna Maria	L	
Brockamp, Maria Josephina	10, May 1857	Heinrich	Lange, Elisabeth	L	
Brockamp, Maria Magdalena	3, Sept 1851	Heinrich	Lange, Elisabeth	A	
Brocker, Agnes Bernardina	19, Nov. 1854	Friedrich	Langkamp, Dina	K	
Bröcker, Anna Elisabeth	23, Feb. 1853	Friedrich	Langenkamp, Bernardina	K	
Bröcker, B. Engelbert Johan	14, May 1857	Gerhard H.	Hinteler, Maria Elisabeth	A	
Bröcker, Joseph	2, June 1851	Heinrich	Streve, Margaretha	A	
Brocker, Maria Elisasbeth	15, Nov. 1856	Frederick	----, Bernardina	R	
Brockhaus, Bernard Joseph	30, Aug. 1853	H. Heinrich	Burrichter, Maria Anna	K	
Brockhaus, Bernard Wilhelm	23, Dec. 1852	A. Theodor	Wolf, Maria Anna	J	20
Brockhaus, Georg Theodor	16, Jan. 1855	A. Theodor	Wolf, Anna Maria	J	30
Brockhaus, Johan Herman	16, Dec. 1850	Anton J.	Rolf, Maria Anna	J	8

Name of Child	Date of Baptism	Father	Mother	Church	Page
Brockhof, A. Maria Francisca	21, Mar. 1858	Johan	---husen, Josephina	T	
Brockhof, Anna Maria Bernardina	3, Feb. 1856	Johan	Lubbehüsen, Josephina	K	
Brockhof, Maria Catharina Elisabeth	2, July 1852	Heinrich	Wentholt, Maria Anna	D	327
Brockhoff, Catharina Josephina	23, Apr. 1858	Julius	Schroer, Elisabeth	L	
Brockhoff, Ernst Ludwig Edward	10, Dec. 1856	Julius	Schroer, Elisabeth	L	
Brockhoff, Heinrich Julius	14, Jan. 1859	Gustav	Rude, Christina	F	
Brockhoff, Johan Heinrich Aloysius	3, Apr. 1855	Julius	Schroer, Elisabeth	L	
Bröcking, Lambert Anton Martin Heinr.	9, Dec. 1850	Lambert	Lütkenhoff, Johanna	A	
Brockkamp, Bernard Heinrich	26, May 1857	Bernard	Austing, M. Agnes	C	
Brockman, Anna Elisabeth	21, Feb. 1858	Bernard	Henke, Anna Maria	Q	26
Brockman, Bernard Herman	31, May 1851	Heinrich	Hümpleman, Dorothea	K	
Brockman, Catharina Dorothea	22, Sept 1852	J. Herman	Hempelman, Dorothea	K	
Brockman, Clement	18, Dec. 1853	Bernard	Henker, Anna Maria	Q	4
Brockman, Elisabeth Dorothea	22, Sept 1852	J. Herman	Hempelman, Dorothea	K	
Brockman, Friedrich Aloysius	7, Nov. 1854	H. Herman	Hempelman, Dorothea	K	
Brockman, Friedrich Stephan Bernard	11, Mar. 1852	Friedrich	Künnen, Catharina Agnes	K	
Brockman, Johan	19, June 1858	Johan	Boecker, Maria	A	
Brockman, Johan Bernard	26, Jan. 1856	H.H.	Torbeck, Catharina	A	
Brockman, Johan Heinrich	13, Apr. 1853	Herman H.	Tollbeck, Catharina	A	
Brockman, Johan Wilhelm Joseph	17, June 1851	J. Dietrich	Ording, Maria Elisabeth	A	
Brockman, Maria	20, Dec. 1857	Johan	Re---, Elisabeth	D	101
Brockman, Maria Angela Carolina	24, May 1859	J. Heinrich	Landwehr, Carolina	N	
Brockman, Maria Catharina	23, Apr. 1851	Heinrich J.	Lakman, Maria Gertrud	D	261
Brockman, Maria Catharina Elisabeth	26, June 1859	Herman H.	Aufderbecke, M. Catharina	A	
Brockman, Maria Theresa	9, Dec. 1856	Johan	Bödeker, Maria	A	
Brockman, Mathias	22, Sept 1855	Bernard	Henke, Anna M.	Q	10
Brockman, Moses Herman Bernard	26, June 1853	Theodor	Ording, Elisabeth	A	
Brockman, Sophia Rosa	30, Apr. 1856	Herman	Hempelman, Dorothea	K	
Brockman, Theodora	4, Sept 1854	Theodor	Ording, Elisabeth	A	
Brockmann, A. Catharina Josephina	4, June 1855	Heinrich	Sund, M. Adelheid	L	
Brockmann, Anna Maria Francisca	4, May 1853	Heinrich	Sund, Anna Adelheid	L	
Brockmann, Bernard Friedrich	11, Mar. 1850	Bernard	Henke, Anna Maria	C	
Brockmann, Catharina Maria Louisa	27, Feb. 1850	Joseph	Schwarz, Elisabeth	C	
Brockmann, Friedrich August	23, Aug. 1855	Joseph	Schwatze, Elisabeth	C	
Brockmann, Gerhard Heinrich	15, Jan. 1857	Heinrich	Sund, Maria Adelheid	L	
Brockmann, Heinrich	3, Jan. 1858	Joseph	Schwarze, Elisabeth	C	
Brockmann, Johan	23, July 1852	Bernard	Henke, Anna M.	C	
Brockmann, Johan Bernard	7, Nov. 1858	J. Heinrich	Sund, Maria	L	
Brockmann, Johan Joseph	5, Apr. 1855	Johan	Boettiger, Maria	F	
Brockmann, Joseph	14, Dec. 1852	Bernard	Schmidt, Gertrud	L	
Brockmann, Joseph	28, Dec. 1851	Joseph	Schwarze, Elisabeth	C	
Brockmann, M. Catharina Bernardina	26, Apr. 1855	Heinrich	Tiemann, M. Theresa	L	
Brockmann, Maria Clara	8, July 1858	Herman	Hempelmann, Dorothea	T	
Brocks, Anna Catharina	4, July 1853	Francis	Bussman, Maria Elisabeth	D	394
Brocks, Anna Maria Catharina	6, Jan. 1859	Francis	Heman, Maria Elisabeth	A	
Brocks, Herman	6, Mar. 1856	Joseph	Feldkamp, Anna	C	
Brockschmidt, Anna	10, Oct. 1858	H.	Tepe, Maria	A	
Brockschmidt, Anna M. Wilhelmina	18, June 1854	Clemens	Moeller, Anna Maria	L	
Brockschmidt, Anna Maria	22, Nov. 1856	Clemens	Moeller, Anna Maria	L	
Brockschmidt, Catharina Josephina	28, Apr. 1851	Christoph	Luening, Gertrud	C	
Brockschmidt, Christoph Heinrich	8, June 1852	Heinrich	Tepe, Anna M.	C	
Brockschmidt, Johan Heinrich	14, June 1856	Heinrich	Tepe, Anna Maria	A	
Brockschmidt, Maria Catharina	19, Mar. 1859	Clemens	Moeller, Anna Maria	L	
Brockschmidt, Maria Elisabeth	2, July 1854	Heinrich	Tepe, Anna	C	
Brockschmidt, Sophia Philippina	26, May 1850	Heinrich	Tepe, Anna Maria	L	
Brodbeck, Amalia Christina	19, Sept 1852	Joseph	Martin, Catharina	F	
Brodbeck, Andreas Nicolaus	4, May 1855	Stephan	Eberenz, Agatha	F	
Brodbeck, August Adolph	28, Apr. 1858	Anastasius	First, Josephina	D	110
Brodbeck, Georg Anton	19, July 1857	Stephan	Emerenz, Agatha	F	

Name of Child	Date of Baptism	Father	Mother	Church	Page
Brodbeck, Maria Amalia	23, Mar. 1856	Anastasius	First, Josephina	D	54
Brodbeck, Martin	19, July 1857	Joseph	Martin, Catharina	D	90
Brodbeck, Stephan Hieronymus	31, Aug. 1851	Stephan	Ebernez, ----	F	
Broddock, Ann Mary	19, Aug. 1855	Michael	Tully, Mary	P	146
Broderick, Anna	17, Mar. 1858	Johan	----, Alice	R	
Broderick, Catharina	14, May 1854	Michael	Costello, Catharina	R	
Broderick, Helena	17, Mar. 1858	Dennis	Mullins, Bridget	J	44
Broderick, Honora	15, July 1855	Dennis	Mullens, Bridget	P	140
Broderick, Jeremiah	10, Nov. 1856	Michael	Tully, Mary	B	36
Broderick, John	20, Nov. 1859	John	McNabe, Elisabeth	R	
Broderick, John	21, May 1854	John	O'Connor, Ann	E	192
Broderick, John	5, Jan. 1856	Michael	Costello, Catherine	R	
Broderick, John	2, Sept 1853	Michael	Tully, Mary	P	50
Broderick, Martin	3, Dec. 1854	William	Coffey, Winefred	P	107
Broderick, Mary	5, Nov. 1854	Michael	Clary, Bridget	P	103
Broderick, Mary	17, Feb. 1856	Michael	Clary, Bridget	P	170
Broderick, Mary Elizabeth	21, May 1856		Broderick, Vina	R	
Broderick, Mary Ellen	30, Nov. 1856	Martin	----, Helen	M	
Broderick, Michael	26, Aug. 1857	Michael	----, Catherine	R	
Broderick, Patrick	12, Oct. 1856	William	Coffee, Winefred	P	195
Broderick, Rosanne	25, May 1859	Martin	----, ----	M	
Broderick, William	19, Sept 1858	Michael	Costello, Catherine	R	
Brodrick, Eliza	18, Sept 1859	Michael	Clary, Bridget	P	296
Brodrick, Sarah	11, Oct. 1857	Michael	Clary, Bridget	P	**226**
Broecherhoff, Louisa	23, Aug. 1857	Johan	Trilling, Magdalena	C	
Broegger, Maria Theresa	4, Mar. 1852	Francis	Fink, Maria	F	
Broeker, Francis Heinrich	6, Mar. 1859	Fr. H.	Kolkmeyer, Catharina Elisabeth	C	
Broeking, Heinrich Joseph	13, May 1854	Lambert	Luetkenhof, Johanna	F	
Broeking, M. Christina Catharina	29, Jan. 1853	Joseph	Haverkamp, Dina	F	
Broering, Emma Margaretha	7, Nov. 1858	Dominick	Trenkamp, Elisabeth	C	
Broering, Maria Bernardina	14, Nov. 1859	Adam	Tapphorn, Wilhelmina	F	
Broering, Maria Philomena	19, July 1858	Arnold	Tappe, Philomena	F	
Broermann, Catharina Philomena	25, Feb. 1853	Adam	Rebbes, Anna Maria	L	
Broermann, Christian	30, May 1858	Friedrich	Busch, Elisabeth	L	
Broermann, Johan Heinrich	16, Nov. 1859	Heinrich	Brune, Elisabeth	C	
Broermann, Maria Elisabeth	22, Nov. 1857	Adam	Rebber, Anna M.	C	
Broermann, Wilhelm	31, Mar. 1850	Adam H.	Rebers, Anna Maria	C	
Brogan, Bernard	13, Nov. 1853	Dennis	Higgins, Ann	E	144
Brogan, Bernard	29, Oct. 1854	Michael	Kilroy, Mary	P	101
Brogan, Bernard	7, July 1850	Peter	Higgins, Catherine	E	229
Brogan, Bridget	28, Dec. 1856	Michael	Kilroe, Mary	P	202
Brogan, Cecilia	24, Mar. 1850	Dennis	----, Ann	E	205
Brogan, Dennis	20, Jan. 1855	Dennis	Higgins, Ann	E	257
Brogan, Ellen	7, Nov. 1852	Peter	----, Ann	E	33
Brogan, James	14, Dec. 1856	Dennis	Higgins, Ann	E	420
Brogan, John	13, May 1855	Brian?	----, Joanne	P	132
Brogan, John	30, Oct. 1858	Michael	Kilroy, Mary	P	265
Brogan, John	17, Feb. 1856	Philipp	Caughlin, Ann	E	345
Brogan, John	2, Apr. 1855	Thomas	Woods, Sarah	P	127
Brogan, Martin	25, June 1853	Michael	Kilroe, Mary	P	45
Brogan, Mary	22, May 1857	Thomas	Woods, Sarah	P	213
Brogan, Mary Ann	16, Jan. 1859	Dennis	Higgens, Ann	T	
Brogan, Sarah	23, Nov. 1851	Dennis	----, Ann	E	361
Broger, Johan Heinrich	21, Sept 1855	Gerhard	Klosterman, Maria	N	
Brokamp, Anna M. Bernardina	9, Nov. 1858	J. Bernard	Austing, Agnes	C	
Brokamp, Anton Bernard	26, Apr. 1857	Francis	Timmer, Maria	C	
Brokamp, Catharina Bernardina	6, Oct. 1855	Fritz	Meyer, Elisabeth	L	
Brokamp, Catharina Elisabeth	26, Dec. 1859	Heinrich	Wilkemeyer, Catharina	L	
Brokamp, Edward Heinrich Anton	14, Jan. 1856	Heinrich	Wilkemeyer, Catharina	L	

Name of Child	Date of Baptism	Father	Mother	Church	Page
Brokamp, Francis	29, Nov. 1857	Friedrich	Meyer, Elisabeth	J	44
Brokamp, Friedrich Johan Bernard	30, Mar. 1851	Heinrich	Wilkemeyer, Catharina	L	
Brokamp, Friedricka Elisabeth	10, Oct. 1858	Heinrich	Wilkemeier, Cath.	L	
Brokamp, Johan Heinrich	19, July 1853	Heinrich	Wilkemeyer, Catharina	L	
Brokamp, Johan Martin	7, Dec. 1858	Bernard	Wategatter, Elisabeth	N	
Brokamp, Maria Catharina Isabella	8, Sept 1857	Heinrich	Stuert, Elisabeth	F	
Brokamp, Maria Elisabeth Josephina	9, Sept 1853	Friedrich	Meyer, Elisabeth	L	
Brokamp, Maria Rosa	8, Aug. 1859	Heinrich	Lange, Elisabeth	F	
Broker, Johan Heinrich Francis	4, Aug. 1851	F. Heinrich	Langkamp, Carolina	K	
Brokhof, Anna Maria Bernardina	1, May 1856	J. Joseph	Tensing, Maria Gesina	F	
Broking, Franz Joseph	24, Nov. 1850	Joseph	Hafercamp, Dina	F	
Bröking, Johan Gerhard	7, Nov. 1856	Lambert	Lütkenhoff, Johanna	A	
Brolag, Margaretha	17, Sept 1851	Anton	Weiss, Elisabeth	Q	1
Brolage, Herman Heinrich	29, Mar. 1854	Anton L.	Weis, Elisabeth	N	21
Bro--man, Joseph Abraham Matthew	23, Jan. 1853	?	Goodan, Ann	B	281
Bromm, Johan Bernard	25, May 1854	Gregor	Beckel, Margaretha	D	11
Bronman, ??	3, Feb. 1850	Friedrich	----, Adelheid	K	
Brook, Josephine Pauline	29, July 1852	William	Cannon, Sophia	B	266
Brooks, Emma Mary	29, Sept 1850	Samuel	adult - 16 years old	B	215
Brophil, James	10, Aug. 1858	Thomas	Quinn, Helen	P	257
Brophy, David	7, Nov. 1858	Joseph	Mullane, Mary	B	66
Brophy, Ellen Rose Agnes	30, Sept 1855	Michael	Meham, Mary	B	20
Brophy, George	18, May 1859	Peter	Naly, Joanne	E	625
Brophy, Helen	11, Sept 1859	Michael	Hayden, Margaret	X	
Brophy, John	27, May 1855	?	Campion, Julia	P	134
Brophy, John Peter	8, July 1855	Joseph	O'Mullane, Mary	B	16
Brophy, Julia Mary	6, Nov. 1853	William	Campion, Julia	P	58
Brophy, Mary	13, Feb. 1853	Michael	Mehan, Mary	B	283
Brophy, Matilda	30, Oct. 1858	John L.	Keating, Margaret	E	574
Brophy, Thomas	26, Jan. 1851	Michael	Mehan, Mary	B	223
Brophy, William Patrick	19, Apr. 1857	John	----, Margaret	E	447
Bror, Jacob Heinrich	26, Mar. 1854	Philip	Catten, Anna	N	21
Brörman, Johan	27, Sept 1858	J. Bernard	Roddinghaus, Anna Maria	A	
Brörman, Johan B. Herman	8, Aug. 1856	J. Bernard	Rottinghaus, Anna Maria	A	
Brörman, Johan Heinrich	7, Oct. 1853	J. Heinrich	Rottinghaus, Anna Maria	A	
Brörman, Maria Josephina Bernardina	1, Nov. 1854	J. Bernard	Rottinghaus, Anna Maria	A	
Brosamer, Philomena	9, Mar. 1851	Lawrence	Lause, Mary Ann	H	
Brosmer, Barbara	2, Feb. 1851	Francis X.	Groh, Clara	F	
Brosmer, Francis Lawrence	30, Jan. 1853	Lawrence	----, Ann Mary	H	
Brosmer, Francisca	13, Jan. 1850	Francis X.	Groh, Clara	F	
Brosmer, Joseph	8, Oct. 1854	Lawrence	----, Mary Ann	H	
Bross, Anthony of Padua	1, Feb. 1852	Charles	----, Cunigunda	H	
Bross, Catharina	6, Jan. 1856	Ferdinand	Goos, Theresa	G	
Bross, Catharina	9, May 1858	Johan	Wiesman, Catharina	H	
Bross, Charles	29, Oct. 1854	Charles	----, Cunigunda	H	
Bross, Francis Xavier	24, May 1857	Ferdinand	Goos, Theresa	G	
Bross, Johan	15, Aug. 1859	Charles	Schott, Cunigunda	H	
Bross, Johan	4, June 1857	Philipp	Matz, Magdalena	G	
Bross, Joseph	2, July 1854	Ferdinand	Goos, Theresa	G	
Bross, Joseph	14, Apr. 1856	Joseph	Junker, Magdalena	G	
Bross, Josephina	17, July 1859	Philipp	Motz, Magdalena	G	
Bross, Louisa	8, July 1855	Philipp	Motz, Magdalena	D	37
Bross, Maria Anna	29, Mar. 1857	Charles	Schott, Cunigunda	H	
Bross, Maria Theresa	31, Mar. 1858	Joseph	Junker, Magdalena	G	
Bross, Mathilda	12, Apr. 1857	Johan	Wiesman, Catharina	H	
Brossack, Peter	23, Feb. 1851	Roger	Kennedy, Margaret	E	286
Brossart, Caecilia Carolina	6, Aug. 1854	Johan	Fricker, Margaretha	J	28
Brossart, Francis	8, Oct. 1853	Ferdinand	Tieler, Catharina	J	24
Brossart, Friedrich	5, July 1857	Johan	Fricker, Margaretha	J	42

Name of Child	Date of Baptism	Father	Mother	Church	Page
Brossart, Johan	15, Mar. 1856	Jacob	Rupp, Magdalena	C	
Brossart, Louisa	1, Feb. 1857	F. Martin	Hermann, Margaretha	C	
Brossart, Margaretha	16, Nov. 1851	Johan	Fricker, Margaretha	C	
Brossart, Peter	6, June 1858	Jacob	Rupp, Magdalena	C	
Brossarth, Margaretha	11, May 1851	Martin	Helferich, Margaretha	D	264
Brossert, Carolina	2, Jan. 1858	Carl	Schwartz, Carolina	T	
Brossert, Johanna Elisabeth	4, Oct. 1857	Ferdinand	Dehoel, Maria Catharina	J	44
Brossmer, Albert Prosper	2, May 1852	Francis X.	G----, Clara	K	
Brotter, Anna Catharina	18, Mar. 1856	Mathias	Schulz, Catharina	N	
Brottman, Maria Philippina	6, Jan. 1850	Ludwig	Hampe, Theresa	D	198
Brouder, Mary	23, May 1852	Dennis	----, Bridget	P	22
Brower, Catherine	5, Nov. 1854	John	Karkan, Ann	P	103
Brown, Ann	17, Feb. 1856	Michael	McEnespy, Rachel	P	170
Brown, Ann	12, Dec. 1858	Peter	Killerolly, Winnefred	E	586
Brown, Ann Elizabeth	21, Aug. 1853	John	Farrell, Mary Ann	P	50
Brown, Arthur Heinrich	20, Mar. 1859	Jacob	Keefe, Margaretha	K	
Brown, Catherine	25, Aug. 1850	James	----, Mary	E	241
Brown, Catherine	28, Apr. 1856	John	Cocke, Helen	E	363
Brown, Catherine	8, May 1852	Peter	----, Winifred	E	409
Brown, Charles	9, Mar. 1851	James	----, Mary	E	289
Brown, Daniel	27, Nov. 1853	Simon	Tuomy, Mary	V	8
Brown, Dennis	28, Aug. 1859	Patrick	O'Neil, Mary	E	650
Brown, Elizabeth	8, June 1856	Thomas	Row, Catherine	E	372
Brown, Francis	11, Apr. 1856	N.	----, Frances	E	358
Brown, Frederick James	26, Jan. 1853	Frederick	Sullivan, Ellen Jane	B	281
Brown, Helen	30, May 1858	John	Corcoran, Honora	E	538
Brown, Helen	10, Mar. 1850	John	Fitzgerald, Mary	B	198
Brown, James	17, July 1853	Michael	----, Joanne	M	
Brown, James	30, July 1854	Michael	McAneshy, Rachael	P	90
Brown, James Franklin	30, Mar. 1858	John	Bell, Elizabeth M.	B	57
Brown, John	15, Aug. 1850	Michael	Haffel, Bridget	B	210
Brown, John	21, Mar. 1853	Michael	McAnassey, Rachel	B	287
Brown, John	8, Mar. 1852	Patrick	Harmany, Joanne	B	254
Brown, John Adam	16, Mar. 1854	Joseph	----, Catherine	U	
Brown, John T.	27, Oct. 1852		adult - 20 years old	B	273
Brown, Joseph Anthony Henry	9, Sept 1854	John A.	Brown, Mary Ann	V	17
Brown, Jsoeph	18, Sept 1858		Brown, Mary	V	50
Brown, Margaret	21, Feb. 1858	Michael	McMahan, Mary	E	518
Brown, Mary	7, Aug. 1858	Thomas	Delaney, Catherine	E	555
Brown, Mary	26, July 1852	James	----, Mary	M	
Brown, Mary	17, Aug. 1856	John	----, Honora	M	
Brown, Mary	2, Oct. 1855	Richard	Kehoe, Mary	P	153
Brown, Mary	17, Dec. 1854	Thomas	----, Elizabeth	M	
Brown, Mary Jane	11, Jan. 1851	Martin	Dogherty, Catherine	B	222
Brown, Mary Jane	10, Jan. 1858	Simon	Toomey, Mary	B	54
Brown, Michael	20, Aug. 1853	Patrick	----, Ellen	E	120
Brown, Michael	10, Aug. 1850	Robert	----, Winefred	E	238
Brown, Peter	19, July 1857	Peter	Kelvarey, Winnefred	E	467
Brown, Richard	30, July 1854	James	----, Mary	M	
Brown, Robert	5, Nov. 1855	Andrew	Carroll, Ann	E	325
Brown, Robert	28, Apr. 1856	John	Cocke, Helen	E	363
Brown, Robert James	13, Jan. 1856	Robert	----, ----	E	337
Brown, Samuel	2, Aug. 1858	Robert	Hagerty, Mary	E	554
Brown, Sarah Mary	28, Apr. 1856	John	Cocke, Helen	E	363
Brown, Simon Henry	8, Apr. 1855	Simon	Tuomy, Mary	V	24
Brown, Terry William	7, Jan. 1850		adult - 25 years old	E	192
Brown, Thomas	30, Aug. 1853	Patrick	Harmon, Joanne	V	5
Brown, Thomas	6, Sept 1857	Thomas	----, Elizabeth	M	
Brown, Thomas Peter	11, July 1858	Michael	McAnessey, Rachel	P	253

Name of Child	Date of Baptism	Father	Mother	Church	Page
Brown, Wiliam	25, Aug. 1856	Morgan	Kramer, H.	V	35
Brown, William	28, Apr. 1856	John	Cocke, Helen	E	363
Brown, William	11, Apr. 1851	William	Cralen, Martha	E	299
Brown, Winneford	7, May 1853	Peter	----, Winnefred	E	87
Brown?, Richard	17, Apr. 1851	Michael	Byrne?, Joanne	M	
Browne, Catherine	23, Mar. 1856	James	----, Mary	R	
Browne, Edward	17, Apr. 1859	James	Kelly, Mary	R	
Browne, Mary	5, July 1859	Elias	----, ----	B	77
Browne, Mary Louise	16, Sept 1855	JOhn	Barrett, Mary Ann	B	19
Browne, Nicolaus	17, Aug. 1854	James	Kelly, Margaret	R	
Brox, Catharina D.	13, Nov. 1854	Francis	Bussman, Maria Elisabeth	A	
Brox, Francis Heinrich	7, June 1857	Francis	Homan, Maria Elisabeth	A	
Brox, Maria Elisabeth	7, May 1856	Francis	Bussman, Maria Elisabeth	A	
Broxtermann, Johan Gerhard	14, July 1850	Johan H.	Becker, Christina	F	
Bruch, Joseph	20, Feb. 1855	Bernard	Mueller, Louisa	F	
Bruch, Maria Louisa	28, June 1854	Heinrich	Schnur, Catharina	D	13
Brücher, Catharina	28, Nov. 1854	Jacob	Miggel, Elisabeth	D	23
Bruck, Catharina Elisabeth	25, July 1858	Heinrich	Schanz, Catharina	D	115
Bruck, Johan	25, Mar. 1856	Heinrich	Schanz, Catharina	D	55
Bruck, Johan	4, June 1859	Johan	Fritz, Elisabeth	D	139
Bruck, Maria Magdalena	18, Mar. 1857	Johan	Fritz, Elisabeth	D	81
Brude, Carl Heinrich	22, Mar. 1855	Heinrich	Aspey, Elisabeth	D	31
Bruder, Georg	11, July 1858	Georg	Rosensteiger, Maria	C	
Bruder, Theresa	12, Mar. 1857	Georg	Steiger, Rosa	C	
Bruegge, Anton Clement	19, Feb. 1857	Heinrich	Lammers, Catharina	Q	20
Bruegge, Johan Edward Florenz	12, July 1851	Andreas	Wyggers, Thersa	L	
Brueggemann, Anna Maria Catharina	10, July 1853	Gerhard H.	Grewe, Maria A.	L	
Brueggemann, Anna Maria Elisabeth	31, Aug. 1856	Mathias	Toennies, A. Elisabeth	L	
Brueggemann, Bernard Heinrich	27, Nov. 1859	Bernard	Luettel, M. Adelheid	L	
Brueggemann, Bernard Heinrich	22, June 1859	Gerhard H.	Grewe, Susanna	L	
Brueggemann, Francisca	28, Jan. 1850	Herman	Elfers, Susanna Anna	C	
Brueggemann, Franz Gerhard	26, Oct. 1856	Gerhard	Grewe, Margaretha	L	
Brueggemann, Georg Joseph	25, June 1851	Johan	Hagemann, Theresa	C	
Brueggemann, Herman Johan Heinrich	20, May 1858	Mathias	Toennis, Anna Elisabeth	L	
Brueggemann, Johan Georg	10, Oct. 1853	Johan	Fischer, Elisabeth	C	
Brueggemann, Johan Gerhard	12, Nov. 1850	Gerhard	Grewe, M. Margaretha	L	
Brueggemann, Maria Anna Theresa	13, Aug. 1854	Mathias	Toennes, Elisabeth	L	
Brueggemann, Maria Elisabeth	12, July 1855	Johan	Fischer, Elisabeth	L	
Brueggemann, Maria Francisca	2, Jan. 1858	Johan	Fischer, Elisabeth	L	
Brueggemann, Maria Theresa	26, Jan. 1850	Heinrich	Schulte, Anna	C	
Brueggemeyer, Bernard Francis	26, Sept 1853	Heinrich	Brolmann, Louisa	C	
Brueggenschmidt, Francis Andreas	8, Feb. 1853	Andreas	Melle, Theresa	C	
Brueggenschmidt, Heinrich	27, June 1858	Heinrich	Theis, Gertrud	T	
Bruegger, Peter Carl	25, July 1859	Wilhelm	Brueg, Anna Maria	T	
Bruehl, Anton Theodor	13, Nov. 1858	Gustav	Reis, Helena	F	
Bruehl, Carl Wilhelm	24, Oct. 1856	Gustav	Reis, Magdalena	F	
Bruehl, Emilia Paulina	27, Sept 1854	Carl	Pfeiffer, Elisabeth	F	
Bruehl, Leo Prosper	27, Aug. 1851	Gustav	Reis, Helena	F	
Bruehl, Leopoldina Josephina	20, Apr. 1851	Carl	Pfeifer, Carolina	F	
Bruehr, Joseph	15, June 1851	Leonard	Heger, Maria	A	
Bruemme, Anna Christina	14, July 1858	Herman B.	Langeland, Theresa	F	
Bruemmer, Johan Bernard	12, Dec. 1856	Johan B.	Hatting, M. Adelheid	F	
Bruemmer, Johan Heinrich	1, May 1856	Herman B.	Langeland, A.M. Theresa	F	
Bruemmer, Joseph Heinrich	20, Mar. 1853	Theodor	Meier, Rosina	A	
Bruemmer, Lena Margaretha	25, Oct. 1854	Johan B.	Hatting, Maria Adelheid	F	
Bruemmer, Maria Adelheid	8, Oct. 1852	J. Bernard	Hatting, Maria Adelheid	A	
Bruemmer, Maria Carolina	25, Dec. 1852	H. Bernard	Langeland, Maria Theresa	F	
Bruemmer, Theodor Heinrich	13, Nov. 1854	Theodor	Meier, Rosina	A	
Bruening, Anna Catharina	17, May 1850	Joseph	Schmidt, A. Catharina	L	

Name of Child	Date of Baptism	Father	Mother	Church	Page
Bruening, Herman Joseph	23, Feb. 1851	Francis	Blome, Francisca	C	
Bruening, Johan Heinrich Gerhard	22, Nov. 1854	Joseph	Schmidt, Catharina	L	
Bruening, Joseph Gerhard Heinrich	17, Dec. 1857	Joseph	Schmidt, Anna Catharina	L	
Bruening, Maria Elisabeth	21, Feb. 1852	Joseph	Schmidt, Catharina	L	
Bruenner, Christina	14, July 1850	Peter	Pauli, Theresa	C	
Bruenning, Anton Christian	25, Dec. 1853	August	Lamping, Josephina	L	
Bruer, James	6, June 1853	John	----, Bridget	M	
Bruer, John	1, Sept 1856	John	----, Bridget	M	
Bruer, Mary Jane	10, Sept 1854	John	----, Bridget	M	
Brueske, Johan	21, Aug. 1859		adult	F	
Brueske, Maria Theresa	13, Nov. 1859	Johan	Auer, Theresa	F	
Bruestle, Maria	7, Sept 1856	Andreas	Litterst, Elenora	G	
Brügeman, Theodora Carolina	31, Oct. 1856	Bernard	Wilderhaus, Elisabeth	N	
Brüger, Anna Maria	19, Feb. 1855	Wilhelm	Fortcamp, Maria Anna	N	27
Brüger, Maria Anna	2, Nov. 1859	Wilhelm	Fortcamp, Maria	N	
Brügge, Anna Maria Elisabeth	30, June 1857	Heinrich	Hülver, Elisabeth	A	
Brügge, Anton Bernard Gerhard	17, Jan. 1852	B. Heinrich	Akamp, Anna Maria	K	
Brügge, Bernard Heinrich Leo	4, Sept 1853	Bernard	Dermeier, Maria Elisabeth	D	403
Brügge, Bernard Joseph	16, Aug. 1855	J. Bernard	Demaer, Elisabeth	D	40
Brügge, Bridget Caroline	20, July 1851	Heinrich	Lambert, Catharina	Q	1
Brügge, Catharina Philomena	3, Jan. 1858	Bernard	Dermeier, Elisabeth	D	102
Brügge, Elisabeth Catharina Maria	25, Nov. 1853	Heinrich	Lambert, Catharina	Q	4
Brügge, Philomena Theresa Adelheid	29, Sept 1854	Heinrich	Akamp, Maria Anna	A	
Brügge, Wilhelmina Maria	19, June 1856	Bernard H.	Akamp, Anna Maria	A	
Brüggel, Francisca Elisabeth	30, Sept 1851	J. Bernard	Termer, Elisabeth	D	285
Brüggeman, Anna Maria	21, Nov. 1855	Johan H.	Ruhe, Wilhelmina	A	
Brüggeman, Bernard Joseph	25, Mar. 1854	B. Theodor	Wildenhaus, Elisabeth	N	20
Brüggeman, Heinrich Anton	14, Mar. 1854	Johan H.	Ruhe, Wilhelmina	A	
Brüggeman, Herman Bernard	21, Mar. 1850	B. Theodor	Wildenhaus, Elisabeth	D	206
Brüggeman, Herman Heinrich	12, Dec. 1853	J. Herman	Elfers, Susanna Adelheid	D	420
Brüggeman, Johan Bernard	5, Sept 1852	Anton	Daming, Adelheid	D	346
Brüggeman, Joseph Heinrich	4, Oct.1857	Heinrich	Letecker, Elisabeth	D	96
Bruggeman, Maria Adelheid Elisabeth	1, Feb. 1854	Bernard	Löttel, Maria Adelheid	K	
Brüggeman, Maria Anna	9, Feb. 1859	Gerhard H.	Klinker, Carolina	A	
Brüggeman, Maria Anna Philomena	2, Feb. 1852	Bernard	Lüttel, Maria Adelheid	K	
Bruggeman, Maria Catharina	13, July 1856	Bernard	Lüttel, Adelheid	K	
Brüggeman, Maria Philomena	8, Sept 1857	Johan H.	----, Susan Adelheid	R	
Brüggeman, Philomena Elisabeth	11, Feb. 1858	Heinrich	Ruhe, Philomena	A	
Brüggemeier, Maria Theresa	24, Feb. 1852	Heinrich	Breierman, Louisa	D	309
Brügger, Wilhelm Anton Heinrich	21, Jan. 1857	Wilhelm	Fortkamp, Maria	K	
Brügler, Carolina	16, Dec. 1854	Georg	Würz, Gertrud	D	24
Brühe, Josephina	5, Jan. 1851	Joseph	Hecker, Carolina	A	
Brüher, Johan	26, Oct. 1856	Jacob	Maiken, Elisabeth	D	70
Bruhl, Catharina Elisabeth	21, Aug. 1859	Georg	Gey---, Elisabeth	D	144
Brühl, Herman	23, Feb. 1852	Heinrich	Andrae, Elisabeth	D	309
Bruhn, Johan Heinrich	20, June 1851	Engelbert	Gossemaier, Maria Angela	D	269
Bruhne, Johan Heinrich	6, Aug. 1859	J. Friedrich	Elbers, Theresa	N	
Brühr, Theresa	30, June 1850	Leonard	----, Marianna	A	
Bruin, Robert	6, Mar. 1853	John	Hearn, Joanne	B	285
Brülle, Wilhelm Albert	17, Apr. 1859	Andreas	Radina, Barbara	A	
Brüllmeyer, Anton	17, May 1857	Anton	Schmidt, Maria	H	
Brumbacher, Heinrich Bernard	18, Mar. 1854	Gottfried	Heitzmann, Christina	C	
Brummer, Anna	11, Mar. 1855	Johan	Gopp, Luitgardis	D	30
Brümmer, Anna Maria	10, Nov. 1854	J. Heinrich	Kemker, Anna Maria	K	
Brümmer, Heinrich Bartholomew	3, Jan. 1859	J. Bernard	Harting, Maria Adelheid	J	48
Brummer, Heinrich Xavier	3, Dec. 1856	J. Bernard	Ahlering, Elisabeth	K	
Brummer, Johan Bernard	13, Apr. 1850	Herman B.	Langeland, Theresa	A	
Brummer, Louisa Francisca	3, Dec. 1856	J. Bernard	Ahlering, Elisabeth	K	
Brummer, Maria Magdalena	8, May 1851	Theodor	Meier, Rosina	A	

Name of Child	Date of Baptism	Father	Mother	Church	Page
Brummer, Wilhelm Joseph Dennis	11, Oct. 1852	J. Bernard	Ahlering, Elisabeth	K	
Brun, Johan Heinrich	11, June 1855	J. Heinrich	Peltin, Maria	K	
Brun, Maria Elisabeth	1, Nov. 1853	Engelbert	Gossemeier, Maria	D	413
Brune, Anna Maria	4, July 1853	Joseph	Tecker, Maria	F	
Brune, Francisca Elisabeth	7, Mar. 1856	J. Heinrich	Ronnebaum, Maria Elisabeth	J	34
Brune, Herman Joseph	2, Dec. 1855	Joseph	Decker, Maria Anna	C	
Brune, Johan Friedrich	8, Mar. 1851	Heinrich	Röneker, Elisabeth	J	10
Brune, Johan Heinrich	21, Mar. 1858	J. Joseph	Fecker, M. Anna	C	
Brune, Maria Bernardina	9, June 1853	J. Heinrich	Rönneke, Maria Elisabeth	J	22
Brune, Rosa Elisabeth	6, Apr. 1859	Heinrich	Rönneker, Elisabeth	J	50
Brunemann, Johan Mathias	12, Dec. 1855	Mathias	Averdick, Marianna	F	
Bruner, Wilhelm	23, May 1851	Johan	Berrinken, Johanna	J	10
Brüning, Bernard Herman Gerhard	17, Oct. 1856	Herman	Hunteman, Maria	A	
Brüning, Theresa Francisca	25, Nov. 1858	Herman	Hunteman, Clara	A	
Brunner, Anna Emilia	27, Mar. 1859	William	Joeg, Anna	D	134
Brunner, Barbara	23, Feb. 1851	Philipp	Schneider, Magdalena	D	254
Brunner, Catharina	19, Oct. 1851	Joseph	Mengemeier, Catharina	A	
Brunner, Edgar	3, Aug. 1855	Johan	Schenk, Sarah	C	
Brunner, Elisabeth	10, Oct. 1858	Johan	Göpp, Luitgardis	D	121
Brunner, Henry	26, Apr. 1857		adult	V	38
Brunner, Johan	4, Jan. 1857	Johan	Plettner, Catharina	K	
Brunner, Johan Sebold	9, July 1854	William	Joeck, Anna	D	13
Brunner, Ludwig	27, Mar. 1859	William	Joeg, Anna	D	134
Brunner, Maria Catharina Helena	16, Aug. 1857	Mathias	VonderWell, Hermina	C	
Brunner, Wilhelm Seibold	22, May 1853	Wilhelm	Gäck, Anna	D	386
Brunner, Winnefeld	3, Aug. 1855	Johan	Schenk, Sarah	C	
Brunnock, Mary Ann	1, Aug. 1852	Roger	Kennedy, Margaret	B	267
Bruns, Anna Catharina	16, Sept 1851	J.B.	Horstman, Anna Maria	K	
Bruns, Anna Maria Elisabeth	24, Sept 1854	J. Herman	Baaman, Maria Elisabeth	N	24
Bruns, Anna Philomena	2, Sept 1853	Joseph	Grawe, Elisabeth	D	403
Bruns, Bernard Heinrich	25, Nov. 1852	Theodor	Wilmes, Maria	J	18
Bruns, Bernard Heinrich Carl	12, Aug. 1856	Johan	Hörstman, Maria Anna	K	
Bruns, Carl Friedrich	17, July 1851	Joseph	Pecker, Anna Maria	F	
Bruns, Elisabeth Philomena	6, Feb. 1857	G. Theodor	Brinkmeyer, Catharina	C	
Bruns, Georg Heinrich	24, July 1851	Joseph	Grawe, Maria Elisabeth	D	274
Bruns, Gustav	20, June 1852	Wilhelm	Benz, Anna Maria	F	
Bruns, Helena Elisabeth	11, Oct. 1859	Anton	Kessens, Angela	K	
Bruns, Herman Heinrich	12, Jan. 1856	Anton	Trimpe, Dina	C	
Bruns, Herman Heinrich	22, June 1855	Gerhard H.	Wobben, Christina	C	
Bruns, Herman Joseph	9, Oct. 1857	Gerhard H.	Wobbe, Christina	C	
Bruns, Johan Heinrich	28, Apr. 1857	J. Herman	Bauman, Maria Elisabeth	N	
Bruns, Johan Heinrich	17, May 1859	Joseph	Meyer, Elisabeth	A	
Bruns, Johan Herman Heinrich	23, July 1854	Herman	Goldschmidt, Theresa	L	
Bruns, Johan Joseph	3, Apr. 1853	Bernard	Wesskamp, Maria Anna	D	379
Bruns, Joseph Stephan	25, Dec. 1853	Johan	Horstman, Maria Anna	K	
Bruns, Ludwig	2, May 1852	Peter	Pauli, Theresa	F	
Bruns, Maria Adelheid Catharina	30, May 1852	J. Herman	Baumann, Elisabeth	L	
Bruns, Maria Anna	18, Apr. 1852	Bernard H.	Goldschmidt, Anna M.	L	
Bruns, Maria Anna	28, Mar. 1852	Theodor	Brinkmeyer, M. Catharina	C	
Bruns, Maria Elisabeth	9, Jan. 1855	Gerhard T	Brinkmeyer, Catharina	C	
Bruns, Maria Josepha	26, Mar. 1854	Wilhelm	Benz, Anna Maria	F	
Bruns, Maria Margaretha	6, May 1856	Joseph H.	Grawe, Maria Elisabeth	F	
Bruns, Peter Bernard Augustin	15, Feb. 1858	Bernard	Growe, M. Elisabeth	T	
Bruns, Theresa Bernardina	13, Nov. 1859	Herman	Bauman, M. Elisabeth	A	
Brunsman, Carl Theodor	14, Jan. 1858	J. Heinrich	Gärdner, Maria Louisa	K	
Brunsman, H.L. Thomas	8, Feb. 1856	Heinrich	Detmer, Elisabeth	K	
Brunsman, Helena Maria	1, Mar. 1852	Albert H.	Stallo, Agnes	K	
Brunsmann, Johan Carl	27, Apr. 1859		Brunsmann, Dorothea	C	
Brunst, Eleonore	24, July 1853	Francis	Tanner, Eva	S	

Name of Child	Date of Baptism	Father	Mother	Church	Page
Brunst, Johan	4, Apr. 1858	Francis	Dauner, Eva	S	
Brunst, Maria Josepha	2, Mar. 1856	Wilhelm	Benz, Maria	F	
Brunst, Marianna	14, June 1857	Wilhelm	Benz, Anna Maria	F	
Bruss, Ferdinand	13, Mar. 1853	Philipp	Motz, Magdalena	L	
Brust, Xavier	27, Mar. 1859	Simon	Neunreiter, Francisca	U	
Bruta, Elisabeth	24, Jan. 1852	John	Conner, Mary	L	
Bryan, Bridget	13, Feb. 1855	James	Londgan, Helen	P	120
Bryan, Bridget	6, Apr. 1855	Thomas	Ryan, Catherine	E	276
Bryan, John	2, July 1852	Dennis	McWilliams, Helen	B	262
Bryant, Catherine	6, Feb. 1855	Daniel	Clark, Bridget	P	119
Bryant, Edward William	26, June 1859	Hiram	Falls, Mary Ann	B	76
Bryant, Ellen Mary	14, Oct. 1855	William	Lynch, Mary Ann	B	20
Bryne, Elizabeth	24, June 1855	Michael	King, Bridget	P	137
Bryne, George Washington	9, Mar. 1851	Patrick	Cole, Rosanne	P	5
Bryne, Thomas	7, Mar. 1854	John	----, Elizabeth	M	
Bryon, John	4, Mar. 1857	John	----, Catherine	E	438
Bryon, William	18, Dec. 1853	Edward	Petry, Mary	R	
Bryson, Patrick	24, Aug. 1857	James	Ward, Joanne	E	476
B---trop, Rosina	11, May 1851	Georg	Roser, Rosina	J	10
Buchanan, Helen Melissa	24, Oct. 1858	William	----, Mary Jane	E	572
Buchanan, Maria Elisabeth	26, Oct. 1851	William	Bhrystig, Mary Ann	K	
Buchanan, Mary Jane	14, Sept 1856	William R.	Christie, Jaen	B	34
Buchanan, William Robert	26, Sept 1853	William	----, Mary Jane	V	6
Buchdrucker, Margaretha	24, May 1853	Carl	Schwarz, Magdalena	D	386
Buchdrucker, Peter Carl	14, Oct. 1855	Carl	Schwarz, Magdalena	C	
Buchdrucker, Valentin Carl	27, Apr. 1851	Carl	Schwarz, Magdalena	D	262
Bucheid, Amelia	20, Jan. 1856	Nicolaus	----, Mary	H	
Bucheid, Mary Magdalene	15, Jan. 1854	Nicolaus	----, Mary	H	
Büchel, Maria Wilhelmina	24, May 1857	Michael	Jören, Magdalena	K	
Bucher, Francis Joseph	19, Jan. 1851	Joseph	Rumpler, Maria	D	249
Bucher, Maria	18, Jan. 1857	Georg	Armel, Josephina	D	77
Bucher, Rosina	1, July 1855	Georg	Armel, Josephina	D	37
Buchert, Carl Heinrich	11, Mar. 1855	Georg	Reiter, Margaretha	F	
Buchert, Catharina Elisabeth	5, Nov. 1854	Anton	Bierenheim, Magdalena	D	21
Buchert, Georg Joseph	16, June 1850	Georg	Reider, Margaretha	F	
Buchert, Johan Edward	17, July 1853	Georg	Reiter, Margaretha	F	
Buchert, John Andrew	25, Apr. 1858	George	Reiter, Margaret	H	
Buchert, Margaretha Amalia	9, Nov. 1856	Georg	Reider, Margaretha	F	
Buchert, Maria Margaretha	22, Feb. 1852	Georg	Reuther, Maria Cecilia	F	
Buchheid, Barbara	2, July 1854	Carl	Kattis, Maria	K	
Buchheid, Joseph Martin	25, Dec. 1858	Nicolaus	Stehle, Mary	H	
Buchheid, Margaretha	22, Feb. 1857	Philipp	Wörtz, Catharina	D	79
Buchheid, Maria Eva	17, Mar. 1852	Simon	Gehring, Anna	D	313
Buchheid, Rosa Carolina	12, Mar. 1856	Simon	Gehring, Anna Maria	D	53
Buchheit, Peter	31, Aug. 1856	Peter	Laudeman, Jacobina	K	
Buchholz, Andreas	29, Dec. 1850	Mathias	Brugger, Maria Anna	D	246
Buchholz, Andreas	25, Dec. 1851	Mathias	Brugger, Maria Anna	D	298
Buchholz, Carolina	4, Oct.1857	Mathias	Bruscke, Mary Ann	D	96
Buchholz, Francis Anton	27, Jan. 1850	Jacob	Jaeger, Magdalena	D	201
Buchholz, Johan Georg	26, June 1853	Mathias	Braugger, Maria Anna	D	392
Buchholz, Maria Anna	3, Mar. 1856	Mathias	Brugger, Maria Anna	D	53
Buchman, Mathias	20, May 1855	Nicolaus	Steuer, Catharina	D	35
Buchman, Peter	28, Nov. 1858	Nicolaus	Steier, Catharina	D	124
Büchner, Margaretha	26, Aug. 1853	Joseph	Höffer, Theresa	D	402
Büchner, Theresa Carolina	7, Oct. 1855	Joseph (+)	Hoeffer, Theresa	D	44
Buchwald, Andrew	5, Nov. 1855	Andrew	----, Anna	H	
Buchwald, Andrew	15, May 1852	Andrew	----, Anna Maria	H	
Buchwald, James Andrew	5, Dec. 1853	Andrew	----, Ann	H	
Buck, Carolina Ottilia	12, May 1858	Ludwig	Bender, Anna	D	111

Name of Child	Date of Baptism	Father	Mother	Church	Page
Buck, Helena Rosalia	4, May 1856	Ludwig	Bender, Anna	F	
Buck, Johan Arnold Heinrich	5, July 1853	J. Herman	Hudepohl, Catharina	C	
Buck, John	13, Mar. 1853	Edward	----, Mary	B	286
Buck, Peter Wilhelm	31, Jan. 1858	Joseph	----, Catharina	R	
Bucke, Johan Bernard	27, Mar. 1851	Bernard C.	Luehl, Anna Maria	F	
Bucke, Johan Heinrich	12, Oct. 1856	Herman H.	Zumdicker, M. Gertrud	L	
Bücke, Wilhelm	24, Oct. 1851	J.	Buninger, Carolina	K	
Buckel, Catharina Philomena	24, May 1858	Michael	Foerst, Barbara	D	112
Buckel, Johan Eberhard	26, Apr. 1853	Jacob	Fiel?, Margaretha	D	382
Buckel, Joseph Matthias	5, Oct. 1856	Michael	Först, Barbara	D	69
Buckel, Maria Magdalena	25, July 1852	Michael	Fürst, Barbara	D	340
Buckel, Peter Joseph	20, Nov. 1853	Michael	F---, Barbara	D	416
Buckereis, Theresa	3, June 1859	Johan	Betzel, Maria Anna	H	
Buckey, Michael	6, Apr. 1850	Patrick	McCarthy, Bridget	E	209
Bucklet, Maria Catharina	1, Dec. 1851	Johan	Riedel, Barbara	D	295
Buckley, Abigail	25, Apr. 1858	Dennis	----, Elisabeth	R	
Buckley, Ann	26, Jan. 1851	John	----, Mary	E	279
Buckley, Ann	22, Mar. 1856	Thomas	O'Brien, Catherine	B	27
Buckley, Catherine	7, Dec. 1857	Daniel	Connell, Ann	B	53
Buckley, Catherine	30, Sept 1855	Jeremiah	----, Mary	E	317
Buckley, Cornelius	5, Apr. 1854	----	----, ----	H	
Buckley, Cornelius	11, July 1859	Michael	Twooney, Helen	R	
Buckley, Dennis	26, Mar. 1854	Dennis	Connell, Margaret	P	76
Buckley, Edward	7, May 1858	John	Gleanon, Mary	B	58
Buckley, Eliza	18, July 1854	Thomas	O'Brien, Catherine	B	3
Buckley, Ellen	22, Jan. 1854	Benjamin	----, Honora	H	
Buckley, Ellen	15, Aug. 1858	Eugene	----, Joanne	M	
Buckley, Frances Josephine	29, May 1859	Francis	Kelley, Josephine	E	628
Buckley, Francis	10, Oct. 1858	Dennis	Connell, Margaret	B	65
Buckley, Honora	23, Mar. 1854	?	----, ----	H	
Buckley, James Arogagh?	28, May 1854	Jeremiah	----, Mary	E	193
Buckley, Jeremiah	12, July 1857	Dennis	Doyle, Mary Ann	H	
Buckley, Jeremiah	15, June 1858	John	Mahoney, Catherine	E	542
Buckley, Jeremiah	25, Nov. 1855	Michael	Hussey, Honora	V	28
Buckley, Jeremiah Daniel	7, Dec. 1856	John	----, Catherine	E	419
Buckley, Joanne	20, Nov. 1853	Dennis	Dorgan, Elizabeth	R	
Buckley, Joanne	8, Jan. 1854	Jeremiah	Laughlin, Mary	E	158
Buckley, John	13, Mar. 1854	Daniel	Maguire, Sarah	B	311
Buckley, John	3, Dec. 1856	Dennis	Connell, Margaret	B	37
Buckley, John	20, June 1855	Eugene	McCarthy, Jane	N	
Buckley, John	13, Aug. 1856	Eugene	McCarthy, Joanne	V	32
Buckley, John	10, Aug. 1857	Jeremiah	Buckly,	P	219
Buckley, John	18, July 1855	John	Glinnon, Mary	P	141
Buckley, John	30, Mar. 1851	John	Murphy, Helen	B	228
Buckley, John Terrence	16, Aug. 1854	John	Mahony, Catherine	V	16
Buckley, Joseph	13, Mar. 1854	Daniel	Maguire, Sarah	B	311
Buckley, Julia	17, Oct. 1858	Patrick	Moroney, Ann	B	65
Buckley, Mary	28, Apr. 1852	Thomas	O'Brien, Catherine	B	258
Buckley, Mary Ann	17, Apr. 1853	John	----, Mary	E	82
Buckley, Mary ann	12, Apr. 1857	Patrick	Moroney, Ann	B	43
Buckley, Mary Jane	15, Nov. 1857	Edward	Walsh, Bridget	B	52
Buckley, Michael	22, Mar. 1852	John	Mahony, Catherine	E	395
Buckley, Michael	4, Dec. 1853	Michael	Hussy, Ann	E	150
Buckly, Column	24, Aug. 1857	James	Kelly, Mary	P	221
Buckman, Maria Catharina Elisabeth	16, June 1853	Friedrich	Ruske, Elisabeth	K	
Buckreis, Cunigunda	5, Feb. 1854	Johan	Betz, Maria Anna	D	3
Buckreis, Johan	14, Jan. 1850	Johan	Betz, Maria Anna	D	199
Buckreis, Maria Cunigunda	4, May 1851	Johan	Betz, Maria Anna	D	264
Budde, Anna Maria Elisabeth	24, June 1854	J. Heinrich	Orlage, Maria Adelheid	D	12

Name of Child	Date of Baptism	Father	Mother	Church	Page
Budde, Herman Friedrich	25, Dec. 1854	Johan	Hoelscher, Maria Engel	F	
Budde, Herman Heinrich	13, May 1853	Herman	Urlage, Adelheid	C	
Budde, Johan Bernard	12, May 1857	Herman	Urlage, Elisabeth	F	
Budde, Johan Heinrich	27, Oct. 1858	Heinrich	Kellker, Elisabeth	A	
Budde, Johan Heinrich	14, Aug. 1853	J. Peter	Stephen, Anna Maria	K	
Budde, Johan Heinrich	29, June 1853	Johan	Hoelscher, Maria Engel	F	
Budde, Johan Herman	30, Dec. 1854	Ludwig	Bueltel, Anna Maria	F	
Budde, Johan Ludwig	7, Dec. 1850	J. Herman	Hoelzker, Engelina	F	
Budde, Ludwig	19, Oct. 1856	J. Herman	Hoelscher, Catharina Engel	F	
Budde, M. Catharina Angela	27, Apr. 1859	Herman	Urlage, Elisabeth	T	
Budde, M. Elisabeth	15, Oct. 1858	Herman	Hoelscher, M. Angela	T	
Budde, Maria Elisabeth	8, Nov. 1855	J. Peter	Stephan, Elisabeth	K	
Budde, Maria Elisabeth Anna	9, Nov. 1856	J. Heinrich	Erpenbeck, Elisabeth	A	
Budde, Marianna	11, Apr. 1857	Ludwig	Bueltel, Marianna	F	
Budde, Peter Herman	23, Nov. 1857	Peter	Steffen, Elisabeth	K	
Buddeke, Heinrich Aloysius	4, Nov. 1850	Heinrich J.	Raterman, Anna Maria	A	
Buddeke, Johan Heinrich Francis Xavier	25, Apr. 1854	H.H.	Raterman, Anna Maria	A	
Buddendick, Anna Maria	7, Sept 1858	Heinrich	Averdick, A. Elis.	L	
Buddick, Maria Magdalena	25, Nov. 1851	Bernard	Schrandt, Gesina	C	
Budenbourg, Friedrich Johan	9, Nov. 1852	J. Bernard	Cona, Antonia Catharina	D	357
Buder, Maria Catharina	15, Sept 1852	Ludwig	Bartel, Marianna	F	
Budke, Josephina	25, Dec. 1851	J. Dietrich	Henning, Maria Elisabeth	A	
Budnick, Emma Theresa	12, Mar. 1854	Ferdinand	Pfoertner, Maria	F	
Budnick, Ferdinand	14, Feb. 1858		adult	F	
Budnick, Ferdinand Franz	29, June 1856	Ferdinand	Pfoertner, M. Agnes	F	
Budnik, Susanna Rosina	29, Aug. 1852	Ferdinand	Pfoertner, Anna Maria	F	
Budte, Carolina Theresa	17, July 1855	J. Heinrich	Erpenbeck, Maria Elisabeth	D	38
Buecker, Anna Maria	12, Apr. 1857	Bernard	Recker, Anna M.	C	
Buecker, Anna Maria	10, Apr. 1854	Christoph	Unnewehr, Angela	C	
Buecker, Anna Maria	26, Aug. 1855	Johan H.	Bartels, Anna M. Cath.	G	
Buecker, Anna Maria Dorothea	20, Aug. 1857	Heinrich	Bader, Catharina	G	
Buecker, Augusta Maria	31, Aug. 1855	Bernard	Reckers, M. Anna	C	
Buecker, Bernard Heinrich	21, Nov. 1854	Francis	Buening, M. Anna	C	
Buecker, Catharina Maria	10, Apr. 1854	Christoph	Unnewehr, Angela	C	
Buecker, Clara Elisabeth	19, Jan. 1855	Heinrich	Blankenmeyer, Elis.	L	
Buecker, Clemens Heinrich	18, Feb. 1856	Heinrich	Blankemeyer, Elisabeth	C	
Buecker, Francis Bernard	26, Feb. 1857	Francis	Buning, M. Anna	C	
Buecker, Francis Martin	14, Apr. 1851	Francis	Dillmann, A.M. Julia	L	
Buecker, Heinrich Franz	21, Mar. 1858	Heinrich	Blankemeier, Elis.	T	
Buecker, Herman Francis Joseph	31, Mar. 1858	Francis	Buening, M. Anna	C	
Buecker, Maria Elisabeth	13, Sept 1859	Bernard	Reker, Maria	C	
Buecker, Maria Theresa	3, Oct. 1853	J. Heinrich	Blakemeyer, M. Elis.	L	
Bueckle, Andreas Johan	16, Apr. 1855	Andreas	Mehr, Catharina	C	
Bueckle, Anna Eva	16, Mar. 1856	Ludwig	Dosenbach, Magdalena	D	54
Buekel, Michael Edmund	2, Oct. 1859	Michael	Fürst, Barbara	AA	
Bueker, Maria	19, May 1850	Friedrich	Schroeder, Angela	C	
Bueker, Mathias Friedrich	14, Feb. 1854	Heinrich	Bartel, Catharina	C	
Buelte, Johan Bernard	4, Dec. 1859	J. Bernard	Huntemann, M. Adelheid	F	
Buelte, Maria Adelheid	4, Oct. 1858	Bernard	Hunten, Adelheid	F	
Bueltel, Maria Rosa	9, Jan. 1855	J. Bernard	Schmidt, M. Theresa	L	
Buelter, Johan Heinrich	20, July 1851	J. Heinrich	Schmitz, Theresa	L	
Buelter, Johan Heinrich Francis	24, Jan. 1850	J. Bernard	Schmitz, Anna Theresa	C	
Buenker, Maria Gesina Philomena	27, Oct. 1859	Wenceslaus	Mestemaker, M. Elisabeth	L	
Buennemeier, Maria Helena	4, Feb. 1858	Herman	Berkert, Elisabeth	D	104
Buennemeyer, Johan Clemens	11, Jan. 1855	Clemens	Wielenberg, M. Agnes	L	
Buennemeyer, Johan Heinrich	18, Dec. 1851	J. Heinrich	Sudbeck, A. Catharina	L	
Buennemeyer, Maria Catharina	10, Jan. 1850	Bernard	Bude, Angela	L	
Buer, Ludwig	3, July 1859	Johan	Elsaso, Catharina	C	
Buer, Maria Anna	13, Apr. 1854	Friedrich	VonderHeide, Maria	C	

Name of Child	Date of Baptism	Father	Mother	Church	Page
Buerger, Eva	9, June 1857	Stephan	Rudolf, Elisabeth	D	87
Buergle, Francis Joseph	10, Apr. 1856	Xavier	Wagner, Agatha	C	
Buergle, Maria Louise	31, Aug. 1851	Xavier	Wagner, Agatha	C	
Buerke, Anna Maria Rosa	30, Aug. 1853	Bernard C.	Luehn, Anna Maria	F	
Buerke, Francis Anton	21, Jan. 1855	Fidel	----, Anna Maria	U	
Buerkle, Johan	8, Feb. 1852	Joseph	Haier, Elisabeth	D	306
Buerkle, Johan Baptist	30, Jan. 1859	Johan	Hofert, Maria	L	
Buerkle, Joseph	9, Apr. 1854	Florenz	Gallus, Catharina	C	
Buerkle, Maria Francisca	25, Sept 1853	Francis	Wagner, Agatha	C	
Buerner, Johan Heinrich	19, Dec. 1852	Maurice	Sievers, Catharina	C	
Buersner, Maria Josephina	12, May 1850	J. Martin	Seemann, Maria Anna	L	
Bues, Johan Bernard Theodor Ludwig	14, Apr. 1851	Wilhelm	Schriber, Agnes	D	260
Bues, Maria Anna Brigitta	8, Oct. 1853	Wilhelm	Schriber, Agnes	D	409
Buescher, Anton Wilhelm	5, Oct. 1856	Anton	Schloebbe, Catharina	C	
Buescher, Margaretha Adelheid	20, Mar. 1853	J. Heinrich	Egbers, M. Christina	L	
Buescher, Maria Catharina Emilia	10, Dec. 1854	Anton	Schlepe, Catharina	C	
Bueschle, Francis Theodor	6, Jan. 1858	Francis X.	She----, Maria Anna	D	102
Buettel, John	18, Jan. 1857	Andrew	Reister, Regina	H	
Buettner, Louis	31, Aug. 1856	Andreas	Krass, Catharina	H	
Buettner, Theresa	30, Oct. 1859	Andreas	Kraus, Catharina	H	
Buggy, Mary Eleanore	6, Mar. 1859	John	Eldrige, Mary	P	278
Bugman, Lawrence	22, July 1855	Georg	Fox, Anna	D	39
Bühl, Catharina	28, Sept 1854	Johan	Seifert, Anna Maria	D	18
Bühl, Johan Conrad	7, June 1857	Johan	Seiter--, Anna	D	86
Bühl, Maria Anna	4, May 1851	Johan	Seiber, Anna Maria	D	263
Bühler, Bertha	7, Dec. 1856	Johan	Hag---, B----	D	73
Bühler, Elisabeth	6, Feb. 1859	Joseph	Müller, Ottilia	A	
Bühler, Francisca	21, Jan. 1855	Johan	Güteman, Francisca	D	27
Bühler, Nicolaus	16, Nov. 1856	Joseph	Müller, Ottilia	A	
Bühn, Catharina	5, July 1857	Andreas	Bart, Elisabeth	D	89
Buhnert, Elisabeth	21, Nov. 1858	Joseph	Türk, Maria	D	124
Buhon, Jacob	6, Aug. 1858	Gregor	Stander, Maria Anna	D	116
Buhr, Anna Philomena	6, Mar. 1853	Joseph	Hellbruner, Regina	J	20
Buhr, Carl	24, May 1857	Joseph	Hellbrunner, Regina	J	40
Buhr, Elisabeth	16, Oct. 1859	Joseph	Hellbrunner, Regina	J	52
Buhr, Johan Baptist	1, Oct. 1850	Joseph	Hellbrunner, Regina	J	8
Buhr, Johan Friedrich Christoph	18, Aug. 1851	Friedrich	Spanhorst, Catharina	L	
Bulger, Mary Ann	15, Nov. 1857	John	Harper, Margaret	E	493
Bullard, William	11, Sept 1853	James	----, Martha	E	127
Bullet, Louise Mary	24, Nov. 1859		adult	B	84
Bullet, Mary Genevieve Judith	1, Jan. 1855	Charles	Winkelman, Louise	B	9
Bülow, Johan Bernard	13, Mar. 1856	Friedrich A.	Richter, Anna Maria	A	
Bulster, Catharina Johanna	12, Oct. 1853	Heinrich	Lageman, Maria	A	
Bültel, Maria Francisca	31, Jan. 1853	J. Bernard	Schmidt, Maria Theresa	K	
Bultel, Maria Regina	4, Dec. 1851	J. Gerhard	Fussgel, Euphemia M.	F	
Bumpus, Mary Ann	14, Aug. 1853		adult	V	5
Büne, Johan Bernard Ferdinand	3, Mar. 1857	Heinrich	Peltin, Maria	K	
Bünger, Anna Maria Bernardina	23, Mar. 1855	Heinrich	----, ----	N	27
Bunger, Elisabeth	21, Jan. 1859	Heinrich	Amenscamp, Maria	N	
Bunger, Helen	28, Sept 1852	J. Heinrich	Amenskamp, Marianna	N	9
Bunger, Josephina	8, Feb. 1857	J. Heinrich	Amenscamp, Anna Maria	N	
Bunger, Maria Agnes	2, Oct. 1850	J. Heinrich	Amenskamp, Maria	N	1
Büning, Anna Christina	6, June 1857	Johan	Durbeck, Theresa	A	
Büning, Catharina Helena	14, Sept 1859	Johan	Durbeck, Theresa	A	
Büning, Francis Jacob	5, Apr. 1859	Francis W.	Ruln--, Theresa	D	135
Büning, Herman	13, Nov. 1851	Herman	Barlage, Catharina	K	
Büning, Theresa Helan	25, Jan. 1857	Francis	Rohne, Theresa	A	
Bunker, Bernard Dietrich	27, Sept 1854	Bernard	Brink, Christina	A	
Bünker, Georg Wilhelm	26, Feb. 1858	Johan	Kobbe, Theresa	A	

Name of Child	Date of Baptism	Father	Mother	Church	Page
Bünker, Herman Heinrich	29, Nov. 1856	J. Dietrich	Brink, Christina	A	
Bunker, Maria	24, June 1855	Christian	Erhart, Maria	K	
Bünker, Maria Elisabeth	16, May 1852	Herman	Kobbe, Maria Theresa	A	
Bunnemaker, Anna Maria Francisca	4, Feb. 1854	J. Heinrich	Sudbeck, Catharina	K	
Bunneman, Johan Philipp	9, Nov. 1856	J.B.	Keimit?, Johanna	K	
Bünnemeier, Johan Francis	24, Feb. 1856	J. Heinrich	Suedback, Anna Catharina	K	
Bünnemeier, Johan Joseph	17, Sept 1855	J. Bernard	Bode, Maria Angela	K	
Bünnemeier, Josepha Maria Elisabeth	7, Jan. 1855	J. Heinrich	Mehring, Louise	R	
Bünnemeier, Maria Catharina	19, Dec. 1856	Heinrich	----, Louisa	R	
Bünnemeyer, Bernard Francis	1, Apr. 1858	Heinrich	Südbeck, Anna	K	
Bünnemeyer, Bernard Heinrich	16, Feb. 1858	Bernard	Butke, Maria Angela	K	
Bünnemeyer, Farncis Aloysius	13, Apr. 1857	J. Bernard	Bode, Maria Anna	K	
Bünnemeyer, Johan Joseph	13, Apr. 1857	J. Bernard	Bode, Maria Anna	K	
Bünnemeyer, Johanna Elisabeth	18, Dec. 1858	John H.	Mohring, Maria L.	R	
Bunnemeyer, Maria Elisabeth	17, July 1857	Clemens	Wielenberg, Maria Agnes	K	
Burbach, Amelia	27, Feb. 1859	August	Penz, Maria Anna	D	132
Burbach, Carolina	17, Aug. 1857	August	Benz, Marianna	F	
Burck, Appolonia	27, Apr. 1856	J. Jacob	Wittinger, Catharina	D	57
Burck, Bertha	24, Oct. 1852	J. Jacob	Witting, Eva Catharina	D	354
Burck, Heinrich	26, June 1859	J. Jacob	Witting, Eva Catharina	D	141
Burck, Johan Baptist	26, Dec. 1858	Christian	Haütle, Regina	D	127
Burck, Johan Michael	18, June 1854	J. Jacob	Wittinger, Eva Catharina	D	12
Bürckel, Joseph	21, Oct. 1855	Joseph	Heil, Elisabeth	D	45
Bürckel, Maria Catharina	20, Dec. 1857	Joseph	Heil, Elisabeth	D	101
Bürckel, Valentin	5, Mar. 1854	Joseph	Heil, Elisabeth	D	6
Burckhard, Francis Adam	24, May 1851	Stephan	Hoffman, Maria Francisca	D	265
Burckhard, Francis Stephan	10, Aug. 1856	F. Stephan	Hofman, Francisca	D	64
Burckhart, Carl Joseph	19, Sept 1853	Francis	Hoffman, Francisca	D	407
Burckhart, Ernst August	13, Jan. 1858	Francis	Hoffman, Francisca	D	102
Burckle, Andreas Peter	1, Jan. 1857	Andreas	Mehr, Catharina	D	76
Bürckle, Barbara Catharina	21, Aug. 1853	Andreas	Mehr, Catharina	D	401
Burdick, Anna Friedrica Josephina	27, Feb. 1856	Francis	Bruns, Bernardina	A	
Burdick, anna Maria	13, May 1885	Francis	Bruns, Bernardina	A	
Burdick, Bernardina	17, Apr. 1859	F.	Brune, Dina	A	
Burdick, Francisca Catharina	6, June 1859	J. Heinrich	Rolfes, Maria	A	
Burdick, Maria Carolina	17, Nov. 1856	J. Heinrich	Rolfes, Anna Maria	A	
Burdick, Maria Josephina	17, June 1854	Heinrich	Rolfes, Maria Anna Elisabeth	A	
Burdick, Mathias	1, Jan. 1856	Heinrich	Schrand, Gesina	C	
Burdig, Gerhard Heinrich	12, June 1850	Heinrich	Schrandt, Gesina	C	
Burdik, Johan Bernard Francis	4, May 1858	J. Friedrich	Hoskamp, Bernardina	K	
Burdley, Margaret	10, Jan. 1856	Michael	White, Catherine	P	166
Burdsell, John	25, June 1857	Henry	Marolle?, Anita	E	462
Burdsol, Ada Cecilia	13, Dec. 1855	Henry	----, Annita	E	333
Burdsol, Mary Theresa	17, Mar. 1854	Henry	----, Ann	E	176
Burehl, Francisca Xaviera	25, Jan. 1853	Gustav	Reis, Magdalena	F	
Burg, Johan	14, Mar. 1858	Nicolaus	Brand, Margaretha	T	
Burg, Johan Georg	16, July 1854	J. Nicolaus	Brand, Margaretha	D	14
Burg, Margaretha	26, Oct. 1856	Nicolaus	Het---, Magdalena	D	70
Burger, Albert	24, Oct. 1858	Albert	Lindauer, Sophia	F	
Burger, Albert	17, Dec. 1854	Hieronymus	----, Mary Ann	U	
Burger, Carl	28, Jan. 1856	Johan	Schell, Barbara	Q	12
Burger, Elisabeth	14, Nov. 1858	Hieronymus	Geiger, Maria Anna	U	
Bürger, Elisabeth	19, June 1859	Stephan	Rudolf, Elisabeth	D	140
Bürger, Emil	8, Feb. 1857	Georg	Wurmel, Josephina	D	78
Burger, Francis	10, Aug. 1851	Heinrich	Muehl, Barbara	C	
Burger, Friedrich	25, Sept 1853	Philipp	Muehl, Barbara	C	
Burger, Gustav	8, July 1855	Valentin	Edler, Maria Anna	F	
Burger, Jacob	1, Jan. 1855	Heinrich	Muhl, Barbara	C	
Burger, Johan	26, Dec. 1858	Johan	Schill, Barbara	Q	30

Name of Child	Date of Baptism	Father	Mother	Church	Page
Burger, Johanna Maria Magdalena	7, Sept 1856	Hieronymus	Geiger, Marianna	F	
Bürger, Josephina	26, Aug. 1855	Stephan	Rudolph, Elisabeth	D	41
Burger, Josephina Antonia	14, Jan. 1856	Francis	---er, Bernardina	D	50
Bürger, Philipp	8, Feb. 1857	Jacob	Fein, Anna	D	78
Burger, Sophia	1, Aug. 1853	Adalbert	Lindauer, Sophia	F	
Burger, Sophia	23, Feb. 1856	Cletus	Geier, Gertrud	F	
Burgermeyer, Anna	11, Sept 1859	Joseph	Sauer, Genofeva	N	
Burgermeyer, Joseph	1, June 1857	Joseph	Sauer, Genofeva	N	
Burgermeyer, Richardina	25, July 1858	Joseph	Sauer, Genofeva	N	
Burgess, Catherine	10, Oct. 1859	Michael	Costello, Joanne	P	300
Burghard, Barbara	5, Oct. 1856	Joseph	Keller, Barbara	D	69
Burghard, Maurice Valentin Bernard	6, Sept 1857	Maurice	Saul, Barbara	D	94
Burghard, Victoria Adelina	1, Dec. 1855	Maurice	Saal, Barbara	D	47
Burghart, Ernst Heinrich	20, Mar. 1859	Maurice	Saul, Barbara	D	134
Burghart, Francis Nicolaus	5, May 1855	Nicolaus	Morio, Catharina	C	
Burghart, Maria Anna	6, Feb. 1854	Georg	Zimmermann, Barbara	C	
Burghoffer, Georg Eugen Carl	10, Mar. 1857	J. Baptist	Lepros, Augustina	K	
Burgin, Honora	17, Apr. 1856	Michael	----, Ann	E	360
Bürgle, Johan	3, Nov. 1853	Arbogast	Grieshaber, Victoria	D	413
Bürgler, Godefried	28, Mar. 1853	Johan	Steimer, Catharina	D	378
Burgoyne, Michael	24, July 1859	Michael	Coony, Joanne	E	642
Burgy, Josepha Bertha	11, Mar. 1855	Gottlieb	Gerschrogler, Josephina	F	
Burhoff, Maria Anna	1, Jan. 1858	Bernard	Göttker, Elisabeth	A	
Buring, Johan	14, Oct. 1851	Peter	Roch, Catharina	C	
Burk, Anna Maria	29, Aug. 1852	Lambert	Bunte, Maria Adelheid	A	
Burk, Bridget	16, June 1853	Thomas	Burke, Catherine	P	44
Burk, Catharina Adelheid	7, Dec. 1857	Jacob	Sutherland, Elisabeth	L	
Burk, Catherine	15, Feb. 1851	Michael	Lamy, Mary	B	225
Burk, Honora	10, Mar. 1853	Patrick	----, Honora	E	71
Burk, Joanne	26, Dec. 1853	John	Fresby?, Catherine	E	155
Burk, John	7, Mar. 1857	James	----, Catherine	E	438
Burk, John James	27, Mar. 1853	Patrick	Storer, Ann	B	287
Burk, John Thomas	5, Aug. 1855	Patrick	McGinsey, Catherine	U	
Burk, Margaret	12, Dec. 1854	Patrick	----, Honora	E	246
Burk, Margaret Telia	1, May 1853	Michael	Daily, Catherine	P	40
Burk, Michael	24, Jan. 1855	Patrick	----, Sarah	E	259
Burk, Thomas	22, July 1857	William	Tracy, Margaret	E	468
Burkard, Georg	12, Sept 1858	Georg	Braun, Maria Anna	D	119
Burke, Ann	28, Jan. 1856	Christopher	----, Mary	E	339
Burke, Ann	17, Apr. 1851	Joseph	Burke, Joanne	M	
Burke, Ann	7, May 1854	Patrick	Conly, Ann	E	188
Burke, Ann	30, May 1857	Patrick	Morris, Sarah	B	44
Burke, Ann	28, Dec. 1851	Thomas	----, Ellen	M	
Burke, Ann	29, July 1852	Thomas	Hatton, Mary	E	1
Burke, Ann	23, Apr. 1854	Thomas	Spain, Ann	P	79
Burke, Ann Mary	18, Apr. 1854	Michael	Kelley, Helen	E	183
Burke, Anna Margaretha	18, Dec. 1859	Bernard	Rakes, Anna Maria	F	
Burke, Anna Maria	16, Aug. 1858	Bernard	Rackers, Margaretha	F	
Burke, Bernard	21, June 1854	Richard	Le---, Margaret	B	1
Burke, Bridget	19, Nov. 1851	Edmund	----, Jane	B	245
Burke, Bridget	22, Oct. 1851	Edmund	Riley, Jane	B	243
Burke, Bridget	18, Apr. 1854	Michael	Kelley, Helen	E	183
Burke, Bridget	21, Aug. 1853	Michael	O'Mara, Mary Ann	B	297
Burke, Bridget	17, June 1855	Patrick	Corlaghan, Mary	P	136
Burke, Bridget	1, Oct. 1854	Patrick	Waldron, Mary	T	
Burke, Bridget	19, Nov. 1853	Tobias	Gilfoyl, Margaret	B	302
Burke, Catherine	29, Jan. 1857	John	Donnelly, Frances	P	204
Burke, Catherine	9, Jan. 1859	Patrick	Colligan, Mary	B	69
Burke, Catherine	19, Dec. 1858	Patrick	McGinsee, Catherine	U	

Name of Child	Date of Baptism	Father	Mother	Church	Page
Burke, Catherine	23, Aug. 1850	Patrick	Walder, Mary	B	211
Burke, Catherine	1, Feb. 1855	Pierce	Connor, Bridget	B	11
Burke, Catherine	1, Apr. 1854	Stephan	Stanton, Mary	V	12
Burke, Cornelius	27, Sept 1857	Tobias	Gilfoil, Margaret	P	**225**
Burke, Edmund	25, Sept 1859	Christopher	Good, Mary	E	658
Burke, Edmund	24, Mar. 1859	Edmund	Dumfield, May	E	613
Burke, Edward	16, Dec. 1856	Dennis	Zandale, Ann	B	37
Burke, Edward	24, Aug. 1851	James	Carthy, Joanne	E	335
Burke, Edward	10, Apr. 1859	Michael	----, Ellen	M	
Burke, Edward	27, Jan. 1856	Michael	Naylor, Mary	R	
Burke, Elizabeth	13, Sept 1852	John	Heily?, Bridget	E	17
Burke, Ellen	8, May 1854	John	----, Ann	M	
Burke, Ellen	1, Apr. 1855	John	----, Catherine	M	
Burke, Francis Xavier	12, Dec. 1851	James F.	Runk, Mary	E	365
Burke, George Patrick	30, Aug. 1857	Patrick	McKinsey, Catherine	U	
Burke, Helen	15, Aug. 1858	Thomas	Spain, Ann	P	257
Burke, Honora	9, Nov. 1856	James	Carthy, Joanne	E	411
Burke, Honora	26, Dec. 1852	William	Welsh, Mary	E	48
Burke, James	27, Feb. 1850	Edmund	Ryan, Jane	B	197
Burke, James	31, Aug. 1856	Edward	Burke, Mary	T	
Burke, James	27, Sept 1857	Francis	----, Bridget	R	
Burke, James	21, Aug. 1859	Michael	Burns, Bridget	P	293
Burke, James	12, Apr. 1851	Michael	Burns, Margaret	E	299
Burke, James	9, May 1852	Patrick	Waldron, Mary	B	258
Burke, James	4, Aug. 1852	Robert	adult - 21 years old	E	2
Burke, James	3, Aug. 1856	Thomas	Spain, Ann	P	187
Burke, James	29, Apr. 1856	Tobias	Gilfoyl, Margaret	P	177
Burke, Joanne	19, Dec. 1852	John	Judge, Laura	B	278
Burke, Joanne	12, Aug. 1855	Thomas	----, Ellen	M	
Burke, Joanne	17, Feb. 1859	Tobias	Guilfoyle, Margaret	E	604
Burke, Johan Bernard Heinrich	21, May 1854	Bernard	Rakers, Margaretha	A	
Burke, Johanne	12, Dec. 1857	Christopher	----, Mary	E	501
Burke, John	9, July 1854	Edmund	Ryan, Jane	B	2
Burke, John	13, Oct. 1852	John	----, Ann	E	27
Burke, John	27, July 1853	John	Davis, Alice	B	296
Burke, John	2, Apr. 1859	Patrick	----, Mary	M	
Burke, John	20, June 1852	Richard	----, Bridget	M	
Burke, John	29, Dec. 1850	Thomas	Lugg, Catherine	E	272
Burke, Joseph	26, Dec. 1857	Edward	Dunphy, Mary	E	503
Burke, Joseph	24, Oct. 1859	Joseph	Carroll, Ann	P	301
Burke, Joseph	6, Nov. 1859	Patrick	Connelly, Ann	E	668
Burke, Joseph Heinrich	26, Aug. 1858	Bernard J.	Luehn, Maria	F	
Burke, Joseph Patrick	26, June 1853	John	----, Catherine	E	101
Burke, Luke	27, Feb. 1855	Thomas	----, Ann	E	268
Burke, Margaret	5, Mar. 1854	James	Carthy, Joanne	E	173
Burke, Margaret	15, Feb. 1852	John	Towrey, Ann	B	252
Burke, Margaret	13, June 1858	Michael	Nestor, Mary	R	
Burke, Margaret	6, Sept 1857	Patrick	Waldron, Mary	B	49
Burke, Maria Elisabeth	15, Oct. 1856	J. Bernard	Rakers, Margaretha	A	
Burke, Mary	28, Dec. 1856	Edmund	Ryan, Joanne	E	422
Burke, Mary	27, May 1854	James	----, Edna	E	193
Burke, Mary	21, May 1854	James	Welsh, Sarah	B	315
Burke, Mary	14, Feb. 1859	John	----, Catherine	M	
Burke, Mary	18, Feb. 1855	John	Condon, Catherine	V	23
Burke, Mary	7, June 1857	Miles	Burke, Bridget	V	39
Burke, Mary	21, Apr. 1859	Patrick	Doran, Catherine	B	74
Burke, Mary	8, Feb. 1857	Pierce	Conners, Bridget	P	205
Burke, Mary Ann	3, Oct. 1852	John	----, Mary	M	
Burke, Mary Ann	28, May 1857	Patrick	----, Margaret	M	

Name of Child	Date of Baptism	Father	Mother	Church	Page
Burke, Mary Ann	8, Mar. 1857	Patrick	Cooligan, Mary	B	41
Burke, Mary Helen	7, Oct. 1855	James	Sudderland, J.	E	319
Burke, Mary Jane	25, June 1854	Michael	Byrne, Margaret	V	15
Burke, Mary Margaret	16, Nov. 1851	Valentin	Murthagh, Mary	B	245
Burke, Michael	24, Apr. 1853	Edmund	Kating, Margaret	E	83
Burke, Michael	13, July 1851	James	Conner, Mary	E	323
Burke, Michael	21, Nov. 1855	Michael	----, Mary	M	
Burke, Michael	10, May 1857	Michael	Burns, Margaret	E	452
Burke, Mina	13, Mar. 1859	Pierce	Connors, Bridget	P	279
Burke, Patrick	28, Sept 1854	Christopher	----, Mary	E	227
Burke, Patrick	29, June 1851	Christopher	Connally, Rose	E	319
Burke, Patrick	23, Nov. 1851	Patrick	Nolent, Ann	E	361
Burke, Patrick	5, Dec. 1853	William	Powers, Catherine	B	303
Burke, Patrick Andrew	5, Feb. 1858	Thomas	----, Ann	E	515
Burke, Peter	22, Feb. 1852	Michael	----, Mary	E	384
Burke, Peter	10, Aug. 1856	Richard	----, Julia	M	
Burke, Richard	30, Aug. 1857	John	----, Catherine	M	
Burke, Richard	7, Aug. 1859	Patrick	Waldron, Mary	B	78
Burke, Richard Thomas	29, Nov. 1852	Patrick	Gallagher, Mary	E	40
Burke, Rosanne	29, May 1853	Thomas	----, Ellen	M	
Burke, Rose Ann	23, Mar. 1856	Patrick	Conly, Ann	E	352
Burke, Thomas	26, Dec. 1857	Edward	Dunphy, Mary	E	503
Burke, Thomas	31, Dec. 1853	John	----, Mary	R	
Burke, Thomas	17, Dec. 1856	John	Farrell, Catherine	U	
Burke, Thomas	5, June 1858	Joseph	Carroll, Ann	P	250
Burke, Thomas	1, Apr. 1854	Michael	Nester, Mary	V	12
Burke, Thomas	27, Feb. 1853	Stephan	Stanton, Mary	V	1
Burke, Thomas	19, Aug. 1855	Stephan	Stanton, Mary	V	26
Burke, Wilhelm	11, June 1859	Edward	Burke, Maria	F	
Burke, William	25, Mar. 1852	John	Brabeng, Bridget	B	255
Burke, William	24, Jan. 1858	Richard	----, Julia	M	
Burke, William	31, May 1859	Richard	Heshen, Julia	Z	
Burke, William	12, Dec. 1858	Stephan	Stanton, Mary	V	52
Burke, William	25, Jan. 1852	William	Power, Catherine	B	251
Burke, Williiam	30, Apr. 1857	Joseph	Carroll, Ann	B	43
Burke, Winnefred	14, July 1855	Michael	Kelly, Ellen	E	299
Burke?, Regina	21, Feb. 1858	Johan	Ess--, Theresa	D	105
Bürkel, Georg Friedrich	28, July 1850	Joseph	Haier, Elisabeth	D	225
Burker, Anna Aloysia	14, Aug. 1859	Valentin	Elder, Anna	F	
Burkett, Sarah Adelia	1, Jan. 1857	William	---bill, Mary Ann	B	38
Burkhard, Anna Maria	10, May 1859	Carl	Kleine, Anna M.	C	
Burkhard, Carolina Clara	19, Mar. 1854	Ferdinand	----, Rosa	H	
Burkhard, Catharine Rose	1, Feb. 1852	Ferdinand	----, Rose	H	
Burkhard, Franz	4, Sept 1853	Basil	Goetz, Catharina	F	
Burkhard, Joseph	27, Jan. 1850	Johan B.	Hugger, Paulina	D	201
Burkhard, Joseph Friedrich	10, May 1857	Nicolaus	Morio, Catharina	Q	22
Burkhard, Margaretha Francisa Maria	26, Dec. 1859	F. Stephan	----, Francisca	D	153
Burkhard, Maria Anna	18, May 1851	Basil	Goetz, Catharina	F	
Burkhard, Maria Elisabeth	15, Aug. 1856	Georg	Braun, Maria	D	65
Burkhard, Michael	1, May 1854	Georg	Braun, Maria Anna	D	9
Burkhardt, Catharina Wilhelmina	6, July 1851	J. Jacob	Schafer, Elenora	A	
Burkhardt, Rosina	25, Dec. 1859	Edward	Orth, Barbara	K	
Burkhart, Francis	14, May 1854	Joseph	Keller, Barbara	C	
Burkhart, Johan	5, Aug. 1855	Joseph	Keller, Barbara	C	
Burkhart, Joseph Peter	17, Jan. 1852	Georg	Braun, Maria A.	D	302
Burkhart, Maria Francisca	22, May 1859	Luke	Wolf, Maria	D	138
Burkhaus?, Maria Philomena	27, Sept 1852	Joseph	Bierman, Catharina	K	
Bürkle, Bernard Joseph	5, Dec. 1852	Florence	Galles, Catharina	D	359
Burkly, Ludwig	19, Aug. 1858	Andreas	----, Catharina	D	117

Name of Child	Date of Baptism	Father	Mother	Church	Page
Burlage, Bernard	21, July 1855	Gerhard	Garre, Lisette	L	
Burlage, Johan Dietrich	12, Aug. 1852	J. Gerhard	Reinke, Maria Adelheid	A	
Burlage, Maria Agnes	15, Oct. 1858	Joseph	Garre, Elisabeth	L	
Burlage, Maria Elisabeth	3, Sept 1856	Gerhard	Reinke, Adelheid	A	
Burlage, Maria Elisabeth	4, Oct. 1853	Joseph	Garre, M. Elisabeth	L	
Burlet, Anna Maria	26, June 1853	Jacob	Lang, Maria Anna	D	391
Burman, Ann Eliza	7, Feb. 1855	Thomas	Gordon, Ann	P	119
Burman, Joseph Abraham	30, June 1851	Thomas	Gorden, Ann	B	237
Burman, Margaret	9, Mar. 1856	Edward	----, Elizabeth	M	
Burman, Mary Ann Eliza	28, Dec. 1856	Thomas	Gordon, Ann	T	
Burmann, Marianna Gertrud	28, Mar. 1858	Ferdinand	Brandhof, Marianna	F	
Burn, Elenore	31, Aug. 1851	Michael	Cruns, Sarah	N	5
Burn, Mary	12, July 1855	N.	Galvin, Helen	E	299
Burne, Ann Mary	3, Sept 1853	William	Brune, Mary	E	125
Burne, Mary	19, Feb. 1859	Hugh	Connell, Sarah	E	605
Burnes, Charles Fleming	28, May 1850	Charles	Tread?, Catherine Adel.	E	223
Burnes, Theresa	30, Apr. 1850	Patrick	Nielden?, Catherine	E	209
Burnes, Thomas Francis	9, Oct. 1853	John	----, Eliza	E	132
Burnes, William	24, Jan. 1857	John	----, Mary	R	
Burnet, Mary	16, July 1855	Patrick	Caughlin, Mary	B	17
Burnett, Catherine	17, Feb. 1850	Patrick	Coghlin, Mary	B	196
Burnett, Elizabeth	3, May 1857	Patrick C.	Coughlin, Mary	B	44
Burnett, Mary Christine	15, Jan. 1854	William	Davis, Elizabeth	B	307
Burnett, Mary Elizabeth	3, Dec. 1850	William	----, Elizabeth	E	265
Burnett, William Charles	6, Dec. 1851	Patrick C.	Coughlin, Mary	P	14
Burney, Mary Jane	27, Oct. 1855	James	Murray, Mary	B	21
Burns, Alice	8, Nov. 1856	James	Kelly, Bridget	E	411
Burns, Catharine	19, Sept 1852	James	Flinn, Rose	L	
Burns, Catherine Ellen	9, Apr. 1859	John	Morogan, Catherine	E	617
Burns, Charles	30, Aug. 1855	James	Beyen, Sarah	R	
Burns, Edward James	3, Jan. 1858	John	Spelman, Honora	B	54
Burns, Elisabeth	29, May 1859	Thomas	Johnston, Mary	U	
Burns, Eliza	25, Dec. 1854	James	Delaney, Mary	B	9
Burns, Elizabeth	5, Dec. 1852	James	----, Ann	E	41
Burns, Elizabeth	14, May 1854	Michael	Jordan, Bridget	P	82
Burns, Elizabeth	15, Aug. 1851	William	Cashan, Elizabeth	B	238
Burns, James	3, July 1853	James	Beehan, Sarah	R	
Burns, James	16, Nov. 1857	John	Summers, Catherine	E	494
Burns, James	12, Feb. 1854	Michael	Burns, Margaret	E	167
Burns, James	24, Mar. 1859	Stephan	Foley, Ann	P	280
Burns, James	24, Mar. 1850	Thomas	----, Ellenore	E	205
Burns, James Patrick	9, Sept 1858	Patrick	Ekers, Mary	E	561
Burns, John	12, Jan. 1853	John	----, Catherine	E	53
Burns, John	25, Aug. 1850	John	----, Margaret	E	242
Burns, John	25, Sept 1857	Lawrence	O'Leary, Honora	P	**225**
Burns, John	14, May 1854	Patrick	Moneghan, Susan	E	190
Burns, John Joseph	16, Oct. 1859	J. Joseph	Spelman, Honora	B	82
Burns, John Patrick	17, Mar. 1858	Louis	Gibeln, Ann	A	
Burns, Louise Agnes	30, Dec. 1855	Edward	Burns, Catherine	P	164
Burns, Margaret	25, Apr. 1858	John	Boland, Hannah	P	247
Burns, Margaret	30, Jan. 1853	John	Summers, Catherine	E	59
Burns, Margaret	12, Dec. 1852	Patrick	Morgan, Sarah	B	277
Burns, Margaret Elizabeth	19, July 1857	Thomas	McGeil, Catherine	E	467
Burns, Maria Alice	15, May 1859	Johan	Trecy, M. Anna	C	
Burns, Mary	8, Sept 1855	James	Burns, Joanne	E	314
Burns, Mary	30, Mar. 1855	John	----, Catherine	E	275
Burns, Mary	5, Mar. 1854	John	Summers, Catherine	E	173
Burns, Mary	28, Jan. 1859	Lawrence	Leary, Hannah	P	273
Burns, Mary	15, June 1858		Burns, Bridget	E	542

Name of Child	Date of Baptism	Father	Mother	Church	Page
Burns, Mary Ann	16, Sept 1856	Christopher	McLaughlin, Ann	P	192
Burns, Mary Ann	28, Feb. 1854	John	Dugles, Ann	E	172
Burns, Mary Ann	16, Aug. 1857	John	Reynolds, Ann	N	
Burns, Mary Ann	9, Sept 1859	Martin	Glenn, Bridget	Z	
Burns, Mary Ann	22, May 1859	Michael	Fitzgerald, Mary	E	626
Burns, Mary Helen	27, Nov. 1853	Edward	Burns, Catherine	P	60
Burns, Matthew	15, Oct. 1856	Stephan	Foley, Ann	P	195
Burns, Michael	30, Aug. 1855	James	Beyen, Sarah	R	
Burns, Michael	21, Jan. 1856	John	Summers, Catherine	E	339
Burns, Michael	16, Mar. 1851	Patrick	Monaghan, Sarah	B	226
Burns, Patrick	9, May 1852	Stephan	----, Ann	E	411
Burns, Richard	28, Mar. 1852	James	Beehan, Sarah	R	
Burns, Stephan	3, Sept 1854	Stephan	Foley, Ann	E	222
Burns, Thomas	6, Feb. 1859	James	Gilligan, Mary	B	70
Burns, Timothy	24, June 1851	Timothy	Babby, Ann	E	318
Burns, Timothy	30, July 1851	Timothy	Barber, Ann	E	334
Burnside, Susan	17, Aug. 1856	John	----, Naneie	E	391
Burrat, Magdalena Philomena	26, May 1853	Nicolaus	Morio, Catharina	C	
Burrell, Edward	12, Oct. 1856	Albert	----, Frances	E	403
Burrows, Margaret Helen	13, Jan. 1855	Silvester	Carroll, Margaret	P	115
Burrus, Maria Antonette	30, May 1858	Ludwig	Wehreng, Catharina	T	
Bursch, Georg	5, Aug. 1855	J. Mathias	----, Agatha	F	
Burt, Alexander	11, Jan. 1857	John	Macauley, Ann	B	39
Burt, John	11, Sept 1859	John	McCalley, Ann	E	653
Burtchi, Maria Josephina	25, July 1859	Columban	Rocklin, Catherine	U	
Burtchi, Mary Rosalia	13, Dec. 1857	Columban	Roglin, Catherine	U	
Burtchy, Francis Anthony	1, Nov. 1855	Columban	Rogling, Catherine	U	
Burtschi, John	28, Mar. 1853	John	----, Agnes	H	
Burwinkel, Gerhard Aloysius	27, Apr. 1852	Gerhard	Stegemann, Bernardina	L	
Burwinkel, Gerhard Joseph	15, Feb. 1858	J. Gerhard	Stegemann, Bernardina	L	
Burwinkel, Johan Heinrich	2, June 1856	Anton	Stegemann, Dina	L	
Burwinkel, Johan Heinrich	21, Jan. 1857	Johan	Overmann, Elisabeth	C	
Burwinkel, Johan Joseph	22, Mar. 1854	Johan	Overmann, Elisabeth	C	
Burwinkel, M. Elisabeth Bernardina	31, Mar. 1854	Anton	Stegemann, Bernardina	L	
Busack, Johan Heinrich Herman	20, Feb. 1853	J. Heinrich	Post, Maria Catharina	K	
Busam, Carl	22, Mar. 1857	Gregor	Pander, Maria Anna	D	81
Busam, Francisca	2, May 1858	Joseph	----, Helen	R	
Busam, Francisca Juliana	1, Feb. 1852	Gregor	Panter, M. Anna	C	
Busam, Joseph	3, Jan. 1857	Joseph	----, Helen	R	
Busam, Maria	27, Nov. 1859	Joseph	Huber, Helen	Q	34
Busam, Rosina	20, Nov. 1853	Gregor	Ponter, M. Anna	C	
Busam, Theresa	30, Sept 1855	Joseph	Huber, Helen	R	
Busbach, August	30, Oct. 1854	August	Benz, Anna	D	21
Buscamp, Maria Elisabeth	27, Feb. 1852	Joseph	Michael, Maria Catharina	A	
Busch, Anna Maria	30, Sept 1855	Carl	Eichelberger, Johanna	F	
Busch, Anotn Jacob Aloysius	9, July 1858	Carl	Witzel, Anna Maria	L	
Busch, Antonia Elisabeth	24, Dec. 1854	Anton	Baumeister, Elisabeth	F	
Busch, Bernard	11, Aug. 1850	Bernard	Kock, Maria Anna	A	
Busch, Clara	5, Nov. 1854	Bernard	Koch, Marianna	F	
Busch, Edward Ludwig	3, Apr. 1854	Edward	Oldenburger, Barbara	C	
Busch, Emilia	5, Apr. 1857	Carl	Eichelberger, Johanna	F	
Busch, Francisca Elisabeth	3, Dec. 1852	Anton	Baumeister, Elisabeth	A	
Busch, Franz Anton	7, Apr. 1857	Anton	Baumeister, Elisabeth	F	
Busch, Franz Georg	2, Jan. 1859	Bernard	Koch, Marianna	F	
Busch, Herman Georg	8, July 1859	Anton	Baumeister, Elisabeth	F	
Busch, Johan Heinrich	12, Mar. 1851	Anton	Baumeister, Elisabeth	F	
Busch, Johan Heinrich	7, Aug. 1859	J. Friedrich	Fierick, Sophia	N	
Busch, Johan Michael	2, May 1852	Bernard	Kock, Maria	A	
Busch, Joseph	1, Feb. 1857	Bernard	Koch, Marianna	F	

Name of Child	Date of Baptism	Father	Mother	Church	Page
Busch, Louisa Regina	13, Sept 1857	Edward	Oldenberg, Barbara	C	
Busch, Maria Theresa	11, May 1855	J. Joseph	Höffer, Maria	D	34
Busch, Paulina	25, June 1854	Christian	Heitler, Regina	C	
Busch, Peter Georg	23, Mar. 1856	Edward	Oldenberg, Barbara	C	
Busche, Bernard Heinrich Rudolph	15, May 1859	Bernard	Marischen, Elisabeth	L	
Busche, Gertrud Josephina	27, Mar. 1854	Bernard	Marischen, Elisabeth	L	
Busche, Rosina Philomena	8, June 1856	J. Bernard	Marischen, Elisabeth	L	
Buschenmühle, Johan Friedrich	31, Mar. 1854	Dietrich	Zurline, Elisabeth	A	
Büscher, Aloysius Xavier	31, Oct. 1858	Anton	Schleppe, Catharina	A	
Buscher, August Hieronymus	22, July 1852	Anton	Schlebbe, Maria Catharina	A	
Büscher, Heinrich	17, July 1853	Friedrich	Wessels, Anna	D	395
Büscher, Johan Friedrich August	2, Jan. 1859	Johan F.	Hausfeld, Elisabeth	K	
Büscher, Theodor	27, Nov. 1850	Anton	Schlebbe, Catharina	A	
Buschermühle, Johan Dietrich	1, June 1857	Friedrich	Kamphaus, Anna Maria	A	
Buschle, Cornelius Theodor	7, Nov. 1852	Gregor	Oker, Catharina	D	356
Buschle, Francis Xavier	19, Oct. 1857	Friedrich	Wike--, Josephina	D	97
Buschle, Friedrich Theodor	13, July 1859	Friedrich	Wittm---, Josephina	D	142
Buschle, Lawrence Ludwig	3, Dec. 1854	Ludwig	Dosenbach, Magdalena	D	23
Buschle, Maria Anna	23, Jan. 1859	Francis X.	S----, Martha	D	129
Buschle, Philippina	27, July 1854	Gregor	Oker, Catharina	D	15
Buschle, Rosina	15, Sept 1856	Gregor	Oker, Catharina	D	67
Buschmann, Joseph	10, Sept 1857	Herman H.	Wiemeler, Anna Maria	L	
Buse, Johan Heinrich	8, Aug. 1858	Martin	Setlage, M. Elisabeth	L	
Bush, Amand	25, Feb. 1854	Francis	Flinn, Catherine	J	26
Bush, Joanne	12, June 1859	Charles	Eikelberger, Ann	B	76
Buskamp, Catharina Rosa	22, Sept 1855	Joseph	Michael, Catharina	A	
Buskamp, Freidrich Wilhelm Joseph	7, Nov. 1857	F. Wilhelm	Michael, Maria Catharina	A	
Buskamp, Heinrich Wilhelm	7, Aug. 1850	Joseph	Michael, Catharina	A	
Buskamp, Johan Bernard	19, Dec. 1853	Joseph	Michael, Catharina	A	
Buskamp, Joseph Johan	4, Apr. 1859	Joseph	Michael, Catharina	A	
Büsken, Luisa Bernarda	24, Aug. 1852	Clemens	Knabbe, Anna	A	
Busker, Catharina Anna M.	13, Dec. 1853	Heinrich	Rehe, Theresa	C	
Büsker, Johan Gerhard	3, Feb. 1857	J.G.H.	Rehe, Anna M. Theresa	A	
Buss, Johan Ludwig	3, Jan. 1859	Wilhelm	Baute, Dina	D	128
Bussan, Anna Maria Theresa	20, Aug. 1852	Herman H.	Weimeler, Anna M. Theresa	L	
Bussan, Theodor Heinrich August	1, Sept 1854	Herman H.	Wiemueller, Anna M.	L	
Busse, Anna Catharina Sophia	18, May 1856	Heinrich	Post, Catharina	K	
Busse, Anna Maria	26, June 1859	Caspar H.	Zinker, Louisa	L	
Busse, Anna Maria	6, Oct. 1858	J. Heinrich	Post, Anna Catharina	K	
Busse, Anna Maria	30, Jan. 1856	Theodor	Horstmann, Bernardina	L	
Busse, Anna Maria Sophia	14, Jan. 1856	J. Mathias	Setlage, Elisabeth	L	
Busse, Francis Joseph	12, Oct. 1856	F. Joseph	Moeller, Elisabeth	C	
Busse, Johan Herman	21, Jan. 1851	Theodor	Horstmann, Bernardina	L	
Busse, Maria Catharina Philomena	14, May 1851	Heinrich	Post, Catharina	K	
Bussjann, Herman Carl August	8, June 1859	Herman	Wiemeler, Anna Maria	L	
Bussman, Anton Heinrich	17, Nov. 1857	Bernard	Bergman, Henrietta	A	
Bussman, Johan Bernard	23, Feb. 1853	J. Bernard	Bergman, Dina Henrietta	A	
Bussman, Maria Elisabeth	21, May 1855	Bernard	Bergman, Henrietta	A	
Bussmann, Heinrich Jacob	8, Mar. 1853		Bussmann, Elisabeth	L	
Bussmann, Maria Anna Thersa	9, June 1850	Herman H.	Wiemueller, Theresa	C	
Busswoeller, Maria Anna Elisabeth	18, Feb. 1851	J. Heinrich	Fortkamp, Gertrud	D	254
Busswoller, Johan Bernard	5, Dec. 1852	J. Heinrich	Fortcamp, Gertrud	D	359
Büstner, Rosina	1, May 1859	Adam	Bergman, Charlotte	D	137
Buten, Carl Leo	3, July 1853		Buten, Bernardina	C	
Butenhorn, Maria Anna	14, July 1850	?	----, Maria	K	
Büter, Anna Margaretha	2, Dec. 1855	J. Bernard	Pellenwessel, Elisabeth	K	
Buter, Elisabeth	21, Apr. 1858	Johan	Pellewessel, Elisabeth	K	
Buter, Johan Heinrich	28, July 1850	Heinrich	Reisinger, Maria Gertrud	K	
Büter, Maria Elisabeth	22, Mar. 1854	J. Bernard	Pellewessel, Maria Elisabeth	K	

Hamilton County, Ohio Roman Catholic Baptism Records -- 1850 - 1859

Name of Child	Date of Baptism	Father	Mother	Church	Page
Butler, Andrew	14, July 1853	William	Ryan, Mary	P	46
Butler, Ann	16, Feb. 1856	Thomas	Flagerty, Bridget	E	345
Butler, Catharina	7, Sept 1855	Michael	Loftus, Margaret	R	
Butler, Catherine	6, June 1856	Patrick	----, Bridget	M	
Butler, Charles	17, June 1854	Thomas	Fox, Bridget	E	198
Butler, David Carroll	19, Apr. 1852	Timothy	Smith, Eliza	B	257
Butler, Eliza	19, Feb. 1859	Columbus	Troy, Ann	P	276
Butler, Elizabeth	31, Aug. 1856	James	----, Bridget	M	
Butler, Ellen	17, Apr. 1858	Thomas	Flagerty, Bridget	E	529
Butler, Ellen Elizabeth	12, Oct. 1856	Nicholas	Lightner, Mary	B	35
Butler, Emilia	4, Dec. 1859	John	Grady, Ellen	B	84
Butler, Esther	28, Aug. 1853	Thomas	Flagerty, Bridget	E	123
Butler, Florence	18, Dec. 1859	Joseph E.	Lafferty, Alice	Z	
Butler, George Henry	16, Feb. 1855	George	----, Mary	M	
Butler, Helen	8, Sept 1856	William	Kerns, Julia	V	33
Butler, James	1, May 1859	James	----, Bridget	M	
Butler, James	30, Oct. 1853	James	----, Ellen	E	139
Butler, James	29, Mar. 1859	James	Kelly, Mary	P	281
Butler, James	25, Aug. 1853	John	Cleary, Ann	B	297
Butler, James	4, Apr. 1853	Nicolaus	McCaid, Mary	P	38
Butler, James	28, Nov. 1852	Patrick	Harris, Ann	E	40
Butler, John	24, Aug. 1851	Columbus	Troy, Ann	B	239
Butler, John	16, Dec. 1855	James	Kelly, Mary	P	163
Butler, John	27, Sept 1857	James	Naughton, Mary Ann	V	41
Butler, John	18, Mar. 1855	Patrick	----, Ann	E	272
Butler, John Kenny	12, May 1856	Joseph	Laverty, Alice	E	366
Butler, Joseph	19, May 1854	Columbus	Troy, Ann	P	83
Butler, Josephine	24, Aug. 1858	James	----, Mary	M	
Butler, Lucy Ann	22, Jan. 1854	James	O'Neill, Mary	V	10
Butler, Margaret	1, Oct. 1854	Bernard	Falen, Mary	E	228
Butler, Margaret	20, Jan. 1850	James	----, Margaret	E	193
Butler, Margaret	30, Nov. 1856	James	----, Mary	M	
Butler, Margaret	6, Jan. 1859	John	Motker, Margaret	E	594
Butler, Margaret Ellen	3, Aug. 1856	George	----, Mary	M	
Butler, Mary	15, Feb. 1852	James	Egan, Honora	B	253
Butler, Mary	24, Jan. 1858	Patrick	----, Bridget	M	
Butler, Mary	23, Mar. 1856	Thomas	Fox, Mary	E	352
Butler, Mary Alice	6, June 1852	James	----, Mary	E	421
Butler, Mary Alice	22, Dec. 1857	Joseph	Larey, Alice	B	53
Butler, Mary Ann	18, July 1858	George	----, Mary	M	
Butler, Mary Ann	23, Oct. 1853	James	----, Bridget	M	
Butler, Mary Helen	10, June 1853	John	Bowl--, Joanne	B	293
Butler, Mary Helen	4, Sept 1859	Richard	Daily, Helen	E	651
Butler, Mary Josephine	28, Mar. 1859	William	O'Connor, Bridget	E	614
Butler, Mary Louise	15, Mar. 1855	James	McDonald, Margaret	V	23
Butler, Mary Louise	29, June 1859	Michael	Burke, Catharine	L	
Butler, Mary Margaret	26, June 1853	Nicholas	Lightner, Mary	B	294
Butler, Mary Susan	28, Apr. 1859	Daniel	Fowler, Emily	E	621
Butler, Patrick	7, Feb. 1858	Patrick	----, Ann Frances	E	515
Butler, Pierce	26, Apr. 1853	Joseph	Hagerty, Alice	B	291
Butler, Thomas	7, Nov. 1852	Bernard	Felan, Mary	B	274
Butler, Thomas	26, Apr. 1854	Thomas	Fox, Mary	E	186
Butler, Thomas	23, May 1858	Thomas	Fox, Mary	E	537
Butler, William	5, Nov. 1850	Patrick	----, Ann	E	259
Butler, William August	22, July 1855	James	----, Mary	M	
Buttemar, Maurice	24, Sept 1855	Maurice	Sullivan, Catherine	V	27
Buttemino, Maria Louisa	3, July 1850	Johan	Laud, Magdalena	D	220
Buttemüller, Eva Isabella	22, Apr. 1853	Johan	Lauth, Maria	D	382
Buttemüller, Georg Sebastian	19, Dec. 1852	Georg	Renz, Maria Theresa	K	

- 80 -

Name of Child	Date of Baptism	Father	Mother	Church	Page
Buttenmueller, Johan	18, June 1854	Georg	Rentz, Maria	K	
Butterby, Ann	24, Oct. 1852	Thomas	Marony, Elizabeth	P	28
Butterhoff, Heinrich	12, Nov. 1857	Johan	Tollner, Anna	L	
Butterly, Michael Bartholomew	2, Dec. 1855	Thomas	M---y, Elizabeth	B	22
Butterman, Sebastian Lewis	18, Jan. 1856	George	Brusz, Mary	B	24
Büttner, Anna Catharina	20, Mar. 1851	Francis	Hoping, Margaretha	A	
Büttner, Anna Maria	20, Mar. 1851	Francis	Hoping, Margaretha	A	
Buttner, Francis Clemens	12, Oct. 1856	Francis C.	Gotke, Anna	A	
Buttomer, Michael	2, May 1853	John	Buckley, Catherine	B	289
Butz, Andreas	18, Apr. 1852	Andreas	Krumholz, Maria Anna	D	317
Butz, Francis	9, Nov. 1853	Andreas	Zimmermann, Maria Anna	Q	3
Butz, Joseph	2, Sept 1855	Andreas	Zimmerman, Maria Anna	Q	10
Butz, Maria Anna	28, July 1850	Andreas	Zimmermann, Maria Anna	C	
Bütz, Maria Bernardina	3, Jan. 1853	Joseph	Höfel, Anna Maria	D	363
Buxan, Maria Philomena	18, Nov. 1858	Theodor	Deppen, Maria	K	
Buxe, Herman Theodor Adolph	9, Sept 1858	Gerhard	Nietfeld, Maria	K	
Buxe, Johan Gerhard	2, June 1856	J. Gerhard	Nietfeld, Maria	K	
Buxe, Johan Herman Heinrich	27, Nov. 1856	H. Theodor	Deppen, Maria Elisabeth	K	
Buxer, Maria Elisabeth	12, Nov. 1854	Theodor	Deppen, Elisabeth	K	
Bymaskiewiz, Wratislaus	21, June 1857	Theophilus	Schindler, Susanna	A	
Byme, Mary	18, May 1851	Patrick	Bryen, Rose	F	
Bymon, Elisa	29, Oct. 1850		adult	E	257
Byon, Emily	1, Mar. 1857	Charles	Hammond, Julia	E	437
Byrel, Michael	5, Dec. 1850	Michael	Farley, Margaret	B	220
Byrne, (girl)	29, May 1853	Thomas	----, Ann	M	
Byrne, Agnes	20, Jan. 1856	Patrick	----, Mary	M	
Byrne, Ambrose	26, June 1853	John	----, Mary	M	
Byrne, Ann	25, June 1854	Hugh	Gibbons, Ann	V	15
Byrne, Ann	14, Feb. 1858	John	----, Mary	M	
Byrne, Ann	17, Mar. 1850	Michael	King, Bridget	B	199
Byrne, Ann Jane	15, June 1851	Edward	Byrne, Catherine	P	9
Byrne, Ann mary	9, Nov. 1857	William	McDowell, Sarah	E	491
Byrne, Bridget	30, Jan. 1853	Joseph	Coogan, Julia	B	282
Byrne, Bridget Ellen	13, Sept 1857	John	----, Mary	M	
Byrne, Catharine	3, Jan. 1855		Byrne, Mary Ann	B	9
Byrne, Catherine	17, Sept 1854	Bryan	Finn, Elizabeth	B	5
Byrne, Catherine	9, Nov. 1858	Christopher	McLaughlan, Nancy	P	266
Byrne, Catherine	10, Feb. 1858	Michael	----, Mary	M	
Byrne, Catherine	24, May 1857	Thomas	Flannery, Julia	U	
Byrne, Catherine Mary	31, Dec. 1850	John	----, Ellenore	E	273
Byrne, Cecilia	15, Feb. 1852	Maurice	Gamann, Rose	B	252
Byrne, Edward	19, June 1859	James	King, Bridget	E	633
Byrne, Edward Arthur	11, July 1858	Edward	Byrne, Catherine	P	253
Byrne, Edward Christopher	7, Jan. 1855	John	Ward, Louise	B	9
Byrne, Eliza	27, Nov. 1857	Bryan	Feeny, Elizabeth	B	52
Byrne, Elizabeth	20, Apr. 1856	John	Hayes, Helen	V	30
Byrne, Ellen	14, Jan. 1859	John	----, Honora	M	
Byrne, Helen	23, July 1854	Michael	Earley, Ann	B	3
Byrne, James	18, July 1853	Bryan	Finn, Martha	B	295
Byrne, James	2, Mar. 1856	James	Dooling, Ann	P	171
Byrne, James	11, Nov. 1858	James	Hennick, Mary	P	266
Byrne, James	20, Aug. 1857	James	King, Bridget	E	475
Byrne, James	15, Feb. 1859	John	----, Ellen	M	
Byrne, James	8, May 1851	Joseph	----, Julia	B	231
Byrne, James	14, Sept 1858	Michael	Finnessy, Alice	P	261
Byrne, James	28, Mar. 1858	Michael	King, Bridget	P	244
Byrne, James	29, Jan. 1855	Owen	Conway, Margaret	B	10
Byrne, John	15, Nov. 1857	George	Molloy, Honora	V	42
Byrne, John	27, Mar. 1856	John	----, Mary	M	

Name of Child	Date of Baptism	Father	Mother	Church	Page
Byrne, John	23, Jan. 1856	Martin	----, Bridget	M	
Byrne, John	6, Feb. 1859	Matthew	----, Mary Ann	E	602
Byrne, John	20, Feb. 1853	Michael	King, Bridget	B	284
Byrne, John Baptist	4, July 1858	Patrick	----, Mary	M	
Byrne, Julia	15, Aug. 1857	Joseph	Coogan, Julia	B	48
Byrne, Mary	27, Apr. 1856	George	Molloy, Honora	V	30
Byrne, Mary	15, Feb. 1857	James	Gilligan, Mary	B	40
Byrne, Mary	25, Dec. 1853	Patrick	----, Mary	M	
Byrne, Mary	18, Feb. 1854	Patrick	----, Rose	M	
Byrne, Mary	28, Apr. 1857	Thomas	Byrne, Ann	P	211
Byrne, Mary Ann	22, June 1854	Thomas	Egan, Bridget	P	85
Byrne, Mary Elizabeth	21, Nov. 1858	Patrick	----, Mary	M	
Byrne, Mary Margaret	30, Jan. 1859	Michael	Hoar, Ellen	E	600
Byrne, Matthew	20, Nov. 1853	James	King, Bridget	E	146
Byrne, Michael	13, June 1850	Edward	Byrne, Catherine	B	204
Byrne, Michael	27, Sept 1859		Byrne, Mary	B	81
Byrne, Patrick	6, Mar. 1853	Bernard	Byrne, Rose	B	285
Byrne, Rose	7, Jan. 1855	James	Haley, Rosanne	B	9
Byrne, Sylvester Joseph	14, Nov. 1852	Patrick	----, Mary	M	
Byrne, Thomas	12, Oct. 1853	Michael	----, Sarah	M	
Byrne, Thomas	11, May 1851	Michael	King, Bridget	B	231
Byrne, Thomas	28, Mar. 1858	Michael	King, Bridget	P	244
Byrne, Thomas	20, Nov. 1853	Peter	Flannigan, Bridget	E	146
Byrne, Thomas	28, Nov. 1852	Thomas	Gallagher, Helen	B	276
Byrne, Timothy	23, May 1850	James	Holand, Margaret	B	203
Byrne, William	25, Dec. 1851	Sylvester	Laughlin, Ann	E	366
Byrnen, Catherine	12, Sept 1858	James	Flynn, Mary	B	64
Byrnes, Ann	30, Dec. 1851	Bernard	Burns, Rose	P	15
Byrnes, Ann Mary	26, Sept 1858	John	Fecherty, Bridget	P	262
Byrnes, Bernard	25, Feb. 1855	James	Flynn, Mary	B	11
Byrnes, Charles	5, Apr. 1857	Thomas	Cunnings, Agnes	B	42
Byrnes, James	14, May 1857	James	Fairy, Bridget	B	44
Byrnes, Martin	28, Sept 1856	James	Flynn, Mary	B	34
Byrnes, Mary	23, June 1851	Brian	Feeny, Elizabeth	B	234
Byrnes, Mary Ann	4, Dec. 1853	Sylvester	Laughlin, Ann	B	304
Byrnes, Mary Ann	27, Feb. 1859	Thomas	Flannery, Julia	U	
Byrnes, Michael	7, Oct. 1853	Michael	----, Elizabeth	E	131
Byrnes, Thomas	20, Mar. 1859	George	Molloy, Honora	V	53
Byrns, Catherine	13, Jan. 1852	H. Francis	Clendening, Catherine	P	16
Byrns, Edward	26, Nov. 1854	James	Dolan, Mary	P	106
Byrns, Mary	21, Dec. 1857	Peter	Laury, Mary	E	502
Byron, Daniel	17, Nov. 1854	John	Mara, Mary	B	7
Byron, Honora	7, Aug. 1852	James	----, Bridget	E	3
Byron, John	13, Oct. 1855	James	----, Bridget	E	320
Bywater, Edward	11, Feb. 1855	Edward	Smith, Mary	B	11
Bywater, James	27, Dec. 1857	Edward	Smith, Margaret	B	53
Bywater, John	1, Nov. 1859	Edward	Smith, Margaret	B	83
Bywater, Margaret Sarah	27, Nov. 1852	Edward	Smith, Margaret	P	30
Bywater, Mary	30, Mar. 1851	Edward	Smith, Margaret	B	228
Ca---, Francis	2, May 1855		adult - 35 years old	P	130
Ca---, Margaret	2, May 1855		adult - 28 years old	P	130
Cabe, Daniel	20, May 1857	Michael	Carney, Margaret	E	454
Caby, Mary Ann	22, Apr. 1851	Matthew	Connolly, Margaret	E	303
Cadamatter, Johan Jacob	4, Feb. 1855	Johan	Cadematters, Rosa	K	
Cadegan, Mary	11, June 1854	Michael	Poggin, Mary	E	198
Cadin, Mary	7, Aug. 1859	Jeremiah	McGloghlin, Rose	R	
Cadmus, William Arbogast	24, Oct. 1858	Charles	Cummins, Mary	B	66
Caffrey, John Edward	3, July 1853	James	----, Mary	E	103
Caffrey, Mary	12, June 1854	John	Lonnergan, Catherine	V	14

Name of Child	Date of Baptism	Father	Mother	Church	Page
Cagney, Martin	15, Oct. 1854	Michael	Stratton, Frances	P	100
Cagney, William	3, July 1856	Michael	Shelton, Frances	B	31
Cahalane, Mary	29, Oct. 1854	Michael	Flynn, Julia	V	19
Cahan, Charles	16, Oct. 1853	James	Connell, Dorcas	E	135
Cahan, Margaret	14, Mar. 1858	Michael	Meely, Catherine	B	56
Cahan, Sarah	14, Mar. 1858	Michael	Meely, Catherine	B	56
Cahellan, Mary Ann	29, Oct. 1854	John	Manion, Helen	P	102
Caher, Thomas	29, Oct. 1854	John	----, Catherine	H	
Cahey, James Conrad	26, Dec. 1852	Patrick	Cunningham, Mary	P	32
Cahill, (girl)	22, Aug. 1852	----	----, ----	E	9
Cahill, Ann Eliza	15, July 1856	John	Doyle, Ann	B	31
Cahill, Catherine	11, May 1851	Bernard	Garvey, Catherine	B	231
Cahill, Catherine	15, Dec. 1853	William	Martin, Susan	P	62
Cahill, Edward	14, Feb. 1858	Edward	Toole, Catherine	B	55
Cahill, Eliza	25, Mar. 1859	John	Manon, Ellen	B	73
Cahill, Ellen	22, Oct. 1854	Michael	O'Mealy, Catherine	B	6
Cahill, Helen	11, Oct. 1854	Hugh	Marshall, Margaret	V	18
Cahill, Helen	6, Feb. 1855	John	----, Bridget	V	22
Cahill, Hugh	21, May 1850	Hugh	Marshall, Margaret	B	203
Cahill, James	2, Sept 1856	John	Magnan, Ellen	B	33
Cahill, James Edward	28, Sept 1851	James	Carrell, D.T.	E	347
Cahill, Johanna	12, Nov. 1852	John	Gorman, Mary J.	B	275
Cahill, John	27, Sept 1857	Thomas	Noonan, Ann	U	
Cahill, John Thomas	18, Dec. 1854	James	Comer, Catherine	Q	5
Cahill, Julia	1, Dec. 1858	Lawrence	Murray, Bridget	R	
Cahill, Lawrence	29, Aug. 1859	John	Gorman, Mary	B	80
Cahill, Mary	25, June 1854	John	Doyle, Ann	B	2
Cahill, Mary	26, Jan. 1856	Michael	Mealy, Catherine	B	24
Cahill, Mary Ann	12, Aug. 1855	Thomas	Nolan, Ann	U	
Cahill, Mary Frances	13, Aug. 1857	John	Clark, Cinthia	B	48
Cahill, Mary Helen	18, Sept 1854	John	Coan, Catherine	B	5
Cahill, Michael	25, May 1856	Patrick	Connor, Catherine	P	181
Cahill, Michael	16, Feb. 1851	Patrick	Haveken, Helen	P	5
Cahill, Patrick Lawrence	15, Sept 1857	John	Gorman, Mary	B	49
Cahill, Sarah	14, Mar. 1858	Hugh P.	Marshall, Margaret	P	242
Cahill, Thomas	10, Nov. 1850	Thomas	Lyons, Catherine	B	218
Cahill, Thomas Franklin	14, Oct. 1859	John F.	Clark, Cynthia	P	300
Cahill, William John	23, Sept 1855	Hugh	Marshall, Margaret	P	152
Cahill?, James	3, Nov. 1850	James	Daley, Catherine	B	217
Cain, Charles Edward	21, Sept 1856	William	Murray, Ann	E	399
Cain, Elizabeth	15, June 1858	James	Brady, Mary	E	541
Cain, George Henry	24, July 1859	Thomas	Duffy, Sarah	R	
Cain, James Lawrence	17, Jan. 1858	John	Sherdan, Mary	E	510
Cain, John	26, May 1856	John	Kelly, Catherine	E	369
Cain, Martin	24, July 1853	Michael	Kenny, Bridget	P	47
Cain, Michael	19, July 1857	John	Gainey, Margaret	E	467
Cain, Patrick	30, July 1850	Thomas	Coan, Sarah	B	209
Cain, William	30, Mar. 1851	Thomas	Cain, Ann	M	
Caldwell, William	30, Sept 1851	William	Biddle, Mary Ann	E	347
Callaghan, Ann	21, July 1852	Thomas	----, Joanne	B	265
Callaghan, Bridget	1, Apr. 1858	Thomas	Payne, Joanne	B	57
Callaghan, Catherine	28, Nov. 1858	James	----, Ann	B	67
Callaghan, Catherine	30, Sept 1858	Patrick	Morgan, Margaret	B	65
Callaghan, Catherine	12, June 1854	Thomas	Pyne, Joanne	B	1
Callaghan, Elizabeth	7, Aug. 1853	Patrick	English, Susan	B	296
Callaghan, Ellen	25, Mar. 1856	Thomas	Pyne, Joanne	B	27
Callaghan, John	10, Apr. 1859	Michael	Feeney, Mary	P	282
Callaghan, John	22, Dec. 1851		Callaghan, Joanne	E	366
Callaghan, John William	7, Oct. 1855	James	Bannon, Bridget	B	20

Name of Child	Date of Baptism	Father	Mother	Church	Page
Callaghan, John William	16, Aug. 1855	Patrick	Hopkins, Margaret	B	18
Callaghan, Joseph	12, July 1850	Michael	----, Ann	E	230
Callaghan, Margaret	20, Aug. 1854	John	Burke, Mary	P	93
Callaghan, Mary	19, Feb. 1854	Bernard	Walsh, Helen	P	69
Callaghan, Mary	4, Oct. 1857	Patrick	Brady, Julia	S	
Callaghan, Mary Ann	25, Feb. 1857	James	Barman, Margaret	B	41
Callaghan, Mary Eliza	9, Sept 1855	Bernard	Walsh, Helen	P	150
Callaghan, Michael	16, Sept 1855	John	Sullivan, Deborah	U	
Callaghan, Michael	4, Oct. 1857	Michael	----, Ann	E	483
Callaghan, Robert	3, Nov. 1858	Dennis	Brady, Catherine	S	
Callaghan, William	19, Oct. 1851	James	McGuin, Margaret	E	352
Callaghan, William John	18, Dec. 1853	Dennis	Callaghan, Mary Ann	P	62
Callahan Margaret	27, June 1852	Ferdinand	Langan, Helen	B	261
Callahan, Amos	5, Dec. 1852	George	Colgan, Mary Elizabeth	B	277
Callahan, Annette	5, Dec. 1852	George	Colgan, Mary Elizabeth	B	277
Callahan, Bridget	15, Nov. 1858	Michael	Kelley, Elizabeth Jane	E	579
Callahan, Catherine	20, Sept 1852	Bernard	Welsh, Ellen	P	27
Callahan, Catherine	27, June 1852	Ferdinand	Langan, Helen	B	261
Callahan, Catherine	16, Oct. 1853	John	----, Ellen	U	
Callahan, Catherine	4, Mar. 1851	Timothy	Buckley, Catherine	P	5
Callahan, Catherine	8, Oct. 1853	Timothy	Buckley, Catherine	P	54
Callahan, Clara Ida	19, May 1859	George	Colgan, Mary E.	B	75
Callahan, Elysean	26, Jan. 1854	?	?	B	308
Callahan, James	25, Dec. 1850	Thomas	Daly, Margaret	B	221
Callahan, James	13, Jan. 1855	Timothy	Curdsto, Ketta	P	115
Callahan, Jeremiah	19, Oct. 1853	Michael	McKellany, Ann	E	136
Callahan, Joanne	6, Jan. 1851	James	Calahan, Sarah	M	
Callahan, John	19, Sept 1850	James	Reed, Henriette	E	248
Callahan, John Patrick	13, Apr. 1856	Timothy	Buckley, Catherine	P	176
Callahan, Margaret Ann	9, Sept 1857	John	Doolan, Bridget	E	479
Callahan, Mary	5, Apr. 1857	Patrick	Morgan, Margaret	B	42
Callahan, Mary	6, Nov. 1856	Thomas	----, Ann	R	
Callahan, Mary Ann	30, Sept 1858	James	Fitzsimmons, Mary	E	565
Callahan, Mary Ann	20, Aug. 1856	John	Burke, Mary	V	32
Callahan, Matilda Elmira	15, June 1854	George	Colgan, Mary Elizabeth	B	1
Callahan, Owen	19, Mar. 1855	James	Finn, Sally	P	126
Callahan, Patrick Henry	3, Mar. 1853	Michael	----, ----	U	
Callanan, Mary	20, July 1856	Patrick	Meara, Elizabeth	E	382
Callanan, William P.	14, Oct. 1858	Patrick	Meara, Elizabeth	E	569
Callanon, Eliza	10, Dec. 1854	Patrick W.	----, Eliza	E	246
Callenson, Michael	29, Apr. 1853	Patrick	Downey, Mary Ann	J	22
Callewell, Rosina	17, Aug. 1854	Joseph	Reilly, Mary	C	
Calligan, Catherine	15, Nov. 1852	Jeremiah	O'Brien, Julia	E	36
Calligan, Catherine	8, Oct. 1856	Michael	Donnelly, Joanne	E	402
Calligan, Cornelius	7, Dec. 1856	Jeremiah	O'Brien, Julia	E	418
Calligan, Ellen	25, Sept 1859	Jeremiah	O'Brien, Julia	E	658
Calligan, Ignatius	1, Apr. 1852	Michael	Calligan, Ann	E	398
Calligan, Jeremiah Michael	29, May 1854	Jeremiah	O'Brien, Julia	E	194
Calligan, Mary Ann	28, Oct. 1855	Michael	McLeary, Ann	E	323
Callin, Franz Gottlieb	20, Nov. 1859	Francis	Frey, Dorothea	T	
Callinan, Alice	6, May 1855	Michael	Power, Mary	V	24
Callinan, Margaret	8, May 1855	Daniel	McCarthy, Honora	E	285
Callinan, Mary	30, Oct. 1853	John	Hissen, Sally	E	138
Callinan, Mary Ann	15, Mar. 1857	Michael	Powers, Mary	V	38
Callinan, Michael	1, Nov. 1857	Daniel	McCarthy, Nanny	E	490
Callinan, Thomas	18, July 1858	Thomas	Morkon, Margaret	E	551
Callinan, Thomas	15, Sept 1856	Thomas	Morton, Margaret	E	398
Callinen, Clara	23, Jan. 1859	Michael	Pauls, Maria	N	
Callinen, Mary	11, Apr. 1851	Thomas	Markon, Margaret	E	298

Name of Child	Date of Baptism	Father	Mother	Church	Page
Callingburn, Charles Fred	6, July 1851	Frederick	Henry, Mary Ann	E	321
Callinin, Margaret	28, May 1854	Thomas	Markan, Margaret	E	194
Caloran, Mary Jane	27, June 1852	Luke	Davy, Bridget	P	24
Calvin, John	6, Apr. 1856	Martin	Roanan, Bridget	E	357
Calvin, John	6, Apr. 1856	Martin	Roanan, Bridget	E	357
Calvin, Mary	5, Oct. 1856	James	O'Brien, Mary	E	402
Caly, Bridget	6, Feb. 1859	John	Felips, Bridget	P	274
Cambers, Catharina	9, Nov. 1851	G. Adam	Rob, Elisabeth	C	
Camble, James	19, Feb. 1853	Peter	McGrau, Martha	P	36
Cambridge, Daniel	6, Mar. 1852	John	Kennedy, Bridget	E	388
Cameron? Ann	15, Oct. 1854	Thomas	Meehan, Bridget	E	232
Campbell, Alice Ann	10, Nov. 1850	Bartholomew	Dowling, Mary	B	218
Campbell, Eliza	27, July 1851	Peter	----, Eliza Mary	E	327
Campbell, Elizabeth	1, July 1853	Daniel	Doyle, Mary	P	46
Campbell, Elizabeth	6, Nov. 1859	John	Cavana, Mary	E	669
Campbell, Frederick Aloysius	9, Oct. 1853	Conrad	Woellern, Catharine	L	
Campbell, George	30, Nov. 1851	Daniel	Doyle, Mary	B	246
Campbell, John	25, Apr. 1857	Patrick	Brown, Mary A.	B	43
Campbell, John August	12, Oct. 1851	Conrad	Wolfel, Catharina	K	
Campbell, John Terrence	4, Apr. 1852	John	Rives, Ann Eliza	B	256
Campbell, Joseph	16, Oct. 1853	Peter	----, Mary	M	
Campbell, Margaret	5, Apr. 1853	John	Ryan, Mary	E	79
Campbell, Matthew	11, Oct. 1854	Patrick	O'Brien, Bridget	D	19
Campbell, Peter	20, Jan. 1850	Charles	McGabe, Martha	B	194
Campbell, Richard	28, July 1852	Bartholomew	Dolan, Mary	B	266
Campbell, Thomas	13, Jan. 1850	Daniel	Doyle, Mary	B	194
Campbell, Thomas	22, Apr. 1855	Daniel	Doyle, Mary	B	14
Campbell, Thomas	20, Jan. 1850	Thomas	Granan, Ann	E	194
Campbell, Walter	19, June 1858	Daniel	Scott, Catherine	B	60
Campell, Margaretha	3, Apr. 1853	Peter	----, Margaretha	C	
Campion, Mary	25, Dec. 1851	Martin	Brown, Catherine	B	248
Camplin, Margaret	16, Oct. 1856	Greenberry	Nichols, Launda	E	404
Can, Amalia	25, Nov. 1855	Jacob	Widet, Helen	K	
Canal, Friedrich	16, Aug. 1857	H. Philipp	Mescher, Catharina	J	42
Canata, Gieronymas	19, Apr. 1857	Giovanni	Brissolari, Celestia	P	210
Canavan, Ellen	7, Nov. 1852	John	----, Jean	E	33
Candon, Michael	24, Aug. 1856	Patrick	Candon, Elizabeth	V	32
Cane, John	2, June 1850	Martin	----, Catherine	E	219
Cane, Mary	28, Jan. 1855	John	Kelly, Catherine	P	117
Cane, Patrick	10, Mar. 1855	Batly	Cahill, Mary	B	12
Cane, Thomas	4, July 1855	Michael	----, Mary	E	297
Canfield, Micahel	20, Feb. 1859	Patrick	Nuttle, Nancy	E	605
Cannal?, John Robert	24, Feb. 1855	Samuel	Cannel, Jane	B	11
Cannaran, Martin	20, Nov. 1853	John	Chambers, Joanne	E	146
Cannavan, John	2, May 1856	John	Chambers, Joanne	V	31
Cannavan, Thomas	16, Mar. 1856	Thomas	Devlin, Bridget	E	350
Cannon, Catherine	11, Apr. 1857	Michael	----, Ellen	E	446
Cannon, Elizabeth	30, Nov. 1856	Bernard J.	McQuillan, Martha	B	37
Cannon, Francis	21, Nov. 1852	Patrick	McAle, Mary	B	275
Cannon, John Francis	9, July 1850	James	Lightner, Elizabeth	B	207
Cannon, Josephine	2, May 1858	Bernard	McQuillen, Elizabeth	P	247
Cannon, Margaret	29, May 1853	James	Kennedy, Bridget	P	43
Cannon, Margaret	21, Sept 1851	John	Moran, Bridget	E	345
Cannon, Mary Alice	17, Sept 1851	Bernard	McQuillan, Martha	B	241
Cannon, Mary Ann	26, Mar. 1854	Patrick	Nolan?, Joanne	B	311
Cannon, Mary Susan	27, June 1853	William	adult - 29 years old	E	102
Cannon, Patrick	30, Apr. 1854	Charles	----, Ann	U	
Cannon, Peter	17, Aug. 1851	Patrick	McHugh, Mary	B	239
Cannon, Peter	7, July 1850	Patrick	McHugh, Mary	B	206

Name of Child	Date of Baptism	Father	Mother	Church	Page
Cannon, William Edward	3, Apr. 1853	James	Lightner, Elizabeth	B	287
Canoli, Maria Theresa Charlotta	27, May 1853	Giovanni	Brisenolari, Celestina	K	
Canry, Hugo	31, Aug. 1851	Michael	Kilrow, Catherine	E	340
Capazza, Maria Louisa	8, Mar. 1856	Andrew	Bernero, Maria	B	26
Caper, Maria Theresa	12, Dec. 1856	Heinrich	Wessel, Theresa	N	
Cappel, Elisabeth	5, Sept 1854	Francis	Rau, Veronica	A	
Cappelle, Maria Anna	5, June 1859	Peter	Zundorf, Margaretha	T	
Caraber?, Mary Ann	7, July 1850	Michael	----, Catherine	B	206
Caragan, William	12, Aug. 1855	Farrell	Quinn, Mary	P	146
Caraghan, Mary Elizabeth	17, Dec. 1855	Michael	Vaughan, Mary	B	23
Caraghan, Michael	24, Apr. 1854	Farrell	Quinn, Mary	P	80
Carans, Ann	30, Jan. 1853	Bartholomew	McHue, Mary	E	59
Carari, Aloysius Jacob Joseph	26, Dec. 1859	Jacob	Carari, Johanna	K	
Caraven, Helen	8, Apr. 1851	John	McDonald, Margaret	E	298
Carbary, Margaret Ann	1, June 1851	Joseph	Eag---, Sarah	P	8
Cardan, Mary Catherine	21, Apr. 1855	J. Baptist	DeBenedette, Angela	B	14
Cardino, Anglas	1, July 1859	J.B.	Debenedetti, Angela	B	77
Carens, John R.	12, May 1857	James	McKue, Margaret	E	453
Carens, Michael	30, Apr. 1854	Lawrence	Kelly, Bridget	E	187
Careny, John	3, Feb. 1856	Patrick	Moran, Winefred	P	168
Carew, James	9, Jan. 1853	Patrick	Boyle, Susan	B	280
Carey, Bridget	8, Aug. 1858	James	Kennedy, Mary	B	62
Carey, Bridget	22, Jan. 1854	John	----, Bridget	B	307
Carey, Bridget	18, Sept 1859	John	Madden, Catherine	Z	
Carey, Henriette	12, June 1852	Thomas	Gallagher, Matilda	B	260
Carey, James	24, Nov. 1856	Edward	Cavanaugh, Joanne	E	415
Carey, Joanne	1, Oct. 1858	Dennis	Corbett, Joanne	E	566
Carey, John	16, May 1852	John	Nestor, Bridget	B	259
Carey, John	11, Aug. 1858	Patrick	O'Neil, Elizabeth	E	556
Carey, Mary	27, Dec. 1857	John	Nester, Bridget	B	53
Carey, Mary Jane	26, Jan. 1851	Edward	Cavanagh, Joanne	B	224
Carey, Thomas	9, Dec. 1855	John	Hester?, Bridget	B	22
Carey, Thomas	6, Apr. 1856	John	Maddin, Catherine	E	356
Carey, Thomas	17, Apr. 1853	John	Murphy, Ann	B	288
Carey, Thomas Edward	19, Oct. 1851	Thomas E.	Reddy, Mary Jane	B	243
Carey, William	9, Feb. 1851	John	Nestor, Bridget	B	224
Carl, Amalia	2, Sept 1855	Friedrich	Haupt, Catharina	Q	10
Carl, Caroline	23, Oct. 1853	Frederick	Ropp, Catharine	Q	3
Carl, Francisca	13, Nov. 1854	Wilhelm	Mesner, Petronella	L	
Carlan, Ellen	7, Dec. 1857	Patrick	----, Mary Ann	E	498
Carley, John	14, Nov. 1858	Michael	Gallagher, Bridget	P	267
Carlin, John	1, Dec. 1850	John	----, Mary	E	264
Carlin, John William	25, Sept 1850	Patrick	Smith, J.	B	214
Carlin, Mary Jane	30, June 1857	Edward	McIntyre, Margaret	P	215
Carlisle, Ellen	30, Oct. 1851	William C.	Quigly, Eliza	E	353
Carlisle, Francis	30, Oct. 1851	William C.	Quigly, Eliza	E	353
Carlisle, James	13, Mar. 1853	James	----, Esther Josephine	E	72
Carlisle, Robert	30, Oct. 1851	William C.	Quigly, Eliza	E	353
Carlton, Margaret	30, Apr. 1855	Hugh	Coll--, Bridget	B	14
Carly, George	27, Sept 1857	Michael	Gallagher, Bridget	V	41
Carly, James	1, June 1856	Michael	Gallagher, Bridget	V	31
Carly, Mary	31, Jan. 1853	Michael	Gallagher, Bridget	V	1
Carmely, Michael	18, Aug. 1855	Anthony	Gannon, Bridget	E	308
Carmody, Michael	3, Nov. 1853	Patrick	----, Bridget	E	140
Carnal, Bernardina Josephina	7, Aug. 1859	Heinrich	Mescher, Catharina	J	50
Carney, Ann	21, June 1857	Thomas	----, Mary	R	
Carney, Ann Josephine	6, Nov. 1859	Daniel	McSorley, Helen	V	62
Carney, Ann Josephine	11, Dec. 1859	Timothy	----, Mary	E	676
Carney, Bridget	24, Oct. 1852	Edward	Toole, Catherine	B	273

Name of Child	Date of Baptism	Father	Mother	Church	Page
Carney, Bridget	7, Oct. 1853	Henry	----, Ann	E	131
Carney, Bridget	31, Aug. 1851	James	Wall, Julia	E	338
Carney, Bridget	14, Aug. 1857	Simon	Coen, Catherine	V	41
Carney, Catherine	1, Nov. 1855	Edward	Toole, Catherine	B	21
Carney, Catherine	20, Feb. 1855	Thomas	King, Winnefred	E	266
Carney, Catherine	17, Dec. 1854	Timothy	Haley, Mary	E	247
Carney, Catherine	28, Oct. 1855	William	McEvilly, Mary	R	
Carney, Daniel William	10, June 1855	Daniel	McSorley, Helen	V	25
Carney, Eliza	26, Apr. 1852	James	McKearnan, Catherine	E	405
Carney, Elizabeth	21, May 1852	Edward	----, Margaret	E	416
Carney, Helen	30, Jan. 1859	Thomas	Ford, Mary	R	
Carney, Helen Ann	23, Nov. 1856	Daniel	McSorley, Helen	V	35
Carney, Honora Joanne	4, Nov. 1853	Edward	----, Margaret	E	140
Carney, James	23, Mar. 1856	Edward	----, Margaret	E	351
Carney, James	13, Feb. 1850		adult - 20 years old	E	199
Carney, Joanne	23, Nov. 1858	James	Wall, Joanne	E	581
Carney, John	7, Aug. 1859	James	Duffessey, Ann	E	644
Carney, John	28, June 1857	Patrick	Connors, Helen	P	215
Carney, John	4, Aug. 1850	Timothy	----, Mary	E	237
Carney, Julia Elizabeth	27, Aug. 1854	Francis	Bulter, Catherine	B	4
Carney, Margaret	8, Sept 1856	James	----, Honora	E	397
Carney, Margaret Ellen	16, Jan. 1853	Timothy	----, Mary	E	54
Carney, Martin	13, Dec. 1853	William	----, Mary	R	
Carney, Mary	26, Mar. 1854	Daniel	McSorley, Helen	V	12
Carney, Mary	23, Mar. 1855	Patrick	Connors, Helen	P	126
Carney, Mary Ann	26, Nov. 1856	William	Harkin, Mary	E	415
Carney, Michael	26, Mar. 1854	Edward	Toole, Catherine	P	76
Carney, Michael	9, Jan. 1859	John	----, Sarah May	E	595
Carney, Michael	22, May 1853	Patrick	Hill, Sarah	P	42
Carney, Nancy	5, July 1858	Thomas	King, Winnefred	E	546
Carney, Patrick	15, Mar. 1859	Owen	Collen, Ellen	P	280
Carney, Patrick	7, Feb. 1858	William	----, Mary	R	
Carney, Paul	25, July 1858	Francis	Boutilier, Catherine	B	62
Carney, Peter	27, Jan. 1857	Francis	Butler, Catherine	B	39
Carney, Samuel Aloysius Patrick	20, Jan. 1856	James	----, Catherine	E	338
Carney, Thomas	26, Aug. 1855	John	Cohen, Catherine	P	148
Carney, Thomas	18, Apr. 1858	John	Flynn, Ann	P	246
Carney, Thomas	3, Dec. 1857	Martin	----, Aster	E	497
Carney, Thomas	10, Dec. 1859	Patrick	Connors, Helen	P	306
Carney, Timothy	25, July 1855	James	----, Joanne	E	303
Carney, William	24, Sept 1859	Martin	Currey, Ann	E	655
Carney, William	16, Aug. 1857	Timothy	Haley, Mary	E	473
Carny, Mary	25, Apr. 1858	John	Carny, Catherine	Q	27
Carolin, Elizabeth	29, Aug. 1852	Anthony	----, Catherine	M	
Carolin, Francis	29, Aug. 1852	Anthony	----, Catherine	M	
Carolin, Harriet Amelia	29, Aug. 1852	Anthony	----, Catherine	M	
Carolin, John	29, Aug. 1852	Anthony	----, Catherine	M	
Carolin, Lawrence	29, Mar. 1851	Hugh	Kating, Mary	E	295
Carpenter, Catherine	17, Nov. 1858	Marion	Ward, Margaret	B	67
Carpenter, James	31, July 1853	Richard	Riley, Helen	B	296
Carpenter, Patrick	30, Mar. 1856	John	Hines, Ann	E	354
Carr, Ann	8, Jan. 1857	Andrew	Smith, Mary	B	39
Carr, Catherine	16, Feb. 1854	John	Kelly, Rose	B	309
Carr, Charles Victor	17, Aug. 1859	Theodore	Gilbert, Eveline	B	79
Carr, Eliza	7, Nov. 1858	Michael	Dempsy, Mary	V	51
Carr, Elizabeth	8, Dec. 1859	Joel	Road, Liddy	E	675
Carr, Emily Mary	16, July 1851	James	Quinn, Margaret	E	324
Carr, James	12, Feb. 1857	Patrick	McFadden, Catherine	B	40
Carr, John	17, June 1852	John	Fenton, Abby	E	425

Name of Child	Date of Baptism	Father	Mother	Church	Page
Carr, John	18, Sept 1859	John	Reddick, Mary	B	81
Carr, John	27, Apr. 1853	John	Stewart, Honora	B	289
Carr, John	22, Apr. 1851	Timothy	Marren, Margaret	E	302
Carr, Lawrence	1, Aug. 1852	John	Kelly, Rose	B	267
Carr, Margaret	15, Nov. 1857	John	Carroll, Margaret	B	52
Carr, Margaret	6, Jan. 1851	Paul	Brophy, Margaret	B	222
Carr, Mary	5, Jan. 1854	Patrick	Tackebary, Bridget	E	158
Carr, Mary Elizabeth	4, Dec. 1859	John	Reardon, Joanne	E	674
Carr, Mary Jane	25, May 1856	Michael	Denison, Mary	E	369
Carr, Rosanne	22, Nov. 1856	John	Kelly, Rosanne	P	199
Carr, Thomas	13, June 1855	John	----, Bridget	E	292
Carr, Thomas	25, Oct. 1857	Peter	Netty, Catherine	E	487
Carr, William Joseph	1, June 1856	John	Carroll, Margaret	P	181
Carr, Winefred	30, Oct. 1853	Patrick	Heslan, Mary	P	57
Carran, Julia	24, Oct. 1852	John	Peckison, Mary	E	30
Carregan, Peter	1, Apr. 1855	Thomas	----, Mary	U	
Carrel, Margaret	28, Sept 1856	James	Corcoran, Mary	Q	16
Carrel, Michael	3, June 1855	Michael	Griffin, Mary	Q	8
Carrell, Bridget	27, May 1855	John	Daugan, Elizabeth	E	289
Carrell, Catherine	29, Sept 1850	Dominick	----, Mary	E	251
Carrell, Catherine	18, May 1851	Patrick	Leahy, Helen	E	309
Carrell, Eliza	29, Oct. 1854	Redmund	Kelly, Eliza	E	236
Carrell, Elizabeth Mary	1, Jan. 1855	Thomas	Sharkey, Catherine	E	252
Carrell, James	5, Oct. 1859	James	Corcoran, Mary	E	660
Carrell, James	12, July 1857	Thomas	Sharkey, Catherine	E	465
Carrell, John	29, Nov. 1857	James	Corcoran, Mary	E	495
Carrell, John	24, Oct. 1853	Michael	----, Joanne	E	137
Carrell, John	10, May 1855	Michael	McGrath, Catherine	E	285
Carrell, Margaret	10, Nov. 1856	Jeremiah	Corcoran, Mary	E	412
Carrell, Mary	10, Mar. 1853	Cornelius	----, Margaret	E	71
Carrell, Mary	22, Apr. 1855	James	Corcoran, Mary	E	281
Carrell, Mary	25, June 1854	Michael	Martin, Ellen	E	201
Carrell, Michael Edward	4, Oct. 1850	Patrick	----, Catherine	E	252
Carrell, Patrick Henry	17, Oct. 1852	Patrick	Burke, Catherine	E	29
Carrelton, Thomas	3, Apr. 1859	Thomas	Cassilly, Elizabeth	E	615
Carrie, Mary	18, Aug. 1850	James	Kernan, Margaret	B	210
Carrigan, Ann	7, Nov. 1858	Thomas	McHanly, Martha	B	66
Carrigan, Charles Lawrence	3, Aug. 1851	Terence	---ff, Mary	B	238
Carrigan, Emiy Frances	12, Apr. 1858	Stephan	Keeshan, Mary Ann	B	57
Carrigan, James	24, Mar. 1851	Michael	Moony, Judith	E	294
Carrigan, John	6, Nov. 1859	Michael	Moony, Julia	E	668
Carrigan, John	20, Feb. 1853	Stephan	Keeshan, Mary Ann	B	284
Carrigan, John	18, July 1858	Thomas	McDermott, Mary	U	
Carrigan, John Thomas	6, Jan. 1858	Michael	Regan, Mary	E	506
Carrigan, Julia	7, Dec. 1856	Thomas	Forlune, Mary Ann	B	37
Carrigan, Mary	2, Mar. 1851	Stephan	Keeshan, Mary Ann	B	228
Carrigan, Mary Ann	28, May 1854	Stephan	Keeshan, Mary Ann	B	315
Carrigan, Mary Josephine	1, July 1855	Stephan	Keeshan, Mary Ann	B	16
Carrigan, Thomas	1, Aug. 1851	James	K----, Margaret	B	237
Carrigan, Thomas	19, May 1850	Thomas	Manning, Joanne	B	202
Carrigan, Thomas	10, Aug. 1856	Thomas	McDermott, Mary	U	
Carrol, Catharina	10, Apr. 1854	Michael	Fuchs, Maria	D	8
Carrol, James	15, Feb. 1857	Patrick	----, Louise	R	
Carrol, John	14, May 1854	Patrick	Binnion, Louise	R	
Carrol, Mary Ann	30, Nov. 1857	Patrick	Martin, Rose	Q	25
Carrol, Thomas	26, Sept 1852	Patrick	Benning, Louise	R	
Carrol, William	13, Mar. 1853	William	Leahy, Mary	R	
Carroll, Ann	11, Feb. 1851	John	Buregan, Elizabeth	E	283
Carroll, Catherine	29, Apr. 1852	John	Dalton, Catherine	B	264

Name of Child	Date of Baptism	Father	Mother	Church	Page
Carroll, Catherine	23, May 1852	Michael	Carroll, Joanne	B	259
Carroll, Catherine	15, Nov. 1857	Michael	Kearney, Mary	B	52
Carroll, Charles Henry	1, Sept 1857	Henry	Gibbons, Mary	B	48
Carroll, Cornelius Stephan	1, Jan. 1855	Cornelius	Brien, Margaret	V	22
Carroll, Elizabeth	1, Oct. 1854	Jeremiah	----, Joanne	M	
Carroll, George Alphonse	23, May 1855	Miles	Kennedy, Catherine E.	P	133
Carroll, James	2, Apr. 1859	Dennis	----, Alice	V	54
Carroll, James	3, Mar. 1850	John	Dalton, Catherine	B	197
Carroll, Joanne	16, Mar. 1850	Thomas	----, Catherine	E	203
Carroll, John	4, Jan. 1852	John	Murphy, Margaret	E	370
Carroll, John	19, Oct. 1856	Patrick	----, Honora	R	
Carroll, John	10, Oct. 1858	Patrick	McCrechlen, Catherine	B	65
Carroll, John	25, Dec. 1853	Timothy	Ryan, Ann	V	8
Carroll, Margaret	27, Jan. 1850	James	Flynn, Bridget	B	195
Carroll, Margaret	30, Nov. 1859	Owen	Corcoran, Ann	P	305
Carroll, Margaret Ann	9, Oct. 1852	Thomas	----, Catherine	E	25
Carroll, Margaretha	13, Dec. 1850	Michael	Fuchs, Maria	D	246
Carroll, Maria Anna Elisabeth	19, Feb. 1856	Michael	Fuchs, Maria	D	52
Carroll, Mary	14, Aug. 1859	John	Ambrose, Margaret	P	292
Carroll, Mary	21, Aug. 1859	Michael	Carney, Mary	B	79
Carroll, Mary	15, Mar. 1856	Michael	Kearney, Mary	B	26
Carroll, Mary	3, June 1851	John	Maher, Bridget	P	8
Carroll, Mary Jane	3, Nov. 1850	Michael	Carroll, Jane	B	218
Carroll, Mary Jane	4, Apr. 1853	Patrick	Laley, Ellen	E	78
Carroll, Owen	10, Jan. 1858	Owen	Corcoran, Elizabeth	Q	26
Carroll, Patrick	22, Jan. 1854	John	McTake?, Mary	E	162
Carroll, Patrick	23, Sept 1857	Patrick	Dunlan, Mena	E	482
Carroll, Sarah	14, Apr. 1850	George	Dooley, Sarah	B	201
Carroll, Sarah	4, Apr. 1858	John	Ambrose, Margaret	P	244
Carroll, Thomas	2, Jan. 1859	Francis	Maloy, Margaret	P	271
Carroll, Thomas	14, July 1850	Thomas	Nugent, Margaret	B	207
Carroll, Timothy	24, Oct. 1859	William	Dobbs, Ann	P	301
Carroll, William	15, Jan. 1853	Michael	Carrell, Elizabeth	E	54
Carroll, William	26, Jan. 1851	Patrick	---nan, Eliza	B	223
Carroll, William Herman	26, June 1859	Bernard	Henly, Eliza	P	286
Carrollton, John Lawrence	17, Feb. 1856	Thomas	Cassilly, Elizabeth	P	170
Carrolton, Catherine	16, Oct. 1852	Thomas	Cassilly, Elizabeth	B	272
Carrolton, James	4, Nov. 1856	Anthony	----, Ann	E	410
Carrolton, James	26, Feb. 1854	Thomas	Cassilly, Elizabeth	P	71
Carrolton, Joseph Francis	2, Aug. 1854	Edward	McIntire, Margaret	P	91
Carrolton, Sarah Ann	31, Jan. 1858	Anthony	McNally, Honora	E	514
Carrolton, Thomas	6, Mar. 1858	Thomas	Caselly, Elizabeth	P	241
Carson, Samuel John	15, Oct. 1857	George	Riley, Eliza	E	486
Carter, Aloysius	16, Dec. 1856	James S.	Chalfant, Susan Mary	B	37
Carter, Ann Eliza	20, Sept 1857	William	Walsh, Bridget	E	481
Carter, Elizabeth	16, Dec. 1856	James S.	Chalfant, Susan Mary	B	37
Carter, Elizabeth Ann	4, Mar. 1850	Bennet	Mustard, Ann	E	201
Carter, James Scott	27, Aug. 1856		adult	B	33
Carter, Joseph	16, Dec. 1856	James S.	Chalfant, Susan Mary	B	37
Carter, Joseph	2, Apr. 1854	Joseph	Flaherty, Mary	B	312
Carter, Joseph Harrison	19, Apr. 1855	Joseph	----, Mary Ann	E	281
Carter, Thomas	24, May 1858	George	Cornelia, Bridget	E	540
Carter, Wiliam Henry	17, Nov. 1855	William	Welsh, Bridget	E	327
Carthwright, Aloysius Heinrich	15, June 1853	Joseph	Sharp, Anna	K	
Carthwright, Stanislaus Thomas	15, June 1853	Joseph	Sharp, Anna	K	
Carthy, Catherine	30, Oct. 1854	William	Fogerty, Catherine	E	237
Cartin, Ellen	28, Sept 1854	William	----, Catherine	E	227
Cartlin, John	30, June 1855	Jeremiah	----, Ellen	E	296
Cartwright, Alonzo William	22, Sept 1853	Chester	McNulty, Catherine	B	299

Name of Child	Date of Baptism	Father	Mother	Church	Page
Cartwright, Edward	19, June 1856	Edward	Fassaille, Mary	E	375
Cartwright, Ira Chester	3, Dec. 1854	Chester	McNulty, Catherine	P	108
Carwe, Margaretha Anna	23, Oct. 1856	Joseph	----, Maria Anna	C	
Cary, Joseph	29, Mar. 1858	John	Gallagher, Jane	P	244
Cary, Mary	27, Apr. 1856	Dennis	Corbit, Joanne	E	362
Casatani, Mary	30, Apr. 1854	John	----, Mary	U	
Case, Agatha Magdalena	27, Apr. 1856	Dominick	Schiemann, Theresa	C	
Case, Catherine Theresa	7, Dec. 1851	Dominick	Scheman, Theresa	B	247
Case, Dominick Charlotte	13, Feb. 1854	Dominick	Schiemann, Theresa	C	
Case, Johan	10, Oct. 1858	Dominick	Schemann, Theresa	C	
Case, Julia	27, Dec. 1857	Michael	Connell, Mary	E	503
Casen, Michael	25, Nov. 1855	Luke	McCormik, Helen	J	34
Cases, Johan	21, June 1857	Luke	McCormick, Helen	J	42
Casey,	20, June 1858	Robert	Sennid, Ellen	B	60
Casey, Ann	17, June 1859	Patrick	Hovel, Margaret	B	76
Casey, Catherine	7, June 1858	James	Butler, Catherine	B	59
Casey, Catherine	6, Nov. 1859	William	Brennan, Catherine	B	83
Casey, Christopher	27, Dec. 1857	Stephan	Senez, Margaret	U	
Casey, Edward	19, Sept 1852	John	----, Bridget	B	270
Casey, Elizabeth	24, Apr. 1852	John	Curtis, Juliana	P	21
Casey, Ellen	3, Apr. 1855	James	----, Ellen	E	276
Casey, Ellen	3, Jan. 1858	Patrick	Hood, Margaret Ann	B	54
Casey, Fanny	5, Dec. 1856	William	Brennan, Catherine	B	37
Casey, Francis Buchanan Breckenridge	26, Oct. 1856	James	Langford, Sarah	V	34
Casey, George Henry	28, June 1857	George H.	Capley, Caroline	B	46
Casey, Henry	1, Aug. 1852	George H.	Capley, Caroline	B	266
Casey, James	19, Apr. 1854	Edward	----, Ellen	E	184
Casey, James	29, Jan. 1854	Matthew	Rohdes, Mary	R	
Casey, James	27, Mar. 1853	Patrick	Brown, Mary	E	77
Casey, James	11, Jan. 1857	Robert	Sennit, Ellen	B	39
Casey, James Francis	16, Jan. 1859	John	Gorgan, Margaret	E	596
Casey, Joanne	5, Oct. 1851	Patrick	Kearney, Bridget	B	242
Casey, John	8, Apr. 1855	Patrick	Probe, Mary	P	127
Casey, Lawrence	9, Jan. 1854	Christopher	Curran, Bridget	V	9
Casey, Maria	25, July 1854	Luke	McCormek, Helen	J	28
Casey, Mary	11, Oct. 1858	James P.	Lenford, Sarah	E	568
Casey, Mary	18, Sept 1853	John	----, Catherine	M	
Casey, Mary Ann	28, July 1850	Cornelius	----, Mary	B	208
Casey, Mary Ann	7, July 1850	Maurice	McCarthy, Catherine	B	206
Casey, Mary Ann	28, Sept 1856	Patrick	Hood, Margaret Ann	B	34
Casey, Mary Ann	16, June 1850	Patrick	Kenneally, Bridget	B	205
Casey, Mary Theresa	8, Nov. 1856	Jeremiah	Sweeney, Ann	E	411
Casey, Michael	30, May 1858	Matthew	----, Mary	M	
Casey, Patrick	20, Jan. 1858	Michael	Reynolds, Ann	B	54
Casey, Richard	22, June 1856	James	Butler, C.	B	30
Casey, Robert	24, Feb. 1857	Patrick	Roach, Mary	E	436
Casey, Rosanne	3, Aug. 1851	James	----ler, Catherine	P	10
Casey, Rosanne	27, Jan. 1855	William	Brennan, Catherine	B	10
Casey, Sarah	5, May 1850	James	----, Sarah	E	211
Casey, Thomas	26, June 1853	Luke	McCormick, Helen	P	45
Casey, Thomas	31, July 1859	Luke	McCormick, Helen	P	290
Casey, Thomas	11, Apr. 1851	Patrick	Fagan, Elizabeth	E	299
Casey, William	20, Feb. 1853	Cornelius	----, Mary	E	63
Casey, Winefred	21, Jan. 1857	John	----, Mary	M	
Cash, Michael	3, Apr. 1853	Thomas	O'Mara, Mary	B	288
Cashan, William Henry	21, Mar. 1858	William	Connelon, Sarah	E	524
Cashels, Christopher	26, Feb. 1854	Edward	Owens, Catherine	E	172
Cashen, Honora	27, Jan. 1854	John	Costello, Honora	E	162
Cashen, John	30, Sept 1851	William	Murphy, Julia	E	347

Name of Child	Date of Baptism	Father	Mother	Church	Page
Cashen, William	7, July 1853	William	Murphy, Julia	E	105
Cashman, Ann	24, Apr. 1859	Thomas	Kane, Anastasia	E	620
Cashman, Charles Thomas	11, Nov. 1852	George T.	----, Ann	E	34
Cashman, James	8, May 1853	James	Bolster, Julia	J	22
Cashman, Mary	22, Sept 1854	George T.	Kane, Anastasia	E	225
Cashman, William Albert	18, Aug. 1850	Thomas	O'Kane, Anastasia	B	211
Cashmann, Edward	23, Jan. 1859	James	Barster, Julia	G	
Cashmon, Michael	7, Sept 1856	Jacob	Bolster, Julia	G	
Casper, Sophia	12, Aug. 1855	Johan	Roger, Maria	D	40
Cass---, Patrick	30, Oct. 1856	Patrick	O'Neill, Margaret	P	196
Cassady, Sarah	27, Sept 1855	Joseph	Kaney, Bridget	P	152
Cassan, John	8, July 1855	John	Clark, Mary	P	139
Cassan, Timothy	17, July 1852	William	Hannaran, Catherine?	E	428
Cassedy, Charles	10, Apr. 1859	John	Conway, Elizabeth	U	
Cassedy, Dorothy	14, May 1853	John	----, Eliza	U	
Casselly, Mary Ann	11, Jan. 1852	Michael	Owen, Margaret	B	250
Cassen, Dennis	27, June 1857	John	Shannahan, Mary	P	215
Cassen, George Washington	22, Apr. 1856	George	Riely, Elizabeth	E	360
Cassen, John	4, July 1859	John	Shannahan, Mary	P	287
Casserly, Bedina	15, Feb. 1854	Michael	Owens, Margaret	P	68
Casserly, Margaret	11, Apr. 1858	Michael	Owens, Margaret	P	245
Casserly, Thomas	20, Jan. 1856	Michael J.	Owens, Margaret	P	167
Cassiday, John	12, May 1852	Michael	McCole, Ann	P	21
Cassiday, Thomas	30, June 1853	Joseph	Kinsella, Bridget	P	45
Cassidy, Alice	15, Mar. 1857	John	Larkin, Bridget	T	
Cassidy, Ann	22, Jan. 1854	John	Carton, Rose	E	161
Cassidy, Catherine	16, Nov. 1856	James	McGarry, Catherine	P	198
Cassidy, Charles Edward	2, Dec. 1851	Henry	----, Susan?	E	363
Cassidy, Eliza Jane	30, July 1853	Andrew	----, Susan	E	113
Cassidy, Eliza Jane	8, Apr. 1855	John	Larkin, Bridget	P	128
Cassidy, Elizabeth	12, July 1856	James	Cronin, Margaret	E	380
Cassidy, Henry	24, Oct. 1858	James	Cronin, Margaret	E	572
Cassidy, James	17, Aug. 1854	Henry	Crowley, Ellen	E	217
Cassidy, James	24, Oct. 1859	James	McGary, Catherine	B	82
Cassidy, James	22, July 1852	John	----, Mary	E	432
Cassidy, James	1, Jan. 1858	Joseph	Kenny, Bridget	P	235
Cassidy, John	10, Mar. 1853	James	----, Margaret	E	71
Cassidy, John	2, Oct. 1853	James	McGarry, Catherine	P	53
Cassidy, John	10, June 1850	Joseph	----, Rosanne	E	221
Cassidy, Joseph	27, June 1859	James	----, Mary	E	635
Cassidy, Margaret	1, July 1851	Henry	----, Ellen	E	320
Cassidy, Margaret	26, Sept 1854	James	Cronen, Margaret	E	226
Cassidy, Margaret	12, Mar. 1854	James	McGarry, Mary	B	310
Cassidy, Margaret	18, Feb. 1850	John	----, Mary	E	197
Cassidy, Mary	30, Dec. 1851	James	Cronan, Margaret	E	369
Cassidy, Mary	28, Oct. 1856	James	McGoum, Mary	E	408
Cassidy, Mary Ann	12, Aug. 1850	Andrew	----, Susan	E	239
Cassidy, Mary Ann	15, Feb. 1857	John	Conway, Lyae	E	433
Cassidy, Sebastian Sylvester	24, Dec. 1854	John	----, Elizabeth	U	
Cassidy, William	15, Feb. 1852	Joseph	Carten, Rose	E	383
Cassidy, William	3, Apr. 1854	Michael	McGuire, Catherine	E	180
Cassilly, Bridget	14, June 1853	Michael	Mealy, Catherine	B	293
Cassilly, Julia	14, June 1853	Michael	Mealy, Catherine	B	293
Cassore, Johan Benedict	29, July 1852		Cassore, Louisa	J	18
Casteler, Matthias	28, July 1850	Peter	----, Maria	A	
Cataiar, Helen	6, May 1851		adult	B	232
Cathariner, Ann Mary Josephine	12, Sept 1854	Anthony	----, Agatha	U	
Catherell, Lawrence	13, Aug. 1854	Michael	Cassidy, Ann	R	
Caton, Alice	8, July 1857	John	Gillet, Catherine	E	464

Name of Child	Date of Baptism	Father	Mother	Church	Page
Caton, Michael	12, Sept 1857	Thomas	Warren, Catherine	E	480
Caton, William	8, Feb. 1852	John	----, Margaret	E	380
Catten, William John	23, May 1852	Thomas	Builder, Amalia	J	16
Catton, James	28, Dec. 1856	James	Asson, Sarah	P	202
Catton, Mary	3, July 1853	Patrick	Fischbach, Catharina	J	22
Caufield, Eliza Jane	12, Dec. 1858	James	Hennessy, Anastasia	P	269
Caufield, John	6, Aug. 1859	James	Kelly, Sarah	E	644
Caufield, John Edward	8, July 1856	Michael	McFedden, Margaret	T	
Caughlin, Edward	9, Nov. 1856	Matthew	Nichols, Mary	B	36
Caughlin, Mary	6, July 1856	Edmund	----, Honora	M	
Caulfield, John H.	31, Dec. 1854	James	Hennesey, Anastasia	E	250
Caulfield, Mary	13, Feb. 1855	Michael	McFadden, Margaret	B	11
Cavanagh, Cornelius	12, Dec. 1857	Patrick	Moran, Winnefred	E	500
Cavanagh, Cornelius	22, May 1853	Roderick	Kilfoyle, Ann	B	292
Cavanagh, Elizabeth	7, Apr. 1856	Dennis	Sullivan, Ellen	B	27
Cavanagh, Elizabeth Frances	21, Sept 1856	John	Horan, Ann	P	193
Cavanagh, Helen	31, July 1853	Dennis	Sullivan, Ellen	B	296
Cavanagh, James	28, May 1857	Dennis	Sullivan, Helen	P	213
Cavanagh, James	9, July 1854	Dennis	Sullivan, Helen	B	2
Cavanagh, Joanne	25, Sept 1853	Thomas	----, Joanne	E	129
Cavanagh, John	13, Dec. 1857	Patrick	Hen---, Elizabeth	V	43
Cavanagh, Margaret	19, Aug. 1850	Andrew	----, Mary	B	211
Cavanagh, Mary	24, June 1858	Patrick	----, Hannah	M	
Cavanagh, Patrick	22, Sept 1852	Miles	----, Eliza	E	19
Cavanagh, Sarah	18, Oct. 1858	John	Curran, Mary	B	65
Cavanagh, Thomas	14, Jan. 1859	Patrick	Mullen, Mary	U	
Cavanaugh, Ann	22, Oct. 1851	John	Kensley, Mary	B	243
Cavanaugh, Catherine	7, Aug. 1859	Patrick	----, Hannah	M	
Cavanaugh, Dennis	18, Nov. 1857	Daniel	Galbeck, Eliza	B	52
Cavanaugh, Edward William	10, Oct. 1858	Daniel	Galvin, Elizabeth	B	65
Cavanaugh, Elizabeth Matilda	9, Mar. 1856	Daniel	Galbelly, Eliza	B	26
Cavanaugh, Isabel	12, Nov. 1854	Dennis	Doyle, Catherine	P	103
Cavanaugh, Margaret Ann	12, Sept 1857	Farrell	Quinn, Mary	B	49
Cavanaugh, Mary	1, June 1851	Thomas	Murphy, Margaret	P	8
Cavanaugh, Mary	29, Mar. 1857	John	Cunningham, Mary	B	42
Cavanaugh, Mary Ann	10, Dec. 1852	Dennis	Doyle, Catherine	B	277
Cavanaugh, Mary Margaret	23, Feb. 1859	Thomas	McCoy, Ann	E	606
Cavans, Maria Barbara	3, Sept 1854	Maurice	Enger, Adelheid	F	
Cavany, Catherine	30, July 1854	Edward	Ryan, Mary	E	211
Cavenaugh, Bridget	22, Aug. 1853	Thomas	McCormick, Mary	J	24
Cavenaugh, Thomas	17, Nov. 1854	Thomas	McCormak, Mary	J	28
Caveny, Patrick	2, Aug. 1850	Patrick	----, Bridget	E	236
Caveny, Thomas	20, Aug. 1854	Patrick	Moran, Winifred	P	93
Cawley, Mary Elizabeth	30, Nov. 1857	John	Philipps, Bridget	P	231
Cawley, Winefred	1, Feb. 1852	Owen	Conway, Win.	P	16
Cedelot, Ann Adelaid	21, Nov. 1852	Michael	----, Ann	M	
Cella, Mary Magdalene	3, Nov. 1850	Antonio	Longinotti, Maria	E	258
Celli, Anton	20, July 1858	Giovanni	Gazzolo, Catharina	K	
Cells, Ann Elizabeth	9, Dec. 1855	James	----, Susan	E	332
Centner, Anna Jacobina	3, Apr. 1853	Philipp	Stubenrauch, Margaretha	F	
Centner, Carl Jacob	25, Mar. 1853	Christoph	Robert, Henrica	F	
Centner, Caspar Heinrich	4, Feb. 1855	Francis H.	Knoblauch, Catharina	F	
Centner, Catharina	10, Feb. 1850	Christoph	Robert, Henrica	F	
Centner, Catharina Carolina	8, Nov. 1857	Francis H.	Koblauck, Catharina	F	
Centner, Johan Philipp	26, July 1857	Philipp	Stubenrauch, Marg.	C	
Centner, Joseph Andreas	29, Oct. 1855	Caspar	Steinhauer, Dominica	C	
Centner, Louisa Margaretha	7, June 1857	Christoph	Robert, Henrietta	F	
Centner, Maria Louisa	18, Feb. 1855	Philipp	Stubenrauch, Marg.	C	
Centner, Rosa Josephina	10, Feb. 1851	Philipp	Stubenrauch, Margaretha	F	

Name of Child	Date of Baptism	Father	Mother	Church	Page
Centner, Wilhelm	22, July 1855	Christoph	Robert, Henrica	F	
Chahe, Mary Hermina Valerie	14, Nov. 1858	Charles A.L.	Parker, Valerie	B	67
Chahy, George Augustus	14, Nov. 1858	Charles A.L.	Parker, Valerie	B	67
Chalfant, Cora Mary	28, Mar. 1858	Francis	----, Martha	E	525
Chalfant, Suan Mary	27, Aug. 1856		adult	B	33
Chambers, Bridget	28, Dec. 1854	Patrick	Brogan, Jane	B	9
Chambers, Charles Theodore	30, Mar. 1852	Theodore	Finley, Susan	B	255
Chambers, Edward	20, Oct. 1850	Theodor	Finley, Susan	B	217
Chambers, Edward	5, July 1857	Theodore	Finley, Susan	B	46
Chambers, George	11, Nov. 1853	Patrick	Brogan, Jane	B	302
Chambers, George Washington	18, Apr. 1852	Pius	Chamberlin, Ann	B	257
Chambers, Martha Elizabeth	11, Oct. 1854	Theodore	Finley, Susan	B	6
Chambers, Mary	16, Oct. 1853	Nicholas	McHale, Julia	B	301
Chambers, Mary	25, Feb. 1856	Patrick	Gorgan, Joanne	V	29
Chambers, Patrick	4, July 1858	Patrick	Brogan, Jane	B	61
Chambers, Richard Henry	18, Apr. 1852	Pius	Chamberlin, Ann	B	257
Chambers, Theodore Henry	24, July 1855	Pius	Louis, Ann E.	B	17
Chambers, William	1, Nov. 1855	Nicholas	McHale, Julia	B	21
Chan, Sarah Ann	13, Feb. 1853	Robert	McCast, Lorita	B	283
Chapelle, Anna Maria Catharina	7, Mar. 1858	Johan	Janzen, Elisabeth	U	
Chapelt, Maria	16, Aug. 1859	Jacob	Williams, Maria	C	
Chapman, Ann	9, Feb. 1852		adult	E	382
Chapman, Eliza	17, Aug. 1856	Henry	Hogan, Ann	B	32
Chapman, Mary Setlla	27, Sept 1859	Henry	Drake, Julia Rosalie	B	81
Charbonnet, Helen Laura Alice	10, Feb. 1856	Benjamin A.	Jackson, Ann E.J.	P	169
Charter, Augustine	9, Sept 1857	George	----, Bridget Cornelia	E	479
Charters, George Asquith	10, Apr. 1850	George	Kenneally, Bridget	B	200
Charters, Mary Eliza	30, Dec. 1852	George	Kenneally, Bridget	B	279
Chatman, Bartha	10, Mar. 1855	Julius	Governeur, M. Josephine	E	270
Chavez, Philomena	23, May 1852	John B.	----, Victoria	E	417
Cheake, Richard Olanzo	29, Aug. 1855	Richard	Pool, Mary Ann	E	312
Cheek, Henry William	24, Dec. 1851	Henry W.	Ross, Sophia	E	366
Chella, Charles Anthony	30, June 1852	Paul	Costa, Catherine	B	262
Chelli, Maria Victoria	27, Oct. 1859	Johan	Gazolle, Catharina	K	
Chems, Maria	2, Apr. 1851	Charles	O'Neil, Mary	K	
Chenworth, Dennis	5, Feb. 1854	Edward	Dolan, Bridget	T	
Chenworth, Mary	15, Aug. 1851	Edward	Dowling, Bridget	B	239
Chenworth, Michael	24, Dec. 1852	Edward	Dolling, Bridget	B	278
Chenworth, William	15, Aug. 1851	Edward	Dowling, Bridget	B	239
Cherlick, Gerhard Heinrich	16, July 1850	Johan M.	Maimann, Elisabeth	C	
Chirsa, Carlo Luigi	11, June 1857	John	Brizzolari, Paula	K	
Chogan, Elisabeth	5, Nov. 1854	Mathias	Donahue, Mary	N	25
Christ, Catharina Laura	3, Feb. 1850	J. Peter	Morgenschweis, Walburga	D	203
Christ, Charda	5, June 1853	J. Peter	Morgenschweis, Walburga	D	388
Christ, Isabel	11, Apr. 1855	John	Walter, Elisabeth	R	
Christ, Isidore	12, Apr. 1857	John	----, Elisabeth	R	
Christ, Jacob Christ.	26, June 1859	Peter	Bittinger, Maria	K	
Christ, Johan	27, Mar. 1853	Johan	Walder, Elisabeth	D	377
Christ, Johan Georg	27, June 1858	Michael	Ri---, Rosina	D	114
Christ, Josephina	1, Mar. 1857	Johan H.	Meyer, Walburga	D	80
Christ, Maria Anna	16, Mar. 1857	Peter	Bidinger, Maria	K	
Christ, Martin	29, Sept 1850	Johan	Waller, Elisabeth	D	235
Christ, Theresa	7, Feb. 1858	Heinrich	Turn, Elisabeth	L	
Christaker, Catharina	15, July 1857	Wilhelm	Wolf, Elisabeth	D	90
Christian, Carl	7, Feb. 1858	Georg	Kaiser, Maria	D	104
Christian, Johan Georg	21, Nov. 1853	J. Georg	Kaiser, Maria	D	416
Christian, Louisa Maria	2, May 1858	Weber	Scherer, Louisa	K	
Christian, Maria Henrietta	2, Sept 1855	Georg	Kaiser, Maria	K	
Christian, Sarah	6, Sept 1853	John	----, Ann	V	5

Name of Child	Date of Baptism	Father	Mother	Church	Page
Christiani, Emil	23, Sept 1855	Theodor	Cornet, Flora	A	
Christiani, Johan	29, Mar. 1857	Johan	Sticke, Elisabeth	K	
Christie, Ann Mary	30, Apr. 1854	Henry	----, Mary	B	314
Christie, John	4, July 1852	Henry	Kelly, Mary	B	265
Christie, Mary	17, Apr. 1859	Henry	Kelly, Mary	B	74
Christman, Heinrich	5, June 1854	Peter	Miller, Maria Anna	D	12
Christofel, Johan	28, Nov. 1855	Michael	Schiff, Catharina	G	
Christofer, Barbara	6, Feb. 1859	Wilhelm	Woll, Elisabeth	D	131
Christofer, Francis	13, Jan. 1856	Wilhelm	G---fka, Marianna	D	50
Christophel, Apollonia	30, June 1850	Michael	Schiff, Catharina	J	6
Christophel, Elisabeth	31, July 1859	Johan	Fus, Maria Anna	D	143
Christophel, Johan	26, Aug. 1855	Johan	Fus, Maria Anna	D	41
Christophel, Louisa Barbara	17, Oct. 1852	Michael	Schiff, Catharina	J	18
Christopher, Georg Jacob	8, Nov. 1857	Johan	Tap---, Maria Dina	D	98
Christopher, James	20, Apr. 1856	Christopher	adult - 16 years old	E	360
Christy, George Burnet	16, May 1857	John	Riley, Caecilia	E	454
Christy, Jane	16, July 1855	Henry	Kelly, Mary	B	17
Christy, John Reilly	14, Aug. 1854	Alexander	Reilly, Mary Ann	B	4
Christy, Mary	22, Dec. 1850	Henry	Kelly, Mary	B	221
Christy, William	4, June 1857	Peter	----, Helen	R	
Christy, William	20, May 1851	William	Besser, Elizabeth	E	309
Chuck, Mary Jane	27, Apr. 1852	Joseph	Wilson, Ann	B	258
Chuck, Robert	9, Feb. 1856	Joseph	Wilson, Ann	B	25
Ciappa, Antonio	10, Apr. 1859	Andreas	Gazzolo, Theresa	K	
Ciappi, Jacob Francis	17, June 1855	Andreas	Gazzolli, Theresa	K	
Ciappi, Maria Rosa	21, June 1857	Andreas	Gazollo, Theresa	K	
Ciarlo, Joseph James	22, Dec. 1858	Joseph	Onetto, Emilia	E	588
Cilhen, Catherine	20, June 1852	Edward	Caner, Helen	Q	2
Claffey, Henry	20, Apr. 1853	Thomas	Rice, Mary	Q	3
Claffey, Thomas	8, June 1851	Thomas	Rice, Mary	B	233
Claffon, Mary	20, Apr. 1856	Thomas	Rice, Mary	U	
Clair, Juliana	4, June 1854	Andrew	Grady, Ann	E	196
Clancey, Mary	9, Aug. 1853	Christopher	Morris, Helen	R	
Clancy, Ann	12, Mar. 1854	Cornelius	Sherlock, Bridget	V	12
Clancy, Ann	16, Oct. 1853	Patrick	----, Ann	E	134
Clancy, Bridget	11, Aug. 1850	John	----, Catherine	E	239
Clancy, Bridget	1, Oct. 1854	John	Lynch, Honora	E	228
Clancy, Bridget	22, Feb. 1857	Michael	----, Helen	R	
Clancy, Catherine	13, Feb. 1853	John	----, Catherine	E	62
Clancy, Cornelius Dennis	17, Feb. 1855	John	----, Catherine	E	265
Clancy, Edward	15, Mar. 1857	John	----, Catherine	E	440
Clancy, James	31, July 1851	James	----, Mary	E	329
Clancy, James	22, July 1855	Michael	Birch, Elisabeth	R	
Clancy, James Francis	19, Dec. 1858	John	Lynch, Honora	P	270
Clancy, Joan	2, Sept 1856	John	Lynch, Honora	E	395
Clancy, John	14, Feb. 1855	Edward	----, Ann	V	23
Clancy, John	15, May 1854	John	----, Elizabeth	E	190
Clancy, John	15, Dec. 1858	Michael	Barrett, Helen	R	
Clancy, John David	16, June 1850	Thomas	----, Mary	E	224
Clancy, Margaret	12, Mar. 1854	Michael	Bradley, Bridget	P	73
Clancy, Margaret	1, June 1856	Patrick	Burns, Ann	E	371
Clancy, Martin Charles	8, Mar. 1859	Michael	Bradley, Bridget	F	
Clancy, Mary	28, Dec. 1856	Michael	Bradley, Bridget	B	38
Clancy, Mary	11, May 1851	Thomas	McCrency, Ellen	P	7
Clancy, Patrick	14, Feb. 1855	Edward	----, Ann	V	23
Clancy, Patrick	6, Nov. 1853	Michael	----, Helen	R	
Clancy, William	4, July 1852	Michael	Bradley, Bridget	P	24
Clancy, William Patrick	16, Mar. 1852	John	----, Elizabeth	E	392
Clansy, John Stephen	2, Jan. 1859	John	O'Donnell, Catherine	E	593

Name of Child	Date of Baptism	Father	Mother	Church	Page
Clare, Daniel	13, Dec. 1851	Andrew	Grady, Nancy	E	365
Clare, Mary Ann	27, May 1852	Michael	----, Bridget	E	418
Clare, Mary Ann	18, Aug. 1853	Thomas	----, Nancy	U	
Clare, Mary Helen	1, July 1853	John	Nolan, Ann	P	46
Clare, Patrick	14, July 1850	John	Nolan, Ann	B	207
Clare, Thomas	2, Nov. 1856	Andrew	----, Ann	E	409
Clare, Timothy	21, Mar. 1855	John	Mullen, Ann	P	126
Clarey, Daniel	24, July 1855	Daniel	Dwyer, Bridget	P	142
Clarey, James	16, June 1856	Daniel	Dwyer, Bridget	P	182
Clarey, John	2, Aug. 1850	Daniel	Dwyer, Bridget	B	209
Clarey, John	3, Aug. 1851	John	Dorn--, Bridget	B	238
Clarey, Mary	16, July 1850	Patrick	Cassidy, Catherine	E	231
Clark, Aloysius	3, June 1855	Dennis	Nugent, Ann	R	
Clark, Ann	30, Oct. 1859	Patrick	Finnigan, Ann	B	83
Clark, Ann	27, Dec. 1857	William	McCadder, Bridget	P	234
Clark, Benedict	28, Aug. 1854	Walter	Speed, Ann	F	
Clark, Bridget	8, Aug. 1853	Eugene	----, Catherine	P	49
Clark, Bridget	28, June 1853	John	Fitzsimmons, Marcella	P	45
Clark, Daniel	5, July 1852	Henry	O'Neal, Margaret	B	263
Clark, Elbert	5, July 1852	Henry	O'Neal, Margaret	B	263
Clark, Helen	27, Mar. 1855	George	14 years old	V	24
Clark, John	28, June 1853	John	Fitzsimmons, Marcella	P	45
Clark, John	10, June 1854	William	----, Sarah	H	
Clark, John	29, June 1851	William	McCarten, Bridget	B	235
Clark, John Edward	12, Oct. 1856	Dennis	Nugent, Ann	E	403
Clark, Margaret	19,Nov. 1854	Eugene	----, Catherine	P	104
Clark, Margaret	2, Mar. 1851	Patrick	Finnegan, Ann	B	225
Clark, Margaret Elizabeth	30, Oct. 1859	Dennis	Nugent, Ann	E	666
Clark, Mary	16, Mar. 1851	Daniel	Driscoll, Margaret	B	226
Clark, Mary	5, Jan. 1851	Thomas	Grady, Catherine	B	222
Clark, Mary Anastasia	20, Apr. 1856	William	McArdle, Bridget	B	28
Clark, Mary Ann	12, Dec. 1857	Dennis	----, Ann	E	500
Clark, Mary Ann	14, Mar. 1858	Patrick	Grove, Anna	T	
Clark, Mary Ulda	9, Dec. 1855	George	----, Ann	E	332
Clark, Rosanne	22, May 1859	Hugh	----, Ann	E	627
Clark, Theresa	10, Dec. 1857	Owen	Ward, Catherine	P	232
Clark, Thomas	15, July 1857	Emil	----, Elizabeth	E	466
Clark, Thomas	26, Apr. 1859	Thomas	Dargan, Eliza	P	282
Clark, William	11, Feb. 1855	John	Fitzsimmons, Marcella	P	120
Clarke, Alice Mary	26, June 1858	John	Nulty, Alice	B	61
Clarke, Ann Mary	23, Jan. 1850	Patrick	Hanlen, Margaret	E	194
Clarke, Bridget	11, Feb. 1859	John	Howley, Bridget	E	603
Clarke, Catherine	21, Apr. 1857	----	----, Mary	M	
Clarke, Catherine	18, May 1858	Hugh	Murphy, Ann	B	59
Clarke, Catherine	5, Oct. 1857	John	Harley, Ann	V	41
Clarke, Daniel	30, June 1850	Patrick	----, Mary	B	206
Clarke, Edward James	18, Feb. 1855	Felix	----, Mary Ann	M	
Clarke, Eliza Mary Helen	7, Sept 1856	Walter	Speed, Ann	T	
Clarke, Elizabeth	9, May 1852	Peter	Shannon, Mary	P	21
Clarke, Fanny Mary	5, Nov. 1858	William	----, Margaret	B	66
Clarke, Helen	8, Apr. 1850		adult	B	200
Clarke, Jane	16, Sept 1855	Patrick	Finnigan, Ann	B	19
Clarke, Joanne Mary	31, Mar. 1859	John	----, Ann	V	53
Clarke, Louise	17, Oct. 1858	----	----, ----	X	
Clarke, Margaret	1, Jan. 1855	John	----, Nancy	E	252
Clarke, Margaret	4, Jan. 1852	Patrick	Mulkern, Mary	B	250
Clarke, Mary	17, Apr. 1853	Hugh	Murphy, Ann	B	289
Clarke, Mary	30, June 1852	Michael	Lynch, Margaret	P	24
Clarke, Michael	11, Oct. 1857	Patrick	Finnigan, Ann	B	50

Hamilton County, Ohio Roman Catholic Baptism Records -- 1850 - 1859

Name of Child	Date of Baptism	Father	Mother	Church	Page
Clarke, Michael Joseph	21, July 1850	Peter	Shanahan, Mary	B	208
Clarman, Carl Wilhelm	25, Jan. 1852	J. Georg	Meier, Theresa	A	
Clary, Elizabeth	6, July 1853	John	Riddle, Margaret	B	294
Clary, James	22, June 1856	Patrick	O'Neil, Elizabeth	E	376
Clary, Margaret	18, Aug. 1851	John	Meade, Helen	M	
Clary, Mary	14, Apr. 1854	Roger	Flynn, Helen	B	313
Clary, Michael	6, July 1853	John	Riddle, Margaret	B	294
Clary, Richard	1, Feb. 1857	Roger	Flynn, Ellen	B	40
Clary, Sarah Ann	6, Apr. 1851	Edmund	Luis, Sarah Ann	M	
Cla-ter, Honora	28, Sept 1851	John	----, Helen	B	242
Clausing, Agnes Helena	4, Feb. 1852	Friedrich	Lasance, Maria	L	
Clausing, Maria Catharina Philomena	17, Feb. 1855	Friedrich	Lasaroe, Maria	K	
Clausing, Maria Philomena E.	17, Jan. 1851	Friedrich	Lasance, M. Gesina	L	
Clausing, Maria Wilhelmina Amalia	12, July 1858	Friedrich	Lasance, Rosina	K	
Clavin, Mary	17, July 1859	Patrick	Daly, Mary	E	640
Clavin, Peter	2, May 1858	James	Crowley, Catherine	P	247
Clear, Thomas	10, Mar. 1859	James	Horn, Mary	T	
Cleare, Mary	24, July 1853	Michael	----, Bridget	U	
Cleary, Bridget	6, Mar. 1856	Thomas	----, Mary	R	
Cleary, Catherine	28, Dec. 1851	Rudolph	Hin---, Ellen	P	14
Cleary, Cecilia	23, Apr. 1854	Patrick	Neale, Eliza	B	313
Cleary, Francis	1, Apr. 1855	Patrick	Cassidy, Catherine	E	276
Cleary, John	12, Sept 1853	Edmund	Forrestet, Margaret	B	299
Cleary, Martin	4, Apr. 1855	Edward	Long, Margaret	P	127
Cleary, Martin	20, Nov. 1859	Michael	Barry, Eliza	B	84
Cleary, Mary	26, Apr. 1855	Edward	Finnly, Ann	R	
Cleary, Mary	28, July 1859	John	----, Margaret	E	643
Cleary, Mary	16, Oct. 1859	Patrick	----, Ellen	E	663
Cleary, Mary Ann	11, Apr. 1852	Edmund	Long, Margaret	P	20
Cleary, Mary Ann	8, Oct. 1854	Robert	----, Catherine	M	
Cleary, Michael	30, Oct. 1858	Cornelius	Dolan, Ellen	E	574
Cleary, Michael	6, Nov. 1853	Daniel	Dwyer, Bridget	P	58
Cleary, Michael	22, May 1856	John	Redman, Margaret	E	367
Cleary, William	29, Feb. 1852	Daniel	Dwyer, Bridget	P	18
Clemens, Johan Jacob	27, Oct. 1850	Johan	Fey, Crescentia	D	240
Clement, Joseph	14, Aug. 1850	Joseph	----, Mary Ann	E	239
Clements, Charles	31, Aug. 1855	Joseph	McLo---, Mary Ann	E	312
Clements, Elisabeth	2, Sept 1854	August	Redinbo, Louise	R	
Cler, John	22, Apr. 1855	Michael	Lally, Bridget	U	
Clerk, Mary	15, May 1852	Patrick	----, Ann	H	
Clifford, Cornelius	26, Jan. 1852	Cornelius	McGinus, Ann	B	251
Clifford, Daniel	3, Apr. 1853	Daniel	----, Margaret	P	39
Clifford, Ellen	28, Nov. 1852	Daniel	Fitzpatrick, Mary	E	38
Clifford, Ellen Bridget	5, Oct. 1856	George	----, Mary	E	401
Clifford, Ellen Julia	4, Nov. 1858	Daniel	Doyle, Joanne	E	575
Clifford, John	13, Aug. 1854	Patrick	----, Mary	E	216
Clifford, John	5, Sept 1859	Patrick	Morris, Jane	B	80
Clifford, John	27, Aug. 1854	Thomas	Geiron, Honora	E	219
Clifford, John	23, May 1852	William	----, Elizabeth	E	418
Clifford, Margaret	6, Dec. 1851	Patrick	----, Catherine	E	364
Clifford, Mary	2, June 1858	George	Powers, Julia	E	539
Clifford, Mary Ann	8, Oct. 1855	Edward	Hand, Mary	B	20
Clifford, Mary Jane	1, Apr. 1854	George	Hamilton, Mary	V	12
Clifford, Patrick	20, Nov. 1850	Derby	Readen, Helen	E	263
Clifford, Sarah	28, Feb. 1854	Michael	Patrick, Sarah	B	310
Clifford, Thomas	3, Apr. 1859	George	----, Mary	E	616
Clifford, Thomas	26, Jan. 1850	Thomas	Herron, Honora	E	194
Clifford, Thomas	8, June 1853	William	----, Elizabeth	E	96
Clifford, William	8, Sept 1854	William	Sweeney, Elizabeth	V	17

Name of Child	Date of Baptism	Father	Mother	Church	Page
Cline, Helen	1, Dec. 1855	Alexander	Keefe, Mary	V	28
Cline, John	31, Oct. 1850	Alexander	Keefe, Mary	E	258
Cline, Mary	6, Mar. 1853	Alexander	Keefe, Mary	E	68
Clinton, Catherine	29, Jan. 1854	John	Clary, Helen	B	308
Clinton, Ellen	19, May 1858	John	Collony, Ellen	B	59
Clinton, George	8, Mar. 1853	Patrick	----, Elizabeth	E	70
Clinton, John	26, Aug. 1855	John	Culleary, Ellen	B	18
Clinton, Mary	20, Apr. 1851	Patrick	Carr, Catherine	P	7
Clinton, Peter	19, Jan. 1854	Patrick	Carr, Catherine	B	307
Clissen, Patrick	7, May 1854	Hugh	Haran, Margaret	V	13
Clitch, Mary Helen	21, Sept 1854	John A.	Clarke, Hulda	V	18
Clo, Maria Philomena	15, June 1856	Mathias	Lichtenberger, Anna Maria	A	
Clo, Mathilda	1, Aug. 1858	Mathias	----, Maria	F	
Clocher, Mary Helen	28, July 1850	John	Cloker, Christine	E	235
Cloid, Henry	13, Mar. 1856	John S.D.	----, Julia	B	26
Cloney, Patrick James	21, July 1852	Thomas	Mulready, Helen	B	265
Close, Sarah Ann	18, July 1852	Richard	McCord, Mary	B	263
Closs, Caecilia Amalia	31, July 1859	Johan	Rickelman, Anna Maria	A	
Closs, Heinrich Carl	30, Nov. 1856	Johan	Rickelmann, Maria	C	
Closs, Johan Heinrich	3, Aug. 1851	Johan	Rickelman, Maria	A	
Closs, Maria Catharina	1, Mar. 1854	Johan	Rickelman, Maria	A	
Closterman, Anna Maria Catharina	28, Apr. 1857	J. Heinrich	Wolfes, Catharina	A	
Closterman, Carl Herman	11, Apr. 1854	J. Heinrich	Kohls, Maria Elisabeth	A	
Closterman, Catharina Josephina	17, Dec. 1851	J. Heinrich	Kohls, Elisabeth	A	
Closterman, Juliana Anna	16, Jan. 1859	Heinrich	Kohls, Maria Elisabeth	A	
Closterman, Maria Catharina Helena	19, Nov. 1853	J. Dietrich	Wulfers, Catharina	A	
Closterman, Maria Clara	3, Sept 1856	Heinrich	Kohls, Maria Elisabeth	A	
Cloud, Clemens August	1, Aug. 1854	Francis	Growe, Wilhelmina	A	
Cloud, Herman Bernard Constantine	9, Dec. 1851	Francis	Grove, Wilhelmina	A	
Cloud, Maria Theresa	27, Mar. 1858	Francis	Grove, Wilhelmina	A	
Cloud, Wilhelmina Carolina Catharina	25, Nov. 1855	Francis	Growe, Wilhelmina	A	
Clynch, Ann	6, Aug. 1856	Francis	----, Ann	M	
Clynch, Catherine	8, Aug. 1858	Francis	----, Mary	M	
Clynch, Francis	2, Sept 1852	Francis	----, Ann	M	
Clynch, Lawrence	16, Apr. 1854	Francis	----, Ann	M	
C---non, Catherine	4, Dec. 1853	Michael	Cavanaugh, Sarah	P	60
Coakely, Helen Honora	21, Feb. 1856	Thomas	Conklin, Margaret	P	170
Coakely, John	2, Oct. 1859	Thomas	Conklin, Margaret	P	298
Coakely, Sarah Helen	25, Nov. 1855	Thomas	Dowd, Bridget	V	28
Coakely, Thomas	29, Dec. 1853	Thomas	Dowd, Bridget	V	9
Coaklely, Mary Ann	19, May 1857	Thomas	Dowd, Bridget	B	44
Coakley, Jeremiah	22, July 1858	Thomas	Conklin, Margaret	P	254
Coakley, Margaret	8, July 1859	Thomas	Down, Bridget	B	77
Coakley, Mary	21, Aug. 1859	William	Cassin, Mary	E	648
Coakley, Thomas	16, May 1852	Thomas	Dowd, Bridget	E	413
Coal, Ann	28, June 1857	Michael	O'Brien, Ann	J	42
Cobb, Charles Burten	5, Nov. 1858	Louis	Reading, Ellen	E	576
Cobb, Louis Albert	1, Aug. 1854	Louis	Reading, Ellen	E	212
Cobb, Mary	31, Dec. 1855	?	?	T	
Cobb, Mary Ann	12, Mar. 1850	Louis	----, Ellen	E	203
Cober, Anna Catharina Elisabeth	1, Apr. 1856	Carl A.	Brueggemann, Antonia	F	
Cochem, Frances	12, June 1853	Caspar	Bachman, Eva	Q	3
Cochlen, Patrick	13, July 1851	Timothy	Carney, Mary	E	323
Cochran, Louise Adele	3, Nov. 1850	Samuel	Cassily, Cecilia	B	218
Cochran, Thomas	18, Sept 1852	Samuel	Dunn, Elizabeth	E	19
Cocke, Helen	28, Apr. 1856	Thomas	adult - 30 years old	E	363
Cockern, Margaretha	20, Oct. 1850	Caspar	Bachman, Eva	D	239
Code, Martin	5, June 1853	Patrick	Murphy, Mary	P	43
Code, Mary	21, Nov. 1855	Patrick	Murphy, Mary	P	160

Name of Child	Date of Baptism	Father	Mother	Church	Page
Cody, Bridget	4, Mar. 1855	William	Rottler, Mary	P	123
Cody, Mary Elizabeth	31, Aug. 1856	John	Larkin, Catherine	V	33
Cody, Richard John	6, Nov. 1853	Patrick	O'Neil, Mary Ann	R	
Coen, Bridget	14, Sept 1851	John	Fitzmorris, Mary	B	241
Coen, Catherine Bridget	5, Aug. 1855	John	Fitzmaurice, Mary	B	17
Coen, James	16, Sept 1857	Thomas	McGarry, Jane	B	49
Coffee, James	12, Sept 1855	James	Ward, Mary	P	151
Coffee, Richard	12, Sept 1858	James	Ward, Mary	P	260
Coffey, Catherine	30, June 1852	James	Ward, Mary	B	262
Coffey, James	15, Nov. 1854	James	Wald, Mary	P	104
Coffey, Joseph	4, Sept 1859	James	Ward, Mary	P	294
Coffey, Mary Ann	4, June 1858	Maurice	----, Mary	M	
Coffey, Michael	27, Nov. 1855	Patrick	Donahue, Mary	E	330
Coffield, Susan Eliza	27, Aug. 1854	John	Rias, Ann Eliza	B	4
Coffy, Helen	17, Nov. 1850	James	Maney, Mary	B	219
Coghlin, James	13, July 1856	Thomas	----, Martha	E	381
Coghlin, Michael	8, Sept 1850	Jeremiah	Cronan, Ann	E	247
Coghtree, Patrick	5, Mar. 1851	Martin	Lavell, Mary	E	287
Coghtry, Mary	5, Apr. 1853	Martin	----, Mary	E	80
Coghtry, Thomas	24, Nov. 1857	Martin	Lavell, Mary	E	495
Coglan, Martin	23, Mar. 1852	John	Fox, Honora	B	254
Coglin, Margaret	13, June 1852	John	McCarpin, Mary	E	424
Coglin, Mary	3, Feb. 1853	William	----, Catherine	E	60
Cohen, James	30, Apr. 1854	Michael	O'Brien, Ann	P	80
Cohen, John	26, Mar. 1854	James	Shanahan, Bridget	P	75
Cohrs, Johan Herman Bernard	22, June 1858	B. Heinrich	Grote, Susan Maria	R	
Cohrs, Maria Anna	16, Jan. 1855	B. Heinrich	Grote, Susan Maria	R	
Cohus, Johan Herman	4, Mar. 1858	Herman	Hinnenbrink, Lisette	K	
Cohus, Johan Ludwig	26, Nov. 1858	Johan	Determan, Veronica	K	
Cokely, Catherine	4, Dec. 1854	William	Lilly, Catherine	V	20
Cole, Ann	26, July 1855	Robin	----, Liddy	E	303
Cole, Henry	16, Apr. 1854	Ernst	----, Mary	E	183
Cole, Honora	15, July 1855	George	O'Donohue, Mary	E	300
Cole, Margret Ellen	19, June 1858	George P.	Donohoe, Mary	B	60
Cole, Mary	2, Jan. 1853	Thomas	Mallan, Mary	P	33
Cole, Mary Martha	13, July 1856	George P.	O'Donohue, Mary	B	31
Cole, William	26, Dec. 1853	William	Garrety, Ann	V	9
Colebb, Margaretha Helena	26, Sept 1852	Johan	Butman, Theresa	D	349
Coleman, Anastasia	24, June 1855	William	----, Mary	E	295
Coleman, Bridget	31, Jan. 1855	John	Cusick, Mary	R	
Coleman, Catherine	11, Sept 1852	Michael	Kelly, Mary	B	270
Coleman, Edward	4, Dec. 1853	Patrick	----, Judith	M	
Coleman, Elizabeth	9, Mar. 1851	Daniel	----, Mary	E	289
Coleman, Elizabeth	19, June 1855	John	Nauchter, Bridget	E	294
Coleman, Frances Angela	4, Feb. 1856	August	O'Shaughnessy, Mary Ann	P	169
Coleman, George	1, Nov. 1853	August	O'Shaunesey, Ann	E	139
Coleman, Helne	20, Aug. 1855	John	Walsh, Bridget	V	26
Coleman, Isabel	14, Aug. 1859	John	Welsh, Bridget	B	79
Coleman, James Henry	25, Sept 1850	Alexander	----, Frances	E	250
Coleman, Jane	16, Jan. 1859	William	Ryan, Mary	E	597
Coleman, Joanne	23, Aug. 1852	John	----, Ann	B	268
Coleman, Joanne	25, May 1851	Lawrence	----, Mary	E	310
Coleman, John	25, Dec. 1850	Patrick	Doran, Judith	M	
Coleman, John Thomas	13, Sept 1857	Thomas	Hays, Mary Ann	P	223
Coleman, Margaret	26, Aug. 1850	Lawrence	Henry, Margaret	B	211
Coleman, Maria Anna	15, June 1857	August	O'Shaughnessy, Anne	A	
Coleman, Mary	5, July 1852	Patrick	McK----, Catherine	P	24
Coleman, Mary	11, July 1851	John	----, Ellen	E	322
Coleman, Mary Ann	14, Mar. 1852	John	----, Bridget	E	391

Name of Child	Date of Baptism	Father	Mother	Church	Page
Coleman, Mary Ann	22, May 1859	John	McNulty, Sarah	B	75
Coleman, Mary Ann	4, Apr. 1852	Patrick	----, Judith	M	
Coleman, Michael	12, Sept 1852	Lawrence	Buckley, Mary	R	
Coleman, Patrick	27, Apr. 1856	William	Connelly, Mary	E	362
Coleman, Peter	4, Mar. 1854	Michael	Kelly, Mary	P	72
Coleman, Richard	24, Nov. 1856	William	Ryan, Mary	E	415
Coleman, Sabina	16, Nov. 1856	Andrew	Walsh, Mary	P	198
Coleman, Sarah Ann	7, Jan. 1855	Michael	Mack, Mary	E	254
Coleman, Thomas	31, Mar. 1850	John	----, Mary	E	205
Coleman, Thomas	27, Jan. 1850	Thomas	McCloskey, Sarah	B	195
Coleman, Walter	27, June 1858	Andrew	Walsh, Mary	P	251
Coleman, William	6, Feb. 1853	Alexander	Martin, Frances	P	34
Coleman, William	6, Mar. 1859	John	----, Mary	E	609
Colerain, Daniel	10, Oct. 1854	Daniel	Carlia, Rose	R	
Colet, Peter	14, Apr. 1850	Joseph	Wiesen, Anna	C	
Colfey?, James	13, July 1856	Luke	Gilligan, Ann	B	31
Colina, Edward Patrick	27, Nov. 1859	Thomas	Mullany, Catherine	B	84
Collega, Catharina	10, Nov. 1850	James	----, Caecilia	L	
Coller, Johan Anton	12, Dec. 1854	Johan	Auer, Magdalena	J	30
Coller, Johan Anton	13, Jan. 1856	Johan	Auer, Magdalena	J	34
Coller, Johan Ignatius	12, Dec. 1854	Johan	Auer, Magdalena	J	30
Coller, Johan Wilhelm	2, May 1858	Constantine	Fruk--, Maria	D	110
Coller, Maria Carolina	6, Dec. 1859	Johan	Auer, Magdalena	J	52
Collert, Maria Elisabeth	28, Nov. 1858	Friedrich	Stumde, Maria Elisabeth	D	124
Collet, Christina	12, Oct. 1851	Peter	Winker, Magalena	D	287
Collet, Elisabeth	25, Apr. 1854	Joseph	Schmidt, Maria Eva	D	9
Collet, Elisabeth Agnes	24, Mar. 1855	Friedrich	Stumpe, M. Elisabeth	C	
Collet, Francis	9, Dec. 1856	Friedrich	Stumpe, M. Elisabeth	C	
Collet, Francis Joseph	14, Nov. 1858	Francis	Liss, Theresa	A	
Collet, Friedrich	13, Dec. 1855	Friedrich	Liesz, Theresa	C	
Collet, Helena	29, May 1859	Peter	Winker, Anna	D	139
Collet, Leo Johan	19, May 1859	Johan	Buschle, Regina	T	
Collet, Maria	19, Aug. 1855	Johan	Buschle, Regina	D	40
Collet, Maria	11, Sept 1854	Peter	Winker, Magdalena	D	17
Collet, Maria Juliana	27, Nov. 1853	Johan	Buschle, Regina	F	
Collet, Mathias	25, Dec. 1851	Joseph	Wisen, Anna	D	298
Collet, Philipp	20, Sept 1857	John	Buschle, Regina	T	
Collet, Wilhelm	29, May 1853	Joseph	Kleeman, Crescentia	D	387
Collier, John	6, May 1853	James	Murphy, Julia	B	290
Collier, Mary	21, Apr. 1855	John	Knightly, Mary	B	14
Colligaer, Mary	23, Sept 1855	Cornelius	Maricar, Bridget	N	
Collin, August	6, Nov. 1853	Peter	Bayer, Elisabeth	F	
Collina, Catherine	8, Jan. 1854	Thomas	Mulvaney, Catherine	B	306
Collina, John	20, Apr. 1851	Thomas	Mulvaney, Catherine	B	230
Collina, Thomas	14, Feb. 1858	Thomas	Mullvany, Catherine	B	55
Collinan, Margaret	11, Jan. 1856	James	----, Joanne	E	337
Colling, Charles John	21, June 1857	John T.	Sowers, Elizabeth	E	460
Collins, Agnes Ann	25, May 1856	John	Sylvester, Emma	B	29
Collins, Angela	30, Dec. 1854	Daniel	----, Mary	M	
Collins, Bartholomew	25, June 1853	Timothy	----, Ellenore	E	100
Collins, Bridget	29, Dec. 1850	Henry	McKue, Mary	E	273
Collins, Bridget	26, Aug. 1855	Jeremiah	Ragan, Catherine	E	310
Collins, Catherine	1, Oct. 1855	John	----, Elizabeth	E	318
Collins, Catherine	2, Dec. 1855	Thomas	Mulvaney, Catherine	B	22
Collins, Charles Benjamin	31, Aug. 1851	Henry	Pearson, Mary	B	240
Collins, Daniel	23, May 1855		adult	B	15
Collins, Dennis	3, Dec. 1854	James	McShane, Bridget	P	107
Collins, Ellen	15, Oct. 1855	John	Door, Antonia	U	
Collins, Herman Louis	8, Jan. 1854	Henry	Lewis, Mary Elizabeth	B	306

Name of Child	Date of Baptism	Father	Mother	Church	Page
Collins, Honora	22, Apr. 1855	Timothy	Lyons, Helen	V	24
Collins, James	4, Aug. 1854	James	Collins, Mary	P	91
Collins, James	10, Feb. 1850	Thomas	Mulvaney, Catherine	B	196
Collins, Joanne	6, Nov. 1859	Michael	Lynch, Mary	B	83
Collins, Joanne	25, Dec. 1859	William	Breen, Catherine	E	679
Collins, John	7, Sept 1852	James	----, Mary	E	15
Collins, John	4, June 1854	James	Murphy, Margaret	E	195
Collins, John	11, Mar. 1855	Maurice	----, Catherine	E	271
Collins, John	25, June 1857	Thomas	Sullivan, Abby	E	462
Collins, John	17, Sept 1850	Timothy	----, Mary	E	247
Collins, John	16, Aug. 1857	William	Breen, Catherine	E	474
Collins, Joseph	8, Mar. 1857	James	McShea, Bridget	B	41
Collins, Julia	14, Dec. 1852	Timothy	Long, Mary	E	43
Collins, Lucy	15, Feb. 1858	?	Collins, Hannah	P	240
Collins, Lula	22, Mar. 1857	Jeremiah	Rogan, Catherine	E	442
Collins, Margaret	12, June 1853	John	McAvoy, Elizabeth	E	98
Collins, Margaret Mary	20, Jan. 1856	Pierce	Brophy, Julia	B	24
Collins, Martha	20, Nov. 1855	John	Meagher, Ann	Q	11
Collins, Martin	6, Dec. 1857	John	----, Helen	R	
Collins, Martin Edward	20, Sept 1857	Pierce	Brophey, Julia	B	50
Collins, Mary	22, July 1854	John	----, Ann	U	
Collins, Mary	28, Dec. 1856	Maurice	Pagan, Catherine	E	422
Collins, Mary	29, June 1852	Michael	Lynch, Mary	B	262
Collins, Mary	15, Aug. 1851	Timothy	Collins, Mary	E	333
Collins, Mary Ann	3, Feb. 1856	Anthony	Gosgrove, Adelia	B	24
Collins, Mary Ann	23, Oct. 1853	Daniel	McCarthy, Helen	B	301
Collins, Mary Ann	2, June 1855	James	16 years old	V	25
Collins, Mary Clare	22, Aug. 1858	Michael	Lynch, Mary	T	
Collins, Mary Elizabeth	17, Feb. 1856	Patrick	Griffin, Mary	B	25
Collins, Mary Margaret	1, Oct. 1856	Andrew	Murray, Bridget	B	34
Collins, Patrick	5, Feb. 1852	Jeremiah	Ryan, Catherine	P	17
Collins, Patrick	22, May 1857	John	Stanton, Helen	E	455
Collins, Sarah	26, June 1854	James	----, Joanne	E	202
Collins, Sarah	7, Sept 1856	John	----, Sarah	E	396
Collins, Thomas	4, Nov. 1855	James	McShea, Bridget	B	21
Collins, Thomas	14, Jan. 1859	Thomas	Sullivan, Abby	E	596
Collins, Thomas	11, Aug. 1856	Timothy	----, Lucy	E	389
Collins, William	30, Sept 1855	Michael	Coulter, Ann	P	152
Collins, William Henry	14, Sept 1856	Daniel	Bradley, Margaret	T	
Collins, William John	23, May 1850	William J.	Hickey, Mary	B	203
Collison, Michael	23, Nov. 1851	Patrick	Tholbert?, Catherine	E	360
Collisson, Catherine	8, Feb. 1854	Patrick	Dalbert, Catherine	E	166
Collisson, John James	13, Oct. 1855	John	Quinlan, Mary	E	320
Collisson, Michael	17, Aug. 1853	John	Quinlan, Mary	E	119
Collopy, Daniel	16, June 1855	Patrick	----, Bridget	U	
Collopy, John	25, Aug. 1850	Michael	Kearny, Mary Ann	B	211
Colman, James	24, July 1854	Lermas?	Wohly, Mary	Q	4
Coltery, Sarah	27, July 1851	Walter	Frenigty, Sarah	E	327
Columbi, Maria Louisa	21, May 1857	Coelestin	Sturla, Antonia	K	
Colwell, Augusta Beatrice	23, June 1853	Andrew	Hammond, Mary Ann	B	294
Colwell, Charles Walter	1, Feb. 1852	Andrew	Hammond, Mary Ann	B	251
Colwell, Ida Louise	15, Jan. 1856	Andrew	Hammond, Mary Ann	B	23
Colwell, John Edward	13, Feb. 1859	Edward	----, Mary	P	275
Comb, Ann	23, Apr. 1857	John	Doud, Sabina	B	43
Comber, Elizabeth	5, Jan. 1854	Martin	Moran, Bridget	V	9
Comeford, Mary Jane	25, July 1858	James	----, Mary Ann	M	
Comer, Ambrose	3, Apr. 1856	Patrick	Flinn, Margaret	R	
Comer, Honora	11, Jan. 1857	Jeremiah	----, Rose	R	
Comer, Honora	25, June 1857	Michael	----, Bridget	R	

Name of Child	Date of Baptism	Father	Mother	Church	Page
Comer, Mary	15, May 1857	Patrick	----, Margaret	R	
Comer, Mary Elizabeth	12, Oct. 1850	William	Pew, Mary	E	253
Comery, George	20, Dec. 1857	James	Roark, Winnefred	E	501
Comfort, Nicolaus John	18, Sept 1856	James	White, Mary Ann	E	398
Commerford, Mary	6, Nov. 1853	Michael	----, Helen	H	
Commerford, Patrick	1, Jan. 1856	John	Hoban, Mary	R	
Comne, Elizabeth	24, Aug. 1851	James	Rourke, Winefred	B	239
Conaghty, Elizabeth	24, May 1857		adult	B	44
Conahan, Catharine	30, May 1858	Michael	Early, Catherine	U	
Conahan, Edward	9 , Jan. 1859	Charles	Whipple, Elizabeth Susan	B	69
Conahan, Eliza	2, Oct. 1852		adult	B	273
Conahan, Henry Aloysius	7, Dec. 1856	Charles	Whipple, Eliza Susan	B	37
Conahan, Mary Jane	8, Sept 1850	Charles	Montfort, Sarah Catharine	B	213
Conahan, Sarah	27, Mar. 1853	Charles	Monfort, Sarah Catherine	B	290
Concannan, Patrick M.	28, Oct. 1859	John	Burret, Mary	J	52
Concannan, Sarah	9, Mar. 1851	Patrick	Rogers, Mary	E	288
Concanning, Francis	4, Jan. 1855	John	----, Mary	M	
Concanning, John	17, Feb. 1857	John	----, Mary	M	
Concannon, Bernard Ignatius	31, July 1859	Michael	Walsh, Sarah	V	57
Concannon, Catherine	2, Oct. 1855	Edmund	Hughes, Sabina	E	318
Concannon, James	5, Apr. 1853	Patrick	Rogers, Mary	E	79
Concannon, John	22, Nov. 1857	Thomas	Walsh, Mary	V	42
Concannon, Michael	3, Oct. 1852	Michael	O'Shaugnesy, Mary	E	23
Concannon, Patrick	2, Aug. 1855	Michael	Walsh, Sarah	K	
Concannon, Sarah	26, June 1859	Thomas	----, Mary	V	56
Condon, Bartholomew	26, June 1858	Patrick	----, Elizabeth	E	543
Condon, Honora	24, Apr. 1853	John	Murphy, Bridget	E	84
Condon, John	14, May 1854	Michael	Moore, Catherine	P	82
Condon, Martin	26, June 1858	Patrick	----, Elizabeth	E	543
Condon, Mary	4, Apr. 1857	Michael	O'Brien, Juliana	E	444
Condry, Mary	25, Mar. 1853	John	----, Elizabeth	B	287
Cone, Eliza	12, Sept 1858	James	Sullivan, Bridget	P	260
Cone, Esther	9, Nov. 1856	James	Shanahan, Bridget	P	197
Cone, Julia	12, Sept 1858	James	Sullivan, Bridget	P	260
Cone, Mary	22, Aug. 1852	James	Thom, Bridget	P	26
Cone, Michael	11, Sept 1854	Patrick	----, Bridget	E	223
Conklin, Michael	6, June 1852	Thomas	----, Ann	P	23
Conkling, Hora Isela Rose	17, Dec. 1854	William M.	----, Frances	E	247
Conkling, Sarah Frances	27, Oct. 1857	William	----, Frances	E	488
Conlan, Bernard	3, Aug. 1857	James	Conley, Susan	E	472
Conlan, Catherine	29, Sept 1850	John	Imney, Sarah	B	215
Conlan, Catherine	22, May 1853	Michael	----, Bridget	E	91
Conlan, Catherine Elizabeth	6, Sept 1855		Conlan, Catherine	B	18
Conlan, Helen	28, Dec. 1851	John	Murphy, Bridget	B	248
Conlan, James	15, Aug. 1854		Conlan, Bridget	U	
Conlan, James Francis	28, May 1858	Michael	Corcoran, Bridget	E	538
Conlan, John	5, Feb. 1854	Thomas	Deane, Catherine	B	309
Conlan, Michael	12, May 1850	Michael	----, Martha	E	213
Conlan, Patrick	2, Nov. 1851	Jeremiah	----, Helen	B	244
Conley, Honora	4, Sept 1852	Dennis	----, Honora	M	
Conley, John	19, Jan. 1858	Michael	----, Ann	E	511
Conley, Mary	5, Mar. 1857	Michael	Matthews, Ann	E	438
Conley, Patrick	11, Dec. 1859	John	Powell, Ann	B	85
Conley, Thomas	23, May 1853	John	----, Catherine	E	92
Conlin, John	25, Oct. 1850		Conlin, Catherine	E	256
Conlin, Martha	5, Dec. 1852	Michael	Duffy, Martha	E	42
Conlin, Michael	24, May 1857	James	Carrigan, Mary	U	
Conlin, Thomas	10, Nov. 1850	James	----, Mary	E	260
Conlin, Thomas	4, Aug. 1850	Michael	Corcoran, Mary	E	236

Name of Child	Date of Baptism	Father	Mother	Church	Page
Conlon, John	21, Oct. 1855	Michael	Corcoran, Bridget	E	321
Conly, Bridget	14, Dec. 1850	Thomas	Kearnan, Ann	E	266
Conly, Elizabeth	13, Jan. 1853	Thomas	Kearnan, Ann	E	53
Conly, M. Ellen	12, Dec. 1857	Francis	----, Ellen	E	500
Conly, Mary	20, Nov. 1853	John	Morissy, Mary	E	145
Conly, Mary Ann	19, Dec. 1852	Joseph	Steward, Winnefred	E	45
Conly, Nicolaus	10, Mar. 1853	Michael	Conly, Sarah	E	70
Conn, Josephine Virginia	19, Mar. 1850	John	White, Mary Eliza	B	198
Connahan, James	9, Mar. 1856	Michael	Harley, Catherine	U	
Connair, Ellen	5, May 1853	Michael	Martin, Mary	E	86
Connally, Bridget	6, Dec. 1856	John	----, Bridget	E	418
Connally, John	18, Sept 1852	John	----, Catherine	E	18
Connaughton, Ann	16, Dec. 1852	Cornelius	Carey, Bridget	B	277
Connaughton, Patrick	2, Mar. 1856	Peter	Shannon, Mary	P	171
Connaughty, Mary Elizabeth	30, Oct. 1858	Hugh	Donnelly, Mary Ann	E	574
Connell, Ann	12, Nov. 1854	Bernard	----, Margaret	M	
Connell, Ann Mary	8, Oct. 1854	William	----, Catherine	U	
Connell, Bridget	24, Oct. 1854	Michael	Brien, Joanne	E	235
Connell, Catherine	5, Sept 1852	Charles	McDonald, Catherine	E	14
Connell, Catherine	20, Sept 1857	James	Reardon, Hanna	B	50
Connell, Charles	25, Aug. 1856	Charles	McDonough, Catherine	V	35
Connell, Charles	16, Jan. 1859	Thomas	Calaghan, Mary	E	596
Connell, Cornelius	24, July 1855	Cornelius	Sullivan, Ellen	U	
Connell, Cornelius	29, July 1857	John	Hinnigan, Mary	P	218
Connell, George Albert	19, Mar. 1856	James	----, Mary	E	350
Connell, Helen	24, Nov. 1855	John A.	Heraghan, Mary	P	160
Connell, Helen	15, Nov. 1857	Michael	Sheehan, Mary	P	230
Connell, James	16, Sept 1852	Andrew	White, Mary	B	270
Connell, James	14, Dec. 1858	James	Rendon, Hannah	B	68
Connell, James	31, Dec. 1854	Michael	----, ----	E	251
Connell, James	17, Apr. 1853	William	Connell, Catherine	U	
Connell, John	18, Sept 1853	Daniel	McCarthy, Margaret	V	6
Connell, John	13, July 1851	Matthew	Byron, Bridget	B	236
Connell, John Charles	10, June 1855	Thomas	Callaghan, Mary	E	291
Connell, Julia	15, Apr. 1856	Patrick	Flynn, Mary	B	28
Connell, Mary	26, Oct. 1856	Michael	Armstrong, Sarah	E	408
Connell, Mary	31, Jan. 1859	Patrick	Flinn, Mary	E	601
Connell, Mary Ann	11, Jan. 1857	Thomas	Callaghan, Mary	V	37
Connell, Maurice	22, Jan. 1854	John	Many, Honora	J	26
Connell, Michael	25, Aug. 1850	Charles	McDonough, Catherine	B	211
Connell, Michael	17, Sept 1852	John	Gra---, Bridget	P	27
Connell, Sarah Jane	15, Dec. 1856	William	Lawler, Catherine	U	
Connell, Thomas	20, Aug. 1854	Charles	McDonough, Catherine	E	217
Connell, William	25, Apr. 1856	John	----, Catherine	E	361
Connell, William Peter	24, Oct. 1859	James	Cummins, Mary	P	302
Connelly, Ann	8, Aug. 1858	Michael	Judge, Bridget	P	257
Connelly, Ann	24, June 1855	Owen	Green, Ann	B	16
Connelly, Ann	19, Apr. 1858	Thomas	Carely, Ann	E	530
Connelly, Bartley	20, Jan. 1859	John	----, Mary	E	597
Connelly, Catherine	5, Jan. 1851	Edward	Bayley, Augusta M.	B	222
Connelly, Catherine	10, Nov. 1850	John	Egan, Mary	B	218
Connelly, Catherine	3, Aug. 1856	Patrick	Curren, Bridget	E	387
Connelly, Dennis	16, June 1859	Daniel	Ryan, Bridget	E	633
Connelly, Elizabeth	16, Oct. 1859	Michael	Rice, Elizabeth	P	300
Connelly, Helen	11, Sept 1853	Owen	Green, Ann	B	298
Connelly, James	28, Apr. 1859	Bartholomew	----, Bridget	E	621
Connelly, James	31, Aug. 1856	Thomas	Morgan, Mary	P	189
Connelly, James	17, May 1851	Walter	----, Mary	E	308
Connelly, James	5, Sept 1859	William	Donlan, Mary	E	651

Name of Child	Date of Baptism	Father	Mother	Church	Page
Connelly, Joanne	1, Feb. 1852	George	Kelly, Mary	E	379
Connelly, Joanne	29, Jan. 1854	Walter	Armstrong, Mary	E	163
Connelly, John	24, Feb. 1850	Owen	Green, Ann	B	197
Connelly, John	23, Apr. 1856	William	----, Margaret	M	
Connelly, John	22, Aug. 1858	William	Murphy, Rose	E	558
Connelly, Margaret	20, Jan. 1858	John	----, Margaret	E	511
Connelly, Martin	20, Nov. 1859	John	Laydon, Margaret	E	672
Connelly, Mary	9, Sept 1856	John	Lyden, Margaret	E	397
Connelly, Mary	14, Sept 1851	Owen	Green, Ann	B	241
Connelly, Mary	14, Dec. 1858	Patrick	Curran, Bridget	E	587
Connelly, Mary	24, Dec. 1858	Thomas	----, Margaret	M	
Connelly, Mary	22, Aug. 1852	Thomas	Curly, Mary	E	8
Connelly, Mary	21, Sept 1852	Walter	----, Mary	E	19
Connelly, Mary	16, Mar. 1851	William	----, Ann	E	
Connelly, Mary Ann	7, Dec. 1856	Gregory	McDonnell, Honora	E	418
Connelly, Mary Ann	10, Feb. 1855	James	----, Winnefred	E	263
Connelly, Michael	4, Sept 1855	Gregory	McDonald, Ann	E	313
Connelly, Michael	12, May 1850	James	----, Catherine	E	212
Connelly, Patrick	30, Sept 1855	Coleman	Mulken--, Mary	B	20
Connelly, Patrick	8, Mar. 1857	F.	Loftis, Mary	E	439
Connelly, Peter	8, June 1856	Thomas	Dolan, Ellen	B	29
Connelly, Richard	28, May 1855	Thomas	Morgan, Mary Ann	P	134
Connelly, Tehresa	6, Nov. 1853	Thomas	McKittrick, Mary	B	302
Connelly, Theresa	22, Sept 1854	Francis	----, Catherine	E	225
Connelly, Walter Joseph	24, Nov. 1855	Walter	Armstrong, Mary	E	328
Connelly, William	12, Jan. 1851	William	Fely, Bridget	F	
Connely, Stanolaus?	10, Dec. 1854	Michael	Brohoney, Bridget	P	109
Conner, Elizabeth	8, Dec. 1859	Francis	Dawson, Margaret	B	85
Conner, Ellen	18, Aug. 1850	Thomas	----, Mary	E	240
Conner, Eugene (Owen)	30, Dec. 1854	John	Gorvan, Helen	P	112
Conner, Francis Michael	25, Dec. 1852	James	----, Mary	E	47
Conner, Helen	4, May 1858	Thomas	Curly, Mary	P	248
Conner, James	12, Aug. 1856	John	Mulvey, Margaret	V	32
Conner, Margaret Elisabeth	31, July 1859	William	Lawler, Catherine	U	
Conner, Mary	15, Nov. 1859	John	Moesy, Mary	N	
Conner, Mary	7, Apr. 1856	Thomas	Curley, Mary	P	175
Conners, Bridget	9, Feb. 1852	Thomas	Curley, Mary	B	252
Conners, Catherine	21, Aug. 1853	Edward	----, Mary	E	121
Conners, John	10, Apr. 1853	Patrick	----, Margaret	E	81
Conners, Patrick	6, Mar. 1859	John	Mown, Mary	P	278
Connerton, Helen Catherine	30, May 1858	Andrew	Tracy, Elizabeth	E	538
Connerton, Joanne	6, Apr. 1856	Andrew	----, Elizabeth	E	357
Connerton, John Patrick Francis	30, May 1858	Andrew	Tracy, Elizabeth	E	538
Connerton, Peter	1, Jan. 1854	Andrew	----, Elizabeth	E	157
Connerty, Ann	16, Jan. 1859	Peter	Sahnnon, Mary	P	272
Connerty, Bernard	30, May 1852	Patrick	Fagan, Bridget	B	264
Connerty, Joseph	15, Feb. 1857	Patrick	Fagan, Bridget	B	40
Connerty, Mary	10, Sept 1854	Patrick	Fagan, Bridget	B	5
Connerty, Mary Josephine	30, Nov. 1859	Patrick	Fagan, Bridget	B	84
Conniff, Mary Ann	6, Jan. 1853	Owen	----, Eliza	E	52
Connoll, Daniel	12, June 1853	Patrick	Planket, Anna	L	
Connolly, Ann	31, July 1855	Edward	Brady, Augusta	B	17
Connolly, August	17, Aug. 1851	Michael	Farrell, Helen	B	238
Connolly, Barbara	26, June 1859	Festus	Loftus, Mary	E	634
Connolly, Catherine	9, Sept 1857	Owen	Green, Ann	B	49
Connolly, David	4, Nov. 1856	Jefferson	Stewart, Winefred	B	36
Connolly, Edward Clifford	26, Dec. 1852	Edward	Bailey, Augusta E.	B	278
Connolly, Felix	22, Oct. 1854	Lawrence	Keenan, Sarah	V	18
Connolly, John	17, Aug. 1851	Brian	Ward, Bridget	B	238

Name of Child	Date of Baptism	Father	Mother	Church	Page
Connolly, John	6, Jan. 1859	John	Lyden, Margaret	B	69
Connolly, Mary	15, Feb. 1857	Coleman	Dunlap, Mary	B	40
Connolly, Mary	1, Oct. 1859	Edward	Bagly, Augusta	V	59
Connolly, Mary	8, Nov. 1855	Francis	Mahoney, Helen	P	158
Connolly, Mary	30, Jan. 1853	Michael	Brahany, Bridget	B	282
Connolly, Mary Helen	23, June 1856	Lawrence	Keenan, Sarah	E	376
Connolly, Patrick	1, Feb. 1857	Patrick	Devanny, Mary	B	40
Connolly, Thomas	12, Oct. 1851	Owen	McAmily?, Margaret	B	242
Connolly, Thomas	15, Feb. 1852	Thomas	Doan, Catherine	B	252
Connolly, Thomas	11, Sept 1853	Thomas	Morgan, Mary Ann	P	51
Connolly, Thomas Jefferson	12, Mar. 1854	Geoffrey	Stewart, Winefred	B	310
Connolly, William	8, May 1850	Thomas	Day, Catherine	B	202
Connolly, Winifred	27, Feb. 1859	Jeffrey	Stewart, Winefred	B	71
Connolly?, Thomas	18, July 1858	Luke	Gilligan, Ann	P	254
Connor, Bridget	7, Dec. 1851	August	----, Bridget	E	364
Connor, Bridget	9, Apr. 1854	Francis	Sheil, Bridget	V	13
Connor, Bridget	1, Feb. 1857	Thomas	Sullivan, Mary	P	205
Connor, Bridget	26, May 1850	William	----, Mary	E	216
Connor, Catherine	1, June 1851	John	----, Ellinor	B	233
Connor, Catherine	10, June 1854	Thomas	Hoban, Mary	P	84
Connor, Daniel	3, Sept 1854	Timothy	Murray, Bridget	P	94
Connor, Eliza	7, Apr. 1851	John	Mulfeatter, Catherine	E	298
Connor, Ellen	18, Sept 1853	Thomas	Sullivan, Mary	E	128
Connor, Francis	7, Dec. 1856	Francis	Shiel, Bridget	V	35
Connor, George	8, Oct. 1858	James	Delany, Helen	P	263
Connor, James	22, July 1855	Michael	Henni, Catherine	N	
Connor, James	16, Oct. 1854	Thomas	Callahan, Bridget	E	233
Connor, James	10, Nov. 1859	William	Gilmore, Mary	V	62
Connor, Joanne	27, Apr. 1851	John	----, Ellen	E	303
Connor, Joanne	1, Nov. 1857	John	Mann, Mary	P	229
Connor, Joanne	29, Dec. 1855	Michael	Fitzgerald, Mary	E	334
Connor, John	18, Feb. 1855	John	Crowley, Mary	B	11
Connor, John	24, Mar. 1853	John	Donovan, Helen	B	290
Connor, John	13, Dec. 1857	Patrick	Leonard, Mary	B	53
Connor, John	2, Aug. 1858	Peter	Magone, Ann	P	256
Connor, John	25, July 1858	Thomas	Sullivan, Mary	P	255
Connor, Jude	26, Oct. 1851	Thomas	Sullivan, Mary	E	353
Connor, Marcella Margaret	16, Oct. 1853	John	Moore, Elizabeth	B	301
Connor, Margaret	23, Mar. 1856	Michael	Judge, Bridget	P	174
Connor, Mary	22, July 1857	Francis	Dawson, Margaret	B	47
Connor, Mary	24, July 1853	John	----, Catherine	M	
Connor, Mary	22, Aug. 1854	Michael	Fitzgerald, Mary	V	16
Connor, Mary	13, Mar. 1859	Peter?	Larkin, Ann	E	610
Connor, Mary	4, Nov. 1855	Thomas	Sullivan, Mary	P	157
Connor, Mary	1, Aug. 1852	William	Gilmore, Mary	E	433
Connor, Mary	4, Feb. 1855	Michael	Feehely, Eliza	B	11
Connor, Mary Ann	30, Oct. 1858	Michael	O'Donnell, mary	P	265
Connor, Mary Ann	26, Mar. 1855	Patrick	McCabe, Catherine	R	
Connor, Mary Helen	20, Sept 1859	Patrick	McGuire, Juliana	E	655
Connor, Michael	15, Sept 1855	Michael	Brean, Joanne	E	315
Connor, Michael	28, Mar. 1858	Michael	Gilmour, Mary	E	525
Connor, Patrick	25, July 1858	Jeremiah	Bresnahan, Ellen	E	552
Connor, Sarah	11, June 1854	Edward	----, Mary	E	197
Connor, Thomas	15, Feb. 1852	Francis	Shegan, Bridget	E	382
Connor, Thomas	1, Apr. 1856	John	----, Catherine	M	
Connor, Thomas	26, Jan. 1853	John	Gorman, Ann	P	33
Connor, Thomas	25, Dec. 1858	John	Heffeld, Helen	P	270
Connor, William	4, July 1854	William	Gilmor, Mary	E	204
Connors, Bridget	10, Aug. 1856	Michael	Morgan, Mary	B	32

Name of Child	Date of Baptism	Father	Mother	Church	Page
Connors, Catherine	28, Apr. 1857	John	----, Eliza	E	449
Connors, Catherine	28, Aug. 1855	John	Delaney, Ann	P	149
Connors, Elizabeth Mary	29, Mar. 1857	John	Sullivan, Elizabeth	B	42
Connors, John Francis	27, July 1855	Martin	----, Sabina	E	303
Connors, John Francis	14, June 1856	William	----, Mary	E	373
Connors, Michael	7, Mar. 1856	Martin	Dillon, Bridget	R	
Connors, Patrick	10, Oct. 1858	John	Concannon, Helen	P	263
Connorton, Anthony	25, Oct. 1855	Patrick	Lyden, Joanne	E	322
Conn---van, Mary	30, Mar. 1852	Walter	Kent, Mary	E	397
Conrad, Catharina	20, Feb. 1859	Caspar	Auberger, Dorothea	T	
Conrad, Francis Seraph	18, Sept 1853	J. Nicolaus	----, Margaret	H	
Conrad, Helena	11, Jan. 1852	Peter	Merl, Helena	D	301
Conrad, Jacob	26, Aug. 1851	Jacob	Kramer, Margaretha	F	
Conrad, Juliana Carolina	1, June 1856	C. Ludwig	Donnersberger, Maria Anna	W	15
Conrad, Louisa Elisabeth	10, May 1858	Carl	Donnersberger, Maria Anna	W	22
Conrad, Margaretha	10, July 1853	Peter	Mehrer, Magdalena	D	394
Conrad, Peter	1, Dec. 1855	Caspar	Auberger, Dorothea	F	
Conrad, Peter	18, Nov. 1859	Peter	Rolf, Gertrud	D	151
Conrad, Philomena Maria	19, Jan. 1851	Johan	King, Maria	C	
Conradi, Agnes	10, Jan. 1858	Peter	Gast, Elisabeth	D	102
Conradi, Elisabeth	13, July 1859	Peter	Gast, Elisabeth	A	
Conradi, Susanna Catharina	22, June 1856	Peter	Gast, Elisabeth	D	61
Conrais, Heinrich	3, Jan. 1850	J. Nicolaus	Spaunagel, Catharina	D	197
Conrais, Maria	3, Jan. 1850	J. Nicolaus	Spaunagel, Catharina	D	197
Conroy, Bernard	3, Aug. 1851	Patrick	Fitzpatrick, Ann	E	329
Conroy, Brian	26, Nov. 1857	John	Carberry, Margaret	P	231
Conroy, Bridget	13, Nov. 1853	James	Garan, Joanne	P	59
Conroy, Daniel	3, Aug. 1851	Patrick	Fitzpatrick, Ann	E	330
Conroy, James Michael	18, Jan. 1852	Martin	Lyle, Margaret	P	16
Conroy, John	18, May 1856	James	Mylan, Catherine	P	180
Conroy, John	20, Nov. 1859	Michael	Hays, Mary	P	303
Conroy, John	20, Mar. 1853	Patrick	----, Helen	B	286
Conroy, John Henry	1, May 1853	Patrick	----, Ann	E	85
Conroy, Julia	2, Feb. 1855	Michael	Sullivan, Margaret	P	118
Conroy, Margaret	30, Nov. 1855	Peter	Burke, Ann	E	330
Conroy, Martin	7, Sept 1856	Martin	Sulivan, Margaret	J	38
Conroy, Mary	17, May 1850	Daniel	Mulready, Honora	B	202
Conroy, Mary	12, June 1852	Henry	----, Winefred	E	423
Conroy, Mary	26, July 1850	Peter	McDermot, Catherine	B	208
Conroy, Mary	22, Feb. 1851		Conroy, Ellenore	E	285
Conroy, Mary E.	18, Dec. 1853	Daniel	----, Honora	P	62
Conroy, Mary Ellen	25, Nov. 1855	Patrick	Britt, Ellen	B	22
Conroy, Patrick	14, Mar. 1852	Daniel	Mulledy, Ann	P	19
Conroy, Peter	28, Oct. 1852	Peter	McDermott, Catherine	P	29
Conroy, Robert Edward	11, May 1856	Daniel	Mulready, Honora	P	179
Conroy, Rosanne	10, Oct. 1858	Daniel	Mulready, Honora	P	263
Conroy, Thomas	23, May 1858	Martin	Sullivan, Margaret	J	46
Conroy, William Joseph	27, Dec. 1854	Patrick	Fitzpatrick, Ann	V	20
Conry, John	27, June 1853	Michael	Mooner, Catherine	N	13
Conry, Margaret	18, Sept 1857	Michael	----, Catherine	M	
Conry, Mary	24, Apr. 1853	Patrick	----, Bridget	M	
Conry, Patrick	22, July 1851	John	Daleysas, Louise	B	236
Conry, Stephen	5, July 1859	Andrew (+)	Hackett, Winnefred	E	637
Considine, Patrick	21, Sept 1852	Patrick	----, Catherine	E	19
Consodine, Mary	15, Jan. 1854	Patrick	Cullen, Catherine	E	160
Convey, Elisabeth	8, Apr. 1851	Lawrence	No---, Maria	K	
Conwae, Catherine	7, Aug. 1859	Thomas	Lynch, Catherine	N	
Conway, Abigail	22, Apr. 1855	Thomas	Lynch, Catherine	N	28
Conway, Ann	9, Nov. 1856	Michael	Courtney, Bridget	E	412

Name of Child	Date of Baptism	Father	Mother	Church	Page
Conway, Bridget Kate	10, Oct. 1855	Andrew	Conway, Bridget	E	320
Conway, Catherine	10, May 1854	John	Clarey, Catherine	P	81
Conway, Catherine	17, June 1857	Matthew	Farrell, Mary	B	45
Conway, Catherine	27, June 1852	Patrick	Guinan, Mary	B	261
Conway, Deborah	17, Apr. 1853	Michael	Conway, Catherine	Q	3
Conway, Edward John	22, Jan. 1854	Walter	Hunt, Mary	V	10
Conway, Elenora	23, Feb. 1852	Lawrence	----, Mary	E	385
Conway, Elizabeth	23, Feb. 1852	Lawrence	----, Mary	E	385
Conway, Helen	1, Aug. 1852	James	Kenny, Mary	B	267
Conway, Honora	25, June 1854	John	Barr, Winnifred	B	2
Conway, James	2, Mar. 1851	James	Good, Mary Rose	P	5
Conway, James	16, Sept 1856	Lawrence	Moore, Catherine	P	192
Conway, James	17, May 1852	Michael	Kalakky, Marianne	E	414
Conway, John	11, May 1850	John	----, Ellen	E	212
Conway, John	11, Aug. 1856	John	Clary, Catherine	B	32
Conway, John	22, Sept 1854	Lawrence	Moore, Catherine	P	96
Conway, John	19, Dec. 1858	Michael	Courtney, Bridget	E	587
Conway, John	29, Nov. 1857	Thomas	Lynch, Catherine	N	
Conway, John Thomas	10, May 1857	John	Fitzpatrick, Winny	E	452
Conway, Joseph	10, June 1855	Thomas	Lynch, Catherine	B	15
Conway, Lawrence	4, May 1856	Lawrence	Mansen, Mary	E	364
Conway, Margaret	27, June 1853	Michael	Fogarty, Mary	V	4
Conway, Margaret	14, Oct. 1856	William	Gardener, Mary	E	404
Conway, Mary	7, Dec. 1853	Cornelius	----, Mary	M	
Conway, Mary	8, May 1859	John	----, Winnefred	E	623
Conway, Mary	1, July 1858	Matthew	Sullivan, Honora	P	252
Conway, Mary	16, Mar. 1856	Stephan	King, Bridget	P	172
Conway, Mary	23, Oct. 1850	Thomas	Lynch, Catherine	E	256
Conway, Mary Jane	4, July 1858	John	Clarey, Catherine	P	252
Conway, Michael	24, Mar. 1855	John	Berton, Catherine	E	274
Conway, Michael	18, Oct. 1856	Matthew	Sullivan, Honora	P	195
Conway, Mosila	27, Feb. 1859	Lawrence	Moore, Kate	B	71
Conway, Sarah	10, Jan. 1858	Lawrence	Mansen, Mary	E	507
Conway, Thomas	25, Mar. 1852	Thomas	Lynch, Catherine	B	255
Conway, Thomas	14, Nov. 1852	Thomas	Lynch, Catherine	E	35
Conway, Thomas Francis	25, July 1858	Michael	Burke, Mary	E	553
Conway, William	14, July 1853	John	Fitzpatrick, Winny	E	106
Conway, William Joseph	27, Nov. 1859	Patrick	Fitzpatrick, Sabina	B	84
Conwell, Ellen	17, Feb. 1853	Donald	Mack, Bridget	P	35
Coogan, Helen	12, Mar. 1854	James	Byrne, Eliza	B	311
Coogan, Mary Catherine	20, Oct. 1850	James	Wi---, Elizabeth	B	216
Cook, Albert	19, Dec. 1852	Sylvan	Cassilly, Elizabeth	B	278
Cook, Ann Catharine	12, Aug. 1855	Andrew	Byrns, Ann	T	
Cook, Edward	21, Sept 1850	Thomas	----, Margaret	E	249
Cook, Ellen	6, Mar. 1859	Edward	----, Mary	E	609
Cook, James	1, Nov. 1853	James	Cook, Mahala J.	E	140
Cook, James	31, July 1853	Thomas	Keegan, Margaret	P	48
Cook, John	29, July 1859	Michael	Mulny, Ann	P	290
Cook, Mary	8, Jan. 1851	Maurice	Cull, Mary	E	274
Cook, Mary	14, Sept 1851	Thomas	Flemming, Bridget	E	343
Cook, Mary Ann	9, June 1856	James	----, Sarah	E	372
Cook, Mary Sarah	5, Nov. 1852		adult	B	274
Cook, Patrick	7, June 1851	Michael	Gannon, Catherine	E	313
Cook, Victoria	25, Oct. 1851	Albert	Weldon, Mary Jane	P	13a
Cook, William Charles	12, July 1857	Joseph	Pratley, Harriet	B	46
Cooke, John	27, Mar. 1853	Michael	----, Catherine	E	77
Cookley, Winnifred	4, Mar. 1858	William	Lally, Catherine	E	519
Cookly, John	12, Jan. 1857	Daniel	Lally, Catherine	E	425
Coolahan, James	7, Mar. 1852	John	Dermody, Honora	B	254

Name of Child	Date of Baptism	Father	Mother	Church	Page
Coon, Margaret	26, May 1850	Thomas	----, Joanne	E	216
Coonen, Jacob	4, May 1856	Wilhelm	Oats, Margaret	U	
Cooney, Andrew	27, June 1858	William	Oats, Margaret	U	
Cooney, Ann	22, Jan. 1854	Patrick	----, Ann	M	
Cooney, Bridget	29, May 1853	David	N----, Margaret	V	3
Cooney, Catherine	13, Jan. 1856	Patrick	----, Ann	M	
Cooney, Joanne	13, Feb. 1859	John	Burk, Mary	P	275
Cooney, John	31, Aug. 1856	John	Burke, Mary	P	189
Cooney, John	26, June 1859	Patrick	----, Ann	M	
Cooney, Joseph	14, Mar. 1858	Patrick	----, Ann	M	
Cooney, Thomas	5, Mar. 1854	John	Burke, Mary	P	72
Cooney, Thomas	10, Dec. 1854	Patrick	----, Ann	M	
Coony, Patrick	5, June 1852	Patrick	Hill, Sarah	F	
Cooper, Andrew	2, Apr. 1853	Caspar	----, Catherine	M	
Cooper, Frederick Henry	18, Dec. 1854	George	Magnes, Charlotte	P	110
Cooper, George	5, Dec. 1853		Cooper, Caroline	B	304
Cooper, Mary	27, June 1859	?	?	B	77
Copeland, Virginia Isabel	26, May 1856	Archibald	Terry, Mary	B	29
Copeland, William	16, Apr. 1859	John	McGrew, Jane	E	618
Copelin, Alice	2, Nov. 1857	Archibald	Terry, Mary	B	51
Coper, Johan Heinrich	9, Mar. 1854	Carl H.	Brüggeman, Antonia	D	6
Copsy, Wilhelm	16, Oct. 1850	Louis	Devine, Margaretha	C	
Corbet, James	27, Sept 1854	John	Kennedy, Bridget	B	6
Corbet, Mary Louise	16, May 1852	James	Caton, Catherine	P	22
Corbet, William	20, Oct. 1856	James	Caton, Catherine	P	196
Corbett, Daniel Francis	19, July 1859	Michael	Finn, Ellen	E	641
Corbett, James	23, Mar. 1851	Ferd?	Pinney, Mary	B	227
Corbett, James	24, Feb. 1856	James	Hoy, Mary	E	347
Corbett, James	18, Oct. 1858	Michael	McCarthy, Elizabeth	B	65
Corbett, Martin	19, Sept 1858	John	Kennedy, Bridget	P	261
Corbett, Mary	23, Feb. 1850	James	Breen, Margaret	E	200
Corbett, Mary	31, Mar. 1851	James	Hoy, Mary	E	296
Corbett, Michael	22, Sept 1856	John	----, Mary	M	
Corbett, Sarah Ann	30, Sept 1855	John	Kennedy, Bridget	P	153
Corbett, Thomas Edward L.	22, Dec. 1857	Michael	Flynn, Ellen	E	502
Corbett, William	19, Oct. 1856	James	Cummins, Mary	V	34
Corbett, William	31, July 1859	John	Brennan, Mary	Z	
Corbil, Honora	12, Feb. 1853	Patrick	Siniokin, Mary	B	283
Corbit, Catherine	25, Dec. 1850	Jeremiah	Caton, Catherine	P	2
Corbley, Elizabeth Ruthven	10, Aug. 1857	Owen	Carlin, Elizabeth	B	48
Corbley, Laura Bell	10, Aug. 1857	Owen	Carlin, Elizabeth	B	48
Corby, Francis Xavier	24, Apr. 1853	Patrick	Farmer, Mary Lucinda	B	289
Corby, Sarah Isabel	26, Oct. 1851	Patrick	Farmer, Mary Lucinda	B	244
Corcoran, Ann	17, July 1856	John	Clark, Ann	E	381
Corcoran, Ann	13, May 1855	Paul	----, Julia	E	286
Corcoran, Ann	23, Aug. 1856	Thomas	Hail, Ann	E	391
Corcoran, Bridget	26, Aug. 1855	John	----, Rose	E	310
Corcoran, Bridget	29, Aug. 1858	Patrick	Layngh, Bridget	F	
Corcoran, Bridget	7, Nov. 1858	Thomas	Syran, Bridget	V	51
Corcoran, Cecilia	10, Nov. 1855	James	Miller, Latty	R	
Corcoran, Dennis	19, Mar. 1854	Dennis	Dyer, Margaret	E	177
Corcoran, Elisabeth	23, Apr. 1854	Christoph	Mihan, Julia	T	
Corcoran, Ellen	22, Aug. 1858	John	Clarke, Ann	E	558
Corcoran, Helen	25, Oct. 1850	John	Barron, Helen	B	217
Corcoran, Henry	18, Sept 1852	Patrick	----, Bridget	E	18
Corcoran, Henry	15, Oct. 1854	Thomas	----, Elizabeth	E	233
Corcoran, Jane	4, Dec. 1851	Dennis	Deal, Margaret	E	363
Corcoran, Joanne	21, July 1850	Thomas	Greer, Ann	B	208
Corcoran, John	5, Sept 1852	Christopher	Megan, Julia	B	269

Name of Child	Date of Baptism	Father	Mother	Church	Page
Corcoran, John	25, Dec. 1855	Edward	Keleher, Helen	V	28
Corcoran, John	14, July 1854	Jeremiah	Corken, Mary	E	208
Corcoran, John	30, July 1854	John	Miller, Mary	P	90
Corcoran, John	9, Feb. 1851	John	O'Neil, Mary	B	225
Corcoran, John	10, Mar. 1851	Patrick	Reynolds, Ann	M	
Corcoran, John	6, Mar. 1853	Paul	Cullony, Mary	E	69
Corcoran, John	16, May 1857	Paul	Kilone, Julia	E	454
Corcoran, John	29, Feb. 1852	Thomas	Bagan, D.	E	386
Corcoran, Margaret	25, Oct. 1850	John	Barron, Helen	B	217
Corcoran, Margaret	5, Apr. 1854	John	Clark, Ann	V	12
Corcoran, Margaret	6, Apr. 1851	Paul	Kiloran, Julia	E	297
Corcoran, Margaret	21, Sept 1850	Thomas	----, Elizabeth	E	248
Corcoran, Mary	7, Feb. 1858	James	----, Ann	M	
Corcoran, Mary	10, Oct. 1856	Patrick	----, Catherine	M	
Corcoran, Mary	28, Sept 1856	Thomas	Syron, Bridget	E	400
Corcoran, Patrick	12, Mar. 1854	Edward	Keleher, Helen	V	12
Corcoran, Patrick	26, Apr. 1857	Michael	----, Mary	E	448
Corcoran, Patrick	10, Feb. 1855	Thomas	Forde, Ann	B	11
Corcoran, Richard	20, Feb. 1859	Michael	Quinn, Mary	E	605
Corcoran, Rose Ann	27, Jan. 1856	Christoph	Meaghan, Julia	T	
Corcoran, Sarah	6, July 1859	Paul	Kilone, Julia	E	637
Corcoran, Thomas	28, June 1857	Edward	Keleher, Helen	V	39
Corcoran, Thomas	22, Oct. 1854	Thomas	Sion, Bridget	B	6
Corcoran, Thomas Richard	25, Dec. 1859	James	Quinlan, Margaret	E	678
Corcoran, William	30, May 1852	John	Clark, Honora	E	420
Cordes, Johan Joseph Christoph	30, Jan. 1857	Christoph	Evers, Agnes	C	
Cordesman, John Joseph	1, July 1855	Henry J.	----, Frances	H	
Cordesman, Rudolph Francis	15, Aug. 1858	Henry J.	Elsesman, Mary Francisca	H	
Cordesmann, A.M. Helena Josephina	1, Jan. 1853	Johan	Elsmann, Francisca	F	
Cordurais, Alphonse	29, Aug. 1855	James	----, Frances	E	312
Corefond, Emil Wilhelm	18, Jan. 1859	Joseph	Frey, Elisabeth	D	129
Coricord, Franz	22, Sept 1854	Joseph	Steinberger, Elisabeth	L	
Cork, Henry Joseph	11, June 1858	George	Garntner, Julia	N	
Corker, Michael	29, June 1854	Patrick	----, Bridget	E	202
Corn, Daniel	25, Dec. 1859	Thomas	Grogan, Ann	U	
Corn, John	25, Dec. 1859	Thomas	Grogan, Ann	U	
Corn, Margaret	18, Jan. 1854	John	Kearnan, Mary	E	161
Cornelius, Anna Margaretha	8, Aug. 1858	Lawrence	----, Magdalena	C	
Cornelius, Georg Jacob	1, May 1859	Georg	Heidl, Catharina	D	137
Cornelius, Heinrich	4, Jan. 1858	Conrad	Haric, Maria	F	
Cornelius, Joseph Herman	26, May 1853	J. Georg	Heidel, Catharina	D	386
Cornelius, Juliana	8, Oct. 1854	Lawrence	Robert, Francisca	D	19
Cornelius, Maria Elisabeth	8, Dec. 1858	Conrad	Harnish, Maria	D	125
Cornelius, Rosina	22, June 1851	Lawrence	----, Magdalena	C	
Cornelius, Theresa Barbara	27, Jan. 1855	Georg	Haidel, Catharina	D	27
Cornell, John Baptist	18, May 1851	George R.	Ward, Mary Ann	B	232
Cornellius, Magdalena	2, Nov. 1856	Georg	Haidt, Catharina	D	71
Corotta, Maria Theresa	26, Mar. 1859	Giovanni	Carotta, Rosa Theresa	K	
Correvond, Leopold Sigmund	29, June 1857	Johan	Zoegelmeyer, Emilia	C	
Correvont, Joseph	10, Oct. 1856	Francis R.	Fenne, Elisabeth	A	
Corrifond, Marianna	7, Oct. 1856	Rudolph	Schmidt, Wilhelmina	F	
Corrifond, Rudolph Franz	30, Oct. 1859	Rudolph	Schmidt, Wilhelmina	F	
Corrifond, Sophia Marianna	10, June 1858	Rudolph	Schmidt, Wilhelmina	F	
Corrifont, Francis Andreas	19, June 1855	Rudolph	Schmidt, Wilhelmina	C	
Corrigan, Ann	30, Mar. 1859	Hugh	Roane, Margaret	B	73
Corrigan, Elizabeth	11, May 1851	John	O'Hara, Bridget	P	8
Corrigan, John	4, Aug. 1850	Thomas	----, Ann	E	237
Corrigan, William	8, June 1856	Martin	Dwyer, Eliza	B	29
Corrotti, Daniel Paul	16, Aug. 1857	J. Baptist	Zambrone, Rosa	K	

Name of Child	Date of Baptism	Father	Mother	Church	Page
Corrotti, Rafael Johan Baptist	19, July 1856	J. Baptist	Zambruner, Theresa	K	
Corte, Johanna Elisabeth	1, Oct. 1852	Friedrich	Brinker, Anna	F	
Corte, Maria Josephina Rosa	9, Sept 1855	Friedrich	Brinker, Anna	F	
Cortes, Maria Elisabeth Agnes	14, Nov. 1858	Christoph	Evers, Agnes	C	
Cortez Bridget	21, Apr. 1850	John	Lynch, Ann	B	201
Corveman, B. Herman	27, May 1850	H.	Flamme, Elisabeth	A	
Corwin, Frances Emily	24, Oct. 1853	Samuel W.	----, Emily	E	137
Cosgroff, Ann Mary	13, Jan. 1855	Michael	----, Susan	U	
Cosgrove, Bridget	9, Sept 1858	James	Slattery, Catherine	E	561
Cosgrove, Edward	21, July 1850	Patrick	Hays, Margaret	B	208
Cosgrove, Elizabeth	8, Nov. 1853	John	----, Rose	E	141
Cosgrove, Ellen	1, Aug. 1858	Peter	Ragan, Mary	E	553
Cosgrove, Frnacis	2, June 1852	Patrick	Camble, Mary	P	22
Cosgrove, James	15, July 1855	Francis	----, Winnefred	E	300
Cosgrove, James	13, Nov. 1854	Peter	----, Ann	E	240
Cosgrove, James Edward	19, Oct. 1856	Otway	Fitzgerald, Catherine	B	35
Cosgrove, Joanne	26, Dec. 1857	Edward	----, Ellen	E	503
Cosgrove, John	7, June 1857	Michael	Penny, Susanna	T	
Cosgrove, John	8, Mar. 1853	Peter	Cahel, Ann	E	70
Cosgrove, Joseph	25, Sept 1859	Peter	McCahill, Ann	E	657
Cosgrove, Margaret	28, Feb. 1858	Peter	Carroll, Ann	E	519
Cosgrove, Mary	5, Apr. 1856	James	----, Catherine	E	356
Cosgrove, Mary	7, Dec. 1856	Peter	Regan, Mary	V	35
Cosgrove, Mary	25, Apr. 1858	john	Madden, Rose	E	532
Cosgrove, Mary Ann	13, May 1856	Peter	----, Ann	E	367
Cosgrove, Mary Catherine	26, Sept 1852	Otway Jos.	Fitzgerald, Catherine	B	272
Cosgrove, Patrick	12, June 1857	James	Slattery, Catherine	E	459
Cosgrove, Philip Purcell	30, Sept 1858	Otway	Fitzgerald, Catherine	B	65
Cosgrove, Philipp	26, Mar. 1854	John A.	Maguire, Rosanne	P	75
Cosgrove, Thomas	19, Aug. 1853	Edward	----, Ellen	E	120
Cosgrove, Thomas	8, Dec. 1851	Thomas	Quinn, Margaret	B	247
Cosgrove, William Peter	28, Oct. 1854	Otway Jos.	Fitzgerald, Catherine	B	6
Cosin, John Henry	4, June 1859	Valentin	Blesker, Anna	D	139
Coss, John	3, Dec. 1859	Daniel	McGrury, Catherine	P	305
Coste, Michael Thomas	9, Oct. 1854	J. Baptist	Zanone, Maria	K	
Costello, Alice	4, May 1856	Michael	Winters, Alice	P	178
Costello, Ann	22, June 1854	Michael	Manough, Margaret	E	201
Costello, Ann Eliza	28, Aug. 1852	John	Gorman, Susan	B	269
Costello, Ann Mary	12, Oct. 1856	Edward	Manick, Elizabeth	E	403
Costello, Anthony	8, Oct. 1854	Anthony	Snively, Mary	P	99
Costello, Bernard	28, Apr. 1850	Thomas	Glinn, Ann	B	201
Costello, Bridget	30, Jan. 1858	Edward	Mannix, Eliza	P	237
Costello, Bridget	1, Feb. 1853	Thomas	Kenny, Mary	R	
Costello, Caroline	1, Jan. 1851	John	Costello, Margaret	B	222
Costello, Catherine	2, Feb. 1851	Anthony	Genavello, Maria	P	4
Costello, Charles	17, Oct. 1852	Timothy	McNealy, Bridget	R	
Costello, Cornelius	14, July 1854	Andrew	Larkin, Bridget	E	207
Costello, Edward	2, Oct. 1859	Edward	----, Elizabeth	E	659
Costello, Ellen	15, Jan. 1858	John	Knightly, Catherine	B	54
Costello, Ellen	13, Nov. 1856	Patrick	Sullivan, Joanne	B	36
Costello, George Edward	7, May 1854	John	Costello, Margaret	P	81
Costello, Helen	25, Nov. 1855	Michael	Mannix, Margaret	E	328
Costello, Helen Theresa	1, Jan. 1859	John	Costello, Margaret	P	271
Costello, Joanne	18, Dec. 1853	William	Hoffman, Eliza	V	8
Costello, John	2, Jan. 1853	John	Costello, Margaret	P	33
Costello, John	23, July 1858	Martin	McGail, Susan	U	
Costello, John Edward	21, Nov. 1858	J. Edward	Fitzsimmons, Catherine	P	267
Costello, John William	12, July 1859	John	Gleeson, Mary	B	77
Costello, Joseph	3, Mar. 1852	Joseph	Dowling, Mary	E	387

Name of Child	Date of Baptism	Father	Mother	Church	Page
Costello, Margaret	7, Sept 1856	Anthony	Snively, Mary	P	190
Costello, Margaret	10, Feb. 1856	John	Knightly, Catherine	B	25
Costello, Margaret	21, Feb. 1855	Michael	Kane, Margaret	P	121
Costello, Margaret	22, Sept 1859	Michael	Manning, Margaret	P	297
Costello, Margaret	11, Dec. 1855	Timothy	----, Winefred	R	
Costello, Mary	12, Dec. 1852	Anthony	Snivelly, Mary	P	31
Costello, Mary	2, Apr. 1854	John	Knightly, Catherine	B	312
Costello, Mary	29, Nov. 1852	Michael	Kane, Margaret	B	276
Costello, Mary	26, July 1857	Michael	Mannix, Margaret	E	469
Costello, Mary	13, Jan. 1850	Michael	Winters, Alice	B	194
Costello, Mary	6, Apr. 1851	Thomas	Fanning, Ann	B	229
Costello, Mary	7, June 1857	Timothy	----, Louise	R	
Costello, Mary Ann	25, Dec. 1854	Francis	Hoffman, Bridget	P	112
Costello, Mary Ann	19, Feb. 1853	John	----, Mary	E	63
Costello, Mary Ann	14, July 1858	William	Karens, Julia	E	549
Costello, Mary Catherine	17, Aug. 1856	John	Costello, Margaret	P	188
Costello, Michael	4, Dec. 1851	Thomas	Cain, Mary	R	
Costello, Michael	5, June 1859	Timothy	----, Winefred	R	
Costello, Peter Francis	5, Oct. 1856	John	Fitzsimmons, Catherine	P	194
Costello, Thomas	13, Jan. 1854	Johan	Walsh, Julia	D	1
Costello, Thomas	25, May 1856	John	Gleeson, Mary	B	29
Costello, Thomas Howard	13, Feb. 1859	Anthony	Snively, Mary Ann	P	275
Costello, William	13, Feb. 1854	Edward	Mannick, Lizzie	E	168
Costello, William	30, Oct. 1859	John	Feo, Julia	U	
Costello, William Henry	12, Mar. 1854	Michael	Winters, Alice	P	73
Costeo, Mary Catherine	6, Jan. 1856	Stephan	Hazelton, Catherine	B	23
Costigan, Joanne	3, Apr. 1855	William	----, Margaret	U	
Costigan, Marianne	6, Jan. 1858	William	Moore, Margaret	P	235
Costillo, Mary Elizabeth	15, May 1853	Thomas	Preston, Helen	B	291
Costillo, Morgan	14, Oct. 1857	John	Leeson, Mary	B	51
Cotter, Michael	19, Oct. 1851	Johan	Aller, Magdalena	J	12
Cotter, Michael	10, July 1859	Michael	Quigley, Mary Ann	P	288
Cotter, Susan	1, Oct. 1856	Patrick	----, Ann	M	
Cottlen, Catherine	10, Nov. 1855	Michael	Cassidy, Ann	R	
Cottrell, John	15, Aug. 1853	Michael	----, Ann	E	118
Coughlan, John Francis	15, Sept 1850	John	----, Mary	E	247
Coughlin, Ann Emma	12, Apr. 1854	John	McCalpin, Mary	E	182
Coughlin, Bridget	22, Jan. 1854	Edward	Dugan, Ann	E	161
Coughlin, Daniel	2, Aug. 1859	Thomas	Coffee, Mary Ann	B	78
Coughlin, Dennis	27, Feb. 1853	Jeremiah	Cronan, Helen	V	1
Coughlin, Elizabeth	7, Mar. 1858	Matthew	Nicholas, Mary	B	56
Coughlin, Helen	3, Apr. 1853	Thomas	Coffee, Mary Ann	B	287
Coughlin, Honora	17, Oct. 1852	Patrick	Butler, Bridget	B	272
Coughlin, John	13, Apr. 1854	Maurice	McKenesy, Joanne	B	313
Coughlin, Mary	10, Feb. 1850	John	Hetry, Julie	E	196
Coughlin, Mary Jane	6, Mar. 1859	Thomas	Cutin, Martha	E	609
Coughlin, Michael	6, May 1855	Thomas	Coffee, Mary Ann	B	14
Coughlin, Thomas	1, Dec. 1850	Thomas	Coffee, Mary Ann	B	219
Coughtry, Bridget	7, Apr. 1850	Matthew	----, Sarah	E	206
Coughtry, Catherine	2, Oct. 1858	Thomas	Haly, Bridget	E	566
Coughtry, Mary	7, Feb. 1857	Thomas	Early, Bridget	B	40
Coughtry, Michael	12, Aug. 1855	Thomas	Early, Bridget	V	26
Coulter, James	26, Oct. 1851	William	Kendall, Mary	B	243
Coun, May	22, Aug. 1858	Patrick	Molwel, Bridget	N	
Courcy, Mary	12, Sept 1859	John	Carver, Margaret	B	80
Courderey, John Patrick	20, Apr. 1851	James	Noel, Joanne Frances	E	301
Courner, Mary	24, June 1855	Henry	Connors, Rose	P	137
Courtney, Bridget	24, Jan. 1858	Michael	Daily, Mary	E	512
Courtney, John	30, Jan. 1857	Michael	Daily, Mary	E	429

Name of Child	Date of Baptism	Father	Mother	Church	Page
Courtney, Mary	11, Dec. 1859	Michael	Daily, Mary	E	676
Couts, John	17, June 1856	John	Young, Rose	T	
Covermann, Anna Maria	5, Jan. 1851		Covermann, Catharina	L	
Cowan, Edward	8, May 1859	James	McGrath, Rose	B	74
Cowan, George Terrence	7, June 1857	James	McGrath, Rose	V	39
Cowan, William	29, Feb. 1856	Anselm	Goren, Amanda	B	26
Cowell, Dennis	20, June 1852	James	----, Joanne	B	261
Cowen?, Isabel	14, Nov. 1856	John	Flaherty, Mary	B	36
Cox, Catherine	15, Aug. 1852		adult	M	
Cox, Charles	1, Sept 1853	Hiram J.	Chamberlain, Sarah	B	298
Cox, Elizabeth	15, Aug. 1852		adult	M	
Cox, Emily	12, June 1853	David	Crawford, Sarah	B	293
Cox, James Daniel Cornelius	15, Aug. 1852		adult	M	
Cox, John	31, Aug. 1855	Richard	Daly, Mary	R	
Cox, Joseph	5, Dec. 1853	Richard	Daly, Mary	R	
Cox, Margaret	5, Dec. 1858	Richard	Daly, Mary	R	
Cox, Martha	15, Aug. 1852		adult	M	
Cox, Mary Ann	12, Dec. 1852	Richard	Daly, Mary	R	
Cox, Mary Ann	4, May 1855		adult - nee Wright	B	14
Cox, Mary Susan	12, June 1851	Hiram	Chamberlain, Sarah	B	234
Cox, Rosetta	4, July 1852	David	Crawford, Sarah	B	265
Cox, Sarah	15, Aug. 1852		adult	M	
Cox, Sarah Ann	19, Mar. 1857	David	Crawford, Sarah	P	208
Cox, William	24, July 1855	James	Murphy, Margaret	P	142
Coyle, Adam Camillus	17, May 1856	Thomas D.	Seal, Henrietta	P	180
Coyle, Apollonia	20, July 1851	Edward	Holcomb, Amanda	B	236
Coyle, Casimir Eugene	20, July 1851	Thomas	Seal, Henrietta A.	B	236
Coyle, Charles	13, July 1853	Cornelius	Dolarty, Sarah	E	106
Coyle, Edward	31, Aug. 1856	John	Cohen, Catherine	P	189
Coyle, Elizabeth	14, Sept 1857	John	Cone, Catherine	B	49
Coyle, Francisca	10, Apr. 1852	Edward	McDonnough, Catharine	F	
Coyle, Harriet	30, July 1854		adult - 26 years old	P	90
Coyle, Hugh Thomas	26, Sept 1852	Hugh	Gilvoy, Mary	S	
Coyle, Margaret	15, Dec. 1850	Philipp	----, Mary	E	268
Coyle, Thomas	19, Sept 1858	John	Shannen, Margaret	R	
Coyle, Thomas Edward	16, Oct. 1859	Thomas	Sear, Henriette	P	300
Coyle, Walter	17, Dec. 1852	Edward	Holten, Amanda Malvina	B	278
Coylen, Mary Caroline	13, Jan. 1856	John	Dogherty, Catherine	J	34
Coyne, Bridget	6, Nov. 1853	Patrick	Flynn, Catherine	E	141
Coyne, Catherine	7, Sept 1853	Martin	Mulvey, Catherine	P	51
Coyne, Honora	31, Oct. 1852	Martin	King, Catherine	B	273
Coyne, James	6, Apr. 1857	James	Sheridan, Bridget	P	209
Coyne, Mary	27, Jan. 1856	Patrick	Flynn, Catherine	P	167
Coyne, Mary	19, Feb. 1854	Patrick	Toole, Catherine	P	70
Coyne, Mary Ann	7, Jan. 1855	Michael	----, Helen	V	22
Coyne, Mary Jane	8, Aug. 1859	James	Sheridan, Bridget	P	291
Coyne, Michael	23, Aug. 1855	Patrick	Toole, Catherine	P	147
Coyne, Thomas	2, Sept 1858	Patrick	Flynn, Catherine	P	259
Coyne, Thomas	10, Jan. 1858	Patrick	Toole, Catherine	P	236
Cracnell, John	4, Apr. 1853	Charles	Welsh, Mary	E	79
Crague, Ann	19, June 1859	Edward	Crane, Ann	P	286
Craig, Ann	14, July 1859	John	Bergin, Joanne	P	288
Craig, John	17, Aug. 1850	John	Hogan, Elizabeth	B	210
Craig, John	7, Oct. 1853	John	Hogan, Elizabeth	P	54
Craig, Julia	15, Feb. 1852	James	Galvin, Mary	B	253
Craig, Louis Joseph	11, May 1856	John	Hogan, Elizabeth	P	179
Craig, Sarah	24, Feb. 1852	Robert	Howard, Margaret	B	253
Craig, William	27, Apr. 1856	James H.	----, Eliza	E	363
Craiger, Elizabeth Agnes	22, Mar. 1857	Charles	Dorr, Mary	B	42

Name of Child	Date of Baptism	Father	Mother	Church	Page
Crain, Bridget	8, Feb. 1852	Michael	Lackin, Barbara	P	17
Crain, Helen	7, Apr. 1856	Michael	Lacken, Barbara	P	175
Crain, Martin	5, Mar. 1854	Michael	Larkin, Barbara	P	73
Crain, Mary	1, Aug. 1858	Michael	Larkin, Barbara	P	255
Cralen, William	11, Apr. 1851		Cralen, Martha	E	299
Crall, Thomas	6, Aug. 1854	William	----, Mary	R	
Cramer, Ann	1, Aug. 1852	Patrick	Milligan, Mary	P	25
Crane, Ann	20, Dec. 1854	Patrick	Cavanaugh, Catherine	P	111
Crane, Ann	1, Nov. 1858	Thomas	Gildea, Helen	P	266
Crane, Bernard	10, Mar. 1850	Thomas	Gildea, Ellen	E	202
Crane, Caroline	25, Dec. 1859		adult	B	85
Crane, James	2, Mar. 1851	Patrick	Cavanaugh, Ellen	P	5
Crane, Joanne	6, Sept 1857	Edward	Brodbeck, Catherine	B	49
Crane, Joanne	30, Nov. 1856	Michael	Collins, Helen	E	417
Crane, John	27, Jan. 1850	Thomas	----, Mary	E	195
Crane, John Edward	30, Dec. 1855	Edward	Broderick, Catherine	B	23
Crane, John Francis	30, Nov. 1857	John	Bergin, Joanne	P	231
Crane, Joseph	9, Jan. 1859	John B.	----, Mary	E	594
Crane, Maria Theresa	17, Mar. 1856		adult - widow of Samuel	K	
Crane, Mary	8, Feb. 1856	John	----, Joanne	E	343
Crane, Mary	18, Sept 1859	Michael	Collins, Helen	E	655
Crane, Mary	14, Jan. 1857	Thomas	Gildea, Ellen	B	39
Crane, Mary Ann	24, Sept 1854	Thomas	Gildea, Helen	B	6
Crane, Michael	22, Mar. 1851	Michael	Collin, Ellen	E	293
Crane, Michael	20, Dec. 1854	Patrick	Cavanaugh, Catherine	P	111
Crane, Samuel Aloysius	28, June 1856	Samuel	Gardener, Mary	E	378
Cranle, Joseph August	30, Oct. 1859	August	Pecheur, Margaret	E	666
Cranle, Louis Augustine	8, Mar. 1857	John	Pruslent, Mary	E	438
Cranley, Margaret	22, Aug. 1852	Michael	Gallagher, Mary	P	26
Crawfield, James	6, Apr. 1856	James	----, Sarah	E	356
Crawford, Joanne	23, Apr. 1854	John	----, Mary	E	184
Crawford, John	22, May 1856	John	Feneran, Catharine	T	
Crawford, Mary	6, Jan. 1852	John	Bradford, Joanne	E	371
Crawford, Mary Ann	24, Mar. 1851	John	Mullady, Mary	E	294
Crawford, Mary Frances	15, Apr. 1858	David	Fenton, Catherine	B	57
Crawford, Robert	28, Feb. 1852	Robert	Morgan, Nancy	E	386
Crawford, William	11, Sept 1853	David	Fenton, Catherine	B	298
Crawley, Daniel	10, Sept 1850	Patrick	Kane, Elizabeth	B	213
Crawley, James	12, Oct. 1851	Patrick	Kane, Elizabeth	P	13a
Crawley, Mary	23, Mar. 1856	Michael	Gallagher, Mary	P	173
Creaghan, Bridget	30, Nov. 1851	Thomas	Gildea, Helen	B	246
Crecy, Michael	22, Oct. 1855	John	Brennen, Ellen	E	322
Credick, Mary	12, Nov. 1857	John	Maloney, Honora	E	492
Creed, Daniel	25, May 1858	Dennis	King, Mary	E	537
Creed, Helen	23, June 1854	Dennis	King, Mary	E	201
Creed, Jeremiah	7, Jan. 1850	Dennis	Reed, Mary	E	190
Creed, John Dennis	15, Sept 1852	Dennis	----, Mary	E	17
Creed, Julia	18, Mar. 1856	Dennis	King, Mary	E	350
Creed, Mary	11, May 1851	Dennis	Reed, Mary	E	307
Creeden, Mary	15, Nov. 1857	Timothy	----, Helen	R	
Creedon, John	22, Jan. 1854	Timothy	Coyle, Helen	R	
Creedon, Margaret	24, July 1859	Timothy	Kallaher, Helen	R	
Creelman, Alice	3, Dec. 1859	Solomon	Finnessy, Bridget	P	305
Creelman, John	1, Mar. 1857	Solomon	Finnessy, Birdget	P	207
Creighton, Frances Elizabeth	13, Dec. 1856	Peter	Wood, Mary Ann	B	37
Creighton, John James	15, July 1852	Peter	Wood, Mary Ann	B	263
Creighton, Martha	29, July 1855	John	----, Catherine	E	305
Creighton, Peter Edward	21, May 1854	Peter	Woods, Mary Ann	B	315
Creighton, William Henry	24, July 1859	Peter	Woods, Mary A.	B	78

Name of Child	Date of Baptism	Father	Mother	Church	Page
Cresta, Theresa Ann	28, Aug. 1851	Emanuel	Larceto, Maria	B	239
Creton, Mary	2, Oct. 1853	Peter	----, Ann	E	130
Creton, William Henry	8, Mar. 1853	John	Coy, Elizabeth	E	70
Crew, John	5, Feb. 1851	Matthew	Lahor, Ann	E	281
Crey, Matthew	16, Sept 1858	Matthew	Canly, Mary	V	50
Crisey, Alice Jane	9, Apr. 1855	Joseph	----, Mary	E	278
Crisey, William John	9, Apr. 1855	Joseph	----, Mary Ann	E	278
Crishe?, John	14, Apr. 1855	James	Gillen, Mary	B	13
Croak, Eliza	17, July 1853		adult - 30 years old	P	46
Croak, William	27, Feb. 1859	William	Burns, Eliza	P	277
Croake, Catherine	22, July 1855	William	Burns, Eliza	P	141
Croften, Margaret	20, May 1852	John	----, Margaret	E	415
Crofton, Bridget	12, May 1850	John	----, Margaret	E	213
Crofton, John	2, Oct. 1853	Patrick	Travers, Mary	P	53
Crofton, Mary	31, Dec. 1854	Patrick	Travers, Mary	B	9
Croke, Mary	26, July 1854	----	----, ----	E	210
Croker, Ann	25, Sept 1853	William	Ames, Ann	P	53
Croker, Catherine	9, Feb. 1851	William	Ames, Ann	P	5
Croker, Helen	29, Dec. 1855	William	Ames, Ann	P	164
Crolahan, John	27, Feb. 1853	John	Cosgrove, Mary	B	285
Crolton, William	8, Aug. 1852	Patrick	Travers, Mary	B	267
Cronan, Catharina	13, July 1855	Martin	Cashmann, Hanna	C	
Cronan, Daniel	18, July 1858	John	Lowry, Margaret	E	550
Cronan, Daniel	27, July 1852	Martin	Cashman, Hannah	B	266
Cronan, Jeremiah	15, Nov. 1851	Dennis	Butler, Ellen	E	357
Cronan, Joanne	14, Mar. 1858	Cornelius	Dugan, Mary	B	56
Cronan, John	17, Oct. 1858	William	Griffin, Mary	E	571
Cronan, Julia	20, Oct. 1851	Timothy	Lehan, Margaret	E	352
Cronan, Margaret	24, Nov. 1859	Cornelius	Dugan, Mary	E	673
Cronan, Mary Ann	17, Apr. 1853	William	Griffin, Mary	E	82
Crone, Arthur James	16, Apr. 1852	Benjamin	Farrell, Gertrude	B	256
Crone, Gerhard Peter	10, Jan. 1859	H. Theobald	Regan, Mary Bridget	J	48
Crone, Johan Heinrich Ludwig	11, Jan. 1854	Ferdinand	Woeremann, Maria	F	
Crone, Johan Heinrich Theobald	14, July 1850	Ferdinand	Woeremann, A. Elisabeth	F	
Crone, Johan Herman August	14, July 1852	Ferdinand	Woeremann, Anna Maria	F	
Crone, Johan Peter Edward	4, June 1856	Ferdinand	Woermann, Anna Maria	F	
Crone, Mary Edith	31, Dec. 1854	Benjamin	Farrell, Gertrude	B	9
Cronin, Agnes	23, Jan. 1855	Daniel	Dolleghan, Mary	E	258
Cronin, Catherine	9, Sept 1855	Dennis	----, Margaret	E	314
Cronin, Catherine	2, May 1852	Patrick	----, Margaret	E	409
Cronin, Catherine	23, Sept 1856	William	----, Mary	E	400
Cronin, Catherine Agnes	1, Nov. 1857	Jeremiah	Mulvey, Josephine	P	229
Cronin, Daniel	3, Oct. 1858	Daniel	Dillahanty, Mary	E	566
Cronin, Daniel	1, Nov. 1853	Dennis	Leonard, Margaret	E	140
Cronin, Daniel	30, July 1854	Timothy	----, Margaret	E	212
Cronin, David	21, Mar. 1858	Timothy	White, Margaret	B	57
Cronin, Dennis	5, July 1853	Cornelius	Butler, Joanne	E	104
Cronin, Dennis	14, Sept 1857	John	Mahony, Bridget	V	41
Cronin, Dennis	28, Jan. 1857	Patrick	Mahoney, Margaret	E	429
Cronin, Edward	27, Jan. 1854	Timothy	White, Margaret	B	308
Cronin, Eliza	15, May 1859	Timothy	Murphy, Johanna	B	75
Cronin, Helen	28, Aug. 1858	Timothy	Layhan, Margaret	E	559
Cronin, Honora	2, Oct. 1855	Dennis	Shea, Catherine	E	318
Cronin, Honora	11, Dec. 1853	Patrick	Mahoney, Margaret	E	152
Cronin, Honora	9, Feb. 1854	Timothy	Murphy, Honora	P	68
Cronin, Jeremiah	15, Jan. 1851	Cornelius	Butler, Joanne	E	276
Cronin, Jeremiah	19, July 1859	Patrick	Maheni, Margaret	E	641
Cronin, Joanne	2, Mar. 1856	Timothy	White, Mary	B	26
Cronin, John	6, Oct. 1854	Dennis	Butler, Ellen	E	230

Name of Child	Date of Baptism	Father	Mother	Church	Page
Cronin, John	28, Sept 1856	John	Denihand, Mary	E	400
Cronin, John	4, Mar. 1855	Thomas	C---, Mary	V	23
Cronin, John	27, June 1850	Timothy	----, Margaret	E	227
Cronin, Joseph	27, May 1852	Daniel	----, Bridget	E	419
Cronin, Joseph	31, Dec. 1854	William	Griffin, Mary	E	251
Cronin, Margaret	15, Feb. 1852	Timothy	White, Margaret	B	253
Cronin, Martin James	21, Sept 1851	William	Griffin, Mary	E	345
Cronin, Mary	17, June 1854	Dennis	Bonny, Elizabeth	P	85
Cronin, Mary	26, May 1853	John	Fox, Bridget	B	292
Cronin, Mary	20, Aug. 1853	Timothy	----, Margaret	E	121
Cronin, Mary	3, Nov. 1857	Timothy	Murphy, Joanne	P	229
Cronin, Mary	30, Nov. 1859	Andrew	Cronin, Catherine	V	63
Cronin, Mary Agnes	22, Aug. 1852	Dennis	----, Margaret	E	8
Cronin, Mary Ann	15, Sept 1855	Daniel	Leonard, Ellen	U	
Cronin, Mary Ann	7, Jan. 1857	John	Walsh, Bridget	V	37
Cronin, Maurice	8, Aug. 1858	Maurice	Reardan, Mary	B	62
Cronin, Michael	19, Dec. 1853	Daniel	Leonard, Ellen	E	153
Cronin, Michael	6, Jan. 1858	Dennis	Shay, Catherine	E	506
Cronin, Sarah Ann	29, Nov. 1859	James	Welsh, Ann	E	673
Cronin, Thomas	20, Aug. 1857	Dennis	----, Margaret	E	475
Cronin, Timothy	1, Sept 1850	Timothy	White, Margaret	B	212
Cronlage, Franz Gerhard	2, Apr. 1859	Francis	Reismann, Clara	F	
Cronn, Ann	20, Oct. 1855	Anthony	McEleer, Bridget	B	20
Cronon, Jeremiah	15, May 1855	Michael	Murphy, Joanne	P	132
Crook, Thomas	10, Oct. 1852	Thomas	----, Elizabeth	B	271
Crosby, James	28, Sept 1857	James	Gilbert, Mary	P	**225**
Crosby, Margaret	7, May 1853	James	Gilbert, Mary	P	40
Cross, John	17, Apr. 1853	Thomas	Murphy, Helen	V	2
Cross, Thomas	2, May 1858	Thomas	Murphy, Helen	E	533
Cross, William	16, Nov. 1851	Thomas	Murphy, Helen	B	245
Cross?, Nicolaus	12, June 1857	Michael	Wood, Mary	E	459
Crotius, Johan Wilhelm	16, May 1856	Georg	Oerfler, Catharina	F	
Crotty, John	27, Dec. 1857	Thomas	Reilly, Elizabeth	P	234
Crotty, Margaret	16, May 1853	Michael	Henry, Joanne	P	41
Crotty, William	18, Sept 1856	Thomas	Riely, Elizabeth	E	398
Crow, Ann	27, Mar. 1859	Patrick	Fealy, Ellen	B	73
Crowe, John	10, Dec. 1854	Patrick	Fehely, Helen	P	108
Crowe, Mary	20, Nov. 1856	Patrick	Fehely, Helen	P	199
Crowley, Catherine	30, Aug. 1854	Cornelius	Conolly, Helen	V	16
Crowley, Cornelius	9, Nov. 1858	John	Mahoney, Margaret	E	577
Crowley, John	30, Sept 1855	James	Franely, Catherine	P	152
Crowley, John	12, Oct. 1856	John	Mahoney, Margaret	E	403
Crowley, John William	17, Aug. 1858	John	White, Honora	E	558
Crowley, Mary	5, May 1856	Cornelius	Conolly, Helen	V	31
Crowley, Mary	27, Nov. 1858	Cornelius	O'Sullivan, Margaret	V	52
Crowley, Mary	24, May 1857	D.W.	Stewart, Mary	B	44
Crowley, Mary	24, July 1853	Jeremiah	Riordan, Mary	V	4
Crowley, Mary	16, Aug. 1853	Patrick	Murphy, Catherine	V	5
Crowley, Mary Ann	30, May 1858	Samuel	----, Elizabeth	E	539
Crowley, Michael Thomas	23, July 1856	C.S.	O'Sullivan, Margaret	E	383
Crowley, Patrick	11, Mar. 1858	Cornelius	Connelly, Helen	E	521
Crowley, William	29, July 1855	Daniel	Stewart, Mary	B	17
Crowley, William	4, July 1858	Michael	Shehan, Julia	E	546
Crowly, Jeremiah	23, Dec. 1854	John	Crowly, Honora	V	20
Crowly, John Joseph Lymore	19, Nov. 1854	Daniel	Mahoney, Mary	B	8
Crowly, Julia Helen	27, Sept 1854	Cornelius	Sullivan, Margaret	B	6
Crowly, Mary	26, Aug. 1850	Daniel	Mahoney, Mary	B	211
Crowly, Thomas	26, Feb. 1854	James	Finley, Catherine	E	171
Crown, Arthur	17, Feb. 1850	Anthony	McAleer, Bridget	B	196

Name of Child	Date of Baptism	Father	Mother	Church	Page
Crown, Thomas	26, Dec. 1852	Anthony	----, Bridget	E	48
Crumly, Mary Ann	9, May 1859	William	McClusky, Bridget	M	
Crummell, Emma	4, Aug. 1857	Charles	Curtiss, Matilda	V	40
Cruse, Josephina Brigitta	4, Feb. 1852	Joseph	Schmidt, Maria Josephina	A	
Cruse, Robert	17, Aug. 1851	Robert	Reddin, Julia	P	11
Cruseau, Mary Isabel	9, Feb. 1854	George	Bailey, Delphine	E	166
Cryan, Mary	30, Nov. 1857	Michael	Dorsy, Helen	P	231
Cryans, Mary	27, Mar. 1853	Bernard	Crians, Ann	B	290
Cryne, Catherine	3, Dec. 1854	Bernard	Cryne, Ann	P	107
Cuhni, Johan	28, Apr. 1850	Ferdinand	Mais, Rosina	D	211
Culkin, John	13, Apr. 1855	Patrick	----, Mary	M	
Cull, Elizabeth	26, June 1858	Adam	Baker, Gertrude	B	61
Cullanan, John	1, Feb. 1857	Michael	Barns, Julia	E	430
Cullen, Ann	18, July 1852	James	----, Elizabeth	M	
Cullen, Bridget	28, Jan. 1855	James	----, Elizabeth	M	
Cullen, Ellen	11, Apr. 1851	Thomas	----, Margaret	E	298
Cullen, James	2, Sept 1853	James	----, Elizabeth	M	
Cullen, John Christopher	27, Jan. 1852	Thomas	Connolly, Mary	P	16
Cullen, Mary	27, Aug. 1854	Thomas	Connolly, Mary	B	4
Cullen, Nathaniel	15, Feb. 1857	James	----, Elizabeth	M	
Cullen, Thomas	20, Aug. 1850	Thomas	Connelly, Mary	B	211
Cullen, Timothy	15, Aug. 1859	James	----, Elizabeth	M	
Cullen, William	23, Nov. 1856	William	Shannon, Mary	B	36
Cullinan, Honora	5, Apr. 1857	Patrick	Kilgariff, Bridget	V	38
Cullon, Andrew	19, Dec. 1858	William	Shannon, Mary	B	68
Cultry, Ann	10, Aug. 1855	Martin	Lavell, Margaret	V	26
Cumbly, George	18, July 1858	Alexander	Howens, Lizzie	E	550
Cumbly, John	18, July 1858	Alexander	Howens, Lizzie	E	550
Cummens, Joseph Ludwig	4, July 1855	Dominick	Kleen, Elisabeth	A	
Cumminch, Johan	17, Oct. 1858	Christ	----, Barbara	D	121
Cumming, Magdalena	3, Aug. 1859	Christian	Spinneweber, Barbara	T	
Cummings, John	25, Jan. 1852	Patrick	Diller, Honora	E	377
Cummings, Mary	23, Mar. 1854	Patrick	Caven, Joanne	E	178
Cummings, Mary	20, May 1855	Patrick	Collen, Bridget	E	287
Cummings, Mary	26, Mar. 1854	William	Roohan, Bridget	T	
Cummins, Catherine	15, May 1851	Martin	----, ----	E	307
Cummins, John	1, Sept 1853	John	Mooney, Joanne	V	5
Cummins, Julia Ann	7, Aug. 1859	William	----, Mary	E	645
Cummins, Margaret	9, Oct. 1859	Martin	Meehan, Mary	V	60
Cummins, Margaret jane	10, Mar. 1857	Patrick	Griffin, Mary	P	208
Cummins, Mary Ann	7, Aug. 1853	Patrick	----, Ann	M	
Cummins, Wilhelm Heinrich	28, Sept 1856	Dominick	Klem, Elisabeth	F	
Cummins, William	5, Aug. 1855	John	Mooney, Joanne	E	306
Cummins, William	12, Jan. 1850	Patrick	Dellon, Honora	B	194
Cummins, William	29, Apr. 1855	Thomas	Mayer, Nancy	P	130
Cummins, William	15, June 1852	William	Muloy, Susan	P	23
Cunady, Frances Josephine	18, Aug. 1852	John	----, Louise	E	7
Cune, Theresa	23, Jan. 1859	Charles	----, Joanne	E	598
Cuni, Elisabeth Theresa	22, Dec. 1859	Ferdinand	Hoffman, Theresa	D	153
Cuni, Ferdinand	18, Oct. 1857	Ferdinand	Hoffman, Theresa	D	97
Cuni, Joseph	25, Oct. 1855	Ferdinand	Hoffman, Theresa	D	45
Cunningham, Alphonse	11, July 1858	John	Murphy, Ellen	B	61
Cunningham, Ann	15, Aug. 1859	Daniel	Fagan, Margaret	P	292
Cunningham, Ann	30, Jan. 1853	James	Cosgrove, Mary	B	282
Cunningham, Ann Gertrude	25, Sept 1859	John	Murphy, Ellen	B	81
Cunningham, Bernard	9, Mar. 1851	Bernard	McCormick, Rebecca	B	226
Cunningham, Bridget	11, Jan. 1852	John	Fennessy, Julia	R	
Cunningham, Bridget	29, Jan. 1859	John	Raney, Margaret	P	273
Cunningham, Bridget	30, June 1850	Miles	Martin, Ann	E	227

Name of Child	Date of Baptism	Father	Mother	Church	Page
Cunningham, Catherine	4, Dec. 1859	Martin	Leonard, Ellen	B	84
Cunningham, Catherine	15, Dec. 1854	Thomas	Haney, Mary	P	110
Cunningham, Catherine	4, Apr. 1859	William	----, Honora	E	616
Cunningham, Christopher Michael	9, Apr. 1856	John	----, Joanne	R	
Cunningham, Daniel	3, Dec. 1859	Thomas	Haney, Mary	P	305
Cunningham, Elizabeth	1, June 1857	William	Kelloy, Ann	E	457
Cunningham, Ellen	13, Mar. 1855	Martin	Pryer, Mary	E	272
Cunningham, George	4, Feb. 1855	James	Cosgrove, Mary	B	11
Cunningham, Helen	6, Mar. 1855	Thomas	McMahon, Sarah	P	124
Cunningham, James	4, Apr. 1852	Henry	McShane,	P	20
Cunningham, James	24, June 1851	James	----, Catherine	E	318
Cunningham, James	16, July 1854	James	McKeown, Mary	B	2
Cunningham, James	15, Aug. 1853	John	Murphy, Ellen	B	297
Cunningham, John	5, July 1857	John	Ennis, Ann	B	46
Cunningham, John	13, July 1856	Michael	Leary, Eliza	B	31
Cunningham, Joseph John	23, Sept 1855	John	Murphy, Ellen	B	19
Cunningham, Josephine	3, Aug. 1851	John	Murphy, Helen	B	238
Cunningham, Margaret	13, Sept 1850	Anthony	----, Margaret	E	247
Cunningham, Margaret	9, Apr. 1856	James	Cosgrove, Mary	T	
Cunningham, Margaret	31, Dec. 1853	John	----, Julia	R	
Cunningham, Mary	13, Apr. 1851	James	Cockery, Mary	B	229
Cunningham, Mary	28, June 1857	John	Murphy, Ellen	B	46
Cunningham, Mary	5, Jan. 1855	William	----, Honora	E	253
Cunningham, Mary	8, May 1850	Thomas	----, Mary	E	212
Cunningham, Mary Ann	21, July 1850	John	Murphy, Helen	B	208
Cunningham, Mary Ann	25, Dec. 1859	Michael	Leary, Elizabeth	B	86
Cunningham, Mary Ellen	14, Nov. 1857	James	McKeown, Mary	B	51
Cunningham, Mary Francis	1, Aug. 1858	Terence	O'Rourke, Jane	B	62
Cunningham, Michael	14, July 1852	Francis	----, Celia	M	
Cunningham, Michael	18, May 1851	James	McKeown, Mary	B	232
Cunningham, Michael	13, July 1850	Michael	----, Margaret	E	231
Cunningham, Michael	1, Oct. 1854	Thomas	Higgins, Bridget	P	97
Cunningham, Patrick	16, Mar. 1856	Thomas	Haney, Mary	P	173
Cunningham, Rosanne	25, Sept 1859	James	McKeon, Mary	B	81
Cunningham, Rose Ann	14, Jan. 1858	Thomas	----, Louise	R	
Cunningham, Thomas	26, Sept 1852	James	McKean, Mary	B	272
Cunningham, Thomas	18, Jan. 1852	Miles	Martin, Ann	E	373
Cunningham, Thomas	27, Dec. 1857	Thomas	Hill, Mary	P	234
Cunningham, William	17, Feb. 1856	James	McKeown, Mary	B	25
Cunningham, William	22, May 1853	John	Cain, Alice	P	42
Cuny, August Alfred	16, June 1850	Nicolaus	Marschal, Rosalia	C	
Curley, Alice	4, Dec. 1858	Daniel	Grert, Mary	E	584
Curley, Andrew	29, Nov. 1857	John	Clinton, Mary	E	496
Curley, Bridget	13, Sept 1857	John	Duffy, Ellen	B	49
Curley, Bridget	14, June 1851	Michael	----, Ellen	E	315
Curley, Catherine Ann	7, July 1854	Michael	----, Ellen	E	205
Curley, Daniel Bernard	11, Nov. 1855	John	O'Conner, Catherine	U	
Curley, Francis Xavier	4, Apr. 1858	John J.	Tranor, Mary Catherine	E	526
Curley, John	31, May 1857	John	----, Mary Sophia	B	44
Curley, John	9, Jan. 1859	John	Clinton, Mary	E	595
Curley, Joseph	27, Feb. 1859	Luke	Conlon, Sarah	E	606
Curley, Luke	10, Nov. 1850	Hugh	----, Sarah	E	260
Curley, Margaret	20, Jan. 1855	Luke	Conlin, Sarah	E	257
Curley, Mary	8, July 1855	John	Duffy, Ellen	B	16
Curley, Mary	22, Mar. 1857	Luke	----, Sarah	E	442
Curley, Mary	9, May 1851	Thomas	Penny, Jane	E	306
Curley, Mary Jane	19, Mar. 1852	D.	Curley, M.	E	393
Curley, Michael	13, Mar. 1853	Luke	Conlin, Sarah	E	72
Curley, Thomas	17, Aug. 1854	Thomas	Kearns, Catherine	P	93

Name of Child	Date of Baptism	Father	Mother	Church	Page
Curley, Thomas James	6, Nov. 1859	John	Loftus, Mary	B	83
Curly, Mary	27, Sept 1857	John	O'Connor, Catherine	B	50
Curly, Michael	27, Mar. 1853	Andrew	----, Mary	E	77
Curly, Peter	26, May 1850	Patrick	Cahill, Margaret	B	203
Curn, Henry	2, Dec. 1855	Patrick	McCarm, Catherine	P	161
Curran, Cornelius	7, Dec. 1856	Cornelius	Fahin, Helen	P	201
Curran, James	23, Dec. 1852	John	McKearnan, Mary	E	46
Curran, John	1, Sept 1850	John	Keernan, Mary	B	212
Curran, Judy	30, Nov. 1851	Daniel	----, Catherine	E	362
Curran, Julia	15, May 1858	Dennis	Spars, Melanie	E	535
Curran, Michael	7, Nov. 1857	John	Kiernan, Mary	V	42
Curran, Michael	23, June 1850	Patrick	McCarthy, Catherine	B	205
Curran, Peter	15, May 1855	John	Kiernan, Mary	V	25
Curran, Thomas	12, July 1859	Thomas	Flinn, Mary	V	56
Curran, Thomas	9, Jan. 1853	Thomas	Morris, Ann	B	281
Curren, Alice	13, Nov. 1853	Patrick	McCarthy, Catherine	P	59
Curren, Mary	6, May 1854	John	Furkenson, Mary	E	188
Curren, Mary	13, Nov. 1853	Patrick	McCarthy, Catherine	P	59
Curri, Anton	10, Mar. 1852	J. Nicolaus	Spaunagel, Catharina	D	311
Curry, Ann	18, Oct. 1857	Hugh	Dunn, Mary	B	51
Curry, David	12, Jan. 1851	Patrick	Condon, Margaret	B	222
Curry, Isabel	4, Oct. 1855	Hugh	Dunn, Mary	P	154
Curry, James	6, Feb. 1854	John	Brown, Bridget	V	10
Curry, John	26, Oct. 1854	Martin	McCormick, Eliza	P	101
Curry, Stephan	18, Aug. 1850	Robert	Sparks, Sophronia	B	212
Curry, William	25, Sept 1859	Martin	McCormick, Eliza	P	297
Curtin, Elizabeth Jane	13, July 1856	Thomas	Cowan, Elizabeth	B	31
Curtis, Florence	26, Aug. 1855	Hershol	----, Julia	E	311
Curtis, Mary Ann	1, Mar. 1853	John	----, Ann	E	67
Curtis, Mary Louise	19, Mar. 1850	John	Wright, Sarah	B	198
Curtis, Thomas Joseph	22, July 1855	John	Rooney, Ann	V	26
Curtiss, Emma	4, Aug. 1857		Curtiss, Matilda	V	40
Cusack, Edward Patrick	23, Mar. 1851	Farrell	Deasey, Joanne	B	227
Cusack, Helen	25, Aug. 1855	Farrell	Dacy, Joanne	V	26
Cusack, James	24, Nov. 1852	Theodore	----, Bridget	E	38
Cusack, John	21, Aug. 1853	Farrell	Dasey, Joanne	V	5
Cushing, John Henry	11, May 1856	Thomas	Kane, Mary	P	179
Cushing, Thomas	31, Oct. 1858	Thomas	Kane, Mary	B	66
Cusick, Michael	3, Oct. 1858	Thomas	McNally, Susan	R	
Cusick, Richard	21, Nov. 1853	William	Gaffney, Bridget	E	146
Cusick, Thomas	28, July 1850	Patrick	Egan, Elizabeth	B	209
Cussen?, Mary	17, Oct. 1858	Garrett	Collins, Elizabeth	B	65
Cutaine, Emily	16, May 1852	Joseph	Stephans, Helen	B	264
Cutaire, Felix August	5, Oct. 1854	Joseph	Stephans, Helen	B	6
Cutaire, Leopold Constantine	31, Dec. 1857	Joseph	Stephens, Helen	B	53
Cutaire, Louise Theresa	31, Dec. 1857	Francis	Love, Louise	B	53
Cutter, John	4, Sept 1857	Michael	Quigley, Mary Ann	U	
C----y, Margaret Jane	18, Dec. 1850	Michael	Browley, Ellen	B	220
Cyder, Francis Wilhelm	12, Feb. 1857	Adam	Ert, Helena	C	
Cynan, Dennis	23, Apr. 1852	Patrick	O'---, Catherine	P	20
D----, Mary	2, Dec. 1856	Patrick	Kissick, Elizabeth	P	200
Da---, Catherine	15, May 1854	John	Davie, Bridget	B	315
Dacey, Catherine	8, Oct. 1855	John	Ley---, Catherine	V	27
Dacey, Edmund	6, June 1852	Henry	Madden, Elizabeth	B	265
Dacey, Elizabeth	23, Sept 1855	Martin	----, Bridget	M	
Dacey, Francis Patrick	14, Apr. 1852	Patrick	----, Bridget	M	
Dacey, James	9, July 1854	Martin	----, Bridget	M	
Dacey, Mary	19, June 1853	Martin	----, Bridget	M	
Dacey, Mary	20, Feb. 1859	Timothy	Buckley, Julia	E	605

Name of Child	Date of Baptism	Father	Mother	Church	Page
Dack, Catharina Maria Josephina	28, Apr. 1858	B. Heinrich	Pagg--, Maria Elisabeth	D	110
Dacy, Bridget	9, Jan. 1852	John	Dacy, Mary	P	15
Dacy, Catherine	9, June 1850	John	----, Ellenore	E	220
Dacy, Cornelius	2, July 1859	Cornelius	Donovan, Bridget	E	635
Dacy, Ellen	28, Mar. 1854	Timothy	Buckley, Julia	E	180
Dacy, John	7, May 1857	Cornelius	----, Bridget	E	142
Dacy, John	9, Nov. 1853	John	Rully, Ellen	E	374
Dacy, John	18, Jan. 1852	Timothy	Buckley, Julia	E	374
Dacy, Mary Ann	12, Feb. 1854	Dennis	Cotter, Margaret	E	167
Dacy, Michael	23, Nov. 1856	Timothy	Buckley, Julia	E	415
Dacy, Timothy	22, Feb. 1850	Timothy	Buckley, Julia	E	198
Dady, Jane	27, Feb. 1853	C.	----, Bridget	E	66
Daffin, Alexander	15, May 1853	Roderick	----, Mary Ellen	M	
Daffin, Thomas Columbus	22, Nov. 1850	Roderick	McKeever, Mary Helen	M	
Dagan, Mary Ann	29, Oct. 1856	Patrick	McMahon, Bridget	E	409
Dagliana, Maria	6, Dec. 1857	Antonio	Gatti, Johanna	K	
Dagliano, Cactano Antonio Adolpho	6, July 1851	Anthony	Gatti, Giovanatti	B	235
Dagliano, John	2, Jan. 1853	John	Gatti, Johanna	B	280
Dagliano, Maria Catharina Johanna	15, Jan. 1855	Antonio	Gatti, Joanna	K	
Daguet, Adelaide	16, Mar. 1856	Alphonse	Codington, Mary	E	349
Dahman, Anna Henrietta	4, Nov. 1857	Heinrich	Moorman, Catharina	A	
Dahman, Catharina	1, Oct. 1850	Heinrich	Moorman, Catharina	A	
Dahman, Maria Catharina	19, Feb. 1852	Heinrich	Moorman, Catharina	A	
Dahman, Maria Catharina	27, Sept 1854	Heinrich	Moorman, Catharina	A	
Dahmann, Johan Wilhelm Anton	4, May 1857	Wilhelm	Kemper, Francisca	C	
Dahmen, Maria Francisca Antonia	4, Oct. 1855	Wilhelm	Kemper, Francisca	C	
Dahnken, Heinrich Carl	9, Feb. 1850	Johan	28 years old	K	
Daier, Johan Andreas	10, Aug. 1852	Wilhelm	Kirerrn, Esther	K	
Dailey, Bridget	8, June 1851	John	Hanlin, Mary	E	314
Dailey, James	1, May 1852	James	Lauwel, Ann	E	408
Dailey, Margaret Helen	21, June 1857	James	----, Ann	R	
Dailey, Michael	12, Jan. 1851	Michael	----, Rose	E	275
Daily, Bridget	25, Jan. 1852	John	Carron, Barbara	E	376
Daily, Dennis	18, Mar. 1854	Dennis?	----, Mary	E	177
Daily, James	21, Aug. 1855	Timothy	----, Joanne	P	146
Daily, John	25, July 1858	John	Hanly, Mary	E	553
Daily, Mary	21, July 1855	Michael	Heart, Sarah	E	300
Daily, Thomas	31, Jan. 1855	Anthony	Howe, Mary	R	
Daley, Ellen	24, July 1858	Carroll	McAuleffe, Julia	B	62
Daley, John	27, Oct. 1850	Dennis	Mulline, Susan	B	218
Daley, Margaret	24, July 1854	Dennis	McGrath, Catherine	E	209
Daley, Mary Ellen	5, July 1857	John	Daley, Ann	B	46
Daley, Susan Ann	20, Mar. 1859	Patrick	Glennan, Susan	B	72
Daley, Timothy	9, Aug. 1859	Timothy	Moroney, Joanne	P	292
Dalheim, Elisabeth Maria	5, May 1858	Jacob	Gohinger, Barbara	F	
Dalheim, Eva Maria	19, Nov. 1855	Jacob	Bonningen, Barbara	F	
Dalheim, Georg	4, Aug. 1850	Jacob	Boning, Barbara	F	
Dalheim, Johan	2, Jan. 1853	Jacob	Bohnengel, Barbara	F	
Dalheim, Maria Theresa	12, Apr. 1858	Johan	Floschner, Paulina	K	
Dalinghaus, Anna Adelheid	30, Jan. 1850	Friedrich	Grower, Adelheid	C	
Dallas, Brdiget	4, Jan. 1852	Michael	Gorman, Elizabeth	B	249
Daller, Amelia	2, June 1854	Clemens	----, Francisca	H	
Daller, Georg	14, June 1857	Jacob	Hunert, Barbara	C	
Daller, Joseph	25, Dec. 1851	Clemens	----, Francisca	H	
Daller, Peter Adam	4, Apr. 1858	Johan	Na---, Catharina	D	108
Dallinghaus, Johan Heinrich Ludwig	24, Jan. 1856	Friedrich	Graver, Adelheid	L	
Dallinghaus, Maria Catharina	28, Feb. 1851	Friedrich	Grote, M. Adelheid	C	
Dallinghaus, Maria Catharina	18, Jan. 1850		Dallinghaus, Elisabeth	C	
Dallinghaus, Maria Clara	8, Dec. 1857	Friedrich	Graber, Maria	N	

Name of Child	Date of Baptism	Father	Mother	Church	Page
Dallinghauser, Elisabeth Henrietta	28, Augs. 1853	Friedrich	Graber, Adelheid	N	15
Dallmann, Wilhelm Heinrich	17, Feb. 1850	Heinrich	Baus, Johanna	C	
Dalton, Ann	16, Feb. 1853	John	Doyle, Ann	P	35
Dalton, James	16, Oct. 1859	James	Rourke, Mary	B	82
Dalton, Mary	11, May 1856	John	Manion, Catherine	P	179
Dalton, Mary	11, Nov. 1855	William	Murphy, Helen	P	158
Dalton, Thomas	28, June 1856	John	Kelly, Honora	E	377
Dalton, Thomas	22, May 1853	John	Manion, Catherine	P	42
Daly, Andrew James	22, Aug. 1858	Matthew	Grogan, Rose	E	558
Daly, Bridget	13, Aug. 1851	John	Dithen, Catherine	E	332
Daly, Bridget	16, Mar. 1856	William	Bluit, Joanne	E	349
Daly, Catherine	23, Apr. 1859	John	Malony, Catherine	E	619
Daly, Catherine	13, Sept 1857	Patrick	----, Joanne	M	
Daly, Catherine	29, May 1859	Thomas	Mullen, Margaret	Z	
Daly, Cornelius	25, Sept 1859	Cornelius	Gary, Margaret	Z	
Daly, Daniel	9, June 1850	James	----, Ann	E	220
Daly, Dennis	21, June 1859	William	Keliher, Mary	Z	
Daly, Elizabeth	1, Jan. 1856	Patrick	----, Joanne	M	
Daly, Ellen	20, Mar. 1859	Dennis	McGrath, Catherine	E	612
Daly, Ellen	6, Nov. 1853	Michael	----, Bridget	E	141
Daly, Francis	4, July 1852	James	----, Esther	B	263
Daly, Hieronymus	18, Sept 1853	Hieronymus	Devlin, Bridget	P	52
Daly, James	10, June 1855	John	Daly, Ann	V	25
Daly, Jeremiah	29, Aug. 1852	Daniel	----, Julia	E	12
Daly, Jeremiah	10, Feb. 1852	James	Daly, Ann	E	381
Daly, Joanne	11, Dec. 1859	Patrick	Kinsella, Joanne	Z	
Daly, Joanne	5, Feb. 1854	Patrick	O'Brien, Honora	B	308
Daly, John	24, Aug. 1856	Dennis	McGrath, Catherine	E	392
Daly, John	31, Aug. 1851	James	----, Mary	E	338
Daly, John	20, Dec. 1854	John	Coughlan, Mary	P	111
Daly, John	4, Feb. 1854	John	Kearney, Barbara	E	165
Daly, John	22, Feb. 1853	Matthew	Grogan, Rose	E	64
Daly, John	1, Nov. 1859	Michael	Boyle, Margaret	P	302
Daly, John	21, Sept 1856	Patrick	Gleenon, Susan	B	34
Daly, John	29, July 1854	John	Kelly, Margaret	B	3
Daly, Margaret	9, Jan. 1858	Daniel	Dwyre, Margaret	P	236
Daly, Margaret	14, Jan. 1857	John	Brien, Ann	B	39
Daly, Margaret	24, Jan. 1858	John	O'Brien, Ann	B	55
Daly, Margaret	11, Dec. 1859	Patrick	Kinsella, Joanne	Z	
Daly, Margaret	8, Mar. 1857	Thomas	----, Margaret	M	
Daly, Mary	25, Sept 1853	Edward	----, Ann	E	129
Daly, Mary	6, Aug. 1854	Patrick	----, Joanne	M	
Daly, Mary	3, Nov. 1854	Thomas	----, Mary	M	
Daly, Mary	15, Jan. 1854	John	O'Brien, Ann	B	307
Daly, Mary Ann	1, June 1853	James	Wyn, Ann	E	94
Daly, Mary Ann	12, June 1859	John	Kelly, Margaret	E	631
Daly, Mary Ann	13, Feb. 1859	Patrick	Moyley, Bridget	E	603
Daly, Mary Eliza	3, Apr. 1853	James	----, Mary	M	
Daly, Mary Eliza	25, Dec. 1853	Michael	Sullivan, Mary Agnes	E	154
Daly, Matthew	16, Jan. 1859	John	Daly, Ann	B	69
Daly, Michael	14, Jan. 1857	John	Brien, Ann	B	39
Daly, Michael	26, Aug. 1855	John	Kelly, Margaret	P	148
Daly, Michael	24, Jan. 1858	Michael	----, Bridget	M	
Daly, Michael	29, Aug. 1854	Patrick	McKnight, Margaret	V	16
Daly, Michael Cornelius	17, Feb. 1856	John	----, Mary	E	345
Daly, Sarah	29, Mar. 1857	John	Kelly, Margaret	E	444
Daly, Thomas	2, Dec. 1858	Andrew	----, Bridget	M	
Daly, Thomas	15, Apr. 1855	Matthew	Brogan, Rose	E	280
Daly, Timothy	18, Jan. 1857	Cornelius	----, Margaret	M	

Name of Child	Date of Baptism	Father	Mother	Church	Page
Daly, Timothy	16, July 1858	William	Cronin, Mary	P	254
Daly, William	14, Feb. 1858	Cornelius	----, Margaret	M	
Damann, Alexander Heinrich	8, Dec. 1850	Heinrich	Rosemeyer, Carolina	C	
Damme, Anna Theresa	25, Jan. 1858	Heinrich	Beckmann, Elisabeth	C	
Damme, Gerhard Heinrich	16, Oct. 1859	Heinrich	Beckmann, Elisabeth	C	
Damme, Margaretha Catharina	20, July 1856	Heinrich	Beckmann, Elisabeth	C	
Damme, Maria Elisabeth	7, Aug. 1854	Heinrich	Baeckmann, Elisabeth	L	
Dane, Francis Adam	7, Oct. 1856	Georg	Celser, Anna Maria	D	69
Danehy, David	17, Oct. 1852	John	----, Catherine	E	28
Danehy, James	3, Oct. 1852	Michael	----, Margaret	E	24
Danhauer, Elisabeth	23, July 1857	Heinrich	Würz, Johanna	D	91
Danhauer, Georg	4, July 1855	Heinrich	Wertz, Johanna	D	37
Daniel, Georg	24, July 1851	Heinrich	Vedder, Catharina	F	
Daniel, Heinrich	24, July 1851	Heinrich	Vedder, Catharina	F	
Daniel, Heinrich Franz	28, Aug. 1857	Heinrich	Bollers, Carolina	F	
Daniel, Johan	24, July 1851	Heinrich	Vedder, Catharina	F	
Daniel, Margaret	21, Mar. 1854	Stephan	----, ----	T	
Daniel, Maria Henrica Friedricka	27, Nov. 1859	Heinrich	Boles, Carolina	F	
Daniel, Mary	14, May 1853	Michael	----, Mary	E	89
Daniels, Anna Maria Elisabeth	11, Apr. 1854	Johan H.	Otte, Anna Maria	F	
Danion, Thomas	17, Sept 1859	Dermod	Fitzgerald, Catherine	V	59
Danner, Caspar	31, Aug. 1856	Bernard	Bogen, Crescentia	D	66
Danner, Maria	7, Sept 1856	Johan	Abin?, Clara	D	66
Danninhold, Francis George	19, July 1857	Balthasar	Powell, Ellen	B	47
Dansch, Catharina	1, Jan. 1856	Jacob	Gutting, Anna	D	50
Danvin, Catherine Jane	31, Aug. 1856	James	Riely, Mary Ann	V	33
Dapp, Francis	17, Nov. 1850	Francis	Jung, Anna	D	243
Dappers, Joseph Georg	18, Nov. 1855	J. Bernard	----,	F	
Daquet, Josephine	16, Mar. 1856	Louis	Magnes, Mary	E	349
Darcy, Catherine	6, Nov. 1859	John	Fahy, Elizabeth	E	668
Darcy, George	25, Nov. 1855	George	Melay, Mary	R	
Dardis, William Thomas	4, May 1856	Andrew	Whelieban, Catherine	V	31
Darenkamp, Bernard Gerhard	4, Sept 1858	J. Gerhard	Grote, Louisa	A	
Dargan, Catherine	9, Aug. 1857	Wilhelm	----, Abby	R	
Dargin, Bridget	31, Jan. 1857	Martin	Morgan, Ellen	B	39
Darling, August Adolph	15, Aug. 1852	Francis X.	Valmer, Caroline	E	5
Darmedy, John	28, June 1854	Joseph	Kilfoyle, Catherine	E	202
Darmody, Joanne	21, June 1857	Andrew	Cashin, Mary	E	460
Darmody, Joseph	15, Apr. 1855	Andrew	Cashen, Mary	E	279
Darmody, Joseph	28, Jan. 1852	Andrew	Cashon, Mary	E	378
Darmody, Mary	28, Dec. 1856	Joseph	Kilfoyle, Catherine	E	423
Darp, Heinrich Joseph	23, Dec. 1855	Heinrich	Bagge, Maria Elisabeth	D	48
Darpel, Antonia Euphemia Elisabeth	1, Jan. 1855	G. Heinrich	Fänger, Catharina	K	
Darpen, Maria Anna Carolina	11, Feb. 1852	Gerhard	Fingers, Catharina	C	
Darr, Blanche Theresa	21, Feb. 1857	Joseph	Armstrong, Catherine	E	435
Darr, Catherine Frances Agnes	23, Apr. 1854	----	----, ----	E	185
Darr, Cecilia	23, Nov. 1851	Joseph	Lohus, Theresa	E	360
Darr, Francis Joseph Andrwe	22, Sept 1859	Francis	Gress, Josephine	B	81
Darr, George Washington	29, May 1853	Joseph	----, Elizabeth	E	93
Darr, Joseph	8, Dec. 1850	Joseph	Armstrong, Catherine	E	265
Darr, Josephine Eugenia	17, Dec. 1857	Francis	Gross, Josephine	B	53
Darr, Mary L.	6, Aug. 1854	Joseph	Wallace, Theresa	E	214
Darr, Robert Henry	10, June 1855	Joseph	Armstrong, Catherine	E	292
Dart, Thomas Heinrich	30, July 1853	Richard	Dart, Helen	K	
Dasey, Mary	19, June 1853	John	Lydan, Catherine	V	3
Dassel, Francis Heinrich	12, July 1857	Anton	Hobe, Johanna	K	
Dassel, Maria Elisa Florentina	14, Nov. 1858	F. Anton	Hoch, Johanna	K	
Dater, Elizabeth	19, Mar. 1854	William	Cartwright, Ann	P	75
Daugherty, Elizabeth	2, Feb. 1851	John	McDonaugh, Bridget	M	

Name of Child	Date of Baptism	Father	Mother	Church	Page
Daum, Barbara	4, June 1854	Michael	Heierich, Margaretha	K	
Daum, Heinrich	17, Feb. 1850	Michael	Heierich, Margaretha	C	
Daum, Margaretha	3, July 1854	Andreas	Rehm, Barbara	K	
Daum, Michael	14, Mar. 1852	Michael	Heierich, Margaretha	K	
Daumnan, Jacob Heinrich	14, Mar. 1852	Heinrich	Becker, Susanna	D	312
Daunt, Elizabeth	29, May 1855	Henry	----, Ellen	M	
Daunt, George	15, June 1854	Robert H.	Williams, Ann	V	15
Daunt, Richard	25, Nov. 1854	Richard	Smith, Helen	V	20
Dauntel, Anna Maria Regina	9, Nov. 1854	Wilhelm	Henke, Regina	K	
Daut, Catherine	8, Sept 1857	Hungerford	----, Elizabeth	M	
Daut, Conrad	13, Apr. 1858	Robert	----, Ann	M	
Daut, Henrietta Jane	8, Sept 1857	Hungerford	----, Elizabeth	M	
Daut, John	1, June 1856	Richard	Smith, Helen	V	31
Daut, Mary Ann	17, Mar. 1853	Robert	----, Ann	M	
Davany, Catherine	19, Nov. 1854	Patrick	----, Catherine	U	
Davenny, Margaret Ann	2, Aug. 1857	James	Harley, Mary	V	40
Davenny, Mary	14, Jan. 1855	James	Harley, Mary	V	22
Davey, Catherine	14, Mar. 1856	Michael	McGann, Bridget	B	26
Davey, Francis	21, Dec. 1856	John	Shields, Ann	P	201
Davey, Martin	9, Feb. 1851	Francis	Gildea, Catherine	B	225
Davey, Michael	6, Feb. 1853	Michael	McGann, Bridget	B	282
David, Benjamin	26, Oct. 1855	Jackson	-armer, Ann	E	322
David, Catherine	17, July 1859	Martin	Levan, Catherine	E	640
David, Elisabeth	15, Jan. 1852	Adam	Watkins, Jean	E	373
David, Joseph	18, Jan. 1855	Jacob	Bräutigam, Catharina	D	27
David, Patrick	22, Apr. 1851	Michael	O'Donnell, Bridget	E	303
David, Sarah	6, Mar. 1850	Andrew	adult - 21 years old	E	202
Davie, Mary	1, Nov. 1859	John	----, Caecilia	E	667
Davin, Helen	30, Jan. 1853	Michael	Ryan, Helen	B	282
Davin, Julia	27, Aug. 1859	Patrick	Mullen, Winnefred	Z	
Davin, Michael	3, Dec. 1854	Michael	Ryan, Helen	V	20
Davins, Patrick	3, Mar. 1855	Patrick	Whahern, Ellen	B	12
Davis, Ann Mary	1, May 1859	Frederick	Keugh, Margaret	J	50
Davis, Bridget	20, Feb. 1859	John	Sheils, Ann	P	276
Davis, Elizabeth	1, Jan. 1852	Patrick	----, Agnes	B	249
Davis, Francis	29, Aug. 1858	Francis	Egan, Bridget	B	63
Davis, John	26, July 1856	Edward	--dings, Mary Ann	E	384
Davis, John	3, Aug. 1851	John	Davis, Catherine	B	238
Davis, John	31, Aug. 1851	John	Godwin, Ann	B	240
Davis, John	5, July 1856	Michael	Dohery, Margaret	B	31
Davis, John	30, Oct. 1851	William	----, Sarah Ann	E	354
Davis, John William	24, July 1859	James	Herman, Clara	S	
Davis, Josephine	7, Sept 1851	John	Plunkett, Margaret	B	240
Davis, Lavina Bell	20, Feb. 1850	William	Shields, Catherine Jane	B	196
Davis, Margaret Jane	24, Apr. 1853	Patrick	----, Agnes	M	
Davis, Mary Ella	6, Mar. 1859	William	Shields, Catherine	B	72
Davis, Thomas	15, July 1852	William	----, Catherine	B	263
Davis, Victoria	5, Aug. 1859	Franklin	Kavanaugh, Alice	B	78
Davis, William	8, May 1855	Patrick	----, Agnes	M	
Davis, William John	27, May 1855	William	Law, Jane	B	15
Davison, (girl)	11, June 1856	Robert	----, Ann	E	373
Davitt, John	23, Dec. 1855	Thomas	Larkin, Margaret	V	28
Davy, Bridget	26, Sept 1852	Daniel	O'Connor, Bridget	E	22
Davy, Bridget	21, Mar. 1858	Michael	McCan, Bridget	E	523
Davy, Catherine	16, Oct. 1853	Francis	Egan, Bridget	B	300
Davy, Helena Anna Maria	18, May 1859	Job	Clifford, Helena	L	
Davy, James	22, May 1859	Thomas	Shenan, Margaret	B	75
Davy, John	27, Nov. 1851	John	----, Bridget	P	13c
Davy, John	22, Oct. 1850	Michael	----, Bridget	E	255

Name of Child	Date of Baptism	Father	Mother	Church	Page
Davy, Maria Carolina	18, May 1859	Job	Clifford, Helena	L	
Davy, Mary	20, Jan. 1856	Francis	Egan, Bridget	V	29
Davy, Matthew	19, June 1851	Francis	Egan, Bridget	B	234
Davy, Patrick	6, Jan. 1850	Daniel	O'Connell, Ann	E	190
Dawler, Mary Ann Crane	6, Aug. 1852	Michael	Collons, Ellen	E	3
Dawnson, Johan	14, May 1857	Johan	Reinhardt, Maria	C	
Dawson, Helen Mary	24, Mar. 1856		adult	B	27
Dawson, Jane Elizabeth Frances	20, June 1858	James J.	Mc----, Jane Frances	B	60
Dawson, John	13, May 1855	John	----, Bridget	E	286
Dawson, Mary Jane	2, Jan. 1855	Robert	----, Ellen	E	252
Dawson, Mary Sophia	6, Jan. 1853	James J.	----, Jane Mary	E	51
Day, Charles	16, Mar. 1857	Robert	Guest, Catherine	E	440
Day, Elizabeth	1, June 1857	Anthony N.	Kearney, Margaret	E	457
Day, Joseph	6, June 1854	Georg	Freund, Anna Maria	W	4
Day, Joseph	17, June 1855	Georg	Freund, Anna Maria	W	9
Day, Joseph Heinrich	20, Mar. 1853	Georg	Freund, Maria Anna	D	376
Day, Ludwig	21, Mar. 1858	Georg	Freund, Anna Maria	W	22
Day, Maria	20, Mar. 1859	Joseph	Mense, Maria	W	25
Day, Maria Eva	11, Apr. 1852	Martin G.	Freund, Maria Anna	D	316
Day, Michael	28, Nov. 1852	Michael	Hennesey, Judy	E	39
Day, Patrick	9, Oct. 1859	James	Biggin, Margaret	B	82
Day, Philipp	25, Sept 1851	----	Armstrong, Ann	E	346
Day, William	27, Apr. 1851	Michael	Maar, Catherine	E	303
De--, John	6, June 1854	Richard	Commons, Margaret	P	84
Dea, John	28, Apr. 1856	Michael	Fitzpatrick, Mary	P	177
Dea, Thomas	23, Sept 1854	Michael	Fitzpatrick, Mary	P	96
Dean, Catherine	30, July 1854	John	Ryan, Catherine	B	3
Dean, Helen	10, July 1853	Patrick	Dean, Bridget	B	295
Dean, Mary Ann	6, Sept 1856	John	Ryan, Catherine	B	33
Dean, Timothy Thomas	5, Nov. 1852	John	Ryan, Catherine	B	274
Dean, William	18, May 1851	John	----, Catherine	B	232
Dean?, Elizabeth	14, Jan. 1855	Frederick	Fitzpatrick, Catherine	B	10
Deane, Ann	13, May 1858	John	Ryan, Catherine	B	58
Deane, Catherine	1, Nov. 1857	Patrick	Feely, Bridget	B	51
Deane, James	13, July 1856	James	Tevin, Catherine	P	185
Deane, John	24, July 1853	James	Seavin, Catherine	P	48
Deane, John Thomas	7, Aug. 1855	Patrick	Fehelly, Bridget	B	17
Deane, Martha	22, Feb. 1854	Peter	Watkins, Ann	B	309
Deane, Mary	3, Aug. 1851	Patrick	Fahelly, Bridget	B	237
Deane, Mary Ann	15, Apr. 1855	James	Tevin, Catherine	P	128
Deane, Mary Ann	14, Mar. 1858	James	Tevin, Catherine	P	242
Deasy, Mary Ellen	17, Nov. 1859	John	Riley, Ellen	E	671
Deben, Maria Francisca	7, Feb. 1853	J. Theodor	Haget, Anna Margaretha	N	12
Deben, Mary Frances	16, Jan. 1855	Theodore	Hagen, Mary Ann	N	26
Debeno, Catharina	10, Mar. 1850	Anton	Kohler, Magdalena	D	205
Debeno, Francisca	9, Mar. 1851	Anton	Kohl, Magdalena	D	256
Debeno, Joseph	17, Dec. 1854	Anton	Kohl, Magdalena	D	24
Debeno, Maria	12, Apr. 1859	Joseph	Lavesch, Magdalena	K	
Deber, Urban	19, Nov. 1852	Johan	Martin, Henrietta	Q	2
Debraen, Maria Agnes Francisca	29, Aug. 1856	Bernard	Schöber, Elisabeth	D	65
Debrein, Maria Agatha Philomena	10, Feb. 1851	Bernard	Schoeber, Cath. Elisabeth	D	253
Debrein, Marianna Rosa	3, Sept 1853	Bernard	Schoeber, Cath. Elisabeth	D	403
Deck, Elisabeth	9, Apr. 1854	Johan	Klein, Helen	Q	4
Deck, Maria Magdalena	20, Dec. 1857	Johan	Klein, Helen	Q	25
Deckelmeier, Rosina	4, Oct.1857	Francis	Gebel, Barbara	D	95
Deckenburg, Heinrich Theodor	6, Mar. 1850	Heinrich	Hinders, Maria Catharina	D	204
Decker, Amelia Romana	31, Jan. 1854	Georg	Schnur, Catharina	D	3
Decker, Anna	21, Feb. 1857	Nicolaus	Grasmeier, Catharina	D	79
Decker, Carl	25, June 1854	Georg	Schebene, Anna	D	13

Name of Child	Date of Baptism	Father	Mother	Church	Page
Decker, Christian	13, June 1854	Christian	Ludwig, Margaretha	D	12
Decker, Francis Joseph	24, July 1851	Francis	Bohnert, Rosina	D	274
Decker, Georg	29, Jan. 1857	Georg	Schenez, Anna	F	
Decker, Gerhard	27, Sept 1857	Heinrich	Hart, Elisabeth	D	95
Decker, Herman	16, Feb. 1851	Christian	Ludwig, Margaretha	D	254
Decker, Jacob	12, Sept 1858	Jacob	Weber, Louisa	T	
Decker, Johan	19, Sept 1852	Christian	Ludwig, Margaretha	D	348
Decker, Johan	7, Apr. 1856	Francis	Bohnart, Rosa	D	56
Decker, Johan	23, Feb. 1851	Georg J.	Menz, Susanna	D	254
Decker, Joseph	20, Mar. 1853	Georg	Schebene, Anna	D	376
Decker, Theodor Heinrich	13, Sept 1858	Gerhard	Ruve, M. Elisabeth	C	
Decker, Wilhelm Johan	20, June 1853	Georg J.	Man---ler, Susanna	A	
DeCruse, Santino Johan	12, Dec. 1856	Anton M.	Bernero, Catharina	K	
Dedel, Louisa Henrietta	14, Sept 1851	Johan	Kessler, Maria	J	12
Dedell, Catharina Theresa	28, June 1859	Joseph	T----, Elisabeth	D	141
DeDonner, Barbara Caecilia	9, June 1851	August	Boullia, Regina	C	
Deer, Louise	26, Dec. 1859	William	Jaques, Esther	E	679
Deest, Ludwig Albert	24, Aug. 1856	Peter	Hamman, Anna	C	
Degan, Mary	28, Nov. 1852	Thomas	McGinnis, Bridget	P	30
Degan, Timothy	29, Jan. 1854	Thomas	McGinnis, Bridget	P	66
Degen, Johan	13, Feb. 1853	Johan	Ostheimer, Barbara	D	371
Degen, Sophia	29, Nov. 1857	Johan	Ostheimer, Barbara	T	
Degenhard, Adam Albert	22, May 1858	Wilhelm	Hartman, Elenora	A	
Degenhard, Maria Barbara	3, Nov. 1850	Johan	Eckert, Maria Eva	F	
Degenhardt, Johan	18, Jan. 1852	August	Winzig, Maria Anna	J	16
Degent, Lucia Louisa	16, Sept 1855	Johan	Ostheimer, Barbara	D	43
Degnan, Ann	15, Feb. 1854	M.	Green, Mary	V	11
Degnan, Margaret	17, Oct. 1852	James	----, Catherine	E	28
Degnan, Mary Ann	9, July 1853	Patrick	Kelly, Mary	V	4
Degnan, Patrick	23, Mar. 1851	Patrick	Kelly, Mary	E	293
DeGrandval, Maria Allai	21, May 1854	Aglau	Landowsky, Theresa	L	
Dehler, Anna Barbara	30, Oct. 1859	Elias	Blum, Barbara	F	
Dehner, Anna Maria	18, Mar. 1855	Hilarius	Bender, Theresa	W	8
Dehner, Daniel Anton	24, Apr. 1853	Daniel	Kehny, Rosina	J	22
Dehner, Elisabeth Crescentia	25, Dec. 1859	Adolph	Greiner, Catharina	G	
Dehner, Johan Anton	3, Aug. 1851	Daniel	Kehny, Rosina	A	
Dehner, Johan Philipp Rudolph	4, July 1858	Daniel	Kaehny, Rosina	G	
Dehner, Johan Rudolph	27, Mar. 1859	Johan	Ott, Maria	F	
Dehner, Joseph Peter	31, Mar. 1859	Hilarius	Bender, Theresa	T	
Dehner, Maria Rosina	31, Jan. 1856	Daniel	Kenny, Rosina	J	34
Dehner, Melchior Heinrich	7, Apr. 1857	Hilarius	Bender, Theresa	F	
Dehner, Melchior Joseph	5, Sept 1852	Hilarius	Bender, Theresa	F	
Dehnker, Johan Heinrich Theodor	16, Mar. 1856	Heinrich	Ploggemann, Theresa	L	
Deho, Friedrich Theodor	9, Apr. 1856	Wilhelm	Ruske, Elisabeth	F	
Deho, Georg Anton	28, May 1854	Jacob	Wellmann, Agnes	F	
Deho, Heinrich	19, Aug. 1856	Jacob	Wellmann, Catharina Maria	F	
Deho, Heinrich August Julius	27, Dec. 1851	Wilhelm	Rusche, Elisabeth A.	F	
Deho, Johan Franz Heinrich	13, Feb. 1858	Wilhelm	Ruske, Elisabeth	F	
Deho, Johan Wilhelm	7, Feb. 1859	Jacob	Wellman, Catharina	K	
Deho, Philomena Agnes	11, Apr. 1854	Wilhelm	Ruske, Elisabeth	F	
Deho, Wilhelm Joseph	7, June 1852	Jacob	Wellmann, Catharina	F	
Dei, Johan Bernard	13, Oct. 1850	Johan	Nöger, Carolina	D	238
Deie, Franz Anton	4, Dec. 1858	Anton	Zumbahlen, Bernardina	L	
Deie, Johan Joseph	14, May 1855	Anton	Zumbahlen, Bernardina	L	
Deie, Maria Elisabeth	19, June 1853	Anton	Zumbahlen, Bernardina	L	
Deierling, Maria Magdalena	13, Mar. 1853	Joseph	Kraul, Barbara	D	375
Deiker, Johan Heinrich	20, Aug. 1857	Herman	Vorgeding, Adelheid	D	92
Deir, Maria Louisa	9, Sept 1857	Johan	Nögler, Carolina	D	94
Deis, Anna Maria	21, Oct. 1857	Heinrich	Wille, Anna Theresa	N	

Name of Child	Date of Baptism	Father	Mother	Church	Page
Deis, Peter Anton	26, Mar. 1859		Deis, Salome	J	50
Deitermann, Anton Joseph	2, Feb. 1856	Anton	Niehaus, Theresa	L	
Deitermann, Josephina Theresa	13, Dec. 1858	Anton	Niehaus, Theresa	L	
Deitermann, Maria Anna	14, Mar. 1853	Anton	Niehaus, Theresa	L	
Deitmering, Maria Adelheid	21, Aug. 1859	Heinrich	Moehle, Emma	C	
DeKamp, Maria Helena	29, July 1858	Francis	Wintmeier, Elisabeth	K	
Delahanty, Bridget	10, Feb. 1856	Thomas	Kane, Catherine	B	25
Delahanty, Henry	12, June 1859	James	----, Mary	M	
Delahanty, James	14, Apr. 1856	Patrick	Meacher, Ann	E	358
Delahanty, John	14, June 1857	Michael	----, Bridget	M	
Delahanty, John	14, Feb. 1855	Patrick	Meagher, Ann	E	264
Delahanty, Mary	16, July 1858	Joseph	Scully, Bridget	K	
Delahanty, Mary	24, July 1859	Michael	----, Bridget	M	
Delahanty, Michael	8, Aug. 1852	Patrick	Meagher, Ann	E	4
Delaney, Ann	15, Feb. 1857	John	Gallagher, Catherine	V	37
Delaney, Arthur	14, Apr. 1850	Bernard	----, Mary	E	208
Delaney, Caroline	25, May 1854	James	Donally, Joanne	E	192
Delaney, Charles Edmund	25, Mar. 1857	John	Mor, Rachael Ann	K	
Delaney, Daniel Joseph	18, Oct. 1857	John	Whelan, Margaret	B	51
Delaney, Edward Richard	31, Aug. 1854	William	----, Jane	U	
Delaney, Ellen	23, Dec. 1854	Patrick	McGrath, Mary	B	8
Delaney, James	20, Apr. 1859	Daniel	Brophey, Margaret	P	282
Delaney, James	14, Feb. 1858	Miles	----, Honora	R	
Delaney, James	8, Dec. 1858	Philip	Burke, Julia	B	68
Delaney, Joh	14, Oct. 1856	Philip	Burke, Julia	B	35
Delaney, John	5, Dec. 1852	John	----, Bridget	E	41
Delaney, John	2, Nov. 1854	John	Daily, Mary	E	237
Delaney, John	15, Aug. 1859	John	Murray, Alice	B	79
Delaney, John	8, Aug. 1858	John	Murray, Alice	B	62
Delaney, Joseph	16, Apr. 1852	James	Donelly, Joanne	E	403
Delaney, Julia	4, Aug. 1856	Daniel	Cooney, Julia	B	32
Delaney, Lawrence	4, Aug. 1858	Thomas	Phelan, Joanne	B	62
Delaney, Mary	10, May 1855	Dennis	Moroney, Mary	R	
Delaney, Mary	26, Mar. 1853	John	----, Catherine	E	76
Delaney, Mary	9, Dec. 1855	Michael	Downs, Honora	R	
Delaney, Mary Jane	5, Mar. 1854	Daniel	----, Mary	E	173
Delaney, Mary Wilhelmina	18, Nov. 1852	Eugene	Colter, Ann	E	36
Delaney, Patrick	8, Jan. 1852	James	Keefe, Margaret	B	249
Delaney, Patrick	18, Mar. 1852	William	----, Jane	Q	2
Delaney, Richard	6, Mar. 1853	Jeremiah	Bradley, Honora	E	69
Delaney, Rose Ann	6, Feb. 1851	Daniel	----, Mary	E	281
Delaney, Thomas	12, Dec. 1859	Miles	Dower, Honora	R	
Delaney, William	6, Feb. 1859	John	Whelan, Margaret	B	70
DelAnge, James Joseph	6, Jan. 1856	Jasper	Crawford, Eliza	B	23
Delany, Helen	18, Sept 1850	William	----, ----	B	214
Delany, Mary	11, May 1856	Michael	Lawless, Margaret	P	179
Delap, Mary	20, Aug. 1851	Patrick	Burns, Ann	P	11
Deleny, Catharine	5, Dec. 1855	John	Wiling, Magdalena	D	48
Dell, Catherine	16, Sept 1855	John	Klein, Magdalena	Q	10
Dell, Margaretha	26, Sept 1858	Nicolaus	----, Catharina	D	120
Dell, Peter	5, Nov. 1854	Anton	Hirt, Elisabeth	A	
Deller, Johan Baptist Eduard	1, July 1855	Johan	Meixner, Eva Catharina	D	37
Deller, Maria Anna	4, Nov. 1856	Johan	Meixner, Eva Catharina	D	71
Deller, Maria Rosina	8, June 1853	Peter	Link, Maria	D	388
Deller, Peter	3, Feb. 1850	Peter	Scherer, Elisabeth	D	202
Dellerman, Anna Carolina	5, Dec. 1858	Andreas	Pitroff, Anna	R	
Dellerman, Anna Margaretha	23, July 1850	Andreas	Pitsof, Anna	D	224
Dellerman, Anna Margaretha	22, Mar. 1855	Andreas	Pittrof, Anna	R	
Dellerman, Elisabeth	22, Mar. 1855	Andreas	Pittrof, Anna	R	

Name of Child	Date of Baptism	Father	Mother	Church	Page
Dellerman, Francis Joseph	30, June 1854	Andreas	Pittroff, Ann	R	
Dellerman, Georg Andreas	17, Mar. 1852	Andreas	Pitroff, Anna	R	
Dellerman, Mary Margaret	22, May 1856	Andrew	Pittrof, Anna	R	
Delmour, Mary	14, May 1858	John	----, Ann	M	
Delter, Margaretha Elisabeth	12, Nov. 1854	Peter	Zipf, Maria Rosina	D	21
Demand, Caroline	6, Dec. 1857	Matthew	Longnecker, Frances	E	497
Demand, Catherine	6, Dec. 1857	Matthew	Longnecker, Frances	E	497
Demand, Cecilia	14, Mar. 1852	Matthew	Longnecker, Frances	E	391
Demand, Charles Edward	20, May 1852	Leopold	Mason, Frances	B	263
Demand, Clara	6, Nov. 1859	Matthew	Laune, Frances	E	668
Demand, Frances Catherine	11, Apr. 1856	Matthew	----, Frances	E	358
Demand, Helen	30, July 1854	Matthew	Leonard, Frances	E	211
Demand, Henry Abraham	25, Mar. 1857	Leopold	Mason, Frances E.	B	42
Demand, Mary Elizabeth	17, Mar. 1850	Matthew	----, Frances	E	203
Demange, Caspar	23, Apr. 1854	Joseph	Birkel, Marianna	F	
Demark, Mary Magdalene	19, June 1858	Andrew	Laversa, Theresa	E	542
Demesy, Maria Elisabeth	18, Nov. 1855	Claude F.	Parmenter, Maria Rosa	L	
Demling, Elisabeth	25, June 1853	Johan	----, Elisabeth	K	
Demmer, Maria Anna	15, June 1855	Carl	Wansink, Maria Anna	D	36
Demming, Heinrich Joseph	8, Jan. 1855	Heinrich J.	Brüggeman, Adelheid	D	26
Demner, Carl Anton	24, Jan. 1858	Carl	Pershink, Maria Anna	D	103
Dempfle, Jacob	8, Dec. 1851	Johan	Gallman, Justina	K	
Dempsey, Bridget	28, Mar. 1856	Michael	----, Catherine	E	354
Dempsey, Catherine	28, Sept 1854	John	----, Ann	E	227
Dempsey, Catherine	28, Mar. 1856	Michael	----, Catherine	E	354
Dempsey, Catherine Maher	17, Oct. 1852	Patrick	Dooley, Mary Ann	B	272
Dempsey, Edward	15, Aug. 1858	John	Brerton, Ann	E	557
Dempsey, James	10, Apr. 1856	John	Brardan, Nancy	E	357
Dempsey, Louis	21, June 1857	John	Reardon, Ann	E	461
Dempsey, Mary	29, Mar. 1857	John	Purcell, Catherine	E	443
Dempsey, Mary Ann	15, Aug. 1850	Dennis	McDonald, Mary Ann	B	210
Dempsey, Mary Ann	2, Apr. 1854	Michael	Finessy, Catherine	P	77
Dempsey, Thomas	18, July 1858	Michael	Hennesey, Catherine	E	551
Demuth, Barbara	18, July 1852	Francis	Wegman, Anna Maria	D	329
Demuth, Francis	10, May 1857	Francis	Wegmann, Anna M.	C	
Demuth, Maria Margaretha	29, Jan. 1854	Francis	Wegman, Anna Maria	D	3
Demuth, Marianna	17, July 1850	Francis	Wegman, Anna Maria	D	223
Den, Michael	24, Feb. 1858	Michael	Folz, Mary	B	56
Denahy, Thomas	12, Oct. 1851	Dennis	Haley, Catherine	B	242
Denedy, James	4, Aug. 1856	Peter	McHenry, Margaret	E	387
Denedy, John Peter	20, Mar. 1858	Peter	McHenry, Margaret	E	523
Denehy, Helen	3, Jan. 1854	Dennis	Haly, Catherine	V	9
Deneil, Francis Thomas	23, Oct. 1853	Thomas	Eaton?, Mary Ann	B	301
Denger, Anna Maria Christina	30, Nov. 1850	J. Theodor	Detters, Anna Adelheid	D	244
Denger, Elisabeth	30, Nov. 1851	Joseph	Graus, Margaretha	D	295
Denger, Joseph Valentin	10, Mar. 1850	Joseph	Graus, Margaretha	D	205
Denger, Maria Alice	31, Aug. 1859	Bernard	Goebel, Catharina	C	
Dengers, Johan Theodor	6, Mar. 1853	J. Theodor	Detters, Anna Adelheid	D	374
Denginger, Josephina	25, Dec. 1859	Francis	Lorens, Victoria	L	
Dengler, Anna Josephina	27, Aug. 1851	Xavier	Küpferle, Maria Josephina	D	279
Dengler, Francis Xavier	11, Dec. 1853	Francis X.	Kipperle, Josephina	D	419
Dengler, George Washington	2, Mar. 1856	Francis X.	Kuepferle, Josephina	F	
Dengler, Magdalena	28, Feb. 1859	Francis X.	Kuepferle, M. Josephina	F	
Denhorn, Heinrich Joseph	12, Dec. 1855	F. Joseph	Thole, Maria Helena	K	
Denier, Agnes	4, Apr. 1852	Anthony	----, Mary	H	
Denier, Elisabeth	16, Feb. 1856	Nicolaus	----, Maria Gertrud	H	
Denier, Henry Albert	8, Dec. 1853	Anthony	----, Anna Maria	H	
Denier, John Anthony	9, Dec. 1855	Anthony	----, Ann Mary	H	
Denier, John Paul	31, July 1853	John	----, Mary	U	

Name of Child	Date of Baptism	Father	Mother	Church	Page
Denier, Joseph	8, July 1855	John	Schuloff, Maria Anna	U	
Denier, Mary	1, June 1850	Nicolaus	----, Mary	H	
Denier, Mary Elizabeth	30, July 1854	Nicolaus	----, Mary Gertrude	H	
Denier, Mary Gertrude	27, Apr. 1854	Lawrence	----, Elisabeth	H	
Denier, Mary Josephine	6, Oct. 1850	Anthony	Memel, Mary	H	
Denier, Mary Theresa	4, July 1852	Nicolaus	----, Mary Gertrud	H	
Denier, Michael Joseph	29, Nov. 1857	Anthony	Memmel, Anna Maria	H	
Denier, Philomena Barbara	20, Jan. 1859	Nicolaus	Missey, Mary	H	
Denier, Veronica	17, June 1855	Florenz	----, Elisabeth	H	
Denier, Veronica Philomena	14, June 1857	Nicolaus	Messing, Maria G.	H	
Denier, William Anthony	31, May 1857	John	Lehnhoff, Mary	H	
Deniger, Johan Ferdinand	24, Sept 1854	Friedrich	Helmich, Catharina	D	18
Deninger, Elisabeth Catharina	3, Jan. 1856	Heinrich	----, Catharina	H	
Denis, Johan Heinrich	20, July 1858	H. Ludwig	Wallman, Catharina Ant.	A	
Denk, Anna Catharina	22, Oct. 1854	Joseph	Hoffmann, Philippina	F	
Denk, August	12, Sept 1854	Francis	Dick, Barbara	C	
Denk, Johan Joseph	20, Apr. 1854	Valentin	Ries, Elisabeth	F	
Denk, Louisa	4, Dec. 1853	Georg (+)	Denk, Magdalena	D	418
Denk, Valentin	23, Feb. 1851	Valentin	Ries, Elisabeth	F	
Denker, Anna Catharina Bertha	22, Aug. 1858	Theodor	Rillmann, Catharina	L	
Denker, Elisabeth Theodora	4, Dec. 1854	Bernard	Meyer, Jenny	C	
Denker, Francisca Hermina	19, Dec. 1858	Bernard	Meier, Johanna	F	
Denker, Johan	31, Dec. 1858	Heinrich	Ploggemann, Theresa	L	
Denker, M. Bernardina Wilhelmina	11, Dec. 1856	Bernard	Meyer, Marianna	F	
Dennan, Edward	1, May 1859	Joseph	----, Catherine	M	
Dennedy, John	11, Jan. 1852	James	Felden, Bridget	E	372
Dennery, Mary	18, Dec. 1858	James	Findley, Catherine	X	
Denney, John	21, Jan. 1854	?	?	B	307
Dennigan, Thomas	11, July 1850	John	Duffy, Margaret	B	207
Dennis, James	19, Nov. 1854	Joseph	Burns, Catherine	P	105
Dennis, John	30, Sept 1858	Joseph	Burns, Catherine	E	565
Dennis, Ludwig	15, Nov. 1857	Ludwig	Wagner, Margaretha	C	
Dennis, William	25, Aug. 1856	Joseph	Byrne, Catherine	V	35
Dennison, Ann Mary	2, Dec. 1855	Joseph	Hamsey, Joanne	E	330
Dennison, Joseph	8, July 1850	Edward	Rowland, Mary	B	206
Dennison, Margaret	20, June 1854	James	Kelleger, Margaret	E	200
Dennison, Mary Ann	14, Sept 1856	Thomas	Flynn, Mary	P	192
Denny, Edward	25, Dec. 1853	Thomas	----, Mary	M	
Denroh, Simon Peter	14, Nov. 1850	Johan	Steppo, Genofeva	K	
Densch, Andreas	10, Dec. 1857	Michael	Schelmorschl, Christina	D	100
Densch, Johan Michael	11, July 1859	Michael	Schnellbeigel, Christina	T	
Denser, Anna Catharina	8, Dec. 1852	Fidel	Schmidt, Catharina	F	
Denser, Maria	12, Apr. 1857	Fidel	Schmidt, Catharina	F	
Denser, Maria	26, Aug. 1855	Martin	Müller, Maria	A	
Dentinger, M. Magdalena	9, Mar. 1851	Francis	Huber, Magdalena	C	
Denver, Rosanne	16, July 1854	James	Cahill, Esther	P	88
Denvir, James	3, Aug. 1851	James	----, Esther	E	331
Denvir, John Joseph	27, Dec. 1859	James	Cahill, Esther	P	307
Denvir, Mary Elizabeth Josephine	23, Nov. 1856	William	Cahill, Esther	P	199
Denwer, Peter Joseph	7, Dec. 1856	Joseph	Muscher, Veronica	D	74
Denz, Carl Friedrich	1, May 1854	Simon	Becker, Catharina	D	9
Denzasse, Carolina Amelia L.	16, Nov. 1856	Carl	Marschall, Josephina	C	
Denzer, Catharina	22, Dec. 1850	Martin	Müller, Maria Eva	A	
Denzer, Heinrich Wilhelm	28, May 1855	Fidel	Denzer, Catharina	A	
Denzer, Joseph	17, Apr. 1853	Martin	Mueller, Maria Eva	A	
Denzler, Johan Heinrich	25, Feb. 1857	Friedrich	Helman, Catharina	D	79
Denzler, Johanna Apollonia	6, Jan. 1854	Valentin	Braun, Margaretha	D	1
Depenbrock, Anna Maria	20, Nov. 1853	Gerhard H.	Kuhl, M. Elisabeth	L	
Depenbrock, Bernard Heinrich	28, July 1850	Rudolph	Klus, Anna Maria	L	

Name of Child	Date of Baptism	Father	Mother	Church	Page
Depenbrock, Herman Heinrich	8, June 1851	Gerhard	Kuhl, M. Elisabeth	L	
Depoel, Gerharda Josephina M.	3, Nov. 1851	Albert	----, Johanna	C	
Depohl, Johan Theodor	2, July 1850	Emmert	Holbers, Johanna	D	220
Depp, Magdalena Johanna	24, Apr. 1859	Johan	König, Elisabeth	D	136
Deppe, Ferdinand Edward	26, Mar. 1855	Heinrich	Thiemann, Catharina	C	
Deppe, Maria Ida	10, Aug. 1856	Heinrich	Tiemann, Catharina	C	
Deppe, Maria Leonora	27, Dec. 1858	Heinrich	Tiemann, Catharina	C	
Deppen, Johan Herman August	5, Mar. 1851	Theodor	Hagert, Maria	A	
Deppenbrock, Johan Georg	10, Oct. 1852	Rudolph	Wibbold, Margaretha M.	L	
Deppenbrock, Johan Gerhard	21, Feb. 1858	Gerhard	Kuhl, Maria Elisabeth	L	
Deppenbrock, Johan Heinrich	7, Aug. 1854	Rudolph	Wibbold, Margaretha	L	
Deppenbrock, Johan Heinrich	2, Aug. 1857	Rudolph	Wibbold, Margaretha	L	
Deppenbrock, Johan Rudolph	15, Apr. 1856	Gerhard	Kuhl, M. Elisabeth	L	
Deppenbrock, Maria Catharina	12, May 1856	Rudolph	Wibbold, Margaretha	L	
Depree, Rosina Carolina	25, June 1859	Nicolaus	Fischer, Margaretha	D	140
Derbeck, Catharina Elisabeth	20, Feb. 1858	Joseph	Gehring, Christina	N	
Derfler, Barbara	5, July 1857	Johan	Werner, Catharina	D	89
Derick, Anna Albina	14, Mar. 1858	Ludwig	Brunner, Amanda	J	44
Derick, Elisabeth Amanda	13, Apr. 1851	Ludwig	Brunner, Amanda	J	10
Derick, Johan Francis	19, Oct. 1856	Ludwig	Brunner, Amanda	J	38
Derick, Joseph Anton Aloysius	24, Sept 1854	Ludwig	Brunner, Amanda	J	28
Derick, Ottilia Christina	8, May 1853	Ludwig	Brunner, Amanda	J	22
Derick, Paulina Catharina	11, Apr. 1852	Ludwig	Brunner, Amalia	J	16
Derick, Philomena Margaertha	2, Oct. 1859	Ludwig	Brunner, Amanda	J	52
Derick, Wilhelm Aloysius	12, Nov. 1854	Joseph	Right, Anna Maria	J	28
Dering, Johan Bernard	21, June 1851	Gerhard B.	Aldemeier, Maria Cath.	F	
Derksen, Johan Heinrich	16, Oct. 1857	Gerhard	Brinkman, Gertrud	J	44
Derksen, Maria	19, Oct. 1851	Johan	VanReh, Gertrud	K	
Derksen, Maria Theresa	2, Jan. 1852	Gerhard	Brinkman, Gertrud	J	16
Derksen, Theresa	9, July 1854	Gerhard	Brinkman, Gertrud	J	28
Derlinde, Anna Maria Catharina	5, July 1857	Anton	Beckhold, Hermina	D	89
Derlinde, Johanna Maria	8, Mar. 1855	Anton	Beckenhaus, Maria	D	30
Derlinde, Wilhelm Heinrich	5, May 1859	Anton	Beckenhorst, Philomena	T	
Dermody, William	20, Nov. 1853	Thomas	----, Eliza	U	
Dermott, Lawrence	11, Apr. 1853	Patrick	Brown, Frances	P	39
Dermott, Margaret	8, Feb. 1852	Patrick	Brown, Frances	P	17
Dermott, Patrick	16, Jan. 1859	Patrick	Brown, Frances	P	272
Derse, Joseph Edward	13, Dec. 1858	Jacob	Bühl---, Marianna	D	126
Dery, Thomas	20, Sept 1857	James	Bingem, Margaret	B	50
Desass, Emil Alexander	12, Feb. 1855	Charles	Marshall, Josephine	E	264
DeShields, Edward	3, Aug. 1852	?	?	B	267
DeShields, Louis	14, May 1850		adult	B	202
DeShields, Louis Barras	23, Apr. 1850	Louis	Anbert, Mary	B	201
Desing, Maria Gertrud Henrietta	14, Apr. 1851	Francis W.	Moorman, Maria Gertrud	D	261
Deskle?, Anton	6, Mar. 1859	Anton	Bladder, Sophia	K	
Desman, Mary Ann	7, Mar. 1858	Joseph	----, Elizabeth	M	
Desmond, Catharine	27, Sept 1857	Humphrey	Borgen, Helen	T	
Desmond, Catharine Helen	5, Oct. 1856	Humphrey	Bergen, Helen	T	
Desmond, Dennis	15, Oct. 1859	Humphrey	Bergin, Ellen	E	662
Desmond, Henry	19, Aug. 1851	Michael	Lehan, Mary	B	239
Desmond, Humphrey Edmond	5, Dec. 1854	Humphrey	Bergin, Ellen	B	8
Desmond, John	5, Jan. 1851	Dennis	----, Margaret	E	274
Desmond, John	12, June 1859	Michael	Lehane, Mary	B	76
Desmond, John Michael	13, June 1852	John	Richards, Julia	B	260
Desmond, Joseph	12, Nov. 1852	Michael	Lehane, Mary	B	275
Desmond, Lucy	25, Sept 1855	Cornelius	Farrell, Lucy	V	27
Desmond, Margaret	8, Feb. 1853	Humphrey	Bergin, Helen	E	61
Desmond, Mary	1, Sept 1854	Cornelius	Farrell, Lucy	V	17
Desmond, Mary Elisabeth	8, Sept 1851	Humphrey	----, Ellenore	E	341

Name of Child	Date of Baptism	Father	Mother	Church	Page
Desmond, Mary Helen	1, Oct. 1854	Michael	Lehane, Mary	T	
Desmond, Patrick	27, Mar. 1851	Thomas	----, Bridget	E	295
Desmond, Rose Joanne	31, Aug. 1856	Michael	Lehan, Mary	T	
Dessart, Victor Eugen Carl	1, Jan. 1858	Louis F.	Bontle, Maria	L	
Dessert, Athanasius	20, Sept 1857	Paul	Abke, Rosina	D	94
Dessert, Maria	1, Dec. 1850	Paul	Abke, Rosina	L	
Deteler, Helena Sibilla	21, Mar. 1858	Clemens	Alder, Maria	L	
Determan, Anna Maria Catharina	28, June 1858	J.H.	Püning, Catharina	A	
Determan, Heinrich Aloysius	1, Oct. 1857	H. Aloysius	Brunsen, Maria Adelheid	K	
Determann, Anna Maria	3, May 1853	Lucas	Gausepohl, Catharina	L	
Determann, Herman Heinrich	12, July 1856	F. Heinrich	Schmidt, Elisabeth	C	
Determann, Maria Anna Josephina	19, Mar. 1858	Heinrich	Smith, M. Elisabeth	C	
Deters, Anna Bernardina Philomena	10, June 1856	H. Arnold	Menke, Maria Anna	K	
Deters, Anna Maria Rosa	21, July 1855	Herman C.	Ortmann, Dina	L	
Deters, Carl Aloysius	2, May 1852	J. Heinrich	Lücken, Maria Josephina	K	
Deters, Carl Joseph	20, May 1853	Heinrich	Wilberding, Maria Agnes	A	
Deters, Clemens Friedrich	21, June 1858	Clemens	Orthman, Bernardina	A	
Deters, Francis Heinrich	1, Sept 1858	Francis H.	Brüning, Anna	A	
Deters, Francis Ludwig	21, May 1854	J. Heinrich	Luken, Josephina	K	
Deters, Franz Joseph Johan	27, Apr. 1859	Francis	Petlin, Maria	L	
Deters, Heinrich Hieronymus	28, Sept 1856	J. Heinrich	Luken, Maria Josephina	K	
Deters, Johan Clemens	28, Nov. 1852	G. Heinrich	Sunneberg, Elisabeth	K	
Deters, Johan Heinrich	12, Nov. 1850	G. Heinrich	Sunneberg, Maria Elisabeth	K	
Deters, M. Catharina Francisca	20, Nov. 1854	Francis H.	Peltin, Maria	L	
Deters, Maria Elisabeth Gertrud	15, May 1858	Heinrich	Menke, Maria	K	
Deters, Maria Francisca Elisabeth	2, Jan. 1856	Francis	Peltin, Euphemia	L	
Deters, Maria Johanna Catharina	22, Mar. 1857	Francis H.	Peltin, Eupheimia	L	
Deters, Wilhelm Eduard	30, Jan. 1859	Johan H.	Lueken, Josephina	F	
Detmer, Johan Heinrich August	25, Aug. 1851	Lucas	Gausepohl, Catharina	C	
Detsinger, Margaretha	21, Sept 1851	Willibald	Brand, Theresa	D	283
Detters, Herman Augustine	26, Jan. 1851	Gerhard H.	Schlichte, Margaretha Maria	D	250
Detters, Johan Aloysius	3, June 1857	Gerhard H.	Schlichte, Maria Margaretha	D	86
Detters, Johan Francis	2, Apr. 1853	Gerhard H.	Schlichte, Maria Margaretha	D	378
Detters, Maria Francisca Rosa	14, Nov. 1855	Gerhard H.	Schlichte, Margaretha Maria	D	47
Dettling, Felicitas	4, Dec. 1859	Johan	Weber, Catharina	F	
Dettling, Franz Joseph	7, Nov. 1858	Johan	Weber, Catharina	F	
Dettling, Georg	22, Jan. 1855	Georg	Weber, Catharina	F	
Dettmer, Bernard Heinrich	15, Sept 1854	Bernard	Luning, Catharina	K	
Dettmer, Elisabeth Carolina	27, Nov. 1851	Joseph	Rusche, Carolina	F	
Dettmer, Josephina Catharina	22, Jan. 1854	Joseph	Ruscher, Carolina	F	
Dettmer, Maria Agnes Rosa	19, Feb. 1856	Joseph	Rusche, Carolina	F	
Dettmer, Maria Francisca	5, Aug. 1858	Joseph	Rusche, Carolina	F	
Dettmers, Maria Rosa	25, Oct. 1857	Bernard	Liening, Catharina	K	
Detzel, Johan Adam	24, Oct. 1858	Michael	Dutenhofer, Maria Eva	K	
Detzel, Maria Anna	9, Nov. 1856	Michael	Dudenhofer, Catharina Eva	K	
Detzel, Wilhelm	19, Aug. 1855	Michael	Duttenhöfer, Eva	K	
Detziner, Elisabeth	17, Feb. 1850	Willibald	Brand, Theresa	D	202
Deubel, Georg	2, Sept 1855	Joseph	Muschle, Veronica	D	41
Deuber, Georg Francis	14, Nov. 1858	Joseph	Muscher, Veronica	D	124
Deus, Francis Bernard	19, Apr. 1853	Gerhard	Nieman, Elisabeth	J	22
Deustch, Margaretha Catharina	26, July 1857	Peter	Knaebele, Mary Ann	D	91
Deutersheim, Magdalena	1, June 1857	Georg	Kotus, Catharina	D	86
Deutsch, Anna Maria Wilhelmina	26, June 1851	Mathias	Breitinger, Anna Maria	A	
Deutsch, Benjamin	23, Feb. 1857	Michael	Bock, Catharina	K	
Deutsch, Catharina Philippina	20, Feb. 1853	Bernard	----, Veronica	D	373
Deutsch, Elisabeth Dorothea	28, Feb. 1853	Mathias	Breitinger, Anna Maria	J	20
Deutsch, Francis Xavier	27, Nov. 1859	Peter	Knaebele, Maria	D	151
Deutsch, Francisca Magdalena	27, June 1858	Peter	Knaeble, Marianna	D	114
Deutsch, Margaretha Elisabeth	6, Mar. 1859	Herman	Wessels, Maria Catharina	D	133

Name of Child	Date of Baptism	Father	Mother	Church	Page
Deutsch, Maria Anna Veronica	20, Apr. 1856	Peter	Knäbele, Maria Anna	D	57
Deva, Anthony	10, Dec. 1859	Anthony	McAndrew, Margaret	P	306
Devane, Michael	3, Mar. 1855	Owen	Kenny, Honora	E	268
Devaney, James	23, May 1857	Odie	Kenny, Honora	E	455
Devaney, Mary	19, Oct. 1856	John	----, Ann	R	
Devaney, Mary Ellen	2, Aug. 1853	James	----, Mary	E	114
Devaney, Thomas	8, Mar. 1857	Patrick	Duffy, Catherine	B	41
Devanney, Julia	30, Sept 1858	Michael	McCail, Bridget	E	565
Devanney, Thomas	20, Jan. 1852	Daniel	----, Ann	E	374
Devanny, Ann	3, June 1859	Patrick	Duffy, Catherine	B	76
Devanny, John	30, Nov. 1856	Patrick	Conrey, Catherine	P	200
Devany, James Hugh	12, Jan. 1851	James	Harley, Mary	E	276
Devareux, Margaret	18, Aug. 1850	Lawrence	Pendergast, Catherine	B	210
DeVase, Anna Maria Josephina	29, Aug. 1852	Carl	Marschall, Josephina	C	
Devenny, Daniel	15, May 1853	Patrick	----, Catherine	B	291
Deveraux, Catherine	8, Feb. 1852	Lawrence	Prendergast, Catherine	B	252
Devid, Henry	7, Feb. 1858	Anthony	McAndrew, Mary	P	238
Devin, John	4, Jan. 1855	Thomas	----, Honora	M	
Devin, Mary	9, Mar. 1856	Thomas	----, Honora	M	
Devin, Thomas	9, July 1857	Thomas	----, Hannah	M	
Devine, Ann	19, Sept 1859	Thomas	Connolly, Joanne	Z	
Devine, Catherine	5, June 1853	James	Connor, Mary	B	293
Devine, Edward	28, May 1854	Edward	Cramer, Bridget	P	83
Devine, Eugene	15, July 1855	Eugene	Keegan, Helen	V	25
Devine, Joanne	12, May 1850	James	Connor, Mary	B	202
Devine, John	29, Aug. 1855	John	Farren, Mary	E	311
Devine, John	17, Sept 1855	M.	Reynolds, Bridget	E	316
Devine, Margaret	26, Dec. 1852	James	Connor, Mary	B	279
Devine, Mary Ellen	5, Oct. 1851	Owen	Keegan, Ellen	E	348
Devine, Timothy	24, July 1850	Michael	O'Neil, Johanna	E	234
Devinery, John	29, Oct. 1854	Michael	McHale, Bridget	B	7
Deviney, John	26, Apr. 1857	Edward	Cremer, Bridget	P	211
Devinn, James	22, Jan. 1856	Michael	Brian, Ellen	B	24
Devinny, Margaret	29, June 1856	Michael	McHall, Bridget	B	30
Devinny, Michael	29, June 1856	Michael	McHall, Bridget	B	30
Devir, Wilhelm	19, Nov. 1858	Wilhelm	Hagerty, Catharina	K	
Devitt, John Francis	10, Mar. 1853	Patrick	----, Catherine	E	71
Devitt, John Francis	12, June 1853	Thomas	----, Margaret	E	97
Devitt, Martin	12, June 1853	Thomas	----, Margaret	E	97
Devitt, Mary Ann	13, Jan. 1856	Anthony	McAndrew, Margaret	P	166
Devlin, Catherine	1, Aug. 1855	Lawrence	----, Ann	E	305
Devlin, Christopher	21, Feb. 1857	Lawrence	Flynn, Ann	E	435
Devlin, Edward	16, Apr. 1854	Edward	----, Ann	U	
Devlin, Elizabeth	16, Mar. 1856	James	Noles, Bridget	E	350
Devoti, Catharina	16, Dec. 1850	Angelo	----, Catharina	C	
Devoto, Edward	9, Mar. 1856	Angelo	Carotto, Theresa	B	26
Devoto, James Bartholomew Aloysius	22, Aug. 1858	Angelo	Corotto, Theresa	B	63
Devoto, John	18, Aug. 1851	John B.	Longinotti, Augustina	B	239
Devoto, John Baptist	6, Nov. 1859	Louis	Mena, Maria	B	83
Devoto, John Louis	4, Apr. 1854	Angelo	Carotta, Theresa	B	312
Devoto, Maria	23, Feb. 1859	Johan	Teritt, Rosa	K	
Devoto, Maria Catharina	12, Nov. 1854	Giovanni B.	Longinotti, Augustina	K	
Devoto, Maria Magdalena	19, Dec. 1858	Giovanni	Longinotti, Augustina	D	126
Devoto, Mary	21, Sept 1856	J. Baptist	Longinatti, Augustina	B	34
Devoto, Mary Louise	3, Apr. 1853	John B.	Longinotti, Augustina	B	287
Devoto, Mary Magdalene Philomena	1, Jan. 1850	Angelo	Caretto, Theresa	B	193
Devoto, Mary Rose	17, Apr. 1853	Louis	Mena, Mary	B	288
Devoto, Nicolaus Stephan Aloysius	13, July 1852	Angelo	Carotto, Theresa	B	263
Devoto, Peter Bartholomew	25, Aug. 1857	Giovanni	Ferretta, Rosa	K	

Name of Child	Date of Baptism	Father	Mother	Church	Page
Devry, John	29, Mar. 1853	John	----, Mary	M	
Dewald, Clara Regina	3, July 1859	Philipp	Doebker, Catharina	T	
Dewald, Heinrich	31, July 1853	Jacob	Schuler, Margaretha	D	397
Dewald, Samuel Edward	23, June 1858	Jacob	----, Kerry	D	113
Dewald, Susanna	24, Dec. 1858	Mathias	Rad, Elisabeth	F	
Dewer, David	5, Aug. 1855	David	----, Ellen	M	
Dewey, Julia	17, Oct. 1852	Edgar	----, Virginia	E	29
Dewis, Paulina	19, June 1859	Carl	Popp, Maria	D	140
Dey, Maria Angelina Clara	6, Feb. 1854	Caspar	----, Elisabeth	A	
Dey, Maria Catharina	21, Mar. 1851	J. Caspar	Ostendorp, Elisabeth	J	10
Deyer, Emilia	6, Nov. 1859	Johan	Weber, Theresa	C	
Deyer, Johan	20, July 1856	Johan	Weber, Theresa	C	
Deyer, Johan Herman	28, Aug. 1853	Johan	Weber, Theresa	C	
Deyer, Maria	25, Apr. 1855	Johan	Weber, Theresa	C	
Deyer, Rosina	22, Feb. 1858	Johan	Weber, Theresa	C	
Dezus, Charles Eubert	6, Nov. 1853	Eubert	----, Mary Josephine	E	141
Dibrauf, Johan Georg	9, Mar. 1851	Francis	Fress, Cunigunda	D	256
Dick, Adolph	1, June 1856	Jacob	Pfeifer, Margaretha	C	
Dick, Anna Maria	27, Aug. 1856	Joseph	Fiet, Catharina	D	65
Dick, Bernard Heinrich	4, July 1851	Heinrich	Fenker, Maria Gesina	F	
Dick, Herman Heinrich	18, Nov. 1853	J. Herman	Abel, Maria Adelheid	D	415
Dick, Joseph Heinrich	28, Aug. 1856	Herman H.	Abel, Maria Adelheid	D	65
Dick, Maria Elisabeth	6, Sept 1851	J. Herman	Abel, Maria Adelheid	D	281
Dick, Maria Elisabeth	3, Jan. 1859	Joseph	Faeth, Catharina	D	128
Dick, Paul	3, Feb. 1857	Johan	----, Jacobina	D	78
Dick, Susanna Louisa	3, Apr. 1859	Jacob	Pfeiffer, Margaretha	F	
Dickenson, John Howard	27, June 1852	Charles H.	Hill, Rosanne	P	23
Dickenson, Rosa Anna Amelia	23, June 1850	Charles E.	Dickeson, Rosa Ann	K	
Dickhaus, Anna Maria Catharina	29, Nov. 1853	Friedrich	Gosemeyer, Friedricka	L	
Dickhaus, Anna Maria Elisabeth	29, Nov. 1856	Friedrich	Huelskamp, Maria	L	
Dickhaus, Bernard	18, Apr. 1858	Bernard	Husman, Gertrud	Q	27
Dickhaus, Catharina Elisabeth	4, July 1859	Bernard	Husman, Gertrud	Q	32
Dickhaus, Clement	21, Dec. 1856	Bernard	Husman, Gertrud	Q	18
Dickhaus, Elisabeth	26, Sept 1851	Heinrich	Emke, Elisabeth	D	284
Dickhaus, Johan Bernard Friedrich	21, Aug. 1851	Friedrich	Kosemeyer, Friedricka	C	
Dickhaus, M. Catharina Elisabeth	25, Mar. 1852	Friedrich	Middendorf, Bernardina	L	
Dickhaus, Margaretha Francisca	4, Jan. 1852	A. Clemens	Hockman, Catharina	D	301
Dickhaus, Maria Elisabeth	3, Jan. 1856	Friedrich	Gossemeyer, Friedricka	L	
Dickhaus, Maria Francisca	1, Aug. 1854	Bernard	Husmann, M. Gertrud	L	
Dickhaus, Maria Magdalena	14, Feb. 1858	Friedrich	Gosemeyer, Catharina	L	
Dickhof, Gerhard Joseph	15, Aug. 1859	Joseph	F---, Elisabeth	D	144
Dickhof, Johan Heinrich	9, Dec. 1854	Heinrich	Weber, Elisabeth	F	
Dickhof, Johan Heinrich	27, July 1857	Johan	Kipp, Elisabeth	F	
Dickhof, Johan Heinrich Joseph	27, Feb. 1855	Bernard	Glins, Elisabeth	F	
Dickhof, Maria Anna Elisabeth	14, July 1859	Heinrich	Weber, Elisabeth	T	
Dickhof, Maria Christina	25, Feb. 1855	Johan	Kipp, Elisabeth	F	
Dickhof, Maria Elisabeth	15, Sept 1852	Johan	Kipp, Maria Elisabeth	J	18
Dickhofer, Anna Maria Catharina	3, Feb. 1851	Bernard	Gliens, Elisabeth	D	252
Dickhoff, Anna Maria	5, May 1850	Heinrich	Timmers, Elisabeth	C	
Dickhoff, Anna Maria	14, Apr. 1850	Johan	Kipp, Elisabeth	D	209
Dickhoff, Bernard Joseph	10, Oct. 1852	Joseph	Timmes, Elisabeth	C	
Dickhoff, Johan Bernard	7, Sept 1851	Heinrich	Webers, Elisabeth	F	
Dickhoff, Johan Heinrich	31, July 1856	Joseph	Vieth, Elisabeth	A	
Dickhoff, Maria Elisabeth	27, May 1853	Bernard	Glins, Elisabeth	F	
Dickkemper, Johan Theodor	15, Dec. 1854	Heinrich	Peistrup, Maria Anna	L	
Dickkemper, Maria Christina	2, June 1856	Heinrich	Beistrup, Anna M.	L	
Dickle, Martin	30, July 1858	James	Nolan, Catherine	E	553
Dickman, Albert Julius	13, July 1851	Herman H.	Feldman, Rebecca Maria	D	272
Dickman, Anna Maria Gertrud	15, Dec. 1851	Heinrich	Rixman, Maria Elisabeth	D	297

Name of Child	Date of Baptism	Father	Mother	Church	Page
Dickman, Bernard	25, Oct. 1858	J. Heinrich	Hackman, Dorothea	A	
Dickman, Bernard Ludwig	12, Dec. 1858	Martin	Tebelman, Margaretha	A	
Dickman, Carl Herman	24, Jan. 1858	Anton	Pulskamp, Maria Catharina	A	
Dickman, Carl Richard	17, Dec. 1856	Herman H.	Feldman, Maria	D	74
Dickman, Catharina Bernardina	30, June 1852	Bernard	Lürs, Maria	A	
Dickman, Catharina Maria	21, July 1859	J. Mathias	We---, Maria Elisabeth	D	142
Dickman, Eberhard Francis	9, Mar. 1851	Mathias	Hortman, Dina	A	
Dickman, Francis Aloysius	12, Mar. 1854	Herman H.	Feldman, Maria Rebecca	D	6
Dickman, Francis Ferdinand	17, Sept 1856	Martin	Tebelman, Margaretha	A	
Dickman, Helena	4, July 1857	J. Heinrich	Hackman, Dorothea	A	
Dickman, Johan Heinrich	5, July 1854	Bernard	Luers, Anna Maria	A	
Dickman, Johan Heinrich Gerhard	22, Feb. 1859	J. Heinrich	Kle---, Anna Maria	D	132
Dickman, Maria Anna	8, Oct. 1859	Herman H.	Feldman, Maria Crescentia	D	148
Dickman, Maria Carolina	22, Mar. 1858	Francis	Franken, Catharina	J	46
Dickman, Maria Catharina	24, Jan. 1857	Ludwig	Westerheide, Gertrud	A	
Dickman, Maria Eva	9, Apr. 1854	Jacob	Saluti, Carolina	D	8
Dickman, Philomena	9, Apr. 1855	Francis	Franke, Catharina	K	
Dickmann, Anna Catharina	25, Aug. 1850	Francis H.	Himmelmeyer, Anna M.	L	
Dickmann, Anna Maria	19, Dec. 1853	Francis	Hemmermeister, Anna M.	L	
Dickmann, Anna Maria	12, Jan. 1852	Wilhelm	Kloevekorn, Anna Maria	L	
Dickmann, Anna Maria	4, Jan. 1857	Wilhelm	Kloevekorn, Maria Agnes	F	
Dickmann, Anna Maria	5, Jan. 1854	Wilhelm	Kloevekorn, Maria Anna	L	
Dickmann, Anna Maria Elisabeth	24, Jan. 1856	Joseph	Brockmann, Gertrud	L	
Dickmann, August Bernard	4, July 1853	Bernard	Munstermann, Sophia	L	
Dickmann, Bernard	28, Apr. 1856	Francis	Himmelmeyer, Anna M.	L	
Dickmann, Francis Bernard	11, Nov. 1858	Bernard J.	Lammers, Elisabeth Catharina	C	
Dickmann, Johan Anton	3, Mar. 1856	Bernard	Munstermann, Sophia	L	
Dickmann, Johan Bernard Wessel	9, June 1851	J. Heinrich	Kellermann, Anna M.	L	
Dickmann, Johan Ferdinand	27, June 1852	Francis	Himmelmeyer, Anna M.	L	
Dickmann, Joseph	19, Jan. 1859	Bernard	Muenstermann, M. Sophia	F	
Dickmann, M. Catharina Henrietta	24, Sept 1856	J. Heinrich	Herbermann, Anna M.	L	
Dickmann, Maria Catharina Johanna	29, July 1855	Christian	Schafendick, Elisabeth	C	
Dickmann, Maria Louisa	19, June 1850	Bernard	Munstermann, Sophia	C	
Dickoner, Michael	5, June 1857	Valentin	Schlo--, Margaretha	D	86
Diebold, Anna Regina	2, Dec. 1852	Michael	Würz, Regina	D	359
Diebold, Anton	20, June 1858	Carl	Ott, Maria	J	46
Diebold, Francis Anton	30, Jan. 1859	Ebrenz	Jäger, Magdalena	D	130
Diebold, Martha	3, Dec. 1858	Michael	Würz, Regina	D	125
Diebold, Rosina Philomena	2, Jan. 1852	Jacob	Dietsch, Marianna	D	300
Diebolt, Johan	14, Nov. 1858	Johan	Merk, Maria	C	
Diebrauf, Johan	25, Dec. 1853	Francis	Fres, Cunigunda	D	421
Dieckhaus, Anna Catharina	25, Nov. 1858	Friedrich	Huelskamp, Anna	L	
Dieckhaus, Maria Gertrud	7, Apr. 1850	Bernard	Hausmann, Gertrud	L	
Dieckman, Bernard Wilhelm	20, Nov. 1856	Heinrich	Sicker, Gesina	A	
Dieckman, Ludwig Francis	22, Mar. 1857	Francis	Klein, Maria	H	
Dieckman, Maria Elisa	4, July 1850	Wilhelm	----, Maria Elisabeth	A	
Dieckman, Martin Ferdinand	30, May 1858	Francis	Kleine, Anna Maria	H	
Dieckmann, Anna Maria	11, Oct. 1857	Francis	Himmelmeier, Maria A.	L	
Dieckmann, Catharina Henrietta	10, Aug. 1853	Gerhard	Schafesdick, Elisabeth	C	
Dieckmann, Christoph Joseph	23, Nov. 1855	Joseph	Lammers, Elisabeth	C	
Dieckmann, Francis Heinrich	17, Aug. 1854	Heinrich	Kellermann, Anna M.	C	
Dieckmann, Gerhard Heinrich	25, Apr. 1853	Gerhard H.	Brehe, A.M. Sophia	L	
Dieckmann, Gerhard Joseph	6, June 1851	Gerhard	Schafendick, Elisabeth	C	
Dieckmann, Herman Heinrich	4, July 1855	Anton	Pulskamp, Catharina	C	
Dieckmann, Johan Heinrich Adolph	29, July 1852	J. Heinrich	Kellermann, Anna Maria	C	
Dieckmann, Maria Anna	10, Sept 1857	Gerhard	Schaferdick, Elisabeth	C	
Dieckmann, Maria Sophia Louisa	24, May 1858	Gerhard H.	Breke, Sophia	L	
Diedmeyer, Alexander	26, Dec. 1859	Michael	Sauer, Richardina	N	
Diedmeyer, Genofeva	2, Oct. 1853	Michael	Sauer, Richarda	N	16

Name of Child	Date of Baptism	Father	Mother	Church	Page
Diedmeyer, Johan	6, Dec. 1857	Michael	Sauer, Richarda	N	
Diedmeyer, Michael	28, Oct. 1855	Michael	Sauer, Richarda	N	
Diedrich, Johan Carl	9, May 1858	Jacob	Al---, Catharina	D	110
Diefenbach, Phillipina	24, July 1859	Peter	Weiri, Catharina	S	
Diehl, Catharina	10, Oct. 1852	Johan	Inn, Theresa	D	352
Diehl, Clara	28, Aug. 1853	Johan	Becker, Sophia	D	402
Diehl, Johan	16, Aug. 1851	Johan	Becker, Sophia	D	278
Dieker, Anna Catharina	25, July 1855	J. Herman	Vögeding, Adelheid	D	39
Dieker, Maria Catharina Philomena	24, Apr. 1859	Wilhelm	Grobman, Maria Catharina	D	136
Diekhaus, Maria Catharina	15, Aug. 1852	Bernard	Husmann, M. Gertrud	L	
Diekman, Matthias Ludwig	11, May 1854	Mathias	Fortman, Bernardina	A	
Dieman, Maria Joseph Anton	13, Dec. 1857	J. Heinrich	Burger, Bernardina	N	
Diener, Anna Magdalena	3, Jan. 1858	Johan	Ott, Maria	F	
Diener, Mary Elizabeth	14, Sept 1856	Joseph	Kraus, Margaret	T	
Dieners, Peter	25, Apr. 1853	Anton	Kinklin, Barbara	D	382
Diepold, Francisca	4, Nov. 1856	Michael	Wurz, Regina	D	71
Diepold, Genofeva	12, Oct. 1856	Lawrence	Jaeger, Magdalena	D	69
Diepold, Georg	24, Nov. 1853	Lawrence	Jäger, Magdalena	D	416
Diepold, Heinrich	13, Oct. 1850	Michael	Würz, Regina	D	237
Diepold, Johan	29, Feb. 1852	Lawrence	Jaeger, Magdalena	D	310
Diepolt, Rosa Margaretha	30, Aug. 1854	Michael	Würz, Regina	D	16
Dier, Susanna Gertrud	7, Mar. 1856	Johan	Hoffman, Anna Maria	A	
Dieringer, Anton	16, Mar. 1856	Marc	Köllman, Antonia	D	54
Dieringer, Catharina	5, June 1853	Marc	Killmeier, Antonia	D	388
Dieringer, Georg Nicolaus	7, Feb. 1858	Marc	Kollman, Antonia	D	105
Dieringer, Jacob	5, June 1853	Marc	Killmeier, Antonia	D	388
Dieringer, Johan	25, Dec. 1854	Coelestin	Worz, Maria Agatha	D	25
Dieringer, Maria Agatha	27, July 1856	Coelestin	Schroeder, Maria Cunigunda	D	63
Dieringer, Maria Carolina	28, Mar. 1858	Coelestin	Schneider, Cunigunda	D	108
Dieringer, Maria Catharina	5, June 1853	Coelestin	Wörz, Maria Agatha	D	388
Dierker, Anna Maria	15, Nov. 1856	Dietrich	Dierker, Maria Catharina	A	
Dierker, Anna Maria Catharina	21, Oct. 1858	J. Dietrich	Dierker, Maria Catharina	A	
Dierker, Johan Bernard	29, Sept 1854	Dietrich	Dierker, Catharina	A	
Dierker, Maria Catharina	29, Oct. 1852	J. Heinrich	Dierker, Anna M. Catharina	A	
Dierker, Maria Elisabeth	24, Oct. 1850	Dietrich	Dierker, Maria Catharina	A	
Dierkers, Maximillian Albert	2, Mar. 1858	Herman B.	Koch, Louisa	F	
Dierks, Heinrich	30, Dec. 1851	B. Herman	Meiners, Catharina	K	
Diers, Herman Heinrich	6, Feb. 1851	Herman H.	Warms, Margaretha	D	252
Diersel, Catharina	30, Nov. 1856	Jacob	Bell, Maria	D	73
Diersi, Jacob	14, May 1854	Jacob	Bell, Anna Maria	D	10
Dietchen, Philomena Henrietta	20, Apr. 1854		adult - 72 years old	K	
Dietmeier, Joseph	24, Apr. 1850	Michael	Sauer, Richardina	C	
Dietmeyer, Bernard	28, Dec. 1851	Michael	Sauer, Richardina	C	
Dietrich, Andreas	4, Dec. 1859	Johan	Meiser, Anna	R	
Dietrich, August Gottlieb	2, Jan. 1859	Gottlieb	Simering, Margaretha	C	
Dietrich, Carolina Cecilia	1, Apr. 1850	Clemens	Walhuser,	L	
Dietrich, Carolina Josephina Cath.	18, Mar. 1855	Mathias	Fest, Catharina	F	
Dietrich, Carolina Magdalena	20, July 1850	Mathias	Fuerst, Catharina	F	
Dietrich, Francis Anton	4, Feb. 1852	Jacob	Reinwald, Regina	D	305
Dietrich, Joseph	14, Nov. 1858	Samuel	Schmitt, Magdalena	K	
Dietrich, Maria Catharina	14, Nov. 1858	Samuel	Schmitt, Magdalena	K	
Dietrich, Mayer August	9, Jan. 1853	Robert	Troy, Bridget	B	281
Dietrich, Sophia	23, May 1858	Robert	Troy, Bridget	B	59
Dietz, Catharina Elisabeth	25, May 1851	Heinrich	Mont, Bernardina	L	
Dietz, Louisa Anna	31, May 1852	Friedrich	Wolf, Margaretha	K	
Diezer, Catharina Elisabeth	16, Feb. 1851	Mathias	Efelein, Kunigunda	F	
Diffley, Bernard	28, May 1854	Edward	Radigan, Joanne	R	
Difley, Mary	20, Nov. 1859	James	Daly, Mary	B	84
Diggens, Mary	10, Dec. 1850	Terence	----, Catherine	E	266

Name of Child	Date of Baptism	Father	Mother	Church	Page
Digman, Elisabeth	22, Feb. 1852	Francis	Franke, Catharina	K	
Digman, Joseph	5, June 1853	Francis	Franke, Catharina	K	
Dignan, Ann	19, Sept 1858	Jeremiah	Crofton, Mary	P	261
Dignan, Ann Louise	18, July 1858	James	Maguire, Catherine	E	549
Dignan, Bernard	8, Apr. 1855	Patrick	Kenny, Ann	T	
Dignan, Catherine	18, June 1854	James	Dolan, Mary	P	85
Dignan, Catherine	6, Aug. 1854	James	McGuire, Catherine	E	214
Dignan, George	4, Sept 1859	John	Hester, Bridget	B	80
Dignan, Helen	15, Oct. 1854	Jeremiah	Crofton, Mary	P	100
Dignan, Hugh	29, July 1854	Hugh	Davy, Mary	V	15
Dignan, James	21, Sept 1856	James	McGuire, Catherine	E	399
Dignan, James	18, Jan. 1857	Patrick	Kinney, Ann	P	204
Dignan, James Edward	13, Apr. 1857	John	O'Connor, Mary	E	446
Dignan, John	14, Sept 1856	Jeremiah	Crofton, Mary	P	191
Dignan, Luke	13, July 1851	James	Doo---, Mary	P	10
Dignan, Margaret	6, Mar. 1853	Jeremiah	Crofton, Mary	P	37
Dignan, Mary	9, Mar. 1851	Jeremiah	Crofton, Mary	E	289
Dignan, Richard	22, Nov. 1851	Hugh	Daley, Mary	B	245
Dignan, Thomas	13, Mar. 1853	John	Joy, Bridget	R	
Dignan, Thomas	14, Feb. 1859	Patrick	Kenney, Ann	P	276
Dignan, William Mat.	31, July 1859	John	Donohue, Margaret	E	643
Dignum, Mary	6, Nov. 1853	John	----, Bridget	E	142
Dilgil, Charles	26, Dec. 1853	Michael	Griller, Mary	B	305
Diller, Mary	30, Nov. 1851	Berthold	Fox, Joanne	R	
Dillinger, Georg Ludwig Friedrich	5, Apr. 1859	Georg	Hunn---, Catharina	D	135
Dillman, Christoph Heinrich	13, Aug. 1854	Heinrich	Ruhe, Maria Agnes	A	
Dillman, Christoph Heinrich	16, July 1853	J. Christoph	Brinkman, Maria Anna	K	
Dillman, Johan Heinrich	14, Apr. 1857	J. Heinrich	Ruhe, Maria Agnes	A	
Dillon, Ann	26, Dec. 1853	John	Wagan, Margaret	E	155
Dillon, Bridget	6, Nov. 1853	Jeremiah	McGannon, Sarah	R	
Dillon, Ellen	28, Mar. 1852	John	Tobin, Catherine	E	396
Dillon, James	29, Nov. 1851	James	Ryan, Catherine	P	13c
Dillon, James	13, Dec. 1857	John	Vaughan, Margaret	V	43
Dillon, James	18, Apr. 1851	Thomas	Carty, Bridget	B	230
Dillon, Jane Ann	16, Mar. 1855	Jeremiah	McGannon, Sarah	R	
Dillon, Jeremiah	25, May 1856	Jeremiah	----, Sarah	R	
Dillon, John	29, June 1851	Christopher	Dillon, Margaret	B	235
Dillon, John	13, July 1856	John	Vaughan, Margaret	V	32
Dillon, John	26, Aug. 1854	Luke	Murphy, Honora	P	94
Dillon, John Joseph	22, Apr. 1854	John	Tobin, Catherine	B	313
Dillon, John Patrick	4, Jan. 1857	Christopher	Halpin, Elizabeth	B	38
Dillon, Margaret	29, July 1855	Michael	Moloney, Ellen	B	17
Dillon, Margaret	3, July 1853	Patrick	Fox, Joanne	R	
Dillon, Mary	29, Feb. 1852	Thomas	Constantin, Mary	R	
Dillon, Mary Ann	21, Sept 1850	John	----, Mary	E	248
Dillon, Mary Ann	5, Mar. 1854	John	Gorman, Ann	B	310
Dillon, Michael	25, July 1850	John	----, Mary	E	233
Dillon, Peter	26, Aug. 1854	Christopher	Halpin, Elizabeth	B	4
Dillon, Peter	15, Nov. 1850	Peter	Camiff, Margaret	M	
Dillon, Peter Thomas	22, Feb. 1852	Peter	----, Joanne	M	
Dillon, Richard	24, Aug. 1853	Patrick	Haley, Bridget	P	49
Dimmick, Coelestin	22, Sept 1850	Wilhelm	Meyer, Josephina	J	6
Dimond, Susan	8, Dec. 1850	Patrick	----, Catherine	E	266
Dinan, William	16, Dec. 1850	William	Lawles, Margaret	E	268
Dineen, Dennis	27, July 1851	Dennis	Murphy, Abigail	B	237
Dinger,	28, Nov. 1858	Joseph	----, Margaretha	T	
Dinger, Albert	5, July 1857	Leonard	Deutsch, Sabina	D	89
Dinger, Carolina	13, Oct. 1851	August	Mayer, Catharina	D	287
Dinger, Catharina	2, Oct. 1853	Leonard	Deutsch, Sabina	D	408

Name of Child	Date of Baptism	Father	Mother	Church	Page
Dinger, Christoph	30, June 1854	Joseph	Kraus, Margaretha	F	
Dinger, Leonard	29, July 1855	Leonard	Deutsch, Sabina	D	39
Dinger, Magdalena	8, Feb. 1852	Bernard	Teitschlert, Sabina	D	306
Dinger, Maria Magdalena	2, Sept 1850	August	Maier, Catharina	D	231
Dingers, Maria Anna	30, Dec. 1858		Dingers, Magdalena	T	
Dinies, Christina Philomena	22, Sept 1850	Martin	Burger, Veronica	D	233
Dinkel, Elisabeth	10, July 1859	Stephan	Gri---, Margaretha	D	141
Dinnies, Elisabeth Amalia	15, May 1853	Martin	Berger, Veronica	D	385
Dinnies, Jacob Aloysius	28, Nov. 1850	J. Heinrich	Enneser, Anna Maria	D	244
Dinsch, Anna Maria Louisa	8, Nov. 1854	Johan	Koch, Elisabeth	D	21
Dinsmore, William	29, May 1853		adult	M	
Dippker, Johan Heinrich	3, Nov. 1850	B. Heinrich	Bohlke, Catharina Maria	K	
Dirfler, Friedrich	4, Apr. 1852	Johan	Weller, Catharina	D	315
Dirig, Josephina Ottilia	15, Feb. 1852	Joseph	Reidt, Anna Maria	F	
Dirk, Johan Georg	28, Dec. 1856	David	Hel---, Catharina Maria	D	75
Dirke, Anna Catharina	20, Nov. 1859	Bernard	Flennink, Lena	C	
Dirker, Martin	15, Dec. 1854	Heinrich	Sprengelmeyer, Elisabeth	D	24
Dirkers, A. Maria Louisa Catharina	13, June 1854	Bernard	Koch, Elisa	F	
Dirkers, Bernard Friedrich Carl	14, Oct. 1855	Bernard	Kock, Elisa	F	
Dirkers, Franz	4, June 1857	Heinrich	Sprengelmeier, Elisabeth	L	
Dirkes, Anna Maria Elisabeth	4, Apr. 1853	Bernard	Schroeder, Bernardina	L	
Dirkes, Caspar Friedrich	4, Aug. 1853	Heinrich	Sprengelmeier, Elisabeth	D	398
Dirkes, Friedrich Wilhelm	22, Apr. 1850	Friedrich	Funcke, Elisabeth	C	
Dirkes, Johan Joseph	17, Dec. 1858	Herman	Greiwe, Clara	L	
Dirks, Bernard Heinrich	7, Oct. 1853	Bernard	Meiners, A. Catharina	L	
Dirks, Johan Bernard	13, Dec. 1855	Bernard	Meiners, Catharina	L	
Dirks, Maria Anna	28, Sept 1854	Gerhard	Tiemann, Gertrud	C	
Dirksen, Anna Elisabeth	4, Oct. 1856	Gerhard H.	Tiemann, Gertrud	L	
Dirksen, Johan Heinrich Friedrich	17, Apr. 1853	Johan	Ree, Gertrud	K	
Dirksen, Maria Louisa	2, May 1858	Heinrich	Tiemann, Gertrud	L	
Dirksmeyer, Joseph Francis	24, Jan. 1850	J. Bernard	Menge, Anna Maria	D	201
Dirr, Georg	25, June 1856	Ludwig	Minder, Theresa	F	
Dirr, Herman Bernard	6, Apr. 1858	Ludwig	Minder, Theresa	F	
Dirr, Joseph	30, Sept 1854	Ludwig	Minder, Theresa	F	
Dirxmeyer, Bernard Jacob	18, July 1851	Bernard	Menke, Maria	D	273
Disch, Heinrich	25, May 1856	Daniel	Laut, Elisabeth	F	
Disching, Johan Adolf	26, June 1853	Raymond	Rister, Maria Anna	D	391
Dischinger, Carolina Adelheid	24, June 1858	Raymond	Rister, Maria Agatha	D	113
Dischinger, Oscar Raymund	9, Mar. 1856	Raymond	Rister, Maria Agatha	D	53
Diskin, Bridget	9, Apr. 1854	John	Winsey, Mary	B	312
Disman, Maria Anna	28, Sept 1858	Heinrich	Störig, Friedrica	K	
Disnan, John James	10, Feb. 1851	John	Early, Catherine	B	225
Diss, Amalia	21, June 1857	Ludwig	Schaefer, Margaretha	C	
Diss, Emil Ludwig	1, Feb. 1852	Ludwig	Schaefer, Margaretha	F	
Diss, Ludwig Joseph	4, Sept 1853	Ludwig	Schaefer, Margaret	C	
Dissel, Anna Maria	9, Jan. 1853	Michael	Theres, Theresa	D	364
Disselhaus, Gerhard Christoph	20, June 1850	Christoph	Beumer, Maria Angela	D	218
Disser, Catherine	10, Nov. 1855	Peter	Racher, Margaret	R	
Disser, Rosina	5, Mar. 1854	Peter	Rachor, Margaret	R	
Dissert, Carolina	12, Dec. 1852	Paul	Abba, Rosina	K	
Dissinger, Margaretha Maria Gertrud	31, May 1853	Peter	Fischer, Philippina	K	
Disstaus, Johan Engelbert	19, Jan. 1855	Bernard	Lücken, Anna	D	27
Distel, Conrad	6, Jan. 1854	Conrad	Ei, Mina	C	
Distler, Anna Maria	23, May 1858	Johan	Zimmerman, Catharina	Q	28
Distler, Barbara	10, Aug. 1854	Johan	Zimmerman, Catharina	Q	4
Distler, Georg	19, Apr. 1857	Johan	Zimmerman, Catharina	Q	21
Distler, Maria Margaretha	28, Aug. 1859	Johan	Zimmerman, Catharina	Q	32
Distler, Mary	12, Mar. 1856	Johan	Zimmerman, Catharina	Q	13
Disz, Ludwig Andreas	2, Sept 1855	Ludwig	Schaefer, Margaretha	K	

Name of Child	Date of Baptism	Father	Mother	Church	Page
Disz, Maria Josephina	29, May 1859	Ludwig	Schaefer, Margaretha	C	
Diterich, Carl Joseph	18, Dec. 1859	Johan P.	Holden, Sarah A.	AA	
Dittman, Carolina	28, Dec. 1852	Jacob	Soluti, Carolina	D	362
Diva, Mary Helen	2, Aug. 1855	David	Mauricy, Alice	P	143
Divenney, Mary	11, May 1851	Daniel	Gurley, Ann	B	231
Diver, Joanne Mary	30, Aug. 1852	Daniel	----, Joanne	M	
Divine, Michael	22, Apr. 1855	James	O'Connor, Mary	B	14
Divine, Sarah Ann	29, Apr. 1855	Thomas	Nolan, Ann	R	
Dixon, Ellen	19, Apr. 1856	Patrick	Kenney, Catherine	E	360
Dixon, James	28, Jan. 1858	Alexander	----, Catherine	M	
Dixon, John	16, Oct. 1858	----	----, ----	P	263
Dixon, John	29, Dec. 1850	James	Carmody, Margaret	B	221
Dixon, Margaret Ann	15, Aug. 1853	Patrick	Keiny, Catherine	B	297
Dixon, Michael	2, Oct. 1853	James	Carmody, Margaret	B	300
Dixon, Peter	18, Dec. 1859	Peter	Kennedy, Catherine	V	65
D-negna, John	22, Mar. 1851	Patrick	Sullivan, Bridget	B	227
Dobanto, Mathias	8, Aug. 1852	Peter	Schaefer, Elisabeth	D	342
Dobbely, Carolina	7, Sept 1856	Xavier	Brogger, Theresa	D	66
Döbben, Anna Christina Francisca	28, Feb. 1854	J. Joseph	Böckeling, Anna Catharina	D	5
Dobbes, Anna Maria Juliana	4, July 1858	J. Bernard	Cortes, Maria Agnes	F	
Doben, Richard	9, July 1855	James	Sielbern, Mary	N	
Dodd, Ann Ellen	30, Oct. 1857	William	----, Cornelia	E	489
Dodd, Mary	2, Mar. 1856	Edward	----, Mary	E	348
Dodd, William	6, June 1858	Edward	Kelly, Mary	E	540
Dodds, Robert Henry	3, Oct. 1858	John	Hiland, Bridget	P	262
Dodt, Bernard Joseph Clemens	24, Mar. 1851	Theodor C.	Wittkamp, Maria Anna	L	
Dodt, Catharina Philomena	13, May 1859	Clemens	Wittkamp, Elisabeth	L	
Dodt, Clemens Heinrich	3, June 1858	Clemens T.	Wittkamp, Elisabeth	L	
Dodt, Johan Bernard Joseph	20, Mar. 1857	Bernard H.	Schulz, Maria Anna	L	
Dodt, Johan Heinrich	25, Oct. 1851	Bernard H.	Schulz, M. Angela	L	
Dodt, Johan Heinrich	7, Mar. 1858	Heinrich	Hiller, Louisa	K	
Dodt, Maria Anna Friedricka	6, Oct. 1850	Heinrich	Schulze, Anna Maria	L	
Dodt, Maria Antonetta	19, Jan. 1853	Bernard H.	Schulze, Maria Anna	L	
Dodt, Maria Bernardina	18, Feb. 1856	Bernard	Schulz, Maria Anna	L	
Dodt, Maria Bernardina Theresa	17, Apr. 1856	Heinrich	Hille, Louisa	L	
Dodt, Maria Elisabeth	10, Jan. 1850	J. Heinrich	Schittmeier, Agnes	K	
Dodt, Maria Elisabeth Josephina	23, Apr. 1855	Clemens	Wittkamp, M. Elisabeth	L	
Dodt, Maria Elisabeth Mathilda	1, Nov. 1854	B.H.	Schulze, M. Anna	L	
Dodt, Maria Elisabeth Matilda	24, Apr. 1854	Clemens	Wittkamp, M. Elisabeth	L	
Dody, James	4, May 1856	Michael	Reilly, Mary	P	178
Doebel, Margaretha	2, Feb.1857	Christoph	----, Barbara	D	78
Doecker, Franz Heinrich	23, Nov. 1851	Francis	Brink, Johanna	F	
Doeggeler, Maria Adelheid	17, Sept 1852	Johan H.	Naber, Maria Engel	F	
Doeke, Johan Franz	18, Jan. 1850	Johan	Baengemann, Anna	F	
Doeker, Gerhard Heinrich	12, May 1854	Francis	Brink, Maria	F	
Doell, Elisabeth	19, June 1853	Nicolaus	König, Catharina	D	390
Doell, Francis Joseph	8, Dec. 1850	Nicolaus	König, Catharina	D	246
Doell, Wilhelm	13, Apr. 1856	Nicolaus	König, Catharina	D	56
Doemmling, Maria Margaretha	23, July 1850	J. Andreas	Silzmann, Josepha	F	
Doenbald, Gerhard Heinrich	28, Sept 1853	Christoph	Hempen, Anna Gesina	F	
Doenewald, Gerhard	14, Nov. 1859	Christoph	Hempe, Anna Gesina	T	
Doennewald, Gerhard Heinrich	4, Sept 1857	Christoph	Hempe, Anna Gesina	F	
Doennewald, Theodor	4, Sept 1857	Christoph	Hempe, Anna Gesina	F	
Doennewalel, Johan Bernard	20, Mar. 1852	Christoph	Hempen, A. Gesina	L	
Doepker, Francis	1, June 1852	Friedrich	Foderlange, Catharina	C	
Doepker, Francisca	30, Aug. 1858	Ferdinand	Tieke, Josephina	T	
Doepker, Heinrich Ferdinand	18, June 1856	Ferdinand	Thiebe, Josephina	C	
Doepker, Johan Franz	28, Dec. 1854	Francis	Messmann, Elisabeth	L	
Doepp, Elisabeth	16, May 1858	Johan	Tochle--, Caecilia	D	111

Name of Child	Date of Baptism	Father	Mother	Church	Page
Doepp, Georg Friedrich	17, May 1857	Johan	Kunz, Elisabeth	D	85
Do---er, Francis Carl Bartholomew	9, Nov. 1859	Gerhard J.	Sch----, Maria Margaretha	D	150
Doerenkamp, Anna Christina	30, Dec. 1857	Conrad	Nordmeier, M. Theresa	F	
Doerle, Catharina	18, Jan. 1857	Mathias	Faller, Walleriana	L	
Doerle, Joseph	12, Feb. 1855	Mathias	Voller, Valeria	F	
Doerle, Philomena	28, Aug. 1859	Mathias	Faller, Waleria	D	145
Doerr, Anna Barbara	7, June 1857	Nicolaus	Morio, Barbara	C	
Doerr, Philipp	16, July 1854	Nicolaus	Moran, Barbara	D	14
Doerr, Philipp	27, Feb. 1853	Nicolaus	Morio, Barbara	D	374
Doersch, Agnes	29, June 1856	Johan	Bedsold, Cunigunda	F	
Doffer, Helena	17, July 1853	Michael	Kynen, Helena	K	
Doffner, Rosina	28, Jan. 1855	John	Gold, Louise	N	26
Dogherty, Ann	1, Apr. 1859	John	----, Jane	E	615
Dogherty, Margaret	29, Sept 1850	Bernard	McBride, Cecilia	B	215
Dogherty, Mary	11, Nov. 1855	James	----, Margaret	E	326
Dogherty, William Anthony	31, Aug. 1856	William	Duklo, Magdalena	J	38
Dohen, Elisabeth	25, Dec. 1858	Patrick	Schlattery, Joanne	U	
Doherty, Bridget	11, May 1851	Charles	Glasco, Ann	E	307
Doherty, Bridget	26, June 1855	Charles	Lynch, Sarah	E	296
Doherty, Catherine	7, Dec. 1853	Charles	Lynch, Sarah	E	150
Doherty, Catherine	5, May 1856	Thomas	Cummings, Julia	E	365
Doherty, Cornelius	14, Apr. 1854	Edward	Gillespie, Bridget	E	182
Doherty, Dennis	12, Dec. 1852	John	Murphy, Sally	E	43
Doherty, Edward	1, Nov. 1857	Cornelius	Sullivan, Catherine	B	51
Doherty, Edward	3, July 1857	James	Walsh, Rebecca	B	46
Doherty, Honora	8, Oct. 1858	Charles	Lynch, Sarah	E	567
Doherty, James	22, Jan. 1856	Patrick	----, Ann	E	339
Doherty, John	31, Aug. 1856	Edward	----, Bridget	E	395
Doherty, John	2, Jan. 1853	James	Walsh, Julia	R	
Doherty, John Francis	7, Dec. 1856	James	Burke, Margaret	V	35
Doherty, Margaret	14, Aug. 1859	John	----, Margaret	E	647
Doherty, Margaret	26, Sept 1858	Michael	McGartley, Ann	E	564
Doherty, Margaret Ann	22, Oct. 1854	John	Gallagher, Mary	B	6
Doherty, Margaret Jane	1, Dec. 1859	James	Burke, Margaret	V	64
Doherty, Mark	1, Jan. 1855	James	Gough, Mary	B	9
Doherty, Mary	21, Feb. 1857	Charles	Lynch, Sarah	E	435
Doherty, Mary Frances	15, Sept 1855	George	Boyle, Mary	E	315
Doherty, Mary Frances	26, Nov. 1856	George A.	----, Mary J.	E	416
Doherty, Mary Helen	21, Nov. 1858	Nicolaus	Commerford, Elizabeth	E	580
Doherty, Michael	2, Sept 1855	John	Murphy, Sally	E	313
Doherty, Nicolaus	24, Feb. 1856	Nicolaus	Commerford, Elizabeth	E	346
Doherty, Sarah	12, Sept 1858	Michael	Langan, Ann	B	64
Doherty, Sarah Ann	26, Sept 1858	John	Baxter, Mary	E	564
Doherty, Susan	3, Nov. 1858	Edward	Gillespy, Bridget	E	575
Doherty, Thomas	31, May 1857	James	----, Joanne	R	
Doherty, Thomas	28, Jan. 1857	John	Gallagher, Mary	B	39
Doherty, Thomas	30, Jan. 1856	Thomas	Ryan, Bridget	E	341
Doherty, William	14, Mar. 1858	George	Boyle, Mary Jane	E	522
Doherty, William	20, Aug. 1854	John	Murphy, Sally	E	218
Dohne, Carl Ferdinand	24, Dec. 1851	Carl	Brokamp, Lisette	F	
Dohrer, Philipp Anton	29, July 1858	Philipp J.	Hartmann, Maria	F	
Döl, Margaretha	18, Dec. 1853	Johan	Inn, Theresa	D	421
Dolan, Charles	26, Nov. 1858	Francis	----, Eliza Mary	E	583
Dolan, Eliza	23, May 1855	John	King, Joanne	P	133
Dolan, Elizabeth Catherine	8, Apr. 1854	John	Bergan, Catherine	E	181
Dolan, James	1, July 1858	John	Galleger, Catherine	E	545
Dolan, James	16, Jan. 1852	Patrick	Cunningham, Ann	B	250
Dolan, James	12, Sept 1858	Patrick	McKenzie, Ann	B	64
Dolan, James John	10, July 1859	Andrew J.	----, Matilda	E	638

Name of Child	Date of Baptism	Father	Mother	Church	Page
Dolan, John Thomas	1, June 1856	Patrick	Kerisey, Ann	B	29
Dolan, Julia	14, Mar. 1853	Patrick	Cunningham, Ann	B	286
Dolan, Margaret	1, Nov. 1853	Michael	----, Alice	E	139
Dolan, Mary	17, May 1857	Patrick	Cunningham, Ann	T	
Dolan, Maurice Patrick	27, Jan. 1856	Patrick	Cunningham, Ann	T	
Dolan, Michael	9, Apr. 1854	Patrick	Cunningham, Ann	T	
Dolan, Patrick Henry	14, Nov. 1858	Patrick	Cunningham, Ann	T	
Dolan, Sarah Mary	19, Aug. 1857	John	Pap---, Matilda	E	475
Dolan, Stephan	1, Jan. 1853	John	----, Ann	M	
Dolan, Timothy	26, Dec. 1854	Patrick	Dolan, Catherine	P	112
Dold, Catharina	20, Apr. 1851	Matthias	Spruer, Catharina	C	
Dole, Carolina Helena	25, Oct. 1857	Francis	Wessendarp, Theresa	C	
Dolf, Bernard Heinrich	23, Oct. 1859	Heinrich	Rolef, Margaretha	D	149
Dolf, Maria Gertrud	14, Feb. 1856	Heinrich	Role, Margaretha	L	
Doll, Anna Catharina	25, June 1854	Samuel	Bauerle, Catharina	C	
Doll, Anna Maria	8, May 1853	Wendelin	Tups, Alberdina	K	
Doll, Carl	14, Dec. 1856	Jacob	Trestel, Apollonia	A	
Doll, Carl Georg	6, June 1852	Samuel	Bauerle, Catharina	C	
Doll, Charles	19, July 1857	Clemens	Aigner, Rosina	Q	23
Doll, Eva Maria	25, Sept 1854	Clemens	Aigner, Rosina	Q	5
Doll, Eva Rosa	26, May 1857	Georg	Dallo, Catharina	L	
Doll, Francisca	14, July 1856	Francis	Berger, Crescentia	L	
Doll, Georg	26, Dec. 1856	Georg J.	Spies, Rosina	D	75
Doll, Georg Jacob	2, Aug. 1853	J. Georg	Dalla, Catharina	L	
Doll, Johan	28, June 1852	J. Jacob	Spies, Rosina	D	327
Doll, Johan Friedrich	31, Jan. 1850	Friedrich	König, Barbara	C	
Doll, Johan Joseph	17, May 1856	Joseph	Bernz, Carolina	F	
Doll, Johan Ludwig	16, May 1852	Lazarus	Götz, Catharina	D	320
Doll, Joseph	7, June 1857	Caspar	Goetz, Catharina	D	86
Doll, Louisa Catharina	8, Apr. 1855	Jacob	Spies, Rosa	D	32
Doll, Ludwig Philipp	11, May 1856	Samuel	Beierle, Catharina	Q	14
Doll, Maria Elisabeth	10, Feb. 1854	Gabriel	Getz, Catharina	D	4
Doll, Maria Magdalena	5, Dec. 1850	Jacob	Spies, Rosa	D	245
Doll, Maria Rosalia	22, Mar. 1855	Wendel	Dubbs, Albertina	K	
Doll, Michael	1, Jan. 1853	Friedrich	Koenig, Barbara	L	
Doll, Nicolaus	9, Nov. 1851	Friedrich	Koenig, Barbara	C	
Doll, Wilhelm	30, Jan. 1859	Lazarus	Goetz, Catharina	C	
Dollatz, Maria Theresa	11, Mar. 1855	Joseph	Herman, Rosa	D	31
Dolle, Francis Heinrich Johan	21, Oct. 1857	Gerhard	Abel, Dina	C	
Dolle, Maria Elisabeth Philomena	6, May 1859	Philip	Diebolt, Philomena Agnes	U	
Dollenmeyer, Francis Sales	21, Mar. 1858	Francis	Schuler, Elisabeth	N	
Dollenmeyer, Georg Peter	6, Apr. 1856	Francis	Schuler, Elisabeth	N	
Doller, Anna Louisa	9, Aug. 1858	Jacob	Rauch, Magdalena	D	116
Doller, Christina	16, Mar. 1852	Jacob	Rauch, Magdalena	D	313
Doller, Georg	3, Feb. 1850	Jacob	Rauch, Magdalena	D	202
Doller, Johan Adam	5, June 1853	Georg	Weishaar, Christina	C	
Doller, Maria	16, July 1854	Leopold	Hoffman, Catharina	D	14
Doller, Maria Magdalena	5, Oct. 1853	Jacob	Rauch, Magdalena	D	409
Doller, Mathias	3, May 1855	Jacob	Rauch, Magdalena	D	34
Dollmaier, Georg	7, Feb. 1853	Mathias	Rosenberg, Anna Maria	D	370
Dollmaier, Johan	28, Aug. 1853	Francis	Schuler, Elisabeth	D	402
Dollman, Johan Peter	13, Dec. 1857	Johan	----, Francisca	R	
Dollman, John William	30, Dec. 1855	John	Mills, Frances	R	
Dollmann, Maria	23, Aug. 1857	Anton	Grone, Maria	C	
Dollmeier, Barbara Wilhelmina	21, Dec. 1856	Mathias	Obeloch, Barbara	D	74
Dollmer, Maria Philomena	16, Dec. 1851	Bernard	Linding, Maria Catharina	K	
Dollweber, Catharina	26, Dec. 1856	Dietrich	Franzmann, Maria	L	
Dollweber, Franz	9, Mar. 1852	Theodor	Franzmann, Maria	L	
Dollweber, Johan Heinrich	2, Mar. 1859	Theodor	Franksmann, A. Angela	L	

Name of Child	Date of Baptism	Father	Mother	Church	Page
Dollweber, Maria Elisabeth	23, Jan. 1854	Theodor	Franksmann, M. Elisabeth	L	
Dölman, Maria Rosanna	18, Apr. 1858	Anton	----, Catharina	K	
Dolphin, Ellen	21, Sept 1851	Michael	White, Catherine	E	346
Dolphin, Joanne	12, Feb. 1854	John	Kelly, Ann	E	167
Dolphin, John	6, May 1855	Michael	White, Catherine	E	284
Dolphin, Mary	13, Feb. 1853	Michael	----, Catherine	E	62
Dolphin, Michael	11, Feb. 1851	John	----, Ann	E	283
Dolton, Mary	21, May 1854	James	Atkinson, Joanne	P	83
Domacher, Johan	22, July 1855	Johan	Briger?, Agatha	D	39
Domigna?, Joseph	26, Mar. 1854	William	----, ----	B	311
Don---, William	21, Oct. 1855	Edward	Laughlin, Sarah	P	156
Donaghue, Ann	22, July 1857	John	Garry, Mary	P	218
Donaghue, Hugh	12, Sept 1858	Martin	Gibbons, Margaret	P	260
Donaghue, Julia Ann	11, July 1853	Martin	Flemming, Catherine	B	295
Donaghue, Juliane	15, July 1859	Martin	Hickey, Catherine	P	288
Donaghue, Margaret	22, July 1858	Michael	Reardon, Margaret	P	254
Donaher, Henry Edward	22, Apr. 1858	James	Kelley, Helen	E	531
Donahoe, Bridget	5, Jan. 1851	Charles	----, Mary	E	274
Donahoe, John	6, Dec. 1854	Patrick	Farrel, Bridget	E	245
Donahoe, Joseph	10, Dec. 1853	Patrick	Doherty, Unity	V	8
Donahue, Catherine	21, June 1857	Walter	Walsh, Alice	J	42
Donahue, Charles Henry	9, July 1854	Charles	Sheehan, Mary	P	87
Donahue, Cornelius	13, Apr. 1851	Daniel	Horrigan, Margaret	J	10
Donahue, Daniel	28, Aug. 1858	Michael	Horgin, Joanne	P	258
Donahue, Joanne	2, Oct. 1853	Florence	Spellman, Helen	P	53
Donahue, John	26, June 1853	Michael	Horgan, Joanne	P	45
Donahue, John	17, Aug. 1856	Michael	Riordon, Margaret	P	188
Donahue, Margaret Helen	9, July 1854	Charles	Sheehan, Mary	P	87
Donahue, Mary	29, Jan. 1855	James	Sullivan, Catherine	P	118
Donahue, Mary Ann	13, July 1858	Francis	Maloy, Mary	E	549
Donahue, Mary Ann	30, July 1854	Michael	Reardon, Margaret	P	90
Donahue, Mary Helen	4, May 1856	Walter	Walsh, Alice	J	36
Donahue, Michael	23, Apr. 1857	Michael	Harrigan, Joanne	P	211
Donahue, Patrick	22, Jan. 1854	John	Gary, Mary	P	66
Donahue, Patrick	24, July 1853	Patrick	Burke, Bridget	V	4
Donahue, Thomas	21, Oct. 1851	Philipp	Laughlin, Elizabeth	B	243
Donahue, William	13, Feb. 1853	Daniel	Horegon, Margaret	J	20
Donahue, William	22, Apr. 1855	Thomas	Herlehy, Mary	P	129
Donalon, Mary	24, Apr. 1852	Patrick	Donalon, Margaret	B	264
Donalty, Timothy	14, Sept 1851	Michael	Stapleton, Bridget	M	
Donat, Ann Phyllis	25, Apr. 1858	Lawrence	Diez, Walburga	H	
Donaty, Ann	27, Sept 1853	P.	Mahar, Ann	E	130
Donaty, Joanne	17, July 1853	Michael	----, Bridget	M	
Donavan, Daniel	18, Dec. 1855	Daniel	Linahan, Helen	R	
Donavan, Helen	12, Sept 1854	Patrick	Quinan, Helen	B	5
Dondaro, Maria	2, Oct. 1859	John	Cassessa?, Theresa	B	81
Donegan, Hugh	26, Dec. 1852	James	Ward, Catherine	P	32
Donelly, Martin	1, Nov. 1857	Martin	Mullen, Margaret	V	42
Donelon, Elizabeth Emilia	8, Feb. 1852	Michael	Picknell, Frances	B	252
Donelon, Patrick Joseph	26, Apr. 1857	James	----, Margaret	E	448
Donieken, Jacob	31, July 1853	Gerhard	Merten, Mary	L	
Don--kin, Martin	4, Jan. 1854	Martin	Gibbons, Mary	P	64
Donna--, Rebecca	3, Oct. 1854	Charles	Mallon, Ann	P	98
Donnacher, Francis Johan	3, Oct. 1858	Johan	Pops---, Laura	D	120
Donnelan, Margaret	3, Oct. 1852	Nicolaus	Walsh, Ellen	Q	2
Donnelen, Helen	14, June 1857	Nicolaus	Walsh, Helen	U	
Donnell, Thomas Bernard	29, May 1859	James	Connors, Ann	E	629
Donnelly, Alexander Levi	7, Mar. 1852	Anthony	----, Esther	M	
Donnelly, Alice Ann	10, Apr. 1850	Francis	Curran, Alice	B	200

Name of Child	Date of Baptism	Father	Mother	Church	Page
Donnelly, Caroline Elisabeth	11, July 1851	Edward	----, Catherine	E	322
Donnelly, Catherine	13, May 1859	Brian	Haily, Bridget	E	624
Donnelly, Catherine	19, July 1850	Charles	Mellon, Ann	B	208
Donnelly, Catherine	1, May 1859	Michael	Hoben, Mary	E	621
Donnelly, Catherine	3, Nov. 1853	Peter	----, Mary	E	140
Donnelly, Daniel	23, July 1852	Edward	----, Charlotte	B	265
Donnelly, Delia	31, July 1859	John	Brennan, Mary	P	290
Donnelly, Edward	26, Jan. 1851	Edward	Ah----, Charlotte A.	B	223
Donnelly, Edward Joseph	11, Dec. 1853	Edward	Esser, Henrietta	B	304
Donnelly, Frances Fanny	15, Oct. 1853	James	----, Margaret	E	134
Donnelly, Helen Mary	2, Mar. 1851	John	Clancy, Catherine	B	225
Donnelly, Henry	7, Oct. 1855	Anthony	Mayer, Esther	E	319
Donnelly, Joanne	3, Oct. 1858	Patrick	Donnelly, Margaret	P	262
Donnelly, Joanne	29, Apr. 1855	Thomas	----, Catherine	E	283
Donnelly, John	23, Sept 1850	John	----, Bridget	E	249
Donnelly, John	1, June 1851	Michael	Higgins, Catherine	B	233
Donnelly, John	19, June 1853	Patrick	Donnele, Margaret	J	22
Donnelly, John	2, July 1853	Thomas	Harran, Mary	B	294
Donnelly, John	7, Aug. 1859	Thomas	Mara, Catherine	E	646
Donnelly, John	19, Jan. 1854	Thomas	Marra, Catherine	E	161
Donnelly, Joseph	3, Sept 1854	Joseph	Collins, Mary	V	17
Donnelly, Letitia	18, Nov. 1853	Anthony	----, Esther	M	
Donnelly, Margaret	14, Dec. 1856	Patrick	Donnelly, Margaret	P	201
Donnelly, Mary	28, Sept 1858	James	Sullivan, Helen	E	565
Donnelly, Mary Alice	5, June 1859	John	McConnell, Margaret	E	630
Donnelly, Mary Frances	24, May 1857	Michael	Hagan, Mary	V	39
Donnelly, Mary Jane	7, Nov. 1857	Anthony	----, ----	E	491
Donnelly, Michael	27, May 1851	Joseph	Collins, Mary	E	310
Donnelly, Michael	11, Feb. 1855	Patrick	Donnelly, Margaret	P	120
Donnelly, Patrick	21, Mar. 1852	John	----, Bridget	E	394
Donnelly, Philip	22, Aug. 1854	Edward	----, Catherine	E	218
Donnelly, Rosanne	17, Oct. 1852	Francis	Curran, Alice	B	272
Donnelly, Rosanne	12, June 1853	James	Donnelly, Rose	B	293
Donnelly, Sarah Mary	3, Jan. 1858	Thomas L.	Williams, Sarah	B	54
Donnelly, Thomas	24, July 1857	Thomas	Mara, Catherine	E	469
Donnelly, Thomas M.	27, Dec. 1857	John	Brennan, Mary	B	53
Donnelly, William	20, June 1853	John	----, Bridget	E	100
Donnelly, William	19,Nov. 1854	Michael	Higgins, Catherine	P	104
Donnelly, William	31, Oct. 1852	Thomas	----, Catherine	E	31
Donnerberger, Louis	11, Sept 1859	Lawrence	Kirch, Maria Rosa	H	
Donnerberger, Maria Anna	22, Nov. 1857	Lawrence	Kirch, Rosa	H	
Donnersberger, Andreas	20, Apr. 1856	Lawrence	----, Maria Rosa	H	
Donnersberger, Anton Jacob	10, Feb. 1856	Johan	Brosemer, Catharina	F	
Donnersberger, M. Magdalena Rosa	4, Dec. 1853	Johan	Brosmer, Catharina	F	
Donnewald, Johan Herman	12, Dec. 1855	Christoph	Hempel, Gesina	F	
Donoghue, Mary Ann	7, Jan. 1855	Francis	Molloy, Mary	B	9
Donohoe, Elizabeth	10, Oct. 1852	?	?	B	271
Donohoe, Francis	10, Oct. 1852	?	?	B	271
Donohoe, Helen	27, June 1852	Hugh	----, Ann	B	262
Donohoe, John	11, Aug. 1850	Hugh	Higgins, Ann	B	210
Donohoe, John	15, Aug. 1852	John	----, Bridget	B	268
Donohoe, Joseph	12, Aug. 1855	Michael	Morgan, Joanne	P	145
Donohoe, Lamuel	27, Aug. 1850	James	----, Bridget	B	212
Donohoe, Margaret	4, July 1856	John	Hannicks, Mary	E	379
Donohoe, Martin	6, Nov. 1851	John?	Garey, Mary	P	13b
Donohoe, Mary	10, Oct. 1852	?	?	B	271
Donohue, Catherine	13, Feb. 1856	John	----, Bridget	R	
Donohue, Charles Farrell	29, Jan. 1854	James	McSullor, Mary	E	163
Donohue, Francis	6, Dec. 1852	Bernard	----, Bridget	M	

Name of Child	Date of Baptism	Father	Mother	Church	Page
Donohue, Helen	22, June 1856	Florence	Spellman, Helen	P	183
Donohue, Helen	7, Aug. 1854	Jeremiah	Crozier, Mary	P	91
Donohue, Helen	24, Jan. 1858	John	----, Bridget	R	
Donohue, James	21, Nov. 1854	James	----, Debora	E	242
Donohue, James	3, Sept 1854	James	O'Laughlin, Bridget	E	221
Donohue, John	26, Jan. 1851	James	McCall?, Mary	E	279
Donohue, Julia	26, Sept 1852	James	McLally, Mary	E	21
Donohue, Margaret	2, Sept 1859	Florence	Spellman, Ellen	P	294
Donohue, Mary	21, Nov. 1854	James	----, Debora	E	242
Donohue, Mary	5, Feb. 1852	John	Murphy, Bridget	P	17
Donohue, Mary Ann	2, Aug. 1857	Bernard	----, Bridget	M	
Donohue, Mary Ann	9, June 1855	Patrick	----, Mary	E	291
Donohue, Michael	14, Sept 1851	Lawrence	Spellman, Ellen	P	12
Donohue, Patrick	16, Oct. 1853	Florenz	----, Eliza	E	135
Donohue, Patrick Joseph	8, Mar. 1858	John	Mannacks, Mary	E	521
Donohue, Susan	24, Nov. 1859	Bernard	----, Bridget	M	
Donohue, Thomas	26, Apr. 1857	James	Sullivan, Catherine	A	
Donohue, William	30, June 1859	James	Sullivan, Catherine	P	287
Donovan, Ann	12, Dec. 1857	Maurice	Cronan, Helen	E	501
Donovan, Catherine	30, July 1854	Dennis	Coleman, Mary	E	211
Donovan, Catherine	18, Dec. 1859	Patrick	Sullivan, Ellen	E	677
Donovan, Catherine	1, Nov. 1856	Timothy	Mahoney, Catherine	E	409
Donovan, Catherine Ann	24, Sept 1853	William	----, Ann	E	129
Donovan, Cornelius	4, Jan. 1856	Daniel	Shenick, Mary	P	165
Donovan, Daniel	3, Oct. 1853	Dennis	Coleman, Mary	E	131
Donovan, Daniel	26, Mar. 1854	Patrick	Rice, Mary	J	26
Donovan, David	10, July 1859	Dennis	----, Mary	E	639
Donovan, Dennis	9, Dec. 1853	Dennis	Durby, Mary	E	151
Donovan, Dennis	11, Nov. 1852	Timothy	Mahony, Catherine	E	34
Donovan, Dennis	7, Jan. 1855	Timothy	Mahony, Catherine	E	255
Donovan, Hannah	25, Aug. 1855	Daniel	Sullivan, Ellen	V	26
Donovan, Helen	8, Mar. 1857	Daniel	Sullivan, Helen	V	38
Donovan, James	26, Apr. 1857	Dennis	Coleman, Mary	E	449
Donovan, James	23, June 1852	Joseph	Quinn, Sarah	P	23
Donovan, Joanne	2, June 1850	Michael	Buckley, Ann	B	204
Donovan, John	2, May 1858	Dennis	----, Mary	E	533
Donovan, John	5, July 1857	Patrick	Commins, Helen	E	463
Donovan, Joseph	27, Dec. 1854	John	McCarthy, Mary	R	
Donovan, Margaret	16, July 1859	Daniel	Shannuck, Mary	P	289
Donovan, Margaret	16, June 1856	Dennis	----, Mary	E	375
Donovan, Mary	19, Oct. 1857	Daniel	Shenig, Mary	P	**227**
Donovan, Mary Ann	18, Jan. 1856	Dennis	----, Mary	E	338
Donovan, Mary Ann	20, July 1851	Dennis	Carran, Elizabeth	E	326
Donovan, Mary Ann	17, Jan. 1855	Timothy	----, Mary	E	257
Donovan, Michael	1, Oct. 1852	Cornelius	Connell, Mary	P	28
Donovan, Patrick Henry	23, Mar. 1853	Timothy	Dunn, Mary	V	2
Donovan, Richard	13, May 1856	Patrick	----, Ellen	E	366
Donovan, Timothy	3, May 1858	Dennis	Coleman, Mary	E	533
Donovan, William	16, Jan. 1851	William	----, Ann	E	277
Donovan, William Edmund	16, Aug. 1857	John	Cotter, Catherine	P	220
Donragan, Patrick	25, Dec. 1852	Patrick	Dowling, Helen	B	278
Donsith, Hugh	9, May 1853	Albert	----, Helen	E	88
Doody, William	5, Sept 1852	Edmund	----, Margaret	E	15
Doolan, Bridget	29, Oct. 1854	Patrick	McKenzie, Honora	B	7
Doolan, Catherine	1, June 1856	Patrick	Crawford, Catherine	P	181
Doolan, Elizabeth	12, Apr. 1857	James	Conway, Catharine	T	
Doolan, James	16, Dec. 1857	James	Haden, Ann	E	501
Doolan, Joanne	30, May 1851	John	Moore, Catherine	E	311
Doolan, John	23, June 1859	John	Keenan, Joanne	E	634

Name of Child	Date of Baptism	Father	Mother	Church	Page
Doolan, John	14, Aug. 1854	Patrick	Foley, Mary	E	216
Doolan, Joseph	14, Jan. 1855	Patrick	Corcoran, Ellen	E	256
Doolan, Margaret	22, Oct. 1854	James	Conway, Catharine	T	
Doolan, Margaret J.	22, May 1859	Patrick	Croffy, Catherine	B	75
Doolan, Mary Ann	1, June 1851	Patrick	Croffy, Catherine	B	233
Doolan, Mary Catherine	9, Apr. 1855	John	Piper, Catherine	E	278
Doolan, Mary Helen	28, Nov. 1852	John	Meagher, Elizabeth	E	39
Doolan, Winifred	8, May 1853	Patrick	Croffey, Catherine	B	290
Dooley, Caecilia Agnes	9, Nov. 1856	Patrick	Livingston, Caecilia	C	
Dooley, Daniel	2, May 1858	Anthony	----, Mary	R	
Dooley, Daniel	28, Oct. 1850	Patrick	Lavery, Ellen	B	217
Dooley, Ellen	21, Dec. 1852	John	----, Catherine	E	46
Dooley, James	10, Jan. 1852	Patrick	Lavary, Helen	B	249
Dooley, James Martin	11, Nov. 1858	Joseph	Brodus, Judith	E	577
Dooley, John	14, Nov. 1857	John	Judge, Mary	P	229
Dooley, John	15, Dec. 1857	Michael	----, Mary	R	
Dooley, John Patrick	8, June 1859	James C.	Hayden, Ann	E	631
Dooley, John William	27, June 1852	Patrick	Livingston, Cecilia	L	
Dooley, Margaret	10, July 1853	John	Judge, Mary	J	22
Dooley, Margaret	18, Feb. 1853	Michael	Barnwell, Mary	P	36
Dooley, Margaret	14, Jan. 1855	Patrick	----, Celia	L	
Dooley, Margaret	23, Sept 1853	Patrick	Lavery, Helen	B	299
Dooley, Mary Ann	8, July 1850	James	----, Ann	E	229
Dooley, Mary Ann	10, Dec. 1859	Patrick	Corcoran, Ellen	E	675
Dooley, Michael	12, Oct. 1856	Anthony	----, Mary	R	
Dooley, Michael	1, Dec. 1850	Michael	----, Julia	E	264
Dooley, Patrick	16, July 1854	James	Gleeson, Margaret	V	15
Dooley, Peter	5, May 1850	Patrick	Livingston, Julia	L	
Dooley, William	3, Aug. 1855	Michael	Burns, Mary	R	
Doolin, John	29, Aug. 1852	John	Moore, Catherine	E	11
Dooling, James	3, Sept 1850	James	Conway, Catharine	L	
Dooling, Joseph	18, Mar. 1855	John	----, Eliza	E	272
Dooling, William	3, Sept 1850	James	Conway, Catharine	L	
Dooly, James	17, Apr. 1853	Patrick	Corcoran, Helen	V	2
Dooly, Joanne	19, Feb. 1856	James	Hader, Ann	E	346
Dooly, Joseph	28, Aug. 1853	James	Flynn, Ann	B	298
Dooly, Mary	17, June 1853	William	Welsh, Margaret	E	98
Doorly, John	6, Aug. 1854	Charles	Hammill, Eliza	B	3
Dopke, August Ferdinand	21, Jan. 1855	Friedrich	Landwehr, Maria	D	27
Döpker, Catharina	26, Feb. 1858	Joseph	Schumacher, Gertrud	A	
Döpker, Maria Elisabeth	26, Aug. 1851	Heinrich	Meier, Anna Maria	A	
Döpler, Anna Maria Catharina	24, Aug. 1857	Joseph	Gude, Maria Anna	A	
Dopper, Bernard Friedrich	17, Mar. 1852	Bernard	Rauh, Agnes	D	313
Dopper, Johan Heinrich	25, Jan. 1857	J. Bernard	Kordes, Maria Clara	F	
Doppes, Francis Ludwig	12, Mar. 1854	J. Bernard	Kortes, Clara	D	6
Doppleier, Maria Anna	7, June 1855	Christian	Wobel, Barbara	D	36
Doppler, Catharina	6, Apr. 1856	Christian	Woll, Barbara	D	55
Doppler, Catharina Euphrosina	27, May 1855	Andreas	Giesler, Monica	F	
Doppler, Georg	26, Dec. 1853	Christian	Woll, Barbara	D	422
Doppler, Johan Andreas	1, Apr. 1850	Christian	Wohl, Barbara	A	
Doppler, Nicolaus	9, Nov. 1851	Christian	Wollen, Barbara	A	
Doppler, Peter	5, Sept 1858	Christian	Woll, Barbara	D	118
Doppler, Regina Carolina	4, Dec. 1853	Andreas	Geisler, Monica	F	
Doragan, John	13, Feb. 1853	Thomas	Cooney, Bridget	B	283
Doran, Alice	21, Sept 1856	John	Dunboyne, Margaret	P	193
Doran, Ann Louise	19, Feb. 1853	Charles	Magee, Catherine	P	36
Doran, Charles	28, Jan. 1855	Charles	McGee, Catherine	P	117
Doran, Dennis	10, June 1854	John	Dunboyne, Margaret	P	84
Doran, Edward	28, Dec. 1850	John	Dunboque, Margaret	P	2

Name of Child	Date of Baptism	Father	Mother	Church	Page
Doran, Emily Agnes	24, Jan. 1858	John	Keenan, Joanne	E	512
Doran, James	23, Mar. 1851	Charles D.	Meyer, Catherine	P	6
Doran, James	9, Oct. 1853	James	Fitzpatrick, Mary Ann	B	300
Doran, James	12, Feb. 1857	James	Lellis, Ann	V	43
Doran, Jeremiah	9, Nov. 1856	John	Gorman, Helen	P	197
Doran, John	2, Dec. 1855	John	King, Mary	P	161
Doran, John William	13, Aug. 1854	James	Brady, Catherine	S	
Doran, Martin	25, Dec. 1859	James	Lellis, Ann	E	678
Doran, Mary	14, Aug. 1859	John	Gorman, Helen	P	292
Doran, Mary Ann	2, Mar. 1856	James	Fitzpatrick, Mary Ann	B	26
Doran, Mary Jane	1, Sept 1852	John	Dunboyne, Margaret	P	27
Doran, Matthew	24, Jan. 1858	James	Fitzpatrick, Mary Ann	P	237
Doran, Michael	30, Nov. 1857	John	Gorman, Helen	P	231
Doran, Owen	21, Oct. 1858	John	Dunboyne, Margaret	P	264
Doran, Patrick	7, Oct. 1855	John	Gorman, Helen	P	155
Doran, William	7, Apr. 1850	John	Sweeney, Helen	E	206
Doran, William	4, July 1855	William	Doran, Catherine	P	138
Dorch, Fridolin	22, Aug. 1852	Johan	Detzold, Cunigunda	D	344
Dorcus, Mary	16, Aug. 1854		adult	V	16
Dore, James	14, Feb. 1858	John	Dignan, Helen	P	239
Dore, John	3, June 1855	John	Dignan, Helen	P	134
Dore, Thomas Edward	26, Dec. 1852	John	Dignan, Ellen	P	32
Dore, Wiliam	19, Sept 1858	Patrick	Sullivan, Honora	P	261
Dorenbach, Catharina Elisabeth	26, July 1858	?	St--ckel, Gertrud	D	116
Dorenkamp, Franz Anton	31, Jan. 1855	Conrad	Nordmeier, Maria Theresa	F	
Dorenkamp, Maria Elisabeth	26, Sept 1852	Conrad	Nordmeier, Maria Theresa	F	
Dorenkemper, Gerhard Heinrich	13, Feb. 1853	Friedrich	Placke, M. Gertrud	L	
Dorenkemper, Johan Albert	17, Oct. 1850	Friedrich	Placke, Gertrud	C	
Dorey, Mary Ann	23, Nov. 1856	Edward	----, Mary	R	
Dorf, Mary Violet	1, Apr. 1853	Samuel	adult - 38 years old	E	78
Dörfer, Catharina	30, Mar. 1856	Johan	Endelein, Catharina	D	55
Dörfler, Catharina	15, Apr. 1855	Johan	Heilman, Catharina	D	33
Dörfler, Eva Margaretha	23, Oct. 1853	Johan	Enderlin, Barbara	D	411
Dörfler, Maria	5, Oct. 1851	Johan	Endres, Barbara	D	285
Dorgan, Catherine Ann	21, Nov. 1854	Michael	Renbird, Eliza	P	105
Dörger, Bernard Heinrich	12, Sept 1859	Johan	Siemer, Anna Maria	A	
Dorger, Gerhard Heinrich	2, Dec. 1852	Gerhard H.	Hölding, Elisabeth	D	359
Dörger, Heinrich August	1, Apr. 1851	Johan	Siemer, Maria	A	
Dörger, Johan Bernard August	22, Jan. 1850	Johan	Siemer, Maria	A	
Dörger, Johan Friedrich	3, May 1855	Johan	Siemer, Maria	A	
Dörger, Maria Magdalena	23, Apr. 1857	Johan	Siemer, Anna Maria	A	
Dorian, Hugh	16, June 1857	John	Tolan, Ann	P	214
Dorian, John	6, Feb. 1854	Michael	Tunny, Catherine	P	67
Dorian, Margaret	21, Dec. 1855	James	McMullen, Hannah	P	163
Doriker, Maria	20, Jan. 1850	Bernard	VonSwin, Helena	J	6
Doris, Margaret	6, Aug. 1854	James	McCabe, Rose	E	214
Doris, Mary Jane	26, June 1853	James	McCabe, Rose	E	101
Doriss, James	9, Feb. 1859	James	McCabe, Rose	E	602
Dorman, Mary	10, May 1855	Richard	King, Mary	E	285
Dormeier, Heinrich	14, May 1852	Heinrich	Steinmetz, Anna Maria Elis.	D	319
Dorn, Johan Heinrich	16, Jan. 1858	Joseph	Behrens, Carolina	F	
Dorn, Mary	3, May 1853	William	Taylor, Margaret	J	22
Dorn, Victoria	18, Dec. 1858	Wilhelm	Becker, Margaretha	D	126
Dornbecker, Elisabeth	27, Feb. 1859	Peter	Stephans, Margaretha	T	
Dornbecker, Helena	11, May 1856	Peter	Stephan, Margaretha	D	58
Dornbecker, M. Magdalena	29, Nov. 1857	Peter	Stephens, Margaretha	T	
Dornbruch, Wilhelm Michael	21, Nov. 1852	Michael	Reinhart, Maria Anna	D	358
Dornbusch, Johan Bernard	21, Jan. 1853	Adolph	Stroeve, Gertrud	D	366
Dornbusch, Maria Catharina	30, Mar. 1855	Adolph	Strobel, Gertrud	D	32

Name of Child	Date of Baptism	Father	Mother	Church	Page
Dörner, Bernardina	11, May 1851	J. Heinrich	Holtmeier, Maria Elisabeth	D	264
Dörner, Francis Heinrich	11, Oct. 1857	Christian	Brockman, Elisabeth	N	
Dorney, William	14, June 1857	Edmund	Toomey, Helen	R	
Dornhoefer, Elisabeth	11, June 1857	Maurice	Loehrlein, Cunigunda	D	87
Dornhoefer, Heinrich Mauritz	18, Sept 1859	Maurice	Loerlein, Cunigunda	D	147
Dornhöfer, Eva Barbara	4, Oct. 1855	Maurice	Löhrlein, Cunigunda	D	44
Dorof, Carolina	13, Nov. 1855	Johan	Walburger, Carolina	S	
Dorr, Carolina	16, Mar. 1855	Christoph	Thiele, Maria	C	
Dörr, Elisabeth	10, Apr. 1859	Georg	Miller, Elisabeth	D	135
Dörr, Rosa	20, July 1856	Georg	Müller, Elisabeth	D	63
Dorr, William	25, Aug. 1850	John	Dignan, Helen	B	211
Dorrey, Nicolaus	8, Mar. 1852	William	Cunningham, Margaret	L	
Dorris, Sarah	20, Feb. 1856	James	Dolen, Sarah	E	346
Dorsch, Heinrich	18, Jan. 1857	Johan	Keck, Francisca	F	
Dorsch, Jacob	13, Aug. 1855	Johan	Keck, Francisca	F	
Dorsch, Jacob Johan	14, July 1853	Johan	Keck, Francisca	F	
Dorsch, Theresa	8, May 1859	Johan	Keck, Francisca	T	
Dorsey, Edward	6, Dec. 1857	James E.	----, Mary	R	
Dorsey, Joanne	25, Jan. 1857	Stephan	Flinn, Bridget	B	39
Dorsey, Margaret	10, Dec. 1857	John	Toway, Elizabeth	E	499
Dorsey, Mary	23, July 1851	John	Creway, Elizabeth	E	326
Dorsey, Mary Ann	10, Aug. 1856	Thomas	Duffy, Margaret	P	187
Dorsey, Michael	27, Nov. 1853	Stephan	Flynn, Bridget	B	303
Dorson, Eliza	7, Aug. 1853	John	----, Eliza	E	115
Dorsy, Elizabeth	4, Apr. 1858	Thomas	Duffy, Margaret	P	245
Dorsy, Helen	28, Mar. 1858	Patrick	Dwer, Mary	P	243
Dorthee, Jacob	9, May 1856	James	Reille, Brigitta	F	
Dorus, Bernard	12, Sept 1857	James	----, Rose	E	480
Dosch, Johan Martin	2, Mar. 1851	Johan	Ballinger, Sophia	C	
Dosin, Mary	13, Mar. 1859	William	Murray, Mary	P	279
Dotel, Johan	20, Jan. 1850	Johan	Detel, Maria	A	
Dothage, Johan Friedrich Wilhelm	10, Oct. 1852	Wilhelm	Staggen, Elisabeth	K	
Dothage, Johan Herman	1, July 1856	Wilhelm	Stagenborg, Elisabeth	K	
Dothage, Maria Gertrud	16, July 1850	Wilhelm	Stagenberg, Elisabeth	K	
Dothman, Gerhard Bernard	18, May 1857	Bernard	Derenkamp, Elisabeth	A	
Dottmeyer, Maria Catharina	7, Oct. 1852	Heinrich	Morwessel, Adelheid	F	
Dotzauer, Jacob	10, Oct. 1858	Friedrich	Kruse, Elisabeth	F	
Dotzauer, Johan Georg Friedrich	3, Aug. 1856	Friedrich	Kraus, Elisabeth	J	36
Dotzauer, Lucia	30, Nov. 1851	Friedrich	Grusi, Elisabeth	D	294
Dotzauer, Margaretha	5, Feb. 1854	Friedrich	Grusi, Elisabeth	D	4
Doud, Bridget	2, July 1854	Thomas	McAndrew, Bridget	E	203
Doud, Catherine	24, Aug. 1855	James	Cohen, Mary	B	18
Doud, George	7, Mar. 1858	Patrick	Kearney, Catherine	S	
Doud, Helen	3, Feb. 1851	John	Calaghan, Catherine	E	280
Doud, James	17, Jan. 1851	Thomas	McAvit, Mary	E	277
Doud, James Patrick	24, July 1855	John	Calagan, Catherine	E	302
Doud, Joseph	2, Oct. 1859	Thomas	----, Bridget	E	659
Doud, Margaret	13, Feb. 1853	James	Cohin, Mary	B	283
Doud, Mary	15, May 1853	Thomas	----, Bridget	E	90
Doud, Sarah	29, July 1855	Thomas	----, Bridget	E	304
Doud, Thomas	3, Aug. 1857	Thomas	McAndrew, Bridget	E	472
Doud, William	6, Mar. 1853	John	Callaghan, Catherine	E	69
Dougherty, Ann	11, Sept 1856	Michael	McGaraghan, Ann	B	34
Dougherty, Ann Mary	24, Aug. 1856	John	Paul, Thomasine	E	392
Dougherty, Catherine	9, Mar. 1851	William	----, Ann	E	289
Dougherty, Charles	17, Apr. 1853	Charles	Glascow, Ann	E	82
Dougherty, Charles	9, May 1853	Charles	Tully, Ann	B	291
Dougherty, Edward	20, Mar. 1852	Edward	----, Bridget	M	
Dougherty, Honora	6, Aug. 1854	Edward	----, Bridget	M	

Name of Child	Date of Baptism	Father	Mother	Church	Page
Dougherty, Honora	5, Oct. 1851	Michael	Connafon, Eliza	E	348
Dougherty, James	4, Dec. 1859	Cornelius	Sullivan, Catherine	B	85
Dougherty, James	19, Jan. 1857	Edward	----, Bridget	M	
Dougherty, John	5, June 1859	Edward	----, Bridget	M	
Dougherty, John	4, Dec. 1853	Nicolaus	----, Elizabeth	M	
Dougherty, John	31, Aug. 1859	Patrick	Burns, Ann	P	294
Dougherty, Joseph Aloysius	27, Mar. 1853	James	Flemming, Mary	B	290
Dougherty, Mary	12, Jan. 1855	Peter	----, Eliza	P	115
Dougherty, Mary Ann	13, June 1852	Bernard	McBride, Cecilia	B	265
Dougherty, Mary Ann	10, Nov. 1856	James	Gough, Mary	B	36
Dougherty, Michael	12, Jan. 1851	Edward	Murphy, Bridget	M	
Dougherty, Michael	1, Feb. 1852	Patrick	---lin, Susan	B	251
Dougherty, Raymond	6, Feb. 1853	William	McCoy, Ann	V	1
Dougherty, Rose Ann	9, Apr. 1852	Thomas	Daugherty, Bridget	E	400
Dougherty, Thomas	11, Dec. 1859	Thomas	Russell, Jane	B	85
Doughtery, Cornelius	30, Dec. 1855	Cornelius	Sullivan, Catharine	T	
Doughtery, Mary	9, Oct. 1855	Michael	Langan, Ann	T	
Douglas, Mary Ann	6, Jan. 1857	Charles?	Dwyer, Abby	B	39
Douglas, William	5, Nov. 1854	Henry	----, Alice	E	238
Dout, Mary Ann	4, Sept 1859	Patrick	Kearne, Catherine	S	
Dout, Thomas Patrick	12, July 1857	Thomas	Devine, Catherine	S	
Dow, Elisabeth Catharina	16, Nov. 1859	Jesse	Storrs, Johanna	K	
Döw, Lucas	18, Dec. 1853	Georg	Sölzer, Anna Maria	D	421
Dowan, Mary	10, Oct. 1852	Thomas	Nolan, Joanne	R	
Dowd, Arthur	25, Oct. 1857	James	Conway, Ann	E	488
Dowd, Catherine	23, June 1850	James	Migewel, Mary	E	226
Dowd, James	24, July 1853	James	Duffy, Bridget	B	295
Dowd, Margaret	29, Oct. 1854	James	Duffy, Bridget	B	6
Dowd, Mary	24, Mar. 1859	James	----, Mary	E	613
Dowd, Sarah	3, Jan. 1858	John	Cooligan, Catherine	E	505
Dowell, Hannah	5, May 1859		adult	B	74
Dowell, Mary Agnes	11, Dec. 1853	Thomas	Pulphry, Mary Ann	E	152
Dowell, William	31, Aug. 1851	Thomas	Pulphry, Mary	E	339
Dower, William	11, Sept 1855	P.	----, Lucy	E	314
Dowling, Bridget	23, Feb. 1851	John	----, Margaret	E	286
Dowling, Catherine	7, Jan. 1853	James	Conway, Catherine	E	52
Dowling, Christopher	17, Dec. 1856	John	Conway, Margaret	B	38
Dowling, Christopher	15, Sept 1850	John	Delehanty, Rosanne	B	213
Dowling, Daniel	20, Jan. 1855	John	Meir, Margaret	E	258
Dowling, Eliza	16, Nov. 1851	Michael	Gibson, Elizabeth	B	245
Dowling, Eliza Ann	9, Jan. 1858	P.	Hayden, Ellen	B	54
Dowling, Elizabeth	19, Dec. 1852	James	----, Mary	E	44
Dowling, James Edward	24, Apr. 1859	James	Riley, Mary	B	74
Dowling, John	14, June 1853	John?	Jennings, Ann	E	98
Dowling, Lilly Theresa	17, Oct. 1856	John	Keating, Joanne	E	405
Dowling, Margaret	24, Jan. 1853	John	Delahanty, Rose	B	281
Dowling, Marianne	20, May 1855	Patrick	Heyden, Ellen	B	14
Dowling, Mary Ann	7, Apr. 1855	Michael	--er, Bridget	E	277
Dowling, Mary Helen	4, May 1856	James	Riley, Mary	T	
Dowling, Michael Patrick	15, June 1851	Patrick	Heyden, Helen	B	234
Dowling, Peter	15, Feb. 1852	John	Whealer, Margaret	E	382
Dowling, William	28, Feb. 1858	John	Norton, Mary	B	56
Downe, Jane	28, July 1850	John	----, Rose	E	234
Downes, Rosanne	27, Feb. 1859	John	Lehehan, Rose	P	277
Downey, Elizabeth	24, June 1852	Moses	adult - 24 years old	P	23
Downey, Helen	7, Aug. 1856	James	----, Mary	R	
Downey, John	17, Dec. 1857	James	----, Mary	R	
Downey, John	17, Dec. 1854	Patrick	Canary, Mary	R	
Downey, Mary Jane	27, Nov. 1851	John	Wellman, Elizabeth	P	13c

Name of Child	Date of Baptism	Father	Mother	Church	Page
Downey, Sarah	1, Mar. 1857	Patrick	----, Mary	R	
Downey, William Patrick	27, Nov. 1851	John	Wellman, Elizabeth	P	13c
Downie, Elizabeth Grace	26, Jan. 1856		adult	B	24
Downs, Ann	23, Apr. 1859	John	McHugh, Catherine	B	74
Downs, Charles	22, Mar. 1857	John	Sweeney, Mary	B	42
Downs, Eliza	14, Jan. 1855	John	Sweeney, Mary	B	10
Downs, Mary Ann	1, Aug. 1852	John	Sweeney, Mary	B	266
Downs, Mary Ellen	29, Mar. 1853	John	----, Rose	E	78
Downs, Philomena	21, Aug. 1859	John	Sweeney, Mary	B	79
Doy, Maurice	27, Sept 1854	John	O'Harn, Mary	N	25
Doyle,	15, Nov. 1857	M.	Rooney, Mary Ann	E	493
Doyle, Alice Agnes	13, Nov. 1853	Michael	Langdon, Mary	E	143
Doyle, Anastasia	30, May 1855	Patrick	Gorman, Catherine	P	134
Doyle, Andrea	20, May 1855	Martin	Mulally, Mary	E	288
Doyle, Ann	23, Apr. 1854	John	Burke, Julia	P	79
Doyle, Ann Mary	24, July 1853	Anthony	Johnson, Bridget	B	295
Doyle, Catherine	30, Nov. 1857	Christopher	Handlin, Catherine	P	231
Doyle, Catherine	28, Oct. 1855	Edward	----, Ann	E	323
Doyle, Catherine	17, July 1853	Edward P.	Gorman, Catherine	B	295
Doyle, Catherine	18, May 1851	Michael	Langdon, Mary	E	308
Doyle, Catherine	15, July 1854	Patrick	----, Elizabeth	M	
Doyle, Daniel	15, May 1853	James	----, Mary Ann	B	291
Doyle, Edmund Henry	12, Aug. 1852	Christopher	----, Catherine	B	268
Doyle, Edward	5, July 1857	Edward	Whelan, Ann	Q	23
Doyle, Elizabeth	2, Jan. 1853	Bernard	----, Margaret	M	
Doyle, Elizabeth	3, Dec. 1857	Patrick	----, Catherine	E	497
Doyle, Elizabeth	20, Apr. 1851	Patrick	Gorman, Catherine	B	230
Doyle, Ellen Frances	30, May 1850	Francis	----, Mary	E	216
Doyle, Esther	8, Apr. 1855	John	Davis, Ann	P	127
Doyle, George	27, Feb. 1851	Daniel	----van, Elizabeth	P	5
Doyle, Helen	22, Dec. 1857	?	Bravey, Mary Ann	E	502
Doyle, Helen	19, Nov. 1851	Daniel	Murphy, Margaret	B	245
Doyle, Henry	8, Feb. 1851	Henry	----, Mary	B	224
Doyle, Henry	9, Nov. 1852	James	Kilfoy, Margaret	E	33
Doyle, James	17, July 1859	Daniel	White, Mary	B	77
Doyle, James	4, Apr. 1852	Edward	Farrell, Eliza	B	256
Doyle, James	25, Mar. 1854	Martin	McHugh, Bridget	P	75
Doyle, James	8, Aug. 1858	Martin	Mulally, Mary	E	555
Doyle, James Thomas	26, May 1851	Andrew	----, Bridget	E	310
Doyle, Joanne	14, Sept 1853	Edward	Farran, Elizabeth	P	52
Doyle, Joanne	10, Dec. 1854	Edward	Farrons, Eliza	P	109
Doyle, John	13, July 1853	Dennis	----, Bridget	E	106
Doyle, John	7, Feb. 1858	Edward	Foran, Eliza	B	55
Doyle, John	16, Mar. 1851	James	Fleming, Mary	B	226
Doyle, John	30, Jan. 1859	John	----, Martha	M	
Doyle, John	29, Mar. 1857	Patrick E.	Gorman, Catherine	P	209
Doyle, John George	16, June 1855	John	----, Ann	U	
Doyle, Julia	14, June 1850	Thomas	Burke, Eliza	B	204
Doyle, Lawrence	26, May 1853	Lawrence	O'Hara, Mary	B	292
Doyle, Luke	16, Oct. 1853	Peter	----, Mary	U	
Doyle, Marcella Ann	10, Dec. 1854	Henry	Hanlon, Margaret	B	8
Doyle, Margaret	15, Oct. 1854	John	Maguire, Ann	P	100
Doyle, Margaret Cecilia	24, Dec. 1854	James	Fleming, Mary	B	9
Doyle, Mary	6, Aug. 1854	Christopher	Hanlon, Catherine	P	91
Doyle, Mary	17, Dec. 1851	Edward	----, Mary	M	
Doyle, Mary	3, Feb. 1856	Edward	Malone, Catharine	T	
Doyle, Mary	7, Jan. 1855	Michael	O'Brien, Ann	P	114
Doyle, Mary	20, Feb. 1859	Patrick	Tainor, Catherine	E	605
Doyle, Mary	3, Jan. 1858	Thomas	----, Ellen	E	505

Name of Child	Date of Baptism	Father	Mother	Church	Page
Doyle, Mary	19, Aug. 1855	Thomas	Behan, Ann	T	
Doyle, Mary Ann	24, Jan. 1851	Edward	Whelan, Ann	B	223
Doyle, Mary Ann	3, May 1851	James	Gilfoil, Margaret	M	
Doyle, Mary Ann	13, Mar. 1853	Martin	----, Maryann	E	72
Doyle, Mary Ann	2, Apr. 1852	Patrick	Brennan, Eliza	B	255
Doyle, Mary Ann	27, Oct. 1858	Thomas	Curley, Ann	E	572
Doyle, Mary Ann	14, Apr. 1850	William	Boyd, Ellen	E	208
Doyle, Mary Ellen	29, Nov. 1851	John	Cook, Margaret	E	362
Doyle, Mary Isabel	15, May 1856	John T.	Jordan, Juliana	B	28
Doyle, Michael	18, Apr. 1858	Patrick	Hennessey, Helen	E	530
Doyle, Michael	25, Mar. 1855	Peter	Tierney, Mary	B	13
Doyle, Patrick	10, Aug. 1859	Aloysius	Brophy, Mary Ann	E	646
Doyle, Patrick	14, Mar. 1858	Jeremiah	Logan, Mary	H	
Doyle, Peter	23, July 1851	Edward	Nevel, Catherine	E	326
Doyle, Richard	22, Oct. 1854	Edward	Malone, Catharine	T	
Doyle, Thomas	3, Mar. 1856	Martin	McHugh, Bridget	P	171
Doyle, Thomas	8, June 1856	Thomas	----, Ellen	E	371
Doyle, Thomas Edward	15, May 1856	John T.	Jordan, Juliana	B	28
Doyle, William	11, Sept 1859	Edward	Hunt, Margaret	B	80
Doyle, William	4, Feb. 1850	Michael	Joh--, Bridget	B	195
Doyle?, Francis	23, Mar. 1855	Anthony	----, Bridget	M	
Drach, Charles Edward	18, Jan. 1857	Louis	Bucher, Ann	E	427
Drach, Louis William	15, May 1859	Louis	Pincher, Ann	E	624
Drach, Maria Mathilda	14, Aug. 1859	Carl	Hu---, Amalia	D	144
Dracheser, Dorothea	19, Nov. 1854	Thomas	Nichtern, Sibilla	D	22
Dracheser, Henrietta	2, June 1850	Thomas	Nichtern, Sybilla	D	215
Dracheser, Jacob	17, June 1859	Thomas	Nichtern, Sybilla	D	140
Dracheser, Johan Georg	18, Sept 1856	Thomas	Nüchtern, Sibilla	D	67
Dracheser, Thomas	15, Aug. 1852	Thomas	Nichter, Sybilla	D	343
Dradey, John	29, May 1859	John	Collins, Ann	E	628
Draeger, Crescentia	4, May 1856	Louis	Huck, Elisabeth	L	
Draeger, Louis Jacob	28, Apr. 1854	Louis	Huck, Elisabeth	L	
Draeger, Theresa Francisca	28, Apr. 1854	Louis	Huck, Elisabeth	L	
Drahan, Mary Jane	9, Aug. 1857	Henry	McCabe, Mary	B	47
Drahman, August	16, Jan. 1858	J. Heinrich	Kessing, Elisabeth	K	
Drahman, Edward	29, Mar. 1857	J. Bernard	Tesing, Theresa	K	
Drahman, Maria Elisabeth	15, June 1854	J. Heinrich	Kessing, Maria Elisabeth	K	
Drahman, Maria Philomena	28, Feb. 1856	Heinrich	Kersing, Maria Elisabeth	K	
Drahman, Rosa	24, Nov. 1859	Heinrich	Kessing, Elisabeth	K	
Drake, George Robert	7, Apr. 1856	David	Shelford, Frances	E	357
Dransman, Herman Heinrich	29, Oct. 1857	?	Kasselman, Catharina	A	
Dransmann, Anna Maria Catharina	6, Sept 1857	Herman	Hehmann, Carolina	C	
Drap--, Margaretha	24, Sept 1850	Michael	Roth, Catharina	D	234
Drap, Nicolaus	18, Mar. 1858	Peter	Kronberger, Margaretha	T	
Draper, Henry	21, Mar. 1853	George	Ryan, Mary	E	74
Draper, Martha	31, Mar. 1850	George	----, Mary	E	205
Draper, Thomas	25, Dec. 1855	George	----, Mary	E	334
Drapp, Johan Georg	24, Apr. 1859	Peter	Kronenberger, Marg.	T	
Dratchar, Alice	23, Sept 1859	Henry	McCabe, Mary	B	81
Drechsler, Magdalena	13, May 1856	Johan	Schweitzer, Genofeva	D	58
Drechzer, Elisabeth	11, July 1858	Aloysius	Dempf, Catharina	D	114
Dreck, Emma Rosa	1, July 1858	Charles	Huber, Maria	C	
Drees, Anna Maria	30, July 1855	Gerhard H.	Stevens, Thecla	C	
Drees, Elisabeth	19, Dec. 1857	Gerhard H.	Stevens, Thecla	C	
Drees, Herman Anton	19, Oct. 1858	Heinrich	Willenborg, Gertrud	A	
Drees, Johan Heinrich	23, May 1856	J. Heinrich	Willenborg, Gertrud	A	
Drees, Maria Christina	11, Aug. 1853	H. Philipp	Willenborg, Maria Gertrud	A	
Dreier, Johan Bernard	1, Nov. 1850	Johan W.	Sanders, Maria Gertrud	F	
Dreier, Maria	30, July 1852	Heinrich	Bensman, Maria Anna	D	341

Name of Child	Date of Baptism	Father	Mother	Church	Page
Dreier, Matthias Heinrich	14, July 1851	Heinrich	Bruns, Bernardina	A	
Dreihman, Bernard	6, Jan. 1859	J. Bernard	Thesing, Sophia	K	
Dreiling, Johan Adam	29, Aug. 1859	Balthasar	Grass, Magdalena	F	
Dreis, Eva	11, Feb. 1851	Philipp	Vogel, Christina	D	253
Dreis, Friedrich	10, Oct. 1855	Philipp	Vogel, Christina	D	44
Dreis, Johan	28, Sept 1858	Philipp	Vogel, Christina	D	120
Dreis, Philipp	9, May 1853	Philipp	Vogel, Christina	D	384
Drennan, James	9, Aug. 1856	James	Mulhall, Ellen	E	388
Drennan, Patrick	17, Mar. 1855	Peter?	----, Mary	E	272
Drennan, Thomas	28, Sept 1851	Pierce	Whelaghan, Mary	B	241
Drennin, Dennis	10, Dec. 1854	James	Malhan, Ellen	B	8
Dres, Catharina	8, Sept 1850	Anton	Wesseling, Adelheid	D	232
Dres, Freidrich Anton	7, Nov. 1854	Anton	Wessling, Maria	F	
Dres, Heinrich Joseph	19, Mar. 1857	Anton	Wessling, Maria Adelheid	D	81
Dres, Herman Johan	19, July 1859	Anton	Wessling, Maria	D	142
Dres, Johanna Margaretha	20, Mar. 1853	Anton	Wessling, Maria	D	376
Dresch, Georg Wilhelm	26, June 1853	Nicolaus	Brunner, Christina	D	391
Dresch, Michael	26, June 1853	Nicolaus	Brunner, Christina	D	391
Drescher, Carl Anton	17, Sept 1854	Carl B.	Pistner, Maria	A	
Drescher, Paulina	3, Feb. 1856	Carl	Pistner, Maria	A	
Dress, Bernard	15, Feb. 1852	Anton	Wessling, Maria	D	307
Drexler, Joseph Heinrich	28, Sept 1853	Anton	Robeloth, Theodora	D	408
Dreyen, James Henry	14, Feb. 1859	Andrew	Murphy, Rosanne	B	71
Dreyer, Anna	1, Nov. 1850	William	König, Gertrud	D	241
Dreyer, Euphemia Bernardina	6, May 1854	Gerhard H.	Bruns, Bernardina	A	
Dreyer, Friedrich Wilhelm	8, Sept 1850	J. Heinrich	Bensmann, Anna Maria	L	
Dreyer, Gerhard Heinrich	5, Dec. 1852	J. Wilhelm	Sanders, Anna Gertrud	F	
Dreyer, Johan Wilhelm	8, May 1855	J. Wilhelm	Sanders, Anna Gertrud	F	
Dreyer, Joseph	19, Mar. 1854	Conrad	Joerger, Helen	G	
Dreyer, Joseph	31, Oct. 1852	Conrad	Jörger, Helena	J	18
Dreyer, Joseph Andreas	5, July 1857	Conrad	Joerger, Helena	W	19
Dreyling, Martin	23, Jan. 1853	Johan	----, Caroline	C	
Drick, John	16, Sept 1850	Frederick	Galvin, Mary Ann	B	214
Driscol, Julia	18, June 1854	Patrick	Murphy, Honora	E	198
Driscol, Timothy	17, Feb. 1859	John	Field, Mary	E	604
Driscoll, Francis	30, Mar. 1859	Henry	Keefe, Catherine	B	73
Driscoll, James	6, July 1856	Michael	Conolly, Mary	V	32
Droitt, Martin	20, Dec. 1852	Michael	McDonnell, Bridget	P	31
Droll, Louisa	25, Sept 1859	Ludwig	Conrad, Theresa	C	
Drömer, Dorothea Philomena	24, Apr. 1851		12 years old	K	
Droppel, Herman	26, Dec. 1858	Bernard	Bussman, Gertrud	A	
Dröppel, Herman	21, Nov. 1856	Herman	Tepe, Elisabeth	A	
Droppelmann, Johan Franz	5, Jan. 1859	Johan H.	Wittkamp, Clara	F	
Droppelmann, M Elisabeth Francisca	9, Aug. 1857	Johan H.	Wittkamp, Clara	F	
Dröscher, Isabella Margaretha	16, May 1852	Carl	Pistner, Maria	A	
Drossel, Maria Anna Elisabeth	4, July 1850	Moses	Schlick, Elisabeth	F	
Drossel, Rosina	3, Dec. 1854	Moses	Schleck, Elisabeth	F	
Droste, Ella Cecilia	2, July 1857	Henry R.	Wagner, Magdalene	B	46
Droste, Francis Heinrich	29, Jan. 1855	Heinrich	Dickmann, Catharina	C	
Droste, Helen	30, Mar. 1858	Friedrich	Mack, Margaretha	T	
Droste, Johan Heinrich	10, Aug. 1851	Heinrich	Dieckmann, Catharina	C	
Droste, Maria Dominica	27, May 1853	Heinrich	Dickmann, Catharine	C	
Drosty, Margaret Frances	11, Dec. 1858	Henry	Wagner, Magdalene	B	68
Drout, John	3, July 1858	Edward	Daly, Ellen	E	545
Drout, Mary	29, July 1853	Edward	Daly, Ellen	E	113
Drout, Thomas	31, Aug. 1851	Conrad	----, Ellen	E	338
Drout, Thomas	6, Jan. 1856	Edward	----, Ellen	E	335
Drucker, Georg Lucas	1, Nov. 1858	Nicolaus	Lautenbach, Elisabeth	A	
Drücker, Johan Bernard	5, May 1856	Nicolaus	Laudenberg, Elisabeth	A	

Name of Child	Date of Baptism	Father	Mother	Church	Page
Druecker, Friedrich Stephan	24, Feb. 1854	Nicolaus	Laudenbach, Maria Elisabeth	F	
Drueker, Maria Elisabeth	26, Jan. 1851	Nicolaus	Laudenbach, Elisabeth	F	
Drum, Edward	31, Aug. 1856	Thomas	Dunn, Mary	P	189
Drury, James	25, Dec. 1856	Thomas	----, Mary	M	
Druss, George Dominick Francis	10, Feb. 1856	Francis X.	----, Clotilda	E	344
Dual, Bridget	17, Mar. 1850	Martin	McKue, Bridget	E	203
Duane, Eliza	29, Mar. 1857	James	O'Connoll, Mary	B	42
Duane, John	6, Feb. 1853	Jeremiah	Nevin, Ellen	V	1
Duane, Michael	15, Apr. 1855	Pierce	Navin, Ellen	V	24
Dubenkop, Maria Elisabeth	6, Dec. 1857	Joseph	Friedrich, Sophia	Q	25
Dubenkrop, Johan	29, Sept 1856	Joseph	Freitag, Sophia	Q	16
Dubenkropf, Maria Theresa	27, May 1852	Joseph	Freitag, Sophia	D	321
Düber, Carl Anton	21, Apr. 1852	Peter	----, Emilia	K	
Dubing, Carolina Hermina	8, Aug. 1850	Joseph	Freitag, Sophia	F	
Duckyou, Thomas	31, Dec. 1854	John	Donnelly, Frances	P	113
Dudei, Anna Margaretha	24, Dec. 1851	Gerhard	Lemmings, Adelheid	L	
Dudei, Gerhard Johan	17, Jan. 1854	Gerhard J.	Limmink, Adleheid	F	
Dudey, Euphemia Wilhelmina	19, Apr. 1858	J. Gerhard	Lemming, Adelheid	F	
Dudey, Gerhard Heinrich	8, Mar. 1857	Johan G.	Lemming, Adelheid	F	
Dudey, Johan Herman	8, Nov. 1850	Gerhard H.	Lemming, Adelheid	L	
Dudey, Maria Adelheid	2, Dec. 1855	Gerhard J.	Lemming, Adelheid	F	
Dudley, Charles	16, Mar. 1850	Robert	McManns, Bridget	B	198
Dudley, Helen	11, Apr. 1854	Robert	McManus, Margaret	P	78
Dudley, John	12, Mar. 1854	Robert	McManus, Bridget	P	73
Dudley, John Henry	14, Feb. 1858	James	H---, Mary	B	55
Dudley, Mary Ann	14, Oct. 1855	James	Knight, Mary	B	20
Dudly, Mary Ann	11, Jan. 1852	Robert	----, Bridget	B	250
Duecker, Johanna Agnes	12, Feb. 1852	J. Bernard	Braegelmann, J.B.H.	L	
Duell, Francis Jacob	18, May 1856	Caspar	Feckel, Mechtilda	W	14
Duellmann, Christoph Friedrich	2, Oct. 1856	Caspar	Schumper, Elisabeth	L	
Duelmann, Bernard	2, Nov. 1855	Joseph	Forsmann, Gertrud	F	
Duelmann, Gerhard Joseph	29, May 1853	Joseph	Fortmann, Gertrud	F	
Duerk, Ida	15, July 1856	Boniface	Minder, Agatha	F	
Duermueller, Johan Heinrich	24, Dec. 1854	Joseph	Buchholz, Maria	F	
Duerr, Caroline	29, Oct. 1858	Boniface	Minder, Agatha	H	
Duerr, Joseph	8, Apr. 1855	Francis	----, Barbara	H	
Duerstock, Anna Maria Catharina	24, Oct. 1858	J. Herman	Gerwing, Anna M.	C	
Duerstock, Anna Maria Theresa	5, Feb. 1859	Bernard	Wendel, M. Theresa	L	
Duerstock, Bernard	26, July 1857	Friedrich	Aklma, Margaretha	T	
Duerstock, Bernard	18, Mar. 1854	Heinrich	Wendel, Anna M.	C	
Duerstock, Bernard	17, May 1850	Herman	Gerwing, Maria	C	
Duerstock, Gerhard Heinrich	30, Sept 1854	Herman	Gerwin, Anna M.	C	
Duerstock, Herman Heinrich	29, Dec. 1852	J. Herman	Gerwin, Maria	C	
Duerstock, Johan	28, Nov. 1858	Friedrich	Huesmann, Anna Adel.	T	
Duerstock, Johan Gerhard	20, June 1851	Heinrich	Kröger, Theresa	A	
Duerstock, Johan Matthias	30, May 1851	Herman	Gervin, Maria	C	
Duerstock, Johan Theodor Ferdinand	7, Feb. 1856	Herman	Gerwin, M. Elisabeth	C	
Duerstock, Johan Wilhelm	26, May 1853	Johan B.	Wendel, M. Theresa	L	
Duerstock, M. Theresa Wilhelmina	3, July 1851	J. Bernard	Wendel, M. Theresa	L	
Duerstock, Maria Henrietta	23, Sept 1855	J. Heinrich	Wendel, M. Anna	C	
Duerstork, Maria Catharina	21, May 1850	J. Heinrich	Kröger, Maria Anna	A	
Duerstrock, M Elisabeth Bernardina	21, July 1855	J. Bernard	Wendel, M. Theresa	L	
Dües, Anna Catharina	11, Nov. 1856	Heinrich	Wehre, Catharina	A	
Dues, Catharina Josephina	9, July 1852	H. Bernard	Wehri, Catharina	A	
Dues, F.	6, Feb. 1850	Heinrich	Wehri, Catharina	A	
Dues, Gerhard Rudolph	18, May 1852	Rudolph	Robers, Gertrud	A	
Dues, Herman Johan	10, June 1854	Heinrich	----, Catharina	A	
Dues, Johan Heinrich	26, Nov. 1857	Friedrich	Teipel, Elisabeth	L	
Dues, Maria Elisabeth	5, May 1858	Heinrich	Wehri, Catharina	A	

Name of Child	Date of Baptism	Father	Mother	Church	Page
Duesing, Maria Theresa	3, May 1859	Francis	Schoppner, Theresa	C	
Duesman, Josephina	17, Mar. 1856	Heinrich	Stoerig, Friedrica	K	
Duesman, Maria Helena	10, Nov. 1853	Heinrich	Heving, Friedrica	K	
Duesman, Philomena Elisabeth	9, Feb. 1851	Heinrich	Moerg?, Friedrica	K	
Duest, Johan Heinrich	4, Mar. 1857	Gerhard	Vogelsang, Maria Anna	J	40
Duetmann, Carl Alphons	18, Aug. 1859	Wilhelm	Handorf, M. Gertrud	L	
Duetmann, Johan Heinrich	6, June 1858	Caspar	Schumpe, Elisabeth	L	
Duetmann, Maria Catharina	28, Apr. 1850	J. Caspar	Schumpe, M. Elisabeth	L	
Duetmann, Maria Catharina	14, Sept 1851	Wilhelm	Handorf, Gertrud	L	
Duetmann, Maria Gertrud	16, Sept 1852	J. Casper	Schumpe, Elisabeth	L	
Duetmann, Maria Philomena	9, July 1854	Wilhelm	Handorf, Gertrud	L	
Duetmann, Wilhelm	17, Sept 1854	Caspar	Schumpe, Elisabeth	L	
Duetsch, Maria Catharina	18, Apr. 1850	Herman	Wessel, Gertrud	C	
Duetz, Anna Maria	1, Feb. 1857	Bernard	Lau, Catharina	L	
Duetz, Johan Bernard	6, Oct. 1854	J. Bernard	Lau, Anna Cath.	L	
Duetz, Johan Bernard	20, May 1858	J. Bernard	Lau, Catharina	L	
Duetz, Maria Anna	26, May 1853	Johan B.	Lau, M. Catharina	L	
Duevel, Aloysius Albert Heinrich	5, Feb. 1854	Herman	Koch, Catharina	L	
Duevel, Anna Maria Bernardina	14, Mar. 1858	Herman	Koch, C.	L	
Duevel, Elisabeth	6, Nov. 1859	Heinrich	Rufers, M. Adelheid	C	
Duevel, M. Anna Henrietta	4, Jan. 1857	Heinrich	Rufers, Maria	C	
Duevel, Maria Anna Philomena	30, Jan. 1856	Herman	Kocks, Anna Maria	L	
Duewel, Anna Maria Josephina	15, Feb. 1852	Herman	Koch, Catharina	L	
Duewel, Johan August Theodor	18, Aug. 1850	Herman	Kock, Maria Catharina	L	
Duffel, Bernard Anton	4, July 1851	Caspar	Meier, Maria Catharina	K	
Duffel, Bernardina Francisca	9, Sept 1855	Caspar	Müller, Catharina	K	
Duffel, Friedrich Caspar	17, Nov. 1857	Caspar	Meyer, Catharina	K	
Duffel, Maria Anna	27, May 1853	Caspar	Meyer, Maria Catharina	K	
Duffey, Charles	25, Dec. 1853	Patrick	Molloy, Bridget	P	63
Duffey, James	7, Mar. 1859	Francis	New, Catherine	B	72
Duffey, John	3, Feb. 1851	Francis	New, Catherine	B	224
Duffey, John	9, Aug. 1856	John	----, Mary	E	389
Duffey, John Edward	30, May 1859	Anthony	Coghen, Ann	F	
Duffey, Lucy	27, Oct. 1853		adult - 22 years old	P	56
Duffey, Mary Ann	19, Oct. 1856	Thomas	----, Margaret	M	
Duffey, Patrick	4, June 1854	Francis	New, Catherine	B	1
Duffey, Thomas	28, Nov. 1858	Thomas	----, Margaret	M	
Duffie, John	13, Mar. 1859	Hugh	----, Bridget	E	611
Duffner, Maria Louisa	27, Nov. 1859	Johan	Goll, Louisa	G	
Duffy, Agnes	13, Aug. 1854	John	----, Mary	E	216
Duffy, Agnes	4, July 1851	Michael	Femly, Catherine	P	9
Duffy, Ann	8, July 1859	John	----, Ann	M	
Duffy, Ann	15, Apr. 1855	William	Duffy, Helen	B	13
Duffy, Blanche Louise	8, Sept 1850	John	Quinn, Bridget	B	213
Duffy, Bridget	23, Mar. 1853	John	----, Bridget	E	76
Duffy, Catherine	2, Oct. 1859	John	----, Cecilia	E	659
Duffy, Catherine	29, Aug. 1858	John	McCabe, Bridget	E	560
Duffy, Catherine Lucy	6, Apr. 1852	Lawrence	----, Mary	E	399
Duffy, Charles Bernard	24, Aug. 1856	Thomas	Haight, Lucy	P	188
Duffy, Charles Edward	24, Mar. 1850	Terence	McCabe, Bridget	B	199
Duffy, Edward	7, Nov. 1852	Peter	----, Margaret	M	
Duffy, Eleanor	23, Jan. 1859	Andrew	Murray, Ellen	B	70
Duffy, Ellen	3, Oct. 1854	John	McCabe, B.	E	229
Duffy, Emma	27, Mar. 1853	Francis	----, Rosanne	E	76
Duffy, Frances	6, Mar. 1859	Terence	McHale, Bridget	B	72
Duffy, Francis	26, Feb. 1854	Edward	Robinson, Mary Jane	P	71
Duffy, Helen	5, Mar. 1854	William	Duffy, Helen	B	310
Duffy, Honora	13, Jan. 1850	Michael	Tinley, Catherine	B	194
Duffy, Hubert	4, July 1852	Patrick	Mc---ne, Bridget	P	24

Name of Child	Date of Baptism	Father	Mother	Church	Page
Duffy, Hugh	13, Sept 1857	Bernard	----, Ann	M	
Duffy, James	19, Oct. 1851	Francis	Rogers, Rose	E	351
Duffy, James	1, Oct. 1854	Michael	Kenny, Elizabeth	P	98
Duffy, Johanna Anna	14, June 1857	Nicolaus	Duffy, Maria	L	
Duffy, John	9, Nov. 1856	John	McCabe, Bridget	V	34
Duffy, John	24, Apr. 1853	John	Quinn, Bridget	B	289
Duffy, John	29, July 1855	Michael	Duffy, Mary	E	304
Duffy, John	6, Mar. 1853	Michael	Kenny, Elizabeth	P	36
Duffy, John	30, Aug. 1858	N.	----, Catherine	E	560
Duffy, John	13, July 1850	William	Redmond, Helen	B	207
Duffy, John Patrick	14, Mar. 1858	William	Duffy, Ellen	B	56
Duffy, Louise Catherine	10, Oct. 1858	Thomas	Hague, Lucy	P	263
Duffy, Margaret	26, Aug. 1855	Bernard	----, Ann	M	
Duffy, Margaret	22, Dec. 1857	Edward	Robinson, Mary J.	B	53
Duffy, Margaret	13, Nov. 1853	John	----, Mary	H	
Duffy, Margaret	17, Apr. 1859	Patrick	Daher, Mary	E	618
Duffy, Martin	21, Nov. 1852	Patrick	Clarke, Bridget	P	30
Duffy, Mary	12, Jan. 1858	Francis	Mahon, Margaret	E	509
Duffy, Mary	25, Aug. 1850	John	----, Mary	E	242
Duffy, Mary	15, Oct. 1854	Terence	McCabe, Bridget	B	6
Duffy, Mary	8, Apr. 1853	Thomas	----, Mary	M	
Duffy, Mary Ann	2, Apr. 1854	Thomas	Haight, Lucy	P	77
Duffy, Michael	26, Aug. 1851	John	----, Bridget	E	336
Duffy, Michael	7, Feb. 1854	Michael	Desmond, Mary	E	166
Duffy, Nicholas	1, Jan. 1859	Nicholas	----, Maria	L	
Duffy, Peter	23, Sept 1852	William	----, Ann	E	19
Duffy, Peter Lawrence	13, Aug. 1854	Lawrence	Quigley, Mary	V	16
Duffy, Robert	26, July 1859	Francis	Rogers, Rose	E	643
Duffy, Robert R.	7, Dec. 1856	Francis	Rogers, Ann	E	418
Duffy, Rosina	7, Apr. 1855	Francis	Rogers, Rosina	E	277
Duffy, Sarah Ann	19, Sept 1852	John	----, Mary	E	18
Duffy, Theresa	3, Apr. 1859	John	Nox?, Mary	E	615
Duffy, Thomas	15, Apr. 1855	John	----, Ann	M	
Duffy, Thomas	14, Sept 1856	Michael	Kenny, Elizabeth	P	191
Duffy, Thomas	9, Mar. 1851	Nicolaus	Peldey, Bridget	L	
Duffy, Thomas	28, Sept 1851	Terence	McCabe, Bridget	B	241
Duffy, Thomas	11, Apr. 1852	Thomas	----, Lucy	B	256
Duffy, Thomas	2, June 1854	Thomas	Cohorn, Ann	E	195
Duffy, Thomas Alexander	15, June 1851	Edward	Robinson, Mary Jane	P	9
Duffy, William Anthony	5, July 1855	Patrick	McLoughlin, Margaret	V	25
Dufley, Catherine	4, Jan. 1854	Thomas	----, Margaret	M	
Dufrain, M. Augustina Josephina	28, Sept 1856	Joseph	Hendricks, Anna	F	
Dugan, Anastasia	11, Sept 1859	John	Gorman, Ann	P	295
Dugan, Andrew James	6, Mar. 1853	Joseph	McKeown, Margaret	B	285
Dugan, Ann	10, Feb. 1854	Daniel	Murray, Joanne	P	68
Dugan, Catherine	9, Dec. 1855	Henry	Langan, Honora	V	28
Dugan, Edward	16, Sept 1855	Mark	Sullavin, Catherine	E	315
Dugan, Ellen	12, Dec. 1852	John	Gorman, Ann	P	31
Dugan, Helen	23, Oct. 1855	John	Gorman, Ann	P	156
Dugan, Joanne Julia	19, June 1853	Timothy	Mulcahill, Mary	E	99
Dugan, John	24, June 1855	Joseph	McKeown, Margaret	B	16
Dugan, Margaret	27, Sept 1857	John	Gorman, Ann	P	**225**
Dugan, Margaret	13, Apr. 1852	William	Kilkennan, Mary	E	402
Dugan, Michael	15, Aug. 1856	Thomas	Lavin, Catherine	P	188
Dugan, Patrick	30, Apr. 1852	Daniel	Mussey, Joanne	B	258
Dugan, Susan	15, Nov. 1857	Henry	Langan, Honora	E	493
Dugan, William	26, Sept 1853	William	Murphy, Helen	P	53
Dugen, Emilia	29, Aug. 1852	Thomas	----, Johanna	F	
Dugen, Michael	3, Dec. 1851	William	Murphy, Helen	B	247

Name of Child	Date of Baptism	Father	Mother	Church	Page
Dugen, Vincent Garrett	3, Sept 1850	Garrett	Beulger, Margaret	B	213
Duggan, Cornelius	8, Jan. 1855	Michael	----, Helen	V	22
Duggan, Joanne	24, Jan. 1857	?	?	T	
Duggan, John	25, Mar. 1855	Henry	----, Margaret	M	
Duggan, Margaret	2, Dec. 1858	Henry	----, Margaret	M	
Duggan, Mary	5, Nov. 1856	Henry	----, Margaret	M	
Duggan, Mary	28, Apr. 1856	James	----, Honora	M	
Duggan, Matthew	16, Aug. 1858	Matthew	Dwyer, Helen	E	557
Duggan, Robert	23, Nov. 1859	Thomas	Huston, Jane	P	304
Duggan, Thomas	21, Aug. 1856	Thomas	Heuston, Joanne	T	
Duggan, Thomas	4, Feb. 1855	Thomas	Hewson, Joanne	T	
Duggen, Ann	12, Sept 1858	James	----, Honora	M	
Duig, Maria Elisabeth	15, Aug. 1858	Heinrich	Sachs, Margaretha	K	
Duke, Ann Jane	24, May 1859	John	Donlon, Jane	E	627
Duke, Catherine	14, Sept 1851	John	Gill, Mary	B	241
Duke, Eliza	24, Sept 1857	John	----, Joanne	E	482
Duke, Mary	24, Sept 1857	John	----, Joanne	E	482
Duke, William Patrick	13, Nov. 1853	John	Donlin, Joanne	E	144
Dukes, John K.	7, June 1857	James	Craner, Elizabeth Ann	E	458
Duklo, Anna Maria	13, May 1855	Lawrence	Hoefer, Paulina	J	32
Duklo, Heinrich Wilhelm	12, Sept 1858	H. Lawrence	Hoefer, Paulina	J	48
Duklo, Johan Matthias Lawrence	23, Sept 1856	Lawrence	Hoefer, Paulina	J	38
Dulap, Mary Jane	13, Feb. 1859	John	Henry, Eliza Jane	E	603
Dulay, Julia Ann	16, Apr. 1854	Dennis	Conklin, Helen	P	79
Düll, Anna Elisabeth	3, June 1855	F. Jacob	Stübing, Friedrica	W	9
Düll, Nicolaus	28, Nov. 1854	Caspar	Fecker, Mechtilda	W	6
Dulle, Bernard Gerhard	5, Sept 1854	Gerhard	Weyering, Helena	C	
Dulle, Catharina Elisabeth Bernardina	10, Nov. 1858	J. Bernard	Folker, Bernardina	C	
Dulle, Gerhard Heinrich	31, Dec. 1855	Gerhard	Abel, Bernardina	C	
Dulle, Maria Elisabeth	10, May 1857	J.B.	Falke, Dina	C	
Dulle, Maria Rosina	2, Feb. 1851	J. Bernard	Gehring, M. Helena	C	
Düllen, Maria	25, Jan. 1857	Michael	Scheit, Anna Maria	D	77
Dullmann, Johan Joseph	6, June 1857	Anton	Roemer, Anna	F	
Dum, Francis Anton	3, Dec. 1854	Heinrich	Henrichs, Elisabeth	D	23
Dum, Johan	20, Feb. 1853	Heinrich	Henrichs, Elisabeth	D	372
Dum, Joseph	6, July 1856	Heinrich	Henrichs, Elisabeth	D	62
Dumann, Johan Theodor	4, Aug. 1852	J. Gerhard	Wörtman, Anna Maria	D	341
Dumans, Mary Elizabeth	7, Jan. 1853	?	?	B	280
Dumaugh, John Benjamin	11, Sept 1853	Benjamin	McEvoy, Rosanne	B	299
Dumay, Honora	30, Mar. 1856	Dennis	----, Helen	R	
Dumbacher, Johan Jacob	4, Apr. 1858	Johan	Grimm, Susan	N	
Dumen, Johan Herman	13, Sept 1850	J. Gerhard	Werner, Anna Maria	D	232
Dumich, Ann Virginia	26, Sept 1852	William	Magen, Josephine	E	20
Dumick, Eugene	27, May 1855	William	Mayer, Josephine	E	288
Dumler, Barbara Margaretha	1, Aug. 1856	Martin	Dinn, Magdalena	F	
Dumler, Margaretha	18, July 1858	Martin	Dimm, Magdalena	F	
Dummhof, Anton	23, May 1858	Heinrich	Sch---, Christina	D	112
Dummich, Joseph Edward	12, Dec. 1858	Wilhelm	Mahieu, Josephina	J	48
Dumphy, Ann Elizabeth	18, Feb. 1850	Patrick	----, Mary	E	197
Dumphy, Mary Helen	2, June 1856	Michael	Landrigan, Helen	E	371
Dunagan, James	5, Mar. 1854	James	Kelly, Ann	P	72
Dunagan, Peter	30, May 1852	James	Kelly, Ann	P	22
Dunat, Catherine	9, Feb. 1853	Patrick	Maloney, Catherine	B	283
Duncan, Albert Charles	18, June 1854	Lawrence	----, Mary Jane	E	199
Duncan, William	1, Mar. 1859	William	----, Catherine	E	607
Dunden, Mary	11, Feb. 1853	William	McAuliff, Joanne	B	283
Dundon, Elizabeth	16, Jan. 1855	William	McAuliff, Joanne	B	10
Dungan, Ann	1, Dec. 1850	Peter	----, Ann	E	264
Dunham, Francis	17, Oct. 1850	Francis	Bloomfield, Mary	E	254

Name of Child	Date of Baptism	Father	Mother	Church	Page
Dunigan, Elizabeth	13, May 1854	John	Duffy, Margaret	P	82
Dunigan, James	8, Mar. 1859	James	Kelly, Ann	P	279
Dunigan, John	1, June 1854	Francis	Dawson, Ann	P	84
Dunigan, Margaret	14, Jan. 1852	William	Kerry, Catherine	B	250
Dunigan, Mary	3, Feb. 1856	Francis	Dorrian, Ann	P	169
Dunigan, Matthew	8, Feb. 1857	James	Kelly, Ann	P	205
Dunigan, Michael	11, June 1853	Francis	Dawson, Ann	P	44
Dunigan, Sarah	14, Jan. 1852	William	Kerry, Catherine	B	250
Dunigan, Thomas	20, Sept 1857	Thomas	Schmidt, Margaret	U	
Duniger, Michael	17, Dec. 1854	Michael	Lyons, Honora	P	110
Dunkens, Joseph Lawrence	30, Mar. 1851	Lawrence	Waller, Maria	K	
Dunker, Anna Margaretha	1, Sept 1858	Anton	Tebbe, Anna Margaretha	F	
Dunker, Anton Adam Adolph	19, Sept 1859	Johan	Danheimer, Rosina	C	
Dunker, Carolina Bernardina	16, Jan. 1851	Johan	Tanheimer, Rosina	D	249
Dunker, Clemens Joseph	15, Mar. 1855	Johan	Danheimer, Rosina	C	
Dunker, Gertrud Elisabeth	18, Jan. 1856	Anton	Tepe, Margaretha	F	
Dünker, Johan	7, Feb. 1858	Stephan	H---, Margaretha	D	104
Dunker, Johan Caspar Heinrich	2, June 1853	Johan	Tanheimer, Rosina	D	387
Dunker, Johan Herman	21, Aug. 1853	Anton	Tepe, Margaretha	F	
Dunker, Joseph	28, Dec. 1854	Joseph	Freitag, Sophia	D	25
Dunker, Michael Johan	13, Sept 1852	Lawrence	Wallers, Maria	K	
Dunlap, Adeline Lousie	2, Sept 1859	Robert	Whiteside, Mary M.	B	80
Dunlap, Ann Lilly	11, Nov. 1855	Daniel	McDonald, Catherine	U	
Dunlap, Bridget	14, Jan. 1850	P.	Ber---, Ann	B	194
Dunlap, Catherine	13, Sept 1857	Joseph	McDonough, Catherine	U	
Dunlap, John	1, Sept 1855	John	----, Elizabeth	E	312
Dunlap, Sarah Elizabeth	9, Apr. 1858		adult	M	
Dunlavy, Catherine	29, Mar. 1853	John	Galleger, Ann	P	38
Dunlavy, Hugh	14, Nov. 1858	James	Scollard, Mary Jane	E	578
Dunlea, James	9, July 1854	James	Regan, Helen	B	2
Dunlea, Johan	11, Aug. 1852	James	Regan, Helen	B	268
Dunlea, Timothy	16, Nov. 1856	James	Regan, Ellen	B	36
Dunlevy, Christopher	23, July 1854	Owen	Maher, Ann	P	90
Dunlevy, Helen	3, Feb. 1856	John	Gallagher, Ann	P	169
Dunlevy, Joseph	21, Dec. 1856	Owen	Meagher, Ann	P	201
Dunlevy, Mary Ann	20, Mar. 1859	Owen	Maher, Ann	P	280
Dunn, Alice	7, Aug. 1850	William	----, Margaret	E	237
Dunn, Anastasia	30, Oct. 1859	John	Ryan, Mary	U	
Dunn, Andrew	4, Apr. 1858	Michael	----, Mary	E	526
Dunn, Ann	26, Dec. 1851	William	Keating, Mary	E	367
Dunn, Ann	1, Oct. 1854	William	Taylor, Margaret	P	98
Dunn, Catherine	20, June 1853	Cornelius	Cassiday, Catherine	P	45
Dunn, Catherine	23, July 1854	Edward	Burns, Catherine	P	89
Dunn, Catherine	3, Oct. 1850	Michael	Mealey, Bridget	B	216
Dunn, Catherine	2, May 1858	Richard	Jenkins, Mary	B	58
Dunn, Charles Albert	25, Aug. 1850	Patrick F.	Moloney, Catherine	B	211
Dunn, Cornelius	30, Apr. 1858	Cornelius	Boyle, Mary	E	532
Dunn, Cornelius	2, Mar. 1859	Peter	Walsh, Bridget	P	278
Dunn, Dennis	20, Feb. 1854	Michael	Farrell, Mary	E	170
Dunn, Edward	11, Nov. 1855	John	Ryan, Mary	U	
Dunn, Eliza	21, Aug. 1851	John	Colter, Joanne	E	334
Dunn, Hannah	5, June 1852	Cornelius	----, Mary	M	
Dunn, Helen	12, Feb. 1854	Bernard	Conklin, Mary	P	68
Dunn, Jaems	27, Jan. 1856	Thomas	Fox, Ann	P	168
Dunn, James	28, Oct. 1855	James	Shanahan, Margaret	P	157
Dunn, James Francis	28 ,Nov. 1858	James	Cassan, Ellen	B	67
Dunn, James Garret	16, May 1852	James	Carsam, Ellen	E	413
Dunn, James William	2, Mar. 1856	Richard	Jenkins, Mary	B	26

Name of Child	Date of Baptism	Father	Mother	Church	Page
Dunn, John	5, Dec. 1852	Bernard	McDonald, Sarah	P	30
Dunn, John	18, Oct. 1857	John	Ryan, Mary	U	
Dunn, John	2, Jan. 1853	Richard	Jenkins, Mary	B	280
Dunn, Margaret	22, Apr. 1855	Daniel	Sullivan, Catherine	E	281
Dunn, Margaret	25, Jan. 1855	John	Corbett, Ann	P	117
Dunn, Margaret	6, Nov. 1853	John	Ryan, Mary	P	58
Dunn, Mary	2, July 1854	Cornelius	----, Mary	M	
Dunn, Mary	20, Apr. 1856	James	Casson, Ellen	B	28
Dunn, Mary	5, Mar. 1854	James	Custen, Ellen	E	173
Dunn, Mary	10, Aug. 1857	James	Shannon, Margaret	P	219
Dunn, Mary	15, Nov. 1859	John	Morrison, Elizabeth	E	671
Dunn, Mary	7, Jan. 1853		adult	B	280
Dunn, Mary Ann	18, July 1850	John	Ryan, Mary	B	207
Dunn, Mary Ann	1, Oct. 1850	Owen	Burns, Margaret	B	215
Dunn, Mary Elizabeth	11, Apr. 1852	Thomas	----, Mary Ann	E	401
Dunn, Mary Helen	27, June 1858	Patrick	McNamara, Bridget	P	251
Dunn, Michael Joseph	21, July 1852	Michael	----, Mary	E	431
Dunn, Peter	19, Oct. 1851	Edward	Byrne, Catherine	P	13a
Dunn, Rose Ann	26, Apr. 1856	Cornelius	Boyle, Mary	E	361
Dunn, Thomas	18, Oct. 1856	Daniel	Sullivan, Catherine	P	195
Dunn, Thomas	20, Feb. 1853	John	----, Ann	E	64
Dunn, Thomas	12, Aug. 1855	Michael	Hogan, Mary	P	145
Dunn, William	7, Jan. 1853	John	Colten, Jane	E	52
Dunn, William	8, Jan. 1858	John	Dunn, Ann	P	235
Dunn, William	7, Sept 1856	William	Brannan, Susan	E	396
Dunn, William	23, Mar. 1851	William	O'Connor, Helen	B	227
Dunn, Winnefred	12, June 1859	James	Shannon, Margaret	P	285
Dunn?, Peter	9, Apr. 1851	John	Ryan, Mary	M	
Dunne, Catharina Mathilda	13, Oct. 1856	J. Heinrich	Bredeler, Gertrud	A	
Dünne, Herman Bernard	23, Apr. 1852	Heinrich	Wegener, Johanna	J	16
Dünne, Johan Herman	25, Mar. 1859	J.H.	Breckeler, Gertrud	A	
Dunne, Johanna Maria	25, Oct. 1852	Heinrich	Bredler, Gertrud	A	
Dünne, Johanna Maria Catharina	4, June 1850	Heinrich	Wegener, Johanna	A	
Dünne, Maria Gertrud	7, Apr. 1855	J. Heinrich	Bredeler, Gertrud	A	
Dunnegan, Elizabeth	25, July 1852	John	----, Margaret	B	266
Dunnegow, Mary	31, May 1855	James	Kelley, Ann	P	131
Dunneham, Michael	24, Apr. 1852	James	Kelley, Ann	P	21
Dunnigan, John	11, Jan. 1857	William	Kelly, Catherine	B	39
Dunnigan, Mary	6, Oct. 1850	Patrick	Dooling, Helen	B	215
Dunphry, John Richard	7, Oct. 1857	Michael	Dunn, Ellen	E	484
Dunphy, Mary Caecilia	1, Feb. 1859	Michael	Dunn, Helen	E	601
Dunrin, Heinrich	15, Mar. 1851	Heinrich	Heinrichs, Elisabeth	K	
Dünsch, Elisabeth	14, Dec. 1856	Johan	Koch, Elisabeth	D	74
Dunsche, August Bernard	14, Nov. 1854	August	Brockmeyer, Antonia	C	
Dunsche, Emilia Maria	22, May 1856	August	Brockmeyer, Gertrud	C	
Dunsche, Ida Josephina	7, Dec. 1857	August	Brockmeyer, Gertrud	C	
Dunworth, Catherine	4, June 1851	John	----, Mary	E	312
Duoner, Carolina	4, July 1858	Wendelin	Braun, Elisabeth	D	114
Duphrene, Mary Louise Maggot	8, Oct. 1854	Isidor	Gardepen, Matilda	P	99
Dupler, Sarah Isabel	10, July 1859	John	Leonard, Sarah	B	77
Duppler, Daniel Ludwig Georg	1, June 1851	Carl	Kopf, Maria Eva	C	
Dupps, Albertina	20, Oct. 1850	Christian	Soesken, Aloysia	C	
Dupps, Ignatz	10, Apr. 1853	Christian	Guerike, Aloysia	C	
Dups, Valentin	18, Apr. 1856	Christian	Joerger, Aloysia	C	
Dupuis, John	24, Jan. 1853	Thomas	----, Jane	E	57
Duran, Mary Josephine	22, Jan. 1856	John	----, Elizabeth	E	339
Durban, James	21, June 1851	----	----, Mary	E	316
Durbin, Margaret	7, Aug. 1853	John	Donnelly, Frances	P	48
Durbin, Owen	28, Mar. 1858	John	Donnelly, Frances	P	243

Name of Child	Date of Baptism	Father	Mother	Church	Page
Durcan, John	26, June 1855	John	Gavin, Helen	P	137
Durchholz, Ann Elisabeth	19, Oct. 1856	Philip	----, Elisabeth	R	
Durchholz, Ann Mary	1, Feb. 1855	John	Genzler, Josephine	R	
Durchholz, Catharina	13, Aug. 1859	Philip	Fischer, Elisabeth	R	
Durchholz, Heinrich	11, Feb. 1858	Johan	----, Josephina	R	
Durchholz, Johan	6, Apr. 1856	Heinrich	Pappenberger, Eva	R	
Durchholz, Joseph	11, Dec. 1859	Heinrich	Pappelberger, Eva	R	
Durchholz, Joseph	8, June 1856	John	----, Josephine	R	
Durchholz, Josephine Elisabeth	28, June 1857	Heinrich	----, Eva	R	
Durchholz, Philip	25, Dec. 1858	Heinrich	Pappenberger, Eva	R	
Dürck, Maria Anna	21, Dec. 1856	Andreas	Koch, Maria	D	74
Durham, Julia	28, Nov. 1852	Patrick	----, Honora	E	39
Durham, Michael	2, May 1852	Dominick	----, Margaret	E	408
Durik, Anna Margaretha	6, Sept 1857	Joseph	Read, Maria	J	42
Düring, Heinrich	3, Nov. 1850	Lawrence	Bovalt, Maria	D	241
Dürk, Carl Wilhelm	27, Jan. 1853	Andreas	Koch, Maria Anna	D	367
Dürk, Georg Eduard	2, Mar. 1851	Andreas	Koch, Marianna	D	256
Dürk, Johan Wilhelm	16, Jan. 1859	Andreas	Koch, Maria Anna	D	129
Dürk, Maria Elisabeth	19, Nov. 1854	Andreas	Koch, Maria Anna	D	22
Durkan, Mary	16, Sept 1858	Patrick	Mulherin, Bridget	E	563
Durken, Helen	21, Sept 1851	John	Ley, Margaret	B	241
Dürker, Johan Gerhard Heinrich	25, Aug. 1850	Heinrich	Buedel, Maria Anna	D	229
Durker?, Michael	1, Dec. 1855	Thomas	O'Neil, Ann	K	
Durkin, Elisabeth Ellen	6, Apr. 1856	Lawrence	----, Mary S.	E	357
Durkin, Michael James	17, Nov. 1856	Thomas	Gavin, Ellen	B	36
Durr, Ann Salome	1, Aug. 1852	Francis	----, Barbara	H	
Durr, Francis James	31, Dec. 1854	John	----, Agatha	H	
Durr, Francis Xavier	29, Dec. 1859	Francis	Ritt, Barbara	H	
Durr, George	25, Sept 1853	George	----, Margaret	H	
Durre, Margaret	25, Mar. 1851	George	Häusler, Margaret	H	
Durren, Margaret	5, Aug. 1854	John	Kirby, Margaret	P	91
Dursch, Theresa	27, Jan. 1850	Johan	Petzold, Cunigunda	D	201
Durst, Heinrich Gerhard	9, Jan. 1852	G. Heinrich	Nieman, Elisabeth	J	16
Durst, Veronica Elisabeth	23, June 1850	Johan	Papp?, Francisca	D	218
Dürstock, Maria Theresa	10, Sept 1852	Heinrich	Kröger, Maria Theresa	A	
Dury, Ann	10, Dec. 1850	Wendel	Freier, Mary	H	
Dury, Barbara	18, May 1856	Wendel	----, Ann Mary	H	
Dury, Catherine	7, Mar. 1858	Wendel	Feldner, Anna Maria	H	
Dury, James	19, Feb. 1854	Wendel	----, Ann	H	
Dury, Peter	2, May 1852	Wendel	----, Ann	H	
Dusch, Johan Michael	9, Oct. 1853	Johan	Bohlinger, Sophia	C	
Duscher, Angela	3, May 1857	Peter	Heinrich, Catharina	F	
Duscher, Maria Elisabeth	19, Aug. 1855	Peter	Heinrich, Catharina	F	
Duscher, Mathias	9, Jan. 1859	Peter	Heinrich, Catharina	F	
Düshauer, Catharina Maria	14, June 1857	Bernard	----, Anna Maria	D	88
Dusolt, Catharina	9, Mar. 1851	Georg	----, Cunigunda	D	257
Dussler, Maria Magalena	11, June 1854	Martin	Meyer, Catharina	K	
Dussour, Catharina	20, Dec. 1857	Martin	Meyer, Catharina	K	
Dussour, Josephina Julia	11, Dec. 1859	Martin	Meyer, Catharina	K	
Düster, Georg	18, July 1858	Georg	Ho----, Carolina	D	115
Dusterberg, Catharina Maria	18, Dec. 1851	J. Heinrich	Himmelmeyer, Elisabeth	C	
Dutenhofer, Louisa	17, Nov. 1856	J. Adam	Schauder, Elisabeth	C	
Dütenhofer, Valentin	10, Feb. 1856	Valentin	Trotman, Helena	K	
Dutlinger, Maria Magdalena	4, June 1854	J. Georg	Kramer, Maria Magdalena	K	
Duttenhoefer, Barbara	19, Nov. 1857	Joseph	Spelz, Margaretha	D	99
Duttenhofer, Barbara	25, Sept 1859	Adam	Me---, Catharina	D	147
Duttenhöfer, Daniel	18, July 1858	Adam	Schaud---, Elisabeth	D	115
Duttenhofer, Michael	10, Sept 1859	Joseph	Spaiz, Margaretha	D	146
Dutthoff, Maria Theresa	8, June 1851	Bernard	Wilbers, Susanna	C	

Name of Child	Date of Baptism	Father	Mother	Church	Page
Duttlinger, Friedrich Bernard	5, Dec. 1858	Johan	Schinzle, Anna	F	
Duttlinger, Georg Francis	6, June 1852	Georg	Kramer, Magdalena	C	
Duttlinger, Maria Sophia	9, Nov. 1856	Johan	Schaezle, Anna	D	71
Dutton, Sarah Mary	2, Feb. 1856	?	Lincoln, Mary	B	24
Duval, Mary	18, Mar. 1853	Matthew	McCann, Bridget	B	286
Duvany, Catherine	17, Feb. 1859	Patrick	Conny, Catherine	B	71
Düvelin, Anna Maria Carolina	23, Sept 1856	Bernard	Dickman, Carolina	A	
Düvelues, Gerhard B. Theodor	8, Mar. 1858	Bernard	Dickman, Maria Carolina	A	
Duvenick, Franz Joseph	10, Jan. 1854	Joseph	Siemers, Catharina	L	
Duvenick, Maria Elisabeth	1, Jan. 1852	Joseph	Siemes, Catharina	C	
Duwald, Margaretha	7, July 1850	Christian	Fischer, Apollonia	D	221
Duweneck, Johan Francis	31, May 1857	Joseph	Siemers, Catharina	K	
Duwenick, Joseph Bernard Friedrich	12, Jan. 1855	Joseph	Siemer, Catharina H.	L	
Dwan, Michael	12, Sept 1853	Patrick	----, Ellen	E	128
Dwire, James	6, Nov. 1859	Patrick	McGroth, Mary	S	
Dwire, John	3, Feb. 1857	Michael	Devine, Joanne	E	431
Dwyer,	14, Sept 1859	John	Keath, Catherine	E	654
Dwyer, Alice	14, Sept 1856	Andrew	Murphy, Rosanne	P	192
Dwyer, Bridget	12, Sept 1852	John	Maher, Mary	E	16
Dwyer, Catherine	28, Oct. 1855	William	Carroll, Catherine	E	323
Dwyer, Edmund	17, Nov. 1856	Edmund	Dwyer, Hannah	E	413
Dwyer, Edward	16, May 1858	Lawrence	Murphy, Mary	P	248
Dwyer, Edward Patrick	29, Nov. 1857	William	Carrell, Catherine	E	496
Dwyer, Elissa	17, Feb. 1850	Patrick	----, Bridget	E	197
Dwyer, Eliza	3, Jan. 1853	Michael	Hodge, Eliza	B	280
Dwyer, Helen	7, Nov. 1859	Patrick	Morisey, Margaret	E	669
Dwyer, Helen	4, Sept 1853	Thomas	Hayes, Mary	P	51
Dwyer, Honora	18, Jan. 1853	Edmund	----, Ann	E	56
Dwyer, James	27, Apr. 1856	Alexander	Halloran, Helen	R	
Dwyer, James	4, July 1858	Edmund	----, Ann	E	546
Dwyer, James	6, Jan. 1854	Edmund	Drayer, Ann	E	158
Dwyer, James	14, Nov. 1856	James	Hodgins, Eliza	B	36
Dwyer, James	25, Aug. 1852	Michael	----, Honora	E	9
Dwyer, James Lawrence	30, Oct. 1859	Lawrence	Murphy, Mary	P	302
Dwyer, Jane	15, Jan. 1853	Patrick	Donovan, Bridget	E	55
Dwyer, Joanne	6, Sept 1857	Patrick	Moracy, Margaret	E	479
Dwyer, John	23, Apr. 1854	Alexander	Hallaner, Ellen	E	184
Dwyer, John	22, June 1855	Edmund	----, Ann	E	295
Dwyer, John	4, Feb. 1855	Lawrence	Reilly, Ann	P	119
Dwyer, John	10, Sept 1854	Michael	Honan, Joanne	P	95
Dwyer, Juliana	18, Nov. 1859	Michael	O'Connell, Mary	E	671
Dwyer, Lawrence	14, Feb. 1852	Thomas	Hays, Mary	P	18
Dwyer, Margaret	29, Dec. 1850	Patrick	----, Bridget	E	272
Dwyer, Martin	15, June 1855	John	Carey, Mary	P	135
Dwyer, Martin	3, Nov. 1854	Patrick	McGreary, Ann	B	7
Dwyer, Martin	19, Oct. 1858	Timothy	Murnaan, Helen	P	264
Dwyer, Mary	2, Nov. 1851	John	----, Eliza	P	13b
Dwyer, Mary	31, July 1859	John	Keilly, Ann	P	290
Dwyer, Mary	23, Mar. 1855	Ron.	Conner, Margaret	E	274
Dwyer, Mary Ann	6, Oct. 1859	Michael	----, Lydia	E	660
Dwyer, Mary Ann	13, Oct. 1853	William	Carroll, Catherine	V	6
Dwyer, Mary Jane	15, Feb. 1854	William	Daley, Catherine	E	169
Dwyer, Matthew	12, July 1857	Alexander	----, Helen	R	
Dwyer, Michael	10, Apr. 1853	John	Carran, Bridget	B	288
Dwyer, Michael	23, May 1851	William	Carroll, Catherine	E	310
Dwyer, Patrick	4, Nov. 1850	Thomas	----, Honora	E	259
Dwyer, Sarah	24, Oct. 1852	Alexander	Halloran, Ellenore	R	
Dwyer, William	3, Oct. 1859	Edmund	----, Ann	E	659
Dyal, Bridget	9, Feb. 1851	Martin	----, Mary	E	282

Name of Child	Date of Baptism	Father	Mother	Church	Page
Dyer, Bridget	1, Mar. 1853	James	----, Bridget	E	67
Dyer, James	19, Aug. 1853	James	Feeny, Catherine	V	5
Dyer, John Andrew	5, Mar. 1851	William	Geroud, Esther	E	287
Eagan, Ann	2, July 1855	John	Bryan, Mary	E	297
Eagan, Ann	2, June 1850	William	----, Joanne	E	219
Eagan, Ellen	30, Dec. 1855	William	Cunningham, Mary	B	23
Eagan, Honora	24, Jan. 1858	John	----, Mary	E	512
Eagan, James	16, Apr. 1858	James	O'Brien, Mary	E	529
Eagan, James	23, Oct. 1854	Martin	Reynolds, Rose	B	6
Eagan, Jeremiah	15, May 1853	William	Cunningham, Margaret	B	291
Eagan, John	16, July 1857	John	Connell, Mary	E	466
Eagan, John	18, Feb. 1856	Martin	Reynolds, Rose	B	25
Eagan, John	19, Apr. 1852	William	O'Brien, Joanne	E	405
Eagan, Margaret Ann	22, May 1859	John	----, Mary	E	627
Eagan, Mary	29, Sept 1850	John	Cullen, Mary	B	215
Eagan, Mary	16, Feb. 1856	Michael	----, Bridget	E	344
Eagan, Mary	3, Dec. 1851	Terence	Flannery, Catherine	P	14
Eagan, Mary Ann	22, May 1853	John	----, Mary	E	91
Eagan, Mary Frances	18, Mar. 1854	William	----, Joanne	E	177
Eagan, Mary Helen	26, Sept 1855	Terence	Flannery, Catherine	P	152
Eagan, Michael	27, Dec. 1857	Martin	Reynolds, Rose	B	53
Eagan, Michael	18, Jan. 1857	Michael	Cl---m, Margaret	E	427
Eagan, Patrick Howard	20, Mar. 1859	Terence	Flannery, Catherine	P	280
Eagan, Stephen Clement	5, Dec. 1858	James	Leonard, Mary Ann	B	68
Eagan, Theresa	19, Feb. 1853	Terence	Flannery, Catherine	P	36
Eagan, Thomas	29, May 1853	John	Brien, Mary	E	93
Eagan, William	28, Feb. 1858	William	Cunningham, Margaret	B	56
Eagan, William John	17, Dec. 1856	William	----, Joanne	E	420
Eagle, Mary Josephine	12, Sept 1858	Joseph	Herzog, Frances	B	64
Eaglehart, John	10, Mar. 1851	John	Colter, Hannah	E	290
Eamss, Mary Elizabeth	9, Jan. 1853	Martin	Pratley, Hannah	B	281
Earley, Charles Carroll	3, June 1855	Peter	Ward, Ann	B	15
Earley, Elizabeth	25, Mar. 1851	Peter	Ward, Honora	B	227
Earley, George Scott	1, Aug. 1852	Peter	Wardery, Ann	B	266
Earley, James	1, May 1859	Michael	McBierty, Bridget	B	74
Earley, Mary Jane	17, Jan. 1858	Bernard	McDermott, Sarah	B	54
Earls, William George	15, May 1859	William	----, Mary	E	624
Early, Catharine	8, June 1856	Bernard	McDermott, Sarah	T	
Early, Clara Elizabeth	19, Oct. 1856	Patrick	Sheridan, Bridget	E	405
Early, John	27, Dec. 1857	Thomas	Ward, Amelia	P	233
Early, Mary	20, Nov. 1853	Thomas	Hart, Ann	E	145
Early, Mary Helen	19, Oct. 1858	Peter	Shay, Ann	E	571
Early, Sarah	28, Jan. 1855	Bernard	McDormott, Sarah	E	260
Earny, Susan Theresa	11, Nov. 1855	Peter	Murray, Bridget	B	21
Easton, Eliza Jane	27, Apr. 1853	William	Howard, Ann	B	289
Eaton, Mary Ann	28, Oct. 1853	Patrick	----, Julia	E	138
Ebbeler, Maria Gertrud	3, Aug. 1851	Joseph	Jacobs, Gesina	D	276
Ebbing, Maria Christina Henrica	1, July 1850	J. Albert	Haneman, Anna Maria	A	
Ebbrig, Clara Amalia Maria	13, Apr. 1858	Johan A.	Enneking, M. Anna	T	
Ebel, Elisabeth Appolonia	9, May 1853	Adam	Falkenstein, Elisabeth	D	384
Ebel, Louisa	26, Apr. 1855	Adam	Wallenstein, Elisabeth	D	34
Ebener, Francis Joseph	16, Nov. 1856	Conrad	Ham---, Carolina	D	72
Eberenz, Anna Maria	4, Aug. 1859	Cosmas	Schmutz, Francisca	F	
Eberenz, Francis	22, Feb. 1857	Cosmas	Schmidt, Francisca	J	40
Eberenz, Maria Francisca	3, Oct. 1858	Johan	Erbstland, Agatha	J	48
Eberhard, Anna Dora	27, Nov. 1859	Mathias	Horn, Elisabeth	T	
Eberhard, Carl	29, Jan. 1854	Johan	Groh, Catharina	R	
Eberhard, Catharine Mary	10, Dec. 1854	Matthew	Horn, Elisabeth	T	
Eberhard, Elisabeth	28, Apr. 1850	Michael	Becker, Margaretha	D	211

Name of Child	Date of Baptism	Father	Mother	Church	Page
Eberhard, Josephine	26, Sept 1856	Matthew	Horn, Elizabeth	T	
Eberharty, Mary Margaret	4, Oct. 1857	Matthew	Seifert, Eva	U	
Eberholdin, Catharina	24, Aug. 1851	Mathias	Kammer, Margaretha	D	279
Eberle, Heinrich	4, Dec. 1855	Heinrich	----, Philomena	C	
Eberle, Julius	22, Aug. 1858	Heinrich	Armbruster, Stephania	C	
Eberle, Mary	1, Jan. 1855	Francis H.	Phillips, Mary	B	9
Eberle, Otto	16, June 1851	Francis H.	Phillips, Mary	B	234
Eberling, Edward	8, Nov. 1858	Edward	Wack, Catharina	C	
Ebert, Maximillian Michael	3, Aug. 1853	Anton	Schraut, Dorothea	D	398
Ebert, Philomena	16, May 1852	Andreas	Willem, Sophia	D	320
Ebert, Walter	22, June 1851	?	Ebert, Mary	E	318
Ebker, Heinrich Joseph	6, May 1859	Johan H.	Tenemberger, Bernardina	F	
Eble, Clemens	21, May 1854	Christoph	Stueve, Clara	C	
Ebmeier, Patrick	24, Mar. 1855	William	----, Sylvia	U	
Ebner, Carl	27, Mar. 1859	Conrad	Hamm---, Carolina	D	134
Ecabert, Peter Claudius	29, May 1853	Peter	Ackermann, Theresa	C	
Echert, Isidor	14, June 1857	Francis	Ackerman, Rosa	J	42
Echinger, Johanna Catharina	24, Dec. 1854	Nicolaus	Stein, Susanna	C	
Echtermann, Bernardina Philomena C	2, July 1854	Bernard	Beckmann, Catharina	L	
Echtermann, Francis	21, Nov. 1852	Bernard	Beckmann, Catharina	C	
Echtermann, Josephina Maria	2, Mar. 1851	Bernard	Beckmann, Catharina	C	
Eckbrink, Anna Maria Gesina Sophia	12, Apr. 1856	Francis	Theders, Catharina	F	
Eckelman, Elisabeth Josephina	17, Oct. 1855	Bernard	Scheppman, Anna Maria	A	
Eckelman, Johan Heinrich	8, Apr. 1859	Johan B.	Schöppman, Anna Maria	A	
Eckelman, Maria Elisabeth	16, Mar. 1857	Johan B.	Scheppman, Maria Elisabeth	A	
Eckelmeier, Bernardina Elisabeth	13, Apr. 1856	Willibrand	Niebolte, Bernardina	D	56
Eckelmeyer, Johan Joseph	24, Apr. 1854	Willibrand	Niebolter Bernardina	D	9
Eckenhorst, Caspar Theodor	28, Oct. 1855	Theodor	----, Elisabeth	A	
Eckenroth, Catharina Barbara	1, Apr. 1855	Valentin	Schlötter, Margaretha	A	
Eckerman, Louise	25, Aug. 1850	Matthew	Schily, Barbara	B	211
Eckert, Adam	9, Apr. 1854	Joseph	Ohnhaus, Maria	D	8
Eckert, Anna Catharina	17, Apr. 1855	Bernard	Latte, Theresa	A	
Eckert, Anna Maria	27, Aug. 1854	Louis	Mueller, Anna M.	C	
Eckert, August	30, Aug. 1858	Joseph	Roth, Rosalia	R	
Eckert, Carolina	20, Mar. 1853	Valentin	Meyer, Carolina	K	
Eckert, Carolina Ruffina	26, Oct. 1856	Valentin	Meyer, Carolina	Q	16
Eckert, Catharina Barbara	29, July 1855	Joseph	Roth, Rosalia	R	
Eckert, Francisca	21, Feb. 1858	Michael	Reis, Elisabeth	T	
Eckert, Johan	21, Nov. 1852	Joseph	Ohnhaus, Maria	D	358
Eckert, Johan	12, Nov. 1854	Valentin	Meyer, Carolina	Q	5
Eckert, Johan Adam	23, May 1857	Joseph	Ohnhaus, Maria	D	85
Eckert, Joseph Ludwig	5, June 1851	Valentin	Meyer, Carolina	K	
Eckert, Josephine	30 , Nov. 1856	Joseph	----, Rosalia	R	
Eckert, Louisa	27, Aug. 1854	Michael	Reis, Elisabeth	F	
Eckert, Ludwig	8, Feb. 1857	Ludwig	Mueller, Anna M.	C	
Eckert, Maria Rosalia	22, Aug. 1854	Georg	Volkmann, Catharina	F	
Eckert, Maria Rosalia Clothilda	23, Feb. 1856	Conrad	Eiert, Susanna	F	
Eckert, Peter	23, Jan. 1854	Francis (+)	Hartman, Christina	K	
Eckert, Regina	24, May 1857	Joseph	Waltz, Ursula	H	
Eckert, Salome Magdalena	5, Jan. 1855	Johan	adult - 35 years old	K	
Eckert, Sophia	1, Nov. 1850	Michael	Reis, Elisabeth	F	
Eckert, Theresa Josephina	4, July 1852	Michael	Reis, Elisabeth	D	328
Eckert, Wilhelm Carl	26, Dec. 1852	August	----, ----	C	
Eckhardt, Augusta	2, Apr. 1853	Joseph	Gänzler, Rosina	R	
Eckly, Francis Joseph	14, July 1856	Arthur	Haas, Justina	A	
Eckman, Edward Henry	7, Oct. 1852	Addison	McGown, Margaret	E	25
Eckman, George	26, Sept 1859	Shanon	----, Margaret	E	658
Eckman, James C.	15, July 1857	----	----, ----	E	465
Eckman, Johan Martin	3, Nov. 1851	M. Johan	Hatcke, Maria	D	291

Name of Child	Date of Baptism	Father	Mother	Church	Page
Eckman, John	19, Feb. 1855	Addison	----, Margaret	E	266
Eckman, John Addison	15, Oct. 1850	Addison S.	----, Margaret	E	254
Eckman, Maria Anna Carolina	9, Nov. 1851	Johan	Erlau, Justina	D	291
Eckman, Philomena	4, July 1859	Johan	Ankauer, Justina	K	
Eckmann, Maria Anna	31, May 1853	Johan	Anlawer, Justina	L	
Eckstein, Albert Georg	6, Aug. 1854	Martin	Schneider, Margaretha	K	
Eckstein, August Friedrich	13, Jan. 1856	Martin	Schneider, Margaretha	K	
Eckstein, Elisabeth	17, Aug. 1851	Paul	Gieringer, Juliana	D	278
Eckstein, Elisabeth Sara	22, Nov. 1857	Martin	Schneider, Margaretha	K	
Eckstein, Helena Kunigunda	15, Apr. 1858	Roman	Poschert, Martina	T	
Eckstein, Rosina	9, Sept 1854	Paul	Geringer, Juliana	D	17
Edelkamp, Cunigunda	28, Dec. 1859	Johan	Vogler, Crescentia	D	153
Edelkamp, Elisabeth	3, Oct. 1858	Johan	Vogler, Crescentia	D	120
Edelkamp, Johan Baptist	22, Apr. 1855	Johan	Vogler, Crescentia	D	33
Edelkamp, Maria Anna	26, Apr. 1857	Johan	Vogler, Crescentia	H	
Edelman, Anna Maria	1, May 1854	Michael	Koessler, Victoria	D	9
Edelman, Gertrud	7, June 1852	Michael	Kessler, Victoria	D	323
Edelmann, Johan Baptist	9, Jan. 1853	Johan B.	Langword, Elisabeth	C	
Edelmann, Wilhelmina	8, Apr. 1855	Johan B.	Landwehr, Elisabeth	C	
Eder, Johan	1, Nov. 1854	Christian	Eder, Maria	K	
Eder, Rosina	31, Aug. 1851	William	Girten, Barbara	D	280
Edge, Samuel	6, Oct. 1850	John	Molloy, Margaret	B	215
Edinger, Mary Ann	24, Nov. 1854	Philipp	Tron, Mary	E	243
Edrich, Christian	23, Apr. 1854	James	----, Frances	H	
Edrich, Peter	2, Aug. 1857	Johan	Klin, Barbara	W	19
Edwards, Catherine	8, Apr. 1855	Kieran	Conway, Mary	P	127
Edwards, Henry	26, Feb. 1857	Hanford	Gleason, Margaret	B	41
Edwards, John Henry	2, June 1851	John	Williams, Mary	E	312
Edwards, Mary	2, Oct. 1859	Thomas	McHugh, Helen	P	299
Edwards, Mary Frances	28, Feb. 1859	Alfred	Gleeson, Margaret	B	71
Effing, Anna Catharina	7, Mar. 1851	J. Heinrich	Blomme, Margaretha	A	
Effing, Anna Maria	21, Apr. 1857	Bernard	Wesk, Adelheid	D	83
Effing, Herman Heinrich	4, June 1853	Heinrich	Blommer, Margaretha	A	
Effing, Maria Margaretha	30, May 1852	J. Heinrich	Blommel, Margaretha	A	
Effinger, August	2, Sept 1855	Francis	Wenzler, Crescentia	F	
Effinger, Catharina	21, Dec. 1851	Francis	Winzler, Crescentia	F	
Effinger, Franz Xaver	14, Aug. 1853	Francis	Winzler, Crescentia	F	
Effinger, Johan	9, June 1850	Francis	Wenzler, Crescentia	F	
Effinger, Maria Agatha	9, May 1858	Francis	Winzer, Crescentia	F	
Efgeman, Johan Bernard	2, Jan. 1851	Johan	Brüning, Margaretha	D	247
Efger, Anna Catharina	1, July 1853	J. Gerhard	Lobbes, Maria Elisabeth	D	392
Efger, Bernard Heinrich Francis	23, Sept 1855	J. Heinrich	Lobert, Elisabeth	D	43
Efkeman, Anna Maria	20, Dec. 1851	J. Gerhard	Wielens, Maria	A	
Efkeman, Johan B.	20, Sept 1857	J.B. Heinr.	Berg, Maria Adelheid	A	
Efkeman, Johan Bernard	28, Sept 1853	Gerhard J.	Wielen, Maria	A	
Efkeman, Johan Joseph	9, Feb. 1851	B. Heinrich	Röshenkamper, Maria	K	
Efker, Anna Maria	27, July 1859	Gerhard	----, Elisabeth	D	143
Efron, Wilhelm Joseph	4, May 1852	Johan	Göder, Louisa Marg. Dorothea	K	
Egan, Ann	10, Mar. 1851	John	Lynch, Joanne	E	290
Egan, Ann Mary	31, Mar. 1854	Anthony	Brown, Mary	B	312
Egan, Bridget	3, Sept 1854	Patrick	Dignan, Bridget	T	
Egan, Catherine	7, Nov. 1852	Patrick	Dignan, Bridget	P	29
Egan, Daniel	30, July 1850	Constantine	Brian, Sarah	B	209
Egan, Daniel	19, Mar. 1854	John	----, Sarah	M	
Egan, Edmond Francis	23, Jan. 1859	John	Fox, Theresa A.	P	272
Egan, Eliza	21, July 1856	Cornelius	O'Brien, Sarah	B	31
Egan, Eliza	16, Dec. 1856		Egan, Bridget	B	37
Egan, Eugene	13, Feb. 1853	Eugene	Singleton, Joanne	B	283
Egan, Eugene	26, Jan. 1853	Eugene	Singleton, Joanne	B	281

Name of Child	Date of Baptism	Father	Mother	Church	Page
Egan, Helen	18, Sept 1852	Michael	Quinn, Margaret	B	270
Egan, Joanne	30, Mar. 1852	John	Connolly, Mary	B	255
Egan, John	1, Oct. 1851	Constantine	Brien, Sarah	B	242
Egan, Julia	23, May 1852	Matthew	Coffin, Julia	B	259
Egan, Louise Jane	22, June 1853	Patrick	----, Elizabeth	B	294
Egan, Margaret	10, June 1851	John	----, Mary	E	315
Egan, Margaret	9, Aug. 1854	John	Connelly, Mary	B	3
Egan, Margaret	20, Feb. 1853	Michael	Carroll, Helen	B	284
Egan, Margaret	2, Jan. 1853	Peter	Mullane, Helen	B	280
Egan, Mary	15, Mar. 1852	John	Lynch, Joanne	B	254
Egan, Mary Ann	14, Mar. 1858	Constantine	O'Brien, Sarah	B	56
Egan, Mary Ann	1, Mar. 1857	Eugene	Singleton, Hannah	B	41
Egan, Mary Jane	11, June 1854	Eugene	Singleton, Hannah	B	1
Egan, Michael	12, Sept 1858	Patrick	Dignan, Bridget	B	64
Egan, Michael	15, Apr. 1855	Peter	Mullane, Ellen	B	13
Egan, Patrick	8, June 1856	Peter	Mullady, Ellen	B	29
Egan, Terrence	1, Feb. 1852	Terence	----, Mary	H	
Egan, Thomas	6, Mar. 1854	Constantine	Brien, Sarah	B	310
Egan, Thomas	27, Aug. 1857	Michael	Dagan, Bridget	T	
Egan, Timothy	31, May 1853	John	Lynch, Joanne	P	43
Egan, William	2, June 1850	Michael	Carroll, Helen	B	204
Egan, William Henry	2, June 1850	Matthew	C---, Julia	B	204
Egbers, Anna Margaretha	30, May 1858	J. Herman	Quaing, Susanna Marg.	F	
Egbers, Carl Ludwig	25, Jan. 1858	J. Gerhard	Keutz, Susanna Adelheid	K	
Egbers, Francis Ludwig	3, Oct. 1850	Gerhard	Keitz, Euphemia Adelheid	K	
Egbers, Johan Bernard	7, Feb. 1853	J. Gerhard	Keutz, Euphemia Aleid	K	
Egbers, Maria Gesina	13, June 1851	J. Herman	Luning, Margaretha	F	
Egbers, Susanna Marianna Adelheid	30, June 1854	J. Herman	Quaing, Susanna M.	F	
Egberts, Maria Magdalena	22, July 1855	J. Gerhard	Keutz, M. Euphemia Adelheid	K	
Egbrink, Franz Bernard	29, June 1854	Francis B.	Tegeder, Maria Cathrina	F	
Ege, Johan Martin Nicolaus	7, Dec. 1857	Joseph	Heimberger, Magdalena	A	
Egelmeyer, Johan Bernard	31, Aug. 1851	Willebrand	Nieporte, Bernardina	L	
Egen, Maria Helena Engel	12, Mar. 1856	Gerhard	Moos, Susanna Maria	F	
Egenroth, Philipp	20, June 1858	Carl	Roland, Anna Maria	A	
Egerle, Maria Josephina	17, Apr. 1854	Xavier	Roth, Martina	L	
Eggelton, Sarah	3, Aug. 1856	Robert	May, Catherine	E	386
Eggemeier, Anna Maria Louisa	7, Mar. 1859	Mathias	Peters, A.M. Louisa	F	
Eggemeier, Friedrich	12, May 1853	Mathias	Peters, Anna Maria	F	
Eggemeier, Johan Heinrich	4, Apr. 1856	Mathias	Peters, Anna Maria	F	
Eggemeier, Maria Anna Francisca	5, Mar. 1859	Georg H.	Bramme, M. Elisabeth	L	
Eggemeier, Maria Elisabeth	4, July 1852	Heinrich	Bramme, M. Elisabeth	L	
Eggemeyer, Catharina Elisabeth	15, May 1856	Georg H.	Bramme, M. Elisabeth	L	
Eggemeyer, Gerhard Georg	8, Dec. 1854	Georg H.	Brame, M. Elisabeth	L	
Egger, Maria Anna	9, July 1858	Bernard G.	Muss, M. Susanna	L	
Eggerle, Francisca	29, Aug. 1858	Heinrich	Nag---, Francisca	D	118
Eggers, Catharina	24, Apr. 1859	Bernard	Kellmann, Carolina	C	
Eggers, Elisabeth Agatha Rosa	20, Oct. 1859	Gerhard	Koch, Sabina	L	
Eggers, Maria Carolina	30, July 1857	Bernard	Kollmann, Carolina	C	
Eggert, Agnes Philomena	12, Sept 1858	Francis	Hölker, Theresa	K	
Eggert, Anna Carolina	17, Sept 1854	Francis	Hoelker, Theresa	L	
Eggert, Francis Bernard	5, Apr. 1857	Francis	Helker, Catharina	K	
Eggert, Joseph Ludwig	14, Feb. 1850	Valentin	Mayer, Carolina	K	
Eggleton, Rudolph	12, June 1854	Robert	May, Catherine	B	1
Eggman, Johan Bernard	24, July 1856	Johan	Anlauer, Justina	D	63
Egle, Edward Wilhelm	7, July 1859	J. Eusebius	Guth, Carolina	N	
Egler, Eugene Constantine Washington	18, Jan. 1852	August	Hank, Lucia	D	303
Egler, Maria Eugenia	15, Aug. 1853	August	Heng, Lucia	D	400
Egli, Carl Albert	5, Aug. 1850	Joseph	Gutt, Carolina	F	
Eglof, Elisabeth Rosina	30, Sept 1857	Carl	Geiner, Veronica	D	95

Name of Child	Date of Baptism	Father	Mother	Church	Page
Eglof, Maria Louisa	24, Oct. 1852	Johan	Doll, Agnes	D	355
Eglof, Mathias Johan	20, Nov. 1859	Gregor	Geiler, Elisabeth	D	151
Egloff, Catharina	19, Sept 1858	Gregor	Giller, Elisabeth	D	119
Egloff, Johan	25, Dec. 1853	Gregor	Giller, Elisabeth	D	422
Egloff, Johan Joseph	25, Mar. 1852	Gregor	Gueler, Elisabeth	F	
Egly, Cornelia Eugenia	13, Sept 1857	Joseph E.	Guth, Carolina	C	
Egly, Guido Johan	29, Sept 1852	J. Eusebius	Gut, Carolina	D	350
Egly, Rosa Augusta	22, Oct. 1854	Joseph	Gut, Carolina	F	
Egman, Joseph	24, Sept 1854	Johan	Ankarger, Justina	N	24
Egner, Barbara	22, May 1859	Johan	Becker, Maria	D	138
Eha, Amalia	21, Feb. 1858	Dominick	Lander, Sophia	F	
Eha, Franz	30, July 1854	Dominick	Lander, Sophia	F	
Eha, Joseph Anton	30, May 1850	Paul	Sahlmueller, Margaretha	C	
Eha, Louisa	2, Dec. 1855	Dominick	Lander, Sophia	F	
Eha, Sophia	11, Sept 1859	Dominick	Lander, Sophia	F	
Ehbauer, Carolina	7, Mar. 1852	Jacob	Hein, Anna Eva	D	311
Eherren, Margaretha Helena	8, Oct. 1852	Cornelius	Brown, Helen	K	
Ehler, Augustine	19, Sept 1858	Benedict	Berwanz, Catharina	D	119
Ehler, Catharina Rosina	27, Oct. 1858	Simon	S----, Margaretha	D	122
Ehlich, Maria Theresa	22, Nov. 1859	Mathias	----, Elisabeth	D	151
Ehlich, Paul	4, July 1858	Mathias	--ter--- Louisa	D	114
Ehling, Johan Bernard	12, Apr. 1856	J. Gerhard	Esken, Catharina	F	
Ehling, Johan Bernard	10, May 1857	Johan G.	Eschen, Catharina	F	
Ehling, Maria Helena	25, Aug. 1850	?	----, Dina	K	
Ehling, Maria Philomena	10, Dec. 1858	Johan	Eschen, Catharina	L	
Ehlinger, Anna Catharina	29, Aug. 1852	Jacob	Feuerback, Sabina	K	
Ehlinger, Barbara	17, Dec. 1854	Jacob	Feuerbach, Sabina	K	
Ehlinger, Johan Jacob	21, Jan. 1858	J. Jacob	Fehlbach, Sabina	K	
Ehlinger, Johan Jacob	12, Oct. 1856	Jacob	Feuerbach, Sabina	K	
Ehlink, Johan Heinrich	1, Apr. 1854	J. Gerhard	Eschen, Catharina	F	
Ehmer, Francisca	9, Jan. 1859	Joseph	Lechner, Margaretha	D	128
Ehmer, Maria Theresa	14, Nov. 1852	Joseph	Lochner, Margaretha	N	10
Ehmer, Theresa	30, Mar. 1851	Joseph	Lechner, Margaretha	D	259
Ehrelecher, Sophia	27, Feb. 1855	F. Xavier	Reichman, Veronica	K	
Ehrenbühl, Elisabeth	10, Apr. 1859	Johan	Mathe--, Margaretha	D	135
Ehrenbühl, Richard	30, Mar. 1856	Johan	Mathe--, Margaretha	D	55
Ehrentraut, Georg Martin	24, July 1859	Ernst	Oberbeck, Anna	D	142
Ehrentraut, Maria Catharina	21, June 1856	Ernst	Obernpik, Anna	L	
Ehret, Philipp	3, July 1853	Francis	Fulgiao, Juliana	D	393
Ehri, Margaretha	27, Jan. 1850	Michael	Kaiser, Anna Maria	D	202
Ehrmantraut, Barbara	2, Jan. 1853	Johan	Adam, Theresa	D	363
Ehrmantraut, Maria Margaretha	23, Sept 1855	Johan	Adam, Theresa	D	43
Ehrmantraut, Michael Joseph	14, Feb. 1858	Johan	Adam, Theresa	D	105
Ehrmantraut, Theresa Margaretha	29, Aug. 1858	Michael	----, Margaretha	D	118
Ehrmentraud, Sophia	15, June 1851	Michael	----, Margaretha	D	268
Ehrmentraut, Margretha Theresa	29, Sept 1850	Johan	Adam, Theresa	D	235
Ehry, Valentin	4, June 1858	Ludwig	Ehry, Theresa	K	
Eibeck, Andreas	1, Nov. 1850	Peter	Freborn, Isabella	D	241
Eibeck, Elisabeth	29, Mar. 1857	Peter	Frepon, Elisabeth	C	
Eibeck, Elisabeth	12, Aug. 1855	Peter	Freppon, Elisabeth	D	40
Eibeck, Maria Magdalena	5, Apr. 1858	Johan	Geisler, Sabina	D	108
Eibeck, Peter	19, Sept 1852	Peter	----, ----	D	348
Eibert, Anna	17, Dec. 1854	Conrad	Bauer, Barbara	D	24
Eibert, Johan	28, Aug. 1854	Maximillian	Burkhart, Theresa	D	16
Eich, Carl Ludwig	8, Feb. 1857	Peter	----, Theresa	R	
Eich, Clara Johanna	1, Mar. 1858	Peter	----, Theresa	R	
Eich, Ferdinand	1, Aug. 1858	Peter	Pistner, Catharina	K	
Eich, Gustav	19, Sept 1856	Peter	Pistner, Catharina	D	67
Eich, Johan	15, Jan. 1854	Peter	Pistner, Catharina	D	2

Name of Child	Date of Baptism	Father	Mother	Church	Page
Eiche, Joseph	24, Apr. 1856	Joseph	Kotterer, Christina	K	
Eichelberger, Carolina	5, Mar. 1854	Wendel	Schwarz, Gertrud	N	20
Eichelberger, Franz	29, June 1856	Joseph	Eck, Eva	F	
Eichelberger, Georg	30, May 1858	Joseph	Eck, Eva	F	
Eichelsbaumer, Magdalena	7, Apr. 1850	Joseph	Schneider, Marcella	D	208
Eichener, Elisabeth	29, June 1856	Nicolaus	Steins, Susanna	D	62
Eichenlaub, Anna Margaretha	28, Oct. 1855	Friedrich	Neurohr, Catharina	F	
Eichenlaub, Catharina	14, Jan. 1855	Francis	Rhein, Theresa	C	
Eichenlaub, Elisabeth	5, June 1851	John Adam	Tuerck, M. Adelheid	C	
Eichenlaub, Elisabeth	3, May 1857	Valentin	Ulziefer, Catharina	D	84
Eichenlaub, Georg Francis	7, June 1857	Georg F.	----, Theresa	D	87
Eichenlaub, Johan	27, Oct. 1850	Friedrich	Neurohr, Catharina	D	240
Eichenlaub, Johan Joseph	1, May 1856	Adam	Diek, Margaretha	D	57
Eichenlaub, Joseph	1, June 1852	Valentin	Wolsiefer, Catharina	C	
Eichenlaub, Joseph Johan	10, June 1857	J. Adam	Dirk--, Margaretha	D	87
Eichenlaub, Louisa	15, May 1859	Friedrich	Neurohr, Catharina	F	
Eichenlaub, Louisa	29, Jan. 1854	Johan	Reling, Agnes	D	3
Eichenlaub, Margaretha	10, Apr. 1853	Francis	Rhein, Theresa	D	380
Eichenlaub, Margaretha	6, Mar. 1853	Friedrich	Neurohr, Catharina	F	
Eichenlaub, Maria	17, Oct. 1858	G. Francis	Rhein, Theresa	D	121
Eichenlaub, Maria Anna	3, Jan. 1850	Valentin	Wolsiefer, Catharina	C	
Eichenlaub, Peter	1, Oct. 1854	Valentin	Wollsiefer, Catharina	C	
Eichenlaub, Sebastian	18, Dec. 1853	Johan	Dirck, Margaretha	C	
Eicher, Caharina Elisabeth	22, Mar. 1857	Friedrich	Tuerck, Elisabeth	H	
Eicher, Johan Jacob	7, July 1859	Friedrich	----, Elisabeth	D	141
Eicher, Rosa	5, Sept 1852	Jacob	Wiedemer, Barbara	K	
Eicher, Simon Jacob	14, May 1854	Jacob	Wiedemer, Barbara	K	
Eichert, Anton	21, Oct. 1850	Francis	Ackerman, Rosa	J	8
Eichert, Elisabeth	14, June 1857	Francis	Ackerman, Rosa	J	42
Eichert, Magdalena	13, June 1852	Francis	Ackerman, Rosa	J	16
Eichert, Michael	1, Apr. 1855	Francis	Ackerman, Rosa	J	30
Eichert, Rosa	20, Nov. 1853	Francis	Ackerman, Rosa	J	24
Eichhorn, Barbara	8, Feb. 1857	Francis	Hettrich, Barbara	D	78
Eichhorn, Georg Andreas Adam Johan	2, Aug. 1859	Georg	Larm, Catharina	F	
Eichhorn, Johan Martin	29, May 1852	Francis	Hetterich, Barbara	F	
Eichhorn, Johan Martin	27, July 1856	Georg	Lern, Catharina	D	63
Eichhorn, Michael	4, July 1855	Francis	Hetterich, Barbara	D	37
Eichner, Georg	22, Dec. 1852	Jacob	Zuberg, Josephina	L	
Eichner, Georg	27, Sept 1859	Johan	Weideler, Francisca	K	
Eichner, Louisa	4, Oct. 1857	Johan	Weidner, Francisca	K	
Eiler, Sophia Mathilda	24, July 1853	Samuel	Heiss, Maria	S	
Eilerman, Heinrich Anton	4, July 1857	B. Heinrich	Hoefel, Maria	Q	23
Eilers, Anna Margaretha Elisabeth	17, July 1859	J. Joseph	Rode, Elisabeth	D	142
Eilers, Anna Maria Theresa	26, Sept 1855	Heinrich	Farlage, Anna Theresa	C	
Eilers, Anna Maria Theresa	5, Feb. 1857	J. Bernard	Flinkers, Anna Maria	A	
Eilers, Bernard Aloysius	11, July 1854	Heinrich	Wellenbrink, Maria Elisabeth	K	
Eilers, Heinrich Wilhelm	12, Feb. 1857	Johan	Koch, Gertrud	D	78
Eilers, Helena Catharina	17, Nov. 1854	J. Bernard	Flinkers, Marianna	A	
Eilers, Herman Heinrich	26, June 1859	Nicolaus	Rademaker, Susanna	J	50
Eilers, Johan Bernard Francis	25, Feb. 1859	Johan B.	Flinke, Maria Anna	A	
Eilers, Johan Bernard Theodor	19, Nov. 1852	J. Bernard	Flinkers, Maria Anna	A	
Eilers, Johan Wilhelm	8, Oct. 1850	J. Herman	Wükenborg, Anna M. Adel.	J	8
Eilers, Johan Wilhelm	11, Sept 1856	Nicolaus	Rademakers, Susanna	J	38
Eilers, Joseph Ludwig	30, Nov. 1852	Heinrich	Willenbring, Elisabeth	K	
Eilers, Maria Adelheid	14, Feb. 1858	Nicolaus	Rademakers, Susanna	J	44
Eilers, Maria Catharina	17, Nov. 1854	J. Bernard	Flinkers, Marianna	A	
Eilers, Maria Christina	9, Aug. 1855	Nicolaus	Rademaker, Susanna	J	32
Eilers, Maria Magdalena Sophia	19, Dec. 1855	Johan	Rode, Maria Elisabeth	D	48
Eilers, Maria Margaretha Rosina	6, Oct. 1856	Heinrich	Wellenbrink, Elisabeth	A	

Name of Child	Date of Baptism	Father	Mother	Church	Page
Eilers, Sophia Maria	21, May 1857	Johan	Rohoe, Elisabeth	D	85
Eilers, Wilhelmina Johanna	14, May 1852	Johan	Brinkman, Francisca	D	319
Eimer, August	30, Jan. 1853	L. Adam	Schaefer, Catharina	Q	2
Eimer, Catherine	24, Sept 1854	August	----, Walburga	H	
Eimer, Francis Heinrich	5, Oct. 1859	Francis	Penzler, Philomena	C	
Eimer, Franz George Washington	27, Feb. 1859	Pius	Bertel, Magdalena	L	
Einsiedl, Victoria	28, Oct. 1855	Joseph	Stadtmüller, Josephina	D	45
Einsiedler, Remigius	23, Feb. 1854	Joseph	Stadmüller, Afra Josephina	A	
Eisele, Barbara Hermina	22, July 1858	Francis X.	Br---, Elisabeth	D	115
Eisele, Gustav Joseph Bernard	9, Apr. 1856	Francis	Brunner, Lisette	L	
Eiselein, Joseph	17, Dec. 1854	Conrad	Siner, Margaretha	D	24
Eiselein, Margaretha	5, Apr. 1857	Conrad	Surrer, Margaretha	D	82
Eisen, Carl Eduard	30, Dec. 1852	Anton	Rapp, Charitas	F	
Eisen, Emma	12, Mar. 1854	Anton	Rapp, Charitas	C	
Eisen, Maria	20, Oct. 1858		adult	F	
Eisen, Maria Louisa	20, June 1858	Anton	Baumann, Francisca	C	
Eisendle, Georg	30, Oct. 1859	Francis	Brunner, Elisabeth	D	150
Eisenhardt, Friedrich Carl	9, Oct. 1859	Carl	Schwarzkopf, Anna	D	148
Eisenhardt, Magdalena Louisa	17, Jan. 1858	Carl	Schweizkopf, Anna	D	103
Eisenhart, Maria Anna	13, Apr. 1856	Carl	Schwarzkopf, Maria Anna	D	56
Eisenhart, Sophia	9, July 1854	Carl	Schwarzkopf, Anna	D	13
Eisenhauer, Herman	16, Dec. 1855	Sebastian	Ulrich, Louise	R	
Eisenhauer, Joseph	12, June 1859	Sebastian	Uhrig, Louisa	R	
Eisenhauer, Lawrence	14, June 1857	Sebastian	----, Louise	R	
Eisenhauer, Maria Paulina	30, June 1854	Sebastian	Uhrig, Louise	R	
Eisenman, Anna Maria	20, Mar. 1859	Jacob	Uhl, Monica	D	134
Eisenmann, Joseph	5, Mar. 1854	Joseph	Uhl, M. Anna	C	
Eisenmenger, Ferdinand	12, Apr. 1855	Peter	Morgensh----, Theresa	D	33
Eiser, Maria Rosina	17, Oct. 1858	Johan	Tuchfärber, Maria	J	48
Eiserman, Josephina	23, July 1859	Bernard	Mer---, Apollonia	D	142
Eisman, Johan Adam	9, Apr. 1854	Daniel	Hach, Francisca	N	21
Eismann, Johan Heinrich	3, Feb. 1858	Friedrich	Stephan, M. Elisabeth	F	
Eismann, Mathias	24, June 1856	Friedrich	Steffen, Maria Elis.	F	
Eith, Carl August	13, Jan. 1856	Bernard	Schauble, Louisa	F	
Eith, Carolina	2, Aug. 1854	Bernard	Schauble, Louisa	F	
Eith, Gustav Adolph	25, Aug. 1858	Bernard	Scheible, Louisa	F	
Ekert, Maria	4, June 1854	August	Boesefelder, Caecilia	K	
Ekle, Francisca	13, Apr. 1859	Francis	Lehle, Anna	F	
Elberg, Maria Eleanora	13, Jan. 1859	J. Bernard	Sievers, M. Adelheid	C	
Elbert, Anna Maria	18, Jan. 1852	Johan	Peter, Elisabeth	D	303
Elbert, Maria Josephina	28, Mar. 1858	Johan	Rufli, Maria	J	46
Elbert, Paul	10, June 1855	Johan	Peters, Elisabeth	F	
Elbke, Maria	23, Mar. 1856	Christoph	Stueve, Clara	C	
Elble, Carl Eduard	19, Mar. 1854	Valentin	Burchert, Apollonia	D	6
Elble, Christoph	22, June 1851	Valentin	Markhorst, Apollonia	A	
Elble, Clara Victoria	2, Mar. 1856	Valentin	Burkhart, Appolonia	D	53
Elble, Francis Ludwig	5, Oct. 1851	Christian	Stüve, Clara	D	286
Elble, Johan	26, Oct. 1856	Joseph	Rudolph, Magdalena	K	
Elbley, Joseph	11, June 1854	Joseph	Rudolf, Magdalena	K	
Elbly, Mary Elisabeth	19, Sept 1858	Joseph	Rudolf, Magdalena	R	
Elbreg, Elisabeth Magdalena	30, Nov. 1854	J. Arnold	Deuble, Elisabeth	F	
Elbreg, George William Henry	10, Feb. 1856	Henry H.	----, Margaret	E	344
Elbreg, Maria Barbara	13, Sept 1852	J. Arnold	Deiwele, Elisabeth	F	
Elbring, Catharina Florentina	4, Nov. 1859	Heinrich	Slu--te, Margaretha	K	
Elder, Barbara	17, Aug. 1851	Rudolph	Brichler, Magdalena	F	
Elder, Jacob	24, July 1853	Rudolph	Brügler, Helena	D	396
Elder, Louisa	17, Dec. 1854	Rudolph	Brugler, Magdalena	D	24
Eldrich, Elizabeth	18, Apr. 1852	Joseph	----, Ann	M	
Elfer, Maria Anna	21, Apr. 1850	Johan	Grunkemeier, Catharina	D	210

Name of Child	Date of Baptism	Father	Mother	Church	Page
Elfering, Johan Herman H.	5, Mar. 1855	Friedrich	Bunte, Maria	A	
Elfering, Maria Gesina	2, Sept 1855	Herman	Schutte, Gesina	A	
Elfers, Anna	23, Dec. 1853	Bernard	Wessling, Susanna	D	421
Elfers, John Bernard	9, Aug. 1857	Bernard	Wesseling, Susan	U	
Elfers, John Henry	9, Dec. 1855	John	Gomer, Catherine	U	
Elfers, Joseph Bernard Clemens	25, Mar. 1859	Anton	Brink, Maria Anna	A	
Elfers, Lawrence	17, Dec. 1850	Wilhelm	Hilbers, Helena	K	
Elfers, Wilhelm	14, Oct. 1853	Wilhelm	Hilbers, Helena	L	
Elgas, Anton	10, Apr. 1853	Anton	Kegler, Catharina	C	
Elgas, Catharina	8, Apr. 1855	Anton	Kegel, Barbara	C	
Elgas, Catharina	21, Mar. 1858	Anton	Kegler, Catharina	C	
Elgas, Francis	2, Mar. 1857	Anton	Koegler, Catharina	C	
Elgas, Johan Jacob	3, Aug. 1851	Anton	Kegel, Catharina	C	
Elgas, Magdalena	4, July 1858	Francis	Diben, Regina	N	
Elgenmüller, Maria Elisabeth	24, May 1852	J. Heinrich	Greiwe, Maria Anna	D	321
Elgetz, Carl	14, Jan. 1855	Francis	Feth, Barbara	D	26
Elitch, Hannah Theresa	3, July 1859	John	----, Hilda	E	636
Elitsch, (girl)	19, Dec. 1852	John	----, Hilda	E	45
Elkel, Wilhelm	16, Dec. 1855	Philipp	Müller, Maria	A	
Elkins, William August	29, May 1853	James	Carey, Eliza	B	293
Ell, Andreas	4, Sept 1854	Peter	Feger, Ottilia	A	
Ell, Catharina	8, Feb. 1852	Peter	Feger, Ottilia	D	306
Ell, Johan Wihelm Adam	25, Aug. 1857	Peter	Feger, Ottilia	C	
Ell, Joseph	17, Mar. 1850	Peter	Feger, Ottilia	C	
Ellas, Johan Gerhard	9, Feb. 1855	Caspar	Bachs, Sophia	D	28
Ellen, Susana Maria	13, Oct. 1850	Albert	Schrane, Angela	K	
Ellenberg, Harriet Ann	30, May 1855	John	----, Harriet Ann	U	
Ellenburger, Johan Ludwig	18, Apr. 1852	Johan	Poudre, Henriette	F	
Eller, Hirlanda	26, May 1856	Leo	Desse, Anna	D	59
Eller, Johan Joseph	20, Jan. 1858	Joseph	Vorlage, Theresa	C	
Eller, Maria Josephina	26, May 1856	Leo	Desse, Anna	D	59
Eller, Otto	24, Feb. 1852	Emanuel	Schneider, Friedricka	C	
Ellerhart, Anna Maria Sophia	28, Dec. 1856	Caspar	Barman, Sophia	D	75
Ellerhorst, Johan Stephen	14, Nov. 1858	Caspar	Balk, Sophia	D	124
Ellerman, Anna Maria	5, Jan. 1851	Friedrich	Paul, Anna	D	247
Ellerman, Anna Sophia Catharina	3, Sept 1854	Friedrich	Schaub, Anna	D	16
Ellerman, Johan Friedrich Conrad	6, Dec. 1852	J. Friedrich	Paul, Anna	D	360
Ellermann, Arnold Martin Friedrich	25, Mar. 1856	Friedrich	Paul, Anna Maria	F	
Ellett, Daniel	14, Aug. 1850	James M.	Johnson, Elizabeth	E	243
Ellett, Martha	14, Aug. 1850	James M.	Johnson, Elizabeth	E	243
Ellett, Thomas	14, Aug. 1850	James M.	Johnson, Elizabeth	E	243
Ellick, Joseph Jacob	23, Apr. 1854	Joseph	Schneider, Maria	D	8
Ellick, Maria Rosalia	16, Nov. 1858	Joseph	Schneider, Maria	T	
Ellig, Francis Carl	14, Sept 1856	Joseph	Schneider, Maria	D	67
Ellig, Joseph	20, Oct. 1850	Joseph	Schneider, Maria	D	239
Ellig, Lucia	11, Mar. 1852	Joseph	Schneider, Maria	D	312
Elliks, Mathias Franz	15, July 1856	Mathias F.	Niederhausen, Louisa	F	
Elliott Thomas Ralph	4, Oct. 1857	Thomas R.	Jones, Hanna Bateman	P	**226**
Elliott, Alexander	6, Dec. 1855	----	----, ----	E	331
Elliott, Catherine Elizabeth	19, Oct. 1856	John	----, Ulda	E	406
Elliott, Joseph	10, June 1852	William	Mannion, Louise	B	260
Elliott, Robert Cudune	4, Oct. 1857	Thomas R.	Jones, Hanna Bateman	P	**226**
Ellis, Caroline	8, Apr. 1855	Edward	Spikin, Elizabeth	B	13
Ellis, Margaret Julia	18, Aug. 1850	Charles	Murphy, Catherine	B	210
Ellis, Thomas	15, June 1851	Patrick	McCormick, Helen	B	234
Ellisheim, Heinrich	16, Mar. 1859		adult - 20 years old	F	
Ellison, George Thomas	19, July 1858	Robert	Luckey, Mary A.	B	61
Ellman, Anna Catharina Josephina	28, Jan. 1857	J. Joseph	Severding, Josephina	K	
Ellman, Maria Elisabeth	4, Apr. 1858	Clemens	Lange, Bernardina	K	

Name of Child	Date of Baptism	Father	Mother	Church	Page
Ellmann, Gertrud	20, Dec. 1853	Bernard	Schuhmacher, Catharina	C	
Ellmann, Helena Francisca	13, Feb. 1858	Bernard	Rolfs, Helena	C	
Elmacker, Barbara Catharina	6, Apr. 1856	Aloysius	Baumgut, Maria	D	56
Elman, Friedrich Wilhelm	19, July 1859	H. Bernard	Rolf, Helena	A	
Elminger, Rosina Theresa	25, July 1858	Aloysius	Baumgärtner, Maria	D	116
Elmore, Charles	7, Oct. 1850	Robert	McClellen, Margaret	E	252
Elpman, Bernard Heinrich	2, July 1859	J. Heinrich	We---, Maria	D	141
Elsasser, Henrietta	24, Feb. 1850	Francis	Schick, Anna Maria	G	
Elsasser, Francis	20, Sept 1857	Francis	Schuck, Anna Maria	U	
Elsässer, Kunigunda	30, July 1854	Francis	Schick, Maria Anna	J	28
Elsbernd, Bernard Heinrich	22, Aug. 1852	G.H.	Hollenberg, Gertrud	D	345
Elsbernd, Francis Leo	13, July 1859	Georg H.	Hollenberg, Gertrud	D	142
Elsbernd, Johan Bernard Albert	25, Jan. 1857	Gerhard H.	Hollenberg, Anna Gertrud	D	77
Elsbernd, Johan Gerhard	23, Oct. 1854	Gerhard H.	Hollenburg, Gertrud	D	20
Elsche, Anton Gerhard	26, Jan. 1856	Heinrich	Husmann, Catharina	C	
Elsche, Johan Heinrich	4, June 1857	Gerhard	Husmann, Catharina	C	
Elsche, Margaretha Catharina	11, Feb. 1854	Gerhard	Husmann, Catharina	C	
Elscher, Bernard Heinric	23, Jan. 1852	Gerhard H.	Husmann, M. Catharina	C	
Elsen, Anna Maria	20, Apr. 1852	Gerhard	Vogel, Maria Gertrud	A	
Elsen, Gerhard Heinrich Francis	9, Nov. 1854	Gerhard	Vogel, Gertrud	K	
Elsenheimer, Heinrich Nicolaus Anna	23, Oct. 1859	Jacob	Grubling, Justina	C	
Elsenheimer, Johan Georg	21, Jan. 1858	Georg J.	Kubling, Christina	C	
Elske, Maria Elisabeth	9, Jan. 1859	Gerhard	Husmann, Catharina	C	
Elsner, Agnes Catharina	7, June 1858	Johan	Kiefer, Maria	T	
Elstro, Philomena	13, Apr. 1852	Francis H.	Brockmann, A.M. Louise	L	
Elstroh, Carolina	12, Jan. 1851	Heinrich	Mittendorp, Anna Maria	D	248
Elstroh, Maria Anna	10, Sept 1850	Francis H.	Brokmann, Maria Louisa	F	
Elstrup, Anna Maria Catharina	15, Jan. 1854	Francis	Brockmann, Cath. Louisa	L	
Elvering, Johan Heinrich	17, July 1853	Friedrich	Bonte, Maria	J	22
Elvers, Anna Maria Carolina	15, Aug. 1852	Johan	Gohman, Catharina	D	343
Elward, Ann	11, Sept 1851	John	Byrne, Ann	B	241
Elwer, Joseph	20, Apr. 1851	F. Wilhelm	Stroetman, Catharina	J	10
Emerent?, Margaretha	12, Sept 1852	?	----, Susanna	D	347
Emge, Andreas	5, July 1857	Valentin	Geppert, Carolina	G	
Emge, Carl Mathias	13, Nov. 1859	Heinrich	Klem, Maria	A	
Emge, Joseph	8, Feb. 1857	Heinrich	Klem, Anna Maria	A	
Emge, Ludwig	3, Apr. 1859	Valentin	Geppert, Carolina	G	
Emge, Wilhelm Heinrich	18, Apr. 1852	Heinrich	Klem, Maria	A	
Emgen, Mathias Carl	29, June 1854	Heinrich	Klene, Maria	A	
Emig, Margaretha Catharina	21, Apr. 1851	Johan	Kroesche, Elisabeth	L	
Emlich, Dominick Christoph	4, Sept 1858	Christoph	Ross--, Bernardina	D	118
Emlich, Mary Barbara	4, Mar. 1855	Christopher	----, Bernardina	H	
Emmerich, Caspar Bernard Francis	9, Oct. 1851	Bernard	Rectine?, Elisabeth	D	286
Emmerich, Maria Elisabeth	9, Jan. 1853	Bernard	Cortina, Maria Elisabeth	D	364
Emmert, Elisabeth	1, Oct. 1856	Wilhelm	Kircher?, E.	D	68
Emmet, William Robert	17, July 1853	Robert	Harney, Margaret	B	295
Emmig, Catharina Christina	10, Dec. 1853	Wilhelm	Brokhof, Ernestina	D	418
Emmig, Wilhelm Heinrich	31, Mar. 1859	Wilhelm	Brockhof, Christina	A	
Emming Johan Heinrich	26, Sept 1851	Bernard H.	Theissen, Anna Catharina	F	
Emming, Anton	19, Sept 1857	Wilhelm	Brockhof, Ernestina	T	
Emming, Anton Julius	16, Oct. 1855	Wilhelm	Brokhof, Ernestina	D	44
Emming, Catharina Maria Elisabeth	6, Mar. 1852	Wilhelm	Brockhof, Angela Augustina	D	310
Emming, Johan Bernard	14, Jan. 1851	Johan	Sturing, Anna	C	
Emminger, Aloysius	23, Feb. 1851	Sebastian	Maurer, Margaretha	A	
Emminger, Justina Francisca	6, Sept 1857	Sebastian	Maurer, Maria	A	
Emminger, Philomena	9, Jan. 1853	Sebastian	Maurer, Margaretha	A	
Emrich, Joseph	20, June 1852	Christopher	----, Bernardina	H	
Emskamp, Johan Heinrich	1, June 1858	Arnold H.	Grote, Anna Maria	A	
Emsken, Heinrich Arnold	18, May 1856	Heinrich	adult - 22 years old	K	

Name of Child	Date of Baptism	Father	Mother	Church	Page
---en, Michael Thomas	19, Apr. 1857	Michael	Nelson, America	P	210
Ender, Margaretha	17, Oct. 1858	Carl	Miller, Margaretha	A	
Enderle, Ludwig	15, Nov. 1857	Johan	Tezack, M. Angela	C	
Enderle, Wilhelm	1, June 1857	Johan	Toerzarn, Maria	C	
Enderling, Francis Joseph	1, Dec. 1850	Theobald	Hege, Barbara	C	
Endres, Maria	8, Aug. 1853	Nicolaus	Miller, Juliana	D	399
Engbart, Johan	23, Nov. 1856	Johan	Schucht, Catharina	F	
Engbart, Maria Elisabeth	19, July 1855	Johan	Schuh, Catharina	F	
Engbers, Anna Maria Elisabeth	30, Sept 1858	Bernard	Behringhaus, Angela	N	
Engbers, Bernard Herman	3, Sept 1854	Bernard	Redinghaus, A. Angela	L	
Engbers, Catharina Elisabeth	12, July 1853	Bernard	Beringhaus, Maria Engel	N	14
Engbers, Herman Heinrich	17, Aug. 1856	Bernard	Berninghauser, Maria Angela	N	
Engbers, Wilhelmina Catharina	19, Jan. 1853	Heinrich	Bauer, Anna	L	
Engbersen, Bernard Heinrich	20, Sept 1857	H. Heinrich	Bauer, Anna Maria	N	
Engberson, Anna Adelheid	7, May 1855	J. Heinrich	Bauer, Johanna	N	
Engbring, Heinrich Anton	21, June 1857	Heinrich	Bötker, Catharina Adelheid	A	
Engel, Anna Maria	3, Sept 1858	Joseph	Vogt, Anna Maria	C	
Engel, Anna Maria	11, Feb. 1859	Simon	Sc---, Carolina	D	131
Engel, Anna Maria Henrietta	17, Aug. 1856	Joseph	Vogt, Elisabeth	C	
Engel, Barbara Margaretha	18, Dec. 1852	Friedrich	Ritter, Barbara	R	
Engel, Carl	27, Aug. 1853	Francis	----, Barbara	R	
Engel, Carolina	20, Feb. 1853	Peter	Goldade, Magdalena	D	372
Engel, Catharina Barbara	20, Dec. 1856	Friedrich	----, Barbara	R	
Engel, Elisabeth	9, Aug. 1858	Edward	----, Barbara	R	
Engel, Emma	14, Nov. 1858	Francis	Eberenz, Susanna	F	
Engel, Franz Simon	20, May 1855	Francis	Eberenz, Susanna	F	
Engel, Georg	9, Aug. 1857	Andreas	Ma---, Margaretha	D	92
Engel, Johan	11, Feb. 1859	Simon	Sc---, Carolina	D	131
Engel, Johan Ferdinand	14, Jan. 1851	Friedrich	Ritter, Barbara	D	249
Engel, Joseph	19, Nov. 1854	Joseph	----, Margaret	H	
Engel, Joseph	20, Apr. 1856	Joseph	----, Margaret	H	
Engel, Joseph	26, May 1850	Peter	Trendel, Regina	D	214
Engel, Margaretha	19, Aug. 1855	Peter	Golde, Magdalena	D	41
Engel, Maria Anna	22, Feb. 1857	Francis	Everenz, Susanna	J	40
Engel, Maria Cunigunda	30, Mar. 1851	Joseph	Barbaret, Margaret	H	
Engel, Michael	28, Mar. 1853	Joseph	----, Margaret	H	
Engel, Vincent	14, Mar. 1858	Joseph	Berdberger, Margaret	H	
Engelbert, Maria Bernardina	19, June 1853	Theodor	Hoffmann, Maria A.	L	
Engelhard, Catharina Elisabeth	26, June 1853	Anton	Urban, Elisabeth	D	391
Engelhard, Elisabeth Catharina Louisa	17, Mar. 1850	Johan	Wiestfeld, Louisa	D	206
Engelhard, Francis Bernard	21, Nov. 1852	Adam	Kracke, Louise	R	
Engelhard, Francis Bernard	21, Nov. 1853	Adam	Krake, Louisa	R	
Engelhard, Friedrich	30, Nov. 1856	Friedrich	----, Maria Louisa	R	
Engelhard, Jacob	15, Aug. 1858	Jacob	Mischler, Louisa	A	
Engelhard, Johan	13, Aug. 1854	Adam	Krake, Louise	R	
Engelhard, Johan Georg	26, Apr. 1857	Lawrence	Otto, Louise	H	
Engelhard, Joseph	10, Nov. 1858	Adam	Krake, Louisa	R	
Engelhard, Magdalena	17, Nov. 1850	F. Joseph	Schmidt, Maria Anna	A	
Engelhard, Otto Lorenz	27, Feb. 1859	Lawrence	Otto, Louisa	T	
Engelhart, Carolina	8, Oct. 1854	Lawrence	Otto, Louisa	Q	5
Engelhart, Jacob Philipp	22, Aug. 1858	Johan	Büchel, Carolina	K	
Engelhart, Johan Joseph	9, Nov. 1851	Lawrence	Otto, Louise	Q	1
Engelhart, Louisa	2, June 1850	Lawrence	Otto, Louise	D	215
Engelhart, Ludwig	29, Aug. 1852	F. Joseph	Schmidt, Maria Anna	A	
Engelhart, Maria Francisca	4, Apr. 1858	Anton	Urban, Elisabeth	D	108
Engelkamp, Johan Joseph	21, Oct. 1859	Johan	Herbert, Elisabeth	L	
Engelkamp, Rosa Maria	30, Aug. 1857	J. Herman	Herbert, M. Elisabeth	L	
Engelke, Johan Anton Friedrich	16, Apr. 1852	J. Friedrich	Helmsing, Catharina	K	
Engelker, Anna Francisca	31, Aug. 1850	Fr.	Helmsing, Catharina	K	

Name of Child	Date of Baptism	Father	Mother	Church	Page
Engels, Heinrich	13, Nov. 1853	Joseph	Vogt, Elisabeth	D	414
Engels, Johan Conrad David	20, Feb. 1855	Joseph	Vocht, Elisabeth	D	29
Enger, Andreas	4, Sept 1859	Joseph	Schadt, Philippina	D	145
Enger, Elisabeth	13, Sept 1857	Nicolaus	Faber, Charlotte	F	
Enger, Franz	13, Sept 1857	Joseph	Schadt, Philomena	F	
Enger, Magdalena	6, Mar. 1859	Jacob	Haumer, Maria Anna	D	133
Engert, Andreas	26, Sept 1858	Andreas	----, Margaretha	D	120
Engert, Dorothea Cunigunda	4, Oct. 1857	Caspar	Langhold, Margaret	H	
Engert, Friedrich Igatius	30, May 1853	Caspar	Heitz, Louisa	D	387
Engert, Joseph	7, Oct. 1855	Joseph	Schadt, Philippina	F	
Engesser, Francisca	12, Dec. 1852	Mathias	Riester, Agnes	C	
Engesser, Joseph	24, Mar. 1855	Mathias	Ocker, Rosina	C	
Engesser, Juliana	12, Dec. 1852	Mathias	Riester, Agnes	C	
Engesser, Rosina	6, July 1856	Mathias	Ocker, Rosina	C	
Enghauser, Anton	18, Jan. 1857	Anselm	Meyer, Johanna	J	40
Enghauser, Elisabeth	10, Oct. 1852	Anton	Meyer, Johanna	J	18
Enghauser, Johan	1, June 1852	J. Georg	Zahner, Maria Anna	J	16
Enghauser, Johan Nepomuck	31, July 1859	Anselm	Meyer, Johanna	J	50
Enghauser, Joseph Georg	24, Feb. 1856	Georg	Lahner, Maria	J	34
Enghauser, Maria Magdalena	17, Sept 1854	Anselm	Meyer, Johanna	J	28
Enginger, Andreas	2, June 1850	Andreas	Hahnhauser, Margaretha	D	215
Enginger, Catharina Elisabeth	12, Sept 1852	Andreas	Hahnhauser, Margaretha	D	347
England, Elizabeth	20, Apr. 1858		adult	B	58
England, Mary Ann Eliza	14, Nov. 1858	John	Darby, Ann	B	67
Engler, Elisabeth	5, Dec. 1852	Jacob	Detomble, Elisabeth	C	
Engler, Georg	1, Feb. 1857	Joseph	Gerteisen, Agatha	J	40
Engler, Jacob	5, Mar. 1854	Jacob	Detampel, Elisabeth	D	5
Engler, Johan	11, June 1853	Joseph	Gardiesen, Agatha	J	22
Englert, Anna Maria	10, Feb. 1854	Johan	Wolfarth, Cunigunda	D	4
Englert, Anna Maria	27, Jan. 1850	Joseph	Rippberger, Louisa	D	201
Englert, Antona Padua	16, Jan. 1859	Francis	Hab, Eva	D	129
Englert, Bernard	24, July 1854	Johan	Brickner, Anna Barbara	R	
Englert, Bernard	25, July 1852	Johan	Brückner, Barbara	R	
Englert, Conrad	18, Jan. 1857	Johan	Staub, Eva	D	77
Englert, Johan Baptist	12, Apr. 1858	Johan	Wolfert, Cunigunda	D	109
Englert, Johan Jacob	2, Mar. 1856	Johan	Wolfert, Cunigunda	D	53
Englert, Joseph	24, Mar. 1858	Georg	Sties--, Cleopha	D	107
Englert, Joseph Bernard	15, Feb. 1852	Joseph	Ripperger, Louisa	D	306
Englert, Maria Anna Philomena	28, July 1850	Gerhard	----, Anna Barbara	D	225
Englert, Maria Catharina	4, July 1858	Anton	Kohp, Anna Maria	R	
Englert, Maria Louisa	31, Mar.1851	Jacob	Freithof, Anna Gertrud	D	259
Englert, Maria Margaretha	9, July 1854	Johan	Brückner, Anna Barbara	R	
Englert, Susanna	13, Mar. 1855	J. Joseph	Staub, Eva	D	31
English, Cecilia	12, Mar. 1852	John	----, Alice	E	390
English, Francis	27, June 1859	John	Lynch, Alice	E	635
English, George	2, Nov. 1856	John	Lynch, Alice	E	409
English, Margaret	14, July 1854	John	----, Alice	E	206
English, Margaret	14, July 1852	Melchesidek	McGrath, Alice	E	427
English, Thomas	7, Mar. 1850	John	Cumming, Elles	E	201
Enkhof, Valentin	15, Feb. 1857	Bartholomew	Nock, Anna Maria	F	
Enneking, Agnes Clara	22, Dec. 1850	J. Bernard	Helmkamp, Elisabeth	A	
Enneking, Anna Louisa	6, Nov. 1855	J. Bernard	Heuer, Elisabeth	C	
Enneking, Anna Maria Rosa	11, Sept 1854	J. Bernard	Schmidt, A. Agnes Theresa	N	24
Enneking, August	28, Feb. 1858	Friedrich	Tiemann, Johanna	L	
Enneking, Bernard	6, Dec. 1857	J. Heinrich	Drahman, Maria Anna	K	
Enneking, Bernard Heinrich Wilhelm	2, Nov. 1856	J. Bernard	Schmidt, Agnes	N	
Enneking, Heinrich	9, Feb. 1856	J. Heinrich	Drahman, Maria Anna	K	
Enneking, Johan Carl	7, Oct. 1859	Friedrich	Tiemann, A. Gertrud	L	
Enneking, Maria Anna	17, Sept 1851	Friedrich	Tiemann, Anna	L	

Name of Child	Date of Baptism	Father	Mother	Church	Page
Enneking, Maria Josephina Carolina	28, Jan. 1858	J. Bernard	Heuber, Elisabeth	C	
Enneking, Maria Theresa Julia	25, July 1858	J. Bernard	Schmidt, Agnes Theresa	N	
Ennis, Ann	22, Mar. 1855	Thomas	McEldown, Catherine	E	274
Ennis, Elisabeth	20, June 1858	Thomas	Murphy, Bridget	T	
Ennis, Henry	29, June 1856	Thomas	Murphy, Bridget	T	
Ennis, James	16, Nov. 1851	Thomas	Murphy, Bridget	B	245
Ennis, John Henry	9, Oct. 1859	Patrick	O'Neil, Bridget	B	82
Ennis, Margaret	16, July 1854	Thomas	Murphy, Bridget	B	2
Ennis, Mary	12, Mar. 1854	John	Losty, Catharine	T	
Ennis, Matthew	15, Feb. 1854	Philipp	McLaughlin, Susan	E	168
Ennis, William Henry	10, Mar. 1850	Martin	Martha, Honora	B	197
Enniss, William	23, Sept 1855	James	Delany, Eliza	P	151
Enoy, Sarah Jane	14, Apr. 1857	Samuel	Hart, Catherine	P	210
Enright, Ann	7, Mar. 1858	John	Mullen, Ann	P	241
Enright, Bridget	7, Sept 1852	Patrick	----, Catherine	E	15
Enright, Catherine	7, Sept 1858	George	Smith, Julia	E	561
Enright, Cecilia Clara	9, Aug. 1852	Theophilus	----, Ann	E	3
Enright, Charles	3, Nov. 1854	Theophilus	Mahon, Ann	B	7
Enright, George	21, Apr. 1851	George	Smith, Juliane	E	302
Enright, John	15, Feb. 1851	Michael	Buckley, Catherine	E	284
Enright, Lucy Ann	22, June 1851	Theophilus	----, Ann	E	317
Enright, Mary	29, May 1859	John	Mullen, Ann	P	285
Entekart, Maria Elisabeth	2, Dec. 1858	Bernard	Hobmeier, Gertrud	D	125
Entele, Sophia	21, Aug. 1859	Johan	Dercep, Maria	F	
Entrup, Francisca	24, Oct. 1857	Christian	Tepe, Maria Catharina	L	
Entrup, Herman Heinrich	22, Aug. 1854	Christian	Teppen, M. Catharina	L	
Entwistle, Andrew	25, Mar. 1852	Andrew	Ainsworth, Helen	B	255
Entwistle, Helen Elizabeth	6, Jan. 1850	Andrew	Ainsworth, Helen	B	193
Eping, Johanna Maria Adelheid	3, Apr. 1859	Anton	Proka---, Johanna Elisabeth	D	135
Epker, Johan Bernard	22, Mar. 1858	Johan H.	Dananberg, Anna Maria	F	
Epker, Johan Bernard Heinrich	14, Oct. 1855	Johan H.	Tenamberg, Bernardina	F	
Eple, Valentin	9, July 1858		Elble, Carolina	T	
Eppel, Georg Carl	18, Sept 1857	Georg	Schneider,	U	
Eppel, Maria Cecilia	26, Dec. 1858	Francis	Schneider, Josephina	U	
Eppich, Joseph	20, Sept 1857	Philipp	Schneider, Catharina	C	
Eppich, Margaretha	21, Nov. 1858	Philipp	Schneider, Catharina	D	124
Epping, Anna Maria	25, Sept 1857	Anton	Brokamp, Elisabeth	T	
Epping, Heinrich Joseph	19, Feb. 1859	Joseph	Brak---, Johanna	D	132
Epping, Johan Bernard	16, Apr. 1857	Johan	Varnhorn, Maria Anna	A	
Epping, Johan Bernard Heinrich	7, Mar. 1855	Bernard H.	Melle, Theresa	L	
Epping, Johan Carl Conrad	1, Jan. 1857	Heinrich	Melle, Theresa	C	
Epping, Marianna Josephina	9, Sept 1859	Johan	Fahrnhorn, Marianna	F	
Eppinger, Herman Engelbert	4, Sept 1856	Herman J.	Benkhof, Johanna	D	66
Eppinghof, Bernard Heinrich	23, Nov. 1854	J. Bernard	Rolfes, Helena Adelheid	D	22
Eppinghof, Johan Bernard	22, Sept 1851	J. Heinrich	Losekamp, Helena Adelheid	D	284
Eppinghof, Johan Bernard Heinrich	8, Sept 1858	B. Heinrich	Rulfer, Adelheid	D	119
Eppinghof, Johan Bernard Heinrich	28, June 1851	Bernard J.	Rolvers, Helena Adelheid	D	270
Eppinghoff, Johan Wilhelm	16, Jan. 1854	Heinrich	Losekamp, Helena Adelheid	D	2
Epple, Judith	9, Mar. 1851	Martin	Volk, Louisa	C	
Erbenstadt, Maria Elisabeth	10, Oct. 1853	Joseph	Rabe, Maria Antonia	F	
Erbenstein, Maria Anna	21, Oct. 1857	Joseph	Rabe, Marianna	F	
Erbenstein, Maria Catharina	25, Oct. 1855	Joseph	Rabe, Catharina	F	
Erbenstein, Rosa	12, July 1859	Joseph	Rabe, Marianna	F	
Erck, Georg	8, Nov. 1855	Martin	----, Margaretha	D	46
Erd, Francis Carl	5, June 1851	F. Ignatius	Lampert, Maria Benedicta	A	
Erd, Jacob Wilhelm	28, Sept 1852	Francis X.	Flemming, Maria	C	
Erd, Maria Henrietta	5, June 1851	F. Ignatius	Lampert, Maria Benedicta	A	
Eret, Elisabeth	27, Oct. 1853	J. Baptist	Burkle, Theresa	C	
Erfkeman, Gerhard Heinrich	29, Oct. 1854	B. Heinrich	Berg, Maria Adelheid	K	

Name of Child	Date of Baptism	Father	Mother	Church	Page
Erhard, Andreas	1, Dec. 1857	Johan	San---, Magdalena	D	100
Erhard, Francis	30, Aug. 1857	Andrew	Spirit, Perpetua	H	
Erhardt, Rosina	28, Mar. 1858	Mathias	----, Magdalena	K	
Erhart, Anna Maria Catharina	8, Aug. 1858	Martin	Bauh, Catharina	Q	28
Erhart, Catharina Barbara	8, Feb. 1852	Johan	Groh, Catharina	D	306
Erich, Anna Elisabeth Margaretha	6, Nov. 1854	Caspar	Stopering, Theresa	D	21
Erich, Catharina	6, Aug. 1854	Joseph	Reuther, Fernandina	A	
Erit, Conrad	25, July 1858	Francis	Deilgiss, Juliana	D	116
Erith, Conrad	23, Nov. 1856	Francis	Fillgis, Juliana	D	72
Erler, Mary	28, Oct. 1852	William	Groyer, Mary	P	28
Ermantraut, Margaretha Theresa	2, Oct. 1853	Michael	Jost, Margaretha	D	408
Ermentraut, Bernard	3, June 1856	Michael	Uth, Margaretha	D	60
Ernestes, Caspar Ludwig	19, Jan. 1852	Caspar	Bedenbecher, Elisabeth	A	
Ernestes, Joseph Heinrich	14, Feb. 1850	Caspar	Bedenbecker, Josephina E.	A	
Ernethal, Carolina	11, July 1853	Adalbert	Scheich, Catharina	C	
Ernsfidel, Maria Elisabeth	23, Jan. 1859	Michael B.	Burnett, Maria Elisabeth	A	
Ernst, Anna Elisabeth	22, Apr. 1858	Georg	Nie---, Maria Anna	D	109
Ernst, Anna Francisca	12, Apr. 1857	Johan	Kurzel, Adelheid	D	82
Ernst, Bertha	24, June 1859	Aloysius	----, Walburga	A	
Ernst, Carl August	3, Oct. 1858	Philipp	Sutt, Josephina	T	
Ernst, Carolina	11, Sept 1855	Conrad	Gerlick?, Elisabeth	R	
Ernst, Elisabeth	21, Dec. 1856	Heinrich	----, Rosina	R	
Ernst, Francis	21, June 1857	Basil	Birenbrand, Carolina	D	88
Ernst, Francis Joseph	2, Oct. 1853	Aloysius	---ch, Agatha	D	408
Ernst, Johan Georg	20, Dec. 1853	Georg	Kühl, Elisabeth	D	421
Ernst, Johan Wilhelm	4, Aug. 1850	Wilhelm	Wessling,	F	
Ernst, Maria Augusta	14, Mar. 1855	Heinrich	Pobst, Regina	R	
Ernst, Maria Catharina Elisabeth	25, June 1851	Georg	Hocks?, M. Cath. Elisabeth	D	270
Ernst, Maria Catharina Theresa	25, Oct. 1853	Conrad	----, Elisabeth	U	
Ernst, Maria Catharina Theresa	27, Feb. 1853	Heinrich	Pabst, Regina	R	
Ernst, Maria Elisabeth	20, June 1855	Georg	Lutz, Anna Maria	D	37
Ernst, Paulina	6, Aug. 1858	Anton	Schmidt, Fridolina	D	116
Ernst, Rosina	29, May 1859	Basil	Riererbergen?, Carolina	N	
Ernst, Rosina	11, Sept 1855	Conrad	Gerlick?, Elisabeth	R	
Ernst, Susanna	5, July 1859	Georg	----, Margaretha	D	141
Ernst, Victoria Magdalena	29, Aug. 1858	Johan	Lang---, Magdalena	D	118
Ersterhof, Johan	6, Aug. 1858	Johan	Fahi, Maria	D	116
Ertel, Margaretha	22, Oct. 1852	Adam	Dor, Catharina	D	354
Ertel, Maria	31, Mar. 1850	Leonard	Horn, Maria	D	207
Ervin, James	12, July 1857	John	Dougherty, Catherine	B	46
Ervin, John	12, July 1857	John	Dougherty, Catherine	B	46
Ervin, Joseph	12, July 1857	John	Dougherty, Catherine	B	46
Erwin, Ellen Cecilia	26, Aug. 1855	James	McCormick, Margaret	E	310
Erwin, Ellen Cecilia	15, Dec. 1850	James	McCormick, Margaret L.	E	267
Erwin, Emma Josephine	19, Dec. 1852	James	----, Margaret Louise	E	45
Erwin, George Washington	7, Mar. 1852	William	----, Martha	E	389
Erwin, James	17, Sept 1854	John A.	----, Frances	V	17
Erwin, James	10, Jan. 1858	Patrick	Maroney, Ellen	B	54
Erwin, John	8, Dec. 1850	John	Brennan, Frances	B	220
Erwin, John	23, Nov. 1856	Thomas	Horan, Theresa	E	415
Erwin, Margaret	22, June 1854	Henry	Duffy, Helen	P	86
Erwin, Mary	7, Dec. 1856	John	Brannan, Fanny	E	418
Erwin, Mary	22, Mar. 1856	Patrick	Murray, Ellen	B	27
Erwin, Thomas	21, Oct. 1855	John	Brannan, F.	E	321
Esbach, Margaretha Theresa	2, Jan. 1859	Seraphin	Schrers, Maria	A	
Esback, Anna Maria Catharina	1, Jan. 1857	Seraphin	Scheis, Anna Maria	A	
Esborn, E.	20, Sept 1850	----	----, ----	E	248
Eschbach, Jacob	22, Aug. 1858	Jacob	Fratz, Catharina	A	
Eschbach, Johan Georg	14, Setp 1856	Jacob	Fratz, Catharina	A	

Name of Child	Date of Baptism	Father	Mother	Church	Page
Eschbach, Louisa	22, May 1859	Joseph	Auer, Maria	T	
Eschback, Sophia	2, Oct. 1859	Michael	----, Maria	D	148
Eschenbach, Anna Maria	13, Sept 1855	Johan	Berling, Agnes	D	42
Eschenbach, Elisabeth	4, Jan. 1857	Johan	Berling, Agnes	D	76
Eschenbach, Johan Michael	25, Dec. 1858	Johan	Berling, Agnes	D	127
Eschenbach, Margaretha	18, Jan. 1858		Eschenbach, Maria	D	103
Eschung, Maria Louisa	20, June 1858	Anthony	Schmeller, Sophia	H	
Eser, Johan	3, Aug. 1851	Martin H.	Nolden, Catharina	C	
Espel, Carl Joseph	23, June 1851	Wilhelm	Jeckel, Helena	D	269
Espel, Gerhard Ludwig	13, Aug. 1852	Heinrich	Auman, Bernardina	K	
Essenbach, Maria Margaretha	23, Oct. 1856	J. Adam	Jacob, Margaretha	D	70
Essenmacher, Joseph	17, Mar. 1850	Carl	Bernari, Maria	H	
Esser, Josephina	25, Aug. 1850	Joseph	Batz, Anastasia	D	229
Esslinger, Barbara	8, Dec. 1850	Peter	Baus, Anna	H	
Esslinger, Christian	17, Feb. 1856	Peter	Baus, Ann	U	
Esslinger, Francis	23, Oct. 1859	Peter	Baus, Ann	U	
Esslinger, Joseph	6, Jan. 1858	Peter	Baus, Ann	U	
Esslinger, Michael	19, Mar. 1854	Peter	----, Ann	U	
Esslinger, Peter	24, Oct. 1852	Peter	----, Ann	H	
Essmann, Elisabeth Anna	19, July 1851	Joseph	Gaertner, Elisabeth	C	
Essmann, Heinrich Johan Philipp	26, Aug. 1859	Joseph	Gaertner, Elisabeth	C	
Essmann, Joseph Anna	27, May 1857	Joseph	Gartner, Elisabeth	C	
Essmann, Maria Anna	19, July 1851	Joseph	Gaertner, Elisabeth	C	
Essmann, Maria Elisabeth	12, May 1853	Joseph	Gartner, Elisabeth	C	
Ester, William	23, May 1855	Nicolaus	----, Margaret	E	288
Estermann, M. Catharina Christina	19, Feb. 1859	Bernard	Riesenberg, Catharina	F	
Etch, Jacob	16, Jan. 1859	Jacob	Henrien, Catharina	C	
Etchworth, James Craft	15, July 1856	Thomas	Workman, Janette	B	31
Etchworth, Mary Ann	15, July 1856	Thomas	Workman, Janette	B	31
Etinger, Catharina Barbara	9, Oct. 1859	Jacob	Seider, Sabina	D	148
Etinger, Joseph	12, Nov. 1854	Jacob	Saeder, Sabina	D	21
Etter, Anna Maria Barbara	24, Aug. 1851	Ludwig	Ducklo, Barbara	J	12
Etter, Carolina	1, Apr. 1856	Wilhelm	Gärten, Barbara	D	55
Etter, Carolina Caecilia	22, Nov. 1857	Ludwig	Duklo, Barbara	J	44
Etter, Catharina Julia	7, May 1854	Ludwig	Duklo, Barbara	J	26
Etter, Magdalena Paulina	22, June 1856	Ludwig	Duklo, Barbara	J	36
Etterer, Johan Georg	3, Oct. 1854	Ambrose	Riedinger, Catharina	J	28
Etterich, Anna Maria	22, Apr. 1855	Francis	Schwarz, Magdalena	J	32
Etterich, Nicolaus	22, Feb. 1857	Francis	Melcher, Maria	J	40
Etterichs, Elisabeth	3, Apr. 1853	Francis	Schwarz, Magdalena	J	20
Euler, Bernard Joseph	13, July 1850	Joseph	Rothland, Louisa	A	
Euler, Catharina	2, June 1850	?	Hurst, Maria Elisabeth	H	
Euler, Johan Heinrich	16, May 1852	Anton	Feldman, Agnes	A	
Euler, John	21, Apr. 1851	Christian	----, Elisabeth	H	
Euler, Mary Elisabeth	2, June 1850	----	adult	H	
Euler, Nicolaus	20, Feb. 1853	Christian	Bord, Elisabeth	D	373
Euler, Wilhelmina	13, Oct. 1851	Joseph	Rothland, Louisa	A	
Eusterkämper, Johan Heinrich	5, Apr. 1853	J. Bernard	Kuhlenberg, Maria Anna	D	379
Eusterkamper, Johan Thomas	7, Mar. 1850	J. Bernard	Kuhlenberg, Maria Anna	C	
Evans, D. Honora	30, Aug. 1853	Edward	Spellman, Ann	B	298
Evans, Edward David	30, Aug. 1853	Edward	Spellman, Ann	B	298
Evans, John Patrick	26, Mar. 1854	Patrick	Boyle, Elizabeth	E	179
Evans, Mary	19, Oct. 1851	Patrick	Boyle, Elizabeth	E	351
Evans, Mary	3, Apr. 1853	Robert	Doyle, Julia	B	287
Evans, Mary Ellen	20, Oct. 1856	George	Melvin, Elizabeth	E	406
Evans, Robert Benjamin	17, Oct. 1855	Edward	Spellman, Ann	B	20
Evans, Thomas	12, Apr. 1855	William	Dempsy, Mary	E	279
Evans, Thomas Francis	5, Sept 1859	Edward	Spelman, Ann	B	80
Evens, Albert Edward	3, Dec. 1858	Francis	Wemhoff, Maria	C	

Name of Child	Date of Baptism	Father	Mother	Church	Page
Evens, Bertha Johanna Eleanora	21, Feb. 1856	Francis	Wemhoff, Maria	C	
Evens, Eduard Bernard Francis	28, Dec. 1851	Francis	Wehmhoff, Maria	C	
Evens, John	10, Jan. 1854	Patrick	London, Margaret	E	160
Evens, Julia Elisabeth	2, Feb. 1854	Francis	Wemhoff, Maria	C	
Evens, Otto Ferdinand Julius	3, Dec. 1858	Francis	Wemhoff, Maria	C	
Evens, Philippina M. Elisabeth	11, May 1850	Francis	Nuelsen, Philippina	C	
Everet, Walter	26, Apr. 1852		adult - 30 years old	E	407
Everfield, Alice Mary	25, Mar. 1856	William	----, Elizabeth	E	352
Everhard, Johan Jacob	29, Nov. 1857	Mathias	Storder, Elisabeth	T	
Everlage, Agnes Catharina Apollonia	9, Feb. 1856	Heinrich	Böckstedte, Elisabeth	K	
Everlage, Anna Elisabeth	16, Mar. 1851	Dietrich H.	Bockerstedte, M. Elisabeth	K	
Evers, Francis Joseph	9, Dec. 1859	Herman	Middendorf, Catharina	C	
Evers, Heinrich Anton	28, Apr. 1854	Bernard H.	Kohne, Maria Angela	A	
Evers, Heinrich Georg	26, Feb. 1856	B. Heinrich	Kohne, Maria	A	
Evers, Heinrich H.	11, Mar. 1851	Herman	Middendorf, Catharina	C	
Evers, Heinrich Joseph Ludwig	26, Aug. 1853	Bernard H.	Middendorf, Catharina	C	
Evers, Herman Heinrich Andreas	11, Nov. 1853	Gerhard H.	Merkhof, Maria Catharina	N	17
Evers, Johan Heinrich Joseph	24, Nov. 1856	Herman	Middendorf, Catharina	C	
Evers, Maria Francisca	13, Dec. 1858	B.H.	Kohne, Maria Angela	A	
Evers, Maria Hermina Catharina	29, Aug. 1851	Gerhard H.	Markoff, M. Catharina	L	
Evers, Maria Philomena	16, Apr. 1858	Gerhard H.	Moemke, Maria Agnes	C	
Evers, Peter Francis	22, May 1859	Bernard	Kiefer, Angela	D	138
Eversfield, Amanda	14, Oct. 1858	William	Cullenan, Mary	E	570
Eversfield, Mary Ellen	25, Apr. 1852	John	----, Mary	E	405
Eversman, Anna Maria	13, June 1852	Joseph	Stieremberg, Anna Maria	A	
Eversman, Anna Maria Theresa	25, Dec. 1854	Peter	Schwerman, Theresa	A	
Eversman, Heinrich	13, June 1852	Joseph	Stieremberg, Anna Maria	A	
Eversman, Johan Gerhard	19, Oct. 1852	Herman P.	Brinkhoff, Carolina	A	
Eversman, Joseph	25 July 1850	Wilhelm	Schwerman, Anna Maria	A	
Eversman, Peter Johan	11, Mar. 1857	Peter	Schwerman, Anna Threresa	A	
Eversmann, Joseph Peter	25, May 1850	Joseph	Sturenberg, Anna M.	C	
Everts, Angela Catharina	25, Dec. 1857	Bernard	Kiefer, Angela	C	
Every, Anna Louisa	12, Sept 1852	Johan	Spiss, Margaretha	D	347
Eveslage, Amelia Margaretha	25, May 1854	Dietrich H.	Boeckerstedde, Elisabeth	K	
Eveslage, Anna Margaretha	27, July 1859	Bernard	Torline, Margaretha	L	
Eveslage, Bernard Heinrich	24, May 1857	B. Godfried	Torline, Margaretha	K	
Eveslage, Catharina Bernardina Joseph.	16, Jan. 1859	Joseph	Bockerstette, Catharina	C	
Eveslage, Georg Heinrich	23, Feb. 1855	B. Godfried	Torliene, Margaretha	K	
Eveslage, Heinrich Carl	14, May 1852	Theodor H.	Boeckstedde, Elisabeth	K	
Eveslage, Herman Heinrich Joseph	14, Nov. 1851	Joseph	Bockestette, Catharina	L	
Eveslage, Maria Gertrud	11, Oct. 1854	Joseph	Boekerstatte, Catharina	K	
Eveslage, Michael Joseph	26, May 1857	Joseph	Bockerstadte, Catharina	C	
Eveslage, Theresa Elisabeth Gertrud	13, Feb. 1853	B. Gottfried	Torliene, Margaretha	K	
Evetly?, Mary Ann	24, Feb. 1856		Evetly?, Mary	B	25
Ewald, Anna Maria Elisabeth	16, June 1855	Joseph	Limberg, Elisabeth	A	
Ewald, Christoph Heinrich	2, Dec. 1855	Heinrich	Kramer, Elisabeth	F	
Ewald, Francis	7, Oct. 1855	Philipp W.	Kopp, Theresa	L	
Ewald, Maria Catharina	3, Jan. 1855	Francis	Helmig, Catharina	L	
Ewald, Maria Catharina Francisca	30, May 1858	Francis	Hallweg, Catharina	L	
Ewald, Maria Clara Elisabeth	9, Oct. 1853	Heinrich	Kramer, Elisabeth	F	
Ewald, Maria Elisabeth	20, Apr. 1856	Heinrich	Eilkers, Elisabeth	A	
Ewald, Maria Margaretha	6, Sept 1857	Joseph	Limberg, Elisabeth	A	
Ewald, Philipp Jacob	22, Nov. 1857	Heinrich	Kramer, Elisabeth	L	
Ewen, Mary Leddy	7, Mar. 1852	John	----, Catherine	E	390
Ewing, Ann	20, Aug. 1857	Thomas	Sullivan, Ann	V	41
Ewing, George Washington	14, Mar. 1859	John	Dougherty, Catherine	B	72
Ewing, William Alexander	18, Jan. 1857	William	Riordan, Joanne	V	37
Exler, Bernard Joseph	2, Sept 1850	Anton	Feldman, Agnes	F	
Exler, Elisabeth Carolina	29, June 1859	Joseph	Niehaus, Carolina	A	

Name of Child	Date of Baptism	Father	Mother	Church	Page
Exler, Johan Francis	14, July 1852	Joseph	Leyedrust, Maria	A	
Exler, Maria Anna	27, Apr. 1853	Gerhard H.	Laukamper, M.A. Elis.	L	
Exler, Maria Elisabeth	30, Nov. 1850	Gerhard H.	Larkemper, Elisabeth	L	
Ey, Johan Heinrich	1, Sept 1859	Johan	Heinz, Emilia	N	
Eymann, Elisabeth Carolina	28, Oct. 1855	Carl	Kuhlmann, Anna M.	L	
Eymann, Henrietta Catharina	12, Nov. 1856	Carl	Kuhlmann, Maria Anna	L	
Eymann, Maria Louisa	5, Dec. 1858	Carl	Kuhlmann, M. Gertrud	L	
Ezal, Rosina	31, July 1854	Johan	Schumacher, Maria Anna	D	15
Ezyn, Georg Jacob	3, June 1858	Lawrence	Kelling, Theresa	K	
F----, Louise	7, Oct. 1855	Francis	Cassassa, Angela	P	154
Faber, Aloysius	20, Apr. 1851		Faber, Maria Anna	D	261
Faber, Anna Maria Magdalena	5, May 1850	Morand	Th--er?, Margaretha	D	212
Faber, Carl	29, July 1855	Boniface	Spitz, Magdalena	D	39
Faber, Maria Anna	30, Jan. 1859	Morand	Ortmann, Barbara	C	
Fackler, Maria Anna	5, Mar. 1854	Georg	Feldschneider, M. Anna	C	
Fackler, Paulina	1, Jan. 1850	Johan	Pillarts, Paulina	C	
Fackler, Philomena	30, Nov. 1851	J. Georg	Poeh, Maria	C	
Faehr, Johan Georg	18, July 1858	Johan	Klevin?, Bridget	Q	28
Faehr, Maria Rosa	1, June 1851	Valentin	Schweizer, Sophia	F	
Faessler, Josephina Johanna	30, Dec. 1855	Louis	Clerk, Maria	C	
Faeth, Bernardina	19, Sept 1858	J. Adam	Helms, Bernardina	T	
Fagan, Ann	19, Oct. 1858	Michael	Hughes, Catherine	E	571
Fagan, Catharine	15, Feb. 1859	Patrick	Kenny, Margaret	E	604
Fagan, Helen	7, Sept 1854	Patrick	Kenny, Margaret	E	222
Fagan, James Patrick	16, Dec. 1855	Patrick	Balfe, Margaret	B	22
Fagan, Margaret	13, June 1852	Patrick	Kenny, Margaret	E	423
Fagan, Mary Ann	3, May 1858	Patrick	Balf, Margaret	B	58
Fagan, Rosanne	22, Mar. 1857	Patrick	Kenny, Margaret	E	443
Fagan, Susan	26, Feb. 1857	Thomas	Brady, Margaret	B	41
Fagin, Mary Ann	24, Dec. 1854	Thomas	Brady, Margaret	P	111
Fahey, Anthony	9, May 1852	Peter	----, Catherine	E	411
Fahey, Bridget	28, Mar. 1853	John	Linsky, Mary	B	287
Fahey, Bridget	29, Aug. 1858	Patrick	----, Sarah	V	50
Fahey, James	22, June 1856	John	Sullivan, May	P	183
Fahey, John	11, Aug. 1857	John	Sullivan, Mary	P	220
Fahey, Mary Ann	20, June 1858	Thomas	----, Catherine	M	
Fahey, Michael	10, Apr. 1855	John	Sullivan, Mary	P	128
Fahey, Patrick	31, Jan. 1854	Michael	Kaley, Bridget	P	67
Fahriebel, Josephina	19, Aug. 1855	Joseph	Klael, Anna	D	41
Fahriel, Carl	11, June 1857	Xavier	Kla--l, Anna	D	87
Fahring, Johan Heinrich	4, Feb. 1856	Johan B.	Buehnker, Adelheid	C	
Fahs, Michael	15, Aug. 1853	Michael	Roth, Catharina	F	
Fahy, Catherine	9, May 1852	William	Mitchell, Catherine	B	258
Fahy, John	29, July 1859	John	Dooly, Mary	B	78
Fahy, Patrick	25, Mar. 1858	Matthew	Murray, Honora	E	524
Fahy, Penelope	3, Sept 1854	James	Fahy, Bridget	T	
Fahy, Peter	21, Mar. 1858	John	Spelman, Margaret	E	523
Fain, John Henry	11, July 1858	Henry	Moran, Mary	E	548
Fais, Anna Catharina	20, Oct. 1850	Georg	Frömmel, Thekla	D	239
Fais, Francisca	6, June 1852	Georg	Schummel, Thecla	D	323
Fais, Francisca Susanna	13, Apr. 1856	Georg	Schrimm, Thecla	D	56
Faiss, Johan Peter	19, July 1857	Georg	Schrim, T.	D	90
Faitsch, Francis Joseph	19, Dec. 1852	Nicolaus	Beckmann, Ephros.	C	
Falada, Victoria	31, Oct. 1858	Francis	Graser, Catharina	C	
Fales, Louise	3, May 1857	William	Lloyd, Catherine	E	450
Falk, Barbara	28, Feb. 1858	Carl	Becht, Margaretha	D	106
Falk, Carolina	18, Jan. 1857	Joseph	Schmeier, Walburga	D	76
Falk, Catharina	15, June 1851	Joseph	Schneider, Walburga	D	268
Falk, Catharina Louisa	5, Jan. 1857	Simon	Zimmer, Lucia	D	76

Name of Child	Date of Baptism	Father	Mother	Church	Page
Falk, Jacob	20, Mar. 1859	Simon	Zimmer, Lucia	D	134
Falk, Joseph	4, Apr. 1856	Carl	Pecher, Margaretha	D	55
Falk, Joseph	15, Aug. 1858	Joseph	Schneider, Walburga	D	117
Falk, Louisa	9, Jan. 1853	Joseph	Schneider, Walburga	D	364
Falk, Maria	28, Jan. 1855	Joseph	Schneider, Walburga	D	27
Falk, Maria	21, June 1859	Michael	Schwab, Elisabeth	U	
Falk, Philipp	5, Nov. 1854	Simon	Zimmer, Lucia	D	21
Falke, Catharina Maria	13, Apr. 1850	Bernard	Fideldei, M. Elisabeth	C	
Falke, Wilhelm Heinrich	21, July 1852	B. Heinrich	Fideldei, Anna Maria	K	
Falkenhahn, Adam Joseph	27, Aug. 1855	Adam	Schwartz, Veronica	L	
Falkenhahne, Sophia	11, Apr. 1858	Adam	Schwartz, Veronica	K	
Falkenstein, Andreas	1, Dec. 1850	Francis	Gut, Maria	K	
Falkenstein, Anna Elisabeth	6, June 1859	Francis	Guth, Maria Anna	K	
Falkenstein, Francisca Carolina	1, Aug. 1852	Francis	Guth, Anna Maria	K	
Falkenstein, Johan Francis	19, Oct. 1856	Francis	Guth, Anna Maria	K	
Falkenstein, Maria Louisa	17, Sept 1854	Francis	Gut, Maria	K	
Falkner, Sarah Isabel	29, Oct. 1851	Charles	Dodson, Sarah	B	244
Fall, Mary Sophia	20, Feb. 1853		adult - 46 years old	B	284
Fallan, Edward James	3, Aug. 1851	Patrick	Waters, Mary	M	
Fallan, Joanne	15, Feb. 1852	Andrew	Filben, Bridget	P	18
Fallen, Bridget	1, Jan. 1854	Patrick	----, Mary	M	
Fallen, Catherine Ellen	8, June 1856	Michael	----, Mary	M	
Fallen, James	27, Jan. 1859	Patrick	----, Margaret	M	
Fallen, John	20, Mar. 1859	Michael	----, Mary	M	
Fallen, John	24, May 1857	Patrick	----, Margaret	M	
Fallen, John	25, July 1858	Patrick	----, Mary	M	
Fallen, Margaret	26, Dec. 1853	Michael	----, Mary	M	
Fallen, Mary	23, Mar. 1856	Patrick	----, Mary	M	
Fallen, Michael	20, Apr. 1854	Patrick	----, Mary	M	
Faller, Amalia	18, Mar. 1856	Anton	Baier, Dorothea	D	54
Faller, Carl Friedrich	3, Oct. 1858	Anton	Beier, Dorothea	D	120
Faller, Rosa	16, Oct. 1858		Faller, Maria	D	121
Fallert, Maria Magdalena	6, Dec. 1858	Anton	Fruh, Apollonia	C	
Fallner, Johan	13, Apr. 1857	Johan	Hernberger, Elisabeth	K	
Fallon, Anastasia	29, Aug. 1858	John	Buttersby, Bridget	E	559
Fallon, Bernard	5, July 1857	Bernard	Kelly, Mary	P	216
Fallon, Catherine	9, Jan. 1859	Jamse	Reding, Catherine	P	271
Fallon, Catherine	20, Mar. 1853	John	----, Bridget	E	75
Fallon, Cornelius	5, July 1851	John	Batterly, Bridget	B	235
Fallon, John	11, Nov. 1855	Andrew	Diwany, Mary	P	159
Fallon, John	19, Aug. 1855	Bernard	Kelly, Mary	B	18
Fallon, John	7, Nov. 1856	John	Butterley, Bridget	E	410
Fallon, John	1, Feb. 1858	Patrick	Jennings, Bridget	P	237
Fallon, Luke	13, Nov. 1859	Bernard	Kelly, Mary	P	303
Fallon, Margaret	13, Dec. 1857	John	Casselly, Margaret	P	232
Fallon, Margaret	24, Aug. 1858	John	Johnston, Catherine	P	258
Fallon, Mary	16, June 1857	James	----, Bridget	E	460
Fallon, Mary	15, July 1855	Patrick	Jennings, Bridget	P	140
Fallon, Susan	28, Oct. 1856	Henry	Woods, Mary	P	196
Fallon, Thomas	5, July 1855	Henry	Woods, Mary	P	138
Fallon, Thomas	2, July 1854	John	Butterly, Bridget	P	86
Fallon, William James	3, Feb. 1855	James	Moran, Bridget	E	261
Falls, Ann	22, Oct. 1851	John	Boyle, Mary	B	243
Falls, Emily	30, Dec. 1852	John	Boylson, Mary	B	279
Falls, William John	12, Mar. 1856	John	Boylson, Mary	B	26
Falvery, Helen	26, Oct. 1854	Jeremiah	Trindeville, Honora	V	18
Falvey, Mary	30, July 1854	James	Brady, Julia	T	
Fanascye, Helen	19, Oct. 1850	Michael	Gilfoil, Mary	E	255
Fäng, Gottfried	13, Jan. 1850	Wilhelm	Kölsch, Solomina	D	199

Name of Child	Date of Baptism	Father	Mother	Church	Page
Fänger, Heinrich Anton	18, Jan. 1852	Heinrich	Schmutte, Agnes	K	
Fanghan, Michael	22, Jan. 1854	Patrick	Thelan, Joanne	B	307
Fangmann, Anna Maria Theresa	4, May 1853	Joseph	Liss, Carolina	L	
Fangmann, Gerhard	28, Oct. 1856	Joseph	Liss, Paulina	L	
Fangmann, Johan Bernard	29, Feb. 1852	Joseph	Liss, Carolina	L	
Fangmann, Joseph Benedict	6, Sept 1855	Joseph	List, Carolina	L	
Fangmann, Joseph Franz Bernard	5, June 1854	Joseph	Liss, Carolina	L	
Fangmann, Maria Catharina	1, Jan. 1858	Joseph	List, Carolina	L	
Fangmann, Wilhelmina	12, May 1859	Joseph	List, Carolina	L	
Faning, Elizabeth	3, Oct. 1852	Brian	Keogh, Eleanore	B	273
Faning, Mary	27, Mar. 1859	Joseph	Moloney, Mary	P	280
Fann, David	24, Jan. 1852	David J.	Allemann, Mary	L	
Fann, Francis	15, Oct.1855	Francis	Lea, Mary	P	156
Fannerty, Mary Ann	25, Jan. 1857	Michael	Quinn, Ellen	B	39
Fanning, Catherine	10, Nov. 1850	Thomas	Reilly, Bridget	B	218
Fanning, Daniel	30, Dec. 1851	John	O'Brien, Mary	E	369
Fanning, John	22, Nov. 1857	Joseph	Maloney, Mary	P	230
Fanning, John	6, July 1856	Michael	----, Mary Ann	M	
Fanning, Joseph James	9, Mar. 1851	Michael	Reynolds, Mary Ann	M	
Fanning, Margaret	18, Aug. 1853	Joseph	----, Joanne	E	120
Fanning, Mary	4, Feb. 1855	John	----, Mary	E	262
Fanning, Mary Ann	15, Aug. 1853	Michael	----, Mary Ann	M	
Fanning, William	20, Sept 1857	Michael	Reynolds, Mary Ann	U	
Fanz, Maria Catharina	13, Dec. 1857	Leopold	----,	T	
Far---, Catherine Leticia	21, June 1857	John	Campbell, Mary	P	214
Fareber, Joseph	18, Sept 1853	Xavier	Hara, Anna	D	406
Farfis, Ann	18, Nov. 1851	James	McCabe, Mary A.	B	245
Farfis, Francis	23, May 1858	James	McCabe, Mary Ann	E	536
Farfis, James	19, Apr. 1856	James	McCabe, Mary Ann	B	28
Farfis, Mary	18, Mar. 1853	James	McCabe, Mary Ann	B	286
Faris, Daniel	9, Aug. 1856	Daniel	Flanun, Mary Isabel	E	389
Faris, Mary Jane	13, Apr. 1855	James	Hanan, Mary Isabel	E	279
Farle, Thomas	10, Sept 1857	James	O'Donnel, Elizabeth	T	
Farley, Ann	26, July 1856	John	Fanan, Catharine	T	
Farley, Ann	17, Aug. 1856	John	Noon, Cecilia	P	188
Farley, Bernard	11, July 1852	John	Fitzpatrick, Ann	R	
Farley, Bridget	5, July 1857	Brian	Monaghan, Rose	B	46
Farley, Bridget	26, Oct. 1856	Charles	Duffy, Julia	B	35
Farley, Catherine	10, Oct. 1856	Jeremiah	Prendivible, Honora	E	403
Farley, Catherine	16, Mar. 1857	Michael	McGinnis, Mary	E	440
Farley, Henry	14, Nov. 1854	Charles	Duffy, Julia	E	240
Farley, James	18, Oct. 1859	James	Donnellan, Eliza	B	82
Farley, James	15, Jan. 1854	James	Sweeney, Ann	E	160
Farley, John William	7, Mar. 1852	Michael	Galligher, Ann	E	389
Farley, Lawrence	11, Apr. 1855	John	Fitzpatrick, Ann	R	
Farley, Margaret	14, Nov. 1858	James	Kelly, Margaret	B	67
Farley, Margaret Ann	13, July 1851	John	Duffy, Margaret	E	323
Farley, Mary	22, May 1859	Brian	Monaghan, Rose	B	75
Farley, Mary	28, Dec. 1856	James	Kelly, Margaret	B	38
Farley, Mary	9, Mar. 1851	Michael	Murtha, Ann	B	228
Farley, Mary Ann	29, June 1854	John	Duffy, Margaret	E	203
Farley, Mary Elizabeth	28, June 1858		Farley, M.	E	547
Farley, Mary Jane	17, Jan. 1858	John	----, Ann	R	
Farley, Sarah	3, Aug. 1851	Hugh	Havern, Sarah	B	238
Farley, Thomas	8, Feb. 1859	John	Keenane, Catheirne	B	71
Farley, Thomas	16, Mar. 1851	Patrick	Kelly, Elizabeth	E	290
Farley, William	19, Jan. 1850	John	Duffy, Margaret	E	193
Farmer, John	12, Jan. 1850	Peter	----, Alice	E	191
Farmer, Marianne	6, June 1852	Patrick	Goodman, Ellen	P	23

Name of Child	Date of Baptism	Father	Mother	Church	Page
Farmer, Mary Jane	4, Feb. 1855	James	Bready, Ann	P	118
Farmer, Otto Jen	5, Aug. 1855	Patrick	Goodmann, Helen	P	144
Farmer, Sarah Ann	11, Oct. 1853	John	Murphy, Bridget	P	54
Farmer, Thomas	30, Nov. 1851	Felix	Dolan, Helen	P	14
Farmer, Thomas	2, Sept 1851	John	Murphy, Bridget	B	240
Farmer, William Oscar	7, Dec. 1851	James	Braider, Joanne	P	14
Farnam, Johan	25, Dec. 1850	Patrick	Nolan, Ann	B	221
Farnam, Peter	4, July 1852	Patrick	Nolan, Ann	B	265
Farney, Bridget	8, Jan. 1854	Michael	----, Helen	B	306
Farnhopp, Bernard Joseph	24, Apr. 1853	Joseph	Toden---, Helena	K	
Farnung, Josephina	18, Apr. 1858	Johan	Dehler, Sybilla	F	
Farr, Johan	1, Oct. 1854	Peter	Leiner, Maria Anna	D	19
Farrad, Thomas	20, Jan. 1855	Edward	Clemer, Marcella	B	10
Farragan, Bridget	8, Aug. 1855	Michael	Gaughan, Ann	E	306
Farrall, Mary	6, Sept 1858	Edward	Cleany, Marcella	B	64
Farran, Edward	11, Mar. 1856	Edward	Clemmer, Marcella	B	26
Farrel, Catherine	26, Nov. 1852	Michael	Tuer, Mary	B	276
Farrell, Andrew	15, Aug. 1851	James	McFall, Mary	B	238
Farrell, Andrew Dennis	10, Apr. 1858	Thomas	Morris, Bridget	E	528
Farrell, Ann	24, Jan. 1858	Francis	Nugent, Margaret	B	55
Farrell, Ann	3, July 1854	Patrick	Dougherty, Honora	B	2
Farrell, Ann	23, Apr. 1854	Thomas	Hogan, Julia	P	80
Farrell, Ann	22, Feb. 1857		Farrell, Eliza	P	207
Farrell, Ann Mary	23, Aug. 1852	Henry	----, Mary Ann	E	9
Farrell, Bernard Francis	30, Oct. 1858	Bernard	Dolan, Ann	E	573
Farrell, Bridget	22, May 1853	Daniel	----, Margaret	B	292
Farrell, Catherine	9, Dec. 1854	Fargus	----, Ann	U	
Farrell, Catherine	13, Feb. 1859	Thomas	Hogan, Julia	P	275
Farrell, Catherine Elizabeth	21, Nov. 1854	James	McFall, Mary	P	105
Farrell, Charles	28, Sept 1857	Francis	Kervin, Ann	E	483
Farrell, Christine Mary	16, Nov. 1851	Michael	Hughes, Christine	B	245
Farrell, Daniel	10, June 1856	Thomas	Morris, Bridget	E	372
Farrell, Dennis	10, Mar. 1854	Henry	----, Mary	E	174
Farrell, Eliza	12, June 1853	James	Cummiskey,	P	44
Farrell, Elizabeth	10, Jan. 1858	John	----, Honora	M	
Farrell, Francis	30, June 1850	Bernard	Shandley, Catherine	B	206
Farrell, Francis	1, June 1857	James	----, Elizabeth	M	
Farrell, Honora	7, Aug. 1859	Richard	Latchford, Honora	P	291
Farrell, James	2, Aug. 1857	Bernard	Leonard, Julia M.	B	47
Farrell, James	31, Mar. 1859	James	Smith, Mary Ann	E	614
Farrell, James	3, Feb. 1857	Richard	Lachford, Honora	B	40
Farrell, James	9, Aug. 1857	William	Jordan, Ellen	B	48
Farrell, James	30, Jan. 1856	William	Jordan, Helen	P	168
Farrell, James Andrew	16, Dec. 1855	Patrick	Livingston, Mary	B	22
Farrell, James Patrick	8, Aug. 1856	Bernard	Doran, Ann	E	388
Farrell, James Timothy	12, Sept 1853	Edward	Cavanaugh, Joanne	P	52
Farrell, Jams	12, Oct. 1859	James	McFall, Mary	B	82
Farrell, Joanne	14, Nov. 1859	James	Costello, Bridget	E	669
Farrell, John	25, June 1854	Daniel	Hannon, Margaret	B	1
Farrell, John	2, Dec. 1855	Francis	Nugent, Margaret	P	161
Farrell, John	21, Nov. 1858	Henry	Woods, Mary	P	267
Farrell, John	5, June 1859	John	----, Honora	M	
Farrell, John	28, Sept 1857	John	Dunlap?, Catherine	B	50
Farrell, John	15, July 1850	John	Hackett, Mary	B	207
Farrell, John	19, Apr. 1856	Michael	----, Margaret	M	
Farrell, John	25, June 1857	Michael	----, Mary	R	
Farrell, John	8, Feb. 1857	Patrick	Dogherty, Honora	E	432
Farrell, John	24, Feb. 1856	Thomas	Cunningham, Lucy	B	25
Farrell, John	16, Mar. 1851	Thomas	Tra---, Bridget	P	6

Name of Child	Date of Baptism	Father	Mother	Church	Page
Farrell, John Hugh	18, Sept 1853	James R.	McFall, Mary	B	299
Farrell, John Joseph	16, Aug. 1854		Farrell, Catherine	E	217
Farrell, Julia	6, Nov. 1859	Patrick	Doherty, Honora	E	668
Farrell, Julia	30, July 1857	Thomas	Hogan, Julia	E	470
Farrell, Livea Caecilia	22, Nov. 1857	Thomas	Shanley, Mary	E	494
Farrell, Lucy	30, Sept 1855	Thomas	Hogan, Julia	P	153
Farrell, Margaret	11, Apr. 1852	James	----, Julia	B	256
Farrell, Margaret	6, Nov. 1852	John	----, Ann	E	32
Farrell, Margaret Jane	11, Sept 1859	Michael	McGory, Ann	P	295
Farrell, Mary	22, Mar. 1857	Fargus	Burke, Ann	U	
Farrell, Mary	5, Feb. 1854	Francis	Nugent, Margaret	P	67
Farrell, Mary	19, June 1857	James	----, Mary	E	460
Farrell, Mary	7, Dec. 1852	James	Smith, Mary	E	42
Farrell, Mary	18, June 1854	John	Burns, Ann	E	199
Farrell, Mary	21, Aug. 1856	John	Duffy, Bridget	E	391
Farrell, Mary	15, June 1852	Martin	Martin, Bridget	B	260
Farrell, Mary	4, Apr. 1853	Thomas	Feeny, Bridget	P	38
Farrell, Mary	26, Dec. 1854		Farrell, Mary	P	112
Farrell, Mary	7, Dec. 1855	James	Hunt, Bridget	P	162
Farrell, Mary Ann	10, May 1857	James	Costello, Bridget	E	452
Farrell, Mary Ann	21, July 1859	Patrick	----, Ann	E	641
Farrell, Mary Ann	27, June 1858	Thomas	Cunningham, Lucy	B	61
Farrell, Mary Ann Elizabeth	13, Aug. 1856	James	Smith, Mary Ann	V	32
Farrell, Mary Ellen	12, May 1858	James	Carroll, Bridget	E	534
Farrell, Mary Ellen	1, May 1859	Richard	Russell, Mary	B	74
Farrell, Mary Jean	25, Dec. 1852	Charles	----, Margaret	E	47
Farrell, Mary Julia	22, Aug. 1852	James	Joice, Bridget	P	26
Farrell, Mary Julia	3, Apr. 1853	Thomas	Hogan, Julia	P	38
Farrell, Mary Virginia	20, Mar. 1857	?	Cusack, Joanne	V	38
Farrell, Michael	7, Apr. 1850	James	Lacy, Mary	B	200
Farrell, Michael	12, Sept 1853	James	Shannan, Catherine	S	
Farrell, Owen	4, July 1855	Thomas	Feney, Bridget	P	138
Farrell, Peter	25, Sept 1859	Bernard	Lenihan, Julia Mary	B	81
Farrell, Robert	2, July 1858	John H.	----, Elizabeth	E	545
Farrell, Rosanne	6, May 1852	James	Shanahan, Catherine	B	258
Farrell, Susan	27, June 1856	Patrick	McGivern, Catherine	B	30
Farrell, Thomas	10, Nov. 1850	Patrick	Dogherty, Honora	B	218
Farrell, Thomas	7, Feb. 1858	Thomas	Feeney, Bridget	P	238
Farrell, Thomas	1, Feb. 1857	Thomas	McGewy, Ann	P	205
Farrell, Thomas	30, July 1854	William	Jordan, Helen	P	90
Farrell, Timothy	31, Aug. 1851	John	----, Ann	N	4
Farrell, William	20, Aug. 1854	James	Smith, Mary Ann	V	16
Farrelly, Catherine	26, Feb. 1855	Bernard	Monahan, Rose	P	122
Farrelly, Margaret	7, Oct. 1857	John	Baumann, Catharina	F	
Farrelly, Mary Elizabeth	23, July 1853	Hugh	----, Sarah	E	111
Farrer, Sarah	3, Apr. 1855		adult	B	13
Farrest, Edward	11, Aug. 1850	Innos	Frenck, Maria	C	
Farrin, James	9, Sept 1852	John	Summers, Elizabeth	B	270
Farrin, James Patrick	4, Dec. 1857	John	Sommers, Elizabeth	B	52
Farrington, James	26, Sept 1858	Peter	Greene, Mary	B	65
Farris, Mary Edith	28, May 1855	Milton	Withers, Eliza	B	15
Farris, Sarah	20, July 1854	James	----, Isabel	E	209
Farrow, Charles Albert	25, Oct. 1859	James	----, Mary Ann	E	665
Farsing, Johan Bernard	19, May 1854	Heinrich	Brockschmidt, Maria	K	
Farsing, Maria Elisabeth Theodora	13, Dec. 1858	Heinrich	Brockschmidt, Maria	K	
Farsing, Wilhelm Herman Heinrich	21, Oct. 1856	Heinrich J.	Brockschmidt, M. Philomena	K	
Farthing, Emily	2, Aug. 1858	Richard	Ryan, Rose	E	554
Farthing, Mary Ann	18, May 1856	Richard	----, Rosanne	E	367
Farthing, Richard	27, Mar. 1853	Richard	----, Mary Ann	E	77

Name of Child	Date of Baptism	Father	Mother	Church	Page
Farthing, Richard	29, Apr. 1855	Richard C.	----, Rose	E	283
Farwick, Catharina	20, Mar. 1859	Bernard	Kuhlmann, Catharina	C	
Farwick, Heinrich	1, Jan. 1855	Bernard	Kuhlmann, Catharina	C	
Farwick, Herman	28, Nov. 1856	Bernard	Kuhlmann, Catharina	C	
Farwick, Maria Anna	20, July 1851	Bernard	Strangenbers, Dina	C	
Fary, William Christopher	5, Jan. 1851	William	Hourigan, Mary	B	222
Fasch, Johan	6, Feb. 1859	J. Baptist	Devot--, Julia	D	130
Faske, Franz Heinrich	20, Aug. 1859	Herman H.	Henners, Anna Maria	F	
Faske, Joseph	29, June 1856	Herman	Hinners, Marianna	F	
Faske, Joseph Bernard	27, Aug. 1857	Heinrich	Hinners, Marianna	F	
Fasker, Johan Heinrich	26, May 1853	Herman H.	Hinners, Marianna	F	
Fastnacht, Carolina	13, Oct. 1858	Linus	Fritsch, Louisa	T	
Fath, Johan	1, Sept 1856	Johan	Geis, Anna Maria	D	66
Fath, Joseph	19, Dec. 1858	Jacob	Peter, Anna	D	126
Fauenkane, Peter	12, June 1853	Heinrich	Fabiaz, Johana	D	389
Faul, Juliana	25, Dec. 1858	Nicolaus	Moor, Francisca	A	
Faulhaber, Anton	19, June 1852	Michael	Roth, Catharina	A	
Faulhaber, Catharina	13, June 1851	Ludwig	Martin, Regina	D	267
Faulhaber, Crescentia	1, Oct. 1854	Michael	Röth, Catharina	A	
Faulhaber, Maria Anna	13, Jan. 1850	Michael	Roth, Catharina	A	
Faulhaber, Michael Bernard	15, May 1853	Ludwig	Martin, Regina	D	385
Faulker, Thomas	28, Feb. 1858	Thomas	----, Ann	M	
Faulkner, Ann Cora	18, Feb. 1855	Charles	----, Sarah	P	120
Faulkner, Catherine	14, July 1854	John	O'Connell, Helen	E	207
Faulkner, James	14, July 1854	John	O'Connell, Helen	E	207
Faulkner, Jeremiah	29, Jan. 1856	John	O'Connell, Helen	E	341
Faulkner, Mary Ann	16, Jan. 1858	John	O'Connell, Helen	E	509
Fautz, Georg	25, Jan. 1853	Joseph	Walter, Barbara	D	367
Fautz, Otto	19, Feb. 1854	Joseph	Walter, Barbara	D	5
Fautz, Theodor	14, June 1855	Joseph	Walter, Barbara	D	36
Fave, Robert	26, Jan. 1851	John	Thomas, Winifred	B	223
Fawcett, Mary	27, June 1852	William	Morgan, Eliza	B	265
Fay, Daniel	25, July 1852	Patrick	Mulloy, Elizabeth	P	25
Fay, James Francis	7, Jan. 1855	Walter	Lyen, Ellen	E	254
Fay, Margaret Elizabeth	7, May 1857	Thomas	----, Catherine	M	
Fay, Maria Louisa	1, Jan. 1859	Mathias	Weiglein, Anna	D	128
Fayl, Ellen	30, June 1856	Patrick	Cettride, Ellen	U	
Feaney, Michael	5, Mar. 1856	Patrick	Caulfield, Ellen	B	26
Febbe, Johan Gerhard	23, Oct. 1856	Herman G.	Wiggmann, Elisabeth	C	
Feber, Carolina	22, Jan. 1854	Martin	Floel, Margaretha	D	2
Feber, Emma Margaretha	10, Feb. 1859	Martin	Floel, Margaretha	D	131
Febiger, John Carson	11, May 1850	John	Ryan, Ann	B	202
Feck, Anna Carolina	31, Sept 1855	August	Risberger, Anna Maria	K	
Fecke, Bertha Anna	22, Feb. 1856	Bernard	Wolf, Theresa	D	52
Fecke, Heinrich Joseph	20, Mar. 1859	Jacob	Wettling, Christina	K	
Fecker, August	23,Sept 1854	Francis X.	Hoch, Crescentia	D	18
Fecker, Johan	11, Oct. 1851	Xavier	Hoch, Crescentia	D	286
Fecker, Louisa	22, Feb. 1859	Francis X.	Hoch, Crescentia	D	132
Fecker, Maria	16, June 1850	Xavier	Hoch, Crescentia	D	217
Feckers, Maria	17, Oct. 1856		Feckers, Maria	K	
Feddern, Heinrich	13, Mar. 1859	Heinrich	Schill, Catharina	Q	31
Feder, Carl Gerhard Johan	15, Aug. 1858	Carl	Schulte, Anna Catharina	A	
Federle, Theresa	5, Sept 1858	Joseph	Schutt, Kunigunda	T	
Federspiel, Augustin	3, Sept 1854	Augustine	Suhr, Maria Clara	L	
Federspiel, Maria Clara	22, Mar. 1857	Ignatius	Suhr, Maria Clara	L	
Federspiel, Maria Magdalena	23, Dec. 1850	August	Suhr, Clara	L	
Federspill, Catharina	2, Oct. 1859	August	Suhr, Clara	L	
Federspill, Josephina	8, Aug. 1852	August	Suhr, Clara	L	
Fee, Elizabeth Ann	11, Dec. 1853	Patrick	----, Elizabeth	E	151

Name of Child	Date of Baptism	Father	Mother	Church	Page
Fee, Mary Helen	15, Jan. 1857	John	Sorley, Josephine	U	
Feene, Peter	21, June 1857	Peter	Connel, Honora	T	
Feeney, Edward	5, Sept 1858	Owen	O'Melia, Helen	P	260
Feeney, Ellen	9, Aug. 1858	Patrick	Flinn, Ellen	B	62
Feeney, Honora	27, Jan. 1852	Marc	Ford, Mary	B	251
Feeney, John	15, Aug. 1858	John	Norton, Mary	P	258
Feeney, Margaret	9, Sept 1852	Patrick	Ryan, Catherine	B	270
Feeney, Thomas	27, Oct. 1851	Michael	Dolan, Elizabeth	P	13a
Feeni, Elisabeth	25, Apr. 1857	John	Kelle, Elisabeth	N	
Feeny, Anthony	17, Sept 1852	Anthony	Flinn, Sarah	P	27
Feeny, Catherine	10, July 1859	Michael	Hughes, Catherine	P	288
Feeny, Daniel	19, Sept 1852	Daniel	White, Mary	R	
Feeny, Daniel	2, Jan. 1853	John	Bartle, Ann	P	33
Feeny, James Edward	9, May 1855	Daniel	White, Mary	R	
Feeny, Joanne	23, Sept 1855	Thomas	Printy, Margaret	U	
Feeny, Johhn	10, Aug. 1859	John	McManus, Margaret	E	646
Feeny, John	27, Aug. 1855	John	Battle, Ann	V	26
Feeny, John	11, Feb. 1852	John	Gildea, Ellen	P	18
Feeny, John	18, Oct. 1858	Thomas	Printy, Mary	U	
Feeny, Mary	2, June 1852	Michael	Mo---, Catherine	P	22
Feeny, Michael Patrick	17, Mar. 1857	Daniel	----, Mary	R	
Feeny, Patrick	17, Mar. 1854	Patrick	Canfell, Helen	B	311
Feeny, Thomas	24, Dec. 1853	Daniel	----, Mary	R	
Fef, Josephina	15, Aug. 1859	Daniel	Breitinger, Eva Dorothea	A	
Feger, Louisa Carolina	6, Nov. 1856	Valentin	Welle, Francisca	C	
Fegh, Mary Ann	15, Apr. 1855	Patrick	Settwright, Helen	P	128
Fehr, Bridget	11, Aug. 1857	John	Clorin, Bridget	U	
Fehr, Carl Friedrich	23, Oct. 1856	Carl	Schible, Emma	D	70
Fehr, Francis	18, Sept 1859	John	Korn, Bridget	Q	33
Fehr, Georg Andreas	13, Mar. 1853	Valentin	Schweizer, Sophia	F	
Fehr, Margaretha	19, July 1851	Simon	Wegeman, Margaretha	A	
Fehr, Theodor Joseph	18, Nov. 1856	August	Fest?, Maria	D	72
Fehrenbach, Maria Anna Carolina	26, Dec. 1851	Theodor	Anselm, Clara	D	298
Fehring, Anna Catharina	27, Sept 1857	J. Theodor	Paul---, Anna Maria	D	95
Fehring, Bernard	13, July 1851	Bernard	Hüsing, Maria	K	
Fehring, Gerhard Herman	12, Aug. 1857	Bernard	Boening, Maria	C	
Fehring, Johan Heinrich	27, Oct. 1852	J. Bernard	Hüsing, Maria Adelheid	K	
Fehring, Johan Herman	6, Feb. 1856	Gerhard B.	Altenmann, M. Catharina	F	
Fehring, Maria Catharina	23, Sept 1854	Bernard	Huesing, Adelheid	C	
Fehring, Maria Margaretha	1, Sept 1853	Gerhard B.	Altenmeier, Maria Catharina	F	
Fehring, Susanna Margaretha	28, May 1859	J. Bernard	Husing, Maria	C	
Fehrkamp, Joseph Bernard	14, July 1858	Gerhard H.	Becker, Anna Maria	F	
Fehrkamp, M. Elisabeth Josephina	16, Nov. 1853	Gerhard	Schmidt, Anna Maria	C	
Fehrkamp, Margaretha Josephina	1, Nov. 1859	Herman	Schuerer, Margaretha	F	
Fei, Georg	14, Dec. 1856	Johan	Selsch, Maria Catharina	D	74
Fei, Johan	6, Mar. 1859	Johan	Selsch, Maria Catharina	D	133
Feibach, Anton	19, Sept 1850	Philipp	Scherer, Sophia	A	
Feie, Anna Maria Elisabeth	14, July 1854	Gerhard B.	Wollkotter, A. Maria	L	
Feie, Catharina Elisabeth	1, Dec. 1850	J. Gerhard	Wulkotten, Anna Maria	L	
Feie, Gerhard Heinrich	27, Apr. 1852	Gerhard	Wulkotten, Anna Maria	L	
Feie, Maria Carolina	22, Mar. 1856	Gerhard	Wollkotter, Anna M.	L	
Feie, Maria Elisabeth	14, July 1857	Bernard G.	Wulkotter, Anna M.	L	
Feiehart, Michael	3, Oct. 1852	Johan	Scheuman, Anna	D	351
Feiger, Catharina	20, Jan. 1850	Johan	Schram, Anna	D	200
Feigh, Margaret Ann	19, Mar. 1854	Patrick	Settright, Helen	P	74
Feigin, John	16, Jan. 1853	Patrick	Settright, Helen	B	281
Feigler, Anna Gertrud	12, Jan. 1854	Theodor	Frering, Anna Maria	L	
Feiler, Adam	22, Feb. 1852	Johan	Peh, Barbara	C	
Feiler, Albert	26, Sept 1852	Christoph	Weidey, Magdalena	D	349

Name of Child	Date of Baptism	Father	Mother	Church	Page
Feiler, Albert Joseph	17, July 1855	Christoph	Weidig, Magdalena	C	
Feiler, Christoph Wilhelm	25, Aug. 1853	Johan	Peer, Barbara	C	
Feiler, Elisabeth	18, July 1858	Christoph	Weiday, Margaretha	D	115
Feiler, Georg	6, Apr. 1856	Johan	Beh, Barbara	C	
Feiler, Magdalena Wilhelmina	12, Nov. 1854	Johan	Beh, Barbara	C	
Feiler, Wilhelmina Barbara	21, Jan. 1854	Christoph	Weiterich, Magdal.	C	
Fein, Andrew	4, Sept 1859	Francis X.	Becker, Helen	H	
Feir, Nicolaus	19, Dec. 1857	Peter	Lein, Maria	D	100
Feis, Batholomew	17, Apr. 1853	Peter	Leien, Maria	D	380
Feiss, Elisabeth Carolina	11, Dec. 1859	Pius	Sch---, Maria	D	152
Feith, Catharina	21, Aug. 1853	Nicolaus	Feller, Susanna	F	
Feith, Nicolaus	5, Jan. 1851	Nicolaus	Feller, Susanna	F	
Fekmar, Marianna	18, Mar. 1858	Joseph	H---, Margaretha	D	107
Feld, Anna Adelheid Elisabeth	7, Mar. 1856	Heinrich	Toennies, Elisabeth	C	
Feld, Clemens Heinrich	5, Nov. 1859	Clemens	Lackman, Carolina	A	
Feld, Francisca Catharina	1, Feb. 1851	Heinrich	Tonnis, Elisabeth	C	
Feld, Georg Heinrich	12, Sept 1853	Gerhard	Doennis, Elisabeth	C	
Feld, Maria Anna	8, Sept 1858	Heinrich	Toennes, Anna Maria	C	
Feldec, George	27, June 1852	Johan	Bohrer, Anna Maria	Q	2
Feldes, Anna Maria	30, Sept 1855	Johan	Bohrer, Anna Maria	Q	11
Feldhake, Johan Friedrich	18, May 1851	Friedrich	Klindkamp, Elisabeth	C	
Feldhaus, Elisabeth	27, Mar. 1854	J. Heinrich	Wessling, Gertrud	A	
Feldhaus, Euphemia Adelheid Cath.	9, Oct. 1850	Johan	Kampemith, Margaretha	F	
Feldhaus, Herman Theodor	28, Nov. 1852	Johan	Kampschmidt, Margaretha	L	
Feldhaus, Johan Heinrich	11, Dec. 1858	J. Heinrich	Wessling, Gertrud	D	125
Feldhaus, Johan Herman	14, Apr. 1856	J. Heinrich	Wessling, Gertrud	A	
Feldhaus, Maria Elisabeth	13, Jan. 1859	Gerhard	Grüter, Maria Elisabeth	A	
Feldhaus, Maria Gertrud Friedrica P.	4, Sept 1857	Bernard	Speckbach, Margaretha	K	
Feldhaus, Theodor Johan Bernard	16, Nov. 1854	Johan	Kampschmidt, Margaretha	F	
Feldick, Friedrich Wilhelm	8, Jan. 1854	F. Wilhelm	Bohrer, Anna Maria	Q	4
Feldkamp, Anna Maria Catharina	23, Dec. 1850	Mathias	Dorrman, Catharina	A	
Feldkamp, Catharina Maria	15, Apr. 1859	Bernard	Moeller, Elisabeth	F	
Feldman, Albert Ferdinand	21, Sept 1856	Herman	Schröder, Elisabeth	A	
Feldman, Anna Margaretha Philomena	29, Sept 1858	Johan	W---, Margaretha Elisabeth	D	120
Feldman, Anna Maria	22, Sept 1858	G.H.	VonderHar, Adelheid	A	
Feldman, Anna Maria	25, Nov. 1858	Theodor	Meier, Maria Adelheid	D	124
Feldman, Anton	8, Feb. 1851	Herman	Schröder, Maria Elisabeth	J	10
Feldman, Francis Heinrich	29, May 1852	Herman	Notebusch, Elisabeth	D	322
Feldman, Francis Heinrich	30, Sept 1856	J. Wilhelm	Steme, Elisabeth	D	68
Feldman, Georg Joseph	1, Mar. 1859	J. Heinrich	Norther---, Maria Elisabeth	D	133
Feldman, Heinrich	26, May 1855	Herman	Notebusch, Elisabeth	D	35
Feldman, Heinrich Bernard	4, Mar. 1852	Heinrich	Bernens, Bernardina	A	
Feldman, Heinrich Francis	16, June 1858	Bernard	Wörste, Anna Maria	N	
Feldman, Herman Heinrich	20, Apr. 1857	J. Heinrich	VanderHaar, Adelheid	A	
Feldman, Herman Heinrich	27, June 1852	J. Herman	Schröder, Elisabeth	J	16
Feldman, Johan Bernard	26, Apr. 1854	J. Herman	Schröder, Maria Elisabeth	J	26
Feldman, Johan Bernard Joseph	30, Oct. 1856	Bernard	Worste, Maria	N	
Feldman, Johan Bernard Wilhelm	1, Feb. 1856	J. Dietrich	Meier, Maria Adelheid	D	51
Feldman, Johan Heinrich	3, Sept 1852	J. Dietrich	Meier, Maria Adelheid	D	346
Feldman, Johan Heinrich Herman	7, Dec. 1858	Johan	Schwering, Elisabeth	D	125
Feldman, Johan Herman	13, June 1852	J. Wilhelm	Stubbe, Maria Elisabeth	D	324
Feldman, Johan Wilhelm	9, Mar. 1852	J. Herman	Frühling, Gertrud	D	311
Feldman, Joseph Herman	27, Jan. 1854	Herman	Frühling, Maria Gertrud	D	3
Feldman, Ludwig Wilhelm	28, May 1858	Herman	Frohling, Gertrud	D	112
Feldman, Maria Adelheid	4, Oct. 1857	Albert	Gausepohl, Maria Elisabeth	A	
Feldman, Maria Carolina	13, June 1855	Bernard	Worste, Maria	N	
Feldman, Maria Catharina	18, Jan. 1854	J. Bernard	Wörste, Anna Maria	N	20
Feldman, Rosa	3, Oct. 1854	Johan	Stoppe, Maria Elisabeth	D	19
Feldman, Wilhelm Herman	30, Oct. 1855	Herman	Frulling, Gertrud	D	45

Name of Child	Date of Baptism	Father	Mother	Church	Page
Feldmann, Anna Maria Bernardina	15, Nov. 1851	Johan	Moeddel, Adelheid	C	
Feldmann, Anna Maria Gertrud	2, Nov. 1853	Johan	Moeddel, Adelheid	C	
Feldmann, Anna Maria Philomena	10, June 1855	Johan	Moeddel, Adelheid	C	
Feldmann, Anton Francis	19, Apr. 1859	Herman H.	Schroeder, Elisabeth	C	
Feldmann, Bernard	28, May 1856	Herman	Dickhaus, Elisabeth	L	
Feldmann, Bernard Herman	23, Apr. 1857	J. Heinrich	Schrichtel, Adelheid	C	
Feldmann, Franz	28, June 1858	Heinrich	Ossenbeck, Elisabeth	L	
Feldmann, Franz Albert	7, Oct. 1858	Herman	Dickhaus, Cath. Elis.	L	
Feldmann, Heinrich	21, Nov. 1852	Herman	Gausepohl, Catharina	L	
Feldmann, Herman Heinrich	31, Aug. 1851	Herman	Dickhaus, Elisabeth	L	
Feldmann, Johan	15, May 1857	Heinrich	Ossenbeck, Elis.	L	
Feldmann, Johan Bernard Heinrich	30, Dec. 1858	Bernard	Borgerding, Maria	L	
Feldmann, Johan Georg	17, July 1853	J. Bernard	Frilling, Maria Elisabeth	F	
Feldmann, Johan Heinrich	19, July 1854	J. Anton	Schrichten, Adel.	C	
Feldmann, Johan Heinrich Franz Bd.	14, Aug. 1859	Francis	Fangmann, A.M. Agnes	L	
Feldmann, Joseph Herman	10, Feb. 1855	Heinrich	Ossenbeck, Elisabeth	L	
Feldmann, M. Catharina Emilia C.	11, Sept 1856	J. Bernard	Borgeding, Maria A.	L	
Feldmann, Maria Adelheid	29, May 1859	Herman	Nietfeld, M. Elisabeth	L	
Feldmann, Maria Agnes	12, Feb. 1854	Heinrich	Ossenbeck, M. Elis.	L	
Feldmann, Maria Agnes	7, Jan. 1857	Herman	Gausepohl, M. Elis.	L	
Feldmann, Maria Anna	14, Sept 1851	Heinrich	Ostenbeck, Elisabeth	C	
Feldmann, Maria Elisabeth	14, Aug. 1855	Albert H.	Gausepohl, Maria A.	L	
Feldmann, Maria Elisabeth	11, Dec. 1853	J. Herman	Dickhaus, M. Elisabeth	L	
Feldmann, Maria Paulina	4, Apr. 1852	J. Anton	Schrichten, M. Adel.	L	
Felher, Adam	21, Nov. 1858	Georg	Neff, Margaretha	C	
Felik, Peter	8, Aug. 1852	James	----, Mary	H	
Felix, Barbara	8, July 1850	Georg M.	Hofreiter, Magdalena	F	
Felix, Carl	8, Jan. 1854	Michael	Hofreiter, Magdalena	D	1
Felix, Carl	11, Mar. 1855	Peter	Sucieta, Barbara	D	31
Felix, Caroline	28, Dec. 1856	Peter	Schissiedort, Barbara	T	
Felix, Catharina	16, Jan. 1858	J. Jacob	Gels, Elisabeth	K	
Felix, Francisca Barbara	28, June 1857	Francis	Meyer, Magdalena	C	
Felix, Franz	16, Jan. 1851	Mathias	Rebold, Catharina	F	
Felix, Georg	25, June 1854	J. Jacob	Kirsch, Elisabeth	D	13
Felix, Johan	27, Jan. 1856	Georg	Flahr, Margaretha	D	51
Felix, Joseph	9, Oct. 1858	Michael	Hoffauter, Magdalena	T	
Felix, Juliana	2, Dec. 1850	Peter	Sucieda, Barbara	D	245
Felix, Louisa	13, Feb. 1859	Peter	Sucieto, Barbara	C	
Felix, Ludwig	18, Jan. 1852	G. Michael	Hofreiter, Magdalena	D	303
Felix, Magdalena	3, Aug. 1851	Francis	Morico, Magdalena	C	
Felix, Magdalena	17, Aug. 1852	Peter	Sucieto, Barbara	D	344
Felix, Mathias	30, May 1851	Friedrich	Weber, Marianna	F	
Felix, Peter	27, Jan. 1856	J. Jacob	Koltsch, Elisabeth	D	51
Felix, Sebastian	10, July 1853	J. Jacob	Koetsch, Elisabeth	D	394
Felix, Sebastian	6, Feb. 1859	Johan	Kelsch, Elisabeth	K	
Felix, William	1, July 1856	Michael	Hofrider, Magdalena	T	
Fell, Eliza	31, Oct. 1856		adult - nee Hagarty	B	35
Fell, Johanna Angela	12, May 1856	Mathias	Köster, Margaretha	D	58
Fell, Ludwig Mathias	20, June 1858	Mathias	Koster, Margaretha	D	113
Feller, Albert	24, Nov. 1850	Johan	Walternath, Sophia	D	244
Feller, Carl	16, Jan. 1853	Carl	Kupper, Barbara	K	
Feller, Margaret	11, Nov. 1855	Anthony	----, Maria	H	
Feller, Michael	19, Aug. 1855	Charles	Kupper, Barbara	U	
Feller, Peter	29, Aug. 1858	Peter	Steffen, Margaretha	C	
Feloy, Margaret	14, Sept 1851	Jeremiah	----, Honora	E	342
Fels, Carolinla	16, Jan. 1853	Johan	Gut, Anna Maria	D	365
Fels, Elisabeth	23, Jan. 1859	Johan	Gut, Maria	T	
Fels, Georg	26, Apr. 1857	Johan	Gut, Anna Maria	D	83
Fels, Johan	6, May 1855	Johan	Gut, Anna Maria	D	34

Name of Child	Date of Baptism	Father	Mother	Church	Page
Fels, Maria Anna	17, Feb. 1852	Johan	Gut, Maria Anna	D	307
Feltmann, Johan Joseph	7, June 1850	Bernard	Trilling, Elisabeth	F	
Fely, Anna Maria	12, May 1850	Wilhelm	Holthaus, Anna Maria	L	
Fend, Maria	8, Dec. 1850	Michael	Roony, Margaretha	F	
Fender, Mathilda	31, July 1858	Martin	Guruck, Maria Anna	C	
Feneran, William	11, May 1856	James	Brennan, Eliza	T	
Fenger, Agnes Elisabeth	18, Sept 1859	Johan	Schmudde, Elisabeth	K	
Fenger, Agnes Elisabeth	10, Apr. 1859	Stephen A.	Mölering, Maria	A	
Fenger, Georg	29, Dec. 1858	Johan	Schmutte, Agnes	A	
Fenger, Johan Wilhelm	30, July 1854	Johan	Schmutte, Agnes	L	
Fenger, Maria Anna Elisabeth	14, July 1856	J. Heinrich	Schmutte, Maria Agnes	A	
Fenker, Johan Bernard	19, Apr. 1856	Heinrich	Feldschneider, Euph.	L	
Fenker, Johan Gerhard	29, Oct. 1854	Anton	----, Agnes	A	
Fenker, Johan Heinrich	29, May 1851	Bernard H.	Feldschneider, Anna M.	L	
Fenker, M. Catharina Bernardina	26, Nov. 1853	Bernard	Feldschneider, Euphemia	L	
Fenker, Maria Angela	16, Sept 1850	J. Bernard	Voss, Maria Catharina	L	
Fenker, Maria Catharina Bernardina	30, Dec. 1852	J. Bernard	Voss, Catharina	L	
Fenlan, Catherine	3, Dec. 1854	Peter	Hogan, Bridget	E	245
Fenlon, Eliza	29, Mar. 1857	Peter	Hogan, Bridget	B	42
Fenlon, Louisa	15, Feb. 1859	Philip	Hogan, Bridget	B	71
Fennedunker, Anna Maria Rosina	7, Sept 1851	Bernard	Baker, Maria Elisabeth	A	
Fennedunker, Heinrich Anton	29, June 1856	Anton	Franzmann, Theresa	F	
Fennedunker, Johan Bernard	5, Apr. 1854	J. Bernard	Bekermann, Maria Elisabeth	F	
Fennedunker, Johan Bernard Wilhelm	4, Apr. 1858	Bernard	Beckermann, Elisabeth	F	
Fennedunker, Johan Heinrich	6, May 1855	Bernard	Beckermann, Elisabeth	F	
Fennedunker, Joseph Anton	11, Jan. 1859	Joseph A.	----, Theresa	F	
Fennedunker, Maria Anna	20, July 1850	Anton	Frankemann, Theresa	F	
Fennel, Elizabeth	4, Oct. 1856	William	----, Bridget	E	401
Fennell, Elizabeth	17, May 1852	William	----, Bridget	E	414
Fenneman, Maria Josephina	15, Oct. 1851	J. Anton	Schwer, Catharina Maria	A	
Fennemann, Johan Heinrich	27, Aug. 1855	J. Gerhard	Grawe, Gertrud	L	
Fennemann, Theodor Clemens	8, Nov. 1857	Gerhard H.	Grefe, Maria Gertrud	L	
Fennen, August	18, Dec. 1851		Fennen, Maria Christina	J	14
Fenner, Margaretha Maria	9, Sept 1859	Aloysius	----, Barbara	D	146
Fennessy, James Edward	14, Nov. 1852	Edward	Keating, Helen	B	275
Fenorn?, John	11, Oct. 1857	Peter	Walders, Ann	B	50
Fentker, Johan Heinrich	20, July 1858	Johan	Grotemeyer, Josephina	A	
Fenton, Bridget	27, Oct. 1850	William	----, Alice	E	256
Fenton, Catherine	9, Sept 1854	John A.	Fitzpatrick, Margaret	V	17
Fenton, Margaret	13, Apr. 1851	Philipp	Bergen, Bridget	B	229
Fenton, Mary	10, Aug. 1850	James	Mahon, Susan	B	209
Fenton, Thomas	29, Aug. 1858	John	Maher, Catherine	E	560
Fenwiggenhorn, Angela Friedrica	17, June 1851	Anton	Bilderman, Catharina	D	268
Fenzel, Anna Barbara	16, May 1858	Caspar	Bruner, Sibilla	D	111
Fenzel, Elisabeth Magdalena	17, Mar. 1855	Caspar	Brunner, Sophia	D	31
Fepman, Theodor Heinrich	12, Jan. 1858	Bernard H.	Wilpe, Maria Anna	D	102
Fera, Adolph Carl	27, Mar. 1853	Christian	Hesing, Lisette	L	
Fera, Antonia Augusta Johanna	13, Mar. 1859	Christian	Hesing, Elisabeth	L	
Fera, Francisca Clara Mathilda	9, Jan. 1855	Adolph	Hesing, Lisette	L	
Fera, Johanna Henrietta	9, Mar. 1851	Adolph	Hesing, Lisette	L	
Fera, Maria Ida	6, Mar. 1857	Christian	Hesing, Lisette	L	
Ferchbeck, Maria Anna	13, Apr. 1855	Jacob	Roak, Sarah	K	
Ferdigham, William Henry	22, Feb. 1857	Charles	O'Brien, Mary	E	434
Fergeson, Joseph	11, Mar. 1855	John	Fitzmaurice, Catherine	V	23
Ferguson, Alice Margaret	10, Nov. 1859	John	Fitzmorris, Catherine	B	83
Ferguson, Charles	16, Nov. 1856	Patrick	McCue, Mary	V	35
Ferguson, Edward Purcell	15, July 1857	John	Fitzmorris, Catherine	B	47
Ferguson, Hugh	15, Jan. 1853	John	----, Catherine	E	55
Ferguson, James	12, June 1859	James	----, Mary	E	632

Name of Child	Date of Baptism	Father	Mother	Church	Page
Ferguson, James	24, Dec. 1854	James	----, Mary	M	
Ferguson, Mary	2, Jan. 1859	Patrick	McKen, Mary	E	593
Ferguson, Mary Helen	24, Nov. 1850	John	Fitzmaurice, Catherine	B	219
Fermann, Anna Maria	15, Aug. 1858	Bernard H.	Brockmann, A. Gertrud	L	
Fermann, Herman Heinrich	12, Feb. 1855	Bernard H.	Brockmann, A. Gertrud	L	
Fermann, Johan Bernard	13, Mar. 1856	Heinrich	Brockmann, M Gertrud	L	
Fermann, Maria Catharina Philomena	11, Aug. 1859	Bernard H.	Brockmann, Anna Maria	L	
Fermann, Maria Engel	22, July 1853	Heinrich	Brockmann, A.M.	L	
Fern, Margaret	5, Jan. 1857	Peter	----, Mary	E	425
Fernbach, Carl Joseph	15, Aug. 1850	Joseph	Fernbach, Catharina	C	
Fernmeier, Louisa Philomena	22, Sept 1857	Joseph	Krisser, Euphemia Maria	D	95
Ferrell, James Henry	28, July 1853	Michael	----, Margaret	M	
Ferrell, William	20, Feb. 1858	Francis	----, Mary	M	
Ferrill, Frederick John	3, July 1859	John	Gold, Mary	B	77
Ferroch, Michael	7, Oct. 1855	Michael	----, Ann	M	
Fessler, Joseph Anton	2, Apr. 1854	Francis A.	Werler, Clothilda	D	7
Fessler, Magdalena Josephina	24, Feb. 1850	Herman	Niederhofer, Catharina	C	
Fessler, Maria Theresa	23, Mar. 1856	Anton	Weller, Clothilda	D	54
Fest, Martin Jacob Bernard	11, Nov. 1851	Johan	Kanters, Christina	A	
Feth, Anna	28, Nov. 1858	Mathias	Busun, Anna Maria	W	24
Feth, Anna Bernardina	1, Oct. 1854	Mathias	Busi, Anna Maria	W	5
Feth, Anna Maria	12, Oct. 1856	Adam	Helmes, Bernardina	D	69
Feth, Elisabeth	26, Aug. 1855	Johan	Schnartz, Margaretha	D	41
Feth, Eva Elisabeth	9, Oct. 1857	Johan	Schnatzman, Margretha	D	96
Feth, Georg	14, July 1850	J. Adam	Helms, Bernardina	D	223
Feth, Johan	5, Oct. 1856	Mathias	Busen, Maria Anna	W	16
Feth, Johan Anton	1, Apr. 1855	J. Adam	Helms, Bernardina	D	32
Feth, Louisa Maria	13, Oct. 1850	Mathias	Büsing, Maria	D	237
Feth, Marianna	30, Nov. 1851	J. Adam	Helms, Bernardina	D	295
Feth, Mathias	31, July 1853	J. Adam	Helms, Bernardina	D	397
Fetsch, Magdalena	12, Mar. 1858	J. Adam	Pistner, Maria	D	107
Fetsch, Margaretha	1, June 1856	Nicolaus	Bruegle, Theresa	D	59
Fetsch, Martha	23, May 1858	Nicolaus	Brügger, Theresa	D	111
Fetsch, Nicolaus	17, Dec. 1854	Nicolaus	Brüchler, Theresa	D	24
Fette, John Frederick Sigismund	6, Nov. 1859	Charles	----, Sophia	E	669
Fetzer, Anthony	17, July 1856	Melchior	Staus, Wily	E	381
Fetzer, Carl Melchior	17, Apr. 1859	Melchior	Strauss, Wilgeford	K	
Fetzer, Johan	29, Aug. 1852	Melchior	Staus, Wielgefrieda	K	
Fetzer, Rosina	28, Sept 1854	Melchior	Staus, Wilgefrieda	K	
Feuerlein, Barbara	25, Nov. 1855	Johan	Wel?, Barbara	D	47
Feuerstein, Carolina Johanna	28, Mar. 1859	Francis	Kunze, Barbara	D	135
Feuerstein, Louisa	18, Oct. 1857	Francis	Kurz, Barbara	D	97
Feulner, Georg	28, Oct. 1859	Johan	Herberig, Elisabeth	K	
Fey, Anna Gertrud	14, Nov. 1852	Nicolaus	Bittlinger, Catharina	F	
Fey, Anna Maria	6, Mar. 1853	Dominick	Mescher, Elisabeth	D	374
Fey, Anna Maria	18, Sept 1859	Felix	Schaibele, Margaretha	G	
Fey, Barbara Laurentia	15, Sept 1858	Jacob	Denzler, Barbara	T	
Fey, Catharina	15, Dec. 1850	Nicolaus	Bittling, Catharina	F	
Fey, Dominick Heinrich	15, Oct. 1858	Dominick	Mescher, Elisabeth	F	
Fey, Eva	15, Oct. 1854	Michael	----, Elisabeth	H	
Fey, Francis	4, Oct.1857	Francis	Gu--, Catharina	D	96
Fey, Johan	23, Nov. 1856	Nicolaus	Bittlinger, Catharina	F	
Fey, Johan Conrad	30, Jan. 1859	Francis	Knebel, Gertrud	D	130
Fey, Johan Heinrich	2, Nov. 1859	Heinrich	Huelsmann, Elis.	T	
Fey, Johan Heinrich	6, Mar. 1857	Johan H.	Huelsmann, Elisabeth	F	
Fey, Johan Herman Heinrich	23, Nov. 1858	Johan H.	Huelsmann, Maria Elis.	T	
Fey, Johan Jacob	28, Jan. 1855	Christoph	Heinrich, Eva	D	27
Fey, Johan Peter	9, Jan. 1859	Nicolaus	Bittlinger, Catharina	T	
Fey, Margaretha Elisabeth	23, Nov. 1856	Jacob	Densel, Barbara	J	38

Name of Child	Date of Baptism	Father	Mother	Church	Page
Fey, Maria	15, Apr. 1855	Nicolaus	Bittlinger, Catharina	F	
Fey, Nicolaus	24, Jan. 1858	Heinrich	Fey, Catharina	T	
Fey, Nicolaus	1, May 1859		Fey, Margaretha	G	
Fey, Peter	21, Oct. 1855	Christian	Frankenbach, Catharina	D	45
Fey, Philip Christian	25, Dec. 1853	J. George	adult - 21 years old	H	
Fey, Theresa Louisa	9, Dec. 1855	Dominick	Mescher, Elisabeth	D	48
Fey, Wilhelm Friedrich	24, Oct. 1858	Friedrich	Quick, Elisabeth	G	
Fezzi, Mary Cecilia	6, July 1851	Bartholomew	Odape, Angelia	B	235
Fibbe, Johan Gerhard	23, Feb. 1852	J. Heinrich	Börger, Maria Agnes	D	309
Fibbe, Johan Heinrich	10, Oct. 1852	Gerhard	Hamberg, Maria	C	
Fibbe, Johan Heinrich	18, Feb. 1853	Herman	Thele, Anna	C	
Fibbe, Johan Herman	5, Oct. 1858	Gerhard H.	Hamberg, M. Anna	C	
Fibbe, Johan Herman Heinrich	4, Dec. 1858	Herman H.	Wichmann, Elisabeth	C	
Fibbe, Johan Ludwig	13, Nov. 1853	J. Heinrich	Bürger, Agnes	D	415
Fibbe, Johan Theodor Aloysius	4, May 1851	Herman H.	Thole, M. Anna	C	
Fibbe, Maria Catharina	6, Aug. 1855	Gerhard	Hamberg, Maria	C	
Fibbe, Maria Elisabeth	20, Oct. 1854	Gerhard	Huelsmann, Elisabeth	C	
Fibich, Joseph August Stanislaus	17, Oct. 1852	Stanilaus	Bender, Maria Anna	F	
Fibig, Maria Helena	6, Oct. 1850	Stanilaus	Bender, Maria	C	
Fibler, Carolina	18, Dec. 1853	Joseph	Dittle, Catharina	D	420
Fichter, Elisabeth	20, Dec. 1857	Lawrence	Walder, Maria S.	F	
Fichter, Rosina	10, Oct. 1858	Gabriel	Meyer, Sarah	J	48
Ficke, Johan Heinrich	22, Aug. 1851	Heinrich	Niemolle, Maria Theresa	K	
Ficker, Anna Catharina	18, Dec. 1856	J. Herman	Pöhling, Euphemia Adelheid	A	
Ficker, Anna Catharina	23, Nov. 1850	Johan	Thöling, Maria Barbara	A	
Ficker, Franz Jacob	7, Feb. 1858	Martin	Ehlen, Maria	T	
Ficker, Heinrich Ludwig	27, July 1853	J. Bernard	Holtmayer, Anna M. Cath.	D	397
Ficker, Johan Gerhard	29, Dec. 1853	J. Gerhard	Pohling, Euphemia Adelheid	A	
Ficker, Johan Herman	28, Oct. 1853	J. Herman	Brueggemann, Clara	L	
Ficker, Maria Clara	30, Nov. 1850	Herman	Brueggemann, M. Clara	L	
Ficker, Maria Elisabeth	19, Feb. 1852	Johan	Pöhling, Euphemia Adelheid	A	
Fickers, Bernard Heinrich	24, Aug. 1857	B. Heinrich	Klei--, Anna Maria	D	93
Fideldai, Catharina Maria	5, Aug. 1856	J. Christian	Janzman, Catharina	D	64
Fideldai, Johan Bernard	4, June 1859	Christian	Janzman, Catharina	D	139
Fideldai, Johan Christian	19, Oct. 1854	J. Heinrich	Johannesman, Anna Cath.	D	20
Fidelday, Caspar Heinrich	12, Oct. 1852	Heinrich	Johannisman, Catharina	D	353
Fideldei, Anna Maria Philomena	8, Mar. 1850	J. Heinrich	Hem, Anna Maria	K	
Fideldei, Bernard Heinrich	23, Nov. 1857	Christian	Stat---ter, Maria	D	99
Fideldei, Christian Wilhelm	7, Nov. 1853	Christian	Lavan, Barbara	K	
Fideldey, Carl Joseph	19, Oct. 1856	J.C.	Lubben, Barbara	K	
Fideldey, Maria Elisabeth	11, Feb. 1851	Heinrich	Johannsman, Maria Cath.	D	253
Fie-alage, Johan Heinrich Theodor	4, Nov. 1857	Heinrich	Ram---, Anna Maria	D	98
Fiedler, Adam Wilhelm	5, Apr. 1858	Johan	Hoefer, Amalia	T	
Fiedler, Anna Maria	7, May 1854	Johan	Höffer, Amalia	D	9
Field, Catherine	13, July 1857	Michael	Malvey, Elizabeth	E	465
Field, Dennis	18, Sept 1851	Dennis	Murphy, Margaret	B	241
Field, Dennis James	22, July 1855	Michael	Mulvey, Elizabeth	V	26
Field, Elizabeth	10, July 1859	Michael	Mulony, Eliza	E	638
Field, Mary	2, June 1850	Dennis	Murphy, Margaret	B	204
Fielding, Thomas Michael	22, Aug. 1853	James	Hover, Hannah Ann	P	50
Fieler, Anna Maria	15, Sept 1858	J. Albert	Fieber, Maria Theresa	K	
Fieler, Anna Maria Elisabeth	15, Dec. 1855	Albert	Hülsing, Theresa	K	
Fieler, Georg Herman	21, Dec. 1857	J. Edward	Bahlmann, Marianna	F	
Fieler, Johan Eberhard	26, July 1855	Eberhard	Bahlmann, Marianna	F	
Fiels, August Friedrich Ludwig	18, Apr. 1858	Johan	Ruehl, Margaretha	F	
Fiener, Theodore William	21, Feb. 1856	William	Wittler, Gertrud	R	
Fierkers, Johan Friedrich	7, Dec. 1855	Bernard	Morian, Anna	L	
Fietler, Maria Elisabeth	3, Aug. 1851	Johan	Hoefer, Amalia	D	276
Fihely,	16, June 1858	John	Hagerty, Mary	B	60

Name of Child	Date of Baptism	Father	Mother	Church	Page
Fikke, Maria Catharina	8, Mar. 1859	Heinrich	Kleinmann, Walburga	F	
Fillbin, Patrick	19, Feb. 1853	John	----, Mary	E	63
Filmore, Thomas	21, Dec. 1852	Michael	----, Julia	E	46
Filzer, Carl	4, July 1858	Peter	Brand, Theresa	D	114
Filzer, Francis	22, June 1856	Peter	Braun, Theresa	J	36
Fimbluck, Mary Ann	20, Feb. 1859	D.W.F.	Ford, Ann	B	71
Finan, Bridget Mary	15, Feb. 1853	Bernard	Barber, Margaret	B	283
Finan, Elias	10, Apr. 1859	Bernard	Bartler, Margaret	B	73
Finan, Michael	18, Oct. 1850		Finan, Mary	E	255
Finan, William	14, Nov. 1850	Bernard	Butler, Mary	B	218
Finane, Bernard	6, Jan. 1856	Bernard	Butler, Margaret	T	
Finch, Caroline	14, May 1854	Charles C.	Farmer, Miranda	B	314
Finch, Edward	30, Aug. 1856	Charles C.	Farmer, Miranda	B	33
Finch, Laura	20, June 1852	Charles C.	Farmer, Miranda	B	261
Finch, Louise Clarke	17, Oct. 1858	----	----, ----	X	
Finch, Mary Elizabeth	8, Jan. 1850		adult - 20 years old	B	193
Finch, Sarah Philomena	21, Mar. 1850	John	Carrigan, Catherine	B	198
Finch, Stephan	18, Jan. 1852	John	Carrigan, Catherine	B	250
Findlay, John	7, Sept 1851	William	Mulcahy, Margaret	J	12
Findling, Johan Ferdinand	8, Apr. 1852	----	----, ----	L	
Finegan, Mary Ann	17, Feb. 1856	Patrick	Ward, Mary	P	170
Finern, Joseph Michael	2, Sept 1858	Michael	Moume?, Mary	B	63
Finessy, John	8, June 1856	Edward	Ryan, Mary	P	182
Finey, Henry	20, Aug. 1854	Michael	----, Elizabeth	U	
Finhage, F. Gerhard Herman	8, Aug. 1850	Joseph	Tieman, Maria Catharina	K	
Finhage, Heinrich Anton	31, Oct. 1856	Joseph	Thieman, Maria	K	
Finhage, Maria Philomena Theresa	27, Sept 1853	Joseph	Thieman, Maria	K	
Finigan, Mary Elizabeth	3, Oct. 1858	Richard	McAndrew, Mary	P	262
Finigan, Rosanne	6, Nov. 1857	William	Blackburn, Bridget	V	42
Finigan, William Joseph	28, Sept 1856	William	Doolan, Helen	P	193
Fink, Anna M. Isabella	19, Feb. 1859	Jacob	Kunz, Maria	C	
Fink, Christoph Albert	4, Feb. 1855	Jacob	Kunz, Maria Anna	C	
Fink, Jacob	8, Mar. 1855	Jacob	Meyer, Barbara	D	30
Fink, Jacob Valentin	1, Nov. 1857	Adam	Wesser, Elisabeth	K	
Fink, Johan	22, Jan. 1854	Francis	Kölsch, Salomea	Q	4
Fink, Joseph	13, Sept 1857	Wilhelm	Koelsch, Salomea	Q	24
Fink, Luke	3, Jan. 1857	Jacob	Kunz, Maria	C	
Fink, Margaretha Elisabeth	18, Apr. 1855	Adam	Wassler, Elisabeth	L	
Fink, Maria	18, Apr. 1854	Jacob	Kunz, Maria	K	
Fink, Maria Helena	12, June 1853	Jacob	Knatz, M. Anna	C	
Fink, Maria Solem.	6, Nov. 1859	Wilhelm	Keltsch, Maria	Q	34
Fink, Wilhelm	2, Jan. 1859	Adam	Fink, Margaretha	K	
Fink, Wilhelm	21, Nov. 1852	Jacob	Meyer, Barbara	D	358
Finke,	31, Jan. 1858	Daniel	Stengfelder, Anna	Q	26
Finke, Bernard	16, Mar. 1853	Johan F.	Debrun, M. Philomena	L	
Finke, Clara	4, Feb. 1854	Francis	Frolken, Maria Elisabeth	R	
Finke, Eva Catharina	8, July 1858	Johan	Jaeger, Maria	F	
Finke, Gerhard Heinrich	9, Sept 1858	Friedrich	Debruige, Wilhelmina	L	
Finke, Johan	20, Apr. 1851	Joseph	Uhlen, Sophia	K	
Finke, Johan Ferdinand	16, Jan. 1851	J. Heinrich	Paul, Louisa	D	249
Finke, John Henry	29, Aug. 1852	Francis	Völker, Maria	R	
Finke, Joseph Clement	30, July 1854	Joseph	Ensfelder, Anna	Q	4
Finke, Joseph Heinrich	6, Sept 1857	Francis	----, Maria Elisabeth	R	
Finke, Joseph Heinrich	11, Aug. 1850	Friedrich	Debruen, M. Philomena	L	
Finke, Maria Anna Elisabeth	23, May 1852	Joseph	Ensfelder, Anna	A	
Finke, Maria Catharina	20, Oct. 1850	Francis	Freulken, Elisabeth	F	
Finke, Maria Catharina	25, Aug. 1850	Joseph	Ensfelder, Anna	A	
Finke, Maria Mathilda	28, Oct. 1855	Friedrich	Debruin, Philomena	L	
Finke, Matthew	22, Feb. 1852	William	Kölsch, Salomea	R	

Name of Child	Date of Baptism	Father	Mother	Church	Page
Finley, Amanda	4, Mar. 1857	Andrew	Cole, Caroline Augusta	B	41
Finley, Ann	23, Aug. 1855	Bernard	Finley, Bridget	E	309
Finley, Ann	31, Dec. 1854	Peter	Gahagan, Bridget	B	9
Finley, Bridget	22, Nov. 1856	Peter	----, Bridget	E	414
Finley, Edward	4, Mar. 1857	Andrew	Cole, Caroline Augusta	B	41
Finley, James Burnet	19, July 1857	John	McCormick, Mary	E	467
Finley, John	4, Oct. 1851	John	Garomly, Mary Ann	E	348
Finley, Margaret	6, May 1854	William	Kelly, Bridget	E	188
Finley, Mary Ellen	25, Aug. 1852	Peter	----, Bridget	E	10
Finley, Patrick	26, July 1859	John	Kane, Ann	B	78
Finley, Thomas	14, Aug. 1853	Peter	----, Bridget	E	118
Finn, August Francis	14, Mar. 1858	Joseph	Resch, Barbara	Q	27
Finn, Caroline	30, July 1859	Joseph	Resch, Barbara	Q	32
Finn, Catherine	30, Nov. 1851	James	----, Sarah	E	362
Finn, Catherine	20, July 1851	John	Burns, Bridget	B	236
Finn, Helen	1, May 1859	Timothy	Ryan, Margaret	J	50
Finn, James	1, Jan. 1854	James	O'M----, Mary	B	306
Finn, John	19, Feb. 1855	John	Dunns, Margaret	R	
Finn, Lawrence	1, May 1853	James	Ryan, Sarah	B	289
Finn, Margaret	21, June 1850	James	Ryan, Sarah	E	225
Finn, Maria Catharina	23, Oct. 1859	J. Adam	Furz, Brigitta	D	149
Finn, Maria Magdalena	3, May 1857	Adam	Duns, Christina	D	84
Finn, Mary	14, Dec. 1856	James	----, Mary Ann	E	420
Finn, Mary	30, Nov. 1854	James	Ryan, Sarah	B	8
Finn, Mary	16, Aug. 1857	John	----, Mary	E	473
Finn, Mary	18, Jan. 1857	John	Battle, Ann	V	37
Finn, Mary	23, May 1859	Patrick	Monks, Ellen	M	
Finn, Mary Ann	9, Mar. 1856	John	----, Helen	R	
Finn, Mary Eva	9, Feb. 1855	Joseph	Resch, Barbara	Q	6
Finn, Michael	7, Sept 1856	Joseph	Resch, Barbara	Q	15
Finn, Thomas	13, May 1858	James	Allman, Mary	E	534
Finn, Thomas	1, Oct. 1854	William	Murray, Ellen	E	229
Finnegan, Agnes	4, Nov. 1856	Miles	----, Agnes	E	410
Finnegan, Ann	28, Jan. 1855	Miles	Finnagan, Agnes	E	260
Finnegan, Caecilia	13, Feb. 1853	Patrick	Kelly, Mary	E	62
Finnegan, Catherine	31, Aug. 1856	Richard	McAndrew, Mary	P	189
Finnegan, Elizabeth Jane	10, June 1855	Patrick	----, Mary	E	291
Finnegan, Hugh Cowan	30, Jan. 1858	Miles	----, Agnes	E	513
Finnegan, James	19, Feb. 1852	Edward	----, Mary	B	253
Finnegan, James	24, Oct. 1852	John	McDonald, Helen	B	273
Finnegan, John	1, Mar. 1857	Michael	----, Helen	R	
Finnegan, Luke	16, Oct. 1853	Patrick	----, Ann	B	300
Finnegan, Margaret Ellen	23, Jan. 1853	Miles	----, Agnes	E	57
Finnegan, Mary Ann	26, Nov. 1854	Thomas	Reagan, Bridget	E	243
Finnegan, Thomas	2, Jan. 1850	John	Moran, Bridget	E	189
Finnegan, Thomas	21, Jan. 1855	Richard	McAndrew, Mary	P	116
Finnel, Mary	4, Dec. 1853	William	Malldare, Mary	E	149
Finnell, Judith	25, June 1850	William	Kelly, Bridget	E	226
Finnell, Margaret Jane	13, July 1855	William	Mulcahy, Mary	V	25
Finnell, William	25, Aug. 1856	William	Mulcahy, Mary	V	36
Finneran, Peter	16, Dec. 1850	John	Finneran, Bridget	B	220
Finnerl, Ann Eliza	18, June 1854	James	Grannand, Eliza	T	
Finnerty, Bridget	10, Feb. 1856	Thomas	----, Honora	E	343
Finnerty, Michael	18, Aug. 1853	Thomas	----, Honora	E	120
Finnerty, Thomas	8, June 1851	Thomas	McKearny, Honora	E	314
Finnerty, William	19, Jan. 1858	Thomas	McDermott, Honora	E	510
Finnery, John	8, Sept 1850	James	Brennan, Eliza	B	213
Finnessy, Edward	8, Dec. 1853	Edward	Ryan, Mary	B	304
Finnessy, Helen	5, Aug. 1856	David	----, Mary	R	

Name of Child	Date of Baptism	Father	Mother	Church	Page
Finnessy, Margaret	13, Aug. 1854	David	Donohoe, Mary Ann	R	
Finney, Bridget	17, Nov. 1850	Patrick	----, Mary	E	262
Finney, Edward	27, Sept 1854	Edward	----, Ellen	E	227
Finnigan, Catherine Ann	20, Mar. 1850	Richard	McAndrews, Mary	B	198
Finnigan, Mary	15, May 1856	Edward	Sullivan, Mary	P	180
Finnigan, Mary Ann	27, Mar. 1855	Michael	Hobans, Helen	R	
Finnigan, Mary Ann	21, Aug. 1853	Richard	McAndrew, Mary	P	50
Finnigan, Thomas	31, Jan. 1850	Francis	Rearnan, Mary	E	195
Finnigan, Thomas	28, Dec. 1851	Richard	McCandles, Mary	B	248
Finnigan, William James	27, May 1855	James	Dowling, Helen	P	134
Finnity, Ellen	17, Oct. 1859	John	Galvin, Mary	B	82
Finoran, James	19, Apr. 1852	James F.	Brannan, Eliza	B	257
Finton, Margaret	27, Feb. 1853	John	Fitzpatrick, Margaret	P	36
Firks, Elisabeth	7, Mar. 1852	Sebastian	Fretsch, Theresa	F	
Firman, Peter	5, Sept 1858	Peter	Whealon, Mary	E	561
Firnbach, Christina Elisabeth	6, Nov. 1853	Joseph	----, Thecla	C	
Firnkaes, Rosalina	9, Apr. 1850	Mathias	Bengert, Magdalena	C	
Fischbach, Elisabeth	1, Aug. 1857	Adolph	Silbereusen, Catharina	L	
Fischbeck, Catharina Philomena	27, July 1851	Adolph	Silbereisen, Catharina	C	
Fische, Gerhard Heinrich	30, Oct. 1851	Gerhard	Overberg, Christina	C	
Fischer, Adelheid Agnes	8, Mar. 1858	Gerhard	Kampschulte, Agnes	L	
Fischer, Aloysius	27, May 1855	Aloysius	Kimmerle, Ottilia	D	35
Fischer, Anna Catharina	14, Mar. 1852	Johan	Herkamp, Magdalena	D	312
Fischer, Anna Catharina	26, Nov. 1855	Joseph	Bauer, Elisabeth	D	47
Fischer, Anna Maria	27, Mar. 1853	Joseph	Bauer, Elisabeth	D	377
Fischer, Anna Maria	17, Feb. 1850	Peter	Schönig, Anna M.	C	
Fischer, Anna Maria Agnes	4, May 1858	Herman H.	Rackers, Anna Maria	L	
Fischer, Anna Maria Christina	13, Dec. 1853	Gerhard L	Kampschulten, Agnes	L	
Fischer, Anna Maria Christina	12, June 1855	Herman H.	Reckers, Anna Maria	L	
Fischer, Anna Maria Elisabeth	16, Apr. 1858	Gerhard	Keller, Monica	F	
Fischer, Anna Maria Louisa	17, Oct. 1852	Martin	Oellen, Maria	D	353
Fischer, Anthony	6, June 1858	Anthony	Laibold, Barbara	Q	28
Fischer, Augustine	27, Oct. 1850	Carl	Reis, Victoria	A	
Fischer, Barbara	24, Sept 1854	Caspar	Scherer, Maria Magdalena	D	18
Fischer, Bernard Heinrich	13, Feb. 1859	Johan	Frohne, M.A. Gertrud	T	
Fischer, Carl	16, Oct. 1853	Boniface	Meier, Marianna	F	
Fischer, Carl	31, May 1857	Caspar	Scherrer, Magdalena	D	86
Fischer, Carl	27, July 1856	Johan	Flerschinger, Anna Maria	F	
Fischer, Carl Wilhelmina	17, Sept 1859	Carl W.	Winzinger, Magdalena	A	
Fischer, Carolina	12, Oct. 1856	Martin	Ehlen, Maria	F	
Fischer, Catharina	7, Sept 1852	Anton	Mueller, Elisabeth	F	
Fischer, Christian	3, July 1853	Michael	Siegwart, Appolonia	D	393
Fischer, Christina Louisa	23, Apr. 1850	Valentin	Mantel, Magdalena	C	
Fischer, Christoher Jacob	25, July 1856	Johan	Schon, Magdalena	H	
Fischer, Conrad Valentin	8, Mar. 1857	Valentin	Mantel, Magdalena	F	
Fischer, Elisabeth	2, Nov. 1851	Friedrich	Neurohr, Catharina	D	290
Fischer, Elisabeth	24, May 1857	Martin	Bittner, Margaretha	D	85
Fischer, Ellen	29, Aug. 1857	John	Fitzpatrick, Margaret	B	48
Fischer, Emma	16, May 1858	Michael	Stegward, Appolonia	D	111
Fischer, Eva	24, Feb. 1850	Jacob	Klingler, Anna	K	
Fischer, Francis	24, Feb. 1859	J. Gerhard	Overberg, Christina	Q	30
Fischer, Francis Heinrich	12, Mar. 1850	Bernard H.	Wiwerich, Anna Catharina	C	
Fischer, Franz	25, Mar. 1855	Valentin	Mantel, Magdalena	F	
Fischer, Friedrich	10, Apr. 1859	Friedrich	Neurohr, Catharina	C	
Fischer, Friedrich Wilhelm	9, Dec. 1855	Christian	Rein, Elisabeth	F	
Fischer, Georg Albert	20, Nov. 1859	Martin	Pittner, Margaretha	D	151
Fischer, Gerhard Bernard Herman	29, Dec. 1851	Gerhard	Kampjans, Engel	L	
Fischer, Gerhard Bernard Herman	15, Feb. 1858	Gerhard H.	Beck---, Euphemia Ad.	D	105
Fischer, Gerhard Heinrich	30, Apr. 1854	Gerhard	Keller, Monica	F	

Name of Child	Date of Baptism	Father	Mother	Church	Page
Fischer, Gerhard Herman	11, July 1855	Gerhard L	Kampschulten, Agnes	L	
Fischer, Gregor William	21, Sept 1851	Ludwig	Buschle, Juliana	D	283
Fischer, Heinrich	14, Jan. 1855	Rudolph	Braun, Ottilia	F	
Fischer, Heinrich August	24, Aug. 1853	August	Froehlich, Anna Margaretha	F	
Fischer, Heinrich Joseph	25, Oct. 1857	Christian	Rein, Elisabeth	D	97
Fischer, Herman Friedrich	28, Nov. 1858	Friedrich	Lasaner, Margaretha	D	124
Fischer, Herman Heinrich	15, Nov. 1853	J. Herman	Lammering, Anna Maria	A	
Fischer, Jacob	29, Feb. 1856	Anton	Leibhold, Barbara	Q	13
Fischer, Jacob	19, Nov. 1854	Johan	Seibert, Anna Maria	D	22
Fischer, Jacob Johan	8, Apr. 1856	Anton	Mueller, Elisabeth	F	
Fischer, Johan	14, June 1857	Leonard	Buschle, Juliana	D	88
Fischer, Johan Friedrich	22, Mar. 1854	Friedrich	Fromm, Maria Gertrud	F	
Fischer, Johan Gerhard	25, Aug. 1850	J. Gerhard	Kampschulte, Maria Agnes	D	229
Fischer, Johan Heinrich	17, Dec. 1857	Francis H.	Hemesaath, Anna Maria	F	
Fischer, Johan Heinrich	12, Sept 1851	Johan	Froh, Gertrud	F	
Fischer, Johan Herman	10, Oct. 1858	Joseph	Bulteman, Catharina	A	
Fischer, Johan Joseph	26, Oct. 1856	J. Joseph	Weigand, Victoria	J	38
Fischer, Johan Joseph	15, Mar. 1858	Jacob	Klein, Anna	T	
Fischer, Johan Ludwig	17, Oct. 1852	Johan	Seberdin, Anna Maria	D	353
Fischer, Johanna Catharina	20, Nov. 1853	Johan	Fleischmann, A. Maria	F	
Fischer, Joseph	3, Jan. 1850	Anton	Mueller, Elisabeth	F	
Fischer, Josephina Catharina	18, June 1851	Joseph	Hagedorn, Maria Elisabeth	F	
Fischer, Leo	21, Mar. 1852	Martin	Pittner, Margaretha	D	313
Fischer, Ludwig	31, May 1857	Aloysius	Kummerle, Ottilia	D	86
Fischer, Ludwig Theodor	20, Aug. 1852	Carl	Reisch, Victoria	F	
Fischer, M. Josephina Clementina	24, Dec. 1853	Bernard	Wiewerth, Catharina	C	
Fischer, Magdalena	16, Aug. 1850	Johan	Seifert, Anna Maria	D	228
Fischer, Margaret Catherine	28, July 1855	Johan	----, Magdalena	H	
Fischer, Margaretha	22, Feb. 1852	Francis	Kamerer, Cunigunda	D	307
Fischer, Margaretha	6, Dec. 1858	Johan	Flachinger, Maria	F	
Fischer, Margaretha Catharina	18, Aug. 1852	Anton	Laibold, Anna Maria	F	
Fischer, Margaretha Maria Gertrud	31, May 1853		Fischer, Philippina	K	
Fischer, Maria	5, Dec. 1858	Ludwig	Kramer, Augusta	D	125
Fischer, Maria Anna	28, Apr. 1858	Bernard H.	Wilerich, M. Catharina	C	
Fischer, Maria Anna	13, July 1856	Leonard	Hafner, Elisabeth	J	36
Fischer, Maria Anna Antonia	21, Sept 1853	Anton	Mueller, Elisabeth	F	
Fischer, Maria Carolina	3, Apr. 1853	Leo	Buschle, Juliana	D	379
Fischer, Maria Catharina	10, Aug. 1855	August	Froehlich, Margaretha	F	
Fischer, Maria Elisabeth	10, Oct. 1858	Anton	Mueller, Elisabeth	F	
Fischer, Maria Elisabeth	12, Oct. 1856	Bernard H.	Wiederich, M. Catharina	C	
Fischer, Maria Elisabeth	5, Oct. 1856	Friedrich	Frohn, Maria Gertrud	F	
Fischer, Maria Francisca	9, Nov. 1851	Bernard H.	Wiwering, Catharina	C	
Fischer, Maria Louisa	1, Jan. 1853	Godfried	Lasance, Margaretha	D	363
Fischer, Maria Louisa	8, July 1855	Leonard	Buschle, Juliana	D	38
Fischer, Maria Magdalena	25, July 1858	Joseph	Bauer, Elisabeth	D	116
Fischer, Maria Theodora	12, Sept 1855	Friedrich	Lausaner, Maria Margaretha	D	42
Fischer, Maria Theresa Monica	5, May 1855	Gerhard	Keller, Monica	F	
Fischer, Martin Nicolaus	11, May 1851	Martin	Oehler, Maria	D	264
Fischer, Mary	30, Oct. 1853	John	----, Magdalena	H	
Fischer, Michael	7, July 1850	Joseph	Bauer, Elisa	D	221
Fischer, Michael	25, Mar. 1855	Martin	Pittner, Margaretha	D	32
Fischer, Nicolaus	31, May 1850	Johan	Sferniaco, Magdalena	H	
Fischer, Nicolaus Joseph	29, May 1854	Martin	Oehlen, Maria	D	11
Fischer, Patrick	1, Apr. 1855	Michael	Parl, Magdalena	R	
Fischer, Paulina	17, July 1859	Christian	Rein, Elisabeth	C	
Fischer, Peter	1, Dec. 1850	Martin	Bittner, Margaretha	H	
Fischer, Peter	27, Nov. 1853	Peter	Schoenberg, Maria Anna	C	
Fischer, Philipp	21, May 1854	Friedrich	Neurohr, Maria Catharina	D	10
Fischer, Philipp	13, July 1851	Johan	Flerchinger, Anna Maria	F	

Name of Child	Date of Baptism	Father	Mother	Church	Page
Fischer, Philipp Carl	8, Aug. 1856	Gerhard	Keller, Monica	F	
Fischer, Philippina Louisa	25, Mar. 1853	Nicolaus	Euler, Barbara	K	
Fischer, Philomena	8, Apr. 1851	Bernard	Schroeder, Carolina	C	
Fischer, Regina	25, Dec. 1858	Mathias	Fischer, Crescentia	D	127
Fischer, Simon	19, Feb. 1854	Valentin	Mantel, Magdalena	F	
Fischer, Sophia	6, Jan. 1852	Friedrich	Reis, Margaretha	D	301
Fischer, Sophia	9, Jan. 1853	J. Friedrich	Reis, Margaretha	D	364
Fischer, Theresa Margaretha	19, Oct. 1857	August	Froehlich, Margaretha	F	
Fischer, Valentin Francis	15, Aug. 1859	Caspar	Scherrer, Magdalena	D	144
Fischhaus, Johan Heinrich	21, Dec. 1852	Bernard	Likers, Anna Maria	D	361
Fishback, James	29, Aug. 1853	James	----, Sarah	E	124
Fishback, Sarah	25, July 1851	John	----, Sarah	E	327
Fisher, Maria Magdalena	18, Mar. 1857	Johan	Siber---, Anna Maria	D	81
Fisher, Mary Eliza	8, May 1853	James	Cline, Ann	E	87
Fisse, Johan Bernard	6, Dec. 1856	J. Gerhard	Overberg, M.A. Christina	Q	18
Fisse, Maria Anna Christina	6, Dec. 1856	J. Gerhard	Overberg, M.A. Christina	Q	18
Fit, Anna Maria	1, Jan. 1855	Jacob	Bat, Maria	D	26
Fitcher, Theodor	24, Aug. 1858	Daniel	Wining, Adelheid	D	117
Fitterer, Carolina	14, May 1853	Joseph	Burkhart, Louisa	D	385
Fitterer, Heinrich	20, June 1854	Joseph	Burkhard, Louisa	D	12
Fitterer, Maria Anna	26, Feb. 1859	Joseph	Burghart, Louisa	D	132
Fitterer, Valentin	25, May 1856	Joseph	Burkhart, Louisa	D	59
Fitton, John	27, Aug. 1854	James	Farrell, Margaret	B	4
Fitton, Mary Ellen	1, Feb. 1857	James	Farrell, Margaret	B	40
Fitton, Thomas	4, Sept 1853	James	Farrell, Margaret	B	298
Fitzer, Jacob	25, Dec. 1859	Peer	Braun, Theresa	J	52
Fitzgerald, Ann	24, Oct. 1852	John	----, Rosanne	E	30
Fitzgerald, Bridget	23, Aug. 1853	Lawrence	----, Bridget	E	122
Fitzgerald, Catherine	9, Jan. 1855	Garret	McCarthy, Catherine	B	10
Fitzgerald, Catherine	25, Aug. 1851	John	McCahil, Sarah	P	11
Fitzgerald, Catherine	6, Aug. 1859	Richard	Kinsella, Elizabeth	B	78
Fitzgerald, Cornelius	25, Apr. 1858	James	Brown, Catherine	P	247
Fitzgerald, Daniel	25, Nov. 1855	James	Brown, Catherine	V	28
Fitzgerald, Dennis	11, Sept 1859	Patrick	O'Mara, Margaret	P	295
Fitzgerald, Edward	24, Jan. 1854	Richard	Lynch, Bridget	E	162
Fitzgerald, Elizabeth	28, May 1853	James	Fitzgerald, Joanne	E	93
Fitzgerald, Elizabeth	5, Aug. 1859	Michael	McCarthy, Helen	X	
Fitzgerald, Ellen	25, Nov. 1855	Richard	----, Elizabeth	E	329
Fitzgerald, Emily	9, May 1852	William	Chambers, Mary	E	410
Fitzgerald, George	20, Sept 1857	Michael	Farran, Hannah	P	224
Fitzgerald, Hannah	4, Apr. 1858	Michael	Dwyer, Ellen	P	244
Fitzgerald, Helen	28, Aug. 1858	David	Ducy, Mary	P	259
Fitzgerald, Helen	12, Aug. 1855	James	Boylson, Ann	R	
Fitzgerald, Helen	19, Dec. 1851	John	Hays, Mary Ann	P	14
Fitzgerald, Honora	30, May 1858	James	Cahill, Sarah	P	249
Fitzgerald, James	31, July 1853	James	Boyle, Ann	B	296
Fitzgerald, James	19, Nov. 1855	Lawrence	Aurns, Bridget	E	328
Fitzgerald, James Francis	28, Dec. 1851	Patrick	Roach, Bridget	B	248
Fitzgerald, John	18, Aug. 1858	James	Eversfield, Elizabeth	E	558
Fitzgerald, John	13, July 1850	Michael	----, Fenna	E	230
Fitzgerald, John	15, Aug. 1854	Patrick	Dwyer, Bridget	B	4
Fitzgerald, John	10, July 1857	Richard	Kinsella, Elizabeth	V	40
Fitzgerald, John	9, Sept 1855	William	Chambers, Mary	B	19
Fitzgerald, John	5, Sept 1851		adult	E	340
Fitzgerald, John Michael	17, Dec. 1856	James	Eversfield, Eliza	E	421
Fitzgerald, John Patrick	24, Mar. 1850	John	----, Ann	E	204
Fitzgerald, Joseph	21, Mar. 1858	James	----, Ann	R	
Fitzgerald, Julia	4, Mar. 1855	Michael	Sullivan, Joanne	P	123
Fitzgerald, Margaret	2, Aug. 1858	Lawrence	Agern, Bridget	E	554

Name of Child	Date of Baptism	Father	Mother	Church	Page
Fitzgerald, Mary	24, June 1851	James	Boyle, Ann	B	234
Fitzgerald, Mary	9, Nov. 1856	James	Cahill, Sarah	P	197
Fitzgerald, Mary	29, July 1856	Michael	Dwyer, Helen	P	186
Fitzgerald, Mary	31, July 1854	Richard	Hayes, Mary	T	
Fitzgerald, Mary	20, Oct. 1851	Richard	Lynch, Bridget	E	352
Fitzgerald, Mary Ann	28, Feb. 1856	John	O'Brien, Rose	P	170
Fitzgerald, Mary Ann	21, Aug. 1855	Michael	Farran, Hannah	P	146
Fitzgerald, Mary Ann	15, Aug. 1854	Patrick	Dwyer, Bridget	B	4
Fitzgerald, Mary Ann	22, May 1859		Fitzgerald, Mary	E	626
Fitzgerald, Mary Jane	30, July 1859	James	McInemy, Bridget	B	78
Fitzgerald, Mary Josephine	29, June 1859	James	Ryan, Elizabeth	E	635
Fitzgerald, Michael	1, Nov. 1857	Michael	----, Helen	S	
Fitzgerald, Patrick	17, Mar. 1854	Edward	----, Abba	U	
Fitzgerald, Patrick	28, July 1856	Richard	Summers, Margaret	E	385
Fitzgerald, Thomas	17, Dec. 1852	Richard	----, Bridget	E	44
Fitzgerald, William	1, Jan. 1854	James	Connors, Joanne	P	64
Fitzgerald, William	14, Dec. 1850	James	Fitzgerald, Joanne	B	220
Fitzgerald, William	7, Jan. 1855	Michael	Dwyer, Helen	P	114
Fitzgerald, William	14, Apr. 1858	Patrick	O'Meara, Margaret	P	246
Fitzgerald, William	9, Nov. 1850	William	----, Mary	E	260
Fitzgerald, Xavier	18, July 1852	David	-----, Margaret	B	263
Fitzgibbon, Catherine	16, Oct. 1854	John	Fox, Catherine	E	233
Fitzgibbon, Catherine Elizabeth	14, Mar. 1850	Patrick	Bradish, Mary	B	198
Fitzgibbon, John	19, Sept 1857	John	Fox, Catherine	E	481
Fitzgibbon, John	7, June 1854	Thomas	----, Helen	H	
Fitzgibbon, Mary Ann	23, Sept 1856	John	Fox, Catherine	E	399
Fitzgibbon, Michael	29, Dec. 1856	Michael	Doody, Mary	E	423
Fitzgibbons, David	23, Aug. 1859	Thomas	Devine, Mary	B	80
Fitzgibbons, Edmund	18, Dec. 1852	John	Fox, Catherine	E	44
Fitzgibbons, Michael	19, Nov. 1859	John	Fox, Catherine	E	671
Fitzharris, Andrew	25, Dec. 1859	Andrew	Hopkins, Mary	P	307
Fitzharris, Mary	1, Jan. 1857	Andrew	Hopkins, Mary	P	203
Fitzharris, Thomas	24, Apr. 1852	Andrew	Hopkins, Mary	P	20
Fitzmaurice, Alfred Pierre	19, Dec. 1858	Nicholas E.	Murray, Ann F.	B	68
Fitzmorris, Bridget	13, July 1855	Michael	McDermott, Mary	B	16
Fitzmorris, Elizabeth	30, Mar. 1851	Michael	McDermott, Mary	B	228
Fitzmorris, Mary Ann	5, June 1853	Michael	McDermott, Ann	B	293
Fitzpatrick, (boy)	21, May 1854	Martin	Shea, Margaret	E	192
Fitzpatrick, Alice	26, Feb. 1851	James	----, Margaret	E	287
Fitzpatrick, Andrew	21, May 1854	Patrick	Elevens, Ann	R	
Fitzpatrick, Ann	28, Mar. 1855	Edward	Geblin, Ann	P	127
Fitzpatrick, Ann Mary	9, May 1852	John	Aiken, Elizabeth	B	259
Fitzpatrick, Bridget	22, Dec. 1850	Michael	----, Mary	E	269
Fitzpatrick, Catherine	2, May 1850	Bryan	Ryan, Mary	B	201
Fitzpatrick, Catherine	10, Dec. 1853	Edward	Mahin, Mary	E	151
Fitzpatrick, Catherine	9, May 1857	John	Barrell, Catherine	E	451
Fitzpatrick, Dennis	7, Dec. 1856	Kieran	Ryan, Mary	B	37
Fitzpatrick, Edmund	24, Dec. 1853	Michael	Kenny, Mary	E	154
Fitzpatrick, Edward	22, Feb. 1857	Edward	Machen, Mary	E	434
Fitzpatrick, Elizabeth	17, Dec. 1858	James	Fitzpatrick, Honora	B	68
Fitzpatrick, Elizabeth	26, Dec. 1857	James	Sullivan, Margaret	P	233
Fitzpatrick, Elizabeth	6, Feb. 1852	Patrick	McAfree, Bridget	P	17
Fitzpatrick, Florant Peter	26, June 1859	Kieran	Ryan, Mary	B	76
Fitzpatrick, Honora	15, Oct. 1854	Dennis	Linehan, Joanne	B	6
Fitzpatrick, James	22, Oct. 1854	Bryan	Ryan, Mary	B	6
Fitzpatrick, John	5, May 1853	James	----, Margaret	E	86
Fitzpatrick, John	12, Oct. 1858	John	Barrett, Catherine	E	569
Fitzpatrick, John	23, Mar. 1851	John	Gleason, Mary	B	227
Fitzpatrick, John	1, Feb. 1852	John	Harrington, Mary	P	16

Name of Child	Date of Baptism	Father	Mother	Church	Page
Fitzpatrick, John	1, June 1853	John	Leeson, Mary	B	293
Fitzpatrick, John	14, Nov. 1852	Matthew	Burke, Margaret	B	275
Fitzpatrick, Julia	17, Oct. 1852	John	Butler, Margaret	B	272
Fitzpatrick, Luke	7, Apr. 1850	Matthew	Burke, Margaret	B	200
Fitzpatrick, Margaret	23, Dec. 1855	Edward	Mahan, Mary	E	334
Fitzpatrick, Margaret	25, May 1856	John	Butler, Margaret	T	
Fitzpatrick, Mary	12, Dec. 1859	Edward	Hynes, Bessy	B	85
Fitzpatrick, Mary	17, Aug. 1858	M.	----, Mary	V	50
Fitzpatrick, Mary	26, Apr. 1857	Michael	Kelley, Mary	E	448
Fitzpatrick, Mary	5, Oct. 1851	Patrick	Quinlan, Catherine	P	12
Fitzpatrick, Mary Ann	12, Apr. 1857	James	Fitzpatrick, Honora	B	43
Fitzpatrick, Mary Ann	15, June 1856	John	Gleeson, Mary	B	30
Fitzpatrick, Mary Ann	6, May 1858	Patrick	----, Mary	E	533
Fitzpatrick, Mary Ann	2, Nov. 1851	Peter	Anderson, Catherine	E	355
Fitzpatrick, Matthew	15, May 1853	Patrick	Quinlan, Catherine	P	41
Fitzpatrick, Michael	26, Nov. 1854	Edward	Morhen, Mary	E	243
Fitzpatrick, Michael	24, Nov. 1850	Patrick	Kane, Margaret	E	263
Fitzpatrick, Michael	3, Oct. 1852	Richard	Ryan, Mary	B	273
Fitzpatrick, Peter	29, Jan. 1854	Peter	Anderson, Catherine	E	164
Fitzpatrick, Richard	5, May 1856	James	Sullivan, Margaret	P	178
Fitzpatrick, Sarah	2, Mar. 1853	Patrick	Welsch, Mary	B	285
Fitzpatrick, Wililam	8, Jan. 1854	John	Harrington, Mary	P	64
Fitzpatrick, William	1, Feb. 1852	Patrick	Kane, Margaret	P	16
Fitzpatrick, William	17, Dec. 1854	Patrick	Walsh, Mary	B	8
Fitzsimmon, William	2, Mar. 1851	Robert	O'Reile, Margaret	K	
Fitzsimmons, Bernard	18, July 1858	Bernard	McCoy, Ann	E	550
Fitzsimmons, Catherine	23, Sept 1853	Patrick	Riley, Catherine	B	299
Fitzsimmons, Charles	23, Sept 1853	Patrick	Riley, Catherine	B	299
Fitzsimmons, Elizabeth	7, Oct. 1855	John	----, Elizabeth	M	
Fitzsimmons, James	12, Apr. 1854	James	Butler, Mary	R	
Fitzsimmons, John	4, Sept 1857	John	Fox, Elizabeth	P	222
Fitzsimmons, John Henry	5, Aug. 1853	Patrick	----, Mary	E	114
Fitzsimmons, Mary	4, May 1856	James?	----, Mary	R	
Fitzsimmons, Mary Ann	16, May 1857	Patrick	Gilligan, Mary	E	454
Fitzsimmons, Patrick	25, Mar. 1851	Patrick	Bauch, Mary	E	295
Fitzsimmons, Susan	22, Sept 1850	Bernard	McCoy, Ann	B	214
Fitzsimmons, Thomas Francis	16, Dec. 1855	Bernard	McCoy, Ann	V	28
Fitzsimmons, Timothy	23, Aug. 1859	Patrick	----, Mary	E	649
Flach, Carl Joseph	24, July 1853	Carl	Jung, Maria	L	
Flach, Francis Johan	11, Jan. 1852	Carl	Jung, Maria	C	
Flach, Maria Louisa	2, Sept 1855	Carl	Jung, Maria	L	
Flack, Anton	10, Oct. 1858	Carl	Jung, Maria	L	
Flagerty, John	29, July 1855	John	Finnigan, Catherine	E	304
Flagerty, John	2, Aug. 1857	Patrick	Moloney, Mary	E	471
Flagerty, Mary	16, Sept 1855	Patrick	Malony, Mary	E	315
Flagerty, Michael	10, Jan. 1858	Patrick	Beckford, Ellen	E	508
Flagerty, Sarah	26, June 1853	Martin	----, Mary	E	102
Flaggerty, Catherine	7, Oct. 1855	Patrick	Begfort, Helen	E	319
Flaggerty, John Francis	11, Apr. 1857	John	Folon, Catherine	E	446
Flagherty, Catherine	2, Nov. 1851	Michael	McDonald, Bridget	E	355
Flagherty, George Thomas	2, Oct. 1859	Thomas	Finnigan, Catherine	P	299
Flagherty, Honora	29, July 1850	Michael	----, Bridget	E	234
Flagherty, James	26, July 1857	Thomas	Finnigan, Catherine	P	218
Flagherty, Mary Ann	24, Apr. 1853	Michael	McDonald, Bridget	E	83
Flaherty, Andrew	7, Apr. 1859	Martin	----, Mary	E	616
Flaherty, Bridget	9, July 1854	Patrick	McDonald, Bridget	B	2
Flaherty, Catherine	1, Jan. 1850	Edmund	Coyle, Nappy	E	189
Flaherty, Charles	14, Aug. 1859	Patrick	----, Bridget	E	647
Flaherty, Joanne	25, Nov. 1855	James	Cummings, Mary	B	22

Name of Child	Date of Baptism	Father	Mother	Church	Page
Flaherty, John	14, Feb. 1858	John	Connell, Catherine	E	517
Flaherty, John	24, Sept 1854	Martin	----, ----	E	225
Flaherty, John	24, Oct. 1853	Michael	----, Joanne	E	137
Flaherty, Margaret	22, Sept 1856	Andrew	Tracy, Catherine	E	399
Flaherty, Martin	14, Aug. 1859	Patrick	----, Ellen	E	647
Flaherty, Mary	3, Mar. 1852	John	D---, Joanne	B	253
Flaherty, Mary	14, Dec. 1856	Martin	Garmaly, Mary	E	420
Flaherty, Michael	22, Dec. 1859	Michael	Higgins, Mary	B	85
Flaherty, Michael	20, July 1853	Patrick	MacDonald, Bridget	B	295
Flaherty, Michael	30, Apr. 1854	William	----, Mary	E	187
Flaherty, Thomas	15, Dec. 1857	James	Cummins, Mary	B	53
Flaherty, William Henry	18, July 1858	Michael	Higgins, Mary	E	550
Flaig, Adolph	3, Aug. 1856	Andreas	Keller, Afra	D	64
Flaig, Joseph	22, Feb. 1854	Andreas	Hessman, Maria Anna	D	5
Flaig, Joseph	12, July 1858	Andreas	Keller, Afra	D	115
Flaig, Ludwig	23, June 1859	Andreas	Keller, Afra	D	140
Flaig, Maria	12, July 1858	Andreas	Keller, Afra	D	115
Flam, Joseph	19, Mar. 1854	Conrad	Gersheimer, Francisca	K	
Flam, Rosa	15, Nov. 1851	Conrad	Kaesheim, Francisca	K	
Flammin, James	17, Nov. 1851	Edward	Correns, Johanna	L	
Flanagan, Ann	23, Dec. 1853	Patrick	Donahue, Catherine	E	154
Flanagan, Bernard	6, July 1856	Martin	Reilly, Helen	P	184
Flanagan, Bridget	19, Nov. 1854	Edward	----, Mary	M	
Flanagan, Catherine	30, Mar. 1856	Henry	McDonnell, Mary	P	174
Flanagan, Catherine	13, June 1858	Martin	Morley, Cecilia	H	
Flanagan, Dennis	22, Aug. 1855	Michael	----, Margaret	E	309
Flanagan, Eliza Ann	11, Aug. 1856	Joseph	Scully, Mary	B	32
Flanagan, George	28, Mar. 1858	John	McCardle, Bridget	E	525
Flanagan, Helen	22, Apr. 1855	Thomas	Quawney, Margaret	P	129
Flanagan, Isabel	9, July 1854	Henry	McDonnell, Mary	P	87
Flanagan, James	24, Apr. 1852	Martin	Connell, Julia	B	264
Flanagan, James	27, Nov. 1853	Michael	McLaughlin, Margaret	E	148
Flanagan, James	28, Dec. 1856	Nicolaus	Plunket, Elizabeth	T	
Flanagan, Joanne	14, May 1857	Michael	McLaughlin, Margaret	E	453
Flanagan, John	23, May 1852	Michael	----, Mary	E	417
Flanagan, John	4, Sept 1858	Michael	Reily, Margaret	T	
Flanagan, John	2, Dec. 1855	Nicolaus	Plunket, Elizabeth	T	
Flanagan, John	12, Oct. 1856	Peter	McAvoy, Ann	P	195
Flanagan, John James	16, Mar. 1856	Martin	----, Cecilia	H	
Flanagan, Joseph Henry	12, Jan. 1853	Michael	----, Mary	E	53
Flanagan, Margaret	14, May 1857	Michael	McLaughlin, Margaret	E	453
Flanagan, Mary	3, Sept 1855	Bartholomew	Mulhall, Mary	P	149
Flanagan, Mary	13, Nov. 1853	Martin	----, Cecilia	H	
Flanagan, Mary Ann	6, July 1856	Patrick	McCarthy, Helen	P	184
Flanagan, Thomas	27, Aug. 1851	Michael	----, Margaret	E	337
Flanery, Catherine	24, Nov. 1851	John	----, Joanne	E	361
Flanery, John	23, July 1857	John	----, Mary	E	469
Flanery, John	17, May 1859	John	Galery, Catherine	P	283
Flanery, Mary Ann	29, Mar. 1857	Thomas	Cummins, Mary	T	
Flanery, Matilda	3, June 1853	John	----, Joanne	E	94
Flanigan, Rose	7, Dec. 1857	Thomas	Coogan, Mary	P	232
Flann---, Mary Ann	30, June 1858	James	Connor, Catherine	P	252
Flannagan, Edward	1, Nov. 1853	Thomas	----, Mary	U	
Flannagan, John	19, Oct. 1857	Michael	Dunigan, Mary	P	228
Flannagan, Mary Ann	16, Jan. 1859	Nicholas	Plunkett, Elizabeth	B	70
Flannery, Alice Mary	2, July 1856	Martin	Kearney, Mary	E	379
Flannery, Ann	28, Oct. 1859	Patrick	----, Honora	E	665
Flannery, Ann	20, Feb. 1858	Patrick	Tracy, Ann	E	517
Flannery, Bridget	9, Dec. 1855	Martin	Fleming, Mary	V	28

Name of Child	Date of Baptism	Father	Mother	Church	Page
Flannery, Catherine	24, Nov. 1857	Martin	Kearney, Mary	E	495
Flannery, Catherine	26, May 1851	Michael	----, Catherine	E	310
Flannery, James	29, Sept 1855	Patrick	Flannery, Ann	B	19
Flannery, John	31, Jan. 1856	John	Mooney, Mary	P	168
Flannery, John	2, Jan. 1859	Martin	Kearney, Mary	E	593
Flannery, John	4, Apr. 1858	Patrick	Flannery, Ann	B	57
Flannery, John	27, May 1856	Thomas	Torpey, Mary	B	29
Flannery, Julianna	7, Aug. 1859	Patrick	Tracy, Bridget	B	79
Flannery, Mary	4, Dec. 1858	Patrick	Kearney, Margaret	E	585
Flannery, Mary	21, Dec. 1851	Patrick	Moloy, Margaret	B	248
Flannery, Mary Ann	14, Feb. 1858	John	Winn, Mary Ann	P	239
Flannery, Mary Ann	30, May 1852		Flannery, Catherine	E	420
Flannery, Mary Frances	28, Feb. 1856	John	Realy, Joanne	E	347
Flannery, Michael	12, July 1857	James	O'Connor, Catherine	P	217
Flannery, Michael	20, Sept 1857	Patrick	Tracy, Bridget	P	224
Flannery, Thomas	24, Apr. 1853	John	Mooney, Mary	B	289
Flannery, Thomas	7, July 1858	Thomas	Torpey, Mary	B	61
Flannery, Timothy	4, July 1858	Patrick	Flannery, Margaret	P	253
Flannery, William	18, Dec. 1859	William	Mangar, Mary	E	677
Flannigan, Elizabeth	16, Oct. 1856		Flannigan, Catherine	E	404
Flannigan, Juliana	19, June 1853	John	Molloy, Mary	L	
Flannigan, Lawrence	28, Jan. 1858	Michael	Marshall, Mary	E	513
Flannigan, Owen Joseph	14, Nov. 1858	Joseph	Scully, Mary	B	67
Flannigan, Thomas	5, July 1857	F.	Quinn, Margaret	B	46
Flannigan, Thomas	23, Dec. 1859	Michael	Reilly, Margaret	B	85
Flannigan, Thomas Joseph	11, July 1858	Peter	Mack, Ann	P	253
Flannigan, William	20, Nov. 1859	Th.	Quinn, Margaret	B	84
Flarity, Joseph	9, May 1852	Joseph	Kegan, Catherine	B	258
Flaspohler, Anna Maria	18, Feb. 1856	Herman	Halmeyer, M. Elisabeth	L	
Flaspohler, Catharina	26, Jan. 1859	Heinrich	Gossmeier, Elisabeth	L	
Flaspohler, Elisabeth	9, Mar. 1851	Heinrich	Holtmeyer, Maria Engel	L	
Flaspohler, Maria Josephina	24, July 1854	Heinrich	Holtmeyer, Catharina	L	
Flately, Ann	11, Sept 1853	Michael	Heston, Sarah	P	52
Flatley, John	18, Nov. 1855	Michael	Hester, Sarah	P	160
Flatly, Thomas	19, Jan. 1857	Michael	Histon, Sarah	B	39
Flattery, John	25, Dec. 1854	Martin	McGlynn, Margaret	P	112
Flattery, Richard	7, Nov. 1852	Martin	McGlenn, Margaret	B	274
Flavin, Edward	11, Oct. 1852	----	----, ----	E	26
Flecher, Johan	12, Mar. 1854	Johan	Straub, Anna Maria	K	
Fleck, Anna Margaretha	19, Nov. 1854	Caspar	Centner, Anna Maria	F	
Fleck, Anton Johan	16, Oct. 1859	Caspar	Centner, Marianna	F	
Fleck, Catharina	23, Nov. 1856	Caspar	Centner, Anna Maria	F	
Fleck, Georg Caspar Franz	11, Apr. 1858	Caspar	Centner, Marianna	F	
Fleck, Georg Christian	1, Mar. 1851	Caspar	Centner, Anna Maria	F	
Fleck, Margaret Jane	29, Sept 1854		adult	V	18
Fleck, Maria Elisabeth	12, Dec. 1852	Caspar	Centner, Maria	F	
Fleckenstein, Adam Joseph	27, Feb. 1854	Johan	Gass, Elisabeth	W	1
Fleckenstein, Andreas	4, Sept 1859	Conrad	Blanke, Catharina	H	
Fleckenstein, Eva R.	26, Oct. 1851	Johan	Goss, Elisabeth	D	289
Fleckenstein, Heinrich	12, Oct. 1856	Johan	Grass, Elisabeth	H	
Fleckenstein, Margaretha Maria	25, Apr. 1859	Johan	Gass, Elisabeth	H	
Fleckenstein, Sebastian	2, June 1852	Lawrence	Ermentraut, Elisabeth	D	323
Fleckstein, Josephina Barbara	28, June 1857	Alexander	Wuest, Margaretha	D	89
Flecksteiner, Alexander C.	30, June 1853	Alexander	Wurst, Margaretha	C	
Flecksteiner, Jacob	23, Feb. 1851	Alexander	Wuest, Margaretha	D	254
Flecksteiner, Maria Catharina	29, July 1855	Alexander	Wuest, Margaretha	D	39
Flecksteiner, Valentin	23, Jan. 1859	Alexander	Wurst, Margaretha	C	
Fledderman, Elisabeth Margaretha	9, Sept 1852	Gerhard	Holbrock, Margaretha	K	
Fledderman, Gerhard Heinrich	30, Aug. 1855	Gerhard	Holbrock, Margaretha	A	

Name of Child	Date of Baptism	Father	Mother	Church	Page
Fledderman, Gerhard Joseph	14, Dec. 1857	Gerhard	Hofbrock, Margaretha	A	
Fleddermann, Catharina Maria	24, Sept 1856	Herman H.	Meinert, Margaretha C.	F	
Fleddermann, J. Joseph Friedrich	4, Dec. 1858	Herman	Memert, Margaretha	F	
Fleddermann, Maria Catharina	13, Mar. 1850	Bernard J.	Rosswinkel, Dorothea	L	
Fleddermann, Maria Elisabeth Dina	4, Dec. 1853	Herman H.	Mehmert, Margaretha C.	F	
Fleg, Maria Josephina	15, May 1858	Benjamin	Burger, Barbara	D	111
Flegel, Elisabeth	19, Apr. 1857	Daniel	Doerzel, Angelina	D	83
Fleger, Johanna	24, Feb. 1854	Johan	Straub, Anna Maria	K	
Flegge, Maria Anna Elisabeth	8, Sept 1850	Bernard	adult - 23 years old	K	
Fleick, Benjamin	7, Sept 1855	Benjamin	Burger, Barbara	C	
Fleid, Josephina	21, Sept 1856	Anton	Hurst, Balbina	D	68
Fleig, Augustine	25, Apr. 1855	Anton	Horst, Balbina	N	28
Fleig, Francis	8, Sept 1850	Anton	Hurst, Balbina	D	231
Fleig, Joseph Anton	4, July 1852	Anton	Hurst, Balbina	D	328
Fleming, Bridget	22, July 1852	James	Carey, Sarah	E	431
Fleming, Bridget	2, Feb. 1853	Michael	----, Bridget	E	60
Fleming, Honora	16, Mar. 1855	Michael	Fox, Bridget	V	24
Fleming, Mary	21, July 1850	James	----, Sarah	E	233
Fleming, Mary	23, May 1850	John	----, Sarah	E	222
Fleming, Patrick	7, Jan. 1855	James	Kavy, Sarah	E	255
Flemman, Ann	27, Jan. 1859	John	----, Sarah	E	599
Flemming, Johan	8, Jan. 1851	Michael	Forke?, Bridget	K	
Flemming, John	4, May 1851	Thomas	O'Hare, Margaret	E	305
Flemming, Mary Ann	10, Mar. 1850	Thomas	O'Hare, Margaret	E	201
Flemming, Peter	11, Sept 1853	Edmund	Kine, Joanne	U	
Flemming, Thomas	4, Oct. 1853	Thomas	O'Hare, Margaret	E	131
Flerlage, Anna Catharina Elisabeth	9, Nov. 1852	Friedrich	Brunsen, M. Gesina	F	
Flerlage, Johan	6, May 1856	Friedrich	Brunsen, Maria Gesina	J	36
Fletcher, Margaret	6, Sept 1857	Charles	Burke, Mary	E	478
Flick, Agnes	5, Sept 1859	Francis	Zimmermann, Helena	F	
Flick, Augustin	3, Oct. 1858	Mathias	Endries, Barbara	D	120
Flick, Carolina	15, Jan. 1852	Joseph	Graf, Francisca	D	302
Flick, Francis	10, Mar. 1855	Francis	Zimmermann, Magdalena	C	
Flick, Georg	12, Nov. 1857	Friedrich	Spencer, Anna Maria	K	
Flick, Georg Friedrich	14, Feb. 1858	Francis	Zimmermann, Helena	C	
Flick, Helena Friedricka	5, Dec. 1852	Francis	Zimmermann, Helena	C	
Flick, Maria	17, Mar. 1856	Francis	Zimmermann, Magdalena	C	
Flick, Maria Barbara	5, Feb. 1854	Francis	Zimmermann, Helena	C	
Flick, Maria Elisabeth	15, June 1851	Georg	Lorenz, Catharina	K	
Flick, Maria Salome	21, Feb. 1858	Peter	Kist, Caecilia	T	
Flick, Mary Margaret	15, Mar. 1852	Martin	Gruber, Margaret	N	6
Flick, Mary Pauline	30, Mar. 1856	Martin	Gruber, Margaret	N	
Flick, Sebastian	23, Dec. 1855	Peter	Kist, Caecilia	D	49
Flick, Wendel	1, Jan. 1854	Martin	Gruber, Margaret	N	19
Flick, Wilhelm Ferdinand	30, Mar. 1856	Francis J.	Graf, Francisca	D	55
Fliege, Maria Louisa	5, Nov. 1850	Heinrich	Richter, Catharina	D	241
Fliegel, Johan Nicolaus	30, June 1850	J. Adam	Wehner, Maria Barbara	A	
Fliese, Anna Elisabeth	5, May 1856	Michael	Karl, Anna Maria	L	
Fliess, Johan	23, Oct. 1853	Michael	Karl, Maria	L	
Flinn, Ann	3, Nov. 1850	Michael	McDermott, Bridget	M	
Flinn, Anthony	29, Aug. 1855	Michael	----, Mary	M	
Flinn, Catherine	15, May 1853	Michael	----, Bridget	M	
Flinn, Catherine	11, Mar. 1854	Michael	Beaty, Catherine	E	174
Flinn, Elizabeth	9, Sept 1855	Michael	----, Bridget	M	
Flinn, Emily Margaret	27, June 1859	Edward	Crily, Ann	B	77
Flinn, Helen	16, July 1851	Michael	McGrane, Bridget	M	
Flinn, Jacob Julius	2, Feb. 1858	James	King, Minerva Jane	B	55
Flinn, James	19, Apr. 1857	John	----, Margaret	M	
Flinn, James	13, July 1857	John	Gill, Bridget	B	47

Name of Child	Date of Baptism	Father	Mother	Church	Page
Flinn, John	22, Jan. 1856	John	----, Mary	E	339
Flinn, John Henry	6, July 1858	John	Martin, Sarah	E	546
Flinn, Margaret	30, Sept 1855	Christopher	Egin, Julia	U	
Flinn, Margaret	14, June 1858	Michael	----, Bridget	M	
Flinn, Mary	28, Sept 1856	Christopher	Hagen, Julia	U	
Flinn, Mary	15, May 1853	Michael	----, Bridget	M	
Flinn, Mary Ellen	18, Dec. 1853	Michael	----, Mary	M	
Flinn, Richard	21, Nov. 1858	John	Boylen, Ann	V	52
Floedde, Maria Elisabeth	10, Sept 1850	J. Bernard	Trentmann, Elisabeth	L	
Floedder, Maria Catharina Agnes	23, July 1854	J. Bernard	Trentmann, Elisabeth	L	
Floedders, Anna Margaretha	18, Apr. 1852	J. Bernard	Trentmann, Anna Maria	L	
Floedders, Franz Joseph	31, May 1856	J. Bernard	Wielenberg, Elisabeth	L	
Floedders, M. Carolina Elisabeth	16, July 1859	J. Bernard	Wielenberg, Elisabeth	L	
Floetker, Maria Louisa	15, June 1858	Gerhard	Hackmann, A. Maria	T	
Flohr, Carl Wilhelm	10, July 1858	Carl	Wolf, Barbara	C	
Flohr, Heinrich	24, Oct. 1852	Carl	Wolf, Barbara	D	355
Flohr, Magdalena	30, June 1850	Carl	Wolf, Barbara	C	
Flohr, Peter	31, Dec. 1854	Carl	Wolf, Barbara	C	
Flood, Charles	4, Jan. 1858	Christopher	O'Meara, Mary Ann	P	235
Flood, Francis	10, Feb. 1850	Patrick	Neil, Ann	E	196
Flood, James	9, Oct. 1853	Hugh	Reynolds, Ann	V	6
Flood, James	10, Mar. 1850	James	Cassidy, Jane	E	201
Flood, John	7, June 1851	John	Murphy, Mary	E	313
Flood, Margaret Ann	19, Mar. 1858	Edward	----, Alice	E	523
Flood, Mary Alice	14, June 1856	Edward	Murphy, Alice	E	374
Flood, Michael	1, Dec. 1850	Hugh	----, Ann	E	264
Flood, Michael	8, May 1853	James	----, Mary	E	87
Flood, Michael	31, Aug. 1858	Patrick	Shay, Mary	E	560
Flood, Patrick	17, Mar. 1857	Patrick	Shay, Mary	E	441
Flood, Richard	27, Jan. 1856	Hugh	Reynolds, Ann	E	340
Flood, William Thomas	27, Mar. 1859	Michael	Lannan, Bridget	B	73
Flor, Anna Susanna	12, Feb. 1851	Friedrich	Bierbon, Maria Anna	D	253
Flotmann, Anna Maria	14, Aug. 1851	Heinrich	Logering, Adelheid	C	
Flotmann, Maria Catharina	14, Aug. 1851	Heinrich	Logering, Adelheid	C	
Flottemesch, Anna Maria Bernardina	22, Jan. 1852	Joseph	Duvel, Anna Maria	L	
Flottmesch, Johan Heinrich	13, Feb. 1855	Joseph	Duevel, M.	C	
Floyd, Christopher	7, Aug. 1853	James	Lar---, Mary	B	296
Flugel, Georg Adam	25, Jan. 1859	Ludwig	Grau, Anna Elisabeth	D	129
Flugel, Johan Georg	15, May 1853	Ludwig	Gnau, Anna Elisabeth	D	385
Fluhr, Andreas	29, Dec. 1854	Donatus	Riche, Eleonore	R	
Flynn, Ann	24, July 1859	Thomas	McK---, Ann	B	77
Flynn, Ann Elizabeth	3, Jan. 1858	Michael	Duffy, Catherine	P	235
Flynn, Bridget	7, May 1854	John	Boylan, Ann	B	314
Flynn, Bridget	13, June 1858	Timothy	O'Donnell, Honora	E	541
Flynn, Catherine	17, July 1853	Hugh	Tully, Ann	P	47
Flynn, Catherine	12, Aug. 1855	John	Rabbit, Mary	E	307
Flynn, Catherine	31, July 1853	Michael	Carroll, Ann	B	296
Flynn, Catherine	17, Aug. 1850	Patrick	----, Mary	E	239
Flynn, Dennis	22, Jan. 1852	Patrick	Midnome, Mary	E	375
Flynn, Dora	19, Nov. 1854		adult - 30 years old	P	104
Flynn, Edward	20, Nov. 1850	John	O'Brien, Mary	E	263
Flynn, Ellen	14, Sept 1854	Patrick	Dehy, Mary	E	224
Flynn, Henry	11, Mar. 1855	Henry	Gillick, Mary	B	12
Flynn, James	4, Nov. 1859	James	----, Helen	E	667
Flynn, Jamse	1, June 1852	Michael	Carroll, Ann	B	260
Flynn, Jeremiah	9, June 1850	Timothy	----, Honora	E	221
Flynn, Joanne	12, Jan. 1852	William	Joyce, Julia	B	250
Flynn, John	30, May 1857	James	----, Ellen	E	456
Flynn, John	9, Oct. 1859	John	Rourk, Margaret	Z	

Name of Child	Date of Baptism	Father	Mother	Church	Page
Flynn, John	4, May 1856	Martin	Cauliffe, Ann	P	178
Flynn, John	21, Oct. 1853	Michael	McAnally, Mary	E	136
Flynn, John	25, Apr. 1852	Patrick	Ervin?, Mary	E	406
Flynn, John	9, Mar. 1851	Thomas	Brown, Ellen	E	288
Flynn, John	5, Sept 1854	William	----, Bridget	U	
Flynn, John Joseph	17, Apr. 1853	Henry	----, Mary	E	82
Flynn, John Robert	21, Dec. 1856	John	Boylan, Ann	V	35
Flynn, John William Dowling	28, Nov. 1858	John	Gill, Bridget	B	67
Flynn, Joseph	3, Apr. 1859	John	Hunt, Sarah	R	
Flynn, Luke	5, Oct. 1856	William	Bird, Bridget	U	
Flynn, Margaret	12, Apr. 1854	James	----, Ellen	E	182
Flynn, Margaret	5, Dec. 1852	John	O'Brien, Mary	E	42
Flynn, Margaret	14, June 1854	William	Joyce, Julia	B	1
Flynn, Mary	25, Nov. 1858	John	O'Brien, Mary	E	582
Flynn, Mary Ann	11, Sept 1859	Patrick	Reagin, Mary	B	80
Flynn, Mary Ann	2, June 1850	Thomas	----, Ann	E	217
Flynn, Mary Ann	23, Oct. 1853	Thomas	McKenna, Ann	P	56
Flynn, Mary Ann	19, Jan. 1850	William	Joyce, Julia	B	194
Flynn, Mary Elizabeth	21, May 1856	Matthew	Broderick, Vina	R	
Flynn, Mary Ellen	19, Aug. 1855	Michael	Duffy, Kate	B	18
Flynn, Mary Helen	9, Oct. 1856	John	----, Sarah	R	
Flynn, Mary Jane	23, Sept 1855	William	Joyce, Julia	B	19
Flynn, Michael	2, May 1858	Christ.	----, Julia	R	
Flynn, Michael	24, Dec. 1854	Thomas	McKenna, Ann	T	
Flynn, Patrick	14, Mar. 1851	Patrick	----, Mary	E	290
Flynn, Patrick	19, Apr. 1859	William	Joyce, Judith	E	619
Flynn, Peter	20, Oct. 1850	Peter	----, Bridget	E	255
Flynn, Sarah	12, Apr. 1854	James	----, Ellen	E	182
Flynn, Sarah Jane	9, Feb. 1853	Thomas	Winston, Ann	V	1
Flynn, Thomas	30, May 1857	James	----, Ellen	E	456
Flynn, Thomas	4, Dec. 1857	Michael	Cayton, Bridget	B	52
Flynn, Thomas	2, Aug. 1857	Thomas	McKenna, Ann	T	
Flynn, William	25, Oct. 1857	John	----, Sarah	R	
Flynn, William	15, May 1853	Thomas	Borwn, Helen	P	41
Flynn, William	24, Oct. 1858	William	Bird, Bridget	U	
Flynn, William	21, Dec. 1856	William	Joyce, Julia	B	38
Fobbe, Johan Bernard	21, Nov. 1851	J. Herman	Eckmann, Elisabeth	C	
Foccacci, Maria Antonia	20, Apr. 1856	John	----, Albina	P	176
Foccaci, Dominick Augustine	3, Apr. 1857	John	Focacci, Carolina	P	209
Focke, Catharina Theresa Philomena	29, Sept 1857	Bernard	Barlage, Margaretha	L	
Föcke, Philomena Gertrud	6, Aug. 1852	Heinrich	Wimler, Theresa	K	
Focke, Theodor Joseph	27, Oct. 1855	Joseph	Massman, Anna	A	
Focker, Johan Bernard	7, June 1857	Bernard	Olgemoeller, Catharina Maria	D	87
Fockler, Johan Georg	12, Oct. 1856	Georg	Boeh, Maria	C	
Fodde, Anna Christina	4, Nov. 1856	Heinrich	Ricker, Louisa	A	
Fodde, Anna Maria Catharina	4, July 1858	Heinrich	Ricker, Francisca	A	
Fodde, Johan Heinrich	6, Aug. 1854	Heinrich	Rickers, Francisca	A	
Fodde, Johan Wilhelm	15, Nov. 1855	J. Heinrich	Ricke, Francisca	A	
Foelker, Margaretha Bernardina	15, Mar. 1851	Gerhard	Gude, Theresa	L	
Foeller, Maria Anna	11, Aug. 1857	Ludwig	Buttelwerth, Christina	C	
Foer, Mary	24, Mar. 1850	Nicolaus	Reitner, Angela	H	
Föerich, Bernard Heinrich	25, Jan. 1859	Clemens	Nattman, Theresa	D	129
Foes, Daniel	4, Apr. 1858	Sales	Streile, Elisabeth	N	
Foes, Thomas	15, Feb. 1852	Thomas	Delany, Ann	P	18
Foet, Adam	26, Dec. 1852	Mathias	Basse, Anna Maria	D	362
Fogan, Joanne	6, June 1858	Patrick	Keegan, Joanne	E	540
Fogarty, Catherine	15, May 1852	Isaac	Rafferty, Bridget	B	259
Fogarty, Catherine	15, Mar. 1856	Martin	Farrell, Elisabeth	R	
Fogarty, Catherine	13, Sept 1850	Martin	Farrell, Elizabeth	B	213

Name of Child	Date of Baptism	Father	Mother	Church	Page
Fogarty, Daniel	3, Mar. 1850	Patrick	Hennessy, Mary	B	197
Fogarty, Joanne	9, Jan. 1853	Martin	Farrell, Elenore	R	
Fogarty, John	18, May 1851	Patrick	----, Bridget	E	308
Fogarty, Martin	14, Nov. 1850	John	----, Margaret	E	261
Fogarty, Mary	22, Nov. 1851	Martin	----, Louise	R	
Fogarty, Michael	12, Dec. 1853	Martin	----, Louise	R	
Fogelmann, Susanna	21, May 1855	Georg	Lawry, Marianna	F	
Fogerty, Margaret	11, July 1853	John	----, Margaret	E	106
Fogt, Michael	14, Sept 1856	Peter	King, Catherine	P	192
Fohle, Andreas Johan	8, Dec. 1857	Wendel	Dups, Albertina	K	
Folbert, Johan Herman	22, Mar. 1854	Theodor	Kettler, Antoinette	L	
Foley, Ann	28, Dec. 1858	Dennis	Lacey, Catherine	X	
Foley, Catherine	3, July 1852	Jeremiah	Smith, Mary	B	262
Foley, Catherine Agnes	7, Sept 1856	John	Leary, Mary	B	33
Foley, Daniel	22, July 1859	John	O'Leary, Mary	B	77
Foley, Dennis	11, Mar. 1857	Dennis	Lacey, Catherine	X	
Foley, Elizabeth	16, July 1854	Daniel	----, Julia	U	
Foley, Elizabeth	8, July 1858	Timothy	Gildea, Margaret	P	253
Foley, Hanna	18, Sept 1853	Patrick	----, Mary	E	128
Foley, Helen	12, Apr. 1857	James	Lynch, Elizabeth	V	38
Foley, James	18, Jan. 1859	Dennis	Buckley, Catherine	H	
Foley, James	28, Jan. 1854	James	Keenan, Bridget	V	10
Foley, James	23, Mar. 1852	Patrick	Moriren?, Margaret	P	19
Foley, James Dennis	5, Feb. 1854	Dennis	Lacy, Catherine	P	67
Foley, John	7, June 1853	Bartholomew	Coffee, Ellen	L	
Foley, John	29, May 1853	Michael	Rooney, Margaret	B	292
Foley, John Henry	14, Nov. 1853	Jeremiah	----, Bridget	B	302
Foley, John Henry	26, May 1854	John	O'Leary, Mary	B	315
Foley, Josephine	17, Feb. 1855	Ellis	----, ----	E	265
Foley, Margaret	19, July 1854	Jeremiah	Smith, Mary	B	3
Foley, Margaret	22, Feb. 1858	Patrick	Neagle, Helen	P	240
Foley, Mary	24, Aug. 1856	Dennis	Buckley, Catherine	H	
Foley, Mary	2, Aug. 1852	James	Lynch, Elizabeth	P	25
Foley, Mary	9, May 1850	Patrick	Morrison, Margaret	B	202
Foley, Mary	28, Mar. 1852	Timothy	Murphy, Mary	E	396
Foley, Mary Ann	26, Feb. 1859	James	Lynch, Elizabeth	V	53
Foley, Mary Ann	15, July 1855	Patrick	Caff, Mary	E	300
Foley, Mary Elizabeth	14, Dec. 1851	John	Leary, Mary	B	248
Foley, Mary Ellen	10, Mar. 1851	Dennis	Lacy, Catherine	P	6
Foley, Michael	27, Oct. 1850	Jeremiah	Smith, Mary Ann	B	217
Foley, Michael	31, July 1856	Timothy	Gildea, Margaret	P	186
Foley, Patrick	13, May 1855	James	King, Bridget	E	285
Foley, Patrick	4, Mar. 1855	James	Lynch, Elizabeth	V	23
Foley, Peter	11, Sept 1854	James	Jacob, Mary	E	223
Foley, Sarah Jane	24, May 1857	James	Keenan, Bridget	V	39
Foley, Thomas	18, Dec. 1853	John	Brun, Ellen	E	153
Foley, Thomas	28, July 1854	Peter	Mathews, Mary	E	211
Foley, William	21, May 1852	William	O'Connor, Kitty	E	416
Foley, William	27, Apr. 1857	William	Ryan, Mary	E	449
Folger, Eva	12, Nov. 1854	Johan	Rigi---, Magdalena	D	22
Folger, Richard Stanislaus	5, May 1850		adult - 15 years old	E	212
Folmer, Juliana	30, Oct. 1855	Daniel	Rorder, Bridget	Q	11
Folz, Clara	15, Feb. 1857	Nicolaus	Kunz, Catharina	G	
Foot, Elisabeth	30, Dec. 1852	Francis	Barlau, Elisabeth	F	
Foot, Heinrich Wilhelm	24, Aug. 1855	Francis H.	Bellard, Elisabeth	F	
Foot, Johan Herman	21, Nov. 1858	Francis J.	Barlage, Elisabeth	F	
Foot, Wilhelm Joseph	12, Mar. 1857	Francis H.	Barlage, Elisabeth	F	
Fopiano, Maria Magdalena	11, Oct. 1855	Jacobo	Retaliata, Theresa	B	20
Foppe, Johan Bernard Heinrich	15, Sept 1850	J. Bernard	Korte, Maria Catharina	K	

Name of Child	Date of Baptism	Father	Mother	Church	Page
Foppe, Maria Bernardina Catharina	13, Sept 1853	Clemens	Korte, Maria Catharina	K	
Foran, Bridget	23, Mar. 1851	Patrick	Fitzsimmons, Catherine	M	
Foran, Catherine	20, Feb. 1854	Patrick	Keegan, Julia	V	11
Foran, Elizabeth	26, Jan. 1853	James	Bulger, Jane	E	58
Foran, Elizabeth	12, Sept 1852	Patrick	Ryan, Julia	E	16
Foran, James	11, June 1859	Patrick	Keegan, Julia	E	631
Foran, Lawrence	14, Oct. 1855	Patrick	Fitzsimmons, Catherine	V	27
Foran, Margaret	22, Nov. 1858	James	Bulger, Jane	E	581
Foran, Margaret	22, Nov. 1857	Patrick	Keegen, Julia	E	495
Foran, Mark	10, Nov. 1855	Patrick	----, Julia	E	326
Foran, Michael	20, June 1858	Patrick	Fitzsimmons, Catherine	E	543
Forbes, Alice Lavina	22, Nov. 1857	Miles	Gleason, Alice	E	494
Forbes, James August	28, Feb. 1858	John	----, Mary	E	519
Forbes, Mary Elizabeth	9, Apr. 1859	Miles	Gleason, Alice	E	617
Ford, Bridget	20, Dec. 1855	Thomas	----, Mary	Q	11
Ford, Ellen	10, May 1851	Dominick	Fanigty, Bridget	E	306
Ford, George W.	27, July 1856	George	Ko--es, Rebecca Jane	E	384
Ford, James	25, Dec. 1859	James	White, Margaret	V	65
Ford, James	9, Sept 1855	John	Noonan, Bridget	P	150
Ford, James	8, Mar. 1857	Michael	Reney, Margaret	T	
Ford, John	22, Sept 1856	Jonathan	----, Genette	E	399
Ford, John	4, June 1856	Patrick	Sullivan, Mary	P	181
Ford, Mary	23, Nov. 1851	John	McDonald, Ann	B	245
Ford, Mary	4, June 1856	Patrick	Sullivan, Mary	P	181
Ford, Mary Ann	8, Apr. 1855	Michael	Raney, Margaret	T	
Ford?, Patrick	1, May 1852	Michael	----, Margaret	B	258
Fordan, Catherine	18, July 1853	Patrick	----, Catherine	E	110
Forde, Elizabeth	27, Nov. 1859	Jonathan	Malone, Bridget	P	304
Forde, John	25, Jan. 1854	John	McDonnell, Honora	P	66
Forge, Mary Jane	11, Sept 1859	Richard	Walsh, Honora	P	295
Förger, Georg	6, Sept 1857	Ignatius	Roth, Magdalena	K	
Fork, Cunigunda	13, Feb. 1859	Carl	Ger---, Catharina	D	131
Forrest?, Elizabeth	16, Aug. 1857	Thomas	Connor, Catherine	B	48
Forrester, Augustine Miller	13, June 1852	Matthew A.	----, Elizabeth	E	424
Forrester, Elizabeth	13, June 1852	Matthew A.	----, Elizabeth	E	424
Forrester, Elizabeth	1, Aug. 1853	Walter	Burke, Margaret	B	296
Forrester, James	24, Apr. 1850	Walter	Burke, Margaret	B	201
Forrester, Sarah	27, Feb. 1859	Thomas	Cannon, Catherine	B	71
Forrester, Thomas Richard	25, Jan. 1852	Daniel	Cameron, Mary	B	251
Forrin, Ann	21, Oct. 1855	William	Ryan, Margaret	V	27
Forst, Catharina	11, Apr. 1852	Enos	Frank, Maria	D	316
Forst, Georg Heinrich	28, Nov. 1858	Georg	Disler, Margaretha	Q	29
Först, Johan	15, June 1851	Georg	Dister, Margaretha	Q	1
Först, Maria Anna	18, May 1856	Georg	Distler, Margaretha	Q	14
Först, Maria Catharina	10, Oct. 1852	Joseph	Heitz, Scholastica	D	352
Först, Michael	23, Oct. 1853	Georg	Disler, Margaretha	Q	3
Forster, Carl	7, Dec. 1851	Georg	----, Margaretha	H	
Forster, Emdeana Winifred	2, Aug. 1858	Henry E.	McGatham?, Winifred	B	62
Forster, Emma	13, Aug. 1855	Henry	McNamara, Winifred	B	18
Forster, Francis	24, Aug. 1857	George	Schmidt, Margaret	H	
Forster, Francis	31, July 1859	George	Schmidt, Margaret	H	
Forster, Francis	13, July 1852	Henry	McNamara, Winifred	B	265
Forster, Magdalena	9, Sept 1855	George	----, Maria Magdalena	H	
Forster, Mary Magdalene	1, May 1853	George	----, Magdalena	H	
Forsthof, Anna Maria Theresa	24, May 1854	Heinrich	Hortman, Theresa	D	11
Forsthof, Philomena Josephina	5, July 1855	Heinrich	Theibe, Theresa	D	37
Forth, Maria Magdalena	2, June 1857	Daniel	Breitinger, Eva	A	
Forthuber, Veronica	6, May 1855	Wilhelm	Goeser, Theresa	G	
Forthuber, Wilhelm	13, Feb. 1859	Wilhelm	Goeser, Theresa	G	

Name of Child	Date of Baptism	Father	Mother	Church	Page
Fortman, Barbara	21, May 1855	Francis	Braun, Elisabeth	K	
Fortman, Clara	25, Apr. 1852	Francis	Schoenenberger, Maria Anna	N	6
Fortman, Clemens Herman	4, July 1858	Johan	Horstman, Bernardina	K	
Fortman, Francis Heinrich Albert	20, Nov. 1853	Francis	Schoenenberger, Maria	N	17
Fortman, Herman August	16, June 1856	Anton	Lamping, Catharina	K	
Fortman, Herman Heinrich	1, June 1857	J. Heinrich	----, Maria	K	
Fortman, Johan Heinrich	2, Oct. 1855	Johan	Horstman, Bernardina	K	
Fortman, Johan Heinrich Christian	9, Mar. 1852	Friedrich	Hoeveler, Catharina	K	
Fortman, Maria Anna	2, Jan. 1851	Clemens	Kottenbrock, Bernardina	K	
Fortman, Maria Elisabeth	28, Apr. 1853	Johan	Horstman, Bernardina	K	
Fortman, Nicolaus Julian	11, Oct. 1857	Francis	Schönberger, Maria	N	
Fortman, Sophia Antonia	18, Oct. 1858	Anton	Lamping, Catharina	K	
Fortmann, Franz Anton	10, Oct. 1853	Anton	Ronnebaum, Anna Maria	L	
Fortmann, Franz Heinrich	3, Jan. 1859	Anton	Ronnebaum, Maria	L	
Fortmann, Johan Heinrich Anton	28, Sept 1856	Anton	Ronnebaum, Maria	L	
Fortmann, Josephina Sophia	25, Mar. 1855	Johan H.	Reiners, Margaretha S.	F	
Fortmann, Maria Elisabeth	3, Jan. 1858	Heinrich	Reiners, Sophia	F	
Fortner, Ellen	28, Mar. 1859	John	Connell, Ellen	E	614
Fortune, Catherine	12, July 1851	Patrick	Slaughter, Elizabeth	B	237
Fortune, Christopher	14, Nov. 1855	Christopher	Troy, Winifred	P	159
Fortune, John	20, Mar. 1859	Christopher	Troy, Winifred	B	72
Fortune, Mary	8, Aug. 1850	George	Tyan, Mary	B	209
Fortune, Mary	15, June 1858	John	Burns, Bridget	E	542
Fortune, Sarah Jane	22, Feb. 1857	Christopher	Troy, Winifred	B	41
Forzer, Josephina	6, Feb. 1853	J. Baptist	----, Josephina	D	370
Fos---, James	7, Aug. 1855	James	Connel, Ann	P	144
Fosgroene, Johan Wilhelm	11, Sept 1856	J. Heinrich	Honebring, Juliana	C	
Fosgrone, Joseph	20, Dec. 1859	Johan	Honebrink, Juliana	C	
Foss, Valentin Liborius	15, Sept 1858	Leopold	Fom---, Catharina	D	119
Foster, Charity Ann	12, Jan. 1859	James	Jenkins, Polly	E	596
Foster, Elizabeth	6, Sept 1853	George	----, Mary	E	126
Foster, George	10, July 1855	George	Collety, Mary	V	25
Foster, George	27, Dec. 1850	George	McCarty, Ellen	E	271
Foster, George	18, Nov. 1850	James D.	McDermond, Elena	B	219
Foster, James	17, May 1851	James	Parle, Elizabeth	B	232
Foster, James Edward	12, May 1853	James	McDermott, Helen	B	291
Foster, John	16, July 1857	George	Colletty, Mary	E	466
Foster, John Hieronymus	18, Nov. 1850	William	Bonnet, Elisabeth Frances	E	262
Foster, Luke	29, June 1851	William L.	Tony, Charlotte	E	318
Foster, Mary	1, Feb. 1858	John	Bets, Matilda	U	
Foster, Mary Hedwig	1, Dec. 1857	James	McDermott, Ellen	B	52
Fosthof, Anna Theresa	5, July 1852	Heinrich	Kortman, Theresa	A	
Foulke, Caretta Ellenore Theresa	16, Feb. 1852	Levi	Foulke, Elizabeth M.	E	383
Foulke, Francis Edward	13, Apr. 1855	Levi	----, Eliza	B	13
Founony?, John	16, Nov. 1855	Jeffrey	Cash, Margaret	P	159
Foutrs, Johan Joseph	26, Jan. 1850	Joseph	Thero, Gertrud	C	
Fowe, Johan Heinrich Aloysius	24, June 1855	J. Heinrich	Kellinghaus, Theresa	K	
Fowle, Maria Emma	14, Dec. 1859	Christoph	Wagener, Maria	K	
Fowler, Elizabeth	29, Feb. 1852	James	Keenan, Bridget	B	253
Fox, Ann	7, Nov. 1852	Francis	Coleman, Sarah	P	29
Fox, Ann	15, May 1853	William	----, Julia	E	89
Fox, Anna Maria	9, June 1852	C. Theodor	Foehr, Susanna	D	323
Fox, Bridget	23, Jan. 1856	Francis	Coleman, Ann Jane	P	167
Fox, Edward	5, June 1853	John	Riley, Bridget	E	95
Fox, Esther	27, Apr. 1851	Alexander	Dempsey, Julia	P	7
Fox, Helen	29, Jan. 1855	Patrick	Burns, Julia	P	118
Fox, James	31, Oct. 1852	Alexander	Dempsey, Julia	B	273
Fox, James Henry	8, Dec. 1850	Thomas	Hyland, Catherine	B	220
Fox, James Patrick	22, May 1856	Thomas	Boyd, Frances	B	29

Name of Child	Date of Baptism	Father	Mother	Church	Page
Fox, Jane	6, Sept 1851	John	McDonough, Sarah	E	340
Fox, Joanne Ann	5, Mar. 1856	Michael	Doley, Johanna	U	
Fox, John	11, May 1856	Alexander	Dempsey, Julia	P	179
Fox, John	1, Mar. 1852	John	Kelly, Catherine	E	387
Fox, John	14, Sept 1851	Michael	Dowling, Joanne	E	343
Fox, John Thomas	16, July 1854	Thomas	Boyd, Frances	B	2
Fox, Leonard	8, Mar. 1858	Thomas	Highland, Catherine	P	241
Fox, Margaret	2, June 1859	John	Butler, Margaret	E	630
Fox, Margaret	30, Nov. 1856	Patrick	Burns, Julia	P	200
Fox, Maria Anna	5, Apr. 1857	Herman	Waldhaus, M. Elis.	L	
Fox, Mary Ann	23, July 1853	John	----, Margaret	E	111
Fox, Mary Ann Frances	13, Apr. 1856	Michael	----, Rosanne	M	
Fox, Mary Elizabeth	28, July 1857	Isaiah	Parker, Helen	E	470
Fox, Mary Frances	8, Dec. 1857	William C.	Thomas, Frnaces C.	B	53
Fox, Mary Jane	23, Jan. 1859	Martin	Cone, Ann	V	52
Fox, Matthew	9, June 1854	Thomas	Hyland, Catherine	P	84
Fox, Michael	20, Sept 1851	John	Reilly, Bridget	E	344
Fox, Michael	21, Dec. 1850	Thomas	----, Bridget	E	269
Fox, Peter	13, June 1858	Alexander	Dempsey, Julia	B	60
Fox, Rose	16, Mar. 1859	Patrick	Burns, Julia	P	280
Fox, Thomas	30, Oct. 1853	Michael	----, Joanne	E	138
Fox, William Henry	13, Dec. 1857	Thomas	Boyd, Frances	B	53
Foy, Ann	14, May 1854	Michael	----, Mary	U	
Foy, Benjamin	9, Oct. 1859	Thomas B.	Boyd, Frances	B	82
Foy, Helen	29, Jan. 1851	Peter	Lennon, Bridget	B	224
Foy, James	11, Sept 1853	Peter	King, Catherine	E	127
Foy, James Henry	3, Oct. 1858	James	Kelly, Ellen	V	51
Foy, John	9, June 1851	John	Maher, Winifred	M	
Foy, John	10, Oct. 1858	William	Mitchell, Catherine	B	65
Foy, Mary	29, May 1853	Philipp	White, Jane	E	93
Foy, William	31, Aug. 1856	William	Mitchell, Catherine	P	189
Foyling, Richard Francis	14, Nov. 1858	James	Farll, Margaret	V	51
Foys, Edward	30, Oct. 1853	William	Mitchel, Catherine	B	301
Foys, Timothy	30, Oct. 1853	William	Mitchel, Catherine	B	301
Fr---, Joseph	25, Mar. 1858		Fr---, Joseph	D	108
Frage, Johan Heinrich	13, Jan. 1854	Joseph	Feldhaus, Marianna	F	
Fragge, Johanna	8, Apr. 1851	J. Joseph	Feldhaus, Maria Gertrud	F	
Fraley, George	12, May 1859	George	Martin, Helen	E	624
Frame, Bernard Herman	12, Sept 1858	J. Heinrich	Niekamp, Catharina	K	
Frame, Johan Clemens	28, Oct. 1856	Heinrich	Niekamp, Catharina	K	
Framme, Anna Catharina	26, May 1859	Meinrad	Wiegman, Maria	A	
Framme, Gerhard Heinrich	22, Apr. 1853	Meinrad	Wiergman, Maria	A	
Framme, Johan Bernard	13, Mar. 1856	Meinrad	Wiegman, Anna Maria	A	
Framme, Maria Elisabeth	12, Jan. 1851	Meinrad	Wiechman, Maria Adelheid	A	
France, William	3, Aug. 1850	William	Dorman, Adele	B	209
Francis, Ellen	19, Jan. 1850	Peter	Ryan, Mary	E	192
Francis, George	19, Jan. 1851	Louis	Coonan, Helen	B	223
Francis, Isabel	5, June 1853	Richard	Coolahan, Helen	P	43
Francis, John	3, Aug. 1851	James	McGrane, Margaret	E	330
Francis, Margaret Elisabeth	22, Feb. 1857	James	----, Margaret	R	
Francis, Mary Ann	3, Aug. 1851	James	----, Margaret	E	330
Francis, Samuel	3, Aug. 1851	James	----, Margaret	E	330
Francis, Thomas	30, July 1854	James	McGray, Margaret	E	211
Francis, William	3, Aug. 1851	James	----, Margaret	E	330
Franconi, Emil Francis	17, July 1859	Heinrich	Berry, Stephania	C	
Franey, Catherine	11, May 1856	John	Huff, Mary Ann	V	31
Frank, Alfred Francis	3, Jan. 1855	Clemens	Wilman, Bernardina	B	9
Frank, Amelia Magdalena	7, Sept 1855	Wilhelm	Weber, Christina	D	42
Frank, Andreas	13, Dec. 1858	Sebastian	Ofer, Rosalia	T	

Name of Child	Date of Baptism	Father	Mother	Church	Page
Frank, Ursula Catharina	13, Feb. 1855	Joseph	Bast, Maria	C	
Franke, Heinrich Ludwig	27, July 1856	Caspar	Brinkman, Clara	D	63
Franke, Imtum Ludwig	23, Mar. 1851	Joseph	Grundei, Maria	D	258
Franke, Johan Gerhard	28, Dec. 1853	Herman	Schülting, Susanna	K	
Franke, Johan Heinrich	28, Feb. 1851	Caspar	Brinkman, Clara	D	255
Frankenberg, Friedrica Elisabeth	22, May 1854	Herman H.	Akemeyer, Theresa Elis.	A	
Frankenberg, Johan Heinrich	10, Aug. 1857	J. Heinrich	Haunert, Maria Gertrud	U	
Frankenberg, Joseph Herman Ludwig	13, Apr. 1852	Herman H.	Schmer, M. Elisabeth	L	
Franklin, Benjamin	29, May 1855	----	----, ----	E	289
Franklin, Cecilia	14, May 1858	Underwood	----, Julia	M	
Franklin, Johan Rudolph	17, Dec. 1854	Joseph	Birg, Juliana	D	24
Franz, Alexander Heinrich	5, June 1854	Kilian	Schneider, Catharina	D	11
Franz, Carolina Sophia	27, Nov. 1858	Georg	Lechner, Clara	T	
Franz, Elisabeth	29, Sept 1850	Kilian	Schneider, Catharina	D	235
Franz, Emilia Magalena	18, June 1854	Johan	Wölfel, Elisabeth	D	12
Franz, Heinrich	19, Apr. 1857	Kilian	Schneider, Catharina	D	83
Franz, Jacob	8, July 1855	Georg	Euler, Catharina	D	38
Franz, Johan Anton	1, Nov. 1852	Johan	Gluepfel, Magdalena	F	
Franz, Johan August	1, June 1856	Conrad	Wehner, Catharina	C	
Franz, Johan Georg	5, Oct. 1856	Georg	Lechner, Clara	F	
Franz, Maria Anna	31, Aug. 1851	Kilian	Schneider, Catharina	D	280
Franz, Philomena	18, July 1858	Conrad	Wena, Catharina	C	
Franzer, Sebastian	28, Apr. 1850	Johan	Feit, Elisabeth	C	
Frapon, Sibilla	25, Dec. 1851	Nicolaus	----, Theresa	D	298
Fräser, Maria Anna Elisabeth	24, Sept 1856	Heinrich	Kesker, Anna	D	68
Frasier, Mary Ann	28, Dec. 1851	Philipp	Manion, Bridget	B	249
Fratz, Anton	2, July 1854	Joseph	----, Barbara	H	
Fratz, Aquilin Julius	24, Apr. 1853	J. Georg	Sandroth, Helena	A	
Fratz, Gertrud Helena	10, May 1851	J. Georg	Sämtrack, Helena	A	
Fratz, Joseph	12, June 1853	Joseph	----, Barbara	H	
Fratz, Maria Anna	9, Mar. 1856	Joseph	----, Barbara	H	
Frauer, Johan Michael	26, Oct. 1851	Johan	Veith, Elisabeth	D	289
Fraun, Maria Catharina	14, June 1850	Francis	Niehaus, Elisabeth	D	217
Fraune, Carl Heinrich	20, June 1858	Francis	Niehaus, Elisabeth	D	113
Fraune, Josephina Gesina	19, Oct. 1851	Francis	Niehaus, Elisabeth	D	288
Fraune, Maria Bernardina	18, July 1855	Francis	Niehaus, Elisabeth	D	38
Frawley, Ellen	16, Jan. 1859	Patrick	Murphy, Ellen	B	70
Frawley, Mary	4, Nov. 1855	Patrick	Murphy, Ellen	B	21
Frawley, William	27, Sept 1857	William	Murphy, Ellen	B	50
Frazer, Helen	12, Dec. 1858	William	Gradley, Helen	E	586
Frazer, Isabel	6, Jan. 1855	William	Bradley, Helen	P	114
Freak, Anna Maria Josephina	24, June 1856	H. Bernard	Schülting, Adelheid	K	
Frebon, Theresa	3, Oct. 1851	Philipp	Eckstein, Catharina	D	285
Frechs, Johan Wilhelm	23, Apr. 1854	Johan	Brueggemann, Elis.	L	
Freckes, Johan Heinrich	28, Jan. 1851	Johan	Brueggemann, M. Elis.	L	
Frecking, Anna Maria Agnes	25, May 1852	Bernard	Ricking, Maria Angela	A	
Frecking, Elisabeth	20, May 1856	Bernard	Ricking, Anna Maria	A	
Frecking, Wilhelm	26, Apr. 1859	B.	Recking, Maria Engel	A	
Freder, Heinrich	26, Mar. 1852	Joseph	Feldhaus, Gertrud	F	
Free, James	25, May 1854	Thomas	----, Margaret	E	193
Freeman, Edward Augustine	16, June 1850	William	----, Margaret	B	205
Freeman, James	9, Jan. 1853	William	Burns, Margaret	B	281
Freeman, Mary Ann	29, Apr. 1855	William	Bruns, Margaret	B	14
Freeman, Mary Augusta	16, Sept 1855	Michael	Moran, Ann	E	315
Freeman, Thomas Alexander	16, June 1850	William	----, Margaret	B	205
Freer, Alice	9, Sept 1855	Barnabas	Cunningham, Elizabeth	P	150
Freher, Maria Catharina	13, Nov. 1856	Bernard	Westrup, Catharina	F	
Freidhof, Ludwig Heinrich	6, Feb. 1853	Johan	Koch, Catharina	D	369
Freiermuth, Joseph	15, Aug. 1852	Joseph	Mueller, Mathilda	C	

Name of Child	Date of Baptism	Father	Mother	Church	Page
Freihofer, Maria Anna	3, Aug. 1856	Jacob	Meyer, Anna Maria	J	36
Freiler, Stephan	22, Feb. 1852	Caspar	Lünneman, Henrietta	D	308
Freis, Carl	8, June 1856	Georg	Beck, Rosina	D	60
Freis, Carolina	6, Mar. 1853	Anton	Kammandl, Catharina	D	374
Freis, Eduard Joseph	28, Mar. 1851	Joseph	Oehler, Maria	F	
Freis, Francisca	19, Dec. 1858	Georg	Beck, Rosina	C	
Freis, Francisca	30, July 1854	Michael	Reiberger, Barbara	T	
Freis, Franz Joseph	7, Apr. 1850	Francis	Oehler, Anna	F	
Freis, Johan	3, Dec. 1854	Georg	Bick, Rosina	D	23
Freis, Johan Michael	15, July 1853	Francis J.	Oehler, Anna Maria	F	
Freis, Maria Catharina	3, Oct. 1852	Georg	Beck, Rosina	D	350
Freis, Maria Louisa	15, Aug. 1858	Joseph	Ehler, Maria	W	23
Freise, Joseph Ludwig	5, Sept 1850	Joseph	Hülsgötter, Louisa	D	231
Freisens, Johan Christoph	30, May 1858	Christoph	Dreis, Barbara	D	112
Freisens, Maria Magdalena	7, Aug. 1853	Christoph	Dreis, Barbara	D	399
Freising, Anna	23, Jan. 1859	Sebastian	Kraus, Ottilia	D	129
Freiss, Carl Ludwig	19, Apr. 1857	Joseph	Oehler, Marianna	W	18
Freisz, Johan Georg	26, Jan. 1851	Georg	Beck, Rosina	D	250
Freisz, Joseph Theodor	27, Apr. 1855	Joseph	Oehler, Maria	W	8
Freisz, Michael	5, Oct. 1851	Jacob	Erlevin, Helena	J	12
Freithof, Andreas	23, Nov. 1856	Johan	Koch, Catharina	Q	18
Freithof, Anna Elisabeth	6, May 1851	Johan	Koch, Catharina	D	264
Freithoff, Elisabeth	2, Mar. 1858	John	Koch, Catharina	Q	27
Frekers, Anna Catharina Charlotte	8, June 1854	Bernard	Mermann, Anna Maria	L	
Frekes, Carl Clemens	28, Dec. 1855	Clemens	Nathman, Theresa	D	49
Freking, Anna Maria Carolina	26, Dec. 1854	Bernard	Keiser, Catharina	J	30
Freking, Gerhard Heinrich	17, Dec. 1858	B. Heinrich	Kaiser, Catharina	J	48
Freking, Johan Heinrich	10, May 1850	J. Bernard	Röhing, Maria	A	
Freking, Maria Catharina Francisca	21, Mar. 1857	B. Heinrich	Kaiser, Catharina	J	40
Freling, Johan Bernard	21, Jan. 1855	Clemens B	Sudmoeller, A. Sophia	L	
Freman, Ellen	23, Jan. 1859	William	Byrne, Margaret	B	70
Fremlen, Theresa Juliana	6, Feb. 1853	Joseph	B---, Juliana	D	369
Frenck, Carolina	15, Jan. 1850	Prosar	----	C	
Frenkle, Joseph	13, Oct. 1850	Joseph	Burg, Juliana	D	237
Frenser, Maria Anna Elisabeth	18, Nov. 1851	Bernard	Hilker, Anna	L	
Frentz, Carl Edward	16, Feb. 1857	Ludwig	Bär, Maria Anna	D	79
Frenzer, Johan Bernard	28, Oct. 1853	J. Bernard	Hilke, Maria Anna	L	
Frericks, Catharina Elisabeth	21, Aug. 1857	Clemens	Nathman, Theresa	D	92
Frerkers, Margaretha Cath. Elis.	15, Nov. 1857	Bernard	Morien, Anna	L	
Frese, Johan Heinrich	1, Sept 1851	Joseph	Hoene, Maria Engel	L	
Frese, Maria Anna Josephina	3, Apr. 1853	Joseph	Hoehne, A.M. Engel	L	
Fresenberg, Catharina Bernardina	10, Sept 1855	Joseph	Brockman, Maria	K	
Fresenberg, Johan Bernard	26, Feb. 1857	Joseph	Brockman, Maria Anna	K	
Freuermund, Johan	1, Sept 1850	Joseph	Müller, Mechtilda	J	6
Freuler, Clara	25, May 1851	Dominick	Linneman, Elisabeth	H	
Freulker, Johan Franz	3, June 1859	Johan H.	Meiering, Elisabeth	F	
Freund, Aloysius	18, Mar. 1853	Georg	Lehman, Maria	J	20
Freund, August	31, Jan. 1858	August	Gfroerer, Ernestina	L	
Freund, Conrad	29, Feb. 1856	Georg	Schmidt, Christina	F	
Freund, Johan	1, Feb. 1853	August	Gfrörer, Ernestina	D	369
Freund, Louisa Wilhelmina	3, Jan. 1854	Joseph	Braun, Anna Maria	D	1
Freund, Magdalena	14, Feb. 1856	Jacob	Zimmerman, Catharina Elis.	D	52
Freund, Magdalena Theresa	19, Mar. 1854	August	Gfroerer, Ernestina	F	
Freund, Maria Anna Francisca	3, Jan. 1854	Joseph	Braun, Anna Maria	D	1
Freund, Maria Eva	24, Mar. 1850	Joseph	Rausch, Anna Maria	D	206
Freund, Maria Mathilda	3, Feb. 1856	August	Gfrörer, Ernestina	D	51
Freund, Peter	16, Nov. 1851	August	Gfroerer, Ernestina	F	
Freund, Susanna Maria	20, Mar. 1851	Georg	Schuman, Maria Helena	A	
Freundt, Edward	15, Dec. 1857	Jacob	Zimmermann, Catharina	C	

Name of Child	Date of Baptism	Father	Mother	Church	Page
Frewer, Caroline Josephine	10, Apr. 1859	A. John	Sall, Maria Theresa	R	
Frey, Dorothy Barbara	7, Apr. 1850	Elias	----, Barbara	H	
Frey, Elisabeth Barbara	27, Mar. 1859	Joseph	Wehrle, Johanna	N	
Frey, Elizabeth	18, Jan. 1857	Elias	Hoffman, Barbara	H	
Frey, Emilian Gustav	14, Sept 1858	Balthasar	Hut, Carolina	N	
Frey, Heinrich Hieronymus Joseph	6, Sept 1856	Heinrich	Heim, Christina	K	
Frey, Johan Baptist	8, Aug. 1852	Elias	----, Barbara	H	
Frey, Louis	25, Apr. 1859	Elias	Hoppman, Barbara	H	
Frey, Margaretha	18, June 1854	Balthasar	Hut, Carolina	K	
Frey, Maria Catharina	25, Mar. 1856	Ubald	Hunt, Catharina	K	
Frey, Martin Elias	19, Nov. 1854	Elias	----, Barbara	H	
Frey, Sigismund Heinrich Carl	1, Jan. 1855	Heinrich	Frischholz, Theresa	D	26
Frey, Wilhelm Jacob Edward	10, Oct. 1858	Heinrich	Heim, Christina	K	
Freye, Peter Christian	3, Sept 1853	Ursus	Zoller, Barbara	K	
Freyhofer, Heinrich	19, Dec. 1858	Jacob	Meyer, Maria	A	
Freyhofer, Jacob Solomon	4, Mar. 1855	Jacob	Meyer, Anna Maria	J	30
Freyne, Edward	26, Sept 1858	Joseph	Gorman, Bridget	B	65
Frick, Anna	20, Mar. 1859	Constantine	Resch, Louisa	D	134
Frick, Bridget	23, Dec. 1855	Joseph	Williams, Ann	P	163
Frick, Margaret Helen	8, Nov. 1857	Joseph	Williams, Ann	P	229
Frick, Martin Johan	30, Jan. 1853	Peter	Lang, Theresa	F	
Frick, Sebastian John	6, Nov. 1853	John	Williams, Ann	P	58
Fricke, Amalia Louisa	16, Aug. 1856	Francis Leo	Linzen, Maria Francisca	A	
Fricke, Francis Albert	24, Sept 1859	Francis	Linsen, Maria	A	
Fricke, Johan Baptist Andreas	14, Apr. 1853	Andreas	Schumacher, Maria	F	
Fricke, Margaretha	10, Aug. 1856	Mathias	Gartner, Margaretha	K	
Fricke, Maria Carolina Amalia	28, Aug. 1858	Francis	Linse, Maria	A	
Fricker, Wilhelm	7, Nov. 1858	Mathias	Gärtner, Margaretha	K	
Frickert, Elisabeth	28, July 1859	Joseph	Honert, Maria	H	
Frickert, Friedrich	26, Apr. 1857	Joseph	Honert, Catharina	H	
Frickert, Joseph Christoph	12, Feb. 1851	Joseph	Honert, Catharina	D	253
Frickert, Margaret	26, Sept 1852	Joseph	Hunet, Catharine	H	
Frickert, Mary	25, Feb. 1855	Joseph	----, Catherine	H	
Frie, Johan	1, Jan. 1858		Frie, Catharina	L	
Frie, Johan Bernard	19, Feb. 1851	Bernard	Sigar, Elisabeth	C	
Frie, Maria Francisca	5, May 1855	Joseph	Müller, Louisa	D	34
Friedel, Caspar	26, Dec. 1850	Johan	Metz, Barbara	D	246
Friedel, Catharina	9, Aug. 1857	Jacob	Strewel, Caecilia	A	
Friedel, John	6, Apr. 1856	Johan	----, Barbara	H	
Friedel, Maria	25, Sept 1859	Jacob	Strebel, Caecilia	A	
Friedel, Maria Catharina	4, Apr. 1859	Johan	Klopf, Dorothea	T	
Friedel, Michael	29, Dec. 1853	Johan	Klopf, Dorothea	D	422
Friedman, Josephina	17, Apr. 1853	Conrad	Schussel, Maria Anna	K	
Friedmann, Amalia	1, Oct. 1857	Anton	Bucher, Crescentia	F	
Friedmann, Elisabeth	29, May 1853	Jacob	Holler, Catharine	C	
Friedmann, Joseph	13, June 1855	Anton	Buche, Crescentia	F	
Friedmann, Margaretha	16, Nov. 1851	Jacob	Holler, Catharina	C	
Friedmann, Maria Magdalena	6, Oct. 1850	Jacob	Holler, Catharina	C	
Friedrich, Barbara Catharina	1, June 1858	Francis	Ruchteschel, Elisabeth	K	
Friedrich, Francis	27, Mar. 1853	Fidel	Wangert, Juliana	C	
Friedrich, Friedrich	28, Dec. 1856	Martin	Nienterheim, Anna	C	
Friedrich, Johan	25, Dec. 1858	Martin	Nenderheim, Constantia	C	
Friedrich, Johanna Maria	16, July 1854	Martin	Nintherlein, Constan.	C	
Friedrich, Margaretha	16, Apr. 1854	Adam	Hoffman, Anna	D	8
Friedrich, Margaretha	15, June 1856	Adam	Hofman, Anna Maria	D	60
Friedrich, Veronica	8, Aug. 1858	Ignatius	Semler, Elisabeth	W	23
Frielich, Catharina	1, June 1856	Ignatius	Frauss, Elisabeth	D	59
Frieling, Johanna Elisabeth	27, Oct. 1858	Herman	Hogeloch, Johanna	A	
Frieling, Maria Elisabeth Josephina	15, Dec. 1859	Bernard	Sudmöller, A.M. Sophia	A	

Name of Child	Date of Baptism	Father	Mother	Church	Page
Friemann, Maria Susanna	13, Feb. 1853	Wilhelm	Wiling, Emilia	L	
Friemann, Wilhelmina	5, May 1859	Anton	Bucher, Crescentia	F	
Friend, John	28, Nov. 1851	Matthew	Berchman, Mary	P	13c
Frierdich, Elisabeth	15, Aug. 1852	Ignatius	Semler, Elisabeth	D	343
Frierdick, Joseph	18, Mar. 1854	Ignatius	Simber, Elisabeth	F	
Fries, Andreas	5, Dec. 1857	Nicolaus	Wolf, Maria	H	
Fries, Carolina	4, May 1851	Amand	Steyert, Maria	J	10
Fries, Catharina	15, Nov. 1857	Balthasar	Ganz, Crescentia	D	98
Fries, Eva Barbara	14, Sept 1856	Balthasar	Janz, Crescentia	C	
Fries, Georg	12, May 1859	Balthasar	Janz, Crescentia	D	137
Fries, Georg	26, Sept 1858	Michael A.	Ripberger, Barbara	T	
Fries, Johan	27, Jan. 1856	Peter	Rief, Maria	N	
Fries, Johan	25, Feb. 1855	Philipp	Hakman, Rosina	D	29
Fries, Johan Georg	8, Oct. 1854	Michael	Scheinhof, Maria Anna	D	19
Fries, Margaretha	27, Sept 1857	Friedrich	Endres, Barbara	C	
Fries, Margaretha	29, Feb. 1852	Michael	Rieberg, Barbara	F	
Fries, Maria Magdalena	19, Jan. 1859	Ferdinand	Wanzhof, Dorothea	T	
Fries, Maria Margaretha	1, Aug. 1852	Michael	Scheinhof, Maria Anna	D	341
Fries, Mary Ann	18, May 1856	Michael	Ripberger, Barbara	T	
Fries, Nicolaus	18, Sept 1859	Nicolaus	Wolf, Maria	H	
Fries, Wilhelm Ferdinand	13, Feb. 1853	Georg	Bless, Amantia	D	371
Friesz, Anna Carolina	21, Oct. 1855	Amand	Steyert, Maria Rosa	J	34
Frigge, Franz Wilhelm	9, Sept 1857	Friedrich	Zepfenfeld, Elisabeth	F	
Frilling, Friedrich Heinrich	24, Sept 1852	Bernard	Sudmoeller, Sophia	L	
Frilling, Maria Catharina	10, July 1855	Friedrich	Rolfes, Gertrud	D	38
Frimoldt, Maria Elisabeth	17, Dec. 1851	J. Conrad	Niebrink, Anna Maria Gertrud	K	
Frimorth, Johan Gerhard Heinrich	6, Nov. 1854	Conrad	Niebruken?, Gertrud	K	
Frimoth, Maria Regina Theresa	9, Sept 1856	J. Conrad	Niebrück, Maria Gertrud	K	
Frisby, Ellen	7, Dec. 1856	Mark	----, Mary	M	
Frisby, Mary	4, Apr. 1858	Mark	----, Mary	M	
Frisch, Carolina Philomena	6, Jan. 1856	J. Joseph	Ott, Marianna	F	
Frisch, Catharina	26, Oct. 1856	Georg	Spreng---, Margaretha	D	70
Frisch, Francisca	31, May 1857	Hieronymus	Emit, Catharina	D	86
Frisch, Maria Louisa	8, Aug. 1858	Joseph	Blank, Marianna	F	
Frisch, Rosa	15, June 1854	Hieronymus	Emit, Catharina	D	12
Frische, Johan Friedrich	19, Oct. 1851	Heinrich	Rehenn, Lisetta	D	288
Frischer, Maria Catharina	10, Feb. 1854	Heinrich	Wippers, Elisabeth	D	4
Frishe, Bernard Christina	6, Aug. 1850	Heinrich	Wibel, Elisabeth	D	227
Friske, Theodora Friedrica	22, Mar. 1857	J. Heinrich	Wibbel, Elisabeth	D	81
Frissen, James	12, Nov. 1853	Dennis	Jagan, Joanne	E	143
Fritsch, Agatha	26, July 1851	Georg	Streubig, Cordille	F	
Fritsch, Anna Barbara	16, Apr. 1854	Francis	Reselag, Clara	F	
Fritsch, Anton	9, Mar. 1851	Anton	Sess, Agnes	K	
Fritsch, Catharina	22, Feb. 1852	Lawrence	Späth, Euphrosina	K	
Fritsch, Erhard	21, Apr. 1850	Simon	Schmer, Regina	D	210
Fritsch, Gertrud	26, July 1851	Georg	Streubig, Cordille	F	
Fritsch, Heinrich	10, May 1854		Fritsch, Magdalena	D	10
Fritsch, Johan Georg	1, Aug. 1858	Francis	Roessler, Clara	C	
Fritsch, Johan Nicolaus	4, Mar. 1855	Nicolaus	Bauman, Elisabeth Catharina	K	
Fritsch, Johan Peter	16, June 1850	Anton	Laux, Felicitas	L	
Fritsch, Joseph Wilhelm	5, June 1853	Nicolaus	Bauman, Elisabeth	K	
Fritsch, Louisa	19, Sept 1852	Francis	Roesler, Clara	C	
Fritsch, Ludwig	24, Aug. 1856	Francis	Resel, Clara	J	38
Fritsch, Maria Caecilia	30, Jan. 1853	Anton	Lins, Felicitas	L	
Fritsch, Maria Kunigunda	2, May 1858	Michael	Roesler, Barbara	F	
Fritsch, Marianna Ottilia	6, Mar. 1853	Francis J.	Ott, Marianna	F	
Fritsch, Michael	25, July 1851	Nicolaus	Peckmann, Euphrosina	C	
Fritsch, Michael Friedrich	2, Aug. 1857	Nicolaus	Bauman, Elisabeth	K	
Fritsch, Nicolaus	15, Dec. 1852	Simon	----, Regina	D	361

Name of Child	Date of Baptism	Father	Mother	Church	Page
Fritsch, Rosina	27, July 1854	Georg	Straubel, Cordula	F	
Fritsche, Maria	9, Dec. 1859	Martin	Roed- -, Barbara	D	152
Fritz, Anna Margaretha	15, Feb. 1857	Joseph	Roehle, Agatha	F	
Fritz, Heinrich	3, Jan. 1852	Carl	Bisel, Elisabeth	F	
Fritz, Josephina	19, Mar. 1858	Friedrich	Renger, Rufina	D	107
Fritz, Ludwig	28, Jan. 1850	Ludwig	Burckhart, Catharina	K	
Fritz, Ludwig Carl	27, Jan. 1856	Friedrich	Renner, Rufina	C	
Fritz, Maria Louisa	8, Sept 1859	Friedrich	Renger, Rufina	D	146
Fritz, Maria Rosa	26, Dec. 1856	Friedrich	Renner, Rufina	C	
Fritz, Maria Theresa	18, July 1858	Mathias	Klein---, Catharina	D	115
Fritz, Simon	24, Oct. 1852		Fritz, Thecla	F	
Fritz, Wilhelm	23, Jan. 1859	Johan	Reinsta---, Walburga	D	129
Fritze, Joseph Wilhelm	7, Feb. 1858	Wilhelm	Gummen, Maria	A	
Frizzel, Bridget	1, Feb. 1858	William	Higgins, Bridget	E	514
Frizzel, John	10, Apr. 1856	William	Higgins, Bridget	E	357
Frizzell, Mary Jane	8, Mar. 1855	William	Higgins, Bridget	E	270
Frizzle, Catherine	15, Nov. 1859	William	----, Bridget	E	671
Frizzle, Patrick	10, Mar. 1859	John	Finn, Bridget	E	610
Fr--ker, Mathias	2, Aug. 1857	Johan	Braun, Johanna	D	92
Froehlich, Anna Margaretha	11, Oct. 1851	Carl	Mueller, Margaretha	F	
Froehlich, Carl Aloysius	10, Oct. 1858	Johan	Brill, Catharina	F	
Froehlich, Catharina	3, July 1853	Carl	Mueller, Margaretha	F	
Froehlich, Clara	18, Apr. 1856	Johan	Brill, Catharina	F	
Froehlich, Johan Adam	29, Oct. 1855	Carl	Mueller, Margaretha	F	
Froehlich, Johan Aloysius	10, May 1854	Johan	Brill, Catharina	F	
Froehlich, Philipp	24, Jan. 1858	Carl	Müller, Margaretha	Q	26
Froehlich, Veronica	19, Jan. 1852	Johan	Brill, Catharina	F	
Froelker, Johan Heinrich	21, Oct. 1856	Heinrich	Meyers, Elisabeth	F	
Froelking, Carl	7, Nov. 1858	August	Marmet, Clementina	T	
Froelking, Paulina Clara	23, Nov. 1856	August	Malmet, Clementina	C	
Froendhoff, Catharina Josephina E.	5, Feb. 1852	J.H.	Hackmann, Theresa	L	
Froendhoff, Friedrich Wilhelm	23, June 1854	Georg	Diestelhorst, M. Engel	L	
Froendhoff, Maria Elisabeth	3, Oct. 1852	Georg	Disselhoff, M. Engel	L	
Fröhle, Bernard Heinrich	21, Aug. 1850	Herman H.	Kleinriths, Elisabeth	D	229
Frohle, Catharina Regina	24, Aug. 1858	Joseph	Koch, Regina	K	
Fröhle, Maria Elisabeth	12, Oct. 1852	Herman H.	Lück, Maria Gertrud	D	352
Frohmueller, Anna Maria	13, June 1859	Thomas	Goetz, Margaretha	F	
Frohmueller, Johan Philipp	15, Apr. 1857	Thomas	Goetz, A. Margaretha	F	
Frohmueller, Michel	6, Aug. 1854	Thomas	Goetz, Anna Margaretha	F	
Fröhmüller, Anna Barbara	29, Jan. 1857	Philipp	Speckner, Barbara	D	77
Frohmüller, Francis Xavier	20, July 1854	Philipp	Speckner, Barbara	D	14
Frohmüller, Johan Thomas	21, Oct. 1855	Philipp	Speckner, Barbara	D	45
Frohmuller, Michael	11, Aug. 1858	Philipp	Speckner, Barbara	D	117
Frohn, Michael	20, Mar. 1858	P.	Vagedes, Catharina	A	
Frohndorf, Catherine	2, Nov. 1852	Francis	----, Mary	H	
Frohndorf, Elisabeth	28, Dec. 1854	Francis	----, Maria	H	
Frohning, Johan Heinrich Florenz	27, Oct. 1850	Bernard	Wehrkamp, Elisabeth	F	
Frohoff, Anna Maria Elisabeth	12, Oct. 1858	Anton	Tarp, Gertrud	A	
Frohoff, Heinrich Anton	13, Dec. 1853	Anton	Darp, Maria Gertrud	D	420
Frohoff, Johan Francis	18, Jan. 1856	Anton	Tarp, Maria Gertrud	A	
Frolicher, Heinrich	28, Apr. 1850	Stephan	Plettner, Maria	K	
Fromm, Anton	12, Sept 1857	Anton	Jons, Elisabeth	A	
Fromm, Maria Elisabeth	10, July 1857	Gerhard H.	Dresmier, Margaretha	D	89
Frommeier, Gerhard Heinrich	9, Aug. 1854	Joseph	Stegman, Maria Anna	K	
Frommel, Peter	4, July 1851	Johan	Schule, Margaretha	K	
Frommer, Johan	1, Feb. 1857	Johan	Schuler, Margaretha	L	
Frommeyer, Angela Catharina	6, Feb. 1853	Friedrich	Straukamp, M. Elis.	L	
Frommeyer, Anna Maria Elisabeth	21, Mar. 1856	Eberhard	Fideldei, Elisabeth	C	
Frommeyer, Catharina	14, Mar. 1856	Heinrich	Melcher, Angela	A	

Name of Child	Date of Baptism	Father	Mother	Church	Page
Frommeyer, Francis Heinrich	10, Aug. 1851	Heinrich	Melcher, Angela	C	
Frommeyer, Francis Heinrich	10, June 1850	Wilhelm	Meers, Elisabeth	A	
Frommeyer, Francisca	12, Mar. 1853	Eberhard	Fideldei, Anna M.	C	
Frommeyer, Johan Joseph	21, Mar. 1857	J. Francis	Straukamp, Maria Elisabeth	A	
Frommeyer, Joseph Johan Heinrich	27, Sept 1853	Herman	Klekamp, Maria A.	L	
Frommeyer, Maria	26, Apr. 1857	Joseph	Stegman, Anna	K	
Frommeyer, Maria Agnes	21, Nov. 1858	Heinrich	Melch, Agnes Maria	A	
Frommeyer, Maria Bernardina	1, Jan. 1854	Heinrich	Melcher, Maria Angela	A	
Frommeyer, Maria Bernardina	15, Jan. 1851	Herman	Klekamp, Anna Maria	L	
Frommeyer, Maria Catharina	21, Mar. 1856	Eberhard	Fideldei, Elisabeth	C	
Frommeyer, Maria Elisabeth	26, June 1859	Joseph	Stegmann, Maria Anna	C	
Frommeyer, Maria Engel	5, Oct. 1851	Eberhard	Fiedeldei, Elisabeth	L	
Frommeyer, Maria Louisa	3, Oct. 1852	Joseph	Steckman, Anna	K	
Frommeyer, Maria Theresa	28, Sept 1858	Eberhard	Fideldei, Maria	C	
Frommeyer, Philomena Cath. Cäcilia	31, Dec. 1850	J. Friedrich	Straukamp, Maria Elisabeth	A	
Frömmling, Anna Maria	11, July 1856	Johan	Wallman, Elisabeth Gertrud	A	
Frommling, Johan Bernard	30, July 1858	Johan	Wallman, Maria Gertrud	A	
Frömmling, Maria Elisabeth	14, July 1854	Johan	Wallman, Gertrud	A	
Frondauf, Carolina	3, May 1857	Francis	Kellin, Maria	D	84
Frondhoff, Cath. Elis. Friedricka	1, Sept 1850	Herman	Hackmann, Theresa	L	
Frondhoff, Catharina Friedricka	19, Dec. 1855	Herman	Hackmann, M. Theresa	L	
Frondhoff, Catharine Elisabeth	6, Feb. 1853	Anton	Balke, Louise	C	
Frondhoff, Franz Anton Herman	21, Sept 1853	Herman	Hackmann, Theresa	L	
Frondhoff, Johan Herman Georg	1, June 1851	Georg	Disterhorst, Maria A.	L	
Frondhoff, Margaretha Emilia	26, Oct. 1857	Herman	Hackmann, Theresa	L	
Frondorf, Barbara	19, June 1853	Philipp	Mill, Eva	C	
Frondorf, Georg	17, Aug. 1851	Francis	Helling, Maria	D	278
Frondorf, Heinrich	31, Mar. 1850	Philipp	Maechl, Maria Anna	C	
Front, Mary Emily	5, Sept 1856		adult - 23 years old	V	33
Frost, Emilia	25, July 1858	Caspar	----, Anna Maria	T	
Frueth, Friedrich	17, Apr. 1853	Valentin	Briederlen, Maria Anna	K	
Frühling, Francis Ferdinand	2, Nov. 1853	Friedrich	Meiers, Elisabeth	D	413
Frühling, Helena	5, Sept 1856	Friedrich	Rof, Gertrud	D	66
Frülling, Johan Friedrich	22, Jan. 1852	Friedrich	Mayer, Maria Elisabeth	D	303
Fruth, Anna Maria Catharina	15, Apr. 1855	Valentin	Bonert, Catharina	K	
Fruth, Carolina	29, Jan. 1859	Eugene	Fruth, Salome	K	
Fruth, Joseph	10, May 1857	Valentin	Bonert, Catharina	K	
Fruth, Maria Margaretha	11, Sept 1859	Valentin	Bonert, Catharina	K	
Fry, Elizabeth	22, Apr. 1855	Francis	Fally, Ann	E	282
Fry, Thomas	15, July 1858	Francis	Farrell, Ann	E	549
Ftizgerald, Honora	27, May 1853	James	Dram, Catherine	P	42
Ftizgerald, Peter	1, June 1856	Peter	Johnston, Joanne	P	181
Ftizpatrick, Mary	5, Sept 1852	Patrick	Elevin, Ann	R	
Fuchs, Anna Maria	27, Feb. 1859	Conrad	Fehr, Susanna	T	
Fuchs, Barbara Paulina	30, Aug. 1850	Martin	Pfeifer, Josephina	F	
Fuchs, Carolina	7, May 1854	Joseph	Griffen, Sara	F	
Fuchs, Francis	7, Aug. 1854	Francis	Bath, Elisabeth	D	15
Fuchs, Francis	5, June 1851	Nicolaus	Schaefer, Catharina	D	267
Fuchs, Francisca Catharina	19, Sept 1857	Nicolaus	----, Catharina	R	
Fuchs, Helen	30, Jan. 1858	Johan	----, Magdalena	R	
Fuchs, Johan	29, Apr. 1855	Johan	Heider, Magdalena	R	
Fuchs, Joseph	23, Mar. 1856	Joseph	Griffen, Sara	F	
Fuchs, Magdalena	5, Mar. 1857	Johan	----, Magdalena	R	
Fuchs, Margaretha	27, Sept 1855	Nicolaus	Schaefer, Cahtarina	R	
Fuchs, Maria Amanda	30, Aug. 1850	Martin	Pfeifer, Josephina	F	
Fuchs, Maria Catharina	7, Feb. 1853	Martin	Pfeifer, Josephina	A	
Fuchs, Maria Margaretha	25, Feb. 1855	Martin	Pfeifer, Josephina	A	
Fuchs, Maria Theresa	29, Sept 1859	Johan	Wolthaus, Elisabeth	C	
Fuchs, Michael	24, Apr. 1851	Johan	Heidel, Magdalena	D	262

Name of Child	Date of Baptism	Father	Mother	Church	Page
Fuchs, Michael	8, Aug. 1858	Joseph	Griffin, Rosalia	G	
Fuchs, Nicolaus	23, June 1856	Francis	Bath, Elisabeth	D	61
Fuchs, Nicolaus	29, Nov. 1853	Nicolaus	Schaefer, Catharina	D	417
Fuchs, Regina	15, Oct. 1854	Conrad	Vehr, Susanna	D	20
Fuchs, Theresa	10, Aug. 1858	Gerhard	----, Theresa	D	116
Fuchs, Theresa	12, Oct. 1851	Peter	Kaufer, Anna Maria	J	12
Fuchs, Wilhelm August	4, Aug. 1852	J. Philipp	Heidel, Magdalena	D	341
Fueglein, Anna Maria	19, Apr. 1859	Andreas	Huber, Theresa	F	
Fueglein, Heinrich	4, July 1856	Andreas	Hubert, Theresa	F	
Fueglein, Johan Heinrich	12, June 1853	Andreas	Huber, Theresa	F	
Fueglein, Joseph	27, Oct. 1850	Andreas	Huber, Theresa	F	
Fueglein, Michael	25, Aug. 1856	Michael	Post, Anna Maria	F	
Fuerst, Adelheid Catharina	20, Nov. 1859	Johan	Busch, Genofeva	C	
Fuerst, Emilia Carolina	28, Mar. 1858	Benedict	Busch, Genofeva	C	
Fuerst, Johan	16, Mar. 1851	Johan	Honert, Cunigunda	C	
Fugassi, Maria Virginia	28, Aug. 1859	Giovanni	Nasani, Maria Rosa	K	
Fuhl, Francisca	27, Oct. 1850	Marc	Kaufman, Christina	D	240
Führing, Catharina Philomena	11, Feb. 1851	B. Theodor	Brommelhaus, Christina	J	10
Fuldner, Heinrich	2, June 1852	Jacob	Oberlander, Clara	F	
Fulert, Johan Heinrich	2, Dec. 1856	J. Heinrich	Holera, M. Elisabeth	L	
Fulert, Maria Elisabeth	10, Mar. 1851	Bernard H.	Holera, Elisabeth	L	
Fullbright, John	19, Jan. 1859	Alfred	----, Mary Jane	E	597
Fullbright, Joseph	19, Jan. 1859	Alfred	----, Mary Jane	E	597
Fullbright, Mary Ann	19, Jan. 1859	Alfred	----, Mary Jane	E	597
Fullbright, Mary Jane	19, Jan. 1859		adult - 43 years old	E	597
Fullenkamp, Bernard	7, Oct. 1859	Heinrich	Thesing, Carolina	K	
Fullenkamp, Johan Heinrich	10, May 1855	Heinrich	Thesing, Catharina	L	
Fuller, Mary	21, Feb. 1853	Patrick	----, Judy	E	64
Fuller, Mary Emily	29, Aug. 1858	William	Barnes, Emma	E	560
Fullert, Johan Wilhelm	2, June 1852	Heinrich	Holera, Elisabeth	L	
Funk, Johan Adam	18, Jan. 1852	Francis	Spaar, Maria	D	302
Funk, Joseph	28, Mar. 1858	Heinrich	Kramig, Louisa	C	
Funk, Maria	13, May 1853	Francis	Spar, Maria	C	
Funk, Maria	30, June 1854	Francis	Spare, Maria	D	13
Funke, August Heinrich	24, Aug. 1856	Heinrich	Kramig, Louisa	D	65
Funke, Francis John	10, Sept 1854	Henry	----, Louise	H	
Furcy, August Anton	29, Feb. 1852	August	Hegel, Augustina	F	
Furlong, Bridget	6, Apr. 1854	Nicolaus	Colliton, Joanne	R	
Furlong, Catherine	23, Nov. 1856	Lawrence	Murphy, Margaret	P	199
Furlong, James	22, June 1856	James	----, Anastasia	M	
Furlong, John	15, July 1856	Nicolaus	----, Joanne	R	
Furlong, Mary Ann	18, Dec. 1853	James	Murphy, Ann	P	62
Furlong, Mary Ann	6, May 1855	James	Murphy, Ann	P	130
Furlong, Mary Ann	20, Oct. 1850	Martin	Templeton, Catherine	B	217
Furlong, Thomas Patrick	29, Nov. 1859	James	Murphy, Ann	P	304
Furlough, James	5, Aug. 1857	James	Murphy, Ann	P	219
Furnis, Emil Eugene	24, July 1853	Johan	Fuss, Josephina	C	
Fury, Mary	17, Aug. 1856	Peter	Henson, Mary	P	188
Fussen, Johan Joseph	31, Oct. 1851	Johan	Krimm, Anna Maria	D	289
Fussner, Margaretha	25, Nov. 1853	Johan	Krämer, Maria Anna	D	417
Fussner, Maria Anna Louisa	20, Jan. 1850	Michael	Miller, Caecilia	D	200
Fusswinkel, Anna Maria	15, Jan. 1852	Johan	Sönchen, Elisabeth	D	302
Fuszner, Mathilda Paulina Adelheid	23, June 1852	Michael	Miller, Caecilia	D	326
Fynn, Helen	22, Dec. 1859	John	Roddin, Mary	E	678
Gabenesch, Anton	28, Mar. 1858	Christoph	Lett, Elisabeth	T	
Gabennesch, Dina	3, Nov. 1850	Christoph	Loth, Elisabeth	K	
Gabennesch, Maria Cathrina	23, Apr. 1854	Christoph	Lett, Elisabeth	F	
Gabriel, Barbara	26, Oct. 1856	Peter	Geissler, Margaretha	F	
Gabriel, Cunigunda	30, Apr. 1854	Peter	----, Margaret	H	

Name of Child	Date of Baptism	Father	Mother	Church	Page
Gabriel, Georg	20, Jan. 1850	Peter	Geisler, Margaretha	H	
Gabriel, Herman	15, June 1851	John	Fischer, Barbara	H	
Gabriel, Jacob	18, May 1852	Mathias	Kruseck, Gertrud	K	
Gabriel, Johan Adam	12, Sept 1858	Johan	Fischer, Walburga	T	
Gabriel, John	5, Feb. 1854	Richard	Sheridan, Margaret	P	67
Gabriel, Maria Barbara	5, Sept 1853	Johan	Fischer, Barbara	F	
Gabriel, Maria Carolina	6, Apr. 1856	Johan	Fischer, Walburga	W	12
Gabriel, Michael	24, Jan. 1852	Peter	----, Margaret	H	
Gabriel, Richard	9, Sept 1855	Richard	Sheridan, Margaret	P	150
Gabriel, Sarah Elizabeth	21, July 1852	John	Sheridan, Nanna	P	25
Gabriel, William	15, Aug. 1854	John	Sheridan, Ann	P	92
Gabriel, William	2, Oct. 1859	Peter	Geissler, Margaretha	H	
Gäcking, Johan	13, Mar. 1859	Johan	Stöky, Anna Maria	D	134
Gaebe, Maria Elisabeth Sophia	27, June 1859	Theodor	Schrader, Mina	U	
Gaecking, Adelheid Catharina	7, Feb. 1855	Gerhard J.	Story, Maria Anna	D	28
Gaertner, Anna Maria	25, Jan. 1857	Conrad	Schott, Elisabeth	F	
Gaertner, Carl	24, Sept 1854	Conrad	Schatt, Elisabeth	F	
Gaertner, Edward Adolph	20, Sept 1858	Sebastian	Weichel, Catharina	C	
Gaertner, Johan	9, Jan. 1853	Conrad	Schardt, Elisabeth	F	
Gaertner, Johan	10, Mar. 1850	Johan	Marfort, Maria	C	
Gaertner, Joseph Alois	18, Mar. 1856	Sebastian	Weigler, Catharina	C	
Gaertner, Theresa	2, Jan. 1859	Conrad	Schirth, Elisabeth	F	
Gaertner, Wilhelm Clemens	3, Nov. 1853	Sebastian	Weigel, Catharina	C	
Gaerty, James	23, July 1854	Bernard	Leighy, Eliza	B	3
Gaffney, Andrew	4, Feb. 1855	John	Fisher, Helen	P	118
Gaffney, Andrew	8, Jan. 1856	Patrick	----, Ann	E	336
Gaffney, Andrew	23, Sept 1850	Thomas	----, Ann	E	250
Gaffney, Ann	21, July 1851	Patrick	Conlin, Ann	E	326
Gaffney, Bernard	21, Feb. 1855	Thomas	Lynch, Ann	P	121
Gaffney, Catherine	12, Sept 1858	Edward	Roony, Catherine	E	562
Gaffney, Ellen	1, June 1851	John	Fisher, Ellen	P	8
Gaffney, Helen	16, May 1853	Thomas	Lynch, Ann	E	90
Gaffney, Isabel	30, Mar. 1858	John	Fisher, Helen	P	244
Gaffney, James	24, July 1853	John	Fisher, Helen	P	47
Gaffney, Mary	7, July 1853	Patrick	Conlan, Ann	B	295
Gaffney, Mary Alice	21, Mar. 1854	Thomas	Cady, Mary	B	311
Gaffney, Mary Jane	11, Mar. 1852	Thomas	Lynch, Ann	E	391
Gaffney, Michael	18, July 1852		Gaffney, Mary	R	
Gaffney, Patrick	2, Apr. 1858	Patrick	Connolin, Ann	P	244
Gaffney, Thomas	3, Feb. 1857	Thomas	Lynch, Ann	E	430
Gafney, John	29, June 1856	Edward	Rooney, Catherine	V	31
Gafney, Thomas	28, May 1854	Edward	Rooney, Catherine	V	14
Gagan, John	13, Apr. 1859	Thomas	Hennessy, Margaret	E	617
Gagan, Thomas	28, Dec. 1855	Michael	Maghen, Joanne	P	164
Gagegan, Mary	9, Feb. 1851	Thomas	----, Margaret	E	282
Gahagan, Joanne	5, Sept 1852	Thomas	Henzey, Margaret	E	14
Gahn, Eva	9, Jan. 1851	Conrad	Stern, Margaretha Eva	D	248
Gahn, Johan	21, Sept 1856	Conrad	Stern, Eva	D	68
Gahn, Maria Anna	23, Oct. 1853	Conrad	Stern, Eva	D	411
Gahr, Johan	28, Sept 1856	Michael	Huber, Maria	D	68
Gahr, Joseph	13, Feb. 1859	Michael	Huber, Maria	D	131
Gahr, Michael	27, Mar. 1855	Michael	Herber, Maria	D	32
Gail, Bridget Rachel	28, May 1854	Peter	McVeigh, Mary	V	14
Gainer, Ann	12, Oct. 1854	Dennis	Dormody, Ellen	E	231
Gaing, Johan Herman	24, Nov. 1850	Heinrich	Vopper, Margaretha	F	
Galbreth, Alexander James	26, May 1859	George	Cunningham, Mary Joanne	T	
Galerest?, Thomas	6, Aug. 1852	James	----, Bridget	M	
Galice, Bernard	6, Apr. 1855	Bernard	----, Cecilia	E	277
Galich, Johan Franz	18, Dec. 1854	J. Mathias	Meiermann, Elisabeth	L	

Name of Child	Date of Baptism	Father	Mother	Church	Page
Gall, Jacob	6, Jan. 1855	Jacob	adult - 27 years old	K	
Gall, Rhoda	30, Mar. 1855		adult	B	13
Gall, Rosa Louisa	12, Aug. 1855	Ludwig	Würmel, Margaretha	D	40
Gallagar, Elisabeth Helen	7, Sept 1859	James	Quinn, Helen	U	
Gallagher, Bridget	29, Sept 1855	Patrick	Boyle, Mary	P	152
Gallagher, Caecila Jane	29, Nov. 1857	Patrick	Kenny, Mary E.	E	495
Gallagher, Catherine	2, Oct. 1859	Patrick	----, Mary	M	
Gallagher, Catherine	2, Oct. 1855	Thomas	McLaughlin, Ann	P	153
Gallagher, Cornelius	11, Oct. 1853	Patrick	Boyle, Mary	P	54
Gallagher, Edward	11, Oct. 1857	Edward	McFarland, Mary	P	**227**
Gallagher, Edward	7, Sept 1856	Francis	McGiveny, Ann	P	191
Gallagher, Edward	19, Feb. 1854	John	Mullen, Joanne	P	69
Gallagher, Elizabeth	22, Mar. 1859	George	Gill, Jane	B	73
Gallagher, Ellen	17, Jan. 1858	Simon	Gallagher, Bridget	B	54
Gallagher, Francis	6, May 1856	John	Mullen, Joanne	P	178
Gallagher, George	22, Apr. 1855	Simon	Gallagher, Bridget	B	14
Gallagher, Helen	1, Jan. 1854	Francis	McGivney, Ann	P	64
Gallagher, Helen	25, June 1854	Patrick	Sweeney, Margaret	P	86
Gallagher, Henry	2, June 1850	John	Fary, Catherine	E	217
Gallagher, James	30, Sept 1859	Edward	McFarland, Mary	P	298
Gallagher, James	13, June 1852	John	Mullen, Joanne	P	23
Gallagher, James	5, Aug. 1855	Michael	Gilson, Catherine	U	
Gallagher, James	29, Mar. 1851	Patrick	McCann, Sabina	B	227
Gallagher, John	4, Dec. 1853	Edward	Carthy, Catherine	B	304
Gallagher, John	13, July 1850	James	Gallagher, Mary	B	207
Gallagher, John	13, June 1858	James	Sweeney, Catherine	P	250
Gallagher, John	22, May 1857	John	Connahan, Joanne	E	455
Gallagher, John	3, Aug. 1856	Patrick	McCann, Sabina	P	186
Gallagher, John	27, Mar. 1854	Peter	Coyne, Mary	P	76
Gallagher, Joseph	7, Aug. 1859	Simon	Gallagher, Bridget	B	79
Gallagher, Joseph	29, Mar. 1858		Gallagher, Jane	P	244
Gallagher, Margaret	30, Jan. 1853	Patrick	Brogan, Catherine	P	34
Gallagher, Margaret	17, June 1859	Patrick	Lawless, Mary	P	286
Gallagher, Mary	30, Mar. 1851	Charles	Nash, Mary	B	228
Gallagher, Mary	13, Aug. 1854	James	----, Ann	M	
Gallagher, Mary	5, Aug. 1855	James	Quinn, Ellen	U	
Gallagher, Mary	8, May 1853	Patrick	McAnn, Sabina	B	290
Gallagher, Mary Ann	4, Feb. 1852	Francis	McGivney, Ann	B	252
Gallagher, Mary Ann	8, May 1857	George	Gill, Jane	B	44
Gallagher, Mary Ann	26, July 1853	James	Gallagher, Mary	P	48
Gallagher, Mary Jane	24, Aug. 1856	Simon	Gallagher, Bridget	B	33
Gallagher, Michael	12, Apr. 1856	James	----, Mary	R	
Gallagher, Patrick	11, Oct. 1853	Patrick	Boyle, Mary	P	54
Gallagher, Peter	16, May 1852	James	Coolikan, Ann	P	21
Gallagher, Rose Ann	20, Feb. 1858	John	Fitzsimmons, Mary	P	240
Gallagher, Seraphina	7, Mar. 1852	James	----, Mary	R	
Gallagher, Thomas	10, Mar. 1850	Patrick	Jordan, Bridget	B	197
Gallagher, Thomas	18, Feb. 1855	Patrick	McCann, Sabina	P	120
Gallagher, Thomas Henry	3, Nov. 1854	Thomas	McCarthy, Ellen	B	7
Gallagher, Thomas William	19, Dec. 1858	Michael	King, Mary	B	68
Gallagher?, Ann	15, May 1855	Thomas	McGrerty, Mary	P	133
Gallaghn, William Charles	9, July 1855	George	Dunn, Jean	B	16
Gallaher, George	20, Feb.1859	John	Fitzsimmons, Mary	P	276
Gallaher, Patrick	10, July 1853	James	Quinn, Helen	B	295
Galland, Maria Anna	1, May 1853	Caspar	Hutzler, Margaretha	D	383
Galland, Michael	12, July 1857	Caspar	Heyler, Margaretha	D	90
Gallane, Mary	2, Apr. 1854	John	Kepple, Mary Ann	B	312
Gallant, Cunigunda	16, Nov. 1851	Caspar	Heyler, Margaretha	D	293
Gallant, Johan Baptist	5, Aug. 1855	Caspar	Hutzler, Margaretha	C	

Name of Child	Date of Baptism	Father	Mother	Church	Page
Gallant, Rosina	13, Mar. 1859	Caspar	Hutzler, Margaretha	T	
Galleno, Christina	18, Oct. 1857	Joseph	Gatty, Mary	E	486
Gallier, Edward Hieronymus	20, Apr. 1856	Edward	McCarthy, Catherine	P	177
Galligan, Ann Mary	7, Mar. 1859	Daniel	Queen, Catherine	P	278
Galligan, Catherine	12, Mar. 1854	Peter	Keown, Mary	P	73
Galligan, Margaret	3, Aug. 1856	Michael	Murphy, Ann	E	387
Galligan, Mary	16, Feb. 1851	Peter	Congan, Mary	B	225
Galligan, Patrick	9, June 1852	Patrick	Smith, Ann	B	260
Galligan, Thomas	30, Nov. 1856	Peter	Keoghan, Mary	P	200
Galligher, John	16, Dec. 1850	John	Griffin, Mary	B	220
Gallino, Peter Louis	15, Jan. 1856	Joseph	Gatti, Maria	P	166
Gallowan, Catherine	25, July 1858	Richard	Murphy, Ann	S	
Galloway, James	12, Dec. 1852	Patrick	Kelly, Mary	B	277
Galloway, Maria Alica	13, July 1856	Joseph	Rielly, Mary Ann	C	
Galvin, Elizabeth	15, Sept 1858	Thomas	Morrarty, Ann	E	563
Galvin, John	29, May 1853	James	----, Honora	M	
Galvin, John	27, July 1853	James	Galvin, Ellenore	E	113
Galvin, John	5, Dec. 1850	Michael	Quinn, Helen	B	220
Galvin, Margaret	21, Jan. 1857	Thomas	----, Ann	E	428
Galvin, Mary	12, July 1855		Galvin, Helen	E	299
Galvin, Maurice	25, Aug. 1855	Thomas	Moriarty, Ann	V	26
Galvin, Michael	15, May 1859	Maurice	Cronin, Ellen	E	625
Galvin, Patrick	8, June 1851	John	Langer, Mary	P	8
Gambel, Catharina Josephina	7, Feb. 1858	J. Peter	Schlichte, Maria Magdalena	D	105
Gamble, Ann Jane	8, Sept 1853	Thomas	Lawler, Catherine	B	298
Gamble, Catherine	29, Dec. 1858	Thomas	Lawler, Catherine	B	69
Gamble, David	5, June 1855	Thomas	Lawlor, Catherine	B	15
Gamble, John	12, Dec. 1859	Maurice	Ducy, Bridget	P	306
Gamble, Mary	5, Sept 1857	Maurice	Ducey, Bridget	P	222
Gamble, Mary Virginia	12, Apr. 1850	John	Ryan, Jane	E	210
Gamble, William	7, Jan. 1857	Thomas	Lawler, Catherine	B	39
Gamm, Maria Elisabeth	2, Nov. 1856	Gerhard	Corte, Catharina	F	
Gammel, Anna Maria	6, Jan. 1855	Peter	Miller, Maria Elisabeth	D	26
Gammel, Catharina Rosa	12, Dec. 1855	J. Peter	Schlichte, Maria Magdalena	D	48
Gammel, Francis Heinrich	29, May 1856	Peter	Müller, Maria Elisabeth	D	59
Gammel, Heinrich Ludwig	25, Oct. 1853	J. Peter	Schlichte, Maria Magdalena	D	411
Gammel, Johan Anton	22, Oct. 1851	Peter	Müller, Elisabeth	D	288
Gammel, Johan Peter	11, June 1851	Johan	Schoepper, Catharina	D	267
Gammel, Maria Magdalena	22, Sept 1852	Johan	Schöpper, Maria Catharina	D	349
Gammel, Maria Magdalena	28, Feb. 1853	Peter	Muller, Maria Elisabeth	D	374
Gammen, Anton	7, Sept 1856	Johan	Schöpper, Catharina M.	D	67
Gance, Daniel	15, Dec. 1850	Dennis	----, Ellenore	E	268
Gander, Georg A.	16, Oct. 1859	Georg	Ebert, Maria Anna	L	
Gander, Josephina	3, Sept 1855	Georg	Eckert, Anna Maria	L	
Gander, Philomena	26, June 1859	Joseph	Rusch--, Cunigunda	D	141
Gandolfa, Angela	25, Nov. 1854	Stephan	Atkins, Sarah	B	8
Gandolfina, Mary Ann	9, Nov. 1856	Stephan	Atkins, Sarah	B	36
Gandolfo, Giovanni Luigi	28, Sept 1856	Francis	Ruperta, Johanna	K	
Ganey, Bridget	3, Nov. 1850	Humprhey	Murphy, Catherine	M	
Ganiland?, Michael Charles	9, May 1859	Bernard	----, Mary	B	75
Ganmeley, Edward	11, Mar. 1855	John	Rumpers, Ann	P	125
Gannan, John Joseph	23, Dec. 1850	John	----, Mary	E	269
Gannan, Mary Ann	13, Mar. 1859	Patrick	Reilly, Bridget	P	279
Gannan, Peter	11, Jan. 1857	John	----, Mary	M	
Ganney, Elisabeth	22, Aug. 1852	Michael	Sahle, Margaretha	J	18
Gannon, Ann	7, May 1854	Michael	----, Catherine	E	188
Gannon, Charles Richard	5, Jan. 1850	Martin	Keegan, Mary Ann	B	193
Gannon, Honora	27, July 1852	James	----, Ellen	E	433
Gannon, Honora	5, Aug. 1855	John	----, Mary	M	

Name of Child	Date of Baptism	Father	Mother	Church	Page
Gannon, James	2, June 1851	Richard	Mulvany, Rose	E	312
Gannon, John	27, Feb. 1853	John	----, Mary	E	66
Gannon, John James	29, Sept 1851	Thomas	Gannan, Bridget	E	347
Gannon, Margaret	20, June 1858	James	Moran, Julia	B	60
Gannon, Marianne	13, May 1856	Patrick	----, Margaret	E	366
Gannon, Michael	26, Sept 1852	James	Farrell, Margaret	E	20
Gannon, Paul	30, June 1858	John	----, Mary	M	
Gannon, Thomas	14, June 1854	John	Fann---, Bridget	B	1
Gans, Francis Gerhard	24, Nov. 1853	Gerhard	Rücken, Carolina	D	416
Ganter, Benjamin	20, Jan. 1853	Casian	Hebel, Catharina	L	
Ganter, Catharina Apollonia	20, Oct. 1850	Caspian	Hubel, Catharina	L	
Ganter, Maria Theresa	27, Sept 1857	Georg	Evert, Anna Maria	L	
Ganter, Martin	8, Nov. 1853	Martin	Gruber, Theresa	N	17
Ganter, Rosalia	20, Oct. 1850	Martin	Huber, Theresa	L	
Gantzer, Daniel	13, May 1855	Michael	Hirzel, Maria Magdalena	D	34
Ganz, Johan	29, Aug. 1854	Lawrence	Ganz, Maria Anna	D	16
Ganzer, Maria Magdalena	30, Oct. 1853	Michael	Hirzel, Maria Magdalena	D	412
Garagan, Margaret	18, Apr. 1852	Peter	----, Catherine	E	403
Garaghan?, Thomas Kennedy	26, Aug. 1854	Patrick	----, Mary	B	4
Garaghty, Joanne	26, Nov. 1854	Thomas	Seery, Mary Ann	P	105
Garaghty, Mary Jane	19, Feb. 1857	Thomas	Heffernan, Mary Ann	P	206
Garaghty, Thomas	26, Apr. 1854	Daniel	Turnan, Margaret	B	313
Garbarini, Antonio	25, Sept 1859	Antonio	Gazzollo, Maria	K	
Garbarini, Joseph Timothy	2, Sept 1855	John	Hays, Mary	B	18
Garberini, Francis Robert	18, July 1854	John	Hays, Mary	B	3
Garbrock, Casper Bernard	8, Mar. 1857	Caspar	Wernke, Elisabeth	L	
Garbrock, Joseph Heinrich	1, July 1854	Caspar	Wernke, Maria Elis.	L	
Garbrock, Maria Elisabeth	17, May 1852	J. Casper	Wernke, M. Adel. Elis.	L	
Garchiner, Elizabeth	3, Dec. 1851	Peter	----, Bridget	B	247
Gardener, Emily Ann	9, Mar. 1853	Hurley	Hurley, Ann	P	37
Gardie?, Mary Jane	13, Mar. 1854	Edward	Holland, Mary	B	311
Gardner, Dennis	15, Dec. 1850	William	McCarthy, Margaret	E	267
Gardner, Emily Catherine	13, July 1857	Francis	Bradley, Catherine	E	465
Gardner, Margaret	25, Feb. 1857	Peter	Glennon, Bridget	T	
Gardner, Mary Theresa	21, Mar. 1859	Walter	Barret, Mary	V	53
Gardner, Peter	4, Apr. 1854	Peter	Glennon, Bridget	T	
Garey, John Baptist	5, Jan. 1857	Anthony	Cannon, Margaret	B	38
Garibaldi, Giovanni Battista Agostina	11, Apr. 1858	Giacomo	Corrotto, Maria	K	
Garibaldi, Giovanni Battista Giacomo	14, Dec. 1856	Jacob	Curotti, Maria	K	
Garibaldo, Mary Catherine Carolina	29, May 1853	James	Carrotta, Maria	P	42
Garling, Jacob Theodor	20, Mar. 1853	J. Mathias	Maymann, Cath. Elis.	L	
Garling, Johan Mathias	16, Nov. 1857	Mathias	Meimann, Elisabeth	L	
Garlorine, Catherine Rose	8, Mar. 1857	Anthony	----, Mary	P	207
Garmeny, James	6, Mar. 1851	James	Connelly, Margaret	E	288
Garragan, James	12, Sept 1857	Patrick	----, Mary	E	480
Garraghty, Helen	4, May 1856	Patrick	----, Catherine	R	
Garraghty, John	25, Apr. 1856	Michael	Moran, Mary	V	30
Garraghty, John	19, Oct. 1856	Thomas	S---ry, Mary Ann	B	35
Garran, Maria	4, Nov. 1855	Johan	Pieper, Catharina	A	
Garratty, Michael	2, July 1855	Patrick	Sheridan, Catherine	B	16
Garraty, Bridget	27, Nov. 1858	Martin	McFadden, Mary	P	268
Garrel, August	22, Feb. 1855	Christian	Hudepohl, Maria	A	
Garrel, Heinrich	26, Oct. 1859	Christian	Hudepohl, Margaretha	A	
Garrel, Johan Bernard	20, July 1857	Christian	Hüdepohl, Maria Anna	A	
Garret, William	25, Sept 1859	Patrick	Coyne, Sarah	B	81
Garrett, August	27, May 1858	August	----, Mary Ann	E	537
Garrett, John	28, May 1856	August	----, Isabel	E	370
Garrett, Mary Ann	5, Sept 1855	James	Kelley, Margaret	P	150
Garrett, Mary Isabel	11, July 1854	George	----, Mary Ann	E	206

Name of Child	Date of Baptism	Father	Mother	Church	Page
Garrigan, Edward Clement	26, Dec. 1859	Michael	----, Mary	V	65
Garrigan, Philip	17, July 1859	Patrick	----, Mary	M	
Garrigan, Thomas	4, Oct. 1858	Thomas	Donnelly, Bridget	E	567
Garry, Catherine	10, Feb. 1855	Thomas	Carey, Mary	B	11
Gart, Michael	1, Mar. 1851		adult	B	225
Gartlan, Catherine	6, Feb. 1854	Thomas	Kearnan, Mary	E	165
Gartmann, Carolina	14, Mar. 1853	Heinrich	Holziger, Elisabeth	F	
Gärtner, Anna	6, Feb. 1855	G. Adam	Hof, Catharina	D	28
Gartner, Elisabeth	24, Jan. 1858	Jacob	Boes, Justina	K	
Gartner, Elisabeth	6, Mar. 1859	Wilhelm	Anger, Maria	K	
Gärtner, Elisabeth	11, Dec. 1859	Jacob	Boes, Justina	K	
Gartner, Heinrich Herman	24, Feb. 1850	F. Joseph	Leppert, Magdalena	D	203
Gärtner, Jacob	22, June 1856	Jacob	Boes, Justina	J	36
Gartner, Louisa	16, Oct. 1853	Francis J.	Leppert, Magdalena	D	410
Gartner, Maria Theresa	17, Mar. 1856	Wilhelm	adult	K	
Gartner, Martin	11, May 1853	Jacob	Boes, Justina	K	
Gärtner, Ottilia	17, July 1859	Peter	Schmidt, Theresa	K	
Gartner, Otto	8, Jan. 1854	Jacob	Adam, Contratina	D	1
Gartner, Stephan	24, Sept 1854	Jacob	Boes, Christina	K	
Garver, Sarah Ann	27, Jan. 1850	Roger	Cornell, Honora	B	195
Garvey, Catherine	8, May 1853	Patrick	Mahony, Mary	E	87
Garvey, Elizabeth	2, Sept 1850	Daniel	----, Elizabeth	E	245
Garvey, James	8, Feb. 1854	Michael	Henry, Bridget	P	68
Garvey, Joanne	10, July 1852	Michael	Henry, Bridget	B	263
Garvey, John	1, June 1857	John	Kearney, Ellen	B	45
Garvey, Mary	12, Feb. 1852	Frederick	Mahony, Mary	E	381
Garvey, Winifred	10, July 1852	Michael	Henry, Bridget	B	263
Garvy, Peter	15, Oct. 1855	Peter	----, Mary	E	321
Gary, Catherine	25, Dec. 1853	William	----, Catherine	B	305
Gas, Georg	15, Feb. 1857	Adam	Meyer, Maria	C	
Gas, Susanna	24, Oct. 1854	Johan	Conrad, Johanna	K	
Gasch, Margaretha	3, July 1853	Heinrich	Hattmann, Christina	C	
Gasper, Maria Louisa	6, Oct. 1850	Johan	Rosche, Louisa	L	
Gasper, Theresa	12, Dec. 1852	Johan	----, Maria	H	
Gass, Adam	26, Jan. 1857	Adam	Theobald, Catharina	D	77
Gass, Adam	25, Dec. 1852	Johan	Kramer, Louisa	D	362
Gass, Christina	22, Mar. 1851	Johan	Kramer, Louisa	D	257
Gass, Francis	2, Sept 1855	Heinrich	Hartmann, Christina	C	
Gass, Johan Adam	26, June 1854	Johan	Kramer, Louisa	D	13
Gass, Mathilda	2, Sept 1859	Adam	Mei---, Maria	D	145
Gass, Susanna	25, Jan. 1859	Adam J.	Theobald, Catharina	D	129
Gassenschmidt, Carolina Elisabeth	27, Aug. 1854	Mathias	Barth, Verena	C	
Gassenschmidt, Catharina Emilia	21, June 1857	Matthias	Barth, Verena	C	
Gassenschmidt, Wilhelmina Verena	3, Apr. 1853	Mathias	Bardt, Verena	C	
Gasser, John Francis	5, Sept 1852	Anthony	Lightner, Theresa	B	269
Gasser, Mary E.C.	14, Feb. 1855	Anthony	Lightner, Theresa	B	11
Gasser, Mary Elizabeth	3, Nov. 1850	Anthony	Lightner, Theresa	B	218
Gassinger, Franz Heinrich	12, Jan. 1858	Francis	Limberg, Josephina	F	
Gassinger, Maria Theresa	1, Aug. 1859	Francis	Polle, Elisabeth	F	
Gastedder, Carolina Margaretha	21, Nov. 1852	Jacob	Schneider, Cecilia	K	
Gastiger, Eva Adelheid	15, Dec. 1857	Robert	Wilson, Agnes	D	100
Gately, James	4, Dec. 1859	Bernard	Hegan, Ann	E	674
Gately, John James	26, Jan. 1853	Bernard	Leonard, Catherine	E	58
Gately, Julia	24, June 1855	Bernard	----, Ann	E	296
Gately, Peter	4, Jan. 1852	Bernard	Fegan, Ann	E	371
Gatens, James	17, Jan. 1854	James	Gallagher, Mary	B	307
Gater, Elizabeth Mary	19, Apr. 1858	Alfred	----, Elizabeth	E	530
Gatler, Walburga	18, Dec. 1858	August	Huber, Lucina	L	
Gatons, Edward	18, Feb. 1855	James	Gallagher, Mary	P	121

Name of Child	Date of Baptism	Father	Mother	Church	Page
Gattermaier, Bernard Herman	7, Sept 1851	Bernard	Höhne, Maria Adelheid	D	281
Gatti, Antonia Maria	8, Sept 1855	J. Joseph	Martin, Sera	K	
Gatti, Johan Baptist Francis	24, Oct. 1858	Joseph	Martin, Sarah	K	
Gatti, John Baptist	8, Apr. 1851	Joseph	Martin, Sarah	E	298
Gatti, Maria	3, Apr. 1858	Lawrence	Gatti, Maria	K	
Gatti, Maria Virginia	12, Apr. 1857	Benedict	----, Maria	K	
Gatting, Catharina	11, Dec. 1853	Joseph	Heilman, Anna	D	419
Gatting, Heinrich	5, Jan. 1851	Joseph	Heilman, Anna	D	247
Gatting, Helena	3, Jan. 1858	Joseph	Heilman, Anna	D	102
Gatting, Johan	28, Dec. 1851	Joseph	Heilman, Anna	D	299
Gatting, Joseph	30, Apr. 1854	Bernard	Hofman, Catharina	D	9
Gattmann, Catharina Josephina E.	23, Mar. 1856	Nicolaus	Hoelscher, M. Elisabeth	F	
Gattmann, Herman Heinrich	20, Nov. 1857	Herman H.	Hoelscher, Elisabeth	F	
Gattmann, J. Franz Joseph Clemens	21, Aug. 1859	Francis	Luchte, Christina	F	
Gattmann, Johan Clemens	17, Jan. 1856	Clemens	Wilke, Agnes	F	
Gatto, Aloysius Jacob	18, Oct. 1858	Benedict	Zelli, Maria	K	
Gatto, Carlo	29, Dec. 1856	Antonio	Gieglia, Maria	K	
Gaughan, Catherine	9, Oct. 1859	Henry	----, Bridget	E	661
Gaughin, Mary	25, Feb. 1857	Henry	----, Bridget	M	
Gaukelbrink, Anna Maria Catharina	4, Jan. 1854	Mathias	Sieme, Anna Maria	L	
Gaukelbrink, Johan Heinrich	11, Sept 1850	Matthias	Lange, M. Bernardina	L	
Gaukelspring, Johan Heinrich	10, July 1859	Mathias	Siems, Maria Catharina	T	
Gaukelspring, Rosalia Barbara	1, Mar. 1857	J. Mathias	Siemes, Anna Maria	F	
Gaule, Emily Mary	11, Sept 1853	Frederick	Foster, Eliza	P	51
Gaule, Louis Frederick	6, Jan. 1855	Frederick	Foster, Eliza	P	114
Gausepohl, Anna Maria	5, May 1850	Heinrich	Stuke, Maria	L	
Gausepohl, Anna Maria Francisca	24, Dec. 1852	J. Bernard	Kroeger, Anna Angela	K	
Gausepohl, Bernard Heinrich August	17, Dec. 1857	J. Bernard	Kroeger, A. Angela	L	
Gausepohl, Johan Franz Joseph	18, Aug. 1859	J. Bernard	Kroeger, A. Angela	L	
Gausepohl, Philomena	4, Nov. 1854	J. Bernard	Kroeger, Anna Maria	L	
Gausing, Johan Bernard Philip	28, Oct. 1858	J. Herman	Goldschmidt, M. Theresa	L	
Gausing, Johan Heinrich	21, July 1855	Herman	Goldschmidt, Theresa	L	
Gausing, Maria Catharina	18, May 1853	J. Herman	Goldschmidt, Theresa	L	
Gausing, Maria Christina	25, Nov. 1851	J. Heinrich	Reckers, Maria Engel	L	
Gausling, Johan Herman Ferdinand	17, Sept 1858	Heinrich	Friele, Maria Catharina	N	
Gausling, Maria Adelheid Catharina	30, Sept 1859	Heinrich	Trahle, Catharina	N	
Gavan, John	8, May 1853	William	Gould, Bridget	B	290
Gavin, Bridget	18, July 1858	Michael	Moran, Catherine	E	550
Gavin, Ellen	1, Mar. 1852	Michael	Moran, Catherine	E	387
Gavin, John	7, July 1859	Michael	----, Mary	E	637
Gavin, Mary	23, June 1850	Michael	Moran, Catherine	E	225
Gavin, Mary	3, Sept 1851		Gavin, Helen	B	240
Gavin, Mary Ann	26, Aug. 1851	Alexander	Reilly, Mary Ann	B	239
Gavin, Mary Ann	12, Nov. 1853	Michael	Moran, Catherine	E	143
Gavin, Michael	2, Aug. 1856	Michael	Moran, Catherine	E	386
Gayner, Bridget	19, Aug. 1852	John	Farley, Ann	P	26
Gaynor, Helen	13, May 1855	John	Byrnes, Mary	R	
Gaynor, Margaret	13, Mar. 1853	John	Bardens, Mary	R	
Gaynor, Martin	14, Dec. 1853	Michael	----, Ann	M	
Gaynor, Matthew	4, Mar. 1855	Patrick	Reilly, Margaret	R	
Gazollo, Carolina	21, Jan. 1854	Dominick	Drofigna, Maria Magdalena	K	
Gazzolli, Aloysius Carl Borromeo	4, Feb. 1856	Dominick	Simoni, Magdalena	K	
Gazzolo, James	24, July 1859	Peter	Rata, Catherine	E	642
Geake, Mary	19, Mar. 1856	William	Shea, Joanne	T	
Gearing, Alice	1, Oct. 1856	John	Murray, Alice	B	34
Gearing, Laura	1, Nov. 1854	John	Murray, Bridget Alice	B	7
Gearing, Mary Helen	6, Oct. 1850	John	Murray, Alice	B	215
Gearson, Ann Elizabeth	23, July 1855	George	Reily, Elizabeth	B	17
Gebbe, Anna Carolina	12, May 1853	J. Heinrich	Brockman, Maria Catharina	D	384

Name of Child	Date of Baptism	Father	Mother	Church	Page
Gebbe, Anton Nicolaus	13, June 1858	J. Heinrich	Brackman, Maria Catharina	D	113
Gebbe, Maria Elisabeth	14, Dec. 1855	J. Heinrich	Baeckman, Maria Catharina	D	48
Gebbe, Theresa Philomena	15, Oct. 1850	J. Heinrich	Brockman, Maria Catharina	D	238
Gebbert, Elisabeth	7, Sept 1851	Andreas	Kaiser, Louisa	D	281
Gebel, Johan	4, Aug. 1850	Christian	Brun, Maria Elis. Philomena	K	
Gebenau, Anton	18, Apr. 1852	Anton	Kohler, Magdalena	F	
Gebenesch, Susanna	16, Mar. 1856	Christoph	Lett, Elisabeth	F	
Gebhard, Anton	28, Feb. 1854	Johan	Reinhard, Theresa	D	5
Gebhard, Catharina Carolina	31, Oct. 1858	Anton	Raim, Louisa	D	123
Gebhard, Joseph Heinrich	17, June 1855	M. Joseph	Wilhelm, Magdalena	N	
Gebhard, Ludwig	24, Jan. 1853	Johan	Reinhart, Theresa	D	367
Gebhard, M. Magdalena	12, July 1857	Joseph	Wilhelm, Magdalena	N	
Gebhard, Margaret	19, Feb. 1854	Joseph	Wilhelm, Magdalena	N	20
Gebhard, Oswald Joseph	19, Oct. 1851	Conrad	Pump, Magdalena	D	288
Gebhardt, Catharina	27, Aug. 1857	Johan	Spi---, Margaretha	D	93
Gebhart, Anton Johan	28, Oct. 1855	Johan	Reinhard, Theresa	D	45
Gebhart, Catharina Louisa	4, Apr. 1858	Johan	Reinhart, Theresa	D	108
Gebhart, Johan Michael	5, Jan. 1851	Heinrich	Reinhart, Thersea	D	247
Gebhart, Maria Elisabeth	29, Aug. 1858	Wendel	Neudocher, Theresa	Q	28
Geckeli, Catharina Josephina	24, Apr. 1859	Andreas	Nicoll, Catharina	F	
Gecks, Maria	20, Nov. 1854	Anton	Binder, Barbara	K	
Geehan, Catharine	16, Apr. 1854	Thomas	Quillinan, Ann	T	
Geerin, Ellen	18, June 1856	Michael	----, Catherine	E	375
Geffert, Johan	22, Aug. 1858	Johan	Higer, Victoria	D	117
Geffigan, Helen	14, Dec. 1851	Patrick	Lawler, Helen	B	248
Gegan, Bartholomew	13, Feb. 1853	John	Richardson, Margaret	B	290
Gegan, Margaret Jane	6, July 1851	John	Richardson, Margaret J.	B	235
Gegeihen, Maria Philomena	26, May 1851		adult - 29 years old	K	
Gegeihen, Oswald Aloysius	26, May 1851		----, Maria Philomena	K	
Gegel, Maria Lisetta Philomena	9, June 1850		adult - 29 years old	K	
Gegges, Jacob Friedrich	29, May 1851	Jacob	Roll, Catharina	G	
Geglein, Anna Margaretha	23, Oct. 1853	Andreas	Knoez, Catharina	D	411
Geglein, Catharina	10, Sept 1857	Andreas	Knoez, Catharina	D	94
Geglein, Georg	17, Aug. 1856	Andreas	Knoetz, Catharina	D	65
Gegnan, John	12, Sept 1855	Bartholomew	Ronan, Bridget	P	151
Gegnan, Margaret Ann	19, Mar. 1854	Bartholomew	Rohan, Bridget	P	74
Gegnan, Mary Helen	17, May 1857	Bartholomew	Ruan, Bridget	P	212
Gegning, Catherine	20, Feb. 1859	Bartholomew	Ruan, Bridget	P	277
Gehan, Edward	28, Jan. 1855	Thomas	Ryan, Ann	B	10
Gehl, Johan Friedrich Anton	1, July 1859	Anton	K---, Maria Anna	D	141
Gehling, Anna Maria Elisabeth	21, Sept 1857	Heinrich	Lammers, Elisabeth	C	
Gehling, Anna Maria Louise	1, Aug. 1852	Heinrich	Hehing, Christina	C	
Gehling, Elisabeth Carolina	11, July 1859	Heinrich	Langers, Elisabeth	C	
Gehling, Maria Elisabeth	16, May 1850	Gerhard	Schmidt, Dina	A	
Gehm, Catharina	20, July 1858	Wilhelm	Kölb---, Catharina	D	115
Gehren, Jacob	2, Feb. 1853	William	Stickeny, Dina	F	
Gehri, Ferdinand	24, Oct. 1858	Cornelius	Fleich, Carolina	J	48
Gehring, Anna Eva	23, Feb. 1857	Heinrich	Keller, Maria	K	
Gehring, Anna Maria	23, Nov. 1858	J. Herman	Gude, Anna Maria	K	
Gehring, Anton Herman Gerhard	1, Aug. 1856	Herman	Gerde, Anna Maria	K	
Gehring, August Carl	25, Oct. 1857	Nicolaus	Suhr, Maria Theresa	L	
Gehring, Bernard Heinrich	27, Apr. 1859	Heinrich	Hulsmann, Bernardina	F	
Gehring, Bernard Heinrich	20, June 1856	Heinrich	Lammers, Elisabeth	C	
Gehring, Carl Ludwig	16, Nov. 1851	Nicolaus	Suhr, M. Theresa	L	
Gehring, Caroline	31, Mar. 1856	Valentin	Geiler, Cunigunda	H	
Gehring, Herman Heinrich	22, Nov. 1858	Heinrich	Keller, Anna Maria	K	
Gehring, Johan Georg	25, Dec. 1853	Nicolaus	Suhr, Theresa	L	
Gehring, Johan Joseph Anton	19, Aug. 1855	Heinrich	Keller, Maria	K	
Gehring, Ludwig	24, Sept 1851	Anton	Blesi, Theresa	D	284

Hamilton County, Ohio Roman Catholic Baptism Records -- 1850 - 1859

Name of Child	Date of Baptism	Father	Mother	Church	Page
Gehring, Maria Anna	22, Jan. 1855	Joseph	Kreier, Maria	F	
Gehring, Maria Bernardina	27, Apr. 1859	Heinrich	Hulsmann, Bernardina	F	
Gehringer, Balthasar	1, July 1855	Nicolaus	Weiss, Barbara	G	
Gehrlich, Anna Maria	12, Oct. 1851	Isidor	Kraft, Susanna Margaretha	J	12
Gehrlich, Catharina	12, Oct. 1851	Isidor	Kraft, Susanna Margaretha	J	12
Gehrling, Eva	2, Mar. 1857	Jacob	Wirnhing, Eva	D	80
Gehrman, Anna Elisabeth	27, Mar. 1853	Carl	Funke, Philomena	A	
Gehrman, Friedrich Carl	16, Jan. 1855	Carl	Funke, Wilhelmina	A	
Gehrman, Johan Bernard	22, Feb. 1853	Bernard	Fortman, Maria	K	
Gehrman, Theresa Philomena	6, June 1851	Carl	Funke, Philomena	A	
Gehsling, Maria Carolina	20, Feb. 1853	J. Heinrich	Denbusch, Bibianna	D	373
Geicher, Elisabeth	27, Jan. 1856	Heinrich	Fischer, Petronella	J	34
Geicher, Peter Anton	27, Mar. 1859	Heinrich	Fischer, Petronella	J	50
Geier, Andreas	5, June 1855	Joseph	Brenner, Anna Maria	D	36
Geier, August	10, July 1859	Francis	Winzeil, Helena	D	142
Geier, Catharina	10, Apr. 1859	Georg	Kraft, Anna Maria	T	
Geier, Georg	15, Dec. 1856	Georg	Kraft, Anna Maria	F	
Geier, Joseph	18, May 1856	C. Joseph	Meisel, Eva	W	14
Geier, Joseph	4, July 1851	Joseph	Brenner, Anna Maria	D	271
Geier, Maria Anna	18, Nov. 1855	F. Magnus	Winzing, Helena	D	47
Geier, Maria Carolina	5, July 1857	Francis	Winzeil, Helena	D	89
Geier, Sarah	25, Jan. 1852	Matthew	Cross, G.	E	377
Geiger, Adam	5, Feb. 1854	Georg	Börtl, Elisabeth	D	3
Geiger, Adolph	6, Apr. 1851	Albert	Kiser, Theresa	K	
Geiger, Anna Maria	22, May 1859	Roman	Nieterhausen, Maria A.	L	
Geiger, Carl	25, Nov. 1857	Johan	Flick, Anna Maria	N	
Geiger, Carl Albert	18, Apr. 1853	C. Albert	Niesen, Theresa	K	
Geiger, Georg	5, Apr. 1858	Christian	Birbreier, Carolina	T	
Geiger, Georg Michael	23, Aug. 1857	Georg	Daum, Catharina	K	
Geiger, Heinrich Jacob	7, Aug. 1853	Heinrich	Fischer, Petronella	J	22
Geiger, Johan Heinrich	14, Jan. 1850	Johan H.	Fischer, Petronella	F	
Geiger, Joseph	18, Oct. 1851	Basil	Götz, Ursula	D	287
Geiger, Joseph	19, June 1859	Johan	Flick, Maria Anna	N	
Geiger, Margaret Catharine	18, Jan. 1855	George	Daum, Catherine	N	26
Geiger, Maria Eva	18, Feb. 1855	J. Georg	Bertel, Elisabeth	D	29
Geiger, Monica	24, May 1855	Jacob	Doll, Carolina	F	
Geiges, Joseph	18, Apr. 1856	Christian	----, Carolina	D	56
Geigher, Barbara	3, May 1857	Heinrich	Fischer, Petronella	J	40
Geil, Wilhelm	2, Feb. 1858	Georg	Kaempf, Catharina	F	
Geile, Johan Caspar	10, July 1856	J. Mathias	Fuchtman, Catharina	D	62
Geiler, Maria Gertrud	14, Jan. 1858	Mathias	Buch---, Maria Elisabeth	D	102
Geiller, Joseph	20, Apr. 1856	Joseph	----, Maria	H	
Geiller, Mary	6, Aug. 1855	Joseph	----, Mary	H	
Geiller, Michael	12, June 1853	Joseph	----, Mary	H	
Geinebach, Maria Anna	15, Oct. 1857	G. Wilhelm	Benkhof, Margaretha	D	97
Geing, Johan Friedrich	18, Mar. 1855	Johan F.	--sch, Maria Catharina	D	31
Geis, Anna Rosa	18, Jan. 1857	Adam	Brand, Apollonia	D	76
Geis, Carolina Apollonia	25, Feb. 1855	Adam	Brand, Apollonia	D	29
Geis, Maria Elisabeth	5, Sept 1852	Adam	Brand, Appolonia	D	346
Geis, Rosa Catharina	25, Dec. 1858	Adam	Brand, Appolonia	F	
Geise, Anna Elisabeth	19, Nov. 1857	David	Lange, Elisabeth	L	
Geise, Anna Margaretha Bernardina	12, Jan. 1856	Bernard H.	Bolke, M. Margaretha	L	
Geise, Anna Maria Catharina	27, Dec. 1851	H. Arnold	Kallage, Theresa	A	
Geise, Anna Maria Elisabeth	12, May 1856	David	Lange, Elisabeth	L	
Geise, Bernard Heinrich	18, Jan. 1851	Bernard	Bolke, Margaretha	L	
Geise, Clemens	25, Feb. 1854	Bernard H.	Bolte, Margaretha	L	
Geise, Heinrich August	28, Apr. 1852	Bernard H.	Bolke, Margaretha	L	
Geise, Maria Sophia	27, Mar. 1859	Bernard	Bohlke, A.M. Margaretha	L	
Geise, Theresa Philomena	22, May 1854	H. Arnold	Kallage, Theresa	A	

Name of Child	Date of Baptism	Father	Mother	Church	Page
Geisendorf, Sophia	14, Oct. 1855	Georg	Volz, Maria	D	44
Geisendorfer, Johan Georg	9, July 1854	Georg	Volz, Margaretha	D	13
Geisendorfer, Magdalena	23, Feb. 1858	Georg	Volz, Maria	D	106
Geiser, Emilia Theresa	14, Mar. 1858	Jacob	Borgen, Cunigunda	D	107
Geiser, Johan	23, Oct. 1859	Jacob	Bergen, Cunigunda	D	149
Geiser, Johan Armleder	2, Dec. 1855		Geiser, Maria	D	48
Geiser, Maria	28, Dec. 1856	Jacob	Berigen, Cunigunda	D	75
Geisler, Barbara Catharina	5, Oct. 1856	Valentin	Herman, Elisabeth	D	69
Geisler, Carolina Margaretha	16, Oct. 1857	Friedrich	Kröger, Francisca	A	
Geisler, Caroline	25, Jan. 1852	Otto	Bryson, Christine	E	376
Geisler, Catharina	14, Mar. 1859	Martin	Borst, Catharina	D	134
Geisler, Freidrich Theodor	2, July 1856	Friedrich	Kröger, Henrica	A	
Geisler, Georg	2, Sept 1855	Valentin	Herman, Elisabeth	D	41
Geisler, Maria Euphemia Gertrud	6, Feb. 1859	Friedrich	Kröger, Henrietta	A	
Geisseldorf, Johan Georg	14, Feb. 1857	J. Georg	M---, Catharina	D	79
Geissendorf, Carl Andreas	10, Oct. 1858	J. Georg	M----, Catharina Maria	D	121
Geissler, Johan	11, Nov. 1855	Martin	Burst, Catharina	D	46
Geissler, Maria Lina Augustina	2, Sept 1856	August G.	Steidel, Maria Catharina	D	66
Geking, Bernard	3, Feb. 1853	Gerhard J.	Stoerich, Marianna	F	
Geldreich, Adolph	25, Oct. 1853	Joseph	Leder, Maria Anna	D	411
Geldreich, Maria Anna	10, Apr. 1859	Joseph	----, Maria Anna	C	
Geldreich, Maria Carolina	27, Apr. 1856	Joseph	Letter, Maria	C	
Gelhaus, Anna Catharina	2, Nov. 1854	Johan	Greve, Gertrud	C	
Gelhaus, Anna Maria Elisabeth	15, June 1851	Otto	Rohe, Catharina	F	
Gelhaus, Johan Heinrich	24, Apr. 1853	Otto	Rohe, Catharina	F	
Gelhorst, Josephina Elisabeth	4, Jan. 1857	Otto	Rohe, Catharina	W	18
Geling, Johan Heinrich Francis	19, Aug. 1854	Heinrich	Hoing, Christina	L	
Gell, Elisabeth	15, Aug. 1852	Wilhelm	Keller, Anna	L	
Gellenback, Maria Anna	26, June 1859	Bernard H.	Langenfels, Anna Maria	D	141
Gellenbeck, Adelheid	4, Oct. 1859	Ferdinand	Ruhkamp, Maria Anna	L	
Gellenbeck, Bernard Clemens	22, July 1856	G. Bernard	Cramer, Maria	C	
Gellenbeck, Bernard Franz	28, May 1855	Ferdinand	Ruhkamp, Maria Anna	L	
Gellenbeck, Elisabeth Philomena	3, Jan. 1854	Gerhard	Kraemer, Maria	C	
Gellenbeck, Francisca Ferdinanda	5, Apr. 1858	B. Heinrich	Langefels, Anna M. Elisabeth	D	108
Gellenbeck, Gerhard Heinrich	27, Aug. 1858	Gerhard	Kramer, M. Anna	C	
Gellenbeck, Herman Joseph	8, Apr. 1850	Gerhard B.	Kraemer, M. Anna	C	
Gellenbeck, Johan Bernard	14, May 1853	Ferdinand	Ruhkamp, Maria Anna	L	
Gellenbeck, M. Friedricka Theresa	6, Mar. 1859	Georg H.	Hellmann, Bernardina	L	
Gellenbeck, Maria Adelheid	1, July 1852	Gerhard	Kraemer, Maria	C	
Gellenbeck, Maria Anna	21, June 1857	Francis	Rohkamp, Maria	L	
Gellenbeck, Maria Elisabeth	20, Mar. 1850	Bernard	Schrage, Elisabeth	L	
Gellenbeck, Rosa	12, Nov. 1852	Bernard	Schrage, Elisabeth	L	
Geller, Heinrich	10, July 1853	Heinrich	Auer, Barbara	D	394
Gelles, Edward	5, July 1857	Edmund	Keller, Gertrud	D	89
Gellhaus, Herman Otto	13, Mar. 1859	Otto	Rohe, Catharina	W	25
Gels, Bernard Heinrich	25, Sept 1859	B. Heinrich	Klönen, Anna Angela	J	52
Gemberlein, Francis Xavier	16, Dec. 1855	Johan	----, Magdalena	H	
Gemberlein, Louis	19, Mar. 1854	Johan	----, Magdalena	H	
Gemeiner, Hieronymus	27, May 1852	Hieronymus	Spinner, Theresa	D	321
Gemeiner, Maria Theresa	2, Sept 1855	Hieronymus	Spinner, Theresa	D	41
Gemeiner, Nicolaus Hieronymus	23, Feb. 1854	Hieronymus	Spinner, Theresa	D	5
Gemeyner, Anna Elisabeth	25, Mar. 1850	Hieronymus	Spinner, Theresa	L	
Gempel, Charlotta Philomena	27, Aug. 1851		adult - 43 years old	K	
Genati, Maria	29, Jan. 1855	Johan	Brizzolari, Coelestina	K	
Gennings, Charles	10, Feb. 1856	Patrick	Gil, Eleanore	V	29
Genocchio, Julia Catherine	7, Nov. 1852	Dominick	Cogni, Catherine	B	274
Genochi, Julia Maria	6, Oct. 1850	Dominick	Conia, Catharina	C	
Genochi, Mary Thersea	1, Mar. 1859	Dominick	----, Catherine	V	54
Genoknapp, Catherine	22, Feb. 1851		Genoknapp, Sarah	E	286

Name of Child	Date of Baptism	Father	Mother	Church	Page
Gensch, Ludwig Johan	28, Aug. 1854	Francis	Berie, Barbara	C	
Gensth, Peter	24, June 1855	Francis L	Perie, Barbara	C	
Gensth, Valentin	26, July 1857	Louis	Pernier, Barbara	C	
Gent---, Francis	2, June 1859	Ludwig	M---, Barbara	D	139
Gentner, Jacob Heinrich	29, Nov. 1857	Heinrich	Clemens, Elisabeth	C	
Gentner, Jacob Philipp Friedrich	4, Dec. 1859		Gentner, Theresa	F	
Gentner, Maria Anna	31, Dec. 1852	Johan	Baumcamp, Maria Anna	N	11
Geoghagan, Helen	8, Dec. 1850	William	Moloney, Joanne	B	220
Geoghagen, Joanne	30, Mar. 1854	John	Kanelly, Anna	L	
Geoghan, Helen	20, Sept 1857	Michael	Meagher, Joanne	P	224
Geoghegan, Catherine Bridget	3, July 1853	William	Mahoney, Joanne	P	46
Geoghegan, Mary	11, Dec. 1856	William	Mahoney, Joanne	B	37
Geoghehan, Edward	24, July 1859	William	Mahoney, Joanne	B	78
Georg, Johan Wilhelm	4, Dec. 1859	Wilhelm	Trefsker, Maria	K	
George, Ernest Philomon	30, Dec. 1851	Henry	Crammer, Agnes	E	369
Geppert, Johan	26, Dec. 1853	Lawrence	Heitz, Magdalena	G	
Geppert, Maria Theresa	2, Oct. 1853	Wendelin	Nautascher, Theresa	D	408
Geraghty, Ann	21, Jan. 1852	James	Dolan, Catherine	B	250
Geraghty, Catherine	1, Apr. 1854	James	Dolan, Catherine	B	312
Geraghty, John	17, Sept 1852	Bernard	Kiernan, Margaret	B	270
Geraghty, John Thomas	2, Jan. 1859	John	Prendergast, Mary	B	69
Geraghty, John Thomas	14, Dec. 1859	Thomas	Heffernan, Mary	B	85
Geraghty, Julia	15, Aug. 1858	James	Dolan, Catherine	B	63
Geraghty, Mary	26, Apr. 1856	James	Dolan, Catherine	B	28
Geraghty, Michael	27, Nov. 1852	James	Mannon, Helen	B	276
Geraghty, Michael	6, Nov. 1856	John	Prendergast, Mary	B	36
Geraghty, Peter	11, Aug. 1858	John	Comer, Mary	R	
Geraghty, Richard	20, June 1855	John	Prendergast, Mary	E	294
Geraghty, Thomas	10, Feb. 1856	James	----, Helen	E	343
Geraldine, Ellen Erwin	2, Jan. 1855	Charles	Higgins, Ellen	B	9
Geraldine, Mary Catherine	1, July 1852	Charles	----, Helen	B	262
Gerard, Margaret	28, Feb. 1858	James	Maig, Bridget	Q	27
Gerard, Otto Richard	20, Oct. 1856	Carl	adult - 21 years old	K	
Gerardin, Margaret Phila	9, May 1859	Henry	Gavillier, Annette	Z	
Gerarty, Elizabeth	24, Jan. 1855	Patrick	----, Catherine	M	
Gerathy, Catherine	24, June 1855	Michael	----, Bridget	M	
Geratiy, William	11, July 1858	Charles	----, Martina	H	
Gerber, Johan	17, Feb. 1856	Johan	Schwalbach, Anna Maria	D	52
Gerber, Johanna	18, Sept 1853	Johan	Schwalbach, Anna Maria	F	
Gerber, Louisa	4, Apr. 1852	Johan	Schwalbach, Maria	D	315
Gerber, Margaretha	25, Feb. 1855	Peter	Barth, Maria	D	29
Gerber, Marianna	23, Dec. 1851	Johan	Guhlberg, Maria Anna	D	297
Gerber, Mathias	4, Apr. 1852	Peter	Barth, Maria	D	315
Gerber, Wilhelm	20, Jan. 1850	Peter	Barth, Maria	F	
Gerbermeier, Bernard Heinrich	29, Sept 1859	Bernard	Broermann, M. Elis.	L	
Gerbes, Bernard Heinrich	10, Jan. 1857	Joseph	Wernke, Maria Anna	L	
Gerbes, Maria Catharina	8, May 1851	Joseph H.	Wernke, M. Anna	C	
Gerbes, Maria Elisabeth	17, Apr. 1854	Joseph	Wernke, M. Anna	C	
Gerbisch, Anna	26, Sept 1858	Nicolaus	Martin, Maria	K	
Gerde, Heinrich	3, Apr. 1859	Francis	Seling, Sophia	C	
Gerdeisen, Anna Maria	18, June 1854	Francis	Hauser, Leopoldina	G	
Gerdeisen, Catharina	17, Oct. 1858	Francis	Hauser, Leopoldina	G	
Gerdeisen, Francis Joseph	23, Nov. 1856	Francis	Hauser, Leopoldina	G	
Gerdeisen, Johan	14, Nov. 1855	Francis	Hauser, Leopoldina	G	
Gerdes, Anna Catharina Helena	3, July 1853	Theodor	Withorn, Agnes	A	
Gerdes, Anna Maria Elisabeth	9, Aug. 1852	J. Dietrich	Wiethorn, Agnes	A	
Gerdes, Johan Dietrich	1, Nov. 1859	Dietrich	Ruhe, Maria Anna	A	
Gerdes, Maria Elisabeth Philomena	24, Feb. 1851	J. Heinrich	Uhlhorn, A. Maria Philomena	A	
Gerding, Johan Herman Heinrich	11, Nov. 1855	J. Heinrich	Holera, Margaretha	L	

Name of Child	Date of Baptism	Father	Mother	Church	Page
Gerding, Louisa	7, Feb. 1858	Heinrich	Hollerah, Margaretha	T	
Gerding, Maria Catharina	24, Jan. 1855	J. Gerhard	Langemeyer, Anna Maria	L	
Gerding, Maria Margaretha	10, June 1859	J. Gerhard	Meyer, Maria	K	
Gerdink, Johan Heinrich	8, May 1851	J. Gerhard	Montel, Anna Maria	L	
Gerhard, Anna Maria Josephina J.	22, Mar. 1858	J. Conrad	Menninger, Rosina	F	
Gerhard, Bertha	11, July 1858	Erasmus	Gast, Anna Maria	D	114
Gerhard, Maria Albertina Elis. B.	16, Dec. 1855	J. Conrad	Menninger, Euphrosina	F	
Gerhart, Francis Bernard	25, July 1853	Johan	Brachman, Maria	N	15
Gering, Friedrich	10, Feb. 1854	Georg	Scharolt, Anna	D	4
Gering, Georg Nicolaus	25, Dec. 1851	J. Georg	Scharold, Anna Maria	D	298
Gering, Johan	24, Feb. 1850	J. Georg	Scharold, Anna Maria	D	203
Gerke, Johan Gerhard	20, July 1850	Johan H.	Gretha, Anna	F	
Gerke, Maria Francisca	22, Oct. 1853		Gerke, Elisabeth	F	
Gerke, Maria Margaretha	27, Feb. 1858	B. Heinrich	Meiners, Maria Gesina	J	44
Gerke, Wilhelm Heinrich	22, July 1851	William	Meier, Maria Elisabeth	F	
Gerken, Georg Amand	8, Nov. 1853	Johan	Ronen, Anna Margaretha	F	
Gerken, Herman Heinrich	14, Oct. 1857	Johan	Kohne, Anna Margaretha	F	
Gerken, Johan Wilhelm	14, Sept 1851	Bernard	Grueter, Margaretha	F	
Gerken, Johan Wilhelm	24, Jan. 1853	Bernard	Grüter, Anna Maria	J	20
Gerken, Johan Wilhelm	14, Oct. 1857	Johan	Kohne, Anna Margaretha	F	
Gerken, Maria Catharina	11, Apr. 1850	Bernard E.	Grueler, Margaretha	F	
Gerken, Maria Elisabeth	30, Oct. 1855	Bernard H.	Meiners, Maria Gesina	J	34
Gerken, Maria Elisabeth	22, Aug. 1851	Johan	Konen, Margaretha	F	
Gerking, Philomena Elisabeth	2, Mar. 1851	J. Gerhard	Sto?, Maria Anna	K	
Gerlach, Apollonia Philomena	14, Apr. 1850	Francis	Brestl, Johanna	D	209
Gerling, Elisabeth	14, Nov. 1852	Jacob	Pfirschin, Eva	D	357
Gerling, Eva	14, Nov. 1852	Jacob	Pfirsching, Eva	D	357
Gerling, Gerhard Herman August	9, Dec. 1851	Gerhard	Schmitz, Bernardina	L	
Gerling, Johan H.	29, Aug. 1850	Johan	Tembusch, Anna	A	
Gerling, Johan Theobald	22, Dec. 1850	Jacob	Pfirsching, Eva	D	247
Gerling, Peter	4, June 1854	Jacob	Pfiersing, Eva	D	11
German, Bernard Ludwig	4, July 1851	Bernard	Fortman, Maria	K	
German, Catharina Angela	6, May 1855	Bernard	Fortman, Maria	K	
Germann, Anna Maria Helena	1, Nov. 1857	Wilhelm	Ort, Anna	G	
Germann, Francisca Theresa	4, Mar. 1855	Wilhelm	Ort, Anna Maria	G	
Germann, Johan Eduard	9, Nov. 1851	J. Bernard	Stefan, Magdalena	L	
Germann, Joseph	24, Nov. 1852	Wilhelm	----, Anna Maria	G	
Germann, Michael Ludwig	8, Dec. 1850	Wilhelm	Ort, Anna Maria	G	
Germer, Roch	16, Aug. 1850	Mathias	Trischtler, Maria Anna	D	228
Gerner, Anna Maria	22, Apr. 1858	Simon	Kennel, Carolina	F	
Gerner, Barbara	24, July 1858	Johan	Altmann, Magdalena	T	
Gerner, Johan	15, July 1855	J. Georg	Altman, Magdalena	D	38
Gernhelder, Andreas Paul	16, July 1854	Johan	Bonz, Cathrina	F	
Geroux, Francis Henry	28, Aug. 1853	Etienne	----, Theresa	E	123
Gerraghty, John Edward	20, Oct. 1855	Bernard	Tieman, Margaret	B	20
Gerraghty, William	15, Feb. 1859	Bernard	Tussey, Mary	B	71
Gerresen, Mary	13, Aug. 1855	James	Mage, Elisabeth	N	
Gerrity, Thomas	5, Sept 1858	Thomas	Leary, Mary A.	B	63
Gersner, Joseph	6, Sept 1857	Nicolaus	Mu---, Magdalena	D	94
Gerstert, Maria Anna	3, Aug. 1857	M.	----, Catharina	D	92
Gerstle, Elisabeth	19, Mar. 1857	Wilhelm	Lichinger, Catharina	D	81
Gerstle, Friedrich Wilhelm	13, Dec. 1855	F. Wilhelm	Lichinger, Catharina	D	48
Gerstle, Maria	15, Jan. 1852	Friedrich	Lieginger, Catharina	C	
Gerstle, Maria Louisa Josephina	13, Mar. 1851	Wilhelm	Liegner, Catharina	C	
Gerstle, Wilhelm	15, Sept 1859	Wilhelm	Lichinger, Catharina	D	146
Gerstle, Wilhelmina	20, Feb. 1855	Wilhelm	Lichinger, Catharina	D	29
Gerten, Elisabeth Dorothea	23, Dec. 1855	Francis	Schrett, Theresa	D	49
Gerten, Francis Napoleon	17, June 1852	Francis	Schrell, Theresa	D	324
Gerten, Maria Johanna	21, Mar. 1858	Francis	Schrell, Theresa	D	107

Name of Child	Date of Baptism	Father	Mother	Church	Page
Gertin, Francis Napoleon	6, June 1853	Francis	Schall, Theresa	D	388
Gerty, Bernard	12, Apr. 1858	Bernard	Leahy, Eliza	P	246
Gerty, Margaret	7, Aug. 1859	Bernard	Leaghy, Eliza	P	291
Gerve, Heinrich Joseph	6, Sept 1857	H. Joseph	Ahaus, Lucia	F	
Gerve, Herman Heinrich	19, Aug. 1859	Heinrich	Ahaus, Lucia	F	
Gerve, Louisa	21, Aug. 1854	Johan	Fot, Elisabeth	K	
Gervering, Anna Maria Catharina	24, Sept 1858	Anton	Hessling, Anna Maria	J	48
Gervering, Francisa	12, Feb. 1854	Anton	Hessling, Maria	J	26
Gervering, Johan Herman	8, Apr. 1856	Anton	Hessling, Anna	J	36
Gervering, Johanna Maria	2, Oct. 1852	Anton	Hessling, Anna	J	18
Gervers, Franz Ludwig Anton	27, June 1854	Johan	Kirchhof, Maria	F	
Gervers, Johan Joseph	1, July 1855	Johan	Kirchhof, Margaretha	F	
Gerves, Bernardina Francisca Marg.	4, Oct. 1856	Johan	Kirchhoff, Margaretha	F	
Gervin, Herman	24, June 1850	Anton	Schroer, Anna M.	C	
Gervin, Joseph Bernard	5, Nov. 1858	Joseph B.	Fellner, Anna M.	C	
Gerwe, Ann	17, Nov. 1853	Martin	Bergan, Ann	B	302
Gerwe, Bernard Heinrich Francis	6, May 1853	J. Heinrich	Funke, Maria Clara	A	
Gerwe, Catharina Josephina	5, Mar. 1857	Joseph	Meierman, Catharina	A	
Gerwe, Francis Aloysius Joseph	9, July 1852	Joseph	Meierman, Catharina	A	
Gerwe, Francis Heinric	4, Sept 1857	Francis A.	Dust, Anna	C	
Gerwe, Francis Herman	24, Feb. 1852	J. Mathias	---owe, Maria Christina	A	
Gerwe, Johan Bernard	7, Mar. 1853	Joseph	Brueggemann, Elisabeth	F	
Gerwe, Johan Franz	4, Oct. 1859	Gerhard	Schopp, Catharina	T	
Gerwe, Johan H. Fr.	10, Dec. 1858	J.H.	Funke, Maria Elisabeth	A	
Gerwe, Johan H. Francis	21, June 1850	J. Heinrich	Funke, Maria	A	
Gerwe, Johan Joseph	24, Nov. 1859	F. Joseph	Meierman, Catharina	A	
Gerwe, Johan Joseph	4, June 1851	Joseph	Brueggemann, Elisabeth	F	
Gerwe, Joseph Friedrich	7, Feb. 1859	Francis	Dust, M. Anna	C	
Gerwe, Maria Anna	13, Mar. 1857	Johan	Voet, Elisabeth	K	
Gerwe, Maria Rosalia	4, Sept 1850	Joseph	Meierman, Catharina	A	
Gerwe, Maria Theresa Bernardina	24, Oct. 1854	Joseph	Meierman, Catharina	A	
Gerwe, Theresa	26, Dec. 1858	Carl	Leich, Theresa	T	
Gerwer, Maria Elisabeth	22, Feb. 1857	Carl	Leik, Theresa	F	
Gerwers, Anna Clara Josephina	14, Oct. 1852	Caspar H.	Gerwe, Anna Margaretha	F	
Gerwers, Franz Johan Ludwig	12, Sept 1851	Johan	Kirkhoff, Maria	F	
Gerwers, Franz Joseph Heinrich	1, Feb. 1850	Heinrich	----, Margaretha	F	
Gerwers, Johan	24, Oct. 1854	Caspar H.	Gerwe, Margaretha	F	
Gerwers, Joseph Heinrich	17, May 1857	Caspar H.	Gerve, Margaretha	F	
Gerwes, Johan Heinrich	6, Oct. 1859	Johan	Pohl, Elisabeth	A	
Gerwes, Margaretha Dina Josephina	5, Dec. 1856	Joseph	Gerwe, Bernardina	F	
Gerwing, Heinrich Bernard	12, Nov. 1850	Anton	----, Maria Anna	F	
Gerwitch, Maria	14, Dec. 1856	Nicolaus	Horton, Maria	K	
Gesell, Robert Friedrich	14, Apr. 1850	Joseph	Weber, Juliana	D	209
Gesike, Herman Heinrich	2, Mar. 1859	Clemens	Waldhaus, Maria Anna	T	
Gessel, Johan	3, Dec. 1859	Johan	Nehring, Catharina	T	
Gessell, Friedrica	15, Feb. 1852	Joseph	Weber, Julia	D	307
Gessen, Johan Heinrich	24, Oct. 1851	Gerhard H.	Ahorst, Maria Anna	A	
Gessert, Anna Catharina Elisabeth	22, Mar. 1855	Heinrich	Sonheimer, Maria Theresa	D	31
Gessert, Heinrich Ludwig	22, May 1857	Heinrich	Danheimer, Theresa	D	85
Gessert, Maria Catharina	10, Feb. 1850	Heinrich	Kanheimer, Theresa	D	203
Gessler, Johan	15, Feb. 1852	Johan	Steckenborn, Margaretha	K	
Gessner, Anna Maria	25, Dec. 1852	Paul	Denk, Anna Maria	F	
Gessner, Johan	15, Aug. 1858	Nicolaus	Stab, Catharina	D	117
Gessner, Susanna	23, Feb. 1851	Paul	Denk, Anna Maria	F	
Gester, Francisca	25, Sept 1859	J. Nicolaus	Ha---, Catharina	D	147
Gestreim, Maria	20, Aug. 1854	Paul	Deutshmann, Anna Cath.	L	
Gestrein, Anna Carolina	20, July 1857	J. Paul	Bockmann, Catharina B.	L	
Gettelman, Ludwig	1, Oct. 1854	Ludwig	Gross, Theresa	D	19
Getti, Joseph	12, July 1853	James	----, Sarah	E	106

Name of Child	Date of Baptism	Father	Mother	Church	Page
Gettman, Maria Elisabeth	3, Oct. 1852	Heinrich	Gehrs, Maria	D	351
Geyer, Amanda Louisa	23, Apr. 1854	Joseph	Basker, Anna Maria	D	8
Geyer, Andreas	10, Mar. 1850	Godfried	Dürk, Catharina	D	205
Geyer, Anna Eva	16, Nov. 1856	Johan	Schwab, Margaretha	D	72
Geyer, Catharina	30, Nov. 1851	Peter	Heban, Anna	D	295
Geyer, Elisabeth	3, Dec. 1854	Johan	Schwab, Margaretha	D	23
Ghiraldelli, Carolyn	28, Jan. 1856	Bernard	Massi, Maria	B	24
Ghirlanda, John Baptist	2, June 1855	Bernard	Binasca, Maria	P	134
Ghirlanda, Mary Louise Paula	14, Apr. 1857	Bernard	Penasca, Mary	P	210
Ghirlanda, Rosa Margaretha	7, Mar. 1853	Bernard	Marina, Maria	K	
Gibbing, Johan Christian	6, Dec. 1859	Johan	Gobbing, Margaretha	A	
Gibbon, Margaret	6, July 1855	John	----, Mary	E	298
Gibbons, Catherine	17, July 1853	Thomas	----, Ann	E	110
Gibbons, Elizabeth	22, Nov. 1857	John	Quinn, Mary	E	494
Gibbons, Jeremiah	2, oct. 1859	John	Daily, Bridget	E	659
Gibbons, John	13, Apr. 1856	John	Chambers, Ellen	B	27
Gibbons, Margaret	17, July 1853	John	----, Mary Ann	E	110
Gibbons, Margaret	30, July 1850	Thomas	----, Ann	E	235
Gibbons, Mary	10, July 1854	John	----, Helen	H	
Gibbons, Mary	17, July 1851	Thomas	Carel, Ann	E	325
Gibbons, Mary Ann	3, Apr. 1852	John	----, Mary Ann	E	398
Gibbons, Mary Ann	11, July 1854	John	Quinn, Mary	P	88
Gibbons, Thomas Joseph	6, May 1859	Thomas	Cole, Honora	E	623
Gibbons, William	2, Feb. 1851	John	Haken, Mary Ann	E	280
Gibbons, William	18, July 1852	John	Ken---, Mary	P	25
Gibbons, William Isaac	8, June 1855	William	Moore, Susan	B	15
Gibbs, Peter	27, Aug. 1853	Henry	----, Sophia	E	123
Giblin, Thomas	16, Sept 1855	John	Dignan, Catherine	B	19
Gibney, Sarah Ann	20, Nov. 1859	William	Hogan, Helen	E	672
Gibson, Mary Ann	25, Dec. 1858	Daniel	Farrell, Honora	E	589
Giegel, Maria Louisa	14, Oct. 1858	Friedrich	Weber, Louisa	C	
Giehlich, Maria Carolina	22, May 1853	Adam	Ripperger, Elisabeth	D	386
Giele, Francisca	9, May 1858	Georg	Meyer, Maria	D	111
Gienant, Peter	16, July 1857	Georg	Telar, Margaretha	D	90
Gier, Johan Joseph	5, Apr. 1858	Johan	Hoffman, Maria Anna	A	
Gier, Wilhelm Heinrich	27, July 1851	Heinrich	Stundebeck, M.	C	
Gieringer, Benedict	10, Apr. 1853	Anton	----, Theresa	H	
Gieringer, Caroline	16, July 1854	Anton	----, Theresa	H	
Gieringer, Maria Theresa	13, June 1858	Anton	Pleisse, Theresa	H	
Gieringer, William	11, Nov. 1855	Anton	----, Theresa	H	
Giese, Anna Bernardina Josephina	15, Feb. 1855	Joseph	Klöman, Anna M. Gertrud	K	
Giese, Clemens Ferdinand	11, July 1855	Ferdinand	Zurliene, Bernardina	K	
Giese, Francis Johan Heinrich	7, June 1853	Francis J.	Kleiman, Maria Gertrud	K	
Giese, Francis Joseph	13, June 1857	Ferdinand	Zurliene, Bernardina	K	
Giese, Francis Joseph	5, Oct. 1851	Ferdinand	Zurliene, Dina	K	
Giese, Franz Ferdinand Joseph	7, Feb. 1850	Francis J.	Kleineman, Anna M. Gertrud	K	
Giese, Johan Joseph Carl	26, Oct. 1858	Joseph	Klüman, Gertrud	K	
Giese, Maria Catharina Philomena	16, Jan. 1857	Joseph	Kleeman, Gertrud	K	
Giese, Maria Helena	12, Sept 1851	F. Joseph	Kluneman, Anna M. Gertrud	K	
Giesing, Johan Gerhard Heinrich	19, Sept 1858	Gerhard	Timpelman, Bernardina	K	
Giesing, Maria Catharina	6, Aug. 1850	Dietrich	Dallinghaus, Maria Gertrud	K	
Gieske, Johan Herman	13, Nov. 1857	Clemens	Holthaus, M. Anna	T	
Giesling, Elisabeth Catharina	2, Aug. 1852	Dietrich	Dalinghaus, Elisabeth	K	
Giesting, Anna Josephina	1, Mar. 1854	Dietrich	Dalinghaus, Elisabeth	K	
Giesting, Anna Louisa	18, Sept 1855	J. Dietrich	Darlinghaus, Elisabeth	A	
Giesting, Clara Elisabeth	4, Nov. 1857	Theodor	Darlinghaus, Elisabeth	A	
Giesting, Johan Heinrich	4, Jan. 1852	Georg	Welage, Maria	C	
Giesting, Johan Theodor	27, Nov. 1859	J. Theodor	Darlinghaus, Maria Elisabeth	A	
Gifford, Julia Frances	7, Oct. 1855	George	Phillips, Eliza	B	20

Name of Child	Date of Baptism	Father	Mother	Church	Page
Gihring, Emilia	21, May 1854	Severin	Ziegler, Louisa	D	11
Gilb, Edward	4, Feb. 1858	Simon	Gilb, Catharina	K	
Gilb, Johan	10, Oct. 1852	Simon	Gilb, Catharina	K	
Gilbering, Anna Gesina	8, Jan. 1859	Johan G.	Dill---, Anna Adelheid	D	128
Gilbert, Anna Maria	17, July 1858	Adam	Hoffman, Catharina	K	
Gilbert, James William	24, Jan. 1851	Thomas	----, Kezar	E	278
Gilbert, Margaret	7, Oct. 1855	Thomas	Cole, Honora	E	319
Gilbert, Mary Elizabeth	15, Feb. 1851	D.	----, ----	E	284
Gilday, Catherine	30, June 1850	Patrick	----, Catherine	E	227
Gilday, Margaret	11, Dec. 1855	James	Hannan, Mary	E	332
Gilday, Mary	15, Dec. 1850	Michael	----, Honora	E	268
Gilday, Mary Ann	1, Sept 1850	James	----, Mary	E	244
Gildea, Edward	30, Jan. 1853	James	Hannan, Mary	B	282
Gildea, Edward	7, Feb. 1858	James	Hannin, Mary	P	238
Gildea, Ellen	11, Jan. 1857	Michael	Keane, Honora	B	39
Gildea, James	13, Aug. 1854	John	McGittrick, Mary	B	4
Gildea, James	22, Jan. 1854	Patrick	Snee, Catherine	B	307
Gildea, John	26, June 1859	Michael	Kaign, Honora	B	76
Gildea, Mary Ann	13, Nov. 1854	Michael	Keane, Honora	B	7
Gilden, Catherine	23, Nov. 1851	?	?	B	246
Gilden, Mary	23, Nov. 1851	?	?	B	246
Gilden, Patrick	23, Nov. 1851	?	?	B	246
Gilderme, Carl	11, Dec. 1859	Carl	Messmer, Petronella	D	152
Gilfoy, Thomas	23, July 1854	Patrick	Ryan, Ann	B	3
Gilfoyl, Mary Ann	16, Mar. 1856	Michael	Garrigan, Mary	P	173
Gilfoyle, Margaret	16, Feb. 1853	John	Keeny, Elizabeth	E	62
Gilfoyle, Mary Helen	5, May 1859	Michael	----, Mary	V	55
Gilke, Elizabeth Caroline	6, Mar. 1856	Adam	Hoffman, Catherine	E	348
Gill, Ann	11, June 1854	James	McHarchy, Helen	P	85
Gill, Ann Elizabeth	25, Apr. 1858	Richard	Grady, Ann	B	58
Gill, Bridget	6, Jan. 1850	James	Malarky, Ellen	B	193
Gill, Charles	7, May 1851	Charles	----, Margaret	E	305
Gill, Charles	22, Feb. 1858	Charles	McHenry, Rose	E	518
Gill, Francis	31, Oct. 1852	John	Lawson, Mary	B	274
Gill, Honora	7, Mar. 1856	Charles	----, Rose	E	348
Gill, James	23, Oct. 1859	John	Whelan, Bridget	B	82
Gill, James	23, Oct. 1852	Martin	Eagel, Clara	E	29
Gill, James Patrick	15, May 1859	Charles	----, Rose	V	55
Gill, John	5, Nov. 1854	Charles	McHin--, Rose	V	19
Gill, John	20, Feb. 1859	George	Doyle, Ellen	B	71
Gill, John	18, Apr. 1852	Robert	Daly, Ellen	E	404
Gill, Juliana Adelaide	15, Oct. 1854	John	Lawson, Mary	B	6
Gill, Mary	2, Mar. 1851	James	McHarkey, Ellen	P	5
Gill, Mary Elizabeth	31, Oct. 1852	John	Lawson, Mary	B	274
Gill, Patrick	1, May 1850	Charles	Moran, Margaret	B	202
Gill, Patrick	21, Mar. 1852	James	Mularky, Helen	B	254
Gillan, Rosanne	11, Feb. 1851	James	----, Mary	E	283
Gillashean, Edmund	19, Dec. 1858	John	----, ----	P	270
Gillean, Rose Ann	31, Oct. 1856	Peter J.	Jacmin, Mary	E	409
Gilleaume, Joseph	8, Nov. 1857	Henry	----, Mary Josephine	E	491
Gillen, Mary Ann	25, Oct. 1857	Archibald	Connery, Margaret	P	228
Gillen, Rosanne	23, Mar. 1851	James	McEntee, Mary	E	294
Gilles, James	3, Feb. 1851	Thomas	Gillis, Margaret	E	280
Gillespie, Ann	24, Sept 1859	Christopher	Burns, Sarah	P	297
Gillespie, Peter	23, Aug. 1855	James	Duggan, Mary	P	147
Gillice, Eliza	20, Sept 1857	Michael	Mulligan, Ann	P	**225**
Gillice, Margaret	17, Aug. 1859	Michael	Mulligan, Ann	P	293
Gilligan, Ann	22, Sept 1850	James	Quinn, Ann	B	214
Gilligan, Catherine	31, Oct. 1852	James	Quinn, Ann	B	273

Name of Child	Date of Baptism	Father	Mother	Church	Page
Gilligan, James	18, May 1851	Patrick	----, Catherine	E	309
Gilligan, Margaret	21, Dec. 1851	Bartholomew	McNulty, Margaret	B	248
Gilligan, Margaret	1, Nov. 1855	John	Kenrick, Cattherine	B	21
Gilligan, Margaret Ellen	21, Sept 1856	Bartholomew	McNulty, Margaret	B	34
Gilligan, Mary	7, Feb. 1858	John	Kenrick, Catherine	B	55
Gilligan, Mary Jane	28, Sept 1859	Michael	Cunnan, Winny	P	297
Gilligan, Matilda Josephine	20, Mar. 1859	Bartholomew	McNulty, Margaret	B	72
Gilligan, Michael	2, May 1852	Michael	Cochran, Ann	P	21
Gilligan, Peter Thomas	5, Feb. 1854	Bartholomew	McNulty, Margaret	B	309
Gilligan, Thomas	17, Aug. 1854	Michael	Corcoran, Ann	P	93
Gilligan, William	19, Aug. 1855	James	Quinn, Ann	P	146
Gillin, John	31, July 1853	John	Dignan, Catherine	P	48
Gillin, Mary Ann	17, Sept 1850	Michael	Mulligan, Ann	B	214
Gillin, Michael	17, May 1857	James	Lally, Cecilia	E	454
Gillis, Mary	8, Oct. 1851	James	Mullaly, Cecilia	E	349
Gillise, Henrietta	29, July 1855	Michael	Mulligan, Ann	P	142
Gillise, Thomas	17, May 1853	Michael	Mulligan, Ann	P	41
Gillivan, Mary	25, June 1854	Richard	----, Ann	U	
Gillon, Joanne	26, Aug. 1855	John	----, Mary	E	310
Gillon, Theresa	13, June 1858	Heinrich	Walz, Margaretha	D	113
Gilman, Mary Helen	2, Jan. 1852	John	Welsh, Mary	B	249
Gilman, Michael	22, May 1859	Patrick	Rider, Sarah	P	284
Gilmann, Anna Maria	25, Feb. 1852	Philipp J.	Horstmann, Anna Maria	L	
Gilmartin, Ann Mary	15, May 1854	James	Gilmartin, Rosanne	P	83
Gilmartin, Eliza Theresa	12, Nov. 1852	James	Gilmartin, Rosanne	P	30
Gilmartin, James	7, Sept 1855	Patrick	Murray, Mary	E	313
Gilmartin, John Baptist	29, Oct. 1858	John	Kilmar, Bridget	E	573
Gilmartin, Margaret Ann	20, Feb. 1858	Hubert	Definny, Harriet J.	P	240
Gilmartin, Michael Francis	11, Apr. 1856	James	----, Rosanne	E	358
Gilmartin, Patrick	15, Feb. 1859	Patrick	Murray, Mary	E	604
Gilmartin, Peter James	18, July 1856	Hubert	Deflenny, Henriette J.	P	185
Gilmor, Margaret	26, Nov. 1852	Patrick	Connell, Ann	P	30
Gilmore, Catherine	27, Jan. 1856	Patrick	Fitzgerald, Mary	P	167
Gilmore, John	25, May 1854	Patrick	Murray, Mary	E	192
Gilmore, John Daniel	1, Sept 1857	Patrick	Murray, Mary	E	477
Gilmore, Mary Letitia	25, Apr. 1853	George	Crancle, Isabel	B	290
Gilmore, Thomas	8, Nov. 1857	Patrick	Reilly, Sarah	P	229
Giloy, John	18, Apr. 1858		Giloy, Carolina	J	46
Gilroy, Bridget	1, Aug. 1854	James	Green, Rose	E	212
Gilroy, Catherine	6, Jan. 1852	James	Green, Rose	E	371
Gilroy, Eleanore	11, June 1850	James	----, Rosanne	E	221
Gilroy, John	23, Sept 1859	Thomas	Garvey, Bridget	E	655
Gilterner, William Friedrich	22, Mar. 1857	Carl	Messmer, Petronela	D	81
Gimpelein, Carl	1, Aug. 1852	Carl	Deiler, Magdalena	D	341
Ginally, Anthony	11, Sept 1852	Anthony	McGraw, Ellen	P	27
Gineley, Mary	12, Mar. 1854	Anthony	McGrath, Helen	P	73
Ginelli, John	20, July 1851	Anthony	McGrath, Ellen	E	325
Ginelly, Anthony	2, Jan. 1857	Anthony	McGrath, Helen	P	203
Gins, Mary Helen	4, May 1859	Thomas	McLenn, Mary	E	622
Ginter, Anna Catharina	13, Aug. 1850	Johan	Bornkamp, Maria	K	
Ginty, Bridget	28, Sept 1856	James	Woods, Bridget	V	34
Ginty, Mary	4, June 1853	John	McCoy, Ann	V	3
Ginty, Mary Ann	28, Mar. 1852	James	Woods, Bridget	E	396
Ginty, Robert	15, Jan. 1854	James	Woods, Bridget	V	9
Gir, Johan Georg	14, Nov. 1852	August	Kaelin, Elisabeth	F	
Giraldelli, Joseph	18, Apr. 1850	Hieronymus	Bianca, Maria	B	201
Girardelli, Mary Louise	12, Oct. 1852	Hieronymus	Brunner, Mary	B	271
Girken, Anna Maria Carolina	22, Sept 1855	J. Heinrich	Kohn, Anna Maria	J	32
Girteman, Maria Margaretha Adelheid	30, Nov. 1850	Heinrich	Me--haus, Adelheid	Q	1

Name of Child	Date of Baptism	Father	Mother	Church	Page
Girtler, Johan Heinrich	27, Oct. 1850	Johan	Gering, Maria	H	
Girtler, John	25, May 1856	Henry	----, Josephine	H	
Girtler, Mary	3, Dec. 1854	Henry	----, Josephine	H	
Gisely?, Mary	11, May 1851	Michael	Maley, Honora	B	231
Giske, Anna Maria Philomena	7, Oct. 1856	Herman	Niemöller, Theresa	J	38
Gisken, Anna Maria Bernardina	24, Apr. 1855	Herman	Niemöller, Theresa	J	32
Gisken, Johan Herman	15, Aug. 1859	Herman	Niemöller, Theresa	J	50
Given, Jacob August	2, Sept 1854	Wilhelm	Bender, Maria Ellen	F	
Giveny, Mary Margaret	21, Aug. 1859	Charles	Cooney, Julia Ann	B	79
Glab, Johan	2, May 1850	Conrad	Steigewald, Gertrud	D	211
Glab, Josephina	20, Nov. 1853	Adam	Mueller, Josephina	C	
Gladen, Herman Bernard	13, July 1852	Bernard	Egbers, Gertrud	L	
Gladen, Johan Heinrich	21, Sept 1856	Heinrich	Kaiser, Theresa	C	
Gladen, Johan Heirnich	17, Dec. 1856	Heinrich	Egbers, Julia	K	
Gladen, Maria Anna Theresa	1, Jan. 1855	Heinrich	Kaiser, Maria Theresa	K	
Gladen, Maria Juliana	5, Sept 1858	Johan H.	Kaiser, Anna Theresa	C	
Glaier, Elisabeth	6, May 1855	Bernard	Bühler, Catharina	D	34
Glancy, William	6, Mar. 1855	John	----, Ann	M	
Glandorf, Gerhard Herman Aloysius	20, Sept 1859	Herman	Klein, Dorothea	T	
Glaran, Johan Georg	16, Oct. 1854	J. Bernard	Egbers, Johanna	K	
Glaren, Juliana Anna	29, Mar. 1859	Bernard	Egbers, Juliana	K	
Glas, Francis	15, Feb. 1852	Joseph	Decker, Elisabeth	Q	1
Glas, Joseph	30, Jan. 1859	Francis	Sche---, Josephina	D	130
Glascow, Bridget	9, Nov. 1856	John	Quinn, Ann	E	412
Glascow, Henry	9, Oct. 1851	James	----, Margaret	E	349
Glaser, Adam	22, Feb. 1857	Adam	Art, Margaret	H	
Glaser, Agnes	9, Sept 1855	Mathias	Fillian, Catharina	D	42
Glaser, Anna Maria	9, June 1850	Mathias	Fillian, Catharina	D	216
Glaser, Balthasar Clemens	17, July 1853	Nicolaus	Andres, Anna Maria	D	395
Glaser, Barbara	23, Aug. 1857	Joseph	Distler, Mary	Q	23
Glaser, Catherine	28, Jan. 1859	Adam	Art, Margaret	H	
Glaser, Johan	12, Mar. 1854	Johan	Wallbichls, Maria	D	6
Glaser, John	25, Dec. 1855	Martin	Frisch, Anna Maria	Q	12
Glaser, Margaretha	11, Apr. 1852	Mathias	Fillian, Catharinar	D	316
Glaser, Martin	5, June 1853	Adam	Art, Margaretha	Q	3
Glaser, Martin	10, July 1853	Mathias	Fillian, Catharina	D	394
Glaser, Michael	15, Apr. 1855	Adam	Art, Margaret	Q	7
Glaser, Michael	17, Sept 1854	Joseph	Glab, Anna	D	18
Glasheen, Helen	28, Aug. 1854	John	Wright, Mary	P	94
Glashine, Mary	1, Aug. 1857	John	Reilly, Mary	P	218
Glasmeier, Johan Friedrich	25, Aug. 1853	Heinrich	Brokamp, Elisabeth	L	
Glasmeier, Johan Heinrich	4, Aug. 1853	Joseph	Stoppelmann, Angela	C	
Glasmeier, Johan Joseph	26, Oct. 1851	Heinrich	Brokamp, Louisa	N	5
Glasmeyer, Bernard Heinrich	11, Apr. 1858	Joseph	Stoppelmann, Angela	C	
Glasmeyer, Johan Christian	4, Nov. 1850	Friedrich	Kleye, M. Catharina	L	
Glasmeyer, Johan Heinrich Francis	19, Aug. 1855	Heinrich	Brockamp, Elisabeth	N	
Glasmeyer, Johan Heinrich Paul	24, Mar. 1850	J. Heinrich	Brockamp, Elisabeth	L	
Glass, Anna Gertrud	20, May 1855	Francis	Ludwig, Maria Anna	D	35
Glass, Caroline	12, Jan. 1859	George C.	O'Hara, Caroline	B	69
Glass, Helena Elisabeth	25, Sept 1859	Lawrence	Wagner, Catharina	A	
Glass, Hieronymus	9, Sept 1855	Lawrence	Wagner, Catharina	A	
Glass, Maria Elisabeth	8, Nov. 1857	Lawrence	Wagner, Catharina	A	
Glass, Mary	15, Feb. 1857	George C.	O'Hara, Caroline	B	40
Glass, William	13, Jan. 1859	William	Kegan, Julia	E	596
Glassmeier, August Heinrich	16, Jan. 1859	Bernard F.	Kle---, Maria Catharina	D	129
Glassmeyer, Johan Bernard	26, Oct. 1859	G. Heinrich	Reling, Elisabeth	N	
Glatthaar, Franz Wilhelm	8, Aug. 1858	Francis J.	Sommer, Theresa	L	
Glaus, Catharina Elisabeth	7, Dec. 1851	Lawrence	Wagner, Catharina	A	
Glaus, Ludwig Philipp	2, Oct. 1853	Lawrence	Wagner, Catharina	A	

Name of Child	Date of Baptism	Father	Mother	Church	Page
Gleason, (boy)	Sept 1855	Michael	Madden, Mary	E	318
Gleason, Agnes	12, Sept 1855	Michael	Blake, Mary	E	314
Gleason, Ann	6, Mar. 1859	Thomas	Hogan, Ann	P	278
Gleason, Catherine	20, May 1857	Michael	Darsey, Mary	E	454
Gleason, Catherine	23, Oct. 1855	Timothy	----, Catherine	E	322
Gleason, Elizabeth	17, Feb. 1856	John	----, Mary	H	
Gleason, Ellen Bridget	5, June 1859	Patrick	Shields, Mary	E	630
Gleason, Helen	8, May 1857	James	McLaughlin, Mary	E	451
Gleason, James	2, Mar. 1859	John	Hayes, Ann	P	278
Gleason, Joanne	18, Jan. 1859	John	Foley, Nancy	P	272
Gleason, John	17, Sept 1855	John	Gilligan, Mary	E	316
Gleason, John	27, Dec. 1858	Timothy	Calvin, Margaret	E	590
Gleason, Margaret	26, Feb. 1857	Timothy	Galvin, Catherine	E	436
Gleason, Mary	28, Jan. 1855	Michael	----, Bridget	E	261
Gleason, Mary	15, July 1855	Patrick	Coffey, Mary	V	25
Gleason, Mary	28, Aug. 1857	Thomas	Hogan, Ann	P	221
Gleason, Michael	1, May 1853	Patrick	Coffee, Mary	V	3
Gleason, Philipp	13, Aug. 1854	James	Cahill, Joanne	E	215
Gleason, Thomas	12, Aug. 1853	James	----, Ellen	E	116
Gleason, William	3, Sept 1857	William	Malcahay, Ann	U	
Gleem?, Mary Ellen	27, Feb. 1859	James	----, Bridget	M	
Gleeson, Alice	9, Aug. 1857	John	Ryan, Ellen	B	47
Gleeson, Andrew	4, Dec. 1859	John	Cunningham, Mary	E	674
Gleeson, Ann	4, Dec. 1859	William G.	Winter, Ann	B	84
Gleeson, Catherine	13, Aug. 1856	Michael	----, Margaret	P	188
Gleeson, Catherine	2, Oct. 1859	Patrick	Gilfoyle, Catherine	B	81
Gleeson, Eliza	31, Dec. 1858	Timothy	McGrath, Mary	E	591
Gleeson, James	4, June 1854	James	----, Nancy	E	196
Gleeson, John	6, Feb. 1859	Dennis	----, Mary	M	
Gleeson, John	11, Sept 1853	John	Hayes, Ann	P	51
Gleeson, Mar Ann	1, Jan. 1859	John	Kyand, Ellen	B	69
Gleeson, Margaret	12, Oct. 1851	Michael	----, Mary	M	
Gleeson, Margaret	7, Oct. 1855	Timothy	McGrath, Mary	E	319
Gleeson, Mary	8, June 1853	Timothy	McGrath, Mary	B	293
Gleeson, Mary Bridget	9, Apr. 1856	Dennis	Delaney, Mary	P	175
Gleeson, Michael	13, Dec. 1852	Michael	----, Mary	M	
Gleeson, Morgan	24, Aug. 1857	Patrick	Kilfoyle, Catherine	B	48
Gleeson, Patrick	19, May1858	Michael	----, Mary	M	
Gleeson, William	20, July 1855	Thomas	Brien, Julia	E	301
Gleis, Anna Margaretha	11, Sept 1853	Joseph	Decker, Elisabeth	Q	3
Glenan, Mary	19, Oct. 1851	John	Dayley, Margaret	P	13a
Glenn, Francis	13, Apr. 1852	Patrick	Smith, Helen	E	402
Glenn, John	6, Jan. 1851	Patrick	Casey, Mary	B	222
Glenn, Margaret	20, July 1858	Martin	----, Catherine	M	
Glenn, Mary Ann	2, May 1858	James	----, Ann	E	533
Glenn, Mary Ann	17, Apr. 1850	Patrick	Hollen, Margaret	E	209
Glenn, Patrick	7, Aug. 1854	William	Whelan, Joanne	B	3
Glennart, John	5, July 1857	James	----, Mary	U	
Glick, Benedict	20, Apr. 1856	Gottlieb	Brand, Catharina	D	57
Gliesen, Thomas	4, June 1854	James	Kint, Margaret	Q	4
Glinn, Catherine	16, Oct. 1859	James	McGuire, Honora	B	82
Glinn, Joseph Francis	31, Mar. 1857	Joseph	Moorman, Theresa	U	
Glins, Anna Maria Catharina	14, Jan. 1852	Joseph	Moorman, Theresa	D	302
Glins, Bernard Heinrich	11, May 1859	Joseph	Moorman, Theresa	U	
Glins, Maria Dina	11, Nov. 1853	J. Joseph	----, Maria Theresa	U	
Glitz, Maria Clara	18, Feb. 1856	Heinrich	Himmelgarn, Elisabeth	N	
Glöckner, Johan	13, Feb. 1859	Johan	Herbert, Margaretha	D	131
Gloeren, Maria Anna Catharina	5, Sept 1856	Jacob	Handley, Anna	Q	15
Gloh, Adelhaid Maria	1, Jan. 1854	Mathias	Emerdinger, Maria	D	1

Name of Child	Date of Baptism	Father	Mother	Church	Page
Glorius, Ferdinand	6, Apr. 1856		Glorius, Barbara	J	34
Glossner, Ludwig Engelbert	29, Aug. 1858	Johan	Busch, Margaretha	F	
Glover, Catherine	14, Apr. 1851	William	Murphy, Catherine	B	230
Glück, Anna Josephina	31, May 1858	Mathias	Wicher, Anna	D	112
Glück, Elisabeth Paulina	23, Sept 1855	Mathias	Wücker, Anna	D	43
Glück, Johan	13, June 1858	Gottlieb	Brand, Catharina	D	113
Gluck, Louisa	24, July 1859	J. Georg	Holber, Maria Anna	D	143
Glück, Margaretha Louisa	7, Nov. 1856	Mathias	C--dres?, Barbara	D	71
Glueck, Anna Maria	12, Apr. 1857	J. Georg	Stubler, Anna Maria	C	
Glueck, Johan	6, Nov. 1859	Nicolaus	Hausel, Barbara	C	
Gluecker, Walburga	11, Sept 1853	Adam	Memmel, Kunigunda	C	
Glueckert, Georg Adam	5, Apr. 1858	G. Adam	Memmel, Kunigunda	C	
Glueckert, Thomas	5, July 1850	Adam	Memmel, Kunigunda	C	
Glynn, Catherine	26, June 1855	John	Hart, Margaret	B	16
Glynn, James	25, Mar. 1856	James	Hall, Mary	T	
Glynn, James	3, Oct. 1852	Patrick	McKenna, Rose	B	271
Glynn, John	1, Mar. 1853	Patrick	Smith, Helen	B	285
Glynn, Martha Joanne	25, Mar. 1856	James	Hall, Mary	T	
Gnau, Barbara Margaretha	16, Mar. 1856	Joseph	Hock, Barbara	J	34
Gnau, Caspar Adam	10, Jan. 1858	Joseph	Hock, Barbara	J	44
Gnau, Friedrich	10, Feb. 1851	Georg A.	Sieber, Anna Maria	F	
Gnau, Johan Chrisian	27, Nov. 1859	Joseph	Hock, Barbara	J	52
Gnau, Maria Francisca	9, June 1850	Joseph	Hock, Barbara	J	6
Gnau, Maria Francisca	21, Dec. 1851	Joseph	Hock, Barbara	J	14
Gnau, Maria Philomena	19, June 1853	Joseph	Hock, Barbara	J	22
Gnut, Catharina	16, Oct. 1853	Johan	Umkehr, Catharina	Q	3
G---o, Columba	27, Aug. 1857	John	Conan, Mary	B	48
Goas, Carolina Helena	15, Sept 1854	Heinrich	Stallo, Maria	D	17
Goas, Carolina Henrietta	7, Aug. 1856	J. Heinrich	Stallo, Anna Maria	D	64
Goas, Georg Joseph	13, July 1859	Johan H.	Stallo, Maria	D	142
Goas, Johan Heinrich Herman Albert	7, Nov. 1852	J. Heinrich	Stallo, Maria	D	356
Goas, Robert	15, Aug. 1858	J. Heinrich	Stallo, Anna Maria	D	117
Göbel, Elisabeth	23, July 1853	Peter	Schumacher, Elisabeth	D	396
Go--bel, Friedrica Helena	20, Oct. 1857	Herman	Huhn, Elisabeth	K	
Göck, Heinrich Augustine	28, Aug. 1854	Bernard	Tempus, Carolina	D	16
Göcke, Anna Maria	27, Jan. 1852	B. Heinrich	Tembusch, Carolina	D	304
Gockel, Barbara Eva	27, July 1856	Christian	Meier, Marianna	F	
Gockel, Maria Magdalena	7, Aug. 1858	Christian	Meier, Maria Anna	T	
Göcken, Francis	1, Nov. 1851	Johan	Feldman, Elisabeth	A	
Gocken, Maria Elisabeth	23, Feb. 1853	Johan	Feldman, Elisabeth	A	
Göckens, Bernard Joseph	30, Jan. 1853	Clemens	Stricker, Catharina	D	368
Goda, Friedrich Herman	11, Dec. 1855	Friedrich	Grote, Friedricka	C	
Godar, Johan Heinrich	18, Apr. 1858	Friedrich	Grute, Friedricka	L	
Gödded, Maria Elisabeth	17, Oct. 1850	Johan	VonderHeide, Margaretha D.	K	
Goddery, Maria Elisabeth	11, May 1856	Georg	Keller, Elisabeth	D	58
Godemann, Joseph Heinrich	14, May 1854	Joseph	Kemker, Margaretha	C	
Gödert, Anna Catharina	26, Sept 1854	Johan	VonderHeit, Margaretha	K	
Goderwis, Conrad	6, Mar. 1859	Libertus	Wingbermil, Anna	C	
Goderwisch, Johan Gerhard	18, Feb. 1855	Libertus	Wingbermühler, Anna M.	A	
Godrey, Catharina	12, Dec. 1858	Georg	Keller, Elisabeth	D	126
Godson, Carl	6, Apr. 1851	Georg	Dickman, Maria	K	
Goebe, Constantin Andreas	6, Aug. 1858	Johan	Boor, Barbara	D	116
Goebel, Amalia Margaretha	19, Feb. 1854	Heinrich	Habig, Maria	L	
Goebel, Carolina	24, Dec. 1854	Leonard	Hess, Regina	F	
Goebel, David	19, June 1859	Leonard	Hess, Regina	F	
Goebel, Francis Michael	20, July 1859	Heinrich	Habig, Maria	C	
Goebel, Heinrich Michael	5, Oct. 1851	Heinrich	Habich, Maria	C	
Goebel, Helena	29, Apr. 1851	Leonhard	Helling, Regina	F	
Goebel, Johan Heinrich	May 1851	Johan	Topp, Anna Maria	S	

Name of Child	Date of Baptism	Father	Mother	Church	Page
Goebel, Josephina	24, Nov. 1857	Leonard	Hess, Regina	F	
Goebel, Leonard	21, May 1853	Leonard	Hess, Regina	F	
Goebel, Maria Anna	26, Apr. 1851	Peter	Schumacher, Elisabeth	D	262
Goebel, Philomena	12, Feb. 1854	Johan	Topp, Anna Maria	S	
Goebel, Wilhelm Edward	30, Nov. 1856	Heinrich	Habig, Maria	C	
Göecke, Anna Maria Theresa	22, Mar. 1853	Heinrich	Schadi, Elisabeth	K	
Goeckel, Rosalia Marianna	5, Nov. 1854	Christian	Meyer, Marianna	F	
Goeckens, Maria Theresa	19, July 1855	Clemens	Stricker, Catharina	L	
Goedeke, Heinrich Wilhelm	6, July 1851	Wilhelm	Hembrock, Theresa	L	
Goedeke, Johan Gerhard	2, Aug. 1853	Wilhelm	Hembrock, Theresa	L	
Goedeker, Anna Maria Theresa	23, Dec. 1855	Wilhelm	Hembrock, Theresa	L	
Goedeker, Wilhelm Joseph	16, Jan. 1858	Wilhelm	Hembrock, Theresa	L	
Goehl, Maria Rosina	9, Aug. 1857	Anton	Kno---, Maria Anna	D	92
Goehling, Clara Elisabeth	14, Sept 1851	Heinrich	Niehaus, Elisabeth	D	282
Goehling, Johan Bernard	15, Nov. 1857	Heinrich	Niehaus, Elisabeth	D	99
Goehm, Catharina	19, July 1857	Wilhelm	Kelb--, Catharina	D	90
Goenner, Heinrich	6, Feb. 1851	Friedrich	Huser, Gertrud	L	
Goepf, Louisa	25, July 1858	Valentin	Wild, Margaretha	D	115
Goerl, Maria Anna	11, June 1857	Georg	Schutt, Catharina	D	87
Goerner, Barbara	6, Aug. 1853	Simon	Kenne, Carolina	D	398
Goers, Agnes	5, Aug. 1851	Herman H.	Debach, Catharina	D	276
Goetke, Francis Anton	25, Sept 1854	Rudolph	Fromin, Anna M.	C	
Goetke, Josephina	20, Apr. 1854	Heinrich	Tapphorn, Margaretha	C	
Goetke, Margaretha Elisabeth	19, Apr. 1852	Heinrich	Tapphorn, Margaretha	C	
Goetke, Maria Bernardina	14, Jan. 1852	Heinrich	Frommeyer, Maria	C	
Goetting, Johan Heinrich	16, Nov. 1851	J. Gerhard	Hausfeld, Catharina	F	
Goettle, Albertina	31, Oct. 1850	Joseph	----, Albertina	C	
Goetz, Andreas Jacob	29, Apr. 1855	Andreas	Geisel, Anna Maria	D	34
Goetz, Carl Theodor	9, Oct. 1859	Carl L.	Kuperschmidt, Wilhelmina	L	
Goetz, Catharina Josephina	25, Apr. 1858	Simon	Kern, Maria Catharina	F	
Goetz, Eva Barbara	16, Oct. 1853	Peter	Wagner, Genofeva	F	
Goetz, Georg	13, June 1850	Philipp	Butzbacher, Barbara	F	
Goetz, Jacob	29, May 1859	Jacob	Walker, Catharina	D	139
Goetz, Johan Georg	19, Sept 1852	G. Anton	Zeil, Elisabeth	D	348
Goetz, Joseph	13, June 1850	Philipp	Butzbacher, Barbara	F	
Goetz, Joseph Balthasar	10, May 1857	Joseph	Mack, Francisca	D	84
Goetz, Joseph Ludwig	26, Feb. 1856	Joseph	Macke, Francisca	D	52
Goetz, Josephina	23, Apr. 1854	Pirmanius	Gut, Friederica	D	8
Goetz, Maria Henrietta	2, Oct. 1859	Johan	Dietz, Elisabeth	N	
Goetz, Peter	11, July 1858	Caspar	Wurzelbacher, Margaretha	H	
Goetz, Rosa	24, May 1857	Tobias	Bauer, Apollonia	D	85
Gogan, Thomas	11, Jan. 1857	John	----, Catherine	R	
Gogerty, James	5, Mar. 1853	Bernard	----, Catherine	M	
Goggin, Michael Robert	3, Oct. 1858	John	Buckley, Catherine	E	566
Goggins, Maria Magdalena	20, Jan. 1850	F. Joseph	Hegele, Maria Magdalena	A	
Goghen, James	3, Aug. 1852	John	----, Ann	E	2
Göglein, Margaretha	24, Aug. 1851	Andreas	Knoest, Catharina	D	279
Gohen, Elizabeth	11, Jan. 1852	Thomas	----, Ann	E	372
Gohen, William	7, Mar. 1858	Thomas	Kenan, Ann	B	56
Göhl, Johan Jacob	6, Dec. 1859	Nicolaus	Bauer, Maria	S	
Göhl, Maria Magdalena	24, Feb. 1854	Nicolaus	Bauer, Maria Anna	S	
Gohl, Peter	31, Oct. 1852	Nicolaus	Bauer, Maria	S	
Gohler, Rosina	29, Aug. 1858	F. Joseph	Weber, Barbara	A	
Göhling, Gerhard Heinrich	21, May 1854	Heinrich	Niehaus, Elisabeth	D	10
Gohman, Johan Gerhard Georg	20, June 1852	J. Heinrich	Barlage, Maria Elisabeth	D	325
Gohman, Maria Elisabeth	9, Sept 1851	J. Theodor	Börger, Maria Elisabeth	D	281
Gohmann, Maria Carolina	29, May 1858	Dietrich	Friemann, M. Anna	C	
Gohmann, Maria Elisabeth	12, Oct. 1856	Joseph	Kemper, Gertrud	C	
Gohmend, Barbara	3, Jan. 1858	Hippolitus	Sonstaedts, Anna	D	102

Name of Child	Date of Baptism	Father	Mother	Church	Page
Gohs, Anna Maria Elisabeth	20, May 1855	Friedrich	Mentrup, Catharina	C	
Gohs, Anton Ferdinand	15, Aug. 1857	Friedrich	----, Catharina	C	
Goigner?, Edward	15, Aug. 1858	James	Griffin, Ellen	B	63
Going, Friedrich Wilhelm	17, Feb. 1858	J. Friedrich	Wuscher, Maria Catharina	D	105
Going, Joseph	22, Dec. 1850	J. Heinrich	Bigers, Anna Maria	D	247
Going, Maria Catharina	10, Nov. 1850	J. Friedrich	Buscher, Maria Catharina	D	242
Going, Maria Mathilda Elisabeth	1, Apr. 1853	Friedrich	Büscher, Catharina	D	378
Göing, Maria Rosa	30, Aug. 1853	J. Heinrich	Bücker, Anna Maria	D	403
Going, Mary Chase	20, Mar. 1850		adult - 22 years old	B	198
Göken, Herman	16, Aug. 1858	Johan	Feldman, Elisabeth	J	46
Göker, Johan	21, Oct. 1858	Bernard	----, ----	D	122
Göking, Anna Maria	19, Oct. 1856	J. Gerhard	König, Anna Maria	D	70
Golagly, Ann	19, Dec. 1859	James	Shields, Ann	E	678
Golatzky, Johan Ludwig	26, May 1859	Anton	Welling, Anna	K	
Goldate, Margaretha	23, Oct. 1855	Johan	Becker, Catharina	D	45
Goldcamp, Maria Anna	7, Mar. 1858	J. Wilhelm	Knemoller, Sophia Friedrica	N	
Golden, Ann	6, Dec. 1852	David	Russell, Ann	E	42
Golden, Catherine	31, Oct. 1854	David	Broslin, Ann	V	19
Golden, Catherine	29, Feb. 1856	James	Sheahan, Julia	E	347
Golden, James	31, May 1859	James	Holly, Mary	P	285
Golden, John	20, Aug. 1852	James	Sheehan, Julia	E	7
Golden, John Anderson	15, Dec. 1856	John	----, Bridget	V	35
Golden, John Edward	31, Aug. 1856	David	Breslin, Ann	V	33
Golden, Mary	16, Aug. 1851	Timothy	Sullivan, Ann	E	333
Golden, Terrence	21, June 1854	James	Sheehan, Julia	E	200
Goldeweyk, Anton	2, Sept 1856	Anton	Zahn, Maria Adelheid	A	
Goldeweyk, Johan Heinrich Francis	21, May 1858	Anton	Zahn, Anna Maria	A	
Goldmeier, Johan Friedrich	5, Feb. 1850		Goldmeier, Maria Angela	D	203
Goldreiner, Johan Albert	6, Dec. 1857	Seraphin	Risch, Francisca	A	
Goldreiner, Johan August	14, May 1854	Seraphin	----, Francisca	A	
Goldreiner, Johan Joseph	9, Mar. 1851	Seraphin	Putsche, Francisca	A	
Goldreiner, Johan Seraphin	22, Aug. 1852	Seraphin	Zeres, Francisca	A	
Goldsberry, Georg	3, Mar. 1855	Samuel	adult	B	12
Goldschmid, Maria Elisabeth	31, May 1857	Bernard	Bringer, Elisabeth	N	
Goldschmidt, Bernard Heinrich	5, Dec. 1852	Albert	Dickhaus, Anna	C	
Goldschmidt, Carl	17, Aug. 1855	Carl	Parrer, Regina	L	
Goldschmidt, Johan Conrad	15, Dec. 1855	Bernard	Dickhaus, M. Anna	C	
Goldschmidt, M. Catharina Angela	14, Oct. 1859	Bernard	Hennekes, Rosina	C	
Goldschmidt, M. Josephina Angela	17, May 1858	Albert	Dickhaus, Anna M.	C	
Goldschmidt, Maria	21, Feb. 1858	Herman	----, Barbara	R	
Goldschmidt, Maria Helena	1, Nov. 1857	Bernard	Hennricks, Helena	C	
Goldschmidt, Maria Louisa	11, May 1856	Herman	----, Eva Barbara	R	
Goldschmidt, Wilhelm	1, Jan. 1854	Herman	Uhrig, Eva Barbara	R	
Goldstädt, Nicolaus	22, Feb. 1852	Johan	----, Maria Anna	H	
Goldweig, Franz Joseph	8, June 1859	Anton	Zahn, Adelheid	F	
Göll, Catharina	12, Mar. 1850	Anton	Pröndl, Catharina	D	205
Goller, Adam Gustavus	20, Jan. 1856	Andreas	Schmitz, Anna Maria	D	51
Gollinger, Catharina	5, Apr. 1857	Friedrich	Müller, Barbara	D	82
Gollinger, Elisabeth	21, Nov. 1858	Friedrich	Mueller, Barbara	T	
Gollinger, Magdalena Francisca	22, Jan. 1854	Friedrich	Miller, Barbara	D	2
Göllman, Vincent	30, Oct. 1853	Wilhelm	Heger, Margaretha	D	412
Gong?, Joanne	20, Jan. 1858	John	Welsh, Catherine	B	54
Gönner, Andreas Cornelius	23, June 1859	Philip	Schwarz, Catharina	Q	31
Gonner, Anna Maria	15, Mar. 1852	Friedrich	Huser, Gertrud	A	
Gönner, Johan Georg	2, June 1852	J. Georg	Alkman, Magdalena	D	323
Gönner, Joseph Heinrich	1, Dec. 1856	Friedrich	Huser, Maria	A	
Gonner, Maria Anna	26, Sept 1854	Friedrich	Huser, Maria	A	
Gonning, Sarah	17, Apr. 1851	Patrick	----, Mary	E	300
Gooden, Francis Mary	21, Aug. 1853	Peter	----, Mary	M	

Name of Child	Date of Baptism	Father	Mother	Church	Page
Goodin, Bridget	25, Jan. 1852	John	----, Catherine	B	251
Goodin, Peter William	31, Aug. 1851	T.	Boudry, Mary	M	
Goodpastor, Sarah Fercella	19, Feb. 1858	Cyril	Hayes,	E	517
Goodwin, Edward	13, May 1858	Richard	----, Mary	E	535
Goodwin, John Francis	6, Nov. 1853	John	McCaffrey, Ann	B	302
Goodwin, Theresa	29, June 1851	John	McCaffrey, Ann	B	235
Goolding, Mary	17, July 1853	John	Hogan, Honora	B	295
Gooley, Sarah	18, June 1854	Thomas	Crowley, Ann	E	199
Gooly, Mary Ellen	26, June 1853	Thomas	----, Ann	E	101
Goos, Anna Maria Friedricka	5, Sept 1852	Johan	----, Catharina	C	
Göpf, Wilhelm	31, Oct. 1854	Valentin	Wess, Margaretha	D	21
Göpfert, Christina Maria	7, Aug. 1859	Michael	Braun, Maria	D	144
Göpfert, Michael	2, June 1857	Michael	Braun, Maria	D	86
Göpner, Michael	12, Jan. 1851	Johan	Rockner, Elisabeth	D	248
Gordela, Mary	24, Apr. 1852	Joseph	----, Magdalena	P	20
Gördert Martha Emilia	16, May 1857	J. Heinrich	Beckers, Maria	A	
Gordon, Ann	1, Sept 1859	James	Farrell, Winefred	B	80
Gordon, Ann	10, Nov. 1858		Gordon, Bridget	B	67
Gordon, Elizabeth	4, Sept 1859	James	McAnessy, Margaret	P	294
Gordon, James	2, Oct. 1853	James	Farrell, Winefred	B	300
Gordon, James	4, Mar. 1858	Luke	Conry, Jane	P	241
Gordon, John	25, Apr. 1857	James	Farrell, Winifred	B	43
Gordon, Joseph	23, Oct. 1854	Peter	----, Mary	M	
Gordon, Luke	19, Oct. 1855	James	Farrell, Winifred	B	20
Gordon, Margaret Ann	10, Sept 1851	John	Mansfield, Ann	E	342
Gordon, Mary	14, Mar. 1858	James	McAnessy, Margaret	P	242
Gordon, Thomas	19, Oct. 1855	James	Farrell, Winifred	B	20
Gordon, Thomas	21, Sept 1856	Luke	Conroy, Jane	B	34
Görg, Joseph	15, Oct. 1854	Wilhelm	Settelmeier, Maria Eva	K	
Gorian, Ann	15, June 1859	Patrick	Harrison, Margaret	B	76
Gorian, Daniel	19, Dec. 1858	Henry	Mullon, Catherine	B	68
Gorien, Mary	20, Sept 1857	Henry	Mullon, Catherine	B	50
Gorke, Maria Theresa Louisa	15, Apr. 1852	Johan	Kottkamp, Maria	K	
Gorman, Alice	15, Mar. 1857	Lawrence	Reilly, Mary Ann	B	42
Gorman, Alice Mary	5, July 1857	John	----, Ann	V	40
Gorman, Ann Augusta	19, Sept 1852	?	----, Mary	B	270
Gorman, Ann Keoun	17, Sept 1854	Peter	McLeary, Frances	B	5
Gorman, Anna Maria	26, May 1859	Johan	Ryan, Elisa	K	
Gorman, Catharina Philomena	12, Apr. 1857		adult - 24 years old	K	
Gorman, Catherine	25, Feb. 1855	John	----, Elizabeth	U	
Gorman, Catherine	28, Aug. 1855	John	Bolan, Catherine	E	311
Gorman, Catherine	25, Feb. 1851	John	Renald, Margaret	E	286
Gorman, Catherine Ellen	27, Aug. 1858	William	Green, Ann	E	559
Gorman, Charles	7, Dec. 1856	Thomas	Galligan, Mary	P	201
Gorman, Clara Elizabeth	15, June 1856	Pierce	O'Leary, Fanny	B	30
Gorman, Edwrad	13, Feb. 1853	Edward	Ward, Alice	P	35
Gorman, Eliza	16, June 1851	William	Russell, Catherine	B	234
Gorman, Ellen	16, June 1851	Lawrence	----, Mary Ann	E	316
Gorman, Frances Honora	9, Mar. 1851	Peter	O'Leary, Frances	B	228
Gorman, Francis	10, Mar. 1855	James	----, Honora	E	270
Gorman, Jaems	25, Sept 1859	Thomas	Galligan, Mary	B	81
Gorman, James	15, Jan. 1854	James	O'Neil, Ann Mary	P	65
Gorman, James	1, Jan. 1854	John	Tracy, Mary	V	9
Gorman, James	7, Sept 1853	Lawrence	----, Sarah	P	51
Gorman, James	2, Mar. 1851	Lawrence	Commen, Elizabeth	E	287
Gorman, James	26, Jan. 1851	Lawrence	Egan, Catherine	B	224
Gorman, James	28, Mar. 1858	Patrick	Caughlin, Ann	B	57
Gorman, James	20, Jan. 1850	Thomas	Galligan, Mary	B	195
Gorman, James	20, May 1856	William	Green, Ann	E	367

Name of Child	Date of Baptism	Father	Mother	Church	Page
Gorman, Jeremiah	15, Nov. 1856	John	----, Mary	R	
Gorman, John	1, July 1856	Bernard	Cavanagh, Sarah	P	184
Gorman, John	18, Aug. 1859	Edward	McKeown, Bridget	B	79
Gorman, John	27, Feb. 1853	James	----, Honora	E	66
Gorman, John	22, Apr. 1855	James	Farrell, Margaret	E	281
Gorman, John	16, Nov. 1851	James	Ockel, Ann Mary	B	245
Gorman, John	28, Mar. 1852	Thomas	Galvin, Mary	B	255
Gorman, John	18, Feb. 1851	Thomas	Harrington, Bridget	B	225
Gorman, John	17, May 1854	Thomas	Landrigan, Joanne	E	190
Gorman, Joseph	23, Jan. 1851	James	Spain, Honora	E	278
Gorman, Joseph	16, Aug. 1857	Joseph	Donohue, Mary	E	474
Gorman, Lawrence	2, July 1854	Lawrence	----, Catherine	U	
Gorman, Lawrence	20, Mar. 1853	Lawrence	Cummins, Elizabeth	V	2
Gorman, Lawrence William	19, July 1857	Michael	Butler, Mary	B	47
Gorman, Margaret	1, Nov. 1857	Charles	----, Mary	E	490
Gorman, Margaret	6, Oct. 1855	John	Foley, Margaret	V	27
Gorman, Margaret	30, Apr. 1854	Thomas	Gallagher, Mary	B	314
Gorman, Margaret Ann	24, Aug. 1856	Patrick	Coughlin, Ann	B	33
Gorman, Martin	6, Nov. 1859	Patrick	Coughlin, Ann	B	83
Gorman, Mary	22, Mar. 1857	James	----, Ann	E	442
Gorman, Mary	10, July 1859	Joseph	----, Mary	V	56
Gorman, Mary	20, Mar. 1853	Lawrence	Cummins, Elizabeth	V	2
Gorman, Mary	29, Aug. 1857	Thomas	----, Joanne	E	476
Gorman, Mary Ann	30, July 1859	Michael	Butler, Mary	B	78
Gorman, Mary Ann	20, Nov. 1859	William	Green, Ann	E	672
Gorman, Mary Hackett	19, Mar. 1853	Pierce	O'Leary, Frances M.	B	286
Gorman, Mary Susan	1, Mar. 1857	John	Ryan, Eliza	B	41
Gorman, Michael	23, Mar. 1851	John	Boran, Catherine	E	293
Gorman, Michael	2, Dec. 1852	Patrick	----, Mary	E	41
Gorman, Michael	7, Sept 1856	William	----, Honora	E	396
Gorman, Patrick	11, May 1851	Edward	Ward, Ann	P	7
Gorman, Patrick	18, Mar. 1853	John	----, Catherine	E	74
Gorman, Stephan	28, Dec. 1853	Thomas	Harrington, Bridget	B	305
Gorman, Thomas	30, Aug. 1852	Lawrence	Keegan, Catherine	B	269
Gorman, Thomas	6, July 1852	Thomas	Ryan, Honora	B	263
Gorman, William	12, June 1857	William P.	----, Ann	E	459
Gormely, Rosanne	13, Sept 1857	Patrick	Gormely, Mary	P	224
Gormley, Bridget	1, Feb. 1852	William	Nestor, Honora	B	251
Gormley, Catherine Ann	24, July 1853	John	Bomphus, Diane	V	4
Gormley, Edward James	27, Apr. 1851	Edward	F----?, Bridget	B	230
Gormley, John	5, Mar. 1854	William	Nister, Honora	V	11
Gormund, Daniel	6, Aug. 1858	Jesse	----, Mary	V	50
Görner, Carolina	16, Sept 1855	Simon	Kell, Carolina	D	43
Gorner, Johan Andreas	18, June 1854	Simon	Kenne, Carolina	D	12
Gorni, Mary Josephine	17, Oct. 1852	John B.	Jeres, Mary J.	B	272
Gorrin, John	25, June 1857	Patrick	Harrison, Margaret	B	45
Görter, Michael Robert	24, Aug. 1856	Christian	Sänger, Maria	K	
Gortha, Maria Louisa	4, Dec. 1859	Johan	Le---, Magdalena	D	152
Gortz, Johanna Carolina	1, June 1856	John	Deitz, Elisabeth	N	
Göseler, Elisabeth	28, Nov. 1858	Johan	Aureden, Margaretha	R	
Gosemeyer, Catharina	5, June 1859	Heinrich	Beumer, Anna Maria	A	
Gosemeyer, Catharina Helena	27, June 1858	Johan	Bohmkamp, Margaretha	J	46
Gosemeyer, Gerhard Joseph	15, Nov. 1859	J. Herman	Baumcamp, Margaretha	N	
Gosemeyer, Johan Herman Heinrich	2, July 1858	G. Heinrich	Beumer, Maria	A	
Goshorn, Michael	23, Aug. 1855	John	----, Winnie	E	309
Gosiger, Maria Josephina	31, Aug. 1852	Friedrich J.	Eversman, Anna Maria	A	
Gosinger, Johan Friedrich	23, Apr. 1850	F. Joseph	Oeverman, Anna Maria	A	
Gosinger, Joseph Anton	12, Apr. 1858	F. Joseph	Oeverman, Anna Maria	A	
Gosinger, Maria Philomena	5, July 1855	F. Joseph	Oeverman, Anna Maria	A	

Name of Child	Date of Baptism	Father	Mother	Church	Page
Gosken, Maria Catharina	15, June 1856	Johan	Feldman, Elisabeth	J	36
Gösker, Anna Catharina	28, Mar. 1854	Joseph	Breitenbach, Anna Catharina	A	
Gösker, Anna Maria	26, Oct. 1856	Joseph	Breitenbach, Anna Catharina	A	
Gösker, Louisa	3, Oct. 1858	Joseph	Breitenbach, Catharina	F	
Goslar, August	14, Oct. 1859	Daniel	Pottner, Wilhelmina	K	
Goslin, Catherine	11, Apr. 1852	James	Boulger, Mary	B	256
Goslin, James	12, July 1855	James	Boulger, Mary	B	16
Goslin, Mary Ann	3, Aug. 1857	James	Boulger, Mary	B	47
Gösling, Bernard Gerhard Friedrich	28, Mar. 1858	Friedrich	Unger, Maria	A	
Gosling, Catharina	23, Apr. 1854	B. Joseph	Kenning, Anna Gertrud	K	
Gösling, Maria Josephina	16, Oct. 1859	Friedrich	Unger, Margaretha	A	
Gosman, Gerhard Heinrich	11, July 1853	Theodor	Berger, Elisabeth	D	394
Gossinger, Elisabeth	13, Oct. 1853	Francis	Limberg, Josephina	A	
Gössinger, Joseph Maximillian	24, Oct. 1852	J. Max	Muth, Gertrud	D	354
Gossinger, Maria Louisa	20, July 1851	J. Herman	Bomcamp, Margaretha	D	274
Gossler, Maria Catharina	30, Oct. 1859	J. Michael	Metz, Carolina	D	150
Gössler, Mathias	26, Oct. 1857	Johan	----, Margaretha	R	
Gossman, Magdalena	6, Nov. 1859	Henry	Honer, Catharina	D	150
Gossmeyer, Johan Heinrich	9, June 1850	J. Heinrich	Fischer, Maria Anna	D	216
Gosting, Bernard Johan	6, May 1856	Joseph	Kenning, Gertrud	K	
Got, Francis Heinrich	27, July 1850	Gerhard	Dösing, Dina	D	225
Gote, Anton Herman	3, Apr. 1859	Herman	Betsche, Philomena	T	
Götke, Bernard	16, Feb. 1859	Wilhelm	Föckers, Margaretha	D	131
Götke, Bernard Heinrich	25, Sept 1856	Wilhelm	Föckers, Margaretha	D	68
Gott, Anna	11, Nov. 1855	Conrad	Monkhaus, Elisabeth	K	
Gott, Anna Maria Friedrica	6, July 1852	Conrad F.	Mönninghaus, Elisabeth	K	
Gott, Catharina Barbara	20, Dec. 1857	Conrad	----, Elisabeth	K	
Gott, Elisabeth Catharina	27, Nov. 1859	H. Andreas	Buhren, Anna	K	
Gott, Heinrich Francis	26, Feb. 1854	F. Conrad	Menkhaus, Elisabeth	K	
Gott, Herman Joseph	17, Dec. 1850	H. Andreas	Busam, Anna Maria	A	
Gott, Hubert Francis	21, Oct. 1852	Andreas H.	Buern, Maria	K	
Gott, Hubert Heinrich	10, May 1857	Heinrich	Buerin, Anna Maria	K	
Gott, Joseph Friedrich Herman	28, Feb. 1856	Joseph H.	Hahnhauser, Catharina	F	
Gott, Juliana	10, Jan. 1858	Herman J.	Hahnhausen, Catharina	F	
Gott, Maria Catharina	11, May 1858	Friedrich	Haar, Marianna	F	
Gott, Maria Francisca Friedrica	23, Apr. 1855	Heinrich	Buhren, Anna Maria	K	
Gottbehöde, Louisa	24, Apr. 1856	J. Heinrich	Hillers, Maria Margaretha	R	
Gottbehode, Maria Elisabeth	12, May 1850	J. Heinrich	Pille, Maria Agnes	C	
Gottbehorde, Maria Agnes	7, Dec. 1853	Johan H.	Helmes, Margaretha	A	
Göttelmann, Maria Anna	15, May 1854	J. Heinrich	Rennecher, Bernardina	D	10
Gottem, Bernard	27, July 1851	Bernard	Hoffman, Catharina	D	275
Götter, Elisabeth	28, Nov. 1858	Carl	Wagner, Maria	A	
Götter, Maria Catharina	21, July 1852	Heinrich	Meier, Maria Catharina	D	340
Gotti, Joanne	14, Jan. 1850	Joseph	----, Sarah	E	192
Göttinger, Margaretha	6, Apr. 1856	Bernard	Steiber, Catharina	D	55
Gottlieb, William John	14, Mar. 1858	William	Donovan, Mary	B	56
Gottmeyer, Johan Bernard	18, Sept 1856	Johan	Bohnkamp, Catharina	L	
Gottschalk, Elisabeth	4, Apr. 1858	Friedrich	----, Theresa	D	108
Götz, adam	5, Feb. 1859	Conrad	Willich, Maria	D	130
Götz, Adam Louis	23, Oct. 1854	Joseph	Mack, Francisca	D	20
Götz, Carolina Philomena	21, Aug. 1859	Tobias	Bauer, Apollonia	J	52
Götz, Catharina	7, Feb. 1857	Andreas	Geisel, Magdalena	K	
Götz, Catharina	3, Feb. 1859	Joseph	Mack, Francisca	D	130
Götz, Catharina	18, Feb. 1855	Tobias	Bauer, Appolonia	D	29
Götz, Johan	9, Mar. 1856	Tobias	Bauer, Appolonia	D	53
Götz, Johan Heinrich	19, Mar. 1854	Johan	Dietz, Elisabeth	K	
Gotz, Maria Magdalena Gertrud	23, Dec. 1855		adult	F	
Gough, Christina	12, Dec. 1854	Patrick	McSheehan, Ann	P	109
Gough, Edward	23, Mar. 1854	John	----, Sarah	B	311

Name of Child	Date of Baptism	Father	Mother	Church	Page
Gough, Helen	17, July 1859	Peter	Hart, Ann	U	
Gough, Mary	23, Dec. 1852	M.	Frain, Ann	B	278
Gough, Michael Joseph	23, May 1852	Christopher	----, Jean	E	417
Gough, Peter William	12, Feb. 1854	Peter	----, Helen	U	
Gough, Thomas	24, Jan. 1851	Patrick	Kilfoy, Mary	E	278
Gou--h, John	30, Nov. 1851	Patrick	Frayner, Ann	B	246
Gould, John Wililam	6, Nov. 1853	William	High, Catherine	B	302
Goun, Jacob	14, Oct. 1850	Jacob	Goan, Elise	D	238
Gourjon, Alina Magdalena	22, Oct. 1853	Edward	Scherier, Magdalena	L	
Gourjon, Andrew Jackson	7, Sept 1856	Edward	Scherier, Magdalena	L	
Gourjon, Maria Louisa Bernardina	14, Nov. 1858	Edward	Schavel, Magdalena	L	
Goury, Charles Leo	31, Dec. 1854	John	Gerry, Margaret	B	9
Gove, Johan Friedrich	5, Feb. 1850	Bernard	Goldmeier, Maria Angela	D	203
Goven, Mary	5, Dec. 1852	Patrick	Langin, Mary	P	31
Grab, Maria Anna	9, July 1855	Ludwig	Glo, Johanna	C	
Grabb, Anna Maria	14, Mar. 1852	Andreas	Fritsch, Crescentia	K	
Grabb, Victoria	25, May 1856	Andreas	Fritsch, Crescentia	K	
Graben, Johan	16, Nov. 1850	Ambrose	Diel, Catharina	D	243
Gräber, Anna Maria	21, Nov. 1852	Johan	Hofman, Anna Maria	D	358
Graber, Daniel	14, May 1850	John	Lockboon, Elizabeth	E	222
Gräber, Joseph	26, Aug. 1851	Johan	Hofman, Anna M.	D	279
Graber, Peter Joseph	29, Apr. 1855	Peter	Schuler, Susanna	K	
Grabinger, Joseph Martin	14, Feb. 1857	Joseph	Timpfel?, Elisabeth Theresa	D	79
Grabman, Joseph	20, June 1858	John	Stiegler, Anna Maria	U	
Grabman, Michael	11, Dec. 1853	Johan	Stogli, Anna Maria	D	419
Grabuth, Maria Catharina	31, Oct. 1858	Georg	Haven, Scholastica	A	
Grace, Thomas	7, Jan. 1854	Martin	Larkin, Judith	B	306
Gradler, Jacob	12, Apr. 1857	Johan	Kern, Christina	D	82
Grady, Daniel	2, Oct. 1853	Timothy	----, Bridget	B	300
Grady, James	21, Dec. 1856	John	Martell, Catherine	V	35
Grady, James Martin	9, Nov. 1859	Timothy	Grady, Ann	B	83
Grady, John	6, Sept 1857	Patrick	----, Catherine	E	479
Grady, John	12, July 1850	Patrick	Nolan, Margaret	E	230
Grady, John	27, June 1858	Timothy	Grady, Ann	B	61
Grady, Julia Ann	25, Sept 1859	Martin	Subler, Julia	E	657
Grady, Julia Mary	8, Sept 1856	John	Carroll, Catherine	V	33
Grady, Margaret	28, Sept 1856	Brian	Grady, Mary	P	193
Grady, Mary	29, June 1851	Bryan	Donnelly, Mary	P	9
Grady, Mary	15, Sept 1851	Daniel	----, Margaret	P	12
Grady, Mary	12, Dec. 1855	L.	Pots, Ann	E	332
Grady, Mary	11, July 1858	Martin	Tabler, Julia	E	548
Grady, Mary	28, June 1856	Patrick	Sullivan, Catherine	E	378
Grady, Mary	30, June 1857	Timothy	Coleman, Bridget	B	46
Grady, Mary Ann	7, Nov. 1858	John	McDowell, Catherine	E	577
Grady, Mary Catherine	23, Dec. 1854	John	----, Catherine	V	20
Grady, Michael	19, Nov. 1854	Brian	Donnelly, Mary	P	105
Grady, Patrick	9, June 1851	William	Smith, Elizabeth	P	8
Grady, Thomas	3, July 1859	Timothy	O'Donnell, Mary	E	636
Grady, Wililam Henry	12, June 1858	William	O'Brien, Ann	B	60
Grady, William	19, Dec. 1856	John	McDonald, Catherine	E	421
Graeb, Carl	12, Dec. 1852	Heinrich	Boehner, Walburga	F	
Graeb, Engelbert	4, Oct. 1857	Hubert	Kiebel, Catharina	F	
Graeman, Johan Heinrich	28, July 1851	J. Bernard	Stahlman, Maria	K	
Graf, Anna Maria	14, Aug. 1859	Adam	Ziegler, Maria Anna	D	144
Graf, Anna Maria	21, July 1850	Philipp	Hammer, Elisabeth	C	
Graf, Carolina Amelia	30, Sept 1855	Jacob	----, Carolina	C	
Graf, Catharina	2, May 1858	Nicolaus	Egli, Gertrud	D	110
Graf, Francis	11, Jan. 1852	Joseph	Graf, Josephina	D	301
Graf, Francisca	24, Sept 1854	Adam	Ziegler, Anna Maria	D	18

Name of Child	Date of Baptism	Father	Mother	Church	Page
Graf, Heinrich	3, Dec. 1854	Ferdinand	Blust, Victoria	D	23
Graf, Henry	25, Jan. 1852	Henry	----, Catharine	H	
Graf, Jacob	13, July 1856	Adam	Ziegler, Anna Maria	D	63
Graf, Johan	16, Nov. 1858	David	Kolet, Lena	C	
Graf, Johan Adam	25, Dec. 1857	Adam	Ziegler, Anna Maria	D	101
Graf, Johan Heinrich	5, Feb. 1854	Heinrich	----, Catharina	H	
Graf, Joseph	8, Apr. 1858	Joseph	Graf, Josephina	D	109
Graf, Josephina	2, Apr. 1854	Joseph	Graf, Josephina	D	7
Graf, Maria Catharina	4, June 1854	Nicolaus	Glaub, Maria	D	11
Graf, Maria Louisa	17, June 1857	Ferdinand	Blust, Victoria	D	88
Graf, Peter Valentin	10, Feb. 1850	Anton J.	Fischer, Maria Anna	D	203
Gräfenhan, Julius Carl	31, July 1859	Julius	Golotzky, Ernestina	K	
Grafenkamp, Anna Maria Agnes	26, July 1858	Heinrich	Kramer, Elisabeth	K	
Gräfenkamp, Bernard Heinrich	13, Nov. 1859	Heinrich	Kramer, Elisabeth	K	
Graff, Anna Magdalena	12, July 1857	David	Collet, Magdalena	T	
Graham, Ann Matilda	27, Feb. 1858	G.	Lary, Honora	E	518
Graham, Catherine	19, July 1857	James	Murtegh, Ann	P	217
Graham, Eliza Jane	25, Nov. 1858	Patrick	----, Elbna	E	582
Graham, Eugene	14, Mar. 1859	John	----, Ann	M	
Graham, James	15, Oct. 1854	James	Riedue, Ann	N	25
Graham, John	12, Nov. 1857	Thomas	----, Margaret	E	492
Graham, Marcellinus	26, Aug. 1855	Patrick	Byrne, Bridget	U	
Graham, Margaret	19, Dec. 1852	Dennis	Curley, Ann	B	278
Graham, Mary	19, June 1853	William	Walsh, Bridget	R	
Graham, Mary Ann	24, June 1855	Patrick	----, Margaret	M	
Graham, Mary Elizabeth	9, July 1853	Patrick	Byrnes, Bridget	V	4
Graham, Mary Ellen	7, Jan. 1855	Patrick	Kately, Ellen	B	9
Graham, Michael	25, Aug. 1855	William	Walsh, Bridget	R	
Graham, Patrick	30, Nov. 1856	Patrick	Kelley, Ellen	B	37
Graham, Phoebe	26, Jan. 1853		adult	B	282
Graham, Thomas	4, Jan. 1852	William	Walsh, Bridget	R	
Grain, William	23, June 1859	Timothy	----, Mary Ann	E	634
Grake, Julia	21, May 1857	William	Shea, Joanne	B	44
Graly, Mary Jane	17, Dec. 1852	Hugh	Maloney, Sarah	P	31
Graman, Johan Friedrich	15, Feb. 1859	Heinrich	Schmidt, Catharina	A	
Graman, Johan Friedrich	19, June 1856	Herman H.	Varnau, Catharina	A	
Graman, Johan Gerhard	1, Dec. 1854	Bernard	Stall, Maria Angela	K	
Gramann, Johan Heinrich	30, Mar. 1859	Heinrich	Olgemoeller, Theresa	L	
Grames, James	31, July 1856	John	Kenny, Bridget	E	385
Gramich, Mathias	20, Oct. 1856	Francis	Hahne, Catharina	C	
Gramke, Arnold Joseph	4, Dec. 1854	Joseph	König, Catharina	D	23
Gramke, Catharina Bernardina	31, May 1859	Joseph	König, Catharina	D	139
Gramke, Johan Bernard Francis	12, Feb. 1857	Bernard	Niemöller, Antonetta	A	
Gramke, Johan Gerhard Bernard	3, May 1852	Joseph	König, Catharina	D	318
Grammen, Johan Dietrich	21, Jan. 1859	Herman	Farenhorst, Catharina	A	
Grammer, Francis Joseph	13, Oct. 1858	Francis	Hae---, Anna	D	121
Grammer, Mary Jane	16, Oct. 1853	Thomas	----, Mary	E	134
Grandidier, John Charles Victor	24, Feb. 1853	John B.	Lodvitz, Mary Ann	E	65
Grandner, Margaretha Mechtildes	2, Nov. 1851	Andreas	Balz, Genofeva	D	290
Graney, Honora Elenore	21, Feb. 1854	Patrick	Manley, Bridget	P	70
Graney, Mary Ann	17, Feb. 1855	Patrick	Manly, Bridget	P	120
Graney, Thomas	9, Nov. 1856	Patrick	Manly, Bridget	P	197
Grann, Robert	17, Oct. 1858	Anton	Gsch---, Gertrud	D	122
Grannan, Helen	30, Mar. 1851	James	Fitzpatrick, Mary	B	228
Grannan, James	8, Aug. 1852	James	Fitzpatrick, Mary	B	267
Grannan, Mary Helen	23, Sept 1855	James	Fitzpatrick, Mary	P	151
Grant, Daniel	15, May 1859	Daniel	Meehan, Mary	E	624
Grant, John	25, Apr. 1859	Dennis	--arner, Josephine	E	620
Grant, Mary Ann	15, Aug. 1853		adult	B	297

Name of Child	Date of Baptism	Father	Mother	Church	Page
Grany, Catherine	11, Dec. 1859	Peter	Keenan, Catherine	E	675
Grany, Edmund	17, Jan. 1858	Peter	Keenan, Catherine	E	510
Grany, Mary Ann	18, July 1856	Peter	Keenan, Catherine	E	382
Grapp, Joseph Andreas	8, July 1854	Andreas J.	Fritsch, Crescentia	K	
Grappi, Barbara	5, June 1852	William	----, Margaret	H	
Grasmuck, Adolph	26, Apr. 1859	John	Kellner, Friedrica	D	136
Grasmuck, Maria Margaretha	18, Dec. 1859	Michael	Marks, Maria	T	
Grass, Anna Louisa	8, Dec. 1858	Godfried	----, Margaretha	D	125
Grass, Anton Mathias	9, Apr. 1854	Anton	Maus, Elisabeth	D	8
Grass, Catharina	29, May 1859	Michael	Oeter, Eva	H	
Grass, Elisabeth	8, Feb. 1852	MIchael	----, Eva	H	
Grass, Francis Johan	30, Nov. 1856	Anton	Maus, Elisabeth	D	73
Grass, Magdalena	3, Oct. 1858	Anton	Maus, Elisabeth	D	120
Grass, Margaret	27, May 1855	Michael	----, Eva	H	
Grass, Margaretha	26, July 1858	Georg	Karre, Barbara	D	116
Grasse, Nicolaus	28, Apr. 1850	William	Werle, Margaret	H	
Grassinger, Carl	12, Aug. 1851	Joseph	Saureiter, Catharina	D	277
Grassinger, Elisabeth	18, May 1854	Joseph	Schreiber, Catharina	K	
Grauss, Catharina	22, Feb. 1857	Carl	Schabbe, Barbara	D	79
Grave, Johanna Angela Elisabeth	25, June 1856	Joseph	Buenker, Carolina	L	
Gravel, Anna Margaretha	25, Oct. 1851	J. Heinrich	Luepken, Maria	C	
Gravel, Johan Bernard	17, Aug. 1856	J. Bernard	Hoelscher, Elisabeth	K	
Gravel, Johan Heinrich	6, Mar. 1855	J. Bernard	Hölscher, Maria Elisabeth	K	
Graven, Susan Mary	24, Aug. 1857	Thomas	Gilmore, Ann	E	475
Graver, John	4, May 1855	Thomas	Gilmore, Ann	E	284
Graver, Maria Catharina	18, Apr. 1856	Peter	Schuler, Susanna	K	
Graves, William Griffin	19, Aug. 1855	Henry	Daly, Ellen	B	18
Gravinger, Elisabeth	22, Jan. 1854	Joseph	Tempfel, Theresa	F	
Grawe, Anna Maria Elisabeth	16, Jan. 1859	Bernard	Schneider, Carolina	C	
Grawe, Johan Francis Bernard	31, Dec. 1854	Bernard	Schneider, Caroline	C	
Grawe, Joseph Bernard	26, Dec. 1858	Joseph	Bunker, M. Carolina	L	
Grawe, Louisa Antonia	16, Nov. 1856	Bernard	Schneider, Carolina	C	
Grawe, Maria Catharina	19, Jan. 1854	J. Heinrich	Wessendorf, Margaretha	C	
Grawel, Anna Maria Elisabeth	1, Aug. 1858	J.B. Heinr.	Hölscher, Elisabeth	A	
Gray, Bridget	4, Apr. 1859	William	Blow, Jane	L	
Gray, Charles Werden	27, Dec. 1851	John D.	Hammond, Eliza Cath.	E	367
Gray, Emma Frances	27, June 1857	John	Lockwood, Ellen	B	45
Gray, James	16, Jan. 1855	James	Corrivan, Honora	R	
Gray, John	22, Jan. 1857	James	Gallagher, Mary	B	39
Gray, Michael	10, July 1852	James	Gallagher, Mary	B	263
Gray, Patrick	29, Oct. 1854	James	Gallagher, Mary	P	101
Gray, William Daniel	5, Feb. 1858	William	Doyle, Catherine	B	55
Gray, William Francis	7, Aug. 1853	Robert	----, Gertrud	E	115
Gready, Margaret	20, Feb. 1853	Bernard	Connellan, Mary	B	284
Grebner, Andreas Eduard	18, Dec. 1859	Johan	Lipps, Maria	F	
Grebner, Anna Maria Clara	19, Apr. 1854	Johan	Lipps, Elisabeth	F	
Grebner, Carolina Elisabeth	22, June 1856	Johan	Lipps, Maria	G	
Grebner, Catharina Wilhelmina	6, June 1858	Johan	Lipps, Maria	G	
Grebner, Franz Joseph	14, Nov. 1852	Johan	Lipps, Marianna	F	
Greece, mary	16, Oct. 1858	Martin	Lackner, Johanna	U	
Greel, Robert	20, June 1855	Francis	Dorsey, Alice	E	294
Green, Ann	6, Apr. 1851	John	Gannon, Helen	B	229
Green, Ann	31, Aug. 1851	Patrick	McKeogh, Mary	E	339
Green, Charles	1, Jan. 1854	Matthew	Mullany, Bridget	B	306
Green, Edward	12, June 1853	John	Gannon, Helen	B	293
Green, James	9, Mar. 1851	Daniel	----, Catherine	E	288
Green, James	30, Jan. 1853	Thomas	----, Elizabeth	M	
Green, James Clarke	23, Jan. 1859		adult	B	70
Green, James Francis	21, June 1857	Matthew	Mullaney, Bridget	B	45

Name of Child	Date of Baptism	Father	Mother	Church	Page
Green, Jeremiah	1, Feb. 1854	James	Tracy, Judith	V	10
Green, Joel Charles	17, Feb. 1856	Joel	Allgeier, Catherine	B	25
Green, John	3, July 1859	John	Gorman, Ann	B	77
Green, John	8, May 1856	Thomas	----, Elizabeth	M	
Green, John	27, Sept 1852	William	Dugan, Sarah Jane	E	22
Green, Julia	4, Jan. 1852	Matthew	Mullaney, Bridget	B	250
Green, Kate	13, Mar. 1859	Joel	Allgaier, Catherine	B	72
Green, Margaret	2, Dec. 1855	James	----, Julia	V	28
Green, Margaret Ann	9, Dec. 1858	John	Lyons, Catherine	E	586
Green, Mary	3, July 1855	Daniel	Hainy, Catherine	E	297
Green, Mary	5, Feb. 1854	Jeremiah	Lynch, Mary	R	
Green, Mary	22, Apr. 1851	John	Fair, Elizabeth	E	302
Green, Mary Almira	28, Jan. 1855	Joel B.	Allgeier, Catherine	B	10
Green, Mary Ann	31, Dec. 1854	George	White, Ann	E	250
Green, Mary Helen	26, Nov. 1854	John	Quinan, Helen	P	106
Green, Mary Jane	15, May 1857	John	Lyons, Catherine	E	453
Green, Mary?	8, Aug. 1858	Thomas	----, Elizabeth	M	
Green, Matthew	15, Aug. 1854	Thomas	----, Elizabeth	M	
Green, Patrick	26, Jan. 1851	Thomas	Tobin, Elizabeth	M	
Green, Thomas	11, Sept 1859	James	Carter, Mary	B	80
Green, Thomas	29, Oct. 1859	John	Spellecy, Mary	V	61
Green, Thomas	21, Aug. 1859	Matthew	Mullanny, Bridget	B	79
Green, William	9, May 1852	James	----, Judy	E	410
Green, William	6, Jan. 1856	Matthew	Mullany, Bridget	B	23
Green, William	8, May 1856	Thomas	----, Elizabeth	M	
Green, William Michael	16, Dec. 1855	James	Holland, Mary	V	28
Greene, Ellen	25, Jan. 1852	Thomas	Coleman, Mary	E	377
Greene, Mary Ann	1, Jan. 1854	Dennis	Quinlan, Brdiget	B	306
Greenrod, Catherine	13, Aug. 1856	Key	Bennett, Mary A.	B	32
Greenrod, George K.	25, Dec. 1856		adult	B	38
Greenrod, Helen	24, Sept 1853	Key	McGinnis, Mary	B	299
Greenrod, James	24, May 1855	Key	Wiggins, Mary Ann	B	15
Greenrod, Mary Ann	26, May 1855		adult	B	15
Greenrod, Mary Jane	13, July 1851	Key	Wiggins, Mary Ann	B	236
Greenwall, John	20, June 1852	John	adult - 23 years old	E	426
Greenwood, George	2, Aug. 1851	William	Duhy, Sarah Jane	E	329
Greever, Patrick	3, July 1853	Patrick	Doherty, Helen	B	294
Greffing, Joseph Bernard	3, Oct. 1851	Anton	Heibring, Catharina	A	
Greifenkamp, Bernard Heinrich	21, Nov. 1858	J. Bernard	Kessing, Agnes	C	
Grein, Francis Xavier	17, Aug. 1859	Martin	----, Maria Anna	J	50
Greiner, Catharina	27, Sept 1856	Johan	Heiob, Maria	C	
Greiner, Catharina Theresa	31, Jan. 1858		Greiner, Catharina	G	
Greiner, Daniel	8, Sept 1850	Johan	Schaumberger, Maria	D	231
Greiner, Ernestina Elisabeth	13, Feb. 1859	Ernst	Schmedding, Christina	C	
Greiner, Meinrad	17, Jan. 1858	Joseph	Beiler, Maria	F	
Greiner, Wilhelm Johan	21, Feb. 1858	Johan	Heiob, Anna Maria	G	
Greis, Johan Mathias	25, Aug. 1850	Francis	Greif, Catharina	J	6
Greive, Thomas	6, Oct. 1850	Joseph	Fink, Catharina	D	236
Greiwe, Adam Heinrich	15, Mar. 1859	Christoph	Wendel, M. Angela	L	
Greiwe, Adam Heinrich	2, Dec. 1852	Eberhard	Hemmelgarn, M. Elis.	L	
Greiwe, Anna Maria	20, June 1853	Adam H.	Littmeier, M. Elisabeth	L	
Greiwe, Anna Maria	19, June 1853	Adam H.	Littmeyer, M. Elis.	L	
Greiwe, Anna Maria Elisabeth	4, Feb. 1852	Georg	Goldmeier, Anna Maria	D	305
Greiwe, Anna Maria Elisabeth	7, Aug. 1857	J. Adam	Lietmeyer, A.M. Elis.	L	
Greiwe, Catharina	29, Aug. 1853	Georg	Goldmaier, Anna Maria	D	403
Greiwe, Everhard Heinrich	16, Sept 1855	Christoph	Wendel, Angela	L	
Greiwe, Franz Heinrich	18, June 1854	J. Heinrich	Tepe, Sophia	L	
Greiwe, Johan	29, Aug. 1853	Georg	Goldmaier, Anna Maria	D	403
Greiwe, Johan Everhard Heinrich	5, June 1855	Adam H.	Littmeyer, M. Elis.	L	

Name of Child	Date of Baptism	Father	Mother	Church	Page
Greiwe, Johan Friedrich	9, Dec. 1857	Christoph	Wendel, M. Angela	L	
Greiwe, Johan Gerhard Heinrich	20, Sept 1851	Heinrich	Tepe, Sophia	L	
Greiwe, Johan Heinrich	4, Apr. 1859	Adam H.	Litemeyer, Elisabeth	L	
Greiwe, Johan Heinrich	3, Feb. 1854	Edward	Hemmelgarn, Elisabeth	L	
Greiwe, Joseph	21, Jan. 1858		Greiwe, Johanna	L	
Greiwe, Maria Louisa	9, Sept 1859	Edward	Hemmelgarn, M. Elis.	L	
Greiwe, Maria Louisa	4, May 1856	J. Heinrich	Tepe, Sophia	L	
Greiwe, Maria Wilhelmina	12, Jan. 1858	Edward	Hemmelgarn, Elisabeth	L	
Greiwe, Regina	25, Mar. 1858	J. Heinrich	Tepe, Maria Sophia	L	
Greiwing, Johan Gerhard	18, Apr. 1851	Gerhard H.	Lanfer, M. Anna	C	
Grell, Maria Francisca	15, Aug. 1858	Theodor	Lechner, Maria	D	117
Gremeis, Francis Anton	6, May 1855	Pantaleon	Brandhuber, Catharina	D	34
Grennan, Mary Jane	18, Mar. 1851	Patrick	Hyens, Catherine	E	292
Grere?, Bridget	1, Jan. 1853	William	Dean, Honora	P	33
Gres, Theresa	7, June 1852	Heinrich	Bauris, Elisabeth	D	323
Grescamp, Anna Maria Elisabeth	3, June 1851	J. Gerhard	Schratz, Christina Elisabeth	D	266
Gresch, Catharina	28, Dec. 1851	Gregor	Maurer, Rosa	J	14
Greschbach,	18, Jan. 1857	Heinrich	Birkle, Justina	F	
Grese, Bridget	15, Dec. 1852	Michael	Coleman, Catherine	P	31
Greskamp, Anton Ferdinand	19, Oct. 1853	J. Herman G.	Schratz, Catharina Christina	D	410
Greskamp, Catharina Christina	24, Feb. 1850	J. Herman	Schratz, Christina Elisabeth	D	203
Greskamp, Wilhelm August	19, Apr. 1857	J. Herman	Schratz, Christina	D	83
Gress, Catharina	4, May 1851	Ludwig	Ulerich, Anna M.	D	263
Gress, Heinrich	6, Jan. 1856	Ludwig	Ulrich, Anna Maria	D	50
Gress, Ludwig	9, May 1852	Ludwig	Ulrich, Anna Maria	D	319
Gresser, Johan	20, Feb. 1859	M. Joseph	Dieckman, Anna Maria	J	48
Greule, Albert Martin	2, Oct. 1859	Lawrence	Grasselli, Theresa	K	
Greule, Francis Joseph	11, Feb. 1857	Lawrence	Grasselli, Theresa	K	
Greuner, Eva Margaretha	12, Oct. 1851	Johan	Spies, Magdalena	L	
Greuter, Edward Alexander	29, Mar. 1857	Jacob	Adam, Constantina	D	81
Greve, Carolina Francisca	12, Nov. 1856	J. Herman	Schmidt, M. Lucia	L	
Greve, Francis Aloysius	16, Mar. 1856	Georg	Korh---, Anna Maria	D	54
Greve, Gerhard Francis	8, Nov. 1850	Gerhard	Fisse, Theresa	C	
Greve, Gesina Maria Josephina	17, June 1857	J. Bernard	Wahoff, Maria Anna	L	
Grever, Maria Francisca Louisa	2, Mar. 1859	Francis	Tangermann, Maria	L	
Greving, Anton	1, Jan. 1856	Herman G.	Landwehr, Anna Maria	L	
Greving, Maria Louisa	17, Jan. 1853	Gerhard H.	Landwehr, Anna Maria	L	
Greving, Nicolaus Joseph Christian	24, Oct. 1858	Nicolaus	Burger, Margaretha	F	
Grewe, Bernard Heinrich August	9, May 1853	Herman	Schmitt, Lucia	L	
Grewe, Clemens August	13, Oct. 1850	Bernard	Herbring, Sophia	L	
Grewe, Gerhard Herman	16, Sept 1858	Johan G.	Wiehof, Catharina	L	
Grewe, Gertrud Elisabeth	22, Apr. 1857	Heinrich	Mönning, G. Bernardina	A	
Grewe, Heinrich Herman	2, Jan. 1856	Joseph	Greivenkamp, Anna	A	
Grewe, J. Elisabeth Bernardina	10, Oct. 1852	Gerhard	Fisse, Theresa	C	
Grewe, Johan Gerhard Bernard	3, Feb. 1854	J. Gerhard	Wiehof, Catharina	L	
Grewe, Johan Heinrich	12, Jan. 1851	Gerhard	Wiehoff, M. Catharina	L	
Grewe, Joseph Bernard Heinrich	10, May 1859	Heinrich	Mönning, Dina	A	
Grewe, Maria Catharina	10, Sept 1853	Bernard J.	Grewenkamp, Anna Maria	A	
Grewe, Maria Catharina Carolina	21, Feb. 1856	J. Gerhard	Wiehoff, Catharina	L	
Grewe, Maria Elisabeth	16, Oct. 1859	Bernard	Ulenbrock, Maria	L	
Grewe, Maria Elisabeth	6, Oct. 1850	Edward H.	Hemmelgarn, M. Elisabeth	L	
Grewing, Christina Josephina	16, Nov. 1856	Nicolaus	Burgert, Margaretha	F	
Grey, Elizabeth	5, July 1850	Anthony	----, Susan	E	228
Grey, Margaret	27, Sept 1856	James	----, Honora	R	
Grey, Mary	28, Oct. 1855	William	Doyle, Catherine	B	21
Grey, Mary Emma	25, Sept 1852	Anthony	----, Susan	E	20
Grey, Sarah Jane	11, May 1858	James	Farrell, Bridget	P	248
Grieb, Martin	29, Feb. 1852	Johan	----, Carolina	H	
Griener, Johan Michael	21, Jan. 1855	Roman	Eckstein, Lucia	F	

Name of Child	Date of Baptism	Father	Mother	Church	Page
Griener, Lucia Anna	9, July 1856	Joseph	Bailer, Maria	F	
Grier, Johan	13, Feb. 1859	Robert	Bauer, Anna Maria	F	
Grier, Robert David	14, July 1854	Robert D.	Bauer, Anna Maria	F	
Grier, Samuel	18, Jan. 1857	Robert	Bauer, Anna	F	
Gries, Adam Johan	18, Apr. 1852	Wigand	Siefert, Maria Anna	K	
Gries, Georg	22, July 1858	Christoph	Pir--, Genofeva	D	115
Gries, Helena	1, Mar. 1853	Francis	Rauch, Helena	F	
Gries, Joseph	22, Mar. 1857	Conrad	Gott, Friedrica	D	81
Gries, Joseph	25, May 1856	Michael	Rauch, Catharina	W	14
Gries, Josephina	14, Aug. 1859	Conrad	Gott, Friedrica	D	144
Gries, Josephina	19, Mar. 1854	Michael	Rauch, Catharina	W	2
Gries, Margaretha	27, June 1852	Michael	Rauch, Catharina	F	
Gries, Maria Catharina	31, Oct. 1858	Michael	Rauch, Catharina	W	24
Gries, Marianna	25, Aug. 1850	Michael	Rauch, Catharina	F	
Griesbaum, Anna Maria	4, Jan. 1855	Johan	Woermel, Barbara	F	
Griesbaum, Augusta	1, Nov. 1858	Johan	Wirmel, Barbara	T	
Griesbaum, Johan	23, Nov. 1851	Johan	Wuermel, Barbara	C	
Griesbaum, Margaretha	1, May 1853	Johan	Würmel, Barbara	D	383
Griese, Anna Carolina Josephina	6, Oct. 1857	Herman	Hulsmann, Elisabeth	C	
Griese, Anna Maria	22, Nov. 1852	Herman	Huelsmann, Elisabeth	C	
Griese, Anna Maria Adelheid	27, Jan. 1852	Johan H.	Schneider, Maria Gertrud	F	
Griese, Bernard Heinrich Joseph	2, Sept 1856	Joseph	Lockmann, Elisabeth	C	
Griese, Catharina Rosina	11, Jan. 1854	Bernard	Hülsman, Maria	K	
Griese, Gerhard Joseph	15, Aug. 1851	Joseph	Jünker, Margaretha	K	
Griese, Johan August Joseph	3, Mar. 1851	Herman	Hulsmann, M. Elisabeth	C	
Griese, Johan Herman Engelhard	19, Aug. 1858	Joseph	Lottmer, Elisabeth	F	
Griese, Margaretha Josephina Philomena	18, Jan. 1852	B. Heinrich	Hülsman, Anna Maria	K	
Griese, Maria Elis. Philomena Christina	8, Feb. 1856	B. Heinrich	Hulsman, Anna Maria	K	
Griese, Maria Elisabeth	27, Oct. 1858	B. Heinrich	Hülsman, Maria	K	
Griese, Rosina Carolina	16, Feb. 1854	Joseph	Tunker, Margaretha	C	
Grieser, Anna Catharina	11, Sept 1859	David	Effinger, Francisca	F	
Grieser, Edward	25, Feb. 1858	David	Effinger, Francisca	F	
Grieser, Joseph	13, May 1855	David	Effinger, Francisca	F	
Grieser, Wendel	29, June 1856	David	Effinzer, Feisca	C	
Grieshop, H. Catharina Josephina	9, Nov. 1852	Heinrich	Schulte, Sophia	A	
Grieshopp, Johan Heinrich	27, Apr. 1855	J. Heinrich	Schulte, Josephina	A	
Griesman, Joseph	2, Mar. 1855	Mathias	Stegman, Rosina	D	30
Griesser, Catharina	26, Apr. 1856	Johan	Neff, Walburga	D	57
Griether, Anna	11, Aug. 1857	Francis	Glorius, Anna Maria	A	
Griffin, Catherine	16, Aug. 1857	Patrick	Daley, Catherine	E	474
Griffin, Daniel	17, Oct. 1858	Daniel	McCauliff, Ellen	E	570
Griffin, Elizabeth	5, Nov. 1852	Nathan	----, Theresa	B	274
Griffin, Emily	5, Nov. 1852	Nathan	----, Theresa	B	274
Griffin, Helen	22, Nov. 1857	Thomas	Holland, Mary	P	230
Griffin, John	23, Aug. 1854	Patrick	Harris, Helen	R	
Griffin, John	7, July 1854	Patrick	McCawly, Helen	E	205
Griffin, John	12, June 1859	Thomas	----, Mary Helen	P	285
Griffin, John	11, May 1856	Thomas	Holland, Mary	P	179
Griffin, Margaret	8, Sept 1856	Patrick D.	McAuliffe,	V	33
Griffin, Mary	5, May 1851	----	----, ----	E	305
Griffin, Mary	18, Apr. 1851	John	Carmack, Ursula	E	300
Griffin, Mary	19, Oct. 1853	Patrick	Harris, Ellen	E	136
Griffin, Mary Ann	21, Jan. 1850	George	VanNess, Mary Dorinda	B	194
Griffin, Mary Ann	25, Apr. 1859	John	Mahan, Mary M.	E	620
Griffin, Mary Ann	14, Dec. 1851	Peter	Lawler, Mary	B	248
Griffin, Mary Constantina	12, Nov. 1853	Apollo	Gillet, Parmelia	V	7
Griffin, Mary Constantina	16, Apr. 1854	Patrick	Faly, Catherine	V	13
Griffin, Mary Elizabeth	19, Dec. 1858	P.J.	Gallagher, Ann	B	68
Griffin, Peter	8, July 1855	Peter	Lawlor, Mary	B	16

Name of Child	Date of Baptism	Father	Mother	Church	Page
Griffin, William	20, Jan. 1850	Peter	Lawlor, Mary	B	195
Griffin, William	6, July 1856	William	McAndrew, Margaret	E	380
Griffin, William Aloysius	5, May 1850		adult - 15 years old	E	212
Griffith, John	23, May 1859	William	Flinn, Margaret	E	627
Grill, Johan Rupert	25, Dec. 1852	Joseph	Laschinger, Theresa	F	
Grim, Genofeva	5, Sept 1852	Jacob	Ripberger, Carolina	N	8
Grim, Johan	13, Dec. 1852	Sebastian	Köhler, Caecilia	D	360
Grim, Maria Anna	30, July 1850	Jacob	Ripperger, Carolina	D	226
Grimes, Martin	31, Dec. 1854	John	Kenney, Bridget	E	250
Grimes, Mary	25, Dec. 1852	Patrick	Philips, Bridget	B	278
Grimes, Patrick	4, Apr. 1856	John	Mealy, Mary	E	356
Grimes, William	19, Feb. 1858	John	----, Mary	E	517
Grimm, Adolph	27, Mar. 1859	Gallus	Effinger, Helena	C	
Grimm, Ann Caroline	11, Sept 1859	Michael	----, Elizabeth	E	652
Grimm, Emma	27, Dec. 1856	Gallus	Effinger, Helena	C	
Grimm, Joseph	7, Oct. 1855	Gallus	Effinger, Helena	C	
Grimm, Joseph	14, May 1854	Ludwig	Brodbeck, Theresa	D	10
Grimm, Ludwig	3, Feb. 1850	Ludwig	Brodweg, Theresa	D	202
Grimm, Maria	18, Dec. 1853	Dominick	Kohler, Caecilia	D	420
Grimm, Paulina	3, Sept 1854	Gallus	Effinger, Helena	C	
Grimm, Sara Elisabeth	27, Feb. 1853	Michael	Reinberger, Elisabeth	F	
Grimm, Schloastica	10, Nov. 1854	Michael	Rennberger, Elisabeth	K	
Grimme, Anna Elisabeth	14, Dec. 1857	Heinrich	Baumer, Bernardina	F	
Grimme, Anna Maria Philomena	4, July 1856	Herman H.	Bohing, Theresa	L	
Grimme, Bernard Heinrich	13, Nov. 1859	Gerhard H.	Bohmann, Bernardina	F	
Grimme, Catharina Louisa	21, Feb. 1854	Herman H.	Buehning, Theresa	L	
Grimme, Dietrich Gerhard	18, Sept 1857	Herman D.	Reckers, Theresa	L	
Grimme, Franz Heinrich	25, Dec. 1856	Dietrich	Lange, Anna	F	
Grimme, Gerhard Theodor	12, Sept 1852	Theodor	Lange, Marianna	F	
Grimme, Herman Heinrich	8, Oct. 1854	Heinrich	Hilbert, Louisa	F	
Grimme, Johan Clemens	20, Sept 1850	J. Heinrich	Rekers, Anna Adelheid	K	
Grimme, Johan Dietrich	8, May 1850	Dietrich	Lange, Anna Maria	F	
Grimme, Johan Georg	23, May 1859	Dietrich	Lange, Marianna	F	
Grimme, Johan Heinrich	7, Jan. 1855	Dietrich	Lange, Anna Maria	F	
Grimme, Maria Catharina	31, Aug. 1851	Michael	Reinberger, Elisabeth	F	
Grimme, Maria Theresa	23, Nov. 1851	Heinrich	Buening, Theresa	L	
Grimmelsman, Angelica Maria	30, Oct. 1850	Francis H.	Storch, Anna Maria	A	
Grimmelsman, Anna Elisabeth	31, Jan. 1858	Francis H.	Storck, Anna Maria	A	
Grimmelsman, Gerhard Heinrich	30, Oct. 1850	Francis H.	Storch, Anna Maria	A	
Grimmelsman, Maria Philomena	25, Jan. 1853	F. Heinrich	Storck, Anna Maria	A	
Grimmelsmann, Carl Heinrich Joseph	20, Mar. 1853	Heinrich	Reiter, Johanna	L	
Grimmelsmann, Gerhard August	24, May 1857	Heinrich	Reuter, Johanna	F	
Grimmelsmann, Johan Franz Georg	22, Aug. 1855	Francis H.	Storch, Anna Maria	F	
Grimmelsmann, Margaretha Johanna H	29, Sept 1850	Heinrich	Reuters, Louisa Lisette	L	
Grimmer, Thomas	27, Mar. 1853	Thomas	----, Hannah	E	77
Grims, Cecilia	24, June 1855	Patrick	Phillips, Bridget	P	137
Grims, Francis	14, June 1853	Jacob	Mulrets, Ann	N	13
Grinkemeyer, Maria Theresa	29, Feb. 1852	Bernard	Moe--g, Maria Anna	D	309
Grinsteiner, Theresa	14, Dec. 1851	Georg	Rieg, M. Anna	C	
Grishman, Maria Barbara	27, July 1852	Peter	Müller, Anna Maria	D	340
Grissman, Margaretha	17, Mar. 1859	Peter	Müller, Anna Maria	D	134
Griswold, Francis Chauncey	17, Apr. 1853		adult	B	289
Griszman, Anna Maria	15, Aug. 1851	Mathias	Stegman, Anna	D	278
Grob, Catharina	10, Sept 1854	Francis	----, Margaret	U	
Grob, Eduard	16, Jan. 1853	Francis	Martin, Margaretha	D	365
Grob, Peter	4, Oct.1857	Adam	----, Margaretha	D	96
Grobenbecker, Magdalena Elisabeth	9, May 1852	Johan	Leibold, Catharina	A	
Grobman, Crescentia	15, Sept 1855	Johan	Stichler, Anna Maria	U	
Grobman, Johan Baptist	7, Dec. 1856	Johan	Stiegler, Anna Maria	U	

Name of Child	Date of Baptism	Father	Mother	Church	Page
Grode, Maria Clara	10, Oct. 1856	Gerhard	Koester, Clara	D	69
Groen, Maria Josephina	26, Sept 1852	Joseph	Bl---, Catharina	K	
Groene, Anna Maria	18, Oct. 1851	Gerhard	Langenkamp, Gertrud	C	
Groene, Gerhard Heinrich	7, Feb. 1859	J.H. Herman	Rediker, A. Maria	T	
Groene, Heinrich	13, Mar. 1856	Herman H.	Recker, Anna Maria	L	
Groene, Johan Heinrich	11, Feb. 1856	Gerhard	Lambers, Maria Anna	L	
Groene, Johan Heinrich Friedrich	7, Oct. 1851	J. Herman	Roetker, Maria Anna	L	
Groene, Johan Herman Heinrich	27, Jan. 1856	J. Heinrich	Kruse, Anna M.	C	
Groene, Maria Anna	17, June 1852	Herman	Kustermeyer, Elisabeth	C	
Groene, Maria Anna	15, June 1853	Herman H.	Roedeker, Anna Maria	L	
Gröer, Robert David	1, June 1851	Robert D.	Bauer, Anna	A	
Groeschel, Barbara	10, Apr. 1853	James	----, Barbara	H	
Groeschel, Elisabeth	25, May 1851	Jacob	Joerg, Barbara	C	
Grogan, Andrew	1, Jan. 1856	Malachai	----, Bridget	M	
Grogan, Ann	29, June 1856	Patrick	Ryan, Bridget	E	378
Grogan, Caroline	6, Apr. 1853	George	----, Mary	H	
Grogan, Charles	24, Oct. 1852	Charles	Corrigan, Mary	B	273
Grogan, Edward	15, Mar. 1857	Patrick	Weatherby, Lucy	U	
Grogan, Emma	4, Sept 1859	Patrick	Whetherbay, Lucy	U	
Grogan, John	17, Sept 1854	Michael	----, Mary	M	
Grogan, Julia	11, July 1852	Patrick	----, Louise	H	
Grogan, Julia Ann	29, Sept 1850	Charles	Corrigan, Mary	B	215
Grogan, Mary	6, Apr. 1853	George	----, Mary	H	
Grogan, Mary	23, Apr. 1854	Malachai	----, Margaret	M	
Grogan, Mary	15, Aug. 1852	Patrick	----, Bridget	E	6
Grogan, Mary Frances	23, July 1854	Patrick	----, Louise	H	
Grogan, Richard	16, Jan. 1859	Richard	Farrell, Sarah	B	69
Grogan, Thomas	11, May 1856	Michael	----, Mary	M	
Groh,	31, Oct. 1857	Georg	Schwarz, Catharina	G	
Groh, Anna Maria	8, Feb. 1852	J. Georg	Schwarz, Catharina	D	305
Groh, Carl	28, Jan. 1855	Christian	Stemmler, Barbara	D	27
Groh, Christoph	8, June 1857	Peter	Tiefel, Kunigunda	C	
Groh, Georg Andreas	8, Aug. 1852	Christian	Stemmel, Barbara	D	342
Groh, Johan	17, Apr. 1857	Christian	Groh, Barbara	D	83
Groh, Johan	24, Mar. 1850	Nicolaus	Burg, Margaretha	D	207
Groh, Joseph	14, July 1853	Georg	Merk, Maria	C	
Groh, Magdalena	24, Feb. 1856	Georg	Schwarz, Catharina	G	
Groh, Nicolaus Francis	30, Oct. 1853	Christian	Stemmer, Barbara	D	412
Groh, Peter	26, June 1853	Georg	Schwarz, Catharina	J	22
Groh, Peter August	23, June 1850	?	Groe, Catharina	A	
Groh, Salome	3, Nov. 1850	Michael	Reis, Anna Maria	F	
Grollmann, Bernard Georg	1, Jan. 1851	Georg	Coreles, Clara	L	
Grombley, Ann	9, Nov. 1851	James	Doyle, Helen	E	356
Gronauer, Georg	30, Jan. 1859	Georg	Schlitz, Carolina	D	130
Gronauer, Juliana	15, June 1856	Georg	Schlitz, Carolina	D	61
Gröne, Johan Bernard Francis	14, July 1858	J.H.F.	Kruse, Maria	A	
Grönefeld, Anna	6, July 1852	Gerhard	Reslage, Maria Agnes	D	328
Gronefeld, August Heinrich	4, July 1857	Herman H.	Greving, M. Helena	L	
Grönefeld, Maria Anna	1, Mar. 1853	J. Bernard	Feldcamp, Maria Anna	D	374
Grönefeld, Maria Catharina	22, June 1857	Wendelin	Dier---, Maria Catharina	D	88
Gronfeld, M. Catharina Bernardina	25, Aug. 1854	Heinrich	Greving, M. Helena	L	
Grönloh, Anna Maria Carolina	29, Feb. 1852	J. Bernard	Ollbrink, Anna Maria	A	
Gronotte, Bernard Joseph	20, Mar. 1859	Bernard H.	Woeste, Elisabeth	L	
Gronotte, Herman Heinrich	24, May 1857	Bernard	Woeste, Cath. Elis.	L	
Gronotte, Johan Bernard	26, Apr. 1854	Bernard	Woeste, Cath. Elis.	L	
Gronotte, Maria Elisabeth	28, Oct. 1855	Bernard	Woeste, Catharina	L	
Gropp, Maria Wilhelmina	23, July 1853	Friedrich	Husmann, Rosina	L	
Groppenbecker, Clara Johanna	8, Apr. 1855	Max. J.	Dunkel, Johanna	D	32
Groppenbecker, Jacob	8, Aug. 1852	Max. J.	Dunkel, Maria	D	342

Name of Child	Date of Baptism	Father	Mother	Church	Page
Gros, Johanna	11, Jan. 1857	Joseph	Stubenrauch, Louisa	C	
Gros, Louisa	11, Jan. 1857	Joseph	Stubenrauch, Louisa	C	
Grosart, Georg	5, Sept 1858	Louis	Dremann, Maria	C	
Grosche, Wilhelm	5, Mar. 1854	Ernst	Rennebaum, Philomena	F	
Gröschel, Johan	19, Aug. 1855	Jacob	----, Barbara	H	
Groskopf, Andreas Johan	28, Mar. 1852	Andreas	Kauper, Barbara	K	
Groskopf, Georg Fidel	17, Jan. 1854	Andreas	Kauber, Barbara	K	
Gross, Andreas	10, Sept 1854	Martin	Elsässer, Gertrud	J	28
Gross, Anna	8, Oct. 1854	Wolfgang	Paper, Ann	Q	5
Gross, Anna Gertrud	14, Dec. 1854	Nicolaus	Deitz, Anna Maria	D	24
Gross, Anna Maria	23, Nov. 1856	Adam	Wobbe, Anna	Q	17
Gross, Anna Maria	28, Jan. 1855	Erasmus	Schilling, Ottilia	D	27
Gross, Charles Edward John Martin	17, Feb. 1850	Andrew	Stickle, Veronica	B	196
Gross, Cunigunda	22, Aug. 1852	Adam	Wobern, Anna	Q	2
Gross, Francis	25, Aug. 1858	Joseph	Stubenrauch, Louisa	D	118
Gross, Johan Martin	24, Mar. 1850	J. Baptist	Habner, Margaretha	H	
Gross, Joseph	1, Nov. 1859	Joseph	Huber, Louisa	D	150
Gross, Kunigunda	29, Sept 1850	Adam	Fisch, Anna	D	235
Gross, Maria Agatha	13, Feb. 1853	Erasmus	Schilling, Maria Ottilia	D	371
Gross, Mechtilda	28, Feb. 1855	Nicolaus	Fecker, Catharina	W	7
Gross, Rosina	21, Aug. 1859	Jacob	Rolf, Agatha	K	
Gross, Wilhelm	12, Dec. 1858	Adam	Wobert, Anna	Q	30
Grossar, Johan Friedrich	4, Feb. 1855	Louis	Niemeyer, Anna M.	C	
Grossart, Heinrich	11, Mar. 1852	Louis	Tiermann, M. Angela	C	
Grossenbrink, Elisabeth Wilhelmina	31, Aug. 1855	Wilhelm	Ortmann, Elisabeth	C	
Grossenbrink, Maria Agnes	27, Mar. 1850	Wilhelm	Ortmann, Elisabeth	C	
Grossenbrink, Wilhelm Heinrich	4, Jan. 1852	Wilhelm	Ortmann, Elisabeth	C	
Grosser, Ann	13, July 1851	Baptist	----, Margaret	H	
Grosser, Anna Margaretha	16, Jan. 1853	John B.	----, Margaret	H	
Grosser, Anna Maria	19, Aug. 1855	Johan B.	----, Margaretha	H	
Grosser, Barbara Maria	15, Mar. 1857	Baptist	Hauptner, Margaret	H	
Grosser, Joseph	26, Mar. 1854	Johan	----, Magdalena	H	
Grossheim, Johan Bernard Heinrich	10, Nov. 1854	Heinrich	Rakers, Elisabeth	A	
Grossheim, Johan Gerhard	11, Jan. 1853	Heinrich	Rocke, Maria Elisabeth	A	
Grossheim, Johan Herman	1, June 1857	J. Heinrich	Raker, Margaretha Elisabeth	A	
Grossman, Barbara Veronica	1, Sept 1850	Simon	Kamp, Barbara	A	
Grossman, Daniel	31, Oct. 1851	Simon	Kamp, Barbara	A	
Grosz, Georg Martin	19, July1850	Anton	Hegel, Magdalena	D	224
Grote, Anna M Josephina Bernardina	28, Sept 1859	J. Gerhard	Fecke, Bernardina	F	
Grote, Anna M. Elisabeth	28, Nov. 1858	Carl	Bültel, Maria	A	
Grote, Anna Maria	4, Oct. 1856	Bernard	Barenkamp, Anna M.	L	
Grote, Anna Maria	29, June 1858	Clemens	Overbeck, M. Catharina	F	
Grote, Anna Maria	31, May 1853	Heinrich	Steinkamp, Anna M.	C	
Grote, Anna Maria Catharina Philomena	11, Oct. 1858	Gerhard H.	Deters, Maria Carolina	K	
Grote, Anna Maria Elisabeth	24, Sept 1858	Anton	Heile, M. Adelheid	L	
Grote, Anna Maria Gertrud	12, Nov. 1857	J. Heinrich	Steinkamp, Anna Maria	L	
Grote, Anna Maria Josephina	2, Dec. 1857	Johan H.	Jaspers, Bernardina	F	
Grote, Anna Maria Margaretha	2, Jan. 1852	Herman H.	Santel, Maria Anna	L	
Grote, Anna Theresa	3, June 1858	Gerhard	Kösters, Anna	A	
Grote, Anton Joseph	27, Aug. 1859	Joseph	Meyer, Anna Maria Gertrud	A	
Grote, Bernard Heinrich	30, Apr. 1858	Bernard	Barenkamp, Carolina	L	
Grote, Bernard Joseph	11, Jan. 1853	Bernard	Brune, Maria Elisabeth	A	
Grote, Bernardina Josephine	23, July 1857	Heinrich	----, Maria Anna	R	
Grote, Francis Heinrich	4, Feb. 1857	Joseph	Meyer, Gertrud	A	
Grote, Georg Bernard	18, June 1855	Joseph	Meyer, Anna Maria Gertrud	A	
Grote, Gerhard Heinrich	5, Feb. 1859	H. Heinrich	Sandel, Maria Anna	R	
Grote, Gerhard Heinrich	18, June 1855	H. Heinrich	Sander, Maria Anna	R	
Grote, Heinrich Anton Franz	21, Feb. 1855	Anton	Heile, M. Adelheid	L	
Grote, Heinrich Clemens	20, June 1858	Bernard	Broxtermann, Elisabeth	F	

Name of Child	Date of Baptism	Father	Mother	Church	Page
Grote, Herman Bernard	20, June 1857	Carl	Bultel, Maria	A	
Grote, Johan Bernard	25, May 1859	Bernard	Barenkamp, Carolina	L	
Grote, Johan Carl	20, June 1857	Carl	Bultel, Maria	A	
Grote, Johan Gerhard	16, July 1854	J. Gerhard	Deters, Maria Carolina	F	
Grote, Johan Heinrich	4, June 1855	Heinrich	Steinkamp, Anna M.	L	
Grote, Johan Herman	2, Mar. 1853	J. Joseph	Meier, Anna Gertrud	A	
Grote, Louisa Elisabeth	17, Aug. 1857	Clemens	Overbeck, Catharina	F	
Grote, Maria Angela Francisca	23, Aug. 1859	Johan H.	Jasper, Bernardina	F	
Grote, Maria Anna	23, Aug. 1856	Anton	Heile, M. Adelheid	L	
Grote, Maria Anna	7, Aug. 1853	H. Heinrich	Sander, Maria Anna	R	
Grote, Maria Catharina Theresa	22, Dec. 1859	Anton	Heile, Maria Adelheid	L	
Grotenkemper, Anna Maria Catharina	10, July 1855	Heinrich	Sandhoff, Catharina	K	
Grotenkemper, Elisabeth Sara	3, Nov. 1857	Heinrich	Sedhoff, Catharina	K	
Grotenkemper, Maria Helena	27, July 1852	Heinrich	Sandhoff, Catharina	K	
Grotenkemper, Philomena Catharina	23, Sept 1850	Heinrich	Sendhof, Catharina	K	
Grothaus, Carolina	2, Dec. 1854	Gerhard	Bönker, Catharina	K	
Grothaus, Catharina Josephina	25, Sept 1852	Gerhard	Rönker, Catharina	K	
Grothues, Gerhard Alex. Ludwig	17, Aug. 1856	Ludwig	Deppe, Elisabeth	F	
Grotmann, Maria Friedricka Louisa	3, Jan. 1851	Gerhard	Mersmann, Maria	L	
Grotus, Anna Maria Susanna	18, Oct. 1858	Ludwig	Tappe, Elisabeth	F	
Growe, Francis	25, Feb. 1856	Charles	Gooding, Ann	B	25
Grower, Anna Adelheid	24, July 1855	H.H.	Mering, Clara	A	
Grower, Francis	9, Nov. 1858	H.H.	Mering, Clara	A	
Grower, Herman Heinrich	29, July 1857	Herman H.	Meiering, Clara	A	
Gru--, Carolina	10, Nov. 1850	Georg	Huber, Louisa	K	
Grube, Anna Louisa	31, July 1853	Heinrich	Margbright, Elisabeth	K	
Grube, Anton Bernard	20, Sept 1851	J. Wilhelm	Hoppenjans, Anna Maria	D	283
Grube, Helen	9, July 1853	Frederick	Grabe, Helen	B	295
Gruber, Dennis	23, Aug. 1853	Dennis	Fries, Margaret	N	15
Gruber, Herman Heinrich	25, Dec. 1858	Fridolin	O'Brien, Helena	D	127
Gruber, Hieronimus	27, Dec. 1857	J. Dennis	Fries, Magaretha	N	
Gruber, Johan	28, Mar. 1852	Fridolin	Hau--held, Helena	D	314
Gruber, Johan	13, Sept 1857	Peter	Schule, Susanna	C	
Gruber, Joseph	23, Nov. 1856	Fridolin	H-air, Helen	D	72
Gruber, Joseph	11, May 1851	J. Dennis	Fries, Margaret	N	3
Gruber, Margaretha Johanna	4, Mar. 1859	David	Miller, Louise	K	
Gruber, Maria	25, Mar. 1854	Fridolin	O'Brien, Ellen	D	7
Gruber, Veronica Agatha	20, Jan. 1856	J. Dennis	Fries, Margaretha	N	
Gruenefeld, Heinrich	26, May 1851	Gerhard	Reslage, Agnes	D	266
Gruener, Joseph	29, May 1853	Roman	Eckstein, Lucia	F	
Gruenwald, Ann	12, June 1853	Thaddeus	----, Cunigunda	H	
Gruenwald, John Otto	24, June 1856	Thaddeus	----, Cunigunda	H	
Gruenwald, Margaret	1, Feb. 1852	Thaddeus	----, Cunigunda	H	
Grueter, Maria Philomena	22, Feb. 1857	J. Heinrich	Deerker, Maria Elisabeth	J	40
Gruh, Barbara	1, Aug. 1851	Johan	Dewald, Maria	D	275
Grumley, Elizabeth	17, July 1853	James	----, Ellen	E	107
Grün, Ludwig	6, Mar. 1854	Conrad	Bachman, Elisabeth	D	6
Grundhoefer, Louisa Carolina	10, June 1855	Ludwig	Wampach, Louisa	F	
Grundhoefer, Wilhelm	11, Sept 1859	Carl	Bücker, Theresa	D	146
Grundhöfer, Carolina Elisabeth	26, Apr. 1856	Peter	Omlor, Margaretha	D	57
Grundhofer, Friedrich Carl	9, Nov. 1856	Carl	Bicker, Theresa	C	
Grundhofer, Margaretha Augusta	2, May 1858	Peter	Omlor, Margaretha	D	110
Grundkäfer, Friedrich	5, July 1857	Ludwig	Wambrock, Lucia	D	89
Gründner, Edward	25, July 1858	Andreas	Waltz, Genofeva	D	115
Grundner, Johan	7, Sept 1856	Andreas	Walz, Genofeva	D	67
Grünefeld, Anna Maria Elisabeth	14, June 1857	Bernard	Feldkamp, Anna Maria	D	88
Grünefeld, Johan Herman	31, Jan. 1855	Bernard	Feldkamp, Anna	D	27
Grünefeld, Maria Catharina	4, Nov. 1859	Bernard	Feldkamp, Anna Maria	D	150
Grüner, Carolina	23, Dec. 1852	Conrad	Bachman, Elisabeth	D	362

Name of Child	Date of Baptism	Father	Mother	Church	Page
Grünkemeyer Johan Bernard	28, Sept 1856	Heinrich	Bettinger, Maria	D	68
Grünstein, Georg	20, May 1854	Georg	Rieke, Maria	A	
Gruntner, Andreas	6, Feb. 1853	Andreas	Walz, Genofeva	D	369
Gruntner, Carl Joseph	3, Dec. 1854	Andreas	Walz, Genofeva	D	23
Grünwald, Johan	6, May 1855	Thaddaeus	Pelz, Cunigunda	D	34
Grünwald, Mathias	18, June 1858	Thaddaeus	Rulz, Cunigunda	D	113
Grupp, Maria Anna	28, Mar. 1854	Joseph	Thessing, Catharina	F	
Gruse, Herman Heinrich	3, Mar. 1858	Heinrich	Bürgerman, Sophia	D	106
Grüter, Anna Maria	28, June 1850	J. Herman	Steltenpohl, Maria Carolina	A	
Grüter, Gerhard Clemens	26, Nov. 1852	Gerhard	Kuhlman, Anna Maria	A	
Grüter, Herman Heinrich	15, June 1852	J. Heinrich	Dirker, Maria Elisabeth	J	16
Grüter, Maria Carolina	22, July 1852	Herman	Steltenpohl, Maria Carolina	A	
Grüter, Maria Elisabeth	9, Oct. 1854	Heinrich	Dirker, Elisabeth	J	28
Grüter, Maria Elisabeth	4, Oct. 1854	Herman	Steltenpohl, Maria Carolina	A	
Gschwenter, Michael	6, Nov. 1854	Georg	Schneider, Thecla	D	21
Gschwentner, Sophia	25, May 1851	Georg	Schneider, Thecla	D	265
Gschwind, Carolina	3, Mar. 1850	Philipp	Mayer, Elisabeth	D	204
Guardair, Mary Rose	27, July 1854	James	Brane, Mary	B	3
Gude, Anna Margaretha	10, Aug. 1859	Joseph	Heidgerdes, Marg.	C	
Gude, Bernard Joseph	31, Oct. 1851	Joseph	Heilges, Margaretha	L	
Gude, Heinrich Anton	24, May 1857	Joseph	Heitgers, Margaretha	L	
Gude, Maria Margaretha	11, Jan. 1850	Joseph	Heitgeist, Euphemia	L	
Gudermann, Carl	31, July 1856	Anton	Bausbacher, Anna	C	
Güdlein, Francisca	22, Mar. 1857	Albert	Hoffman, Barbara	D	81
Guelker, Anna Maria Elisabeth	22, Oct. 1854	Heinrich	Doepker, Catharina	K	
Guelker, Cath. Josephina Philomena	29, Sept 1850	Heinrich	Döbker, Catharina	K	
Guelker, Catharina Philomena	26, July 1852	Heinrich	Döpker, Maria Catharina	K	
Guelker, Heinrich Ferdinand	7, Feb. 1857	Heinrich	Dobker, Maria Catharina	K	
Guenn?, Mary	17, Apr. 1853	Patrick	----, Mary	M	
Guentman, Bernardina Josephina	23, Apr. 1855	Wilhelm	Kunk, Theresa	C	
Guerant, Emil Louis Henry L.	5, Sept 1858	Louis G.	Hubert, Amelia	E	560
Guertler, Caroline	2, May 1858	Heinrich	Nickle, Josephine	H	
Guertler, Wilhelm	30, Oct. 1859	Heinrich	Wickle, Josephina	H	
Guetermann, Carl	9, Sept 1858	Anton	Bauschbach, Anna M.	F	
Guetermann, Eduard	15, Nov. 1859	Anton	Bausbacher, Maria	F	
Guetlein, Heinrich	13, Nov. 1859	Albert	Hoffmann, Barbara	F	
Guhan, Adeline Bridget	30, Mar. 1856	Thomas	Cullinan, Ann	T	
Guildy, Margaret	2, Jan. 1853	Michael	Keene, Ann	B	280
Guilfoyle, Elizabeth	12, Mar. 1854	James	----, Catherine	E	175
Guilfoyle, James	5, May 1854	Daniel	Murphy, Joanne	E	188
Guilfoyle, James	5, Dec. 1857	James	----, Catherine	E	497
Guilfoyle, John	27, Mar. 1856	Daniel	----, Joanne	E	353
Guilfoyle, John	24, Sept 1852	Michael	----, Mary	E	20
Guilfoyle, Joseph	26, Mar. 1851	John	----, Elizabeth	E	295
Guilfoyle, Margaret	29, Aug. 1852	James	Hennesey, Catherine	E	11
Guilfoyle, Mary Ann	13, Jan. 1856	James	Hainy, Catherine	E	337
Guilfoyle, Timothy	8, Feb. 1858	Daniel	Meagher, Joanne	E	516
Guillerme, Maria Magdalena	1, May 1853	Carl	Mesmer, Petronella	J	22
Guinan, Christopher	2, Aug. 1856	Edward	Kenny, Elizabeth	E	386
Guinan, Edward	26, Nov. 1859	Edward	Kenny, Lizzie	E	673
Guinan, James	19, June 1858	Edward	Kenny, Lizzie	E	542
Guinan, James	16, Dec. 1855	James	Gafney, Ellen	B	22
Guinan, Margaret	28, Dec. 1852	James	Garahan, Helen	B	279
Guinan, Thomas	18, Apr. 1858	William	Dougherty, Joanne	B	57
Guinan, William	29, July 1855	William	Dougherty, Joanne	B	17
Guinons, Mary	10, May 1855	James	Tompkins, Mary	R	
Guirard, Henry Eugene	9, Jan. 1853	Adolph	Chabrier, Mary	E	52
Guiraud, Jean William Gustave	8, May 1853	Louis G.	Herbert, Elizabeth Amelia	E	87
Guiroud, Mary Louise Antonette	6, Apr. 1856	Adolph	----, Mary	E	356

Name of Child	Date of Baptism	Father	Mother	Church	Page
Gulick, John Walker	24, June 1850		adult	B	205
Gulick, Joseph Aiken	9, Apr. 1850	John	Aiken, Elizabeth	B	200
Gülker, Johan Heinrich	3, Feb. 1850	Johan	Hervers, Margaretha	K	
Gullaney, Patrick	4, Dec. 1854	Patrick	Downey, Mary Ann	P	108
Gunch, Ann Adalaide	30, Oct. 1853	Anthony W.	McLaughlin, Ann	B	301
Gunckel, Johan Casimer	26, May 1850	Johan	Steffen, Helena	A	
Gunkel, Maria Elisabeth	13, Nov. 1853	Johan	Stephan, Helena	F	
Gunkel, Susanna Rosina	26, Sept 1855	Johan	Stephan, H.	F	
Gunkeler, Jacob	1, Jan. 1852	Johan	Stephans, Magdalena	F	
Günker, Johan Bernard Gerhard	18, July 1850	Gerhard G.	Kuhlman, Anna Maria	A	
Gunning, John	17, Mar. 1852	Patrick	----, Mary	E	392
Gunning, Margaret Sarah	25, June 1854	Daniel	----, Ann	E	201
Gunning, Patrick	19, Apr. 1854	Patrick	Scanlan, Mary	E	184
Guntenberg, Joseph Heinrich	17, Oct. 1858	Bernard	Lechleitner, Sophia	A	
Guntenberg, Paulina Mechtilda	19, Apr. 1851	Bernard	Lechleitner, Sophia	A	
Günther, Conrad	6, Dec. 1859	Francis	Pist---, Helena	D	152
Günther, Magdalena	9, Jan. 1859	Nicolaus	Holler, Margaretha	D	128
Günther, Michael	12, Sept 1854	Nicolaus	Holler, Margaretha	D	17
Günther, Thecla	2, Sept 1853	Nicolaus	Holler, Margaretha	D	403
Gunthman, Joseph Bernard Wilhelm	23, Apr. 1851	Wilhelm	Kunk, M. Theresa	C	
Guntmann, Catharina Bernardina	20, Aug. 1857	Wilhelm	Kunk, Theresa	C	
Guntmann, Johanna Philomena	17, Jan. 1853	Wilhelm	Kunk, Theresa	C	
Gunzelman, Anotn	3, May 1855	Michael	Maus, Helena	D	34
Gurnlevan, Mary	13, July 1851	Patrick	Kennedy, Bridget	E	323
Gusker, Maria Anna	27, Mar. 1853	J. Gottfried	Schloer, Rosina	R	
Gustavus, Mina	27, Feb. 1859	Charles	Wooster, Catherine	E	606
Gut, Barbara Elisabeth	6, Sept 1857	Andreas	Rewald, Elisabeth	F	
Gut, Carl	3, Aug. 1855	Carl	Veal, Maria Anna	D	39
Gut, Catharina Ottilia	19, May 1850	Herman H.	Engel, Adelheid	D	213
Gut, Francis Joseph	25, Nov. 1855	F. Peter	Gebhart, Catharina Barbara	N	
Gut, Friedrich	5, Apr. 1858	Philipp	Die---, Maria Catharina	D	108
Gut, Georg	29, Aug. 1855	Mathias	Beck, Catharina	D	41
Gut, Honora	4, Sept 1853	Francis P.	Gebhart, Barbara	N	16
Gut, Isabella Philomena	5, Sept 1852	Ferdinand	Bühler, Margaretha	D	346
Gut, Johan	28, Apr. 1850	Ferdinand	Buehler, Margaretha	D	211
Gut, Margaretha	1, Nov. 1853	Mathias	Beck, Catharina	D	412
Gut, Maria Francisca	13, July 1851	Mathias	Beck, Catharina	D	272
Gut, Rosa	17, Aug. 1856	Jacob	Klem, Barbara	D	65
Gut, Rosina	26, Apr. 1857	Matthias	Beck, Catharina	C	
Gute, Franz	18, Jan. 1858	Herman	Batsche, Wilhelmina	F	
Gute, Heinrich Joseph	12, Aug. 1855	Joseph	Haidgaas, Margaretha	C	
Güteman, Louisa	12, Oct. 1851	Anton	Bausbacher, Anna Maria	D	287
Gutendorf, Joseph	15, Aug. 1855	Friedrich	Linz, Elisabeth	D	40
Guteower, Heinrich Wilelhm	4, Jan. 1857	Johan	Wimpermühle, Anna Maria	K	
Güterman, Anna Maria Louisa	4, Nov. 1852	Anton	Bausbacher, Anna Maria	D	356
Guterman, August	17, Oct. 1854	Anton	Bausbach, Anna Maria	D	20
Guth, Clara	23, July 1854	Adam	Wapterin, Maria Eva	Q	5
Guth, Elisabeth	9, Mar. 1851	Francis	Gebhardt, Barbara	C	
Guth, Elisabeth	19, Mar. 1858	Friedrich	----, Elisabeth	D	107
Guth, Francis Albert	17, Dec. 1854	Friedrich	Bühler, Margaretha	D	24
Guth, Francisca	17, Sept 1851	Adam	Weinlam, Maria Eva	Q	1
Guth, Johan	1, Jan. 1857	Johan	Schwartz, Elisabeth	D	76
Guth, Johan Georg	22, Nov. 1859	Johan	Schwarz, Elisabeth	C	
Guth, Peter Martin	17, July 1859	Mathias	Beck, Catharina	D	142
Güthlein, Peter Joseph	17, Dec. 1854	Albert	Hoffman, Barbara	D	24
Gütleiin, Cunigunda	15, Nov. 1853	Albert	Hoffman, Barbara	D	415
Gutmann, Veronica Elisabeth	12, Mar. 1853	Xavier	Wankhorst, Agatha	C	
Gutt, Maria Anna	7, Mar. 1852	Herman	Engel, Adelheid	D	311
Gutto, John Charles	19, Dec. 1858	Paulo	Bedrick, Maria	B	68

Name of Child	Date of Baptism	Father	Mother	Church	Page
Gutzendorf, Joseph	21, Dec. 1852	Joseph	Braun, Anna Maria	D	361
Gutzweiler, Anna Margaretha	29, Nov. 1857	Joseph	Kunz, Maria	D	99
Gutzweiler, Anna Maria	26, May 1850	Joseph	Kunz, Anna Maria	D	214
Gutzwiller, Anton	24, Jan. 1859	Remidgius	Schott, Bridget	H	
Gutzwiller, Elisabeth	9, Dec. 1855	Joseph	Kunz, Anna Maria	D	48
Gutzwiller, Johan	21, Mar. 1858	Fridolin	Hauer, Theresa	H	
Gutzwiller, Joseph	11, Dec. 1853	Fridolin	----, Theresa	H	
Gutzwiller, Joseph	24, Jan. 1859	Remidgius	Schott, Bridget	H	
Gutzwiller, Joseph Anton	30, Oct. 1859	Joseph	Kuntz, Maria	D	150
Gutzwiller, Joseph Anton	27, June 1852	Joseph	Kunz, Anna Maria	D	327
Gutzwiller, Maria Anna	24, July 1852	Fridolin	----, Theresa	H	
Gutzwiller, Maria Philomena	3, Apr. 1859	Joseph	Re---ter, Magdalena	D	135
Gutzwiller, Rosina	27, Jan. 1856	Fridolin	----, Theresa	H	
Gutzwyler, Ludwig Franz Xavier	19, Mar. 1854	Joseph	Kunz, Anna Maria	F	
H----, Margaret	30, Nov. 1856	Cornelius	Beecher, Mary	P	200
Ha---, Emilia	4, Sept 1859		Ha---, Catharina	D	145
Haag, Catharina	21, June 1853	Johan	Jonte, Catharina	D	390
Haag, Johan	23, Nov. 1856	Johan	Jentes, Catharina	K	
Haag, Johan Jacob	11, Dec. 1859	Jacob	Haselbeck, Catharina	D	152
Haag, Maria Amalia Justina	30, July 1859	Andreas	----, Catharina	D	143
Haag, Mathias	11, Feb. 1855	Jacob	Haselbeck, Catharina	D	28
Haag, Thomas	25, Feb. 1858	Andreas	Ruhl, Catharina	F	
Haake, Johan Bernard	23, Oct. 1859	Anton	Neuhaus, Elisabeth	C	
Haaker, Maria Louisa	15, Feb. 1857	Anton	Niehaus, Elisabeth	C	
Haap, Barbara	8, Dec. 1850	Adam	Campeis, Rosina	D	245
Haar, Georg	30, May 1854	Johan	Schmidt, Marianna	A	
Haar, George Edward	30, June 1856	John	Smith, Mary	B	30
Haarman, Louisa Mechtildis	3, Mar. 1858	Heinrich	Burlage, Anna	A	
Haarman, Wilhelmina Louisa	23, Dec. 1855	Heinrich	Burlage, Anna	A	
Haarmann, Anna Maria Philomena	4, May 1857	Bernard	Barlage, Louisa	L	
Haarmann, Anna Veronika	30, Dec. 1855	Bernard	Barlage, Louisa	L	
Haarmann, Bernard Heinrich	6, Jan. 1859	Bernard	Burlage, Louise	L	
Haarmann, Johan Heinrich	22, Sept 1856	Gerhard H.	Westerhaus, Cath.	L	
Haarmeier, Anton	10, May 1855	Herman	Dellman, Maria Elisabeth	K	
Haarmeyer, Maria Elisabeth	17, Feb. 1855	G. Heinrich	Kemper, Anna Maria	K	
Haas, Anna Maria	1, May 1851	Jacob	Bürkle, Elisabeth	D	263
Haas, Anthony	10, Apr. 1853	George	----, Luitgarda	H	
Haas, Carl Gottfried	18, Dec. 1859	Gottfried	Sellmer, M. Barbara	L	
Haas, Carolina	20, Mar. 1859	Ferdinand	Schmidt, Carolina	C	
Haas, Ferdinand	20, Apr. 1856	Johan	Weirich, Thecla	W	13
Haas, Francis	24, July 1859	Nicolaus	Mi---, Helena	D	142
Haas, Francisca	14, Dec. 1850	Georg	Detch, Louisa	D	246
Haas, Frederick	26, Dec. 1855	George	----, Luitgarda	H	
Haas, Georg	14, Mar. 1859	Ignatius	Gruner, Elisabeth	K	
Haas, Johan	9, July 1854	Nicolaus	Muller, Magdalena	C	
Haas, Johan	4, May 1852	Nicolaus	Pelz, Margaretha	L	
Haas, Joseph	6, Sept 1854	George	----, Luitgarda	H	
Haas, Joseph Ferdinand	6, Aug. 1852	Ferdinand	Schmidt, Carolina	C	
Haas, Joseph Ferdinand	9, Sept 1853	Ferdinand	Schmidt, Carolina	C	
Haas, Joseph Michael	19, Mar. 1854	Philipp	Weirich, Thecla	W	2
Haas, Josephina Carolina	12, Oct. 1856	Georg	Hatten, Catharina	D	69
Haas, Louisa	15, Mar. 1857	Nicolaus	Mueller, Helena	C	
Haas, Ludwig	5, Feb. 1854	Jacob	Fess, Carolina	K	
Haas, Maria Christina	22, Aug. 1858	Gervasius	Williams, Josephine	J	46
Haas, Maria Louisa	2, Nov. 1859	Johan	Weirich, Thecla	T	
Haas, Maria Walburga	3, Jan. 1858	George	Dietz, Louisa	H	
Haas, Otto	1, June 1856	Ferdinand	Schmidt, Carolina	C	
Haas, Pius	24, Jan. 1858	Johan	Weirig, Thecla	W	21
Haas, Theodor	27, July 1856	Joseph	Geier, Barbara	D	63

Name of Child	Date of Baptism	Father	Mother	Church	Page
Haas, Wilhelm	2, Sept 1851	Georg	Detsch, Louise	Q	1
Habain, Caroline	10, Oct. 1852	Heinrich	Fredewes, Catherine	Q	2
Habekotte, Heinrich Wilhelm	23, Jan. 1859	Wilhelm	Pabst, Regina	R	
Habel, Otto Fridolin	11, Nov. 1857	August	Kaminzer, Magdalena	K	
Habelberger, Philipp	22, Nov. 1857	Valentin	Schneider, Francisca	N	
Habening, Maria Adleheid	16, Oct. 1854	Philipp	Bockweg, Maria Anna	D	20
Habening, Philipp	9, July 1856	Philipp	Bockweg, Adelheid	D	62
Haber, Johan Stephan	7, Jan. 1855	Andreas	Lorer, Bertha	D	26
Haber, Maria Mathilda	2, May 1852	Carl Jos.	Boffinger, Mathilda	F	
Haber, Peter	30, Sept 1850	Benedict	Stifel, Elisabeth	L	
Haberbusch, Catharina Friedricka	20, Nov. 1859	Dennis	Hyndmann, Maria	G	
Haberecht, Jacob	29, Jan. 1854	Leonhard	Bauendistel, Lenore	L	
Haberes, Johan Bernard	28, Nov. 1856	J. Bernard	--grat--, Gertrud	D	73
Haberhof, Johan	12, Apr. 1857	J. Herman	Koch, Maria	D	82
Haberkern, Francis Anton	25, Mar. 1856	Carl J.	Bofinger, Mathilda	D	54
Haberkorn, Rosina Ottilia	7, Aug. 1853	Benedict	Stiefel, Louisa	D	399
Haberland, Maria	22, Sept 1850	Johan	----, Margaretha	D	233
Habermäher, Robert	14, Aug. 1859	Johan	Ulrich, Catharina	H	
Haberman, Joseph	30, Nov. 1858	Philip	Langhausen, Juliana	U	
Haberman, Wilhelm	11, Feb. 1855	Johan	Rau, Elisabeth	D	28
Haberthur, Georg Jacob	12, June 1859	Jacob	Spiess, Catharina	T	
Habethin, Jacob	20, Nov. 1856	Jacob	Spiess, Catharina	D	72
Habich, Maria Elisabeth	11, Oct. 1857	Friedrich	Hiller, Appolonia	D	96
Habichhorst, Clement	21, Mar. 1853	Heinrich	Weber, Elisabeth	Q	3
Habickhorst, Bernard Heinrich	18, Aug. 1859	Heinrich	Weber, Elisabeth	L	
Habicost, Georg Heinrich	16, Aug. 1850	Herman	Francis, Catharina	D	228
Habig, Anna Maria	20, July 1850	Michael	Hauer, Kunigunda	J	6
Habig, Carl	18, Dec. 1859	Michael	Auer, Kunigunda	G	
Habig, Catharina	29, Sept 1850	Wendelin	Krug, Kunigunda	J	8
Habig, Heinrich	25, Jan. 1852	Michael	Auer, Kunigunda	F	
Habig, Johan	2, Apr. 1854	Michael	Auer, Kunigunda	F	
Habig, Johan Michael	5, Dec. 1852	Wendelin	Krug, Cunigunda	J	18
Habig, Michael Philipp	14, May 1857	Michael	Auer, Kunigunda	F	
Habig, Wendelin Michael	14, May 1854	Wendelin	Krug, Cunigunda	J	26
Habighaus, Anna Maria	14, Jan. 1856	Heinrich	Weber, M. Elisabeth	L	
Habighorst, Johan Aloysius	6, Nov. 1850	Philipp	Weber, Maria Elisabeth	K	
Habighorst, Theresa Josephina Elis	29, Dec. 1857	Heinrich	Weber, Elisabeth	L	
Habikhorst, Maria Cath. Philomena	23, Oct. 1851	Heinrich	Weber, Elisabeth	K	
Habler, Heinrich Theodor	12, Sept 1852	Johan H.	Franzmann, Marianna	F	
Habner, Barbara Maria	22, Jan. 1850	Michael	Streberol, Barbara	H	
Habner, Michael	21, Mar. 1850	George	Hamerle, Mary	H	
Habrecht, Anna Dorothea	23, Mar. 1856	Leonard	Sendel, Anna Dorothea	A	
Habson, August	15, Dec. 1859	Simon	Hirsch, Maria	F	
Hach, Catharina	28, Mar. 1858	Jacob	Hack, Catharina	D	108
Hack, Elisabeth	9, Jan. 1853	Johan	----, Elisabeth	C	
Hack, Franz	9, June 1850	Peter	Deck, Victoria	F	
Hack, Heinrich	28, May 1857	Heinrich	Küglin, Margaretha	A	
Hack, Maria Anna	5, June 1852	Peter	Dick, Victoria	F	
Hack, Peter Wilhelm	8, Aug. 1854	Peter	Dick, Victoria	F	
Hacke, Francis	19, Mar. 1854	Anton	Neuhaus, Elisabeth	C	
Hacke, Johan	30, Oct. 1853	Anton	Siefert, Elisabeth	C	
Hacke, Johan Heinrich	3, Mar. 1856	J. Heinrich	Heleke, Anna Maria	L	
Hacke, Johan Herman Heinrich	3, June 1850	F. Wilhelm	Reverman, Helena	K	
Hacket, Henry William	26, Feb. 1854	William	Henry, Ann	P	71
Hackett, Josephine	25, Aug. 1856	William	Henry, Ann	P	189
Hackman, Francis Xavier	3, Dec. 1851	Heinrich	Bäumer, Maria Anna	A	
Hackman, Gerhard Heinrich	24, Jan. 1858	Gerhard	Hemmelgarten, Theresa	A	
Hackman, Gerhard Heinrich	2, Mar. 1853		Hackman, Maria	D	374
Hackman, Herman Heinrich	21, Sept 1855	J. Gerhard	Hemmelgarn, Theresa	A	

Name of Child	Date of Baptism	Father	Mother	Church	Page
Hackman, Johan Bernard	12, Mar. 1854	J. Gerhard	Ruthers, Catharina	A	
Hackman, Joseph Herman	14, July 1856	Heinrich	Baumer, ----	A	
Hackman, Maria Anna Elisabeth	14, Oct. 1859	J.H.	Baumer, Maria Anna	A	
Hackman, Maria Antonette Josephina	9, Feb. 1854	Heinrich	Bäumer, Anna Maria	A	
Hackman, Maria Gertrud	20, Sept 1853	Gerhard	Hemmelgarn, Theresa	A	
Hackman, Wilhelm Heinrich	11, Apr. 1852	Gerhard	Rothus, Maria Adelheid	A	
Hackmann, Agnes	16, Oct. 1850	Friedrich	Borger, Maria	C	
Hackmann, Anna Marg't Josephina	22, Feb. 1859	Nicolaus	Helms, M. Anna	C	
Hackmann, Anna Maria	2, Dec. 1855	Nicolaus	Herens, M. Anna	C	
Hackmann, Anna Maria	24, Feb. 1859		Hackmann, M. Angela	L	
Hackmann, Anna Maria Catharina	14, Mar. 1859	Friedrich	Boerger, M. Catharina	L	
Hackmann, Christoph Bernard	10, Sept 1853	Friedrich	Boerger, A.M. Catharina	L	
Hackmann, Gerhard Everhard	16, Sept 1857	Gerhard	Bruemmer, Margaretha	C	
Hackmann, Johan Heinrich	15, Mar. 1857	Friedrich	Boerger, Maria	L	
Hackmann, Joseph Nicolaus Heinrich	25, Aug. 1850	Gerhard	Luesken, Margaretha	C	
Hackmann, Maria Anna	18, Apr. 1852	Gerhard E.	Bruemmer, Margaretha	C	
Hackmann, Maria Catharina Angela	6, Oct. 1854	Gerhard E.	Bruemer, Margaretha	C	
Hadley, Charles	3, July 1859	George D.	Hennessy, Mary	P	287
Hadley, Clara Isabel	20, Sept 1857	John	Burnside, Susan	P	225
Hadley, Cuba Ann	3, Feb. 1856	James A.	Burnside, Mary Ann	P	168
Hadley, James Alexander	11, Oct. 1857	George D.	Hennessy, Mary E.	P	**227**
Haeffling, Maria	13, July 1851	Georg	Riff, Maria	F	
Haeffner, Johan Heinrich	18, July 1857	Andreas	Bechtel, Johanna	K	
Haekle, Johan	6, Aug. 1858	Caspar	Wie---bau--, Crescentia	D	116
Haemerle, Othmar	26, Jan. 1850	Joseph	----, Anna Magdalena	D	201
Haemmerle, Francisca	24, Apr. 1859	Johan	Hasler, Josephina	D	136
Haemmerle, Sophia	30, Sept 1856	Johan	Hasler, Josephina	C	
Haensler, Maria Anna	21, Nov. 1858	Valentin	Her---, Maria Elisabeth	D	124
Haeny, Catherine	28, Dec. 1851	James	Grey, Bridget	E	368
Haessler, Carl Ferdinand	2, Jan. 1857	Ferdinand	Dieterling, Theresa	F	
Haf, Anna Rosa	4, Sept 1859	Jacob	----, Magdalena	D	145
Haf, Carl Jacob	24, May 1857	Jacob	Jupenlatz, Magdalena	F	
Haf, Catharina	24, Oct. 1852	Jacob	Juppenlatz, Magdalena	D	354
Haf, Elisabeth	18, Mar. 1855	Jacob	Jupenlotz, Magdalena	F	
Haf, Maria Elisabeth	4, Sept 1859	Jacob	----, Magdalena	D	145
Hafey, Patrick	10, Mar. 1855	Matthew	O'Brien, Catherine	V	23
Haffin, Edward	29, Feb. 1852	Edward	Roner, Catherine	B	253
Haffner, Anna Maria	17, July 1853	Urban	Schelaf?, Agatha	D	395
Haffner, Johan	25, Jan. 1857	Stephan	Pau---, Augusta	D	77
Haffner, Stephan	27, Feb. 1859	Stephan	Bernh---, Augusta	D	132
Hag, Mathias	25, Apr. 1855	John	Tentes, Catherine	N	28
Hagan, Ann	15, June 1855	John	Gater, Mary	E	293
Hagan, Bridget	26, Jan. 1850	John	Carroll, Catherine	E	194
Hagan, Catherine	15, June 1855	John	Gater, Mary	E	293
Hagan, Ellen	29, Aug. 1857	Patrick	McCarey, Mary	E	477
Hagan, James	20, Feb. 1853	Thomas	Murray, Rose	E	64
Hagan, William	17, Oct. 1852	John	Lyons, Sarah	E	27
Hagand, William	23, Feb. 1851	Patrick	Dignum, Bridget	P	5
Hagarty, Anthony	10, May 1853	Anthony	----, ----	P	41
Hagarty, Anthony	2, Oct. 1852	Patrick	Flynn, Winnefred	E	23
Hagarty, Daniel	4, Feb. 1855	Anthony	Brown, Helen	P	119
Hagarty, James	6, Apr. 1851	Anthony	Brown, Ellen	P	6
Hagarty, Mary Bridget	17, June 1855	Robert	Troy, Mary	P	136
Hagarty, Patrick	25, Aug. 1854	Patrick	Flynn, Winefred	V	16
Hagarty, Thomas	21, Dec. 1851	Robert	Troy, Mary	B	248
Hage, Catharina	10, Jan. 1855	Friedrich	Fillian, Appollonia	D	26
Hage, Wilhelm	4, Jan. 1854	Joseph	Fideldai, Catharina Maria	D	1
Hagedorn, Anna Gesina Philomena	2, July 1856	Heinrich	Toennies, Gesina A.	L	
Hagedorn, Anna Maria	12, Sept 1852	Johan	Halterman, Elisabeth	D	347

Name of Child	Date of Baptism	Father	Mother	Church	Page
Hagedorn, Anna Maria Gertrud	19, Mar. 1856	Bernard	Schlemann, Elisabeth	F	
Hagedorn, Gerhard Joseph Heinrich	12, Dec. 1851	Gerhard	Toenies, Gesina Adel.	L	
Hagedorn, Johan Bernard	18, Apr. 1853	Bernard	Schlemann, Elisabeth	C	
Hagedorn, Johan Heinrich	2, Feb. 1858	Bernard	Schleman, Elisabeth	A	
Hagedorn, Johan William	10, Dec. 1854	J. Wilhelm	Hahneman, Elisabeth	D	23
Hagedorn, Maria Adelheid Catharina	18, May 1854	Gerhard	Toennes, M. Adelheid	L	
Hagedorn, Maria Catharina	24, Apr. 1853	Heinrich	Krappe, Anna Catharina	F	
Hagedorn, Maria Elisabeth	1, Dec. 1850	Herman	Grabbe, Marianna	F	
Hagedorn, Maria Elisabeth	16, Aug. 1850	Johan	Hallerman, Elisabeth	D	228
Hagel, Gerhard	12, Sept 1858	Bernard	Fangman, Catharina	A	
Hagel, Maria	12, Sept 1858	Bernard	Fangman, Catharina	A	
Hagel, Mary	26, Aug. 1855	Bernard	Donovan, Catherine	P	148
Hageman, Francis Heinrich	28, July 1857	Ferdinand	Engelbert, Maria Catharina	K	
Hageman, Gerhard Bernard	22, Mar. 1857	Bernard	Wilmsen, Theresa	U	
Hageman, Maria Anna Theresa	11, Oct. 1858	Bernard	Wilmsen, Theresa	U	
Hagen, Anna Maria	11, Apr. 1854	Johan	Diman, Catharina M.	D	8
Hagen, Catharina	26, Nov. 1854	Johan	Rinck, Elenora	G	
Hagen, Louisa Juliana	27, Oct. 1854	Nicolaus	Schmidt, Juliana	D	20
Hagen, Maria Anna	23, July 1854	Joseph B.	Hagel, Crescentia	D	14
Hagen, Matthias	21, June 1857	Friedrich	Fillian, Appollonia	D	88
Hagen, Peter	23, Mar. 1856	Johan	Hirchner, Catharina	C	
Hagen, Peter	6, Jan. 1857	Johan	Ring, Elenora	G	
Hagenhofer, Johan Georg	7, Nov. 1858	Johan	Koch, Maria	D	123
Hageny, George	14, Apr. 1859	Nicolaus	Rösch, Elisabeth	H	
Hageny, Joseph Herman	11, July 1859	Wilhelm A.	Deschering, Francisca	F	
Hager, Anna Maria	19, Jan. 1853	Johan	Specht, Magdalena	D	365
Hager, Martin	12, Feb. 1851	Johan	Specht, Magdalena	D	253
Hager, Peter	3, Sept 1854	Johan	Specht, Magdalena	D	17
Hagerty, Alexander	10, Nov. 1853	Alexander	Kelly, Ann	B	302
Hagerty, Ann	8, Sept 1850	Alexander	Kelly, Ann	B	213
Hagerty, Ann	13, June 1858	Robert	Troy, Mary	B	60
Hagerty, Ann	5, Sept 1858	William	McManus, Rose	B	64
Hagerty, Charles	26, June 1853	Patrick	Crier, Mary	E	101
Hagerty, Dora Margaret	16, Mar. 1857	Robert	Troy, Mary	B	42
Hagerty, Elizabeth	29, Oct. 1856		adult - 33 years old	V	34
Hagerty, Hugh	13, Aug. 1858	Alexander	Kelly, Ann	B	62
Hagerty, James	29, Mar. 1858	Patrick	Flynn, Winny	E	525
Hagerty, James	19, Dec. 1854	Thomas	Rafferty, Helen	P	111
Hagerty, Joanne	17, June 1852	Alexander	Kelly, Ann	B	261
Hagerty, John	11, Aug. 1850	Robert	Troy, Mary	B	209
Hagerty, Margaret	3, Feb. 1856	James	----, Catherine	E	342
Hagerty, Mary	21, Sept 1856	Alexander	Kelly, Ann	B	34
Hagerty, Mary Ann	12, Aug. 1855	Alexander	Kelly, Ann	B	18
Hagerty, Mary Ann	21, July 1851	James	Hurley, Catherine	B	237
Hagerty, Mary Ann	27, Nov. 1853	Robert	Troy, Mary	B	303
Hagestege, Maria Gertrud	22, Apr. 1854	Johan	Niehaus, Anna Catharina	D	8
Hagge, Mathias	13, Feb. 1859	Friedrich	Filian, Apollonia	D	131
Haggerton, John	24, Aug. 1853	James	Hurley, Catherine	B	297
Haggerty, Joanne	8, Feb. 1852	Patrick	Donohoe, Catherine	P	18
Haggerty, Mary	19, June 1853	Patrick	Donovan, Catherine	P	44
Haggerty, Mary Ann	18, Nov. 1858	Patrick	Cryer, Mary	E	579
Hagherty, Edmund	8, Feb. 1854	Edmund	Carrell, Margaret	E	166
Hagherty, Thomas	20, Sept 1855	Patrick	----, Winnifred	E	316
Hagi, Mary Ann	21, Nov. 1858	Andrew	Collins, Catherine	N	
Hagins, Mary	9, Aug. 1852	Bernard	McCran, Mary	E	4
Haglage, Anna Maria Friedrica	12, June 1857	Joseph	Hoedebeke, Catharina	K	
Haglage, Joseph	24, July 1852	Joseph	Woedebeck, Maria Catharina	K	
Haglage, Maria Carolina	13, Mar. 1859	Joseph	Hodebecke, Catharina	K	
Haglage, Maria Catharina	16, Aug. 1854	Joseph	Hoedebeke, Maria Catharina	K	

Name of Child	Date of Baptism	Father	Mother	Church	Page
Hahenleitner, Carolina	3, Sept 1858	Joseph	Waiand, Carolina	D	118
Haher, John Edward	5, Apr. 1855	Edward	Moroney, Helen	P	127
Hahn, Agatha Louise	8, Aug. 1852	John	----, Regina	H	
Hahn, Anna Maria	11, June 1850	John	----, Rose	H	
Hahn, Anna Maria	16, Feb. 1850	Valentin	Mueller, Elisabeth	L	
Hahn, August	10, Sept 1854	Philipp	Guth, Rosina	C	
Hahn, Catharina	8, Feb. 1857	Nicolaus	Schmid, Juliana	D	78
Hahn, Catharina Josephina	28, Nov. 1852	Max.	Heide, Theresa	D	358
Hahn, Emilia Isabella	25, Sept 1859	Philipp	Guth, Rosalia	C	
Hahn, Eva Catharina	6, Apr. 1856	Johan	----, Rosina	H	
Hahn, Francis	22, Oct. 1854	Wilhelm	Baumegger, Carolina	D	20
Hahn, Friedrich Francis Xavier	15, May 1858	Friedrich	Zi---, Salomea	D	111
Hahn, Heinrich	18, Sept 1859	Wilhelm	Baumhekel, Catharina	C	
Hahn, Helena	28, Mar. 1852	Friedrich	Becker, Elisabeth	D	314
Hahn, Johan Adam	20, June 1852	Philipp	Gut, Rosina	C	
Hahn, Johan Christoph Wilhelm	1, Aug. 1850	Maximilian	Haite, Theresa	D	226
Hahn, Joseph	1, Oct. 1854	Valentin	Amen, Maria	A	
Hahn, Juliana	12, Mar. 1854	Friedrich	Becker, Louisa	D	6
Hahn, Louise	14, Mar. 1858	John	Wagner, Rosa	H	
Hahn, Magdalena	16, Dec. 1855	Ludwig	Jansen, Elisabeth	D	48
Hahn, Michael	26, Apr. 1857	Wilhelm	Baumkeckl, Catharina	D	83
Hahn, Rosina	11, June 1854	John	----, Rosina	H	
Hahne, Johan Arnold	23, Jan. 1857	Arnold	Pelzer, M. Theresa	L	
Hahnhausen, Joseph	18, Oct. 1855	Jacob	Müller, Francisca	D	44
Hahnhauser, Anton	6, Nov. 1853	Anton	Hartmann, Catharina	C	
Hahnhauser, Anton	22, July 1855	Anton	Hartmann, Catharina	C	
Hahnhauser, Carl Wilhelm	20, Mar. 1859	Anton	Hartmann, Catharina	C	
Hahnhauser, Emilia	22, Feb. 1857	Anton	Hartmann, Catharina	C	
Hahnhauser, Theodor	14, Mar. 1855	Johan	Juerger, Magdalena	L	
Hahnlen, Ella	12, May 1856	Aaron	Ceyrode, Louise	P	180
Hai, Catharina	6, Dec. 1850	Nicolaus	Schmidt, Louisa	D	245
Hai, Maria	23, May 1852	Nicolaus	Schmidt, Louisa	D	321
Haidegger, Bernardina Henrietta	27, Aug. 1855	Wilhelm	Siemer, Elisabeth	D	41
Haiger, Sophia Amalia	11, July 1858	Benedict	Baerz, Theckla	D	114
Hailey, Mary	18, Aug. 1850	Daniel	----, Catherine	E	240
Hailey, Mary	21, Oct. 1850	John	----, Mary	E	256
Haily, Catherine	20, July 1854	Daniel	Murphy, Catherine	E	208
Haily, Catherine	30, Apr. 1853	Jeremiah	Clary, Julia	E	85
Haily, Catherine	5, Mar. 1858	Patrick	----, Joanne	E	520
Haily, Dennis Francis Xavier	6, Jan. 1858	Thomas	Sullivan, Bridget	E	506
Haily, James	31, July 1859	Cornelius	Starr, Catherine	E	644
Haily, James	12, July 1857	Daniel	----, Catherine	E	464
Haily, Joanne	5, Mar. 1858	Patrick	----, Joanne	E	520
Haily, John Philipp	23, Apr. 1854	Daniel	Groom, Ann	E	184
Haily, Mary	19, Oct. 1856	Thomas	Sullivan, Bridget	E	405
Haily, Mary Ann	18, Mar. 1855	Thomas	----, Bridget	E	273
Haily, Timothy	6, Aug. 1854	Daniel	Cronan, Catherine	E	214
Haimer, Johanna Catharina	16, June 1850	William	Rieder, Catharina	D	217
Hain, Anna Margaretha	8, Feb. 1857	Jacob	Entres, Apollonia	D	78
Haindl, Bridget	4, Aug. 1854	Michael	Doe, Bridget	N	23
Hainy Ann	25, Feb. 1857	Patrick	Ready, Mary	E	436
Hainy, Cecilia	16, Mar. 1851	James	----, Mary	E	291
Hainy, Mary	24, Apr. 1857	Thomas	Nicholson, Honora	E	447
Hainy, Patrick	24, Apr. 1857	Thomas	Nicholson, Honora	E	448
Hainz, Barbara	1, Oct. 1854	Michael	Beis, Margaretha	D	18
Haiob, Jacob	12, Apr. 1856	Henry	Stahl, Charlotte	U	
Haiop, Catharina	11, Apr. 1852	Heinrich	Stahl, Carolina	D	315
Hair, Ann	25, June 1854	John	Faith, Mary	B	2
Haire, Helen	8, Jan. 1854	Edward	Moroney, Helen	P	64

Name of Child	Date of Baptism	Father	Mother	Church	Page
Haire, Robert	1, Oct. 1854	Johan	Spies, Magdalena	L	
Haiss, Catharina Christina	8, Apr. 1855	Ludwig	Betscher, Maria Anna	D	33
Hak, Maria Anna	26, Dec. 1852	Heinrich	Kisling, Margaretha	K	
Hake, Maria Elisabeth	13, Mar. 1859	Anton	Siefers, Elisabeth	H	
Hake, Peter	21, Sept 1856	Anthony	Siefers, Elisabeth	H	
Hakes, William	29, Jan. 1854	John	O'Connell, Joanne	P	67
Haldeman, Charles Jefferson	26, Jan. 1851	Thomas J.	Gilman, Sarah Ann	B	224
Halden, Mary	13, Aug. 1852	Daniel	----, Nora	E	5
Halder, Joseph Ludwig	27, May 1850	Joseph	Hoping, Margaretha	L	
Halenkamp, Heinrich	26, July 1851	Wilhelm	Bischer, Elisabeth	A	
Halenkamp, J.H. Gerhard	25, June 1858	J. Gerhard	Lübbers, Maria Elisabeth	A	
Halenkamp, Johan Wilhelm	8, Jan. 1854	Wilhelm	Henghold, Julia	A	
Hales, Werner	14, Sept 1859	Heinrich	Thiele, Bernardina	C	
Haley, Barbara Helen	10, Dec. 1855	Daniel	Clifford, Mary	E	332
Haley, Catherine	13, Nov. 1850	Patrick	Ryan, Abby	E	261
Haley, Dennis	10, Feb. 1851	John	Purcell, Joanne	B	225
Haley, Helen	30, Jan. 1852	Daniel	----, Ann	B	251
Haley, Helen	3, Aug. 1851	Luke	Dunn, Julia	B	238
Haley, James	14, May 1854	Henry	McCarthy, Sarah	P	82
Haley, James	6, Feb. 1853	John	Goghin, Ann	E	61
Haley, James	25, Jan. 1852	Patrick	Ryan, Abie	E	377
Haley, Joanne Mary	31, Oct. 1852	John	Purcell, Joanne	B	273
Haley, Mary	28, Sept 1856	Patrick	----, Bridget	R	
Haley, Mary	18, Mar. 1859	Patrick	Ryan, Abby	E	611
Haley, Mary	22, July 1859	Sylvester	Sullivan, Honora	E	642
Haley, Mary Ann	15, June 1851	Henry	McCarthy, Sara Ann	P	9
Haley, Mary Ann	15, Feb. 1857	Henry	McCarthy, Sarah	P	206
Haley, Matthew	2, June 1850	Charles	----, Catherine	E	218
Haley, Michael	10, Oct. 1853	Patrick	Ryan, Abbie	E	133
Haley, Patrick	29, Apr. 1857	Patrick	Ryan, Adelaide	E	449
Haley, William	2, May 1854	Patrick	Mitchell, Johanna	C	
Hall, Aloysius	14, Aug. 1856	John	10 years old	K	
Hall, Ann	23, Nov. 1859	Kieran	Shaw, Mary	E	673
Hall, Ann	8, Sept 1851	William	Whalen, Margaret	B	240
Hall, Catherine	11, June 1854	Christopher	----, Joanne	M	
Hall, Catherine	24, Sept 1854	Henry	----, Ann	M	
Hall, Catherine	20, Nov. 1853	William	Whelan, Margaret	P	59
Hall, Daniel	2, Apr. 1854	James	Hurley, Mary	B	312
Hall, Elizabeth	22, Mar. 1857	Kieran	----, Ann	M	
Hall, Francis	11, Dec. 1853	William	Whelan, Margaret	P	61
Hall, George	19, Sept 1859	Ebenezer	Borgess, Helen	E	655
Hall, Helen	11, Dec. 1853	William	Whelan, Margaret	P	61
Hall, Henry	29, Mar. 1855	Henry	Smith, Martha	E	275
Hall, Honora	30, Mar. 1856	Christopher	----, Julia	M	
Hall, Joseph	7, Nov. 1853	William	----, Margaret	P	58
Hall, Lilly Mary	30, Dec. 1851	Thomas	adult - 45 years old	E	369
Hall, Margaret	23, Nov. 1850	Bernard	Harney, Helen	B	219
Hall, Margaret	21, Sept 1851	James	----, Ann	E	345
Hall, Margaret	11, Dec. 1853	William	Whelan, Margaret	P	61
Hall, Maria Theresa	16, Feb. 1858	?	?	A	
Hall, Martin Anton	25, July 1858	Anton	Back, Elisabeth	C	
Hall, Mary	14, Aug. 1856		adult - 32 years old	K	
Hall, Regina Josephine	10, Oct. 1858	James	Francis, Martha	P	263
Hall, Robert	11, Dec. 1853	William	Whelan, Margaret	P	61
Hall, Thomas	17, Oct. 1858	Christopher	----, Jane	M	
Hall, Thomas	16, Mar. 1856	Kieran	----, Ann	M	
Hall, Thomas	8, Aug. 1858	Thomas	Hickey, Catherine	P	256
Hallahan, Mary	12, Oct. 1851	Patrick	----, Hannah	E	350
Hallan, Maria Johanna	22, May 1852	Michael	Wink, Maria Appolonia	D	320

Hamilton County, Ohio Roman Catholic Baptism Records -- 1850 - 1859

Name of Child	Date of Baptism	Father	Mother	Church	Page
Hallen, James William	21, Aug. 1850	John C.	Roach, Julia	B	211
Hallenan, John	26, Dec. 1859	Daniel	Doran, Ann	B	86
Hallenan, Julia	26, Dec. 1859	Daniel	Doran, Ann	B	86
Hallenbeck, Anna Maria Emilia	15, Aug. 1851	Herman G.	Ertel, Maria Elisabeth	F	
Hallenbeck, Ernst August	23, Feb. 1854	Herman	Ertel, Maria Elisabeth	F	
Hallenbeck, Herman Georg	11, Oct. 1857	Herman G.	Ertel, Maria	F	
Hallenkamp, August	5, July 1857	Wilhelm	Roberg, Juliana	F	
Haller, Josephina Theresa	20, Apr. 1851	Anton	Brodwick, Catharina	D	261
Haller, Julius	25, May 1859	Christian	Singlair, Maria	D	138
Halleran, Thomas	26, Dec. 1858	Thomas	Maginnes, Catherine	B	69
Halley, Joseph Mary	13, July 1851	Samuel	Mallon, Susan	B	236
Halley, Mary Ann	15, Feb. 1854	?	?	B	309
Halley, Michael	19, May 1856	Michael	Londrigan, Margaret	E	367
Halligan, Edward	14, Aug. 1859	Patrick	----, Eliza	E	647
Halligan, Elizabeth	17, Jan. 1855	James	----, Mary	E	257
Halligan, Henry	15, Mar. 1853	James	McLaughlin, Mary Ann	E	73
Halligan, Margaret	17, Jan. 1858	Patrick	Sweeney, Elizabeth	B	54
Halligan, Mary	20, July 1856	James	McLaughlin,	E	383
Halligan, Mary Ann	30, Oct. 1851	John	Churchill, Mary	B	244
Halligan, Michael	26, July 1853	John	----, Honora	E	112
Hallighan, Mary Ann	21, Nov. 1852	Patrick	Sweeney, Elizabeth	B	276
Hallinan, Daniel	25, Dec. 1851	William	Byrne, Elizabeth	B	248
Hallinan, John	15, May 1853	William	Byrne, Elizabeth	B	291
Halloran, James	29, Apr. 1859	William	Meeshan, Margaret	E	622
Halloran, John	23, Oct. 1859	Daniel	Stableton, Mary	Z	
Halloran, John	12, Mar. 1854	John	Finnegan, Ann	E	175
Halloran, Margaret	25, Jan. 1857	Michael	----, Honora	M	
Halloran, Mary Ann	23, May 1858	Daniel	----, Mary	M	
Halloran, Thomas	17, Dec. 1854	Francis	Forrester, Mary	B	8
Hallran, Mary Ann	22, June 1850	Robert	----, ----	E	225
Hall-son, Margaret	17, Feb. 1850	William	Burns, Elizabeth	B	196
Halper, Mary Helen	14, Oct. 1856	Thomas	Fitzgerald, Mary	J	38
Halpin, Ann	19, Jan. 1858	John	King, Ann	E	510
Halpin, Catherine	3, Mar. 1856	Anthony	Dignan, Bridget	P	171
Halpin, Catherine	22, July 1853	Michael	----, Ann	M	
Halpin, Dennis	21, Jan. 1851	Patrick	Britton, Elizabeth	B	223
Halpin, Eliza	2, Nov. 1853	Edward	----, Mary	E	140
Halpin, Elizabeth	30, Jan. 1853		adult - 50 years old	B	282
Halpin, Helen	8, Nov. 1857	Thomas	Fitzgerald, Mary	J	44
Halpin, Honora	11, Oct. 1858	Dennis	----, Bridget	M	
Halpin, John	30, Jan. 1859	Anthony	Degnan, C.	P	273
Halpin, John	13, Oct. 1851	Jeremiah	----, Elizabeth	B	242
Halpin, Joseph	25, Mar. 1855	Edward	----, Mary	E	274
Halpin, Mary	3, Sept 1854	Thomas	Fitzgerald, Mary	P	94
Halpin, Mary	14, Jan. 1855	William	----, Julie	U	
Halpin, Mary Ann	31, Dec. 1854	Michael	----, Ann	M	
Halpin, Michael	6, Mar. 1859	John	King, Ann	B	72
Halpin, Patrick	10, Apr. 1853	William	Hollers, Susan	B	288
Halpin, Thomas	28, Jan. 1852	Thomas	Fitzgerald, Mary	B	251
Halpin, William	9, Oct. 1853	Patrick	Britton, Elizabeth	B	300
Halstead, Mary Elizabeth	12, Jan. 1851	David Curtis	Sheridan, Ann	E	275
Halstead, Paige Curtis	4, Sept 1853	David	----, Ann	E	125
Halter, Catharina	21, Nov. 1858	Anton	Lang---, Catharina	D	124
Haltermann, Johan Clemens	18, July 1851	J. Clemens	Harmann, Regina	F	
Halton, Charles Alexander	14, Dec. 1856	Thomas	Morragh, Ann	T	
Haly, Catherine	26, Oct. 1856	John	Gaughan, Ann	V	34
Haly, Thomas	6, July 1857	Michael	Forde, Bridget	V	40
Hamacher, Maria Margaretha Magdalena	11, Jan. 1850	Michael (+)	Schmitz, Catharina	D	198
Hamann, Anna Maria	11, Dec. 1853	Heinrich	Frehle, Catharina	C	

Hamilton County, Ohio Roman Catholic Baptism Records -- 1850 - 1859

Name of Child	Date of Baptism	Father	Mother	Church	Page
Hamann, Johan Bernard	3, Apr. 1856	Bernard	Wernsing, Anna Maria	C	
Hambacher, Jacob	20, Oct. 1852	Jacob	Matthus, Elisabeth	C	
Hamberg, Anna Maria	20, Jan. 1856	Ferdinand	Bochmann, Catharina	F	
Hamberg, Franz Ferdinand	29, Aug. 1856	Heinrich	Kruemberg, Anna M.	F	
Hamberg, Johan Georg	11, Aug. 1859	Heinrich	Dinkel, Anna Catharina	K	
Hamberg, Johan Heinrich	22, Dec. 1851	Ferdinand	Borgmann, Anna Catharina	F	
Hamberg, Theodor	9, Nov. 1857	Johan H.	Krumberg, Marianna	F	
Hamberg, Theodor Herman	1, July 1859	Heinrich	Krumberg, Anna	F	
Hamberger, Anna Maria	14, Feb. 1854	Ferdinand	Borgmann, Maria Catharina	F	
Hambler, Francis Joseph	1, Jan. 1857	Francis	Putz, Maria	D	76
Hambler, Henriette	9, Apr. 1854	Heinrich	Kessens, Josephina	F	
Hambo, Stephan	21, Apr. 1850	Stephan	Scheible, Anna	C	
Hamen, Thomas	27, Sept 1854	Thomas	Cashan, Margaret	P	97
Hamerle, Carl	6, Apr. 1856	Adolph	Beiler, Crescentia	D	56
Hämerle, Maria Rosa	10, Oct. 1858	Adolph	Bailer, Crescentia	D	121
Hamilton, Elizabeth	15, Mar. 1853	Richard	Tyge, Bridget	E	73
Hamilton, James William	13, Aug. 1854	Nicolaus	Lamb, Susan	P	92
Hamilton, John	31, Jan. 1850	John	----, Ellen	E	195
Hamilton, John	11, June 1854	John	Harnson, Bridget	P	85
Hamilton, Nicolaus George	22, Sept 1857	Nicolaus	Lamb, Susan	P	**225**
Hamilton, Sarah	9, Feb. 1850		adult	B	196
Hamilton, Sarah	2, Dec. 1855		adult	V	28
Hamilton, Thomas Peter	9, July 1851	Nicholas	----, Susan	E	322
Hamman, Johan Christoph	21, Mar. 1858	Johan	Kehrer, Rosa	D	107
Hamman, Wilhelm Theodor Heinrich	29, July 1851	Christoph	Pund, A.M. Josephina	A	
Hammann, Anton Heinrich	11, Oct. 1859	Anton H.	Keller, Justina	C	
Hammann, Johan Anton	7, Jan. 1852	Heinrich	Froele, Catharina	C	
Hammann, Johan Christoph	9, May 1858	Heinrich	Frohle, Catharina	C	
Hammann, Johan Heinrich	9, Dec. 1851	Heinrich	Stewer, Anna Maria	C	
Hammann, Johan Heinrich Herman	28, June 1858	Herman B.	Wernsing, Maria	C	
Hammann, Justina Friedricka	3, Aug. 1859	Heinrich	Froehle, Catharina	C	
Hammann, Maria Catharina	2, Mar. 1856	Heinrich	Froelen, Catharina	C	
Hammann, Willibold	2, Jan. 1859	Mathias	Schills, Catharina	C	
Hammant, George	5, Oct. 1851	Lambert	Bordeau, Mary	E	348
Hammant, Maria Julia	15, Nov. 1859	Lambert	Bardo, Maria	T	
Hammel, Johan	15, June 1856	Jacob	Ast, Magdalena	D	61
Hammel, Magdalena	29, May 1858	Jacob	Ast, Magdalena	D	112
Hammelman, Barbara	21, Dec. 1856	Friedrich	Müller, Elisabeth	D	74
Hammelman, Johan Michael	27, Aug. 1854	Friedrich	Miller, Elisabeth	D	16
Hammend, Clara	29, Jan. 1854	Joseph	Bards, Catharina	D	3
Hammer, Anna Magdalena	16, June 1850	Jacob	Little, Anna Maria	J	6
Hammer, Anna Maria	11, July 1858	J. Peter	Vollmer, Maria	D	114
Hammer, Anna Maria	20, Oct. 1850	Peter	Wirte, Anna Maria	J	8
Hammer, Anna Philomena	24, July 1856	Jacob	Little, Anna Maria	J	36
Hammer, Anton	13, Nov. 1853	Peter	Wirtz, Anna Maria	J	24
Hammer, Benjamin	21, Apr. 1854	Johan	Wirtlin, Rosina	K	
Hammer, Bernard	1, Sept 1850	Peter F.	Haring, Philomena	D	231
Hammer, Catharina Elisabeth	7, June 1858	Peter	Wuertz, Anna Maria	T	
Hammer, Elisabeth	20, Sept 1857	Adam	Pfenning, Anna Maria	D	95
Hammer, Elisabeth	19, Nov. 1854		Hammer, Carolina	A	
Hammer, Francis Anton	29, June 1857	Wilhelm	Ahler, Elisabeth	D	89
Hammer, Francis Joseph	30, May 1852	P. Joseph	Wirtz, Anna Maria	J	16
Hammer, Heinrich	25, Jan. 1852	Peter	Akergrues, Wilhelmina	F	
Hammer, Johan	25, May 1856	J. Adam	Pfenning, Anna Maria	C	
Hammer, Johan	4, May 1856	Johan	Werdling, Rosina	N	
Hammer, Johan Jacob	4, Sept 1855	P. Joseph	Wirtz, Anna Maria	J	32
Hammer, Joseph	12, July 1858	Joseph	Henninger, Maria Anna	G	
Hammer, Margaretha	5, Oct. 1851	Jacob	Little, Anna Maria	J	12
Hammer, Maria Josephina	26, Dec. 1859	Peter	Wuertz, Anna Maria	T	

Name of Child	Date of Baptism	Father	Mother	Church	Page
Hammer, Maria Magdalena	7, May 1854	Adam	Pfennig, Maria	D	10
Hammer, Maria Margaretha	26, Dec. 1859	Peter	Wuertz, Anna Maria	T	
Hammer, Peter	1, Feb. 1857	J. Leopold	Schmidt, Anna	D	77
Hammer, Peter Jacob	6, Dec. 1857	Jacob	Little, Anna Maria	J	44
Hammer, Regina	23, Jan. 1853	Jacob	Litdel, Anna Maria	D	367
Hammer, Wilhelm Jacob	23, Nov. 1851	Johan	Wörtline, Rosina	K	
Hammerer, Francis Anton	7, June 1857	Benedict	----, Anna Maria	R	
Hämmerle, Georg Engelbert	18, Apr. 1858	Wendelin	Hammerle, Margaretha	J	46
Hammerle, Maria Eva	11, June 1856	Joseph	Mad, Anna	D	60
Hämmerle, Wilhelmina	31, Dec. 1854	Johan	Hassler, Josephina	J	30
Hammers, Anna Maria	20, Apr. 1854	Heinrich	Groenefeld, Adel.	L	
Hammill, James	18, Sept 1853	John	Diegan, Helen	B	299
Hammon, John	17, Oct. 1852	Prosper	Burtheau, Catherine	E	27
Hammond, Catherine M.	8, Dec. 1857		adult - 37 years old	E	499
Hammond, Emily Catherine	7, Oct. 1855	Roper	Bardo, Catherine	E	318
Hammond, John	3, Mar. 1855	John	Dehan, Ellen	B	12
Hammond, John Henry	4, Apr. 1857	Lambert	Bordeau, Mary	E	445
Hammond, Lambert Ed.	1, Mar. 1857	Prosper	Bordeau, Catherine	E	437
Hampe, Heinrich	7, Feb. 1851	Daniel	Sachteleben, Regina	C	
Hampe, Heinrich Wilhelm	21, Sept 1858	Heinrich	Kessens, Josephina	F	
Hampe, Johan Heinrich	20, Apr. 1851	Heinrich	Kessens, Josephina	C	
Hampe, Maria Margaretha	11, June 1856	Heinrich	Kessens, Josephina	F	
Hampe, Theodora Elisabeth Antonia	18, June 1852	Heinrich	Kessner, Josephina	F	
Hamps, Josephina Sophia	30, June 1856	Bernard	Ruf, Carolina	D	62
Hanagan, Francis	14, June 1853	Patrick	Borphy, Catherine	B	293
Hanaghan, Michael	30, Mar. 1851	Michael	Doyle, Mary	P	6
Hanbut, Elisabeth	8, Sept 1858	John	Gorman, Susan	U	
Hand, Jeremiah	8, Apr. 1855	Benjamin	Kerdoff, Margaret	B	13
Hand, Johan Georg	16, Aug. 1857	Silvester	Orth, Elisabeth	F	
Hand, Margaret	7, Aug. 1859	Benjamin	Kerdolf, Margaret	B	79
Hand, William Benjamin	15, Oct. 1850	Benjamin	Kerdolff, Margaret	B	216
Handerner, Anna Dorothea	6, Feb. 1859	Friedrich	Eckstein, Carolina	N	
Handfelt, Carolina Bernardina	22, Jan. 1853	Wilhelm	Schroeder, Margaretha	D	366
Handlon, Daniel	1, Dec. 1850	John	Haney, Mary	B	219
Handlon, Margaret	11, Oct. 1857	Andrew	----, Mary	R	
Handlon, Martin	5, Sept 1852	Andrew	Clancy, Mary	R	
Handlon, Patrick	4 Nov. 1855	Andrew	Clancey, Mary	R	
Handlon, Thomas	24, July 1854	Andreas	Clancey, Mary	R	
Handman, Albert Heinrich	21, Oct. 1859	Anton	Kühn, Margaretha	K	
Handman, Anna Maria Catharina	30, Jan. 1858	Johan H.	Pruss, Maria Elisabeth	A	
Handman, Carl Edward	20, Aug. 1857	Anton	Kuhn, Margaretha	K	
Handman, Georg Anton	11, Apr. 1853	Anton	Kuhn, Margaretha	K	
Handmann, Elisabeth Eleanora	10, Apr. 1851	Anton	Kuhr, Margaretha	L	
Handorf, Catharina Elisabeth	11, June 1859	Anton	Wilkemeier, Gertrud	L	
Handorf, Maria	9, Nov. 1851	Bernard	Wilhausen, Anna Maria	L	
Handorf, Maria Gertrud	8, Aug. 1853	Anton	Wilkenmeyer, M. Gertrud	L	
Handorf, Wilhelm	14, Dec. 1855	Anton	Wilkemeyer, Gertrud	L	
Handragan, James	6, May 1853	James	----, Helen	E	86
Handrigan, James	2, Aug. 1854	John	----, Ann	E	213
Handrigan, Richard	14, July 1852	Cornelius	----, Catherine	E	427
Handschmidt, Maria Elisabeth Margaret	31, July 1859	Arnold	Pruss, Maria Elisabeth	A	
Handwerk, Gregor	3, Oct. 1852	J. Adam	Decker, Elisabeth	D	351
Handwett, Maria Elisabeth	2, Feb. 1851	William	Schröder, Margaretha	D	251
Haney, Catharine	2, Jan. 1853	Michael	Newman, Ann	B	280
Haney, Catherine	26, Jan. 1854	Bernard	Brady, Catherine	P	66
Haney, Daniel	16, Aug. 1853	James	----, Bridget	E	119
Haney, Elizabeth	21, Nov. 1858	Martin	Gilroy, Bridget	P	267
Haney, James	21, May 1850	John	Conlan, Elizabeth	B	203
Haney, John	21, Dec. 1856	George	Moran, Mary	B	38

Name of Child	Date of Baptism	Father	Mother	Church	Page
Haney, Martin	8, Sept 1851	Martin	----, Ellenore	E	341
Haney, Mary	25, Aug. 1850	John	Maken, Bridget	M	
Haney, Mary Margaret	29, July 1855	Dennis	Heagheny, Mary	P	143
Haney?, Mary Ann	22, Mar. 1857	Mark	Kilroe, Bridget	P	208
Hanfbauer, Anna Maria	27, June 1858	Conrad	Heimkreuter, Anna Maria	D	114
Hanfeld, Christopher Henry	11, Oct. 1857	William	Schröder, Margaret	U	
Hanfeld, Margaretha Maria	27, Jan. 1859	Wilhelm	Schroeder, Maria	U	
Hanhauser, Ann	1, Feb. 1852	Bernard	Martin, Mary	E	379
Hanhauser, Edward Joseph	25, Oct. 1857	Bernard	Martin, Mary	E	487
Hanhauser, Joseph Edward	20, Aug. 1854	Bernard	Martin, Ann Mary	E	218
Hanhauser, Mary Margaret	25, Sept 1859	Bernard	----, ----	E	657
Hanhauser, Michael Jacob	5, Oct. 1851	Jacob	Mueller, Francisca	L	
Hanhauser, Rosa Johanna	24, Jan. 1858	----	Jaeger, Magdalena	L	
Hanigbauer, Magdalena	5, Mar. 1854	Conrad	Heimkreider, Maria Anna	D	5
Hank, Heinrich	5, Apr. 1857	Lawrence	Burkhard, Rufina	F	
Hankel, Johan Jacob	17, June 1855	Valentin	Breitigam, Rosina	K	
Hankenbauer, Johan Adam	29, Oct. 1854	Johan	Kemper, Anna Maria	A	
Hankong, Wilhelm Anton	9, Aug. 1851	Anton	Clausen, Elisabeth	C	
Hanks, August Ludiwg	25, Dec. 1853	Joseph	Enderle, Catharina	D	422
Hanks, William Francis	11, Sept 1853	Felden	----, Martha	E	127
Hanlan, David	12, June 1859	Michael	Butler, Mary	E	632
Hanlen, Margaret Mary	30, Mar. 1857	John	Gorman, Susan	U	
Hanley, Ann	30, Jan. 1853	Patrick	Lynch, Ann	P	34
Hanley, Bridget	14, Dec. 1851	Dennis	Madden, Mary	P	14
Hanley, Charles Joseph John	10, Sept 1857	Joseph	----, Theresa	E	480
Hanley, Edward William	23, Sept 1856	Thomas	----, Mary	E	400
Hanley, John	23, Oct. 1851	Michael	Ryan, Ann	P	13a
Hanley, Mary	9, May 1851	Timothy	----, Margaret	B	231
Hanley, Mary	13, Aug. 1850		Hanley, Bridget	E	239
Hanley, Mary Josephine	6, Apr. 1851	Joseph C.	----, Theresa	E	297
Hanley, Theresa	28, Mar. 1853	Joseph	----, Theresa	E	78
Hanlin, Helen	5, Sept 1857	Thomas	Norris, Joanne	U	
Hanlin, Mary Ann	8, Dec. 1850	Timothy	English, Margaret	E	265
Hanlin, Thomas	20, Mar. 1859	Thomas	Handlan, Joanne	U	
Hanlon, Ann Margaret	9, Oct. 1854	Cornelius	----, Mary	E	230
Hanlon, Ellenore	7, Aug. 1853	Timothy	----, Margaret	E	115
Hanlon, Hanna Mary	23, Aug. 1852	James	----, Hanna	E	9
Hanlon, Margaret	4, Apr. 1859	Timothy	----, Margaret	E	616
Hanlon, Mary Cora	1, June 1857	Aaron	Serron?, Louise	B	45
Hanlon, Maurice	7, Jan. 1858	Michael	Butler, Mary	E	507
Hanlon, Michael Edward	16, May 1855	John	----, Susan	H	
Hanlon, Richard	25, June 1854	Thomas	----, Joanne	U	
Hanlon, Susan	20, Mar. 1856	Timothy	English, Margaret	V	30
Hanly, Charles	20, Oct. 1859	Joseph C.	Lanigan, Theresa	E	664
Hanly, Edward Francis	25, July 1858	Patrick	Lynch, Ann	P	255
Hanly, Elizabeth	30, Sept 1852	Peter	Gill, Catherine	B	271
Hanly, James	9, Oct. 1852	Bartholomew	Tugy, Honora	E	25
Hanly, James	28, Sept 1856	Patrick	Lynch, Ann	P	193
Hanly, John	1, Mar. 1857	Michael	Davis, Joanne	B	41
Hanly, Joseph Charles	9, Apr. 1856	Joseph C.	Lanigan, Theresa	P	175
Hanly, Julia	6, Nov. 1854	Peter	Gill, Catherine	B	7
Hanly, Mary	20, May 1855	Patrick	Lynch, Ann	P	133
Hanly, Michael	22, Oct. 1854	Thomas	Cary, Mary	E	234
Hanly, Nicolaus	21, Aug. 1853	Michael	Ryan, Honora	P	49
Hanly, Peter	4, Apr. 1851	Peter	Gill, Catherine	B	228
Hanly, Robert Francis	11, Oct. 1857	Thomas	Cary, Mary	E	485
Hanly, Thomas	1, Jan. 1854	Patrick	Lynch, Ann	P	64
Hanly, William	7, Jan. 1857	Robert	O'Neil, Bridget	E	425
Hanna, John	14, Oct. 1859	John P.	Egan, Bridget	B	82

Name of Child	Date of Baptism	Father	Mother	Church	Page
Hannagan, Nicolaus	7, May 1854	Patrick	Sweeney, Elizabeth	B	314
Hannagan, Patrick	10, Nov. 1850	Patrick	Fahey, Catherine	B	218
Hannaher, Patrick	25, Mar. 1853	August	Moran, Honora	P	37
Hannan, Abigail	18, July 1856	Dennis	Murphy, Dora	P	185
Hannan, Daniel	16, Apr. 1854	Dennis	Murphy, Dora	P	79
Hannan, John	19, June 1859	Dennis	McCarn, Ann	U	
Hannan, John	25, Mar. 1854	James	----, Helen	P	75
Hannan, John	24, Apr. 1853	Patrick	Hannan, Catherine	B	290
Hannan, Luke	28, Jan. 1855	Bartholomew	Meagher, Margaret	P	118
Hannan, Mary	6, Nov. 1853	James	----, Ellen	E	141
Hannan, Mary Isabel	13, Apr. 1855	John	adult - 32 years old	E	279
Hannan, Mary Jane	11, May 1856	Edward	Henrigan, Mary	E	366
Hannan, Thomas	6, Jan. 1850	Bartholomew	Dial, Ann	E	190
Hannan, Thomas	25, Dec. 1854	Michael	Denedy, Jane	B	9
Hannan, Thomas	12, Nov. 1854	Patrick	Hannan, Catherine	P	103
Hannan, Thomas Stephen	27, July 1851	Thomas	----, Elizabeth Ann	E	328
Hannan, William	30, Aug. 1851	Patrick	Jackson, Margaret	E	337
Hannegan, Bridget	7, Feb. 1855	Patrick	----, Mary	E	263
Hannegan, Mary	3, July 1859	Thomas	----, Frances	M	
Hannen, Bridget	17, Aug. 1851	Bartholomew	Maher, Margaret	B	239
Hannen, Michael	17, July 1850	James	Coleman, Helen	B	207
Hanney, Daniel	20, Feb. 1853	Patrick	Egan, Bridget	B	284
Hanney, Mary	8, Mar. 1857	Patrick	Egan, Bridget	B	41
Hanney, Mary Alice	11, May 1851	Martin	----, Margaret	B	231
Hannigan, Henriette	23, Jan. 1858	John	----, Catherine	E	511
Hannigan, Richard	20, Jan. 1856	Patrick	Sweeney, Elizabeth	B	24
Hannigan, Thomas	19, May 1850	Edmund	Tobin, Helen	B	202
Hanninger, Johan Georg	9, Apr. 1855	Joseph	Kraft, Louisa	K	
Hannon, Ann	5, Dec. 1858	Michael	Denedy, Jane	B	68
Hannon, Ann	8, Aug. 1853	Patrick	----, Margaret	E	116
Hannon, Bridget	30, Nov. 1856	Michael	Denedy, Jane	B	37
Hannon, Charles	1, Jan. 1858	Edward	Henrigan, Mary	E	505
Hannon, Edward	9, May 1852	Dominick	----, Honora	M	
Hannon, Francis	18, May 1851	Patrick	Bartly, Catherine	P	8
Hannon, Joanne	17, July 1854	Edward	----, Mary	E	207
Hannon, Johanna	9, May 1857	----	----, ----	G	
Hannon, Maria Anna	21, July 1859	Michael	Kelly, Catharine	G	
Hannon, Mary Elizabeth	8, Oct. 1857	John F.	Bell, Sarah	B	50
Hannon, Thomas	23, Jan. 1859	John	Bell, Sarah	P	273
Hanny, Joseph	13, May 1855	Edward	Bacon, Rose Ann	R	
Hanny, Michael	17, Dec. 1854	Patrick	Egan, Bridget	B	8
Hanofbauer, Elisabeth	2, Mar. 1856	Conrad	Heimkrauter, Anna M.	C	
Hanraham, Maria Anna	26, Aug. 1854	Jacob	Donovan, Catharine	C	
Hanrahan, Catherine	24, Sept 1854	James	Dooly, Catherine	E	225
Hanrahan, Catherine	22, Aug. 1852	Michael	----, Bridget	B	268
Hanrehan, Johan Carl	18, June 1857	Jacob	Donovan, Catharine	C	
Hans, Francis	16, July 1854	Januarius	Michel, Catharina	D	14
Hans, Heinrich	6, Oct. 1857	Georg	Braun, Juliana	K	
Hansman, Ferdinand	14, Jan. 1855	Aloysius	Hoffman, Ursula	W	7
Hansman, Jacob	27, Jan. 1850	Aloysius	Hofman, Ursula	D	201
Hansman, Margaretha	1, Nov. 1851	Aloysius	Hoffman, Theresa	D	290
Hanson, Delia Mary Elizabeth	28, Mar. 1859	Robert A.	----, Eliza	E	614
Hantle, James	28, Aug. 1858	James	Malone, Bridget	K	
Hany, Catherine	31, July 1859	Daniel	Dunn, Mary	P	290
Happman, Johan Peter	17, Nov. 1858	Francis	Gruen, Elisabeth	D	124
Haran, Virginia	10, Sept 1854	John	McCauley, Mary Jane	B	5
Harbaugh, Mary Ann	5, Apr. 1859	Christian	adult - 51 years old	E	616
Harcey, Johan Joseph	20, May 1853	Hugh	12 years old	K	
Hard, Mary	4, Dec. 1853	James	Rint, Mary	Q	4

Name of Child	Date of Baptism	Father	Mother	Church	Page
Harden, John	4, Mar. 1855	John	Finneran, Mary	P	123
Harden, Mary	9, Aug. 1854	Edward	Murty, Ann	B	3
Harding, Helen	15, June 1856	John	Feneran, Mary	T	
Harding, John Thomas	6, Dec. 1857	Edward	Murray, Ann	P	232
Harding, Lucinda	16, May 1858	William	Chamberlain, Margaret	B	59
Harding, Martha Jane	15, July 1855	William	Chambers, Margaret J.	B	16
Harding, Mary Eldora	5, Feb. 1854	William	Chambers, Margaret	B	309
Harding, Richard	21, Dec. 1851	John	Finnern, Mary	B	248
Harding, Thomas	1, Aug. 1858	John	Fennellon, Mary	B	62
Hardinger, Maria	28, May 1858	Michael	Spieckenleiter, Margaretha	H	
Hardinghaus, Heinrich Edward	21, Jan. 1855	Heinrich	Messmann, Elisabeth	C	
Hardinghaus, Johan Clemens	31, July 1852	Heinrich	Messmann, M. Elisabeth	C	
Hardinghaus, Joseph August	4, Aug. 1850	Heinrich	Mesmer, Elisabeth	C	
Hardinghaus, M. Elisabeth Rosa	14, Jan. 1857	Heinrich	Messmann, Elisabeth	C	
Hardy, Ann	26, July 1855	Robin	----, Liddy	E	303
Hardy, William	2, Jan. 1850	Patrick	Dams, Ann	E	189
Hare, Andreas Georg	17, Sept 1854	Anton	Oculi, Catharina	L	
Hare, Carl Johan	24, Jan. 1850	Anton	O'Kuli, Catharine	L	
Hare, Catharina Carolina	6, May 1852	Anton	Oculi, Catharina	L	
Hare, Franz Georg	3, Dec. 1855	Anton	Oculi, Catharina	L	
Hare, Helen	24, Nov. 1854	Michael	Conroy, Mary Ann	P	105
Hare, James	5, Aug. 1850	James	----, Catherine	E	237
Hare, Johan Anton	12, Oct. 1851	Conrad	Bachmann, Elisabeth	L	
Hare, Johan Bernard	19, Aug. 1853	Anton	Oculi, Catharina	L	
Hare, Joseph	7, Feb. 1851	Anthony	O'Kuli, Catharine	L	
Hare, Josephina	4, Apr. 1857	Anton	Oculi, Catharina	L	
Hare, Marianne	4, Jan. 1852	Edward	Marony, Ellen	P	15
Hare, Mary	6, Apr. 1852	Michael	Haely, Mary Ann	E	399
Hare, Matthew	11, May 1850	Edward	Malone, Ellen	E	212
Hare?, Joseph	24, Nov. 1853	Absolom	Dwyer, Ann	B	303
Harenberg, Conrad Wilhelm	14, Apr. 1850	Conrad H.	Kaufmann, Dorothea	F	
Harens, Daniel	18, June 1854	Michael	McGuire, Eliza	E	199
Harens, James	12, Sept 1859	John	Feghery, Catherine	E	653
Harens, Mary Ellen	25, Apr. 1855	Patrick	----, Mary	E	282
Harford, Ann	7, Aug. 1859	Christopher	----, Margaret	E	645
Harford, Michael	2, Oct. 1853	Christopher	Tully, Margaret	B	300
Hargen, David	25, July 1858	Daniel	Binicer, Anna	N	
Harig, Anna Maria	7, Apr. 1859	Johan	Weber, Elisabeth	F	
Harig, Heinrich	7, June 1857	Johan	Weber, Elisabeth	F	
Harig, Philipp	15, Apr. 1855	Johan	Weber, Elisabeth	A	
Härigfeld, Benedict Heinrich	23, Feb. 1852	Francis	Hesterman, Maria	D	308
Harken, Martin	9, Mar. 1856	John	Gallagher, Sarah	P	172
Harken, Patrick	19, Mar. 1854	John	Gallagher, Sarah	P	74
Harkens, John	8, Aug. 1858	John	Gallagher, Sarah	P	256
Harkin, Bridget	24, May 1857	Peter	Reilly, Bridget	P	213
Harkin, Rosanne	23, May 1852	John	Galagher, Sarah	P	22
Harkin, Thomas	20, Apr. 1851	John	Gilligan, Catherine	B	230
Harknett, Mary	22, Apr. 1852		Harknett, Mary	B	257
Harl, George	8, Feb. 1857	Joseph	----, Crescentia	R	
Harlacher, Carolina	27, July 1856	Jacob	Jasser, Veronica	C	
Harlon, Thomas	9, Sept 1855	Michael	----, Mary	M	
Harlow, Bridget	3, Oct. 1852	John	----, Mary	M	
Harly, Daniel	20, July 1854	Daniel	Leonard, Catherine	E	208
Harly, Ellen	7, Oct. 1855	Daniel	Leonard, Catherine	E	319
Harly, Julia	6, June 1852	Daniel	Leonard, Catherine	E	422
Harman, Ann Elizabeth	17, Feb. 1850	John H.	Toby, Catherine	B	196
Harman, Edward	22, Apr. 1850	Patrick	Jackson, Mary	B	201
Ha--rman, Francisca	7, Jan. 1858	Mathias	Ziegler, Francisca	D	102
Harman, J. Heinrich	10, Sept 1851	J. Anton	Back, Maria Elisabeth	K	

Name of Child	Date of Baptism	Father	Mother	Church	Page
Harman, Johan Herman Ferdinand	4, July 1858	Stephan	Meigler, Theresa	N	
Harman, Johanna Catharina	14, Oct. 1854	Joseph	Woiring, Antonia	D	19
Harman, Sarah Ann	24, May 1857		adult	B	44
Harman, Thomas	18, Aug. 1850	Patrick	Harman, Sarah	E	240
Harmann, Herman Joseph	15, Mar. 1857	Joseph	Weihring, Philomena	F	
Harmann, Joseph Heinrich	23, Dec. 1858	Joseph	----, ----	T	
Harmann, Maria Elisabeth	9, Feb. 1853	Heinrich	Westerhaus, Catharina	L	
Harmeier, Bernard Felix	4, Mar. 1855	Bernard F.	Niemers, Catharina	D	30
Harmeier, Catharina Elisabeth	25, Dec. 1850	Herman	Dollen, Elisabeth	K	
Harmeier, Johan Joseph	14, Apr. 1853	J. Joseph	Spiekers, Helena Maria	K	
Harmeier, Maria Agnes	3, Oct. 1854	Joseph	Spieker, Maria Helena	K	
Harmeier, Vanna Maria	11, Feb. 1851	Joseph	Spicker, Maria Helena	A	
Harmeyer, Anna Maria Elisabeth	3, Feb. 1857	G. Heinrich	Kemper, Anna Maria	K	
Harmeyer, Anna Maria Louisa	29, July 1852	H. Heinrich	Döllman, Maria Elisabeth	K	
Harmeyer, Johan Heinrich	21, July 1858	H. Heinrich	Döllman, Maria Elisabeth	K	
Harmeyer, Johanna Francisca	29, Dec. 1856	Francis	Vrocklage, Gertrud	C	
Harmeyer, Louisa Christina Josephina	12, Apr. 1858	Georg H.	Kemper, Anna Maria	K	
Harn?, Thomas	29, Dec. 1850	Michael	Kinney, Bridget	B	221
Harnett, James	21, Mar. 1858	Daniel	Herd, Bridget	B	57
Harnett, Theresa	25, May 1856	Daniel	Heard, Bridget	B	29
Harney, Ann Mary	6, Dec. 1857	James	Grubbs, Joanne	B	52
Harney, Henry	5, Feb. 1856	William	----, Olive	E	342
Harney, Joanne	6, Dec. 1857		adult - nee Grubbs	B	52
Harney, Robert	7, Jan. 1850	John	Donohue, Jane	E	190
Harney, Robert	8, Dec. 1857	Robert	----, Margaret	E	498
Harney, Thomas	25, Mar. 1851	James	Bliss, Ann	E	295
Harnold, Georg Michael	1, Sept 1850	Jacob	Groh, Barbara	D	231
Harnrigan, Edward	5, May 1858	Edward	----, Ellen	E	534
Harpenau, Maria Elisabeth	28, Dec. 1859	Conrad	Coors, Catharina	F	
Harrety, Winnifred	6, Feb. 1852	John	Foy, Winnifred	P	17
Harrig, Maria Paulina	3, July 1853	Johan	Weber, Elisabeth	J	22
Harrigan, Cecilia	11, Nov. 1854	Michael	----, Bridget	M	
Harrigan, Charles	10, Sept 1859	Patrick	----, Catherine	E	652
Harrigan, Dennis	29, Apr. 1855	John	Hartigan, Honora	E	282
Harrigan, Edward	11, Nov. 1855	William	Aldrich, Mary	B	21
Harrigan, Honora	26, July 1850	John	Hartigan, Honora	E	234
Harrigan, James	20, Feb. 1851	D.	Cameron, Isabel	B	225
Harrigan, Jeremiah	19, July 1851	John	----, Honora	E	325
Harrigan, Joanne	17, Nov. 1853	Peter	----, Isabel	M	
Harrigan, Margaret	5, Jan. 1858	John	Hartigan, Mary	E	506
Harrigan, Margaret Ann	5, Feb. 1854	William	Aldridge, Mary	B	308
Harrigan, Mary	3, Aug. 1856	Peter	----, Isabel	M	
Harrigan, Mary	14, May 1853	Thomas	McLaughlin, Rose	E	89
Harrigan, Patrick	17, Mar. 1857	Michael	Fitzgerald, Mary	E	441
Harrigan, Peter	11, Aug. 1850	Patrick	Brophy, Catherine	B	209
Harrigan, Peter	30, Jan. 1859	Peter A.	----, Isabel	M	
Harrigan, Peter Alexander	30, Jan. 1859	Roderick	----, Bridget	M	
Harrigan, Rosanne	11, Nov. 1854	Michael	----, Bridget	M	
Harrigan, Rose	27, Apr. 1856	James	Laverty, Ellen	U	
Harrigan, Thomas	24, Nov. 1851	Bernard	Brennan, Mary	P	13c
Harrigan, William	26, July 1857	William	Aldrige, Mary	B	47
Harringson, Patrick	20, Feb. 1853	Patrick	----, Bridget	M	
Harrington, Ann	8, Mar. 1857	Roderick	----, Bridget	M	
Harrington, Catherine	30, June 1850	Daniel	----, Mary	E	227
Harrington, Catherine	15, Jan. 1856	Jeremiah	Murphy, Ann	V	29
Harrington, Charles August	26, Oct. 1851	James	Spalding, Caroline Cecilia	B	244
Harrington, Christopher	9, Oct. 1852	John	Carty, Bridget	B	271
Harrington, Clara Isabel	26, Sept 1858	James S.	Spalding, Caroline	B	64
Harrington, Elizabeth	14, Mar. 1853		adult	E	73

Name of Child	Date of Baptism	Father	Mother	Church	Page
Harrington, Helen Honora	7, Oct. 1854	James	Conklin, Julia	P	98
Harrington, James	17, Jan. 1858	James	Turner, Bridget	B	54
Harrington, James Dennis	13, Sept 1857	Dennis	Hassett, Helen	P	223
Harrington, James Edward	21, Aug. 1853	James T.	Spalding, Caroline	B	297
Harrington, Joanne	29, Nov. 1857	Daniel	Hagerty, Catherine	E	496
Harrington, John	13, July 1855	Daniel	Hagarty, Catherine	P	140
Harrington, John	18, Sept 1857	Daniel	O'Connor, Mary	E	481
Harrington, John	9, Oct. 1859	Dennis	Hasset, Ellen	P	299
Harrington, John	10, May 1857	James	Conchlin, Julia	E	452
Harrington, John	12, Apr. 1858	Jeremiah	----, Ann	E	528
Harrington, Lawrence	4, Feb. 1854	Matthew	Harrington, Mary	B	308
Harrington, Lelia Ann	Aug. 1850	James S.	Spalding, Virginia	B	212
Harrington, Margaret	19, Sept 1858	Michael	----, Bridget	M	
Harrington, Mark	15, June 1856	Mark	Harrington, Mary	B	30
Harrington, Mary Ida	4, Mar. 1855	James	Spalding, Caroline	B	12
Harrington, Minnie Edith	25, Apr. 1857	James	Spalding, Caroline	B	43
Harrington, Thomas	30, Sept 1855	Daniel	O'Connor, Mary	E	317
Harrinson, John Joseph	14, Apr. 1857	John	Heffernan, Anastasia	P	210
Harrinson, Joseph	28, Aug. 1853	John	Heffernan, Anastasia	P	50
Harrinson, Lawrence	22, Apr. 1855	John	Heffernan, Anastasia	P	129
Harrinson, Louis Thomas	4, Dec. 1859	John	Heffernan, Anastasia	B	84
Harrinson, Margaret	1, Nov. 1851	John	Heffernan, Anastasia	B	244
Harris, Charles	22, Jan. 1850	John D.	Crone, Mary W.	E	194
Harris, Elisabeth	25, Mar. 1855	Michael	----, Mary	U	
Harrison, Ann	1, Sept 1851	Robert	Bons, Elisabeth	D	280
Harrison, Caroline	8, June 1851	Charles	Cranston, Mary Ann	E	314
Harrison, Catherine	1, Sept 1851	Robert	Bons, Elisabeth	D	280
Harrison, Daniel	11, July 1850	Daniel	Dunleavy, Hannah	B	207
Harrison, Joanne	12, May 1854	Walter	Hanlan, Ellen	E	189
Harrison, John	30, Oct. 1859		adult	B	83
Harrison, Robert	27, Jan. 1853	Robert	Bons, Louisa	D	367
Harrold, Alice	7, July 1858	John	Dunn, Joanne	E	546
Harser, Joseph	27, Mar. 1859	Stephan	Weis, Sabina	D	134
Harson, James	11, Apr. 1852	Bernard	Whitney, Bridget	B	256
Härstke, Anna Maria Adelheid	1, May 1856	J. Heinrich	Schulte, Mina	D	57
Hart, Ann	13, Apr. 1854	Patrick	Barron, Bridget	B	313
Hart, Ann	22, Feb. 1857	Patrick	Farrell, Eliza	P	207
Hart, Ann	11, Jan. 1857	Thomas	Bragheny, Mary	B	39
Hart, Ann	26, July 1852	Thomas	Kitchen, Rebecca	E	433
Hart, Augustine	4, Dec. 1853	Matthew	Moreland, Mary Ann	E	149
Hart, Bernard Heinrich	14, Dec. 1856	Carl J.	Kurz, Margaretha	D	74
Hart, Caroline	25, Feb. 1855	Thomas	Shafer, Emily Jane	P	121
Hart, Catharine	31, Apr. 1854	John	Toy, Mary	Q	4
Hart, Catherine	20, Nov. 1853	Anthony	Madden, Margaret	E	145
Hart, Catherine	14, Sept 1856	Henry	----, Mary	E	398
Hart, Catherine Ann	5, Feb. 1854	Thomas	Dunn, Olivia	B	308
Hart, Clara Ellen	22, Aug. 1852	Thomas	Schaefer, Emily J.	P	26
Hart, Cordelia	20, June 1858	Thomas	Dunn, Olivia	B	60
Hart, Edward	1, Nov. 1858	Matthew	Monlord, Ann	E	574
Hart, Eliza	6, Feb. 1853	Patrick	----, Mary	E	61
Hart, Eliza Monica	30, May 1852	Thomas	Dunn, Olivia	B	264
Hart, Ellen Louise	21, June 1852	Patrick	----, Ellen	E	426
Hart, Emma	28, May 1851	Matthew	Morland, Mary Ann	E	311
Hart, Francis	25, Sept 1859	Anthony	Madden, Margaret	V	59
Hart, Helen Mary	29, June 1856	Thomas	Dunn, Olivia	B	30
Hart, Honora	29, Oct. 1856	Thomas	Craven, Bridget	V	34
Hart, James	3, June 1852	Neil	Wood, Joanne	B	264
Hart, John	15, May 1855	Thomas	Craven, Bridget	V	25
Hart, John	12, Apr. 1851	Thomas	Hart, Elizabeth	B	230

Name of Child	Date of Baptism	Father	Mother	Church	Page
Hart, John	18, Sept 1858	Thomas	Tool, Margaret	U	
Hart, John Patrick	31, Oct. 1858	Henry	O'Brien, Mary	B	66
Hart, Margaret	13, Feb. 1859	Thomas	Craven, Bridget	E	603
Hart, Mary	12, Sept 1857	Anthony	Madden, Margaret	E	480
Hart, Mary	17, Sept 1854	Thomas	Judge, Mary	B	5
Hart, Mary Ann	2, Aug. 1858	John	McGinnes, Mary	U	
Hart, Mary Elizabeth	22, Mar. 1857	Thomas	----, Margaret	U	
Hart, Michael	2, May 1852	Anthony	----, Margaret	E	408
Hart, Michael	23, May 1852	James	Torte, Mary	B	264
Hart, Olivia Jane	20, Oct. 1850	Thomas	Dunn, Olivia	B	217
Hart, Thomas	21, Aug. 1855	Anthony	Madden, Margaret	E	309
Hart, William	19, Oct. 1851	James	Byrne, Mary Ann	E	351
Hart, William	18, Aug. 1855	Patrick	----, Bridget	E	308
Hartens, Margaretha Elisabeth	1, May 1858	G.H.	Holthaus, Maria Elisabeth	A	
Harter, Anna Maria	9, Mar. 1857	Joseph	Weigen, Agnes	D	80
Harter, Anna Maria	6, Jan. 1856	Joseph	Weiger, Agnes	D	50
Harter, Benedict	5, Sept 1852	Benedict	----, Victoria	H	
Harter, Benedict	25, May 1854	Benedict	----, Victoria	H	
Harter, Bertha	30, Sept 1855	Mathias	Merk, Rosina	D	43
Harter, Caroline	30, Dec. 1855	Benedict	----, Victoria	H	
Harter, Johan	27, May 1852	Heinrich	Mertz, Eleanora	L	
Harter, Josephina	21, Aug. 1859	Joseph	Weicher, Agnes	T	
Harter, Maria Anna Veronica	9, Feb. 1851	Benedict	Müller, Victoria	H	
Harter, Maria Barbara	2, Feb. 1854	Joseph	Weiger, Agnes	D	3
Harter, William	13, Dec. 1857	Benedict	Müller, Victoria	H	
Harterrauf, Sebastian	1, Jan. 1857	Leonard	Weiskopf, Margaretha	A	
Hartford, Bridget	24, Mar. 1858	Christopher	Cummelton, Margaret	E	524
Hartford, Mary	11, Nov. 1855	Christopher	Tomelty, Margaret	E	326
Hartgerken, Johan Bernard	23, Sept 1859	Johan G.	Klenke, M. Elisabeth	C	
Hartgerken, Maria Elisabeth	5, May 1858	J. Gerhard	Klenke, M. Elisabeth	C	
Hartig, Barbara Genofeva	17, Jan. 1854	Adam	Aulbach, Elisabeth	C	
Hartig, Georg	29, June 1856	Adam	Albach, Elisabeth	C	
Hartig, Johan	30, Apr. 1851	Peter	Bachman, Eva	D	263
Hartigan, Mary	24, Aug. 1856	Michael	Doyle, Mary	P	188
Hartigan, Mary	6, Mar. 1858	Michael	Doyle, Mary	P	241
Hartigan, Michael	22, July 1854	John	Ryan, Joanne	E	209
Harting, Frederick William	4, Mar. 1857		adult	B	41
Harting, Gerhard Heinrich	29, Nov. 1857	Wilhelm	Schomakers, M. Elisabeth	L	
Hartke, Georg Bernard	10, Feb. 1858	J. Heinrich	Henneker, Maria Anna	L	
Hartke, Johan Theodor	4, Mar. 1858	J. Gerhard	Winkeljohan, Anna Maria	D	106
Hartke, Maria Catharina Elisabeth	28, Apr. 1859	Joseph	Staudtberg, M. Catharina	L	
Hartley, Mary	27, Nov. 1853		15 year old	P	60
Hartling, Catharina Margaretha	18, July 1858	Francis	----, Catharina	F	
Hartling, Francis Michael	21, Sept 1851	Michael	Halbich, Eva	D	283
Hartling, Franz	23, July 1854	Francis	Hartling, Catharina	F	
Hartling, Georg	26, Sept 1858	Michael	Halbrey, Eva	T	
Hartling, Johan Michael	14, Sept 1856	Johan	Eckstein, Louisa	F	
Hartling, Michael	27, May 1855	Johan	Eckstein, Louisa	D	35
Hartling, Michael	16, Oct. 1853	Michael	Halwig, Eva	L	
Hartlop, Mary Ann	10, Feb. 1858	Patrick	McLaughlin, Ann	E	516
Hartman, Adam	18, July 1854	Anton	Holzmeister, Margaretha	D	14
Hartman, Adam	24, Aug. 1858	Anton	Holzmeister, Margaretha	D	118
Hartman, Alexander	28, Aug. 1859	Johan	Hümmelmeyer, Anna Maria	K	
Hartman, Anna Maria	24, Mar. 1850	Leopold	Eyring, Anna Maria	D	206
Hartman, Barbara Dorothea	7, Feb. 1856	Anton	Holzmeister, Margaretha	D	51
Hartman, Benjamin	23, Feb. 1855	Francis	----, Elizabeth	M	
Hartman, Bernard	26, July 1853	J. Heinrich	Hömmelmeier, Catharina	K	
Hartman, Catharina	3, Aug. 1856	Valentin	Kiel---, Margaretha	D	64
Hartman, Catharina Elisabeth	6, May 1858	Peter	Krein, Catharina	D	110

Name of Child	Date of Baptism	Father	Mother	Church	Page
Hartman, Emil	23, Jan. 1859	Michael	Strets, Margaretha	D	129
Hartman, Francis Friedrich	1, Aug. 1851	Peter	Grün, Catharina	D	275
Hartman, Francis Wilhelm	31, July 1856	Francis	Gretner, Elisabeth	D	63
Hartman, Francis Xavier	20, Feb. 1859	Valentin	----, Margaretha	D	132
Hartman, Johan Francis	18, Feb. 1855	Johan	Hummelmeier, Caharina	K	
Hartman, Johan Friedrich	14, Feb. 1857	Johan	Hummelmeier, Maria Elis.	K	
Hartman, Johan Jacob	20, Dec. 1857	Valentin	Rül----, Margaretha	D	101
Hartman, Joseph	10, Sept 1857	Francis	Greiter, Elisabeth	D	94
Hartman, Louisa	9, Feb. 1858	Conrad	Wimm---, Helena	D	105
Hartman, Maria	15, Dec. 1850	J. Peter	Scherer, Magdalena	J	8
Hartman, Maria Margaretha	25, Sept 1853	Anton	Holzmeister, Margaretha	D	407
Hartman, Matilda	26, Apr. 1855	Peter	----, Catherine	M	
Hartman, Michael	8, June 1856	Michael	Stretz, Margaretha	D	60
Hartman, Peter William	19, June 1853	Peter	Krön, Catharina	D	390
Hartman, Philipp	4, May 1856	Anton	Amrain, Anna Maria	D	57
Hartman, Rosa	24, Mar. 1850	Peter	Grün, Catharina	D	206
Hartman, Susanna Magdalena	21, Sept 1851	Michael	Ziegler, Barbara	D	283
Hartman, Theresa	15, Dec. 1850	J. Peter	Scherer, Magdalena	J	8
Hartmann, Herman Heinrich	2, Nov. 1851	Heinrich	Niemers, Maria Anna	L	
Hartmann, Johan E.	29, Sept 1850	J. Georg	Gabelgel, Magdalena	C	
Hartmann, Johan Ferdinand	25, June 1851	Johan	Haemelmeyer, Catharina	C	
Hartmann, Joseph Felcian	9, June 1859	Carl	Hansratjens, Johanna	L	
Hartmann, Marianna Elisabeth	4, July 1853	Johan H.	Niemer, Marianna	F	
Hartnagel, Carl	3, July 1855	Joseph	Butz, Juliana	C	
Hartnagel, Carl Friedrich Joseph	26, Oct. 1851	Joseph	----, Juliana	C	
Hartnagel, Carolina	5, Oct. 1856	Joseph	Putz, Juliana	C	
Hartnell, Ellen	20, Mar. 1859	Jeremiah	Kelly, Ellen	B	72
Hartnet, Agnes	1, July 1855	Daniel	Herd, Bridget	B	16
Hartnett, Elizabeth	27, Dec. 1859	Daniel	Herd, Bridget	B	86
Harton, Elizabeth Ann	4, May 1856	James	McDowall, Ann	V	31
Harton, John	29, Nov. 1857	James	McDowall, Ann	V	42
Harton, Mary	13, Feb. 1859	James	McDonoue, Ann	V	52
Hartschneider, Johan August	24, Sept 1858	Theodor	Schupohl, Maria	F	
Hartung, Anna Maria	11, Oct. 1857	Fr.	O'Brien, Nancy	K	
Hartwich, Anton	23, Sept 1855	J. Baptist	Pecht, Martha	D	43
Hartwich, Barbara	7, Sept 1856	J. Baptist	Pecht, Martha	D	66
Hartwich, Johan Baptist	1, Nov. 1858	J. Baptist	Beckt, Martha	D	123
Harty, Daniel	31, Dec. 1854	Daniel	Carty, Mary	E	251
Harty, Ellen	23, May 1856	Daniel	Carthy, Mary	E	368
Harty, Georg Anton	5, Feb. 1854	Anton	Henneching, M. Anna	C	
Harty, Michael	14, Apr. 1858	Daniel	----, Mary	M	
Harty, Thomas	11, Dec. 1853	John	Flagerty, Ann	E	152
Harvey, Catherine	11, Nov. 1855	Francis	McLaughlin, Susan	E	326
Harvey, Edward	25, Mar. 1857	Edward	McBrian, Catherine	P	208
Harvey, Elizabeth	11, Aug. 1856	William	Richards, Susan	V	32
Harvey, Margaret	19, Sept 1852	Robert	----, Margaret	M	
Harvey, Mary	30, Oct. 1859	Robert	Burthor, Margaret	E	666
Harz, Friedrich Joseph	17, June 1857	August	Fromoore, Elisabeth	J	42
Hascker, Johan Heinrich	21, Nov. 1857	G. Heinrich	Thole, Anna Maria	D	99
Hascon, Thomas	1, Oct. 1854	Thomas	Hickey, Mary	E	228
Hasebacher, Catharina Elisabeth	4, Jan. 1859	Joseph	Höck, Christina	D	128
Haselacher, Francis Carl	14, Apr. 1856	Joseph	H--k, Christina	D	56
Haselmann, Johan Joseph	23, July 1851	Theodor	Beimer, Catharine	C	
Haselton, Bernard	19, Nov. 1853		adult - 50 years old	E	145
Hasenard, Michael	16, June 1850	Johan	----, Anna Maria	F	
Hasenau, Johan Adam	5, Dec. 1852	Johan	Wenzel, Anna Maria	F	
Hasenstab, Cunigunda	25, June 1854	Johan	Edelman, Anna Maria	D	13
Hasenstab, Johan	17, Mar. 1853	Johan	Edelman, Anna Maria	D	375
Hasenstab, Johan Georg	20, Mar. 1859	Johan	Edelman, Anna Maria	D	134

Name of Child	Date of Baptism	Father	Mother	Church	Page
Hasenstab, Maria	28, Sept 1856	Johan	Edelman, Anna Maria	D	68
Haslam, James Christopher	10, Feb. 1858	James W.	McCarthy, Catherine	E	516
Haslan, John	14, June 1852	James	Gallagher, Ann	E	425
Haslan, Mary Alice	9, Apr. 1854	James	Gallagher, Ann	E	181
Haslon, Mary Ellen	7, Aug. 1859	James	----, Catherine	E	645
Hassagen, Lucas	1, Jan. 1855	Johan	Warell, Clara	F	
Hasse, Johanna	29, May 1855	Wilhelm	Kriech, Francisca	F	
Hasse, Josephina	29, May 1855	Wilhelm	Kriech, Francisca	F	
Hasse, Maria Antonia	29, May 1855	Wilhelm	Kriech, Francisca	F	
Hassel, Mathilda	1, Jan. 1852	Peter	Lange, M. Anna	C	
Hassel, Peter Georg Francis	22, Sept 1850	Peter	Schmidt, Mathilda	C	
Hasselback, August	25, Oct. 1857	Johan	Felix, Catharina	D	97
Hasselback, Francis Michael	24, Aug. 1857	Johan	Rebold, Catharina	D	93
Hasselback, Michael	8, Aug. 1852	Johan	Felix, Catharina	D	342
Hasselbeck, Anna Catharina	12, Aug. 1855	Peter	Rebold, Catharina	F	
Hasselbeck, Heinrich	9, Oct. 1853	Peter	Rebold, Catharina	F	
Hasselbeck, Johan	11, Feb. 1855	Johan	Felix, Catharina	D	28
Hasselbeck, Peter	1, Nov. 1857	Peter	Ling, Catharina	D	98
Hasselbeck, Wilhelm	6, Apr. 1851	Peter	Rebold, Catharina	D	259
Hasselberger, Franz	18, Aug. 1850	Francis	Schneider, Francisca	F	
Hasselinger, Anna Carolina Angela	22, Sept 1851	J. Herman	Elsen, Anna Catharina	D	284
Hasselwander, Anna Barbara	27, Nov. 1859	Heinrich	Bach, Anna Maria	H	
Hasselwander, Francis Joseph	20, June 1858	Henry	Bach, Anna Maria	H	
Hasselwuth, Rosa Isabella	1, July 1855	Thomas	----, Sarah	F	
Hasser, Maria Louisa	30, Dec. 1855	Joseph	Müller, Theresa	A	
Hasshagen, Anna Maria	1, Feb. 1852	Johan	Warel, Clara	C	
Hassin, Dorcas Ann	10, Feb. 1850	Thomas	Crouse, Sophia	B	197
Hassing, Johan Philipp	3, Oct. 1855	Gerhard H.	Ferley, Elisabeth	L	
Hassman, Gertrud	25, July 1858	Adam	Spuler, Maria	K	
Hastetter, Maria Anna	10, Sept 1854	Francis	Jorers?, Maria Anna	D	17
Hasting, Michael	9, May 1856	John	Burke, Margaret	E	365
Hates, Frances John	25, Aug. 1851	James	Funker, Henriette	E	336
Hatke, Anna Maria Catharina	25, Oct. 1858	Johan	Ortmann, Maria	T	
Hatke, Catharina Friedrica	2, Dec. 1855	Gerhard	Kroeger, Maria	D	48
Hatke, Johan August Gerhard	9, Nov. 1855	Gerhard	Winkeljohan, Anna Maria	D	46
Hatke, Johan Gerhard Benedict	21, Mar. 1852	Gerhard	Winkeljohan, Anna Maria	D	313
Hatke, Johan Joseph	30, June 1854	J. Joseph	Schoppman, Catharina	D	13
Hatke, Margaretha	21, Dec. 1856	Gerhard	Winkeljohan, Anna Maria	D	74
Hatke, Matthias	30, Oct. 1858	Gerhard	Kroeger, Maria	C	
Hatling, Michael Johan	8, June 1856	Michael	Halbich, Eva	F	
Hatter, Michael	8, Oct. 1854	Thomas	Morrow, Ann	T	
Hatter?, William	19, Jan. 1851	Patrick	Mullen, Elizabeth	B	223
Hattig, Anna Maria	28, Dec. 1851	Adam	Aulbach, Elisabeth	C	
Hatting, Johan Herman Dietrich	30, Oct. 1854	Herman D.	Ott, Gesina	F	
Hattke, Johan Heinrich Joseph	19, Nov. 1856	Johan	Artmann, Marianna	F	
Hatzell, James William	2, Apr. 1851	James	Milligan, Mary	B	228
Haubner, James Louis	12, Sept 1852	Michael	----, Barbara	H	
Haubner, Joseph	4, Mar. 1855	Michael	----, Barbara	H	
Haubner, Rose Amelia	6, Aug. 1855	Gregory	----, Mary	H	
Hauck, Anna Catharina	10, Feb. 1850	J. Georg	Weigand, Anna	C	
Hauck, Anna Maria	1, Feb. 1857	Bernard	Wind, Elisabeth	D	78
Hauck, Anna Maria	11, Nov. 1855	Lawrence	Unser, Sibilla	D	46
Hauck, Carl	25, Apr. 1859	Ignatius	Mauzan, Catharina	H	
Hauck, Catharina	10, May 1857	Ignatius	Mausart, Catharina	H	
Hauck, Catharina	24, Jan. 1858	Lawrence	Unser, Sibilla	D	103
Hauck, Catherine	9, Apr. 1854	Ignatius	Mausard, Catherine	H	
Hauck, Elisabeth	18, June 1853	Johan	Reis, Eva	C	
Hauck, Franz Xavier	5, Feb. 1854	Lawrence	Unser, Sibilla	F	
Hauck, Johan	30, Sept 1859	Michael	Klingbe--, Anna	D	147

Name of Child	Date of Baptism	Father	Mother	Church	Page
Hauck, John B.	20, May 1855	Ignatius	----, Catherine	H	
Haucke, Anna Maria Gertrud	30, Mar. 1851	J. Georg	Weigand, Maria Anna	D	259
Hauckter, Mary Jane	19, Aug. 1857	Michael	Moloy, Rose	P	221
Hauenhorst, Anna Josephina	12, Sept 1858	Albert	Bruns, Maria Engel	A	
Hauenhorst, Anna Maria	12, Sept 1858	Albert	Bruns, Maria Engel	A	
Hauenhorst, Paul Theodor	26, Mar. 1852	Albert	Bruns, Angela	A	
Hauer, Bernard Eduard	27, Sept 1857	Johan	Bau---, Maria Anna	D	95
Hauer, Carl	19, Sept 1858	Michael	Fair, Theresa	T	
Hauer, Fidel	1, Jan. 1854	Michael	Fehr, Theresa	F	
Hauer, Friedrich Francis	11, May 1856	Michael	Fehr, Theresa	D	58
Hauer, Rosina	25, May 1851	Michael	Faehr, Theresa	F	
Haughton, Mary Ann	9, May 1857		adult - 44 years old	E	453
Haumos, Nicolaus	27, Feb. 1859	Jacob	Wetstein, Maria Anna	T	
Haund, Laurenz Alexander	29, Feb. 1852	Lawrence	Burghart, Rufina	C	
Haunert, Maria Gertrud	27, Dec. 1857	Heinrich	Glassmeier, Maria Catharina	Q	25
Haungs, Johan Martin	8, Jan. 1854	Lawrence	Burkhardt, Rufina	C	
Haupt, Anna Maria Louisa	3, Oct. 1858	Heinrich	Fleik, Elisabeth	D	120
Haupt, Friedrich Heinrich	27, May 1855	F. Heinrich	Sauders, Anna	C	
Haupt, Georg Francis Ludwig	5, Oct. 1851	Georg	Sanders, Anna	C	
Haupt, Georg Johan Joseph	10, July 1853	Georg	Sanders, Anna Elisabeth	C	
Haupt, Ludwig Conrad	28, Feb. 1858	G. Joseph	Sanders, Anna Maria	C	
Hauptmann, Franz Xavier	22, Nov. 1859	Georg J.	Regnei, Anna	T	
Haus, Anna Maria	23, Sept 1852		Haus, Anna	D	349
Haus, Barbara Walburga	28, Oct. 1855	Philip	----, Louise	H	
Haus, William	22, May 1853	Philip	----, Louise	H	
Hausacker, Wilhelm Heinrich	5, Oct. 1856	Wilhelm	Sime--, Luisa	D	69
Hausener, Catharina Margaretha	8, Aug. 1858	Johan	Lädoker, Magdalena	J	46
Hausener, Johan Jacob	26, Feb. 1856	Johan	Lädogar, Magdalena	J	34
Hausener, Joseph	4, June 1854	Johan	Lüdebar, Magdalena	J	26
Hausenrieder, Anna Catharina	29, Dec. 1854	Nicolaus	Ruhle, Margaretha	A	
Hauser, Carolina	23, Jan. 1859	Ferdinand	Meyer, Martina	C	
Hauser, Carolina	11, May 1853	Friedrich	Gürtler, Anna Maria	J	22
Hauser, Ferdinand	8, Feb. 1857	Ferdinand	Meyer, Martina	C	
Hauser, George Anthony	23, Apr. 1851	Fridolin	Girtler, Mary	H	
Hauser, Maria Anna	30, Jan. 1851		Hauser, Louisa	F	
Hauser, Maria Elisabeth	3, June 1855	Ferdinand	Meyer, Martina	C	
Hausfeld, Carolina Philomena	29, Apr. 1855	H.	Hembrock, Catharina	C	
Hausfeld, Gerhard Heinrich	1, Jan. 1853	Heinrich	Hembrock, Catharina	L	
Hausfeld, Johan Bernard	13, May 1856	Johan H.	Hembrock, Catharina	C	
Hausfeld, Johan Georg Bernard	24, Aug. 1858	J. Heinrich	Hembrock, Maria	C	
Hausfeld, Johan Heinrich	3, Mar. 1859	Bernard	Nieman, Elisabeth	A	
Hausfeld, Maria Francisca	19, June 1853	J. Joseph	Fischer, M. Engel	L	
Hausfeld, Philomena	10, Nov. 1850	Joseph	Fisher, Angela	L	
Hausfert, Carl Ludwig	16, Apr. 1851	?	?	K	
Häusler, Anna Maria	21, Oct. 1859	Sebastian	Bertr---, Margaretha	D	149
Hausman, Friedrich Wilhelm	20, Feb. 1859	Friedrich	Huber, Christina	J	48
Hausman, John	27, Mar. 1859	Joseph	Horman, Elisabeth	R	
Hausman, Joseph	20, Sept 1857	Joseph	Hurman, Elisabeth	R	
Hausman, Mary Ann	9, Aug. 1855		adult - 40 years old	P	144
Hausmann, Anna Catharina	2, Nov. 1852	Ferdinand	Mueller, Catharina	G	
Hausmann, Johan	5, Jan. 1851	Martin	Ziegler, Francisca	L	
Hausmann, Johan Bernard	26, Feb. 1854	Martin	Ziegler, Francisca	L	
Hausmann, Josephina	11, May 1851	Ferdinand	----, Catharina	G	
Hautman, Anna	21, May 1857	Xavier	Hasman, Francisca	D	85
Hautman, Philipp	15, May 1854	Francis X.	Hasman, Francisca	D	10
Hautz, Johan	11, Oct. 1857	Philip	Riester, Louise	H	
Hautz, John Peter	6, Aug. 1854	Philipp	----, Louise	U	
Hautz, Theresa	16, Jan. 1859	Philip	Riester, Louise	H	
Hauz, Anna Maria	25, Dec. 1855	Johan	----, Gretchen	H	

Name of Child	Date of Baptism	Father	Mother	Church	Page
Hauz, Catherine	25, Sept 1853	John	----, Wilhelmina	H	
Hauz, John	22, Nov. 1857	John	Moses, Wilhelmina	H	
Hauz, Louise	25, Sept 1853	John	----, Wilhelmina	H	
Have, Louisa	10, Apr. 1854	Carl	Herzog, Agnes	K	
Havercamp, Anna Margaretha	12, Dec. 1855	Heinrich	Rolfes, Elisabeth	D	48
Haverkamp, Anna Maria	16, Jan. 1859	J. Heinrich	Marischen, Carolina A.	L	
Haverkamp, Anna Maria Elisabeth	13, Aug. 1854	Clemens	Zurliene, Theresa	K	
Haverkamp, Anna Maria Elisabeth	8, Dec. 1859	Heinrich	Rolvers, Elisabeth	T	
Haverkamp, Anna Maria Josephina	11, Dec. 1851	Clemens	Zurliene, Theresa	K	
Haverkamp, Bernard Joseph	7, Oct. 1856	J. Heinrich	Marischen, Carolina A.	L	
Haverkamp, Carl	26, Feb. 1854	Carl	Boffinger, Mathilda	D	5
Haverkamp, Catharina Adelheid	6, Jan. 1854	Heinrich	Rolfers, Elisabeth	D	1
Haverkamp, Catharina Theresa	24, Oct. 1858	Clemens	Zurliene, Theresa	K	
Haverkamp, Gerhard Heinrich	25, Sept 1856	Clemens	Zurliene, Theresa	K	
Haverkamp, Gerhard Heinrich Martin	10, Feb. 1855	Martin	Stecker, Dina	F	
Haverkamp, Johan Bernard	24, Oct. 1853	J. Heinrich	Marischen, Carolina A.	L	
Haverkamp, Johan Georg	14, Dec. 1859	Joseph	Gauksterd, Luisa	K	
Haverkamp, Johan Heinrich	26, Nov. 1857	Herman H.	Rolfers, M. Elisabeth	T	
Haverkamp, Johan Wilhelm	20, May 1852	Friedrich	Rothes, Gertrud	L	
Haverkamp, M. Carolina Elisabeth	9, Sept 1851	J. Heinrich	Marischen, Carolina	L	
Haverkamp, Margaretha Elisabeth	17, June 1859	J. Heinrich	Riesenberg, Maria Elisabeth	U	
Haverkamp, Maria Elisabeth	6, Jan. 1852	H. Heinrich	Rolfers, Maria Elisabeth	D	301
Haverkamp, Maria Philomena	17, Jan. 1850	Mathias	Wendt, Maria Anna	K	
Haverland, Gerhard Henry	13, Sept 1857	Gerhard	Behrens, Euphemia M.	H	
Haverland, Johan Herman Joseph	28, Dec. 1851	J. Georg	Krickmann, Anna Carolina	C	
Haverland, Johan Wilhelm	15, Apr. 1855	J. Gerhard	Behrens, Euphemia Margaret	K	
Haverland, John Gerhard	1, Feb. 1853	J. Gerhard	Behrens, Euphemia Maria	R	
Havertepe, Johan Bernard	8, Apr. 1857	Johan H.	Losekamp, Catharina	F	
Havertepe, Johan Theodor Joseph	6, Nov. 1859	Heinrich	Losekamp, Catharina	F	
Haverty, John	18, Dec. 1858	Thomas	Farrell, Margaret	R	
Haverty, Margaret	27, Dec. 1856	John	----, Mary	R	
Haverty, Patrick	15, Feb. 1859	John	Cusick, Mary	R	
Hawerkost, Anna Maria	25, Jan. 1851	Friedrich	Ellerhorst, Maria Elis.	L	
Hawey, Susan	7, Jan. 1850	Francis	----, Susan	E	191
Hawkins, Francis	1, Aug. 1852	Peter	Reilly, Bridget	P	25
Hawkins, John Baptist	15, Aug. 1852	John	Whelan, Julia	P	26
Hawks, Helen	19, Oct. 1858	Henry	Walsh, Helen	P	264
Hawley, John	20, Apr. 1850		adult	B	201
Hawley, Mary	7, Nov. 1852	John	----, Mary	M	
Hawley, Sarah Jane	29, Aug. 1853	John	Divine, Catherine	V	5
Hay, Ann	5, Dec. 1852	Richard	Kelly, Margaret	P	30
Hay, Catherine	2, Sept 1854	Patrick	Angel, Bridget	R	
Hay, John	12, Apr. 1856	Dennis	Sullivan, Margaret	U	
Hay, Thomas	19, May 1852	Bernard	----, Catherine	E	415
Hay, William	25, June 1854	Stephan	Hannan, Ann	R	
Hayden, Mary Emily	15, Aug. 1857	Lawrence	----, Theresa	E	473
Hayden, Theresa Ann	6, July 1856	Lawrence	Kelly, Theresa	E	380
Hayden, William	15, Aug. 1854	Lawrence	Kelly, Theresa	E	216
Hayes, Ann Mary	30, June 1850	Patrick	Jordan, Ann	B	206
Hayes, Bridget	17, June 1851	Patrick	Fitzgerald, Alice	E	316
Hayes, Bridget Mary	15, Feb. 1856	Patrick	Marery, Margaret	B	25
Hayes, Cajetan	4, May 1854	Patrick	----, Ann	B	314
Hayes, Catherine	5, Dec. 1854	James	Ryan, Margaret	P	108
Hayes, Catherine	1, Sept 1850	John	----, Mary	E	245
Hayes, Catherine	3, Dec. 1857	Philip	Bannan, Bridget	E	497
Hayes, Catherine	15, May 1859	William	----, Julia	E	624
Hayes, Daniel	22, Sept 1853	John	----, Julia	E	128
Hayes, Daniel	16, Nov. 1853	Philipp	Fannan, Bridget	E	145
Hayes, Ellen	5, Oct. 1856	Thomas	Crawley, Mary	B	34

Name of Child	Date of Baptism	Father	Mother	Church	Page
Hayes, Helen	21, Sept 1851	William	McCarthy, Helen	E	346
Hayes, Henry	11, May 1856	William	McCarthy, Helen	E	365
Hayes, James	9, July 1858	John	Connor, Julia	E	547
Hayes, James	6, May 1853	Thomas	Logan, Ann	B	290
Hayes, Joanne	22, Jan. 1852	John	Hickey, Joanne	E	375
Hayes, John	22, Jan. 1854	John	O'Donnell, Mary	B	307
Hayes, John	22, Sept 1855	Lawrence	Kirwin, Ann	B	19
Hayes, John	17, June 1852	Thomas	----, Mary	M	
Hayes, Julia	17, Apr. 1850	John	Hickey, Joanne	B	201
Hayes, Julia	8, Aug. 1858	Thomas	Crowley, Mary	B	62
Hayes, Margaret	19, Oct. 1856	James	Ryan, Margaret	P	195
Hayes, Margaret	1, Apr. 1855	John	O'Donnell, Mary	B	13
Hayes, Martin	5, Apr. 1857	Lawrence	Kerwin, Ann	B	42
Hayes, Mary	13, May 1853	Dennis	----, Margaret	M	
Hayes, Mary	7, Jan. 1855	Francis	Dugan, Ann	B	9
Hayes, Mary	12, May 1856	John	Connor, Judith	E	366
Hayes, Mary	29, May 1853	John	Halligan, Mary	E	94
Hayes, Mary	27, Juen 1854	Thomas	----, Mary	M	
Hayes, Mary	22, Feb. 1855	William	Small, Julia	E	267
Hayes, Mary	1, Feb. 1854	Patrick	Banden, Joanne	E	164
Hayes, Mary	22, Oct. 1853	William	McCarthy, Helen	E	137
Hayes, Mary Ann	19, Oct. 1856	Thomas	Logan, Ann	P	196
Hayes, Mary Catherine	29, Dec. 1859	Bernard	Frechen, Mary Catherine	K	
Hayes, Michael	16, Mar. 1856	John	----, Elizabeth	M	
Hayes, Michael	21, July 1855	John	Hooligan, Mary	E	300
Hayes, Sarah	3, Jan. 1857	William	Small, Julia	E	424
Hayes, Stephen	11, Sept 1859	Lawrence	Kerwin, Ann M.	B	80
Hayes, Stephen	30, Dec. 1859	Philip	----, Bridget	E	680
Hayes, Thomas	13, Nov. 1854	Thomas	Logan, Ann	B	7
Hayes, William	27, Mar. 1859	William	McCarthy, Ellen	E	613
Hayes, William Edward	15, Aug. 1851	Thomas	Logan, Ann	B	239
Haynes, John	16, Nov. 1854	Patrick	Cain, Bridget	R	
Haynes, Josephine Mary	20, Jan. 1859	Mason	----, Belinda	E	598
Hays, Ellen Ann	1, Jan. 1853	John	Te--lin, Ann	P	33
Hays, Helen	8, Aug. 1858	James	O'Brien, Margaret	P	256
Hays, Joanne	27, Oct. 1851	Patrick	Murray, Margaret	P	13a
Hays, John	4, July 1850	James	Hays, Mary	B	206
Hays, John Francis	4, July 1853	Patrick	----, Mary	M	
Hays, Joseph	18, Apr. 1858	Patrick	----, Mary	M	
Hays, Margaret	16, Dec. 1853	Patrick	Murray, Margaret	P	62
Hays, Marianne	13, Feb. 1853	James	Ryan, Margaret	P	35
Hays, Mary	3, Feb. 1851	Matthew	----, Joanne	B	224
Hays, Mary	28, Jan. 1855	Michael	Carroll, Catherine	B	10
Hays, Mary Ann	18, Jan. 1852	Patrick	----, Mary	M	
Hays, Sarah	9, Mar. 1856	Stephan	----, Ann	R	
Hays, William James	30, Nov. 1851	Richard	McElhany, Mary	P	13c
Haywood, Mary	1, Nov. 1850	Richard	----, Ann	E	258
He---, Mary Helen	1, May 1852	Michael	----, Joanne	B	258
Heafy, John	14, July 1850	Michael	Desmond, Margaret	B	207
Healey, Catherine	23, Aug. 1855	Michael	Gallagher, Mary	P	147
Healey, Helen	12, July 1855	Martin	Nolan, Nancy	P	139
Healey, Michael	17, July 1850	Patrick	Riley, Catherine	B	207
Healion, Helen	14, Nov. 1858	James	Woods, Rose	P	267
Healion, Julia	30, Nov. 1856	James	Woods, Rosanne	P	200
Healion, Mary	23, July 1854	James	Woods, Rosanne	P	89
Healy, Bridget	15, Nov. 1857	James	Quinlan, Mary	P	230
Healy, Elizabeth	19, Nov. 1857	Martin	Nolan, Nancy	B	52
Healy, Ellenore	16, Mar. 1851	John	----, Honora	E	291
Healy, Henry	6, Nov. 1853	Cornelius	McEnery, Helen	V	7

Name of Child	Date of Baptism	Father	Mother	Church	Page
Healy, James	1, Nov. 1857	Michael	Gallagher, Mary	B	51
Healy, Joanne	26, July 1853	Patrick	Mitchell, Joanne	B	296
Healy, Joanne	5, Mar. 1854	Timothy	Kennedy, Bridget	R	
Healy, Johan Herman Albert	3, May 1857	Johan N.	Simper, Maria Bernardina	D	84
Healy, John	1, Jan. 1850	John	----, Ann	B	193
Healy, John	26, July 1853	Patrick	Mitchell, Joanne	B	296
Healy, Julia	24, Oct. 1850	Michael	----, Margaret	E	256
Healy, Lawrence	12, Aug. 1855	Patrick	Mitchell, Jane	B	18
Healy, Margaret Ann	12, Dec. 1858	Martin	Nolan, Ann	B	68
Healy, Mary	22, May 1859	Anthony	Walsh, Catherine	P	284
Healy, Mary	13, Nov. 1856	Martin	----, Nancy	B	36
Healy, Mary Ann	14, Mar. 1852	James	----, Catherine	E	392
Healy, Mary Jane	13, Nov. 1859	Michael	Gallagher, Mary	B	83
Healy, Thomas	29, Jan. 1859	Bartholomew	McGowen, Margaret	P	273
Healy, Thomas	13, Oct. 1851	Patrick	----, Catherine	B	243
Healy, Thomas John Joseph	21, Nov. 1858	John	O'Connell, Mary	B	67
Heaney, Margaret	6, Sept 1854	James	----, Mary	M	
Heany, Ann	23, Nov. 1856	James	----, Ann	E	414
Heard, John	2, Sept 1852		adult	B	269
Hearry?, Hugh	11, Feb. 1852	Michael	McGonigal, Margaret	P	18
Heath, Martin	22, Aug. 1858	Michael	Foy, Bridget	B	63
Heathen, Elizabeth	17, July 1854	Patrick	Fisbach, Catharina	J	28
Heaton, Mary	26, May 1850	Patrick	O'Brien, Elizabeth	B	203
Hebauf, Anna Catharina	27, Nov. 1850	Johan	Schweigel, Magdalena	H	
Hebauf, Anna Maria	20, Nov. 1859	Johan	Giesler, Magdalena	T	
Hebauf, Anna Maria Magdalena	26, July 1855	J. George	----, Magdalena	H	
Hebauf, Franz Joseph	27, Sept 1857	J. Georg	Giesler, Magdalena	T	
Hebauf, John B.	17, Apr. 1854	John	----, Magdalena	H	
Hebauf, Magdalena	3, Aug. 1852	John	----, Catharina Magdalena	H	
Hebauf, Mary Magdalen	6, Jan. 1857	John	Schweigel, Catharina	H	
Hebel, August Ludwig	14, Sept 1855	August	Kamintzier, Magdalena	K	
Hebel, Herman Joseph	17, Apr. 1859	Conrad	Bailer, Francisca	D	136
Hebel, Jacob	12, Aug. 1855	Conrad	Beiler, Francisca	C	
Hebel, Johanna	1, Feb. 1857	Conrad	Buhler, Francisca	D	78
Hebel, Maria	28, Aug. 1853	Andreas	Kunz, Margaretha	D	402
Hebeler, Anton	15, May 1850	Heinrich	Franzmann, Marianna	F	
Hebenhart, Maria Elisa	29, Dec. 1859	J. Heinrich	----, Maria	D	153
Hebenstreit, Clemens	23, Dec. 1859	Philip	Keelen, Gertrud	R	
Hebenstreit, Xavier Philip	4, Dec. 1859	Philip	Karlin, Gertrud	R	
Heber, Johan Gerhard	9, Feb. 1856		Heber, Maria Carolina	K	
Hebler, Johan Bernard	30, June 1857	Johan H.	Fanzmann, Marianna	F	
Heblich, Appollonia	23, Apr. 1850	Michael	Herfel, Margaretha	D	210
Hechinger, Carl Francis	29, Aug. 1852	Protasus	Lawrence, Maria	J	18
Hechinger, Gertrud	4, Aug. 1850	Thomas	Runser, Gertrud	F	
Hechinger, Sarah Johanna	13, July 1856	Protasus	Lawrence, Maria	J	36
Hechinger, Thomas Heinrich	1, Aug. 1852	Thomas	Nunzer, Gertrud	F	
Hechler, Magdalena	26, Feb. 1854	Peter	Hehrhager, Barbara	F	
Hechler, Maria Christina	9, Mar. 1856	Peter	Baubach, Barbara	F	
Hechler, Peter	23, June 1851	Peter	Behrhagen, Barbara	D	269
Hecht, Georg Martin	8, Dec. 1850	Martin	Kraus, Margaretha	D	245
Hecht, Joseph	29, Feb. 1852	Martin	Kraus, Margaretha	D	310
Hecht, Veronica	20, Oct. 1850	Johan	Eder, Veronica	J	8
Heck, Carl Ludwig	25, Jan. 1853	J. Georg	Beierlein, Catharina	D	367
Heck, Clemens Herman Anton	25, May 1854	Anton	Ostendorf, Elisabeth	C	
Heck, Clemens Herman Joseph	13, Sept 1858	Anton	Ostendorf, Elisabeth	C	
Heck, Elisabeth	24, July 1859	Ludwig	Lett, Catharina	T	
Heck, Francis Peter	10, May 1858	J. Georg	Becklein, Catharina	D	111
Heck, Johan Francis Heinrich	24, Mar. 1856	Anton	Ostendorf, Elisabeth	C	
Heck, Theresa Louisa	24, Oct. 1852	Edward	Sensbach, Helena	D	355

Name of Child	Date of Baptism	Father	Mother	Church	Page
Heckbonner, Anna Maria	11, July 1855	Nicolaus	Harg, Anna Maria	D	38
Heckel, Anna Maria	24, June 1855	Caspar	Wittenbauer, Crescentia	F	
Heckel, Joseph	2, Mar. 1856	Caspar	Wittenbauer, Crescentia	F	
Hecker, Caspar	21, Oct. 1857	Johan	----, Rosina	R	
Hecker, Heinrich Anton	11, Sept 1859	F. Heinrich	Hoch, Florentina	K	
Hecker, Joseph	2, Aug. 1856	J. Gottfried	----, Rosina	R	
Heckert, Elisabeth Florentina	3, Sept 1857	Francis H.	Hoog, Florentina	K	
Heckert, Georg Fidel	29, Jan. 1854	Francis	Hoch, Florentina	C	
Heckert, Heinrich Johan	15, Dec. 1855	F. Heinrich	Hoag, Florentina	K	
Heckinger, Clara Magdalena	2, Apr. 1854	Thomas	Runsel, Gertrud	T	
Heckinger, Henry Leopold	10, May 1857	Thomas	Ransom, Ruth	T	
Hecklenborg, Johan Bernard	24, July 1850	Joseph	Schulte, Anna Maria	C	
Heckman, Maria Catharina	24, Feb. 1856	J. Bernard	Nader?, Elisabeth	R	
Heckmann, Georg Heinrich	29, Jan. 1854	Heinrich	Loebbe, Maria Anna	F	
Heckmann, Marianna Elisabeth	1, Aug. 1852	Johan H.	Lubbe, Anna Maria	F	
Heckmayer, Lawrence	6, Feb. 1859	Anton	Leite-, Maria Anna	D	130
Heckmeyer, Jacob	2, Sept 1857	Anton	Leile-, Anna Maria	D	93
Heder, Johan Anton	22, May 1859	Johan	Koppman, Gertrud	D	138
Heders, Johan Bernard	20, July 1850	Johan	Kockmann, Gertrud	F	
Hedgelan, Mary Emma	13, Oct. 1857	James	Adams, Amanda	P	**227**
Hedgelen, Martha Elizabeth	31, May 1858	James	Adams, Amanda Catherine	P	249
Hedole, Alexander	3, July 1854	Patrick	Keannon, Bridget	J	28
Hedrick, Edward	23, Nov. 1851	Clemens	----, Catherine	E	360
Hee, Anna Maria	6, Jan. 1856	Peter	Wenger, Eva Catharina	W	11
Hee, Barbara	8, Aug. 1858	Peter	Wenger, Eva Catharina	C	
Hee, Johan	2, Mar. 1851	Peter	Wenger, Eva Catharina	D	255
Hee, Louisa	23, Oct. 1853	Peter	Wenger, Catharina Eva	C	
Hee, Maria Magdalena	6, Jan. 1856	Peter	Wenger, Eva Catharina	W	11
Heed, Johan Heinrich	24, July 1851	Anton	Luttel, Maria Anna	C	
Heeger, Johan Jacob	8, Sept 1854	J. Heinrich	Roe, Anna M. Philomena	C	
Heeger, Julia	25, Feb. 1855	Anton	Riefenstahl, Elisabeth	C	
Heeley, James	20, July 1852	----	----, ----	E	431
Heely, William	19, July 1854	William	----, Mary	M	
Heenan, William	27, Oct. 1850	John	Curran, Margaret	B	217
Heeny, Elizabeth	26, Oct. 1856	William	----, Mary	M	
Heeny, Patrick	18, Dec. 1854	Martin	----, Ellen	M	
Heet, Anna Maria Sophia	6, May 1854	Lucas	Belken, Anna M.	C	
Heet, Christina Theresa	3, Mar. 1851	Gerhard	Mollenkamp, Elisabeth	C	
Heet, Johan Gerhard	28, Apr. 1859	Anton	Littel, Maria Anna	L	
Heet, Johanna Christina	25, July 1853	Anton	Lietel, Maria Anna	L	
Heet, Maria Anna	15, Apr. 1856	Gerhard	Moellenkamp, Elisabeth	C	
Heet, Maria Theresa	3, June 1852	Lucas	Benken, M. Anna	C	
Heeth, Johan Heinrich	27, Sept 1855	Anton	Luettel, M. Anna	C	
Heffern, Catherine	20, Feb. 1850	Richard	Dunn, Ellen	E	198
Heffern, Patrick	12, Feb. 1850	John	Coughlin, Winny	E	196
Heffernan, Bridget	24, July 1859	Miles	O'Connell, Bridget	B	78
Heffernan, Catherine	25, July 1852	Dennis	Stanley, Alice	E	432
Heffernan, Helen	5, Feb. 1856	Thomas	Tierney, Mary	V	29
Heffernan, John	27, Jan. 1856	Michael	Gormly, Sabina	V	29
Heffernan, John	25, June 1855	Miles	O'Donnell, Bridget	P	137
Heffernan, John	15, Aug. 1858	Thomas	Tierney, Mary	V	50
Heffernan, Louis	29, May 1853	Thomas	Martin, Mary	E	93
Heffernan, Mary Ann	3, Sept 1859	Michael	Kelley, Ann	E	651
Heffernan, Thomas	6, Apr. 1852	Michael	---han, Alice	P	20
Heffernan, Thomas	27, Jan. 1857	Miles	O'Donnell, Bridget	P	204
Heffernan, Thomas William	8, July 1858	Thomas	Martin, Mary	E	547
Heffernen, Theresa Mary	29, Nov. 1855	Thomas	Martin, Mary	E	330
Heffler, Catherine	22, July 1855	John	Coghlan, Winifred	B	17
Heffler, Mary	22, July 1855	John	Coghlan, Winifred	B	17

Name of Child	Date of Baptism	Father	Mother	Church	Page
Hefner, Daniel	27, June 1850	Thomas	----, Mary	E	226
Hegarty, John	7, May 1854	Patrick	Craig, Elizabeth	V	13
Hegel, Anna	4, July 1852	M.	----, Maria	K	
Hegel, Johan	19, July 1857	Johan	Kulohn, Barbara	A	
Hegel, Johanna Aloysia Paulina	3, Oct. 1855	Lawrence	Elfers, Theresa	L	
Hegel, Joseph	27, Sept 1857	Joseph	Zimmerer, Carolina	C	
Hegel, Joseph Lorenz	6, Dec. 1857	Lawrence	Elfers, Henrica	L	
Hegel, Kunigunda	25, Apr. 1852	Michael	Scheider, Josepha	F	
Hegel, Maria Adelheid	4, Apr. 1852	Lawrence	Elfers, Bernardina	C	
Hegemann, Herman Gerhard	9, Dec. 1850	Theodor H.	Kollmann, Catharina	L	
Hegener, M. Theresa	26, Oct. 1852	Anton Th.	Kollmann, Theresa C.	L	
Hegeny, Mathew	6, Feb. 1853	Lawrence	Connor, Rose	P	34
Heger, Anna Maria Wilhelmina	28, Jan. 1851	Heinrich	Rothe, Maria	A	
Heger, Catharina Philomena	18, June 1854	Friedrich	Revers, Adelheid	A	
Heger, Herman Bernard	26, June 1859	Bernard	Schumacher, Theresa	C	
Heger, Herman Heinrich	12, Aug. 1856	J. Heinrich	Rohen, Philomena	C	
Heger, Johan	19, Mar. 1854	Michael	Scheidler, Josephina	D	6
Heger, Joseph Clemens	30, June 1854	Clemens	Schweding, Clara	F	
Heger, Joseph Dennis	2, Nov. 1856	Friedrich	Revers, Adelheid	A	
Heger, Josepha	7, Nov. 1852	Adam	Gensheimer, Elisabeth	F	
Heger, Kunigunda Margaretha	10, Feb. 1851	Adam	Genzheimer, Elisabeth	F	
Heger, Maria Angela Longina	31, Jan. 1852	Friedrich	Revers, Adelheid	A	
Heger, Maria Anna Elisabeth	14, Nov. 1852	Heinrich	Rahm, Philomena	C	
Heger, Maria Cecilia	20, Jan. 1856	Adam	Gehensheimer, Elisabeth	F	
Heger, Maria Louisa	12, June 1853	Joseph	Karch, Theresa	F	
Heger, Martin	8, Nov. 1857	Adam	Gensheimer, Elisabeth	F	
Hegerty, John	22, Dec. 1857	Nicolaus	----, Elisabeth	K	
Hegg, Ludwig	8, Mar. 1857	Ludwig	Lett, Catharina	F	
Hegger, Anna Maria Catharina	8, Jan. 1857	Friedrich	Uphoff, Maria Catharina	K	
Hegger, Johan Bernard	6, Sept 1852	Friedrich	Uphoff, Catharina	K	
Hegger, Johan Gerhard Edward	2, Oct. 1859	J. Friedrich	Uphoff, Catharina	K	
Hegling, Johan Heinrich	27, July 1851	Friedrich	Kleine, Maria	C	
Hegner, Anton	20, Nov. 1859	Friedrich	Gebhard, Barbara	T	
Hegney, Catherine	4, Oct. 1851	Lawrence	Connor, Rose	E	348
Hegney, James	11, July 1858	Lawrence	Connors, Rose	P	253
Hegney, John	9, Apr. 1854	Lawrence	Connor, Rose	P	78
Hehe, Maria Catharina	3, Mar. 1859	Clemens	Schure, Catharina	T	
Heheman, Herman Heinrich	1, Nov. 1858	Wilhelm	Döpker, Maria Agnes	A	
Heheman, Johan Philipp Wilhelm	4, June 1855	Wilhelm	Doepker, Maria	K	
Heheman, Maria Agnes	15, Jan. 1857	Wilhelm	Döpker, Maria Agnes	A	
Hehey, Catherine	26, Feb. 1854	Francis	Carr, Alice	P	71
Hehir?, Rose Ann	14, Apr. 1850	Michael	----, Mary Ann	E	207
Hehl, Johan	29, Oct. 1854	Francis	Leutpolt, Sophia	D	21
Hehman, Francis Martin	10, Mar. 1854	F. Wilhelm	Wendt, Clara	K	
Hehman, Johan Ludwig	8, Sept 1851	F. Wilhelm	Wendt, Clara Elisabeth	K	
Hehmann, Catharina Wilhelmina	17, Jan. 1859	Friedrich	Brinkmann, Helena T.	L	
Hehmann, Heinrich Gustav	21, June 1859	Lambert	Henneke, Catharina	C	
Hehmann, Maria Mathilda	12, June 1859	Andreas	Brokamp, Catharina	F	
Hehmann, Robert Ignatz	8, Mar. 1856	Lambert	Hennecke, Catharina	C	
Hehn, Francis Xavier	11, July 1851	?	----, Catharina	D	272
Hehner, Thomas	7, Nov. 1858	Balthasar	Briegler, Elisabeth	G	
Heiberger, Barbara Christina	30, Jan. 1853	Raymond	Unger, Barbara	J	20
Heid, Maria Anna	7, Feb. 1858	Tobias	Forstmann, Philippina	C	
Heid, Philomena	12, Feb. 1859	Johan	Leonhard, Elisabeth	C	
Heidacher, Bernard Heinrich	24, June 1851	Heinrich	Siemer, Bernardina	C	
Heidacher, Herman Heinrich	28, Aug. 1853	Eberhard	Siemer, Bernardina	C	
Heidacker, Edward Heinrich	29, Aug. 1858	Edward	Siemer, Bernardina	C	
Heidacker, Robert Wilhelm	17, Jan. 1855	Ludwig	Heobi, Rosa	D	27
Heidacker, Wilhelm Heinrich	3, Aug. 1856	Heinrich	Siemer, Bernardina	C	

Hamilton County, Ohio Roman Catholic Baptism Records -- 1850 - 1859

Name of Child	Date of Baptism	Father	Mother	Church	Page
Heide, Anna Barbara	8, Sept 1850	J. Baptist	Hoffman, Magdalena	A	
Heidel, Joseph Martin	28, Apr. 1855	Michael	Buck, Ottilia	D	34
Heidel, Michael Francis	16, Oct. 1859	Michael	Buck, Ottilia	D	149
Heidel, Wilhelm Christoph	26, July 1857	Michael	Buck, Elisabeth	D	91
Heidelberger, Ferdinand	27, June 1851	Roman	Unger, Barbara	J	12
Heidelberger, Maria	21, Mar. 1852	Wendelin	Schwarz, Gertrud	K	
Heidelberger, Maria Anna	30, Mar. 1856	Roman	Unger, Barbara	J	34
Heidelman, Johan Bernard	14, Oct. 1850	Arnold H.	Klatte, Maria Elisabeth	A	
Heider, Anna Barbara	20, Sept 1856	Christoph	Mack, Louisa	D	67
Heider, Anna Catharina	13, Nov. 1859	Christoph	Mack, Louisa	D	150
Heider, Carolina	31, Jan. 1858	Christoph	Mack, Louisa	D	104
Heider, Maria Theresa	1, Dec. 1850	Jacob	Clemens, Catharina	F	
Heiderick, Carolina	6, Nov. 1850	Christian	Heinz, Elisabeth	D	241
Heidkamp, Bernard Edward	24, Feb. 1859	Ferdinand	Schuh, Elisabeth	L	
Heidkamp, Franz August	25, Apr. 1859	Friedrich	Beckmann, Maria Anna	L	
Heidkamp, Heinrich Martin	12, Nov. 1859	Bernard	Kloenne, Anna Maria	L	
Heidkamper, Johan Bernard	5, May 1857	J. Gerhard	Strüwing, Lisetta	D	84
Heidle, Elisabeth	21, Sept 1851	Johan	Hormeler, Veronica	C	
Heidler, Anna Maria	30, Jan. 1853	Johan	Hermueller, Veronica	C	
Heidmeier, Caspar Ludwig August	25, Mar. 1853	Caspar	Warnesmann, Anna Sophia	F	
Heier, Anna Maria Catharina	6, Feb. 1850	Herman L.	Asbree, Maria Catharina	C	
Heier, Catharina	22, Sept 1850	Johan	Aignus, Maria	C	
Heier, Johan Heinrich	8, Jan. 1856	Johan	Vonberger, Maria Anna	D	50
Heier, Margaretha	19, Dec. 1858	Mathias	Buchman, Margaretha	N	
Heier, Maria Catharina Elisabeth	3, Nov. 1851	J. Heinrich	Keller, Maria Catharina	A	
Heier, Sophia	18, Jan. 1858	Christian	Wild, Rosa	D	103
Heiert, Johan	1, Jan. 1850	Pancratz	Menninger, Anna Maria	A	
Heigman, Peter	12, Aug. 1855	J. Adam	Englert, Catherine	R	
Heiing, Anna Maria	6, Mar. 1857	Heinrich	Kürsen, Regina	A	
Heiing, Christina	1, Feb. 1859	J.H.	Kniven, Gesina	A	
Heiing, Johan Bernard	18, May 1853	Gerhard	Littel, Maria	A	
Heiing, Johan Gerhard	18, May 1853	Gerhard	Littel, Maria	A	
Heiker, Johan F. August	15, May 1853	Friedrich	Fussner, Barbara	L	
Heiker, Magdalena Catharina	23, July 1858	Friedrich	Pfaschner, Barbara	F	
Heiker, Theodor Mathias	29, July 1855	Friedrich	Fusner, Barbara	A	
Heil, Carolina	21, Aug. 1853	Leonard	Bonnert, Anna Maria	D	401
Heil, Catharina	4, Nov. 1855	Leonard	Bonnert, Maria Anna	D	46
Heil, Elisabeth Francisca	25, Dec. 1853	Valentin	Renck, Francisca	S	
Heil, Francisca	3, Nov. 1857	Leonhard	Bonnert, Marianna	F	
Heil, George Martin	2, Sept 1857	William B.	Catine, Cecilia	B	49
Heil, Hieronymus	23, Mar. 1856	Jacob	----, ----	D	54
Heil, Jacob	10, Feb. 1854	Jacob	Becker, Maria	D	4
Heil, Johan	20, July 1851	Valentin	Renk, Francisca	L	
Heil, Johan Georg Aloysius	11, Dec. 1859	Valentin	Reichling, Clara	F	
Heil, Joseph	26, Dec. 1858	Joseph	----, Theresa	T	
Heil, Joseph Jacob Valentin	11, July 1858	Valentin	Reichling, Clara	F	
Heil, Josephina	8, Aug. 1852	Johan	Hiegel, Ottilia	F	
Heil, Margaretha	6, July 1851	Jacob	Becker, Maria	D	271
Heil, Maria Anna	15, June 1851	Leonard	Bonett, Maria Anna	F	
Heil, Simon	12, Nov. 1851	Johan	Draper, Lucia	D	292
Heil, Valentin	13, June 1849	Valentin	Renk, Francisca	S	
Heile, Bernard Heinrich	9, Apr. 1856	Francis	Korte, Clara	L	
Heile, Herman	7, Sept 1858	Francis	Korte, Clara	L	
Heile, Johan Bernard Heinrich	4, Nov. 1857	Herman	Growe, Maria Theresa	A	
Heile, Johan Gerhard	28, Aug. 1859	Francis	Korte, Clara	L	
Heileman, Anton Bernard	25, May 1850	J. Bernard	Duddei, Maria Elisabeth	D	214
Heileman, Margaretha Henrietta	11, Apr. 1852	J. Bernard	Tuddel, Susanna Elisabeth	D	316
Heileman, Susanna Adelheid Christina	12, Feb. 1858	J. Gerhard	Widde, Gertrud	D	105
Heilemann, Anna Gesina	9, Oct. 1854	Herman H.	Thoeter, Maria Helena	F	

- 264 -

Name of Child	Date of Baptism	Father	Mother	Church	Page
Heilemann, Anna Helena	20, Nov. 1857	Herman H.	Tegeder, Maria Helena	F	
Heilemann, Johan Bernard Alexander	1, Mar. 1857	J. Bernard	Dudei, Elisabeth	C	
Heilemann, Maria Elisabeth	11, Oct. 1852	Herman H.	Tegeter, Helena	C	
Heilers, Anna Maria Antonia	8, Nov. 1853	Theodor	Feldkamp, Antonette	A	
Heilers, Maria Catharina	17, Feb. 1856	Theodor	Feldkamp, Antonetta	A	
Heilman, Barbara	28, June 1857	Adam	Dollman, Helena	D	88
Heilman, Helena	3, Apr. 1859	Adam	Trollman, Helena	D	135
Heilman, Johan Bernard Heinrich	30, June 1851	J. Bernard	Vorholt, Margaret Adelheid	A	
Heilman, Maria	29, Jan. 1852	Joseph	Rech, Anna Maria	D	304
Heilman, Susanna Adelheid	6, Jan. 1855	J. Herman	Dudey, Susanna Elisabeth	D	26
Heilmann, Anna Maria Margaretha	13, June 1852	Bernard	Vorholt, Maria	C	
Heilmann, Magdalena Bernardina	20, June 1850	Heinrich	Frohning, Lena	F	
Heim, Barbara	1, July 1854	Wilhelm	Busalt, Barbara	C	
Heim, Carolina	28, May 1854	Leonhard	Stein, Margaretha	C	
Heim, Catharina	23, Mar. 1851	Herman	Hut, Margaretha	D	258
Heim, Georg	20, Mar. 1859	Philipp	Sellir, Maria Anna	D	134
Heim, Johan Philipp	10, Dec. 1854	Philipp	Deller, Anna Maria	D	23
Heim, Margaretha	21, July 1850	Wilhelm	Bussalt, Barbara	C	
Heim, Maria	8, Mar. 1859	Wilhelm	Buserd, Barbara	D	133
Heim, Maria Anna	3, Feb. 1850	Philipp	Deller, Anna Maria	D	202
Heim, Maria Magdalena	16, Aug. 1857	Ludwig	Misler, Anna Maria	A	
Heim, Theresa	27, July 1856	Wilhelm	Busard, Barbara	D	63
Heim, Valentin	2, Nov. 1856	Philipp	Deller, Anna M.	D	71
Heim, Wilhelm Philipp	29, Aug. 1852	Wilhelm	Busalt, Barbara	C	
Heimbach, Carolina Francisca	15, Mar. 1856	J. Adam	Höbner, Anna Maria	D	54
Heimbach, Elisabeth	6, Mar. 1852	J. Adam	Hibner, Anna Maria	D	310
Heimbach, Elisabeth	8, Dec. 1850	Peter	Will, Elisabeth	D	246
Heimbach, Francis Xavier	28, Mar. 1858	Johan	Hübner, Maria Anna	D	108
Heimbach, Johan Adam	26, Sept 1852	Peter	Will, Elisabeth	F	
Heimbach, Joseph	2, Apr. 1854	Johan	Hibner, Maria Anna	D	7
Heimbach, Lorentz	26, Sept 1852	Peter	Will, Elisabeth	F	
Heimfeld, Francis Herman	23, July 1850	Francis	Hasselman, Maria Anna	D	224
Heimler, Leonard	13, Sept 1857	Leonard (+)	Stein, Margaret	H	
Heimmel, Bartholomew	7, Mar. 1852	Michael	Gottard, Magdalena	D	311
Heimrod, Wilhelm	4, Aug. 1850	Adolph	Engel, Carolina	C	
Heinbach, Johan	3, Mar. 1850	Johan	Höbler, Maria	D	204
Heind, Barbara	8, Aug. 1852	Philipp	Hebler, Anna Maria	D	342
Heine, Heinrich Joseph	1, Mar. 1857	Bernard	Ewing, Margaret	N	
Heineke, Anna Maria	25, Sept 1856	Francis J.	Ries, Anna Maria	A	
Heineke, Catharina	29, Sept 1851	Joseph	Fries, Anna Maria	J	12
Heineke, Johan Francis	6, July 1854	Francis J.	Riers, Anna Maria	A	
Heinel, Maria Catharina	28, Jan. 1850	J. Michael	Godar, Magdalena	D	202
Heineman, Anna Catharina	11, Sept 1858	Magnus	Macke, Catharina	A	
Heinemann, Maria Agnes	12, Nov. 1850	Anton	Emeholt, Agnes	C	
Heinemann, Maria Anna Agnes	28, July 1852	Anton	Imholte, Agnes	C	
Heinen, Maria Regina	13, Dec. 1852	Theodor	Roeser, Maria Margaretha	F	
Heiney, Abraham	17, July 1853	Joseph	----, Elizabeth	M	
Heiney, Louise	18, Feb. 1855	Joseph	----, Elizabeth	M	
Heiney, Martha	4, June 1858	Joseph	----, Elizabeth	M	
Heing, Johan	28, Oct. 1856	Francis	Wambach, Maria	N	
Heing, Johan Bernard Heinrich	22, Aug. 1851	Johan	Tennenfeld, Maria	A	
Heing, Maria Elisabeth	12, Dec. 1852	Bernard	Tewing, Margaretha	N	10
Heing, Martin	28, Oct. 1855	Francis	Wambach, Maria	N	
Heink, Anna	7, May 1859	Bernard	Ludgebruns, Maria	N	
Heink, Carolina	7, Nov. 1852	Heinrich	Wensing, Clara	C	
Heinlein, Appolonia	26, Oct. 1851	Heinrich	Friels, Barbara	D	289
Heinlein, Barbara	9, Jan. 1850	Heinrich	Hilz, Barbara	D	198
Heinrich, Anna Maria	15, Aug. 1850	Francis	----, Juliana	H	
Heinrich, Elisabeth	4, Jan. 1857	Anton	Rescher, Friedrica	K	

Name of Child	Date of Baptism	Father	Mother	Church	Page
Heinrich, Elisabeth	15, July 1852	Jacob	Plaetner, Maria	C	
Heinrich, Elisabeth Magdalena	29, Dec. 1859	Jacob	Blettner, Magdalena	C	
Heinrich, Jacob	22, May 1856	Jacob	Blettner, M. Anna	C	
Heinrich, Johan	6, Sept 1853	Andreas	Krieg, Anna Maria	D	405
Heinrich, Joseph	7, Nov. 1854	Jacob	Blettner,	C	
Heinrich, Joseph	1, Oct. 1858	Jacob	Plettner, Maria	C	
Heinrich, Magdalena Josephina	23, Oct. 1859	Georg	Sittel, Elisabeth	C	
Heinrich, Peter	22, Sept 1850	Andreas	Krieg, Anna Maria	C	
Heinrich, Rosina	7, Aug. 1858	Nicolaus	Fritsch, Margaretha	T	
Heinrichfeld, Johan Bernard	8, June 1854	Bernard	Henschitman, Maria Anna	D	12
Heinrichman, William Paul	8, Feb. 1857	Bernard	Kemper, Elisabeth	D	78
Heinrichs, Elisabeth Theresa	13, Aug. 1852	G. Heinrich	Grosheim, Antonia	A	
Heinrichs, Maria Louisa Antonette	17, June 1854	J. Gerhard	Grossheim, Antonette	A	
Heinrichs, Seraphina Wilhelmina Ther.	6, Sept 1859	Gerhard	Grossheim, Antonette	A	
Heinrichsman, Eduard Boniface	19, June 1853	Bernard	Campbell, Elisabeth	D	389
Heinricks, Johan Gerhard	31, Aug. 1856	Gerhard H.	Grossheim, Antonetta	A	
Heins, Margaretha Philomena	12, Sept 1852	Heinrich	Sauerbier, Elisabeth	K	
Heinsen, Anna Maria	13, Nov. 1854	Theodor	Kaiser, Margaretha	F	
Heinser, Johan Herman	16, Feb. 1851	Theodor	Kaiser, Margaretha	F	
Heintz, Eduard Wilhelm	25, July 1851	Joseph	Klausman, Christina	D	275
Heintz, Michael	23, Jan. 1853	Valentin	Rotti, Maria Anna	K	
Heinz, Anna Eva	5, Feb. 1854	Valentin	Roth, Maria Anna	K	
Heinz, Catharina Ottilda	1, June 1856	Peter	Clemens, Magdalena	J	36
Heinz, Heinrich	11, Dec. 1851	Philipp	----, Maria	C	
Heinz, Helena Maria	9, June 1858	August	Hennel, Magdalena	F	
Heinz, Johan	20, Sept 1858	Johan	Manning, Maria	F	
Heinz, Maria	25, May 1856	Jacob	----, Francisca	H	
Heinz, Maria	28, Feb. 1858	Jacob	Knab, Francisca	H	
Heinz, Maria Elisabeth	13, Nov. 1859	Peter	Loebe, Dorothea	D	150
Heinz, Peter	31, Aug. 1859	Peter	----, Gertrud	D	145
Heinz, Peter	28, Apr. 1858	Peter	Löbe, Dorothea	D	109
Heinz, Peter Vincent	30, Jan. 1859	Peter	Clemens, Magdalena	J	48
Heinz, Rosa Josephina	10, Apr. 1856	Joseph	Klausman, Christina	D	56
Heinz, Wilhelm	20, Dec. 1855	Valentin	Roth, Maria Anna	K	
Heir, Anna	20, Dec. 1859	Nicolaus	Kern, Elisabeth	K	
Heirich, Maria Barbara	20, July 1856	Michael	Helfrich, Barbara	W	15
Heis, Conrad Johan	19, Sept 1858	Conrad	Hammer, Gertrud	T	
Heis, Johan Francis	26, Jan. 1858	Johan	Linneman, Maria Catharina	A	
Heis, Maria Mathilda	9, May 1852	Andreas	Volk, Mathilda	D	319
Heisel, Joseph Gerhard	24, Apr. 1858	Gerhard	Niehaus, Francisca	D	109
Heiser, Gerhard Heinrich	15, Aug. 1851	Gerhard	Niehaus, Francisca	D	278
Heiser, Johan Heinrich	10, July 1854	J. Gerhard	Niehaus, Francisca	D	13
Heiser, Theodor Gerhard	23, Aug. 1856	Gerhard	Niehaus, Anna Friedrica	D	65
Heising, Emilia	23, Jan. 1853	H. Anton	Lamping, Louisa	L	
Heising, Maria Sophia	4, July 1854	William	Patscher, Christina	D	13
Heisman, Anna Maria	5, Feb. 1854	J. Heinrich	Schutte, Theresa	K	
Heisman, Johan Heinrich	5, Feb. 1854	J. Heinrich	Schutte, Theresa	K	
Heiss, Maria Louisa	24, July 1853	Andreas	Volk, Mathilda	S	
Heiss, Maria Magdalena	22, Dec. 1857	Sebastian	Petscher, Anna Maria	T	
Heiss, Nicolaus	17, Oct. 1858	Andreas	Volz, Helena	D	122
Heister, Heinrich	31, Jan. 1858	Heinrich	Vogelsang, Catharina	L	
Heister, Heinrich	27, Oct. 1856	Michael	Linden, Gertrud	K	
Heister, Peter	16, Sept 1858	Michael	Linden, Gertrud	C	
Heistler, Johan	2, Mar. 1856	Johan	Heleninger, Veronica	D	53
Heit, Gerhard Heinrich	19, Feb. 1854	Gerhard	Mullenkamp, Elisabeth	C	
Heitbrink, Anna Maria Elisabeth	2, Aug. 1855	J. Heinrich	Steinke, Maria Angela	D	39
Heitgers, Euphemia Margaret	12, Oct. 1858	Heinrich	Roling, Catherine	R	
Heitgers, Johan Bernard	4, Sept 1855	Heinrich	Roling, Elisabeth Catharina	R	
Heitgers, Maria	14, Sept 1854	Heinrich	Roling, Euphemia	R	

Name of Child	Date of Baptism	Father	Mother	Church	Page
Heithaus, Genoveva Elisabeth	3, Jan. 1859	Bernard	Willeke, Maria	L	
Heitig, Georg Friedrich	25, June 1854	G. Adam	Meister, Johanna Susanna	D	13
Heitkamp, Anna Maria	8, Apr. 1852	Joseph	Grewe, Catharina	L	
Heitkamp, Anna Maria Elisabeth	28, Apr. 1854	Ferdinand	Schow, A.M. Elis.	L	
Heitkamp, Franz	10, Jan. 1854	Francis	Puthoff, Elisabeth	L	
Heitkamp, Franz Joseph	20, Mar. 1856	Joseph	Grewer, Carolina	L	
Heitkamp, Heinrich Ferdinand	11, May 1856	Francis	Puthoff, Elisabeth	J	36
Heitkamp, Maria Helena	8, Sept 1856	Ferdinand	Schug, Elisabeth	L	
Heitkamp, Maria Margaretha	9, Oct. 1850	Francis	Puthoff, Elisabeth	L	
Heitkemper, Anna Catharina	17, July 1851	J. Gerhard	Stroecking, Elisabeth	D	273
Heitkemper, Anna Maria	28, Apr. 1859	J. Gerhard	Strasing, Elisabeth	D	137
Heitkemper, Johan Gerhard	29, June 1853	J. Gerhard	Strüving, Elisabeth	D	392
Heitlen, Philomena	25, July 1858	Johan	Kerrminge, Veronica	D	115
Heitler, Philomena	25, June 1854	Johan	Hermueller, Veronica	C	
Heitman, Anton Friedrich	4, Dec. 1859	Francis H.	Heheman, Louisa	D	152
Heitman, Bernard Heinrich	28, Nov. 1850	Francis	Heheman, Louisa	D	244
Heitman, Catharina Louisa	5, Aug. 1855	Francis H.	Heheman, Louisa	D	40
Heitman, Johan Bernard	18, July 1854	Francis	Brinkers, Helena	D	14
Heitman, Johan Philipp Wilhelm	19, Feb. 1853	Francis H.	Heheman, Elisabeth	D	372
Heitmeier, Johan Bernard	20, Mar. 1855	Caspar	Herzog, Anna Maria	K	
Heitschneider, Maria Elisabeth	24, Nov. 1856	Theodor	Schohstoppel,	F	
Heitzelman, Carolina	3, Sept 1854	Gregor	Uhl, Carolina	D	17
Heitzelman, Euphrosina	28, Apr. 1858	Gregor	Uhl, Carolina	D	110
Heitzelman, Louisa	10, Aug. 1856	Gregor	Uhl, Carolina	D	64
Heitzmann, Margaretha	10, Apr. 1859	Joseph	Sattler, Anna	G	
Heiwick, Josephina	23, Aug. 1857	Michael	Sievermann, Magdalena	L	
Hekel, Andreas	20, July 1858	Jacob	Rose, Margaretha	C	
Hekle, Louisa Amalia	16, Jan. 1851	Joseph	German, Helena	D	249
Held, Anna Maria	5, Sept 1858	Johan	Klaus, Anna	D	118
Hel--d, Barbara	23, Nov. 1856	Philipp	----, Margaretha	D	73
Held, Josephina	27, June 1858	Georg	Hoe---, Christina	D	114
Held, Leonard	7, Nov. 1852	Paul	----, Barbara	H	
Held, Margaret	7, Dec. 1852	Andrew	----, Catherine	H	
Held, Margaret	29, Sept 1850	Paul	Mercel, Barbara	H	
Held, Mary Ann	31, May 1850	Andrew	Mahler, Catherine	H	
Held, Peter	7, Dec. 1852	Andrew	----, Catherine	H	
Held, Peter	22, July 1855	Paul	----, Barbara	H	
Held, Peter	17, Jan. 1858	Paul	Mecklin, Barbara	H	
Held, Peter	9, July 1856		Held, Margaret	H	
Held, Rose of Lima	31, May 1850	Andrew	Mahler, Catherine	H	
Helde, Catharina Amalia	5, Oct. 1851	Jacob	Emminger, Crescentia	F	
Helde, Rosina	4, June 1856	Jacob	Eminger, Crescentia	F	
Helde, Thomas	12, May 1850		adult	F	
Helder, Charitas Josephina	1, Jan. 1854	Jacob	Emminger, Agnes	F	
Helfel, Francisca	25, May 1855	Adam	Theil, Catharina	D	35
Helferich, Adalbert	20, Feb. 1859	Francis	Gost, Rosina	C	
Helfrich, Heinrich Friedrich	6, Apr. 1856	Johan	Hof, Magdalena	D	55
Helfrich, Maria Magdalena	24, Jan. 1858	Johan	Hof, Magdalena	D	104
Helfrig, Margaretha	3, Feb. 1853	Johan	Riek, Francisca	L	
Helft, Johan Mathias	19, Aug. 1859	Caspar L.	Hold---, Anna Maria	D	144
Heli, Jacob	9, June 1850	Anton	Trondel, Catharina	C	
Helker, Francisca	1, Feb. 1855	Herman	Hess, Elisabeth	F	
Helker, Joseph Heinrich	26, June 1851	Joseph	Kabelkemper, Theresa	D	270
Helker, Laurentz	18, Mar. 1858	Herman	Hess, Elisabeth	F	
Helker, Leonard	14, Feb. 1850	Herman	Herz, Elisabeth	F	
Helker, Maria Magdalena	25, Apr. 1852	Herman	Hess, Elisabeth	F	
Helle, Heinrich Bernard	10, May 1854	Herman H.	Bahlman, Angela	A	
Hellear, Catherine	1, Feb. 1852	Charles	Costello, Catherine	E	379
Hellebusch, Elisabeth Amalia	21, July 1857	Clemens	Specker, Elisabeth	A	

Name of Child	Date of Baptism	Father	Mother	Church	Page
Hellebusch, Maria	19, May 1856	B.H.F.	Putthoff, Catharina Maria	A	
Hellebusch, Maria Anna Francisca	6, Feb. 1856	Clemens	Specker, Lucia Elisabeth	A	
Hellebusch, Maria Elisabeth	17, Oct. 1858	B.H.H.	Putthoff, Catharina Maria	A	
Helleman, Johan Bernard Heinrich	20, Nov.1859	J. Gerhard	Witte, Maria	D	151
Hellenthal, Peter Anton	17, Apr. 1859	Peter	Kessler, Maria Anna	D	136
Heller, Anna Maria	8, Feb. 1857	Herman H.	Bahlman, Angela	A	
Heller, Elisabeth	15, Aug. 1858	Johan	Wittenbauer, Catharina	D	117
Heller, Elizabeth Jane	25, Nov. 1850	Francis R.	Bower, Ann	B	219
Heller, Helen	6, Jan. 1853	John	Bowers, Ann	B	280
Heller, Herman Heinrich	1, Dec. 1859	Herman H.	Bahlman, Engel	A	
Heller, Herman Heinrich	5, July 1857	Herman H.	Doppes, Anna Maria	D	89
Heller, Johan Bernard	7, Dec. 1852	Herman	Bahlman, Angela	A	
Heller, Johan Bernard	26, Feb. 1854	J. Bernard	Doppes, Anna Maria	D	5
Heller, Johan Bernard	22, Aug. 1859	Bernard	Doppes, Anna Maria	D	145
Heller, Johan Herman	22, Aug. 1855	J. Bernard	Doppes, Anna Maria	D	41
Heller, Joseph August	3, Oct. 1856	Francis	Bowers, Ann	P	194
Heller, Mary Caroline	3, Nov. 1858	Francis P.	Bowers, Anna E.	B	66
Heller, Thomas George	23, May 1858	Benedict	Fries, Barbara	S	
Hellerich, Anna Francisca	26, Sept 1852	Benedict	Fries, Barbara	S	
Hellerich, Benedict	2, July 1853	John	Barry, Mary	B	294
Hellernan, Margaert	18, July 1856	F. Christ	Klenne, Adleheid	C	
Hellich, Wilhelm Albert	5, May 1850	J. Heinrich	Massman, Anna Sophia	D	212
Hellick, Johanna Elisabeth	16, May 1852	J. Heinrich	Mossman, Sophia	D	320
Helling, Anna Maria Henrietta	19, Sept 1854	Heinrich	Massman, Sophia	D	18
Helling, Johan Herman Heinrich	3, June 1858	Caspar H.	Bussman, Maria Catharina	A	
Hellman, Bernard	27, Dec. 1851	Gerhard	Meiers, Maria Elisabeth	D	298
Hellman, Gerhard Stephan	15, Oct. 1854	Adam	Geiger, Anna Maria	D	20
Hellman, Jacob	21, Oct. 1857	Joseph	Lohlin, Clementina	K	
Hellman, Johan Heinrich	4, July 1852	H. Joseph	Schlief, Clementina	D	328
Hellman, Mathias Herman Joseph	17, Sept 1854	Friedrich	Dickmann, M.A.	L	
Hellmann, Anton Ferdinand	19, Nov. 1852	Friedrich	Diekmann, Maria Anna	L	
Hellmann, Bernard Joseph	26, Feb. 1856	Friedrich	Rullmann, Agnes	C	
Hellmann, Carl Friedrich	29, Aug. 1858	Friedrich	Dieckmann, Maria Anna	L	
Hellmann, Johan Georg	21, Sept 1856	Friedrich	Dickmann, Maria Anna	L	
Hellmann, Joseph Friedrich	19, Oct. 1856	G. Adam	Geiger, Maria Anna	L	
Hellmann, Theresa	19, Jan. 1854	Joseph	Grief, Maria	D	2
Hellmund, Eva	15, Feb. 1856	Joseph	Graef, Anna Maria	D	52
Hellmuth, Anna Maria	16, Dec. 1857	Joseph	Graef, Maria	D	100
Hellmuth, Catharina	30, Nov. 1851	Joachim	Nunner, Catharina	D	295
Hellstern, Carolina	22, Sept 1850	Joseph	Haar, Barbara	D	234
Hellstern, Elisabeth	2, June 1855	Joachim	Nuner, Catharina	C	
Hellstern, Eva	19, Oct. 1851	Christian	Merz, Agatha	D	288
Hellstern, Jacob	24, Oct. 1858	Michael	----, Catherine	D	122
Hellstern, Johan Nepomuck	19, Mar. 1857	Joachim	Nonner, Catharina	D	81
Hellstern, Joseph	25, Aug. 1850	Christian	Marz, Agatha	D	229
Hellstern, Maria Anna	7, Jan. 1853	Christian	Marz, Agatha	D	363
Hellstern, Maria Anna	17, Apr. 1853	Joachim	Lunering, Catharina	D	380
Hellstern, Walburga Catharina	30, Apr. 1858	August	----, Mary	E	532
Helm, Henry Francis	15, Oct. 1854	Joseph	Schlief, Clementine	A	
Helman, Anna Maria	13, Aug. 1852	H. Heinrich	---man, Dina	K	
Helman, Herman Francis	22, June 1856	Aloysius	Bernard, Maria	K	
Helmbacher, Aloysius	18, Dec. 1853	Herman	Oerly, Catharina	L	
Helmeg, Georg Herman	26, Dec. 1858	Herman	Krissler, Anna Maria	D	127
Helmers, Anna Maria	6, June 1852	Herman	Krüseler, Anna Maria	D	323
Helmers, Anton Bernard	2, Mar. 1856	Bernard H.	Kriesser, Anna Maria	D	53
Helmes, Anna Maria Francisca	3, Feb. 1856	Herman	Kohl, AnnaT.	C	
Helmes, Anna Theresa	16, Mar. 1858	Herman	Kople, Theresa	C	
Helmes, Herman Heinrich	28, June 1857	J. Anton	Taphorn, Bernardina	A	
Helmes, Johan Heinrich	25, June 1859	Bernard H.	Fideldei, M. Angela	T	
Helmes, Maria Catharina					

Name of Child	Date of Baptism	Father	Mother	Church	Page
Helmich, Elisabeth Louisa	30, July 1857	Joseph	Schultz, Maria Anna	D	91
Helmich, Johan Bernard	28, June 1855	Joseph	Schulte, Maria Margaretha	D	37
Helmich, Johan Georg	10, Aug. 1851	J. Heinrich	Schulte, M. Margaret Angela	D	277
Helmich, Johan Heinrich	8, Oct. 1858	Heinrich	Nonb---, Christina	D	121
Helmich, M. Elisabeth Phil. Catharina	23, Feb. 1854	Gerhard	Maier, Elisabeth	D	5
Helmich, Margaretha Rosina	5, May 1853	J. Joseph	Schulte, Margaretha Angela	D	384
Helmich, Maria Theresa	15, Aug. 1850	J. Gerhard	Messmair, Marianna	D	228
Helmig, Bernad Mathias	26, Sept 1858	Bernard	Tepe, M. Catharina	T	
Helmig, Euphemia Margaretha	25, Nov. 1858	Johan	Schroeder, Agnes	C	
Helmig, Gerhard Heinrich	14, Sept 1855	Heinrich	Vonhollen, Christina	D	42
Helmig, Maria Catharina	23, Aug. 1859	Joseph	Schulte, M. Angela	T	
Helmig, Maria Elisabeth	17, Sept 1859	Gerhard	Riehemann, Maria Elis.	T	
Helming, Anna Theresa Philomena	6, Apr. 1859	Herman	Hilvert, Maria	L	
Helming, Bernard Heinrich	31, Aug. 1856	Bernard H.	Hülfert, Anna Maria	D	66
Helming, Bernard Herman Gerhard	29, Mar. 1854	Bernard H.	Hilfort, Maria Anna	A	
Helming, Johan Herman	15, Oct. 1856	Georg J.	Schroeder, Agnes	C	
Helming, M. Bernardina Clara	13, Dec. 1859	Johan	Schroeder, Agnes	C	
Helmkamp, Anna Agnes	11, May 1856	C. Heinrich	Eberle, Elisabeth	R	
Helmkamp, Bernard Heinrich	26, July 1854	Christ. H.	Eberle, Elisabeth	R	
Helmkamp, Bernard Heinrich	25, July 1852	Christopher	Eberle, Elisabeth	R	
Helmkamp, Florenz	14, Aug. 1854	Christopher	Eberle, Elisabeth	R	
Helms, Adam Anton	2, Oct. 1859	Anton	Taphorn, Bernardina	A	
Helms, Johan Anton	6, May 1857	J. Heinrich	Kraus, Marianna	A	
Helms, M. Elisabeth	19, Apr. 1859	Heinrich	Kraus, A. Maria	T	
Helmstadt, Herman	27, Feb. 1859	Francis	Findel, Barbara	R	
Helmstadt, Maria Catharina	5, June 1853	Francis	Friedel, Barbara	F	
Helmstadt, Susanna	19, Nov. 1854	Francis	Friedel, Barbara	F	
Helmstatter, Anna Maria	7, Sept 1856	Stephan	Wilzbach, Margaretha	C	
Helmstätter, Catharina Margaretha	19, Jan. 1851	Johan	Wildsbach, Margaretha	D	249
Helmstedt, Ann Mary	12, Oct. 1856	Francis	----, Barbara	R	
Helmstedt, Francis	23, Oct. 1853	Johan	Willsbey, Margaretha	K	
Helmuth, Wilhelm Ferdinand	18, July 1852	Joseph	Graef, Maria	C	
Heltel, Wilhelmina	7, June 1857	Michael	Heck, Theresa	F	
Heltman, Leonard	27, Oct. 1851	George	----, Maria Theresa	H	
Helweg, Carl Heinrich	17, Nov. 1858	Herman	Earley, Catharina	L	
Helweg, Joseph Herman	25, Sept 1859	Joseph	Rufin, Barbara	L	
Helweg, Joseph Ludwig	23, Dec. 1855	Heinrich	Erly, Catharina	L	
Heman, Anna Maria Antonetta	9, Mar. 1856	Joseph A.	Deville, Anna Margaretha	A	
Heman, Johan Friedrich	28, Mar. 1858	J. Anton	Deville, Anna Margaretha	A	
Heman, Laura Catharina Bernardina	7, Aug. 1853	J. Anton	Deville, Anna Margaretha	A	
Heman, Marianna	15, Jan. 1853	F. Heinrich	Brox, Marianna	D	364
Hemann, Agnes Catharina	29, Aug. 1857	Lambert	Henneke, Catharina	C	
Hemann, Anna Elisabeth	8, Dec. 1850	Heinrich	Schoetmann, Theresa	C	
Hemann, Georg Heinrich	5, Nov. 1857	Herman	Schuttmer, Theresa	C	
Hemann, Herman Bernard	17, Oct. 1855	Herman	Schoettmer, Theresa	C	
Hemann, Johan Heinrich	19, Dec. 1858	Heinrich	Runte, Louisa	C	
Hemann, Joseph Anton	20, July 1851	Joseph	Deville, A. Margaretha	L	
Hemann, Josephina Sophia	15, Nov. 1857	Tobias H.	Stricker, M. Gertrud	C	
Hemann, Lambert Andreas H.	20, Mar. 1854	Lambert	Heneke, Catharina	C	
Hemann, Maria Angela	27, May 1853	Herman	Schoetmer, Theresa	C	
Hemann, Maria Catharina Johanna	5, Feb. 1856	Heinrich	Stricker, Gertrud	C	
Hemberger, Francis Joseph	31, Oct. 1858	Joseph	Milz, Rosa	R	
Hembrock, Anna Maria	12, Oct. 1851	Gerhard H.	Bolte, A. Margaretha	L	
Hembrock, Georg Heinrich	5, Jan. 1854	Heinrich	Bueltel, Anna Maria	F	
Hembrock, Maria Theresa Angela	18, Aug. 1859	Joseph	Lueben, M. Adelheid	L	
Hemker, Clara Maria	9, June 1859	Heinrich	Steckmann, M. Cath.	L	
Hemmelmeier, Johan	1, Nov. 1853	J. Bernard	Wehmeier, Cath. Elisabeth	L	
Hemmelmeier, Maria Elisabeth	28, Jan. 1855	Friedrich	Gallhaus, Antonia	D	27
Hemmes, Maria	5, Oct. 1851		adult	F	

Name of Child	Date of Baptism	Father	Mother	Church	Page
Hempe, Elisabeth Gertrud	9, Dec. 1857	Herman	Henke, Elisabeth	A	
Hempe, Joseph	18, Nov. 1855	John	Mandly, Mary	B	22
Hempelman, Bernard Herman	18, Feb. 1856	Bernard	Engel, Catharina Maria Elis.	D	52
Hempelmann, Dorothea Elisabeth	1, Apr. 1858	Bernard	Grafe, Elisabeth	T	
Hempelmann, Friedrich Bd. Eduard	27, Oct. 1859	Bernard	Grafe, Elisabeth	T	
Hempen, Maria Magdalena	20, Aug. 1855	Herman	Henke, Elisabeth	A	
Hemsaat, Heinrich	14, Feb. 1857	Heinrich	Froehlinghaus, Catharina	C	
Hemsath, Bernardina Theodora Henr.	15, Nov. 1855	Heinrich	Robbeloth, Henrietta	L	
Hemsath, Josephina Henrietta	21, Jan. 1858	Heinrich	Robbeloth, Henrietta	L	
Hemsteger, Alphonse Joseph	2, Mar. 1856	Joseph	Dobmeyer, Theresa	R	
Henahan, Honora	4, Mar. 1854	Michael	Moreghan, Bridget	P	72
Henahan, Mary Ann	20, July 1856	Michael	Flinn, Mary	B	31
Henderick, James	3, Oct. 1855	Michael	Dawrow, Mary	P	154
Henderson, James	14, June 1856	James	Colbert, Catherine	E	374
Henderson, Mary	8, Oct. 1857	George	----, Julia	E	484
Hendrick, John	1, Dec. 1859	Miles	Doran, Mary	P	305
Hendrick, Martin	7, Feb. 1858	Miles	Doran, Mary	P	238
Hendricks, August Edward Anton	23, Sept 1858	J. Gerhard	Berger, Maria Elisabeth	K	
Hendricks, Johan Heinrich	11, Jan. 1854	J. Heinrich	Bagge, Elisabeth	K	
Hendricks, Joseph	23, Nov. 1856	Johan	Bagge, Maria	K	
Hendricks, Maria Elisabeth Bernardina	27, Dec. 1857	Heinrich	Schürman, Catharina	A	
Hendricks, Sarah Jane	30, May 1850		adult - 14 years old	B	203
Hendy, Adelaide Elizabeth	17, Mar. 1858	Samuel	Hart, Kate	B	56
Henekes, Maria Catharina	11, Dec. 1852	J. Gerhard	Going, Maria Anna	C	
Henessmann, Maria Elisabeth	11, Mar. 1855	J. Bernard	Kemper, M. Elisabeth	L	
Heney, Edward	1, Dec. 1852	William	Mulfether, Mary	B	277
Heney, Francis	11, Jan. 1852	Francis	Carr, Ellen	P	16
Heney, Mary Ann	11, Jan. 1852	Francis	Carr, Ellen	P	16
Heng, John Nicolaus	18, June 1854	J. George	----, Josephine	H	
Hengehold, Anna Maria Adelheid	30, Jan. 1857	Wilhelm H.	Windmeyer, Anna Maria	L	
Hengelad, Herman Friedrich	27, Apr. 1851	Friedrich	Krake, Louisa	D	263
Henges, Adam Jacob	14, Nov. 1858	Adam	Haas, Catharina	A	
Henges, Carl	28, Sept 1856	Adam	Haas, Catharina	A	
Henges, Heinrich	29, July 1855	Adam	Haas, Catharina	A	
Henges, Johan	15, Mar. 1857	Johan	Meyer, Christina	A	
Henges, Maria	13, Nov. 1853	Johan	Meyer, Christina	A	
Henghold, Bernard Heinrich	19, July 1859	Wilhelm	Wiedmeyer, Anna Maria	L	
Henig, Maria Elisabeth	7, June 1852	Theodor	Botig, Anna Maria	F	
Henigan, Stephen	13, June 1852	John	----, Bridget	E	423
Henigge, Francis Joseph	14, Dec. 1858	Francis	Ross, Anna Maria	D	126
Henke, Aloysius	14, Apr. 1853	Peter Paul	Froelich, Elisabeth	D	380
Henke, Catharina	21, Aug. 1859	Vincent	Handeschak, Anna	D	144
Henke, Ignatius	23, July 1854	Paul	Fröhlich, Elisabeth	D	14
Henke, Johan Heinrich	25, Mar. 1855	Heinrich	Krieger, Anna Elisabeth	D	32
Henke, Josephiina	14, Dec. 1856	Paul	Froehlich, Elisabeth	D	74
Henke, Margaretha	27, July 1856	Vincent	Handeschak, Anna Friedrica	D	63
Henke, Maria	7, Sept 1856	Balthasar H.	Krieger, Anna Elisabeth	D	67
Henke, Maria	9, Nov. 1851	Peter Paul	Fröhlich, Elisabeth	D	291
Henke, Maria Gertrud	15, May 1859	Balthasar	Speckman, Anna Elisabeth	D	138
Henke, Peter Paul	16, Jan. 1859	Peter Paul	Fröhlich, Elisabeth	D	129
Henke, Philomena	4, Feb. 1855	Vincent	Handeschek, Anna	D	27
Henke, Theodor Johan	1, Nov. 1857	Vincent	Hoeg, Anna Friedrica	D	98
Henkel, August Joseph	4, July 1858	Leopold	Müller, Rosina	R	
Henkel, Constantine	12, Sept 1858	August	Eckert, Margaret	R	
Henkel, Joseph	1, Feb. 1853	August	Eckhardt, Margaretha	R	
Henkel, Maria Catharina Margaretha	4, Mar. 1858	Valentin	Bräutigam, Rosina	K	
Henkin, Rosanne	16, June 1850	Peter	Reilly, Bridget	B	205
Henkmann, Catharina Anna Elisabeth	23, Oct. 1859	Bernard	Mette, Catharina	F	
Henley, Bridget	28, Nov. 1852	John	----, Bridget	M	

Name of Child	Date of Baptism	Father	Mother	Church	Page
Henn, Barbara	25, May 1855	Anton	Reich, Maria	K	
Henne, Eduard Constantin	28, Dec. 1851	Carl	Schwer, Josephine	C	
Hennehan, Bridget	14, Jan. 1853	Thomas	McDonald, Ann	B	281
Hennehan, John Patrick	20, Jan. 1856	Thomas	McDonald, Ann	B	24
Hennehan, John Thomas	30, Mar. 1858	Thomas	McDonald, Ann	B	57
Hennehan, Mary Ann	22, June 1854	Thomas	McDonald, Ann	B	1
Hennehan, Mary Ann	15, Mar. 1857	Thomas	McDonald, Ann	F	
Hennel, Andreas	4, Feb. 1855	Peter	----, Margaretha	U	
Hennel, Burchard	1, Mar. 1857	Peter	Pennua, Margaret	Q	20
Hennel, Catharina	11, May 1851	Jacob	Brusy, Barbara	D	264
Hennel, Catharina	2, Feb. 1851	Peter	Bennoa, Margaretha	J	10
Hennel, Peter	3, Apr. 1853	Peter	Bennoa, Margaretha	J	20
Hennelly, Eliza	6, July 1851	John	Dowling, Winefred	B	235
Hennes?, Elizabeth	26, Feb. 1850	George	Casey, Caroline	B	197
Hennesey, Margaret Louise	9, Nov. 1856	William	Murphy, Bridget	E	412
Hennessey, Elizabeth	3, Nov. 1859	William	Rogers, Catherine	E	667
Hennessey, Henry	17, Feb. 1858	James	Scully, Ann	E	517
Hennessey, Mary	12, Feb. 1859	William	Murphy, Bridget	E	603
Hennessy, Catherine	19, Jan. 1850	Patrick	Cotter, Bridget	B	194
Hennessy, Cecilia	5, Dec. 1855	Thomas	Springin, Jane	B	22
Hennessy, Elizabeth	29, Oct. 1854	Joseph	McBride, Margaret	P	101
Hennessy, Helen	18, May 1853	John	Heasity?, Mary	B	291
Hennessy, John	6, Nov. 1853	Andrew	Welsh, Ellen	E	141
Hennessy, John	17, Aug. 1856	James	Lawler, Mary	V	32
Hennessy, John	20, Apr. 1851	John	Hanley, Mary	B	230
Hennessy, John	13, Apr. 1851	Patrick	Cutter, Bridget	B	229
Hennessy, John	2, May 1858	Thomas	Spinken, Jane	B	58
Hennessy, Laura Ann	16, Jan. 1858	John	Mandly, Mary	B	54
Hennessy, Margaret	15, Oct. 1850	Richard	Holahan, Catherine	B	216
Hennessy, Margaret	3, Dec. 1854	William	Coleman, Mary	E	245
Hennessy, Margaret Ann	20, June 1852	----	----, ----	P	23
Hennessy, Mary	22, Aug. 1858	Andrew	Welsch, Ellen	B	63
Hennessy, Mary	5, Sept 1852	Martin	Ryan, Mary	E	14
Hennessy, Mary	14, Sept 1854	Patrick	Rony, Ann	E	224
Hennessy, Mary	19, Apr. 1854	Thomas	Springer, Jane	B	313
Hennessy, Mary Catherine	11, Oct. 1857	Robert	Anderson, Adaline	P	**227**
Hennessy, Mary Theresa	22, May 1856	Joseph	McBride, Margaret	P	180
Hennessy, Maurice	28, June 1857	William J.	Byrne, Bridget	B	46
Hennessy, Richard	20, Feb. 1853	Richard	Holahan, Catherine	B	284
Hennessy, Richard	19, June 1859	William	Nagle, Joanne	B	76
Hennessy, William	16, May 1858	Edmund	Ryan, Mary	P	248
Hennessy, William	20, May 1852	Joseph	McBride, Margaret	P	22
Hennessy, William	3, Apr. 1853	Patrick	----, ----	U	
Hennesy, John	4, May 1855	James	Lawler, Mary	B	14
Hennigan, John	15, Apr. 1855	Michael	Corcoran, Winnefred	E	280
Hennigan, Mary Ann	5, June 1853	Michael	Corcoran, Winny	E	95
Hennigan, Michael	2, Aug. 1857	Michael	Corcoran, Winifred	B	47
Henniger, Johan	15, July 1855	Thomas	Schüttelmeyer, Magdalena	J	32
Henniger, Martin	4, Apr. 1858	Thomas	Schindelmaier, Magdalena	W	22
Henniger, Peter	14, Sept 1856	Thomas	Schindermeier, Magdalena	D	67
Hennikes, Anna Maria	1, Dec. 1857	Gerhard	Hoing, Maria	C	
Henning, Anna Adelheid	15, June 1858	Wilhelm	Hagenhoff, Maria Anna	A	
Henning, Charles	9, Sept 1855	Charles	----, Louise	H	
Henning, Johan Carl	5, Oct. 1851	Carl	Pabst, Louise	C	
Henning, Maria	22, June 1850	Thomas	Schindelmeier, Magdalena	D	218
Henning, Mary Catherine	2, Oct. 1853	Charles	----, Louise	H	
Henning, Wilhelm	18, Sept 1853	Thomas	Schindelmeier, Magdalena	D	406
Henny, Bridget	4, Sept 1859	Michael	Widney, Catharine	G	
Henny, Cecilia	14, Dec. 1851	William	----, Honora	B	247

Name of Child	Date of Baptism	Father	Mother	Church	Page
Henny, Ellen Margaret	17, Aug. 1856	John	Malony, Ellen	B	32
Henny, Patrick	28, July 1853	Patrick	Towey, Isabell	B	296
Henretty, Maria	23, Aug. 1857	Peter	----, Maria Anna	R	
Henretty, Martha Ann	27, May 1855	Peter	Dillon, Mary A.	R	
Henrety, Margaret Elisabeth	8, May 1859	Peter	Dillon, Ann Mary	R	
Henri, Stephan	6, Dec. 1857	Patrick	Costeler, Margaret	Q	25
Henrich, Heinrich	11, Dec. 1853	Michael	Helfering, Barbara	L	
Henrich, Johan	21, Nov. 1858	Michael	Helfrich, Barbara	T	
Henrich, Ludwig	8, Sept 1851	Michael	Helfrich, Barbara	L	
Henrichs, Agnes Elisabeth	22, Dec. 1850	G. Heinrich	Bagge, Elisabeth	K	
Henrichs, Catharina Elisabeth Philomena	4, Aug. 1856	Heinrich	Schürman, Catharina	A	
Henrichs, Heinrich	14, Jan. 1855	Heinrich	adult - 37 years old	K	
Henrichsmann, Johan	24, Aug. 1851	Bernard	Kemper, Elisabeth	F	
Henriden, Mary	17, July 1858	Felix	Lamb, Mary	E	549
Henrigan, Catherine	23, Aug. 1851	James	McCann, Ellen	E	334
Henrigan, Joanne	7, July 1855	John	Early, Ann	E	299
Henrigan, Mary	7, July 1855	John	Early, Ann	E	299
Henrigsman, Maria Anna Catharina	7, Sept 1858	Bernard	Kemper, Elisabeth	T	
Henry, Bridget	13, Nov. 1853	William	Hayden, Sarah	P	59
Henry, Catherine	17, June 1855	John	Molony, Ellen	B	16
Henry, Charles	27, Aug. 1852	Patrick	Tracy, Mary	E	10
Henry, Elizabeth	17, July 1853	Michael	----, Bridget	E	110
Henry, George	9, Feb. 1851	George	----, Caecilia	E	281
Henry, John	29, Aug. 1854	Alexander	Rinn, Mary	V	16
Henry, John	13, June 1855	Bartholomew	Gallagher, Bridget	B	15
Henry, Margaret	20, July 1851	Patrick	Tracy, Mary	E	325
Henry, Mary	8, Mar. 1857	Bartholomew	Gallagher, Bridget	B	41
Henry, Mary	11, Sept 1853	Patrick	Tracy, Mary	E	127
Henry, Michael	23, Feb. 1851	John	McDonough, Bridget	B	225
Henry, Patrick	17, Dec. 1858	Bartholomew	Gallagher, Bridget	B	68
Henry, William	12, Nov. 1856	Henry	Holighan, Joanne	E	413
Henry, William	12, Aug. 1852	Michael	----, Bridget	E	4
Henschen, Wilhelm August	13, Apr. 1851	Heinrich	Lubbe, Maria	K	
Henscher, Francis Joseph	14, Sept 1856	Heinrich	Lubbe, Anna Maria	A	
Henscher, Maria Anna	26, Oct. 1853	Heinrich	Lübbe, Maria Anna	A	
Hense, Christina Elisabeth	21, Aug. 1859	Johan J.	Knob, Gertrud	C	
Henseler, Johan	2, Mar. 1858	Peter	Moore, Maria	G	
Henseler, Peter	16, Oct. 1856	Peter	Moure, Maria	G	
Hensen, Anna Maria Elisabeth	16, May 1851	Bernard	Timpe, Maria	C	
Hensen, Anna Maria Theresa	26, Apr. 1850	Herman	Meyermann, Theresa	C	
Hensen, Bernard Heinrich Gustav	6, Oct. 1853	Bernard	Timpe, Maria	C	
Hensen, Georg Ludwig	6, Mar. 1859	Bernard	Timpe, Anna Maria	F	
Hensen, Ludwig Anton	29, Mar. 1857	Bernard	Timpe, Anna M.	C	
Hensen, Maria Amalia	20, Sept 1855	Bernard	Timpe, Anna Maria	C	
Hensey, Mary Ann	28, Nov. 1854	Michael	Cavanaugh, Bridget	P	106
Hensler, Anna Francisca	24, Sept 1854	J. Nepomuck	Piper, Bernardina	D	18
Hensler, Johan August	26, Dec. 1852	Johan N.	Piper, Bernardina	D	362
Hensler, Josephina	9, May 1850	J. Heinrich	Tepe, Gertrud	A	
Hensler, Ludwig Wilhelm	10, July 1859	Johan	Ordenberg, Maria	T	
Hensohn, Ann Mary	11, June 1854	John	----, Magdalena	H	
Hensohn, Maria Magdalena	10, July 1857	Georg	Otwein, Maria Gertrud	D	89
Henson, Mary	5, Aug. 1851	Peter	Fallon, Mary	B	238
Henson, Peter	13, Nov. 1852	Peter	Fallon, Mary	B	275
Hentjes, Heinrich	12, May 1850	Johan	Meier, Christina	J	6
Hentjes, Johan	27, May 1851	Johan	Meier, Christina	J	12
Henton, John	11, Mar. 1855	Peter	Farrell, Mary	P	125
Hentschen, Christina	21, Nov. 1852	J. Georg	Heitz, Christina	C	
Hentz, Maria Louisa	26, Oct. 1851	Joseph	Frischholz, Maria A.	K	
Hentzer, Rosalia	25, July 1859	Heinrich	Tinn, Eva	H	

Name of Child	Date of Baptism	Father	Mother	Church	Page
Henvin, John	15, Feb. 1857		Henvin, Ann	E	434
Henz, Carl	15, Aug. 1858	Ludwig	Beutel, Catharina	F	
Henz, Peter Wendelin	16, Oct. 1859	Georg	Duls, Juliana	K	
Henzerling, Carl Bernard	30, Nov. 1856	Conrad	Waldbillig, Eva	F	
Henzerling, Catharina	26, Sept 1858	Conrad	Waldbillig, Eva	F	
Heough, Sarah Mary	12, May 1850	Patrick	McCane, Margaret	B	202
Hepp, Johan	19, Nov. 1854	Johan	Frank, Margaretha	A	
Hepp, Louisa	7, June 1857	Johan	Gasig, Anna Margaretha	A	
Heppenheimer, Dorothea Carolina	11, June 1854	Louis	----, Christine	H	
Heppenheimer, Elisabeth	17, May 1857	Louis	Graf, Christina	H	
Heppenheimer, Louis	25, Sept 1859	Louis	Graf, Christina	H	
Heppenheimer, Maria Anna	18, July 1852	Louis	----, Christine	H	
Hepperger, Philoeman	11, Apr. 1851		Hepperger, Elisabeth	D	260
Heppert, Johan Joseph	13, Sept 1852	Georg	Kufel, Barbara	C	
Hepperton, Charlotte Elizabeth	30, Apr. 1852	John	Lane, Charlotte	B	258
Herb, Eva	6, Jan. 1854	Aloysius	Stern, Agatha	G	
Herb, George	14, Oct. 1855	Charles	----, Agatha	H	
Herb, James	27, July 1857	Charles	Hanselman, Agatha	H	
Herb, Maria	13, Oct. 1850	Aloysius	Stern, Agatha	F	
Herb, Peter	20, May 1859	Charles	Hanselman, Agatha	H	
Herbe, Adam	22, Aug. 1852	Aloysius	Stern, Agatha	Q	2
Herbeler, Maria Josephina	27, Sept 1859	Herman	Hölterman, Margaretha	A	
Herber, Heinrich	17, Jan. 1854	Francis M.	Linder, Elisabeth	L	
Herber, Walburga Monica	19, Nov. 1851	Joseph	Kies, Walburga	J	12
Herberding, Josephina Catharina	1, Oct. 1850	Francis H.	Brinkmann, Bernardina	L	
Herberding, Maria Anna	1, Aug. 1854	Francis	Brinkmann, Bernardina	C	
Herberding, Rosa Catharina	17, Jan. 1858	Francis	Brinkmann, Bernardina	C	
Herberger, Johan	19, Dec. 1852	Michael	Linder, Elisabeth	L	
Herberger, Philomena	22, Dec. 1850	Francis M	Linder, Elisabeth	C	
Herberling, Francis Heinrich	10, Dec. 1856	Francis	Brinkmann, Bernardina	C	
Herbermann, Franz Theodor	24, Nov. 1851	Heinrich	Grotmann, Maria Anna	L	
Herbermann, Heinrich Franz	12, Sept 1856	J. Heinrich	Grotmann, Maria A.	L	
Herbers, Gerhard Heinrich	23, Nov. 1852	J. Heinrich	Jaspers, Maria Angela	K	
Herbers, Herman Wilhelm	9, June 1859	Heinrich	Jaspers, Maria Angela	K	
Herbers, Johan Heinrich	13, Feb. 1856	J. Heinrich	Jaspers, Maria Angela	K	
Herbers, Johan Joseph	1, Apr. 1853	J. Bernard	Linnemann, Maria	F	
Herbers, Maria Elisabeth	27, Feb. 1858	J. Gerhard	Tengemann, Bernardina	L	
Herbers, Maria Elisabeth Philomena	10, Aug. 1854	Heinrich	Jaspers, Maria Angela	K	
Herbert, Andrew	11, July 1859	Jeremiah	Lindy, Catherine	P	288
Herbert, Charles	6, Nov. 1853	Charles	Riley, Mary	E	142
Herbert, John Henry	10, Mar. 1858	Heinrich	----, Louisa Friedrica	R	
Herbert, Josephina Regina	14, Jan. 1857	Heinrich	----, Louisa	R	
Herbert, Lucy	1, Jan. 1852	Patrick	Ireland, Matilda	B	249
Herbert, Luke	21, May 1854	Michael	Connell, Honora	P	83
Herbert, Mary Josephine	19, May 1850	Patrick	----, Matilda Ann	E	215
Herbert, Sarah	12, Feb. 1854	Patrick	Johnson, Matilda Ann	B	309
Herbig, Wilhelmina	25, Sept 1859	Johan K.	----, Apollonia	D	147
Herbst, Maria Elisabeth	17, July 1859	Henry	Borlt, Louise	R	
Herbst, Maria Elisabeth	11, Apr. 1855	J. Mathias	Rensen, M. Elisabeth	L	
Herbstreit, Emma	11, June 1856	Francis	Kanzler, Theresa	F	
Herbstreit, Georg	9, Nov. 1851	Johan	Strecke, Rosina	C	
Herbstrith, Edmund	27, Aug. 1858	Francis	Kanzler, Theresa	D	118
Herby, Andreas August	28, Aug. 1853	Johan B.	Hoffmann, Magdalena	F	
Herders, Anna Sophia	28, Apr. 1853	Johan	Kockman, Gertrud	A	
Herders, Heinrich Georg	30, Aug. 1854	Johan	Kockman, Gertrud	A	
Herdes, Charles Thomas	20, Nov. 1853	Charles	----, Helen	B	302
Herdhoff, Johan Heinrich	8, Apr. 1858	J. Heinrich	Kuhlman, Maria Anna	N	
Herfel, Appolonia	10, Apr. 1853	Francis	Schwarz, Anna	D	379
Herfett, Jacob	11, Oct. 1857	Francis	Schwarz, Anna	W	20

Name of Child	Date of Baptism	Father	Mother	Church	Page
Herfl, Johan August	11, May 1857	Caspar	Holtmeier, Maria	D	84
Herfort, Johan Caspar	20, May 1855	Caspar	Holdhaus, Catharina	D	35
Herft, Johan Mathias	16, Jan. 1853	J. Mathias	Rensen, Elisabeth W.	F	
Herft, Marianna	1, Nov. 1859	J. Mathias	Renzen, Maria Elisabeth	F	
Hergel, Heinrich Carl	9, Mar. 1856	Heinrich C.	Bach, Theresa	A	
Hergel, Theresa Francisca Carolina	25, Feb. 1855	Carl	Bach, Theresa	A	
Herger, Catharina	30, Mar. 1856	Francis	Dick, Elisabeth	Q	14
Herger, Jacob	12, Oct. 1851	Francis	Dick, Elisabeth	Q	1
Herget, Maria Theresa Emilia	31, May 1857	Heinrich	Bach, Theresa	C	
Hergin, Julia Ann	27, Dec. 1857	Dennis	Ward, Ann	P	233
Hergis, Timothy	2, May 1853	Edward	Williams, Mary	P	40
Hericks, Anna Maria	20, Mar. 1856	Caspar	Stockbrings, Theresa	D	54
Herins, William	24, Jan. 1858	John	Feghery, Catherine	B	55
Herlehy, Bridget	10, Dec. 1858	David	Sullivan, Ellen	B	68
Herler, Philomena Louisa	18, Apr. 1852	Jacob	Recher, Maria Elisabeth	K	
Herley, Dennis Ignatius	31, July 1850	Dennis	----, Catharina	K	
Herlich, Jacob	14, July 1855	Johan	Collet, Theresa	D	38
Herlich, Maria	17, Sept 1857	Johan	Collet, Theresa	D	94
Herlich, Peter	22, June 1851	Johan A.	Collet, Theresa	D	269
Herlick, Jacob Washington	27, Feb. 1854	J. Napoleon	Collet, Theresa	D	5
Herlihy, Daniel	31, Aug. 1859	John	Ring, Mary	E	651
Herlinger, Franz Carl Edward	24, June 1857	Mathias	Ege, Maria	F	
Herlinger, Louisa Charlotte	29, Aug. 1858	Mathias	Ege, Maria Charlotte	F	
Herman, Adam	28,, Apr. 1850	Jacob	Pfarr, Catharina	H	
Herman, Anthony	6, Apr. 1856	James	----, Mary	E	356
Herman, Carolina	7, Aug. 1853	Friedrich	----, Frances	U	
Herman, Catharina	10, Apr. 1853	Sigmund	Brandt, Maria Anna	L	
Herman, Francisca	8, Jan. 1855	Friedrich	Folzenlagen, Francisca	D	26
Herman, George	30, May 1858	Xavier	Mattis, Ottilia	U	
Herman, Henry James	31, July 1853	James	----, Catherine	H	
Herman, Jacob	29, July 1855	Sigmund	Braun, Maria Anna	R	
Herman, John	13, Jan. 1857	Francis X.	Mattis, Ottilia	Q	19
Herman, Joseph	10, Jan. 1858	Conrad	Schaller, Francisca	D	102
Herman, Joseph	17, May 1857	Sigmund	----, Maria Anna	R	
Herman, Louisa	29, Apr. 1858	Friedrich	Folzenlohen, Francisca	D	110
Herman, Maria	6, July 1856	Conrad	Schäfer, Francisca	D	62
Herman, Maria Magdalena	28, June 1857	Valentin	Spaeth, Catherine	R	
Herman, Mary Theresa	25, Mar. 1858	John H.	Tooby, Kate	B	57
Herman?, Elisabeth	9, Aug. 1857	Johan	Margner, Margaretha	D	92
Hermann, Carolina	3, May 1858	Joseph	Gehring, Agatha	F	
Hermann, Catharina	9, Apr. 1854	Joseph	Bogner, M. Anna	C	
Hermann, Elisabeth	14, Dec. 1854	Joseph	Gehring, Maria Agatha	F	
Hermann, Emma	13, Oct. 1856	Joseph	Gehring, Maria Agatha	F	
Hermann, Franz Michael	4, Aug. 1856	Lawrence	Philipp, Sophia	F	
Hermann, Georg	2, Apr. 1854	Jacob	Gruensteiner, Magd.	C	
Hermann, Georg Herman	18, Mar. 1855	Herman	Holtermann, Margaretha	F	
Hermann, Heinrich Georg	23, Feb. 1858	Joseph	Jung, Susanna	F	
Hermann, Johan Herman	31, Aug. 1856	Joseph	Bogner, M. Anna	C	
Hermann, Johanna	21, Aug. 1859	Adam	Wagner, Anna	C	
Hermann, Josephina Maria	12, Nov. 1854	Joseph	Jung, Susanna	F	
Hermann, Louise	27, Feb. 1853	Gabriel	Adams, Meta	C	
Hermann, Maria Anna	2, May 1858	Joseph	Bogner, M. Anna	C	
Hermann, Maria Louisa	3, July 1850	Jacob	Grunsteiner, Magdal.	C	
Hermann, Michael Otto	5, Dec. 1852	Lawrence	Philipp, Sophia	F	
Hermann, Philomena	23, Apr. 1854	Gabriel	Adams, Johanna	C	
Hermann, Susanna Magdalena	3, Oct. 1852	Joseph	Jung, Susanna	F	
Hermann, Theresa	19, Oct. 1856	Adam	Wagner, Anna	C	
Hermbeck, Maria Margaretha	25, Dec. 1858	Bernard W.	Benkhof, Margaretha	D	127
Hermeling, Gerhard Bernard Franz	28, Oct. 1859	J. Bernard	Welling, Anna Maria	F	

Name of Child	Date of Baptism	Father	Mother	Church	Page
Hermeling, Johan Theodor Herman	6, June 1851	J. Bernard	Willing, Anna Maria	F	
Hermeling, Maria Elisabeth	13, Mar. 1854	J. Bernard	Welling, Maria Anna	F	
Hermeling, Marianna	25, Nov. 1855	Bernard	Willing, Anna Maria	F	
Hermeling, Marianna Agnes	18, June 1858	Bernard	Welling, Anna Maria	F	
Hermers, Anna Maria Christina	10, Oct. 1855	Gerhard	Mueller, Gesina S.	L	
Hermers, Johan Gerhard	11, July 1858	J. Gerhard	Moeller, Gesina Sophia	L	
Hermers, Maria Anna	18, May 1854	J. Gerhard	----, ----	L	
Hermes, Augusta Clara Johanna	19, July 1857	Anton	Dierix, Henrietta	F	
Hermes, Maria Theresa	4, Dec. 1859	Anton	Dierichs, Henrietta	F	
Hern, Joseph	1, Mar. 1857	Simon	Wetter, Catharina	D	80
Hern, Mary Josephine	23, June 1857	John	----, Ellen	E	461
Hernan?, Mary Caroline	5, June 1853	Samuel	----, Emma	E	95
Herold, Alfred	15, Mar. 1856	Michael	Englasley, Catherine	B	26
Herold, Andreas	7, Sept 1856	Andreas	Barbich, Susanna	D	67
Herold, Anna Barbara	27, Jan. 1850	Johan	Wutke, Paulina	K	
Herold, Anna Maria	14, Apr. 1850	Johan	Barbich, Christina	D	209
Herold, Elisabeth	1, Oct. 1854	Adam	Kunzmann, Margaretha	F	
Herold, Ellen	20, Feb. 1859	Michael	Inglasley, Catherine	B	71
Herold, Ferdinand August	8, June 1854	August	Bertke, Maria	C	
Herold, Georg	18, Dec. 1853	Andreas	Barbich, Susanna	D	421
Herold, Georg	30, May 1852	Andreas	Barbick, Susanna	D	322
Herold, Georg Adam	26, Dec. 1859	Adam	Kunzmann, Margaretha	F	
Herold, Johan	28, July 1850	Andreas	Barbich, Susanna	D	225
Herold, Mathias	6, Mar. 1859	Andreas	Barbich, Susanna	D	133
Herold, Victor Thomas	22, June 1854	Michael	Inglasley, Catherine	B	1
Heroltz, Johan Martin	21, Mar. 1852	Johan	Wutke, Paulina	K	
Heron, Mary	24, June 1852	James	O'Brien, Alice	B	265
Herran, Ellen	19, Feb. 1853	John	McCawley, Mary Jane	P	36
Herrer, Francis Xavier	13, Sept 1857	Jacob	Binder, Rosina	W	20
Herrhi, Catherine	30, Apr. 1854	Andrew	----, Sophia	H	
Herrier, Anna Francisca	25, Dec. 1859	Jacob	Binder, Rosina	D	153
Herrier, Jacob Philipp	11, Sept 1854	Jacob	Binder, Rosina	W	5
Herrier, Joseph	2, Mar. 1856	Jacob	Binder, Rosina	W	11
Herrier, Peter	20, Apr. 1858	Peter	Dielman, Elisabeth	H	
Herrier, Rosa	9, Nov. 1856	Peter	Dollman, Elisabeth	H	
Herrlich, Theresa	1, Aug. 1852	Johan	Collet, Theresa	F	
Herrn, Elisabeth	24, Nov. 1853	Wilhelm	Kief, Helen	N	18
Herron, Catherine	7, Apr. 1856	James	Cooligan, Helen	P	175
Herron, Mary	28, Feb. 1855	James	Coligan, Ellen	B	12
Herron, Mary Helen	25, Mar. 1858	James	Cooligan, Helen	P	243
Herron, Michael	21, Apr. 1857	James	Coligin, Ellen	B	43
Herron, William	31, Oct. 1852	John	Brennan, Frances	E	31
Herschede, Anna Maria Mechtildis	9, June 1858	Heinrich	Limberg, Maria Anna	A	
Herschede, Franz	30, July 1857	Johan	Linnemann, Maria	L	
Herschede, Franz Johan	11, Sept 1853	Johan	Linnemann, Maria	F	
Herschede, Johan Friedrich	11, Feb. 1855	Johan	Linnemann, M. Elis.	L	
Herschede, Maria Gertrud	5, Feb. 1854	Heinrich	Limberg, Maria	F	
Herschfeld, Johan Paul	2, Aug. 1857	Joseph	Hoffmann, Catharina	C	
Hersel, Elisabeth	1, Nov. 1855	Francis	Schwarz, Anna	F	
Hershede, Anna Margaretha Lisette	13, Jan. 1851	Heinrich	Limberg, Anna Maria	A	
Hertig, Maria Francisca	10, Sept 1850	G. Adam	Meistler, Susanna	D	232
Hertlein, Anna Maria	19, Sept 1858	Georg	Scherpf, Elisabeth	T	
Hertwig, Henrietta Magdalena	14, Oct. 1855	Johan	Helferich, Catharina	C	
Herweg, Johan Gerhard	15, Nov. 1850	Herman	Morhermann, M. Anna	L	
Herwich, Anna Barbara	31, Dec. 1854	J. Friedrich	Heller, Apollonia	D	25
Herwig, Anna Margaretha	28, Feb. 1855	J. Francis	Kalthof, Maria	F	
Herwig, Gerhard	23, June 1857	Francis J.	----, Mary	R	
Herz, Franz	12, Apr. 1857	Vincent	Koenig, Euphemia	F	
Herzog, Adelgunda	29, Jan. 1854	Fridolin	Dumolin, Catharina	C	

Name of Child	Date of Baptism	Father	Mother	Church	Page
Herzog, Anna Maria	1, Oct. 1854	Bernard	Putthof, Christina	K	
Herzog, Anna Maria	5, May 1851	J. Heinrich	Stallo, Elisabeth	F	
Herzog, Anna Maria Clara	27, June 1858	J. Heinrich	Braumes, A.M. Clara	L	
Herzog, Bernard	21, Feb. 1856	Heinrich	Meyer, Agnes	L	
Herzog, Bernard	9, Sept 1858		Herzog, Elisabeth	L	
Herzog, Bernardina	13, Sept 1857	Heinrich	Meier, Maria Anna	L	
Herzog, Catharina Margaretha	9, Nov. 1856	Aloysius	Gilb, Maria Eva	K	
Herzog, Emil Valentin	1, Nov. 1859	Emil	Brosemer, Theresa	F	
Herzog, Herman	1, Dec. 1855	Bernard	Fehr, Anna Maria	F	
Herzog, Johan Clemens	20, Aug. 1853	Bernard H.	Stallo, Maria Elisabeth	F	
Herzog, Johan Franz Heinrich	30, Dec. 1859	J. Heinrich	Braumes, A.M. Elisabeth	L	
Herzog, Johan Heinrich	16, Aug. 1858	Johan B.	Puthoff, Christina	K	
Herzog, Johan Herman Bernard	26, Dec. 1859	Bernard	Vehr, Anna	L	
Herzog, Lisetta Maria	19, Mar. 1859	Anton	Pellewessel, Elisabeth	K	
Herzog, Maria Anna	13, Sept 1857	Bernard	Vehr, Anna Maria	L	
Herzog, Maria Elisabeth	26, Oct. 1852	Bernard	Potter?, Christina	J	18
Herzog, Valentin	3, Nov. 1853	David	Maixner, Josephina	D	413
Herzog, Veronica Carolina	4, Apr. 1858	Aloysius	Gilb, Maria Eva	K	
Hesan, James	12, Dec. 1852	Cornelius	Everight, Joanne	B	277
Hesbacher, Martin	3, Mar. 1850	Cornelius	Walter, Anna Maria	D	204
Hesch, Martin	28, Nov. 1852	Johan	Berwanger, Barbara	D	359
Hesch, Mathias	10, Oct. 1858	Johan	Berwanger, Barbara	U	
Hesch, Sarah	25, Dec. 1859	Johan	Lehnhoff, Sarah	H	
Hescho, Albert Nicolaus	30, Dec. 1855	Anthony	----, Sophia	H	
Hesdorfer, Anna Maria	26, Sept 1854	Michael	Thea, Catharina	D	18
Hesel, Georg	22, Jan. 1857	Francis	Schneberger, Walburga	K	
Heser, Anna	30, Sept 1855	Johan	Karch, Theresa	F	
Heser, Joseph	25, Mar. 1857	Joseph	Karch, Theresa	F	
Hesing, Emil Clemens	23, Nov. 1851	C. Anton	Lamping, Louisa	L	
Hesing, Henrietta Josephina	14, Nov. 1858	Caspar	Friend, Barbara	C	
Heskamp, Bernard Rudolph	5, Feb. 1853	Bernard	Hacke, Euphemia Maria	A	
Heskamp, Johan Bernard Albert	19, Nov. 1857	Gerhard H.	Huelsmann, Anna Maria	L	
Heskamp, Johan Gerhard	23, Aug. 1857	J. Gerhard	Brinker, Gesina	L	
Heskamp, Johan Heinrich	18, Dec. 1856	J. Herman	Büter, Margaretha	K	
Heskamp, Johan Herman	4, May 1853	Johan	Büter, Margaretha	K	
Heskamp, Maria Catharina	13, Mar. 1855	J. Herman	Buter, Anna Margaretha	K	
Heskamp, Maria Elisabeth	25, Aug. 1858	Herman	Koors, Margaretha	K	
Heskamp, Maria Margaretha Elis.	3, Mar. 1859	J. Gerhard	Brinkel, M. Gesina	L	
Hesling, Carl Andreas	27, Nov. 1859	Adam	Menninger, Maria	F	
Heslop, Mary Charlotte	15, Aug. 1859	George	Storms, Mary	P	293
Hesman, Veronica	17, Sept 1855	H. Heinrich	Graf, Amelia	K	
Hesping, Anna Rosalia	19, May 1855	Herman	Ahlert, Margaretha	F	
Hesping, Maria Agnes	22, Jan. 1857	Herman	Helmes, Adelheid	F	
Hess, Agnes	2, Nov. 1856	John	Globen, Elizabeth	T	
Hess, Anna Maria	26, Nov. 1854	Johan	Hepp, Elisabeth	D	22
Hess, Anton Constantin	13, May 1857	Anton	Volz, Helena	D	85
Hess, Carl	22, July 1855	Caius	Merz, Theodosia	D	39
Hess, Carolina	31, Oct. 1858	Caius	Mertz, Theodosia	T	
Hess, Catharina	26, Sept 1852	Anton	Fey, Margaretha	D	349
Hess, Elisabeth	8, May 1859	Johan	Zern, Elisabeth	T	
Hess, Francis Joseph	1, Jan. 1853	Caspar	Heimkreiden, Elisabeth	D	363
Hess, Georg	25, Oct. 1850	Caspar	Heimkreuter, Elisabeth	D	240
Hess, Johan	21, Aug. 1859	Caspar	Heimkreuter, Elisabeth	D	144
Hess, Johan Joseph	1, Jan. 1850	Johan	----, Catharina Elisabeth	D	197
Hess, Louisa	30, Jan. 1859	Johan	Hepp, Elisabeth	T	
Hess, Magdalena	26, Nov. 1854	Johan	Hepp, Elisabeth	D	22
Hess, Maria	12, Apr. 1851	Johan	Hepp, Elisabeth	F	
Hess, Maria Josephina	21, Nov. 1852	Johan	Hepp, Elisabeth	D	358
Hess, Maria Wilhelmina	5, July 1857	Caius	Mertz, Theodosia	D	89

Name of Child	Date of Baptism	Father	Mother	Church	Page
Hess, Michael	16, Mar. 1851	Michael	Little, Maria	D	257
Hessbacher, Bernard	12, Jan. 1852	Alexander	Scheibers, Catharina	D	301
Hesse, Carl Friedrich	23, Mar. 1851	Francis	Gengel, Catharina	F	
Hesse, Carolina	26, Mar. 1850	Jacob	Weber, M. Barbara	C	
Hesse, Francis Joseph	27, Sept 1857	Francis J.	Koehle, Catharina	D	95
Hesse, Gerhard Anton	20, July 1851	F. Anton	Lohman, Anna M. Bernardina	K	
Hesse, Johan	15, May 1853	Joseph	Kenkel, Catharina	D	385
Hessel, Herman Heinrich Gerhard	22, Oct. 1859	J. Heinrich	Vogt, Maria Anna	L	
Hessel, Ludwig (Emil)	20, Nov. 1859	August	Karringer, Margaretha	K	
Hessel, Maria Elisabeth	6, Nov. 1859	Johan	Lindemann, M. Elis.	L	
Hesselbach, Francis	3, Apr. 1854	Friedrich	Klein, Elisabeth	C	
Hesselbach, Georg Peter	8, Oct. 1850	Friedrich	Klein, Elisabeth	C	
Hesselbach, Johan	8, July 1856	Friedrich	Klein, Elisabeth	C	
Hesselbach, Josephina	19, Sept 1852	Friedrich	Kleine, Josephina	C	
Hesselbrock, Anna Maria Theresa	27, Oct. 1850	Herman	Hopsters, Anna Maria	L	
Hesselbrock, Gerhard Heinrich	10, Mar. 1855	Joseph	Husman, Theresa	D	30
Hesselhaus, Bernard Jacob	28, May 1851	Jacob	Siemer, Catharina	C	
Hesseling, Elisabeth Philomena	28, June 1854	Johan H.	Elsen, Catharina G.	A	
Hesser, Georg	13, Nov. 1854	Nicolaus	Reinhart, Maria Anna	D	22
Hesser, Johan Lawrence	1, July 1855	Joseph	Kenker, Catharina	D	37
Hessessy, Emily	10, Apr. 1854	Joseph	----,	T	
Hessing, Anna Maria	30, Apr. 1854	Conrad	Farley, Elisabeth	L	
Hessler, Anna Maria	9, Dec. 1855	Bernard	Luettmer, Anna M.	C	
Hessler, Anna Maria Dorothea	15, Aug. 1853	J. Herman	Taphorn, Margaretha	F	
Hessler, Anna Maria Elisabeth	13, Oct. 1850	Joseph	Wanstrodt, Maria	L	
Hessler, Friedrich August	22, May 1859	Joseph	Wanstroth, Maria	L	
Hessler, Joseph	28, Mar. 1853	Bernard	Lutmer, Maria	C	
Hessler, Joseph Heinrich	29, Jan. 1854	Joseph	Wanstrate, Gertrud	L	
Hessler, Maria Josephina	10, Jan. 1857	Joseph	Wanstrot, M. Gertrud	L	
Hessler, Mary	30, Mar. 1851	Cornelius	Everet, Gesina	L	
Hessler, Michael	13, Jan. 1856	Heinrich	Vogelsang, Catharina	J	34
Hessler, Pius	16, Dec. 1855	Philipp	Fleckenstein, Catharina	D	48
Hessler, Susanna	2, Jan. 1859	Philipp	Flekenstein, Catharina	F	
Hessler, Wilhelm	30, Nov. 1856	Wilhelm	Duniter, Maria	K	
Hessling, Margaretha Josephina E.	18, Oct. 1857	Herman	Farley, Elisabeth	L	
Hessling, Maria Catharina	6, May 1850	Johan	Elsen, Catharina	D	212
Hessling, Maria Catharina Louisa	5, Jan. 1857	Bernard	Sickman, Catharina	A	
Hessmann, Franz Anton	7, Sept 1859	Francis	Schonekamp, Philomena	L	
Hessmann, Wilhelm Franz	6, May 1857	Francis J.	Schoneweg, Wilhelmina	L	
Hester, Bridget	4, Mar. 1855	Patrick	McCarton, Bridget	P	123
Hester, James	20, Feb. 1853	Patrick	----, Elizabeth	M	
Hester, John	3, Jan. 1858	Patrick	Benke, Mary	P	235
Hester, John	4, July 1852	Peter	Brannan, Margaret	B	262
Hester, John	28, June 1857	Thomas	Donnelon, Mary	B	46
Hester, Margaret	13, Dec. 1858	Michael	Keenan, Margaret	E	586
Hester, Mary Ann	24, Sept 1857	John	Callaghan, Ellen	B	50
Hester, Mary Ann	17, Dec. 1858	Thomas	Donnolly, Mary	B	68
Hester, Stephen	5, July 1857	Patrick	McCarthy, Bridget	B	46
Hester, Thomas	3, Mar. 1855	John	Callaghan, Helen	P	122
Hester, Thomas	7, Aug. 1853	Thomas	----, Ann	M	
Hester, Wililam	24, Apr. 1853	Patrick	McCarthy, Bridget	E	84
Hetmann, Bernard Wilhelm	27, Feb. 1854	J. Bernard	Vedder, Elisabeth	L	
Hett, Anna Maria	11, Feb. 1851	Adam	Lechner, Clara	F	
Hett, Louisa	7, Jan. 1853	Adam	Lechner, Clara	F	
Hett, Mathilda Jacobina	22, Mar. 1855	Adam	Lechner, Clara	F	
Hettel, Elisabeth Cordula	27, Aug. 1854	Michael	Heck, Theresa	F	
Hettel, Johan	2, Jan. 1853	Michael	Heck, Theresa	D	363
Hetterman, Bernard	30, Jan. 1859	Paul	Verkamp, Margaretha Adel.	K	
Hetterman, Herman Anton Peter	25, Aug. 1855	P. Paul	Vehrkamp, Margaretha	K	

Name of Child	Date of Baptism	Father	Mother	Church	Page
Hetterman, Herman Heinrich	9, May 1857	Peter P.	Vehrkamp, Margretha	K	
Hettesheimer, Barbara	9, Nov. 1856	William	Hessel, Elizabeth	T	
Hettesheimer, Daniel	13, Sept 1854	Wilhelm	Haseler, Elisabeth	D	17
Hettlich, Anna Louisa	24, Sept 1854	Friedrich	Klenne, Adelheid	C	
Hettlich, M. Elisabeth Wilhelmina	30, Jan. 1853	Friedrich	Klene, Adelheid	C	
Hettrich, Paulina	8, June 1851	Carl	Ollier, Magdalena	C	
Heuer, Anna Clara	7, Nov. 1852	Gerhard	Eigennutz, Maria	C	
Heuer, Bernard	17, Feb. 1852	Bernard	Hammer, Catharina	C	
Heuer, Bernard	26, July 1857	Carl F.	Dups, Augusta	A	
Heuer, Catharina Elisabeth	9, July 1854	Bernard	Hammer, Catharina	C	
Heuer, Catharina Theresa	22, Feb. 1850	Bernard	Hammer, Catharina	C	
Heuer, Gerhard Heinrich Wilhelm	11, Dec. 1853	Johan	Borntrager, Maria Anna	D	419
Heuer, Johan Joseph	5, Oct. 1856	Bernard	----, Catharina	F	
Heuer, Ludwig	23, Oct. 1859	Johan	Dec---, Maria Anna	D	149
Heuer, Ludwig Friedrich	14, Oct. 1858	Bernard	Hammer, Catharina	F	
Heuer, Marianna Carolina	6, Jan. 1854	Heinrich	Kaeller, Catharina	F	
Heuer, Mathias	16, Nov. 1851	Mathias	Buchman, Margaretha	D	292
Heuer, Wilhelm Heinrich	25, Oct. 1855	Johan	Hammer, M. Agnes	C	
Heuerman, Anna Maria	4, June 1851	J. Bernard	Schrömmeier, Lucia	K	
Heuerman, Catharina	9, Mar. 1856	J. Heinrich	Torphy, Catharina	D	53
Heuerman, George Joseph	31, Mar. 1858	J. Gerhard	Heheman, Henrietta	A	
Heuerman, Johan Theodor	1, Feb. 1850	J. Bernard	Schrommeier, Lucia	K	
Heuerman, Maria Carolina	23, Sept 1852	J. Gerhard	Heheman, Henrietta	K	
Heuerman, Maria Catharina	31, Jan. 1854	Bernard	Schrotmeier, Lucia	A	
Heuerman, Maria Dorothea Henrietta	1, Feb. 1855	Johan	Heherman, Dorothea Henr.	A	
Heuerman, Maria Theresa	10, Mar. 1855	Bernard	Schrömeyer, Lucia	A	
Heuermann, Bernard Heinrich	24, Oct. 1858	J. Bernard	Schermeyer, Lucia	C	
Heuermann, Maria Louisa	25, Dec. 1853	Heinrich	Torpe, Catharina	C	
Heuermann, Wilhelm Heinrich	20, Nov. 1859	J. Heinrich	Torpy, Catharina	C	
Heufl, Anna Maria	22, Aug. 1859	Adam	Der---, Catharina	D	145
Heuk, Georg Otto	2, Jan. 1855	J. Georg	Bäunlein, Catharina	D	26
Heul, Francisca Philomena	4, Mar. 1850	Peter	----, Maria Elisabeth	H	
Heutacker, Johan Heinrich	9, May 1858	Wilhelm	----, Elisabeth	D	111
Heuyer, Catharina	26, Aug. 1855	Mathias	Buchman, Margaretha	D	41
Heuyer, Johanna	8, Jan. 1854	Mathias	Buchman, Margaretha	D	1
Hevekehr, Herman Heinrich	14, June 1853	Christian	Witteriede, Maria Catharina	D	389
Heveker, Catharina Friedrica	1, Feb. 1857	Christian	Witteriede, Catharina	D	78
Heverkühr, Herman Christian	7, Nov. 1854	Christian	Witteride, Maria K.	D	21
Hewes, Theresa Magdalene	26, Nov. 1853	John	Dis, Magdalene	B	303
Hewett, George Daniel	24, Oct. 1858	George	Moran, Elizabeth	B	66
Hewiker, Barbara Theresa	13, June 1859	Bernard	Ihl, Theresa	A	
Hewit, Thomas Francis	6, Apr. 1851	John	Austin, Bridget	P	6
Hewitt, Rebecca Mary	29, Aug. 1854	Richard	Lean, Susan	E	220
Heyer, Anna Maria	16, Aug. 1857	Dominick	Kroll, Maria Anna	A	
Heyer, Carl August Adam	9, Dec. 1855	Carl F.	Dupps, Augusta	A	
Heyer, Wilhelm Amand	15, Sept 1859	Carl F.	Dupps, Augusta	D	146
Heying, Anna Maria	27, Aug. 1850	Heinrich	Wensing, Clara	C	
Hibb, Lilly	7, Sept 1858	James	King, Margaret	P	260
Hibele?, Johan Heinrich	6, May 1850	Edward	Wessels, Johanna Martha	A	
Hickel, Maria Anna	11, Sept 1859	Ludwig	Meiker, Maria Elisabeth	A	
Hickert, Joseph	9, Jan. 1853	Anthony	----, Elizabeth	H	
Hickey, Alice	6, Dec. 1859	Edward	Ryan, Mary Ann	P	305
Hickey, Alice Augusta	21, Sept 1856	Patrick	Meagher, Margaret	P	192
Hickey, Ann	1, Jan. 1854	Richard	Fagy, Catherine	E	157
Hickey, Ann Bridget	16, Feb. 1854	Michael	Costello, Ann	E	168
Hickey, Catherine	21, Aug. 1855	Daniel	Williams, Honora	E	309
Hickey, Catherine	21, Apr. 1857	John	----, Mary	M	
Hickey, Catherine	24, July 1853	William	Hollahan, Joanne	B	295
Hickey, Daniel	4, Sept 1852	Thomas	Ward, Catherine	E	14

Name of Child	Date of Baptism	Father	Mother	Church	Page
Hickey, Edmund	7, Dec. 1851	John	Conlan, Bridget	B	247
Hickey, Edward Patrick	8, Mar. 1859	Patrick	Staunton, Joanne	B	72
Hickey, Elizabeth	14, Sept 1856	John	Kenne---, Ann	V	33
Hickey, Ellen	1, Apr. 1855	John	----, Mary	M	
Hickey, Ellen	21, June 1857	Richard	Fahey, Catherine	E	461
Hickey, Honora	14, Aug. 1853	Daniel	----, Honora	E	118
Hickey, Honora	1, Mar. 1853	Patrick	Maher, Margaret	P	36
Hickey, Honora	22, June 1853	Patrick	Sherlock, Sarah	B	294
Hickey, James	22, Dec. 1852	John	Fegaly, Mary	E	46
Hickey, James Lawrence	5, June 1853	John S.	Conlan, Bridget	B	293
Hickey, James Patrick	4, Dec. 1858	Patrick	Maher, Margaret	P	269
Hickey, John	3, May 1854	----	----, ----	E	187
Hickey, John	16, Oct. 1857	Daniel	Williams, Honora	E	486
Hickey, John	16, Feb. 1854	Michael	Costello, Ann	E	168
Hickey, John	29, Dec. 1853	Thomas	Wall, Catherine	E	155
Hickey, Julia	1, Sept 1850	John	Conlan, Bridget	B	212
Hickey, Margaret	16, Feb. 1854	Miles	Burke, Mary	B	309
Hickey, Margaret	20, July 1855	Patrick	Sherlock, Sarah	E	301
Hickey, Margaret	17, June 1859	Thomas	Wall, Catherine	E	633
Hickey, Mary	10, Oct. 1850	John	Fogerty, Mary	E	253
Hickey, Mary	14, Dec. 1858	Michael	Lachnan, Mary	E	587
Hickey, Mary	3, May 1851	Richard	----, Catherine	E	304
Hickey, Mary Ann	26, May 1850	James	Hoffam, Mary Ann	B	203
Hickey, Mary Ann	29, Oct. 1855	Richard	----, Catherine	E	324
Hickey, Mary Ann	19, Nov. 1854	Thomas	Ward, Catherine	E	241
Hickey, Mary Ann	25, Feb. 1853	William	Doolin, Ann	B	284
Hickey, Michael	3, May 1854	----	----, ----	E	187
Hickey, Richard	7, Apr. 1850	William	Doolan, Ann	B	200
Hickey, Robert	2, Dec. 1859	Daniel	Wililams, Honora	E	674
Hickey, Sarah	7, Dec. 1851	John	Gleedy, Honora	E	364
Hickey, Sarah Elizabeth	30, Oct. 1858	John	Conlan, Bridget	P	266
Hickey, Theresa Jane	26, Nov. 1854	John	Conlan, Bridget	B	8
Hickey, Thomas	27, Apr. 1855	John	Foley, Margaret	B	13
Hickey, Thomas	19, Mar. 1851	Michael	Naud, Bridget	E	292
Hickey, Thomas	26, Sept 1858	Thomas	Fahey, Catherine	E	565
Hickey, Thomas Simon	6, Oct. 1856	John S.	Conlan, Bridget	B	35
Hickey, William	25, May 1856	William	Hoolihan, Jane	B	29
Hickey, William David	9, Sept 1857	Patrick	Stanton, Joanne	B	49
Hickey?, John	15, Aug. 1856	Andrew	----, Catherine	M	
Hicks, James	7, Sept 1856	?	Wright, Mary Ann	B	33
Hicks, John	7, Sept 1856	?	Wright, Mary Ann	B	33
Hiem, Joseph Conrad	9, Mar. 1856	Caspar	Kelle, Walburga	U	
Hien, Ann Mary	13, Dec. 1857	Caspar	Keller, Walburga	U	
Hien, Michael	16, Oct. 1859	Caspar	Keller, Walburga	U	
Higgerson, John	1, Nov. 1851	Bath.	Shire, Joanne	E	354
Higgins, Bridget	26, Mar. 1854	Hugh	Gilmore, Mary	V	12
Higgins, Catherine	12, Apr. 1856	Patrick	Flannery, Margaret	U	
Higgins, Catherine	31, Mar. 1851	Peter	Luddy, Margaret	E	296
Higgins, Catherine	23, Oct. 1859	Thomas	McDonald, Ann	B	82
Higgins, Catherine Ann	11, Dec. 1853	Peter	Moffet, Mary	E	151
Higgins, Daniel	12, Feb. 1855	John	Hooligan, Catherine	E	264
Higgins, Dennis	23, Nov. 1857	John	Holligan, Catherine	E	495
Higgins, Eliza	18, Feb. 1853		adult - 30 years old	P	36
Higgins, Helen	8, June 1851	Michael	O'Donnell, Margaret	B	233
Higgins, Helen	15, July 1856	Miles	----, Mary	R	
Higgins, Honora	29, Jan. 1855		Higgins, Honora	E	261
Higgins, James	24, Oct. 1858	Oda	Gilmartin, Helen	E	571
Higgins, John	8, Feb. 1853	Michael	O'Donnell, Margaret	P	34
Higgins, Margaret	25, Oct. 1854	Michael	O'Donnell, Margaret	P	101

Name of Child	Date of Baptism	Father	Mother	Church	Page
Higgins, Margaret Helen	23, June 1850	George	Fanning, Isabell	B	206
Higgins, Mary	16, Oct. 1851	Owen	Gilmore, Mary	P	13a
Higgins, Mary	14, Nov. 1852	Patrick	Flannery, Margaret	B	275
Higgins, Mary Catherine	21, Dec. 1856	Michael	O'Donnell, Margaret	P	201
Higgins, Mary Helen	25, July 1858	James	O'Connor, Mary	E	552
Higgins, Michael	4, Nov. 1854	John	Bien, Catherine	R	
Higgins, Michael	14, May 1854	Patrick	----, Mary	U	
Higgins, Patrick	1, Apr. 1858	Patrick	Flannery, Margaret	U	
Higgins, Phillip	3, Aug. 1851	Peter	----, Mary	E	331
Higgins, Susan	2, Jan. 1859	Michael	O'Donnell, Margaret	P	271
Higgins, Thomas	19, Nov. 1854	John	Cahill, Ann	B	8
Higgins, Timothy	19, Mar. 1851	John	Coughlin, Winnefred	E	292
Higgins, William	25, July 1850	Peter	----, Mary	E	234
Higginson, John Bartholomew	31, Oct. 1852	Michael	Fitzsimmons, Ann	E	31
Higginson, Joseph Henry	14, Sept 1854	Michael	Fitzsimmons, Ann	E	224
Hilbert, Otto Wilhelm	7, May 1852	Edward	Storz, Maria Anna	D	318
Hilbuerger, Carl	18, Apr. 1853	Simon	Petz, Margaretha	A	
Hilburger, Anna Maria	21, Aug. 1850	Simon	Pelz, Margaretha	A	
Hilburger, Maria Francisca	25, Oct. 1857	Simon	Petz, Margaretha	A	
Hildebrand, Francis Joseph	9, Apr. 1852	Joseph	Hulsmeier, Maria Anna	A	
Hildebrand, Francis Joseph	1, July 1853	Joseph G.	Heidkamp, Anna Maria	A	
Hildebrand, Johan Heinrich	22, Nov. 1850	J. Heinrich	Lehe, Maria Elisabeth	L	
Hildebrecht, Otto Theodor Carl	11, Feb. 1850	Theodor	Resz, Henrietta	D	202
Hildebreidel, Francisca	31, May 1857	Johan	Hof, Catharina	D	86
Hildenbeutel, Wilhelmina	6, Aug. 1858	Johan	Hof, Catharina	D	116
Hildwein, Joseph Albert	7, Apr. 1859	Carl	----, ----	A	
Hildwein, Maria Emilia	7, Apr. 1859	Carl	----, ----	A	
Hilferd, Johan Herman	27, Aug. 1851	Herman	Holfels, Anna Engel	L	
Hilgefort, Bernard Heinrich	24, May 1855	Heinrich	Uchtman, Elisabeth	K	
Hilgefort, Carolina Elisabeth	4, July 1852	Heinrich	Sading, Catharina	F	
Hilgefort, Catharina Elisabeth	7, Sept 1859	Heinrich	Upmann, Elisabeth	L	
Hilgefort, Clemens Heinrich	7, Nov. 1850	Heinrich	Suding, Catharina	F	
Hilgefort, Joseph Francis	7, June 1857	Heinrich	Uchtman, Elisabeth	K	
Hilgefort, Maria Anna	13, Feb. 1853	H.	Ochtman, Elisabeth	K	
Hilgenhold, Johan	16, Sept 1856	J. Heinrich	LüdkeKlanneman, Adelheid	N	
Hilgert, Elisabeth	20, Feb. 1859	Peter	Gross, Elisabeth	D	132
Hilgert, Magdalena	1, May 1853	Peter	Gross, Elisabeth	D	383
Hilgert, Mathias	22, June 1856	Peter	Gross, Elisabeth	D	61
Hilker, Johan Theodor Bernard	9, Apr. 1859	J.B.	---eun, Theresa	A	
Hill, Anna Maria	29, Mar. 1857	Carl	Wolf, Margaretha	L	
Hill, Carl	8, Mar. 1857	Johan	Hill, Ottilia	D	80
Hill, Catharina	22, Nov. 1858	John	Hill, Ottilia	K	
Hill, Georgina	24, Mar. 1850	Georg	Kunckel, Catharina	D	206
Hill, Ida Grace Victoria	12, May 1850	U. Carrell	Philips, Lucy Grace	E	214
Hill, Jacobina Augusta	2, Oct. 1853	Johan	Hiegel, Odilia	L	
Hill, John	5, Dec. 1858	Patrick	Philips, Margaret	B	68
Hill, John William	27, Nov. 1859	Johan	Hiel, Maria Ottilia	K	
Hill, Joseph	30, Sept 1855	Johan	Gigel, Odilia	L	
Hill, Mary	11, Oct. 1851	Andrew	Welsh, Ann	E	349
Hill, Mary Adelaide	1, May 1853	Patrick	Harbison, Sarah	E	85
Hill, Urel Carrell	12, May 1850		adult	E	214
Hillan, Catherine	22, Mar. 1854	James	Stanton, Mary	P	75
Hillan, Mary	12, Mar. 1856	James	Stanton, Mary	P	172
Hillbarth, Josephina Amelia	4, Aug. 1850	Edward	Stortz, Maria Antonia	D	227
Hillebrand, Anna Maria Bernardina	9, Aug. 1853	Bernard	Diercks, Bernardina	L	
Hillebrand, Anna Maria Theresa	16, July 1858	Bernard	Dirks, Bernardina	A	
Hillebrand, Caspar Eduard	24, Aug. 1856	Bernard	Dieker, Bernardina	A	
Hillebrand, Casper Franz Joseph	27, Feb. 1851	Bernard	Wellers, Bernardina	L	
Hillebrand, Francis Conrad	4, May 1858	Francis	Loehr, Elisabeth	C	

Name of Child	Date of Baptism	Father	Mother	Church	Page
Hillebrand, Maria Anna Karolina	15, Sept 1850	Joseph	Heitmeier, Maria Anna	A	
Hillebrandt, Heinrich David	10, June 1855	Francis	Laehr, Elisabeth	C	
Hillebrandt, Maria Elisabeth	9, May 1853	J. Francis	Loers, Maria Elisabeth	C	
Hiller, Margaretha	27, Feb. 1859	Adolph	Schau---, Elisabeth	D	132
Hillers, Mary Catherine Elizabeth	9, Dec. 1855	Henry	Repking, Anna Maria	R	
Hillgenholt, Gesina	19, May 1858	Heinrich	Glaneman, Adelheid	K	
Hilmer, Bernard Joseph	17, Feb. 1856	Joseph	Schnier, Anna	A	
Hilmer, Heinrich Bernard	12, July 1852	Joseph	Schnier, Maria Anna	A	
Hilmer, Maria Magdalena	25, Aug. 1853	Joseph	Schnier, Anna Maria	A	
Hilmers, Johan Anton	21, Dec. 1857	Joseph	Schnier, Maria Anna	A	
Hilsmann, Herman Johan	26, June 1854	Bernard	Beckers, Maria Gertrud	F	
Hilsmeier, Johan Bernard	27, Aug. 1852	Bernard	Beckers, Gertrud	F	
Hilsmeier, Maria Helena	9, Aug. 1850	Bernard H.	Becker, Maria Gertrud	F	
Hilton, Albert	24, May 1859	David	Laughlin, Mary	P	284
Hilton, George Lafferty	2, Apr. 1850	George H.	Laferty, Honora	B	199
Hilton, Honora Mary	31, Dec. 1853	George H.	Laverty, Honora	B	305
Hilton, James Frederick	3, Apr. 1856	George H.	Laverty, Honora	B	27
Hilton, John	31, May 1854	William	Crowly, Ellen	V	14
Hilton, Joseph B.	29, Oct. 1859	George	Lafferty, Alice	B	83
Hilton, Mary Elizabeth	24, May 1859	David	Laughlin, Mary	P	284
Hiltrob, Bernard Anton	26, May 1850	Bernard	Muenstermann, Catharina E.	F	
Hilvert, Johan Gerhard	29, Mar. 1855	Herman	Hoewel, Anna Engel	L	
Hilzleider, August Wilhelm	4, Feb. 1855	Georg	Roeslein, Gertrud	G	
Himmelmeyer, Johan Bernard	6, Dec. 1857	Friedrich	Gellhaus, Antoinette	C	
Himmer, August	12, June 1858	Joseph	Lurz, Maria Anna	D	113
Himmer, Johan	3, June 1855	Joseph	Lurz, Maria Anna	D	36
Himmer, Josephina Elisabeth	18, Jan. 1857	Joseph	Lurz, Maria Anna	D	77
Himpfner, Anna Maria	8, Sept 1851	Michael	Hofman, Anna Maria	H	
Himpfner, John	24, Dec. 1854	Michael	----, Maria	H	
Hinderlang, Maria Eva	2, Mar. 1858	Martin	Hornberger, Anna Maria	Q	27
Hines, Ellen	15, June 1856	John	----, Mary	M	
Hines, John	31, Jan. 1858	Lawrence	Manion, Mary	B	55
Hines, John	16, Dec. 1852	Thomas	----, Bridget	M	
Hines, Mary	4, Mar. 1855	Thomas	----, Bridget	M	
Hines, Mary Sabley	12, May 1850	John	Hagan, Catherine	E	213
Hines, Michael	6, Apr. 1856	Lawrence	Mannion, Mary	B	27
Hines, Patrick	9, Oct. 1859	Lawrence	Manion, Mary	B	82
Hingsberger, Maria Catharina	31, Sept 1855	Conrad	Sommermeyer, Helena	K	
Hinkebeen, Johan Theodor	27, Sept 1850	Gerhard	Behrer, Anna M.	K	
Hinkeberin, Euphemia M. Philomena	16, Apr. 1855	Meinrad	Behrens, Maria Anna	K	
Hinkel, John	18, May 1854	August	Eckhardt, Margaretha	R	
Hinkel, Lawrence	8, June 1856	August	----, Margaret	R	
Hinkeler, Angela	30, July 1854	Johan	Hass, Elisabeth	F	
Hinkeler, Theodor	25, May 1856	Johan	Huss, Susanna Elisabeth	F	
Hinkler, Angela	24, Oct. 1858	Johan	Huss, Elisabeth	T	
Hinkler, Georg Carl	5, July 1857	Johan	Segler, Rosina	F	
Hinley, Mary	31, Jan. 1854	Patrick	Burke, Bridget	V	10
Hinson, Nathaniel	15, Apr. 1853	Nathaniel	adult - 41 years old	E	83
Hinson, Robert A.	5, Nov. 1857		adult	B	51
Hinteis, Anna Maria	Feb. 1853	John	----, Barbara	H	
Hinterberg, Jacob	21, Sept 1852	Martin	Hornberger, Maria	D	348
Hintereck, Gottlieb	11, Feb. 1856	Bernard	Faller, Rosa	D	52
Hinterek, Bernard	26, Apr. 1854	Bernard	Faller, Rosa	D	9
Hinterlang, Johan Martin	25, Dec. 1850	Martin	Hohenberg, Maria	D	246
Hinterlang, Maria Magdalena	1, Oct. 1854	Martin	Hornberger, Anna Maria	G	
Hinterlange, Johan Heinrich	27, Mar. 1857	Martin	Horn, Maria	Q	20
Hintermesch, Anna Maria Carolina	4, Mar. 1850	J. Bernard	Rehe, Maria Catharina	L	
Hintermesch, Edward Heinrich	4, Nov. 1855	Friedrich	Sifke, Gertrud	F	
Hintermesch, Georg Franz Ludwig	1, Nov. 1857	Friedrich	Siefke, Gertrud	F	

Name of Child	Date of Baptism	Father	Mother	Church	Page
Hinternesch, Franz Heinrich	26, Feb. 1852	Francis	Rehe, A.M. Catharina	L	
Hinternesche, August Bernard Eduard	23, Oct. 1859	Friedrich	Siefke, Gertrud	A	
Hinternesche, Louise Gertrud	4, Oct. 1855	Bernard	Rehe, Catharina	C	
Hintheis, Anton	5, Dec. 1850	Johan	Hippolsteiner, Barbara	H	
Hintz, Johan Georg Anton	30, Nov. 1857	Bartholomew	Oster, Rosina	D	100
Hio, Johan Jacob	27, June 1857	Nicolaus	----, Elisabeth	K	
Hiop, George	7, Feb. 1854	H.	----, Charlotte	U	
Hipner, Johan Conrad	30, Aug. 1857	Johan	Meier, Sophia	D	93
Hippoldsteiner, Francis Xavier	10, Oct. 1858	Francis X.	Wiesman, Margaretha	H	
Hippoldsteiner, Michael	28, May 1855	Michael	----, Anna Maria	H	
Hippoldsteiner, Walburga	16, Dec. 1858	Joseph	Wittmer, Walburga	H	
Hippoltsteiner, Anna Margaretha	5, Dec. 1856	Francis X.	Wiesman, Magdalena	H	
Hippoltsteiner, Anna Maria	8, Dec. 1852	Joseph	----, Walburga	H	
Hippoltsteiner, Anna Maria	19, Apr. 1852	Willibald	----, Theresa	H	
Hippoltsteiner, Barbara	19, Nov. 1854	Joseph	----, Walburga	H	
Hippoltsteiner, Joseph	20, Nov. 1853	Michael	----, Maria	H	
Hippoltsteiner, Joseph	24, July 1856	Willibald	Mayer, Theresa	H	
Hippoltsteiner, Michael	22, Feb. 1859	Francis	Kremel, Maria Anna	H	
Hippoltsteiner, Philomena	5, Dec. 1856	Joseph	Wittman, Walburga	H	
Hippoltsteiner, Sebastian Johan	13, Feb. 1859	Willibald	Meyer, Theresa	H	
Hippoltsteiner, Willibald	21, May 1854	Willibald	----, Theresa	H	
Hirbe, Johan	1, Dec. 1850	Francis	Freund, Maria	F	
Hirbe, Lorenz	11, Apr. 1859	Lawrence	Frey, Maria	T	
Hirby, George	26, July 1857	Lawrence	Freund, Maria	H	
Hireman, James Rufus	23, Nov. 1851	J. Heinrich	Torpyn, Catherine	B	246
Hirpe,	6, Apr. 1855	Lawrence	----, Mary	H	
Hirpe, Helena	15, June 1856	Lawrence	Freund, Maria	D	60
Hirpe, Maria Agatha	5, Dec. 1852	Lawrence	Freund, Maria	F	
Hirpe, Maria Anna	26, Oct. 1851	Lawrence	Freund, Maria	F	
Hirpe, Maria Theresa	19, Mar. 1854	Lawrence	Freund, Maria	W	2
Hirsch, Anton Valentin	14, Sept 1854	Anton	Kleinman, Carolina	A	
Hirsch, Carola Theresa	9, Oct. 1859	Johan	Oster, Eva	C	
Hirsch, Catharina Philomena	6, Mar. 1852	Anton	Kleinman, Carolina	D	310
Hirsch, Johan Jacob	17, Aug. 1852	Jacob	Martz, M. Anna	C	
Hirsch, Katharina Eva	17, Jan. 1858	Johan	Oster, Eva	D	103
Hirsch, Martin	26, June 1855	Johan	Oster, Eva	D	37
Hirsch, Wilhelm Heinrich	9, Nov. 1856	Anton	Kleinman, Carolina	D	72
Hirschauer, Carl Joseph	18, July 1858	Philipp	Schiwener, Elisabeth	K	
Hirschauer, Catharina	22, Feb. 1857	Paul	Marx, Susanna	D	79
Hirschauer, Ludwig Philipp	26, Mar. 1854	Philipp	Schewene, Elisabeth	K	
Hirschauer, Maria	9, Sept 1855	Paul	Marx, Susanna	D	42
Hirschauer, Nicolaus	4, Apr. 1858	Johan	Bauer, Catharina	S	
Hirschauer, Peter	7, Nov. 1858	Carl	Mey---, Susanna	D	123
Hirschener, Nicolaus	5, Dec. 1858	Nicolaus	Meyer, Maria Anna	K	
Hirschhauer, Ludwig	25, Dec. 1851	Philipp	Schenning, Elisabeth	K	
Hirshman, John	25, Dec. 1859	Joseph	Maher, Ann	B	85
Hirt, Rosa	18, Oct. 1857	Carl	Stierer, Theresa	F	
Hirtz, Maria Genofeva	11, Sept 1859	Carl	Stierer, Theresa	F	
His, Johan	11, Sept 1853	Johan	Kern, Elisabeth	D	405
Hisch, Joseph	20, Oct. 1850	Johan	Heig, Cholastica	D	239
Hislop, Charles	15, Dec. 1850	George	Harb, Mary	B	220
Hitcher, Maria Magdalena	13, Feb. 1859	Francis	Bachmann, Margaretha	T	
Hixon, Elizabeth	14, Aug. 1850	----	----, ----	E	243
Hoar, Bridget	9, Oct. 1853	James	Murphy, Margaret	B	300
Hoar, James Michael	27, Mar. 1859	James	Murphy, Margaret	B	73
Hoar, John Thomas	15, Mar. 1857	James	Murphy, Margaret	B	42
Hoar, Mary Ann	30, May 1852	James	----, Margaret	E	420
Hoar, Mary Ann	4, Dec. 1858	Patrick	Garden, Mary	E	585
Hoare, Catherine	20, Aug. 1854	Bartholomew	----, Elisabeth	H	

Name of Child	Date of Baptism	Father	Mother	Church	Page
Hoare, Margaret	13, May 1855	Francis	Murphy, Margaret	B	14
Hoarz, Rosa	28, Aug. 1859	Anselm	Sailer, Elisabeth	D	145
Hob, Catharina	3, July 1859	Bernard	Sebastian, Apollonia	N	
Höb, Johan Thomas	13, Apr. 1856	Thomas	Dorn, Margaretha	D	56
Hoban, Bridget	1, Feb. 1857	Patrick	Purcell, Catherine	E	430
Hoban, Bridget Mary	8, Feb. 1857	Martin	Murray, Catherine	P	205
Hoban, Catherine	1, Oct. 1854	Patrick	Purcell, Catherine	E	228
Hoban, Eliza	12, July 1854	Martin	Murray, Catherine	B	2
Hoban, Helen	4, Dec. 1857	Thomas	Havey, Mary	P	231
Hoban, Joanne	25, May 1856	John	Moran, Bridget	P	181
Hoban, John	30, Oct. 1858	John	Moran, Bridget	P	265
Hoban, John	3, Aug. 1854	Michael	----, Catherine	R	
Hoban, John	13, July 1851	Thomas	Havey, Mary	P	10
Hoban, John Martin	13, Nov. 1859	Patrick	Purcell, Catherine	E	670
Hoban, Margaret	6, Feb. 1852	Patrick	Jordan, Bridget	P	17
Hoban, Mary	15, June 1855	Thomas	Havey, Mary	P	136
Hoban, Nicholas	12, Sept 1850	Patrick	----, Catherine	E	247
Hoban, Thomas	16, Jan. 1859	Martin	Murray, Catherine	P	272
Hobbs, Jacob Heinrich	6, Oct. 1859	Jacob	Rolinson, Maria	C	
Hobbs, Wilhelm Anton	21, Feb. 1858	Jacob	McDormat, M. Anna	C	
Hobin, James	26, Sept 1858	John	----, Catherine	M	
Hobin, Ludwig August	11, Aug. 1850	Francis	Gendret, Justina	F	
Hobin, Mary	10, Oct. 1852	Patrick	----, Catherine	E	26
Hobin, Nicolaus	26, July 1857	John	----, Catherine	M	
Höbing, Clara Agnes	1, Mar. 1850	J. Heinrich	----er, Anna Maria	D	203
Höbing, Elisabeth Catharina	14, Mar. 1852	Bernard	Bornhorst, Catharina B.	A	
Hobing, Maria Carolina	2, Apr. 1854	J. Heinrich	Tembusch, Anna Maria	A	
Höbing, Maria Susanna Philomena	29, Apr. 1853	Bernard	Barenhorst, Maria Bernardina	K	
Höbing, Rosa Mina	14, Mar. 1852	Heinrich	Tembusch, Anna Maria	A	
Hobmaier, Maria Louisa	30, Jan. 1853	Heinrich	Kemaier, Catharina	D	368
Hoch, Francis	26, Sept 1853	Georg	Anger, Rosa	D	407
Hoch, Maria	7, Oct. 1855	Lawrence	Aigner, Elisabeth	D	44
Hocheluch, Johan Gerhard Herman	1, Nov. 1856	J. Gerhard	Remsing, Elisabeth	N	
Hochelucht, Johan Herman Heinrich	20, Feb. 1859	J. Herman	Halmsing, Elisabeth	N	
Hochelucht, Johanna Maria Elisabeth	28, Oct. 1856	J. Herman	Böhmer, Maria Anna	N	
Hochgreve, Francis Victor	11, Mar. 1859	Francis	Fisting, Carolina	C	
Hochstuhl, Anna	13, Apr. 1856	Martin	Lorenz, Rosina	F	
Hochstuhl, Martin	17, Apr. 1859	Martin	Lorenz, Rosina	D	136
Hock, Carl	24, July 1855	Adam	Alexander, Catharina	F	
Hock, Catharina	1, Apr. 1855	Heinrich	----, Margaretha	K	
Hock, Elisabeth	21, Sept 1856	Carl	Alexander, Catharina	F	
Hock, Francis	6, June 1852	Georg	Ostheimer, Lucia	D	323
Hock, Gustav	24, Oct. 1858	Georg	Ostheimer, Lucia	T	
Hock, Johan Adam	4, Apr. 1858	Peter	Zahn, Catharina	T	
Hock, Johan Ernest	30, May 1852	Johan	----, Anastasia	H	
Hock, Joseph August	8, Sept 1856	Georg	Bauerlein, Catharina	D	67
Hock, Mathias	3, Nov. 1850	Lawrence	Eichler, Elisabeth	D	241
Höcker, Catharina Adelheid	1, Dec. 1854	H. Bernard	Greskamp, Catharina Adelheid	K	
Höcker, Christina Philomena Friedrica	2, Feb. 1852	Bernard	Greskamp, Catharina	K	
Hocks, Johan Herman	2, Apr. 1853	J. Gerhard	VanGroeninger, Adelheid	J	20
Hockzema, Anton Francis Clemens	3, July 1854	Anton	Holthaus, Elisabeth	C	
Hockzema, Antonia Josephina F.	3, Oct. 1852	Anton	Holthaus, Lisette	C	
Hockzema, Barbara Francisca	8, Apr. 1856	Anton	Holthaus, Lisette	C	
Hockzema, Everhard Carl Juliuss	18, Feb. 1851	Anton	Holthaus, Elisabeth	C	
Hockzema, Gertrud Barbara Johanna	4, Apr. 1858	Anton	Hollhaus, Elisabeth	C	
Hocter, Ann	17, July 1853	Patrick	Burke, Mary	P	47
Hocter, John	10, Aug. 1858	John	Tinley, Honora	P	257
Hocter, Sarah	2, Sept 1855	Patrick	Burke, Mary	P	149
Hoctor, Elizabeth	3, Dec. 1854	Thomas	----, Margaret	M	

Name of Child	Date of Baptism	Father	Mother	Church	Page
Hoctor, Emma Ann	13, Apr. 1854	John	----, N.	E	182
Hoctor, John	3, July 1853	Thomas	----, Margaret	M	
Hoctor, Margaret	10, July 1859	Thomas	----, Margaret	M	
Hoctor, Mary Ann	3, May 1857	Thomas	----, Margaret	M	
Hoctor, Sarah	2, Feb. 1851	Patrick	Burke, Mary	P	4
Hocum, Sarah Ellen	6, Sept 1856	Thaddeus H.	King, Caroline	B	33
Hodapp, Joseph	12, Oct. 1856	Wendel	----, Magdalena	R	
Hodapp, Maria Anna	3, Apr. 1853	Wendel	Paunder, Magdalena	Q	3
Hodapp, Wendelin	19, Nov. 1854	Wendel	Paunder, Magdalena	Q	5
Hodd, Stephan	17, Apr. 1855		adult - 45 years old	P	129
Hode, Joseph Bernard Gerhard	31, Aug. 1851	Gerhard	Steinge, Anna Maria	D	280
Hode?, Caspar Francis Wilhelm	3, Feb. 1851	Caspar	Hülsen, Gertrud	A	
Hodel, Maria Theresa Francisca	22, Mar. 1859	Georg	Schlick, Catharina	A	
Hodgman, Lancing Henry	6, May 1857	Leonard	Cronin, Elizabeth	E	450
Hödru, Maria Philomena	17, June 1855	J. Baptist	Turen, Maria	K	
Hoeb, Johan	18, Apr. 1854	Thomas	Dorn, Margaretha	D	8
Hoeb, Maria Anna	24, Sept 1858	Thomas	Dorn, Margaretha	D	119
Hoebeler, Johan Gerhard	12, Oct. 1851	Gerhard	Schaefer, Clara	C	
Hoeck, Mary	4, Dec. 1853	John	----, Mary	H	
Hoeck, Peter	11, Dec. 1853	Peter	----, Magdalena	H	
Hoedebeck, M. Elisabeth Josephina	3, July 1859	Joseph	Memmert, Catharina B.	L	
Hoef, Bernard Heinrich	16, Jan. 1859	Heinrich	Reh---, Maria	D	129
Hoeferman, Maria Louisa	1, Jan. 1851	J. Heinrich	Ahors, Maria Louisa	D	247
Hoeffer, Anna Henrietta	15, Mar. 1857	Heinrich	Sohnchen, Anna Maria	F	
Hoeffer, Anna Maria	6, Feb. 1858	Georg	Elbert, Margaretha	D	104
Hoeffer, Anna Maria	17, Apr. 1859	Heinrich	Sohnchen, Anna Maria	F	
Hoeffer, Barbara	19, Oct. 1859	Francis	Blaesi, Marianna	F	
Hoeffer, Catharina	1, Aug. 1852	Heinrich	Soehchen, Anna Maria	F	
Hoeffer, Elisabeth	19, Dec. 1854	Heinrich	Sohneken, Anna Maria	F	
Hoeffer, Georg Heinrich	2, Aug. 1857	Georg F.	Blaesi, Anna Maria	F	
Hoeffer, Jacob	8, Feb. 1852	Georg Fr.	Blessy, Anna Maria	F	
Hoeffer, Maria Anna	15, Aug. 1854	Francis	Blaesy, Anna Maria	F	
Hoeffer, Martha	26, Mar. 1854	Georg	Elbert, Margaretha	D	7
Hoeffer, Simon	17, Sept 1853	Georg Fr.	Blaesy, Maria	F	
Hoeffer, Simon Peter	15, Dec. 1850	Francis	Blaesi, Maria	F	
Hoeffler, Maria Gertrud	10, July 1853	J. Gerhard	Schepen, Clara	C	
Hoeffner, Agatha	18, Dec. 1853	Anton	Kessler, Louisa	C	
Hoefling, Amalia Margaretha	11, Oct. 1857	Michael	Albrecht, Catharina	F	
Hoefling, Anna Catharina	13, Nov. 1853	Michael	Albrecht, Anna Catharina	F	
Hoefling, Anna Maria	25, Apr. 1852	Georg A.	Meininger, Anna Maria	F	
Hoefling, Catharina Josephina	26, Nov. 1854	Adam	Meininger, Maria	F	
Hoefling, Georg Franz	4, Apr. 1852	Michael	Albrecht, Catharina	F	
Hoefling, Joseph	11, Nov. 1855	Michael	Albrecht, Catharina	F	
Hoefly, Anna Gertrud	23, Jan. 1859	Paul	Eicher, Crescentia	D	129
Hoefly, Catharina Elisabeth	23, Jan. 1859	Paul	Eicher, Crescentia	D	129
Hoegemann, Maria Bernardina	16, Jan. 1850	J. Heinrich	Bahlmann, Bernardina	L	
Hoeger, Louisa Dorothea	22, Feb. 1856	Benedict	Merz, Thecla	D	52
Hoeger, Maria Magdalena	4, Aug. 1850	Anton	Beivenstuhl, Elisabeth	C	
Hoehn, Aloysius	4, Dec. 1853	Michael	Braun, Margaretha	F	
Hoehn, Anna Maria	8, Apr. 1855	Michael	Braun, Margaretha	F	
Hoehn, Georg Michael	21, Dec. 1851	Michael	Braun, Margaretha	F	
Hoehn, Margaretha	28, June 1857	Michael	Braun, Margaretha	F	
Hoeing, Joseph Bernard	6, May 1855	Joseph	Westel, Rebecka	A	
Hoelker, Bernard Heinrich Martin	6, Mar. 1857	Francis	Schomaker, Elisabeth	L	
Hoelker, Catharina Carolina	16, May 1852	Dietrich	Kleine, Elisabeth	L	
Hoelker, Catharina Sophia Maria A.	5, Mar. 1858	Joseph	Vogelsang, Sophia	F	
Hoelker, Franz	18, Dec. 1854	Francis	Schuhmacher, Elisabeth	L	
Hoelker, Franz Theodor	11, Feb. 1855	Dietrich	Kleine, M. Elisabeth	L	
Hoelker, Heinrich Franz	7, Apr. 1856	Francis	Ossinger, Elisabeth	L	

Name of Child	Date of Baptism	Father	Mother	Church	Page
Hoelker, Johan Franz	5, Dec. 1858	Francis	Ossel, Elisabeth	L	
Hoelker, Johan Joseph	28, Dec. 1854	Francis J.	Vogelsang, Sophia C.	F	
Hoelker, Juliana	30, May 1850	Dietrich	Kleine, Elisabeth	L	
Hoelker, Maria Elisabeth	15, Mar. 1857	Dietrich	Kleine, Elisabeth	L	
Hoelker, Maria Helena	8, Feb. 1859	Francis	Schoemaker, Elisabeth	L	
Hoelker, Maria Veronica	20, Jan. 1856	Joseph	Vogelsang, Sophia Cath.	F	
Hoelscher, Herman Heinrich	26, Nov. 1850	Bernard H.	Hoespling, Theresa	C	
Hoelscher, Josephina Wilhelmina	15, Dec. 1850	Heinrich	Lohmann, A. Margaretha	L	
Hoelscher, Maria Clara Veronica	19, Nov. 1854	Wilhelm	Schomann, A. Margaret	L	
Hoelscher, Mathias Augustin	15, Oct. 1857	Mathias	Metger, M. Elisabeth	T	
Hoelscher, Nicolaus Heinrich	31, Jan. 1858	Friedrich	Kampmeier, Cath. Elis.	T	
Hoeltz, Marianna	22, Mar. 1857	Jacob	Knaup, Josepha	F	
Hoelz, Sophia	6, Mar. 1859	Jacob	Haug, Sophia	F	
Hoemig, Clara Rosalia	1, Aug. 1858	Francis	Huehner, Sophia	T	
Hoening, Franz Wilhelm Bernard	29, Feb. 1852	Gerhard F.	Bach, Wilhelmina C.	L	
Hoenschemeier, Johan Heinrich	31, May 1859	Francis H.	Huepel, M. Elisabeth	F	
Hoenschemeyer, Elisabeth Theresa	18, Sept 1858	Heinrich	Fischer, Theresa	F	
Hoerner, Maria Anna	10, Sept 1856	Michael	Goetz, Barbara	K	
Hoerner, Valentin	2, May 1858	Michael	Götz, Barbara	K	
Hoernschemeier, Anna Maria Theresa	13, July 1853	Johan H.	Fischer, Theresa	F	
Hoernschemeier, Johan Heinrich	28, Aug. 1856	Johan H.	Fischer, Theresa	F	
Hoernschemeier, Maria Elisabeth	18, July 1850	Johan	Mayers, Maria Elisabeth	F	
Hoersting, A. Margaretha Francisca	19, May 1858	Heinrich	Kraemer, Gertrud	F	
Hoersting, Anton Heinrich	2, Oct. 1853	Anton	Eilermann, M. Anna	C	
Hoersting, M. Elisabeth Bernardina	20, May 1859	Heinrich	Kraemer, Gertrud	F	
Hoersting, Maria Catharina	21, Nov. 1855	Heinrich	Kraemer, Gertrud	L	
Hoespling, Maria Catharina	1, Oct. 1851	Herman	Luehn, Margaretha	F	
Hoess, Eleanora Sabina	2, Mar. 1857		Hoess, Martha	D	80
Hof, Catharina	14, Mar. 1858	Edward	Schmidlin, Margaretha	C	
Hof, Francis	5, Aug. 1855	Francis	Groh, Francisca	R	
Hof, Johan Thomas	2, Mar. 1851	Georg	Adam, Elisabeth	A	
Hof, Maria Ann	18, July 1857	Francis	----, Francisca	R	
Hof, Maria Anna	3, Aug. 1851	Valentin	Hohn?, Anna Maria	D	276
Höf, Wilhelm David	19, Sept 1852	David	Müller, Catharina	D	348
Hofacker, Maria Elisabeth	17, Apr. 1855	Martin	Burge, Elisabeth	C	
Hofele, Mathias	31, July 1853	Bernard	Hosses, Maria	D	398
Hofeling, Georg Joseph	29, Aug. 1854	Georg J.	Klüpfel, M. Magdalena	A	
Hofer, August	13, Dec. 1857	Ignatius	Habecht, Magdalena	T	
Hofer, Johan Joseph	31, Oct. 1858	Joseph	Eble, Maria Anna	T	
Hoff, Catharina	7, Feb. 1858	Jacob	Lang, Magdalena	D	104
Hoff, Jacob Francis	11, Sept 1853	Jacob	Lang, Magdalena	D	405
Hoff, Johan	9, Dec. 1855	Jacob	Lang, Magdalena	D	48
Hoff, Johan	9, Jan. 1853	Valentin	Käffer, Agnes	K	
Hoff, Mary Ann	26, Dec. 1851	Isaac	Crane, Catherine	P	14
Hoff, Michael	1, Apr. 1851	Jacob	Lang, Magdalena	D	259
Hoffart, Gregor	1, June 1856	Johan	Deisig, M. Anna	C	
Hoffart, Gregor	23, Sept 1854	Johan	Thersing, Maria	C	
Hoffart, Joseph	23, May 1858	Wilhelm	Meyer, Elisabeth	K	
Hoffart, Martin Johan Joseph	3, Oct. 1852	Hyacinth	Deisig, M. Anna	C	
Hoffart, Philomena Barbara	9, Feb. 1851	H.	Thersing, Anna	C	
Höffer Barbara	30, Apr. 1854	Nicolaus	Birkle, Maria M.	D	9
Hoffer, Carl	22, Aug. 1858	Carl	Feder, Wilhelmina	A	
Höffer, Catharina	31, Oct. 1852	Georg	Elbers, Margaretha	D	355
Höffer, Nicolaus	8, Feb. 1856	G. Nicolaus	Elbers, Margaretha	D	51
Hoffhaus, Clemens August	25, Dec. 1850	Anton	BeiderMütke, Maria Theresa	A	
Hoffhaus, Dietrich	25, Apr. 1852		Hoffhaus, Catharina	C	
Hoffhues, Anna Catharina Elisabeth	19, Dec. 1858	Theodor	Schulten, Maria	L	
Hoffkamp, Johan Bernard Albert	27, Oct. 1851	Bernard	Huke, Euphemia Maria	A	
Höffler, Georg Francis	6, Apr. 1851	Georg	Elbers, Margaretha	D	260

Name of Child	Date of Baptism	Father	Mother	Church	Page
Höffling, Maria Elisabeth Gertrud	4, Aug. 1858	Bernard	Sickman, Catharina	A	
Hoffman, Anna Catharina Francisca	15, Apr. 1855	Jacob	Morsch, Anna	A	
Hoffman, Anna M. Bernardina	21, Aug. 1850	Heinrich	Evers, Anna	A	
Hoffman, Anna Maria	24, Aug. 1851	Friedrich	Gütterman, Barbara	D	279
Hoffman, Bernard Wilhelm	11, Feb. 1857	Wilhelm	Mayer, Anna	A	
Hoffman, Carl Joseph	24, June 1855	J. Adam	Burkart, Anna Maria	D	37
Hoffman, Carl Ludwig	18, Sept 1859	J. Adam	Feist, Carolina	D	147
Hoffman, Catharina Amelia	8, Nov. 1857	Friedrich	Schweiz---, Catharina	D	98
Hoffman, Catharina Maria	25, Aug. 1850	Herman	Warensman, Anna Maria	D	230
Hoffman, Charles	5, Oct. 1851	Philipp	Hackmeyer, Mary	P	12
Hoffman, Eva	27, Feb. 1853	Friedrich	Giderman, Barbara	D	374
Hoffman, Francis	6, Mar. 1853	Johan	Frank, Maria	D	374
Hoffman, Francis Heinrich	31, Oct. 1858	Heinrich	Evers, Maria Anna	A	
Hoffman, Francis Joseph	6, Jan. 1854	Johan	Rutz, Magdalena	D	1
Hoffman, Francisca Magdalena	27, Sept 1857	J. Adam	Feist, Carolina	D	95
Hoffman, Georg	15, Aug. 1854	Peter	Reis, Veronica	D	15
Hoffman, Jacob	6, May 1853	Georg	Helam, Elisabeth	A	
Hoffman, Jacob	28, Apr. 1857	Michael	Kapp, Maria	D	84
Hoffman, Jacob	19, Nov. 1855	Michael	Rapp, Maria Anna	D	47
Hoffman, Johan	30, Mar. 1851	Johan	----, Magdalena	H	
Hoffman, Johan	1, Jan. 1850	Peter	Reis, Veronica	D	197
Hoffman, Johan August	5, June 1857	Johan	---man, Maria	D	86
Hoffman, Johan Georg	11, Sept 1850	Friedrich	Giderman, Barbara	D	232
Hoffman, Johan Herman August	14, June 1857	J. Heinrich	Frotman, Maria Anna	N	
Hoffman, Joseph Pius	3, May 1858	Johan	Siegman, Anna Elisabeth	D	110
Hoffman, Margaretha	21, July 1851		Hoffman, Margaretha	D	274
Hoffman, Maria Anna	28, Aug. 1852	Gerhard H.	Efers, Maria Anna	A	
Hoffman, Maria Anna	24, Oct. 1858	Peter	Bettrich---, Rosina	D	122
Hoffman, Maria Apollonia	4, Sept 1859	J. Adam	Burkhart, Maria Anna	A	
Hoffman, Maria Barbara	11, June 1852	Johan	Appelman, Margaretha	D	324
Hoffman, Maria Catharina	24, Mar. 1850	Georg	Wegener, Anna Maria	K	
Hoffman, Maria Catharina	26, Dec. 1850	Johan	Redelberger, Margretha	D	246
Hoffman, Maria Elisabeth	13, Nov. 1859	Adolph	Engel, Maria Anna	D	150
Hoffman, Maria Elisabeth	17, July 1854	H. Bernard	Evers, Maria	A	
Hoffman, Mendora Macready	20, Apr. 1856	Jacob	Gabel, Louisa	B	28
Hoffman, Michael Sebastian Caspar	9, July 1854	Caspar	Wolpert, Catharina	D	13
Hoffman, Peter	12, July 1850	Peter	Tat, Barbara	K	
Hoffman, Philipp	31, July 1851	Georg P.	Graf, Marianna	D	275
Hoffman, Philipp	9, Apr. 1855	Philipp	Hechinger, Maria	J	32
Hoffman, Phillip	30, Aug. 1850	Philipp	Haskinger, Mary A.	B	212
Hoffman, Thomas Edward	26, July 1857	Johan	Burkart, Anna Margaretha	D	91
Hoffman, Wilhelm	29, Nov. 1857	Carl	----, Catharina	R	
Hoffmann, Adam Friedrich	23, June 1858	Jacob	Geeser, Anna	L	
Hoffmann, Anna Maria	29, Aug. 1858	Friedrich	Hirck, Catharina	T	
Hoffmann, Carl	9, Oct. 1859	Peter	Daul, Barbara	C	
Hoffmann, Carl Joseph	10, July 1854	Heinrich	Fordmann, M. Anna	C	
Hoffmann, Carolina	4, Nov. 1855	Adam	Feiss, Carolina	F	
Hoffmann, Casper Sebastian Theodor	21, Sept 1851	Caspar	Wolbert, Catharina	L	
Hoffmann, Catharina	3, Apr. 1857	Peter	Daub, Barbara	C	
Hoffmann, Francis Heinrich	9, Mar. 1853	Heinrich	Fortmann, Anna	C	
Hoffmann, Francis Peter	26, Aug. 1855	Peter	Pottichheimer, Regina	C	
Hoffmann, Friedricka	6, Apr. 1856	Michael	Hirsch, Catharina	C	
Hoffmann, Genofeva	8, Nov. 1857	Peter	Reis, Francisca	T	
Hoffmann, Georg Heinrich	24, Oct. 1852	Adam	Tenech, Margaretha	L	
Hoffmann, Georg Jacob	20, Nov. 1853	Jacob	Gruber, Barbara	L	
Hoffmann, Georg Michael	27, May 1855	Carl	Kuhn, Agnes	C	
Hoffmann, Heinrich	16, Mar. 1851	Jacob	Gruber, Barbara	C	
Hoffmann, Jacob	18, Apr. 1855	Adam	Denk, Margaretha	L	
Hoffmann, Johan	1, Oct. 1854	Adam	Flerchinger, Barbara	C	

Name of Child	Date of Baptism	Father	Mother	Church	Page
Hoffmann, Johan	25, May 1851	Peter	Reis, Veronica	F	
Hoffmann, Johan Adam	17, Sept 1854	Peter	Daut, Barbara	C	
Hoffmann, Joseph	7, Sept 1856	Jacob	Gruber, Barbara	L	
Hoffmann, Joseph Heinrich	21, Feb. 1856	Heinrich	Fortmann, M. Anna	C	
Hoffmann, Maria Angela	11, July 1859	Herman	Warnsmann, Anna Maria	F	
Hoffmann, Maria Josephina	11, May 1853	Herman	Warnsmann, Anna Maria	F	
Hoffmann, Maria Josephina	12, Jan. 1858	Johan	Frank, Maria	F	
Hoffmann, Peter Wendel	9, Aug. 1857	Peter	Boettigheimer, Regina	C	
Hoffmann, Susanna Elisabeth	13, Sept 1852	Peter	Daut, Barbara	C	
Hoffner, Georg	16, Jan. 1859	Aloysius	Behrman, Anna	U	
Hoffroge, Maria Agnes	27, Nov. 1859	J. Gerhard	Dexel, Marianna	F	
Hoffrogge, Anna Theresa	24, May 1857	Bernard H.	Winter, A. Angela	L	
Hoffrogge, Bernard	22, Aug. 1858	Herman	Herzog, Catharina M.	F	
Hoffrogge, Franz Friedrich	21, Oct. 1859	J. Heinrich	Reiter, Wilhelmina	L	
Hoffrogge, Gerhard Bernard	10, Nov. 1855	Bernard H.	Winters, Anna Engel	L	
Hoffrogge, Gerhard Heinrich	22, Feb. 1858	J. Heinrich	Dirksen, Maria Anna	K	
Hoffrogge, Gerhard Heinrich	9, Dec. 1857	J. Heinrich	Reiter, Wilhelmina	L	
Hoffrogge, Henrietta Gertrud Mech.	17, Mar. 1857	Anton	Post, Gertrud	A	
Hoffrogge, Herman Heinrich	16, July 1856	Gerhard H.	Herzog, Maria Anna	F	
Hoffrogge, Hugo Francis Xavier	1, Apr. 1854	J. Anton	Post, Gertrud	A	
Hoffrogge, J. Bernard Heinrich	6, June 1857	Gerhard B.	Cohors, M. Th.	C	
Hoffrogge, Johan Eduard	27, Sept 1859	Joseph A.	Post, Gertrud	A	
Hoffrogge, Johanna Josephina	1, Oct. 1851	Anton	Post, Gertrud	A	
Hoffrogge, Maria Angela	24, Apr. 1859	Bernard H.	Winters, Anna Angela	L	
Hofgesang, Barbara Margaretha	4, Dec. 1859	Caspar	Hoffmann, Margaret	C	
Hofgesang, Catharina	15, Feb. 1857	Caspar	Hoffmann, Margaretha	C	
Hofgesang, Elisabeth	5, Jan. 1851	Caspar	Hoffmann, Margaretha	C	
Hofgesang, Josephina	17, Apr. 1853	Caspar	Hoffmann, Margaretha	L	
Hofhaus, Carl	30, Dec. 1852	Anton	Wilke, Agatha	A	
Hofhaus, Maria Theresa	12, Nov. 1856	Gerhard T	Schulte, M. Gesina	L	
Höfken, Johan Bernard	2, Feb. 1853	B. Herman	Rademaker, Susanna	J	20
Höfker, Johan Herman	9, Jan. 1852	Herman	Rademaker, Susanna	J	16
Höfle, Johan	6, Apr. 1856	Paul	Eicher, Crescentia	D	55
Hofling, Georg Anton	7, Sept 1856	Georg	Klippel, Maria Magdalena	D	67
Hofman, Adolph	13, Oct. 1850	Xavier	Bechtel, Barbara	D	237
Hofman, Barbara	15, Dec. 1850	Mathias	Ludman, Christina	N	2
Hofman, Carolina	3, May 1857	Mathias	Lutman, Christina	N	
Hofman, Catharina Crescentia Apol.	15, Dec. 1857	Caspar	Wohlpert, Catharina	D	100
Hofman, Christina	23, Apr. 1854	Lawrence	Sauer, Genofeva	N	21
Hofman, Daniel	19, June 1856	Carl Anton	Kihn, Anna Maria	N	
Hofman, Georg	5, Sept 1852	Mathias	Ludman, Christina	N	8
Hofman, Georg	24, Sept 1854	Mathias	Ludman, Christina	N	24
Hofman, Heinrich	26, Apr. 1857	Adam	Herching, Barbara	D	84
Hofman, Johan	21, Oct. 1859	Mathias	Ludman, Christina	N	
Hofman, Sales Nicolaus	1, July 1858	Heinrich	Fortman, Maria Anna	N	
Hofreider, Anton	19, May 1850	Johan	Effger, Maria Catharina	D	213
Hofreiter, Eva Maria Magdalena	7, June 1852	Sebastian	----, Crescentia	H	
Hofreiter, Johan Sebastian	24, June 1853	Sebastian	Rittinger, Crescentia	D	391
Hofreiter, Philomena Victoria	14, July 1850	Sebastian	Rittinger, Crescentia	D	223
Hofstädler, Anna Maria	7, July 1851		adult - 49 years old	K	
Hofstätter, Anna Euphemia Elisabeth	8, Sept 1858	B. Heinrich	Frihler, Elisabeth	N	
Hog, Elisabeth	5, Sept 1858	John	Jentes, Catharine	N	
Hog, Wilhelm	23, Mar. 1856	Peter	Zahn, Catharina	D	54
Hogan, (boy)	13, Nov. 1859	Patrick	----, Joanne	M	
Hogan, Ann	25, Feb. 1853	?	Ryan, Joanne	V	1
Hogan, Ann	19, Oct. 1851	Anthony	Small, Julia	P	13a
Hogan, Ann	29, Apr. 1855	Michael	Russell, Eliza	E	283
Hogan, Ann	15, Jan. 1853	Patrick	McKenney, Mary	E	54
Hogan, Ann Mary	4, Oct. 1855	Michael	Woods, Mary	P	154

Name of Child	Date of Baptism	Father	Mother	Church	Page
Hogan, Bridget	17, Apr. 1859	Peter	Fox, Mary	E	618
Hogan, Bridget	23, Aug. 1854	Michael	Woods, Mary	B	4
Hogan, Catherine	16, Feb. 1850	Daniel	Hogan, Bridget	E	197
Hogan, Catherine	9, Sept 1856	Jeremiah	----, Catherine	E	397
Hogan, Catherine	30, Oct. 1859	Patrick	Purcell, Margaret	P	302
Hogan, Catherine	29, Oct. 1854	Thomas	Hennessy, Margaret	V	19
Hogan, Dennis John	11, Aug. 1856	Michael	Ryan, Helen	P	187
Hogan, Edward	20, Sept 1855	Patrick	Fincesey, Honora	R	
Hogan, Eliza	25, May 1859	Patrick	Flagherty, Ann	P	285
Hogan, Elizabeth	29, Dec. 1850	James	Dooly, Joanne	M	
Hogan, Ellen	13, Nov. 1853	Thomas	Kelly, Sarah	E	144
Hogan, Francis Christopher	1, Jan. 1859	Michael	Martin, Bridget	E	592
Hogan, Helen	19, Mar. 1858	Michael	Woods, Mary	P	243
Hogan, Honora	29, Mar. 1859	Patrick	McCanna, Mary	P	281
Hogan, Honora	7, Feb. 1855	Patrick	McDonough, Sabina	P	119
Hogan, James	5, Dec. 1857	James	Molony, Ann	V	42
Hogan, James	14, July 1854	Jeremiah	----, Catherine	E	207
Hogan, James	18, July 1858	John	Handly, Ann	P	254
Hogan, John	10, Feb. 1856	James	Malony, Ann	E	344
Hogan, John	8, May 1857	Jeremiah	Welsh, Eliza	E	451
Hogan, John	19, Dec. 1857	Michael	Ryan, Helen	P	233
Hogan, John	6, July 1856	Patrick	McNeary, Mary	E	379
Hogan, John	18, July 1852	Thomas	----, Elizabeth	E	429
Hogan, John	1, May 1859	Thomas	Kelly, Sally	E	622
Hogan, John Joseph	22, Oct. 1857	Patrick	McDonnell, Catherine	B	51
Hogan, John Thomas	5, Mar. 1858	Peter	----, Margaret	E	519
Hogan, Joseph	3, June 1853	Thomas	Harey, Mary	P	43
Hogan, Margaret	12, Aug. 1855	Michael	Ryan, Helen	P	145
Hogan, Mary	6, Sept 1852	M.	Woods, Mary	P	27
Hogan, Mary	13, Feb. 1856	Peter	Farrell, Julia	R	
Hogan, Mary	21, Sept 1856	Peter	Flood, Ann	P	193
Hogan, Mary	26, July 1858	Richard	King, Catherine	B	62
Hogan, Mary	5, Feb. 1854	Thomas	----, Mary	E	165
Hogan, Michael	16, Jan. 1859	Michael	Ryan, Ellen	P	272
Hogan, Michael	11, Aug. 1854	Patrick	Brien, Ann	P	92
Hogan, Patrick	20, Feb. 1853	Thomas	Gleason, Mary	E	63
Hogan, Peter Augustine	1, Nov. 1859	Patrick	McDonough, Catherine	B	83
Hogan, Prudence	19, May 1851	Arthur	Quinn, Juliana	B	232
Hogan, Sarah	3, June 1853	Thomas	Harey, Mary	P	43
Hogan, Susan Telia	26, Apr. 1853	Patrick	Camel, Ann	P	40
Hogan, Thomas	1, Nov. 1859	James	----, Ann	E	667
Hogan, Thomas	8, July 1855	James	Hannigan, Catherine	E	298
Hogan, Thomas	30, Apr. 1857	Thomas	Kelley, Sarah	E	450
Hogan, Thomas Dennis	29, Dec. 1857	Jeremiah	----, Catherine	E	504
Hogan, Wilhelm	23, July 1855	Patrick	----, Joanne	E	302
Hogan, William James	12, Oct. 1856	Andrew	Mara, Catherine	P	195
Hogarty, Martin	8, Apr. 1855	Martin	Frazier, Mary	B	13
Hogarty, Martin Henry	31, Aug. 1851	Michael	Flannelly, Isabel	B	240
Hogarty, Mary	16, May 1853	Martin	Hegarty, Mary	B	291
Hogarty, Mary	5, Feb. 1854	Michael	Flannelly, Isabel	B	308
Hogarty, Mary Ann	2, Dec. 1852	Michael	Flannery, Isabel	B	277
Hogeback, Bernard Heinrich	13, Nov. 1851	J. Heinrich	Tinkenker, Maria Adelheid	D	292
Hogeback, Gerhard Heinrich	16, Aug. 1857	Heinrich	Tinkler, Maria Anna	C	
Hogeback, Josephina Elisabeth	14, Aug. 1853	J. Heinrich	Tinckers, Maria Adelheid	D	400
Hogeback, Maria Anna	7, July 1850	J. Heinrich	Tinker, Maria Adelheid	D	221
Hogebuch, Maria Josephina	1, Mar. 1855	Georg H.	Tinker, Maria Adelheid	D	30
Hogeluch, Gerhard Herman Heinrich	24, Mar. 1855	H. Heinrich	Böhmer, Maria	K	
Högeman, Gerhard Heinrich	25, Dec. 1858	Herman H.	Püning, Anna Sophia	A	
Höger, Maria Carolina	9, June 1850	Joseph	Geisler, Walburga	A	

Name of Child	Date of Baptism	Father	Mother	Church	Page
Hoghan, James	18, Aug. 1858	Thomas	Quinlan, Joanne	P	258
Hogin, Jeremiah	20, Apr. 1853	Jeremiah	Riordi, Catherine	E	82
Hogin, John	24, June 1855	William	Murphy, Elizabeth	U	
Hohenbrink, Anna Maria	2, July 1853	Joseph	Bonte, Maria Gesina	J	22
Hohenegger, Johan Georg	27, Aug. 1854	Peter	Fromm, Catharina Maria	D	16
Hohenleitner, Joseph	27, July 1856	Joseph	Weyand, Carolina	F	
Hohenleitner, Maria	20, Feb. 1853	Joseph	Weyand, Carolina	F	
Hohler, Philipp	24, Mar. 1850	Johan	Rob, Margaretha	D	206
Hohman, Albert Herman Heinrich	23, Oct. 1857	T. Herman	Friehler, Margaretha	N	
Hohman, Carolina Louisa	21, Dec. 1856	Francis	Breitenbach, Maria	D	74
Hohman, Herman Albert	8, Nov. 1858	Albert	Benolgen, Catharina	N	
Hohman, Maria Francisca	26, Aug. 1858	Francis	Breitenbach, Maria Louisa	D	118
Hohmann, Johan Franz	23, Mar. 1851	Johan H.	Dressler, Maria	F	
Hohmann, Maria Margaretha	26, Apr. 1856	Herman H.	Ackermann, Margaretha	F	
Hohn, Georg Michael	2, Oct. 1853	Francis L.	Marschall, Anna Maria	A	
Hohn, Heinrich	30, Sept 1855	F. Lothar	Marschal, Anna Maria	A	
Hohneck, Friedrich August	4, Feb. 1852	Valentin	Pfleger, Elisabeth	D	305
Hohnegger, Francis Anton	22, Aug. 1852	Peter	Fromm, Catharina M.	D	344
Hohnhorst, Anna Maria Elisabeth	11, June 1852	Joseph	Raber, Maria Gertrud	K	
Hohnhorst, Anna Philomena	2, July 1850	Theodor	Heheman, Charlotte Dorothea	K	
Hohnhorst, Bernard Heinrich	8, Apr. 1858	Joseph	Rave, Maria Gertrud	K	
Hohnhorst, Johan Friedrich Wilhelm	19, June 1853	J. Theodor	Heheman, Charlotte Dorothea	K	
Hohnhorst, Joseph	20, May 1856	Georg	Rabe, Gertrud	K	
Hohnhorst, Maria Gertrud	2, Feb. 1854	Joseph	Rabe, Maria Gertrud	K	
Hohnhorst, Wilhelm Theodor	15, May 1856	J. Theodor	Heheman, Carolina Dorothea	K	
Hoin, Joseph	13, Apr. 1856	Johan	Menker, Catharina	D	56
Hoing, Bernard Joseph Anton	20, Feb. 1859	Alexander	Brökerhoff, Elisabeth	A	
Hoing, Francis C. Anton Herman	11, Mar. 1851	Anton	Meyer, Margaretha	J	10
Höing, Heinrich Ludwig	30, Oct. 1854	Johan	Ostendorf, Elisabeth	D	21
Höing, Maria Elisabeth	22, Jan. 1857	Alexander	Bröckhoff, Elisabeth	A	
Höker, Bernard Wilhelm	7, Feb. 1858	Johan B.	Greskamp, Catharina	K	
Hölcher, Bernard Mathias	23, Feb. 1852	Francis	Schuhmacher, Elisabeth	A	
Holcker, Elisabeth	9, June 1853	Francis	Schuhmacher, Elisabeth	C	
Holcomb, Thomas	20, Feb. 1853		adult	B	284
Hold, Johan	5, Apr. 1858	Johan	Benninger, Elisabeth	C	
Holden, Daniel	18, Sept 1858	Johan	Riley, Margaret	U	
Holden, James	18, Sept 1853	William	Stokes, Margaret	B	299
Holden, Mary	11, Nov. 1855	John	Reilly, Margaret	U	
Holden, Mary Elizabeth	13, Nov. 1854	William	Stokes, Margaret	B	7
Holden, William Joseph	1, May 1859	William	Stokes, Margaret	B	74
Holdkamp, Bernard Francis	10, Apr. 1853	Joseph	Husman, Theresa	D	380
Holdkamp, Johan Joseph	18, Sept 1850	Joseph	Husman, Theresa	D	233
Holdmeier, Anna Elisabeth	3, Feb. 1855	Gerhard C.	F----, Anna E.	D	27
Holdmeyer, Catharina Maria	20, Nov. 1850	Francis H.	Deppe, Maria Elisabeth	D	243
Holdmeyer, Eberhard Heinrich	22, June 1859	Christian	Kutman, Elisabeth	D	140
Holfel, Johan Christoph	15, Aug. 1850	Adam	Tar, Catharina	D	228
Holgreber, Adelheid Amalia Gertrud	13, Jan. 1858	Joseph	Ortmeyer, Amalia	N	
Hölker, Johan Martin	1, Sept 1858	Ferdinand	Egbers, Helena	A	
Hölker, Johan Theodor	16, May 1853	Ferdinand	Egbers, Helena	A	
Hölker, Joseph Wilhelm	27, May 1855	J. Heinrich	Egbers, Maria Helena	A	
Holker, Maria Helena	14, Nov. 1851	Ferdinand	Egbers, Helena	L	
Hollaender, Adam Francis	3, Dec. 1854	Adam	Flersinger, Christina	C	
Hollahan, Elizabeth	24, May 1859	Michael	----, Margaret	E	628
Holland, (girl)	17, Feb. 1852	Hugh	Kelley, Mary	E	384
Holland, Catherine	19, Sept 1858	Morris	Camedy, Mary	E	564
Holland, Daniel John	19, July 1857	James	Delaney, Margaret	V	40
Holland, Elizabeth	25, July 1857	Thomas	Bird, Julia	E	469
Holland, James	5, Feb. 1854	John	Moran, Mary	E	165
Holland, John	24, Sept 1859	Thomas	Bird, Julia	E	656

Name of Child	Date of Baptism	Father	Mother	Church	Page
Holland, Mary Ann	13, Sept 1857	John	Wacker, Mary	V	41
Holland, Michael	3, Oct. 1852	Thomas	----, Fahoe?	E	23
Holland, Michael	6, May 1855	Thomas	Birds, Julia	E	284
Holland, Patrick	13, Oct. 1852	Patrick	----, Bridget	E	27
Holland, Richard	19, Nov. 1853	Patrick	Hearby, Bridget	E	145
Holländer, Anna Maria	21, Feb. 1857	Adam	Fleckinger, Christina	D	79
Hollander, Emma	1, Dec. 1859	Gregor	Gleich, Eva	F	
Holländer, Peter	1, Jan. 1859	Adam	Fleckinger, Christina	D	128
Hollbrach, Anna Maria Catharina	29, Apr. 1854	Heinrich	Schuhmacher, Catharina	C	
Holle, Christopher Anthony	2, July 1854	Francis	----, Christine	H	
Holle, John B.	2, Sept 1855	Francis	----, Christine	H	
Holle, John Francis	3, Aug. 1852	Francis	----, Christine	H	
Hollen, Anna Catharina	6, Mar. 1854	Stephan	Freicking, Elisabeth	C	
Hollen, Bernard	18, Mar. 1858	Stephan W.	Frecking, Elisabeth	A	
Hollen, Herman Joseph	18, Nov. 1855	Stephan	Freking, Maria Elisabeth	C	
Hollen, Johan Heinrich	8, June 1851	B. Heinrich	Fleckterkotter, Theresa	K	
Hollenbeck, Johan Gustav	24, Mar. 1859	Johan	----, Louisa	C	
Hollenbrink, Johan Bernard	11, July 1858	Johan	Pleking, Marianna	F	
Hollencamp, Francis Joseph	26, Oct. 1851	H. Bernard	Grüter, Maria Elisabeth	A	
Hollenkamp, Gerhard Francis	3, Sept 1854	G. Heinrich	Reinke, Maria Gertrud	J	28
Hollenkamp, Gerhard Heinrich	2, Nov. 1850	Herman H.	Wellmeyer, Theresa	L	
Hollenkamp, Johan Herman	27, Aug. 1850	Bernard	Grüter, Elisabeth	A	
Hollenkamp, Joseph Bernard	7, Nov. 1850	Gerhard H.	Reinken, Maria Gertrud	A	
Hollenkamp, Maria Anna Catharina	11, Aug. 1851	J. Gerhard	Depweh, Maria Elisabeth	F	
Hollenkamp, Maria Bernardina	9, Oct. 1859	J. Heinrich	Rechtin, Maria	C	
Holler, Anna Thecla	22, May 1859	Joseph	Wolf, Barbara	A	
Holler, Bertha	6, Dec. 1857	Andreas	Schmidling, Anna Maria	D	100
Holler, Catharina	1, Oct. 1854	Johan	Rupp, Margaretha	C	
Holler, Heinrich	11, May 1856	Sebastian	Schmalholz, Margaretha	D	58
Holler, Jacob	24, Oct. 1852	Adam	Reising, Anna Maria	D	354
Holler, Johan	4, Apr. 1857	Johan	Rapp, Margaretha	D	82
Holler, Johan Heinrich	29, Apr. 1852	Stephen W.	Freking, M. Elisabeth	C	
Holler, Joseph	18, June 1854	Adam	Reising, Anna Maria	D	12
Holler, Magdalena	24, Mar. 1852	Johan	Rapp, Margaretha	D	314
Holler, Maria Albertina	20, Apr. 1851	Adam	Reising, Anna Maria	D	261
Holler, Maria Elisabeth	22, Apr. 1855	Heinrich	Fisse, Marianna	F	
Holler, Maria Eva	12, Oct. 1851	Peter	Grösch, Margaretha	D	286
Holler, Rosina	14, Aug. 1853	Peter	Greser, Margaretha	D	400
Holler, Valentin	1, Nov. 1857	Joseph	Wolf, Barbara	C	
Holleran, Ellen	7, Nov. 1858	John	Finnigan, Ann	E	577
Holleran, Patrick	27, Apr. 1856	John	Finnigan, Ann	E	362
Hollerbach, Johan	22, Sept 1856	Johan	Scherer, Louisa	K	
Hollermann, Anna Maria Elisabeth	9, May 1850	Bernard	Paske, Gertrud	F	
Hollermann, Anton Herman	27, Sept 1852	Bernard	Paske, Gertrud	F	
Hollermann, Bernard	9, May 1850	Bernard	Paske, Gertrud	F	
Hollermann, Elisabeth	10, May 1857	Wilhelm	Schneider, Elisabeth	F	
Hollermann, Wilhelm Bernard	25, Dec. 1859	Wilhelm	Schneider, Elisabeth	F	
Holling, Johan Herman	7, Feb. 1859	J. Herman	Beumer, Theresa	K	
Hollinger, Adelheid	10, Apr. 1859	Alexander	Eckstein, Ludgardis	N	
Hollinger, Carolina	21, Mar. 1852	Alexander	Exstein, Lucata	K	
Hollinger, Joseph Wendel	23, Nov. 1856	J. Wilhelm	Regelsperger, Magdalena	N	
Hollinger, Louisa	22, Sept 1856	Alexander	Eckstein, Lugarda	N	
Hollinger, Mathilda Genofeva	21, Feb. 1858	Joseph	Regelsperger, Magdalena	N	
Hollivan, Edward James	24, Nov. 1859	James	Delany, Margaret	P	304
Hollman, Catharina Elisabeth	5, July 1859	Bernard	Brinkmeyer, Maria Elisabeth	A	
Hollmann, Clara Elisabeth	4, June 1850	Heinrich	Stockhof, Clara	F	
Hollmann, Franz Heinrich	22, Jan. 1852	Heinrich	Stockhof, Clara	F	
Hollmann, Heinrich Aloysius	3, Apr. 1854	Heinrich	Stockhof, Clara	F	
Hollmeier, Georg Heinrich	30, Oct. 1857	Gerhard	Riessing, Maria Elisabeth	D	98

Name of Child	Date of Baptism	Father	Mother	Church	Page
Holloran, Mary	13, Mar. 1853	Francis	Forrester, Mary	B	286
Holloran, Thomas	31, Dec. 1854	James	Delany, Margaret	B	9
Holly, Elizabeth	6, June 1852		adult - 25 years old	B	260
Hol--ly, James	25, Nov. 1851	Patrick	Davis, Ann S.	B	246
Holly, John	24, Jan. 1859	Michael	----, Margaret	E	599
Holly, Margaret	19, Dec. 1854	John	----, Winnefred	E	248
Holly, Michael	30, Aug. 1853	John	----, Winneford	E	124
Holly, Robert John	30, Oct. 1859	Robert	----, Bridget	E	666
Holly, William	31, Aug. 1856	John	Gibbens, Winny	E	394
Holm---, Gerhard Heinrich	17, Nov. 1856	Gerhard H.	----, Maria Elisabeth	D	72
Holman, Jane Louise	12, May 1853	John	McFeeley, Joanne	B	291
Holmes, Catherine	24, Sept 1854	Nicolaus	Flaherty, Mary	V	18
Holmes, Eliza	21, May 1859		adult - 25 years old	E	626
Holmes, Francis Edward	15, July 1857	William	Roberg, Sophia	D	90
Holmes, George William	15, July 1857	William	Roberg, Sophia	D	90
Holmes, Johan Edward	12, July 1855	Wilhelm	Ruberg, Sophia	K	
Holmes, John	21, Apr. 1854	Eugene	McHale, Ann	B	313
Holmes, John	10, May 1857	Martin	Hannaghan, Judith	P	212
Holmes, Juliana Margaretha	6, Mar. 1853	William	Ruberg, Sophia	K	
Hölmes, Maria Elisabeth	3, Feb. 1854	Bernard H.	Kriesel, Anna Maria	D	3
Holmes, Mary	17, Mar. 1855	Eugene	McHale, Ann	P	125
Holmes, Mary Ann	28, June 1858	Owen	McHale, Nancy	P	252
Holmes, Mary Eliza	7, June 1851	Ezekiel	----, Mary Eliza	B	233
Holmes, Neal	10, Nov. 1859		adult - 21 years old	E	670
Holmes, Patrick	4, Feb. 1855	Martin	Hanahoe, Julia	P	118
Holmes, Stephen	8, Feb. 1853	James	Johnson, Elizabeth	E	61
Holmes, Walter William	17, Aug. 1858	Ezekiel	Golden, Bridget	E	558
Holms, Thomas	17, Apr. 1859	Martin	Hanehy, Julia	P	282
Holscher, Elisabeth Theresa	18, Dec. 1851	Herman	Hessling, Theresa	A	
Hölscher, Francis Anton Bernard	16, Sept 1854	Bernard	Hoing, Francisca	A	
Hölscher, Francis Mathias	21, Sept 1853	Mathias	Mitges, Maria Elisabeth	D	407
Holscher, Franz Anton	30, June 1850	Francis C.	Reiser, Rosina	L	
Hölscher, Johan Alexander	21, Sept 1856	Bernard	Höing, Francisca	A	
Hölscher, Johan Gerhard Heinrich	14, Oct. 1855	J. Mathias	Mitges, Maria Elisabeth	D	44
Hölscher, Johan Heinrich	12, Dec. 1854	Friedrich	Kumpmeyer, Elisabeth	A	
Hölscher, Johan Joseph	5, Apr. 1857	Francis	Klein, Maria	A	
Hölscher, Maria Christina	1, Mar. 1853	Herman F.	Kolkmeier, Catharina Elis.	A	
Hölscher, Maria Josepha	4, Dec. 1859	Francis H.	Klein, Maria Anna	A	
Holstermann, Bernard Clemens	21, July 1859	Clemens	Hamer, Regina	T	
Holstermann, Bernard Heinrich	8, June 1853	Clemens	Haarmann, Regina	F	
Holstermann, Johan Bernard	22, Nov. 1855	Clemens	Harman, Maria Regina	F	
Holt, Ann Mary	11, Dec. 1853		adult - 19 years old	P	61
Holt, Maria Catharina	7, Aug. 1859	Gerhard	Gruening, Maria	L	
Holt, Maria Josephina	9, Dec. 1855	Joseph	Deppe, Maria	D	48
Holt, Maria Rosalia	20, Feb. 1854	Joseph	Deppe, Maria	D	5
Holt, Philomena	9, Apr. 1858	Joseph	Deppe, Maria	D	109
Holte, Maria Catharina	9, Apr. 1850	Gerhard B.	Dirker, Maria Elisabeth	A	
Holtel, Anna Christina	12, Oct. 1854	G. Bernard	Lübbers, Maria Adelheid	D	19
Holtel, Bernard Francis	10, Apr. 1853	Gerhard H.	Nägel, Anna Christina	D	380
Holtel, Heinrich Ludwig	17, Aug. 1856	Gerhard H.	Naegel, Anna Christina	D	65
Holtel, Johan Wilhelm	26, July 1858	Gerhard H.	Naegel, Christina	D	116
Holtel, Maria Elisabeth	13, Nov. 1854	Gerhard H.	Nägel, Anna Christina	D	22
Holten, Euphemia Maria Catharina	9, June 1852	G. Bernard	Luppers, Maria Adelheid	D	323
Holtenreider, Friedrich Michael	30, Apr. 1854	Tobias	Eiser, Catharina	D	9
Holtermann, Cath. Philomena Marg.	6, Sept 1851	J. Herman	Taphorn, Margaretha	L	
Holters, Anna Catharina Rosa	23, Dec. 1853	Heinrich	Wilke, Maria Catharina	A	
Holters, Catharina Philomena	21, Jan. 1851	J. Bernard	Stuerwald, Helena	A	
Holters, Georg Heinrich	10, Oct. 1854	J. Gerhard	Borgers, Bernardina	C	
Holters, Johan Bernard	14, Nov. 1855	J. Bernard	Sturwald, Maria Magdalena	A	

Name of Child	Date of Baptism	Father	Mother	Church	Page
Holters, Johan Francis	7, June 1857	J. Heinrich	Wilke, Catharina	A	
Holters, Maria Bernardina Philomena	13, Mar. 1851	J. Heinrich	Wilke, Maria Catharina	A	
Holters, Maria Catharina Josephina	6, June 1859	Gerhard	Börger, Anna Maria	A	
Holters, Maria Elisabeth	18, Oct. 1859	Heinrich	Wilke, Catharina	A	
Holters, Maria Helena	20, July 1853	Bernard	Stuerwold, Maria Helena	A	
Holters, Wilhelm Heinrich	19, June 1858	Bernard	Sturwald, ----	A	
Holtes, Joseph Bernard	19, Oct. 1856	Gerhard	Borger, Maria Johanna	C	
Holtgraeve, Maria Catharina	8, July 1852	Conrad	Naegle, Gertrud	K	
Holthaus, A. Maria	26, Dec. 1857	Eberhard	Baute, A. Maria	T	
Holthaus, Anna Elisabeth	31, Jan. 1856	Heinrich	Flege, Elisabeth	A	
Holthaus, Anna Maria	19, Feb. 1854	B. Heinrich	Brune, Maria Elisabeth	K	
Holthaus, Anna Maria Elisabeth	19, Mar. 1852	J. Bernard	Brune, Anna Maria	K	
Holthaus, Bernard Ludwig	10, Oct. 1852	Bernard	Baumer, Elisabeth	L	
Holthaus, Catharina Josephina	14, Nov. 1855	B. Heinrich	Prune, Anna Maria	K	
Holthaus, Elisabeth	23, Oct. 1851	Heinrich	Flege, Elisabeth	K	
Holthaus, Friedrich Wilhelm	25, June 1853	Bernard	Dierks, Anna M.	C	
Holthaus, Gesina Philomena	17, Aug. 1857	B. Heinrich	Bruns, Anna Maria	K	
Holthaus, Heinrich	6, Apr. 1856	Eberhard	Baute, Anna Maria	F	
Holthaus, Johan Bernard	13, June 1850	J. Bernard	Brune, Anna M. Elisabeth	C	
Holthaus, Johan Bernard	25, Jan. 1858	J. Heinrich	Flege, Elisabeth	A	
Holthaus, Johan Caspar	28, Sug. 1859	F. Heinrich	Grave, Maria Elisabeth	K	
Holthaus, Johan Heinrich	15, Dec. 1858	J. Heinrich	Broerman, Maria Elisabeth	A	
Holthaus, Johan Heirnich	30, Apr. 1857	Francis H.	Grafe, Maria Elisabeth	K	
Holthaus, Maria Elisabeth	8, Nov. 1854	Eberhard	Bauten, Anna Maria	F	
Holthaus, Maria Theresa	3, Aug. 1859	Eberhard	Baute, Anna Maria	T	
Holthaus, Maria Theresa	16, Oct. 1853	Heinrich	Flege, Anna Regina Elisabeth	A	
Holthaus, Philomena Elisabeth	29, Sept 1850	J. Bernard	Böhmer, Elisabeth	K	
Holtheide, Catharina Margaretha	19, Jan. 1853	Heinrich	Kellermann, Catharina	C	
Holtheide, Johan Bernard Heinrich	6, Aug. 1857	Herman H.	Kellermann, Catharina	C	
Holtheide, Johan Clemens August	25, Jan. 1851	Herman H.	Kellermann, A. Catharina	L	
Holtheide, M. Elisabeth Francisca	8, Sept 1854	Herman	Kellermann, Catharina	C	
Holtkamp, Anna Gertrud	4, Nov. 1856	Heinrich	Tieke, M. Elisabeth	C	
Holtkamp, Anna Maria Catharina	15, Apr. 1850	Joseph	Tillman, Anna Catharina	K	
Holtkamp, Anna Philomena	2, Jan. 1857	B. Joseph	Thelen, Anna Angela	K	
Holtkamp, Caspar Heinrich	29, July 1857	J. Friedrich	Kleimeier, Maria	K	
Holtkamp, Gerhard Joseph	10, Dec. 1854	Joseph	Harsman, Theresa	D	23
Holtkamp, Johan Heinrich	29, Nov. 1851	J. Heinrich	Dieke, Maria Elisabeth	D	294
Holtkamp, Mathias Joseph	24, Feb. 1854	Heinrich	Tieker, Elisabeth	A	
Holtman, Bernard Anton	2, Jan. 1859	Bernard	Nienaber, Maria	K	
Holtman, Philipp	7, July 1850	Georg	Block, Theresa	D	221
Holtmann, Everhard Heinrich	17, Oct. 1858	J. Francis	Baute, Maria	L	
Holtmann, Francis Heinrich	3, Feb. 1850	Francis	Bauten, M. Elisabeth	L	
Holtmann, Franz Heinrich	11, Sept 1856	Francis H.	Baute, M. Elisabeth	L	
Holtmann, Johan Friedrich	1, Feb. 1852	Francis H.	Bauten, Elisabeth	L	
Holtmann, Maria Angela	14, June 1854	Francis H.	Baute, Elisabeth	L	
Holtmeier, Elisabeth	16, Jan. 1853	Christian	Kortman, Elisabeth	D	365
Holtmeier, Francis Bernard	8, Feb. 1854	Francis	Tepe, Maria Catharina	D	4
Holtmeier, Francis Heinrich	15, Dec. 1857	Francis H.	Tepe, Maria Elisabeth	D	100
Holtmeier, Heinrich	23, Aug. 1857	Christian	Kothmeier, Elisabeth	D	93
Holton, George	7, Aug. 1856	Thomas	----, Ann	E	388
Holweg, Johan Friedrich	18, Feb. 1852	Jacob	Schildering, Adelheid	C	
Holweg, Maria Friedricka	27, Mar. 1851	Jacob	Schildering, Adelheid	C	
Holz, Adam	9, Jan. 1853	Joseph	Stephani, Catharina	D	364
Holz, Elisabeth	1, May 1856	Johan	Lorenz, Maria Anna	N	
Holz, Georg	12, Feb. 1850		adult	F	
Holz, Johan Wilhelm	15, Nov. 1857	Johan B.	Lorenz, Maria	N	
Holz, Pauline	6, May 1854	Johan	Koch, Gertrud	N	22
Holz, Valentin	18, Jan. 1859	Johan	Lorenz, Maria	N	
Holzbach, Veronica	26, Nov. 1854	William	Schlosser, Anna Maria	D	22

Name of Child	Date of Baptism	Father	Mother	Church	Page
Holzbach, Wilhelm	24, Oct. 1852	Wilhelm	Schleper, Anna Maria	A	
Holzback, Maria Elisabeth	12, May 1850	Wilhelm	Schlosser, Anna Maria	L	
Holzleder, Anna Maria	24, Apr. 1853	Georg	Röslein, Gertrud	J	22
Holzlin, Catharina Beata	5, July 1857	Georg	Ahlers, Elisabeth Catharina	D	89
Holzman, Johan Christian	5, Nov. 1854		Holzman, Cunigunda	D	21
Holzmann, Albert Franz Robert	6, Mar. 1857	Johan	Rebold, Clara	L	
Holzmann, Georg Rudolph	12, Sept 1858	Johan	Rebold, Clara	L	
Holzmann, Johan	21, Oct. 1854	Johan	Rebold, Clara	L	
Holzmann, Margaretha Emilia	4, Nov. 1855	Johan	Rehbold, Clara	L	
Holzmeister, Carl	30, May 1858	Jacob	Schreck, Eva	D	112
Homan, Johan Bernard	16, Feb. 1854	Johan	Daie, Anna Maria	D	4
Homan, Johan Bernard Heinrich	9, July 1852	Albert	Benölcken, Catharina	N	8
Homan, Maria Catharina	13, Jan. 1852	Johan	Daie, Maria Anna	D	302
Homan, Maria Elisabeth	28, Feb. 1856	Albert	Benolgen, Catharina	N	
Homann, Amalia Bernardina	11, Dec. 1853	Heinrich	Ackermann, Margaret	C	
Homann, Anna Catharina	17, Feb. 1858	Joseph	Greiwe, Anna	C	
Homann, Anna Philomena	5, June 1859	Francis	Brock, M. Anna	C	
Homann, Francis Xavier	3, Dec. 1851	Heinrich	Ackermann, Margaretha	C	
Homann, Johan Albert	24, Oct. 1851	J. Heinrich	Brinkmann, Theresa	L	
Homann, Martha Elisabeth	11, Nov. 1858	Herman H.	Ackermann, Margaretha	C	
Homberg, Johan Gerhard	29, Nov. 1857	Heinrich	Dinker, Anna Maria	A	
Homberg, Louisa	15, Oct. 1859	Wilhelm	Dre---, Catharina	D	149
Home, William	19, Feb. 1854	Solomon	adult - 36 years old	E	169
Hommelmeyer, Ferdinand	3, Mar. 1850	Friedrich	Gelhausen, Antonia	C	
Hommelmeyer, Maria	7, Dec. 1851	Friedrich	Gelhaus, Antonette	L	
Honberger, Florenz	12, Sept 1858	Lawrence	Tresner, Johanna	K	
Hone, Peter	10, Apr. 1853	Peter	----, Ann	E	80
Honeck, Maria Louisa	27, Jan. 1850	Johan	Moser, Catharina	C	
Honelage?, Johan Joseph Theodor	20, Mar. 1859	Joseph	Wesselman, Anna Maria	D	134
Hönemeier, Maria Catharina	18, Aug. 1859	Gerhard H.	Rusche, Maria Agnes	A	
Honer, Albert	1, Mar. 1857	J. Baptist	Bock, Anna	A	
Honer, Amalia	24, July 1853	Xavier	----, Catharina	D	396
Honer, Johan Francis	16, Jan. 1859	J. Baptist	Bock, Anna	A	
Honfund, Maria Magdalena	10, Sept 1855	Joseph	Fennie, Elisabeth	L	
Honig, Friedrich	6, July 1854	Valentin	Pfleger, Elisabeth	D	13
Honig, Heinrich	11, Mar. 1858	Valentin	Pfleger, Elisabeth	D	106
Honigfort, Herman Heinrich	6, Mar. 1854	H. Bernard	Müller, Anna Margaretha	R	
Honigfort, Maria Margaretha	24, Nov. 1852	Herman B.	Moeller, Anna Margaret	F	
Honkamp, Anna Bernardina	4, Oct. 1856	Heinrich	Hausfeld, Anna M.	L	
Honkamp, Bernard Lawrence	9, Jan. 1851	Friedrich	Rabe, Anna Maria	A	
Honkomp, Anna Maria	29, July 1859	Heinrich	Hausfeld, Anna Maria	L	
Honkomp, Arnold	23, Nov. 1856	Anton	Klausing, Elisabeth	C	
Honkomp, Bernard Joseph	19, June 1853	Anton	Klausing, Elisabeth	C	
Honkomp, Bernardina	29, May 1851	Herman H.	Hausfeld, Anna Maria	L	
Honkomp, Francis Johan	16, Sept 1856	Friedrich	Rabe, Bernardina	A	
Honkomp, Heinrich Joseph	7, Apr. 1855	Anton	Klausing, Elisabeth	C	
Honkomp, Joseph Lorenz	20, Feb. 1854	Herman H.	Hausfeld, Maria	L	
Honkomp, Maria Catharina Emilia	2, Oct. 1852	Friedrich	Rabe, Bernardina	K	
Honkum, Anna Maria Elisabeth	15, Aug. 1858	Anton	Klausing, Elisabeth	C	
Hönner, Anna Maria	11, Feb. 1855	Michael	Gotz, Barbara	K	
Honuld, Caspar	15, Dec. 1856	Joseph	Weh---, Maria A.	D	74
Honzert, Rosina Magdalena	21, June 1857	Stephan	Weis, Sabina	K	
Hood, Edward	27, Oct. 1850	Jonathan	----, Mary	B	217
Hood, James	4, Nov. 1856	James	Rielly, Ann	B	36
Hood, John	14, Nov. 1858	John	Reilly, Ann	B	67
Hood, Margaret	18, Jan. 1856		adult	B	24
Hood, Margaret Ann	12, Mar. 1854	John	Briling, Ann	B	311
Hood, Sarah	15, Feb. 1852	Benjamin	adult - 22 years old	E	382
Hoog, Carolina	25, Dec. 1858	Bernard	Doll, Monica	F	

Name of Child	Date of Baptism	Father	Mother	Church	Page
Hoog, Francisca	17, Aug. 1856	Bernard	Doll, Monica	F	
Hoog, Maria Anna	23, Aug. 1857	Sebastian	Wagener, Maria Anna	K	
Hook, Anastasia	28, Nov. 1855	J. Aloysius	Wolff, Mary	P	161
Hook, James Abrose	29, Nov. 1857	Daniel	Wolf, Mary A.	B	52
Hook, John Francis	14, Dec. 1859	John A.	Wolf, MaryA.	B	85
Hook, Mary	25, Mar. 1854		adult - 27 years old	P	75
Hoolahan, Elizabeth Frances	13, Apr. 1851	John	Jones, Elizabeth	B	229
Hoolahan, Mary Ann	28, Nov. 1852	Bartholomew	----, Ellen	E	39
Hoolahan, Sarah Jane	13, Apr. 1851	John	Jones, Elizabeth	B	229
Hooley, Edward	8, Oct. 1855	Patrick	Ryan, Barbara	E	320
Hooligan, Alma	25, Mar. 1858	Michael	Hoctor, Margaret	E	524
Hooligan, Dennis	18, May 1855	Bartholomew	Keefe, Ellen	E	287
Hooligan, William	29, June 1856	Michael	Hocter, Margaret	E	378
Hoolihan, Helen Mary	4, May 1856	Bartholomew	Keefe, Helen	E	364
Hoolihan, John	21, July 1856	Cornelius	Daily, Catherine	E	383
Hoolihan, John	24, July 1854	Henry	Hector, Margaret	E	210
Hoolihan, Margaret	2, Apr. 1854	Thomas	Raspe, Ann	R	
Hoover, Francis Joseph	12, Mar. 1850	Joseph	Able, Rose Ann	E	203
Hopf, Barbara	25, Jan. 1852	Peter	Schaefer, Maria	C	
Hopf, Christine	15, Apr. 1858	Michael	Wagenhäuser, Maria Anna	H	
Hopf, Conrad	17, Feb. 1856	Peter	Schaefer, Maria Anna	C	
Hopf, Johan	29, Sept 1850	Valentin	Rank, Maria Eva	F	
Hopf, Johan Adam	4, Apr. 1858	Peter Jos	Schaefer, M. Anna	C	
Hopf, Johan Baptist	7, Apr. 1850	Michael	Wagner, Anna Maria	H	
Hopf, Johan Georg	13, Nov. 1853	Peter J.	Schaefer, M. Anna	C	
Hopf, Louis Joseph	30, Oct. 1859	Joseph	Schaefer, M. Anna	C	
Hopf, Magdalena	13, June 1852	Michael	----, Anna Maria	H	
Hopf, Maria	9, Dec. 1854	Heinrich	Becker, Maria	F	
Hopf, Mary Magdalene	Jan. 1854	Michael	----, Anna Maria	H	
Hopf, Peter	8, Feb. 1852	Valentin	Rau, Eva	C	
Hopf, Theobald	17, Mar. 1856	Michael	----, Ann	H	
Hoping, Franz Heinrich	1, Dec. 1856	Johan H.	Buettner, M. Bernardina	F	
Hoping, Johan Bernard	3, Dec. 1854	Johan	Buettner, Bernardina	F	
Höpink, Elisabeth Philomena	22, June 1859	Bernard	KleineBornhorst, Bernardina	K	
Höpink, Francis Bernard	22, June 1859	Bernard	KleineBornhorst, Bernardina	K	
Hopkins, Andrew	25, Dec. 1855	Joseph	----, Eliza	E	334
Hopkins, Ann	25, Aug. 1854	Martin	----, Bridget	E	219
Hopkins, Anthony	23, Mar. 1856	Martin	----, Bridget	E	352
Hopkins, Catherine	22, Feb. 1854	Patrick	Fitzpatrick, Helen	P	70
Hopkins, Catherine	7, May 1854	Thomas	O'Brien, Catherine	P	81
Hopkins, Edward	9, Sept 1855	Michael	Morgan, Catherine	B	18
Hopkins, Edward Henry	6, Oct. 1859	Edward	Robinson, Juliana	E	660
Hopkins, Elizabeth	13, Mar. 1859	Patrick	Fitzpatrick, Ellen	P	279
Hopkins, Elizabeth	4, Sept 1858	Thomas	O'Brien, Catherine	P	259
Hopkins, Helen	13, June 1857	Patrick	Fitzpatrick, Helen	P	214
Hopkins, John	28, Dec. 1857	Martin	----, Bridget	E	504
Hopkins, John	2, Oct. 1859	Patrick	Carroll, Caroline	E	659
Hopkins, John	29, Oct. 1854	Peter	Reily, Bridget	B	7
Hopkins, John Edward	28, Feb. 1854	Thomas	Kelly, Helen	B	310
Hopkins, John Washington	24, Apr. 1858	Edward	----, Julia	E	531
Hopkins, Mary Ann	25, July 1858	John	Farrell, Catherine	P	255
Hopkins, Mary Ann	5, Aug. 1855	Patrick	Fitzpatrick, Helen	P	143
Hopkins, Mary Jane	2, Mar. 1856	Thomas	O'Brien, Catherine	P	171
Hopkins, Mary Josephine	1, Jan. 156	Edward	Robinson, Julia	E	335
Hopkins, Sophia Margaret	12, Jan. 1859	Michael	Meyan?, Catherine	B	69
Hopp, Anna Maria Lisette	26, Apr. 1854	Heinrich	Kroesche, Maria	C	
Hopp, Maria Anna	2, Mar. 1856	Herman H.	----, Maria	C	
Hoppe, Johan Heinrich	31, July 1856	Dominick	Dusterberg, Catharina	C	
Hoppe, Martin Johan Nicolaus	3, Oct. 1858	Heinrich	Gresche, Maria	F	

Name of Child	Date of Baptism	Father	Mother	Church	Page
Hoppe, Theodor Wilhelm	18, Dec. 1859	Dominick	Dusterberg, Elisabeth	C	
Hopper, James Robert	25, June 1851	Jonathan	Perry, Eliza Ann	B	235
Hopser, Herman Heinrich Joseph	14, Jan. 1856	Herman H.	Mescher, Catharina M.	L	
Hopster, Elisabeth	13, Feb. 1856	Heinrich	Rohe, Maria Angela	K	
Hopster, Johan Herman	17, Feb. 1858	Herman	Merscher, Catharina	L	
Hopster, Maria Angela	3, May 1852	Heinrich	Rohe, Anna Maria	K	
Horack, Joseph Johan	3, July 1859	Johan	Pikawa, Anna	L	
Horag, Joseph Wilhelm	4, Apr. 1857	Francis	Cli--yn, Anna	D	82
Horan, Ann	20, Mar. 1853	Thomas	Cowlin, Ellen	E	75
Horan, Honora	31, Aug. 1856	James	Graham, Ann	E	394
Horan, John	25, Oct. 1850	Edward	King, Bridget	B	217
Horan, John	6, Sept 1857	Thomas	----, Elisabeth	R	
Horan, Margaret	16, Oct. 1853	Patrick	Jennings, Mary	P	55
Horan, Mary	10, June 1855	Patrick	Jennings, Mary	P	135
Horan, Mary Ann	31, Jan. 1855	J.	Hynes, Winefred	P	118
Horan, Patrick	13, Oct. 1858	Patrick	----, Elisabeth	U	
Horan, Thomas	17, Jan. 1858	Patrick	Jennings, Mary	P	236
Horan, Thomas	24, July 1859	Thomas	Tierney, Margaret	P	289
Hore, Catherine	25, Dec. 1858	John	----, Mary	B	69
Hore, Mary	3, Oct. 1856	John	Linihan, Mary	B	34
Hore, Matthew	27, Apr. 1854	John	Lennon, Mary	B	313
Horgan, John	4, Feb. 1851	Dennis	Donohue, Sarah	E	281
Horgan, Martin	14, Sept 1856	Cornelius	Dennis, Mary	V	33
Horn, Carolina	24, Feb. 1850	Johan	Schwab, Philippina	D	203
Horn, David John	30, Aug. 1856	John	Corr, Mary	B	33
Horn, James August	3, Nov. 1859	John	----, Theresa	E	667
Horn, Johan Philipp	30, Mar. 1851	Johan	Schwab, Philippina	D	258
Horn, John Isaac	30, Nov. 1856	Nicolaus	Hay, Mary Jane	U	
Horn, Mary Ann	16, Oct. 1859	Nicolaus M.	Hays, Mary Jane	U	
Horn, Peter	21, Feb. 1853	Johan	Schwab, Philippina	F	
Hornbach, Ludwig	28, Sept 1858	Aloysius	Walter, Christina	D	120
Hornbach, Michael	21, Sept 1856	Aloysius	Walter, Christina	D	68
Horne, Mary Adda	14, Sept 1858	William	Moran, Sarah Jane	P	261
Hörneman, Johan Heinrich	2, May 1859	Johan H.	Winkelhorst, Gertrud	D	137
Horner, Bernard	20, Nov. 1859	Francis	Wagener, Theresa	T	
Hornitz, James	15, Aug. 1854	Moritz	Conlan, Bridget	U	
Hornung, Anna Maria	29, Mar. 1854	Johan	Elbert, Anna M.	C	
Hornung, Anna Maria Catharina	14, Nov. 1858	Eberhard	Schers, Theresa	C	
Hornung, Carl Friedrich Wilhelm	27, Aug. 1854	Peter	Mueller, Dorothea	C	
Hornung, Eduard Francis	8, Oct. 1855	Philipp	Untersinger, Clara	D	44
Hornung, Francis Johan	12, May 1850	Francis	Beckermann, Anna	C	
Hornung, Johan Everhard	18, May 1856	Johan	Elbert, Maria	C	
Hornung, Johan Michael	7, June 1857	Peter	Mueller, Dorothea	C	
Hornung, Johan Wilhelm	28, Feb. 1858	Johan	Elpert, Anna Maria	C	
Hornung, Peter	13, Apr. 1856	Peter	Mueller, Dorothea	C	
Hornung, Peter Aloysius	15, Aug. 1852	Johan	Elbert, Anna	C	
Hornung, Valentin Albert	8, Aug. 1852	Peter	Mueller, Dorothea	C	
Horr, Elizabeth	11, Sept 1858		adult	P	260
Horragan, Daniel	13, Mar. 1853	Dennis	Donahue, Sarah	B	286
Horst, Elisabeth Catharina	31, Dec. 1854	Heinrich	Tumbrink, Elisabeth	K	
Horst, Friedrich	29, Apr. 1851	Heinrich	Woehlfort, Kunigunda	F	
Horst, Joseph Anton	27, Feb. 1859	Carl	Grein, Elisabeth	R	
Horst, Maria Anna Catharina	19, May 1850	Roch	Hartman, Maria Anna	D	213
Hörstein, Ottilia	19, Nov. 1854	Ludwig	Reir, Catharina	D	22
Horsting, Bernard Heinrich	21, July 1858	Bernard	Hagel, Francisca	C	
Hörsting, Maria Theresa	17, Oct. 1858	Anton	Eilerman, Maria Anna	J	48
Horstman, Francis Heinrich	21, Sept 1853	J. Heinrich	Krone, Bernardina	A	
Horstman, Johan Gerhard	24, Oct. 1858	Heinrich	Krone, Bernardina	A	
Horstman, Margaretha Francisca	5, Oct. 1856	Heinrich	Krone, Bernardina	A	

Name of Child	Date of Baptism	Father	Mother	Church	Page
Horstman, Paul Heinrich	22, Oct. 1854	J. Herman	Krone, Bernardina	A	
Horstman, Thomas	28, Aug. 1851	Bernard	----, Sophia	E	337
Horstmann, Bernard August	5, Nov. 1856	August	Vison, Lisette	L	
Horstmann, Carl Nicolaus	21, Nov. 1857	Nicolaus	Bruns, Charlotte	C	
Horstmann, Catharina	9, Aug. 1855	Gerhard	Froehling, Sophia	C	
Horstmann, Herman Heinrich	25, Aug. 1856	Anton	Poos, Catharina	L	
Horstmann, Johan	24, Nov. 1859	J. Heinrich	----, Catharina Engel	L	
Horstmann, Johan Heinrich	17, May 1859	J. Heinrich	Tegler, Agnes	L	
Horstmann, Joseph August	25, Dec. 1858	Bernard	Cort, Elisabeth	F	
Horstschneider, Johan Heinrich	21, Jan. 1857	Joseph	Pape, Bernardina	A	
Horstschneider, Maria Elisabeth	16, June 1859	Joseph	Pape, Dina	A	
Horstschneller, Johan Joseph	27, Mar. 1853	J. Joseph	Pape, Maria Bernardina	A	
Horton, Elizabeth	18, Dec. 1859	Frederick	O'Brien, Ann	V	64
Horton, Elizabeth	5, Aug. 1855	John	Dailey, Jane	P	144
Horton, Nicolaus Quinn	1, July 1851	Smith W.	Cassidy, Elizabeth	B	235
Horton, Pauline	5, Nov. 1851	John	Dayley, Joanne	P	13b
Horweg, Joanne Theresa	14, Oct. 1859	J. Francis	Kollhof, Maria	R	
Hoser, James	14, June 1855	James	Grugen, Rose	E	293
Hosey, John	11, July 1858	James	Rogan, Rose	B	61
Hosler, William	26, May 1850	Eli	Divine, Mary	E	216
Hossman, Johan Heirnich	16, Mar. 1858	Heinrich	Kram---, Maria	D	107
Host, Johan Friedrich	13, Sept 1859	Heinrich	Wilfert, Cunigunda	D	146
Hösting, Johan Bernard	31, May 1855	Anton	Eilerman, Maria Anna	A	
Hotapp, Juliana	18, Dec. 1859	Georg	Pond---, Juliana	D	153
Hotke, Bernard Herman Joseph	28, July 1852	Joseph	Schuhmann, Catharine	C	
Hotler, Philipp	4, Sept 1859	Johan	Schumacher, Catharina	T	
Hötzke, Christian Lawrence	4, Sept 1853		adult	K	
Houley, Edmund	16, Aug. 1857	Edmund	Donaghue, Margaret	P	220
Houli, Augustine Foster	27, Jan. 1850	Frederick	Foster, Elizabeth	B	195
Houseman, John Francis	13, Jan. 1856	James	Ripple, Elizabeth	B	23
Houston, Elizabeth	14, Mar. 1853	Samuel	Semple, Mary Ann	E	73
Houston, Martha	14, July 1857	Robert	Grubs, Elisabeth	U	
Houston, Martha	1, July 1851	Samuel	Sample, Mary Ann	B	235
Houston, William	21, Nov. 1854	Samuel	Semple, Mary Ann	B	8
Hoverstadt, Catharina Maria Henrietta	6, Jan. 1859	Herman	Stolz, Christina	K	
How, Lucy Ann	26, Apr. 1858	Peter	Jones, Mary Frances	P	247
Howard, Charles	12, Mar. 1851	Michael	Tynan, Bridget	E	290
Howard, Gary Andrew	22, May 1859	John	Sweeney, Ann	B	75
Howard, George Washington	22, Feb. 1852	Timothy	----, Bridget	B	252
Howard, James Henry	27, Jan. 1850	Timothy	Horn?, Bridget	B	195
Howard, Margaert	16, Oct. 1851	Roger	Murphy, Margaret	B	243
Howard, Margaret	3, Sept 1854	Timothy	Wood, Bridget	B	5
Howard, Mary Ann	4, Jan. 1857	Timothy	----, Bridget	E	424
Howard, Mary Ellen	21, June 1857	William	Dowry, Ellen	E	461
Howard, Michael	27, Apr. 1852	Timothy	----, Margaret	E	406
Howell, Edward	25, Apr. 1852	James	----, Mary	B	257
Howell, James	1, Mar. 1857	James	Hudy?, Mary	B	41
Howels, Bethse	17, Jan. 1853	Abner	adult - 50 years old	E	55
Howley, Helen	6, Nov. 1851	Thomas	Barr---, Margaret	P	13b
Howley, James	18, Dec. 1859	James	Donoghue, Margaret	P	306
Howley, Thomas	8, Apr. 1855	John	Donoho, Margaret	P	127
Hox, Johan	23, Nov. 1853	Heinrich	Dunlnoy, Helen Ellen	N	18
Hoy, Daniel	31, July 1853	John	Cronin, Ann	R	
Hoy, James	23, Nov. 1851	John	Cronin, Ann	R	
Hoyer, Johan Wilhelm	24, Feb. 1850	Friedrich	Rebe, Adelheid	A	
Hoyi, John William	22, Oct. 1859	George	Hamilton, Ann	E	665
Hoyland, Helen	24, Sept 1859	John	Flinn, Mary	E	656
Hraky?, John	21, Oct. 1851	William	----, Ann	B	243
H--sel, Wilhelm	13, Aug. 1855	Christian	Schmidt, Regina	N	

Name of Child	Date of Baptism	Father	Mother	Church	Page
Hubbard, John	10, July 1852		adult - 74 years old	E	427
Hubbel, Ludwig	29, Oct. 1851	Francis	Nölle, Maria Philomena	K	
Hubbell, Phebe Jane	24, Oct. 1853		adult	B	301
Huber, Aloysius	16, Mar. 1851	Heinrich	Baur, Barbara	J	10
Huber, Amalia	1, Aug. 1854	Johan	Arns, Maria Magdalena	K	
Huber, Andreas	28, Nov. 1852	Andreas	Wedemer, Baldewina	L	
Huber, Andreas	18, July 1854	Johan	Schilling, Carolina	D	14
Huber, Ann Elizabeth	3, Mar. 1850	Joseph	McCabe, Mary	E	200
Huber, Anna Maria	26, Aug. 1855	Andreas	Burger, Barbara	Q	10
Huber, Anna Maria	5, July 1858	Thomas	Goldschmidt, Anna Maria	D	114
Huber, Anton	23, Nov. 1852	Wendelin	Görth, Regina	K	
Huber, Bernard	14, Aug. 1853	Hilarius	Goert, Rosina	K	
Huber, Bernard	25, Dec. 1858	Johan	Schilling, Carolina	F	
Huber, Carl Edward	2, Aug. 1857	Andreas	Huber, Rosina	D	91
Huber, Carolina	6, Jan. 1856	Andreas	Huber, Theresa	D	50
Huber, Carolina	6, Jan. 1854	Joseph	Keiseler, Walburga	A	
Huber, Catharina	17, Sept 1854	Andreas	Burger, Anna Maria	Q	5
Huber, Catharina	27, May 1855	Andreas	Spinner, Agatha	D	35
Huber, Catharina Carolina	26, June 1856	Friedrich	Oswald, Elisabeth	C	
Huber, Elisabeth	25, Dec. 1859	Andreas	Spinner, Agatha	D	153
Huber, Elisabeth	19, July 1857	Joseph	Scher, Margaretha	C	
Huber, Elisabeth Agatha	15, Sept 1858	Johan	Arnold, Magdalena	K	
Huber, Emily Cacilia	26, May 1850	James	Citmey, Adeline	B	203
Huber, Francis Seraphin	19, Oct. 1851	Francis X.	Danheimer, Louisa	D	288
Huber, Francis Xavier	19, Oct. 1856	Francis X.	Dannheimer, Louisa	D	70
Huber, Francis Xavier	24, Oct. 1852	Thomas	Goldschmidt, Anna	D	355
Huber, Francisca	23, Nov. 1856	Xavier	---ff, Catharina	D	72
Huber, Georg Xavier	1, Nov. 1857	Clemens	Beckle, Catharina	A	
Huber, Helen Maria Magdalena	31, Jan. 1858	George	Ramstein, Theresa	H	
Huber, Jacob Wilhelm	11, Oct. 1857	Jacob	Cetini, Adelheid	C	
Huber, Johan	21, Sept 1856	Johan	Schilling, Carolina	D	68
Huber, Johan	18, Oct. 1857	Thaddeus	----, Maria	S	
Huber, Joseph	9, Jan. 1859	Joseph	Ramstein, Theresa	H	
Huber, Josephina	2, Apr. 1854	Thomas	Goldschmidt, Maria Anna	D	7
Huber, Josephina Brigitta	19, Oct. 1856	Anton	Huegel, Anna M.	C	
Huber, Louis	13, Mar. 1859	Joseph	Schäl,	X	
Huber, Ludwig	13, Feb. 1859	Anton	Hüger, Anna Maria	K	
Huber, Magdalena	14, Mar. 1855	Zacharias	Werner, Walburga	G	
Huber, Maria Barbara	31, Jan. 1858	George	Ramstein, Theresa	H	
Huber, Maria Carolina	3, June 1855	Anton	Hugel, M. Anna	C	
Huber, Maria Francisca	3, June 1856	Johan	Arnold, Magdalena	K	
Huber, Maria Josephina	22, Nov. 1853	Joseph	Jung, Christina	C	
Huber, Maria Magdalena	30, Apr. 1854	Francis X.	Dannheimer, Louisa	D	9
Huber, Maria Rebecca	1, Jan. 1854	Joseph	McKraf, Mary	K	
Huber, Michael Ludwig	27, Mar. 1853	Friedrich	Oswald, Elisabeth	C	
Huber, Otto	13, Feb. 1859	Francis X.	Dannheimer, Louisa	D	131
Huber, Philipp Aloysius	29, Mar. 1856		12 years old	K	
Huber, Philomina	12, Dec. 1851	Friedrich	Oswald, Elisabeth	C	
Huber, Rosalia	29, Nov. 1857	Theobald	Gilmer, Catharina	C	
Huber, Rosina	7, Mar. 1858	Hilarius	Gerb, Rosina	K	
Huber, Simon Bernard	14, Oct. 1855	Hilarius	Görth, Rosina	K	
Huber, Sophia Maria	24, Jan. 1854	Peter	Morin, Charlotte	C	
Huber, Stephen	17, Mar. 1856	Stephan	Ernst, Victoria	C	
Huber, Theresa	20, Feb. 1853	Jacob	----, Catharine	C	
Hubert, Christina Johanna	23, Oct. 1852	Wilhelm	Haverkamp, Catharina	K	
Hubert, Elisabeth Gertrud	16, June 1853	Heinrich	Love, Elisabeth	C	
Hubert, Georg Eduard	19, July 1853	J. Georg	Kampson, Catharina	L	
Hubert, Theresa Catharina	28, Aug. 1853	J. Georg	Böllinger, Theresa	D	403
Hubert, Wilhelm Johan	29, July 1851	Heinrich	Lewe, Elisabeth	L	

Name of Child	Date of Baptism	Father	Mother	Church	Page
Huberti, Margaretha	27, Dec. 1858	Joseph	Schilz, Margaretha	F	
Hubing, Anna	13, Mar. 1854	Friedrich	Miltenberger, Maria	C	
Hubing, Anna Catharina Philomena	28, Oct. 1850	Anton	Schapke, Catharina	A	
Hubing, Anton	5, Sept 1855	Anton	Schapker, Catharina	R	
Hubing, Catharina Margaretha	13, Sept 1858	Anton	Schapker, Catharina	R	
Hubing, Gesina Adelheid	31, Dec. 1858	Wilhelm	Bosen, Gesina Adelheid	A	
Hübing, Johan Stephan	11, Aug. 1858	Heinrich	Tenbusch, Anna Maria	A	
Hubing, Johanna Maria	21, Nov. 1854	J. Wilhelm	Bosen, Gesina Adelheid	A	
Hubing, Johnna Margaretha	8, Jan. 1852	Johan	Jansen, Maria	A	
Hubing, Maria Adelheid	5, Dec. 1852	Wilhelm	Bosen, Gesina Adelheid	A	
Hubing, Maria Rosina	24, May 1858	Friedrich	Mietensberger, Maria	C	
Hubing, Martha Margaretha	29, July 1857	Wilhelm	Bosen, Gesina Adelheid	A	
Hubing, Wilhelm Anton	3, Jan. 1853	Anton	Schapker, Maria Catharina	A	
Hübner, Francis Julius	4, July 1859	John	Meyer, Sophia	D	141
Hübner, Johanna Maria	1, Oct. 1854	Johan	Meyer, Sophia	D	19
Huck, Carolina	13, Nov. 1859	Gottlieb	Hech, Martha	T	
Huck, Catharina	20, Nov. 1859	Jacob	Meier, Barbara	D	151
Huck, Johan	3, Jan. 1850	Forman?	Bogenschultz, Regina	D	197
Huck, Martin	10, Apr. 1859	Georg Adam	Scheld--, Elisabeth	D	135
Huck, William	8, June 1856	John	Finley, Honora	P	182
Hück?, Carl Bartholomew	11, Apr. 1851	Johan	Huck, Regina	K	
Hucter, Michael	26, Feb. 1854	John	Finley, Honora	P	72
Hudelbrink, Anna Maria	15, Aug. 1855	J. Heinrich	Polking, Maria Anna	L	
Hudelbrink, Catharina M.	21, Mar. 1857	J. Heinrich	Poelking, Anna Maria	L	
Hudelbrink, Franz Xavier	6, Nov. 1853	J. Heinrich	Polking, Maria Anna	L	
Hudelbrink, Johan Heinrich	12, Apr. 1852	J. Heinrich	Poelking, Anna Maria	L	
Hudepohl, Bernard Heinrich	25, Dec. 1850	Bernard	Schmidt, Maria	L	
Hudepohl, Herman Heinrich	4, Nov. 1855	Bernard	Bergfeld, Elisabeth	L	
Hudepohl, Herman Heinrich Wilhelm	4, Mar. 1858	Bernard	Bergfeld, M. Elisabeth	L	
Hudepohl, Johan Herman	15, June 1853	Bernard	Schmidt, Maria	L	
Hudepohl, Maria Angela	30, May 1850	Francis H.	Flaspohler, Gertrud	C	
Hudman, Francis	3, June 1850	Bernard	Meier, Maria Anna	A	
Hudson, Catherine	3, Jan. 1850	John	----, Mary	B	193
Hudson, Catherine	1, Aug. 1858	Peter	Caren, Ann	E	553
Hudson, Elizabeth	5, Dec. 1852	Peter	Kearns, Ann	E	42
Hudson, Mary Ann	3, Sept 1854	Peter	----, Ann	E	222
Hudson, Sarah Jane	21, Sept 1856	Peter	Caren, Elizabeth	E	398
Huebel, Joseph Heinrich	10, Nov. 1859	Joseph	Putthoff, Louisa	L	
Huebner, Franz Anton	21, Apr. 1858	Francis	Sertel, Catharina	T	
Hueger, Maria Magdalena	15, Feb. 1857	Anton	Riefenthal, Elisabeth	F	
Hueker, Theresa	6, Dec. 1857	Carl	Keller, Catharina	D	100
Huellmann, Rosa Elisabeth	1, Jan. 1857	Theodor	Boellner, Anna M.	C	
Huellmann, Theodor Heinrich	19, Sept 1853	Theodor	Boelner, Maria	C	
Huels, Franz	7, Nov. 1852	Ulrich	Schumann, Margaretha	F	
Huelsebeck, Catharina	31, July 1855	Gerhard H.	Hugenberg, Gertrud	L	
Huelsebeck, Josephina	31, July 1855	Gerhard H.	Hugenberg, Gertrud	L	
Huelsing, Johan Gerhard	22, Aug. 1854	J. Gerhard	Muellering, M. Catharina	F	
Huelsmann, Anna Catharina	16, Aug. 1857	Bernard	Stegmann, M. Catharina	F	
Huelsmann, Francis Ferdinand	18, Aug. 1850	Joseph	Roenker, Elisabeth	L	
Huelsmann, Franz Heinrich	21, Oct. 1854	Conrad	Asbree, M. Catharina	L	
Huelsmann, Gerhard Johan Bernard	17, Aug. 1856	Bernard	Becker, Maria	F	
Huelsmann, Herman Joseph	7, Sept 1858	H. Anton	Fiehoff, M. Anna	C	
Huelsmann, Johan Ferdinand	10, Sept 1858	J. Heinrich	Schloemann, Catharina	L	
Huelsmann, Johan Heinrich	29, Oct. 1852	Conrad	Wander, Elisabeth	L	
Huelsmann, Johan Heinrich	18, Dec. 1858	Ferdinand	Rottinghaus, Anna	L	
Huelsmann, Maria Elisabeth	25, June 1855	Bernard H.	Stegmann, M. Catharina	F	
Huelsmann, Maria Elisabeth	19, Nov. 1850	Conrad	Lange, M. Elisabeth	L	
Huelsmeier, Johan Heinrich	6, Sept 1858	Bernard	Becker, Gertrud	F	
Huenefeld, Anna Maria Elisabeth	24, Oct. 1854	Conrad D.	Steffen, Clara M.	L	

Name of Child	Date of Baptism	Father	Mother	Church	Page
Huenefeld, Johan Martin	19, Oct. 1856	Conrad D.	Steffens, Clara Maria	F	
Huenemann, Anna Maria	8, Feb. 1859	Gerhard H.	Depenbrock, Catharina	C	
Huenemann, Johan Heinrich	31, Aug. 1856	Heinrich	Depenbrock, Catharina	C	
Huening, Bernard Heinrich	25, Feb. 1852	Heinrich	Twente, Elisabeth	L	
Huening, Maria Catharina Elisabeth	6, Jan. 1851	Herman	Tuent, Elisabeth	L	
Huennemann, Elisabeth Catharina	17, Mar. 1850	Johan H.	Rolvers, Angela	C	
Huerling, Emilia	15, Sept 1859	Friedrich	Büs, Martina	A	
Huermann, Anna Clementina	20, Sept 1858	Gerhard H.	Enneking, Angela	C	
Huermann, Anna Maria Josephina	14, Feb. 1857	G.H.	Enneking, Angela	C	
Huermann, Maria Rosa Francisca	1, Sept 1855	Gerhard	VonderHeide, Angela	C	
Huerst, Johan Gerhard Heinrich	1, June 1851	Herman	Kramer, Maria Catharina	F	
Hues, Carolina	25, June 1854	Ignatius	Kramer, Elisabeth	K	
Hues, Maria Magdalena	4, Jan. 1857	Ignatius	Kramer, Elisabeth	K	
Huesbacher, Francis Jacob	11, Dec. 1853	Elias	Strubbel, Rosina	K	
Hueser, Anna Maria Theresa	8, May 1856	Bernard	Vroklage, Theresa	L	
Hueser, Herman Heinrich August	11, Feb. 1853	Bernard	Vrocklage, Theresa	L	
Hueser, Victor Bernard Heinrich	25, Feb. 1850	Bernard	Vrocklage, Theresa	L	
Huesing, Bernard Herman Michael	29, Sept 1859	Herman	Beck, Ursula	T	
Huesing, Marianna	12, Sept 1855	J. Wilhelm	Wennemann, Gesina A.	F	
Huesling, Johan Bernard	25, Mar. 1852	J. Gerhard	Moellering, Catharina	F	
Huesmann, Anna Maria	6, Mar. 1857	Heinrich	Vormbrock, Gertrud	L	
Huesmann, Franz	13, Sept 1857	Louis	Bleckschmidt, Maria	L	
Huesmann, Johan Casper	26, Dec. 1853	Heinrich	Vornbroke, Gertrud	L	
Huesmann, Johan Joseph	30, Dec. 1859	Heinrich	VordemBroke, Adelheid	L	
Huesmann, Ludwig	30, Oct. 1852	Heinrich	Timmers, Maria	L	
Huesmann, Maria Adelheid	4, Oct. 1857	Bernard	Roberts, Maria	L	
Huesmann, Maria Anna	11, Feb. 1856	Bernard	Robbers, Maria Anna	L	
Huesmann, Maria Elisabeth	2, May 1852	Heinrich	VondenBrocke, Gertrud	L	
Huest, Theresa	9, June 1852	Johan	Patten, Brigitta	C	
Huestmann, Theodor Heinrich	16, Apr. 1850	Heinrich	Dammann, Friedricka	L	
Huetscher, Philipp	17, May 1857	Francis	Volkmann, Margaretha	F	
Huever, Johan Georg	12, Feb. 1855	Nicolaus	Panthoefer, Catharina	F	
Huevert, Johan Gerhard Herman	30, Aug. 1856	Gerhard H.	Kramer, Maria Catharina	F	
Huevet, Maria Catharina	21, Mar. 1859	Gerhard H.	Kraemer, M. Catharina	F	
Huewel, Wilhelm Heinrich	29, Mar. 1857	Joseph	Puthoff, Louisa	L	
Huey, Mary Ann	8, Apr. 1855	George	Moran, Mary	B	13
Hufmeister, Maria Louisa	23, Jan. 1858	Francis H.	Burk--, Maria Anna	D	103
Hufnagel, Josephina	20, Nov. 1851	Andreas	Peter, Caecilia	A	
Hug, Valentin	27, July 1856	Mathias	Weiglein, Anna	D	63
Huger?, Andreas	27, Apr. 1852	Daniel	Holscher, Susanna	D	318
Hugh, Elizabeth	10, Aug. 1856	Thomas	Ryan, Catherine	U	
Hugh, John	2, Sept 1853	Patrick	----, Joanne	E	125
Hughes, Albert	23, June 1856	John	McCalester, Ann	P	183
Hughes, Alice	17, Feb. 1852	George	Murray, Margaret	B	252
Hughes, Alice	28, Feb. 1857	James	----, Ellen	E	436
Hughes, Ann	30, Jan. 1853	Thomas	----, Catherine	M	
Hughes, Blanche Bertha	7, Feb. 1853	Edward	Lewis, Elizabeth	P	34
Hughes, Bridget	7, Nov. 1852	Anthony	Cook, Ann	E	33
Hughes, Catherine	7, Jan. 1855	Arthur	O'Brien, Sarah	E	255
Hughes, Catherine	19, June 1852	Michael	----, Alice	E	426
Hughes, Catherine Florence	16, Jan. 1853	James	Tierney, Catherine	B	281
Hughes, Charles	15, Apr. 1851	Edward J.	Lewis, Elizabeth	B	230
Hughes, Edith	21, Mar. 1858	Edward J.	Lewis, Elizabeth	B	57
Hughes, Elizabeth	30, Nov. 1856	James	Bywaters, Eliza	B	37
Hughes, Ellen	3, Jan. 1858	James	Bywater, Eliza	B	54
Hughes, Emma	28, Nov. 1854	Samuel	Rössel, Maria	D	23
Hughes, Florence	9, June 1852	Leopold	Lewis, Mary	P	23
Hughes, Helen	28, May 1852	John	----, Bridget	E	419
Hughes, Helen	27, May 1853	Martin	Moloney, Mary	B	292

Name of Child	Date of Baptism	Father	Mother	Church	Page
Hughes, Henry Dermont	1, Jan. 1859	Henry W.	Dermont, Elizabeth H.	B	69
Hughes, Honora	9, Mar. 1855	Martin	----, Catherine	M	
Hughes, James	29, Aug. 1858	Anthony	Earley, Mary	B	63
Hughes, James	29, May 1857	Thomas	----, Bridget	M	
Hughes, John	8, Feb. 1852	Michael	Hughes, Ann	E	380
Hughes, John	4, Jan. 1855	Thomas	----, Bridget	M	
Hughes, John	28, Oct. 1851	Thomas	Moore, Elizabeth	B	244
Hughes, John	6, July 1853	William	O'Connor, Catherine	E	105
Hughes, John Charles	13, June 1858	Thomas	McKenna, Susan	E	541
Hughes, John Edward	11, Jan. 1857	Thomas	Connor, Bridget	V	37
Hughes, John Knox	26, Mar. 1853	William B.	adult - 24 years old	E	76
Hughes, Louis Edward	16, Jan. 1856	Edward	Lewis, Elizabeth	P	166
Hughes, Margaret	30, Apr. 1858	William	Connor, Catherine	B	58
Hughes, Martin	26, Oct. 1859	Patrick	Foley, Margaret	P	302
Hughes, Mary	23, Aug. 1853	Arthur	O'Brien, Sarah	E	122
Hughes, Mary	3, July 1856	Patrick	Cassily, Sarah	E	379
Hughes, Mary	2, Mar. 1850	Patrick	Curley, Bridget	E	200
Hughes, Mary	14, Nov. 1852	Thomas	----, Bridget	M	
Hughes, Mary Ann	10, Mar. 1850	Anthony	Cook, Ann	E	202
Hughes, Mary Ann	6, Mar. 1859	Edward	Williams, Mary	P	279
Hughes, Mary Ann	9, Feb. 1855	James	Bywaters, Eliza	B	11
Hughes, Mary Ann	18, Nov. 1853	James	Bywaters, Elizabeth	B	302
Hughes, Mary Ann	14, Feb. 1851	Michael	Meckenly, Alice	E	284
Hughes, Mary Ann	3, Oct. 1858	Thomas	Conner, Bridget	E	566
Hughes, Mary Helen	23, Mar. 1851	James	Kearney, Catherine	B	228
Hughes, Matilda	28, July 1850	Thomas	Cunningham, Mary	B	208
Hughes, Michael	15, Mar. 1852	Michael	Jo---, Bridget	B	254
Hughes, Reuben Francis	20, Aug. 1850	Leopold	Lewis, Mary	B	211
Hughes, Sarah	21, Mar. 1852	Patrick	Cassidy, Sarah	E	393
Hughes, Terrence	26, July 1853	Michael	McCarty, Alice	E	112
Hughes, Thomas	1, Nov. 1855	Michael	Hughes, Ann	E	324
Hughes, Thomas	20, July 1859	Thomas	----, Bridget	M	
Hughes, William	2, June 1859	James	Tyrall, Ellen	E	630
Hughes, William	12, Mar. 1854	Michael	----, Ann	E	175
Hughes, Winnefred	15, May 1853	Thomas	Leonard, Anastasia	V	3
Hughey, Isabel	13, Oct. 1853	James	----, Mary	E	134
Hugle, Gideon	16, Jan. 1859		adult	P	271
Hühlefeld Georg Aloysius	15, May 1851	Gerhard H.	Wöpkenberg, Maria Angela	D	265
Hühn, Johan	1, Feb. 1852	Sebastian	Guatte, Magdalena	Q	1
Hühn, Johan Lothar	24, Aug. 1851	F. Lothar	Marschal, Anna Maria	A	
Hühnefeld, Maria Catharina	27, Mar. 1859	Conrad	Steffens, Maria Elisabeth	J	50
Hühnefeld, Maria Louisa	13, Feb. 1855	Gerhard	Wipkenberg, Maria Angela	D	28
Huhning, Maria Anna	1, May 1853	Heinrich	Tweenta, Elisabeth	R	
Huhning, Maria Anna	8, Dec. 1859	Heinrich	Twens, Elisabeth	R	
Hulings, Mary	1, Mar. 1856	Samuel	Bu---, Louise	B	26
Hull, George Frederick Hieronymus	29, Mar. 1852	Michael	Russell, Isabel	B	255
Hülle, Francis Ludwig	23, May 1852	J. Conrad	Stüve, Anna M. Elisabeth	K	
Huller, Alexander	20, June 1858	Adam	Reising, Anna Maria	T	
Huller, Catharina	23, Nov. 1856	Adam	Reising, Anna Maria	D	72
Huller, Joseph Georg	15, Sept 1850	J. Georg	Schnebergel, Walburga	K	
Huller, Margaretha	25, Sept 1855	Peter	Grösser, Margaretha	D	43
Huller, Valentin	26, July 1857	Peter	Grosser, Margaretha	D	91
Hüllman, Maria Elisabeth	25, Nov. 1850	Heinrich	Tobe, Maria Anna Christina	K	
Hulls, Joseph Andreas Conrad	23, Nov. 1852	Conrad	Wedding, Anna	C	
Huls, Bernardina Carolina	15, Mar. 1850	Johan	Harmeier, Theresa	K	
Huls, Carl Heinrich	25, Nov. 1855	Conrad	Wedinger, Anna	C	
Hüls, Gerhard Heinrich	19, Jan. 1851	Heinrich	Kemper, Theresa	K	
Huls, Johan Bernard	11, Oct. 1857	Conrad	Wedding, Anna	C	
Hüls, Johan Joseph	22, Apr. 1853		Hüls, Anna Maria	A	

Name of Child	Date of Baptism	Father	Mother	Church	Page
Huls, Peter Arnold	13, Mar. 1854	Conrad	Wetting, Anna	C	
Hulshorst, Johan Heinrich	31, Jan. 1852	J. Friedrich	Grewen, Clara	D	304
Hülsman, Catharina Elisabeth	8, Feb. 1852	Johan	Nordloh, Maria Gertrud	K	
Hülsman, Catharina Maria	31, Oct. 1852	Joseph	Grasen, Maria Angela	D	355
Hulsman, Herman Heinrich	8, Mar. 1858	Herman	Nordlohn, Gertrud	K	
Hülsman, Herman Heinrich	13, Aug. 1852	H. Anton	Thiehof, Maria Anna	D	343
Hülsman, Johan Anton	20, June 1851	Anton	Diar, Marianna	D	269
Hülsman, Juliana	15, Dec. 1850	Joseph	VonGrasse, Anna Catharina	D	246
Hülsman, Juliana Theresa	11, Jan. 1858	Wilhelm	Weisskittel, Elisabeth	K	
Hülsman, Maria Bernardina Philomena	15, Oct. 1853	Herman	Nordlohn, Helena	K	
Hulsman, Maria Carolina	3, Dec. 1859	Francis	Brack, Margaretha	K	
Hülsman, Maria Catharina	4, Mar. 1855	Herman A.	Thierhof, Anna Maria	D	30
Hülsman, Maria Elisabeth	10, Mar. 1854	Heinrich	Spillbrink, Marianna	A	
Hülsman, Theodor Herman	30, Oct. 1858	F. Heinrich	Brake, Margaretha	K	
Hulsmann, Anna Maria Elisabeth	8, Dec. 1856	Anton	Diehoff, Anna Maria	C	
Hulzberger, Anna	13, Feb. 1857	Johan	Hulzberger, Anna	A	
Humbers, Herman Friedrich	13, July 1856	Heinrich	Grünfeld, Maria Adelheid	A	
Humbert, Anna Maria	29, Nov. 1856	Bernard	Egbers, M. Adelheid	F	
Humbert, Gerhard Heinrich	21, June 1853	Gerhard	Hölscher, Anna	A	
Humbert, Herman Heinrich	25, Nov. 1853	T. Herman	Girleman, Adalheid	Q	3
Humbert, Johan Bernard	30, Jan. 1852	J. Heinrich	Grönfeld, Maria Adelheid	D	304
Humbert, Johan Friedrich	7, June 1856	J. Wilhelm	Nieman, Anna Maria	D	60
Humbert, Johan Friedrich Wilhelm	8, June 1854	J. Wilhelm	Nieman, Maria Anna	D	12
Humbert, Johan Heinrich	21, Sept 1850	Herman H.	Brinker, Anna Maria	D	233
Humbert, Johan Heinrich	13, May 1858	J. Heinrich	Grönefeld, Maria Adelheid	A	
Humbert, Maria Bernardina	28, Oct. 1859	Herman	Borgerding, Maria Elisabeth	J	52
Humbert, Maria Catharina	8, Dec. 1856	Herman	Bogerding, Elisabeth	J	38
Humbert, Maria Christina Henrietta	11, Mar. 1852	J. Wilhelm	Nieman, Maria Catharina	D	312
Humbert, Maria Josephina	16, Mar. 1859	Heinrich	Egbers, Anna	F	
Humbert, Theresa	13, Jan. 1850	Joseph	Spieger, Angela Maria	D	199
Humbert, Valentin Bernard Heinrich	16, Feb. 1856	Theodor	Messing, Adelheid	Q	13
Humbler, Alphons	18, Feb. 1855	Francis	Putz, Maria	D	29
Hümler, Peter	12, Aug. 1855	Johan	Park, Felicitas	A	
Hummel, Augustine	19, Oct. 1851	Johan	Fehr, Elisabeth	A	
Hummel, Edward	27, Jan. 1850	Johan	Feher, Elisabeth	A	
Hummel, Franz Ludwig Ernst	20, Mar. 1859	Johan	Fehr, Elisabeth	F	
Hummel, Jacob August	2, Nov. 1853	Theodor	Neinreiter, Carolina	Q	3
Hummel, Johan Baptist	7, Oct. 1853	Johan	Fehr, Elisabeth	F	
Hummel, Johan Ernst	28, June 1855	Anton	Lauth, Catharina	L	
Hummel, Johan Friedrich	9, May 1858	Anton	Lauth, Catharina	L	
Hummel, Maria	7, Jan. 1855	Michael	Schmutz, Josephina	D	26
Hummel, Maria Elisabeth	11, Oct. 1857	Johan	Fehr, Elisabeth	F	
Hummel, Maria Josephina	18, Apr. 1852	Theodor	Neunreiter, Carolina	D	316
Hummel, William Hieronymus	13, Sept 1855	Johan	Fehr, Elisabeth	F	
Hummelmeier, Adam Heinrich	18, Apr. 1857	Bernard	Wiemeier, Catharina	L	
Hummelmeier, Herman	25, Jan. 1859	Bernard	Wiemeier, Catharina	L	
Hummelmeyer, Johan Heinrich	20, Apr. 1852	Bernard H.	Wiemeyer, Cath. Elis.	L	
Hummelmeyer, Maria Cath. Elisabeth	7, Dec. 1850	----	----, ----	L	
Hummelmeyer, Maria Elisabeth	11, Oct. 1855	Bernard	Wiemeyer, Catharina	L	
Hund, Maria Louisa	27, Sept 1857	Francis X.	Kramer, Maria Anna	T	
Hund, Pancratz	22, Oct. 1854	Sylvester	Orth, Elisabeth	F	
Hunefeld, John Adolph	6, Nov. 1858	Adolph	Ludler, Mary	E	576
Hunefort, Bernard Herman	27, Mar. 1851	Bernard H.	Mueller, Margaretha	F	
Hüneman, Maria Anna Elisabeth	4, June 1850	Eberhard	Pörtner, Anna	A	
Hunemeier, Anna Maria	23, Nov. 1856	Tobias	----, Catharina	D	73
Hunert, Friedrich	4, Oct.1857	Heinrich	Hilmich, Elisabeth	D	95
Hungeling?, Johan Herman Heinrich	24, Sept 1851	J. Gerhard	Lempker, Anna Maria	D	284
Hunheger, Bernard Joseph	12, July 1851	Anton	Tenker, Francisca	L	
Hüning, Johan Heinrich	4, Mar. 1857	Heinrich	----, Elisabeth	R	

Name of Child	Date of Baptism	Father	Mother	Church	Page
Hunkege, Bernardina	9, Dec. 1853	Anton	Tonker, Francisca	C	
Hunkler, Barbara	5, June 1853	Gallus	Eckert, Francisca	F	
Hunkler, Catharina Maria	9, Nov. 1851	Johan	Schopp, Catharina	C	
Hunkler, Johan	17, Feb. 1850	Andreas	Hercourt, E.	F	
Hünkler, Maria Catharina Elisabeth	11, Sept 1859	Heinrich	Lon---, Maria Adelheid	D	146
Hunkler, Theresa	29, Apr. 1855	Johan	Sigler, Theresa	F	
Hunnkamp, Heinrich Friedrich Joseph	6, Nov. 1851	F. Joseph	Flederman, Maria Elisabeth	A	
Hunt, (boy)	15, Jan. 1854	Martin	Bowen, Ann	B	307
Hunt, Ann	15, Oct. 1854	Thomas	Higgins, Eliza	P	100
Hunt, Bridget	23, Aug. 1854	James	Bland, Mary	E	219
Hunt, Catherine	6, Sept 1852	Martin	Bolls, Ann	E	15
Hunt, Charles	17, June 1855	Frederick	Young, Caroline	P	136
Hunt, Eliza	25, Mar. 1856	Thomas	Higgins, Eliza	P	174
Hunt, Francis Joseph	3, Nov. 1850	F. Xavier	Kramer, Maria Anna	D	241
Hunt, Francis Ludwig	26, Sept 1852	Francis X.	Braun, Maria Anna	D	349
Hunt, Franz Xavier	12, May 1850	Silvester	Ott, Elisabeth	F	
Hunt, James	18, May 1851	Andrew	Owen, Catherine	B	232
Hunt, James	15, June 1856	Michael	Brannan, Mary	P	182
Hunt, John	28, June 1857	James	Dougherty, Joanne	B	46
Hunt, John	5, Apr. 1855	Peter	Connor, Honora	B	13
Hunt, John	3, June 1857	Thomas	Connor, Mary	P	214
Hunt, John	27, June 1852	Thomas	Hunt, Eliza	B	261
Hunt, John Thomas	18, Aug. 1857	Patrick	Kellet, Mary	B	48
Hunt, Julia	1, Nov. 1857	Thomas	Higgins, Eliza	P	228
Hunt, Margaret	6, Mar. 1853	Thomas	Connor, Mary	V	2
Hunt, Maria Magdalena	25, Mar. 1855	Xavier	Kramer, Maria Anna	D	32
Hunt, Mary	26, July 1857	Martin	Ball, Ann	B	47
Hunt, Mary Jane	28, Aug. 1858	Michael	Brennan, Mary	P	258
Hunt, Patrick William	13, July 1856	Patrick	Philips, Winifred	T	
Hunt, Peter	19, Jan. 1851	Thomas	Higgins, Eliza	B	223
Hunt, Thomas	8, Nov. 1857	Patrick	----, Catherine	E	491
Hunt, Thomas	14, May 1855	Thomas	O'Connor, Mary	P	132
Hunteman, Heinrich	12, July 1859	Friedrich	Kenkel, Bernardina	D	142
Huntemann, Anna Maria Catharina	2, Oct. 1856		Theising, Catharina	L	
Huntemann, Clementina Friedricka	16, Nov. 1853	Friedrich	Kenkel, Bernardina	L	
Huntemann, Elisabeth Bernardina	5, Sept 1852	Friedrich	Kenkel, Dina	L	
Huntemann, Franz	7, Apr. 1856	Fritz	Kenkel, Bernardina	L	
Huntemann, Friedrich Joseph	7, Feb. 1858	Friedrich	Kenkel, Bernardina	L	
Huntemann, Johan Bernard	20, Sept 1852	J. Conrad	Theising, Cath. Adel.	L	
Huntemann, Johan Heinrich Conrad	28, Aug. 1854	J. Heinrich	Theising, Cath. Adel.	L	
Huntemann, Maria Catharina	13, Jan. 1859	Conrad	Theising, Anna Cath.	L	
Hunter, Mary Ann	4, July 1859	James	----, Ann Mary	D	141
Huntinger, Catharina	1, June 1851	Anton	Süg--, Marianna	D	266
Huntner, Catharina	15, Mar. 1857	J. Baptist	Winds, Anna Maria	C	
Hunziger, Anna	4, Oct.1857	Jacob	Schmidt, Eva	D	95
Hup, Maria Anna	19, Aug. 1855	Johan	Scharf, Anna Maria	D	41
Hup, Peter	14, Aug. 1857	Johan	Scharf, Maria Anna	D	92
Hupp, Barbara	29, Mar. 1853	Joseph	Depp, Eva	F	
Hupp, Johan	17, Nov. 1854	Peter	Schmidt, Marianna	F	
Hupp, Johan	2, July 1856	Peter	Schmidt, Monica Louisa	F	
Hurd, John	11, May 1856		adult	B	28
Hüring, Heinrich Bernard Anton	27, Jan. 1859	H. Anton	Hülsman, Maria Catharina	A	
Hurley, Catherine	24, Aug. 1854	Daniel	Cronin, Helen	B	4
Hurley, Catherine	6, Oct. 1850	Dennis	Middleton, Ann	B	216
Hurley, Catherine	10, Oct. 1853	Richard	Donovan, Catherine	E	133
Hurley, Edward	31, July 1850	Michael	----, Bridget	E	236
Hurley, Elizabeth	2, Dec. 1858	Michael	White, Hannah	P	269
Hurley, Elizabeth	9, Aug. 1859	Richard	----, Catherine	E	646
Hurley, Helen	3, July 1853	Dennis	----, Ann	B	294

Name of Child	Date of Baptism	Father	Mother	Church	Page
Hurley, James Francis	3, June 1853	Francis	Mulvey, Honora	E	94
Hurley, Jerusha Mary Jane	19, Sept 1858	Daniel	Sasser, Jane	B	64
Hurley, Margaret	11, Apr. 1852	Daniel	----, Helen	B	256
Hurley, Margaret	9, Nov. 1856	Michael	White, Hannah	P	197
Hurley, Mary	23, Nov. 1850	Daniel	----, Helen	B	219
Hurley, Mary	2, Jan. 1857	Richard	Donovan, Catherine	E	424
Hurley, Owen Clar.	20, Nov. 1852	Patrick	Shea, Mary	E	37
Hurley, Peter Joseph	22, Oct. 1859	John	----, Ellen	E	665
Hurley, Philipp	29, Apr. 1855	Michael	White, Hannah	P	130
Hurley, Thomas	30, May 1850	Thomas	Hurley, Margaret	E	217
Hurley, Timothy	19, Oct. 1857	Michael	White, Catherine	P	228
Hürling, Maria Francisca	27, Dec. 1858	Friedrich	Boos, Martina	A	
Hurly, Francis	5, Nov. 1853	Daniel	----, Bridget	M	
Hurly, Francis	30, Jan. 1855	Francis	Mulvey, Honora	V	22
Hurly, Margaret Ann	17, Apr. 1859	Francis	Mulvey, Honora	P	282
Hurly, Martin	5, Nov. 1853	Daniel	----, Bridget	M	
Hurly, Mary Ann	10, Feb. 1858	James	----, Mary Ann	M	
Hurly, Thomas	1, Feb. 1857	Daniel	Cronan, Ellen	E	430
Hurly, William Henry	13, Aug. 1857	Francis	Mulvey, Honora	P	220
Hurm, Carl	4, July 1857	Wendelin	Oehler, Carolina	D	89
Hurm, Johan Eduard	1, Jan. 1851	Wendelin	Oehler, Carolina	D	247
Hurn, Bridget	31, Oct. 1852	Peter	Guire, Mary	Q	2
Huser, Anna Elisabeth	4, Oct. 1853	J. Heinrich	Schuering, Johanna	L	
Huser, Franz Heinrich Herman	17, May 1858	Heinrich	Schuering, Johanna	L	
Huser, Johan Gerhard	12, July 1856	Heinrich	Schuring, Johanna	L	
Huser, Johan Heinrich	23, Jan. 1852	Gerhard H.	Schiering, Maria Anna	A	
Huser, Maria Catharina	4, Oct. 1853	J. Heinrich	Schuering, Johanna	L	
Hushion, Mary	3, June 1850	Dennis	Riordan, Helen	B	204
Hüsing, Bernard Herman	3, Feb. 1851	Bernard	Weitzel, Maria Gertrud	A	
Hüsing, Johan Heinrich	24, Apr. 1859	J.D. Theodor	Niemeyer, Margareth Adel.	A	
Hüsing, Johan Herman Wilhelm	5, Dec. 1856	J. Theodor	Niemeyer, Maria Adelheid	A	
Hüsing, Margaretha Philomena	26, Aug. 1858	Wilhelm	Wünneman, Gesina Adelheid	K	
Huskamp, Herman Joseph	14, Oct. 1858	Joseph	Borgerding, Agnes	C	
Huslage, Anna Maria Elisabeth	16, Oct. 1853	Heinrich	Jansen, Margaretha	C	
Husman, Anna Maria Gertrud	12, Jan. 1859	Bernard	Thaman, Catharina	A	
Husman, Bernard	20, Jan. 1854	H. Andreas	Wiemöller, Maria Anna	A	
Husman, Johan Francis	9, Mar. 1854	H. Tobias	Nuree, Maria Elisabeth	D	6
Husman, Josephine	28, Apr. 1858	Joseph	Maher, Ann	E	532
Husman, Maria Carolina	21, May 1856	Andreas	Wiemöller, Anna Maria	A	
Husmann, Anna Carolina Philomena	13, Mar. 1856	Heinrich	Mescher, M Catharina	L	
Husmann, Anna Maria Francisca	28, Mar. 1852	Friedrich	Schulte, M. Catharina	L	
Husmann, Bernard Joseph	27, Aug. 1854	Bernard	Rober, Maria	C	
Husmann, Bernardina Carolina	9, Nov. 1851	Johan H.	Beckschmidt, Anna M.	L	
Husmann, Francis Heinrich	25, Jan. 1854	Heinrich	Dreyer, Maria	C	
Husmann, Franz Herman	5, Oct. 1854	Friedrich	Schulte, Catharina	L	
Husmann, Friedrich Bernard	15, Apr. 1850	Friedrich	Schulte, Catharina	L	
Husmann, Georg Bernard	23, Feb. 1856	Francis	Gauspohl, Anna Maria	L	
Husmann, Herman Heinrich	2, Oct. 1855	Ludwig	Beckschmidt, Maria	C	
Husmann, Johan Bernard Franz	15, Mar. 1857	Friedrich	Schulten, Catharina	L	
Husmann, Johan Ludwig Bernard	31, Oct. 1852	Ludwig	Beckschmidt, Maria	C	
Husmann, Johan Mathias	26, June 1853	Anton	Schildmeyer, Margaretha	L	
Husmann, Maria Bernardina	14, Jan. 1851	Francis	Gausepohl, Maria	L	
Husmann, Maria Catharina Louisa	27, July 1856	Heinrich	Viterere, M. Anna	C	
Husmann, Maria Elisabeth Paulina	13, Mar. 1856	Heinrich	Mescher, M Catharina	L	
Husmann, Maria Francisca Josephina	7, Nov. 1852	Francis	Gausepohl, Maria Anna	L	
Husmann, Maria Josephina	14, Feb. 1852	Thomas	Nurre, Elisabeth	C	
Husser, Louise	27, Jan. 1850	Jacob	Scheuer, Margaretha	C	
Hussey, Honora	17, July 1856	John	Henrigan, Ellen	E	382
Hussey, James	22, Oct. 1854	John	Handrigan, Helen	E	234

Name of Child	Date of Baptism	Father	Mother	Church	Page
Hussey, James	18, Sept 1853	Thomas	Loftus, Elizabeth	V	6
Hussman, Heinrich Andreas	16, Oct. 1858	Andreas	Biemöller, Mariana	A	
Hussman, Maria Theresa	8, Oct. 1850	Andreas	Wiemöller, Maria	D	237
Hussmann, Catharina Josephina	13, Nov. 1859	Anton	Kloenne, Anna Maria	F	
Hussmann, Franz Ignatz	15, June 1856	Anton	Kloenne, Maria	F	
Hussmann, Maria Elisabeth	28, June 1851	Anton	Kloenne, Anna Maria	F	
Hussmann, Maria Philomena	17, Feb. 1855	Anton	Kloenne, Maria	F	
Husson, Johan Peter	29, Oct. 1851	Friedrich	Greif, Johanna	C	
Hussong, Joseph Friedrich	16, Jan. 1853	Friedrich	Greif, Johanna	D	365
Hussy, Edward	13, Sept 1857	Martin	Foley, Mary	P	223
Hussy, Mary	21, Mar. 1859	Martin	Foley, Mary	P	280
Hussy, Michael	7, Dec. 1856	James	Crogan, Rose	E	419
Hussy, Patrick	1, July 1856	Martin	Foley, Mary	P	183
Hust, Anna Maria	28, Jan. 1852	Adam	Gaist, Anna Maria	D	304
Hust, Bernardina	22, July 1850	Johan	Bron, Bernardina	D	224
Hustedde, Anna Maria Elisabeth	11, Dec. 1859	J. Gerhard	Dreyer, M. Elisabeth	L	
Huster, Bernard Heinrich	28, June 1859	Heinrich	Middendorf, M. Elisabeth	C	
Huster, Bernardina Elisabeth	9, May 1857	Heinrich	Middendorf, Elisabeth	C	
Huster, Francis Herman	28, Sept 1855	Heinrich	Middendorf, Elisabeth	C	
Huster, Johan Bernard	27, Apr. 1851	Francis	Beckschulte, Maria Anna	D	263
Huster, Johan Heinrich	13, Nov. 1853	Heinrich	Middendorf, Elisabeth	C	
Huster, Maria Philomena Elisabeth	27, Sept 1851	J. Heinrich	Middendorf, Elisabeth	C	
Huston, Amanda Mary	23, Oct. 1852	Francis	----, Catherine	E	30
Hutapp, Carl	16, Aug. 1850	Wendelin	Pander, Magdalena	D	228
Hutapp, Wilhelm	21, Mar. 1858	George	----, Juliana	R	
Hutchinson, Thomas	2, Dec. 1855	John	Corcoran, Margaret	B	22
Huth, Barbara	30, Nov. 1851	Jacob	Klein, Barbara	D	295
Huth, Jacob	14, May 1854	Jacob	Klein, Barbara	D	10
Huth, Joseph	20, Jan. 1850	Jacob	Klein, Barbara	D	200
Hütker, Catharina Josephina	17, Oct. 1858	Jacob	Kich---, Maria	D	122
Hutscheson, Ann jane	1, June 1858	Joseph	Wynn, Bridget	B	59
Hutsebant, Julia Francisca	16, Sept 1852	Roger B.	Kloph, Anna Helena	L	
Huttel, Ernst Aloysius	9, June 1850		4 years old	K	
Huttel, Maria Christina Philomena	9, June 1850		adult - 32 years old	K	
Hüttelberg, Heinrich Albert	23, Nov. 1851	Albert	Huttelberg, Margaretha	A	
Huttinger, Elisabeth	19, Oct. 1851	Johan	Scheid, Catharina	C	
Huttinger, Peter	23, Oct. 1853	Johan	Scheid, Catharina	C	
Hüttner, Catharina	20, Jan. 1856	F. Anton	Sertel, Catharina	D	50
Hutzler, Marcus	3, Dec. 1854	Georg	Seibold, Veronica	F	
Hüve, Antonia Elisabeth	13, Mar. 1854	Heinrich	Hempelman, Elisabeth	K	
Hüve, Elisabeth Josephina	3, Mar. 1852	J. Heinrich	Hempelman, Elisabeth	K	
Hüve, Emma Maria	12, Dec. 1858	Herman	Pape, Francisca	D	125
Huvelroder, Joseph Gottfried	6, July 1858	Joseph	Ulrich, Barbara	C	
Hüvet, Gerhard Heinrich	2, June 1856	Heinrich	Hempel, Elisabeth	K	
Hüwe, Caspar Edward	22, Oct. 1858	Heinrich	Hempelman, Lisetta	K	
Huy, Catharina	24, Sept 1859	Joseph	Eicher, Catharina	H	
Huy, Charles Francis	8, June 1857	Joseph	Gestimenor?, Magdalena	H	
Huy, Eugene August	20, Aug. 1854	Joseph	----, Magdalene	H	
Huy, Ignatius	27, Oct. 1851	Joseph	----, Magdalena	H	
Huy, Maria	30, Nov. 1856	Philip	Rothenkirch, Regina	H	
Huyey, John	2, Mar. 1853	John	----, Helen	E	67
Huzel, Maria	14, Feb. 1855	Johan	--irsch, Margaretha	D	28
Hyde, Bridget	24, Sept 1854	William	Lynch, Helen	E	226
Hyde, Charles Whipple	14, Apr. 1856	Charles	Whipple, M.T.	B	28
Hyde, Josephine Frances	30, Jan. 1859	Charles	Whipple, Margaret T.	B	70
Hyde, William	30, June 1857	Charles	Whipple, Margaret	B	46
Hyland, Catherine	8, Oct. 1854	John	Kearney, Catherine	P	99
Hyland, Mary Jane	9, Jan. 1853	John	Kearney, Catherine	V	1
Hyland, Michael	11, Oct. 1855	John	Fanaghy, Ellen	E	320

Name of Child	Date of Baptism	Father	Mother	Church	Page
Hyland, William	25, Apr. 1855	James	----, E.	E	282
Hyman, Mary Ellen	7, June 1857	John	Gentile, Mary	E	458
Hyne, Bridget	12, Jan. 1851	Thomas	Hogan, Margaret	E	275
Hynes, Bridget	2, Feb. 1854	Patrick	Walsh, Catherine	E	164
Hynes, Bridget	25, Dec. 1853	Thomas	McKensy, Margaret	E	155
Hynes, Caroline	28, Sept 1856	Thomas	Trainor, Mary Jane	E	400
Hynes, Catherine	17, Oct. 1855	John	Manyon, Catherine	E	321
Hynes, Cornelia Emma Jane	2, Aug. 1857	William J.	Statin, Ann	E	471
Hynes, Elizabeth	27, Nov. 1859	Thomas	Trainor, Mary Jane	E	673
Hynes, James	28, Dec. 1851	Patrick	Egan, Catherine	B	248
Hynes, John	16, Nov. 1854	John	Hayes, Mary	E	240
Hynes, John	25, June 1857	John	Manyan, C.	E	462
Hynes, John	14, Aug. 1855	Michael	Kelly, Mary	B	18
Hynes, John	6, Feb. 1853	Patrick	Egan, Catherine	B	283
Hynes, John C.	28, Aug. 1852	Thomas	Tranor, Mary Jane	E	11
Hynes, Martin	24, Feb. 1856	Patrick	Cain, Bridget	R	
Hynes, Mary	23, June 1859	John	Manyon, Catherine	E	634
Hynes, Mary Ann	28, July 1850	William	Heins, Catherine	E	235
Hynes, Mary Theresa	5, June 1855	Edward	Warre, Caroline	E	290
Hynes, Patrick	26, June 1853	Stephan	----, Mary	E	102
Hynes, Sarah	19, Mar. 1854	Thomas	Cramer, Mary Jane	E	177
Hynes, Timothy	21, Nov. 1853	Timothy	Hyens, Bridget	E	146
Hynes, William	4, Sept 1853	William	----, Mary	E	126
Idelhoff, Maria Rosina	26, July 1857	Georg	Konert, Elisabeth	C	
Idensol, Magdalene	3, Aug. 1856	Georg J.	Ottmeier, Maria	U	
Igelbrink, Catharina Elisabeth	6, May 1855	Heinrich	---, Cath. Elis.	L	
Igelkamp, Anna Maria	28, Sept 1856	Francis	Vit, Paulina	L	
Igo, Ellen	14, Nov. 1858	Martin	Maguire, Margaret	B	67
Igo, Honora	10, Aug. 1856	Martin	----, Margaret	M	
Ihle, Anton	22, June 1856	Anton	Brecht, Barbara	D	61
Ihle, Bernard	12, Dec. 1858	Anton	Brechtel, Barbara	T	
Ihmen, Maria Carolina Elisabeth	1, Dec. 1851	Eberhard	Eyman, Maria	A	
Iking, Bernard Gerhard	2, July 1859	Gerhard	Kaiser, Carolina	J	50
Iking, Maria Johanna Catharina	14, Mar. 1858	Gerhard	Kaiser, Carolina	J	44
Iland, Johan Wilhelm	22, June 1859	J. Albert	Stub---, Anna Margaretha	A	
Ilg, Otto	31, Mar. 1855	Anton	Mans, Charitas	D	32
Ilg, Wilhelm	3, May 1853	Anton	Manz, Charitas	D	383
Ilg, Wilhelm Georg	30, Mar. 1851	Anton	Menz, Charitas	D	259
Ilich, Jacob	24, Nov. 1850	Ferdinand	Deutsch, Theresa	D	244
Ilig, Johan	21, Nov. 1852	Ferdinand	Deutsch, Theresa	F	
Ill, Joseph Bernard	12, July 1857	Bernard	Brucker, Agatha	C	
Ill, Wilhelm	24, Feb. 1856	Bernard	Brucker, Agatha	C	
Ill, Wilhelmina	19, Feb. 1854	Bernard	Brucker, Agatha	C	
Imbusch, Maria Adelheid Francisca	27, June 1859	J. Bernard	Gesker, Catharina	L	
Imbusch, Maria Elisabeth	5, Dec. 1856	Bernard	Geschen, Catharina	L	
Imbusch, Maria Philomena	8, Feb. 1854	Bernard	Jocker, Catharina Maria	K	
Imbusch, Wilhelm	6, Mar. 1850	Bernard	Schefers, Catharina	K	
Imbush, Helena Emma	28, Nov. 1858	Caspar	Schmitz, Maria	D	124
Imheld, Herman Heinrich	8, Aug. 1856	H. Anton	Runer, Anna Maria	D	64
Imhof, Barbara Elisabeth	22, Dec. 1856	J. Jacob	Zentner, Barbara	D	74
Imhof, Francisca	7, May 1854	Martin	Scherer, Magdalena	D	9
Imhof, Georg Anton	18, May 1856	Johan	Wagner, Cunigunda	D	59
Imhof, Heinrich	5, Mar. 1852	Herman	Ropke, Elisabeth	F	
Imhof, Heinrich Wilhelm	23, Mar. 1851	Joseph	Ohlenbrock, Maria	F	
Imhof, Johan	18, May 1856	Michael	Gessel, Maria Anna	D	59
Imhof, Johan Heinrich	20, Sept 1857	J. Herman	Robker, Elisabeth	F	
Imhof, Martin Georg	25, Jan. 1852	Martin	Scherrer, Magdalena	D	303
Imhof, Peter Heinrich	14, Mar. 1858	J. Jacob	Zentner, Barbara	D	107
Imhoff, Anna Maria Louisa	26, Aug. 1854	Herman	Robke, Elisabeth	F	

Name of Child	Date of Baptism	Father	Mother	Church	Page
Imhoff, Magdalena	20, Jan. 1850	Martin	Sherer, Magdalena	C	
Imholde, Friedrich Sebastian	16, Feb. 1857	Johan	Schroff, Elisabeth	G	
Imholte, Antonia Elisabeth	21, May 1851	Johan	Schrothe, Elisabeth	A	
Imholte, Friedrich Heinrich	24, Oct. 1858	Johan	Schrote, Elisabeth	G	
Imholte, Johan Christian	19, July 1855	Johan	Schroten, Maria Elisabeth	G	
Imholte, Johan Friedrich Anton	24, Jan. 1854	Anton	Kemker, Maria	C	
Imholte, Maria Henrica Wilhelmina	31, Oct. 1852	Johan	Schroten, Maria Elisabeth	A	
Imholte, Maria Henrietta Friedrika	10, June 1852	Anton	Kempker, M. Anna	C	
Imig, Anna Catharina	26, Nov. 1857	Nicolaus	Kroescher, Elisabeth	C	
Imig, Henrietta Elisabeth	23, May 1854	Nicolaus	Krosche, Elisabeth	C	
Imig, Maria Elisabeth	16, Mar. 1856	Nicolaus	Kroesche, Elisabeth	C	
Imm, Carl	28, Jan. 1859	Carl	Jäger, Catharina	D	130
Imm, Rosina	10, June 1855	Carl	Jaeger, Catharina	D	36
Immäng, Bernardina Philomena	15, July 1857	Bernard	Brescher, Anna Maria	K	
Immert, Catharina	1, Nov. 1858	Heinrich	Rund, Anna Maria	D	123
Immig, Maria Margaretha Elisabeth	6, Jan. 1853	Nicolaus	Kraesche, Lisette	L	
Imming, Anna Maria Catharina	15, Dec. 1851	Bernard	Büske, Anna Maria	K	
Imming, Francis Wilhelm	24, Aug. 1858	Bernard	Bösker, Maria Anna	K	
Imming, Johan Bernard	14, Oct. 1853	Bernard	Büscher, Anna Maria	K	
Imming, Johan Heinrich	26, Sept 1855	J. Bernard	Buscher, Anna Maria	K	
Imorde?, Maria Catharina	5, Dec. 1850	Heinrich	Nichter, Maria Adelheid	A	
ImseeFeeln, Elisa Maria	23, June 1850	Jacob	----, Maria	K	
Imsike, Johan Franz	30, Jan. 1859	Joseph	Ennekind, Marianna	F	
Imsike, Johan Heinrich	12, May 1851	Joseph	Enneking, Maria	F	
Imsike, Joseph	28, Aug. 1853	Joseph	Enneking, Anna Maria	F	
Imwalde, Bernard Wilhelm	22, Sept 1856	Herman H.	Markus, Susanna	L	
Imwalde, Elisabeth Emma	14, Nov. 1852	Heinrich	Beumer, Theresa	L	
Imwalde, Herman N.	5, Sept 1852	Herman	Markes, Christina	L	
Imwalde, Johan Albert	2, June 1850	Herman	Markus, Anna Maria	L	
Imwalde, Joseph	10, Oct. 1854	Herman	Markus, Susanna M.	L	
Imwalde, Josephina Elisabeth	18, Feb. 1855	Heinrich	Baimer, Theresa	K	
Imwalde, Ludwig Heinrich	12, Dec. 1850	Heinrich	Baumer, Theresa	L	
Imwalde, Maria Adelheid	10, Dec. 1858	Herman	Marcus, Maria	L	
Imwalde, Maria Elisabeth	29, Aug. 1858	Georg	Kaiser, Catharina	L	
Imwalde, Rosa	21, Dec. 1856	Heinrich	Baumer, Theresa	F	
Imwalle, Georg Heinrich	26, Oct. 1856	Georg	Kaiser, Maria Elisabeth	K	
Indelkofer, Carolina	28, Dec. 1856	Edward	Pohl, Gertrud	D	75
Indelkofer, Elisabeth	15, Aug. 1858	Edward	Pohl, Gertrud	D	117
Indelkofer, Francisca	2, Mar. 1856	Edward	----, Francisca	D	53
Indelkofer, Francisca	14, Jan. 1855	Edward	Pohl, Gertrud	D	26
IndemWalle, Dietrich Joseph	13, Mar. 1859	Wilhelm	Taphorn, Anna Margaretha	A	
Inderriede, Johan Dietrich	16, Oct. 1852	J. Heinrich	Wehmhoff, Elisabeth	K	
Inderrieden, Heinrich Francis	13, Dec. 1850	Anton	Decker, Agnes	C	
Inderrieden, J. Herman Friedrich	5, Jan. 1856	Friedrich	Gausepohl, Gertrud	C	
Inderrieden, Johan Bernard Friedrich	11, Oct. 1859	Friedrich	Gausepohl, Adelheid	D	148
Inderrieden, Johan Heinrich	17, Jan. 1854	Friedrich	Gausepohl, Adelheid	C	
Indli, Kunigunda	3, July 1853	J. Georg	Kaise, Genofeva	C	
Ingermenn, Joseph	21, June 1855	Adolph	Koffler, Walburga	K	
Inickhover, Joseph	30, Nov. 1854	Caspar	Kramer, Genofeva	C	
Inkrod, Joseph	18, Aug. 1851	Bernard	Folly, Mary	D	279
Inloes, Edward Hieronymus	19, June 1851	Edward	Sp---, Sarah	B	234
Innis, Ann	8, Aug. 1852	John	Losty, Catherine	B	267
Inoldigerd?, Herman Heinrich	22, May 1859	Johan	Schmidt, Maria	D	138
Insert, Joseph Bernard	13, Apr. 1856	Richard	Wilhelmi, Catharina	D	56
Insold, Anna Margaretha	6, Nov. 1853	Georg	Lieb, Cunigunda	D	414
Ipalit, Barbara Leopoldina	8, June 1856	Gaumond	Sakstetter, Anna M.	F	
Ireland, Alexander Thomas	4, Aug. 1854	Thomas	Keck, Louise	A	
Ireland, Charles George	12, June 1859	Thomas	Keck, Aloysia	T	
Ireland, Edward Lawrence	9, May 1852	Thomas	Keck, Louise	A	

Name of Child	Date of Baptism	Father	Mother	Church	Page
Ireland, George N.	4, Sept 1859	George N.	Ryan, Mary	C	
Ireland, James	4, Apr. 1857	George	Ryan, Mary	E	445
Ireland, James Louis	7, Aug. 1856	Thomas	Keck, Louise Anna	A	
Ireland, Joseph	12, May 1854	George H.	----, Mary	E	189
Ireland?, James	29, Oct. 1854	John	----, Mary	M	
Irion, Catharina Magdalena	6, Aug. 1850	Thomas	Jacoby, Barbara	L	
Irion, Thomas Johan	31, July 1856	Thomas	Jacobi, Barbara	C	
Irione, Peter	30, Jan. 1853	Thomas	Jacobi, Barbara	L	
Irvin, Mary Ann	15, Aug. 1852	Henry	Duffy, Ellen	P	26
Irwin, Emanuel	22, Feb. 1857	Alexander	Reilly, Mary Ann	B	41
Irwin, Helen	22, Feb. 1852	Thomas	Prile, Ann	B	252
Irwin, William	27, Apr. 1852	Patrick	Wright, Helen	B	258
Isaak, Catharina	25, July 1859	Johan	He---, Maria Agatha	D	143
Isaak, Christopher	1, Mar. 1857	John	Hirk, Agatha	H	
Isaak, Maria Catharina	7, June 1857	Michael	Wiedeman, Veronica	D	87
Ischer, Margaret Elisabeth	1, Nov. 1859	John	Smith, Elisabeth	Q	33
Isphording, Catharina Elisabeth	30, Sept 1852	Anton	Deipel, Elisabeth	D	350
Isphording, J. Friedrich Francis	7, Mar. 1858	Anton	Teipel, Elisabeth	C	
Isphording, Johan	18, June 1856	Anton	Teipel, Elisabeth	C	
Isphording, Peter Francis Albert	7, July 1850	Anton	Teipel, Elisabeth	D	222
Isphording, Theresa	6, Nov. 1854	Anton	Deubel, Elisabeth	C	
Israel, Anton Bernard	12, Dec. 1850	Bernard	Kock, Elisabeth	C	
Issler, Catharina Elisabeth	26, Mar. 1854	Chrysostum	Diezen, Elisabeth	W	3
Issler, Johan Peter	29, Feb. 1852	Chrysostum	Dietz, Elisabeth	F	
Issler, Nicolaus	13, Sept 1857	Chrysostum	Hülser, Elisabeth	W	19
Ivers, Mary Christine	22, Dec. 1853	Thomas	Ryan, Margaret	B	305
Ives, Charles	6, June 1852	Charles	----, Elisha	E	421
Iws, Anna	18, Mar. 1851	Patrick	Jarle, Bridget	L	
Jack, Edmund	1, Jan. 1859	John W. G.	Kennedy, Catherine	E	592
Jackmer, John James	7, Jan. 1858	John J.	Holden, Francis	E	506
Jackmer, Richard Edward	7, Jan. 1858	John J.	Holden, Francis	E	507
Jackson, Andrew	2, Dec. 1855	John	Hyens, Mary Ann	E	331
Jackson, Catherine	27, Mar. 1853	Hugh	----, Mary	E	77
Jackson, Charles Francis	18, Sept 1857	Charles	----, Anna Maria	L	
Jackson, Eliza	22, June 1856	Hugh	Sheridan, Fanny	E	376
Jackson, George	27, Apr. 1851	?	----, Catharina	D	262
Jackson, George	13, Oct. 1850	Hugh	----, Mary	E	253
Jackson, George	28, Dec. 1851	John	Gorman?, Julia	E	368
Jackson, George	21, June 1858	John	McGryon, Julia	E	543
Jackson, Henry Sales	14, Jan. 1852	George	Merganey, Mary	K	
Jackson, John	31, Oct. 1855	John	----, Julia	E	324
Jackson, John	20, Apr. 1851	John	Brunner, Margaretha	K	
Jackson, John	12, June 1853	John	Hynes, Mary	E	97
Jackson, Mary	29, Apr. 1853	John	McSoron, Julia	E	85
Jackson, Mary Ann Elizabeth	22, July 1857	John	----, Mary Ann	E	468
Jackson, Robert	17, Sept 1857	James	----, Catherine	E	481
Jackson, Samuel Joseph	27, Apr. 1852	John	Hyens, Mary	E	407
Jackson, Sarah Elisabeth	13, Feb. 1859	John	Klein, Elisabeth	G	
Jackson, Thomas Andrew	1, Mar. 1859	John	Hynes, Mary Ann	E	607
Jackson, Vincent de Paul	30, Apr. 1854	Henry	Jones, Elizabeth	B	314
Jacob, Andreas	1, Jan. 1854	Adam	Pfarrer, Anna M.	D	1
Jacob, Anna Maria	19, July 1857	Clemens	Fischer, Anna Margaretha	D	90
Jacob, Anna Maria	7, July 1850	Johan	Brandt, Maria Anna	D	221
Jacob, Anna Maria Catharina	18, Feb. 1855	Georg	Schad, Catharina	D	29
Jacob, Anna Rosina	8, Feb. 1852	J. Clemens	Fischer, Anna	D	305
Jacob, Anton	8, Jan. 1854	Heinrich	Hartman, Elisabeth	D	1
Jacob, Bernard Heinrich	4, June 1854	Joseph	Wingbermühle, M. Elisabeth	D	11
Jacob, Bernardina	12, June 1859	Christian	Horst, Bernardina	F	
Jacob, Carl Thomas	19, Sept 1854	Clemens	Fischer, Anna Maria	D	18

Name of Child	Date of Baptism	Father	Mother	Church	Page
Jacob, Elisabeth	9, Feb. 1859	Clemens	Fischer, Maria Anna	D	131
Jacob, Eva	15, Nov. 1857	David	----, Catharina	D	99
Jacob, Francis	2, Apr. 1857	Georg	Schath, Catharina	D	82
Jacob, Francis Joseph	17, Oct. 1858	Joseph	Wingbermuhle, Elisabeth	D	122
Jacob, Georg Anton	11, Sept 1859	Georg	Schat, Catharina	D	146
Jacob, Johan	24, Apr. 1853	Clemens	Fischer, Maria Anna	D	382
Jacob, Johanna Margaretha	10, Feb. 1856	Joseph	Wingbermühle, Elisabeth	D	52
Jacob, Joseph	9, Dec. 1855	Clemens	Fischer, Anna Maria	D	48
Jacob, Josephina	2, July 1852	Joseph	Winkelmühle, Elisabeth	D	327
Jacob, Margaretha	30, May 1858	Heinrich	Hartman, Elisabeth	D	112
Jacob, Maria Barbara	3, Oct. 1858	J. Theodor	Thamann, Margaretha	F	
Jacob, Maria Elisabeth	17, Nov. 1850	Joseph	Wingbermile, Maria Elis.	D	243
Jacob, Michael	11, Sept 1853	Georg	Schat, Catharina	D	405
Jacob, Peter	15, Nov. 1857	Johan P.	Weindel, Margaretha	F	
Jacob, Peter Christoph	30, July 1854	Peter	Wittkamp, Maria	C	
Jacobi, Johan	20, Nov. 1855	Peter	Egner, Anna Maria	F	
Jacobi, Johan Nicolaus	3, Nov. 1856	Johan	Schwarz, Margaretha	C	
Jacobi, Margaretha	22, Aug. 1858	Peter	Egner, Anna Maria	F	
Jacobi, Maria	5, Oct. 1856	Peter	Egner, Maria	F	
Jacobi, Nicolaus	28, Jan. 1855	Peter	Egner, Anna Maria	F	
Jacobman, Magdalena	30, July 1854	August	Armbruster, Stephani	D	15
Jacobs, Anna Maria Elisabeth	9, Sept 1852	Carl C.	Busken, Maria Thecla	A	
Jacobs, Carl Marion	13, July 1856	Carl	Busken, Maria	A	
Jacobs, Catherine Ann	27, Mar. 1859	John	O'Brien, Elizabeth	P	280
Jacobs, Christian Jacob	28, Oct. 1857		adult - 31 years old	F	
Jacobs, Flora Ellen	25, Jan. 1852	William H.	Luca, Jean	E	376
Jacobs, Isabella Maria	27, Oct. 1854	Clemens	Busken, Maria	A	
Jacobs, James William	6, Apr. 1854	William H.	Green, Lucy Jane	E	181
Jacobs, John	26, June 1853	James	Adams, Emily	E	101
Jacobs, Maria Anna	2, May 1858	Conrad	Hut, Margaretha	J	46
Jacobs, Maria Elisabeth	3, Mar. 1851	Peter	Boen, Barbara	D	256
Jacobs, Mary Elizabeth	15, Feb. 1857	John	Ryan, Elizabeth	P	206
Jacobs, Mary Ellen	5, Nov. 1850	James	----, Emelia	E	259
Jacobs, Peter	15, Feb. 1853	Peter	Driel, Barbara	D	371
Jacobs, Philipp	8, Oct. 1858	Philipp	Tru---, Catharina	D	121
Jacobs, Richard	13, Feb. 1856	Peter	Wittkamp, Maria	F	
Jacobus, Friedrich Alexander	30, Aug. 1857	Ludwig	Frondhoff, Catharina	C	
Jacquemet, Francis Xavier	15, Apr. 1852	Louis	adult - 27 years old	E	403
Jacquemin, Caroline	8, Feb. 1852	Felix	Gerard, Mary	E	380
Jacques, Elizabeth Ellenore	21, June 1851	John	----, Elizabeth	E	316
Jaeger, Anna	14, Feb. 1855	Johan	Winter, Barbara	D	28
Jaeger, Anna Maria Catharina	15, May 1859	Friedrich	Lueke, Helena	F	
Jaeger, Carl Michael	6, Apr. 1851	Peter	Knecht, Anna	Q	1
Jaeger, Elisabeth	17, Sept 1851	Christian	Schaetzmann, Margaretha	F	
Jaeger, Francis Henry	2, Aug. 1854	Peter	Knecht, Anna	R	
Jaeger, Friedrich Wilhelm	12, Apr. 1855	Friedrich	Luecke, Helena	F	
Jaeger, Georg	19, Jan. 1853	Christian	Schatmann, Margaretha	C	
Jaeger, Jacob	9, Apr. 1854	Francis A.	Ripperger, Genofeva	D	8
Jaeger, Johan	17, Dec. 1854	Georg H.	Kibl, Francisca	C	
Jaeger, Johan	16, Feb. 1851	J. Joseph	Meyer, Elisabeth	D	254
Jaeger, Johan Anton	22, Feb. 1856	Francis A.	Ripperger, Genofeva	D	52
Jaeger, Johan August	16, Dec. 1856	Friedrich	Lueke, Helena	F	
Jaeger, Johan Baptist	23, Jan. 1859	Johan	Dih---, Maria	D	129
Jaeger, Joseph	20, Jan. 1850	Georg H.	Kiel, Francisca	C	
Jaeger, Joseph	2, May 1852	Heinrich	Kiel, Francisca	C	
Jaeger, Joseph	27, Feb. 1856	Peter	----, Anna	R	
Jaeger, Ludwig	31, Aug. 1851	Francis	Ripperger, Genofeva	D	279
Jaeger, Maria	31, Aug. 1856	Joseph	Leppert, Louisa	K	
Jaeger, Maria Magdalena	15, Aug. 1858	Francis A.	Ripperger, Genofeva	D	117

Name of Child	Date of Baptism	Father	Mother	Church	Page
Jaeger, Theresa	27, July 1856	Johan	Winter, Barbara	D	63
Jaeger, Victor Peter	13, Dec. 1852	Peter	Knecht, Ann	R	
Jäger, Andreas	9, Oct. 1859	Joseph	Schmidlin, Josephina	D	148
Jäger, Carl	11, Oct. 1857	Carl	Grob, Catharina	H	
Jäger, Carl	3, Dec. 1857	Heinrich	Stephan, Juliana	D	100
Jager, Catharina Maria A. Elisabeth	29, Jan. 1854	Heinrich	Stephan, Juliana	D	3
Jäger, Christiana	28, Apr. 1850	Christian	Schutzman, Margaretha	A	
Jäger, Jacob Friedrich	23, Nov. 1851	Heinrich	Stephan, Juliana	D	293
Jäger, Joseph Wilhelm	4, June 1854	Joseph	Leppert, Louisa	K	
Jägering, Catharina Elisabeth	1, Mar. 1854	Georg	Klüman, Maria Elisabeth	D	5
Jägering, Ephemia Maria	1, Mar. 1854	Georg	Klüman, Maria Elisabeth	D	5
Jahle, Eduard	20, Apr. 1856	Edward	Renner, Edeltraud	W	13
Jahnsen, Maria Adelheid	1, Sept 1856	Heinrich	Kuhr, Anna	C	
Jaiconet, Eduard Jacob	26, Apr. 1857	Joseph	Berger, Catharina	A	
Jako, Maria	9, Nov. 1857	Vincent	Balof, Anna	D	98
James, Christopher	21, Apr. 1850	Hugh	Dunn, Margaret	B	202
James, John	15, Aug. 1853	?	?	B	297
Janbaptist?, Francis Ludwig	25, Oct. 1857	Bernard	Rosehorz, Christina	D	97
Janemann, Herman Joseph	12, July 1851	Joseph	Bunker, Maria Anna	C	
Janing, Joseph	6, Nov. 1858	William	Spielmayer, Catharina	D	123
Janmair, Maria Louisa	2, Apr. 1850	Theodor	Hannebaum, Louisa	D	208
Janmeier, Johan Wilhelm	30, Aug. 1850	Johan	Borman, Maria Anna	K	
Janner, Friedrich Bernard	18, Apr. 1849	Bernard	Bogenschuetz, Crescentia	S	
Janning, Bernard Heinrich	10, Apr. 1856	Herman H.	Fangman, Anna Maria	L	
Janning, Bernard Joseph	27, Dec. 1853	Herman H.	Fangmann, Anna Maria	L	
Janning, Heinrich August	18, Sept 1850	Herman	Wortmann, Gertrud	F	
Janning, M. Elisabeth Bernardina	8, Nov. 1859	J. Heinrich	Fangmann, Anna Maria	L	
Janning, Maria Catharina Josephina	31, Dec. 1851	Herman	Woerkmann, Maria Gertrud	F	
Janning, Maria Gertrud Rosina	18, Mar. 1857	Herman	Woertmann, Gertrud	F	
Janning, Marianna Philomena	25, Mar. 1855	Herman	Wortmann, Anna M. Gertrud	F	
Janno, Elizabeth	20, Jan. 1856	Henry	----, Mary	M	
Jans, Theresa	18, June 1857		Jans, Gertrud	D	88
Jansbrucker, Maria Barbara	30, Mar. 1851	Michael	Zackmeier, Monica	D	259
Jansbrucker, Maria Rosina	20, Feb. 1853	Michael	Zachmeier, Monica	D	372
Jansen, Anna	26, Aug. 1856	Heinrich	Bauer, Margaretha	F	
Jansen, Anna Maria Carolina	25, May 1856	Bernard H.	Mette, Bernardina	L	
Jansen, Anna Maria Elisabeth	21, May 1852	Arnold	Rechtine, Theresa	A	
Jansen, Anna Maria Theresa	6, Aug. 1856	Arnold	Rechtine, Anna M. Theresa	A	
Jansen, Anton	1, Mar. 1858	Joseph	Ronnebaum, Agnes	L	
Jansen, Catharina	5, Mar. 1854	Jacob	Richter, Elisabeth	A	
Jansen, Franz Anton	18, Apr. 1858	Heinrich	Mette, Bernardina	L	
Jansen, Gerhard Heinrich	19, Feb. 1850	Heinrich	Mette, Bernardina	L	
Jansen, Heinrich	11, June 1854	Jacob	Fischer, Dina	D	12
Jansen, Heinrich Anton	27, Aug. 1856	Heinrich	Sickman, Elisabeth	A	
Jansen, Heinrich Joseph Anton	2, Aug. 1856	Joseph	Ronnebaum, M. Agnes	L	
Jansen, Helena M. Christina	15, Feb. 1852	Heinrich	Schwinging, Carolina	D	307
Jansen, Jacob	21, Aug. 1856	Jacob	Richter, Elisabeth	A	
Jansen, Jacob	7, July 1850	Jacob	Richter, Elisabeth	A	
Jansen, Johan	15, Aug. 1854	Heinrich	Mette, Bernardina	L	
Jansen, Johan	28, Oct. 1852	Johan	Wintering, Susanna M.	L	
Jansen, Johan Bernard	8, Oct. 1853	Herman	Deppe, Catharina	D	409
Jansen, Johan Heinrich	14, Aug. 1854	Arnold	Rechtine, Theresa	A	
Jansen, Johan Heinrich	27, Feb. 1859	Jacob	Richter, Maria Elisabeth	A	
Jansen, Johan Heinrich Theodor	18, July 1858	J. Heinrich	Siekmann, Maria Anna	L	
Jansen, Johan Herman Heinrich	21, Feb. 1858	Johan	V---, Anna Catharina	D	105
Jansen, Johan Joseph	24, June 1857	Wilhelm	Sibeling, Maria Anna	D	88
Jansen, Johan Wilhelm	7, Apr. 1855	Johan	Winterberg, Susanna	L	
Jansen, Josephina	26, May 1853	Wilhelm	Sieverding, Maria A.	L	
Jansen, Josephina Elisabeth	10, June 1852	Heinrich	Mette, Bernardina	L	

Name of Child	Date of Baptism	Father	Mother	Church	Page
Jansen, Margaretha	11, June 1852	Martin	Abke, Wilhelmina	D	324
Jansen, Maria Catharina Elisabeth	17, May 1850	Johan	Wintering, Anna Maria	D	213
Jansen, Maria Elisabeth	1, Jan. 1856	Martin	Abke, Wilhelmina	D	50
Jansen, Maria Theresa	10, July 1850	Herman	Debe, Carolina	F	
Jansen, Martin	10, July 1859	Christian	Witter, Elisabeth	D	141
Jansen, Martin	23, Apr. 1852	Jacob	Richter, Elisabeth	A	
Jansen, Mathilda Barbara	28, Nov. 1858	Joseph	Mueller, Elisabeth	T	
Jansen, Wilhelm B.K.	31, Oct. 1852	William	Höfler, Elisabeth	D	355
Janser, Philomena	27, Nov. 1853	Joseph	Müller, Elisabeth	K	
Janson, Barbara	15, Oct. 1850	Heinrich	Bauer, Margaretha	F	
Janson, Georg	1, Feb. 1854	Heinrich	Bauer, Margaretha	F	
Janson, Jacob	3, Apr. 1853	Nicolaus	Broak, Magdalena	C	
Janson, Johan	16, Apr. 1854	Martin	Abke, Wilhelmina	D	8
Janson, Maria Margaretha	18, Mar. 1858	Christian	Witter, Maria Elisabeth	D	107
Janson, Martin	17, Oct. 1850	Martin	Abke, Wilhelmina	D	238
Janz, Johan	16, Nov. 1856	Anton	----, Gertrud	D	72
Janzen, Francisca Carolina	30, Sept 1851	Herman	Durtige, Helena	K	
Jasper, Herman Heinrich	30, May 1858	Wilhelm O.	Hembrock, M. Anna	C	
Jaspers, Elisabeth	16, Aug. 1855		Jaspers, Anna	A	
Jaspers, Gerhard Bernard	3, Apr. 1859	J. Bernard	Schele, Dorothea	K	
Jaspers, Johan Bernard	28, Mar. 1858	H. Theodor	Emke, Anna Maria	J	46
Jaspers, Johan Heinrich	18, May 1856	H. Theodor	Emke, Carolina	J	36
Jaspers, Johan Heinrich	28, Apr. 1858	J. Herman	Torliene, Dorothea	K	
Jaspers, Maria Josephina	3, Apr. 1859	J. Bernard	Schele, Dorothea	K	
Jaspes, Maria Carolina	5, Aug. 1854	Dietrich	Emke, Carolina	F	
Jaun, Philipp	25, Oct. 1850	Michael	Matz, Maria	C	
Jauss, Josephine	6, Apr. 1856	Michael	Jack, Mary Ann	U	
Jauss, Maria Louisa	30, Jan. 1853	Michael	Jaeg, Anna Maria	F	
Jauss, Michael	2, Sept 1853	Michael	----, Mary Ann	U	
Jauss, Michael	27, May 1850	Michael	Jaeg, Anna Maria	K	
Jauss, Sophia Maria	4, Aug. 1851	Michael	Jäck, Maria Anna	Q	1
Jaw, Johan	12, Jan. 1851	Jacob	Calleo, Helena	J	10
Jeck, Cunigunda	14, June 1857	Martin	Ditsch, Margaretha	D	87
Jeck, Martin	8, Dec. 1850	Martin	Ditschen, Margaretha	D	246
Jeckel, Anna Maria	22, Dec. 1852	J. Herman	Kramer, Elisabeth	D	361
Jeckel, Elisabeth Josephina Louisa	21, Apr. 1858	Joseph	Kramer, Elisabeth	A	
Jeffers, Ann	10, Nov. 1853	James	Kenny, Mary	E	143
Jeffers, Anthony	15, Sept 1850	Thomas	McCaffrey, Mary	B	213
Jeffers, Anthony	21, Sept 1851	Thomas	McCaffrey, Mary	B	241
Jeffers, Catherine	10, May 1857	Thomas	McCaffrey, Mary	B	44
Jeffers, James	25, May 1856	James	Kenny, Mary	E	369
Jeffers, Mary	30, May 1855	Thomas	McCaffrey, Mary	B	15
Jeffers, William	22, Aug. 1858	John	Karney, Ellen	B	63
Jefferson, Bridget	22, May 1853	Thomas	----, Mary	B	292
Jefferson, Mary Frances	3, Mar. 1853	John	Adams, Helen	B	285
Jeffries, John	22, Feb. 1857	John	Kearney, Ellen	B	41
Jegelbrink, Catharina Elisabeth	20, Mar. 1859	Christian	Bensmann, Elisabeth	L	
Jehling, Jacob	8, May 1859	Edward	Reinard, Helena	G	
Jelges, Johan David	22, Dec. 1858	B. Heinrich	Fisbeck, Maria Catharina	K	
Jelges, Johan Heinrich	2, Feb. 1854	B. Heinrich	Fisbecks, Maria Catharina	K	
Jelich, Catherine	17, June 1855	John	----, Caroline	H	
Jelich, Christina	20, Nov. 1859	Johan	Bentz, Carolina	H	
Jelich, Francis James	1, July 1853	John	----, Caroline	H	
Jelich, Johan Baptist	15, June 1851	Johan	Benz, Carolina	D	268
Jelich, Maria Victoria	26, July 1857	John	Bins, Caroline	H	
Jendes, Anna Maria	11, Mar. 1855	Mathias	Werner, Catharina	C	
Jendes, Mathias	26, July 1853	Mathias	Werner, Catharina	C	
Jenes, Isabella	26, June 1857	Samuel	Williams, Elisabeth	L	
Jenewein, Nicolaus	12, July 1857	Ludwig	Jung, Elisabeth	D	90

Name of Child	Date of Baptism	Father	Mother	Church	Page
Jenjohn, John	12, Dec. 1858	George	Cordmeyer, Maria Gertrud	H	
Jennewein, Anna	15, Feb. 1857	Peter	Kirchner, Louisa	D	79
Jennewein, David	7, Aug. 1858	Ludwig	Jung, Elisabeth	T	
Jennewein, Jacob	4, Mar. 1854	Peter	Kirchner, Louisa	D	5
Jennewein, Magdalena	12, June 1855	Peter	Ragge, Catharina	D	36
Jennewein, Margaretha	17, Mar. 1858	Peter	Racke, Catharina	D	107
Jennigan, Martin	5, Mar. 1854	Joseph	Doran, Helen	B	310
Jenning, Bridget	25, July 1852	Patrick	----, Mary	M	
Jennings, Edward	16, Oct. 1853	Patrick	Geblen, Margaret	P	55
Jennings, Henry	3, June 1855	Alexander	Duff, Sarah	P	135
Jennings, Lydia Frances	16, June 1859	Thomas	Clary, Mary Ann	E	633
Jennings, Margaret	29, Feb. 1852	Martin	Coolickin, Mary	P	18
Jennings, Martin	29, Mar. 1854	John	----, Honora	E	180
Jennings, Mary	14, Apr. 1850	Raymond	Morron, Bridget	B	201
Jennings, Mary Ann	16, May 1858	John	Harringan, Amy	B	59
Jennings, Michael	19, Feb. 1854	Patrick	Gill, Helen	B	309
Jennings, Patrick	2, Feb. 1851	Patrick	Gillin, Margaret	P	4
Jennings, Rose	14, Mar. 1852	Raymond	Moran, Bridget	B	254
Jennings, Thomas	3, July 1853	Alexander	Duff, Sarah	B	294
Jens, Georg	9, Feb. 1857	Samuel	Wilhelms, Elisabeth	L	
Jentes, Catharina	13, Dec. 1856	Mathias	Werner, Catharina	F	
Jentes, Jacob	27, Dec. 1857	Mathias	Werner, Catharina	F	
Jentz, Charles	6, May 1851	Samuel	Williams, Elizabeth	B	231
Jerane, Elisabeth	6, Dec. 1857	Johan	Paulin, Catharina	D	100
Jerg, Cunigunda Margaretha	14, Feb. 1853	Martin	Ditsch, Margaretha	D	371
Jerg, Georg	14, Feb. 1853	Martin	Ditsch, Margaretha	D	371
Jergen, John	10, Mar. 1850	Francis	Balican?, Margaret	B	198
Jewell, Abigail Mary	16, Aug. 1852	Silas	adult - 30 years old	E	6
Jilges, Anna Maria Catharina	26, Aug. 1855	Heinrich	Fisbecks, Maria Catharina	K	
Jinder, Joseph Bernard Oswald	27, Nov. 1859	Oswald	Briche, Johanna	K	
Jirgis, Bernard Francis	12, Dec. 1851	Bernard H.	Fischbecks, Maria Catharina	K	
Joachim, Johan	5, Sept 1853	Jacob	Bauer, Maria Anna	D	404
Joachim, Joseph Ludwig	3, Apr. 1856	Johan	Pfarer, Maria Anna	D	55
Joachim, Maria Elisabeth	20, May 1858	Jacob	Bauer, Maria Anna	D	111
Joannes, Christina	10, Feb. 1854	Thomas	Weimer, Barbara	D	4
Jobert, Alexander Victor	29, Aug. 1852	Joseph	Roy, M. Francisca	C	
Jobert, Felicitas	13, June 1854	Joseph	Roy, Maria	A	
Jobert, Flora Josephina	23, Sept 1855	Joseph	Roy, Francisca	A	
Jobert, Justina	23, Sept 1855	Joseph	Roy, Francisca	A	
Joerg, Anna Susan	25, Sept 1859	Johan	Alban, Susan	H	
Joerg, Elisabeth Josephina	29, Mar. 1857	Francis	Ostheimer, Elisabeth	F	
Joerg, Johan Bernard	20, May 1855	Francis	Ostheimer, Elisabeth	F	
Joergen, Maria Agnes	5, June 1859	Wilhelm	Schmidinghof, Catharina	F	
Joergens, Joseph	1, Sept 1850	Lawrence	----, Catharina	H	
Joergens, Joseph Ferdinand	24, June 1857	Wilhelm	Schmittinghof, Catharina	F	
Joerger, Barbara	13, Mar. 1859	Charles	Grab, Catharina	H	
Joerger, Helen	11, May 1856	Charles	----, Catherine	H	
Joerger, Johan	11, Oct. 1857	Aloysius	Resch, Maria Anna	D	96
Joerger, John	15, Oct. 1854	Charles	----, Catherine	H	
Joerger, Maria	11, May 1856	Charles	----, Catherine	H	
Joering, Anna Maria	21, Mar. 1858	Ferdinand	Reuter, Friedricka	L	
Joering, Dorothea	1, Apr. 1852	Georg	Beckmann, Elisabeth	L	
Joering, Johan Bernard	4, Nov. 1853	Jurgen	Beckmann, Elisabeth	L	
Joering, Johan Herman Heinrich	21, Aug. 1855	J. Bernard	Stautberg, M. Elis.	L	
Jöger, Thomas Ludwig	2, Oct. 1853	Aloysius	Resch, Maria	D	408
Johan, Elisabeth	30, Mar. 1851	Friedrich	Hermkrauter, Ottilia	C	
Johan, Elisabeth Julia	1, Sept 1851	Bernard	Westner, Magdalena	C	
Johan, Friedrich	4, June 1850	Joseph	Martin, Veronica	C	
Johan, Joseph	27, Sept 1856	Friedrich	Krauter, Ottilia	C	

Name of Child	Date of Baptism	Father	Mother	Church	Page
Johanchen, Margaretha	6, July 1851	Georg	Heitz, Christina	C	
Johann, Edward	7, Aug. 1859	Friedrich	Handgrever, Ottilia	C	
Johannes, Maria	20, Oct. 1853	Caspar	Gessner, Maria Anna	D	410
Johannesman, Johan Heinrich	7, Dec. 1854	Caspar H.	Kenkel, Catharina	D	23
Johannesman, Maria Elisabeth	7, Dec. 1851	Caspar H.	Meyer, Anna Maria	D	296
Johannigman, Anna Maria	11, Mar. 1854	Mathias	Hatke, Maria Catharina	D	6
Johannigman, Bernardina Clementina	4, Nov. 1856	J. Heinrich	Könkel, Catharina	D	71
Johannigman, Elisabeth Carolina	21, Apr. 1858	Mathias	Hatke, Anna Maria	D	109
Johannigman, Maria Josephina	29, Apr. 1856	Mathias	Hatke, Catharina	D	57
Johannisman, Maria Catharina	11, Sept 1853	Heinrich	Meyer, Maria	D	405
Johe, Elisabeth	26, Sept 1858	Joseph	Ruff, Elisabeth	H	
Johe, Maria Barbara	2, May 1858	Peter	VonderElle, Elisabeth	H	
Johentgen, Anna Maria	27, Jan. 1850	Peter	Lemix, Maria Paulina	D	201
John, Barbara	4, Feb. 1856	Joseph G.	Pohl, Elisabeth	C	
John, Juliana Amalia	4, Aug. 1859	Ludwig	Donnersberger, Rosina	F	
John, Marianna	11, Sept 1856	Ludwig	Donnersberger, Rosina	F	
John, Mary Jane	30, July 1850	Michael	Callahan, Mary Ann	B	209
Johns, Maria Elisabeth	30, Apr. 1854	James H.	Brooks, Mary	A	
Johnson, Alice Helen	9, Aug. 1857	William	McGuire, Catherine	E	473
Johnson, Ann	9, Aug. 1852	Henry	Connelly, Julia	B	267
Johnson, Ann	13, Mar. 1859	William	Bannalson, Ann	E	611
Johnson, Bethse	17, Jan. 1853		adult - 50 years old	E	55
Johnson, Bridget	16, Mar. 1851	Nicolaus	Nonner, Helena	J	10
Johnson, Catherine	26, Aug. 1855	Henry	Connelly, Julia	B	18
Johnson, Charles Thomas	17, Dec. 1854	William	----, Honora	V	20
Johnson, Edward	10, June 1850		adult - 40 years old	E	223
Johnson, Elizabeth	12, May 1855	William	----, Julia	U	
Johnson, Emanuel Julius	9, Mar. 1851	John	Rankin, Elizabeth	B	226
Johnson, George Sample	22, May 1859	William	Sample, ann	B	75
Johnson, Harriet Melissa	19, Jan. 1859	Samuel	Brown, Elizabeth	B	70
Johnson, James C.K.	4, July 1858	William	Kenny, Catherine	E	545
Johnson, John Henry	20, Mar. 1856	Richard R.	Potter, Julia	B	27
Johnson, Julietta L.	30, Sept 1857	Richard	Potter, Julia	B	50
Johnson, Mary	19, May 1852	George	Musy?, Fanne	E	415
Johnson, Mary	7, Mar. 1852	John	Reilly, Joanne	B	254
Johnson, Mary Ann	6, Dec. 1855	James	Mourron, Bridget	P	162
Johnson, Mary Ellen	11, May 1859	John	Kennedy, Eliza	E	624
Johnson, Mary Jane	20, Oct. 1853	Samuel	----, Bridget	E	136
Johnson, Sarah Mary	12, Sept 1856	Charles	Caxon, Lucinda	E	398
Johnson, Thomas	25, Dec. 1853	John	Riley, Joanne	B	305
Johnson, William Francis	21, May 1851	James	Buckley, Margaret	P	8
Johnston, Ann	24, Aug. 1851	Thomas	Hall, Mary	E	335
Johnston, Catherine	20, July 1857	Edward	Hagerty, Ann	P	217
Johnston, Catherine	21, Aug. 1853	William	Eversfield, Honora	E	122
Johnston, Catherine Elizabeth	31, July 1857	William	Everfield, Honora	E	470
Johnston, Henry	7, Apr. 1858		Johnston, Mary A.	P	245
Johnston, James	1, Jan. 1858	William	Brenner, Ann	E	505
Johnston, James Henry	21, Mar. 1852	William	Eversfield, Honora	E	393
Johnston, John	10, June 1852	John	----, Elizabeth	E	422
Johnston, Louise Jane	6, Dec. 1855	Adam	Blair, Ann	E	331
Johnston, Margaret Jane	12, Apr. 1851	William	McGuire, Catherine	E	299
Johnston, Mary Ellen	9, Dec. 1851	James	Lehens, Mary	E	365
Johnston, William	23, Dec. 1852	Nathan	Whelan, Margaret	B	278
Joice, John	29, Aug. 1855	Patrick	----, Catharine	T	
Jonas, Johan Anselm	19, Jan. 1859	Johan	Doecker, Carolina	F	
Jonas, Johan Bernard Peter	16, Aug. 1858	Jacob	Schulte, Elisabeth	F	
Jonas, Maria Adelheid	18, Jan. 1857	Jacob	Schulte, M. Euphemia	F	
Jones, Ann	6, Sept 1853		adult	B	298
Jones, Catherine	27, Mar. 1851	David	Hughes, Mary	E	295

Name of Child	Date of Baptism	Father	Mother	Church	Page
Jones, Charles	6, Mar. 1859	James	Connell, Margaret	E	609
Jones, Edward Joseph	14, Feb. 1858	Robert	Nolan, Catherine	E	517
Jones, Francis Carl Ludwig	31, July 1859	Louis	Frondhoff, Francisca	C	
Jones, George Albert	4, Aug. 1857	James V.	O'Donnell, Ann	P	219
Jones, Helen	30, Oct. 1855	Samuel	McEntyre, Elizabeth	E	324
Jones, Henrietta Charlote Carolina	25, Nov. 1855	Ludwig	Frundhoff, Catharina	C	
Jones, James Henry	9, Mar. 1851	James	----, Margaret	E	288
Jones, James Thomas	18, Nov. 1855	James	O'Donnell, Ann	B	21
Jones, John	4, Feb. 1855	Patrick	Stokes, Mary	B	11
Jones, John	1, July 1851		adult - 40 years old	E	320
Jones, John Henry	3, Sept 1858	Peter	Ennis, Elizabeth	B	63
Jones, Joseph	2, Sept 1855	William	Bonney, Catherine	P	149
Jones, Joseph William	21, Sept 1856		adult	M	
Jones, Josephine	2, Apr. 1850	Charles T.	Chambers, Margaret	B	200
Jones, Margaret	28, Feb. 1854		adult	M	
Jones, Martha	5, Mar. 1851	Hiram	----, Mary	E	287
Jones, Martha Elizabeth	17, Oct. 1852	Charles T.	Chambers, Margaret	B	272
Jones, Mary Agnes	19, Feb. 1857		adult	B	40
Jones, Mary Ann	12, Oct. 1856	Peter	Ennis, Elizabeth	B	35
Jones, Mary Ann	18, Dec. 1857	William	Bonny, Catherine	P	232
Jones, Mary Jane	22, May 1852	John	Gallagher, Ann	B	263
Jones, Mary Josephine	19, Feb. 1857		adult	B	40
Jones, Michael	19, Apr. 1852	Charles	Cu---, Bridget	B	257
Jones, Peter	26, Jan. 1856	Od.	----, Mary	E	340
Jones, Richard	17, Nov. 1854	Peter	Ennis, Elizabeth	B	7
Jones, Robert	12, Aug. 1851	Robert	Ellis, Elizabeth	E	332
Jones, Thomas	21, Aug. 1853	James	----, Margaret	E	121
Jones, Thomas	4, Oct. 1852	Walter	Weber, Levina	E	24
Jones, Wililam	27, Jan. 1858	Daniel	Foster, Mary J.	B	55
Jordan, Agnes	5, Sept 1858	David	Ashby, Martha	B	64
Jordan, Agnes	1, May 1856	Nicholas	Hendricks, Rebecca	B	28
Jordan, Bernard William	21, June 1859	Martin	Cunningham, Bridget	B	76
Jordan, Bridget	18, July 1855	Martin	Cunningham, Bridget	B	17
Jordan, Charlotte	12, May 1852	Richard	Campbell, Mary	B	259
Jordan, Daniel	18, Apr. 1852	Nicholas	Hendricks, Rebecca	B	257
Jordan, David	4, Dec. 1853	David	Ashby, Martha Ann	B	304
Jordan, Dennis	13, Nov. 1859	Thomas	Nethercote, Mary	B	83
Jordan, Edward Daniel	7, Jan. 1855	Richard M.	Campbell, Mary Ann	E	254
Jordan, John	13, Apr. 1856	David	Ashby, Martha Ann	B	27
Jordan, John	17, Feb. 1855	Simon	----, Alice	E	265
Jordan, Louis	27, Nov. 1853	Martin	Cunningham, Bridget	B	303
Jordan, Louisa Wilhelmina H.	26, Apr. 1853	Theodor	Bessling, Maria	D	382
Jordan, Margaret	30, Sept 1858	Patrick	Gavin, Bridget	E	565
Jordan, Martha	22, May 1854		adult	B	315
Jordan, Mary	30, July 1859	Charles	Brown, Bridget	B	78
Jordan, Mary Ann	23, Apr. 1851	Martin	Cunningham, Bridget	B	230
Jordan, Richard Michael	21, Mar. 1851	Michael	Campbell, Mary Ann	E	293
Jordan, Robert	4, Apr. 1858	Thomas	Merit, Mary	P	245
Jordan, Susan Ann	29, Sept 1859	James	Thompson, Mary Ann	E	658
Jordan, Thomas	24, Feb. 1851	James	M----,	B	225
Jordan, William	16, Nov. 1851	David	Ashby, Martha	B	245
Jörg, Johan Heinrich	30, May 1858	Johan	Alban, Susan	H	
Jorg?, Maria Louisa Philippina	6, Feb. 1853	Francis	Ostheimer, Elisabeth	D	370
Jörgens, Jacob	8, June 1851	Philipp	Steffen, Maria	J	12
Jörgens, Maria Elisabeth	15, Aug. 1853	Philipp	Stephen, Maria	J	24
Jörger, Carolina	27, Jan. 1856	Anton	Bender, Christina	D	51
Jörger, Maria	22, July 1855	Aloysius	Resch, Maria	D	38
Jöring, Friedrich	1, Apr. 1858		Jöring, Anna Maria	A	
Jos?, Christian Martin	28, July 1850	Christian	Blocher, Marina	K	

Name of Child	Date of Baptism	Father	Mother	Church	Page
Jost, Ottilia	16, Mar. 1856	Jacob	Weingärtner, Wilhelmina	A	
Jostarnd, Anna Louisa	26, Nov. 1856	J. Joseph	Schulte, Anna M.	D	73
Jostarnd, Gerhard Heinrich Joseph	19, Oct. 1852	J. Joseph	Schulte, Elisabeth Anna M.	D	353
Jostarnd, Maria Anna	3, Oct. 1858	Joseph	Schulte, Maria Anna	U	
Jostarnd, Maria Anna Elisabeth	5, June 1851	Joseph	Schulte, Anna Maria	D	267
Jostarnt, Maria	18, Sept 1853	Joseph	Schulte, Maria Elisabeth	D	406
Jostworth, Gerhard Heinrich	7, Sept 1858	Wilhelm	Rademaker, Elisabeth	A	
Jostworth, Johan Wilhelm	21, Aug. 1856	Wilhelm	Rademaker, Maria Elisabeth	A	
Joy, Elizabeth	16, Nov. 1851	Michael	Parker, Mary	B	245
Joy, Martin	4, Feb. 1855	Peter	----, Catherine	E	262
Joy, Mary	31, Mar. 1856	Thomas	Cary, Bridget	E	355
Joy, Robert	22, Mar. 1858	Patrick	----, Catherine	E	524
Joy, Robert	3, Dec. 1854	Thomas	Cary, Bridget	E	244
Joy, Thomas	29, Oct. 1859	Thomas	Cary, Bridget	E	665
Joyce, Ann	27, Apr. 1854	Patrick	----, Catherine	B	313
Joyce, Ann	8, Oct. 1854	Timothy	Ahern, Elizabeth	P	99
Joyce, Catherine	27, Apr. 1854	Patrick	----, Catherine	B	313
Joyce, Charles	22, July 1856	Charles	Reilly, Judith	E	383
Joyce, Edward James	9, Mar. 1853	John	----, Mary	B	285
Joyce, Elizabeth	3, Aug. 1851	Timothy	Ahern, Elizabeth	B	238
Joyce, Ellen	20, Aug. 1854	Charles	Reiley, Julia	E	218
Joyce, Ellen	24, Aug. 1853	Peter	----, Rose	E	122
Joyce, Helen	20, Oct. 1850	Edward	Kennedy, Mary	B	216
Joyce, Helen	13, Apr. 1856	Henry	McEvilly, Helen	R	
Joyce, Honora	26, Sept 1852	John	Kelly, Ann	E	20
Joyce, John	5, Oct. 1851	John	----, Mary	E	349
Joyce, Margaret	27, Feb. 1853	Michael	Carolton, Mary	E	66
Joyce, Mary	4, Aug. 1853	Anthony	----, Ann	M	
Joyce, Mary Ann	10, Jan. 1858	Charles	Reilly, Julia	E	507
Joyce, Patrick	26, Feb. 1854	Thomas	Gill, ----	B	309
Joyce, Thomas	5, Feb. 1856	Thomas	Gi---, Margaret	V	29
Joyce, Timothy	20, Sept 1857	Timothy	Ahern, Elizabeth	P	224
Jüdeman, Maria	29, May 1850		adult - 31 years old	D	215
Judge, Ann Mary	8, Aug. 1852	Patrick	Moran, Ann	E	3
Judge, Catherine	26, July 1857	Mark	----, Catherine	M	
Judge, John	16, June 1850	Patrick	----, Ann	E	223
Judge, John	16, Oct. 1853	William	----, Catherine	M	
Judge, Mary Ann	6, Mar. 1859	William	----, Catherine	M	
Judge, Sarah	22, May 1853	Patrick	----, Margaret	B	292
Juelg, Carl	15, Aug. 1852	Michael	Speck, Maria Anna	D	343
Juelg, Emma	4, May 1851	Michael	Speck, Maria Anna	C	
Jueneman, Jacob	11, Mar. 1855	Heinrich	Hageman, Theresa	W	7
Juergens, Anton Joseph	7, Aug. 1859	Joseph	Fasbinder, Catharina	C	
Juergens, Franz Joseph	15, June 1856	Joseph	Fassbinder, Catharina	F	
Juerger, Carl Wilhelm	14, Mar. 1855	Ignatius	Rott, Magdalena	L	
Jülg, Johanna Friedrica	7, Feb. 1858	Michael	Speck, Maria Anna	D	104
Jülg, Michael	22, Oct. 1854	Michael	Speck, Maria Anna	D	20
Julien, John Edward	10, Mar. 1857	James	Reoret, Mary	E	439
July, John Dennis	2, July 1850	Bernard	Gestes, Mary	E	228
Juncker, Anna Maria	20, Oct. 1859	Joseph	Oldenhagen, Anna Maria	G	
Jüneman, Maria Magadalena Theresa	13, Mar. 1859	Heinrich	Hageman, Theresa	W	25
Jung, Adam	19, Oct. 1856	Erhard	Heine, Helena	F	
Jung, Andreas	22, July 1855	Ignatius	Rapp, Maria Anna	D	39
Jung, Andreas	12, June 1859	Jacob	Kellermann, Catharina	T	
Jung, Anna Maria	19, May 1850	Johan	Rauh, Barbara	C	
Jung, Anna Maria	15, Sept 1850	Nicolaus	Jennewein, Anna Maria	J	6
Jung, Anna Maria Juliana	23, Aug. 1857	Peter	Dickman, Margaretha	Q	23
Jung, Antonia Elisabeth	11, Aug. 1850	Theobald	Bloom, Thecla	F	
Jung, Barbara	18, Feb. 1859	Heinrich	Blümberg, Catharina	D	132

Name of Child	Date of Baptism	Father	Mother	Church	Page
Jung, Carl	18, Oct. 1857	Wendel	Ziegler, Francisca	N	
Jung, Catharina	27, Mar. 1853	Christian	Miller, Magdalena	D	377
Jung, Catharina	12, Apr. 1857	Jacob	Schum, Catharina	D	82
Jung, Christoph	28, Aug. 1853	Heinrich	Bluemlein, Catharina	F	
Jung, Elisabeth	10, Jan. 1858	Heinrich	Blumlein, Catharina	D	102
Jung, Elisabeth	12, Apr. 1857	Joseph	Fleckenstein, Elisabeth	D	82
Jung, Elisabeth Amalia	6, Aug. 1854	Jacob	Schum, Catharina	D	15
Jung, Friedrich	18, Feb. 1855	Nicolaus	Volz, Margaretha	D	29
Jung, Genofeva	5, Dec. 1858	Wendel	Ziegler, Francisca	N	
Jung, Georg	9, Jan. 1853	Nicolaus	Jennewein, Anna Maria	F	
Jung, J. Heinrich	21, Feb. 1858	Joseph	Greis, Margaretha	T	
Jung, Johan	14, Dec. 1851	Johan	----, Catharina	D	297
Jung, Johan Christian	11, Oct. 1857	Christian	Müller, Magdalena	D	96
Jung, Johan Georg	20, Apr. 1856	Joseph	Kreis, Margaretha	F	
Jung, Joseph	31, Mar. 1859	Johan	Rauh, Barbara	C	
Jung, Magdalena Carolina	3, Apr. 1853	Johan	Rau, Barbara	C	
Jung, Magdalena Carolina	24, May 1855	Johan	Rau, Barbara	C	
Jung, Margaretha	27, Feb. 1859	Ignatius	Rapp, Maria Anna	D	133
Jung, Margaretha	9, Oct. 1856	Johan	Rau, Barbara	C	
Jung, Margaretha	9, Nov. 1851	Theobald	Blum, Thecla	F	
Jung, Maria Dorothea	18, Mar. 1857	Ignatius	Rapp, Maria	D	81
Jung, Maria Elisabeth	18, May 1856	Johan	Moritz, Maria Anna	K	
Jung, Maria Henrietta Elisabeth	6, Aug. 1859	Peter	Dickman, Magdalena	D	143
Jung, Nicolaus	23, Sept 1855	Heinrich	Blümlein, Catharina	D	43
Jung, Peter	5, Oct. 1851	Heinrich	Bluemlein, Catharina	F	
Jung, Philippina	29, May 1859	Christian	Moller, Maria	D	139
Jung, Philippina	23, June 1850	Johan	Martin, Catharina	D	218
Jungblut, Aloysius Edward	14, Nov. 1858	Stephan	Bitter, Johanna Francisca	N	
Jungblut, Francisca Amalia	3, May 1857	Stephan	Piter, Johanna Francisca	N	
Jungblut, Frank Stephen	10, July 1853	Stephan	Bitter, Francisca	C	
Jungblut, Georg Michael	8, July 1855	Nicolaus	Stocker, Maria	N	
Jungblut, Johan	30, Mar. 1857	Nicolaus	Stocker, Maria	N	
Jungblut, Johan	14, May 1855	Stephan	Peter, Johanna Francisca	K	
Jungblut, Joseph	28, Dec. 1853	Nicolaus	Stocker, Maria	N	19
Jungblut, Leonard	3, July 1859	Nicolaus	Stöger, Maria	N	
Jungblut, Magdalena	3, Nov. 1852	Nicolaus	Steckel, Marianna	N	9
Jungman, Bernard Heinrich	15, Mar. 1852	Joseph	Schemmel, Anna Gertrud	K	
Jungmann, Francis	7, Sept 1853		Jungmann, Maria	C	
Junk, Johan	10, Apr. 1854	Johan	Moritz, Anna Maria	K	
Junk, Johan Georg	7, Nov. 1858	Johan	Moritz, Anna Maria	K	
Junker, Anna Margaretha	24, Oct. 1852	Michael	Ziegler, Catharina	D	354
Junker, Anton Edward	13, Apr. 1854	Michael	Ziegler, Catharina	G	
Junker, Catharina	27, June 1858	Benedict	Lipps, Theresa	J	46
Junker, Catharina	16, July 1854	Wendelin	Bathalder, Euphrosina	K	
Junker, Georg	19, Dec. 1858	Joseph	Oldenhagen, Anna Maria	G	
Junker, Heinrich	10, July 1857	Wendel	Battenlter, Euphemia	L	
Junker, Joseph Valentin	14, June 1857	Joseph	----, Anna	G	
Junker, Maria Francisca	16, Nov. 1856	Fidel	Motz, Eva	J	38
Junker, Maria Magdalena	26, Nov. 1854	Fidel	Metz, Eva	J	30
Junker, Valentin	23, Dec. 1855	Benedict	Lipps, Theresa	J	34
Junneman, Carl	1, Mar. 1857	Heinrich	Hageman, Theresa	D	80
Jünneman, Heinrich	2, Feb. 1851	Heinrich	Hageman, Theresa	D	251
Jurgens, Lawrence	23, Apr. 1854		Jurgens, Elisabeth	H	
Ka---, Mary Ann	25, Dec. 1850	Michael	McGeharty, Bridget	M	
Kabbes, Anna Maria Catharina	8, June 1854	Gerhard	Zurliene, Maria Anna	K	
Kabbes, Johan	26, Nov. 1856	Gerhard	Zurliene, Maria Anna	K	
Kabbes, Maria Elisabeth	11, Feb. 1852	Gerhard	Zurliene, Maria Anna	K	
Kabbes, Maria Wilhelmina Rosa	26, May 1859	Gerhard	Zurliene, Maria Anna	K	
Kaegen, Johan	6, Feb. 1853	Polycarp	Gaegler, Magdalena	F	

Name of Child	Date of Baptism	Father	Mother	Church	Page
Kaegen, Maria Magdalena	15, Dec. 1850	Polycarp	Goetler, Maria Magdalena	F	
Kaehne, Maria Louisa	11, May 1856	Johan	Dehner, Anna	G	
Kaelen, Aloysius Johan	12, June 1859	Aloysius	Meier, Maria	T	
Kaelin, Carl Sales	17, Jan. 1858	Maurice	Koelin, Augusta	D	103
Kaeling, Maurus Georg	23, Mar. 1856	Maurice	Diringer, Augusta	D	54
Kaemmerer, Francis	25, Apr. 1852	Valentin	Kramer, Barbara	D	317
Kaempf, Marianna	16, Jan. 1853	Joseph	Brett, Catharina	F	
Kaennan, Edward	2, Feb. 1852	James	Murray, Honora	B	252
Kaes, Franz Joseph	4, July 1854	Joseph	Master, Elisabeth	F	
Kaes, Maria	27, May 1855	Joseph	Stecher, Agnes	D	35
Kaes, Maria Elisabeth	23, Sept 1855	Joseph	Mattis, Elisabeth	F	
Kaess, Joseph	7, Feb. 1858	Joseph	Stecher, Agnes	D	104
Kaferman, Andreas Ludwig	6, Nov. 1855	Heinrich	Drees, Maria Elisabeth	A	
Kaferman, Christina	25, Mar. 1852	Heinrich	Drees, Elisabeth Anna M.	A	
Kaferman, Francis Joseph	17, Dec. 1859	Heinrich	Drees, Elisabeth	A	
Kaferman, Johan Heinrich	8, Nov. 1853	Heinrich	Drees, Elisabeth	A	
Kaferman, Johan Mathias	4, Nov. 1857	Heinrich	Drees, Elisabeth	A	
Kaffell, Anthony	8, Sept 1852	Martin	Filpin, Elizabeth	B	270
Kahlhofer, Bernard	31, Mar.1851	Anton	Kern, Victoria	D	259
Kahlmeier, Herman Heinrich	9, Sept 1854	Herman H.	Meistermann, Catharina	F	
Kahlmeier, M. Elisabeth Philomena	14, Jan. 1858	Herman H.	Schulte, Maria Adelheid	F	
Kahlmeyer, Friedrich Aloysius	7, June 1859	Herman H.	Schulte, Adelheid	F	
Kahn, Mary	29, Aug. 1858	John	Wachter, Sophia	S	
Kaihn, Peter	3, June 1855	Peter	Bayer, Elisabeth	F	
Kail, William August	19, Nov. 1854	James W.	Carrol, Mary	B	7
Kailin, Elisabeth	14, May 1857	Peter	Bayer, Elsiabeth	F	
Kain, Ann Elizabeth	21, July 1850	Arthur	----, Elizabeth	E	233
Kain, Anthony	10, Apr. 1859	Patrick	Ford, Mary	B	73
Kain, Bernard	18, Aug. 1853	John	Toolan, Mary	U	
Kain, Bridget	11, Dec. 1853	Patrick	Ford, Mary	B	304
Kain, Mary	17, Sept 1856	Patrick	Ford, Mary	B	34
Kain, Michael	5, May 1853	Michael	Alley, Margaret	E	86
Kaiser, Amelia Theresa	19, Oct. 1856	Mathias	Biehle, Elisabeth	C	
Kaiser, Anna Maria	4, Feb. 1855	Johan	Bockhold, Anna Maria	D	28
Kaiser, Carl	18, Nov. 1855	Benjamin	Hoffmann, Catharina	C	
Kaiser, Carl	4, July 1853	Heinrich	?	D	393
Kaiser, Carl Heinrich	30, Apr. 1858	Friedrich	Toelke, Johanna	L	
Kaiser, Carolina Rosina	5, Aug. 1855	Mathias	Bahler, Elisabeth	C	
Kaiser, Catharina Elisabeth	15, Jan. 1854	Conrad	Schneider, Barbara	D	2
Kaiser, Elisabeth Philomena	16, July 1851		adult - 25 years old	K	
Kaiser, Emerentiana	31, July 1859	Valentin	Kierberger, Carolina	D	143
Kaiser, Francis Anton	17, Feb. 1856	Conrad	Schneider, Barbara	D	52
Kaiser, Francis Joseph	17, Aug. 1856	Valentin	Kiemberger, Carolina	W	15
Kaiser, Francisca	3, June 1858	Conrad	Schneider, Barbara	D	112
Kaiser, Gerhard Georg	2, Mar. 1852	Gerhard G.	Haverkamp, Bernardina	F	
Kaiser, Heinrich Joseph	19, Oct. 1855	Gerhard G.	Haverkamp, Bernardina	F	
Kaiser, Herman Clemens	27, Sept 1859	Bernard	Cramer, M. Anna	C	
Kaiser, Herman Heinrich	10, July 1853	Gerhard	Ungrund, Maria Catharina	F	
Kaiser, Hermina	7, Mar. 1858	Valentin	Kierberger, Carolina	J	44
Kaiser, Johan	23,Dec. 1850	Anton	Linder, Anna	D	247
Kaiser, Johan	25, Oct. 1853	Francis X.	Eder, Maria Anna	D	411
Kaiser, Johan Heinrich	17, Feb. 1851	J. Gerhard	Ungrund, Maria Catharina	F	
Kaiser, Johan Herman	13, Aug. 1855	Johan G.	Wilbers, Anna Maria	F	
Kaiser, Johan Joseph	31, Jan. 1859	J. Gerhard	Wilbers, Anna Maria	F	
Kaiser, Johan Mathias	20, Feb. 1859	Mathias	Meyer, Maria Anna	T	
Kaiser, Joseph Theodor	14, Sept 1851	H. Joseph	Schnyder, Agnes C.	C	
Kaiser, Josephina Maria	6, Mar. 1855	Caspar	Schnieders, Maria	C	
Kaiser, Maria Anna	19, Sept 1852	Mathias	Buchholt, Anna M.	C	
Kaiser, Maria Anna Josephina	12, June 1856	Caspar	Meyer, Maria Anna	D	60

Name of Child	Date of Baptism	Father	Mother	Church	Page
Kaiser, Maria Catharina	17, Dec. 1851	Gerhard	Wilbers, Anna Maria	F	
Kaiser, Maria Elisabeth	26, May 1858	Georg	Haverkamp, Bernardina	T	
Kaiser, Maria Elisabeth	27, Nov. 1859	Gerhard H.	VonBrink, Maria	C	
Kaiser, Maria Elisabeth	25, Dec. 1850	Matthias	Buchholz, Anna M.	C	
Kaiser, Maria Johanna	10, Sept 1852	Caspar T.	Schneider, M. Clara	C	
Kaiser, Maria Rosalia	22, Feb. 1857	Theodor H.	Weber, Maria Anna	L	
Kaiser, Peter Fortunatus	5, June 1853	Fortunatus	Faber, Magdalena	D	387
Kaiser, Theodor Heinrich	24, Feb. 1858	Theodor	Schneider, Maria	C	
Kaiser, Theodor Heirnich	13, Dec. 1857	Mathias	Meier, Maria	D	100
Kaiser, Wilhelm Georg Anton	22, May 1853	Georg	Haverkamp, Bernardina	F	
Kaisser, Johan Georg	5, Oct. 1853	Benjamin	Hoffmann, Catharina	C	
Kakenge, Helena Maria Anna	27, Nov. 1851	H.	Meyrose, A. Maria	L	
Kala, John	8, Dec. 1850	James	Delaney, Mary	B	220
Kalb, Francis Joseph	10, July 1858	Friedrich	Schenk, Eleonora	D	114
Kaleher, Cornelius	11, Apr. 1852	Cornelius	Murphy, Elizabeth	P	20
Kaleher, Maria	19, May 1850	Cornelius	Murphy, Elizabeth	J	6
Kaley, Ann	29, Feb. 1852	James	Byers, Helen	B	253
Kalin, Christina	4, July 1852	Lawrence	Schoenbechler, Benedicta	D	328
Kallage, Gerhard Joseph Clemens	22, Mar. 1854	Joseph	Foppe, Christina	K	
Kallage, Maria Anna Catharina	13, Jan. 1851	Joseph	Voppe, Christina	A	
Kallaher, Daniel	2, Apr. 1854	Matthew	O'Connell, Margaret	P	77
Kallehan, Alice	31, Oct. 1858	Edward	Moore, Alice	U	
Kallen, Mathias	13, Oct. 1857	Aloysius	Meyer, Maria	T	
Kalling, Johan Theodor	18, Oct. 1858	J. Theodor	Sauer, Elisabeth	F	
Kallmeier, Francis Boniface	13, July 1851	Friedrich	Schwan, Maria Catharina	A	
Kallmeier, Heinrich Aloysius	25, Jan. 1853	G. Heinrich	Kleinmeier, Carolina	K	
Kallmeier, M. Catharina Philomena	21, Feb. 1852	Gerhard H.	Droppelmann, Maria	F	
Kallmeyer, Alphons Herman	24, Feb. 1857	Jacob	Kleinmeyer, Elisabeth	C	
Kallmeyer, Anna Maria Elisabeth	20, Apr. 1854	Friedrich	Schwan, Maria	C	
Kallmeyer, Friedrich Wilhelm Anton	13, June 1854	Gerhard	Kleinmeyer, Carolina	C	
Kallmeyer, Maria Catharina	24, Dec. 1859	Friedrich	Schwane, M. Catharina	C	
Kallmeyer, Maria Philomena	25, Jan. 1857	Friedrich	Schwane, M. Catharina	C	
Kaltenbaum, Anton	25, June 1854	Anton	Nogg, Magdalena	D	13
Kaltenbrand, Sophia Theresa	6, July 1856	Anton	Nogg, Magdalena	D	62
Kaltenbrand, Theodor	12, Sept 1858	Anton	Nock, Magdalena	D	119
Kaman, Anton	7, Aug. 1856	Eberhard H.	Richter, Catharina Elisabeth	H	
Kaman, Rosina	5, Oct. 1851	Georg	Meisachner, Cunigunda	D	286
Kambeitz, Johan Baptist	23, Sept 1853	Wilhelm	Fettig, Francisca	C	
Kamer, James	17, May 1857	Matthew	Hack, Mary	T	
Kamerer, Crescentia	20, Feb. 1854	Joseph	Ruel, Theresa	F	
Kamerer, Theresa	10, Sept 1856	Joseph	Ruehl, Theresa	D	67
Kammer, Angela	15, Oct. 1855	Peter	Back, Susanna	F	
Kammer, Balthasar	18, Sept 1859	Jacob	Hilgert, Katharina	W	27
Kammer, Barbara	3, Feb. 1850	Jacob	Hillgerd, Catharina	D	202
Kammer, Barbara	13, Feb. 1859	Peter	Barkes, Susanna	W	25
Kammer, Catharina Carolina	19, Sept 1858	Jacob	Hilger, Catharina	W	23
Kammer, Daniel	7, Feb. 1857	Jacob	Hilgert, Catharina	W	18
Kammer, Ignatz	29, Jan. 1854	Peter	Weber, Elisabeth	F	
Kammer, Jacob	29, Jan. 1854	Jacob	Helgert, Catharina	W	1
Kammer, Johan	24, Feb. 1852	Peter	Weber, Elisabeth	D	309
Kammer, Josephina	26, June 1859	Mathias	Heck, Maria	F	
Kammer, Margaretha	9, June 1850	Peter	Weber, Elisabeth	D	216
Kammer, Maria	14, Dec. 1852	Mathias	Heck, Maria	F	
Kammer, Maria	15, Oct. 1855	Peter	Backangel, Susanna	F	
Kammer, Mathias	2, Feb. 1851	Jacob	Hilger, Catharina	F	
Kammer, Mathias	5, Dec. 1852	Jacob	Hilgert, Catharina	F	
Kammer, Mathias	27, May 1855	Mathias	Heklage, Maria	F	
Kammer, Mathias	12, Oct. 1856	Peter	Bakes, Susanna	F	
Kammer, Susanna	2, Sept 1855	Jacob	Hilget, Catharina	W	10

Name of Child	Date of Baptism	Father	Mother	Church	Page
Kammerer, Albuinus	17, July 1853	David	Hofer, Xaverina	D	395
Kammerer, Friedrich Wilhelm	20, Nov. 1854	J. David	Hofer, Xaverina	D	22
Kammerer, Gottfried Theodor	22, Feb. 1857	J. David	Hofer, Xavierina	D	79
Kammerer, Joseph Rupert	11, Apr. 1852	J. David	Hofer, Xavierina	D	316
Kammerer, Maria Josephina	4, May 1856	Wendelin	Hafener, Rosina	J	36
Kammerer, Maria Sophia	27, Dec. 1850	David	Hofer, Xaverina	D	246
Kammerer, Maria Theresa	11, Apr. 1858	Wendelin	Hafner, Rosina	J	46
Kammerer, Theodor Engelbert	25, July 1858	J. David	Hofer, Xavierina	D	115
Kamp, Anna Maria Philomena	17, June 1851	Philipp	Backhaus, Catharina	C	
Kamp, Bernardina Josephina	28, June 1850	Joseph	Mescher, Gertrud	L	
Kamp, Clara Josephina	13, Aug. 1854	Philipp	Backhaus, Catharina	C	
Kamp, Gerhard W. Heinrich	31, Dec. 1859	Gerhard H.	Wittrock, Catharina	A	
Kamp, Herman Bernard Ludwig	5, June 1859	Philipp	Kramer, Anna Maria	C	
Kamp, Itta Catharina	25, June 1850	Peter	Schepner,	F	
Kamp, Johan Heinrich	24, Oct. 1851	Joseph	Mescher, Gertrud	L	
Kamp, Johan Joseph	25, June 1852	Philipp	Backhaus, Catharina	C	
Kamp, Joseph Heinrich	11, Dec. 1859	Joseph	Pundsack, Antonia	F	
Kamp, Maria Agnes Catharina	7, July 1859	Joseph H.	Mescher, Maria	L	
Kamp, Maria Catharina Elisabeth	20, Jan. 1854	Joseph	Mescher, M. Gertrud	L	
Kamp, Maria Elisabeth	12, June 1856	Joseph	Mescher, Maria	L	
Kamp, Maria Elisabeth	23, Apr. 1858	Joseph	Pundsack, Antonette	L	
Kamp, Maria Helena	23, Aug. 1852	Peter	Schoepner, Adelheid	F	
Kamp, Maria Louisa	20, July 1859	Herman	Uhlenberg, Theresa	K	
Kamp, Peter Heinrich	6, Jan. 1857	Peter	Schoepner, Adelheid	F	
Kampe, August Ludwig	2, Mar. 1851	August H.	Frech, Anna Maria	D	255
Kämpe, Francis	28, July 1857	Johan	Kuhlenberg, Maria	D	91
Kampeitz, Albert	13, Dec. 1855	Wilhelm	Fettich, Francisca	C	
Kampelman, Maria Anna Wilhelmina	5, Dec. 1859	Herman	Schrill, Adelheid	R	
Kamper, Gerhard Heinrich	22, Mar. 1855	Gerhard H.	Strifing, Lisetta	D	31
Kämpf, Caspar Heinrich	13, July 1851	Francis J.	----, Catharina	N	4
Kamphauer, Johanna M. Rosa J.	30, Aug. 1850	Joseph	Goos, Maria	F	
Kamphaus, Carolina	15, Mar. 1856	Georg	Feld, Helena Adel.	C	
Kamphues, Maria Elisabeth	13, Jan. 1858	Georg	Feed, Adelheid	C	
Kamphues, Maria Helena Carolina	4, Apr. 1853	Joseph	Goos, Anna Maria	F	
Kampman, Anna Maria Chrstina	18, Mar. 1852	Georg	Lühn, Maria Adelheid	J	16
Kampman, Johan Gerhard	21, Jan. 1851	Bernard G.	Lüher, Maria Adelheid	D	250
Kampmann, Bernard Heinrich	2, Dec. 1853	Georg	Luehn, Maria Adelheid	F	
Kampmann, Johan Bernard	11, Oct. 1857	Gerhard	Luehn, Maria Adelheid	F	
Kampmann, Margaretha	9, Mar. 1855	Georg	Luehn, M. Adelheid	F	
Kampmeier, Johan Heinrich	29, June 1859	Heinrich	Lage, Maria	F	
Kampmeier, Maria Elisabeth	6, May 1857	Johan H.	Lage, Anna Maria	F	
Kampris, Florentina	11, Nov. 1855	J. Heinrich	----, Elisabeth	Q	11
Kams, Heinrich Francis	12, Mar. 1852	Francis	Homelars, Johanna	K	
Kamstock, Elisabeth Adelheid	26, Jan. 1852	Jacob	Hamilton, Caroline	D	304
Kander, Carolina	7, June 1852	Aloysius	Grube, Theresa	K	
Kane, Alexander	30, Jan. 1852	William	Rielly, Ann	P	16
Kane, Andrew James	19, June 1857	John	Doyle, Joanne	B	45
Kane, Catherine	20, Feb. 1858	Thomas	----, Margaret	M	
Kane, Clara	2, Oct. 1855	William	Reilly, Nancy	P	153
Kane, Dennis	24, May 1853	Dennis	----, Bridget	E	92
Kane, Elizabeth	23, Nov. 1852	Richard	Jordan, Elizabeth	B	276
Kane, Emily	25, Jan. 1857	Thomas	----, Margaret	M	
Kane, Emily Agnes	1, Jan. 1854	Bartholomew	Hakly, Adrean	E	156
Kane, Frances Jane	20, Apr. 1851	John	Doyle, Joanne	B	230
Kane, Francis	21, Feb. 1850	Francis	Timmins, Margaret	B	197
Kane, Helen	17, Mar. 1850	John	Delaney, Margaret	B	199
Kane, James	19, Nov. 1853	John	Case, Honora	E	145
Kane, James	29, Dec. 1859	Patrick	Daly, Mary	P	307
Kane, James Henry	29, Feb. 1852	Arthur	Lennan, Elizabeth	E	386

Name of Child	Date of Baptism	Father	Mother	Church	Page
Kane, Margaret	29, July 1855	---ry	Heffernan, Margaret	P	142
Kane, Mary	13, Oct. 1854	John	Doyle, Joanne	B	6
Kane, Mary	17, Apr. 1856	Michael	----, Mary	E	359
Kane, Mary	27, June 1858	Philip	Hallinan, Catherine	E	544
Kane, Mary	19, June 1853	William	Reilly, Ann	P	44
Kane, Mary Ann	19, Feb. 1854	Richard	Forde, Elizabeth	V	11
Kane, Mary Elizabeth	4, Mar. 1855	Thomas	----, Margaret	M	
Kane, Mary Jane	16, Aug. 1857	Michael	----, Bridget	E	474
Kane, Michael	25, May 1856	Richard	Forde, Elizabeth	V	31
Kane, Patrick	14, Jan. 1853	Patrick	----, Margaret	M	
Kane, Patrick	7, Mar. 1850	Patrick	Crowley, Bridget	E	201
Kane, Susan	4, June 1851	James	Martin, Theresa Elizabeth	E	312
Kane, Theresa Elizabeth	6, Jan. 1856	James	Martin, Theresa Elizabeth	E	335
Kane, Theresa Elizabeth	20, Sept 1857	James	Martin, Theresa Elizabeth	E	481
Kane, Thomas	28, Mar. 1858	Michael	----, Rose	M	
Kane, William Francis	9, Nov. 1852	William	----, Ann	E	33
Kane, William Patrick	3, Oct. 1852	John	Doyle, Joanne	B	273
Kanet, Maria Anna	7, Sept 1851	Michael	Bauer, Maria Anna	D	281
Kanet, Maria Elisabeth	2, June 1850	Michael	Bauer, Maria Anna	D	215
Kanfert, Elisabeth Johanna	6, July 1851		Kanfert, Christina	D	271
Kannan, John	16, May 1852	William	Prendergast, Bridget	P	21
Kannan, William	30, Mar. 1854	William	Prendergast, Bridget	P	76
Kansy, John	8, June 1856	Jeremiah	----, Honora	H	
Kant, Patrick James John	27, Oct. 1853	Patrick	McCarty, Ellen	L	
Kany, Honora	1, Feb. 1855	Jeremiah	----, Honora	H	
Kapp, Johan Thomas	11, Dec. 1859	Johan	Meyer, Maria	C	
Kapp, Louisa	20, Mar. 1853	Johan	Meyer, Maria Anna	D	376
Kapp, Maria Louisa	11, Nov. 1855	Johan	Meier, Maria	D	46
Kappel, Caspar Philipp	12, Jan. 1858	Heinrich	Volmeke, Clara	A	
Kappel, Heinrich Jacob	25, July 1854	Herman	Börmig?, Laura	D	15
Kappel, Joseph Heinrich	16, Sept 1855	Heinrich	Völmeke, Maria Clara	A	
Kappel, Maria Josephina Clara	10, Nov. 1856	Heinrich	Völmeke, Clara	A	
Kappertz, Maria Adelheid	15, Aug. 1856	Heinrich	Richter, Anna M. Magdalena	A	
Kappler, Heinrich	28, Feb. 1854	Thomas	Leiz, Johanna	D	5
Karbel, Maria Appolonia	28, July 1850	Johan	----, Theresa	D	225
Karhof, Bernard Heinrich	16, Jan. 1858	Bernard	Heit, Francisca	F	
Karhof, Catharina Maria Josephina	31, July 1853	Heinrich	Engelbert, M. Cath.	L	
Karhof, Elisabeth Louisa Maria	1, Jan. 1850	Heinrich	----, Maria	K	
Karhof, Herman Heinrich	7, Aug. 1855	J. Heinrich	Engelbert, Anna M.	L	
Karhof, Johan Heinrich Franz	10, Jan. 1858	Heinrich	Engelbert, Maria	L	
Karhoff, Gerhard Heinrich	9, June 1859	Bernard	Heit, Francisca	C	
Karhoff, Johan Heinrich Franz	14, Sept 1851	Heinrich	Engelbert, Maria	L	
Karl, Anna Maria	25, Mar. 1850	Friedrich	Rupp, Katharina	D	207
Karl, Eugenia Clementina	4, July 1858	Johan	Hemke, Barbara	L	
Karman, Robert Friedrich	5, Nov. 1858	Andreas	Neurohr, Elisabeth	S	
Karne, Margaret	12, Oct. 1850	Edmund	Habker, Helena	K	
Karp, Angela	22, Feb. 1856	Georg	Colla, Angela	F	
Karp, Johan	18, Nov. 1859	Georg	Coller, Angela	T	
Karp, M. Elisabeth	16, Aug. 1857	Georg	Coller, Angela	T	
Karp, Maria	10, Sept 1854	Georg	Koller, Angela	F	
Karp, Philipp	31, Oct. 1858	Georg	Coller, Angela	T	
Karrs, Catharina	7, Sept 1854	Johan	Dreschers, Catharina	D	17
Kartus, Heinrich Friedrich	20, Jan. 1856	Heinrich	Geiger, Theresa	D	50
Kary, Francis Joseph	17, June 1855	Aloysius	Mayer, Anna Maria	D	36
Käs, Johan Georg	9, Jan. 1852	Joseph	Gebhardt, Barbara	A	
Käs, Joseph	20, Nov. 1853	Joseph	Stecher, Agnes	D	415
Kasher, Johan Peter	1, Aug. 1850	B.	Klocke, Christina	A	
Kasker, Anna Margaretha	25, Sept 1859	Heinrich	Schulte, Hermina	F	
Kasker, Hermina	11, June 1858	J. Heinrich	Schulte, Hermina	D	113

Name of Child	Date of Baptism	Father	Mother	Church	Page
Kaspers, Catharina Caecilia	1, June 1851	Gerhard	Havertepe, Catharina	D	266
Kasselmann, Johanna Elisabeth	27, Dec. 1857	Friedrich	Huennighake, Maria A.	L	
Kasselmann, M. Henrietta Paulina	1, Nov. 1859	Anton	Huninghake, Maria Anna	L	
Kasser, Albert	8, June 1856	Benedict	Klocke, Alvina Christina	A	
Kasser, Elisabeth Maria	15, Aug. 1858	Benedict	Klocke, Christina	A	
Kasser, Herman Wilhelm	11, June 1855	Benedict	Klocke, Christina Albina	A	
Kassler, Louisa	3, Nov. 1851	Nicolaus	Volz, Thecla	F	
Kast, Catharina	7, Mar. 1852	Christian	Wolf, Catharina	F	
Kast, Francis Bernard	13, Oct. 1850	Christian	Wolf, Catharina	C	
Kast, Otto	15, Oct. 1854	Christian	Wolf, Catharina	W	6
Kastelman, Anna Elisabeth	6, Feb. 1852	Francis	Gonersman, Maria Elisabeth	D	305
Kastler, Maria Barbara	7, Dec. 1853	Nicolaus	Vols, Thecla	D	418
Kastner, Peter Daniel	7, Aug. 1857	Peter	Munchenbach, Cacilia	L	
Kastner, Theresa	25, Dec. 1858	Peter	Munchenbach, Caecilia	L	
Katheiser, Maria Elisabeth	7, Nov. 1852	Friedrich	Zink, Helena	F	
Katherer, Johan	16, Sept 1855	Joseph	Meyer, Christina	N	
Kathman, Anna Margaretha	10, Apr. 1853	J. Bernard	Konst, Anna Margaretha	K	
Kathman, Catharina Anna	21, Sept 1854	Herman	Holied, Theresa	A	
Kathman, Catharina Elisabeth	27, Oct. 1852	Clemens	Schierberg, Catharina	A	
Kathman, Catharina Josephina	17, Oct. 1857	Gerhard	Kemper, Gertrud	J	44
Kathman, Christina Josephina	22, Feb. 1855	Clemens	Schierberg, Maria Catharina	A	
Kathman, Francis Joseph Bernard	5, Aug. 1856	Herman H.	Holied, Theresa	A	
Kathman, Gerhard Everhard	10, May 1852	Gerhard	Kemper, Maria Gertrud	A	
Kathman, Herman Heinrich	7, Oct. 1858	H.B.	Hilling, Maria Gesina	A	
Kathman, Herman Heinrich Bernard	7, May 1856	Bernard	Rittman, Louisa	A	
Kathman, Johan Bernard	1, Feb. 1858	Joseph	Flacke, Elisabeth	A	
Kathman, Johan Heinrich	1, Mar. 1854	H.H.	Schürman, Maria Elisabeth	A	
Kathman, Johan Heinrich	23, Oct. 1850	Heinrich	Schierberg, Catharina	A	
Kathman, Johan Heinrich	12, Sept 1854	J. Heinrich	Schillmöller, Anna Elisabeth	K	
Kathman, Johan Heinrich Clemens	19, June 1856	Heinrich	Schürman, Elisabeth	A	
Kathman, Johan Herman Joseph	20, Oct. 1853	Joseph	Flacke, Maria Elisabeth	A	
Kathman, Johan Joseph	25, Dec. 1857	Clemens	Schierberg, Catharina	A	
Kathman, Johan Joseph	13, Sept 1852	J. Clemens	Ortman, Anna Catharina	K	
Kathman, Joseph Arnold	27, Nov. 1858	Heinrich	Schürman, Elisabeth	A	
Kathman, Longinus	15, Mar. 1853	Herman	Hilling, Maria Gesina	J	20
Kathman, Maria Adelheid Louisa	17, Dec. 1855	Herman	Hilling, Gesina	A	
Kathman, Maria Catharina	25, Mar. 1856	J. Heinrich	Schillmöller, Maria Elisabeth	K	
Kathman, Maria Louisa	17, Sept 1858	Herman	Holied, Maria Theresa	A	
Kathman, Peter Francis	21, Oct. 1854	Gerhard	Kemper, Gertrud	A	
Kathmann, Anna Maria Josephina	10, Apr. 1858	Clemens	Ortmann, Catharina	C	
Kathmann, Bernard	26, Sept 1859	Heinrich	Reckel, Margaretha	T	
Kathmann, Herman August	7, Jan. 1858	Clemens	Beckel, Euphemia	F	
Kathmann, Johan David Clemens	13, Jan. 1854	Clemens	Wilkemaker, Agnes	F	
Kathmann, Maria Christina	14, May 1858	Heinrich	Schillmoeller, Elis.	L	
Katon, Joanne	2, July 1854	John	----, Joanne	H	
Katon, Thomas	31, Dec. 1854	James	Hatman, Sarah	P	113
Katterkamp, Marianna	1, Feb. 1856	Herman H.	Zolloh, Marianna	F	
Kattis, Carl	18, Sept 1859	Ferdinand	Schweitzer, Bernardina	D	146
Kattmann, Georg Heinrich	20, Aug. 1855	Clemens	Ortmann, Catharina	F	
Kattmann, Heinrich Joseph	29, Apr. 1852	Clemens	Wilkemeier, Maria Agnes	F	
Kattrauch, Anton	10, Dec. 1857	Sebastian	Wohlapp, Maria	D	100
Kattus, Anna Maria	4, Apr. 1858	Valentin	Schweitzer, Catharina	D	108
Kattus, Carolina	17, July 1853	Valentin	Schweitzer, Catharina	D	395
Kattus, Ferdinand	16, Nov. 1856	Valentin	Schweizer, Catharina	D	72
Kattus, Jacob	10, Jan. 1858	Ferdinand	Schweitzer, Bernardina	D	102
Kattus, Joseph	10, Dec. 1854	Valentin	Schweitzer, Catharina	D	23
Katzenstein, Anna Maria Theresa	20, Feb. 1856	Theodor	Schab, Maria Elisabeth	D	52
Katzenstein, Francis Heinrich	12, Sept 1850	Theodor	Schap, Anna Maria	L	
Katzenstein, Johan Theodor	24, Feb. 1853	Theodor	Schab, Anna Maria	D	373

Name of Child	Date of Baptism	Father	Mother	Church	Page
Katzenstein, Maria Elisabeth	6, Jan. 1855	Theodor	Schab, Maria	D	26
Kaucher, Jacob	1, May 1859	Ludwig	Oelgass, Margaretha	D	137
Kaucker, Maria Josephina	11, Jan. 1857	Ludwig	Elgas, Margaretha	C	
Kauffman, Margaret Louise	15, Aug. 1852	Louis	Barrett, Ann	B	268
Kauffman, Mary Emma	25, May 1856	Louis	Barrett, Hanna	B	29
Kaufhold, Carl	13, Sept 1857	Johan	Salzmann, Theresa	C	
Kaufhold, Elisabeth Ottilia	29, May 1854	Johan	Salzman, Theresa	D	11
Kaufholt, Johan Philipp	13, Apr. 1856	Johan	Salzman, Theresa	D	56
Kaufholt, Maria Anna	14, Sept 1851	Johan	Salzman, Theresa	D	282
Kaufman, Carl	1, May 1859	Vincent	Meisener, Carolina	W	26
Kaufman, Catharina	21, Sept 1856	Johan	Eichenlaub, Maria A.	D	68
Kaufman, Francis Wilhelm	21, May 1859	Francis	Brandhuber, Maria	Q	31
Kaufman, Georg	30, May 1858	Peter	Acker, Francisca	D	112
Kaufman, John Louis	10, Sept 1856		adult	B	33
Kaufman, Martin Johan	17, May 1857	Francis	Brandhuber, Maria Anna	Q	22
Kaufman, Wilhelmina	9, Apr. 1859		Kaufman, Maria Josephina	D	135
Kaufmann, Anna Catharina	13, Feb. 1855	Georg	Benzinger, Amalia	F	
Kaufmann, Anna Maria	22, Jan. 1855	Francis	Bradhuber, Maria	L	
Kaufmann, Francis	12, July 1852	Johan	Baar, Anna Maria	L	
Kaufmann, Francis Balthasar	28, June 1857	Georg J.	Pfeiffer, Antonia	C	
Kaufmann, Franz Joseph	3, Apr. 1853	Francis	Brandhuber, Maria A.	L	
Kaufmann, Jacob Anton Georg	15, Jan. 1854	Johan	Pfeifer, Antoinette	C	
Kaufmann, Johan Franz Rudolph	25, July 1858	Johan	Eichenlaub, Maria	L	
Kaufmann, Johan Jacob Michael	24, Feb. 1850	Johan	Ball, Anna Maria	L	
Kaufmann, Margaretha	25, Dec. 1852	Johan	Eichenlaub, Maria A.	L	
Kaufmann, Maria Clara	22, Jan. 1855	Francis	Bradhuber, Maria	L	
Kaufmann, Maria Elisabeth	12, Jan. 1855	Johan	Eichenlaub, M. Anna	C	
Kaugh, Edmund	15, Feb. 1854	Edmund	O'Neely, Catherine	E	169
Kaugh, Mary	29, July 1851	Edmund	Neil, Catherine	E	329
Kaupel, Anna Margaretha	10, Feb. 1851	Heinrich	Rohring, Adelheid	C	
Kaupel, Herman Heinrich	16, Oct. 1853	Heinrich	Rolmig, Adelheid	C	
Kaups?, Maria Margaretha	28, Jan. 1858	Carl	Schrocek, Maria Anna	D	104
Kaus, Eva	21, Feb. 1858	Johan	----, Catharina	D	105
Kaus, Michael	27, Nov. 1859	Adam	Res, Catharina	T	
Kauser, Maria Magdalena	15, Jan. 1854	Jacob	Becht, Eva	D	2
Kausser, Bernard Ahler	27, Aug. 1852	Bernard	Klocke, Christina	A	
Kautz, Catharina Elisabeth	12, Aug. 1855	Johan	Jung, Eva Rosina	F	
Kautz, Jacob	29, July 1858	Johan	Jung, Rosina	T	
Kautzman, Carl	11, Mar. 1855	Georg	Fischer, Maria Anna	D	31
Kavanagh, Elizabeth	24, Dec. 1853	Miles	Esmond, Eliza	B	305
Kavanagh, James Joseph	15, Aug. 1855	Daniel	Hyde, Elizabeth	B	18
Kavanagh, Joanne	5, Dec. 1858	Patrick	Connor, Joanne	B	68
Kavanagh, Mary Ann	22, May 1853	Daniel	Hyde, Elizabeth	B	292
Kavanaugh, Daniel John	28, Oct. 1858	Daniel	Hyde, Elizabeth	B	66
Kavanaugh, James Hyde	19, Apr. 1857	Daniel	Hyde, Elizabeth	B	43
Kavanaugh, James Joseph	23, Dec. 1858	Michael A.	Scanlon, Lucy	E	589
Kavemann, Francis Georg	1, Feb. 1853	Carl	Speckmann, Anna M.	C	
Kavemann, Heinrich Edward	26, May 1858	Carl	Speckmann, Maria	F	
Kavemann, Maria Clara	8, Sept 1855	Carl	Speckmann, Anna Maria	F	
Kaveny, Charles	17, Dec. 1851	Charles	Corcoran, Ann	B	248
Keagan, Catherine	13, Oct. 1854	John	----, Mary	E	231
Keagan, John	14, Oct. 1855	Michael	Flannigan, Mary	R	
Keagan, Michael	22, Feb. 1859	Matthew	Donahoe, Mary	E	606
Keagan, Nathan	20, Jan. 1857	Matthew	Donohue, Mary	E	428
Keahan, Caroline	4, Mar. 1858	Michael	Coffee, Mary	E	519
Keahan, Michael	23, Nov. 1854	Michael	Coffee, Mary	E	243
Kealty, Catherine	16, Feb. 1853	Patrick	McCormick, Margaret	P	35
Kealy, James	8, Sept 1850	Patrick	----, Ann	E	246
Keanan, William	3, Oct. 1853	James	----, Ann	E	131

Name of Child	Date of Baptism	Father	Mother	Church	Page
Keane, Margaret	2, Dec. 1855	John	Hayes, Margaret	E	330
Keane, Mary	7, May 1854	Daniel	Sheahan, Margaret	V	13
Keane, Thomas Henry	22, Dec. 1850	Michael	Coffey, Mary	E	269
Keanes, John Francis	15, Oct. 1858	Michael	----, Bridget	E	570
Kearn, Bridget	1, June 1857	Daniel	May, Sarah	E	457
Kearn, Thomas	27, Jan. 1850	Johan	Smith, Johanna	C	
Kearnan, Margaret	10, Mar. 1852	Michael	Ryan, Catherine	E	390
Kearnan, Mary	26, Dec. 1859	Thomas	Shanahan, Honora	B	86
Kearnan, Michael	19, Dec. 1852	Michael	----, Margaret	M	
Kearne, Catherine	17, Dec. 1854	Patrick	McCue, Mary	E	247
Kearney, Andrew	16, Mar. 1851	James	Farley, Mary	P	6
Kearney, Ann	13, June 1852	Patrick	Barth, Elizabeth	B	260
Kearney, Anthony	15, Jan. 1853	Edward	Burns, Honora	E	55
Kearney, Bernard	7, Oct. 1850	James	Kearney, Bridget	M	
Kearney, Bridget	26, Mar. 1857	Edward	----, Catherine	M	
Kearney, Bridget	11, Sept 1855	Patrick	Finnigan, Helen	P	151
Kearney, Catherine	30, Nov. 1851	John	McDonnel, Bridget	P	13c
Kearney, Catherine	3, Jan. 1854	John	Ryan, Bridget	V	9
Kearney, Cecilia	18, Feb. 1855	Francis	Mahoney, Helen	P	121
Kearney, Charles	14, Nov. 1858	Thomas	Williams, Bridget	V	51
Kearney, Daniel	10, Feb. 1857	John	Ryan, Bridget	E	432
Kearney, Eustacia	20, Sept 1851	James	McFallen, Catherine	E	344
Kearney, George	4, Feb. 1855	George	Knox, Helen	P	119
Kearney, Harriet	13, May 1855	Edward	----, Catherine	M	
Kearney, Helen	12, Oct. 1851	Francis	Mahoney, Helen	B	242
Kearney, Henry	12, Sept 1858	Michael	Early, Mary	E	562
Kearney, James	10, Dec. 1852	James	McFarland, Catherine	E	43
Kearney, James	20, Nov. 1852	James W.	Donohue, Joanne	E	36
Kearney, John	26, Nov. 1854	John	McDonnell, Bridget	P	106
Kearney, John Joseph	7, Aug. 1853	Thomas J.	Power, Mary	B	296
Kearney, John Philip	9, Mar. 1856	William	Buckley, Honora	B	26
Kearney, John Thomas	30, Aug. 1857	Francis	Mahoney, Ellen	B	48
Kearney, Joseph Edward	9, June 1851	Joseph	Rhodes, Elizabeth	M	
Kearney, Liza	2, Jan. 1859	John	Ryan, Bridget	E	593
Kearney, Louise	1, Jan. 1854	Edward	----, Catherine	M	
Kearney, Louise Ann	5, June 1853	Francis	Maloney, Helen	P	43
Kearney, Mary	16, Aug. 1850	Michael	Knox, Helen	B	210
Kearney, Mary	7, Apr. 1850	William	Rock, Winifred	B	200
Kearney, Mary Alice	9, Sept 1855	Thomas	----, Mary	B	19
Kearney, Mary Ann	22, Feb. 1857	James	Hanley, Ann	P	207
Kearney, Michael	24, Jan. 1854	Michael	Early, Mary	E	162
Kearney, Michael	7, Nov. 1852	Michael	Knox, Helen	P	29
Kearney, Owen	20, Nov. 1859	Patrick	----, Winnefred	E	671
Kearney, Philipp	13, May 1852	Thomas	Roarke, Bridget	B	259
Kearney, Prudence	10, Mar. 1850	William	Buckley, Honora	B	197
Kearney, Sophia	18, Jan. 1855	Patrick	Apjohn, Sophia	E	257
Kearney, Thomas	31, Oct. 1853	James	----, Honora	E	138
Kearney, Thomas	6, Jan. 1850	John	McDonnell, Bridget	B	193
Kearney, Thomas	19, Jan. 1851	Michael	Early, Mary	E	277
Kearney, Thomas John	16, Mar. 1851	Thomas	Power, Mary	B	226
Kearney, William	25, Oct. 1859	Dennis	Shea, Mary	B	82
Kearney, William	9, Feb. 1855	James	Hanly, Ann	P	119
Kearney, William Francis	30, Aug. 1857	Francis	Mahoney, Ellen	B	48
Kearney, William Lemon	8, Nov. 1857	Thomas J.	Powers, Mary	B	51
Kearns, Ann Eliza	31, July 1859	Thomas	Quirk, Honora	P	291
Kearns, Eugene	22, Jan. 1854	John	Keenagh, Mary	P	66
Kearns, Francis	8, May 1859	John	Keenen, Mary	P	283
Kearns, James	5, Oct. 1856	Thomas	Quirk, Honora	V	34
Kearns, John	29, Feb. 1852	John	Keenan, Mary	P	18

Name of Child	Date of Baptism	Father	Mother	Church	Page
Kearns, John	17, Sept 1855	Michael	O'Donnell, Helen	E	316
Kearns, Margaret	8, Oct. 1854	Thomas	Quirk, Honora	P	99
Kearns, Mary	27, Sept 1859	John	Delany, Catherine	R	
Kearns, Mary	8, Oct. 1854	Thomas	Quirk, Honora	P	99
Kearns, William	25, Jan. 1857	John	Keenagh, Mary	P	204
Kearny, Bridget	25, July 1854	Michael	Power, Mary	E	210
Keasy, Catherine	25, Apr. 1858	Terence	Doyle, Honora	H	
Keath, Elisabeth Ursula	3, Sept 1854	Carl	Keath, Barbara	D	16
Keating, Alice	19, Aug. 1855	Michael	Cranny, Elizabeth	P	146
Keating, Ann	23, July 1850	Edmund	Kinsella, Catherine	B	208
Keating, Ann	2, July 1858	Michael	McCormick, Mary	E	545
Keating, Catherine	14, Sept 1851	John	Shea, Alice	E	343
Keating, Catherine	25, Dec. 1850	Thomas	Kennedy, Mary	E	271
Keating, Catherine	12, Oct. 1859	William	Miles, Helen	E	662
Keating, Cornelius	16, Jan. 1857	Michael	Shea, Mary	E	426
Keating, Dennis	26, Jan. 1855	Michael	----, Mary	E	260
Keating, Edmund	12, May 1850	James	McGrath, Catherine	E	214
Keating, Helen Mary	9, Jan. 1858	John	Shay, Alice	E	507
Keating, James	9, Apr. 1859	Andrew	----, Bridget	E	617
Keating, James	20, Jan. 1853	John	Shea, Alice	E	56
Keating, James	24, Nov. 1857	Thomas	Burke, Margaret	E	495
Keating, John	5, Aug. 1857	Andrew	Conway, Bridget	E	472
Keating, John	16, Mar. 1851	James	Pyne, Joanne	B	226
Keating, John	23, May 1856	John	Laucier, Alice	E	368
Keating, John	23, Dec. 1853	John	May, Sarah	E	154
Keating, John	8, June 1856	Thomas	Burck, Margaret	E	372
Keating, Joseph Patrick	6, Aug. 1855	Joseph	Edwards, Mary	V	26
Keating, Mary	29, Oct. 1857	Joseph	----, Mary	E	489
Keating, Mary	23, Feb. 1851	Michael	Croney, Elizabeth	P	5
Keating, Mary	1, June 1858	Patrick	Sheran, Barbara	B	59
Keating, Mary	8, Apr. 1859	Thomas	----, Ellen	E	617
Keating, Mary	19, Sept 1852	Thomas	----, Mary	E	18
Keating, Mary Ann	7, Jan. 1854	Henry	Conway, Bridget	E	158
Keating, Mary Ann	8, May 1857	William	Miles, Ann	E	451
Keating, Mary Jane	28, Aug. 1856	Benjamin	Clark, Jane	E	393
Keating, Michael	2, July 1854	Thomas	Kennedy, Mary	E	203
Keating, Patrick	14, Oct. 1855	John	May, Sarah	E	320
Keating, Patrick	17, Mar. 1851	Michael	----, Mary	E	292
Keating, Patrick	18, Mar. 1855	Thomas	----, Honora	E	273
Keating, Robert	18, Apr. 1858	Michael N.	Cranny, Elizabeth	P	246
Keating, Robert	26, Dec. 1852	Thomas	----, Honora	E	48
Keating, Thomas	15, Oct. 1857	Michael	Keley, Honora	E	486
Keating, Thomas	3, Dec. 1854	Thomas	Parke, Margaret	E	244
Keating, William	15, Feb. 1852	John	May, Sarah	E	383
Keating, William	15, July 1854	John	Shay, Helen	E	207
Keaton, Mary	29, Mar. 1853	Michael	----, Mary	E	78
Kebel, Margaretha	26, Sept 1852	Adam	Weitman, Catharina	D	349
Keberschlag, Carolina Theresa	7, Apr. 1858	Joseph	Klori, Theresa	K	
Kebler, Barbara Wilhelmina	22, Jan. 1854	Joseph	Troll, Cunigunda	D	3
Keck, Carolina	30, Jan. 1853	Johan	Theiring, Anna Maria	F	
Keck, Elisabeth	23, Nov. 1854	Johan	Theiring, Anna Maria	F	
Keck, Gottfried	7, Mar. 1858	Georg	Satta, Maria Anna	N	
Keck, Theodor Georg	17, Feb. 1856	Georg	Sather, Anna Maria	D	52
Kecks, Barbara	17, Sept 1857	Anton	Winter, Barbara	K	
Kecks, Francis Joseph	16, Nov. 1856	Anton	Winter, Barbara	K	
Kedders, Mary Ann	2, May 1855	William	Riley, Ann	E	283
Keefe, Ann	2, June 1850	Arthur	----, Ann	E	219
Keefe, Bridget	7, Mar. 1858	Dennis	Sheehan, Catherine	B	56
Keefe, Catherine	21, Oct. 1853	Daniel	----, Margaret	E	137

Name of Child	Date of Baptism	Father	Mother	Church	Page
Keefe, Cornelius	7, Mar. 1857	Cornelius	----, Mary	E	438
Keefe, Daniel	29, May 1853	Arthur	----, Ann	E	93
Keefe, Daniel	6, Sept 1855	Cornelius	Reardon, Margaret	B	18
Keefe, Daniel	7, Feb. 1850	Daniel	McCarthy, Margaret	E	195
Keefe, David	15, Feb. 1852	Daniel	Shehan, Catherine	B	252
Keefe, Edward	21, May 1859	Cornelius	Ryan, Mary	E	626
Keefe, Ellen	11, Jan. 1857	Joseph	Pepper, Rosanne	B	39
Keefe, Eugene	21, Dec. 1856	Cornelius	Riarden, Margaret	B	38
Keefe, Honora	2, May 1852	Michael	Dorney, Margaret	E	408
Keefe, James	29, July 1855	Daniel	Shehan, Catherine	B	17
Keefe, James	25, Mar. 1850	Hugh	Keefe, Catherine	B	199
Keefe, John	17, Nov. 1855	Cornelius	Ryan, Mary	E	327
Keefe, John	1, Aug. 1858	Daniel	McCarthy, Margaret	E	554
Keefe, John	7, Apr. 1858	Dennis	----, Margaret	E	528
Keefe, John	6, Nov. 1853	Dennis	Sheehan, Catherine	B	302
Keefe, John	10, Aug. 1852	Hugh	Ahern, Catherine	B	267
Keefe, John	23, Oct. 1853	John	Hayes, Margaret	B	301
Keefe, Joseph	7, Jan. 1855	Joseph	Heffert, Rosanne	B	9
Keefe, Julia	22, June 1851	John	----, Margaret	E	317
Keefe, Lawrence	4, Feb. 1855	Michael	----, Margaret	U	
Keefe, Margaret	16, Apr. 1856	Daniel	----, Catherine	R	
Keefe, Margaret	22, June 1855	Michael	Darney, Margaret	E	295
Keefe, Mary	2, July 1851	Daniel	----, Elizabeth	E	320
Keefe, Mary	30, Oct. 1854	John	----, Henriette	E	236
Keefe, Mary	17, Feb. 1856	Luke	Burke, ----	E	345
Keefe, Mary Ann	9, Feb. 1854	Dennis	Dalton, Mary	U	
Keefe, Mary Ann	8, Nov. 1857	Michael	Curran, Margaret	B	51
Keefe, Sarah Elisabeth	30, July 1859	Cornelius	Cratty, Ann	U	
Keefe, Thomas	10, Feb. 1856	Daniel	McC---, Margaret	V	29
Keefe, Thomas	24, Dec. 1854	Dennis	----, Margaret	E	249
Keefe, Thomas	17, Apr. 1859	Joseph	Peppard, Rosanne	B	74
Keefe, Thomas	25, Jan. 1852	Michael	Curreng, Margaret	E	377
Keefe, Thomas	22, June 1855	Michael	Darney, Margaret	E	295
Keefer, Georg Valentin	15, Feb. 1852	Jacob	Meier, Anna Maria	J	16
Keeffe, John	25, June 1854	Luke	----, Ellen	E	201
Keeffe, Robert	28, June 1857	Kieran	Cahill, Mary	B	46
Keegan,	16, June 1858	John	Dunn, Catherine	B	60
Keegan, Anastasia	27, Sept 1857	Patrick	Connally, Joanne	E	482
Keegan, Catherine	28, Feb. 1858	Thomas	Leddy, Mary	B	56
Keegan, Elizabeth	16, Oct. 1853	Thomas	----, Ellen	M	
Keegan, Frances Josephine	16, Mar. 1856	Joseph	Byrne, Mary	V	30
Keegan, George	6, Sept 1857	John	Moran, Ann	B	49
Keegan, James	28, Nov. 1858	James	Costigan, Margaret	P	268
Keegan, James Edward	5, May 1850	John	Moran, Ann	B	202
Keegan, John	18, Sept 1853	John	Dunn, Catherine	P	52
Keegan, John	5, June 1857	Matthew	----, Mary	E	457
Keegan, Joseph	14, Sept 1851	John	Moran, Ann	B	241
Keegan, Julia	11, Sept 1859	Patrick	----, Joanne	E	652
Keegan, Julia Ann	10, Feb. 1856	John	Dunn, Catherine	P	169
Keegan, Mary	23, Oct. 1859	John	Moran, Ann	B	82
Keegan, Mary Ann	23, July 1854	Joseph	Byrne, Mary	B	3
Keegan, Matthew	16, Mar. 1855	Matthew	Kearney, Mary	V	23
Keegan, Robert	30, May 1852	Matthew	Kearny, Mary	E	419
Keegan, Rosanne	13, Mar. 1853	John	Moran, Ann	B	286
Keegan, Thomas	31, Aug. 1851	Thomas	Riley, Ellen	P	11
Keeghan, Julia Agatha	20, Feb. 1853	Michael	Coffee, Mary	V	1
Keehan, Emma Louise	11, Jan. 1857	Thomas	Walley, Caroline	V	37
Keehan, Sarah Ann	20, Jan. 1855	Thomas	Moony, Caroline	E	258
Keehan, Thomas Francis	25, Sept 1859	Thomas	Whaley, Caroline	B	81

Name of Child	Date of Baptism	Father	Mother	Church	Page
Keeler, Ann Jane	7, Apr. 1855	Thomas	Shepher, Sarah	E	278
Keeler, Cornelius	25, July 1852	Matthew	O'Connor, Margaret	P	25
Keeler, Mary	9, Sept 1857	Patrick	Lawless, Mary	P	222
Keeler, Rebecca	6, Oct. 1856	Thomas	Ward, Sarah	E	402
Keely, Ellen	27, July 1856	Patrick	----, Ann	E	385
Keely, Francis	23, Mar. 1854	Patrick	Kensaler, Ann	E	178
Keely, John	29, June 1851	Michael	Kennedy, Catherine	E	319
Keely, Joseph	23, Mar. 1854	Patrick	Kensaler, Ann	E	178
Keely, Margaret	15, Feb. 1852	Patrick	Kensaler, Ann	E	383
Keely, Thomas	28, Mar. 1859	Thomas	Kearon, Mary	B	73
Keen, Francis	28, Feb. 1858	Thomas	Dunphy, Sarah	Q	26
Keenan, Bridget	5, Mar. 1857	Lawrence	McHugh, Margaret	P	207
Keenan, Edmund	12, Sept 1852	John W.	Baer, Helen	B	270
Keenan, Ezra James	30, Dec. 1855	John W.	Baer, Ellen	B	23
Keenan, Francis	25, Feb. 1859	James	Karney, Bridget	P	277
Keenan, Hamilton Foy	1, Dec. 1853	John	Baer, Helen	P	60
Keenan, James	3, Feb. 1853	Lawrence	Meldal, Margaret	B	282
Keenan, James	29, Apr. 1857	Nicolaus	Devalin, Margaret	P	211
Keenan, John	13, Feb. 1854	Michael	Lane, Ann	V	11
Keenan, Margaret	13, Mar. 1856	Eugene	Rennick, Mary Ann	P	172
Keenan, Mary	26, July 1859	Matthew	Hughes, Sarah	B	78
Keenan, Mary Jane	5, Dec. 1857	John	Crilly, Ann	P	232
Keenan, Mary Jane	10, Sept 1859	Lawrence	McHugh, Margaret	P	295
Keenan, Michael Hamilton	30, Dec. 1855	John W.	Baer, Ellen	B	23
Keenan, Nicholas	16, May 1859	Nicholas	Devlin, Margaret	B	75
Keenan, Robert	29, Apr. 1855	Lawrence	McHugh, Margaret	P	129
Keene, Richard	1, May 1855	Nicholas	Devlin, Margaret	B	14
Keenon, Rose	21, May 1854	Frederick	Welsh, Bridget	E	192
Keernan, James	19, May 1858	Henzi	Keernan, Bridget	P	249
Keernan, Mary Frances	17, Oct. 1852	James	McBride, Margaret	B	272
Keeshan, Agnes	27, Apr. 1856	John	Carrigan, Honora	B	28
Keeshan, Albert	1, Jan. 1854	John	Madagan, Catherine	E	157
Keeshan, Edward	27, July 1856	Edward	Fitzpatrick, Catherine	B	31
Keeshan, Francis	24, Apr. 1859	John	----, Dora	E	620
Keeshan, Joanne	9, July 1854	Edward	Fitzpatrick, Catherine	B	2
Keeshan, Mary	19, Dec. 1852	Edward	Fitzpatrick, Catherine	B	278
Keeshan, Mary	27, Nov. 1853	John	Coregan, Bridget	B	303
Keeshan, Mary Ellen	25, July 1858	Edward	Fitzpatrick, Catherine	B	62
Keeshan, ---nell	16, June 1858	John	Carrigan, Hannah	B	60
Keeshan, William	25, May 1856	John	Costelle, Odora	E	369
Kefering, Johan Herman	6, June 1853	Herman	Brueggemann, Maria	C	
Kehl, Andreas	20, Apr. 1851	Francis	Doll, Anna Maria	A	
Kehl, Bernard Joseph	6, July 1851	Joseph	Götz, Maria	D	271
Kehl, Bernard Wilhelm	4, Nov. 1852	Francis	Doll, Anna Maria	A	
Kehl, Francis	30, Nov. 1851	Francis	Schmid, Catharina	D	295
Kehler, Maria Catharina	13, Oct. 1850	Johan	Luft, Elisabeth	N	1
Kehler, Mary	17, Nov. 1853	Jeremiah	----, Mary	U	
Kehler, Mathias	25, Feb. 1855	Balthasar	Gehringer, Barbara	D	29
Keho, Catherine Ann	5, Mar. 1858	Thomas	----, Ann	M	
Keho, Margaret	29, Apr. 1857	John	Keleher, Catherine	V	38
Kehoe, Edward	9, July 1854	Peter	----, Mary	M	
Kehoe, Joanne	5, Apr. 1858	John	----, Mary	M	
Kehoe, John	17, Nov. 1850	John	----, Catherine	E	262
Kehoe, John	24, July 1858	Patrick	----, ----	E	551
Kehoe, Joseph	16, Sept 1855	Thomas	----, Margaret	M	
Kehoe, Margaret	17, Sept 1854	John	Dempsey, Mary	P	96
Kehoe, mary	16, Sept 1856	Patrick	----, Mary	M	
Kehoe, Mary	15, June 1854	Thomas	----, Margaret	M	
Kehoe, Mary Elizabeth	19, Nov. 1850	John	----, Mary	E	263

Hamilton County, Ohio Roman Catholic Baptism Records -- 1850 - 1859

Name of Child	Date of Baptism	Father	Mother	Church	Page
Kehoe, Matthew	22, July 1855	Matthew	----, Honora	E	301
Kehoe, Peter	31, Oct. 1858	Peter	----, Mary	M	
Kehoe, Timothy	1, Oct. 1855	James	----, Margaret	M	
Kehoe, William	25, May 1851	James	Conroy, Honora	P	8
Kehoe, William	29, Apr. 1856	John	----, Mary	M	
Kehr, Johan Adam	19, Oct. 1851	Michael	Bär, Maria	D	287
Kehr, Maria Genofeva	15, Jan. 1854	Michael	Baer, Maria	D	2
Kehrer, Maria	13, June 1858	Anton	Steph---, Catharina	D	113
Kehrer, Maria Agatha	30, Apr. 1859	Anton	Papp--, Catharina	D	137
Kehring, Franz Heinrich	11, Jan. 1852	Francis H.	Bottler, Catharina	L	
Keifer, John Edward	24, July 1859	Anthony	----, Felicity	S	
Keiger, Theresa	2, Aug. 1857	J. Georg	Zimmermann, M. Elis.	L	
Keigman, Richard Bartholomew	27, Oct. 1857	F. Heinrich	Hohen---, Maria Elisabeth	D	97
Keil, Anna Maria	29, May 1852	Georg	Zacharias, Sophia	C	
Keil, Catharina	11, June 1857	Georg	Zacharias, Sophia	C	
Keil, Georg	3, Sept 1854	Georg	Zacharias, Sophia	C	
Keiley, Patrick	1, May 1859	James	Finn, Margaret	E	622
Keilty, Mary	10, June 1855	Thomas	Bregany, Ellen	E	292
Keily, John	20, May 1858	Anthony	McHugh, Elizabeth	E	536
Keim, Regina	16, May 1858	Heinrich	Stauder, Christina	U	
Keimel, Johan Friedrich	23, Apr. 1858	Michael	Bauer, Anna Maria	A	
Keiner, Anna Elisabeth C.	9, Jan. 1857	Georg	Gruber, Agnes	D	76
Keisel, Elisabeth	22, Feb. 1857	Friedrich	Mohr, Sibilla	C	
Keisen, Joseph Bernard	19, Aug. 1857	Henry	Ahaus, A. Maria	T	
Keiser, Andrew	18, Aug. 1850	John	Mitchell, Rebecca	B	211
Keisker, Mary Ann Louise	14, July 1851	Henry W.	Burke, Alice R.	B	236
Keitel, Georg	20, Aug. 1854	Georg	Guetlein, Barbara	F	
Keitel, Johan M.	8, June 1856	Georg	Guetlein, Barbara	F	
Keith, Mary	1, Nov. 1851	William	Davenport, Mary	E	354
--kel, Maria Adelheid	3, Aug. 1857	Herman	Ton---, Maria A.	D	92
Kelahar, Dennis	16, Oct. 1859	John	Sullivan, Abby	U	
Kelaher, Julia	11, Oct. 1857	John	Sullivan, Abigail	U	
Kelaher, Mary	5, Mar. 1854	John	----, Abby	U	
Keleher, Ellen	28, July 1855	Daniel	----, Ellen	M	
Keleher, Honora	14, Dec. 1855	Charles	Meu--, Elizabeth	B	22
Keleher, James	2, May 1852	Daniel	----, Ellen	M	
Keleher, John	3, Dec. 1854	Daniel	Keleher, Helen	V	20
Keleher, Julia	3, Sept 1854	Daniel	Drislane, Margaret	V	17
Keleher, Julia Ellen	2, Mar. 1858	Daniel	----, Mary	M	
Keleher, Margaret	20, June 1858	Daniel	----, Ellen	M	
Keleher, Mary	6, Nov. 1855	Daniel	----, Mary	M	
Keleher, Michael	2, Nov. 1856	Edward	Moore, Alice	B	35
Kell--, Isabel	13, May 1856	Peter	Boyd, Susan E.	B	28
Kelle, Carolina	23, Jan. 1853	Anton	Klinge, Paulina	C	
Kelle, Heinrich Wilhelm	4, Mar. 1850	Heinrich	----, Maria	K	
Keller, A. Maria Bernardina Agnes	11, Nov. 1855	Johan H.	Lange, Anna M. Agnes	F	
Keller, Anna Maria	5, July 1858	Heinrich	Segbers, Clara	L	
Keller, August	3, Sept 1854	August	Wirmel, Anna Maria	F	
Keller, Balthasar	17, Jan. 1854	Balthasar	Gehringer, Barbara	D	2
Keller, Barbara	22, Aug. 1852	Balthasar	Geringer, Barbara	D	345
Keller, Barbara	14, Sept 1850	Francis A.	Meyer, Elisa	D	232
Keller, Barbara Aloysia Francisca	17, June 1856	Friedrich	Bien, Barbara	F	
Keller, Barbara Carolina	28, Mar. 1852	Stephan	Krapp, Margaretha	C	
Keller, Barbara Philomena	23, Nov. 1856	Francis A.	Meier, Elisabeth	D	72
Keller, Burchard	3, Feb. 1850	Stephan	Krapp, Margaretha	C	
Keller, Carl August	25, Feb. 1855	Constantine	Trücker, Elisabeth	D	29
Keller, Carl Heinrich	9, July 1851	Johan H.	Lange, Agnes Maria	F	
Keller, Carolina	6, Nov. 1853	Sebastian	Holzhammer, Maria	J	24
Keller, Carolina Paulina	28, Mar. 1852	Friedrich	Hans, Rosalia	D	314

Name of Child	Date of Baptism	Father	Mother	Church	Page
Keller, Cath. Johanna Friedricka	3, June 1858	Friedrich	Bien, Barbara	F	
Keller, Catharina	19, Oct. 1856	Johan	Wittenbauer, Catharina	F	
Keller, Edward	25, Nov. 1854	Anton	Klingler, Paulina	C	
Keller, Elisabeth	18, July 1853	J. Adam	Klingler, Maria	C	
Keller, Elisabeth	12, May 1856	Johan	Höhn, Elisabeth	D	58
Keller, Elisabeth Margaretha	1, Aug. 1858	Adam	Blass, Margaretha	F	
Keller, Francis Philipp	1, May 1853	Francis A.	Meyer, Elisabeth	D	383
Keller, Friedrich	19, Sept 1852	Valentin	Braun, Catharina	D	348
Keller, Georg	15, June 1854	Francis	Schneider, Gertrud	C	
Keller, Georg	13, Aug. 1856	Georg	Popp, Elisabeth	F	
Keller, Georg Joseph	12, Nov. 1854	Friedrich	Bien, Barbara	F	
Keller, Heinrich Joseph	18, Apr. 1858	Joseph	Bauer, Maria Eva	W	22
Keller, Helen	31, May 1855	John	O'Connor, Mary Ann	P	131
Keller, Jacob	6, Apr. 1853	Jacob	Pfeister, Dorothea	D	379
Keller, Johan	19, Feb. 1854	Jacob	Pfeifer, Margaretha	C	
Keller, Johan	23, Mar. 1855	Johan	Willenbauer, Maria	D	31
Keller, Johan Francis	3, May 1857	G. Jacob	Pfeifer, Margaretha	C	
Keller, Johan Friedrich	17, Dec. 1854	Friedrich	Henz, Rosalia	D	24
Keller, Johan Heinrich	3, May 1850	J. Heinrich	Wiesman, Maria Theresa	D	211
Keller, Johan Heinrich	6, Mar. 1855	J. Heinrich	Wissman, Theresa	D	30
Keller, Johan Heinrich Victor	20, July 1853	Johan H.	Lange, Anna Maria	F	
Keller, Johan Herman	24, Dec. 1858	Gerhard	Peters, Helen	T	
Keller, Johan Jacob	25, Mar. 1858	Anton	K---, Magdalena	D	108
Keller, Joseph	23, Sept 1855		Keller, Margaretha	C	
Keller, Leonard	29, July 1854	Heinrich	Bauer, Elisabeth	W	4
Keller, Lucia	13, May 1855	J. Adam	adult - 19 years old	K	
Keller, Margaretha	8, Mar. 1857	John Adam	Klingler, M. Anna	C	
Keller, Margaretha	20, Apr. 1853		Keller, Barbara	D	381
Keller, Margaretha	30, Aug. 1857	Johan	Haehn, Elisabeth	K	
Keller, Maria	28, Apr. 1859	David	Seitz, Maria	D	137
Keller, Maria Anna	4, Nov. 1855	Adam	Klingler, Maria Anna	D	46
Keller, Maria Anna	14, Oct. 1855	August	Wirmel, Anna Maria	D	44
Keller, Maria Anna	26, Sept 1858	Gregor	Popp, Elisabeth	D	120
Keller, Mary	8, Dec. 1854	Francis	Barrela, Ann Elizabeth	P	108
Keller, Mary Ann	8, Sept 1857	Joseph	----, Rose	M	
Keller, Mary Frances	4, Feb. 1851	Matthew	Conners, Margaret	B	224
Keller, Mathias	17, Jan. 1854	Balthasar	Gehringer, Barbara	D	2
Keller, Mathilda	17, Feb. 1856	Constantine	Fricker, Elisabeth	D	52
Keller, Michael	20, Jan. 1856	Francis	Schneider, Gertrud	D	50
Keller, Ottilia	28, Dec. 1856	Valentin	Braun, Carolina	Q	19
Keller, Peter	1, Nov. 1857	Patrick	Spahler, Magdalena	N	
Keller, Rosa	28, Dec. 1856	Heinrich	Wichman, Theresa	D	75
Keller, Sophia	6, Mar. 1859	Stephan	Grab, Margaretha	C	
Keller, Sophia Bertha	25, Dec. 1853	Stephan	Krapp, Margaretha	C	
Keller, Theodor	19, Oct. 1856	Stephan	Krapp, Margaretha	C	
Kellerman, Heinrich Joseph	1, Feb. 1857	Heinrich	Behrens, Helen	J	40
Kellerman, Helena Francisca	9, May 1858	Heinrich	Recen--, Helena	D	110
Kellerman, Johan Joseph	3, Jan. 1856	Johan	Koors, Francisca	J	34
Kellerman, Joseph Otto	9, June 1859	Johan	Koors, Maria Francisca	J	50
Kellerman, Josephina Carolina	29, Jan. 1854	Johan	Koors, Francisca	J	26
Kellerman, Maria Anna Francisca	26, Aug. 1857	Johan	Koors, Francisca	J	42
Kellerman, Maria Elisabeth	9, Oct. 1852	Johan	Kohrs, Francisca	J	18
Kellermann, Anna Maria Elisabeth	11, Sept 1851	Francis J.	Pundsack, Anna Maria	F	
Kellermann, Franz August	4, Dec. 1853	Francis H.	Pundsak, Anna Maria	F	
Kellermann, Johan Gerhard	4, Mar. 1858	Francis H.	Pundsack, Anna Maria	G	
Kellermann, Maria Agnes	5, Sept 1852	Joseph	Maringer, Catharina	F	
Kellermann, Maria Catharina	14, Feb. 1856	Francis H.	Pundsack, Anna Maria	F	
Kelley, Alice	14, Jan. 1855	James E.	----, Mary A.	E	256
Kelley, Bridget	30, July 1854	Daniel	Erwin, Mary	E	211

Name of Child	Date of Baptism	Father	Mother	Church	Page
Kelley, Ellenore	25, May 1856	Thomas	Ryan, Catherine	U	
Kelley, Helen	3, Sept 1854	Anthony	Buress, Honora	E	221
Kelley, James	7, Dec. 1857	John	----, Ann	E	498
Kelley, James	11, Mar. 1858	Thomas	Coolahan, Helen	E	521
Kelley, John	7, Sept 1856	John	----, Joanne	E	395
Kelley, Mary	10, Mar. 1850	James	Cormoly, Ann	B	197
Kelley, Mary	2, Oct. 1851	Patrick	Kane, Mary	B	242
Kelley, Mary	3, Sept 1856	Thomas	Calaghan, Helen	E	395
Kelley, Mary Ann	31, May 1855	Patrick	----, Catherine	E	290
Kelley, Mary Ann	29, Mar. 1857	Thomas	----, Bridget	G	
Kelley, Robert Anthony	5, Mar. 1856	Michael	King, Ellen	U	
Kelley, Sarah	23, Nov. 1856	Anthony	----, Honora	E	414
Kelley, Sarah	11, Aug. 1854	Patrick	----, Bridget	E	215
Kelley, Thomas	1, Mar. 1854	Thomas	----, Joanne	E	172
Kellinger, Catharina Rosina	5, Nov. 1852	Anton	Wörtlin, Johanna	K	
Kellinger, Clara Johanna	16, June 1850	Anton	Wörtlen, Maria Johanna	K	
Kellinger, Johanna Catharina Francisca	23, Aug. 1857	Anton	Wirthlin, J.	K	
Kellinger, Maria Magdalena	28, Jan. 1855	Anton	Wirthlin, Johanna	K	
Kellkerry, William	7, June 1853	James	----, Bridget	E	96
Kellner, Maria Agnes	22, July 1852	Bernard	Grotmann, Angela	C	
Kelloran, Mary Ann	8, Sept 1850	Eugene	Davis, Catherine	B	213
Kelloran, Thomas	12, Aug. 1855	John	Scanlan, Bridget	P	145
Kelly, Alice Mary Ann	29, Apr. 1857	Patrick J.	Fox, Bridget	B	43
Kelly, Andrew	19, May 1850	Martin	----, Margaret	E	215
Kelly, Ann	21, Feb. 1851	John	----, Mary	E	285
Kelly, Ann	15, Feb. 1857	John	Ryan, Bridget	E	433
Kelly, Ann	20, Jan. 1855	Matthew	Reilly, Margaret	E	258
Kelly, Ann	5, Mar. 1852	Michael	Lyons, Mary	B	254
Kelly, Ann	16, Sept 1850	Patrick	Rawle, Ann	B	214
Kelly, Ann	19, July 1857	Thomas	Brooder, Ann	E	468
Kelly, Archibald	6, Feb. 1859	Michael J.	McClerin, Isabel	B	70
Kelly, Barbara	16, Feb. 1851	Anthony	Buress, Honora	P	5
Kelly, Bernard	10, June 1856	Thomas	Kelly, Mary	E	373
Kelly, Bernard Walter	12, Dec. 1857	Thomas	Kelly, Mary	E	500
Kelly, Bridget	5, Feb. 1854	John	Bohan, Catherine	B	309
Kelly, Bridget	29, Oct. 1854	John	McCormick, Elizabeth	B	7
Kelly, Bridget	8, Apr. 1855	Patrick	----, Bridget	M	
Kelly, Bridget	23, July 1854	William	----, Rosanne	M	
Kelly, Bridget Honora	7, Dec. 1851	John	Lynch, Catherine	B	247
Kelly, Catharine	8, Feb. 1859	Thomas	Kelly, Bridget	G	
Kelly, Catherine	3, June 1858	Anthony	----, Margaret	E	539
Kelly, Catherine	9, Mar. 1851	Daniel	----, Julia	E	289
Kelly, Catherine	27, Aug. 1853	Dennis	----, Catherine	E	123
Kelly, Catherine	13, May 1850	James	----, Bridget	E	214
Kelly, Catherine	18, Dec. 1858	John	Latimir, Joanne	E	587
Kelly, Catherine	20, Nov. 1859	John	Shannon, Margaret	P	303
Kelly, Catherine	31, Dec. 1853	Michael	----, Bridget	R	
Kelly, Catherine	20, Apr. 1850	Michael	Burke, Margaret	B	201
Kelly, Catherine	18, Mar. 1855	Patrick	----, Catherine	M	
Kelly, Catherine	24, Jan. 1858	Patrick	Gahan, Catherine	E	512
Kelly, Catherine	21, Mar. 1853	Patrick	Kane, Mary	B	287
Kelly, Catherine	10, Feb. 1858	Patrick	Maher, Bridget	E	516
Kelly, Catherine	27, Feb. 1853	Patrick	O'Donnell, Bridget	B	284
Kelly, Catherine	11, May 1851	Thomas	Lalley, Ann	P	7
Kelly, Catherine	26, Oct. 1856	William	Abbott, Cecilia	E	407
Kelly, Catherine	12, Mar. 1855	William	McCann, Sarah	E	271
Kelly, Catherine	30, Mar. 1856		Kelly, Elizabeth	P	174
Kelly, Catherine Louise	4, Nov. 1855	William	Long, Helen	V	28
Kelly, Columbus	27, Mar. 1859	John	Dolin, Margaret	P	281

Name of Child	Date of Baptism	Father	Mother	Church	Page
Kelly, Daniel	2, Sept 1857	Daniel	Cooney, Julia	B	49
Kelly, Daniel	8, Dec. 1850	Daniel	Erwin, Mary	B	220
Kelly, Daniel J.	27, Nov. 1850	Thomas	----, Mary	E	263
Kelly, Edith Helen	13, July 1856	Henry	Kelley, Mary	E	381
Kelly, Edmund	29, Apr. 1855	Patrick	Gilmartin, Ann	B	14
Kelly, Edward	30, Dec. 1857	Dennis	----, Catherine	R	
Kelly, Edward	21, Aug. 1859	Dennis	Byrne, Bridget	B	79
Kelly, Edward	31, Jan. 1858	James	Cannon, Margaret	B	55
Kelly, Edward	19, Aug. 1852	James	Troy, Mary Ann	B	268
Kelly, Edward	20, Apr. 1856	Richard	Kelly, Catherine	P	177
Kelly, Edward	22, Nov. 1853	Thomas	Cunningham, Mary	V	8
Kelly, Edward James	30, Jan. 1853	John	Curran, Bridget	S	
Kelly, Eliza	26, Oct. 1855	Thomas	Fahy, Bridget	B	21
Kelly, Eliza Jane	2, Sept 1852	Thomas	Hanly, Mary Ann	E	13
Kelly, Elizabeth	21, Jan. 1855	James	Schway, Mary	P	116
Kelly, Elizabeth	29, Jan. 1854	Lawrence	----, Mary	U	
Kelly, Elizabeth	11, Nov. 1852	Michael	Coghlan, Helen	B	275
Kelly, Elizabeth Jane	9, July 1856	Thomas	Lackey, Rosanne	P	184
Kelly, Ellen	14, Dec. 1850	John	Swift, Mary	E	267
Kelly, Ellen	13, Apr. 1852	Owen	Murphy, Ellen	E	403
Kelly, Ellen	29, Oct. 1854	Martin	Busker, Ann	E	236
Kelly, Francis	18, Sept 1854	Thomas	Haley, Mary Ann	E	224
Kelly, Francis Xavier	21, Sept 1850	Michael	----, Ellen	E	249
Kelly, George Levata	19, June 1856	John	McCormack, Elizabeth	B	30
Kelly, Georgina	23, Nov. 1856	John	Doyle, Dora	B	36
Kelly, Helen	6, Jan. 1855	Anthony	----, Margaret	V	22
Kelly, Helen	31, Dec. 1853	Michael	Coughlan, Helen	P	63
Kelly, Helen	11, Aug. 1850	William	Dunbar, Mary	B	210
Kelly, Helen Louise	25, Sept 1853	William	----, Helen	E	129
Kelly, Henry	23, Sept 1855	Henry	Gavakin, Ann	B	19
Kelly, Henry	3, Jan. 1855	Henry	Kelly, Mary	E	253
Kelly, Henry	24, Oct. 1854	John	----, Ellen	V	18
Kelly, Henry	31, Oct. 1854	John	Kelly, Ellen	V	19
Kelly, Honora	2, Jan. 1853	Anthony	----, Honora	E	49
Kelly, Honora	4, Jan. 1853	John	Swift, Mary	B	280
Kelly, Hugh	27, Mar. 1853	James	----, Mary	B	287
Kelly, Isabel	5, Nov. 1854	Henry	Kelly, Mary	V	19
Kelly, Isabel	9, Aug. 1857	Henry	Kelly, Mary	K	
Kelly, James	4, Apr. 1856	Anthony	Kelly, Margaret	V	30
Kelly, James	3, Feb. 1855	James	Brannon, Louise	B	11
Kelly, James	7, Apr. 1850	James	Dolen, Mary Ann	B	200
Kelly, James	29, Oct. 1854	James	Lambert, Bridget	P	102
Kelly, James	5, Apr. 1857	James	Molloy, Margaret	B	42
Kelly, James	13, Oct. 1851	John	----, Alice	B	242
Kelly, James	19, Mar. 1853	John	----, Mary	E	74
Kelly, James	12, Sept 1858	John	Ryan, Bridget	E	562
Kelly, James	27, July 1856	Martin	Byrne, Ann	B	32
Kelly, James	23, July 1854	Michael	Burk, Margaret	E	209
Kelly, James	2, Oct. 1856	Michael	Casey, Mary	P	194
Kelly, James	11, Feb. 1855	Michael	Monaghan, Mary	P	120
Kelly, James	4, July 1858	Patrick	McGuire, Bridget	E	546
Kelly, James	1, Aug. 1858	James	McCabe, Julia	B	62
Kelly, James Patrick	23, Oct. 1851	Martin	----, Ann	E	353
Kelly, Joanne	2, July 1853	Xavier	Wickert, Rose	D	393
Kelly, Johan	19, Feb. 1854	Bernard	Noon, Bridget	P	69
Kelly, John	29, Aug. 1857	Christopher	Cary, Catherine	E	476
Kelly, John	16, July 1855	Dennis	Field, Ellen	B	17
Kelly, John	2, Mar. 1856	Edward	Pennifeather, Mary	B	26
Kelly, John	11, Feb. 1855	James	McCabe, Julia	P	120

Name of Child	Date of Baptism	Father	Mother	Church	Page
Kelly, John	12, Nov. 1857	John	McCormack, Elizabeth	B	51
Kelly, John	4, Apr. 1858	Martin	McCormick, Ellen	B	57
Kelly, John	29, Nov. 1853	Michael	Cosgrove, Margaret	B	303
Kelly, John	24, Feb. 1855	Michael	McElerin, Isabel	B	12
Kelly, John	12, June 1853	Patrick	----, Catherine	M	
Kelly, John	13, July 1856	Patrick	Britt, Bridget	E	381
Kelly, John	28, Oct. 1851	Patrick	Crosby, Bridget	E	353
Kelly, John	7, Nov. 1858	Patrick	Mary, Margaret	G	
Kelly, John	16, Sept 1850	Patrick	Rawle, Ann	B	214
Kelly, John	17, Aug. 1856	Thomas	Haly, Mary Ann	E	390
Kelly, John	28, Feb. 1859	Thomas	Ryan, Catherine	U	
Kelly, John	4, Jan. 1857	Thomas	Scully, Ann	P	203
Kelly, John	2, Apr. 1850	Timothy	----, Margaret	B	199
Kelly, John	15, Feb. 1857	Webb	Henvin, Ann	E	434
Kelly, John	21, June 1857	William	Cro---, Mary	V	39
Kelly, John	23, May 1855		adult	B	15
Kelly, John Jeremiah	20, July 1856	John	Cummings, Catherine	B	31
Kelly, John Joseph	20, Mar. 1859	Matthew	----, Margaret	M	
Kelly, John Michael	13, Oct. 1851	Michael	----, Helen	B	242
Kelly, John Smith	3, Apr. 1853	Daniel	Irwin, Mary	V	2
Kelly, John Thomas	22, Aug. 1854	John	Swift, Mary	B	4
Kelly, Joseph	27, May 1858	John	Murphy, Helen	E	537
Kelly, Joseph James	11, Dec. 1853	Joseph	O'Toole, Mary M.	B	304
Kelly, Joseph William	20, Nov. 1858	Thomas	----, Mary Ann	E	580
Kelly, Josephine	17, July 1853	Brian	----, Barbara	E	107
Kelly, Julia	1, Oct. 1854	Dennis	----, Honora	M	
Kelly, Julia	16, Feb. 1853	James	Kelly, Mary	P	35
Kelly, Julia	2, Oct. 1853	John	Lynch, Catherine	B	300
Kelly, Julia	12, Dec. 1850	Patrick	Flannegan, Mary	E	267
Kelly, Julia	20, Apr. 1851	Patrick	Nowlan, Catherine	M	
Kelly, Julia Mary	25, Apr. 1858	Luke	Murray, Margaret	B	58
Kelly, Lawrence	7, Aug. 1853	Matthew	----, Margaret	E	114
Kelly, Louis? Stephen	26, Dec. 1859	James	McCarthy, Catherine	E	679
Kelly, Louise	1, Nov. 1856	Edward	----, Catherine	E	409
Kelly, Lucy Ann	31, May 1857	Thomas	Nolan, Marcella	P	213
Kelly, Malachai	25, June 1859	Francis	Kelly, Bridget	Z	
Kelly, Margaret	26, Oct. 1856	Edward	Molan, Catharine	L	
Kelly, Margaret	9, May 1852	James	----, Bridget	E	411
Kelly, Margaret	22, June 1851	John	----, Ann	E	317
Kelly, Margaret	9, Mar. 1856	John	McCormick, Elizabeth	B	26
Kelly, Margaret	9, June 1850	Lawrence	----, Mary	B	204
Kelly, Margaret	12, Sept 1858	Martin	Manon, Bridget	E	562
Kelly, Margaret	4, Nov. 1855	Martin	McCormick, Ellen	B	21
Kelly, Margaret	8, Jan. 1854	Patrick	Mack, Bridget	E	159
Kelly, Margaret	28, Mar. 1851	Patrick	Maher, Bridget	K	
Kelly, Margaret	10, July 1853	Patrick	Rawle, Ann	B	295
Kelly, Margaret	9, May 1852	Thomas	Howland, Marcella	P	21
Kelly, Margaret	23, Aug. 1856	William	----, Margaret	B	33
Kelly, Margaret Ann	18, Apr. 1853	Edward	Pennifeather, Margaret	B	289
Kelly, Maria Dorothea	25, Feb. 1854	Patrick	Welsh, Elisabeth	L	
Kelly, Martin	28, Apr. 1856	Eugene	Curley, Margaret	V	31
Kelly, Martin	25, Nov. 1852	John	----, Bridget	M	
Kelly, Martin	18, Mar. 1858	Martin	Lamore, Emily	E	523
Kelly, Martin	13, Feb. 1859	Richard	Kelly, Catherine	B	71
Kelly, Mary	15, Feb. 1852	Bernard	Noon, Bridget	P	18
Kelly, Mary	14, Oct. 1855	Dennis	McNamara, Catherine	R	
Kelly, Mary	5, Dec. 1852	Henry	Gorman, Elisabeth	F	
Kelly, Mary	29, May 1853	Henry	Kattenn, Mary	K	
Kelly, Mary	23, Oct. 1854	John	----, Bridget	M	

Name of Child	Date of Baptism	Father	Mother	Church	Page
Kelly, Mary	18, Dec. 1853	John	Cary, Catherine	E	153
Kelly, Mary	7, Feb. 1858	John	Lambert, Mary	P	238
Kelly, Mary	19, Dec. 1858	Michael	Cosgrove, Margaret	U	
Kelly, Mary	9, July 1858	Michael	Ging, Ellen	B	61
Kelly, Mary	27, Mar. 1853	Patrick	Kilmarten, Mary Ann	B	287
Kelly, Mary	5, May 1856	Patrick	Machen, Bridget	E	365
Kelly, Mary	22, Aug. 1850	Patrick	McKeow, Bridget	E	241
Kelly, Mary	7, July 1850	Thomas	Gilligan, Bridget	E	229
Kelly, Mary	8, Nov. 1855	Michael	Coughlan, Helen	P	158
Kelly, Mary Agnes	13, Mar. 1853	Michael	Casey, Mary	B	286
Kelly, Mary Ann	24, May 1857	Francis	----, Bridget	M	
Kelly, Mary Ann	24, Sept 1853	Henry	Feeney, Ann	B	300
Kelly, Mary Ann	17, Aug. 1856	James	McMinamy, Bridget	V	33
Kelly, Mary Ann	4, Aug. 1850	John	Lynch, Catherine	B	209
Kelly, Mary Ann	21, Aug. 1859	John	McCormick, Elizabeth	B	79
Kelly, Mary Ann	21, Dec. 1855	John	Shannon, Margaret	P	163
Kelly, Mary Ann	12, Feb. 1854	Patrick	Tracy, Margaret	P	68
Kelly, Mary Ann	20, Nov. 1853	Richard	Kelly, Catherine	B	303
Kelly, Mary Ann	19, May 1850	Thomas	Lackey, Rosanne	B	202
Kelly, Mary Ann	7, Mar. 1858	William	Abbott, Celia	E	520
Kelly, Mary Augusta	2, Nov. 1856	William	Derby, Catherine	P	197
Kelly, Mary Catherine	26, Jan. 1851	John	----, Ann	B	223
Kelly, Mary Eliza	9, May 1852	John	Bohan, Catherine	B	258
Kelly, Mary Eliza	16, May 1852	John V.	Doyle, Dora	B	259
Kelly, Mary Eliza	4, July 1852	Michael	Burke, Margaret	B	262
Kelly, Mary Frances	11, May 1856	James	Connor, Margaret	B	28
Kelly, Mary Frances	15, Feb. 1857	Matthew	----, Margaret	E	433
Kelly, Mary Helen	22, Aug. 1852	Alfred	----, Ann	B	268
Kelly, Mary Helen	30, Nov. 1853	William	----, Mary	H	
Kelly, Mary Louise	10, July 1852	Joseph M.	O'Toole, Mary	B	263
Kelly, Matthew Thomas	28, Dec. 1851	Matthew	Duncan?, Mary	P	14
Kelly, Michael	4, May 1856	Christopher	Noon, Bridget	P	178
Kelly, Michael	7, June 1859	Hugh	Boyle, Mary	Z	
Kelly, Michael	25, July 1859	James	Lambert, Bridget	P	289
Kelly, Michael	24, Apr. 1854	Martin	McCormick, Ellen	E	185
Kelly, Michael	30, Apr. 1854	Michael	Gooden, Mary	E	187
Kelly, Michael	6, Dec. 1852	Michael	Lynch, Ann	R	
Kelly, Michael	6, July 1853	Patrick	----, Bridget	E	105
Kelly, Michael	14, Apr. 1850	Patrick	Grier, Margaret	B	200
Kelly, Michael	4, Aug. 1852	Thomas	Kelly, Hannah	B	267
Kelly, Michael	14, Mar. 1855	Thomas	Nolan, Marcella	P	125
Kelly, Michael	7, Dec. 1855	Patrick	Lawless, Barbara	B	22
Kelly, Michael	3, Oct. 1852	Thomas	Manion, Bridget	P	28
Kelly, Miles	1, Aug. 1852	Patrick	----, Bridget	M	
Kelly, Patrick	10, Oct. 1852	Lawrence	Flannery, Mary Catherine	Q	2
Kelly, Patrick	7, Jan. 1851	Martin	Cormac, Helen	B	222
Kelly, Patrick	27, Mar. 1859	Patrick	Dawb?, Barbara	E	613
Kelly, Patrick	14, Jan. 1855	Patrick	Rawle, Ann	B	10
Kelly, Patrick	2, Nov. 1856	Patrick	Tracy, Margaret	P	197
Kelly, Peter	9, June 1850	John	----, Ellenore	E	220
Kelly, Peter	23, Apr. 1857	John	Murphy, Ellen	E	447
Kelly, Peter	1, Aug. 1858	Martin	Byrne, Ann	B	62
Kelly, Peter	9, June 1851	Patrick	Linn, Margaret	E	314
Kelly, Richard	7, Dec. 1856	Michael	Monahan, Mary	V	35
Kelly, Richard	17, Jan. 1858	Owen	Dunkin, Mary Ann	P	236
Kelly, Richard	29, June 1851	Richard	Kelly, Catherine	B	235
Kelly, Robert	21, Nov. 1858	Patrick	Tracy, Margary	B	67
Kelly, Rosanne	17, Mar. 1856	Owen	Duncan, Mary Ann	P	173
Kelly, Rosanne	4, Apr. 1852	Thomas	Lackey, Rosanne	P	20

Name of Child	Date of Baptism	Father	Mother	Church	Page
Kelly, Susan	14, Feb. 1859	James	MacMinamie, Bridget	E	604
Kelly, Thomas	4, Apr. 1858	Bernard	Noonan, Bridget	P	245
Kelly, Thomas	12, Feb. 1854	Daniel	Cooney, Julia	V	10
Kelly, Thomas	10, Mar. 1855	George	----, Alice	E	270
Kelly, Thomas	5, Sept 1852	James	McCabe, Julia	B	269
Kelly, Thomas	31, May 1857	James	Milample, Bridget	P	213
Kelly, Thomas	27, Nov. 1859	Martin	Manion, Bridget	E	673
Kelly, Thomas	6, Nov. 1853	Patrick	----, Bridget	M	
Kelly, Thomas	11, Nov. 1854	Patrick	Hinchy, Ellen	B	7
Kelly, Thomas	7, June 1859	Patrick	Nolan, Catherine	Z	
Kelly, Thomas	5, Apr. 1857	Patrick	Rawle, Ann	B	42
Kelly, Thomas	18, July 1858	Thomas	Kelly, Bridget	G	
Kelly, Thomas James	25, May 1851	Henry	----, Mary	B	232
Kelly, Thomas Owen	18, Apr. 1852	Patrick	Tracy, Margaret	B	257
Kelly, Timothy	3, Jan. 1855	Henry	Kelly, Mary	E	253
Kelly, Timothy	31, July 1854	Thomas	Lackey, Rosanne	P	90
Kelly, Timothy	28, Aug. 1859	Thomas	Lackey, Rosanne	P	294
Kelly, Tomas	5, Oct. 1859	Thomas	Kelly, Mary	E	660
Kelly, Vincent	8, Jan. 1854	John	Doyle, Dora	P	65
Kelly, William	20, July 1859	Edward	Pennifeather, Margaret	B	77
Kelly, William	4, Aug. 1855	James	Molloy, Margaret	B	17
Kelly, William	9, Apr. 1859	Michael	Manohan, Mary	E	617
Kelly, William	31, May 1857	Patrick	----, Catherine	M	
Kelly, William Henry	24, Oct. 1859	William	Derby, Catherine	P	301
Kelly, Winefred	4, Mar. 1855	Thomas	Brodrick, Ann	B	12
Kelmann, Lina	18, Feb. 1855	Vincent	Knapp, Louisa	C	
Keloran, Andrew	24, Oct. 1852	John	Scanlin, Bridget	P	28
Kelsch, John George	10, Aug. 1856	Peter	Roll, Margaret	U	
Kelsch, William	2, Dec. 1855	Balthasar	Conrad, Eva	Q	11
Kelso, James	27, Jan. 1852	James	McGrew, Mary Jane	E	378
Keltler, Johan B.	29, Sept 1854	Gerhard R	Schipper, Anna Maria	L	
Kelty, Patrick	17, Mar. 1850	Peter	Kearney, Winny	E	204
Kelty, Timothy	12, Oct. 1857	Thomas	----, Ellen	E	485
Kembel, Josephina Clara	24, Oct. 1852	Conrad	Wolfel, Catharina	D	354
Kemker, Anna Maria	10, Nov. 1854		Kemker, Anna Maria	K	
Kemker, Maria Elisabeth Catharina	15, Mar. 1854	Johan	Holenkamp, Catharina	C	
Kemme, Catharina Elisabeth	25, Feb. 1859	Heinrich	Reinermann, M. Theresa	T	
Kemme, Georg August	30, Aug. 1857	Francis J.	Klene, Anna	A	
Kemme, Johan	14, Sept 1854	Heinrich	Reineman, Theresa	J	28
Kemme, Maria Catharina Francisca	28, Sept 1856	Heinrich	Reinemann, M. Theresa	F	
Kemme, Maria Elisabeth	28, June 1855	Francis J.	Kleen, Anna	A	
Kemmerer, Catharina	13, July 1858	Benedict	Gerlach, Anna Maria	R	
Kemmy, Joseph Anton	21, Sept 1856	F. Joseph	Clehm, Francisca	J	38
Kemmy, Maria Josephina	27, Nov. 1859	F. Joseph	Klene, Maria	A	
Kemmy, Michael Adolph	21, Sept 1856	F. Joseph	Clehm, Francisca	J	38
Kemna, Alexander Johan Heinrich	16, Sept 1856	J. Heinrich	Feldman, Agnes	A	
Kemna, Catharina Bernardina	1, Apr. 1858	Heinrich	Feldman, Agnes	A	
Kemna, Herman	15, Oct. 1854	Heinrich	Feldman, Agnes	A	
Kemner, Maria Agnes	16, June 1853	Heinrich	Feldmann, Agnes	L	
Kempel, Carl Edward	23, Sept 1850	Conrad	Wolfel, Catharina	K	
Kempel, Gallus Francis	3, June 1855	Conrad	Wölfel, Catharina	D	36
Kempel, Joseph Anton	17, Oct. 1858	Conrad	Wölfel, Catharina	D	122
Kempel, Josephina Catharina	26, Aug. 1855	Heinrich	Lorenz, Eva	C	
Kempel, Maria Elisabeth	7, May 1855	Johan	Kulenberg, Maria Anna	D	34
Kempel, Martha Anna	22, Feb. 1857	Conrad	Wolfer, Catharina	D	79
Kemper, Cornelius Vincenz	16, Oct. 1859	Heinrich	Duffner, Maria	C	
Kemper, Heinrich Joseph	30, June 1856	Gerhard H.	Klosterman, Margaretha	D	62
Kemper, Johan	8, Feb. 1852	Joseph	König, Catharina Elisabeth	K	
Kemper, Johan Heinrich	13, Oct. 1852	Heinrich	Klosterman, Margaretha	A	

Name of Child	Date of Baptism	Father	Mother	Church	Page
Kemper, Johan Joseph	8, Mar. 1859	Joseph	Schuhmacher, Catharina	J	50
Kemper, Johan Philipp Anton	23, Nov. 1859	Arnold	Droppelmann, Anna M.	L	
Kemper, Johan Philipp Anton	14, Oct. 1858	Philipp	Thiemann, Elisabeth	C	
Kemper, Johan Philipp Anton	5, Dec. 1859	Philipp	Thiemann, Elisabeth	C	
Kemper, Maria Elisabeth	26, June 1858	Heinrich	Klosterman, Margaretha	D	114
Kempf, Anna Margaretha	9, Nov. 1858	Philipp	Albert, Appolonia	F	
Kempf, Christian Joseph	4, June 1859	Lawrence	Peter, Gertrud	D	139
Kempf, Elisabeth	11, May 1856	Johan	Peter, Gertrud	D	58
Kempf, Gertrud	16, Apr. 1854	Lawrence	Peter, Gertrud	D	8
Kempf, Johan Georg	2, Mar. 1851	Lawrence	Peder, Gertrud	D	255
Kempf, Margaretha Elisabeth	26, Oct. 1857	Lawrence	Peter, Gertrud	D	97
Kempf, Maria Elisabeth	19, Dec. 1852	Lawrence	Peter, Gertrud	D	361
Kempf, Michael	11, Nov. 1857	Philipp	Albert, Appononia	F	
Kempf, Theodor Georg	9, Apr. 1854	Francis	Feldy, Catharina	L	
Kemphaus, Johan Heinrich	15, Oct. 1854	J. Heinrich	Bogerding, Elisabeth	J	28
Kemphues, Anna Maria Catharina	1, Oct. 1858	Joseph	Wetteriede, Elisabeth	A	
Kemphues, Catharina Francisca	29, Jan. 1857	Joseph	Wiederiede, Elisabeth	A	
Kemping, Johan Bernard	22, Jan. 1857	J. Bernard	Rahm, M. Elisabeth	L	
Kemping, Maria Josephina	11, Nov. 1854	Bernard	Rahe, M. Elisabeth	L	
Kempker, Johan Heinrich	20, June 1850	J. Heinrich	Hoeveler, Adelheid	C	
Kemple, Winifred	4, Mar. 1857	Thomas	Leonard, Sarah	B	41
Kendelin, Maria	15, May 1855	Maximillian	Eberle, Augusta	K	
Keneally, Catherine	1, July 1854	Patrick	Deba--, Mary	B	2
Keneally, Catherine	17, Feb. 1853	Patrick	Garrett, Bridget	P	35
Kenelly, John	18, May 1855	Thomas	Corley, Mary	V	25
Kenick, Rosa	10, May 1857	Albert	Gross, Catharina	D	84
Kenigan, Margaret	2, May 1852	Peter	Donahue, Catherine	B	264
Kenkel, Clemens Anton	10, July 1857	Anton	Brauer, Elisabeth	C	
Kenkel, Francisca Bernardina	24, June 1858	Heinrich	Ronker, Bernardina	C	
Kenkel, Gerhard Heinrich	7, Jan. 1857	Heinrich	Roenker, Bernardina	C	
Kenkel, Johan Bernard	9, Oct. 1854	Clemens	Vornholt, Anna M.	C	
Kenker, Johan Clemens	19, Dec. 1858	Clemens	Fornos, Anna M.	C	
Kenker, Maria	25, Oct. 1856	Clemens	Fahrenhorst, Maria	C	
Kenna, John	18, Aug. 1850	Malachai	Doyle, Mary	E	239
Kenna, William Edward	29, Aug. 1859	William	Kain, Mary	B	80
Kennebeck, Anna Catharina	7, July 1856	J. Wilhelm	Penkhof, Anna Margaretha	D	62
Kennedy, Agnes	7, Feb. 1858	Michael	Bulfin, Alice	P	238
Kennedy, Albert	7, Apr. 1853		adult	B	288
Kennedy, Ann	17, Mar. 1858	Michael	----, Ann	M	
Kennedy, Ann	7, Feb. 1851	Michael	Kating, Ann	E	281
Kennedy, Anna	18, May 1854	Michael	O'Neil, Bridget	L	
Kennedy, Bridget	9, Jan. 1856	James	Roach, Ann	E	336
Kennedy, Bridget	26, Jan. 1851	Thomas	Flynn, Catherine	E	278
Kennedy, Bridget	28, June 1854	William	Foley, Ellen	E	202
Kennedy, Catherine	15, Feb. 1857	Daniel	Corne, Margaret	B	40
Kennedy, Catherine	27, Jan. 1856	John	Kennedy, Catherine	P	167
Kennedy, Catherine	15, Apr. 1855	Michael	Kating, Ann	E	279
Kennedy, Catherine	18, Dec. 1853	Patrick	Karney, Catherine	B	304
Kennedy, Catherine	21, Feb. 1859	Patrick	Kennedy, Margaret	E	605
Kennedy, Catherine	13, Apr. 1852	Patrick	Wise, Mary	E	402
Kennedy, Charles	14, June 1857	Albert	Kane, Mary Ann	E	459
Kennedy, Charles	17, Feb. 1857	Daniel	----, Roseanne	E	434
Kennedy, Charles	21, Dec. 1852	James	McKenna, Mary	P	31
Kennedy, Charles	6, June 1856	Michael	----, Joanne	E	371
Kennedy, Daniel	25, Jan. 1853	James	Gleeson, Ann	E	58
Kennedy, Edward	25, Aug. 1856	James	----, Elizabeth	E	393
Kennedy, Ellen	6, Sept 1852	William	----, Ellen	E	15
Kennedy, Ellen Elizabeth	22, Aug. 1858	Patrick	Harney, Catherine	B	63
Kennedy, Francis Joseph	28, Feb. 1859	John	----, Catherine	E	607

Name of Child	Date of Baptism	Father	Mother	Church	Page
Kennedy, Helen	19, Mar. 1854	Michael	Bulfin, Alice	P	74
Kennedy, Helen	16, Jan. 1853	Thomas	Penny, Joanne	B	281
Kennedy, James	15, June 1851	James	----, Elizabeth	E	316
Kennedy, James	5, Feb. 1852	James	Scanlin, Ellen	P	17
Kennedy, James	9, Mar. 1856	Martin	King, Margaret	B	26
Kennedy, James	30, Oct. 1855	Patrick	Collins, Winefred	B	21
Kennedy, James	11, Mar. 1852	Thomas	----, Ellen	E	390
Kennedy, Jane	30, Jan. 1853	Michael	Kating, Ann	E	59
Kennedy, Jane	27, Feb. 1859	Michael	O'Neil, Bridget	B	71
Kennedy, Joanne	22, July 1853	John	Kennedy, Catherine	P	47
Kennedy, Joanne	20, Feb. 1853	Michael	Meaken, Mary	B	284
Kennedy, Joanne	10, Mar. 1858	Michael	Walsh, Joanne	E	521
Kennedy, John	18, June 1854	James	Haugh--, Margaret	B	1
Kennedy, John	8, Oct. 1854	James	Keatey, Helen	E	230
Kennedy, John	2, Apr. 1854	Martin	King, Margaret	B	312
Kennedy, John	10, June 1850	Michael	----, Alice	E	221
Kennedy, John	22, June 1856	Patrick	Carman, Mary	E	375
Kennedy, John	15, Mar. 1857	Patrick	Conroy, Mary	V	38
Kennedy, John Augustine	28, Aug. 1859	Michael	O'Gara, Catherine	V	58
Kennedy, John Francis	30, Apr. 1854	Albert	Keane, Mary Ann	B	314
Kennedy, John James	18, Apr. 1852	John	Regan, Catherine	B	258
Kennedy, John James	25, Apr. 1852	Patrick	----, Catherine	B	257
Kennedy, Joseph	29, Mar. 1857	Michael	----, Ann	M	
Kennedy, Joseph Charles	7, Nov. 1855	John	Marshall, Louise	E	325
Kennedy, Louise	18, Apr. 1858	James	Murphy, Margaret	B	57
Kennedy, Margaret	23, Sept 1850	James	Murphy, Margaret	B	214
Kennedy, Margaret	7, Mar. 1858	John	Kennedy, Catherine	P	241
Kennedy, Margaret	3, Sept 1857	Michael	O'Gara, Catherine	V	41
Kennedy, Margaret	27, Dec. 1854	Patrick	Kennedy, Margaret	V	20
Kennedy, Margaret	20, July 1855	William	Foley, Helen	E	300
Kennedy, Martin	5, Dec. 1858	Michael	Scullin, Mary	B	67
Kennedy, Mary	10, Oct. 1852	Hugh	Cavanagh, Mary	B	271
Kennedy, Mary	21, Dec. 1851	James	Murphy, Margaret	B	247
Kennedy, Mary	27, Apr. 1851	John	Schwab, Mary	P	7
Kennedy, Mary	7, Feb. 1858	Michael	Hefferden, Joanne	E	515
Kennedy, Mary	6, Apr. 1856	Michael	Meeghan, Mary	B	27
Kennedy, Mary	13, Apr. 1856	Michael	O'Neil, Bridget	B	27
Kennedy, Mary	22, May 1855	Michael	Walsh, Joanne	E	288
Kennedy, Mary	28, Nov. 1852	Patrick	----, Mary	B	276
Kennedy, Mary Ann	4, Nov. 1857	James	Honbigan, Margaret	E	491
Kennedy, Mary Ann	5, July 1855	Nicolaus	Cooney, Ann	V	25
Kennedy, Mary Ann	20, Nov. 1853	Patrick	----, Catherine	M	
Kennedy, Mary Ann	6, Feb. 1857	Patrick	----, Margaret	V	37
Kennedy, Mary Ann	27, July 1856	Patrick	Harney, Catherine	B	32
Kennedy, Mary Ellen	9, Sept 1858	Owen	Carroll, Margaret	E	561
Kennedy, Mary Jane	16, Aug. 1859	Daniel	Leonard, Rose Ann	E	648
Kennedy, Mary Louise	1, Jan. 1854	James	Foulon, Mary	E	156
Kennedy, Michael	4, Apr. 1858	James	Conway, Sarah	E	527
Kennedy, Michael	30, May 1858	James	Houghy, Margaret	B	59
Kennedy, Michael	30, Jan. 1853	Martin	King, Bridget	B	282
Kennedy, Michael	29, May 1859	Michael	Walsh, Joanne	E	629
Kennedy, Nicolaus	4, Nov. 1856	James	Reason, Helen	E	410
Kennedy, Nicolaus	2, Mar. 1853	Nicolaus	Coony, Ann	E	67
Kennedy, Patrick	30, Jan. 1858	James	Keating, Ellen	E	513
Kennedy, Patrick	26, Jan. 1852	Nicolaus	----, Ann	E	378
Kennedy, Patrick	24, May 1857	Patrick	----, Mary	R	
Kennedy, Philipp	14, Oct. 1857	Patrick	Fahy, Joanne	E	486
Kennedy, Richard	7, Oct. 1857	Nicolaus	----, Ann	E	484
Kennedy, Robert	5, Mar. 1854	Patrick	Wise, Mary	R	

Hamilton County, Ohio Roman Catholic Baptism Records -- 1850 - 1859

Name of Child	Date of Baptism	Father	Mother	Church	Page
Kennedy, Sarah	17, Sept 1854	Patrick	Conory, Mary	P	96
Kennedy, Thomas	22, Feb. 1850	Hugh	Cavanagh, Mary	B	197
Kennedy, Thomas	29, June 1859	John	Kennedy, Catherine	P	287
Kennedy, Thomas	16, Apr. 1856	Michael	Rolfen, Alice	P	176
Kennedy, Thomas	26, Aug. 1854	Patrick	Geraghan, Mary	B	4
Kennedy, William	10, June 1851	Hugh	Cavanagh, Mary	B	234
Kennedy, William	29, Mar. 1856	Hugh	Cavanagh, Mary	P	174
Kennedy, William	2, Nov. 1851	James	----, Ellen	E	354
Kennedy, William	24, July 1853	James	Conway, Elizabeth	V	4
Kennedy, William	3, Dec. 1854	James	Conway, Elizabeth	V	20
Kennedy, William	30, Nov. 1854	James	Murphy, Margaret	P	107
Kennedy, William	1, Nov. 1854	John	Regan, Catherine	B	7
Kennedy, William	28, Mar. 1852	Michael	Balfan, Alice	E	397
Kennedy, William Edward	24, Aug. 1851	Edward	Carr, Ann	B	239
Kennell, Bernard	14, May 1854	Bernard	----, Mary	U	
Kenner, Maria Anna	17, July 1857	Gerhard	Heidenb--, Maria	D	90
Kenney, Helen	13, May 1853	Timothy	Whelan, Mary	B	291
Kenney, Michael	13, Jan. 1850	Michael	McCahill, Mary	B	194
Kenney, Michael	3, Sept 1851	Owen	Fitzpatrick, Jane	E	340
Kenney, Patrick	8, Dec. 1855	Michael	----, Mary	E	331
Kenney, Peter	18, Jan. 1856	Peter	----, Bridget	E	337
Kenney, Sarah	28, July 1858	John	McGreevy, Sarah	P	255
Kenney, Thomas	15, Aug. 1858	Patrick	Gallagher, Ann	P	258
Kenny, Ann	11, Oct. 1857	Dennis	Tague, Ann	E	485
Kenny, Ann	5, July 1857	Patrick	----, Catherine	V	40
Kenny, Ann	14, Mar. 1859	William	Mulfeather, Mary Elizabeth	M	
Kenny, Anna Crescentia	24, Oct. 1858	Johan	Dihner, Anna	J	48
Kenny, Bridget	6, Feb. 1851	James	Jeffers, Sabina	B	224
Kenny, Bridget	15, July 1855	Michael	Shea, Margaret	P	140
Kenny, Bridget Catherine	6, Feb. 1853	Patrick	Morris, Ann	E	61
Kenny, Catherine	7, Jan. 1854	James	----, J.	E	158
Kenny, Catherine	18, Dec. 1856	James	Scully, Ann	E	421
Kenny, Catherine	5, Feb. 1854	John	Crimmins, Catherine	P	67
Kenny, Catherine	25, Apr. 1858	John	Gorden, Mary	B	58
Kenny, Catherine	17, Oct. 1850	Patrick	----, Ann	E	254
Kenny, Catherine	12, Jan. 1851	Thomas	Curley, Mary	P	3
Kenny, Dennis	20, Jan. 1853	Michael	McCalisas, Bridget	E	56
Kenny, Edward	4, Mar. 1855	Dennis	Lagg?, Ann	E	268
Kenny, Edward	4, Dec. 1853	Peter	Kenny, Bridget	E	148
Kenny, Eliza Jane	6, Nov. 1859	Christopher	Fitzgerald, Mary	P	303
Kenny, Elizabeth	18, Apr. 1857	James	Jeffers, Sabina	E	446
Kenny, Ellen	30, Sept 1855	John	Gordon, Mary	B	20
Kenny, Ellen	27, Mar. 1855	Patrick	Costello, Margaret	B	13
Kenny, Helen Ann	31, Aug. 1851	Anthony	Gill, Margaret	B	240
Kenny, James	20, Apr. 1851	Dennis	McCue, Mary	M	
Kenny, James	23, Feb. 1852	James	Jeffere, Sabena	E	385
Kenny, James	13, July 1851	John	Cummins, Catherine	P	10
Kenny, James	30, Oct. 1853	Patrick	----, Mary	E	139
Kenny, Johan Anton	9, Jan. 1853	Johan	Dehner, Anna	J	20
Kenny, John	30, May 1852	James	Smith, Catherine	E	419
Kenny, John	7, Sept 1851	John	Navin, Margaret	B	240
Kenny, John	18, Dec. 1853	Michael	Shea, Margaret	P	62
Kenny, John	21, Dec. 1851	Patrick	----, Ann	M	
Kenny, John	28, Mar. 1858	Thomas	Curley, Mary	P	243
Kenny, Margaret	11, Dec. 1853	James	Smith, Catherine	P	61
Kenny, Margaret	12, Nov. 1854	Michael	Sears, Margaret	V	19
Kenny, Margaret	17, Jan. 1855	Patrick	----, Catherine	E	257
Kenny, Martin	30, Oct. 1853	James	Jeffers, Sabina	P	57
Kenny, Mary	16, July 1851	Dennis	Cayne, Ann	E	324

Name of Child	Date of Baptism	Father	Mother	Church	Page
Kenny, Mary	19, Sept 1858	James	Halay, Bridget	T	
Kenny, Mary	27, June 1854	Thomas	----, Mary	M	
Kenny, Mary	6, June 1855	Thomas	Curly, Mary	P	135
Kenny, Mary	12, Apr. 1857	William	Kane, Mary	B	43
Kenny, Mary Ann	19, July 1856	Michael	McCabe, Bridget	E	382
Kenny, Mary Ann	17, Mar. 1853	William	----, Sarah	E	74
Kenny, Mary Helen	28, Aug. 1859	Edward	Leddy, Bridget	P	294
Kenny, Michael	9, Oct. 1853	Dennis	----, Ann	E	133
Kenny, Michael	20, Oct. 1850	John	Gordan, Mary	B	216
Kenny, Michael	9, Aug. 1856	John	McCabe, Nancy	E	388
Kenny, Michael	20, Nov. 1859	Thomas	Moriarty, Catherine	P	303
Kenny, Patrick	31, Oct. 1857	Edward	Kenny, Ann	E	490
Kenny, Patrick	13, Oct. 1854	James	Connolly, Mary	E	231
Kenny, Patrick	11, Nov. 1854	Michael	----, Bridget	E	239
Kenny, Sabina	17, Dec. 1854	James	Jeffers, Sabina	P	110
Kenny, Sarah	7, Aug. 1859	Thomas	Mason?, Sabina	B	78
Kenny, Thomas	5, Feb. 1853	Thomas	Curley, Mary	P	34
Kenny, Wilhelm Daniel	15, Nov. 1854	Johan	Dehner, Anna	J	28
Kenny, William	21, Nov. 1852	John	Gordon, Mary	B	275
Kenny, William	4, Mar. 1855	John	Sweeney, Margaret	P	123
Kenny, William	11, Sept 1856	William	McCann, Sarah	E	397
Kenny, William Edward	24, July 1857	Edward	Leddy, Bridget	P	218
Kenrick, Thomas	27, July 1855	Dennis	----, Ann	E	303
Kent, George	9, July 1850	Morel?	----, Mary	E	230
Kent, Henry Alonzo	17, July 1857	Alonzo	Bloomfield, Elizabeth	E	466
Kent, James	25, Dec. 1859	Patrick	----, Ellen	E	679
Kent, James	4, Dec. 1856	Pierce	McEtey, Mary Liza	E	417
Kent, Laura	27, Oct. 1858	Alonzo	Bloomfield, Eliza	E	572
Kent, Mary Ann	7, June 1859	Pierce	Migolin, Mary Elizabeth	E	630
Kent, Mary Helen	1, Feb. 1857	John	Davis, Elizabeth	E	430
Kent, William	23, Nov. 1855	Patrick	----, Ellen	E	328
Kentrup, Elisabeth Philomena	9, Apr. 1851	Heinrich	Greve, Gertrud	K	
Kentrup, Francis Heinrich	25, Nov. 1852	Heinrich	Grewe, Maria Gertrud	K	
Kentrup, Maria Anna	14, July 1855	Heinrich	Greve, Gertrud	K	
Kenzeimer, Susanna	22, Aug. 1858	Wilhelm	Hessel, Elisabeth	D	117
Keobel, Adam	4, Aug. 1850	Adam	Weitman, Catharina	D	226
Keogh, James	8, Nov. 1852	John	----, Mary	E	33
Keogh, Michael	30, July 1859	Michael	Brophy, Bridget	B	78
Keogh, Patrick	14, Mar. 1852	Patrick	----, Mary Ann	E	391
Keon, Philip	5, Aug. 1857	Andrew	Keon, F.	S	
Keone, Mary Ann	9, June 1850	Bernard	----, Catherine	B	204
Keough, James	13, Sept 1857	Michael	----, Bridget	M	
Keough, Mary	25, May 1854	James	----, Mary	M	
Keown, Helen	29, June 1851	August	Belechm?, Ann	E	319
Keown, Hugh Samuel	21, May 1854	Hugh	Belchan, Ann	V	14
Keown, Joseph	8, Apr. 1859	Hugh	Belchamp, Margaret Ann	V	54
Keown, Margaret	6, Feb. 1853	Hugh	Belcham, Ann	V	1
Keown, William Eugene	16, June 1850	Hugh	Belcham, Margaret Ann	B	205
Kepner, Ludwig	20, Feb. 1859	Francis X.	Sa---, Theresa	D	132
Kerbel, Francisca	8, Aug. 1852	J. Adam	Ginglin, Catharina	D	342
Kerber, Francisca	28, July 1850	J. Georg	Stang, Eva	D	225
Kerber, Johan Weigant	27, Mar. 1853	Georg	Stab, Eva	D	377
Kerdolf, Amanda Jane	12, Oct. 1852	John	Jelleff, Amanda	B	271
Kerdolff, Catharina	18, Apr. 1858	Johan A.	Wader, Catharina	F	
Kerer, Carolina	20, Nov. 1853	Anton	Antoni, Maria Anna	D	415
Kerger, Maria Elisabeth	15, Nov. 1857	Peter	Berger, Clara	N	
Kerkner, John	8, Mar. 1857	Francis	McKane, Elizabeth	E	439
Kerler, Alexander	30, Aug. 1859	Thomas	----, Sarah	E	650
Kern, Edward Eberhard	3, Nov. 1852		Kern, Catharina	K	

Name of Child	Date of Baptism	Father	Mother	Church	Page
Kern, Franz Carl	25, Oct. 1857	Francis	----, Maria	T	
Kern, Joseph Anton	24, July 1859	Francis	Braun, Maria Antonia	T	
Kern, Martha	21, Mar. 1858	Michael	Wagner, Anna Maria	H	
Kernan, James	5, June 1851	James	Meehan, Ellen	P	8
Kernbach, Maria Catharina	14, Feb. 1854	Gerhard H.	Klosterman, Margaretha G.	D	4
Kernebeck, Anna Maria Catharina	20, Apr. 1855	Gerhard W	Benkhof, Margaretha	F	
Kerner, Johan	10, Apr. 1859	J. Conrad	Wuest, Elisabeth	T	
Kerns, Andrew	6, Dec. 1855	James	----, Margaret	M	
Kernstein, Theresa	5, July 1857	Ludwig	Rein, Catharina	D	89
Kerr, James	17, Oct. 1859	Stephan	Jacobs, Susan	E	663
Kerry, Catharina Elisabeth	16, Jan. 1859	Samuel	Kramer, Magdalena	T	
Kerry, Edward Jacob	9, Nov. 1856	Samuel	Kramer, Magdalena	D	71
Kerry, Maria Theresa	16, Jan. 1859	Samuel	Kramer, Magdalena	T	
Kerry, Salomea	16, Aug. 1850	Samuel	Kramer, Magdalena	D	228
Kerschner, John	7, Sept 1858	John	Septel, Rosa	X	
Kersker, Anna Maria Adelheid	27, Mar. 1858	H. Heinrich	Robben, Maria Adelheid	D	108
Kersker, Gerhard Heinrich	8, May 1856	Herman H.	Robben, Maria Adelheid	D	57
Kersker, Johan Baptist	8, June 1859	Heinrich	Robben, Maria Adelheid	D	139
Kersting, Casper Heinrich	1, Dec. 1850	Herman	Farenhorst, Catharina	L	
Kersting, James	22, May 1859	Thomas	Wanrans, Sarah	E	626
Kersting, Johan Heinrich	8, Oct. 1854	J. Heinrich	Farnhorst, M. Cath.	L	
Kersting, Maria Philomena	26, May 1857	Herman	Fahrenhorst, Maria	L	
Kerth, Franz Joseph	27, Nov. 1856	Carl	Goetz, Barbara	F	
Kerth, Georg	8, May 1859	Carl	Goetz, Barbara	T	
Kerth, Johanna	14, July 1852	Carl	Götz, Barbara	D	328
Kertner, Johanna Regina	21, Aug. 1859	Johan	Stad---, Walburga	D	144
Kerwan, Patrick	29, Aug. 1853	Michael	Noonan, Joanne	V	5
Kerwan, Thomas	24, Feb. 1854	Martin	----, Mary	M	
Kerwick, James	15, Nov. 1857	Patrick	Hogan, Honora	B	52
Kerwin, Helen	29, June 1851	August	Belechm?, Ann	E	319
Kerwin, James	18, Aug. 1850	Jeremiah	----, Catherine	E	240
Kerwin, James	14, Jan. 1850	Thomas	Murphy, Margaret	E	192
Kerwin, Jean	13, Aug. 1857	Michael	Noonan, Jane	P	220
Kerwin, John	27, Apr. 1851	Michael	Ryan, Catherine	E	303
Kerwin, Margaret Ann	14, Jan. 1850	Thomas	Murphy, Margaret	E	192
Kerwin, Mary	27, Apr. 1851	Michael	----, Catherine	E	304
Kerwin, Mary Jane	3, Jan. 1850	Michael	----, Catherine	E	189
Kerwin, Michael	25, Sept 1859	Michael	Noon, Jane	B	81
Kesheimer, Francis Joseph	9, Feb. 1851	Sebastian	Streile, Loretha	K	
Kesheimer, Joseph	1, Jan. 1855	Sebastian	Streile, Loretta	N	26
Kesheimer, Maria Adelheid	4, Oct. 1857	Sebastian	Streile, Loretto	N	
Kesheimer, Maria Juliana	23, Jan. 1853	Sebastian	Straile, Maria Loretto	N	11
Kesker, Gerhard Heinrich	10, May 1850	J. Gerhard	Robben, Anna Maria	D	212
Kesker, Johan Gerhard	4, June 1854	J. Gerhard	Robben, Anna Maria	D	11
Kesker, Johan Gerhard	16, Aug. 1852	J. Gerhard	Robben, Maria Anna	D	344
Kesker, Johan Herman	6, Oct. 1856	J. Gerhard	Röbben, Anna Maria	D	69
Kesker, Maria Adelheid	4, Oct. 1854	Gerhard H.	Tole, Anna Adelheid	D	19
Kesker, Maria Catharina	10, Feb. 1859	J. Gerhard	Robben, Anna Maria	D	131
Kesler, Philomena Veronica	28, Jan. 1855	Johan	Steckenborn, Margaretha	K	
Kessart, Rosa Maria Magdalena	1, Aug. 1858	Joseph	----, Theresa	C	
Kessel, Georg Blasius	4, Oct. 1857	Peter	Lortz, Josephina	S	
Kesselbach, Johan	6, May 1859	Johan (+)	Grun---, Catharina	D	137
Kessen, Andreas Johan	11, June 1858	Johan	Kall, Theresa	K	
Kessen, Anna Helena Carolina	10, Oct. 1859	Johan H.	Ahaus, Maria Anna	T	
Kessen, Anton Bernard	17, May 1852	J. Theodor	Kollman, Maria Theresa	A	
Kessen, Catharina Wilhelmina	6, Feb. 1858	J. Herman	Bump, Wilhelmina	K	
Kessen, Elisabeth Paulina Maria A.	13, Feb. 1855	Gerhard H.	Ahaus, Marianna	F	
Kessen, Johan Clemens	14, Jan. 1851	J. Theodor	Kulman, Theresa	A	
Kessen, Johan Gerhard	11, Nov. 1856	Johan	Kallman, Theresa	K	

Name of Child	Date of Baptism	Father	Mother	Church	Page
Kessen, Johan Joseph	1, Mar. 1854	J. Theodor	Kahlman, Theresa	K	
Kessen, Maria Elisabeth	16, June 1859	J. Gerhard	Brodbeck, Anna	F	
Kessen, Maria Helena	8, May 1859	J. Herman	Rump, Josephina Philomena	K	
Kessen, Maria Theresa	26, Jan. 1853	Gerhard H.	Ahaus, Marianna	F	
Kessener, Anna Maria	17, Feb. 1850	Jacob	Bokhof, Barbara	A	
Kessing, Francis Heinrich	9, Aug. 1852	Heinrich	Brockmann, M. Elisabeth	C	
Kessing, Herman Heinrich	26, Mar. 1854	Johan	Brokamp, Elisabeth	C	
Kessing, Maria Catharina Agnes	23, Jan. 1851	H. Heinrich	Schroeder, Maria Elisabeth	K	
Kessing, Sarah	20, Nov. 1859	William	----, Sarah	E	671
Kessler, Anton Ludwig	21, Apr. 1854	Valentin	Hubert, Catharina	A	
Kessler, Barbara Magdalena	4, Aug. 1850	Balthasar	Ankenbauer, Dorothea	D	226
Kessler, Carolina Maria	6, Apr. 1856	Valentin	Hubert, Catharina	A	
Kessler, Catharine	22, Apr. 1855	Balthasar	Ankenbauer, Dorothea	Q	7
Kessler, Georg Jacob Heinrich	18, Nov. 1856	J. Heinrich	Mittreder, Anna	Q	17
Kessler, Johan Valentin	22, Aug. 1852	Valentin	Hubert, Catharina	A	
Kessler, Joseph	2, Dec. 1855	Joseph	Brehm, Catharina	W	11
Kessler, Maria Catharina	25, Oct. 1857	Joseph	Brehm, Catharina	W	20
Kessler, Maria Clara Elisabeth	29, Aug. 1858	Valentin	Hubert, Catharina	A	
Kessler, Maria Magdalena	19, Oct. 1851	Balthasar	Ankenbauer, Theresa	D	287
Kessler, Michael	26, Sept 1852	Anton	Warner, Clothilda	R	
Kessler, Valentine	10, Aug. 1850	Valentin	Hubert, Catharina	A	
Kessling, Maria Catharina	21, Jan. 1855	Heinrich	Berling, Catharina	F	
Kessling, Maria Elisabeth	5, May 1853	Heinrich	Berling, Anna Maria	F	
Kessling, Maria Mathilda	5, Aug. 1858	H. Joseph	Berling, Maria Catharina	F	
Kestler, Anna Catharina	5, Apr. 1858	Balthasar	Ankenbauer, Dorothea	Q	27
Kestler, Margaretha	2, Feb. 1854	Balthasar	Ankenbauer, Dorothea	Q	4
Ketchum, George H.	23, Sept 1857	George H.	Ryan, Fanny	B	50
Ketchum, Henry Michael	23, Aug. 1856	George	Ryan, Fanny	B	33
Ketorin?, Joseph Maurice	5, Nov. 1854	Maurice	----, Joanne	P	103
Ketschum, Johan Wilhelm	15, May 1859	Wilhelm	Franz, Catharina	D	138
Kettelary, Johan Heinrich	20, Feb. 1850	Heinrich	Laake, Maria Anna	C	
Kettelary, Maria Elisabeth	20, Feb. 1850	Heinrich	Laake, Maria Anna	C	
Kettelen, Peter	19, Oct. 1851	Sebastian	Reif, Maria	K	
Ketteler, Johan Bernard	15, Oct. 1850	J. Bernard	Lansing, Gertrud	D	238
Kettelman, Johan Francis	15, Dec. 1859	Heinrich	Renecker, Bernardina	D	153
Kettelman, Maria Magdalena	9, Sept 1855	Heinrich	Renecker, Dina	D	42
Kettelmann, Johan Heinric	13, May 1852	Heinrich	Reidt, Catharina	C	
Kettels, Anna Catharina Christina	1, May 1853	Heinrich	Windmeyer, Theresa	C	
Kettels, Anna Maria Philomena	27, Feb. 1851	Heinrich	Windmeyer, Theresa	C	
Kettels, Gerhard Andreas	5, Nov. 1856	Gerhard	Timmer, Anna Maria	F	
Kettels, Johan Heinrich	3, Oct. 1851	F. Wilhelm	Deter, Anna Maria	K	
Kettels, Johan Herman	10, Oct. 1854	Wilhelm J.	Deters, Anna Maria	K	
Kettels, Maria Catharina	1, Aug. 1854	Gerhard	Knapmeyer, Maria G.	A	
Kettels, Maria Elisabeth	12, Nov. 1857	Wilhelm	Deiters, Catharina	K	
Kettels, Wilhelm Gerhard Theodor	27, Mar. 1852	Gerhard	Knappmeyer, Maria Gesina	K	
Ketter, Charles	5, Apr. 1852	Charles	Gallagher,	P	20
Ketterer, Joseph Ignatz	16, May 1859	Joseph	Birele, Luitgarda	F	
Ketterer, Maria Josephina	21, Mar. 1858	Joseph	Pigerer, Luitgarda	F	
Ketterer, Maria Louisa	2, July 1853	Nicolaus	Durst, Anna Maria	J	22
Ketterer, Sibilla	1, June 1857	Andreas	Dickman, Regina	D	86
Kettle, Mary Louise	13, Dec. 1859	Peter	Boyd, Susan	B	85
Kettle, Robert Emmett	2, Aug. 1857	Robert?	Boyle, Susan	B	47
Kettler, Anna Maria	27, Dec. 1855	J. Heinrich	Schaber, Anna Maria	D	49
Kettler, Anna Maria Louisa	20, Sept 1858	J. Heinrich	Schaf, Maria	D	119
Kettler, Bernardina Elisabeth	6, July 1851	Carl	Schroeder, M.A. Elis.	L	
Kettler, Johan Gerhard	9, Sept 1852	Gerhard R	Schipper, Margaretha	L	
Kettler, Johan Heinrich	8, Sept 1854	Carl	Schroeder, Elisabeth	L	
Kettler, Louisa	2, Mar. 1856	Sebastian	----, Maria	J	34
Keultz, Catherine	6, June 1852	Peter	---rey, Winefred	P	22

Name of Child	Date of Baptism	Father	Mother	Church	Page
Keusch, Wilhelm	26, May 1858	Wilhelm	----, ----	D	112
Keuter, Anna Maria Rosa Euphemia	26, Oct. 1858	Herman T.	Honigfort, Anna Maria	L	
Keuter, Johan Herman Heinrich	13, Feb. 1856	Theodor	Honigfort, Maria Anna	L	
Keuter, Margaretha Rosina	25, Dec. 1857	Georg	Guetlein, Barbara	F	
Keutz, Bernard Heinrich	15, June 1856	B. Heinrich	Hüneman, Elisabeth	K	
Keutz, Heinrich Ludwig	31, Aug. 1855	B. Heinrich	----, Elisabeth	K	
Keutz, Johan Bernard	6, Jan. 1854	B. Herman	Ferneding, Elisabeth	K	
Keutz, Johan Herman	11, Oct. 1857	Herman	Ferneding, Elisabeth	K	
Keutz, Margaretha Elisabeth	20, Dec. 1859	Herman	Ferneding, Elisabeth	K	
Kevecordes, Helena Francisca	19, Sept 1852	Theodor	Mueller, C. Carolina	F	
Kevecordes, Wilhelm Theodor	24, Sept 1854	Theodor	Mueller, Carolina	F	
Kevil, Thomas	20, Mar. 1853	Dominick	Cullen, Mary	V	2
Kevil, Winefred	9, Mar. 1856	Dominick	Cullin, Mary	V	30
Kewering, Anna Maria	4, Apr. 1850	Herman	Brueggemann, Maria	C	
Key--, Helen	8, Jan. 1854	William	Butler, Catherine	P	64
Keys, George	27, Nov. 1852	George	Diller, Ann	B	276
Keys, John	7, Mar. 1856	George	Dillon, Ann	P	172
Keys, Thomas	9, May 1854	George	Dillon, Ann	P	81
K---gh, Michael	16, June 1850	William	Whelan, Elizabeth	B	204
K---gh, Thomas	16, June 1850	William	Whelan, Elizabeth	B	204
Kibbs, Bernard Joseph	6, Jan. 1855	Joseph	Overmatt, Maria	F	
Kick, Anna Margaretha	30, Oct. 1853	J. Bernard	Kramer, Anna Margaretha	D	412
Kick, Maria Elisabeth	30, Dec. 1857	J. Bernard	Kramer, Margaretha	D	101
Kieber, Francisca	19, Nov. 1854	Adam	Oehri, Ursula	D	22
Kieber, Johan	8, Feb. 1857	Adam	Oehry, Ursula	D	78
Kieber, Johan Ludwig	5, Dec. 1852	Adam	Oehri, Maria Ursula	D	359
Kieber, Maria Barbara	2, Mar. 1851	Adam	Oehri, Ursula	D	256
Kiefer, Ferdinand August	26, Dec. 1858	Ferdinand	Steinführer, Catharina	D	127
Kiefer, Francis August	23, Aug. 1857	Ferdinand	Steinfihrer, Catharina	D	93
Kiefer, Francis Joseph	4, Jan. 1857	Georg	Stork, Coelestina	D	76
Kiefer, George Joseph	24, Dec. 1858	George	Hoetzlern, Elisabeth	H	
Kiefer, Jacob	20, June 1852	Adolph	Lindi, Maria	J	16
Kiefer, Johan Andreas	19, Dec. 1858	Georg	Stork, Coelestina	D	126
Kiefer, Joseph	2, Dec. 1851	Ignatius	Schoebele, Catharina	F	
Kiefer, Louisa	22, Apr. 1855	Ignatius	Schewne, Catharina	F	
Kiefer, Maria	12, Mar. 1858	Ignatius	Schevene, Catharina	F	
Kiefler, Francis Seraph	2, Sept 1855	George	----, Elisabeth	H	
Kiefmeier, Johan Joseph	6, June 1858	J. Joseph	Niemeier, Bernardina	L	
Kiefmeyer, Johan Herman	20, Apr. 1854	Joseph	Niemeyer, Catharina	L	
Kiefmeyer, Maria Engel	22, Oct. 1856	Joseph	Niemeyer, Bernardina	L	
Kieger, Carolina	14, Apr. 1857	Arnold	Bussart, Margaretha	D	82
Kiel, Carolina	18, Apr. 1858	Jacob	Rich, Maria	C	
Kiel, Joseph	25, May 1856	Jacob	Rich, Anna M.	C	
Kientz, Francis	26, Oct. 1856	Andreas	Kistner, Louisa	D	70
Kientz, Joseph	5, May 1850	Andreas	Kistner, Louisa	D	212
Kientz, Louisa	19, Jan. 1854	Andreas	Kistner, Louise	C	
Kieny, Godofried	15, July 1855	Sebastian	Gumly, Magdalena	Q	9
Kienz, Johanna Rosa	27, Mar. 1859	Andreas	Kistner, Louisa	C	
Kienzler, Maria Louisa	24, Feb. 1856	Ferdinand	Duffner, Judith	C	
Kiernan, Julianna	12, Apr. 1857	James	Nolan, Mary	B	43
Kiernan, Terence	13, Jan. 1850	Thomas	Dougherty, Mary J.	B	194
Kiernan, William	18, Dec. 1858	Bernard	Reynolds, Ann	B	68
Kierns, Mary J.	6, May 1851		adult	B	232
Kiersey, Lawrence	16, Dec. 1852	John	----, Mary	M	
Kiez, Francis Ignatius	31, Oct. 1858	Richard	Fanz, Paulina	T	
Kiggen, Heinrich Adam	1, May 1853	Nicolaus	Schoen, Josephina	F	
Kiggin, Josephine Angela	4, Apr. 1852	Nicholas	Shane, Josephine	B	255
Kihn, Johan Herman	6, Feb. 1858	J. Gerhard	Klempering, Wilhelmina	N	
Kihne, Johan Bernard	27, June 1856	Johan	Wilhelmy, Wilhelmina	N	

Name of Child	Date of Baptism	Father	Mother	Church	Page
Kihner, Carl Ludwig	27, Mar. 1853	Jacob	Kihner, Louisa	D	378
Ki---ich, Caecilia Rosalia	18, Oct. 1858	Aloysius	Griess, Elisabeth	D	122
Kilb, Carolina Victoria	5, Mar. 1854	Johan	Hofreider, Maria Anna	D	6
Kilby, William James	12, Dec. 1859	William	Keatty, Margaret	B	85
Kilcary, Edward	5, June 1851	Patrick	----, Mary	E	313
Kilcoyn, Mary Ann	12, Feb. 1854	Patrick	Gaffney, Mary	B	309
Kilcoyne, Bridget	22, Feb. 1857	Patrick	Gafney, Mary	V	37
Kilday, Mary Ann	1, July 1855	Patrick	Kane, Honora	E	297
Kildea, John	11, Sept 1859	John	Toohy, Hannah	P	295
Kildea, Mary Ann	5, Oct. 1857	John	Toohy, Hannah	P	**226**
Kildea, Thomas	20, Mar. 1856	John	Toohey, Hannah	P	173
Kilduff, Mary	8, Oct. 1852	Peter	Moran, Margaret	B	271
Kilduff, Peter	17, Oct. 1850	Peter	----, Margaret	E	255
Kilduff, Thomas	22, Nov. 1855	Peter	Moran, Margaret	B	22
Kilfellan, Ann	7, Feb. 1859	William	Corcoran, Margaret	P	274
Kilfellan, John	7, Sept 1853	William	Corcoran, Margaret	P	51
Kilfellan, William	15, Dec. 1854	William	Corcoran, Margaret	P	110
Kilfethan, Mary	18, Jan. 1857	William	Corcoran, Margaret	P	204
Kilgallin, Mary	19, Apr. 1855	Daniel	McCabe, Ellen	B	14
Kilgaran, Daniel	1, Jan. 1857	Daniel	Cahill, Ellen	B	38
Kilgaren, Bridget	5, Aug. 1858	Daniel	McHale, Ellen	B	62
Kilgary, John	11, Apr. 1850	Patrick	Murray, Bridget	E	207
Kilkarey, Michael	3, May 1851	James	Clare-, Bridget	B	231
Kilkary, William	27, July 1852	Patrick	----, Mary	E	433
Kilkeary, Cecilia	14, Feb. 1854	Patrick	Dolphy, Mary	E	168
Kilkelly, Ann	7, Sept 1856	Patrick	Kennedy, Margaret	P	190
Kilkelly, Catherine	29, May 1853	Edward	Martin, Margaret	P	42
Kilkelly, James	16, Sept 1857	Patrick	Kennedy, Margaret	B	49
Kilkelly, James Joseph	8, Apr. 1855	Edward	Martin, Margaret	T	
Kilkelly, Mary Helen	17, June 1857	Edward	Martin, Margaret	T	
Kilkelly, Timothy	13, Apr. 1851	Edward	Martin, Margaret	B	229
Kilkenny, John	3, July 1852	Anthony	Robertson, Bridget	B	262
Kilkenny, Mary	26, May 1854	Edward	----, Joanne	E	193
Kilkenny, Patrick	18, Apr. 1852	Patrick	Meagher, Bridget	E	404
Kilkerry, Margaret	6, Jan. 1856	James	Clear, Bridget	E	335
Killbright, Mary	19, Sept 1852	John	Waldron, Catherine	B	270
Killeran, James	23, Mar. 1851	James	Hanley, Ann	B	227
Killeran, James	31, Oct. 1852	Michael	Patton, Margaret	B	273
Killerean, Michael	16, Dec. 1855	Thomas	Conroy, Ann	P	163
Killi, Anton Pat.	28, June 1850	Vincent	Gratt, Susanna	D	219
Killian, Adam	23, May 1858	Jacob	Staet, Barbara	D	111
Killian, John	21, June 1854	Michael	Moran, Bridget	B	1
Killian, John	27, Feb. 1853	Thomas	Moran, Sabina	E	67
Killian, Joseph	17, July 1853	Jacob	Stet, Barbara	D	395
Killian, Luke	31, Oct. 1858	Michael	Moran, Bridget	B	66
Killian, Patrick	23, Jan. 1855	Edward	Earley, Catherine	E	259
Killian, Patrick	7, Dec. 1851	Thomas	Moran, Sabina	E	364
Killian, Theresa Elisabeth	29, Sept 1856	Andreas	--ensch, M.	D	68
Killian, Thomas	17, Jan. 1855	Thomas	Moran, Sabina	E	257
Killigan, Thaddeus	26, Feb. 1852	John	Lungan, Catherine	E	385
Killoran, Margaret	26, Jan. 1851	Thomas	Kenny, Mary	E	279
Killoran, Michael	8, Mar. 1854	James	Hanly, Ann	P	73
Killroy, Mary Helen	21, June 1857	Thomas	Conroy, Ann	Q	22
Kilmeyer, Johanna Theresa	8, Aug. 1858	Joseph	Gerke, Etha	K	
Kilone, Michael	10, Aug. 1857	Michael	Pattan, M.	E	473
Kiloran, Thomas	5, Jan. 1851	John	----, Susan	E	274
Kilroy, Bridget	11, Feb. 1853	Patrick	Burk, Honora	E	61
Kilroy, James	10, Aug. 1857	Patrick	Davy, Mary	V	40
Kilroy, Mary Ann	20, Nov. 1859	John	Murphy, Bridget	B	84

Name of Child	Date of Baptism	Father	Mother	Church	Page
Kilroy, Mary Ann	30, Apr. 1857	Patrick	----, Honora	E	450
Kilroy, Thomas	26, Aug. 1855	Patrick	----, Honora	E	310
Kilty, Mary	16, Feb. 1850	Patrick	McCormick, Margaret	E	197
Kimmes, Magdalena	3, Nov. 1853	Melchior	Schulmerich, Margaretha	D	413
Kinan, Ellen	27, Sept 1857	Francis	Walsh, Atty	E	482
Kindel, Caecilia	29, May 1859	Gabriel	Herkommer, Maria Anna	T	
Kindel, Georg Johan	4, Mar. 1855	Gabriel	Herkman, Maria Anna	D	30
Kindel, Maria Anna	11, June 1856	Gabriel	Herkman, Maria Anna	D	60
Kindel, Maria Margaretha	15, July 1858	Georg	Keble, Margaretha	A	
Kinder, Elisabeth	31, Aug. 1856	Johan	Wellman, Apollonia	A	
Kindl, Joseph	6, Jan. 1850	Simon	Lintner, Ursula	D	198
Kindle, Rudolph	7, Aug. 1859	Michael	Zeil, Blandina	C	
Kine, Catherine	9, July 1859	Patrick	Mullen, Bridget	E	638
King, Ann	29, May 1856	Patrick	----, Mary	E	370
King, Anna Maria	19, Aug. 1853	John	Dewald, Maria	D	401
King, Bridget	29, Aug. 1852	James	----, Mary	B	269
King, Catherine	25, July 1856	James	Connelly, Mary	E	384
King, Catherine	16, Aug. 1857	Michael	Howall, Mary Ann	P	220
King, Charlotte Louise	25, Feb. 1859		adult	B	71
King, David	27, June 1857	Robert	McCoy, Margaret	B	46
King, Elisabeth	6, Jan. 1853	Joseph	W----, Catharina	D	363
King, Elisabeth	8, Feb. 1852	Patrick	Pohlen, Catherine	Q	2
King, Eliza	17, Mar. 1854	Joseph	Whealan, Mary	E	176
King, Emily Louise	14, May 1854	John	----, Elizabeth	M	
King, James	30, Dec. 1854	William	Miles, Ellen	E	250
King, John	18, June 1854	David	----, ----	U	
King, John	16, Mar. 1851	Joseph	Whelan, Mary	E	291
King, John	12, July 1855	Peter	----, Nancy	E	299
King, Margaret	26, June 1853	Alexander	----, Ann	B	294
King, Margaret	23, May 1854	Patrick	Bohlen, Catherine	Q	4
King, Mary	8, Feb. 1852	Patrick	Pohlen, Catherine	Q	2
King, Mary	10, Apr. 1853	Robert	Lonnergin, Catherine	B	288
King, Mary Angela	12, July 1857	James	McGlone, Mary Ann	P	217
King, Mary Ann	12, Jan. 1851	James	----, Mary	E	275
King, Mary Ann	29, June 1854	James	Camble, Ann	E	202
King, Mary Ann	27, Sept 1858	Michael	Howell, Mary Ann	P	262
King, Mary Ann	14, Feb. 1859	Robert	McKoy, Margaret	B	71
King, Mary Ann	29, June 1856	James J.	McGlone, Mary	P	183
King, Mary Helen	1, Oct. 1854	James J.	----, Elizabeth Mary	E	228
King, Mary Julia	15, Aug. 1852	Joseph	----, Mary	E	5
King, Michael	29, Sept 1850	Michael	Anderson, Mary	B	215
King, Michael	9, May 1852	Michael L.	----, Ellen	E	411
King, Michael Gabriel	30, Jan. 1853	Thomas	McDonough, Sarah	B	282
King, Sarah Elizabeth	29, Oct. 1850	----	----, ----	E	258
King, William	12, Dec. 1858	G. Heinrich	Elfers, M. Anna	C	
Kinker, Johan Bernard	25, May 1856	Heinrich	Elfers, Maria	C	
Kinker, Johan Francis	3, Sept 1850	J. Heinrich	Lintmeier, Anna Maria	J	6
Kinker, Johan Heinrich	3, Apr. 1859	J. David	Meyer, Catharina	X	
Kinkle, John Adam	27, Feb. 1859	Johan	Brausch, Elisabeth	D	132
Kinkler, Helena	28, Dec. 1851	Michael	Hackmann, Catharina	C	
Kinne, Maria Angela	27, Nov. 1854	James	----, Mary	M	
Kinsella, Bridget	29, Jan. 1854	James P.	Tarelton, Helen	B	308
Kinsella, Catherine Agnes	24, Oct. 1852	James	----, Mary	M	
Kinsella, Lawrence	29, June 1856	James	----, Mary	M	
Kinsella, Martin	25, Mar. 1855	Michael	----, Ann	M	
Kinsella, Mary	2, Mar. 1851	James P.	Dunn, Helen	B	225
Kinsella, Rosanne	23, May 1852	James P.	Torlington, Helen	B	264
Kinsella, Theresa	23, May 1858	James	----, Mary	M	
Kinsella, Thomas	6, Mar. 1853	Patrick	Lucas, Catherine	E	68
Kinsley, Catherine					

Name of Child	Date of Baptism	Father	Mother	Church	Page
Kinzbach, Emma	1, Jan. 1856	Georg	----, Maria	D	50
Kipgen, Adelheid	9, Jan. 1855	Michael	Stumpf, Catharina	L	
Kipgen, William	6, Nov. 1853	Michael	Stumpf, Catharina	F	
Kipp, John	16, Sept 1855	John	Kuderer, Magdalena	Q	10
Kipp, Maria Elisabeth	4, Nov. 1857	Joseph	Avermull, Maria	F	
Kippenberger, Anna Catharina Fransica	30, May 1852	Philipp	Corten, Maria	D	322
Kippenberger, Anna Louisa	25, Sept 1857	Jacob	L---, Louisa	D	95
Kippenberger, Catharina	30, May 1852	Philipp	Schneider, Margaretha	D	322
Kippenberger, Elisabeth	30, May 1852	Philipp	Corten, Maria	D	322
Kippenberger, Francisca	30, May 1852	Philipp	Corten, Maria	D	322
Kippenberger, Henrietta	30, May 1852	Philipp	Corten, Maria	D	322
Kippenbrock, Anna Elisabeth	20, Nov. 1856	Bernard	Exler, Elisabeth	L	
Kippenbrock, Johan Bernard	24, Nov. 1858	Bernard	Exler, Elisabeth	L	
Kippenbrock, Johan Bernard	25, Mar. 1859	Johan	Punt, Josephina	L	
Kippenbrock, Maria Elisabeth	12, Mar. 1855	Bernard	Exler, Elisabeth	L	
Kippes, Johan	18, July 1852	Johan	Sauer, Barbara	D	329
Kippner, Theresa Mathilda	6, July 1856	Jacob	Hein, Louisa	F	
Kirbeck, Bridget	27, Jan. 1854	Patrick	Hogan, Honora	B	308
Kirby, Daniel	25, Aug. 1856	Daniel	Gaho, Mary	V	36
Kirby, Honora	1, Apr. 1851	Jeremiah	Kirby, Margaret	B	228
Kirby, Mary Ann	4, July 1851	Daniel	----, Mary	E	320
Kirby, Michael	3, Apr. 1854	James	Foley, Winefred	B	312
Kirby, William	1, Jan. 1854	Daniel	Rayheart, Mary	E	156
Kirch, Anna Maria	6, Sept 1853	Godfried	Koester, Margaretha	D	405
Kircher, Catharina Theresa	27, July 1851	Adam	Imm, Catharina	L	
Kircher, Ferdinand Philipp	20, Sept 1857	Carl	Brum, Ernestina	D	94
Kircher, Francis S.	2, June 1850	Francis	Siefert, Monica	C	
Kircher, Johan Martin	22, Aug. 1852	Francis	Siefort, Monica	C	
Kircher, Michael	7, Apr. 1850	Adam	Imm, Catharina	L	
Kirchmer, Johan	27, Feb. 1851	Jacob	Steinbron, Margaretha	L	
Kirchner, Anna Maria	17, Apr. 1854	Michael	Ams, Anna Maria	C	
Kirdolf, Catharina	21, May 1857	Johan A.	Poritz, Margaretha	F	
Kirk, Elizabeth	9, Feb. 1851	James	Winters, Elizabeth	E	282
Kirk, Elizabeth	2, May 1852	James	Winters, Elizabeth	E	408
Kirk, Johan	16, Dec. 1857		adult - 25 yeas old	F	
Kirk, Thomas	21, Dec. 1851	Thomas	Gill, Honora	B	247
Kirken, Michael	18, Aug. 1854	Michael	----, ----	B	4
Kirkpatrick William	11, July 1856		adult - 24 years old	B	31
Kirkpatrick, John	26, June 1859	William	Gorman, Joanne	E	634
Kirkpatrick, William	5, July 1857	William	Gorman, Joanne	E	463
Kirner, Josephina	23, Jan. 1859	Seraphin	Mohr, Anna Maria	D	129
Kirschner, Maria Amalia	29, July 1855	Johan	Zaepfel, Rosina	G	
Kirschner, Philipp	12, Oct. 1859	Johan	Zepfel, Rosina	G	
Kirschner, Theresa	12, Oct. 1859	Johan	Zepfel, Rosina	G	
Kirstein, Anton	31, Dec. 1854	Anton	Forster, Maria	D	25
Kirstein, Margaretha Anna	14, Sept 1850	Anton	Foerster, Maria Caecilia	D	232
Kirstein, Maria Anna	31, Oct. 1852	Anton	Förster, Maria Anna Caecilia	D	355
Kischner, Rosina	29, Mar. 1857	Joseph	Jaeger, Maria	D	81
Kisker, Anna Gertrud Elisabeth	5, May 1854	Heinrich	Hanke, Theresa	C	
Kisker, Anna Maria	14, June 1851	Heinrich	Hanker, Theresa	C	
Kisker, Anton Heinrich	15, Apr. 1856	Heinrich	Hanken, Theresa	C	
Kisker, Maria Elisabeth	16, Feb. 1859	Heinrich	Hanke, Theresa	C	
Kisselmacher, Anna Maria	15, May 1859	Georg	Fritzinger, Anna Maria	D	138
Kist, Anna	27, Nov. 1859	Bernard	Wagner, Catharina	T	
Kister, John	25, May 1855	Mark	Carrell, Regina	N	
Kisterer, Johan	4, Nov. 1856	Wilhelm	Lux, Magdalena	F	
Kisting, Anna Maria Clara	23, Feb. 1858	Herman B.	Reckers, Anna Elis.	L	
Kisting, Anna Maria Elisabeth	25, Jan. 1856	Bernard	Reckes, Anna. Elisabeth	L	
Kistner, Aloysius	12, Dec. 1850	Joseph	Jaeger, Maria Anna	D	246

Name of Child	Date of Baptism	Father	Mother	Church	Page
Kistner, Carl	18, Dec. 1859	Wilhelm	Lux, Magdalena	F	
Kistner, Emma Catharina	7, Mar. 1858	Godfried	Schmidt, Maria	D	106
Kistner, Johan Adam	11, Jan. 1857	Johan	Friedmann, Rufina	F	
Kistner, Johan Gregor	24, Mar. 1850	Theodor	Schell, Maria Anna	C	
Kistner, John Louis	21, May 1854	Theodor	----, Mary	H	
Kistner, Magdalena	5, July 1858	Wilhelm	Lueke, Magdalena	F	
Kistner, Maria Barbara	16, Feb. 1856	Theodor	----, Maria Anna	H	
Kistner, Wilhelm	28, Nov. 1852	Joseph	Jäger, Maria Anna	D	358
Kistner, Wilhelm	21, Nov. 1854	Wilhelm	Lux, Magdalena	F	
Kistner, Wilhelm Friedrich	7, Nov. 1858	Johan	Friedman, Rosina	D	123
Kites, Ambrose	26, June 1853	Joseph	----, Mary	E	102
Kitt, Maria Appolonia	28, Dec. 1851	Balthasar	Durein, Elisabeth	D	299
Kitt, Maria Elisabeth	21, May 1854	Balthasar	Durein, Elisabeth	D	11
Kitt, Maria Elisabeth	31, Mar. 1856	Balthasar	Durein, Elisabeth	D	55
Kitte, Anna Elisabeth	3, Jan. 1859	Bernard	Menemann, Catharina	C	
Kitte, Elisabeth	29, July 1851	Johan	Forst, Maria	C	
Kitte, Heinrich	31, Oct. 1858	Johan	Fuchs, Maria	C	
Kitte, Johan Bernard	21, July 1853	Johan	Voss, Catharina	C	
Kitte, Johan Heinrich	14, Feb. 1851	Heinrich	Fibbe, Elisabeth	C	
Kitte, Maria Elisabeth	12, Sept 1853	J. Bernard	Fibbe, Elisabeth	C	
Kitte, Marianna	5, Nov. 1856	Bernard	Mennemann, M. Catharina	F	
Kittel, Alexander	25, Dec. 1858	Alexander	Beil, Catharina	D	126
Klaap, Adam	10, Aug. 1856	Philipp	Muller, Josephina	K	
Klab, Adam	14, July 1852	J. Adam	Weiss, Maria Anna	D	329
Klab, Johan Wilhelm	14, July 1852	J. Adam	Weiss, Maria Anna	D	329
Klamp, Francis Jacob	28, Aug.1859	Jacob	Buss---, Carolina	D	145
Klaphage, Gerhard Heinrich	24, Dec. 1852	J. Gerhard	VonderWellen, M. Catharina	A	
Klaphake, Johan Heinrich	22, Aug. 1859	G. Heinrich	VonderWellen, Catharina	A	
Klaphake, Maria Elisabeth	19, Apr. 1856	Gerhard	VanderWellen, Catharina	A	
Klar, Joseph Ignatz	15, Sept 1850	Ignatius	Fruh, Christina	C	
Klär, Maria	21, Nov. 1852	Georg	Vetter, Maria	J	18
Klarenaar, Anna	1, Apr. 1856	J.F.	Goris, Mathilda	C	
Klarenaar, Anna Maria Mathilda	4, Mar. 1853	Johan	Goris, Mathilda	C	
Klarenaar, Johan Ludwig	4, Mar. 1853	Johan	Goris, Mathilda	C	
Klarenaar, Theodor	18, Jan. 1852	J. Francis	Goris, Mathilda	C	
Klarenaar, Wilhelmina	27, Oct. 1850	J.F.	Goris, Mechtiletis	L	
Klarenaer, Ida Louise	5, July 1859	Charles H.	Norris, Margaret	B	77
Klarer, Paul	9, May 1852	Wendel	Eha, Walburga	C	
Klas, Maria Anna	6, Feb. 1859	Carl	Ludwig, Anna Maria	D	131
Klasen, Johan Heinrich	25, Feb. 1855	Herman	Rump, Helena	C	
Klasen, Johan Herman H.	10, Dec. 1858	J. Heinrich	Rump, Helena	C	
Klasmeier, Ferdinand Edward	1, Nov. 1853	Friedrich L.	Darlinghaus, Maria Elisabeth	A	
Klasmeier, Maria Elisabeth Carolina	3, Dec. 1851	Friedrich L.	Darlinghaus, Elisabeth	A	
Klass, Magdalena	20, Sept 1857	Francis	Ludwig, Anna	D	95
Klassen, Johan Heinrich	7, Mar. 1850	Herman H.	Rump, Helena	C	
Klassen, Maria Josephina	15, Aug. 1852	Herman H.	Rump, Helena	C	
Klatt, Ludwig	4, Apr. 1858	Joseph	Erbert, Theresa	K	
Klaub, Maria Esther	3, Sept 1850		adult	F	
Klaus, Alexander August	26, May 1850	Francis	Groter, Mina	A	
Klaus, Anna Friedrica	20, Jan. 1855	Dominick	Hoppenjans, Anna Catharina	A	
Klaus, Catharina Elisabeth	18, Sept 1852	Dominick	Hoppenjans, Catharina	A	
Klaus, Christina	12, Jan. 1851	Andreas	Seemüller, Eva	D	248
Klaus, Johan Dietrich	2, Oct. 1851	Bernard	Trentmann, Catharina	C	
Klaus, Maria Agnes	1, Aug. 1854	Bernard	Trentmann, Anna Maria	F	
Klaus, Maria Anna	26, July 1850	Dominick	Hoppengans, A. Catharina	A	
Klaus, Maria Catharina	19, Dec. 1852	J. Bernard	Trentmann, Elisabeth	F	
Klauser, Margaretha	20, Aug. 1854	Martin	Prisch, Anna Maria	Q	5
Klausing, Bernard Clemens	25, Dec. 1850	Clemens	Holther, Margaretha Elisabeth	K	
Klausing, Bernard Clemens	10, July 1854	Joseph	Rabe, Catharina	K	

Name of Child	Date of Baptism	Father	Mother	Church	Page
Klausing, Bernardina Philomena	30, May 1850	Heinrich	Upheuer, Gertrud	K	
Klausing, Catharina Elisabeth	6, Sept 1852	Bernard	Rude, Anna Maria	K	
Klausing, Clemens Herman Bernard	28, Aug. 1859	Clemens	Holthaus, Margaret	C	
Klausing, Johan Heinr. August Lawrence	29, Aug. 1858	Johan	Rabe, Catharina	K	
Klausing, Joseph Heinrich	11, June 1856	Joseph	Rabe, Catharina Maria	K	
Klausing, M. Catharina Clementina	5, Sept 1852	Clemens	Holthaus, Margaretha	C	
Klausing, Margaretha Catharina	14, Sept 1854	Clemens	Holthaus, Margaretha	C	
Klausmaeier, Johan	28, Dec. 1856	Friedrich	Kleis, Catharina	D	75
Klausmeier, Carl August Wilhelm	28, May 1853	Wilhelm	Strobel, Emilia	D	387
Klausmeier, Emma Louisa Carolina	12, Sept 1854	Wilhelm	Strobel, Amelia	D	17
Klausmeier, Oscar Wilhelm Ludwig	16, July 1856	Wilhelm	Strobel, Emilia	D	63
Klausmeyer, Alfred Wilhelm	25, Nov. 1858	Wilhelm	Strobel, Emilia	C	
Klausmeyer, Anna Maria Henrietta	14, Aug. 1852	Friedrich	Kleis, Catharina	D	343
Klaverkamp, Gerhard Joseph	17, Feb. 1852	Joseph	Rakel, A. Adelheid	L	
Klebe, Maria Josephina	28, Apr. 1850	Wenceslaus	Stocker, Sarah Louise	C	
Kleber, Jacob	3, July 1857	Jacob	Hetesheimer, Elisabeth	D	89
Kleber, Johan	13, Nov. 1858	Jacob	Hettesheim, Elisabeth	C	
Kleber, Margaretha Magdalena	12, Apr. 1854	Jacob	Heteshaimer, Elisabeth	W	3
Kleckner, Jacob	2, Dec. 1855	Johan	Weller, Catharina	L	
Kleckner, Thomas Edward	31, Aug. 1851	Balthasar	Vogel, Catharina	K	
Klee, Elisabeth	22, Aug. 1858	Johan	Matt, Apollonia	K	
Klee, Johan	8, Aug. 1854	Johan	Maack, Apollonia	C	
Klee, Johan	27, Dec. 1855	Johan	Mack, Apollonia	C	
Klee, Johan Theodor	13, June 1850	Nicolaus	Hardig, Margaretha	L	
Klee, Rudolph	8, Aug. 1854	Johan	Maack, Apollonia	C	
Kleeforten, Maria Catharina	29, Dec. 1857	Heinrich	Lange, Angela	C	
Kleeman, (boy)	8, Dec. 1857	J. Theobald	Fey, Crescentia	W	21
Kleeman, Anton	10, Dec. 1854	Heinrich	Woerman, Anna Maria	D	23
Kleeman, Joseph	23, May 1852	J. Theobald	Fey, Crescentia	D	320
Kleeman, Louisa Catharina	12, Mar. 1854	J. Theobald	Fey, Crescentia	W	2
Kleeman, Magdalena	25, Mar. 1856	J. Theobald	Fey, Crescentia	W	12
Kleemann, Catharina	28, May 1857	Heinrich	Wehrmann, Anna Maria	F	
Kleemann, Maria Elisabeth Anna	1, May 1859	Anton	Westrich, Catharina	F	
Kleemann, Marianna	27, May 1859	Heinrich	Woermann, Anna	F	
Kleibecker, Johan Joseph	3, Sept 1856	Anton	Flotemesch, Maria	A	
Kleiber, Caspar	17, Oct. 1850	Joseph	Zwislein, Margaretha	D	238
Kleiböcker, Bernard Anton	4, Jan. 1859	Anton	Flottemesch, Maria	A	
Kleibocker, Maria Elisabeth	1, Aug. 1858	Joseph	Haverbeck, Maria Anna	L	
Kleiböker, Georg Heinrich	17, June 1854	J. Anton	Flotemersch, Maria Gertrud	A	
Kleier, Maria Elisabeth	5, Sept 1852	Gerhard	Recamp, Catharina	F	
Klein, Anna Maria	14, Aug. 1851	Bernard	Torbeck, Gertrud	A	
Klein, Catharina	29, May 1853	David	Rade, Maria	D	387
Klein, Catharina	11, Nov. 1851	Johan	Reichert, Theresa	D	291
Klein, Conrad August	29, Apr. 1855	Peter	Stanz, Anna Maria	D	34
Klein, Elizabeth	3, Apr. 1854	Patrick	Moore, Ann	P	77
Klein, Francis Joseph	7, Aug. 1859	Francis D.	Collet, Barbara	D	144
Klein, Friedrich	24, Mar. 1853	Georg	Wilhelm, Walburga	D	377
Klein, Georg	17, July 1857	Georg	Wilhelm, Walburga	D	90
Klein, Georg	8, Mar. 1859	Georg	Wilhelm, Walburga	F	
Klein, Helena	31, July 1859	Nicolaus	Merl, Gertrud	D	143
Klein, Jacob Eduard	3, Dec. 1854	Anton	Schue, Catharina	A	
Klein, Johan	16, July 1850	G. Peter	Krock, Margaretha	D	223
Klein, Johan	26, Oct. 1856	G. Peter	Kroll, Margaretha	D	70
Klein, Johan	16, July 1855	Georg	Wilhelm, Walburga	D	38
Klein, Johan Adam	1, Feb. 1852	Georg	Knochner, Margaretha	D	305
Klein, Johan Francis	11, Mar. 1855	Francis	Collet, Anna Barbara	D	30
Klein, Johan Georg	14, Nov. 1859	Francis	Collet, Barbara	D	150
Klein, Johan Herman	4, June 1851	J. Herman	Wichman, Maria Elisabeth	K	
Klein, Johan Peter	6, July 1856	Francis	Collet, Barbara	D	62

Name of Child	Date of Baptism	Father	Mother	Church	Page
Klein, Johanna	13, July 1857	Francis	Collet, Barbara	D	90
Klein, Juliana Rosina	23, Aug. 1857	Francis D	Braun, Elisabeth	C	
Klein, Magdalena	8, Dec. 1850	Nicolaus	Merl, Gertrud	D	245
Klein, Margaretha	10, Oct. 1852	Nicolaus	Merl, Gertrud	D	351
Klein, Margaretha Gertrud	25, Nov. 1855	Nicolaus	Maerl, Gertrud	D	47
Klein, Maria	2, Mar. 1851	David	Rad, Maria Anna	D	255
Klein, Maria Catharina	11, Sept 1853	Francis	Collet, Anna Barbara	D	405
Klein, Maria Margaretha	11, Dec. 1851	Friedrich	----, Walburga	D	296
Klein, Mathilda Barbara	6, May 1859	Georg P.	Knocher, Margaretha	D	137
Klein, Nicolaus	30, Aug. 1857	Nicolaus	Mürl, Gertrud	D	93
Klein, Otto	20, Nov. 1853	G. Peter	Keschler, Margaretha	D	416
Klein, Peter	18, Aug. 1850	Heinrich	Buegelberger, M.	C	
Klein, Philipp	25, Aug. 1851	Caspar	Schulz, Elisabeth	D	279
Kleinback, Johan Adam	26, Oct. 1856	Joseph	Nussbaum, Regina	D	70
Kleinbeck, Barbara	6, Aug. 1854	Joseph	Nussbaum, Regina	D	15
Kleinbeck, Joseph	2, Nov. 1852	Joseph	Nussbaum, Regina	D	355
Kleine, Bernard Heinrich Aloysius	7, Aug. 1858	Heinrich	Schoeppe, Elisabeth	C	
Kleine, Carl Peter	5, Sept 1856	Johan	Wegman, Carolina	A	
Kleine, Carolina	15, Feb. 1855	Meinrad	----, Magdalena	F	
Kleine, Catharina Friedrica	20, Oct. 1853	Bernard	Torbecke, Gertrud	A	
Kleine, Daniel Edward	28, Mar. 1853	Heinrich	----, ----	C	
Kleine, Fortuna Magdalena	4, Sept 1852	Herman	Kestner, Dorothea	C	
Kleine, Francis Heinrich	10, July 1853	Friedrich	Linnenkugel, Elisabeth	N	14
Kleine, Francis Joseph	9, Nov. 1856	Anton	Schue, Catharina	A	
Kleine, Friedrich	28, Mar. 1853	Heinrich	----, ----	C	
Kleine, Georg	28, Mar. 1853	Heinrich	----, ----	C	
Kleine, Heinrich Anton	28, July 1854	J. Herman	Wigman, Elisabeth	K	
Kleine, Herman Heinrich	1, May 1850	----	----, ----	L	
Kleine, Johan Friedrich	19, Sept 1850	Heinrich	----, Maria	H	
Kleine, Johan Heinrich	12, June 1850	Johan	Lening, Maria	L	
Kleine, Johan Nep. Joseph Alphonse	25, Aug. 1855	Friedrich	Linnenkugel, Elisabeth	N	
Kleine, Joseph	17, Feb. 1855	Meinrad	Buerkle, Josepha	F	
Kleine, Maria Anna Josephina	3, Nov. 1859	Friedrich	Linnenkugel, Elisabeth	N	
Kleine, Maria Edward Joseph	27, Aug. 1857	Friedrich	Linnenkugel, Elisabeth	N	
Kleine, Maria Elisabeth	21, Feb. 1851	Herman H.	Wittholter, M. Elisabeth	L	
Kleine, Maria Elisabeth Agnes	12, Jan. 1851	Friedrich	Linnenkugel, Maria Elisabeth	N	2
Kleine, Maria Veronica	4, Feb. 1854	Heinrich	Schepper, Elisabeth	C	
Kleine, Mary Elizabeth	12, Oct. 1853	Henry	----, Mary	H	
Kleine, Regina	5, Sept 1856	Johan	Wegman, Carolina	A	
Kleine, Sophia Catharina	16, Mar. 1856	Bernard	Torbeck, Gertrud	A	
Kleineberg, Anna Bernardina	27, July 1858	Theodor	Henssler, Bernardina	F	
Kleineberg, Carolina Francisca A.	12, Dec. 1853	Gerhard J.	Hengen, Anna Maria	F	
Kleineberg, Clara Regina	4, July 1856	Gerhard	Lampert, Elisabeth	F	
Kleineberg, Daniel Gerhard Herman	15, Feb. 1854	Gerhard T	Hinschlage, Bernardina	F	
Kleineberg, Elisabeth Bernardina	7, May 1852	Theodor	Hengster, Bernardina	F	
Kleineberg, Franz Herman	15, Nov. 1850	Theodor	Hengske, Bernardina	F	
Kleineberg, Herman	5, July 1859	Herman	Nuxoll, Sophia	F	
Kleineberg, Herman	10, Aug. 1850	Joseph	Henker, Anna Maria	F	
Kleineberg, Johan Dietrich	24, Sept 1857	J. Gerhard	Theders, Anna Gesina	F	
Kleineberg, Johan Gerhard Joseph	3, Apr. 1852	Gerhard J.	Hinken, Anna Maria	F	
Kleineberg, Joseph	15, July 1859	Gerhard	Tillich, Christina	F	
Kleineberg, Maria Barbara	16, Dec. 1855	Theodor	Hingslage, Bernardina	F	
Kleineberg, Theodor Filbert	11, Aug. 1854	Gerhard	Lampe, Maria Elisabeth	F	
Kleineberg, Xavier Joseph Gerhard	20, June 1852	Gerhard	Lampe, Elisabeth	F	
Kleinemann, Maria Anna	27, May 1857	Johan	Lehmkuhl, M. Catharina	C	
Kleiner, Bertha	8, July 1859	Fridolin	Birkle, Josephina	F	
Kleinfelder, Carl Heinrich	11, Mar. 1858	Michael	Huesmann, Elis. Gertrud	C	
Kleinfelter, Joseph Johan	26, Oct. 1851	Johan	----, Gertrud	K	
Kleinman, Georg	8, Mar. 1857	Wilhelm	Durr, Josephina	D	80

Name of Child	Date of Baptism	Father	Mother	Church	Page
Kleinman, Josephina Elisabeth	31, July 1859	Wilhelm	Döhl, Josephina	D	143
Kleinmann, Adolph Joseph	4, Oct. 1854	Johan	Lehmkuhl, Catharina	C	
Kleinmann, Angela Anna	1, Mar. 1851	Johan	Lehmkuhl, Catharina	C	
Kleinmann, Anna Maria Catharina	29, July 1853	Johan	Lehmkuhl, Catharina	C	
Kleinmann, Bernard	14, Apr. 1852	Johan	Lehmkuhl, Catharina	C	
Kleinmeier, Francisca Maria	20, Nov. 1852	Heinrich	Sanner, M.	F	
Kleinmeier, Johan Heinrich	8, Dec. 1854	Gerhard H.	Sander, Maria	F	
Kleinmeier, Philomena Luisa	15, Dec. 1850	Heinrich	Sander, Maria	A	
Kleinsandermann, Bernard	6, Dec. 1850	Francis	Rechtin, Elisabeth	C	
Kleinsandermann, Francis	31, Dec. 1853	Francis	Rechtin, Elisabeth	C	
Kleinsandermann, Franz	6, Jan. 1853	Heinrich	Kloenne, Maria Anna	L	
Kleintank, Herman	16, July 1854	Johan	Ostendorf, Sophia Maria	A	
Kleintank, Herman Joseph	12, May 1855	Anton	Messink, Adelheid	A	
Kleintank, Johan Heinrich	12, Jan. 1851	Johan	Ostendorf, Maria Sophia	A	
Kleintank, Lambert Wilhelm	15, Aug. 1857	Anton	Messing, Aleida	A	
Kleintank, Maria Magdalena	28, June 1858	Johan	Ostendorf, Sophia	A	
Kleintank, Philomena	26, Aug. 1852	Johan	Ostendorf, Sophia Catharina	A	
Kleit, Johan	27, Apr. 1851	Georg	Burgard, Augusta	C	
Klem, Elisabeth	23, Jan. 1859	Johan	Seitz, Johanna	T	
Klem, Johan Heinrich	14, Sept 1853	Florian	Ritter, Martha	A	
Klem, Michael	28, June 1857	John	Letz, Johanna	T	
Klemann, Anna Catharina	10, Feb. 1856	Anton	Weinrich, Catharina	F	
Klemann, Heinrich Everhard	19, Sept 1858	Friedrich	Ballmann, Anna Maria	L	
Klene, Johan Anton Bernard	17, Oct. 1856	J. Herman	Wiegmann, Elisabeth	L	
Klenke, Anna Elisabeth	21, July 1855	J. Heinrich	Trentmann, Elisabeth	L	
Klenke, Johan Heinrich	9, Jan. 1851	Heinrich	Trentmann, Elisabeth	C	
Klenke, Johan Heinrich	7, May 1859	J. Heinrich	Trentmann, Elisabeth	L	
Klenke, Maria Elisabeth	3, Aug. 1858	Friedrich	Bonhaus, Anna Sophia	T	
Klenke, Maria Elisabeth	14, June 1857	J. Heinrich	Trentmann, M. Elisabeth	L	
Klenke, Maria Engel	25, Dec. 1852	Heinrich	Trentmann, Elisabeth	L	
Klenn, Maria Juliana	14, Oct. 1855	Johan	Leitz, Johanna	F	
Klern, Roman	20, Jan. 1850	Roman	Weber, Magdalena	C	
Kleshan, Mary Ann	4, Jan. 1853	Thomas	McDonnell, Bridget	B	280
Kliebing, Elisabeth Francisca	14, Oct. 1857	G. Johan	Wilming, Maria Adelheid	N	
Kline, Catherine	19, Sept 1858	Francis	Cormick, Catherine	E	564
Kline, Francis	27, Apr. 1856	Francis	McCormick, Catherine	E	362
Klinepeter, Jerome	16, Jan. 1853	Josiah	Mudd, Caroline	E	54
Kling, Carl	23, June 1850	Heinrich	Haug, Maria Catharina	K	
Kling, Johan Georg	18, Sept 1853	J. Nepomuck	Hoffman, Catharina Dorothea	J	24
Kling, Johan Martin	14, Sept 1851	Johan	Hoffmann, Catharina	F	
Kling, Lawrence	11, Mar. 1855	Johan	Hoffman, Catharina	J	30
Kling, Maria Francisca	17, Jan. 1858	Johan	Hoffman, Catharina	J	44
Klingenberg, Elisabeth Carolina	31, Aug. 1859	Gerhard	Dudei, Gertrud	L	
Klingenberg, Elisabeth Johanna	14, Feb. 1858	J. Gerhard	Dudey, Gertrud A.	L	
Klingenberg, Johan Gerhard	20, May 1851	J. Heinrich	Kuhlmann, Theresa	L	
Klingenberg, M Margaretha Adelheid	13, Apr. 1853	Gerhard	Dudei, Gertrud	L	
Klinger, Anton	11, Sept 1859	Anton	Mo---, Magdalena	D	146
Klinger, Heinrich	31, Sept 1855	Georg	Alendorf, Christina	K	
Klinghamer, Anna Maria	10, Oct. 1857	H. Heinrich	Feldman, Elisabeth	N	
Klingler, Agnes	22, Mar. 1851	Georg	Aldorf, Christina	K	
Klingler, Georg	2, Jan. 1853	Georg	Huth, Christina	K	
Klingler, Jacob	6, Jan. 1850	Georg	----, Christina	K	
Klingler, Johan	2, Nov. 1857	Georg	Ahlenberg, Christina	K	
Klingler, Maria Anselina	14, Sept 1856	William	----, Mary	R	
Klinkenberg, Anna Carolina	26, Jan. 1855	J. Gerhard	Dudei, Gertrud A.	L	
Klinker, Bernard Heinrich	25, Dec. 1859	Bernard	Rademaker, Catharina	A	
Klinkhamer, Herman Heinrich	1, Mar. 1854	H. Heinrich	Feldman, Elisabeth	Q	4
Klinkhamer, Johan Heinrich	21, July 1859	Friedrich	Meyer, Anna Maria	K	
Klinkhammer, Heinrich Friedrich	15, Mar. 1856	Heinrich	Feldman, Elisabeth	Q	13

Name of Child	Date of Baptism	Father	Mother	Church	Page
Klins, Johan Gerhard Heinrich	18, July 1850	J. Heinrich	Wellinghof, Catharina	D	223
Klintemeier, Anna Margaretha	31, Mar. 1856	Johan H.	Roetgers, Anna Maria	F	
Klister, Anna Maria	13, Mar. 1857	Herman	Bickmann, Catharina	L	
Klister, Bernard Wilhelm Herman	13, Feb. 1859	Herman	Brockmann, Catharina	L	
Klister, Elisabeth Gertrud	13, Sept 1851	Herman	Schoten, Elisabeth	C	
Klister, Johan Gerhard	5, June 1853	Herman	Schaden, Elisabeth	C	
Klister, Josephina	13, Mar. 1857	Herman	Bickmann, Catharina	L	
Klitz, Anna Maria Elisabeth	11, Sept 1857	Heinrich	Hemmelgarn, Anna M.	L	
Klitz, Franz	23, Jan. 1855	Heinrich	Hemmelgarn, Elisabeth	L	
Klitz, Herman Heinrich	7, Sept 1859	Heinrich	Hemmelgarn, Elisabeth	C	
Klitz, Johan Anton	23, Aug. 1853	Heinrich	Hemmelgarn, Elis.	L	
Klitz, Johan Heinrich	5, Oct. 1852	Heinrich	Hemmelgarn, M. Elisabeth	L	
K---lmuth, Francis David	26, Aug. 1859	Johan	Collet, Helena	D	145
Klobb, Maria Elisabeth	12, Oct. 1852	Francis	Reidt, Elisabeth	L	
Klock, Ernst Heinrich	31, May 1857	J. Albert	Stembrink, Louisa	F	
Klock, Francis Xavier	9, May 1852	Johan	Klingler, Maria Magdalena	K	
Klock, Johan	20, Aug. 1854	Johan	Klingler, Magdalena	K	
Klock, Maria Anna	21, Aug. 1859	Albert	----, Louisa	J	52
Kloekner, Christian	21, May 1857	Johan	Weller, Catharina	L	
Kloekner, Johan	21, Sept 1853	Johan	Weller, Catharina	L	
Kloenne, Maria Adelheid	24, Jan. 1853	Johan H.	Lauenberg, Anna Maria	F	
Kloep, Anna Philomena	9, Aug. 1851	Johan	Geist, Emilia	L	
Kloke, Christina Louise	20, June 1852	J. Peter	Graf, Elisabeth	C	
Kloke, Christina Philomena	25, Oct. 1857	Peter	Graef, Elisabeth	C	
Kloke, Maria Helena	22, Apr. 1855	Peter	Graef, Elisabeth	C	
Kloman, Maria Anna	8, Nov. 1857	Johan	Kleman, Agnes	D	98
Klomann, Clara	18, Apr. 1858	Adam	Alfron, Elisabeth	F	
Klönne, Herman	12, July 1857	B.H.	Gausepohl, M.E.	A	
Klönne, Johan	5, June 1851	Bernard H.	Gausepohl, Catharina M.Elis.	A	
Klönne, Joseph	4, May 1853	Bernard H.	Gausepohl, Maria Elisabeth	A	
Klönne, Maria Anna	20, Sept 1854	B.H.	Gausepohl, Elisabeth	A	
Klopf, Catharina	10, Apr. 1859	Francis	Kessler, Catharina	D	135
Klopp, Catharina Elisabeth	7, Oct. 1857	Joseph	Mueller, Margaretha	D	96
Klopp, Jacob	22, Dec. 1858	Joseph	Müller, Margaretha	D	126
Klopp, Sebastian Adelbert	28, Dec. 1856	Johan	Klingler, Magdalena	K	
Kloppenburg, Maria Catharina Elis.	11, Dec. 1853	Johan H.	Hausfeld, Catharina E.	F	
Klopper, Wilhelm	8, Mar. 1857	Wilhelm	Niesel, Anna M.	L	
Kloppner, Augusta Maria Theresa	1, Nov. 1854		adult - 18 years old	H	
Klösener, Johan Heinrich	6, Jan. 1857	Heinrich	----, Maria	A	
Klosner?, Crescentia	10, Jan. 1857	Johan	----, Margaretha	D	76
Klössner, Joseph Adam	31, Oct. 1852	Heinrich	Reissner, Maria Anna	R	
Klosterman, Bernardina Elisabeth	25, Oct. 1857	Anton	Cotte, Maria Elisabeth	N	
Klosterman, Carl Anton	4, Sept 1853	C. Anton	Hardae, Maria	N	16
Klosterman, Francisca Rosalia	18, Dec. 1859	Heinrich	Hüllman, Maria	J	52
Klosterman, Heinrich Paul	23, June 1850	Heinrich	Hüllman, Maria Elisabeth	J	6
Klosterman, Johan Anton	25, May 1859	Johan	Freneg---, Elisabeth	D	138
Klosterman, Johan Victor	1, Jan. 1857	J. Heinrich	Hülsman, Maria Angela	J	40
Klosterman, Maria Elisabeth	2, Feb. 1853	Heinrich	Schürman, Maria Angela	J	20
Klosterman, Philomena	9, Apr. 1851	Carl Anton	Korte, Maria	N	3
Klostermann, Anna Maria Elisabeth	6, May 1850	J. Joseph	Busch, Elisabeth	F	
Klostermann, Friedrich Joseph	18, Apr. 1852	Joseph	Steinemann, Anna M.	C	
Klostermann, Johan Gerhard	20, Sept 1858	Gerhard	Eilers, M. Magdalena	F	
Klostermann, Johan Theodor	24, Aug. 1852	J. Joseph	Busse, Elisabeth	F	
Klostermann, Maria Catharina	13, Sept 1854	Joseph	Steinemann, Anna M.	L	
Klostermann, Marianna	2, Aug. 1859	Carl A.	Korte, Anna Maria	F	
Kloverkamp, Gesina Margaretha E.	2, July 1856	Joseph	Kuhr, Anna Adelheid	L	
Kloverkamp, Maria Anna	25, Jan. 1859	Joseph	Kuhr, Anna Adelheid	L	
Kluba, Maximillian	12, Oct. 1857	Paul	Gau---, Elisabeth	D	97
Kluck, Anna Maria	4, July 1853	Johan	Klingler, Helena	K	

Name of Child	Date of Baptism	Father	Mother	Church	Page
Klueber, Johan	22, Feb. 1852	Johan	Baus, Barbara	L	
Klueber, Joseph	29, July 1855	Joseph	Menzer, Christina	F	
Kluemper, Johan Bernard Ferdinand	7, Mar. 1853	J. Ferdinand	Kröger, Dora	K	
Kluewer, Johan Aloysius	17, Apr. 1855	Johan	Baus, Barbara	L	
Klug, Barbara	10, Dec. 1855	Valentin	----, Catharina	H	
Klug, Caspar	7, Aug. 1851	Valentin	----, Catharina	H	
Klug, Catharina	18, May 1856	Johan	Schaub, Gertrud	F	
Klug, Catharina Louisa	18, Feb. 1855	Joseph	Boess, Barbara	C	
Klug, Francis Xavier	13, Dec. 1857	Valentin	Brontel, Catharina	H	
Klug, Georg	17, Feb. 1853	Valentin	----, Catharina	H	
Klug, John	1, Oct. 1854	Valentin	----, Catharina	H	
Klug, Joseph	6, Mar. 1859	Valentin	Bendel, Catharina	H	
Klug, Lawrence	24, Feb. 1850	Valentin	Bendel, Catharina	H	
Klug, Theresa	9, June 1853	Johan	Schaup, Gertrud	F	
Kluman, Michael	15, June 1856	Johan	Kluman, Agnes	D	61
Klump, Amalia	30, Oct. 1859	Anton	Stukert, Eva	C	
Klump, Anton	30, Aug. 1857	Anton	Stugart, Eva	C	
Klump, Catharina	30, Mar. 1856	Peter	Boos, Louisa	D	55
Klump, Eleonora	7, July 1850	Peter	Stegreier, Susanna	D	222
Klump, Francisca	22, June 1851	Joseph	Burst, Agatha	D	269
Klump, Joseph	23, Jan. 1853	Joseph	Post, Agatha	D	366
Klump, Maria	26, Sept 1852	Anton	Geiger, Maria	D	349
Klümper, Bernard Samuel	18, Jan. 1858	Ferdinand	Kroeger, Dorothea	K	
Klümper, Carolina Wilhemina Josephina	10, May 1855	Joseph	Brüggeman, Angela	A	
Klümper, Herman Bernard	25, July 1856	Gerhard	Kruse, Anna Maria	A	
Klümper, Joseph August Gerhard	30, May 1852	Joseph	Bruggeman, Angela Maria	A	
Klümper, Maria Rosina	1, June 1851	Ferdinand	Feldman, Maria Adelheid	A	
Klümper, Maria Theresa	6, Feb. 1858	Gerhard	Kruse, Maria Josephina	A	
Knab, Albertina	27, Aug. 1854	Peter	Reising, Elisabeth	F	
Knab, Augustine	25, Oct. 1858	Peter	Reise, Elisabeth	H	
Knab, Bernard	3, Feb. 1850	Adam	Beer, Ida	D	203
Knab, Eva Rosina	2, Sept 1855	Adam	Beer, Eva	D	41
Knab, Johan	10, July 1853	Adam	Beer, Eva	C	
Knab, Peter	1, Mar. 1850	Peter	Reiling, Elisabeth	D	203
Knabbe, Anna Maria Amalia	4, Feb. 1856	Bernard	Bürger, Lucia	K	
Knabbe, Anna Maria Christina	26, Dec. 1851	Bernard	Bürger, Maria Lucia	A	
Knabe, Jacob	1, Oct. 1858	Jacob	Wolter, Elisabeth	D	120
Knäbel, Louisa	8, June 1851	Georg	Knarr, Elisabeth	D	267
Knäbel, Maria	20, Feb. 1856	Johan	Jansen, Margaretha	D	52
Knaber, Agnes Louisa	11, Nov. 1855	Georg	Krebs, Barbara	C	
Knaber, Rosina Amalia	9, Jan. 1859	Georg	Krebs, Barbara	D	128
Knaebel, Georg	30, Dec. 1852	Georg	Knors, Elisabeth	C	
Knaebel, Maria Antoni	8, Oct. 1854	Georg	Erhart, Friedrica	D	19
Knaebel, Maria Elisabeth	13, Feb. 1859	Georg L.	Knoer, Elisabeth	D	131
Knaebel, Maria Louisa Josephina	28, Dec. 1851	Georg	Erhart, Friedrica	D	298
Knaebel, Philomena	30, Oct. 1859	Georg	Erhart, Friedrica	D	150
Knagge, Bernard Heinrich	24, Oct. 1853	Theodor	Carnal, Agnes	C	
Knagge, Emilia Elisabeth Catharina	8, May 1859	J. Theodor	Carnal, Maria	D	137
Knagge, Francis Heinrich	23, June 1852	Theodor	Carnal, Agnes	C	
Knagge, Francis Heinrich	17, Mar. 1850	Theodor H.	Husmann, Catharina M.	C	
Knagge, Maria Anna	22, May 1856	Theodor	Carnal, M. Agnes	C	
Knaggs, Ann	28, Sept 1856	Robert	Corcoran, Catharine	T	
Knaggs, Robert James	18, Mar. 1855	Robert	Corcoran, Catherine	P	125
Knaggs, Theresa	11, Sept 1859	Robert	Corcoran, Catherine	P	295
Knaggs, Thomas	29, May 1853	Robert	Corcoran, Catherine	P	43
Knapke, Anna Maria	30, July 1854	Bernard A.	Froring, Anna Maria	L	
Knapke, Georg	16, Jan. 1859	Engelbert	Bayer, Maria	S	
Knapke, Johan Joseph	6, Mar. 1853	Bernard	Brundiers, Anna M.	L	
Knapke, M. Bernardina Francisca	29, Aug. 1852	Heinrich	Trotick, M. Catharina	L	

Name of Child	Date of Baptism	Father	Mother	Church	Page
Knapmeier, Anna Maria Theresa	8, July 1858	J. Theodor	Gausing, M. Catharina	L	
Knapp, Agatha	2, Oct. 1859	Joseph	Felger, Theresa	H	
Knapp, Anna Clara Josephina	9, Oct. 1858	Francis	Rowekamp, Christina	F	
Knapp, Anna Maria	22, Nov. 1857	Nicolaus	Schmidt, Catharina	K	
Knapp, Bernard Heinrich	8, Apr. 1855	Heinrich	Huntmann, Josephina	F	
Knapp, Carolina	16, May 1858	Leonard	Tricke--, Caecilia	D	111
Knapp, Elisabeth	23, July 1854	Nicolaus	Schmidt, Maria	K	
Knapp, Franz Heinrich	1, Nov. 1855	Caspar	Greive, Maria	F	
Knapp, Heinrich	23, Feb. 1853	Caspar	Gerwe, Anna Maria	F	
Knapp, Johan Caspar	17, Dec. 1858	Caspar	Grewe, Maria	F	
Knapp, Joseph	31, Jan. 1856	Johan	Hügenberg, Elisabeth	A	
Knapp, Joseph Heinrich	20, Dec. 1857	Caspar	Grewe, Maria	F	
Knapp, Joseph Heinrich	2, Mar. 1852	Heinrich	Huntemann, Josephina	F	
Knapp, Maria	26, June 1853	Gerhard	Becker, Anna Maria	F	
Knapp, Maria Catharina	26, June 1859	Nicolaus	Schmidt, Catharina	J	50
Knapp, Maria Margaretha	6, May 1855	Leonard	Wetzel, Maria Margaretha	F	
Knapp, Mary	25, Oct. 1857	Joseph	Feyer, Theresa	H	
Knapp, Mary Cornelia	25, July 1852	William J.	McGinn, Helen	B	266
Knapp, Michael	17, July 1859	Francis	Sei, Theresa	Q	32
Knapp, Peter	18, Nov. 1855	Nicolaus	Schmidt, Catharina	F	
Knapp, Theresa Francisca	7, Oct. 1858	Heinrich	Huntermann, Josephina	F	
Knath, Herman Bernard Francis	12, July 1851	Herman B.	Hofman, Maria	K	
Knau, Francis	7, Feb. 1858	Heinrich	Traeger, Anna Catharina	D	104
Knaubel, Peter	22, Jan. 1854	Johan	Jansen, Margaretha	D	2
Knauber, Barbara	27, Apr. 1851	Jacob	Walder, Elisabeth	D	262
Knauber, Carolina	10, Apr. 1853	Francis	Katz, Anna Maria	D	380
Knauber, Christina	30, May 1852	Jacob	Walder, Elisabeth	D	322
Knauber, Conrad Edward	17, May 1857	Francis	Katz, Maria	D	85
Knauber, Elisabeth	3, June 1855	Francis	Katz, Anna Maria	D	36
Knauber, Maria	7, Nov. 1858	Johan	Banzer, Barbara	T	
Knauber, Maria Elisabeth	20, Feb. 1855	Jacob	Walter, Elisabeth	D	29
Knaubler, Maria Anna Carolina	17, Jan. 1850	F. Joseph	Schweizer, Maria Magdalena	A	
Knauper, Ferdinand Francis	10, Nov. 1856	Jacob	Haller, Elisabeth	D	72
Knaupf, Jacob	18, Dec. 1853	Jacob	Walter, Elisabeth	D	420
Knebel, Elisabeth	6, Jan. 1855	Georg	Knerr, Elisabeth	C	
Knecht, Anna Elisabeth	5, Aug. 1855	Jacob	Renner, Josephina	A	
Knecht, Anton	21, Apr. 1853	Jacob	Renner, Josephina	D	381
Knecht, Carolina Catharina	5, Sept 1859	Adam	Korb, Veronica	F	
Knecht, Catharina	4, July 1858	J. Adam	Hahn, Veronica	A	
Knecht, Catharina Josephina	16, July 1857	Jacob	Renner, Josephina	A	
Knecht, Friedrich	22, Mar. 1851	Jacob	Renner, Josephina	D	258
Knecht, Johan Ernest	17, Dec. 1854	Johan	Gerth, Helena	D	24
Knecht, Maria Catharina	28, Feb. 1858	Michael	Gadet, Helena	D	106
Knecht, Maria Josephina	22, Sept 1850	Ludwig	Engelhard, Catharina	A	
Kneip, Anna Maria	25, June 1854	Philipp	Heim, Anna M.	C	
Kneip, Francis	10, May 1857	Peter	König, Carolina	N	
Kneip, Johan Jacob	25, Dec. 1858	Peter	König, Carolina	N	
Kneipp, Carl	29, Apr. 1855	Peter	König, Catharina	N	28
Kneipp, Maria Theresa	17, Apr. 1853	Peter	Koenig, Carolina	K	
Kneller, Sophia	8, May 1856	Philipp	Schell, Caroline	U	
Knese, Eberhard Washington	15, Mar. 1856	Bernard	Unkraut, Cornelia	A	
Knese, Egon?	20, Dec. 1853	J. Bernard	Unkraut, Francisca Cornelia	A	
Knese, Marcellus Joseph Johan	27, Sept 1850	Bernard	----, ----	A	
Knessman, Rosina Maria Catharina	24, Apr. 1853	Adam	Conrad, Maria Lucia	K	
Knies, Bernard Heinrich	12, Dec. 1855	Bernard	Feders, Euphemia	L	
Knies, Johan Heinrich	16, May 1852	J. Bernard	Kleinsandermann, Agnes	L	
Knight, Bridget	18, May 1859	Michael	Cornely, Catherine	B	75
Knight, Michael	21, Aug. 1853	Michael	Connelly, Catherine	B	297
Knight, Philipp	1, May 1853	Philipp H.	Hochter, Sarah	B	289

Name of Child	Date of Baptism	Father	Mother	Church	Page
Knight, Richard Michael	17, Sept 1850	Michael	Connoly, Catherine	B	214
Knight, Thomas	14, Dec. 1851	Michael	Cornelia, Catherine	P	14
Knightly, Mary	26, Mar. 1854	William	Sheehan, Joanne	B	311
Knipper, Franz Joseph	24, Sept 1856	Francis J.	Schmitt, Elisabeth	L	
Knipper, Heinrich	15, Nov. 1854	Herman H.	Schmidt, M. Elisabeth	L	
Knipper, Maria Agnes Anna	29, Oct. 1858	Herman A.	Schmidt, M. Elisabeth	L	
Knittel, Catharina	16, Dec. 1855	Peter	Weissberg, Margaretha	D	48
Knobbe, Francisca Lucia Wilhelmina	3, Aug. 1850	Bernard H.	Burger, Maria Lucia	A	
Knobbe, Maria Lucia	15, Sept 1858	Bernard	Börger, Lucia	K	
Knobel, Maria Catharina	3, Dec. 1852	Georg	Siehling, Maria Anna	K	
Knoblach, Carl Martin	30, Oct. 1859	Francis	Todtenbier, Elisabeth	C	
Knoblauch, Margaretha	20, Aug. 1854	Jacob	Guetlein, Maria	F	
Knoblaugh, Georg	16, Dec. 1855	Jacob	Guetlein, Maria	F	
Knobloch, Andreas Johan	19, July 1857	Francis	Dodenbier, Elisabeth	C	
Knoe, Maria Catharina	12, Mar. 1855	Anton	Wolwers, Maria	L	
Knoeger, Maria Bernardina	19, Aug. 1856	G. August	Hoppenjans, Maria	C	
Knofloch, Helena Amalia	19, Aug. 1855	Francis	Todtenbier, Elisabeth	D	40
Knolb?, Carl Ludwig	31, Octt. 1857	Joseph	Ric---, Josephina	D	98
Knollman, Gerhard Heinrich	30, Dec. 1851	Gerhard	Attermeyer, Theresa	D	299
Knollman, Johan Mathias	21, Feb. 1858	August	H---, Maria Eva	D	105
Knollman, Theresa Louisa	17, Feb. 1856	Gerhard	Attermayer, Theresa	D	52
Knollmann, Andreas Stephen	26, Dec. 1853	Gerhard	Attermeyer, Theresa	C	
Knopf, Johan Nicolaus	1, June 1851	Francis	Hechstul, Margaret	H	
Knopf, Maria Anna	4, Jan. 1852	Peter	Engel, Anna Margaretha	D	300
Knöpfer, Francis	23, May 1858	Michael	Oberlin, Elisabeth	C	
Knöpfler, Francisca	26, June 1855	Michael	Oberle, Elisabeth	A	
Knöpfler, Maria Elisabeth	12, Mar. 1854	Michael	Oberle, Elisabeth	A	
Knöpfler, Maria Elisabeth	26, June 1855	Michael	Oberle, Elisabeth	A	
Knöpflesch, Wilhelm	9, Feb. 1851	Michael	Oberle, Elisabeth	D	252
Knopp, Anna Catharina	13, May 1858	Bernard	Kemper, Catharina	J	46
Knosp, Catharina	17, Oct. 1855	Joseph	Gardiser, Magdalena	C	
Knostman, Herman Heinrich	20, Dec. 1857	Carl	Niehaus, Maria	K	
Knostman, Maria Catharina	18, Nov. 1851	Carl H.	Niehaus, Catharina	K	
Knoth, Joseph	7, Feb. 1858	Leonard	Hasel, Christina	T	
Knoth, Maria Anna	21, Jan. 1855	Amand	Huefner, Catharina	F	
Knoth, Michael	7, Sept 1859	Leonard	Hasel, Christina	T	
Knowles,	11, Feb. 1850	----	----, ----	E	199
Knox, Andrew Francis	13, Sept 1857	Canny	----, Helen	P	223
Knox, Barbara	29, Nov. 1857	Andrew M.	--in, Rebecca	B	52
Knue, Bernard Wilhelm	8, Feb. 1852	J. Bernard	Fangman, Dorothea	A	
Knue, Theodor Francis	19, Oct. 1850	Bernard	Fangman, Theodora	A	
Knuewe, Clemens Bernard	21, Dec. 1858	Bernard	Kenkel, Margaretha	L	
Knuewe, Johan Bernard	28, Oct. 1856	Bernard	Kenkel, Margaretha	L	
Knuf, Johan Gerhard	20, Feb. 1851	J. Herman	Hoefer, Maria	L	
Knuf, Maria Theresa	4, Jan. 1854	J. Herman	Hovels, Maria Anna	L	
Knuhe, Bernard Heinrich	29, Aug. 1852	Anton	Wolf, Anna Maria	L	
Knuwe, Gerhard August	1, Jan. 1859	G. August	Huppenjan, Anna Maria	K	
Knüwer, Johan August Eduard	9, Jan. 1858	Clemens	Schrolüken, Elisabeth	A	
Köbbe, Johan Bernard	28, May 1858	J.H. Sistus	VanHagen, Elisabeth	A	
Kobblitz, Susanna Margaretha	30, Sept 1853		Kobblitz, Margaretha	A	
Kobicker, Philipp	6, Oct. 1850	Balthasar	Gütlein, Cunigunda	D	236
Kobiger, Rosalia	26, Nov. 1854	Balthasar	Guetlein, Kunigunda	F	
Kobricher, Heinrich	12, Dec. 1852	Balthasar	Gutlein, Cunigunda	D	360
Kocen, Elisabeth	4, Jan. 1854	Bernard	Mayrose, Francisca	C	
Koch, Adolph	19, Feb. 1854	Johan	Meyer, Rosina	C	
Koch, Albert Herman	8, Apr. 1858	Bernard H.	Unluecke, A. Catharina	L	
Koch, Anna M. Christina	7, June 1857	Georg	---ter, Anna Maria	D	86
Koch, Anna Maria	11, Dec. 1859	Michael	Hettesheimer, Philomena	D	152
Koch, Bernard Heinrich	11, Dec. 1856	Adolph J.	Bussman, Anna Maria	D	74

Name of Child	Date of Baptism	Father	Mother	Church	Page
Koch, Bernard Jacob	20, Nov. 1852	Bernard	Steinshulz, Magdalena	D	357
Koch, Bernard Joseph	8, Mar. 1853	Adolph J.	Buschman, Maria Anna	D	375
Koch, Carolina	4, Sept 1859	Jacob	Hirtl, Theresa	C	
Koch, Carolina	9, June 1850	Nicolaus	Garth, Maria Antonia	D	217
Koch, Carolina Genofeva	13, Jan. 1856	Johan	Bramberger, Angela	C	
Koch, Catharina	30, Sept 1855	Johan	Meyer, Rosina	C	
Koch, Catharina	16, Jan. 1853	Johan	Runegger, Magdalena	D	365
Koch, Catharina	10, Feb. 1854	Michael	Hetteshümer, Philippina	D	4
Koch, Clara Maria	6, Nov. 1851	Wilhelm	Moenning, Elisabeth	C	
Koch, Francis Joseph Anton	15, May 1859	Francis	Knittel, Paulina	D	138
Koch, Friedrich	28, July 1850	Georg	Ostheimer, Lucia	F	
Koch, Georg	14, Nov. 1858	Francis	Meier, Francisca	D	124
Koch, Georg Bernard	2, Feb. 1851	J. Baptist	Vormair, Magdalena	D	251
Koch, Georg Franz	28, Apr. 1859	Bernard	Steinschulz, Magdalena	T	
Koch, Georg Joseph	14, Dec. 1856	Georg	Ostheimer, Lucia	F	
Koch, Gerhard Joseph	8, Mar. 1857	Herman T.	Kuhl, Maria Louisa	F	
Koch, Herman Bernard	1, Nov. 1853	Herman T.	Kuhl, Louisa	L	
Koch, Herman Heinrich	25, Sept 1859	Friedrich	Rechtin, Elisabeth	C	
Koch, Ida Gertrud	22, Oct. 1856	Joseph	Mönning, Maria Elisabeth	Q	16
Koch, Jacob	31, May 1851	Johan	Meyer, Rosina	C	
Koch, Johan	9, Oct. 1859	Friedrich	Span---, Anna Maria	D	148
Koch, Johan	6, June 1858	Heinrich	Schroten, Maria	G	
Koch, Johan	18, Dec. 1853	Johan	Braunberg, Angela	C	
Koch, Johan	24, June 1851	Johan	Ronnegger, Magdalena	D	269
Koch, Johan	20, Aug. 1854	Nicolaus	Clark, Ellen	D	16
Koch, Johan Bernard	9, Nov. 1857	Bernard	Bahlmann, Elisabeth	L	
Koch, Johan Bernard	16, Feb. 1855	Joseph	Bussman, Maria Anna	D	29
Koch, Johan Christian	7, Sept 1855	Francis	Meier, Francisca	D	42
Koch, Johan Gerhard	28, Apr. 1852	J. Gerhard	Barlage, Catharina	A	
Koch, Johan Herman	20, May 1855	Herman	Kohl, Louisa	D	35
Koch, Joseph Eduard	25, Sept 1859	Joseph	Drettly, Henrica	F	
Koch, Magdalena	21, June 1857	Michael	Hettesheimer, Philomena	D	88
Koch, Maria	13, Apr. 1857	Francis	Meier, Friedrica	D	82
Koch, Maria Adelheid	12, Feb. 1854	Joseph	Mening, Maria Elisabeth	Q	4
Koch, Maria Agnes	10, Aug. 1851	Adolph J.	Buszman, Maria Anna	D	277
Koch, Maria Anna	30, Jan. 1859	Johan	Eslinger, Louisa	T	
Koch, Maria Antonia	2, Feb. 1854	Johan	Ronnegger, Magdalena	D	3
Koch, Maria Appolonia	13, Feb. 1859	Herman T.	Kuhl, Louisa	F	
Koch, Maria Catharina Philomena	15, Sept 1850	Heinrich	Koch, Catharina Marg.	C	
Koch, Maria Clara	24, Sept 1854	Friedrich	Rechtin, Elisabeth	C	
Koch, Maria Elisabeth	11, Apr. 1850	Johan F.	Rechtin, Elisabeth	C	
Koch, Maria Elisabeth	10, Dec. 1859	Joseph	Moenig, Maria Elisabeth	Q	34
Koch, Maria Paulina Antonia	17, Jan. 1858	Francis	Knote, Paulina	D	103
Koch, Maria Theresa	4, Jan. 1859	Joseph	Bussman, Maria	D	128
Koch, Maria Veronica	25, Mar. 1856	Johan	Riebel, Elisabeth	K	
Koch, Martin	21, Nov. 1854	Bernard	Steinschulz, Magdalena	C	
Koch, Paul	7, Oct. 1855	Michael	Hetteseimer, Philomena	D	44
Koch, Theresa Helena	25, July 1858	Jacob	Heidel, Theresa	C	
Koch, Thomas Nicolaus	5, Sept 1852	Nicolaus	Gerth, Maria Antonia	D	346
Koch, Urban	1, Nov. 1855	Johan	Dingmeier, Louisa	D	46
Koch, Wilhelm Johan	30, Jan. 1852	Friedrich	Rechtin, M. Elisabeth	C	
Kocher, Francis	9, Mar. 1856	Georg	Volz, Maria	Q	13
Kocher, Johan	1, Mar. 1852	Georg	Julz, Maria	Q	1
Kocher, Maria Elisabeth	13, Feb. 1859	Georg	Vo---, Anna Maria	D	131
Köck, Andreas	11, Jan. 1852	Georg	Sutor, Maria	D	301
Kock, Anna Margaretha	18, Aug. 1855	Heinrich	Schroten, Maria Adelheid	A	
Kock, Anna Maria Angela	28, July 1853	Herman H.	Steinke, Anna Maria	D	397
Kock, Bernard Heinrich	22, Jan. 1855	Bernard	Beelmann, Elisabeth	L	
Kock, Bernard Herman Heinrich	8, Nov. 1852	Herman W.	Overberg, Elisabeth	L	

Name of Child	Date of Baptism	Father	Mother	Church	Page
Kock, Bernardina Maria Catharina	27, June 1859	Herman H.	Steinke, Maria	D	141
Kock, Euphemia Maria Catharina	7, Oct. 1855	J. Bernard	Bruns, Anna Adelheid	F	
Kock, Georg Augustine	16, July 1850	Georg	Sutter, Marianna	D	223
Kock, Gerhard Heinrich	13, Nov. 1857	Bernard H.	Bruns, Anna Adelheid	F	
Kock, Herman Heinrich	13, Feb. 1850	Herman H.	Steinke, Anna Maria Angela	D	202
Kock, Herman Heinrich Joseph	29, July 1855	Herman H.	Steinke, Maria Anna	D	39
Kock, Johan Gerhard	5, Mar. 1856	Anton	Hussmann, Lisette	F	
Kock, Maria Adelheid	1, Sept 1853	Heinrich	Schroten, Maria Adelheid	A	
Kock, Maria Anna Euphemia	18, Feb. 1856	Bernard H.	Unluecken, A. Cath.	L	
Kock, Maria Christina	18, June 1854	Georg	Ostheimer, Lucia	F	
Kock, Maria Elisabeth	14, Nov. 1851	Gerhard H.	Schroeter, Maria Adelheid	A	
Kock, Sophia Genofeva	9, Oct. 1859	Michael	Wiedeman, Veronica	D	148
Kock, Valentin	18, Dec. 1853	Georg	Sutter, Anna Maria	D	420
Kockenge, Bernard	18, Mar. 1850	J. Bernard	Neirose, Maria Anna	C	
Kockfoet, Bernardina Dorothea	10, Feb. 1851	Heinrich	Uhlenbrink, Christina	D	253
Kockman, Anna Maria	16, Sept 1855	Heinrich	Bulter, Gertrud	D	43
Kockman, Bernard Ludwig	31, Dec. 1853	Heinrich	Bülter, Gertrud	D	423
Kockman, Johan Heinrich	30, Jan. 1859	Heinrich	Bilsch, Gertrud	D	130
Kockman, Maria Gertrud	31, May 1857	Heinrich	Bulter, Gertrud	D	86
Kockmeyer, Johan Bernard Heinrich	4, May 1853	Bernard H.	Pott, Elisabeth	L	
Kocks, Anna Julia	22, Feb. 1850	H. Heinrich	Bagge, Maria Anna	K	
Koddenberg, Johan Georg	9, July 1854	J. Heinrich	Gerdes, Catharina Maria	A	
Kodi, Patrick	23, Jan. 1859	John	Galli---, Sarah	D	129
Koebbe, Anna Maria	25, Sept 1856	J. Albert	Kopmann, A. Maria	L	
Koebbe, August Andreas	14, May 1858	Andreas	Kohes, Elisabeth	L	
Koebbe, Franz Andreas	17, Feb. 1855	Albert	Kopmann, Anna Maria	L	
Koebbe, Johan Albert	28, Nov. 1855	Andreas	Kurs, Elisa	F	
Koebbe, Maria Carolina	21, Jan. 1859	J. Albert	Kopmann, Anna Maria	L	
Koebel, Johan	2, Sept 1851	Joseph	Loge, Margaretha	C	
Koebel, Joseph	16, Jan. 1853	Joseph	Loge, Maria	F	
Koech, Andreas Carl	27, Feb. 1859	Johan	Theiring, Anna Maria	D	133
Koechler, M. Catharina Josephina	18, Aug. 1859		Koechler, Maria	C	
Koeck, Maria Catharina	18, June 1854	David	Schlick, Catharina	D	12
Koegler, Catharina	24, July 1851		Koegler, Barbara	C	
Koehl, Bernard	11, Sept 1859	Heinrich	Konig, Rosina	T	
Koehl, Elisabeth	17, Nov. 1850	Francis	Sibery, Margaretha	Q	1
Koehler, Carl Joseph	8, July 1857	Christian	Kuechler, Maria	F	
Koehler, Carolina Philippina	16, Oct. 1859	Philipp	Wettengel, Barbara	C	
Koehler, Johan Georg	7, Aug. 1856	Heinrich	Stenk, Anna Maria	D	64
Koehler, Joseph Franz	22, May 1855	Francis J.	Gaeser, Francisca	F	
Koehler, Julia Elisabeth	22, Oct. 1850	Christian	Kuchler, Maria	F	
Koehler, Juliana Maria	28, Oct. 1855	Joseph	Krebs, Rosina	F	
Koehler, Maria Catharina	8, Aug. 1850	Arnold	Moritz, Gertrud	F	
Koehler, Peter	8, Dec. 1855	Joseph	----, Catharina	K	
Koehler, Sophia Elisabeth	26, Dec. 1859	Heinrich	Renk, Anna Maria	D	153
Koehler, Wilhelm Adam	31, July 1853	Christian	Kuechler, Maria	F	
Koehn, Carolina	2, May 1858	Johan	Hoff, Margaretha	D	110
Koel, Peter	27, Feb. 1853	Francis	Siwee, Margaretha	D	374
Koelble, Maria Victoria	9, Oct. 1859	Joseph	Schonach, Agatha	T	
Koelch, Heinrich	12, Oct. 1856	Nicolaus	Appleman, Anna Maria	U	
Koelker, Anton Heinrich	8, Nov. 1859	Herman B.	Kraemer, Catharina	F	
Koelker, Clemens	7, Dec. 1856	Herman B	Kraemer, M. Catharina	F	
Koelker, Franz Joseph	24, Jan. 1854	Herman B.	Kremer, Maria Catharina	F	
Koelker, Johan Bernard	11, Oct. 1851	Herman B.	Kraemer, Maria Catharina	F	
Koell, Francis	14, June 1857	Heinrich	Koenig, Rosina	D	87
Koelner, M. Carolina Wilhelmina	4, Dec. 1854	Bernard	Grotmann, M. Engel	L	
Koelsch, Anna Elisabeth	28, Mar. 1858	Nicolaus	Appelmann, Anna Maria	G	
Koelsch, Johan	20, May 1852	Balthasar	Conrad, Eva	R	
Koelsch, Johan Heinrich Wilhelm	28, Apr. 1857	Johan H.	Kroeger, Elisabeth	F	

Name of Child	Date of Baptism	Father	Mother	Church	Page
Koelsch, Johan Stephan	30, Aug. 1857	Johan	Miller, Margaretha	D	93
Koelsch, Joseph	18, Sept 1859	Michael	Messman, Catharina	D	147
Koelsch, Maria	23, Aug. 1855	Nicolaus	Appelman, Anna Maria	D	41
Koelsch, Sophia Elisabeth	12, Oct. 1855	Johan	Kroeger, Lisetta	F	
Koembel, Maria Josephina Carolina	14, Nov. 1852	Peter	Lips, Francisca	C	
Koenig, Adam Joseph	28, Nov. 1858	Vitus	Nichte, Julianna	F	
Koenig, Anna Maria Gertrud	21, Jan. 1855	Joseph	Wehlage, Elisabeth	F	
Koenig, Barbara	17, June 1855	Peter	Fasse, Maria Anna	D	36
Koenig, Heinrich	27, Jan. 1852	Herman H.	Boberg, A. Gertrud	L	
Koenig, Helena	24, July 1853	Peter	DeFoser, Maria Anna	D	396
Koenig, Johan	23, Sept 1856	Fidel	Nuechter, Julianna	F	
Koenig, Johan Casper	25, Aug. 1856	Herman	Boberg, Gertrud	C	
Koenig, Johan Friedrich	9, Apr. 1856	Joseph	Wehlage, Elisabeth	F	
Koenig, Johan Joseph	4, May 1859	Joseph	Wehlage, Elisabeth	F	
Koenig, Joseph Friedrich	8, Aug. 1856	Friedrich	Renneker, Gertrud	L	
Koenig, Louisa	18, July 1858	Peter	Defoset, Maria	T	
Koenig, Maria	3, Aug. 1851	Peter	Devoset, Maria Anna	D	276
Koenig, Maria Anna	29, June 1854	Herman H.	Boberg, Gertrud	C	
Koenig, Maria Catharina	24, Dec. 1859	Friedrich	Renneger, A.M. Gertrud	L	
Koenig, Maria Catharina	22, Feb. 1858	Friedrich	Renneker, Anna Maria	L	
Koeninger, Anna Eva	13, Dec. 1854	Bernard	Stegman, Catharina	D	24
Koennen, Friedrich Joseph	16, Mar. 1853	Andreas S.	Wehmeier, Maria Engel	F	
Koepfer, Michael	15, Mar. 1857	Andreas	Weidner, Magdalena	G	
Koepman, Maria Magdalena	15, Sept 1858	J. Heinrich	Wessel, Rebecca	D	119
Koers, Francis	18, Apr. 1856	J. Friedrich	Tobe, Wilhelmina	K	
Koerz, Maria	27, Sept 1858	Wilhelm	Hannes, Clara	T	
Koeth, Elisabeth	16, Jan. 1859	Valentin	Wolf, Veronica	D	129
Koeth, Valentin	31, Aug. 1856	Valentin	Wolf, Veronica	D	66
Koetter, Anna Maria Bernardina	30, July 1855	Bernard	Bergmann, Dina	L	
Koetter, Anton Wilhelm Edward	7, May 1856	J. Heinrich	Grevenkamp, Anna Maria	K	
Koetter, August Eduard	8, June 1854	August	Schwarz, Maria Anna	L	
Koetter, Bernard Ferdinand	12, Oct. 1852	Bernard	Schnier, Theresa	F	
Koetter, Gerhard Heinrich	14, Aug. 1858	Joseph	Gehring, M. Anna	C	
Koetter, Johanna Sophia Theresa	8, Aug. 1852	Theodor	Riegelmeyer, Clara	C	
Koetter, Maria Bernardina	4, Feb. 1855	Joseph	Gering, Maria Anna	L	
Koetter, Maria Henrietta	15, Aug. 1853	J. Bernard	Bergmann, Dina	L	
Koetter, Marianna Theresa	19, Oct. 1855	Bernard P.	Schnuer, Theresa	F	
Koettner, Valentin	26, Dec. 1858	Georg	Schoenauer, Juliana	C	
Koetz, Francis Joseph	19, Apr. 1857	J. Philipp	Gatt, Maria	D	83
Koetz, Georg	19, Apr. 1857	J. Philipp	Gatt, Maria	D	83
Koferman, Maria	6, Dec. 1855	Eberhard	Niemaier, Clara	D	48
Kofermann, Anna Sophia	10, Nov. 1852	Eberhard	Niemeyer, Clara	C	
Kofermann, Maria Elisabeth	27, June 1858	Eberhard	Niemeyer, Clara	C	
Kohaus, Anna Maria	23, Sept 1852	Heinrich	Haus, Anna	D	349
Koher, Edward	1, June 1857	Nicolaus	----, Antonia	C	
Köhl, Johan	8, Apr. 1855	Heinrich	König, Rosina	D	33
Kohl, Johan Heinrich Bernard	17, Jan. 1858	J. Bernard	Lange, Elisabeth	C	
Kohl, Johan Mathias	9, Nov. 1856	Johan	Fell, Anna	D	72
Kohl, Johan Philipp Jacob	26, June 1859	Johan	----, Angela	D	141
Kohl, Maria	31, Jan. 1858	Francis	Kraus, Margaretha	D	104
Kohl, Peter	31, Jan. 1858	G. Francis	Masch, Barbara	D	104
Kohle?, Anna Maria	23, Oct. 1859	Joseph	----, Rachael	K	
Köhler, Alexander	23, Sept 1853	Joseph	Krebs, Rosina	D	407
Kohler, Anna Maria	25, Nov. 1855	Michael	Hafenbradel, Christina	D	47
Kohler, Carolina	14, Jan. 1855	Joseph	Dorzbach, maria	R	
Köhler, Elisabeth	20, Feb. 1859	Caspar	Volpert, Catharina	D	132
Kohler, Francis	14, Oct. 1855	Caspar	Volpert, Catharina	D	44
Kohler, Friedrich August	22, Dec. 1859	Bernard	Hoger, Barbara	D	153
Köhler, Johan	27, June 1852	Johan	Luft, Elisabeth	Q	2

Name of Child	Date of Baptism	Father	Mother	Church	Page
Kohler, Joseph	24, Sept 1854	Michael	Hafenbraidel, Christina	D	18
Kohler, Louisa	2, June 1857	Bernard	Hügel, Barbara	D	86
Köhler, Louisa	28, Feb. 1854	Joseph	Krane, Catharina	K	
Köhler, Margaretha Philomena	24, Mar. 1858	Eustachus	Kripp, Gesina Maria	K	
Köhler, Maria Anna	11, May 1856	Bernard	Heger, Barbara	D	58
Köhler, Maria Francisca	4, Apr. 1852	Heinrich	Renk, Anna Maria	D	315
Köhler, Maria Louisa	19, July 1854	Heinrich	Renk, Maria Anna	D	14
Kohler, Maria Magdalena	7, July 1850	Bernard	Huger, Barbara	D	222
Köhler, Maria Magdalena	31, July 1853	Bernard	Hüger, Barbara	D	397
Kohler, Maria Theresa	10, Aug. 1851	Joseph	Krebs, Rosina	D	277
Kohler, Michael	29, Sept 1851	Michael	Hafenbradel, Christina	D	285
Köhler, Paulina Carolina	23, Aug. 1857	Francis J.	Weber, Barbara	A	
Kohles, Johan Herman Heinrich	31, Aug. 1859	Bernard	Lange, Elisabeth	C	
Kohlhumer, Anna Maria	23, June 1856	Ignatius	Kehl, Anna Maria	D	61
Köhling, Johan August	8, Nov. 1851	J. Herman	Wessels, Anna Maria	K	
Kohlman, August	15, Mar. 1857	Peter	Lenneman, Margaretha	J	40
Kohlman, Bernard Heinrich	8, Feb. 1850	J. Bernard	Ossendorf, Catharina Maria	A	
Kohlman, Herman Heinrich	13, Dec. 1853	J. Heinrich	Grubing, Maria Magdalena	N	19
Kohlmann, Gerhard Everhard	30, Jan. 1853	Johan	Hackmann, Angela	C	
Kohls, Anna Maria Catharina	18, Apr. 1854	Heinrich	Wübbeler, Catharina	A	
Kohls, Catharina Helena	31, Oct. 1858	Heinrich	Burrichter, Elisabeth	A	
Kohls, Maria Elisabeth Paulina	26, Apr. 1856	J. Bernard	Lange, M. Elisabeth	L	
Kohlsdorf, Anna Sophia Catharina	13, Nov. 1859	Johan	Breitenstein, Maria Elisabeth	D	150
Kohlsdorf, Johan	11, Aug. 1858	Johan	Breitenstein, Maria Elisabeth	D	117
Kohlsdorf, M. Catharina Francisca	16, Jan. 1859	Francis	Weisbrick, Catharina	T	
Kohlsdorf, Peter Joseph	15, July 1855	Francis	Weisbruch, Catharina	D	38
Kohlstätt, Catharina	11, Aug. 1850	Johan	Listerman, Maria	H	
Kohlstorf, Sophia	14, June 1857	Johan	Breitenstein, Maria	D	87
Kohmescher, Elisabeth Mathilda	9, Aug. 1851	Johan D.	Hemmelgarn, Anna M.	L	
Kohmescher, Johan Theodor Herman	5, Nov. 1853	Theodor	Hemmelgarn, Maria	L	
Kohmescher, Theresa Agnes Louisa	19, Dec. 1855	Dietrich	Hemmelgarn, Anna M.	L	
Kohne, Anna Catharina Elisabeth	10, Sept 1854	Heinrich	Burwinkel, Elisabeth	L	
Kohne, Anna Margaretha	24, Jan. 1857	Conrad	Honigfort, Margaretha	L	
Kohne, Franz Heinrich	14, Sept 1858	Conrad	Honigfort, Anna M.	L	
Kohne, Susanna Margaretha	24, Apr. 1859	Heinrich	Bawinkel, Gertrud	C	
Kohnen, Anna Margaretha	1, Feb. 1857	Peter	Liebgott, Anna Maria	A	
Köhnen, Margaretha	10, Feb. 1855	Peter	Liebgott, Anna Maria	A	
Kohnen, Theodor	22, Oct. 1852	Heinrich	Burwinkel, Elisabeth	F	
Kohnle, Anton Carl	11, Aug. 1859	Peter	Herzog, Francisca	A	
Kohnly, Maria Barbara	10, Aug. 1854	Anton	Fischer, Maria	C	
Kohorst, Eberhard Heinrich	20, Dec. 1850	Heinrich	Holtkamp, Elisabeth	C	
Kohorst, Francis Heinrich	10, Oct. 1858	Herman	Hoffmann, Dina	C	
Kohorst, Heinrich	23, Oct. 1850	Theodor	Reverman, Margaretha	A	
Kohorst, Johan Casper Heinrich	6, Jan. 1856	Herman	Hoffmann, Bernardina	C	
Kohorst, Johan Herman Heinrich	21, Apr. 1853	Herman H.	Hoffman, Dina	A	
Kohorst, Maria Josephina	24, Oct. 1852	Herman H.	Holtkamp, M. Louise	C	
Kohus, Maria Anna	27, Jan. 1857	H. Heinrich	Determan, Veronica	K	
Koke, Elisabeth Maria Catharina	13, Mar. 1858	Joseph	Pohlmeyer, Catharina	K	
Koke, Heinrich Joseph	14, Sept 1853	B. Heinrich	Moellerhues, Maria Elisabeth	K	
Koke, Herman Joseph Heinrich	29, Sept 1854	Joseph	Höwel, Bernardina	K	
Koke, Maria Elisabeth	10, Aug. 1856	Heinrich	Mollers, Elisabeth	K	
Koke, Maria Gertrud Josephina	28, July 1856	Joseph	Howel, Dina	K	
Kokenbrink, Anna Maria	5, Oct. 1854	Bernard	Natrup, Leonora	L	
Kokenbrink, Johan Bernard	24, Apr. 1857	J. Bernard	Natrup, Clara	L	
Kokenbrink, Johan Bernard Heinrich	17, May 1859	Bernard	Natrup, Eleanora	C	
Kokeng, Francisca Josephina	14, Aug. 1856	Bernard	Mairose, Maria Anna	C	
Kolafrath, Catharina	6, Jan. 1850	Francis	----, Maria	K	
Kölb, Anna Maria Margaretha	30, June 1857	Sebastian	Flick, Catharina	D	89
Kolb, Catharina	7, Apr. 1855	Sebastian	Flick, Catharina	D	32

Name of Child	Date of Baptism	Father	Mother	Church	Page
Kolb, Christina	15, May 1859	Adam	Becker, Gertrud	A	
Kolb, Emilia Mathilda	15, May 1859	Adam	Becker, Gertrud	A	
Kolb, Francisca	2, Jan. 1859	Georg	Brem, Dorothea	T	
Kolb, Georg Adam	15, May 1859	Adam	Becker, Gertrud	A	
Kölb, Johan Baptist	15, Aug. 1853	Sebastian	Flick, Catharina	D	400
Kolbel, Agatha	15, Mar. 1855	Joseph	Schonach, Agatha	D	31
Kölbel, Jacob	6, Aug. 1857	Joseph	Schoenach, Agatha	D	92
Kolbinzky, John Martin	8, July 1855	Martin	Kersten, Dorothy	U	
Kölk, Amadeus	23, Dec. 1856		adult	D	74
Kölker, Anna Philomena Francisca	27, Apr. 1853	J. Gerhard	Nichting, Anna Maria	A	
Kölker, Anna Philomena Josephina	27, Feb. 1854	J. Joseph	Vaske, Catharina	A	
Kölker, Catharina	13, June 1857	Adam	Hoffman, Catharina	A	
Kölker, Johan Anton	20, Apr. 1852	J. Gerhard	Nichting, Anna Maria	A	
Kölker, Johan Heinrich	16, July 1858	J. Joseph	Vaske, Catharina	A	
Kölker, Joseph Gerhard	10, May 1852	J. Joseph	Vaske, Maria Catharina	A	
Kölker, Maria Catharina Francisca	18, Apr. 1856	J. Joseph	Vaske, Maria Catharina	A	
Kölker, Maria Juliana	23, June 1850	Gerhard	Nichting, Maria	A	
Kolkmeier, Bernard Heinrich	26, Jan. 1851	Bernard	Pott, Elisabeth	L	
Kolkmeyer, Anna Francisca	18, Sept 1856	Bernard	Pott, Elisabeth	L	
Kolkmeyer, Anna Maria Catharina	16, Oct. 1853	Heinrich	Frommeyer, Catharina	C	
Kolkmeyer, Elisabeth	27, Nov. 1855	F. Heinrich	Stockhoff, Elisabeth	C	
Kolkmeyer, Friedrich	10, Mar. 1852	Heinrich	Stockhoff, Elisabeth	C	
Kolkmeyer, Georg Friedrich	6, Nov. 1857	Johan H.	Frommeyer, Catharina	C	
Kolkmeyer, Johan Francis	15, Oct. 1850	Francis H.	Stockhoff, Elisabeth	C	
Kolkmeyer, Johan Heinrich	7, Aug. 1857	Francis	Stockhoff, Elisabeth	C	
Kolkmeyer, Johan Heinrich	7, Mar. 1854	Francis H.	Stockkop, Elisabeth	C	
Koll, Carl Heinrich	27, June 1858	Johan	Jecker, Anastasia	A	
Kolle, Anna Maria	28, Mar. 1851	Heinrich	Kuhlmann, A. Margaretha	L	
Kollefrath, Anna Maria	9, May 1858	Jacob	Unger, Catharina	T	
Kollefrath, Francis Carl	10, June 1855	Jacob	Nampher, Catharina	K	
Kollefrath, Maria Ursula	19, June 1857	Jacob	Umper, Catharina	D	88
Kollet, Peter	25, Dec. 1856	Peter	Mücke, Magdalena	D	75
Kollhof, Johan Heinrich	27, Aug. 1852	Joseph	Bremer, Catharina	A	
Kollhof, Joseph	17, Feb. 1850	Joseph	Bremer, Maria Catharina	A	
Kollhoff, Heinrich Francis	20, Oct. 1857	Joseph	Bremer, Maria Catharina	A	
Kollhoff, Johan Bernard	9, Apr. 1855	Joseph	Bremer, Maria Catharina	A	
Kollman, Catharina Rosa	21, Dec. 1851	August	Stanger, Maria	D	297
Kollman, Maria Elisabeth	9, June 1850	Johan	Hackman, Elisabeth	D	216
Kolm, Aloysius	21, June 1850	Jacob	Beer, Theresa	K	
Kölman, Valentin	1, Jan. 1854	Vincent	Knapp, Louisa	D	1
Kölp, Rosa	1, Nov. 1859	Sebastian	Flink, Catharina	D	150
Kölsch, Johan	15, Nov. 1857	Michael	Messman, Catharina	D	98
Kölsch, Josephina	13, Oct. 1852	Nicolaus	Apelman, Anna Maria	Q	2
Kölsch, Maria Eva	8, Apr. 1855	Johan	Miller, Margaretha	D	32
Kölsch, Mathias	8, Jan. 1854	Balthasar	Conrad, Eva	D	1
Kombrink, Bernard Heinrich	8, Nov. 1853	Bernard H.	Droppelmann, M Gertrud	L	
Kombrink, Catharina Francisca	14, Sept 1859	Bernard	Droppelmann, Gertrud	F	
Kombrink, Elisabeth Johanna	29, Dec. 1856	Bernard	Droppelman, Gertrud	C	
Komens, Francis Wilhelm	14, Apr. 1859	Wilhelm	Moemke, Maria	C	
Köne, Caspar Heinrich	14, Sept 1855	Joseph H.	Wacker, Maria Anna	A	
Köne, Catharina Philomena Dorothea	20, Feb. 1852	Joseph	Wacker, Anna Maria	A	
Köne, Johan Joseph	5, Mar. 1858	Joseph	Dreyer, Catharina	A	
Köne, Joseph Benedict	16, Aug. 1853	Joseph H.	Wocke, Anna Maria	A	
Konen, Johan Heinrich Bernard	28, Aug. 1859	Bernard	Klinker, Angela	A	
Konerman, Anna Maria Theresa	1, Oct. 1855	Herman H.	Kruse, Anna Maria	A	
Konerman, Maria Catharina Philomena	24, Aug. 1857	H.H.	Kruse, Anna Maria	A	
Konermann, Anton Herman H.	26, July 1859	Anton	Hilling, Elisabeth	C	
König, Anna Maria Philomena	5, Mar. 1850	Heinrich	Behrens, Maria Gertrud	K	
König, Maria Elisabeth	25, Nov. 1859	J. Heinrich	Buscher, Maria Catharina	D	151

Name of Child	Date of Baptism	Father	Mother	Church	Page
König, Rosina	25, Dec. 1856	Peter	----, Maria	D	75
Köninger, Eva Catharina	20, Oct. 1859	Bernard	Steigerwald, Catharina	D	149
Konne, Rudolph Heinrich	2, Feb. 1856	Heinrich	Deppenbrock, Antonette	L	
Konneman, Heinrich Anton Dennis	18, July 1857	Anton H.	Beulman, Maria Anna	D	90
Konnerman, Albert Bernard	31, Dec. 1855	Anton	Böhmer, Maria Anna	D	49
Konnerman, Joseph Bernard	9, Aug. 1858	Anton	Boehnle, Maria Anna	D	116
Konslar, Johan	20, Nov. 1859	Nicolaus	Scheibel, Catharina	F	
Konst, Maria Elisabeth	26, Dec. 1858	J. Herman	Kolder, Martha	D	127
Koo, Bernard Heinrich	23, Mar. 1856	Wilhelm H.	Bricke, Gesina Engel	A	
Koo, Herman Heinrich	1, Nov. 1858	W.H.H.	Brink, Angela	A	
Koo, Wilhelm Gerhard Heinrich	20, Sept 1853	Wilhelm H.	Brink, Gesina Angela	A	
Koob, Anna Maria	6, Nov. 1858	Herman	Schaefer, Elisabeth	L	
Koons, Maria Anna	4, Dec. 1853	Friedrich	Tobe, Philomena	K	
Koons, Maria Bernardina	2, Dec. 1852	Friedrich	Toben, Bernardina Wilhelmina	K	
Koop, Anna Maria	21, Oct. 1854	Jacob	Bol, Anna Julia	A	
Koop, Carl Wilhelm Joseph	10, Jan. 1851	Joseph	Faske, Anna Maria	A	
Koop, Jacob	7, Dec. 1853	Herman	Farkenberg, Maria	C	
Koop, Jacob Herman	23, Mar. 1859	Jacob	Boor, Anna Julia	C	
Koop, Johan Wilhelm	25, June 1850	Herman	Schuhmacher, Helena	A	
Koop, Maria Francisca	18, Jan. 1857	Heinrich	Bode, Julia	C	
Koop, Maria Helena	5, Jan. 1852	Herman	Schumacker, Maria Helena	A	
Koopman, Maria Bernardina	14, Feb. 1858	Herman	Schuhmacher, Helena	N	
Koors, Anna Margaretha	7, June 1858	Friedrich	Tobe, Josephina	K	
Koors, Anton Bernard	24, Sept 1857	Bernard	Ferneding, Maria Anna	K	
Koors, Anton Joseph	5, Aug. 1851	J. Joseph	Rackel, Maria Elisabeth	A	
Koors, Francis Joseph	5, Nov. 1859	B.L.	Ferneding, Maria Anna	A	
Koors, Johan Herman	23, May 1853	J. Joseph	Rakel, Maria Elisabeth	K	
Koors, Margaretha Philomena	14, Nov. 1850	Friedrich	Tobe, Euphemia	K	
Koors, Maria Anna	8, Sept 1850	Bernard	Becker, Margaretha Anna	K	
Koors, Maria Catharina Francisca	28, June 1854	Bernard	Ferneding, Maria Anna	K	
Koors, Maria Elisabeth Francisca	19, Aug. 1854	Clemens	Brueggemann, Angela	L	
Koors, Maria Juliana	22, July 1852	Clemens	Bruegge, Angela	L	
Koper, Herman Clemens	1, Nov. 1858	Carl	Brueggemann, Antonia	F	
Kopf, Carl	1, Mar. 1851	Carl	Vitt, Rosa	F	
Köpfer, Seraph	21, Nov. 1858	Andreas	Weidener, Magdalena	J	48
Kopman, Charlotte Catherine	14, Apr. 1855	J. Bernard	Lindeman, Anna Catharina	Q	7
Kopman, Herman Heinrich	9, Nov. 1859	J. Herman	Schuhmacher, Helena	N	
Kopman, Johan Bernard Friedrich	31, Jan. 1857	J. Bernard	Lindeman, Catharina	Q	19
Kopman, Maria Theresa Carolina	27, Oct. 1858	J. Bernard	Linneman, Anna Catharina	N	
Kopmann, Bernard Heinrich	4, Sept 1851	Bernard H.	Kroeger, Euphemia	C	
Kopmann, Herman Heinrich Franz	7, May 1853	Bernard	Kroeger, A. Margaretha	L	
Kopmann, Maria Anna Philomena	19, June 1850	J. Bernard	Boier, Anna Maria	F	
Kopp, Elisabeth	11, May 1856	Georg	Vitt, Rosa	D	58
Kopp, Johan Frederick	26, Sept 1858	George	Vitt, Rosa	H	
Kopp, Maria Rosalia	19, Oct. 1856	Valentin	----, Maria	D	70
Kopp, Marianna	14, Mar. 1852	Georg	Vitt, Rosa	F	
Kopp, Rosa	27, Aug. 1854	Georg	Vitt, Rosa	D	16
Kopp, Wilhelm Herman	25, Apr. 1852	Constantine	Huber, Caecilia	C	
Kopper, Elisabeth Maria	3, June 1858	Theodor	Kolkman, Bernardina	A	
Kopriwa, Johan Wilhelm	1, June 1855	Johan	----, Maria	C	
Korb, Adam Carl	21, July 1850	Joseph	Vornwald, Francisca	D	224
Korb, Catharina	13, July 1856	Adam	Huetinger, Catharina	F	
Korb, Franz	29, June 1851	Adam	Hettinger, Catharina	F	
Korb, Joseph	19, Sept 1858	Adam	Hettinger, Catharina	F	
Korb, Margaretha	12, July 1857	Francis	Greider, Catharina	D	90
Korb, Maria Catharina	11, Sept 1853	Adam	Huetlinger, Catharina	F	
Korb, Maria Magdalena	13, Mar. 1859	Francis	Kreider, Catharina	D	134
Körbel, Anton	26, Feb. 1857	Albert	----, Magdalena	D	79
Körber, Georg Joseph	12, Feb. 1854	Johan	Herman, Catharina	J	26

Name of Child	Date of Baptism	Father	Mother	Church	Page
Körber, Johan Wilhelm	11, Apr. 1852	Johan	Herman, Catharina	J	16
Korber, Joseph	16, Dec. 1855	Johan	Herman, Catharina	J	34
Körber, Maria Wilhelmina	29, Dec. 1856		Körber, Justina	A	
Korderman, Clemens August	6, Aug. 1850	H. Joseph	Elseman, Maria Francisca	K	
Korders, Maria Anna	23, June 1856	J. Friedrich	Steinkamp, Maria Elisabeth	D	61
Kordes, Juliana	1, Mar. 1857	Carl	Meier, Carolina	D	80
Kordes, Rosalia	16, Oct. 1853	Heinrich	Geiger, Theresa	D	410
Korf, Johan Heinrich	15, Mar. 1855	Heinrich	Tiemann, Maria	C	
Korf, Maria Catharina	27, June 1857	Heinrich	Tiemann, Maria	C	
Korfhage, Anna Maria Gertrud	2, Nov. 1859	Heinrich	Lohman, Bernardina	A	
Korfhage, Johan Joseph	2, June 1851	Dietrich	Lohman, Bernardina	A	
Korfhage, M.A. Catharina Philomena	8, Apr. 1853	Dietrich	Lohman, Bernardina	A	
Korfhage, Maria Angela Bernardina	17, Nov. 1857	J. Dietrich	Lohman, Maria Anna	A	
Korfhage, Maria Anna	17, June 1855	Dietrich	Lohman, Bernardina	A	
Korher, Wilhelm	17, July 1859	Nicolaus	Reitmeyer, Antonia	C	
Korhoff, Johan Heinrich	26, Aug. 1855	Gerhard H.	Buden---, Maria Anna	D	41
Korhumer, Alexander	30, Apr. 1854	Ignatius	Köel, Anna	D	9
Korman, Johan	2, Aug. 1857	Conrad	Mil--ese, Elisabeth	D	91
Korn, Herman Bernard	8, June 1859	Jacob	Reb, Elisabeth	T	
Kornman, Margaretha Elisabeth	11, Dec. 1859	Cornelius	Milden---, Elisabeth	D	152
Kornmeier, Maria Theresa	10, Aug. 1856	August	Schneider, Louisa	D	64
Kornmeyer, Francis	7, Sept 1851	Carl	Friedmann, Elisabeth	C	
Kornmeyer, Georg	8, July 1856	Carl	Friedmann, Elisabeth	C	
Kornney, Jacob	6, Aug. 1854	Lawrence	Henning, Mary	K	
Kornwanz, Antonia	28, Aug. 1854	Johan	Siegelmeyer, Emilia	C	
Korre, Heinrich Bernard	2, May 1855	Bernard H.	VonderHeide, Elisabeth	C	
Korsenborn, Ludwig	30, Mar. 1851	Georg	Walter, Eva	A	
Korsmeier, Margaretha Catharina	11, Dec. 1856	Bernard	KleinSextro, Margaretha	F	
Korsmeyer, Bernardina	11, June 1858	Bernard	KleineSextro, Margaretha	A	
Korte, Anna Maria Christina	1, July 1853	Johan	Sarpe, Maria Adelheid	A	
Korte, Anna Maria Josephina	31, Dec. 1851	Gerhard	Dessing, Bernardina	D	299
Korte, Bernard Heinrich Aloysius	3, Oct. 1858	Heinrich	Boelschers, Maria Anna	L	
Korte, Bernard Heinrich Jacob	18, Sept 1858	B. Heinrich	VonderHeiden, Elisabeth	C	
Korte, Francis	23, May 1852	Friedrich	Macke, Elisabeth	K	
Korte, Heinrich Joseph	27, Sept 1850	Johan	Brenker, Anna	F	
Korte, Helena Elisabeth	2, Dec. 1851	Heinrich	Tepen, Bernardina	C	
Korte, Herman Heinrich	20, Sept 1853	Bernard H.	Mescher, Anna Catharina	D	407
Korte, Johan B. Alexander	15, Mar. 1859	Johan	Brinker, Anna	A	
Korte, Johan Bernard Heinrich	12, July 1854	Heinrich	Boelscher, M.A.	L	
Korte, Johan Gerhard	20, Jan. 1857	J. Heinrich	Boelscher, Maria Anna	L	
Korte, M. Agnes Mathilda Philomena	21, Jan. 1851	B. Heinrich	VonderHeide, Maria Elisabeth	K	
Korte, Maria	2, Mar. 1856	Johan	Voss, Maria Elisabeth	L	
Korte, Maria Angela	22, Feb. 1853	Mathias	Ronker, Elisabeth	A	
Korte, Maria Anna	6, May 1855	J. Heinrich	Roenneker, Lisette	L	
Korte, Maria Carolina	14, July 1853	Bernard	VonderHeide, Elisabeth	C	
Korte, Maria Elisabeth	26, May 1850	Heinrich	Borgeding, Angela	D	214
Korte, Maria Elisabeth	21, July 1857	J. Bernard	Berlage, Elisabeth	L	
Korte, Maria Elisabeth	11, Sept 1858	J. Bernard	Berlage, Elisabeth	L	
Korte, Maria Elisabeth Henrietta	19, Nov. 1857	Mathias	Roennker, Elisabeth	L	
Korte, Maria Philomena	3, Nov. 1850	Friedrich	Werke, Elisabeth	K	
Kortes, Anna Margaretha	17, Jan. 1852	Heinrich	Geiger, Theresa	D	302
Korthaus, Anna Bernardina	6, May 1853	Wilhelm	Stopperman, Elisabeth	D	384
Kortis, Mathias	10, Apr. 1859	Heinrich	Schor---, Rosina	D	135
Kortman, Anna Maria	20, Jan. 1859	Dietrich	Krusling, Anna Margaretha	K	
Kortman, Anna Maria Elisabeth	15, Apr. 1851	J. Heinrich	Meier, Maria Gertrud	A	
Korzenbaum, Anna	15, Aug. 1855	Friedrich	Latz, Elisabeth	W	9
Korzenborn, Ernestina	18, Oct. 1853	Friedrich	Laty, Elisabeth	C	
Korzenborn, Joseph	25, Jan. 1853	Georg	Walter, Eva	D	367
Korzenborn, Maria Louise	1, May 1852	Friedrich	Latz, Elisabeth	C	

Name of Child	Date of Baptism	Father	Mother	Church	Page
Kösler, Margaretha Elisabeth	2, Aug. 1852	Heinrich	Wirmer, Theresa	D	341
Kosmeier, Marianna	15, Mar. 1850	Johan	Bomkamp, Margaretha	D	205
Kossalman, Friedrica Angela	27, Nov. 1851	J. Wilhelm	Rütemayer, Maria Elisabeth	D	294
Köster, Joseph	21, Feb. 1852	Peter	Munzinger, Anna Maria	D	307
Kosterman, Carolina	14, Oct. 1858	Heinrich	N---, Josephina	D	121
Kosters, Anna Elisabeth	20, Mar. 1856	Bernard	Kottman, Elisabeth	A	
Kösters, Anna Maria Margaretha	29, Aug. 1857	Francis	Averdonk, Maria Gesina	A	
Kösters, Johan Bernard	26, Feb. 1859	Francis	Averdonk, Maria Gesina	A	
Kösters, Joseph Bernard	12, Oct. 1853	Bernard	Kottman, Elisabeth	A	
Kösting, Georg Bernard	3, Apr. 1859	Bernard	Schabing, Gertrud	D	135
Koter, Maria Carolina	3, Dec. 1856	Herman	B---gen, Agnes	D	73
Kots, Herman Heinrich	1, Jan. 1853	Heinrich	Rotering, Johanna	A	
Kots, Johanna Gertrud	30, Dec. 1856	Heinrich	Rotering, Johanna	A	
Kottenbrock, Bernard Heirnich	18, Apr. 1856	Heinrich	Kellerman, Gertrud	K	
Kottenbrock, Carl Heinrich	1, Apr. 1858	Heinrich	Kellerman, Maria Gertrud	K	
Kottenbrock, Heinrich Bernard	12, Nov. 1853	Heinrich	Kellerman, Maria Gertrud	K	
Kottenbrock, Maria Anna Josephina	14, Dec. 1851	Heinrich	Kellerman, Gertrud	K	
Kotter, Anna Maria Catharina	10, July 1850	G. Heinrich	Grevenkamp, Anna Maria	K	
Kötter, Bernard Joseph	2, Apr. 1857	Joseph	Möllering, Anna	A	
Kötter, Elisabeth Catharina	5, Nov. 1850	Heinrich	Meyer, Catharina	D	241
Kotter, Herman Heinrich Joseph	24, Nov. 1859	Joseph	Mollering, Anna	C	
Kötter, Johan Bernard	10, Mar. 1852	Gerhard	Kamping, Maria	A	
Kötter, Maria Agnes Louisa	2, Aug. 1859	Heinrich	Grevenkamp, Anna Maria	K	
Kötter, Maria Anna Catharina	28, Oct. 1856	Gerhard	Kamping, Maria	A	
Kötter, Maria Carolina	19, Jan. 1854	Heinrich	Meyer, Catharina	D	2
Kötter, Maria Josephina Bernardina	2, July 1854	Gerhard	Kamping, Marianna	A	
Kötter, Maria Louisa	1, May 1853	G. Heinrich	Grevenkamp, Maria Anna	K	
Kötter, Veronica	26, Jan. 1853	August	Schwarz, Maria Anna	K	
Kotters, Johan Bernard H.	16, Oct. 1856	J. Bernard	Imholt, M. Anna	C	
Kötting, Johan Gerhard	15, Jan. 1851	J. Gerhard	Romb, Maria Adelheid	D	249
Kottman, Maria Francisca Louisa	15, Sept 1851	Bernard	Rittman, Louisa	D	282
Kottmann, Anna Maria	23, Nov. 1853	J. Bernard	Fering, A. Margaretha	L	
Kottmann, Carl Ludwig	19, Dec. 1853	Philipp	Billian, Francisca	C	
Kottmann, Catharina Francisca	7, July 1853	Heinrich	Stelz, Catharina	C	
Kottmann, Emma	6, Apr. 1856	Heinrich	Stelz, Catharina	C	
Kottmann, Johan Gerhard	17, June 1855	Bernard H.	Fering, Margaretha	L	
Kottmann, Ludwig	6, Apr. 1856	Heinrich	Stelz, Catharina	C	
Kottmann, Margaretha Philomena	11, Aug. 1857	Bernard	Fehring, Margaretha	L	
Kottmann, Mathilda	14, Feb. 1858	J. Heinrich	Stelz, Catharina	C	
Kottmeier, Genofeva	30, July 1859	Christian	Danner, Christina	T	
Köttner, Elisabeth Catharina	20, Jan. 1851	Bernard H.	B---, Maria Adelheid	D	250
Kotz, Johan Heinrich	28, Nov. 1850	Heinrich	Rotering, Johanna Catharina	A	
Kotzenborn, Maria Theresa	20, Jan. 1858		Latz, Elisabeth	T	
Koverman, Johan	31, Aug. 1851	Edward	Niemeier, Clara	D	279
K---per, Dominica	29, Nov. 1857	Francis J.	Track, Theresa	D	99
Krab, Johan	14, Nov. 1852	Johan	Käfer, Rosina	N	10
Krabi?, Johan Jacob	27, July 1854	Johan	Dullman, Gesina Maria	K	
Kracht, Francis Heinrich	20, Dec. 1851	Wilhelm	Doepker, Catharina	A	
Kracht, Johan Wilhelm	23, Oct. 1850	Wilhelm	Doepker, Catharina	A	
Kracht, Maria Catharina Agnes	19, Jan. 1856	Wilhelm	Döpker, Catharina	A	
Kracht, Maria Elisabeth	4, Sept 1853	Wilhelm	Döpker, Anna Catharina	A	
Kracke, Herman Heinrich	9, Jan. 1852	Herman	Koenig, Elisabeth	C	
Kracke, Anna Maria Rosalia	27, Apr. 1857	Herman	Koenig, Elisabeth	L	
Kracke, Franz Herman	21, Jan. 1855	Heinrich	Pasmann, M. Elisabeth	L	
Kracke, Franz Joseph	4, Jan. 1857	Heinrich	Bussmann, Maria	L	
Kracke, Heinrich Andreas	30, Nov. 1853	Herman	Koenig, M. Elisabeth	L	
Kracke, Heinrich Clemens	26, Feb. 1856	Herman	König, Elisabeth	D	52
Kracke, Maria Elisabeth	30, Nov. 1858	Heinrich	Bussmann, M. Elisabeth	L	
Kraemer, Anton	19, Jan. 1857	Johan	Rasch, Maria	D	77

Name of Child	Date of Baptism	Father	Mother	Church	Page
Kraemer, Bernard Theodor	11, Nov. 1859	J. Gerhard	Hopman, Maria	K	
Kraemer, Bernard Wilhelm	7, Apr. 1858	Gerhard H.	Blömer, Catharina Gertrud	D	109
Kraemer, Carl Joseph	19, July 1850	Ferdinand	Wehming, M. Gertrud	L	
Kraemer, Catharina Francisca	4, Nov. 1854	Bernard	Wehming, Catharina	F	
Kraemer, Franz Xavier	2, Dec. 1854	Wilhelm	Wellen, Marianna	F	
Kraemer, Heinrich	15, July 1856	Friedrich	Kleinesextro, Catharina	K	
Kraemer, Heinrich Friedrich	25, Feb. 1851	Friedrich J.	Kleinesextro, Catharina	K	
Kraemer, Jacob	12, Jan. 1858		adult - 20 years old	T	
Kraemer, Johan Bernard	2, Aug. 1857	Ferdinand	Wehmenke, Gertrud	F	
Kraemer, Johan Bernard	9, July 1850	Herman	Kahlenberg, Adelheid	C	
Kraemer, Johan Felix	29, May 1854	Felix	Borntraeger, Elisabeth	D	11
Kraemer, Johan Ferdinand	19, July 1850	Ferdinand	Wehming, M. Gertrud	L	
Kraemer, Maria Anna	29, May 1851	Anton	Schwärzler, Rosalia	J	12
Kraemer, Maria Anna Philomena	2, Mar. 1851	Felix	Bonreicher, Elisabeth	L	
Kraemer, Maria Wilhelmina	9, July 1850	Herman	Kahlenberg, Adelheid	C	
Kraemer, Valentin	18, Sept 1859	Felix	Borntraeger, Anna Elisabeth	D	147
Kraemer, Wilhelm	24, Jan. 1857	Wilhelm	Wellen, Angela	F	
Kraf, Francis	26, Jan. 1851	Ignatius	Brickler, Christina	D	250
Kraf, Ignatius	27, Apr. 1856	Ignatius	Breichler, Christina	D	57
Kraf, Johan	16, Nov. 1851	J. Adam	Faulhaber, Catharina	D	292
Krafeld, Elisabeth Theresa	4, Apr. 1852	Herman	Roh, Louise	C	
Krafeld, Johan Heinrich Herman	5, Mar. 1854	Herman	Ruhe, Elisabeth	C	
Krafeld, Maria Anna	16, Apr. 1856	Herman	Ruh, Elisabeth	C	
Krafsack, Johan	9, Nov. 1857	Paul	Lamber--, Sophia	D	98
Krafsay, Albert	20, Apr. 1859	Paul	Lamber---, Sophia	D	136
Kraft, Barbara Josephina	11, Sept 1849	Nicolaus	Klaab, Marianna	S	
Kraft, Catharina	7, Oct. 1855	Nicolaus	Mathion, Regina	J	32
Kraft, Dorothea	16, Mar. 1856	Johan	Faulhaber, Catharina	D	54
Kraft, Ignatius	5, July 1857	Ignatius	Brubacker, Christina	D	89
Kraft, Jacob	28, Nov. 1858	Nicolaus	Glas, Maria	D	124
Kraft, Johan Baptist	16, Nov. 1851	Nicolaus	Plass, Anna Maria	D	292
Kraft, Joseph	3, Jan. 1853	Ignatius	Brüchler, Christina	D	363
Kraft, Magdalena	18, Sept 1859	Ignatius	Brichler, Christina	A	
Kraft, Margaretha Julia	26, May 1853	J. Adam	Faulhaber, Catharina	D	386
Kraft, Maria Anna	25, Mar. 1852	Johan	Reis, Carolina	D	314
Kraft, Maria Barbara	14, Mar. 1858	Nicolaus	Mathion, Regina	J	44
Kraft, Maria Elisabeth	5, Oct. 1857	Johan	Reiss, Carolina	L	
Kraft, Nicolaus	10, Dec. 1854	Johan	Reis, Carolina	F	
Kraft, Theresa	21, Sept 1856	Nicolaus	Klass, Maria	D	68
Krager, Anna Maria Elisabeth	24, June 1858	Ludwig	Wessellar, Catharina	D	113
Krakenberg, Franz	4, Dec. 1859	Ludwig	Meier, Maria	F	
Krall, Anton	9, Mar. 1857	Michael	Eck, Barbara	L	
Kramer, Adolph Heinrich	11, Jan. 1857	Adolph	Helmkamp, Agnes	C	
Kramer, Alfred Francis	24, Feb. 1859	Adolph	Helmkamp, Agnes	C	
Kramer, Amalia	18, Jan. 1857	Francis	He-bel, Anna	D	77
Kramer, Anna Francisca	6, Feb. 1859	Joseph	Kramer, Francisca	D	131
Kramer, Anna Maria	31, Feb. 1852	Arnold	Helmkamp, A.	K	
Kramer, Anna Maria Angela	26, Nov. 1856	Gerhard	Drahman, Maria Anna	A	
Kramer, Anton	12, Aug. 1856	Sebastian	Kraft, Sophia	J	36
Kramer, Bernard	2, July 1850	Herman H.	Kramer, Maria Magdalena	D	220
Kramer, Bernard Heinrich	23, Nov. 1858	J. Herman	Meyer, Maria Agnes	A	
Kramer, Bernard Herman Heinrich	4, July 1856	Theodor	Keller, Maria Anna	C	
Kramer, Bernard Theodor Heinrich	20, Aug. 1857	Gerhard	Weinel, Catharina Elisabeth	C	
Kramer, Bernardina	15, Oct. 1854	J. Wilhelm	Becker, Maria Agnes	A	
Kramer, Catharina Bernardina	21, June 1854	J. Bernard	Moormann, Bernardina	L	
Kramer, Elisabeth	23, Sept 1850	Heinrich	Brokamp, Elisabeth	N	1
Krämer, Elisabeth	3, Feb. 1850	Mathias	Brausch, Angela	D	202
Kramer, Emma Amelia	11, Mar. 1855	Johan	Meyer, Maria	K	
Krämer, Ferdinand	4, Apr. 1852	Ferdinand	Wenning, Maria Gertrud	D	315

Name of Child	Date of Baptism	Father	Mother	Church	Page
Krämer, Francis	6, Feb. 1853	Felix	Borntraeger, Elisabeth	D	369
Kramer, Francis Bernard	16, June 1859	Friedrich	Kleinesextro, Maria Catharina	K	
Kramer, Francis Heinrich	15, Feb. 1852	Heinrich	Kalvelage, Catharina	C	
Kramer, Francis Herman	30, Dec. 1853	Gerhard H.	Blömer, Gertrud	D	422
Kramer, Francis Wilhelm	4, June 1852	J. Heinrich	Meyer, Anna Maria	K	
Kramer, Friedrich Theodor	9, Nov. 1851	Bernard	Moormann, Bernardina	L	
Kramer, Heinrich August	26, Aug. 1855	J. Heinrich	Speckmann, Angela	C	
Kramer, Helena	18, Mar. 1857	Gottlieb	Tost, Elisabeth	D	81
Kramer, Johan	13, Mar. 1853	Sebastian	Kraft, Sophia	J	20
Kramer, Johan Gerhard	5, Oct. 1857	J. Bernard	Edelbr---, Maria Adelheid	D	96
Kramer, Johan Heinrich	17, Aug. 1851	J. Gerhard	Drahman, Maria Anna	A	
Kramer, Johan Heinrich	29, Sept 1856	J. Heinrich	Meyer, Maria Agnes	A	
Krämer, Johan Wilhelm Bernard	7, Aug. 1853	J. Bernard	Drahman, Marianna	A	
Kramer, Johanna Elisabeth	13, Oct. 1850	Bernard	Dreppe, Maria Catharina	F	
Kramer, John	20, Oct. 1850	Patrick	Mulligan, Mary	B	217
Kramer, Joseph Heinrich	28, Nov. 1858	Joseph	Rombach, M. Agnes	C	
Kramer, Louisa	4, Oct. 1855	Joseph	Kramer, Francisca	D	43
Krämer, Ludwig Eduard	28, Apr. 1858	Felix	Bornträger, Anna Elisabeth	D	110
Kramer, Maria	17, Sept 1854	Gottlieb	Gobmüller, Constantina	Q	5
Kramer, Maria	6, May 1852	Heinrich	Brokamp, Elisabeth	N	7
Kramer, Maria Agnes	30, Mar. 1853	Heinrich	Droppelmann, M. Catharina	F	
Kramer, Maria Anna	4, May 1856	Bernard	Moormann, Bernardina	L	
Krämer, Maria Anna	9, Nov. 1856	Joseph	Franzen, Maria Anna	D	71
Krämer, Maria Anna	13, May 1856	Gerhard H.	Blömer, Catharina Gertrud	D	58
Kramer, Maria Carolina	28, Feb. 1858	Sebastian	Kraft, Sophia	J	44
Kramer, Maria Catharina	18, Feb. 1852	G. Herman	Blömer, Gertrud Catharina	D	307
Kramer, Maria Christina Henrietta	25, Dec. 1859	August	Helmer, Elisabeth	F	
Kramer, Maria Clara Agnes	1, Oct. 1854	Adolph	Hellenkamp, Maria	C	
Kramer, Maria Elisabeth	4, Sept 1853	Bernard	Munsch, Louisa	D	404
Krämer, Maria Elisabeth	9, Apr. 1853	Friedrich	Kleinesextro, Catharina Maria	K	
Kramer, Maria Friedrica	14, Nov. 1856	Heinrich	Brokamp, Elisabeth	N	
Krämer, Maria Louisa	1, Oct. 1850	G. Herman	Blömer, Catharina Gertrud	D	236
Krämer, Maria Margaretha	18, Sept 1859	Johan	Engelbre--, Maria	D	147
Krämer, Mathias	19, Oct. 1851	Mathias	Brausch, Angela	D	287
Kramer, Philomena	6, Mar. 1859	Heinrich	Rocamp, Elisabeth	N	
Kramer, Robert	5, Aug. 1855	Francis	Hengel, Anna	C	
Kramer, Sophia Josephina	10, Aug. 1851	Francis	Sobers, Margaretha	A	
Kramer, Theresa Louisa	1, Nov. 1858	Carl	Hoenitz, Catharina	D	123
Kramer, Thomas	27, July 1851	Lawrence	McKew, Margaret	P	10
Kramer, Wilhelm Heinrich	25, Apr. 1858	Johan B.	Meyer, Mary	K	
Kramer, Wilhelm Joseph	28, Mar. 1859	Joseph	Kramsen, Maria Anna	D	135
Kramering, Gerhard Herman	19, Mar. 1856	Bernard	Heskamp, Anna	L	
Kramig, Christopher	20, Nov. 1851	Francis	Hehn, Catharina	A	
Kramig, Elisabeth	28, May 1854	Francis	Hana, Catharina	C	
Kramig, Francis Anton	3, Mar. 1859	Francis	Hersen, Catharina	C	
Kramker, Johan Joseph	26, Nov. 1858	Bernard	Nieman, Antonia	D	124
Kramper, Joseph Anton	6, May 1854	Joseph	Lichterich, Elisabeth	F	
Kramper, Marianna Magdlena	6, Apr. 1858	Joseph	Lechterich, Elisabeth	F	
Kramschuster, Barbara	22, Dec. 1859	Peter	Fruder, Barbara	D	153
Kramschuster, Francis	13, Sept 1857	Peter	Fruder, Barbara	D	94
Kramschuster, Margaretha	22, Dec. 1859	Peter	Fruder, Barbara	D	153
Kramschuster, Maria Louisa	13, Nov. 1853	Peter	Frut, Barbara	C	
Kramschuster, Peter	1, July 1855	Peter	Fruth, Barbara	C	
Kranning, Maria Anna Elisabeth	1, June 1856	Georg J.	Dirk, Catharina	D	59
Krantman, Theresa	19, Sept 1852	Johan	----, Anna Maria	H	
Kranz, Anna	4, July 1856	Anton	Rueters, Catharina	C	
Kranz, Bernard Heinrich Anton	19, Feb. 1857	Zacharius	Stegemann, Anna Maria	C	
Kranz, Carl	17, Apr. 1859	Anton	Rutker, Catharina	C	
Kranz, Johan Heinrich	10, Aug. 1853	Anton	----, Catharina	C	

Name of Child	Date of Baptism	Father	Mother	Church	Page
Kranz, Maria Gertrud	20, Apr. 1859	Zacharias	Stegemann, Anna M.	C	
Krassel, Francis Joseph	7, Apr. 1850	Johan	Dickman, Cunigunda	D	208
Krasser, Elisabeth	23, Jan. 1859	Carl	Gruch, Elisabeth	D	129
Kraua, Francis	30, Sept 1855	Johan	Trendl, Margaretha	D	43
Kraus, Adam Philipp	3, Jan. 1858	Adam	Haus, Elisabeth	F	
Kraus, Adam Philipp	23, May 1859	Adam	Hausch, Elisabeth	F	
Kraus, Agnes Margaretha	12, Aug. 1856	Andreas	Seemüller, Eva	D	64
Kraus, Amelia Francisca	9, Apr. 1851	Conrad	Fleisman, Theresa	A	
Kraus, Andreas	4, Sept 1853	Johan	Trendl, Margaretha	D	404
Kraus, Barbara Eva	23, Apr. 1854	Carl	Schwaebel, Barbara	D	8
Kraus, Carl Georg	14, Oct. 1855	Carl	Schwaebel, Barbara	D	44
Kraus, Catharina	21, Feb. 1858	Johan	Trendl, Margaretha	D	105
Kraus, Catharina	25, Nov. 1855	Michael	Nehring, Elisabeth	F	
Kraus, Georg Michael	29, Nov. 1858	Conrad M.	Stüsman, Theresa	A	
Kraus, Herman Heinrich Mathis	15, Jan. 1858	J. Friedrich	Hobman, Maria Anna	D	102
Kraus, Johan	25, Mar. 1855	Andreas	Seemüller, Eva	D	32
Kraus, Johan Michael	13, Nov. 1853	Conrad M.	Bleichman, Theresa	A	
Kraus, Joseph	6, Nov. 1853	Georg	Clark, Sara	D	414
Kraus, Magdalena	20, Oct. 1850	Georg	Grindel, Margaretha	D	239
Kraus, Margaretha	3, June 1858	Carl	Schwaebel, Barbara	D	112
Kraus, Michael	24, Sept 1854	Johan	Kraft, Catharina	D	18
Kraus, Michael	29, Sept 1850	Michael	Neuring, Maria Elisabeth	D	235
Krauss, Johan	14, June 1857	Johan	Braun, Margaretha	D	87
Krautheimer, Johan Georg	5, Feb. 1855	Johan	Gallenstein, Barbara	K	
Krautwasser, Theresa	24, July 1856	Johan	Gallenstein, Barbara	K	
Krebs, Anna Catharina	20, Jan. 1856		Krebs, Rosina	D	51
Krebs, Anna Elisabeth	5, Sept 1858	Joseph	Staab, Anna Maria	D	118
Krebs, Anna Eva	31, May 1852	Joseph	Einloth, Margaretha	D	322
Krebs, Antonia	6, May 1851	Caspar	Reinsen, Anna Johanna	C	
Krebs, Gerhardina Catharina	30, July 1854	Caspar	Reinsing, A. Johanna	L	
Krebs, Johan Francis	16, Oct. 1853	Wilhelm	Gasser, Theresa	C	
Krebs, Johan Paul	7, Sept 1855	J. Paul	Meber, Maria Anna	K	
Krebs, Joseph	16, Apr. 1853	Caspar	Reinzen, Anna Johanna	K	
Krebs, Ludwig	12, June 1853	Johan	Abbes, Anna Maria	K	
Krebs, Margaretha	25, Feb. 1855	Wilhelm	Gasser, Dorothea	C	
Krebs, Maria	10, Sept 1854	Johan	Bauer, Catharina	F	
Krebs, Maria Amelia Louisa	25, Mar. 1859	Caspar	Reinze, Johanna	K	
Krebs, Maria Catharina Philomena	30, Nov. 1856	Caspar	Reinzen, Theresa Johanna	K	
Krebs, Maria Margaretha	1, Sept 1850	Ludwig	Bechl, M. Anna	C	
Krebs, Paul Philipp	31, Jan. 1858	Wilhelm	Gasser, Dorothea	C	
Krebs, Peter Paul Lawrence	18, July 1858	J. Paul	Abba, Maria	K	
Krebs, Susanna	18, July 1852	Joseph	Walles, Maria Anna	D	329
Krebsbach, Anna Margaretha	16, Oct. 1854	Johan	Sery, Margaretha	F	
Krebsbach, Jacob Oswald	21, Nov. 1858	Johan	Jerry, Margaretha	T	
Kreckler, Bernard	11, Sept 1853	Bernard	Siemes, Elisabeth	C	
Krehenbrink, Johan Bernard Joseph	2, Mar. 1854	Herman	Grotjohan, Elisabeth	C	
Krehenbrink, Johanna Gertrud	25, Nov. 1857	Bernard	Hesskamp, Helena	C	
Krehenbrinks, M. Josephina Elisabeth	4, Dec. 1851	Heinrich	Grotjohan, Elisabeth	C	
Kreher, Anton	19, June 1859	Michael	Hertlin, Maria	T	
Krehming, Johan Heinrich Aloysius	3, Aug. 1856	Heinrich	Grotian, Anna M.	C	
Krehn, Johan Carl	22, Aug. 1858	Peter	Diringer, Jacobina	D	117
Kreidenweiss, George	13, May 1855	Frederick	----, Catherine	H	
Kreider, Josephina	3, Oct. 1852	J. Joseph	Fang, Catharina	D	351
Kreideweiss, Ursula Barbara	26, July 1857	Friedrich	wermuth, Catharina	H	
Kreienbaum, Georg Heinrich	22, Sept 1850	Georg H.	Erdmann, Catharina	C	
Kreienbaum, Maria Catharina	19, Apr. 1857	Georg H.	Erdmann, M. Catharina	L	
Kreienbaum, Maria Catharina	27, Apr. 1853	Heinrich	Erdmann, M. Catharina	L	
Kreiennest, Anna Elisabeth	1, June 1852	Heinrich	Brockman, Elisabeth	A	
Kreighead, George	20, Sept 1850	----	----, ----	E	248

Name of Child	Date of Baptism	Father	Mother	Church	Page
Kreinert, Maria Elisabeth	7, Apr. 1851	J. Heinrich	Beckman?, Maria Elisabeth	A	
Krekeler, Herman Heinrich	3, Sept 1855	Bernard	Ziener, M. Elisabeth	F	
Krekeler, Joseph	24, Nov. 1850	Bernard	Siemer, Elisabeth	C	
Krekler, Francis Bernard	14, Dec. 1851	Bernard	Siemer, M. Elisabeth	C	
Krelin, Nicolaus	12, Jan. 1852	Nicolaus	Eberlin, Barbara	L	
Kreling, Heinrich Wilhelm Joseph	12, Sept 1858	August	Rettman, Friedrica	A	
Kreling, Maria Clara	4, Apr. 1856	August	Redmann, Friedricka	C	
Kremer, Heinrich Theodor	10, May 1852	Johan D.	Wichmanns, M. Catharina	F	
Krempe, Barbara Maria	11, Apr. 1856	Thomas	Brachle, Maria	A	
Krempelman, Josephina Bd. Helena	26, Jan. 1859	Joseph	Gertrud, Maria Anna	C	
Krennan, Christine	22, Aug. 1852	Patrick	Heinz, Mary	B	268
Krenz, Anna Maria	31, Aug. 1856	Carl	Christ, Catharina	D	66
Krenz, Jacob Carl	11, Apr. 1858	Carl	Christ, Catharina	D	109
Kresbenk, Anna Maria Angela	7, Oct. 1851	Bernard	Meik, Elisabeth	D	286
Kresser, Catharina Augustina	7, Feb. 1858	Johan	Berger, Margaretha	A	
Kresser, Emerentiana Catharina	3, Feb. 1856	Johan	Berger, Margaretha	A	
Kressman, Peter Wilhelm	14, Dec. 1854	Adam	Conrad, Maria	K	
Krettenhemer, Henriette	6, Oct. 1850	John	----, Mary	E	252
Kreuser, Margaretha	12, Sept 1852	Francis	Kink, Anna	L	
Kreutz, Catharina	6, Nov. 1858	Daniel	Kr---, Margaretha	D	123
Kreutz, Eugene Peter Maria	23, Apr. 1857	Jacob	Lier, Carolina	A	
Kreutz, Johan M. Joseph	25, Dec. 1858	Jacob	Lier, Carolina	D	127
Kreutz, Maria Louisa	27, Aug. 1854	Jacob	Lier, Carolina	D	16
Kreutzburg, Joseph Maria	4, Aug. 1853	Peter M.	Nurre, Gertrud	D	398
Kreutzjohan, Maria	20, Aug. 1850	Christian	Lindeman, Maria	K	
Kreuz, Alphons Maria	28, Nov. 1852	Jacob	Lier, Carolina	D	358
Kreuz, Maria Antonia Josephina	22, Sept 1850	Jacob	Lier, Carolina	D	234
Kreuzburg, Maria Cyprian	16, May 1856	Peter M.	Nurre, Maria Gertrud	D	58
Kreuzdorn, Johan Wilhelm	12, July 1857	Johan	Thomas, Christina	G	
Kreuzjohan, Maria Helena	7, Oct. 1852	Christian	Linneman, Maria	K	
Kreuzmann, Maria Catharina	13, Apr. 1851	Joseph	Knapke, Elisabeth	L	
Kreyer, Carl	20, May 1858	Carl	Merker, J. Friedricka	F	
Krie, Johan Martin	29, June 1851	Caspar	Krie, Maria	K	
Krie--bock, Maria Elisabeth	24, Oct. 1859	Rudolph	----man, Maria Anna	D	149
Krieche, Mathilda	20, Sept 1857	Johan	Becker, Maria	D	94
Krieg, Adam	28, Sept 1856	Jacob	Gross, Anna Maria	J	38
Krieg, Anna Maria Gertrud	10, Oct. 1852	Johan	Fey, Elisabeth	D	352
Krieg, Carl	19, Mar. 1854	Johan	Fey, Elisabeth	J	26
Krieg, Johan	28, Sept 1856	Jacob	Gross, Anna Maria	J	38
Krieg, Johan Martin	30, June 1850	Johan	Fey, Elisabeth	D	219
Krieg, Joseph	13, Mar. 1853	Benedict	Welsch, Johanna	J	20
Krieg, Martin	19, Aug. 1855	J. Joseph	Sutter, Joanne	N	
Krieg, Wilhelmina	9, Apr. 1850	Benedict	Welsch, Johanna	A	
Kriege, Maria Josephina	2, Feb. 1851	Jacob	Marixen, Magdalena	G	
Krieger, Bernardina	9, Feb. 1851		Krieger, Bernardina	D	252
Krieger, Dina Elise	1, Apr. 1854	Johan H.	Talken, Carolina Elisabeth	F	
Krieger, Johan	18, July 1852	Robert	Bauer, Maria Anna	F	
Krieger, Johan Joseph	13, June 1858	Johan	Rothhaus, Magdalena	F	
Krieger, Maria Theresa	23, Mar. 1856	Johan	Becker, Anna Maria	D	54
Krieger, Philomena	20, July 1856	Johan	Rothan, Magdalena	F	
Krig, Martin	24, July 1859	Martin	Renz, Margaretha	Q	32
Krilb, Julia	14, July 1858	Joseph	Krilbach, Johanna	C	
Krim, Francis Anton	29, Jan. 1854	Jacob	Berger, Carolina	D	3
Krinkemeier, Maria Elsabeth	17, Sept 1850	J. Heinrich	Bethinghaus, Maria Catharina	D	233
Krinkenmieer, Anna Maria Elisa	13, Nov. 1851	Heinrich	Brinkhaus, Maria Anna	D	292
Kristel, Ferdinand	3, Sept 1852	Sebastian	Mühleisen, Genofeva	D	346
Kristmann, Joseph	27, Dec. 1853	Ignatius	Baiel, Maria	C	
Kritzelmann, E. Francisca Augusta	14, Sept 1853	Georg	Wipenberg, Elisabeth	C	
Kroder, Johan Friedrich	2, Sept 1855	Friedrich	Schau, Kunigunda	C	

Name of Child	Date of Baptism	Father	Mother	Church	Page
Kroder, Margaretha	21, Sept 1851	Friedrich	Scharholt, Kunigunda	C	
Kroeger, Adam Heinrich	26, Sept 1859		Kroeger, Susanna M.	T	
Kroeger, Anna Maria	26, Sept 1856	August	Imholt, Anna Maria	C	
Kroeger, Bernard August Anton	5, May 1858	August	Imhoff, Theresa	C	
Kroeger, Bernard Heinrich	27, Apr. 1851	J. Heinrich	Massman, Agnes	D	262
Kroeger, Catharina Elisabeth	21, May 1855	August	Sextro, Elisabeth	F	
Kroeger, Christoph Edward	20, Dec. 1857	Heinrich	Schlebbe, Maria	F	
Kroeger, Dorothea Elisabeth	17, Aug. 1856	Heinrich	Brömlage, Elisabeth	K	
Kroeger, Edward Herman	26, June 1855	Bernard	Hüls, Bernardina	K	
Kroeger, Georg Wilhelm	16, Sept 1855	Johan H.	Schlebbe, M. Gertrud	F	
Kroeger, Heinrich Joseph	9, Apr. 1857	Johan H.	Massmann, Maria Agnes	F	
Kroeger, Helena Philomena	7, Apr. 1854	J. Herbert	Wilken, Helena	K	
Kroeger, Johan Albert	24, Apr. 1859	Bernard	Hüls, Bernardina Christina	K	
Kroeger, Johan Aloysius	12, Oct. 1855	Herman	Wilke, Anna Helena	K	
Kroeger, Johan Friedrich	22, Oct. 1854	Johan H.	Massmann, Maria Agnes	F	
Kroeger, Johan Heinrich	27, Apr. 1851	J. Heinrich	Massman, Agnes	D	262
Kroeger, Johan Joseph	7, Sept 1859	J. Herbert	Wilken, Helena	K	
Kroeger, Johan Theodor	27, Nov. 1853	Johan H.	Schlebbe, M. Gertrud	F	
Kroeger, Joseph	30, Jan. 1859	Heinrich	Bromlage, Elisabeth	K	
Kroeger, Maria Anna Veronica	4, Aug. 1850	Bernard	----, Maria Veronica	K	
Kroeger, Maria Elisabeth	2, May 1852	J. Heinrich	Massman, Maria Agnes	D	318
Kroeger, Wilhelm Heinrich August	25, Jan. 1853	August	Sextro, Maria Elisabeth	F	
Kroene, Maria Catharina	26, Oct. 1851	Bernard H.	Janning, Anna Catharina	C	
Kroenes, Johan Anton	22, Mar. 1855	Johan	Beid, Jacobina	D	31
Kroenes, Wilhelm	26, Dec. 1852	Johan	Beit, Jacobina	D	362
Kröger, Anna Maria	31, July 1859	Bernard	Egbers, Anna Veronica	K	
Kröger, August B. Heinrich	29, Nov. 1858	Heinrich	Grieshopp, Margaretha	A	
Kröger, Bernard Christoph	28, Sept 1854	Heinrich	Bramlage, Catharina Elisabeth	K	
Kröger, Bernard Friedrich	21, Aug. 1857	Bernard	Huls, Bernardina	K	
Kröger, Carolina Bernardina	6, Apr. 1851	Bernard	Huer, Bernardina	K	
Kröger, Elisabeth Bernardina Friedrica	6, Feb. 1853	Heinrich	Bramlage, Elisabeth	K	
Kroger, Georg Friedrich	4, Feb. 1850	Bernard	Hülls, Dina	K	
Kröger, Heinrich Joseph Friedrich	2, May 1858	Joseph	Bramlage, Wilhelmina	A	
Kröger, Herman Heinrich	2, July 1851	Heinrich	Bramlage, Elisabeth	K	
Kröger, Johan August	23, Nov. 1851	Johan	Gerding, Elisabeth	K	
Kroger, Johan Bernard	4, Feb. 1850	Bernard	Hülls, Dina	K	
Kröger, Johan Heinrich	7, Dec. 1859	J. Heinrich	Wünneman, Anna Maria	K	
Kröger, Maria Catharina	20, Mar. 1851	Dietrich	Hausman, Julia	A	
Kröger, Maria Catharina	1, Sept 1856	Heinrich	Grieshopp, Margaretha	A	
Kröger, Maria Elisabeth	27, June 1859	J. Bernard	Vahle, Maria Anna	R	
Kröger, Maria Emma Elisabeth	9, Sept 1853	Bernard	Hüls, Bernardina	K	
Kröger, Maria Josephina	2, July 1854	J. Herman	Greishop, Margaretha	A	
Kröger, Maria Rosina	30, Jan. 1856	Bernard	Egbers, Veronica	K	
Kröger, Maria Wilhelmina	15, Jan. 1853	Bernard	Egbers, Veronica	K	
Kroger, Romana Maria	24, Feb. 1858	Herbert	Wilken, Helena	K	
Krogman, Catharina Theresa	28, Oct. 1857	Anton	Brinkmeyer, Maria Catharina	A	
Krohn, Catharina Elisabeth Engel	18, Aug. 1850	Wilhelm	Brinke, ----	A	
Krohn, Francisca	5, Dec. 1859	Peter	Lieringer, Jacobina	D	152
Krolage, Anna Catharina Elisabeth	26, Sept 1857	Heinrich	Wolker, Elisabeth	C	
Krolage, Benjamin Francis	9, Nov. 1858	Bernard	----, ----	C	
Krolage, Bernard Heinrich	7, Nov. 1855	Bernard H.	Walke, Anna M. Louisa	C	
Krolage, Maria Catharina Francisca	18, Dec. 1859	Heinrich	Walke, Catharina Gertrud	C	
Kronlage, Anna Maria	12, Apr. 1855	Friedrich	Peddenpohl, Anna M.	L	
Kronlage, Anna Maria	8, Feb. 1852	Heinrich	Setlage, Dorothea	L	
Kronlage, Franz Heinrich	22, July 1857	Francis	Weismann, Clara	F	
Kronlage, Wilhelm Heinrich Friedr.	29, Oct. 1857	Friedrich	Peddenpohl, M. Elis.	L	
Kronmüller, Maria Theresa	17, Mar. 1850	Johan	Baier, Luikart	A	
Krör, Johan Theodor	23, July 1854	C. Heinrich	Weber, Elisabeth	J	28
Krosmeyer, Anna Maria Elisabeth	10, Oct. 1857	Gerhard H.	Ott, A.M. Elisabeth	T	

Name of Child	Date of Baptism	Father	Mother	Church	Page
Krote, Georg	21, May 1854	Friedrich	Scharholt, Kunigunda	C	
Krottmann, Maria Agnes	20, Oct. 1850	Heinrich	Stuewe, M. Gertrud	C	
Krouter, Maria Francisca	2, Jan. 1859	Friedrich	Scharholt, Kunigunda	C	
Krozinger, Wilhelmina	20, May 1850	Georg	Waltel, Elisabeth	D	213
Krueb, Gerhard Heinrich	31, Aug. 1852	J. Gerhard	Thi, Anna Maria	F	
Krueb, Maria Philomena	18, Jan. 1850	Gerhard	Thi, Anna Maria	F	
Krueker, Maria Gertrud	30, June 1856	Anton	Mertens, Elisabeth	F	
Kruempelmann, Carolina Catharina	3, Jan. 1858	Georg	Thiemann, Elisabeth	F	
Krueschel, Johan Bernard	19, July 1850	J. Bernard	Ruettermann, Anna Maria	F	
Kruesling, Johan Heinrich	6, Dec. 1857	J. Bernard	Ruetermann, Anna Maria	F	
Kruesling, Margaretha Agnes	18, Jan. 1855	J. Bernard	Ruettermann, Anna M.	F	
Kruesling, Maria Catharina	14, Nov. 1852	J. Bernard	Ritterman, Anna Maria	F	
Krug, Amalia Theresa	19, Dec. 1858	Jacob	Schulz, Maria	D	126
Krug, Anna Maria Elisabeth	17, Aug. 1856	Adam	Hoefer, Henrietta	J	38
Krug, Carl Jacob	9, Jan. 1854	Jacob	Schulz, Maria	D	1
Krug, Catharina	13, Feb. 1854	Johan	Fritz, Elisabeth	D	4
Krug, Cunigunda	18, Apr. 1858	Adam	Hoefer, Henrietta	J	46
Krug, Edward	9, Nov. 1856	Jacob	Schulz, Maria	D	71
Krug, Francis	13, June 1850	Georg	Riss, Barbara	D	217
Krug, Franz	6, Apr. 1851	Dagobert	Sictinger, Genofeva	F	
Krug, Hubert	12, May 1850	Dagobert	Sickinger, Genofeva	F	
Krug, Johan	28, Mar. 1855	Jacob	Scholz, Maria	J	30
Krug, Johan Georg	26, Nov. 1851	Georg	Riss, Barbara	D	294
Krum, Ann	20, Mar. 1856	Thomas	Lucas, Mary	E	351
Krumberg, Johan Herman Theodor	6, Aug. 1853	Herman	Menke, Elisabeth	C	
Krumberg, Maria Josephina	25, Dec. 1850	Herman	Menke, Elisabeth	C	
Krumberg, Maria Philomena	26, Sept 1850	Theodor	Moellmann, Elisabeth	C	
Krumbusch, Anna Maria	11, July 1858	Carl	Geiger, Theckla	D	114
Krumme, Bernard Franz	5, Oct. 1859	Francis B.	Huelskamp, Elisabeth	F	
Krumme, Christina Elisabeth	6, Sept 1854	Bernard	Hilsken, Elisabeth	F	
Krumme, Heinrich Franz	26, Feb. 1857	Bernard	Huelskamp, Elisabeth	F	
Krumme, Maria Elisabeth	16, July 1857	Herman F.	Kamp, Theresa	F	
Krumme, Rosa Catharina	5, Sept 1859	Francis	Kamp, Theresa	F	
Krummen, Herman	5, Apr. 1857	J. Bernard	Grewers, Margaretha	C	
Krummen, Johan Heinrich	18, July 1859	J. Bernard	Grevers, Margaretha	C	
Krümpelbeck, Augustine Ludwig	20, Nov. 1855	Francis H.	Quatman, Carolina	D	47
Krümpelbeck, Johan Bernard	26, May 1851	Francis	Quatman, Maria Carolina	D	266
Krümpelbeck, Maria Rosalia	28, June 1853	Francis H.	Quartman, Carolina	D	392
Krümpelman, Bernard Heinrich	17, Mar. 1858	Christian	Jansen, Catharina Elisabeth	A	
Krümpelman, Johan Heinrich Anton	1, Aug. 1855	Johan	Jansen, Elisabeth	A	
Krumpelman, M. Philomena Elisabeth	3, Dec. 1850	Christian	Jansen, Elisabeth	A	
Krumpelmann, Elisabeth	11, Sept 1855	Georg	Schaefer, Maria	C	
Krumpholz, Daniel	23, Nov. 1858	Herman	Knoll, Anna	K	
Krup, Ferdinand Clemens	20, Sept 1857	Francis	Korte, Anna Maria	L	
Krüp, Johan Bernard	12, Jan. 1854	Francis	Korte, Maria Anna	D	1
Kruse, Albert	14, Sept 1852	Heinrich	Brüggeman, Sophia	D	347
Kruse, Albert Heinrich August	17, Sept 1856	Heinrich	Aschman, A. Francisca	D	67
Kruse, Anna Catharina	22, June 1852	Heinrich	Backe, Anna Maria	L	
Kruse, Anna Gertrud	3, Nov. 1859	Heinrich	Brüggeman, Sophia	D	150
Kruse, Anna Maria Clara	13, July 1859	Heinrich	Wilmer, Maria Agnes	L	
Kruse, Anna Sophia	23, May 1856	J. Heinrich	Brüggeman, Sophia	D	59
Kruse, Carl Friedrich	4, Feb. 1855	J. Bernard	Ubert, A. Maria	K	
Kruse, Catharina Hermina	8, Oct. 1856	J. Heinrich	Wilmer, Agnes	A	
Kruse, Gustav Adolf	26, Dec. 1858	Heinrich	Aschman, Francisca	D	127
Kruse, Johan Bernard	21, Jan. 1850	Joseph	Bolles, Maria Agnes	L	
Kruse, Johan Gerhard Friedrich	6, Oct. 1852	Arnold	Heekmann, Bernardina	L	
Kruse, Maria Bernardina	28, Jan. 1851	Arnold	Hackmann, Bernardina	L	
Kruse, Maria Catharina Agnes	18, Jan. 1853	Heinrich	Wilmer, Agnes	L	
Kruse, Maria Catharina Elisabeth	18, Jan. 1855	J. Heinrich	Wilmer, Maria Agnes	L	

Name of Child	Date of Baptism	Father	Mother	Church	Page
Kruse, Maria Rosalia	17, Jan. 1854	J. Heinrich	Brüggeman, Sophia	D	2
Kruse, Otto Heinrich	29, Sept 1854	Heinrich	Ausmann, Francisca Dina	F	
Kruse, Philipp Heinrich	13, July 1859	Heinrich	Wilmer, Maria Agnes	L	
Krusemeier, Anna Maria	26, Dec. 1853	Heinrich	Otto, Elisabeth	F	
Krusemeier, Bernard Heinrich	27, Jan. 1856	Heinrich	Ott, Elisabeth	F	
Krusemeier, Casper August	29, Aug. 1850	Conrad	Brockamp, Elisabeth	A	
Krusemeyer, Anna Maria	8, Jan. 1855	Herman	Schromeyer, Dina	C	
Krusemeyer, Herman Bernard	10, Sept 1850	Herman	Schroenmeyer, Dina	C	
Krusemeyer, Herman Heinrich	20, Dec. 1855	Conrad	Eilerman, Anna Maria	A	
Krusemeyer, Johan Joseph	28, Nov. 1858	Joseph	Broermann, Louisa	C	
Krusemeyer, Maria Adelheid	19, Aug. 1854	Conrad M.	Eilerman, Anna Maria	A	
Kruthaup, Anna Maria	23, Aug. 1856	Joseph	Lange, Maria	Q	15
Kruthaup, Anna Maria Josephina	19, Sept 1857	J. Herman	Ricking, Anna M. Bernardina	K	
Kruthaup, Bernard Edward	24, Oct. 1855	J. Herman	Reicking, Maria Bernardina	K	
Kruthaup, Bernard Friedrich	14, Dec. 1858	Friedrich	Laing, Dina	K	
Kruthaup, Joseph Heinrich	5, Aug. 1859	Joseph	Lang, Maria	Q	32
Kruthaupt, Heinrich	26, June 1853	J. Herman H.	Bis---, Maria A. Bernardina	K	
Kruthof, Maria Philomena	8, May 1851	H. Heinrich	Ricking M. Agnes Bernardina	K	
K---th, Leonard	18, Dec. 1856	Leonard	----, Christina	D	74
Kuball, Emma Margaretha	10, Jan. 1854	Adolph	Seibert, Elisabeth	C	
Kübel, Joseph	4, Aug. 1853	Carl	Ruschman, Rosalia	D	398
Kübel, Rosina	29, Aug. 1850	Carl	Rueschman, Rosalia	D	230
Kubisch, Anna Maria	3, Oct. 1858	Francis M.	Jung, Maria Anna	G	
Kucher, Heinrich	16, Oct. 1853	Georg	Fuls, Maria	Q	3
Kuckman, Charlotta Catharina Henr.	9, June 1850	Heinrich	Nieman, Maria Catharina	D	216
Kuckman, Nicolaus	12, Apr. 1857	Nicolaus	Klein, Catharina	D	82
Kuckmeyer, Anna Maria Francisca	15, Apr. 1856	Heinrich	Niemann, M. Cath.	L	
Kuckmeyer, Wilhelm Joseph	8, Aug. 1852	Heinrich	Niemann, M. Catharina	L	
Kuderer, Johan	6, Nov. 1859	Bartholomew	Oberle, Veronica	Q	34
Kuebing, Catharina Bernardina	15, Feb. 1850	Joseph	Tiemann, Catharina	C	
Kueffler, George	13, Apr. 1851	George	Hoelzlein, Elisabeth	H	
Kuehlenberg, Anna Angela Maria	29, Nov. 1857	Johan	Rechtin, M. Gesina	F	
Kuehlenberg, Gesina Elisabeth	28, Sept 1859	Johan	Rechtin, Gesina	F	
Kuehlenburg, Barbara Wilhelmina	29, Apr. 1856	Johan	Rechtin, Maria Gesina	F	
Kuehne, Mary Magdalene	9, Apr. 1855	John B.	----, M. Magdalena Barbara	H	
Kuemmel, Johan	30, Jan. 1857	Vincent	Knapp, Louisa	L	
Kuemmerling, Gerhard	5, Aug. 1855	Bernard	Gerwers, Catharina	F	
Kuemper, Catharina Elisabeth	30, July 1855	J. Bernard	Boeckmann, Elisabeth	L	
Kuemper, Maria Elisabeth	10, Mar. 1857	Bernard	Bockmann, Elisabeth	L	
Kuemper, Maria Elisabeth	2, Nov. 1859	J. Bernard	Bockmann, Elisabeth	L	
Kuenne, Andreas Stephan	18, Apr. 1851	Andreas	Wiemeyer, M.	C	
Kuennen, Maria Catharina	18, Dec. 1855	Stephan A.	Wehmeier, Maria Engel	F	
Kuennen, Maria Theresa	11, Dec. 1857	Stephan	Wiemeier, Maria	F	
Kues, Anna Elisabeth	21, Apr. 1858	Herman	Reiss, Anna Adelheid	U	
Kues, Christina Josephina	14, Mar. 1854	Bernard	Buening, Elisabeth	L	
Kues, Johan Herman Bernard	19, June 1855	Bernard	Buening, Elisabeth	L	
Kues, Johanna Josephina	14, Apr. 1859	J. Gerhard	Weitzel, Anna Maria	L	
Kues, Maria Anna Francisca	23, Dec. 1855	Johan	Weitzel, Margaretha	L	
Kues, Maria Anna Theresa	13, Nov. 1851	Bernard	Buening, Elisabeth	L	
Küfer, Magdalena	15, Apr. 1854	Johan	Dahlheimer, Catharina	K	
Küfer, Simeon	13, Jan. 1850	Jacob	Meier, Maria	J	6
Kugh, Charles	28, Apr. 1856	Edmund	O'Neil, Catherine	E	363
Kugler, Francis Joseph	5, Dec. 1852	Peter	----, Ann	H	
Kuhal, Anna Maria	28, Oct. 1856	Adolph	Seefert, Elisabeth	C	
Kuhal, Emilia	9, Nov. 1858	Adolph	Seibert, Elisabeth	C	
Kuhen, Elisabeth	10, Mar. 1850	Wilhelm	Jansen, Rosina	K	
Kuhl, Anna Maria	3, Mar. 1858	Bernard	Hof---, Anna Angela	D	106
Kuhl, Anna Maria Elisabeth	24, Apr. 1851	Philipp	Engel, Anna	C	
Kuhl, Bernard Heinrich	14, Mar. 1857	J. Heinrich	Doerpel, Euphemia	D	80

Name of Child	Date of Baptism	Father	Mother	Church	Page
Kuhl, Herman Francis	4, Nov. 1853	J. Bernard	Niehoff, Angela	C	
Kuhl, Johan August Hieronymus	23, Aug. 1853	H. Michael	Darpel, Euphemia	D	402
Kuhl, Johan Bernard	18, Sept 1856	Herman	Fortmann, Carolina	C	
Kuhl, Maria Antonia Carolina	15, Aug. 1851	Heinrich	Darpel, Euphemia Adelheid	D	278
Kuhlenberg, Anna Catharina	30, Mar. 1853	J. Heinrich	Götke, Elisabeth	D	378
Kuhlenberg, Johan Heinrich	13, Aug. 1854	J. Albert	Hafner, Magdalena	F	
Kuhlenberg, Johan Heinrich	9, Sept 1855	J. Heinrich	Götke, Elisabeth	D	42
Kuhlenberg, Josephina	2, Feb.1857	Gerhard H.	Rolfeson, Elisabeth	D	78
Kuhlenberg, Maria Catharina Elisabeth	19, Oct. 1854	Gerhard H.	Rolferz, Maria Elisabeth	D	20
Kühling, Bernardina Josephina	17, Sept 1856	Heinrich	Döbler, Helena	A	
Kuhling, Maria Elisabeth	12, Sept 1858	Heinrich	Döbbler, Helena	A	
Kuhlman, Anna Catharina	9, Jan. 1855	Joseph	Wessling, Maria Anna	J	30
Kuhlman, August Gerhard	27, Nov. 1851	Hieronymus	Reising, Helena Theresa	D	294
Kuhlman, Catharina	31, May 1857	Martin	Schneider, Margaretha	D	86
Kuhlman, Elisabeth	9, Nov. 1856	Lawrence	----, Mary	R	
Kuhlman, Elisabeth Philomena	15, May 1857	Joseph	Wessling, Anna Maria	A	
Kuhlman, Friedrich Johan Heinrich	9, Mar. 1853	Friedrich	Meyer, Maria Catharina	K	
Kuhlman, Johan Albert Philipp	9, Aug. 1855	Carl	Huseler, Catharina	A	
Kuhlman, Johan Heinrich	6, Nov. 1853	Bernard	----, Elisabeth	R	
Kuhlman, Johan Heinrich	12, Sept 1856	Bernard	----, Elisabeth	R	
Kuhlman, Johan Heinrich	8, Aug. 1853	Herman	Rotering, Adelheid	A	
Kuhlman, Johan Herman	13, Aug. 1855	J. Herman	Rotering, Adelheid	A	
Kuhlman, Johan Joseph	17, Oct. 1859	Joseph	Schierberg, Bernardina	A	
Kuhlman, Lucia Gertrud	1, Feb. 1855	H. Dietrich	Huser, Maria	K	
Kuhlman, Maria Anna	30, Apr. 1859	Johan	Geibing, Maria Magdalena	N	
Kuhlman, Maria Anna	5, Dec. 1852	Joseph	Wessling, Maria	J	20
Kuhlman, Maria Catharina	28, June 1853	H. Dietrich	Huser, Anna Maria	K	
Kuhlman, Maria Catharina Francisca	18, Nov. 1852	Joseph	Kohls, Catharina	A	
Kuhlman, Maria Elisabeth	21, Oct. 1857	Carl	Huser, Catharina	K	
Kuhlman, Maria Gertrud Catharina	13, Aug. 1854	Carl	Huser, Catharina	K	
Kuhlman, Maria Sophia	4, Apr. 1858	Peter	Timmers, Margaretha	A	
Kuhlman, Theresa Bernardina	16, Nov. 1853	Hieronymus	Reisinger, Helena Theresa	D	415
Kuhlman, Wilhelm Joseph	3, July 1859	Joseph	Wesseling, Maria	A	
Kuhlman, Wilhelm Theodor	6, Apr. 1856	Johan	Gaubing, Magdalena	N	
Kuhlmann, Anna Catharina Louisa	7, Oct. 1858	Clemens H.	Horstmann, Adelheid	F	
Kuhlmann, Anna Maria	2, Jan. 1853	Heinrich	Neubauer, Elisabeth	C	
Kuhlmann, Bernard Heinrich	4, Feb. 1856	Johan	Niehoff, Angela	C	
Kuhlmann, Carl Joseph	26, Dec. 1853	Clemens H.	Horstmann, Maria Adelheid	F	
Kuhlmann, Carl Theodor	17, Dec. 1854	Heinrich	Neubauer, Marg. Elisabeth	C	
Kuhlmann, Catharina	10, July 1853	Friedrich	Kraming, Caecilia	C	
Kuhlmann, Catharina Carolina	18, Jan. 1857	Heinrich	Neubauer, Elisabeth	C	
Kuhlmann, Franz	19, Apr. 1852	Wilhelm	Speckmann, Anna Maria	L	
Kuhlmann, Georg Heinrich	2, Aug. 1850	Clemens	Horstmann, Maria	F	
Kuhlmann, Gerhard Heinrich	8, Sept 1850	Heinrich	Diegmann, Catharina	F	
Kuhlmann, Heinrich Matthias	30, Nov. 1859	Herman H.	Kaiser, M. Elisabeth	L	
Kuhlmann, Johan Georg	13, Jan. 1851	Heinrich	Neubauer, Elisabeth	C	
Kuhlmann, Johan Heinrich	1, Jan. 1859	J. Heinrich	Neubauer, Marg. Elisabeth	C	
Kuhlmann, Johan Heinrich	19, Nov. 1858	Martin	Schneider, Margaretha	T	
Kuhlmann, Johan Joseph	15, July 1852	Clemens H.	Horstmann, Maria Adelheid	F	
Kühn, Alexander	2, June 1855	Valentin	Miller, Anna Maria	D	36
Kuhn, Anna Francisca	3, Mar. 1855	Francis J.	Schneider, Margaretha	F	
Kuhn, Anna Maria	3, June 1854	J. Adam	Fussner, Susanna	D	11
Kuhn, Anna Maria Carolina	15, Aug. 1858	Herman	Fortmann, Carolina	C	
Kuhn, Catharina Elisabeth	2, Oct. 1859	Johan	Weitz, Magdalena	A	
Kuhn, Catharina Philomena	13, Mar. 1853	Georg	Stein, Magdalena	K	
Kühn, Clara Carolina	1, Dec. 1859	Valentin	Meininger, Anna Maria	D	152
Kuhn, Ferdinand Wilhelm	20, Mar. 1859	Godfried	Lamart---, Barbara	D	134
Kuhn, Georg	3, Feb. 1856	Georg	Rebel, Margaretha	F	
Kuhn, Herman Heinrich	4, July 1856	Johan	Ludmer, Bernardina	C	

Name of Child	Date of Baptism	Father	Mother	Church	Page
Kuhn, Jacobina	9, Aug. 1857	Joseph	Remmi, Margaretha	C	
Kuhn, Johan	25, Jan. 1852	Johan	Weitz, Magdalena	F	
Kuhn, Johanna	2, May 1858	Georg	----, Margaretha	T	
Kuhn, Lawrence Valentin	19, Jan. 1858	Valentin	Meininger, Anna Maria	D	103
Kuhn, Margaretha	9, Feb. 1851	Georg	Bebel, Margaretha	D	252
Kuhn, Margaretha	22, Dec. 1850	Johan	Weitz, Magdalena	F	
Kuhn, Maria Josephina	13, Nov. 1853	Georg	Rebel, Margaretha	F	
Kuhn, Maria Louisa	9, Mar. 1851	Georg	Rein, Magdalena	K	
Kuhn, Maria Margaretha	31, Sept 1855	Georg	Stein, Magdalena	K	
Kuhn, Maria Margaretha	9, Nov. 1851	Joseph	Remi, Margaretha	C	
Kuhn, Maria Rosalia	25, Apr. 1859	Wilhelm	Springer, Carolina	D	136
Kuhn, Maria Sophia	19, Apr. 1857	Wilhelm	Springer, Carolina	D	83
Kuhn, Peter	4, Mar. 1855	Joseph	Remmig, Margaretha	C	
Kühn, Peter	18, Sept 1853	Valentin	Miller, Anna Maria	D	406
Kuhn, Peter Joseph	22, Mar. 1852	Martin	Reising, Barbara	D	314
Kuhn, Philipp	2, July 1854	Johan	Weitz, Magdalena	F	
Kühne, Johan B.	24, Feb. 1852	Johan B.	----, Maria Barbara	H	
Kühne, Johan Baptist	9, Aug. 1857	J. Baptist	Klaus, Maria Barbara	H	
Kühne, Johan Constantine	27, Nov. 1857	Georg	Stein, Magdalena	K	
Kuhne, Joseph Marcell	10, Apr. 1859	Baptist	Klaus, Barbara	H	
Kuhne, Mary Jennifer	6, Mar. 1853	John	----, Barbara	H	
Kühne, Theresa	20, Feb. 1853	Sebastian	Quarter, Magalena	Q	3
Kühnel, Mathias Aloysius	5, Mar. 1859	Aloysius	Kieffler, Catharina	Q	31
Kuhnen, Johan Peter	8, Dec. 1850	Cornelius	VanBade, Margaretha	C	
Kuhnert, Emilia Sophia	7, Mar. 1858	Robert	Regneri, Anna M.	C	
Kuhnle, Constantine	19, Sept 1857	Johan	Garnert, Barbara	K	
Kuhr, Anna Maria Elisabeth	5, Apr. 1859	Johan	Evens, Maria	C	
Kuhr, Gerhard Bernard	3, Mar. 1857	Johan H.	Evers, Maria Anna	C	
Kuhr, Johan Heinrich	3, Sept 1855	J. Heinrich	Evers, M. Anna	C	
Kuhr, Johan Joseph	27, Nov. 1854	Herman	Luettmer, Dina	C	
Kuhwinkel, Maria Philomena	9, July 1852	F. Anton	Schroeder, Bernardina	A	
Kulkey, Catherine	12, Oct. 1851	Patrick	Ansbury, Mary	E	350
Kullenkam, Maria Johanna Josepha A	27, Feb. 1851	Carl	Koch, Anna Maria	F	
Kuller, Catharina	9, Aug. 1857	Bernard	Lill, Maria	D	92
Küneman, Heinrich Jacob	8, Aug. 1852	Heinrich	Otto, Theresa	D	342
Küninger, Heinrich	19, July 1858	Joseph	Gries---, Maria	D	115
Kunk, Anna Margaretha Adelheid	29, Feb. 1856	Francis	Hoffman, Anna Maria	K	
Kunk, Anna Maria Catharina	2, Dec. 1858	Gerhard	Mescher, Elisabeth	L	
Kunk, Anna Maria Elisabeth	31, Dec. 1853	Gerhard	Mescher, Elisabeth	L	
Kunk, Anna Maria Elisabeth Adelheid	16, Feb. 1856	B.H.	Reilmann, Theresa	C	
Kunk, Bernard Gerhard	15, Feb. 1857	Gerhard	Mescher, Elisabeth	L	
Kunk, Bernard Heinrich	21, Dec. 1852	Francis	Hoffman, Maria	K	
Kunk, Bernard Heinrich Joseph	28, June 1851	Gerhard	Mescher, Elisabeth	L	
Kunk, Herman Bernard Francis	28, Mar. 1858	Francis	Hoffman, Maria	J	46
Kunk, Herman Gerhard Franz	28, Jan. 1851	Herman	Menners, Gesina	F	
Kunk, Maria Anna Adelheid	13, Nov. 1852	Gerhard H.	Meinders, Gesina	F	
Kunk, Maria Elisabeth	23, May 1850	Francis	Hoffmann, Maria	C	
Kunk, Maria Theresa	11, Sept 1854	H. Bernard	Hoffman, Anna Maria	K	
Kunkel, Adelheid	27, Sept 1857	J. David	Meyer, Catharina	D	95
Kunkel, Amalia	27, Mar. 1859	Theodor	Mayer, Agatha	D	134
Kunkel, Carolina	12, July 1857	Theodor	Mayer, Agatha	D	90
Kunkel, Herman Ludwig	15, Sept 1850	J. Gerhard	Krafeld, Catharina	C	
Kunkel, Jacob	15, July 1858	Constantine	Imhof, Margaretha	D	115
Kunkel, Joseph	9, Aug. 1854	Johan	Pusch, Catharina	W	4
Kunkel, Josephina	20, Apr. 1851	Johan	Busch, Catharina	F	
Kunkel, Louisa Helena	13, Sept 1853	Georg	Mueller, Barbara	C	
Kunkel, Nicolaus	20, Jan. 1856	Constantine	Imhof, Margaretha	D	50
Kunkel, Nicolaus	15, Aug. 1850	Kilian	Stengel, Anna Maria	D	228
Kunkel, Peter	13, July 1855	Theodor	Meyer, Agatha	D	38

Name of Child	Date of Baptism	Father	Mother	Church	Page
Kunkelmiller, Christoph Wilhelm	2, Dec. 1855	Wilhelm	Lamping, Francisca	C	
Kunkler, Johan Aloysius	8, Oct. 1852	Francis J.	Schweitzer, Magdalena	C	
Kunst, Anna Maria	24, June 1854	J. Bernard	Dobbelhof, Maria Elisabeth	D	12
Kunst, Johan	16, Nov. 1856	Herman B.	----, Anna Maria	D	72
Kunst, Johan Bernard Herman	24, June 1852	J. Bernard	Doppelhof, Maria Elisabeth	D	326
Kunst, Theresa Magdalena	17, May 1857	Francis	Werbit?, Catharina	D	85
Künstler, Michael	30, Aug. 1857	Adam	Ohr, Elisabeth	H	
Kunstner, Louisa Barbara	1, June 1856	Wilhelm	Mueller, Sophia	K	
Kunstner, Peter	12, May 1857	Wilhelm	Miller, Sophia	K	
Kuntz, Anna	24, Feb. 1854	?	?	A	
Kuntz, Anna	23, Jan. 1859	Nicolaus	Müller, Hannah	W	24
Kuntz, Augusta Barbara	30, Jan. 1859	Joseph	Neuschwender, Catharina	C	
Kuntz, Barbara Johanna	16, Oct. 1859	Ignatius	Schwarzenberg, Johanna	D	149
Kuntz, Catharina	23, Mar. 1851	Adam	Beer, Eva	D	258
Kuntz, Francis Joseph	22, Feb. 1857	Joseph	Neuschwander, Catharina	K	
Kuntz, Francisca	17, Aug. 1851	Ignatius	Schwarzenberg, Johanna	D	278
Kuntz, Herman	22, May 1854	Ignatius	Schwarzenberger, Johanna	D	11
Kuntz, Johan	28, Aug. 1853	Peter	Niederer, Catharina	K	
Kuntz, Maria Elisabeth	24, July 1856	Ignatius	Schwarzenberg, Johanna	D	63
Kuntz, Maria Elisabeth	4, July 1858	Marc	Buk---, Wilhelmina	D	114
Kuntz, Maria Louisa	21, Apr. 1850	Joseph	Wernet, Magdalena	D	210
Kuntz, Peter	1, Nov. 1855	Peter	Nieder, Catharina	K	
Kuntzler, Barbara	12, Oct. 1856	Nicolaus	Freib, Margaretha	A	
Kuntzler, Johan Oswald	27, June 1858	Nicolaus	Freib, Margaretha	A	
Kunz, Catharina	16, Jan. 1853	Nicolaus	Miller, Johanna	D	365
Kunz, Francis	28, Apr. 1858	Peter	Niederer, Catharina	K	
Kunz, Franz Mathias	15, Feb. 1858	Francis J.	Kelsch, Barbara	F	
Kunz, Jacob	28, Apr. 1850	Adam	Volz, Louisa Maria	D	211
Kunz, Jacob	20, July 1854	Jacob	Herb, Josephina	A	
Kunz, Joseph	17, July 1853	Jacob	Heeb, Josephina	A	
Kunz, Ludwig	9, Oct. 1859	Jacob	Sieg---, Maria Anna	D	148
Kunz, Magdalena	16, Jan. 1853	Nicolaus	Miller, Johanna	D	365
Kunz, Maria Louisa	14, Dec. 1851	Adam	Volz, Louisa Maria	D	297
Kunz, Mathias	20, June 1852	Johan	Meiers, Catharina	D	325
Kunz, Nicolaus	12, Feb. 1854	Nicolaus	----, Joanne	H	
Kunz, Theresa	21, May 1854	G. Francis	Masch, Barbara	D	10
Kunz, Veronica	8, Jan. 1857	Georg F.	Muge---, Barbara	D	76
Kunz, Wendel	1, Nov. 1856	Nicolaus	Miller, Johanna	G	
Kunzler, Johan	20, May 1855	Nicolaus	Treib, Margaretha	F	
Kunzmann, Heinrich	18, Mar. 1855	Lawrence	Stiksel, Elisabeth	F	
Kunzmann, Johan	15, Sept 1850	Johan	Stiksel, Elisabeth	F	
Kunzmann, Maria Eva	21, Nov. 1852	Lawrence	Stiksel, Elisabeth	F	
Kupferschmidt, Emil	16, Aug. 1857	Leo	Zumeister, Josephina	D	92
Kupferschmidt, Johan Peter Richard	8, Oct. 1854	Leo	Zumpfnäster, Josephina	D	19
Kupisch, Johan Heinrich	21, May 1854	Francis M.	Jung, Maria Anna	G	
Kupmeier, Carolina Margaretha Friedrica	11, Nov. 1857	J. Heinrich	Nieman, Maria Catharina	D	98
Kupp, Ferdinand	10, Jan. 1858	Johan	Kuderer, Magdalena	Q	26
Kuppel, Catharina	28, Mar. 1858	Caspar	Daut, Catharina	C	
Kupper, Casper	12, Apr. 1857	Caspar	Daut, Catharina	C	
Kurre, Anna Maria Elisabeth	17, Aug. 1851	Clemens	Kef, Helena Adelheid	F	
Kurre, Georg	16, Apr. 1856	Martin	Kresbach, Catharina	C	
Kurre, Johan Bernard	20, Mar. 1854	Bernard	Winzel, Maria	F	
Kurre, Maria Catharina Euphemia	22, Sept 1850	Arnold H.	Beck, Anna Elisabeth	L	
Kurre, Maria Helena	15, June 1858	Bernard	Rump, Antonia	F	
Kurtz, Francis Arthur	27, July 1856	George W.	Doyle, Mary	B	31
Kurwinkel, Friedrich Anton	19, July 1855	Anton	Schröder, Bernardina	A	
Kurz, Francis	20, Apr. 1856	Wilhelm	----, Clara	D	57
Kurz, Georg Peter	20, Aug. 1858	Christian	Müller, Catharina	D	117
Kurzenborn, Eva Elisabeth	4, July 1859	Friedrich	Lotz, Elisabeth	T	

Name of Child	Date of Baptism	Father	Mother	Church	Page
Kurzendorf, Elisabeth	2, July 1854	Heinrich	Bachman, Eva	R	
Kurzendorfer, Johan	5, Mar. 1854	Joseph	----, ----	H	
Kurzendorfer, Joseph	5, Mar. 1854	Joseph	----, ----	H	
Kurzendorfer, Maria Crescentia	14, Apr. 1857	Joseph	Braun, Anna Maria	H	
Kurzendorfer, Michael	1, Aug. 1852	Heinrich	Bachman, Maria Eva	R	
Kusgaerd, Josephina Catharina Elisabeth	1, Dec. 1853	Anton	McGinnes, Ellen	A	
Kusgoerd, Alexander Johan	27, Apr. 1852	F. Anton	McGinnis, Ellen	A	
Kuss, Edward Carl	23, Dec. 1855	Carl	Pflum, Christina	C	
Küstner, Caspar	4, Apr. 1858	Theodor	Schelle, Maria	H	
Kutschenreiter, Anna Maria	13, Jan. 1859	Johan	Stahr, Sophia	H	
Kutschenreiter, Johan	29, Mar. 1857	Johan	Stahl, Sophia	H	
Küttner, Anton	3, June 1856	J. Michael	Sch---, Magdalena	D	60
Kybrain?, Joseph	4, July 1858	John	Boughan, Bridget	B	61
Kylius, Barbara	11, Dec. 1851	Ferdinand	Schmidt, Apollonia	C	
Kylius, Barbara Carolina Henrietta	21, Dec. 1852	Ferdinand	Schmidt, Apollonia	C	
Kylius, Georg Heinrich	22, Aug. 1858	Ferdinand	Schmidt, Apollonia	C	
Kylius, Heinrich Ferdinand	10, Nov. 1850	Ferdinand	Schmidt, Apollonia	C	
Kylius, Johan Jacob	1, Nov. 1856	Ferdinand	Schmidt, Apollonia	C	
Kylius, Maria Catharina	9, Apr. 1855	Ferdinand	Schmidt, Apollonia	C	
Kyne, Ann Mary	30, July 1850	Dennis	Vailen, Theresa	E	236
Kyte, Elizabeth	14, Apr. 1859	Joseph	Reedy, Mary	E	618
Kyte, Helen	5, Apr. 1857	Joseph	Reedy, Mary	V	38
Kyte, Mary Ann	23, Feb. 1855	Joseph	Reedy, Mary	E	267
Laa, Wilhelm Franz	2, Aug. 1855	Joseph	Stemann, Maria Catharina	F	
Laacke, Maria Margaretha Adelheid	15, Apr. 1856	Bernard H.	VonHandorf, Margaret Elis.	D	56
Laage, Herman Bernard	10, Aug. 1858	Joseph	Stehmann, Maria	F	
Laage, Johan Bernard	28, Jan. 1857	Gerhard H.	Niehaus, Maria Elisabeth	D	77
Laage, Maria	2, Mar. 1855	Gerhard H.	Niehaus, Maria Elisabeth	D	30
Laage, Maria Francisca	8, June 1851	Bernard H.	VonHandorf, Maria Elisabeth	D	267
Laage, Maria Francisca	8, Apr. 1853	Gerhard H.	Niehaus, Maria Elisabeth	D	379
Laake, Bernard Heinrich	13, Sept 1853	Bernard	VonHandorf, Elisabeth	D	406
Laake, Bernard Heinrich	10, Feb. 1851	Gerhard H.	Niehaus, Elisabeth	D	252
Laake, Maria Amalia Philomena	14, Nov. 1858	B.H.	Handorf, Maria Elisabeth	A	
Laake, Maria Anna	4, Oct. 1852	Heinrich	Backhaus, M. Anna	C	
Laake, Maria Elisabeth	13, Apr. 1856	J. Bernard	Vehrmann, Elisabeth	C	
Laboyteaux, Robert (Riley)	18, Oct. 1857	Isaac	McLenan, Margaret	B	51
Lacey, Edward	25, June 1850	William	Vanson, Ann	B	205
Lacey, Francis Edward	5, Sept 1859	Edward	----, Joanne	E	651
Lacey, Mary Jane	21, Feb. 1858	Edward	----, Joanne	E	518
Lach, Anna Theresa	15, Oct. 1851	Friedrich	----, Anna	N	5
Lach, Francisca Rosina	4, Aug. 1856	Friedrich	Drisch, Anna	C	
Lach, George	4, Apr. 1858	Peter F.	----, Ann	R	
Lach, Margaretha	23, Apr. 1855	Peter F.	Desch, Anna	D	33
Lacher, Heinrich Joseph	28, Nov. 1858	Wilhelm	Schrick, Josephina	N	
Lacher, Johan	26, Feb. 1853	Martin	Borger, Catharina	F	
Lacher, Johan Heinrich	7, Dec. 1856	Martin	Berger, Catharina	G	
Lacher, Joseph Sebastian	5, Nov. 1854	Martin	Berger, Catharina	G	
Lacher, Wilhelm	29, Mar. 1857	Wilhelm	Schreig, Josephina	N	
Lachmeyer, Anton	2, Apr. 1854	Anton	----, Isabel	U	
Lack, Amalia Philomena	3, Sept 1850	Friedrich	Drerch, Anna	K	
Lack, Louisa	17, Apr. 1853	J. Friedrich	Dresch, Anna	D	380
Lacke, Maria	26, Nov. 1854	Heinrich	Hebauf, Anna Maria	D	22
Lackey, Hugh	31, Jan. 1858	George	McCabe, Isabel	E	514
Lacy, Patrick	11, Oct. 1857	Patrick	Sanders, Sarah	E	485
Ladenkotter, Francisca Catharina	18, May 1852	Joseph	Weyers, M. Catharina	L	
Laderkotter, M. Elisabeth Paulina	5, Apr. 1857	Francis	Weibers, Anna M.	L	
Laffley, John	6, July 1851	Daniel	Kane, Ann	B	235
Lafontaine, Mary	12, Feb. 1854	Peter	----, Catherine	H	
Lafontaine, Nicolaus	6, Sept 1857	John	Schäfer, Catherina	U	

Name of Child	Date of Baptism	Father	Mother	Church	Page
Lafontaine, Nicolaus	27, Jan. 1856	Peter	----, Catherine	H	
Lafontayne, Charles Edward	16, Nov. 1856	Claude	Hendricks, Sarah J.	B	36
Lafontne, Helena	2, Jan. 1859	?	Hendricks,	F	
Lagamarsin, Mary Angela	30, Nov.1852	Paul	Riccie, Catherine	B	277
Lagany, Mary Margaret	3, Apr. 1851	Patrick	McCormick, Mary	E	299
Lagario, Maria Theresa Matilda	4, May 1854	Joseph	Filliberti, Maria	P	81
Lage, Herman Joseph	14, Apr. 1859	H. Gerhard	Niehaus, Maria Elisabeth	D	136
Lagemann, Anna Maria	24, Jan. 1855	J. Bernard	Wieghaus, M. Catharina	L	
Lagemann, Anna Maria	12, Aug. 1855	Joseph	Putthoff, Anna M.	C	
Lagemann, Bernard Clemens	29, Dec. 1856	Bernard	Wieghaus, Catharina M.	F	
Lagemann, Bernard Joseph	5, Jan. 1859	Bernard	Wieghaus, Catharina M	T	
Lagemann, Bernardina	23, Aug. 1857	Joseph	Puthoff, Maria	C	
Lagemann, Joseph	20, Jan. 1859	Joseph	Putthoff, Anna M.	C	
Lagemann, Joseph	27, Oct. 1853	Joseph	Putthoff, Maria	C	
Lagers, Francis Alois	6, Apr. 1851	Francis	Laglig?, Appolonia	D	260
Laghtes, Juliana	14, June 1850	James	Thus, Margaret	L	
Lahan, Helen	28, May 1854	Matthew	Cronin, Elizabeth	E	194
Lahan, Margaret	25, Dec. 1850	Matthew	Cronan, Elizabeth	E	270
Lahan, Mary	29, Apr. 1857	Matthew	Cronin, Elizabeth	V	38
Lahaney, Michael	27, Oct. 1851	James	Collins, Catherine	E	353
Lahany, Catherine	17, Jan. 1858	Thomas	Madden, Mary	E	510
Lahey, Catherine	13, Oct. 1851	John	Flaherty, Mary	E	350
Lahey, Margaret	27, Nov. 1853	Michael	Scandlan, Mary	E	147
Lährman, Johan Bernard	14, Jan. 1855	J. Gerhard	Rickelman, Theresa Anna	A	
Lahy, Patrick	9, Dec. 1854	Timothy	----, Lucy	E	246
Laid, John	12, May 1858	John	O'Neil, Margaret	E	534
Laird, William J.	14, Feb. 1852		adult - 85 years old	E	381
Laiser, Maria	22, Feb. 1857	J. Adam	Fing, Julia	N	
Lake, Johan Gerhard Bernard	31, Mar. 1854	Bernard	Fermann, Elisabeth	C	
Lake, Maria Catharina Rosina	4, May 1858	Herman	Fehrmann, Lisette	C	
Lallmane, Lawrence	19, Feb. 1854	John	Volemme, Elisabeth	D	5
Lally, Ann	10, Nov. 1859	John	Leonard, Joanne	E	669
Lally, Bridget	21, Aug. 1853	John	Kelly, Bridget	P	50
Lally, Catherine	7, Dec. 1858	Thomas	O'Brien, Catherine	E	585
Lally, Ellen Rose	6, Apr. 1856	Malachai	Scott, Mary	U	
Lally, Francis	6, Oct. 1850	Thomas	Kelly, Mary	B	215
Lally, Honora	27, Apr. 1854	M.	----, Bridget	U	
Lally, Honora	29, Jan. 1854	William	----, Catherine	M	
Lally, James	6, Jan. 1855	John	----, Joanne	E	254
Lally, James	11, Apr. 1854	Thomas	Farrell, Eliza	B	312
Lally, John	4, Aug. 1856	John	----, Joanne	E	387
Lally, Margaret	14, Aug. 1859	John	----, Bridget	E	647
Lally, Mary	17, Apr. 1858	John	Maloy, Bridget	E	529
Lally, Mary	28, Dec. 1851	Malachai	Scott, Mary	Q	1
Lally, Mary	22, Apr. 1852	Patrick	Harknett, Mary	B	257
Lally, Mary Ann	30, Mar. 1856	William	----, Catherine	M	
Lamas, Emil Georg	11, Sept 1859	Nicolaus	----, Rosa	T	
Lamb, Mary	27, Oct. 1855	William	Featherston, Mary	T	
Lamb, Mary Eliza	14, Feb. 1853	Andrew	Duffy, Elizabeth	B	290
Lamb, Mary Helen	14, Feb. 1853	Andrew	Duffy, Elizabeth	B	290
Lamb, Michael	10, Feb. 1856	Michael	Power, Mary	E	343
Lamb, Patrick	28, Oct. 1853	William	Featherstone, Mary	P	57
Lamb, William Patrick	13, Dec. 1857	James	Collins, Joanne	V	43
Lamber, Anna Maria	2, Aug. 1851	J. Heinrich	Flotemesch, Anna Maria	K	
Lambers, Anna Margaretha Rosa	10, Jan. 1857	Herman T.	Sack, Maria Anna	L	
Lambers, Bernard Heinrich	5, June 1851	Gerhard	Wilkamp, Theresa	F	
Lambers, Catharina Elisabeth	4, Sept 1854	Dietrich	Huenemann, Elisabeth	C	
Lambers, Elisabeth	29, Dec. 1850	Johan	Neurohr, Maria	D	246
Lambers, Gerhard H.	7, Sept 1850	B.	Kemper, Helena	A	

Name of Child	Date of Baptism	Father	Mother	Church	Page
Lambers, Herman Heinrich	11, Sept 1858	J. Herman	Sack, Maria Anna	L	
Lambers, Johan Bernard	17, May 1855	J. Bernard	Kemper, Helena	A	
Lambers, Maria Catharina	25, July 1858	Gerhard	Detmer, Catharina	L	
Lambers, Maria Helena	15, Nov. 1856	Gerhard J.	Knueven, Helena	L	
Lambert, Adelheid	23, Jan. 1859	Jacob	Schagge, Maria Anna	D	129
Lambert, Carolina Catharina	12, Sept 1854	Georg	Meyer, Susanna	A	
Lambert, Eva Catharina	6, June 1852	Vincent	Ball, Louise	C	
Lambert, Francis	5, Apr. 1857	Jacob	Schagge, Maria Anna	D	82
Lambert, Hannah	15, July 1855	Thomas	Keleher, Honora	P	140
Lambert, Heinrich Francis	8, Mar. 1857	Bernard H.	Huenemann, Elisabeth	C	
Lambert, Jacob	26, Sept 1852	Jacob	Schaggi, Maria	D	349
Lambert, Johan	5, Jan. 1851	Jacob	Jacob, Anna Maria	D	247
Lambert, Johan Adam	25, Jan. 1857	Vincent	Ball, Louisa	F	
Lambert, John	6, Aug. 1857	James	Birmingham, Margaert	P	219
Lambert, John	8, Aug. 1858	James	Birmingham, Margaret	P	257
Lambert, John	2, Dec. 1852	Thomas	----, Honora	E	40
Lambert, Joseph	12, Feb. 1855	Jacob	Schage, Maria Anna	D	28
Lambert, Margaret	25, June 1851	Thomas	Kelliger, Honora	E	317
Lambert, Maria Anna	26, Dec. 1852	August	Winter, Johanna	N	10
Lambert, Maria Barbara	24, Sept 1854	Vincent	Baal, Louisa	W	5
Lambert, Martin Joseph	5, Jan. 1851	Anton	Riehle, Theresa	D	247
Lambert, Mary	18, Feb. 1855	John	Gallagher, Bridget	T	
Lambertson, Mary Frances Ann	22, June 1856	John	Dain, Felicia	E	376
Lambertson, Sarah Jane	16, May 1852	John	Dean, F.	E	414
Lambour, Barbara	20, June 1858	Louis	Kirsch, Anna Maria	H	
Lambour, Louis	22, June 1856	Louis	Kirch, Maria Anna	H	
Lambour, Mary Rose	18, Feb. 1855	Louis	----, Mary Ann	H	
Lambur, Anna Maria Catharina	18, Dec. 1853	Hubert	Wagner, Catharina	F	
Lambur, Anton Francis Xavier	30, Dec. 1852	Anton	Bender, Anna Margaretha	A	
Lambur, Eduard	9, June 1850	Hubert	Wagner, Catharina	F	
Lambur, Elisabeth	6, July 1851	Anton	Bender, Margaretha	A	
Lambur, Joseph	22, Aug. 1856	Anton	Bender, Anna Margaretha	A	
Lambur, Mathilda	19, Oct. 1856	Hubert	Wagner, Catharina	F	
Lambur, Philipp	22, Aug. 1856	Anton	Bender, Anna Margaretha	A	
Lamerding, Barbara	28, Oct. 1857		adult - 17 years old	F	
Lammeier, Maria Elisabeth	21, Sept 1857	J. Heinrich	Brinkman, Angela	D	95
Lammering, Anna Elisabeth	2, Nov. 1854	Bernard	Terwelp, Maria Elisabeth	D	21
Lammering, Bernard Heinrich	20, Mar. 1853	Bernard	Dörtel, Elisabeth	D	376
Lammering, Johan Anton	5, Oct. 1850	Bernard	Terwelp, Elisabeth	D	236
Lammers, Anna Catharina	30, May 1859	Bernard	Huenemann, Anna	C	
Lammers, Anna Maria	21, Mar. 1853	Gerhard H.	Feldmann, Anna Maria	L	
Lammers, Anna Maria	13, Aug. 1850	Herman H.	Deye, Gertrud	L	
Lammers, Anna Maria Catharina	16, Aug. 1857	Carl	Spiekermeyer, Anna M.	C	
Lammers, Anna Maria Gertrud	18, May 1858	Bernard J.	Deie, Theresa	L	
Lammers, Bernard Carl Joseph	26, Dec. 1859	Carl	Speckmeier, Maria	Y	
Lammers, Catharina Maria Bernardina	19, June 1851	Joseph	Stratman, Gertrud	D	268
Lammers, Christopher	13, Sept 1855	Heinrich	Kellerman, Wilhelmina	A	
Lammers, Euphemia Maria	4, Apr. 1857	H.H.	List, Maria Agatha	A	
Lammers, Gerhard Herman	29, May 1855	Gerhard H.	Liss, Agatha	A	
Lammers, Gerhard Joseph	23, Oct. 1855	Joseph	Deie, Theresa	L	
Lammers, Heinrch Johan	12, Mar. 1858	J. Gerhard	Feldmann, Anna Maria	C	
Lammers, Johan Bernard	7, Mar. 1858	Francis J.	----,	T	
Lammers, Johan Bernard Heinrich	27, Jan. 1852	B. Theodor	Huenemann, Catharina Elis.	C	
Lammers, Johan Gerhard Heinrich	4, Aug. 1850	Gerhard	Feldmann, Maria	C	
Lammers, Johan Joseph Heinrich	8, May 1856	Joseph	Feldmann, Anna	C	
Lammers, Joseph Bernard	19, July 1856	Bernard H.	Deie, A.M. Gertrud	L	
Lammers, Juliana	29, Oct. 1856	Francis	Wehring, A. Catharina	F	
Lammers, Maria Angela	7, Mar. 1858	Francis J.	Holtkamp, A. Catharina	T	
Lammers, Maria Anna	15, Sept 1853	J. Bernard	Kempen, Maria Helena	A	

Name of Child	Date of Baptism	Father	Mother	Church	Page
Lammers, Maria Anna	12, Mar. 1858	J. Gerhard	Feldmann, Anna Maria	C	
Lammers, Maria Catharina Magdalena	19, July 1858	Joseph	Fehr, Maria Catharina	F	
Lammers, Maria Elisabeth	31, May 1853	Heinrich	Reckelhoff, M. Elis.	L	
Lammers, Maria Gertrud Josephina	15, Oct. 1850	Carl R.	Spiker, Maria Catharina	D	238
Lammers, Maria Theckla	28, Sept 1855	J. Wilhelm	Guggelmeyer, Susanna	L	
Lammers, Maria Theresa	15, Oct. 1852	Heinrich	Deie, M. Gertrud	L	
Lammers, Victoria Maria Anna	23, Dec. 1858	J. Herman	Liss, Maria Agatha	A	
Lammert, Bernard Heinrich	25, Aug. 1858	Francis	Macke, Maria Agnes	K	
Lammert, Elisabeth Helena	19, Oct. 1856	Joseph	Egner, Maria	C	
Lammert, Francis Heinrich	19, Aug. 1851	Ferdinand	Vascke, Agnes	K	
Lammert, Gesina	3, Mar. 1856	F. Ferdinand	Macke, Agnes	K	
Lammert, Heinrich Ludwig	5, June 1859	Joseph	Egner, Maria	C	
Lammert, Maria Carolina	21, Nov. 1853	F. Ferdinand	Macke, Agnes	K	
Lamoth, Catharina	2, Feb. 1851	Georg J.	Fräri, Catharina	J	10
Lamoth, Cunigunda	2, Feb. 1851	Georg J.	Unger, Maria Anna	J	10
Lamoth, Georg Joseph	23, Oct. 1859	G. Jacob	Rari, Catharina	J	52
Lamoth, Jacob	27, May 1855	Nicolaus	Ungar, Maria Anna	J	32
Lamoth, Joseph	27, Jan. 1850	Cyril	Vogt, Magdalena	J	6
Lamoth, Louisa	26, Oct. 1851	Cyril	Mäkli, Magdalena	J	12
Lamoth, Margretha	27, Sept 1857	Nicolaus	Ungar, Maria Anna	J	42
Lamoth, Maria Anan	24, Jan. 1853	Nicolaus	Ungar, Maria Anna	J	20
Lamoth, Maria Magdalena	30, Mar. 1856	Georg J.	Ferazi, Catharina	J	34
Lampe, Anna Dorothea	9, Jan. 1854	Francis	Greiven, Anna Maria	F	
Lampe, Anna Maria	26, Apr. 1857	Friedrich	Fleg, Francisca	A	
Lampe, Bernard	24, Jan. 1850	Friedrich	Dedick, Elisabeth	C	
Lampe, Bernard Ludwig	11, Mar. 1857	Gerhard H.	Trentmann, M. Angela	C	
Lampe, Carl Edward	28, Apr. 1858	Christian	Higer, Magdalena	A	
Lampe, Francisca Margaretha	27, May 1855	J. Friedrich	Fleger, Francisca	A	
Lampe, Georg Bernard	18, Jan. 1858	Bernard	Moehlenkamp, Angela	C	
Lampe, Herman Heinrich	25, Feb. 1855	J. Bernard	Osterhus, Anna Maria	L	
Lampe, Johan	29, Sept 1859	Francis	Greve, Maria	F	
Lampe, Johan Bernard Christian	18, May 1854	J. Bernard	Mollenkamp, Angela	C	
Lampe, Johan Friedrich	12, June 1859	Friedrich	Fleg, Francisca	D	140
Lampe, Johan Heinrich	5, June 1853	Bernard	Mollenkamp, Angela	C	
Lampe, Johan Heinrich	1, Dec. 1853	Friedrich	Fleige, Francisca	A	
Lampe, Johan Heinrich	24, Mar. 1853	Heinrich	Trentmann, Angela	C	
Lampe, Maria Clara	10, May 1857	Francis	Greiwe, Maria Elisabeth	F	
Lampe, Maria Elisabeth	26, Jan. 1855	Gerhard H.	Trentmann, Angela	C	
Lampe, Maria Louisa	14, May 1854	Heinrich	Flotemesche, Louisa	K	
Lampe, Mathilda	3, Oct. 1857	Christian	Higger, Magdalena	J	42
Lampert, Bernard	31, Oct. 1858	Carl	Menke, Maria Elisabeth	L	
Lampert, Johan Gerhard Anton	14, July 1859	Gerhard	Trentmann, M. Angela	C	
Lampert, Maria Carolina	6, Apr. 1850	Vincent	Bahl, Louisa	F	
Lamping, Anna Maria Elisabeth	6, May 1851	J. Bernard	Zahe, A. Maria Margaretha	A	
Lamping, Anna Maria Elisabeth	14, Jan. 1853	J. Bernard	Zahen, Maria Margaretha	A	
Lamping, Anna Maria Gertrud	20, July 1851	Heinrich	Bunte, G. Carolina	C	
Lamping, Anton Carl	12, June 1855	Bernard	Westerkamp, Elisabeth	C	
Lamping, Anton Heinrich	24, Aug. 1854	Heinrich	Bunte, Gertrud	C	
Lamping, Carl	22, Oct. 1854	Joseph	Deters, M.	C	
Lamping, Carolina Elisabeth Barb.	5, Oct. 1859	Friedrich	Reichling, Elisabeth	C	
Lamping, Clemens Heinrich	4, Jan. 1857	Bernard H.	Westerkamp, Josephina	C	
Lamping, Francis Ferdinand	16, Nov. 1856	Joseph	Deters, Maria Anna	C	
Lamping, Friedrich August	20, Oct. 1858	Bernard	Westerkamp, Elisabeth	C	
Lamping, Friedrich Joseph	19, Dec. 1858	Joseph	Deters, Maria Anna	C	
Lamping, Johan Bernard	9, July 1856	J. Bernard	Zahn, Anna Maria Margaretha	A	
Lamping, Johan Gerhard	30, Apr. 1858	Johan H.	Brunklaus, Anna M.	A	
Lamping, Johan Heinrich	8, Apr. 1858	Johan	Koatschl, Maria Sophia	L	
Lamping, Johan Heinrich	16, May 1853	Johan H.	Brunklaus, Maria M.	A	
Lamping, Joseph	4, Sept 1855	J. Heinrich	Branklaus, Maria Adelheid	A	

Name of Child	Date of Baptism	Father	Mother	Church	Page
Lamping, Josephina Elisabeth	6, Oct. 1857	Anton	Bunte, Carolina G.	C	
Lamping, Maria Antonia	6, Jan. 1853	Joseph	Deters, Catharina	C	
Lamping, Maria Sophia	4, Sept 1855	Johan	Korte, Sophia	L	
Lamping, Maria Sophia	12, Apr. 1854	Johan	Kortsehl, Sophia	C	
Lamping, Wilhelmina	15, Dec. 1850	Joseph	Deters, M. Anna	C	
Lamy, Margaretha	19, Nov. 1854	Peter J.	Waner, Anna	D	22
Lanahan, Catherine	18, Nov. 1850	Patrick	Welsh, Bridget	B	219
Lancaster, Charles Henry	26, Feb. 1854	Josiah?	Finley, Sarah	E	171
Lancy, William	9, May 1852	Patrick	----, Bridget	B	259
Land, Julie Ann	15, Jan. 1850	Michael	O'Brien, Rachel	E	192
Landau, Heinrich	7, July 1856	Leonard	Stoker, Magaretha	N	
Landau, Heinrich	11, Sept 1859	Leonard	Stocker, Margaretha	N	
Landau, Maria	25, Oct. 1857	Leonard	Stöcker, Margaretha	N	
Lande, Leo Carl	20, May 1855	Carl Anton	Caufeld, Anna	N	
Landenweg, Elisabeth	22, Apr. 1852	Andreas	Thybil, Maria Anna	D	317
Landenwetsch, Johan Michael	24, June 1855	Anton	Lang, Francisca	D	37
Landenwetsch, Joseph	12, June 1853	Anton	Lang, Francisca	D	389
Landenwitsch, Carolina	26, Mar. 1854	Andreas	Deuber, Maria	W	3
Landenwitsch, Louise	9, Aug. 1857	Anton	----, Francisca	R	
Landers, Catherine Jane	9, Feb. 1858	James	Hickey, Mary J.	P	239
Landers, David Mary	26, Aug. 1855	William	Cane, Mary	E	311
Landers, Eleanora	23, Sept 1852	William	Teen, Mary	L	
Landers, Mary	11, Apr. 1858	William	Taigan, Mary	E	528
Landes, John Felix	20, Oct. 1859	John	----, Matilda	E	664
Landes, Margaret Elizabeth	20, Oct. 1859	John	----, Matilda	E	664
Landes, Martha Jane Frances	20, Oct. 1859	John	----, Matilda	E	664
Landes, William Henry	27, Oct. 1859	John	----, Matilda	E	665
Landewitsch, Jacob Andreas	27, Sept 1857	Andreas	Daubel, Maria Anna	W	20
Landewitsch, Michael	30, Oct. 1859	Anton	----, Catharina	Q	33
Landieck, Catharina	21, Mar. 1858	Thomas	Fortringler, Barbara	K	
Landman, Veronica Atilia Aurelia	8, Apr. 1852	Johan	Puntage?, Catharina	A	
Landrigan, Bridget	22, July 1855	Edward	Palmer, Helen	P	142
Landrigan, Edmund	4, Apr. 1858	Edward	Palmer, Ellen	P	245
Landrigan, Elisabeth	1, Sept 1854	Paul	Fitzpatrick, Mary	R	
Landrigan, Eliza	5, May 1853	John	White, Bridget	E	86
Landrigan, Ellen	19, May 1855	John	White, Bridget	E	287
Landrigan, Margaret	24, Oct. 1858	Paul	Fitzpatrick, Mary	R	
Landrigen, Mary	9, Nov. 1856	Paul	----, Mary	R	
Landrigran, Charles	18, Dec. 1859	Patrick	Griffin, Mary	R	
Landwehr, Anna Maria	25, Apr. 1853	Bernard	Fromme, Catharina	L	
Landwehr, Franz Anton	22, Feb. 1855	Anton	Lanser, Bernardina	L	
Landwehr, Georg Vitus	29, Aug. 1852	J. Balthasar	Miller, Anna Maria	D	345
Landwehr, Johan Heinrich	17, Nov. 1856	Bernard	Fromme, Catharina	L	
Landwehr, Johan Joseph	24, May 1857	Anton	Lanfers, Bernardina	L	
Landwehr, Johan Wilhelm	29, Dec. 1854	Bernard	Fromme, Catharina	L	
Landwehr, Louisa	23, Dec. 1850	Anton	Langfen, Bernardina	K	
Landwehr, Maria Anna	4, Mar. 1858	Bernard	Fromme, Catharina	L	
Landwehr, Maria Bernardina	21, Dec. 1852	Anton	Lanffer, Bernardina	L	
Landwehr, Maria Gertrud	30, Aug. 1857	Sebastian	Denk, Margaret	H	
Landwehr, Maria Josephina	29, Dec. 1859	Friedrich	Meinschatz, Maria Elisabeth	A	
Landwir, Maria Elisabeth	5, Aug. 1855	Ernst	Nieman, Elisabeth	D	40
Lane, Cornelius	20, July 1851	Patrick	O'Connor, Margaret	E	326
Lane, David	15, July 1851	William	Goy, Sarah	E	324
Lane, Eliza	24, Dec. 1857	Michael	Mullins, Eliza	B	53
Lane, Emily Frances	27, Oct. 1856	Charles	----, Mary	E	408
Lane, Helen	19, Oct. 1853	Maurice	Donavan, Helen	P	56
Lane, John	20, Dec. 1854	Michael	Mullin, Eliza	P	111
Lane, John	30, Mar. 1856	Patrick	----, Margaret	E	354
Lane, John Joseph	20, May 1850	George	----, Mary	E	215

Name of Child	Date of Baptism	Father	Mother	Church	Page
Lane, Margaret	1, July 1855	Maurice	Donovan, Helen	P	138
Lane, Mary	6, July 1856	Michael	----, Elizabeth	X	
Lane, Mary Ellen	10, Jan. 1854	George	Arthur, Mary	E	159
Lane, Michael	5, Oct. 1851	Peter	Donovan, Elizabeth	P	12
Lane, Samuel	28, Nov. 1851	Samuel	adult - 23 years old	E	361
Lane, Timothy	19, Apr. 1857	Maurice	Donivan, Helen	P	210
Lanehan, Mary	4, Apr. 1857	Joseph	Bogan, Ann	E	445
Laney, Francis	1, June 1851	Patrick	Burns, Ann	E	311
Lanfermann, Antonia Carolina J.	22, Dec. 1857	Heinrich	Riedemann, Catharina M.	F	
Lanfermann, Johan Heinrich	19, Sept 1852	J. Heinrich	Riemann, Catharina M.	F	
Lang, Albert Francis	23, Aug. 1857	Paul	Held---, Maria Anna	D	93
Lang, Andreas	28, Mar. 1858	Peter	Machinot, Magdalena	F	
Lang, Anna Maria	24, Nov. 1858	Arbogast	Sehr, Scholastica	D	124
Lang, Anton	1, Mar. 1857	Anton	Berger, Catharina	D	80
Lang, Carl Anton	14, May 1854	Leonard	Schemmel, Christina	D	10
Lang, Catharina	27, Sept 1854	Anton	Berger, Catharina	D	18
Lang, Catharina	9, Nov. 1856	Johan	Paehl, Catharina	D	71
Lang, Catharina Maria	30, Dec. 1850	Herman	Kuhlman, Margaretha	A	
Lang, Eliza Sarah	6, Mar. 1850	James	----, Jane	E	201
Lang, Elizabeth	1, July 1856	Patrick	Stern, Bridget	P	184
Lang, Francis	15, Oct. 1854	Arbogast	Vehr, Scholastica	D	20
Lang, Francis Michael	15, Aug. 1855	Francis	Heide, Carolina	D	40
Lang, Francisca Elisabeth	24, Oct. 1852	Francis	Hollinger, Elisabeth	K	
Lang, Heinrich	5, Feb. 1852	Anton	Berger, Catharina	D	305
Lang, Heinrich Carl	7, May 1854	Erhard	Ebler, Helena	D	9
Lang, Johan	4, Aug. 1859	Anton	Berger, Catharina	D	143
Lang, Johan	25, Jan. 1857	Arbogast	Sehr, Scholastica	D	77
Lang, Johan	10, Dec. 1854	Georg	Beile, Cunigunda	D	23
Lang, Johan	24, Mar. 1859	Johan	Buckheit, Elisabeth	K	
Lang, Johan	8, June 1856	Johan	Döberin, Catharina	D	60
Lang, Johan Baptist	28, July 1859	Georg	Blank, Walburga	D	143
Lang, Johan Georg	7, Dec. 1856	Georg	Baile, Cunigunda	D	73
Lang, Johan Georg	20, Sept 1854	Georg	Blank, Walburga	D	18
Lang, Johan Jacob	12, Feb. 1854	Georg	Klein, Philomena	J	26
Lang, John	27, May 1851	Michael	----, Bridget	E	311
Lang, Joseph	4, Apr. 1858	Gervasius	Langbein, Magdalena	F	
Lang, Josephina	6, Mar. 1856	Johan	Amman, Catharina	D	53
Lang, Kilian	8, June 1851	Johan	Oberly, Charitas	F	
Lang, Ludwig	13, Aug. 1853	Ludwig	----, Elisabeth	F	
Lang, Magdalena	31, July 1850	Johan	Ammann, Catharina	F	
Lang, Margaret Philomena	7, Mar. 1852	John	Uhrig, Margaret	R	
Lang, Margaretha	21, July 1851	Georg	Hoffman, Margaretha	D	274
Lang, Margaretha	8, Oct. 1854	Peter	----, Magdalena	F	
Lang, Maria Elisabeth	3, Feb. 1850	Francis	Otz, Appolonia	D	203
Lang, Maria Josephina Helena	12, June 1852	Georg	Blank, Walburga	D	324
Lang, Maria Prisca	30, Apr. 1854	John	Uhrig, Margaret	R	
Lang, Maria Theresa	13, Feb. 1852	Johan N.	Amand, Catharina	F	
Lang, Peter	26, Oct. 1855	Johan	Bahl, Catharina	D	45
Lang, Peter	29, Oct. 1854	Johan	Buchheit, Elisabeth	K	
Lang, Philomena	6, Jan. 1854	Francis	Holinger, Elisabeth	N	19
Lang, Wilhelm	8, June 1856	Johan	Döberin, Catharina	D	60
Lang, Wilhelm	7, June 1857	Leonard	Schemmel, Christina	D	87
Lang, Wilhelm Anton	23, June 1858	Johan	Amand, Catharina	D	113
Langan, Bridget	7, June 1854	Thomas	Hunt, Ann	P	84
Langan, Catherine	20, Feb. 1856	Martin	Moley, Helen	V	29
Langan, Michael	25, Jan. 1852	Thomas	----, Ann	B	251
Langan, William	1, June 1856	Michael	McGrath, Elizabeth	V	31
Langdon, Jane	29, May 1859	George	Lawler, Margaret	E	629
Lange, Anna Catharina	31, Aug. 1859	Bernard	Franke, Anna Maria	A	

Name of Child	Date of Baptism	Father	Mother	Church	Page
Lange, Anna Francisca	21, Dec. 1855	J. Heinrich	Rühbusch, Anna Catharina	A	
Lange, Bernard Franz	4, Mar. 1857	Ferdinand	Lampe, Bernardina	L	
Lange, Carolina Elisabeth	28, Aug. 1853	Carl	Keller, Maria	F	
Lange, Catharina	13, Jan. 1859	Anton	Oliva, Maria	F	
Lange, Catharina Elisabeth	28, Aug. 1859	J. Heinrich	VonderHeide, Catharina	L	
Lange, Catharina Louisa Anna	12, Dec. 1852	Martin	Niechter, Maria Anna	L	
Lange, Catharina Margaretha Dina	25, Aug. 1856	Johan	VonderHeide, Cath.	L	
Lange, Clemens	10, Jan. 1850	Herman	Lamping, Francisca	L	
Lange, Dorothea Dina	18, Jan. 1851	Anton	Rolfsen, Agnes	F	
Lange, Ferdinand	22, July 1853	Bernard	Franke, Anna Maria	A	
Lange, Francis Carl	9, May 1859	Paul	Helmer, Maria	A	
Lange, Friedrich Georg	10, Sept 1858	Johan H.	Ruebusch, Catharina	A	
Lange, Gerhard Carl	6, Mar. 1852	Carl	Keller, M. Theresa	L	
Lange, Gerhard Dietrich	26, Sept 1856	Gerhard	Hille, M. Elisabeth	F	
Lange, Heinrich Aloysius	1, June 1854	H. Joseph	Fischer, Margaretha Adelheid	K	
Lange, Helena Elisabeth	16, Apr. 1854	Heinrich	Rubusch, Catharina	A	
Lange, Jacob	26, Apr. 1857	Johan	Bucheit, Elisabeth	K	
Lange, Johan	22, Dec. 1850	Johan	Bricke, Maria Elisabeth	K	
Lange, Johan Gerhard	3, Sept 1855	Ferdinand	Lampe, Catharina W.	L	
Lange, Johan Heinrich	27, Dec. 1858	Ferdinand	Lampe, Wilhelmina	L	
Lange, Johan Heinrich Francis	31, Aug. 1851	J. Bernard	Franke, Maria	A	
Lange, Johan Heinrich Theobald	2, Sept 1852	J. Gerhard	Hille, Anna Maria	F	
Lange, Johan Herman Gerhard	27, Feb. 1856	Gerhard	Thele, Maria Anna	L	
Lange, Joseph Theobald	12, Oct. 1858	Joseph	Rufin, Maria	L	
Lange, Louisa Francisca	22, Nov. 1858	Gerhard	Obler, Helena	F	
Lange, Ludwig August	29, Sept 1854	Martin	Nichter, Mary	L	
Lange, Maria	12, Dec. 1852	Johan	Buchheid, Elisabeth	K	
Lange, Maria Anna	15, Feb. 1858	Gerhard	Telen, Maria Anna	L	
Lange, Maria Catharina Elisabeth	5, July 1856	Bernard	Franke, Maria Elisabeth	A	
Lange, Maria Catharina Wilhelmina	31, Aug. 1859	Bernard	Franke, Anna Maria	A	
Lange, Maria Christina	18, Nov. 1853	J. Anton	Rolfsen, Maria Agnes	F	
Lange, Maria Elisabeth	18, July 1856	Anton	Rolfsen, Agnes	F	
Lange, Maria Elisabeth Magdalena	10, Nov. 1850	Martin	Nuechter, Maria	L	
Lange, Maria Francisca	21, Dec. 1859	Gerhard	Theilen, Maria Anna	L	
Lange, Maria Johanna Jeanette	7, Aug. 1854	Heinrich	Early, Anna	L	
Lange, Maria Philomena Bernardina	1, Oct. 1850	Carl H.	Keller, Maria Anna	L	
Lange, Mary	24, July 1854	Jeremiah	Hennessy, Margaret	R	
Lange, Matilda	28, Dec. 1854	Thomas	Collins, Helen	R	
Lange, Wilhelm Heinrich	28, Mar. 1852	H. Joseph	Kunst, Maria Catharina	K	
Langefeld, Francisca Maria Theresa	21, Mar. 1855	J. Heinrich	Holzstage, Francisca	K	
Langelage, Anna Maria Elisabeth	26, Dec. 1852	Joseph	Reinerman, Anna	D	362
Langelage, Johan Gerhard Joseph	27, June 1854	J. Joseph	Rainerman, Anna	D	13
Langelage, Margaretha Philomena	25, May 1856	Joseph	Rainerman, Anna	D	59
Langelage, Maria Francisca	29, Jan. 1859	Joseph	Reinerman, Anna	D	130
Langeland, Maria Angelina	20, Feb. 1859	J. Joseph	Frie, Maria Elisabeth	A	
L'Angelier, Louisa Catherine	20, Feb. 1859	Charles	Sweeney, Joanne	B	71
Langemeier, Gerhard Friedrich	27, June 1859	Gerhard	Kemker, Theresa	L	
Langemeier, Gerhard Heinrich	23, Aug. 1859	J. Heinrich	Bruening, Gesina M.	L	
Langemeier, Johan Heinrich	9, Dec. 1857	Gerhard	Kemker, Theresa	L	
Langemeyer, Anna Friedrica	15, July 1856	Heinrich	Faske, Angela	A	
Langemeyer, Anna Maria	24, Apr. 1859	Heinrich	Faske, Anna Maria	A	
Langemeyer, Heinrich	23, Mar. 1859	Joseph	Rott, Gertrud	A	
Langemeyer, Herman	4, Apr. 1856	Joseph	Rott, Gertrud	A	
Langemeyer, Johan Heinrich	18, Oct. 1857	Herman H.	Faske, Maria Angela	A	
Langemeyer, Maria Anna	9, June 1857	Joseph	Rott, Gertrud	A	
Langemeyer, Maria Catharina	12, May 1853	Gerhard	Kemker, Theresa	C	
Langemeyer, Maria Elisabeth	27, Sept 1854	Herman	Faske, Angela	A	
Langen, Johan Bernard	24, Sept 1850	Fritz	Schulten, Gesina Adel.	L	
Langenfels, Theodor Heinrich	3, Feb. 1859	Theodor	Ostendorf, Theresa	A	

Name of Child	Date of Baptism	Father	Mother	Church	Page
Langenstroer, Maria Elisabeth	2, Feb. 1858	Caspar	----,	F	
Langferman, Anna Maria Josephina	5, July 1852	Joseph	Lübbelhusen, Josephina	K	
Langhold, Anna Maria	14, Sept 1850	Fridolin	Bauerle, Christina	D	232
Langhorst, Georg	16, Oct. 1853	Michael	----, Anna	C	
Langin, Catherine	27, June 1858	Thomas	Hunt, Ann	P	251
Langley, John Ludwell	10, Nov. 1851	Ludwell J.	Arnold, Ann	B	245
Langonetti, Edward	23, July 1855	John B.	----, Margaret	E	302
Langstermann, Maria Elisabeth	30, Nov. 1851	David	Engel, Maria	F	
Langtry, Catherine	3, Oct. 1852	Francis	Curry, Mary	B	271
Langtry, James	10, Sept 1854	Francis	Curley, Mary	P	95
Langtry, Mary	25, Aug. 1858	Patrick	Horan, Bridget	P	258
Langtry, Thomas	12, Nov. 1854	Patrick	Horan, Bridget	P	103
Lanigan, Mary	26, Dec. 1852	Martin	Pendergast, Catherine	P	32
Lanigan, Richard	4, Apr. 1852	Timothy	Sweeney, Mary	B	256
Lanser, Catharina	13, Feb. 1859	Heinrich	----, Christina	A	
Lanser, Heinrich P.	6, Dec. 1857	Peter	Pusch, Clara	A	
Lanser, Heinrich Peter	26, Oct. 1856	Heinrich	Meyer, Christina	A	
Lansing, Johan Bernard	25, Dec. 1852	Bernard H.	Kessler, Ursula	D	362
Lanz, Carl	6, May 1859	Peter	Grunbaum, Catharina	D	137
Lanz, Johanna Catharina	20, May 1856	Peter	Grunebaum, Catharina	D	59
Lanzer, Carl Pius	12, July 1859	Peter	Busch, Clara	F	
Lanzing, Anna Maria Gertrud	22, Sept 1858	Anton	Bielacher, Maria	D	119
Lapense, Mary Adalaide	5, Jan. 1855	Francis	----, Ann	E	253
LaPoint, Mary	25, July 1852	John	----, Mary	B	266
Laponsy, Ann	10, May 1853	Francis	----, Ann	E	88
Larale, Aloysia Mary	23, July 1856	Edward	Blache, Aloysia A.	E	384
Larcher, Peter	31, Aug. 1851	Martin	Berger, Catharina	D	279
Larg, Bernard Heinrich	7, Oct. 1855	Bernard	Gehring, Catharina	N	
Larg, Ellen	16, Sept 1855	Dennis	Cochlan, Catherine	U	
Larg, Maria Christina	2, May 1857	Bernard	Gehring, Catharina	N	
Largy, John Patrick	19, May 1858	John	Largy, Ellen	E	535
Larick, Sarah Elizabeth	18, May 1859	John	----, Mary Elizabeth	E	626
Lärk, Joseph	1, May 1859	Bernard	Gehring, Catharina	N	
Larke, Maria Elisabeth	8, Aug. 1858	G. Herman	Brockman, Maria	N	
Larken, Thomas	17, Nov. 1852	Thomas	Clarke, Ann	P	30
Larken, William	9, June 1850	John	Lochen, Bridget	H	
Larkey, Mary Alice	28, Mar. 1856	John	Meagher, Helen	E	353
Larkin, Ann Emily	15, June 1856	James	Colter, Elizabeth	E	375
Larkin, Bridget	30, May 1853	Thomas	Kane, Mary	E	94
Larkin, Eliza Helen	26, Dec. 1853	James	----, Eliza	E	155
Larkin, Francis	9, Feb. 1856	Peter	Ricke, Leontine	B	25
Larkin, Helen	3, Aug. 1856	Michael	Lawless, Mary	P	186
Larkin, James Edward	23, June 1850	James	Colter, Elizabeth	B	205
Larkin, John	15, Feb. 1854	James	Hennessy, Catherine	B	309
Larkin, John	23, Feb. 1851	James	Sereeney, Margaret	B	227
Larkin, John Henry	5, Feb. 1855	James	Cotter, Elizabeth	E	262
Larkin, Joseph	22, Jan. 1854	Maurice	Clark, Ann	V	10
Larkin, Leontine	9, Feb. 1856	Peter	Ricke, Leontine	B	25
Larkin, Mary Elizabeth	30, Mar. 1858	James	----, Ellen	E	526
Larkin, Patrick	20, Dec. 1859	John	Connors, Joanne	R	
Larkin, Patrick	9, Feb. 1856	Thomas	Kelly, Mary	E	343
Larkin, Thomas	10, Jan. 1852	James	Cotter, Eliza	E	372
Larman, Joseph Johan	3, Nov. 1850	Joseph	Stalkamp, Agnes	D	241
Larny, Elizabeth	26, Jan. 1856	Thomas	Bann, Mary	E	340
Larson, David	15, June 1857	William	McGuire, Catherine	E	459
Lartura, Augustine	8, Sept 1851	Francis	Reggio, Magdalena	E	341
Läry, Anna Catharina	25, Nov. 1853	J. Bernard	Gehring, Catharina	N	18
Lasance, Bernard Friedrich	31, Mar. 1856	Bernard	Schaeper, Adelheid	C	
Lasance, Christoph Jacob	3, Apr. 1854	Bernard	Scheper, Adelheid	C	

Name of Child	Date of Baptism	Father	Mother	Church	Page
Lasance, Christopher Alexander	19, July 1857	August	Detert, M. Wilhelmina	A	
Lasance, Gerhard Heinrich	11, Feb. 1855	August	Deters, Maria Wilhelmina	A	
Lasance, Margaretha Friedricka	8, Feb. 1852	Bernard	Scheper, Adelheid	C	
-laskleist, Maria Anna	2, Oct. 1859	?	----, Catharina	D	148
Lass, Eduard	24, June 1856	Ignatius	Scherer, Theodosia	D	61
Lass, Mary	1, Aug. 1858	Ignatius	Habersack, Theresa	H	
Lass, Mary Frances	4, Sept 1859	Ignatius	Habenzettel, Theresa	S	
Lassmeier, Heinrich	22, Oct. 1854	Friedrich	Klair, Maria Catharina	D	20
Latsch, Johan Baptist	21, July 1850	Peter	---rns, Felicitas	D	224
Latscha, Carl	10, Dec. 1858	Carl	Suhr, M. Magdalena	L	
Laube, Johan Friedrich	18, Mar. 1851	Francis	Gree, Maria	F	
Laubs, Mary	24, May 1856	John	Donlan, Elizabeth	E	368
Laucamp, Bernard Heinrich	15, May 1852	Bernard	Niehaus, Elisabeth	A	
Lauday, George William H.	15, Nov. 1850		adult	E	261
Lauday, Theresa Josephine	13, Mar. 1855	George	Dumick, Josephine	E	271
Laudenbach, Johan Joseph	15, Oct. 1852	J. Heinrich	Beckers, M. Catharina	L	
Laudenbach, Maria Cath. Susanna	26, June 1854	Joseph	Evers, Susanna	L	
Laudenbach, Maria Catharina	3, Dec. 1854	Heinrich	Becker, M. Catharina	L	
Laudener, Johanna Francisca	18, Feb. 1855	Maximilian	Winter, Francisca	A	
Lauderer, Anna Catharina	25, Apr. 1859	Maximilian	Winter, Johanna E.	A	
Lauderer, Martha	15, Feb. 1857	Maximilian	Winter, Johanna	A	
Lauders, Arnold Wilhelm	3, Nov. 1850	Max M.	Winter, Johanna Francisca	A	
Lauenhauer, Magdalena	2, Oct. 1859	Heinrich	----, ----	D	148
Lauenstein, Anna Maria	31, May 1857	Ernst	Teggekamp, Rosalia	J	40
Lauenstein, Francis August Friedrich	30, June 1859	Ernst	Tegenkamp, Elisabeth	A	
Lauer, Carl	10, May 1857	Lawrence	Lauer, Catharina	D	84
Lauer, Friedrich Ignatius	27, Jan. 1850	Andreas	Dier, Elisabeth	A	
Lauer, Johan Adam	1, Nov. 1857	Paul	Herzog, Catharina	D	98
Lauer, Joseph	3, May 1855		Lauer, Maria	F	
Lauer, Juliana	18, Sept 1859	Peter	Hetzog, Carolina	D	147
Lauer, Ludwig	23, June 1850	Johan	Heri?, Marianna	D	218
Lauer, Maria Josephina	1, Jan. 1855	Paul	Herzog, Catharina	D	26
Lauer, Maria Magdalena	18, Mar. 1857	Martin	Berger, Veronica	D	81
Lauf, Anna Elisabeth	16, Aug. 1854	Ernst	Schwenger, Maria	A	
Lauf, Johan Ernst	6, Nov. 1852	Ernst	Schwengel, Maria Anna	A	
Lauf, Johan Wilhelm	11, Apr. 1850	Ernst	Schwengel, Luisa	A	
Lauf, Maria Catharina E.	11, Apr. 1850	Ernst	Schwengel, Luisa	A	
Laufer, Josephina	4, Feb. 1855	Mathias	Krebs, Maria	C	
Laugel, Anton Johan	14, July 1851	Anton	Jachtefuchs, Maria Anna	D	273
Laugel, Francis Xavier	1, May 1859	Anton	Würz, Margaretha	D	137
Laugel, Jacob Johan	24, July 1853	Anton	Würz, Margaretha	D	396
Laugel, Peter Joseph	24, May 1855	Anton	Würtz, Margaretha	D	35
Laugen, Anton	4, July 1857	Anton	Würtz, Margaretha	D	89
Laughan, Mary Helen	30, Sept 1855	Michael	Lowrey, Mary Ann	P	153
Laughlan, Ellen	17, Apr. 1859	Michael	Hector, Ann	P	282
Laughlan, John	14, Oc.t 1855	Michael	Hector, Ann	P	155
Laughlan, Mary	13, Nov. 1854	John	Kane, Ann	T	
Laughlan, Mary Ann	7, Mar. 1858	Thomas	Dea, Margaret	P	241
Laughlan, Peter	19, Aug. 1857	Michael	Lowrey, Mary Ann	P	221
Laughlin, Connor	21, Dec. 1856	Patrick	Nestor, Sarah	V	35
Laughlin, Edward	25, Oct. 1857	Michael	Hector, Ann	P	228
Laughlin, James	28, Nov. 1853	James	Doherty, Joanne	E	148
Laughlin, John	2, Sept 1850	James	----, Mary	E	245
Laughlin, John	27, Dec. 1857	James	Brodrick, Ann	P	233
Laughlin, John	24, Oct. 1859	Michael	Lowrey, Mary	P	301
Laughlin, Julia	7, Nov. 1852	James	Doyle, Sarah	E	32
Laughlin, Margaret	26, Oct. 1855	Patrick	Maher, Margaret	E	323
Laughlin, Mary	13, Oct. 1850	Michael	Hector, Ann	B	216
Laughlin, Michael	23, May 1852	Michael	Hoctor, Ann	P	22

Hamilton County, Ohio Roman Catholic Baptism Records -- 1850 - 1859

Name of Child	Date of Baptism	Father	Mother	Church	Page
Laughlin, Sarah	15, Nov. 1857	Daniel	Maloy, Catherine	P	230
Laughlin, William	26, Feb. 1854	Michael	Hector, Ann	P	71
Laughnan, Andrew	19, Nov. 1854	Andrew	----, Rose	M	
Lauman, Johan Bernard	10, July 1856	J. Bernard	Spellmeier, Maria	D	62
Lauman, Joseph Heinrich	31, Oct. 1858	Joseph H.	Spellman, Catharina Maria	D	123
Laumann, Anna Elisabeth Catharina	24, Nov. 1855	Heinrich	Schomaker, Maria	L	
Laumann, Franz Aloysius	29, Mar. 1858	Heinrich	Schomachers, Maria	L	
Laumann, Johan Heinrich	23, May 1850	Bernard	Spellmann, Cath. Elis.	L	
Laumann, Johan Heinrich	25, July 1853	Heinrich	Schomacher, Margaretha	L	
Laun, Catharina	26, June 1850	Andreas	Laun, Elisabeth	K	
Laurent, Elisabeth Theresa	11, May 1856	Philipp	Beck, Philippina	D	58
Laurent, Leonard	21, Mar. 1858	Philipp	You---, Philppina	D	107
Laurent, Mary	19, Dec. 1855	Daniel	Diggan, Ann	P	163
Laury, Catherine	5, Dec. 1858	James	Callahan, Mary	S	
Lauser, Elisabeth	6, Mar. 1859	Adam	Fink, Julia	N	
Lautemann, Christian	23, Aug. 1857	Christian	Petsch, Magdalena	L	
Lauter, Carolina	2, May 1859	Carl	Flug, Stephania	D	137
Lauth, Carolina Dorothea	7, Sept 1856	Jacob	Walz, Maria Genofeva	D	67
Lauth, Catharina	24, June 1855	Jacob	Walz, Maria Genofeva	D	37
Lauth, Friedrich	27, Feb. 1851	Johan	Hanselmann, Dorothea	L	
Lauth, Maria Eva	27, Feb. 1851	Johan	Hanselmann, Dorothea	L	
Lauth, Maria Louisa	31, July 1853	Jacob	Walz, Maria Genofeva	D	397
Laux, Francis Joseph	7, July 1853	Valentin	Kress, Elisabeth	C	
Laux, Margaretha Elisabeth	31, Dec. 1854	Valentin	Kretz, Elisabeth	F	
Laux, Maria Magdalena	4, May 1859		Laux, Appolonia	D	137
Lauxtermann, Maria Gertrud	27, May 1855	David	Goeske, Maria Helena	F	
Lavale, Edward Nathaniel	28, Aug. 1856	Edward	----, Amanda	E	394
Lavall, Wililam John	16, June 1850	Andrew	----, Catherine	B	205
Lavan, John	31, Dec. 1854	John	Roddy, Mary	B	9
Lavan, William	28, Nov. 1852	Thomas	----, Mary	E	39
Lavas--, Charles Francis	1, Nov. 1851	Amand	Taylor, Louise	P	13b
Lavay, William	11, Oct. 1858	Edward	Haily, Winnefred	E	568
Lavazzi, Angela Mary	6, May 1859	John	----, Catherine Benedicta	E	623
Lavelle, Mary Ann	17, Oct. 1858	Joseph	Christy, Louise Ann	E	570
Lavender, Catherine	13, Apr. 1851	Thomas	McNulty, Catherine	P	7
Lavender, Edward	8, Aug. 1850	Michael	----, Mary	E	238
Lavender, Edward	21, Nov. 1852	Thomas	McDonald, Dilia	P	30
Lavender, George	10, Feb. 1850	Thomas	McNulty, Catherine	B	197
Lavender, Marianne	19, Feb. 1853	Thomas	McNulty, Catherine	P	36
Lavender, Mary Ann	9, Sept 1855	Michael	Tonston?, Mary	E	314
Lavender, Michael H.	15, Jan. 1857	Michael	----, Mary	E	426
Lavender, Thomas	5, Sept 1853	Robert	Reordan, Helen	P	51
Lavender, Thomas Francis	30, Nov. 1854	Thomas	McNulty, Catherine	P	107
Lavender, William	2, Feb. 1853	Michael	Johnson, Mary	V	1
Laveng, Daniel	2, June 1850	Daniel	Sweeney, Jane	B	203
Lavers, Charles Gregory	4, Jan. 1852	Daniel	Sweeney, Jane	B	249
Lavery, Edmund Francis	5, Feb. 1854	Daniel	Sweeney, Jane	B	308
Lavery, John	4, Feb. 1850	John	----, Margaret	E	195
Lavill, Patrick	16, Feb. 1851	Thomas	Peyal, Helen	B	225
Lavin, Ann	20, Mar. 1855	John	Owens, Sarah	B	12
Lavin, Catherine	3, Dec. 1852	John	Roddy, Mary	B	277
Lavin, Catherine	6, Mar. 1854	Thomas	Kelly, Mary	B	310
Lavin, Helen Theresa	8, Feb. 1859	Peter	Walsh, Julia	P	274
Lavin, James Martin	14, Nov. 1856	Peter	Walsh, Julia	P	198
Lavin, Margaret Catherine	6, Aug. 1854	Peter	Walsh, Julia	P	91
Lavin, Mary	26, July 1857	John	Owens, Sarah	P	218
Lavin, Mary	25, Dec. 1852	Peter	Welsh, Julia	P	32
Lavin, Thomas	6, June 1858	Thomas	Kelly, Mary	B	59
Law, Andrew	14, June 1852	Andrew	Ayars, Margaret	E	423

- 378 -

Name of Child	Date of Baptism	Father	Mother	Church	Page
Law, William John	27, May 1855		Law, Jane	B	15
Lawarre, Johan Heinrich	30, May 1858	Johan	Albertzart, Margaretha	L	
Lawday, Charles Joseph	24, Aug. 1851	George W.	Mayer, Celestine?	E	335
Lawday, Lucy Mary	5, Dec. 1852	George	Magen, Celestine	E	42
Lawdy, Edward Wilhelm	1, Mar. 1858	G. Wilhelm	Ma---, Maria Christina	D	106
Lawler, Ann	26, Sept 1853	James	Burns, Mary	E	129
Lawler, Ann	22, Apr. 1859	John	Donnelly, Elizabeth	E	619
Lawler, Dennis	10, Aug. 1851	Daniel	Fitzpatrick, Sarah	P	11
Lawler, Eleanor	7, July 1851	Daniel	----, Ann	E	321
Lawler, Francis	19, May 1859	Francis	Roach, Mary	B	75
Lawler, Hieronymus	23, Apr. 1851	Edward	Miller, Emeline	B	230
Lawler, James	3, Dec. 1857	James	McCoy, Mary Jane	V	42
Lawler, John	2, Sept 1853	Daniel	----, Ann	M	
Lawler, John	5, Aug. 1851	James	Byrnes, Mary	E	331
Lawler, John	23, June 1857	John	Donaghue, Catherine	P	215
Lawler, John James	30, May 1858	thomas	Collins, Mary	B	59
Lawler, Margaert	12, Jan. 1851	Joseph	Clare, Mary	P	3
Lawler, Mary	19, Mar. 1854	James	Dady, Mary	V	12
Lawler, Mary	15, Aug. 1859	James M.	McCoy, Mary J.	B	79
Lawler, Sarah	10, Aug. 1851	Daniel	Fitzpatrick, Sarah	P	11
Lawless, Ann	6, Nov. 1859	Edward	Keegan, Ann	E	668
Lawless, Catherine	9, Oct. 1859	Patrick	Owens, Mary	E	661
Lawless, John Francis	16, Jan. 1852	Dennis	Haidman, Mary	B	250
Lawless, Margaret	15, Oct. 1854	Edward	Malony, Catherine	E	232
Lawless, Margaret	30, Mar. 1856	Patrick	Owens, Mary	L	
Lawless, Margaret	28, Jan. 1855	William	----, Mary	E	261
Lawless, Martin	9, Nov. 1854	Michael	Cutt, Sarah	P	103
Lawless, Mary	25, Aug. 1856	John	Boylan, Hannah	V	36
Lawless, Mary Ann	27, July 1857	Patrick	Owens, Mary	E	470
Lawless, Patrick	23, Feb. 1855	Joseph	----, Mary	E	267
Lawless, Sarah Mary	3, Feb. 1858	John	Boyle, Ann	E	515
Lawless, Thomas	3, Dec. 1854	James	----, Ann	M	
Lawless, Thomas	12, Mar. 1856	Patrick	Tracy, Ann	B	26
Lawless, Thomas Joseph	2, June 1854	Dennis	Harman, Mary	B	1
Lawless, William Nic.	2, Aug. 1857	William	Brennan, Mary	E	471
Lawlor, Sarah Jane	11, Sept 1859	Thomas	Collins, Mary	B	80
Lawny, Eliza Louise	4, Sept 1851	Jasper	Crawford, Eliza	P	11
Lawny, Sarah Ellen	4, Sept 1851	Jasper	Crawford, Eliza	P	11
Lawrence, Anthony	28, July 1850	Michael	----, Catherine	E	235
Lawrence, David	12, Sept 1852	David	Connell, Margaret	B	270
Lawson, James	26, Oct. 1856	James J.	McCormack, Joanne	E	407
Lawson, Laura Mary	29, June 1856	Thomas	Cobb, Eveline	T	
Lay, Catharina	1, Sept 1859	Jacob F.	Roel, Catharina	L	
Layhan, Timothy	12, Oct. 1858	Matthew	Cronin, Elizabeth	E	569
Leady, John	19, Feb. 1854	Patrick	Leahy, Mary Ann	B	309
Leaghy, Helen	7, Aug. 1859	Patrick	Leaghy, Helen	P	291
Leaghy, Margaret	22, Aug. 1858	Timothy	Purcell, Mary	P	258
Leahan, Timothy	23, Jan. 1857	John	Cronin, Joanne	V	37
Leahey, Ann	19, July 1857	Patrick	Hogan, Mary Ann	B	47
Leahy, Ann	26, Dec. 1856	Dennis	Dea, Bridget	P	202
Leahy, Daniel	30, Jan. 1853	Patrick	Higgins, Mary Ann	B	282
Leahy, Emmett Eugene	14, Aug. 1859	Jeremiah	Hustes, Charlotte	P	292
Leahy, Frances	6, Jan. 1856	Patrick	Higgins, Mary Ann	B	23
Leahy, John	14, Jan. 1853	Dennis	Day, Bridget	P	33
Leahy, John	2, July 1856	Timothy	Kennedy, Lucy	P	184
Leahy, Margaret	20, Aug. 1854	Dennis	Dea, Bridget	P	93
Leahy, Mary	20, Aug. 1854	Dennis	Dea, Bridget	P	93
Leahy, Mary Catherine	24, Aug. 1859	Timothy	Kenny, Lucy	P	294
Leahy, Mary Elizabeth	15, May 1859	Patrick	Hogan, Mary Ann	B	75

Name of Child	Date of Baptism	Father	Mother	Church	Page
Leahy, William	2, May 1857	Patrick	Handly, Helen	P	212
Leahy, William	14, Nov. 1852	William	Lenehan, Mary	B	275
Lean, Morris	14, Feb. 1859	Morris	Lean, Helen	P	276
Leany, Bridget Mary	17, Oct. 1858	John	----, Ann	P	264
Lear, Alice Georgia Ann	29, Oct. 1858	George	Morgan, Ann J.	E	573
Learned, Mary	6, May 1851		adult	B	232
Leary, Albert	24, Jan. 1858	Jeremiah	----, Charlotte	E	512
Leary, Ann Eliza	8, Nov. 1853	Patrick	Cashly, Catherine	E	142
Leary, Ann Mary	24, Apr. 1859	John	McGills, Catherine	B	74
Leary, Cornelius	27, Aug. 1858	Jeremiah	Gronin, Ann	E	559
Leary, Dennis	18, Aug. 1859	Cornelius	----, Ellen	E	648
Leary, Helen	9, Apr. 1854	James	Ryan, Ann	B	312
Leary, Joanne	21, Mar. 1857	Cornelius	----, Ellen	E	441
Leary, John	20, Nov. 1859	Dennis	Cronin, Catherine	B	84
Leary, John	11, Mar. 1856	Michael	----, Mary	E	349
Leary, John	28, Mar. 1852	Michael	Kearney, Mary	B	255
Leary, Joseph	12, Sept 1851	Matthew	----, ----	P	12
Leary, Margaret	2, Nov. 1851	Patrick	Cassidy, Catherine	E	355
Leary, Mary Helen	22, Apr. 1854	Michael	Kearney, Mary	B	313
Leary, Timothy	7, Jan. 1858	Dennis	Cronin, Catherine	P	235
Leary?, Helen	26, Mar. 1854	Patrick	Glennon, Catherine	P	75
Lease, Catherine	23, May 1853	James	----, Cecilia	E	92
Leathercott, Mary	18, July 1852	John	Gafferty, Ann	B	263
Lebbert, Georg Lawrence	28, Aug. 1859	Nicolaus	Zoller, Maria Anna	J	52
Lebbert, Louisa Agatha	26, Apr. 1857	Nicolaus	Zoller, Maria Theresa	J	40
Leber, Johanna	26, Dec. 1851	Wilhelm	Zoller, Margaretha	F	
Lechinger, Catherine Margaret	21, June 1857	Martin	Fries, Barbara	H	
Lechinger, Frances Romana	11, Feb. 1855	Martin	----, Barbara	H	
Lechinger, Rose Mary	30, Jan. 1853	Martin	----, Barbara	H	
Lechinger, Theodora Barbara	11, Sept 1859	Martin	Fries, Barbara	H	
Lechleichner, Johan Mathias	25, Oct. 1855	Mathias	Grundorf, Anna Maria	L	
Lechleitner, Nicolaus Albert	10, Dec. 1857	Mathias	Gundorf, Anna Maria	L	
Lechler, Josephina Margaretha	31, May 1852	Michael	Wolf, Anna	K	
Lechler, Leona Maria	16, Oct. 1859	Michael	Wolf, Anna	K	
Lechlere, Ludwig	1, Apr. 1850	Michael	Wolf, Anna	D	207
Lechner, Amalia	29, Sept 1852	Simon	Hauck, Eva	C	
Lechner, Anna Catharina	15, May 1851	Simon	Hauck, Eva	L	
Lechner, Johan	19, Aug. 1856	Johan	Burger, Francisca	D	65
Lechner, Johan	23, July 1854	Simon	Haack, Eva	C	
Lechner, Johan Georg	4, Dec. 1859	Johan	Bürger, Francisca	D	152
Lechner, Maria Franisca	17, Jan. 1858	Johan	Burger, Francisca	D	103
Lechting, Carl Christian	13, June 1858	Carl	Hoelster, Maria	C	
Leddy, Daniel	12, Jan. 1857	Daniel	Gafen, Rose	E	426
Leddy, Julia	24, Aug. 1856	Michael	McGinnis, Bridget	R	
Leddy, Thomas	31, July 1853	Daniel	----, Rose	E	114
Ledeler, Adam Wilhelm	7, May 1854		Ledeler, Caecilia	C	
Lederer, Johan	8, Aug. 1852	Anton	Donauer, Margaretha	F	
Ledogar, Maria Juliana	7, Feb. 1858	Jacob	Künsler, Rosina	A	
Ledretta, Virginia	2, Jan. 1856	Francis	McDonald,	B	23
Lee, Alice	25, Aug. 1854	Matthew	----, Ann	E	219
Lee, Ann	13, Dec. 1853	Patrick	Farris, Margaret	E	152
Lee, Catharine	9, Aug. 1857	James	Geller, Catharine	T	
Lee, Catherine	23, May 1852	John	----, Bridget	E	418
Lee, Charles	13, Nov. 1853	Michael	----, Margaret	E	143
Lee, James Albert	2, Apr. 1856	Thomas	----, Joanne	E	355
Lee, Jane	11, Sept 1856	William	Regan, Ann	B	34
Lee, Mary	25, Dec. 1854	James	Hestor, mary	E	249
Lee, Mary	2, May 1852	Matthew	----, Ann	E	408
Lee, Mary Ann	5, May 1850	Matthew	----, Ann	E	211

Name of Child	Date of Baptism	Father	Mother	Church	Page
Lee, Mary Catherine	13, Nov. 1853	Michael	----, Margaret	E	143
Lee, Patrick	6, Feb. 1852	Patrick	Barrett, Margaret	P	17
Lee, Robert Henry	28, Aug. 1852	Thomas	----, Jean	E	10
Lee, Thomas	8, July 1853	John	----, Helen	B	295
Lee, Thomas Joseph	25, Dec. 1856	Thomas	----, Joanne	E	422
Lee, William	8, Oct. 1853	James	----, Mary	E	132
Leeds, Eliza Clara	14, May 1854	Lafayette	McSweeney, Mary	B	315
Leeds, Francis Eugene	11, Apr. 1852	Lafayette	McSweeney, Mary Ann	B	256
Leeds, Francis Eugene	15, Jan. 1852	Lafayette	McSweeney, Mary Ann	B	250
Leeds, John	3, July 1859	John	Morgan, Mary	P	287
Leeds, Mary Ann	19, Oct. 1858	Lafayette	McSweeney, Mary Ann	B	66
Leeds, Thomas Lafayette	25, Feb. 1856	Lafayette	McSweeney, Mary Ann	B	25
Leehany, James	30, June 1854	Thomas	O'Neil, Ellen	B	2
Leen, (boy)	8, Oct. 1854	Michael	----, Mary	M	
Leen, Bernard	22, June 1856	Bernard	----, Joanne	M	
Leen, Caroline	14, Sept 1856	Michael	----, Ellen	M	
Leen, David	7, May 1854	John	----, Mary	M	
Leen, Ellen	28, Jan. 1855	Bernard	----, Joanne	M	
Leen, James	22, July 1858	Bernard	----, Joanne	M	
Leen, Joanne	5, Dec. 1858	John	----, Mary	M	
Leen, Magdalena	19, Jan. 1851	B.	Butlers, Johanna	L	
Leen, Mary	19, Oct. 1851	John	----, Mary	M	
Leen, Maurice	4, Feb. 1853	Bernard	----, Joanne	M	
Leen, Thomas	20, Feb. 1853	Michael	----, Ellen	M	
Leeny, John	18, Feb. 1855	Jeremiah	Bradley, Honora	V	23
Leeny, Mary Ann	20, Jan. 1856	Bryan	McWilliams, Helen	P	167
Leeny, Thomas Steele	12, Jan. 1854	Brian	McWilliams, Helen	P	65
Leeron, Michael	15, Aug. 1855	Thomas	Horley, Ann	E	307
Leeson, Thomas	3, Aug. 1852	William	Savage, Ann	B	267
Leet, John	30, Apr. 1850		adult - 25 years old	E	210
Leewe, Bernard Herman Heinrich	1, May 1855	Heinrich	Schroeder, Anna M.	F	
Lefebvre, Nicolaus Heinrich	22, Mar. 1855	Heinrich	Wielinger, Ida	D	31
Lefevre, Dennis	13, Mar. 1855	Oliver	McMannus, Bridget	E	271
Lefken, Joseph Wilehlm	15, Sept 1850	Wilhelm	Meyerhoff, M. Anna	C	
Lefled, Bernard Heirnich	22, Aug. 1854	Herman	Beckman, Elisabeth	K	
Legel, Vincent	19, Sept 1858	Ludwig	Martin, Margaretha	W	23
LeGras, Edward John	6, Sept 1854	Edmund	Egle--, Mary	B	5
Lehan, Daniel	2, Mar. 1859	John	----, Jane	E	608
Lehany, Ann Eliza	24, Feb. 1853	Bernard	McElroy, Ann	E	65
Lehi, Henry Christopher	7, Oct. 1855	J. Adam	----, Mary	H	
Lehkamp, Anna Maria	13, Jan. 1859	J. Adam	Schmidt, Anna Maria	L	
Lehman, Anna Maria Nicola	30, Mar. 1851	Herman	Lohman, Maria Anna	A	
Lehman, Francis Joseph	16, Oct. 1853	Herman	----, Maria Anna	H	
Lehman, Freidrich	14, Apr. 1850	Friedrich	Maringer, Susanna	D	209
Lehman, Johan	14, Sept 1854	Simon	Schwendeman, Carolina	D	17
Lehman, Maria	9, May 1852	Stephan	Freye, Carolina	K	
Lehman, Maria Elisabeth	24, Apr. 1859	Ferdinand	Burt, Bridget	R	
Lehman, Peter Carl	27, Nov. 1856	Herman	Wiederstäter, Maria Anna	H	
Lehman, Philipp	29, June 1856	Simon	Schwendeman, Carolina	D	61
Lehman, William Albert Anthony	16, Dec. 1858	Herman	Widderstett, Maria Anna	H	
Lehmann, Anna Maria Catharina	28, Mar. 1854	Herman	Varer, Anna Maria	C	
Lehmann, Herman Gerhard	14, Oct. 1859	Anton	Wuebel, Francisca	C	
Lehmann, Maria	24, Apr. 1853	Stephan	Freye, Carolina	L	
Lehmer, Clara Carolina	13, Dec. 1853	Friedrich	Zimmerman, Barbara	D	420
Lehmer, Georg	9, Oct. 1859	Wilhelm	Walter, Catharina	C	
Lehmes, Maria	5, May 1856		adult - 33 years old	K	
Lehmeyer, Johan Bernard	16, Jan. 1859	Joseph	Schromeyer, Theresa	C	
Lehmeyer, Joseph Theodor	17, Feb. 1856	Joseph	Schroenmeyer, Theresa	C	
Lehmeyer, Maria Emilia	11, Dec. 1853	Joseph	Schroermeyer, Theresa	C	

Name of Child	Date of Baptism	Father	Mother	Church	Page
Lehmeyer, Maria Sophia	16, Dec. 1850	Joseph	Schroermeyer, Theresa	C	
Lehmkuhl, Anna Maria Magdalena	22, May 1857	Bernard	Borges, Anna M.	C	
Lehmkuhl, Anton Bernard	13, Feb. 1851	Anton	Westbrock, Anna M.	C	
Lehmkuhl, Johan Dietrich	5, Feb. 1854	Dietrich	Hoffhaus, Catharina	C	
Lehmkuhl, Joseph Heinrich	23, Feb. 1851	Dietrich	Hofhaus, M. Catharina	C	
Lehmkule, Bernard Theodor	22, Dec. 1858	Dietrich	Hofhaus, Gertrud	N	
Lehnbeuter, Johan	20, June 1858	Christopher	Stadelman, Catharina	H	
Lehnhardt, Joseph	1, Nov. 1851	Johan	Konradt, Theresa	J	12
Lehnhof, Margaretha	3, Mar. 1850	Friedrich	Oestler, Margaretha	H	
Lehnhoff, Henry	9, July 1854	Mathias	----, Barbara	H	
Lehnhoff, Joseph Anselm	24, Jan. 1858	Frederick	Esslinger, Margaret	H	
Lehnhoff, Margaretha Veronica	23, June 1859	Peter	Braun, Maria Veronica	H	
Lehnhoff, Mary	25, Apr. 1852	Frederick	----, Margaret	H	
Lehnhoff, Veronica	6, Aug. 1854	Frederick	----, Margaret	H	
Lehnter, Anna Maria G.	15, Aug. 1852	Caspar	Steinhauer, Dominica	C	
Lehrman, Anna Maria	20, Nov. 1859	Michael	Oldenberg, Josephine	R	
Lehrman, Anna Philomena	20, Oct. 1850	G. Herman	Varell, Anna Maria	K	
Lehrman, Christopher	9, July 1854	John	----, Gertrud	H	
Lehrman, Margaret Francisca	18, Mar. 1855	Michael	Oldenburg, Jsoephina	R	
Lehrman, Nicolaus	1, Mar. 1857	George	----, Josephine	R	
Lehsnick, Bernard Ludwig	16, Aug. 1857	Mathias	----, Margaretha	D	92
Leib, Francis	2, June 1850	Caspar	Schneider, Barbara	K	
Leib, Joseph Michael	29, Sept 1851	Michael	Schnetzer, Francisca	J	12
Leib, Lucia Anna	4, July 1853	Caspar	Schmidt, Barbara	K	
Leibe, Adam Georg	2, Aug. 1857	Xavier	Leibe, Francisca	D	91
Leibeck, Bernard	14, Dec. 1851	Sebastian	Staubach, Rosina	F	
Leibeck, Carolina	25, Dec. 1855	Sebastian	Staubach, Rosina	F	
Leibeck, Gertrud	22, Oct. 1853	Sebastian	Staubach, Rosina	F	
Leibeck, Rosina	12, Jan. 1850	Sebastian	Staubach, Rosina	F	
Leiber, Joseph	10, July 1853	Albin	----, Agnes	H	
Leibhold, Carl	1, Jan. 1850		Leibhold, Margaretha	A	
Leibhold, Carl Matthias	27, Oct. 1850	Christian	Halblich, Catharina	A	
Leich, Anton	6, July 1856	Peter J.	Naegele, Sophia	F	
Leich, Maria	21, Feb. 1858	Caspar	Kramer, Genofeva	D	105
Leich, Martin	2, May 1858	Peter J.	Naegel, Sophia	A	
Leichen, Maria Euphemia	26, Mar. 1855	Bernard H.	Reilman, Christina	A	
Leicht, Maria	23, Oct. 1859	Caspar	----, Genofeva	D	149
Leick, Carl Eduard	2, Oct. 1859	Peter	Tomeny, Mary	T	
Leidecker, Christina	22, May 1856	Michael	Paulus, Catharina	D	59
Leidegger, Joseph	13, Mar. 1859	Michael	Paulus, Catharina	D	133
Leidenheimer, Elisabeth	28, Feb. 1854	Jacob	Hoffman, Elisabeth	D	5
Leidenheimer, Eva	28, Mar. 1852	Jacob	Hoffmann, Elisabeth	C	
Leideralbert, Anton Heinrich	9, Feb. 1854	Herman H.	Bockmann, Maria Anna	L	
Leideralbert, Heinrich	19, Oct. 1856	Herman H.	Bockmann, Anna	L	
Leideralbert, Joseph	24, Nov. 1859	Herman	Bockmann, Maria Anna	L	
Leideralbert, Maria Gertrud	9, May 1855	Herman	Bockmann, Maria Anna	L	
Leidinger, Jacob	22, Feb. 1852	Jacob	Thoma, Catharina	D	308
Leidinger, Johan	10, Feb. 1856	Jacob	Thoma, Catharina	D	51
Leidinger, Maria	13, Dec. 1857	Jacob	Thamma, Catharina	C	
Leierer, Dorothea	1, June 1856	Francis	----, Barbara	H	
Leifeling, Francis	22, Mar. 1853	Herman	Hausterup, Maria Gertrud	K	
Leifling, Johan Bernard	8, June 1859	Heinrich	Austrup, Gertrud	L	
Leifling, Johan Gerhard	29, Oct. 1854	Herman	Austrup, M. Gertrud	L	
Leifling, Maria Elisabeth	1, Apr. 1857	Heinrich	Austrup, Gertrud	L	
Leihnick, Walter E. Burrags	29, Apr. 1857	Francis	Conand, Mary Elisabeth	H	
Leik, Ludwig Edward	22, Nov. 1857	Peter	Thoming, Maria	F	
Leike, Philipp	22, Apr. 1853	Peter	Tomney, Mary	B	289
Leike, Theresa	6, Jan. 1856	Peter	Tomeny, Mary	T	
Lein, Johan Peter	13, Jan. 1850	Johan (+)	Schütz, Maria	D	199

Name of Child	Date of Baptism	Father	Mother	Church	Page
Leiner, Johan Melchior	4, May 1850	----	----, ----	A	
Leiner, Wilhelm	21, Nov. 1858	Francis	Holslager, Barbara	A	
Leininger, Adam	30, Mar. 1851	Adam	Stemmler, Magdalena	K	
Leininger, Anna Angela	5, Nov. 1854	Carl	Berst, Angela	C	
Leininger, Johan Ferdinand	4, Sept 1859	Georg	Wetter, Maria	K	
Leipold, Anna Maria Theresa	29, Jan. 1854	Carl	Schmid, Anna Eva	D	3
Leipold, Carl	10, June 1855	Carl	Schmitt, Maria Eva	D	36
Leipold, Elisabeth	9, Nov. 1856	Carl	Schage, Maria	D	71
Leipold, Heinrich Albert	23, Sept 1855	Anton	Riger, Maria	D	43
Leipold, Valentin	8, Dec. 1858	Carl	Schmidt, Maria Eva	D	125
Leis, Ferdinand	1, June 1856	Peter	Forster, Cunigunda	J	36
Leis, Maria Margaretha	5, June 1853	Peter	Keil, Cunigunda	A	
Leiser, Anna Sabina Angelica	9, Mar. 1856	Georg	Braunwarz, Margaretha	D	53
Leiser, Catharina	14, May 1854	Georg	Braunworth, Margaretha	D	10
Leiser, Francisca Philomena	4, Mar. 1855	J. Adam	King, Julia	N	27
Leiser, Georg Edward	10, Oct. 1858	Sebastian	Duerck, Catharina	D	121
Leiser, Johan Valentin	12, Apr. 1857	Georg	Braunworth, Margaretha	D	82
Leiser, John	19, Nov. 1854	Timothy	McGrath, Mary	E	241
Leiser, Maria	2, June 1850	Sebastian	Dürk, Catharina	D	215
Leiser, Maria Elisabeth	21, Oct. 1855	Sebastian	Dirck, Catharina	D	45
Leiser, Martin	3, Oct. 1852	Sebastian	Dürk, Catharina	D	351
Leising, Johan Herman	13, June 1857	Wilhelm	Ahaus, Francisca	F	
Leist, Anna Maria Magdalena	25, Dec. 1853	Georg	Burkhart, Augusta	D	422
Leist, Clara Martha	17, May 1857	Georg	Burkhard, Augusta	C	
Leist, Francis Carl	27, Mar. 1859	Georg	Burkhard, Augusta	C	
Leist, Francis Joseph	21, Apr. 1850	Georg	Burghart, Augusta	D	210
Leist, Joseph Lawrence	21, Jan. 1855	James	----, Magdalene	H	
Leist, Maria Anna Magdalena	10, June 1855	Georg	Burkhard, Augusta	C	
Leitinger, Francis Joseph	11, Sept 1859	Jacob	Tama, Catharina	A	
Lejeune, Stephan	30, Oct. 1853	Stephan	Knebel, Anna Maria	F	
Lekteich, Emilia	23, Nov. 1853		Lekteich, Catharina	C	
Lell, Ann	24, Nov. 1856	George	Warmuth, Anna	H	
Lell, Barbara	25, Mar. 1859	George	Wermuth, Ann	H	
Lell, Philip	15, June 1851	George	----, Margaret	H	
Lell, Philip	22, Oct. 1854		Lell, Ann	H	
Lelly, Mary	28, Oct. 1855	Patrick	McCormick, Ellen	B	21
Lemcole, Ann	10, Mar. 1855	Henry	McLaughlin, Ellen	E	271
Lemcole, Mary	15, Mar. 1857	Henry	McLaughlin, Ellen	E	440
Lemcole, Michael	4, Dec. 1853	Henry	Laughlin, Ellen	E	150
Lemcole, Sarah	30, Jan. 1859	Henry	McLaughlin, Ellen	E	600
Lemkers, Anna Maria	25, Aug. 1852	Bernard H.	Bruening, M.	C	
Lemkheim, Johan Georg	10, Mar. 1854	Johan	Zweigardt, Elis.	L	
Lemkheim, Johan Joseph	10, Jan. 1853	Johan	Zweighard, Elisabeth	L	
Lemkheim, Maria Elisabeth	10, Mar. 1854	Johan	Zweigardt, Elis.	L	
Lemme, Johan Bernard	8, June 1853	Caspar	Osfort, Gertrud	L	
Lemme, Maria Catharina	17, Jan. 1855	Caspar	Oswald, Gertrud	L	
Lemmen, Georg Wilhelm	3, Aug. 1856	Heinrich	Kuhlman, Maria	K	
Lemming, Franz Laurentius	10, Aug. 1855	Johan	Wiegmann, Elisabeth	L	
Lemming, Johan Bernard	29, Oct. 1855	Johan	Gieseke, Maria	L	
Lemming, Johan Paul Herman	27, June 1858	Johan	Wieckmann, Adelheid	L	
Lemming, Johanna Philomina Adel.	7, May 1859	Gerhard	Wieckmann, Helena	L	
Lemmink, Johan Wilhelm	1, Jan. 1853	J. Gerhard	Wichmann, Gesina Adel.	L	
Lemmon, Johan Heinrich	10, Aug. 1854	Heinrich	Kuhlman, Maria Anna	K	
Lemon, Emma Theresa	27, Apr. 1859	Henry	----, Mary Ann	E	621
Lemper, Anna Elisabeth	19, Mar. 1856	Joseph	Haarman, Anna	A	
Lemper, Bernard Heinrich	16, Dec. 1850	Bernard	Strotkamp, Anna	C	
Lemper, Carolina Josephina	29, July 1858	Joseph	Haarman, Anna	A	
Lemper, Carolina Philomena	19, Sept 1853	Joseph	Haarmann, Maria Anna	L	
Lemper, Gertrud Rosalia	28, Nov. 1856	Ferdinand	Wortman, Elisabeth	A	

Name of Child	Date of Baptism	Father	Mother	Church	Page
Lemper, Johan Heinrich	23, Mar. 1853	J. Bernard	Strocamp, Maria Anna	D	377
Lemper, Josephina	16, Dec. 1850	Bernard	Strotkamp, Anna	C	
Lempker, Arnold	10, Mar. 1858	Heinrich	Kampschmidt, Maria	A	
Lempker, Bernard Joseph	23, May 1856	Bernard H.	Kampschmidt, Maria	A	
Lenagan, Bridget	1, Feb. 1853	Patrick	Welsh, Bridget	E	60
Lenaghen, Cornelius	1, Jan. 1854	James	----, Catherine	U	
Lenahan, John	19, May 1851	Philipp	McGowen, Catherine	B	232
Lenahan, Richard	28, Aug. 1856	Patrick	----, Bridget	R	
Lenan, Agnes	10, Oct. 1852	Thomas	----, Ann	E	26
Lengners, Anna Maria Gertrud	4, Aug. 1853	Engelbert	Egart, Gertrud	N	15
Lennan, Honora Ellen	2, Jan. 1859	Patrick	Clay--, Honora	B	69
Lennay, William	27, Dec. 1852	Alfred	10 years old	B	279
Lenneman, Eliza	3, May 1859	Henry	McFarland, Margaret	E	622
Lennen, Castodius Washington	20, June 1858	Hezen	Deuders, Maria Clementina	N	
Lennen, Euchenius Wachin	20, June 1858	Hezen	Deuders, Maria Clementina	N	
Lennon, Ann	13, Feb. 1853	James	Casey, Ann	P	34
Lennon, Bridget	6, Jan. 1850	James	Casey, Ann	B	193
Lennon, Catherine	19, Oct. 1851	Henry	Ward, Elizabeth	E	350
Lennon, Egemus?	7, Aug. 1855	Owen	Brady, Bridget	E	306
Lennon, Eliza Mary	17, Nov. 1856	William	Hogan, Julia	B	36
Lennon, Elizabeth	24, Aug. 1851	Michael	----, Elizabeth	E	336
Lennon, Helen	19, July 1857	James	Casey, Ann	P	217
Lennon, John	7, Sept 1851	James	Casey, Ann	P	12
Lennon, John	7, Mar. 1858	William	Hogan, Julia	B	56
Lennon, John William	18, Apr. 1852	Owen	Brady, Bridget	E	404
Lennon, Margaret Elizabeth	17, Nov. 1859	James	Hawkins, Margaret Ann	B	83
Lennon, Marianne	14, Nov. 1852	Henry	Coleman, Mary	P	30
Lennon, Mary	20, July 1855	James	Casey, Ann	P	141
Lennon, Mary	16, Oct. 1859	Michael	----, Eliza	E	663
Lentel, Crescentia	9, Oct. 1859	Sebastian	Eda, Crescentia	U	
Lentz, Emilia Louisa	28, Aug. 1859	Julius	Terwinski, Catharina	C	
Lentz, Joseph	12, Sept 1858	Georg	Glorius, Barbara	G	
Lenz, Johan Heinrich	25, June 1857	Georg	Glorius, Barbara	A	
Lenz, Maria Wanda Stephania	6, Aug. 1855	Julius	Cwerwinska, Cath.	L	
Leon, Carolina	12, Jan. 1851	Joseph	Doll, Gertrud	F	
Leon, Francisca	18, Dec. 1859	Joseph	Tolin, Gertrud	G	
Leon, Joseph Bernard	5, Oct. 1856	Joseph	Doll, Gertrud	F	
Leon, Maria Justina	6, Feb. 1853	Joseph	Doll, Gertrud	F	
Leon, Sebastian	15, Oct. 1854	Joseph	Doll, Gertrud	F	
Leonard, Ann	8, Jan. 1856	Andrew	McGrath, Catharine	T	
Leonard, Ann	18, Mar. 1859	John	----, Alice	E	611
Leonard, Ann	15, Jan. 1853	Patrick	Larkin, Elizabeth	B	281
Leonard, Ann	6, Apr. 1850	Richard	----, Margaret	E	207
Leonard, Bernard	6, June 1857	Bernard	Mallon, Ellen	B	45
Leonard, Bridget	28, Apr. 1850	Bernard	Leonard, Bridget	B	201
Leonard, Catherine	19, Oct. 1856	Bernard	Opton, Sophia	E	406
Leonard, Catherine	18, Nov. 1855	John	Meed, Mary	E	328
Leonard, Catherine	15, July 1858	Matthew	Cavanaugh, Sarah	B	61
Leonard, Cornelius	28, Nov. 1858	Patrick	Cronin, Mary A.	P	268
Leonard, Edward	24, Oct. 1858	James	O'Neil, Ann	P	264
Leonard, Edward	29, Apr. 1859	Patrick	McDonough, Honora	B	74
Leonard, Elisabeth	12, Dec. 1858	Bernard	Casey, Ann	T	
Leonard, Elizabeth	10, Oct. 1852	Richard	Daly, Margaret	B	271
Leonard, Ellen	28, Feb. 1856	James	----, Catherine	E	347
Leonard, Francis	9, Mar. 1851	William	Dougherty, Catherine	B	226
Leonard, Helen	27, Oct. 1850	Andrew	McGarty, Catherine	B	217
Leonard, James	10, Sept 1854	Bernard	Knox, Ellen	B	5
Leonard, James	1, Jan. 1854	James	Maher, Catherine	E	156
Leonard, John	4, Jan. 1857	Bernard	Casey, Ann	B	38

Name of Child	Date of Baptism	Father	Mother	Church	Page
Leonard, John	18, Aug. 1857	Francis	Poul, Bridget	T	
Leonard, Julia Helen	29, May 1853	Bernard	Knox, Ellen	B	292
Leonard, Margaret	1, May 1853	Andrew	McGarty, Catherine	B	289
Leonard, Margaret	20, Sept 1852	Matthew	Cavanaugh, Sarah	P	27
Leonard, Margaret	12, Mar. 1854	Richard	Daly, Margaret	B	310
Leonard, Mary	15, Dec. 1852	Dennis	Hughes, Rose	E	43
Leonard, Mary	7, Feb. 1853	James	----, Ann	M	
Leonard, Mary Ann	22, Dec. 1851	Patrick	----, Honora	E	366
Leonard, Mary Ann	10, Apr. 1859	Robert	Nolan, Ann	P	281
Leonard, Mary Ellen	26, Dec. 1852	William	Leonard, Mary Ann	E	48
Leonard, Mary Jane	11, June 1856	Bernard	Knox, Ellen	B	30
Leonard, Mary Jane	29, Mar. 1857	Thomas	Crowly, Catherine	E	444
Leonard, Michael	29, May 1855	Bernard	Casey, Ann	B	15
Leonard, Michael	4, Dec. 1858	James	Maher, Catherine	E	584
Leonard, Patrick	22, Jan. 1856	Edward	Scollen, Ann	T	
Leonard, Rosanne	17, June 1855	Matthew	Cavanagh, Sarah	B	15
Leonard, Sarah	5, Sept 1858		adult	B	63
Leonard, Thomas	21, Dec. 1857	Edward	Scoller, Ann	T	
Leonard, Thomas	31, Aug. 1856	Patrick	McDonough, Honora	P	189
Leonard, William Edward	11, Dec. 1859	Andrew	McGrath, Catherine	B	85
Leonett, Johan Peter Jacob	28, Apr. 1850	Philipp J.	Freis, Maria	F	
Leonhard, Catharina Theresa	28, Feb. 1858	Johan	Mazette, Ursula	J	44
Leonhart, Carolina	20, July 1853	Georg	Salomon, Maria Dorothea	K	
Leopold, Georg	26, Sept 1858	Francis	Stricker, Francisca	D	120
Leopold, Johan	19, Aug. 1855	Michael	Arbogast, Francisca	C	
Leopold, Johan	10, July 1853	Michael	Arbogast, Francisca	D	394
Leopold, Johan	28, Sept 1859	Michael	Arbogast, Francisca	D	147
Leopold, Johan Jacob	13, Mar. 1859	Joseph	Schmid, Anna	D	134
Leopold, Louisa	7, June 1857	Michael	Arbogast, Francisca	D	87
Leopolt, Francis	18, Jan. 1856	Friedrich	Gesler, Louisa	K	
Lepoint, Susan	14, May 1853	John	----, Catherine	E	89
Leppert, Carl Ludwig	4, May 1851	Carl	Pfeifer, Francisca	K	
Leppert, Edward Jacob	27, May 1853	Nicolaus	Solert, Maria Theresa	K	
Leppert, G. Wilhelm	22, Dec. 1850	Nicolaus	Soler, Maria Theresa	K	
Leppert, Georg Jacob	13, Aug. 1854	Carl	Pfeifer, Francisca	K	
Leppert, Joseph Simon	7, Aug. 1859	Joseph	Herman, J.	K	
Leppert, Maria Francisca	26, July 1857	Carl	Pfeifer, Maria Francisca	K	
Leppert, Maria Magdalena	15, Nov. 1857	Joseph	Herman, Susanna	K	
Leppert, Maria Theresa	15, July 1855	Nicolaus	Soler, Theresa	K	
Lerch, Carolina Maria Augusta	17, May 1857	Michael	Spitzmüller, Maria	D	85
Lerch, Maria Josephina	3, Apr. 1859	Michael	Spitzmüller, Maria	D	135
Lerry, Daniel	23, Feb. 1855	Dennis	Moriarty, Bridget	E	267
Lerte, Mary Caroline	5, Aug. 1855	Francis	Cherotta, Mary	E	305
Lertora, John	3, Apr. 1853	Francis	Cherotta, Maria	B	287
Lertura, Maria Catharina Angela	11, Oct. 1857	Francis	Conotti, Maria	K	
Lesaint, Catharina	6, Aug. 1858	Francis	Rink, Catharina	D	116
Lesaint, Christoph	1, Sept 1850	Francis	Rinck, Catharina	D	231
Lesaint, Elisabeth	15, Nov. 1854	Francis	Rinck, Catharina	D	22
Lesaint, Johan	28, Nov. 1852	Francis	Rinck, Catharina	C	
Lesbach, Francis	11, Feb. 1855	Michael	Schmitt, Victoria	K	
Leseke, Catherine	16, Oct. 1859	Henry	Madden, Elizabeth	B	82
Leseke, Eliza	6, June 1857	Henry	Madden, Elizabeth	B	45
Leseken, John Henry	4, Mar. 1855	Henry	Madden, Elizabeth	B	12
Leser, Carl Christian	30, Mar. 1856	Carl C.	Dietz, Philippina	D	55
Lessel, Johan	2, Jan. 1858	Peter	Wolsiefer, Elisabeth	L	
Lessel, Maria Catharina	2, June 1850	Peter	Wolsifer, Elisabeth	L	
Lessel, Maria Elisabeth	7, Mar. 1853	Peter	Wolsiefer, Elisabeth	L	
Lessel, Peter Paul	12, Aug. 1855	Peter	Wolsiefer, Elisabeth	L	
Lessenich, Johan Gerhard August	26, June 1853	Mathias	Schmitz, Margaretha	D	391

Name of Child	Date of Baptism	Father	Mother	Church	Page
Lessenig, Catharina Philomena	18, Apr. 1852	Mathias	Schmitz, Margaretha	D	316
Lessenig, Mathias Joseph	15, Aug. 1850	Mathias	Schmitz, Margaretha	C	
Lessing, Ludwig	25, Dec. 1859	Anton	Kirchner, Maria	F	
Lessner, Dorothea	19, Feb. 1855	Johan	Knoflach, Anna Maria	D	29
Lessnick, Josephina Margaretha	19, June 1855	Mathias	Schmitz, Margaretha	D	37
Lethscher, Heinrich	15, June 1852	Heinrich	Scheerer, Maria	K	
Leues, Barbara Francisca	10, Dec. 1854	Peter	Sommer, Cunigunda	J	30
Leuffert, Anna Maria Ursula	7, Mar. 1852	Andreas	Reinhart, Catharina	D	311
Leuhmert, Francis	14, Aug. 1859	Francis	Reinhart, Catharina	D	144
Leuner, Albert J. Leonard	27, Jan. 1850	Nicolaus	Pedel, Rosina	D	202
Leurert?, Maria Magdalena	11, June 1857	Joseph	Guhlel, Maria Elisabeth	D	87
Leuser, Barbara	14, Feb. 1858	Peter	Sommer, Cunigunda	A	
Leutenheimer, Josephina	4, Apr. 1852	Gerhard	Bapst, Catharina	F	
Lev---, William	29, Jan. 1854	Michael	Mondfort, Mary Jane	P	66
Levi, August Lewis	22, Aug. 1857	Aaron	adult - 21 years old	K	
Levin, Edward	7, May 1854		Levin, Rose	B	314
Levin, Mary Catherine	27, Nov. 1859	Thomas	Howley, Ann	V	63
Levin, Mary Jane	1, Dec. 1857	John	----, ----	B	52
Levins, Agnes	23, Aug. 1852	Charles	----, Mary	M	
Levoy, Margaret	25, Jan. 1852	Michael	Munford, Mary Jane	E	376
Levy, Helen	14, Mar. 1858	David	Connell, Margaret	B	56
Levy, Julia Eliza	16, June 1859	Dennis	Brennan, Mary	P	286
Levy, Mary Ann	7, May 1856	Dennis	Brennan, Mary	P	178
Lewe, Friedrich Anton Clemens	18, Jan. 1852	Heinrich	Schroeder, Anna	L	
Lewe, Heinrich Bernard Joseph	6, May 1850	Christian	Schulte, Anna	F	
Lewe, Heinrich Joseph	22, Mar. 1853	Heinrich	Schroeder, Anna	L	
Lewe, Johan Heinrich	18, Apr. 1852	Christian	Schulte, Anna	F	
Lewe, Maria Anna	19, Jan. 1855	Christian	Schulte, Marianna	F	
Lewin, Catherine Louise	6, June 1852	Frederick	Daley, H.	B	260
Lewis, Adelhaid	14, Sept 1851	Richard	Moorman, Helen	B	242
Lewis, Ann	10, July 1856	Michael	----, Catherine	E	380
Lewis, Charles	27, Mar. 1853	Richard	Moorman, Helen	B	290
Lewis, Esther Louise	13, Aug. 1854	William	Marks, Annette	B	3
Lewis, Joseph L.	28, Jan. 1850	Ashel	----, Jean	E	195
Lewis, Mary Emily	14, Sept 1851	Richard	Moorman, Helen	B	242
Lewis, Mary Ursula	6, June 1854	Richard	Moorman, Helen	B	1
Lewissey, Catherine	27, Aug. 1854	Cornelius	Toomey, Julia	P	94
Lewud, Anna Christina	5, Apr. 1855	Johan	Quaing, Maria	F	
Lewud, Anna Margaretha Elisabeth	31, Jan. 1857	Johan	Quaing, Anna Maria	F	
Lewud, Johan Herman Heinrich	23, June 1850	Johan	Quaing, Anna Maria	F	
Lewud, Louise Engel	18, Jan. 1853	Johan	Quaing, Maria	F	
Lewud, Maria Anna	4, Aug. 1851	Johan	Quaing, Anna Maria	F	
Ley, Heinrich	17, Apr. 1853	Heinrich	Brecht, Maria Anna	J	22
Ley, Heinrich	20, Nov. 1856	Heinrich	Brett, Anna Maria	J	38
Ley, Margaretha	19, Dec. 1858	Heinrich	Brett, Anna Maria	J	48
Ley, Simon	1, Oct. 1854	Heinrich	Brett, Maria Anna	J	28
Ley, Susanna	11, Aug. 1850	Heinrich	Brett, Maria Anna	J	6
Leyden, John	11, Jan. 1857	Michael	Gillespie, Honora	P	203
Leyfelt, Maria Catharina	15, Jan. 1856	Theodor	Werneke, Wilhelmina	J	34
Leyney, Rosalie	31, Mar. 1856	Bernard	McElroy, Ann	B	27
Libberman, Anna Maria	4, Oct. 1859	Bernard	Vo---, Anna Maria	D	148
Libberman, Johan Bernard Joseph	8, Nov. 1852	Bernard	Schmitt, Anna M.	D	356
Libert, Magdalena	14, Nov. 1858	Georg	Haberb---, Margaretha	D	124
Libig, Emil Ferdinand	24, Feb. 1851	Johan	Hauser, Maria Anna	L	
Licher, Johan Heinrich	19, June 1853	J. Casper	Brinkmeyer, M. Cath.	L	
Licher, Maria Catharina Elisabeth	15, Apr. 1850	J. Caspar	Brinkmeier, M. Cath.	L	
Lichtenberg, Bernard Heinrich	9, Aug. 1850	Clemens A.	----, Theresa G.	L	
Lichtenberg, Franz Edward	17, Oct. 1852	August	Gehrs, A.M. Theresa	L	
Lichtenberg, Herman Anton	22, Oct. 1856	Herman	Bolster, Maria	A	

Name of Child	Date of Baptism	Father	Mother	Church	Page
Lichtenberg, Herman Ignatius	31, July 1858	Herman	Bolster, Maria	A	
Lichtenberg, Johan Bernard	12, Feb. 1855	Heinrich	Gerdes, M. Theresa	L	
Lichtenberg, Johan Bernard	15, Aug. 1852	Herman	Bolster, Maria	A	
Lichtenberg, Johan Heinrich	16, June 1854	Herman	Bolster, Johanna Maria	J	26
Lichtendieck, Clara Eva	8, Feb. 1856		Lichtendieck, Catharina	C	
Lichtenfeld, Maria Carolina	27, June 1858	Jacob	Keicher, Francisca	N	
Lichtenwald, Joseph	5, June 1854	Adam	Baller, Theresa	D	11
Liddy, Mary	17, May 1858	Hugh	Kearney, Rose	B	59
Lidin, Amalia Paulina Henrica	19, Mar. 1855	Johan	Gehrik, Johanna	K	
Lidin, Amelia	12, Sept 1858	Johan	Gehrig, Johanna	C	
Lidin, Johan Georg	10, Aug. 1856	Johan	Gehrig, Johanna	K	
Lieber, Rosina Francisca	31, Oct. 1858	Thomas	Lühr, Maria Anna	D	123
Lieberman, Johan Gregor	4, July 1850	J. Bernard	Beyer?, Anna	D	220
Liebert, Anna Maria	20, June 1858	Sebastian	Wagner, Cunigunda	D	113
Lieberth, Catharina Margaretha	14, Dec. 1856	Sebastian	Wagner, Kunigunda	C	
Lieberth, Johan	10, Dec. 1854	Sebastian	Wagner, Cunigunda	D	24
Liebick, Anna	9, May 1858	Johan	Krampfert, Sibilla	N	
Liebig, Carl Victor	4, May 1856	Johan	Krampfer, Sibella	L	
Liebler, Maria Josephina	17, Feb. 1852	Thomas	Lier, Anna Maria	L	
Liedebrand, Theresa	14, Mar. 1857	Heinrich	Koldstädt, Christina	J	40
Liederbrand, Ann	4, July 1853	Heinrich	----, Christina	H	
Liederbrand, Heinrich Joseph	21, Apr. 1850	Heinrich	Cholstaet, Christina	H	
Liederbrand, Peter	16, Nov. 1851	J. Heinrich	----, Christina	H	
Liederbrandt, Georg	8, Apr. 1855	Heinrich	Gold, Christina	J	30
Lienhan, Daniel	22, Oct. 1854	Dennis	Goran, Ann	B	6
Liening, Johan Heinrich	18, Dec. 1858	J. Arnold	Schalend, Friedricka	L	
Liererl, Johan Mathias	23, May 1858	Mathias	Pfaller, Walburga	T	
Lies, Johan Baptist	31, Aug. 1852	Bernard	Altenschulten, Engel	F	
Lieser, Maria Agnes	20, Nov. 1859	Johan	----, Christina	K	
Liest, Johan Heinrich	7, Oct. 1855	Ferdinand	Scherder, Elisabeth	C	
Liest, Maria Elisabeth	27, May 1856	Benedict	Heger, Margaretha Elisabeth	D	59
Liever, A. Maria Johanna	29, May 1854	Ludwig	Kerkhof, Agnes	D	11
Liever, Agnes Maria Margaretha	25, Jan. 1852	Ludwig	Kerkhoff, Maria Agnes	D	303
Liever, Catharina	3, Sept 1856	Ludwig	Kerhof, Agnes	D	66
Liever, Maria Elisabeth	10, June 1851	Bernard	Moehlenkamp, Maria Gesina	F	
Lievre, Bernard	31, July 1854	Bernard	Tonies, Antonia	F	
Lievre, Bernard Franz	2, Sept 1850	Ludwig	Fennemann, Agnes	F	
Lievre, Johan Herman	2, July 1856	Bernard	Tennies, Antonia	F	
Lievre, Maria Helena	10, Oct. 1852	Bernard	Termies, Antonia	F	
Ligarri, Paul John	2, Sept 1855	Luigi	Nasagna, Olivia	B	18
Ligberti, Mary Catherin	14, Jan. 1851	Engelbert	Egarch, Gertrud	M	
Light, Maria Theresa	14, Oct. 1858	Peter	Light, Mary D.	A	
Lightfoot, Mary	10, Sept 1857	William	Donnager, Ann	E	480
Lihwehr, August Joseph	19, Apr. 1852	Joseph	Herold, Elisabeth	C	
Lilfle, Maria	29, May 1850	Thaddeus	adult - 31 years old	D	215
Liller, Johan Georg	3, July 1854	Joseph	Nusslein, Anna	D	13
Lillie, Bridget	23, Aug. 1850	Patrick	Crary, Ann	E	241
Lillis, David	10, July 1853	Patrick	----, Ann	E	105
Lillis, Helen	13, Mar. 1858	Patrick	McCormick, Helen	P	242
Lillis, John	26, July 1851	Henry	Sullivan, Mary	E	327
Lillis, Martin	17, Dec. 1859	Patrick	Tracy, Ann	B	85
Lilly, Angelina	27, Feb. 1855	John	----, Mary	V	23
Lilly, Ann	7, Jan. 1855	Henry	Hesbrum?, Catherine	E	255
Lilly, James Thomas	8, Dec. 1859	Hugh	Carney, Rose	B	85
Lilly, Johan Andreas	12, Nov. 1854	Wilhelm	Causfill, Elisa	F	
Lilly, Mary	29, Apr. 1854	Terence	----, Mary	E	186
Lilly, Mary Ann	21, Aug. 1853	John	----, Mary	E	121
Lilly, Thomas	28, Dec. 1851	George	adult - 27 years old	E	367
Lilly, Thomas	20, Sept 1851	Terence	----, Mary	E	345

Name of Child	Date of Baptism	Father	Mother	Church	Page
Lim, Helena	22, Sept 1850	Michael	Keller, Catharina	K	
Limberger, Johan Wilhelm	20, June 1858	Wilhelm	Day, Bernardina	J	46
Limbers, Maria Catharina Elisabeth	5, Feb. 1856	Bernard	Beckman, Maria	K	
Limke, Anna Maria	27, May 1850	Clemens	Grote, Maria Anna	D	214
Limke, Caspar Heinrich	12, Aug. 1855	Clemens	Grote, A.Maria Engel	Q	9
Limke, Gertrud Wilhelmina	22, Aug. 1852	Francis	Schlieper, Louisa	A	
Limke, Herman Martin	20, Aug. 1858	Francis	----, Louisa	A	
Limke, Johan Anton Bernard	4, June 1854	Francis	Schlieper, Louisa	A	
Limke, John Frederick	11, Oct. 1857	Clemens	Grote, Angela	U	
Limke, Maria Catharina Carolina	4, May 1856	Francis	Schipper, Louisa	K	
Limpke, Johan Bernard	23, Nov. 1852	Clemens	Grote, Maria Angela	D	358
Lincett, Amanda Griffin	13, Sept 1852	Peter	Huston, Amanda	E	16
Lincett, Loranda Jean	13, Sept 1852	Peter	Huston, Amanda	E	16
Lincett, Mary Catherine	13, Sept 1852	Peter	Huston, Amanda	E	16
Linch, Rose	25, Oct. 1854	John	----, Susan	U	
Lincoln, Charlotte Elizabeth	23, Sept 1855	Timothy D.	Clark, Mary	B	19
Lincoln, Florence	24, Jan. 1858	Timothy	Quinn, Mary	B	55
Lincoln, Helen	9, Oct. 1853	Timothy	Clarke, Mary	B	300
Lincoln, Mary Lucy	29, Dec. 1850	Timothy	----, Mary	B	221
Lind, Adam	31, Aug. 1856	Johan	Schaefer, Barbara	F	
Lind, Eva Margaretha	9, May 1852	Johan	Schaefer, Barbara	F	
Lind, Johan Simon	23, July 1854	Johan	Schaefer, Barbara	F	
Lind, Maria Magdalena	17, Apr. 1859	George	Hörst, Clotilda	R	
Lindauer, Carl	2, Nov. 1856	Meinrad	Zender, Meinrada	A	
Lindauer, Francisca Benedicta	31, Aug. 1854	Joseph M.	Zehnter, Minrada	L	
Lindauer, Franz Carl	14, Mar. 1859	Meinrad	Zehnder, Meinrada	F	
Lindeman, Francis Heinrich	7, Oct. 1854	Christian F.	Röckelman, Maria Elisabeth	D	19
Lindeman, Friedrich Joseph	2, Aug. 1857	Joseph	Rie---, Catharina	D	91
Lindeman, Johan Heinrich	31, Mar. 1857	F. Christian	Rickelman, Maria Elisabeth	D	82
Lindeman, Maria Angela	6, Aug. 1857	Clemens	Grote, Maria Angela	D	92
Lindeman, Maria Magdalena	9, Feb. 1851	Joseph	Loiting, Christina	J	10
Lindemann, Joseph Heinrich	18, Sept 1859	J. Heinrich	Ossenbeck, Clara	L	
Linden, Ernst	21, Aug. 1859	Thomas	Hirigoben, Catharina	D	144
Linden, Ferdinand	25, July 1858	Thomas	Hirigoben, Catharina	C	
Linden, John	23, Nov. 1856	William	Keegan, Mary	E	414
Linder, Andreas	16, July 1854	Joseph	Felix, Catharina	W	4
Linder, Johan Aloisius	2, Nov. 1856	Joseph	Felix, Catharina	W	17
Linder, Wilhelm	13, Feb. 1859	Joseph	Felix, Catharina	T	
Lindlevy, Ellen	26, Nov. 1855	Peter	Hogan, Bridget	B	22
Lindner, Anna Margaretha	19, Sept 1852	Michael	Förster, Margaretha	A	
Lindner, Elisabeth	20, Nov. 1856	Michael	Voshorn, Margaretha	A	
Lindner, Louisa	7, June 1858	Joseph	Sailer, Margaretha	T	
Lindner, Margaretha	24, June 1854	Michael	Forster, Margaretha	A	
Lindner, Maria Cunigunda	16, June 1850	Michael	Förster, Margaretha	A	
Linehan, Mary Josephine	3, Oct. 1853	Dennis	O'Brien, Helen	B	300
Linfer, Maria Gertrud	1, Aug. 1854	Johan	Wenthold, Maria Anna	D	15
Linfert, Anna Elisabeth Antonette	13, Feb. 1855	J. Heinrich	Lüker, Marianna	A	
Linfert, Bernardina Anna Maria	5, Oct. 1858	Wilhelm	Duesing, Bernardina	D	120
Linfert, Dina Bertha	6, May 1854	Wilhelm	Desing, Dina	D	9
Linfert, Heinrich	4, June 1857	Johan	Wendhold, Maria Anna	D	86
Linfert, Herman Heinrich	20, Dec. 1857	Heinrich	Lueker, Anna Maria	F	
Linfert, Johan	12, Sept 1859	Johan	Wentholz, Maria Anna	D	146
Linfert, Johan Anton Francis	16, Sept 1855	Johan	Wentholz, Maria Anna	D	43
Linfert, Maria Francisca	17, July 1857	Wilhelm	Duesing, Dina	D	90
Linfert, Maria Gertrud	31, May 1853	Heinrich	Lücker, Maria Anna	D	387
Linfert, Regina	6, May 1854	Wilhelm	Desing, Dina	D	9
Linfert, Wilhelm Heinrich	18, Oct. 1855	Wilhelm	Desing, Bernardina	D	44
Lingan, Mary	21, Aug. 1859	James	O'Connor, Julia	E	648
Lingemann, Anna Maria Elisabeth	24, Apr. 1851	Joseph	Gelhaus, Helena	F	

Name of Child	Date of Baptism	Father	Mother	Church	Page
Lingen, James	11, May 1854	James	O'Connor, Julia	E	189
Lingen, Jeremiah	8, Feb. 1857	James	O'Connor, Julia	E	431
Linger, Georg Bernard	12, Sept 1859	J. Gerhard	Feigert, Maria Anna	D	146
Linger, Johan Heinrich	17, Oct. 1850	J. Gerhard	Fenger, A.M. Dorothea	L	
Linger, Stephan Anton	10, Feb. 1853	J. Gerhard	Fenger, Anna Maria	D	370
Lingin, Edward	2, June 1859	William	Keagan, Mary	E	629
Lingraff, Maria Louisa	10, Jan. 1853	Peter	Fries, Barbara	N	11
Lings, Anna Maria Elisabeth	18, Oct. 1859	Jacob	Esketter, Maria Elisabeth	Q	33
Lings, Francis	4, Oct. 1853	Jacob	Esgetter, Maria Elisabeth	Q	3
Liningen, Julia Helen	25, Dec. 1857	Jacob	Künsle, Sarah	Q	25
Link, Elisabeth Barbara	12, Dec. 1852	Francis	Feigert, Susanna	D	360
Link, Johan	5, Dec. 1858	Johan	Reis, Maria Anna	D	125
Link, John	1, July 1857	John	Denk, Anna Maria	H	
Link, John Wesley	8, Mar. 1859	Joseph	----, ----	D	133
Link, Lazarus Carl	18, Mar. 1855	Johan	Reis, Maria	D	31
Link, Louise	6, Apr. 1856	John	----, Anna Maria	H	
Link, Ottilia	28, Sept 1856	Francis	Behmer, Catharina	D	68
Link, Peter	4, July 1852	Johan	Reis, Maria Anna	D	328
Linker, Anna Maria Elisabeth	4, Sept 1857	J. Gerhard	Ell--berger, Anna Maria	D	93
Links, Philomena	29, Sept 1850	Jacob	Esker, Maria Elisabeth	K	
Linneman, Anna Christina	17, Dec. 1857	Heinrich	Paskes, Maria Catharina	J	44
Linneman, Georg August	5, June 1853	Heinrich	Bilke, Maria Elisabeth	J	22
Linneman, Johan Joseph	26, June 1859	Bernard	Packet, Maria Catharina	J	50
Linnemann, Bernard Johan	29, Sept 1850	Gerhard	Stockhoff, Margaretha	L	
Linnemann, Franz Heinrich	27, Feb. 1852	Gerhard	Stockmann, Margaretha	L	
Linnemann, Franz Stephan	7, Nov. 1850	Gerhard H.	Birken, Elisabeth	F	
Linnemann, Friedricka Bernardina	16, Nov. 1859	Gerhard H.	Stockhoff, Margaretha	L	
Linnemann, Henrietta Catharina	6, Jan. 1857	Gerhard H.	Birke, Maria Elisabeth	G	
Linnemann, Johan Dietrich	3, Nov. 1855	Gerhard	Stolker, Maria	L	
Linnemann, Johan Heinrich	24, Dec. 1854	Gerhard H.	Birke, Maria Elisabeth	G	
Linnemann, Johan Herman	1, Jan. 1854	J. Theodor	Wellering, Helena	L	
Linnemann, Maria Catharina	20, Feb. 1854	Gerhard H.	Stockhof, A.M. Marg.	L	
Linnemann, Maria Elisabeth	25, Dec. 1857	Gerhard	Stockhoff, Margaretha	L	
Linnemann, Maria Gesina	4, Oct. 1857	J. Theodor	Woltering, M. Helena	L	
Linnemann, Peter	7, Nov. 1850	Gerhard H.	Birken, Elisabeth	F	
Linnemann, Susanna	24, Apr. 1859	Gerhard	Birke, Maria Elisabeth	G	
Linnen, George Washington	4, Aug. 1852	Washington	Deiters, Maria	L	
Linnen, Heinrich Wilhelm	4, Aug. 1852	Washington	Deiters, Maria	L	
Linnen, Maria Theresa	4, Aug. 1852	Washington	Deiters, Maria	L	
Linnenkugel, Anna Maria	9, June 1853	Joseph	Erskeman, Anna Margaretha	K	
Linnenkugel, Johan Bernard	22, Aug. 1851	Friedrich J.	Efkeman, Margaretha	A	
Linnenkugel, Johan Francis	10, Dec. 1854	Joseph	Efkeman, Margaretha	K	
Linnenkugel, Maria Louisa	7, Oct. 1856	Joseph	Efkeman, Margaretha	K	
Linnert, George Washington	17, Jan. 1858	Georg	Ge--t, Alwina	D	103
Linnert, William Edward	19, June 1859	Georg	H---, Albina	D	140
Linnes, Alice	6, Jan. 1854		adult	B	306
Linnon, John	31, Jan. 1859	Washington	Deiters, Maria Elisabeth	N	
Lins, Margaret	8, Dec. 1855	Michael	Conohon, Bridget	P	162
Linsch, Margaert	13, June 1858	James	Bretsbet, Bridget	N	
Linwig, Philippina	29, June 1856	Peter	Weiss, Catharina	C	
Linz, Gertrud	30, Nov. 1856	Pius	Lang, Aloysia	F	
Linz, Johan Sebastian	13, Feb. 1859	Pius	Lang, Aloysia	F	
Lippehüsen, Johan Heinrich	9, June 1853	Heinrich	Stahlkamp, Elisabeth	D	388
Lippehüsen, Joseph August	17, July 1851	J. Heinrich	Stahlcamp, Elisabeth	D	273
Lippehüsen, Joseph Heinrich	11, Mar. 1850	J. Heinrich	Stalkamp, Maria Elisabeth	D	205
Lippert, Joseph Herman	25, Mar. 1854	Wilhelm	Voss, Magdalena	D	7
Lippert, Josephina	11, June 1852	Wilhelm	----, Magdalena	D	324
Lippert, Maria	9, Aug. 1852	Philipp	Groh, Maria Anna	F	
Lipps, Anna Clara	28, Jan. 1855	Andreas	Grebner, Catharina	G	

Name of Child	Date of Baptism	Father	Mother	Church	Page
Lipps, Barbara	11, Dec. 1853	Ferdinand	Thennis, Catharina	F	
Lipps, Bernard	4, Jan. 1852	Andreas	Grebner, Catharina	F	
Lipps, Carolina	27, Apr. 1856	Wilhelm	Reselage, Bernardina	J	36
Lipps, Catharina Maria	13, May 1858	Georg	Krieg, Theresa	G	
Lipps, Edward	2, Oct. 1853	Wendelin	Wagener, Elisabeth	K	
Lipps, Francisca	10, Nov. 1850	Andreas	Grevener, Catharina	J	8
Lipps, Johan	2, Oct. 1853	Andreas	Grebner, Catharina	G	
Lipps, Johan	19, Oct. 1856	Ferdinand	Thinnes, Catharina	W	17
Lipps, Joseph	19, Oct. 1856	Andreas	Grebner, Catharina	G	
Lipps, Maria Elisabeth	25, Nov. 1858	Andreas	Grebner, Catharina	G	
Lipps, Maria Wilhelmina	16, Aug. 1857	Wilhelm	Resellage, Elisabeth B.	G	
Lipps, Regina	16, Nov. 1851	Ferdinand	Thennis, Catharina	F	
Lipps, Simon Dominick	12, June 1859	Johan	Karch, Magdalena	G	
Lipps, Theodora Agnes	25, Sept 1854	Wilhelm	Reselage, Bernardina	F	
Lipps, Theresa	10, Apr. 1859	Ferdinand	Thinnes, Catharina	G	
Lipps, Wilhelm Andreas	21, Aug. 1859	Wilhelm	Reselage, M. Elisabeth	G	
Lippus, Joseph Albert	3, Nov. 1850	Sebastian	Koch, Antonia	D	241
Lippus, Maria Theresa	5, Feb. 1854	Sebastian	Koch, Antonia	D	3
Lips, Andreas	2, Oct. 1859	Ferdinand	Stadtmiller, Catharina	J	52
Lirup, Aloysius Heinrich	31, Aug. 1851	Gerhard	Schwane, Theresa	L	
Lirup, Friedrich Joseph	15, Jan. 1854	Gerhard	Schwane, Theresa	L	
Lisch, Christian	5, May 1850	Johan	Derr, Catharina	D	212
List, Gerhard Ferdinand	20, July 1858	Ferdinand	Scherder, Elisabeth	L	
List, Herman Franz	12, Nov. 1858	J. Herman	VanGuelek, Johanna Christ.	L	
Listen, Edward	28, Apr. 1857	Thomas	Hogan, Margaret	B	43
Listerman, Catharina	23, Nov. 1851	J. Adam	----, Catharina	H	
Listerman, Catherine	2, June 1850	William	Mock, Mary	H	
Listerman, Henry Nicolaus	20, May 1855	William	----, Mary	H	
Listerman, Joachim	7, Apr. 1850	Carl	----, Christina	H	
Listerman, Michael Louis	14, Feb. 1858	Wilhelm	Wang, Maria Anna	H	
Listin, Thomas	23, Nov. 1856	James	Ward, Margaret	P	199
Liston, Michael	9, Sept 1855	Thomas	Hogan, Margaret	P	150
Liston, William	8, Aug. 1859	James	Ward, Margaret	P	291
Lisz, Johan Bernard	18, Oct. 1858	Benedict	Hegger, Margaretha Anna	K	
Litilot, William Henry	10, Sept 1854	Michael	O'Brien, Ann	N	24
Litmer, August Bernard	13, Oct. 1856	Caspar	Huesmann, Dina	L	
Litmer, Cath. Bernardina Louisa	30, Oct. 1850	Caspar	Huesmann, Bernardina	L	
Litmer, Johan Casper	10, July 1851	J. Herman	----, ----	L	
Litmer, Johan Friedrich	11, May 1858	Caspar	Huesmann, Bernardina	L	
Litmer, Joseph August	13, Aug. 1856	Herman H.	Beimke, Christina	L	
Litmer, Maria Josephina	21, Dec. 1854	Caspar	Huesmann, Bernardina	L	
Litmer, Sophia Christina	17, Nov. 1852	Caspar	Huesmann, Bernardina	L	
Litsch, Anna Sophia	14, Feb. 1855	Bernard	Ziegler, Sophia	A	
Litsch, Elisabeth Louisa	23, May 1852	Bernard	Ziegler, Sophia	A	
Litsch, Emma Justina	15, Mar. 1857	Xavier	Berger, Walburga	F	
Litsch, Emma Sophia	5, June 1853	Wilhelm B.	Ziegler, Sophia	F	
Litsch, Johan Bernard	17, Oct. 1858	Xavier	Berger, Walburga	F	
Litsch, Maria Magdalena	25, June 1850	Bernard	Ziegler, Sophia	A	
Litsch, Paul Herman	7, Sept 1856	Bernard	Ziegler, Sophia	A	
Litsch, Wilhelm	14, Mar. 1858	Bernard	Ziegler, Sophia	A	
Litsler, Jacob	2, May 1858	Jacob	Buckener, Susanna	A	
Litteken, Catharina Christina	27, Jan. 1850	J. Michael	Vogel, Barbara	A	
Littel, Anna Maria Helena	12, Jan. 1854	J. Bernard	Diers, Maria Catharina	D	1
Littel, Barbara	23, Mar. 1856	Mathias	Faller, Walpurga	J	34
Littel, Marthias Joseph	25, Apr. 1858	Theodor	Maret, Elisabeth	K	
Litticken, Anna Maria Margaretha	11, Feb. 1855	Ludwig	Gerlein, Catharina	D	28
Litticker, Christina	28, Sept 1851	Ludwig	Gerlein, Catharina	D	284
Littiken, Johan Heinrich	4, Apr. 1853	Ludwig	Gerlein, Catharina	D	379
Little, Elisabeth Felicitas Lucia	22, Oct. 1859	Theodor	Maret, Elisabeth	K	

Name of Child	Date of Baptism	Father	Mother	Church	Page
Little, Helen	29, Sept 1850	John	Ames, Catherine	B	215
Little, Johan	21, Jan. 1851	Wilhelm	Roc, Maria	J	10
Litzinger, Johan	20, June 1852	Johan	----, Anna Maria	H	
Litzinger, Martin	11, Sept 1853	John	----, Anna Maria	H	
Livell, Thomas	13, July 1850	Martin	King, Mary	B	207
Livellere, Mary Louise	19, May 1852	John	Corrotta, Mary Magdalene	B	259
Livingston, Mary	26, Mar. 1854	John	----, Mary	E	179
Livingston, William	9, Mar. 1859		Livingston, Mary	E	610
Livrow, John	2, Aug. 1852	John	adult - 43 years old	E	2
Lloyd, Edward Francis	18, Oct. 1859	John	Burke, Margaret	E	663
Lloyd, Sarah	8, June 1857	John	Burk, Margaret	E	458
Lobbe, Adelheid, M. Clementina	9, Oct. 1859	Heinrich	Fels, Elisabeth	C	
Lobbe, Carolina Hermina	29, Aug. 1854	Heinrich	Fels, Elisabeth	C	
Lobeck, Johan Dietrich	27, June 1857	J. Heinrich	Gehrs, Maria Anna	A	
Lobeck, Maria Catharina	3, Feb. 1856	Heinrich	Gehrs, Maria Magaretha	A	
Lobecke, Anna Maria	16, Mar. 1853	Heinrich	Gers, Anna Maria	A	
Lober, Johan Herman	3, Feb. 1859	Anton	Sendker, Margaretha	L	
Lobesch, Anna Maria Elisabeth	18, Apr. 1856	Heinrich	AusdemMohre, Maria Elis.	A	
Löbke, Gerhard Heinrich	4, Apr. 1854	Gerhard H.	Deiters, Anna Maria	A	
Lobke, Maria Margaretha	5, Apr. 1857	Heinrich	Fels, Elisabeth	C	
Löbke, Venna Margaretha	9, Apr. 1854	Gerhard H.	Gerke, Gesina	A	
Löbker, Anna Carolina	31, Jan. 1857	Heinrich	Fehe, Maria	A	
Löbker, Johan Georg	20, Jan. 1856	B. Heinrich	Gerken, Anna Gesina	A	
Löbker, Johan Theodor	4, Dec. 1859	Gerhard	Lammers, Anna Margaretha	A	
Löbker, Maria Elisabeth	22, Feb. 1859	Gerhard H.	Gerke, Gesina	A	
Lobwasser, Christina	11, Sept 1855	Wilhelm	Barsda, Catharina	D	42
Löchtefeld, Heinrich	3, Aug. 1859	Bernard	Kratte, H.N.	A	
Locklan, Margaret	15, Dec. 1855	Daniel	Locklan, Catherine	P	163
Lodeman, Mary Matilda	13, July 1851	Marc	Magee, Sarah	B	236
Loebbeker, Anna Maria Catharina	21, May 1854	Clemens	Klausing, Henrietta	L	
Loebke, Heinrich Wilhelm	5, Nov. 1856	Clemens J.	Klasen, Henrietta	L	
Loebker, Anna Maria Philomena	21, Apr. 1858	Anton	Grose, Louisa	L	
Loebker, Bernard Heinrich	30, Mar. 1858	J. Bernard	Steinriede, Anna Maria	F	
Loebker, Gerhard Herman	8, Mar. 1859	Bernard H.	Boergers, Gesina Adel.	L	
Loebker, Gerhard Herman	29, Jan. 1856	Herman	Steinriede, Anna Maria	F	
Loebker, Helena Catharina	21, Feb. 1858	Gerhard H.	Lambers, A. Margaretha	L	
Loebker, Herman Heinrich	18, May 1856	Gerhard	Lambers, A. Margaret	L	
Loebker, M. Helena Euphemia	17, Jan. 1853	Bernard	Borges, Adelheid	L	
Loebker, Margaretha	12, July 1855	Bernard	Boerger, Susanna	L	
Loebker, Margaretha Adelheid	2, Oct. 1850	Gerhard	Schulten, Helena	F	
Loebker, Maria Euphemia Margaretha	5, Sept 1852	Gerhard	Fehe, Anna Maria	L	
Loeffler, Anna Maria	20, Feb. 1857	Theodor	Radens----, Carolina	D	79
Loehr, Johan Bernard	25, Apr. 1859	J. Conrad	Thele, M. Anna	C	
Loehr, Johan Francis	17, Oct. 1857	J. Conrad	Thele, Maria	C	
Loepker, Clemens Louis	18, Feb. 1856	Anton	Groser, Louisa	L	
Loer, Maria Elisabeth	11, Sept 1855	J. Conrad	Toehler, Maria Anna	C	
Loering, Joseph Andreas	16, Dec. 1852	Heinrich	Timmerwilke, Anna M.	L	
Loery, Carolina	30, Oct. 1859	Carl	Nesselhaus, Leopoldina	D	150
Loesch, Carl	7, Nov. 1858	Carl	Wes---, Carolina	D	123
Loesch, Catharina	4, July 1853	Johan	Schlaufner, Philippina	D	393
Loesch, Johan	4, July 1853	Johan	Schlaufman, Philippina	D	393
Loesch, Margaretha	2, July 1852	Johan	Dörr, Catharina	D	327
Loesch, Philippina	4, July 1853	Johan	Doerr, Catharina	D	393
Loesey, Joanne	22, Feb. 1852	Cornelius	Toomy, Julia	P	18
Loewen, Friedrich Wilhelm	17, Jan. 1858	Christoph	Weinburg, Maria	D	103
Löfer, Anna	24, Feb. 1850	Andreas	Dothinger, Elisabeth	K	
Löffler, Anton Francis	16, Oct. 1859	Theodor	Raden---, Carolina	D	149
Löffler, Theresa	16, Oct. 1859	Theodor	Raden---, Carolina	D	149
Loftus, Ann	1, May 1855	Michael	Hessian, Sarah	V	24

Name of Child	Date of Baptism	Father	Mother	Church	Page
Loftus, Catherine	12, Sept 1858	Michael	Hessian, Sarah	B	64
Loftus, James	5, Aug. 1852	Martin	Furgison, Catherine	E	2
Loftus, James	30, May 1852	Timothy	Hanly, Margaret	B	259
Loftus, Laura	17, Feb. 1856	James	----, Eliza	E	345
Loftus, Margaret	7, Sept 1856	Michael	Heshum, Sarah	B	33
Loftus, Margaret Ann	25, May 1859	Timothy	Hanly, Margaret	P	284
Loftus, Margaret Jane	14, Sept 1856	Martin	Ferguson, Margaret	P	191
Loftus, Mary Eliza	25, Mar. 1857	James	Noonan, Liza	E	443
Loftus, Thomas	26, Nov. 1858	James	Noonan, Lizzie	E	583
Loftus, William	27, May 1854	Martin	Forbes, Margaret	B	315
Logan, Catharine Margaret	25, Jan. 1852	Christopher	Daley, Catherine	B	251
Logan, Daniel	22, June 1857	James	----, Julia	R	
Logan, Elizabeth Catherine	17, July 1853	Christopher	Logan, Catherine	P	47
Logan, James	17, June 1852	James	Green, Elizabeth	B	260
Logan, Joanne	10, Aug. 1854	John	Rogers, Elizabeth	P	92
Logan, Margaret	11, Dec. 1852	Daniel	Charters, Mary	J	20
Logan, Marietta	20, Apr. 1851	James	Green, Elizabeth	B	230
Logan, Mary	26, Nov. 1854	Andrew	Joy, Juliane	E	243
Logan, Mary	21, Oct. 1855	John	Rogers, Elizabeth	P	156
Logan, Robert	22, Sept 1853	Robert	----, Susan	E	129
Logan, William Charles	26, May 1850	Christopher	Daley, Catherine	B	203
Logue, August	6, Feb. 1859	George	McCabe, Isabel	E	602
Logue, Bridget	8, Oct. 1853	John	----, Mary	E	132
Logue, Phillip James	14, Oct. 1850	John	----, Mary	E	254
Lohle, Anna Maria Elisabeth	25, Nov. 1856	Theodor	Wessel, Anna M. Rebecca	F	
Lohle, Bernard Theodor	6, Sept 1854	Theodor	Wessel, Rebecca	C	
Lohli, Johan Bernard	25, Oct. 1859	J. Theodor	Wessel, Rebecca	C	
Lohli, Johan Heinrich Eusebius	15, Aug. 1852	Johan	Wessel, Rebecca	C	
Lohli, Johan Herman B.	28, May 1851	Johan	Wessel, Barbara	C	
Lohli, Rebecca Severina	9, Jan. 1850	Johan	Wessel, Rebecca	C	
Lohman, Anna Catharina	4, Apr. 1858	Dietrich	Graman, Maria Theresa	A	
Lohman, Anna Catharina	24, Oct. 1858	Melchior E.	Groll, Caecilia	D	122
Lohman, Anton Heinrich	14, Dec. 1852	Gerhard	Graman, Catharina	K	
Lohman, Bernard Johan	28, Sept 1856	Melchior E.	Groll, Caecilia	D	68
Lohman, Emma Frances	12, Apr. 1857	Ferdinand	Birt, Bridget	Q	21
Lohman, G. Heinrich	27, Apr. 1851	G.	Grelman, Catharina	K	
Lohman, Gerhard Anton	5, Sept 1852	J. Gerhard	Renne, Maria Anna	K	
Lohman, Johan Herman Heinrich	18, Jan. 1855	J. Theodor	Graman, Maria Theresa	A	
Lohman, Johan Theodor	2, Dec. 1852	J. Dietrich	Grahman, Theresa	A	
Lohman, Maria Elisabeth	4, Oct. 1855	G. Heinrich	Graman, Maria Catharina	K	
Lohmann, Anna Bernardina	20, Nov. 1859	Bernard	Roth, Anna M.	C	
Lohmann, Anna Maria	16, Mar. 1856	Herman	Roth, Anna M.	C	
Lohmann, Anton	30, Dec. 1857	Anton	Wubbel, Francisca	C	
Lohmann, Bernard Herman	27, Aug. 1857	Bernard H.	Roth, Anna M.	C	
Lohmann, Josephina Elisabeth	17, Oct. 1850	J. Gerhard	----, Anna M.	C	
Lohmann, Maria Anna	3, Jan. 1850	Herman H.	Fels, Elisabeth	C	
Lohmeier, Francis	16, Oct. 1856	Heinrich	Brinkman, Maria A.	D	69
Lohmeier, Heinrich	16, Oct. 1856	Heinrich	Brinkman, Maria A.	D	69
Lohmeier, Maria Magdalena	30, Oct. 1859	Henry	Brinkman, Maria Engel	D	150
Lohmeier, Maria Wilhelmina	30, Aug. 1857	Johan	Lohre, Helena	F	
Lohmiller, Elisabeth Francisca	24, Sept 1850	J. Bernard	Meyer, Gertrud	D	234
Lohmueller, A. Maria Friedricka	18, Jan. 1857	Heinrich	Fallo, M. Elisabeth	L	
Lohmueller, Franz Heinrich	27, May 1855	Heinrich	Vallo, Elisabeth	L	
Lohmueller, Heinrich	19, June 1853	J. Heinrich	Fallo, M. Elisabeth	L	
Lohmueller, Maria Elisabeth	22, Sept 1850	J. Heinrich	Fallo, Maria Elisabeth	L	
Lohr, Heinrich Georg	22, Sept 1859	J. Heinrich	Gut, Barbara	L	
Lohrer, Francis Xavier	16, Oct. 1853	Pantaleon	Zimmerman, Elisabeth	D	409
Lohrer, Louisa	15, June 1851	Pantaleon	Zimmerman, Elisabeth	D	268
Lohrer, Maria Elisabeth	23, Aug. 1857	Roman	Lipps, Maria Anna	K	

Name of Child	Date of Baptism	Father	Mother	Church	Page
Lohrer, Maria Theresa	31, May 1857	Pantaleon	Zimmerman, Elisabeth	D	86
Löhrlein, Cunigunda	3, Sept 1854	Johan	Barenschmidt, Eva	D	17
Löhrlein, Heinrich	26, June 1859	Johan	Bauer, Eva	D	141
Löhrlein, Johan	14, Sept 1856	Johan	Bauernscheider, Eva	D	67
Löhrlein, Johan	15, Sept 1851	Johan	Baumiller, Eva	D	282
Löhrlein, Maria Anna	2, Aug. 1857	Johan	Baurenschmidt, Eva	D	92
Löhrlein, Michael	14, Nov. 1852	Johan	Baurenschmidt, Eva	D	357
Loibl, Apollonia	2, July 1854	Francis X.	Stricker, Francisca	D	13
Loibl, Elisabeth	22, Aug. 1852	Francis X.	Stricker, Francisca	D	344
Lollihen, James H.	6, July 1850	Patrick	----, Jane	D	221
Lombrorwk, Theodor	27, Dec. 1853		adult - 28 years old	K	
Lommers, Heinrich Aegidius	16, Sept 1850	Johan	Brand, Catharina	C	
Lonagan, Anna Maria	5, Oct. 1856	Jacob	Renzler, Sarah	Q	16
London, Mary Jane	2, Sept 1852	James	----, Bridget	E	13
Londrigan, Honora	2, Aug. 1859	Edward	Ryan, Catherine	B	78
Londrigan, Margaret	15, Oct. 1859	James	Dalton, Mary	P	300
Londrigan, Mary	16, Aug. 1853	John	Buckley, Joanne	B	297
Lonergan, Albert	2, July 1853	Patrick	Driscoll, Helen	P	46
Lonergan, Catherine	25, June 1853	William	McGrath, Honora	E	100
Lonergan, Robert Patrick	18, Nov. 1854	Patrick F.	Driscoll, Helen	P	104
Lonergan, William	6, May 1855	William	McGrath, Honora	V	24
Long, Barbara Walburga	20, Feb. 1851	Georg	Klein, Philomena	J	10
Long, Bartholomew	15, May 1855	William	Mullen, Joanne	P	133
Long, Elizabeth	30, May 1854	James	Murphy, Mary	E	194
Long, James Henry	5, Oct. 1856	Henry	Earley, Ann	E	401
Long, John	15, June 1856	David	Connell, Margaret	T	
Long, John	29, Jan. 1854	Michael	Ryan, Sabina	V	10
Long, Mary	20, Nov. 1853	David	O'Connor, Margaret	U	
Long, Mary Ann	10, Aug. 1856	William	Mullen, Joanne	B	32
Long, Mary Jane	22, Jan. 1856	James	Fitzpatrick, Ann	E	339
Long, Patrick	7, Feb. 1856	John	Dolan, Bridget	E	342
Long, Peter	6, June 1852	Peter	Weis, Barbara	D	323
Long, Richard L'Hommedieu	6, Nov. 1859	Charles L.H.	Fitzgibbon, Josephine	B	83
Long, Samuel	15, Apr. 1853		adult - 28 years old	E	83
Longinotti, John	21, Mar. 1853	John B.	Botta, Carolina	B	287
Longinotti, John Anthony	26, Apr. 1852	John B.	Batto, Carolina	B	257
Longinotti, Maria Elisabeth	14, Mar. 1857	Antonio	Gatti, Maria	K	
Longmeyer, James Albert	23, Mar. 1857	John G.	Lackey, Julia	P	208
Longniere, John George	28, Nov. 1859	John	----, Julia	M	
Longschur, Cunigunda Helena	30, Oct. 1859	John	Hergenröther, Barbara	D	150
Longshore, Cornelia Frances	6, Apr. 1851	Abner	O'Neill, Mary Ann	B	229
Longshore, Jane	17, Mar. 1858	Abner	O'Neil, Mary Ann	P	242
Longshore, John	24, Dec. 1854	John	adult - 22 years old	P	111
Longshore, Margaret	10, July 1853	Abner	O'Neil, Mary Ann	P	46
Lonigan, William Francis	8, Feb. 1852	Bartholomew	Moran, Marianne	P	17
Lonston, Alexander	25, May 1856	Alexander	Simpson, Elizabeth	E	369
Look, Henry	14, Aug. 1859	Peter	Mathews, Mahala	B	79
Loonay, John	12, Dec. 1858	William	Dorgan, Margaret	E	586
Looney, John	18, Sept 1853	Patrick	Quinlen, Mary	Q	3
Loos, Anna Barbara	1, Nov. 1853	Georg	Diener, Elisabeth	D	413
Loos, Anna Maria	26, Feb. 1857	Georg	Dennies, Elisabeth	D	80
Loos, Carl	28, Oct. 1855	Georg	Dinnies, Elisabeth	D	45
Loos, Catharina Josephina	7, July 1850	Georg	Dennies, Elisabeth	D	222
Loos, Conrad Georg	24, Oct. 1852	Georg	Dinnies, Elisabeth	D	354
Lopel, Joseph	31, Jan. 1850	Heinrich	Hohmeier, Bernardina	K	
Lopker, Elisabeth Adelheid	8, July 1859	Johan	Klausing, Elisabeth Henrietta	K	
Lorberg, Maria Catharina	24, Jan. 1858	J. Heinrich	AusdemMoor, Maria Elis.	D	103
Lorch, Johan	26, Oct. 1856	Peter	Kloss, Catharina	D	70
Lorch, Peter	24, May 1854	Peter	Glaser, Catharina	D	11

Name of Child	Date of Baptism	Father	Mother	Church	Page
Lorch, Peter	20, Feb. 1859	Peter	Glass, Catharina	D	132
Lord, John	24, Feb. 1855	Martin	Bergin, Ann	B	11
Lord, Mary	22, Feb. 1856	John	O'Neill, Margaret	V	29
Lorenz, Andreas	18, Jan. 1858	Johan	Mennig, Elisabeth	D	103
Lorenz, Catharina	12, June 1859	Adam	Trunk, Louisa	K	
Lorenz, Catharina	4, Mar. 1850	Donatus	Titsch, Walburga	C	
Lorenz, Francis Xavier	23, Jan. 1858	Carl	----, Josephina	D	103
Lorenz, Francisca	21, Apr. 1850	Basil	Leppert, Catharina	K	
Lorenz, Frederick	26, Mar. 1855	Donald	----, Walburga	H	
Lorenz, Johan Caspar	12, Apr. 1856	Johan	Mennig, Elisabeth	D	56
Lorenz, Johan Georg	19, Oct. 1851	Georg	----, Margaretha	C	
Lorenz, Louise	19, Mar. 1853	Donatus	----, Walburga	H	
Lorenz, Magdalena	27, Oct. 1850	Peter	Schillinger, Cecilia	D	240
Lorenz, Margaretha	20, July 1853	Carl	Radler, Margaretha	D	396
Lorenz, Maria	10, June 1855	Carl	Bartl, Josephina	D	36
Lorenz, Maria Barbara	17, Nov. 1850	Donatus	Deutsch, Walburga	C	
Lorenz, Maria Magdalena	18, July 1855	Michael	Laex, Magdalena	D	38
Lorenz, Regina Magdalena	30, Jan. 1852	Basil	Leppert, Catharina	K	
Lorenz, Rosa Catharina	2, Oct. 1859	Joseph	Wuermel, Magdalena	F	
Lorenz, Theresa	19, Dec. 1858	Francis L.	Kahler, Margaret	R	
Lorett, William	15, Apr. 1850		adult	E	209
Lorigny, Rosy	20, June 1850	----	----, ----	E	232
Lorink, Anna Maria	15, July 1856	Joseph	Timmerwilke, Anna Maria	L	
Lorkarn, Margaretha	28, Apr. 1850	Johan	Jack, Maria	K	
Lorkarn, Peter	28, Apr. 1850	Johan	Hack, Maria	K	
Lorkerder, Andreas	27, May 1853	Johan	Heck, Maria Anna	K	
Losan, Patrick	2, Mar. 1851	John	Hayes, Ann	P	5
Losano, Mary Theresa	29, May 1859	John B.	Laverun, Catherine	E	629
Lösch, Francisca	9, Jan. 1857	Mathias	Torbeck, Carolina	D	76
Lösch, Johan	8, Apr. 1855	Johan	Derwarf, Barbara	D	32
Lösch, Joseph	9, Aug. 1855	Mathias	Wesbecke, Carolina	D	40
Lösch, Peter	14, Mar. 1858	Anton	Herb---, Maria	D	107
Losekamp, Anna Bernardina	21, Aug. 1853	Heinrich	Brink, M. Agnes	C	
Losekamp, Bernard	30, Dec. 1851	G. Heinrich	Decker, Elisabeth	D	299
Losekamp, Gerhard Heinrich	3, Jan. 1859	Heinrich	Brink, Agnes	F	
Losekamp, Johan Heinrich	29, June 1855	Bernard H.	Brink, Maria Agnes	F	
Losekamp, Maria Anna	25, Dec. 1853	J. Gerhard	Decker, Elisabeth	D	422
Losekamp, Maria Catharina	16, Jan. 1857	Heinrich	Brink, Maria Agnes	F	
Losekamp, Maria Elisabeth	6, Nov. 1850	J. Heinrich	Rolfes, Anna Maria	C	
Losekamp, Wilhelmina	13, Feb. 1856	Gerhard H.	Decker, Maria Elisabeth	D	52
Losenkamp, Johan Gerhard	24, July 1857	Johan G.	Tecke, Maria Elisabeth	D	91
Loseny?, William	19, July 1857	William	Dorgen, Margaret	E	467
Loth, Elenora Louisa	5, May 1857	Georg	Schoenmann, Maria	D	84
Loth, Friedrich Jacob	16, Jan. 1859	Joseph	Tannenhofer, Magdalena	D	129
Loth, Georg Franz	21, Nov. 1853	Michael	Michelo, Elenora	F	
Loth, Johan	29, Feb. 1852	Joseph	Tannenhofer, Magdalena	D	309
Loth, Jonas Washington	24, Mar. 1856	Michael	Mischlo, Elenora	F	
Loth, Joseph Cyprian	7, Apr. 1850	Michael	Mischle, Elenora	F	
Loth, Magdalena Clara	4, July 1856	Joseph	Tannenhofer, Magdalena	D	62
Loth, Margaretha	17, Dec. 1854	Joseph	Tannenhofer, Magdalena	D	24
Loth, Maria	10, Apr. 1859	Michael	Michelo, Elenora	F	
Loth, Maria Josephina	10, Apr. 1859	Georg	Chemetzner, Maria	F	
Loth, Michael	13, Feb. 1855	Georg	Schimmotzler, Maria	F	
Loth, Rosina	7, June 1852	Michael	Michels, Elenora	F	
Loth, Theresa	7, June 1852	Michael	Michels, Elenora	F	
Lothan, Mary Julia	5, Nov. 1852	Thomas	adult	B	274
Loths, Maria Catharina Elisabeth	29, Oct. 1853	Carl	Hodson, Elisabeth	L	
Löthscher, Maria	17, May 1854	Heinrich	Scherer, Maria	D	10
Lotter, Joseph	12, Oct. 1859	Johan	Hut, Margaretha	A	

Name of Child	Date of Baptism	Father	Mother	Church	Page
Lottmann, Bernard Heinrich	16, Dec. 1855	J. Bernard	Kleine, Agnes	F	
Lottmann, Johan Heinrich	10, Dec. 1852	J. Bernard	Kleine, Maria Agnes	F	
Lotz, Anna Maria	29, June 1858	Peter	Henning, Anna Maria	D	114
Lotz, Eduard	21, July 1856	Peter	Henning, Maria	D	63
Lotz, Herman Ludwig	28, June 1857	Ludwig	Beckmann, Margaretha	F	
Lotz, Johan	22, Jan. 1854	Johan	Voglin, Barbara	F	
Lotz, Magdalena Louise	31, July 1852	Adolph	Behring, Magdalena	C	
Lotz, Margaretha	17, June 1851	Lawrence	Glueck, Eva	C	
Lotz, Maria	15, May 1859	William	Tapf, Margaret	R	
Lotz, Maria Elisabeth	31, Jan. 1853	Peter	Henning, Anna Maria	D	368
Lotz, Marianna	16, Dec. 1855	Johan	Vogel, Barbara	F	
Lotz, Mathias Christian	12, Jan. 1851	Adolph	Behring, Magdalena	C	
Lötz, Nicolaus Anton	1, Nov. 1857	Wilhelm	----, Margaretha	R	
Lotz, Peter	17, Aug. 1851	Peter	Henning, Anna Maria	D	279
Lotze, Balthasar Friedrich	15, Jan. 1854	Adolph	Behring, Margaretha	C	
Lotze, Franz Laurentz	2, Oct. 1859	Lawrence	Ernst, Maria	F	
Lotze, Maria Magdalena	19, Aug. 1858	Lawrence	Ernst, Anna	F	
Loud, Mary	6, May 1851		adult	B	232
Loudan, William	23, May 1852		adult	M	
Loughen, John	4, July 1854	James	Ward, Margaret	P	87
Loughlan, Elizabeth	8, Apr. 1855	----	adult	V	24
Loughlin, Ellen	25, Apr. 1858	Patrick	Lane, Cecilia	B	58
Loughlin, Mary	11, Jan. 1854	Daniel	Molloy, Catherine	P	65
Loughlin, Mary	10, Aug. 1854	Patrick	Cain, Cecilia	B	3
Loughlin, Michael	6, Mar. 1853	James	Joyce, Mary	V	2
Loughman, Patrick	24, Jan. 1853	Thomas	----, Mary	M	
Louis, Catharina	21, Oct. 1855	Christian	Schneider, Jetta	C	
Louis, Maria Eugenia	23, Mar. 1851	Peter	Gauche, Catharina	C	
Louis, Theresa	29, Feb. 1852	Christian	Schneider, Jetta	C	
Louns, Josephina Carolina	2, Mar. 1856	F. Carl	Ratler, Margaretha	R	
Lovin?, Edward	21, Nov. 1858	Edward	McMacken, Jane	B	67
Low, Ann	8, June 1856	Michael	Dunn, Sarah	E	372
Lowe, Ann	24, Feb. 1856	James	Bergen, Catharine	T	
Lowe, Catharina Maria	17, Aug. 1858	James	Bergen, Catharine	T	
Lowe, James	13, Sept 1857	James	Bergen, Catharine	T	
Lowe, Jane Elizabeth	15, Oct. 1859	James	Bergen, Catherine	X	
Löwe, Johan Georg	2, Sept 1859	Joseph	Weinbach, Maria	D	145
Löwe, Johan Gerhard Ludwig	30, Jan. 1851	J. Caspar	Lienesch, Anna Maria	D	251
Lowe, John	11, July 1853	James	Bergen, Catherine	B	295
Lowe, Lawrence	26, Aug. 1854	James	Bergen, Catharine	T	
Lowe, Lawrence	13, July 1856	Martin	Bergen, Ann	T	
Lowell, Mary	6, July 1850	Matthew	Conlan, Mary	B	206
Lowry, Ann	4, Sept 1858	John	McGinnis, Margaret	R	
Lowry, James	17, June 1853	John	McGinnis, Margaret	R	
Lowry, Martin	27, Mar. 1851	John	McGinnis, Margaret	P	6
Lowry, Mary	30, Mar. 1856	John	McGinnis, Margaret	R	
Lowry, Mary Ann	20, Dec. 1857	Thomas	Keogh, Julia	B	53
Loyd, Mary Ann	13, Feb. 1853	Wesley	Mulligan, Eliza	E	62
Loyering, Maria Margaretha	18, July 1855	J. Herman	Wübben, Anna Maria	A	
Lua, Christian	22, Sept 1850	Nicolaus	Bollom, Margaretha	J	6
Lübbe, Francis Georg	5, Feb. 1850	Rudolph	Duvenick, Anna	A	
Lübbe, Francis Rudolph	23, Dec. 1851	Georg	Zusanne, Anna Maria	A	
Lübbe, Johan Georg	2, June 1857	Rudolph	Duweneck, Bernardina	A	
Lübbe, Johan Heinrich	1, Jan. 1852	Rudolph	Duveneck, Dina	A	
Lübbe, Sophia Josephina	1, Oct. 1854	Rudolph	Duveneck, Bernardina	A	
Luberman, Maria Theresa	14, Oct. 1854	Bernard	--nad, Anna	D	19
Lübke, Bernard Herman	20, July 1850	Joseph	Kühl, Margaretha	A	
Lübke, Catharina Maria	25, Mar. 1852	Joseph	Kuhl, Maria	J	16
Lübke, Georg	8, Oct. 1855	Gerhard H.	Fehe, Euphemia	A	

Name of Child	Date of Baptism	Father	Mother	Church	Page
Lübke, Maria Elisabeth	8, Oct. 1854	Joseph	Kühl, Margaretha	A	
Lubkeser, Bernard Francis	11, June 1857	Bernard	Sch---, Anna Maria	D	87
Luby, John	6, Feb. 1859	John	Gleeson, Eliza	E	602
Luby, Patrick	20, July 1851	John	Connor, Alice	B	237
Lucas, Catherine Mary	12, July 1857	William	O'Neil, Mary	P	216
Lucas, Christian	9, Oct. 1853	Andrew	----, Margaret	H	
Lucas, Honora	20, Dec. 1854	John	Daily, Honora	E	248
Lucas, Louise	22, May 1853	John	----, Ellen	E	91
Lucas, Margaret	22, May 1856	Andrew	Rau, Margaret	U	
Lucas, Margaretha	25, Oct. 1857	Andreas	Rauch, Margaretha	W	20
Lucas, Mary	6, Apr. 1851	Andrew	Rau, Margaret	H	
Lucher, Carl	5, July 1858	Philipp	Müller, Agatha	A	
Luchs, Mary	16, Feb. 1852	Nicolaus	----, Margaret	H	
Luchte, Anton Joseph	1, Jan. 1855	Johan	Bierbutze, Theresa	F	
Luchte, Johan Heinrich	16, Nov. 1851	Johan	Bierbuesse, Theresa	F	
Lücken, Ludwig Philipp	28, Feb. 1851	Bernard H.	Hartlaub, Maria Christina	A	
Lucken, Susanna	15, Nov. 1857	J. Heinrich	Hartlaus, Maria M.	K	
Lücken, Wilhelm Maurice	16, Sept 1859	Gerhard	Brockman, Anna Maria	N	
Lückener, Johan Francis	15, Sept 1859	Joseph	Doepper, Maria Theresa	D	146
Lückener, Joseph Bernard	29, July 1857	Joseph	Döppers, Maria Theresa	D	91
Luckener, Maria Theresa	18, May 1856	Joseph	Dobber, Anna Maria Theresa	D	59
Luckey, Ann Elizabeth	31, Dec. 1854	James	McCoy, Rose	B	9
Lücking, Maria Henrietta Philomena	7, Sept 1856	Joseph	Tangeman, Gertrud	A	
Lückmers, Maria Anna	13, Sept 1852	Heinrich	Wöllenbrink, Catharina	K	
Lucy, Daniel	18, Aug. 1855	Patrick	----, Sarah	E	308
Lucy, John	15, May 1856	Michael	Foley, Joanne	E	366
Ludbert, Johan	13, Nov. 1850	Heinrich	----, ----	K	
Luddan, Helen	2, Apr. 1854	Francis	Kenny, Mary	E	180
Luddon, James	10, July 1859	Francis	Kenny, Mary	E	638
Ludinger, Jacob	20, Feb. 1851	Jacob	Hammann, Catharina	C	
Ludlow, James	26, June 1853	Walter	----, Catherine	M	
Ludman, Francis Johan	10, Apr. 1859	J. Francis	Op---, Anna Maria	D	135
Ludwig, Adam	1, Oct. 1856	Philipp	Kohl, Elisabeth	D	69
Ludwig, Anna Catharina	2, Apr. 1854	Sebastian	Schaupp, Catharina	D	7
Ludwig, Anna Maria	17, Aug. 1856	Mathias	Schuh, Angela	D	65
Ludwig, Barbara	7, Dec. 1851	Sebastian	Schaub, Catharina	D	296
Ludwig, Elisabeth	19, Sept 1854	Philipp	Kohl, Elisabeth	D	18
Ludwig, Friedrich William	25, Feb. 1855	Mathias	Schuh, Angela	D	29
Ludwig, Georg Valentin	28, Dec. 1851	L. Philipp	----, Elisabeth	D	299
Ludwig, Heinrietta	7, Nov. 1858	Peter J.	Weiss, Catharina	D	123
Ludwig, Herman	11, Mar. 1852	Herman	Mekey, Martha	D	312
Ludwig, Rosina Barbara	5, Jan. 1854	Herman	McGee, Martha	D	1
Ludwig, Wilhelm	28, Dec. 1856	Herman	Mechy, Martha	D	75
Luebbe, Georg Heinrich	11, Mar. 1855	Georg	Rake, M. Anna	C	
Luebben, Anna Maria Gertrud	22, Jan. 1858	J. Herman	Lohmann, Anna M.	C	
Luebbermann, Bernard August	28, Mar. 1850	Gregor	Hetlage, M. Sophia	C	
Luebbermann, Francis Clemens	14, Mar. 1852	Gregor	Hetlage, Sophia	C	
Luebbermann, Hieronymus Theodor	19, Oct. 1854	Gregor	Hetlage, Sophia	C	
Luebbermann, Johan Heinrich	19, Nov. 1855	Heinrich	Exler, M. Anna	C	
Luebbermann, Joseph Albert	1, Dec. 1859	Gregor	Hetlage, Sophia	C	
Luebbermann, Lucia Emma	7, Jan. 1857	Gregor	Hetlage, Sophia	C	
Luebbermann, Maria	2, Jan. 1854	Heinrich	Exler, Maria	C	
Luebbermann, Maria Bernardina	9, May 1858	B. Heinrich	Exler, M. Anna	C	
Luebbermann, Maria Sophia	2, Feb. 1852	Heinrich	Exler, M. Anna	C	
Luebbers, Johan Gerhard	24, Apr. 1856	J. Albert	Muntel, Adleheid	L	
Luebbers, Maria Anna	20, May 1853	Albert	Muntel, Marg. Adel.	L	
Luebel, Ludwig	17, Nov. 1850	Xavier	Stricker, Francisca	C	
Luebke, Anna Maria Adelheid	29, July 1852	Herman	Lohmann, Maria	C	
Luebke, Bernard Herman	27, July 1855	J. Herman	Lohmann, Anna Maria	C	

Name of Child	Date of Baptism	Father	Mother	Church	Page
Luechter, Johan	25, July 1850	Johan	Barbasch, Theresa	F	
Luechter, Joseph	25, July 1850	Johan	Barbasch, Theresa	F	
Luecke, Johan Heinrich	7, Mar. 1853	J. Gerhard	Pund, Maria Elisabeth	F	
Luecken, Johan Herman	16, Aug. 1854	J. Bernard	Seger, Anna Maria	F	
Luecker, Martin Heinrich	15, Nov. 1850	Gerhard	Brockman, Anna Maria	N	2
Luecking, Bernard Heinrich	28, Jan. 1855	J. Ernst	Menke, Anna Elisabeth	L	
Luecking, Bernardina Gertrud	27, Sept 1853	Joseph	Tangemann, Gertrud	C	
Luecking, Carl Rudolph	17, Apr. 1859	Ernst	Menke, Elisabeth	L	
Luecking, Johan Heinrich	4, May 1851	Joseph	Tangemann, Gertrud	C	
Luecking, Maria Engel	6, Apr. 1856	Ernst	Menke, Elisabeth	L	
Lueckmann, Joseph Arnold	4, May 1857	Johan G.	Pung, Elisabeth	F	
Lueckmann, Paulina Maria	29, June 1855	J. Gerhard	Punt, Elisabeth	F	
Luedmann, Maria Josephina	5, Nov. 1853	Carl H.	Bergkotter, Helena	L	
Luehn, Anna Catharina	7, Dec. 1852	Bernard	Duetz, Maria Adelheid	F	
Luehn, Anna Maria	12, July 1855	Heinrich	Franz, Maria	F	
Luehn, Johan Bernard Heinrich	11, Feb. 1854	Johan H.	Gersen, Anna Maria	F	
Luehn, Johan Heinrich Ludwig	4, Feb. 1853	Johan H.	Gessen, Anna Maria	F	
Luehn, Maria Anna	12, Dec. 1850	J. Bernard	Duetz, Maria Adelheid	F	
Luehn, Maria Louisa	26, May 1851	J. Heinrich	Gersen, Anna Maria	F	
Luehn, Maria Magdalena	28, May 1856	Johan H.	Franz, M. Adelheid	F	
Luehr, Johan Heinrich	3, Apr. 1853	Johan	Grewe, Gertrud	C	
Lueke, Joseph Herman	17, Feb. 1855	Joseph	Tecker, Carolina	K	
Lueken, Bernard Heinrich	18, July 1851	Bernard	Liggers, Maria	F	
Lueken, Catharina Maria	7, Feb. 1855	Gerhard	Brockmann, Anna M.	C	
Lueken, Francis Joseph	19, Feb. 1857	J. Gerhard	Brockmann, Maria	C	
Lueken, Gerhard August	12, Jan. 1852	H. Heinrich	Ortman, Maria Elisabeth	K	
Lueken, Johan Heinrich Friedrich	23, Apr. 1855	B. Heinrich	Hartlaub, Christina Maria	K	
Lueken, Maria Catharina	21, June 1859	Bernard	Segers, Maria	F	
Lueken, Maria Catharina	10, Apr. 1852	Gerhard	Gertes, Maria Adelheid	F	
Luenemann, Elisabeth Francisca	28, Apr. 1850	Heinrich	Moormann, Catharina	C	
Luening, Anna Maria Josephina	2, Mar. 1852	Heinrich	Hulsmann, M. Anna	C	
Luening, Agnes Josephina	25, Aug. 1858	Friedrich	Broering, Gertrud	C	
Luening, Anna Bernardina Henrietta	22, Mar. 1853	Heinrich	Huelsmann, Catharine	C	
Luening, Bernardina Louisa Regina	29, Nov. 1857	Heinrich	Hulsmann, Anna	C	
Luening, Catharina Henrietta Elisabeth	9, Apr. 1856	Joseph	Imwalde, Lisette	C	
Luening, Elisabeth	24, Oct. 1850	Francis	Krone, Catharina	C	
Luening, Georg August	16, Feb. 1858	Joseph	Imwalde, Elisabeth	F	
Luening, Joseph Heinrich Casper	6, Jan. 1853	Joseph	Imwalle, Lisette	C	
Luening, M. Bernardina Josephina	7, May 1854	Joseph	Imwalle, Elisabeth	C	
Luening, Maria Catharina Amalia	1, Apr. 1856	Friedrich	Broering, Gertrud	C	
Luening, Mathilda	15, July 1851	Joseph	Imwalle, Elisabeth	C	
Luennemann, Johan Herman	14, Mar. 1854	Stephan	Kloppenberg, Euphemia	L	
Luenning, Wilhelm Nicolaus	8, June 1859	Joseph	Imwalde, Elisabeth	F	
Luepker, Johan Joseph Herman	2, Dec. 1851	Bernard	Burgers, Susanna Adel.	L	
Lueppemeyer, Heinrich Joseph	4, Nov. 1854	Joseph	Fallo, Jenne	L	
Luer, Nicolaus	10, Jan. 1858	Nicolaus	Bethus, Margaretha	D	102
Luerman, Freidrich Wilhelm	3, Feb. 1856	Jacob	Rübel, Philippina	K	
Luers, Anna Maria	27, Aug. 1859	Francis	Hölscher, Anna Maria	A	
Lüers, Anna Maria	21, Jan. 1856	Francis	Hölscher, Anna Maria	A	
Lüers, Francis Heinrich	1, Mar. 1850	Francis	Hölscher, Maria	D	203
Luers, Gertrud Elisabeth	27, Aug. 1859	Francis	Hölscher, Anna Maria	A	
Luers, Johan Heinrich	28, Apr. 1852	J. Bernard	Roberg, Theresa	K	
Luers, Julia Theresa	27, Nov. 1856	J. Bernard	Ruberg, Theresa	K	
Lüers, Maria Anna Carolina	8, Sept 1851	Francis	Hölzger, Anna Maria	D	281
Lüers, Maria Gertrud	10, Jan. 1855	Francis H.	Hölscher, Anna Maria	A	
Luers, Sophia Henrietta	1, May 1859	J. Bernard	Ruberg, Theresa	K	
Luers, Theresa Sophia	9, May 1854	Bernard	Roberg, Theresa	K	
Luetkehaus, Louisa	21, Aug. 1859	Ludwig	Gerlein, Catharina	F	
Luetkenhaus, Anna Catharina	4, Apr. 1857	Ludwig	Vitrok, Marianna	F	

Name of Child	Date of Baptism	Father	Mother	Church	Page
Luetkhaus, Franz Ludwig	10, Apr. 1858	Francis W.	Vedder, Catharina	F	
Luetmer, Catharina Bernardina	1, May 1859	Joseph	Kroeger, M. Gertrud	L	
Luetmer, Heinrich Joseph	6, Nov. 1851	Joseph	Kroeger, M. Gertrud	L	
Luetmer, Heinrich Julius	21, Feb. 1858	Ferdinand	Krumpelbeck, Anna M.	L	
Luetmer, Johan Gerhard Francis	16, Apr. 1856	Joseph	Kroeger, Gertrud	L	
Luetmer, Maria Anna	6, Jan. 1854	Joseph	Kroeger, M. Gertrud	L	
Luetmers, Anna Maria Elisabeth	31, Aug. 1856	Francis F.	Krumpelbeck, Anna M.	L	
Luette, Anna Maria	5, June 1859	Thomas	Schmidt, Anna Maria	T	
Luettmann, Maria Elisabeth	15, Sept 1850	Gerhard H.	Fund, Maria Elisabeth	F	
Luettmer, Bernardina Mathilda	24, Apr. 1854	J. Heinrich	Baunker, Regina Chris.	L	
Luettmer, Heinrich	23, Nov. 1856	Joseph	Wustefeld, Margaretha	C	
Luettner, Herman Joseph	10, Jan. 1858	Joseph	Wustefeld, Margaretha	C	
Luford, Anna Elisabeth	1, Dec. 1850	J. Baptist	Lang, Barbara	N	2
Luft, Anna Maria Carolina	22, Sept 1853	Johan	Bless, Anna Maria	D	407
Lugel, Francisca	8, Feb. 1854	Joseph	Weiss, Catharina	C	
Lugel, Gertrud	13, Apr. 1856	Joseph	Weiss, Catharina	C	
Lüger, Magdalena	26, Dec. 1858	Anton	Henne, Josephina	D	127
Lühn, Anna Catharina	1, June 1858	J.H.	Gersen, Marianna	A	
Lühn, Anna Margaretha	29, Nov. 1858	Benedict	Dietz, Maria Adelheid	D	125
Lühn, B.H.	15, June 1856	B. Herman	Reelman, Christina	A	
Luhn, Carl Wilhelm	4, Nov. 1854	H. Johan	Keller, Maria Elisabeth	K	
Lühn, Clemens Wilhelm	17, Feb. 1856	J. Heinrich	Gerven, Anna Maria	A	
Lühn, Johan Heinrich	23, May 1852	J. Heinrich	Köller, Maria Elisabeth	K	
Lühn, Johan Wilhelm	20, Mar. 1858	J. Wilhelm	Hamer, Theresa	K	
Lühn, Johan Wilhelm	11, Sept 1854	Wilhelm	Hamer, Theresa	K	
Lühn, Maria Carolina	10, Dec. 1854	J. Bernard	Dietz, Maria Adelheid	D	24
Luhn, Maria Elisabeth Adel, Christina	1, Jan. 1857	Heinrich	Käller, Maria Elisabeth	K	
Luhn, Philomena Maria Margaretha	4, Dec. 1856	Bernard	Dietz, Maria	D	73
Luhweise?, Leander Francis	9, Mar. 1859	Anton	Clarken, Rose	K	
Luigatt, Josephina	5, June 1855	Joseph	Schmutz, Francisca	D	36
Luisterman, Ann	6, July 1856	Christopher	Felix, Catherine	H	
Luisterman, Charles William	10, Aug. 1852	Joachim	----, Thersa	H	
Luisterman, Dorothea	12, Sept 1858	Christopher	Felix, Catharine	H	
Luisterman, Johan	12, Feb. 1854	Christopher	----, Ursula	H	
Luitgard, Gustav	15, June 1858	Joseph	Baumgärtner, Catharina	D	113
Luitgard, Johan	15, June 1858	Joseph	Baumgärtner, Catharina	D	113
Lüken, Adolph	15, Nov. 1857	Herman	Reutman, Christina	A	
Lüken, Anna Christina	11, Sept 1853	Heinrich	Hartlaub, Christina	K	
Luken, Anna Maria Philomena	2, Jan. 1850	J. Bernard	Gosepohl, Maria Agnes	K	
Luken, Anna Maria Rosina	24, Nov. 1858	Bernard	Gausepohl, Agnes	K	
Luken, August Gerhard	27, Nov. 1856	Bernard	Gausepohl, Maria Agnes	K	
Luken, Francis Heinrich	21, Aug. 1858	Joseph	Sanders, Angela	K	
Luken, Josephina	23, Dec. 1851	J. Bernard	Gauspohl, Agnes	K	
Luken, Maria Elisabeth Carolina	24, Jan. 1854	J. Bernard	Gosepohl, Maria Agnes	K	
Luker, Mary	10, July 1859	Samuel	Carroll, Bridget	E	638
Lump, Maria	8, Dec. 1853	Traugatt	Becker, Magdalena	A	
Lun, Catharina	6, July 1856	Nicolaus	Pattong, Margaretha	F	
Lündeman, Louisa	16, Aug. 1858	J. Friedrich	Moor----, Anna Maria	D	117
Lunderer, Maria Anna Theresa	29, May 1853	Maximillian	Winter, Johanna Francisca	J	22
Lundigran, James	29, Mar. 1859	James	Monk, Bridget	B	73
Lundy, George Henry	30, Jan. 1853	Charles	Carofield, Ann	E	59
Lundy, Wilhelm	25, Oct. 1857	Carl A.	Caufield, Ann	N	
Lüneman, Anna Friedrica	14, Aug. 1856	Friedrich	Moser, Maria	D	64
Lüning, Catharina Friedrica	25, Oct. 1857	J. Arnold	Schauland, Catharina Friedr.	K	
Luning, Christoph Heinrich	6, Aug. 1855	Heinrich	----, Anna	C	
Lünneman, Johan Gerhard	22, Dec. 1850	Theodor	Volstring, Maria Helena	D	247
Lunvigenda, Sarah Mary	10, Sept 1854	James	----, Sarah	U	
Luny, Mary Ann	7, Oct. 1855	William	----, Margaret	M	
Luny, Thomas	9, Apr. 1852	Patrick	Guindle, Mary	Q	2

Name of Child	Date of Baptism	Father	Mother	Church	Page
Lür, Margaretha	15, Oct. 1857	Joseph	Liebler, Francisca	D	97
Lurrand, Joseph Anthony Adolph	3, Jan. 1858	Adolph	Shubert, Mary	E	505
Lüsman, Anna Maria	25, Feb. 1855	Jacob	Ruebol, Philippina	K	
Lust, Johan Christoph	22, Jan. 1850	Christoph	Bless, Anna Maria	D	200
Lust, Maria Anna	8, July 1855	Johan	Teil, Maria Anna	D	38
Lustig, Friedrich	27, Jan. 1856	Nicolaus	Volz, Christina	D	51
Lustig, Georg	27, Nov. 1853	Nicolaus	Volz, Christina	D	417
Lustre, Elizabeth	11, Dec. 1859		adult	M	
Lustre, John	11, Dec. 1859	Francis	----, Elizabeth	M	
Luteshen, Nicolaus	7, Feb. 1856		Luteshen, Christina	N	
Lutiger, Margaretha	21, Aug. 1853	Christian	Brunhart, Francisca	D	401
Lutkemeyer, Anna Maria Elisabeth	7, Aug. 1854	Herman	Siemer, Maria Anna	L	
Lütkenhof, Johan Bernard	1, Aug. 1852	Engelbert	Bus, Gertrud	D	341
Lütkenhof, Maria Francisca	23, Oct. 1851	J. Gerhard	Fruhling, Maria Francisca	A	
Lutkenhoff, Johanna Gertrud	7, June 1850	Engelbert	Bus, Gertrud	D	216
Lütkenhoff, Maria Elisabeth	24, Dec. 1856	Johan	Frieling, Maria Francisca	A	
Lütmerding, Anna Maria Francisca	20, Aug. 1852	Ferdinand	Ahlering, Susanna	A	
Lütmerding, Heinrich	26, Mar. 1856	Ferdinand	Ahlering, Susanna	A	
Lütmerding, Louisa Bernardina	24, Feb. 1855	Ferdinand	Ahlering, Susanna	A	
Lütmerding, Maria Hermina	2, Oct. 1857	Ferdinand	Ahlering, Susanna	A	
Lutschberg, Joseph	7, Dec. 1851	Sigismund	Meier, Magdalena	J	14
Lutterbeck, Anna M. Catharina Elis	11, Dec. 1857	Bernard	Biedenharn, Anna M.	L	
Lutterbeck, Anna Maria Carolina	29, Aug. 1853	Bernard	Bittenabend, A.Maria	L	
Lutterbeck, Johan Bernard	30, Mar. 1851	J. Bernard	Niehaus, Elisabeth	L	
Lüttman, Anna Maria	23, Aug. 1854		adult	A	
Lutz, Andreas	27, June 1858	Johan	----, Barbara	T	
Lutz, Anna Maria	24, May 1857	Lawrence	Glick, Maria Eva	D	85
Lutz, Bernard Joseph	29, Aug. 1858	Peter A.	Zimmer, Catharina	D	118
Lutz, Catharina Theresa Wilhelmina	26, Apr. 1857	Johan	Rorsch, Theresa	D	84
Lutz, Eduard	23, Oct. 1859	Johan	Resch, Theresa	T	
Lutz, Emma Theresa	23, Oct. 1859	Anton	Moser, Crescentia	D	149
Lutz, Johan	19, May 1850	Johan	Wittman, Barbara	K	
Lutz, Johan Georg	20, June 1855	Lawrence	Glueck, Eva	C	
Lutz, Joseph August	5, May 1855	J. Georg	Eberlin, Charlotte	D	34
Lütz, Margaretha	18, Jan. 1857		adult	A	
Lutz, Maria Kunigunda	1, Aug. 1851	Johan	Bach, Barbara	F	
Lutz, Maria Louisa	9, Aug. 1857	Xavier	Vorschula, Maria	C	
Lutz, Martin	15, Oct. 1854	Peter A.	Zimmer, Catharina	D	20
Lutz, Theresa Francisca	24, May 1858	Francis	Re---, Theresa	D	112
Lutzenberg, Elisabeth	20, Apr. 1851	Rudolf	Küer, Anna Gertrud	A	
Lutzenberger, Maria Crescentia	15, June 1853	Rudolph	Ruewe, Anna Gertrud	F	
Lützinger, Johan	30, June 1850	Christian	Kraner, Catharina	D	219
Lux, Johan Nicolaus	19, May 1855	Nicolaus	Batton, Margaretha	A	
Lüx, Margaretha	30, Oct. 1853	Nicolaus	----, Margaret	U	
Luxenberger, Gerhard Heinrich	16, Aug. 1857	Peter	Lüske, Catharina	J	42
Luxenburger, Heinrich	17, June 1855	Peter	Lubke, Catharina	J	32
Luxenburger, Johan B.	27, May 1850	Peter	Haberhaus, Catharina	A	
Luxenburger, Joseph Bernard Herman	19, Oct. 1851	Peter	Lübke, Catharina	J	12
Luxenburger, Peter	6, Mar. 1853	Peter	Lübke, Catharina	J	20
Luy, Peter	3, Apr. 1850	Christian	Schneider, Henrietta	D	208
Lwellari, Aloysius Stephan	26, Sept 1850	J. Baptist	Venne, Mary	B	214
Lydan, Mary Ann	23, Aug. 1857	William	Buckly, Bridget	P	221
Lyden, Patrick	12, Dec. 1856	Francis	----, Mary	E	419
Lydon, John	21, Nov. 1858	William J.	Buckly, Bridget	P	267
Lydon, Stephan	10, July 1859	Stephan	McGinly, Helen	P	287
Lymon, Ann	2, Sept 1850		adult - 19 years old	E	248
Lynagh, Ann Elizabeth	24, Apr. 1853	Peter	McGrann, Ellen	V	3
Lynan, Ann	24, June 1851	John	McCabe, Mary	B	234
Lynan, Charles	20, June 1852	John	McCabe, Mary	B	261

Name of Child	Date of Baptism	Father	Mother	Church	Page
Lynan, William	18, Nov. 1855	John	McCabe, Mary	B	22
Lynch, (boy)	21, May 1854	James	White, Bridget	E	191
Lynch, Andrew	28, Dec. 1858	James	Ring, Elizabeth	E	590
Lynch, Ann	13, Sept 1857	John	O'Brien, Mary	J	42
Lynch, Ann Jean	17, Nov. 1850	Patrick	Lynch, Bridget	E	262
Lynch, Bridget	26, Jan. 1851	John	McCarty, Ann	B	224
Lynch, Bridget	3, Nov. 1852	Patrick	----, Bridget	E	32
Lynch, Bridget	12, Mar. 1858	Patrick	Ryan, Bridget	E	521
Lynch, Catherine	24, May 1857	Patrick	Cunningham, Mary	P	213
Lynch, Catherine	8, Mar. 1853	Patrick	Delaney, Catherine	E	70
Lynch, Catherine	26, Oct. 1856	Patrick	Ryan, Bridget	E	408
Lynch, Catherine Margaret	9, Nov. 1852	Christopher	Moore, Catherine	B	275
Lynch, Cornelius	17, Mar. 1851	Dennis	Dacy, Mary	E	291
Lynch, Cornelius	16, May 1852	Michael	----, Sarah	P	21
Lynch, Ellen	15, Mar. 1857	James	----, Bridget	E	440
Lynch, Ellen	2, Mar. 1856	John	Kellan, Bridget	E	348
Lynch, Ellen	29, June 1856	Patrick	Conly, Bridget	E	378
Lynch, Ellen	29, Aug. 1859	William	Savage, Margaret	E	650
Lynch, Eugene	8, Aug. 1852	Michael	----, Mary	M	
Lynch, Francis	1, Jan. 1859	Thomas	----, Ann	E	592
Lynch, George	13, Sept 1857	John	O'Brien, Mary	J	42
Lynch, Helen	28, Oct. 1855	Humphrey	Sweeney, Mary	P	157
Lynch, Helen	14, Dec. 1851	Terence	Keenan, Catherine	B	247
Lynch, Henry	27, July 1851	Peter	Judd, Ann	B	237
Lynch, James	25, Jan. 1857	John	McDonald, Susan	U	
Lynch, James	18, June 1855	Michael	----, Ann	M	
Lynch, James	4, Oct. 1856	Michael	----, Mary	M	
Lynch, Jeremiah	8, June 1856	John	----, Honora	H	
Lynch, John	17, Feb. 1853	Dennis	Dacey, Mary	P	35
Lynch, John	2, Jan. 1853	James	White, Bridget	E	50
Lynch, John	23, Oct. 1859	John	McDonald, Susan	U	
Lynch, John	22, Aug. 1858	Michael	White, Sarah	X	
Lynch, John	7, Oct. 1855	Patrick	Cunningham, Mary	B	20
Lynch, John	26, Jan. 1856	Peter	----, Ann	E	340
Lynch, John William	11, July 1852	Arthur	O'Brien, Mary	A	
Lynch, Julia Ann	31, Aug. 1854	Michael	----, Bridget	E	220
Lynch, Lauretta Julia	20, Aug. 1854	Christopher	Moore, Catherine	E	218
Lynch, Linus	10, Apr. 1855	Edward	Smith, Margaret	P	128
Lynch, Louis	14, July 1850	Timothy	Longhmon, Catherine	B	207
Lynch, Margaret	25, May 1854	Michael	Wight, Sarah	J	26
Lynch, Margaret	8, Nov. 1858	Thomas	Sullivan, Joanne	B	66
Lynch, Martha Ann	24, Apr. 1852	Thomas	----, Mary	E	405
Lynch, Mary	24, July 1853	Daniel	Haily, Catherine	E	112
Lynch, Mary	21, Feb. 1852	Hugh	Kelly, Mary	E	384
Lynch, Mary	26, Oct. 1851	James	McLaughlin, Catherine	B	243
Lynch, Mary	6, Nov. 1853	John	----, Bridget	E	141
Lynch, Mary	18, Nov. 1853	Michael	----, Mary	M	
Lynch, Mary	19, July 1858	Michael	Flannagan, Winifred	B	61
Lynch, Mary	17, Sept 1854	Nicolaus	Russell, Catherine	V	17
Lynch, Mary	14, Mar. 1854	Patrick	Conly, Elizabeth	E	176
Lynch, Mary	28, Sept 1855	Thomas	Winston, Ann	V	27
Lynch, Mary	14, Jan. 1858	William	Savage, Margaret	E	509
Lynch, Mary Ann	30, Nov. 1857	James	King, Elizabeth	E	496
Lynch, Mary Jane	11, Sept 1858	John	Grinele, Honora	H	
Lynch, Michael	20, Jan. 1855	James	Brady, Ellen	E	258
Lynch, Michael	18, Nov. 1853	Michael	----, Mary	M	
Lynch, Michael	17, Nov. 1856	Michael	Flannigan, Winifred	B	36
Lynch, Michael	10, Sept 1851	Michael	Manough, Ann	E	342
Lynch, Michael	20, May 1859	Michael	McCauliff, Ellen	E	626

Name of Child	Date of Baptism	Father	Mother	Church	Page
Lynch, Michael	28, June 1856	Michael	McMahan, Ann	E	378
Lynch, Patrick	22, Feb. 1857	Michael	White, Sarah	X	
Lynch, Patrick	17, Nov. 1850	Terence	----, Catherine	E	261
Lynch, Sarah Jane	9, Oct. 1853	Timothy	Laughlin, Catherine	E	132
Lynch, Susan	26, Oct. 1856	Lawrence	Scanlan, Margaret	E	407
Lynch, Thomas	3, Apr. 1853	Michael	Flanagan, Winifred	B	287
Lynch, Thomas	31, May 1854	Peter	Judge, Ann	E	195
Lynch, William	29, Dec. 1858	Lawrence	----, Margaret	M	
Lynch, William	29, Aug. 1857	Michael	McCallis, Ellen	E	477
Lynch, William	21, July 1850	Thomas	Winstald, Ann	B	208
Lynch, William	23, June 1857	William	Gee, Mary	E	461
Lynch, William Christopher	20, Jan. 1851	Christopher	Moore, Catherine	E	278
Lynn, Mary Elizabeth	15, Apr. 1858	William	Hill, Fanny	P	246
Lyon, James	28, Sept 1856	James	Lane, Ann	E	400
Lyon, Mary Helen	30, Jan. 1855	Dennis	----, Margaret	V	22
Lyons, Anthony	23, Oct. 1853	John	Cunningham, Mary	B	301
Lyons, Catherine	18, Dec. 1859	Michael	Kennan, Bridget	P	306
Lyons, Dennis	14, Dec. 1853	Jeremiah	Walsh, Mary	V	8
Lyons, Edward	29, Jan. 1852	Edward	----, Bridget	M	
Lyons, Elizabeth	11, Apr. 1852	Patrick	----, Elizabeth	M	
Lyons, Francis John	8, Sept 1850	William	Meagher, Mary Ann	B	213
Lyons, Helen	11, Sept 1859	Patrick	Griffin, Bridget	Z	
Lyons, James	27, June 1858	John	----, Mary	M	
Lyons, John	15, Feb. 1857	Jeremiah	Walsh, Mary	V	37
Lyons, John	25, Mar. 1855	John	----, Mary	M	
Lyons, John	10, Feb. 1858	John	Tolson, Mary	E	516
Lyons, John	10, June 1852	Michael	----, Catherine	E	421
Lyons, John	26, Feb. 1854	Michael	Keenahan, Bridget	P	71
Lyons, Joseph	12, Mar. 1854	Thomas	----, Catherine	M	
Lyons, Margaret	7, Oct. 1855	Patrick	Ruffen, Bridget	E	318
Lyons, Maria Anna	12, July 1853	Edward	O'Connell, Bridget	K	
Lyons, Martha Ann	12, June 1859	Isaac	O'Keefe, Ellen	E	631
Lyons, Mary	29, Aug. 1855	David	Flinn, Honora	U	
Lyons, Mary	20, Nov. 1859	Jeremiah	Walsh, Mary	V	63
Lyons, Mary	16, Aug. 1857	Michael	Carran, Bridget	J	42
Lyons, Mary	13, Feb. 1854	Timothy	Doyle, Joanne	V	11
Lyons, Mary	8, Aug. 1858	William	Fitzsimmons, Margaret	E	555
Lyons, Mary	9, Mar. 1856	Jeremiah	Sheehey, Bridget	P	172
Lyons, Mary Ann	16, Aug. 1857	Patrick	----, Bridget	M	
Lyons, Mary Lucy	25, Dec. 1854	Edward	----, Bridget	M	
Lyons, Michael	11, Aug. 1850	Dennis	----, Margaret	E	238
Lyons, Michael	3, Dec. 1854	Michael	Kelly, Catherine	E	244
Lyons, Patrick	24, Mar. 1851	Timothy	Doyle, Joanne	E	294
Lyons, Sarah	19, Apr. 1857	John	----, Mary	M	
Lyons, Sarah Louise	25, Jan. 1858	Richard	Hogan, Mary	E	513
Lyons, Thomas	9, Apr. 1854	James	Hefferen, Catherine	E	181
Lyons, Thomas	9, Nov. 1856	Michael	Kelly, Catherine	E	411
Lyons, Timothy	29, Oct. 1855	Timothy	----, Joanne	E	323
Lyons, Timothy	16, May 1852	Timothy	Doyle, Joanne	E	414
Lyons, William	25, June 1853	James	----, Catherine	E	100
Lyons, William	18, Mar. 1852	John	adult - 30 years old	E	392
Lyons, William	21, Nov. 1858	John	Dwyer, Catherine	E	580
Lyons, William	4, Sept 1854	William	Cunnigham, Mary Ann	B	5